KU-097-676

The **Rough Guide** to

Tuscany & Umbria

written and researched by

Tim Jepson, Jonathan Buckley, and Mark Ellingham

additional research by

Nicholas Harrison

ROUGH
GUIDES

NEW YORK • LONDON • DELHI
www.roughguides.com

Contents

Michelangelo insert
following p.120

The Siena Palio insert
following p.408

Landscape insert
following p.472

3

◁◁ Monteriggioni ◁ Cypress trees, Val d'Órcia

N

Ravenna

Faenza
Forlì
Cesena

Rimini

ADRIATIC SEA

SAN MARINO

Urbino

Ancona

Stia
Poppi
Bibbiena

Sansepolcro
Monterchi
Arezzo
Città di Castello

Umbertide
Gubbio

MARCHE

Cortona
Lago Trasimeno

PERUGIA
Assisi

Montepulciano
Castiglione
del Lago
Pienza

UMBRIA

Foligno
Bevagna

Monte Amiata

Montefalco
Trevi
Norcia

MONTI SIBILLINI

Monte Vettore

Todi
Spoleto

Sant'Anatolia
di Narco
Arquata del Tronto

Orvieto

Pitigliano

Terni

LAZIO

Lago di Bolsena

Narni

ABRUZZO

L'Aquila

Viterbo

Rieti

0   25 km

Rome   Rome

5

Introduction to

Tuscany & Umbria

Tuscany and Umbria harbour the classic landscapes of Italy, familiar from a thousand Renaissance paintings, with their backdrop of medieval hill-towns, rows of

cypress trees, vineyards and olive groves, and artfully sited villas and farmhouses. It's a stereotype that has long held an irresistible attraction for northern Europeans. Shelley referred to Tuscany as a "paradise of exiles", and ever since his time the English, in particular, have seen the region as an ideal refuge from a sun-starved and overcrowded homeland.

The expatriate's perspective may be distorted, but the central provinces – and especially Tuscany – are indeed the essence of Italy in many ways. The national language evolved from Tuscan dialect, a supremacy ensured by Dante, who wrote the *Divine Comedy* in the vernacular of his birthplace, Florence. Other great Tuscan writers of the period – Petrarch and Boccaccio – reinforced its status, and in the nineteenth century Manzoni came to Tuscany to purge his vocabulary of any impurities while working on *The Betrothed*, the most famous of all Italian novels. But what makes this area pivotal to the culture not just of Italy but of all Europe is, of course, the **Renaissance** period, whose masterpieces of painting, sculpture and architecture are an intrinsic part of any tour. The very name by which we refer to this extraordinarily creative era was coined by a Tuscan, Giorgio Vasari, who wrote in the sixteenth century of the "rebirth" of the arts with the humanism of Giotto and his successors.

Nowadays Tuscany and Umbria are among the wealthiest regions of the modern Italian state, a prosperity founded partly on agriculture and tourism, but largely on their industrial centres, which are especially conspicuous in the Arno valley. Nonetheless, both Tuscany and Umbria are predominantly **rural** provinces, with great tracts of land still looking much as they did half a millennium ago. Just as the hill-towns mould themselves to the summits, the terraces of vines follow the lower contours of the hills and open fields spread across the broader valleys, forming a distinctive balance between the natural and human world.

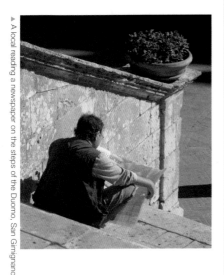

◢ A local reading a newspaper on the steps of the Duomo, San Gimignano

Where to go

Florence was the most active centre of the Renaissance, flourishing through the patronage of the all-powerful Medici, of a multitude of religious bodies and of the guilds, whose merchants and manufacturers laid the foundations of the city's prosperity. Every eminent artistic figure from Giotto onwards – Masaccio, Brunelleschi, Alberti, Donatello, Botticelli, Leonardo, Michelangelo – is represented here, in an unrivalled gathering of churches, galleries and museums.

Fact file

Tuscany

• **Tuscany** (Toscana) has a **population** of around 3.5 million, with some 400,000 in Florence, its capital.

• It is bordered by the **sea** to the west, and by the Apennine **mountains** to the east; in the north lie the Alpi Apuane (where Monte Prado reaches 2054m), while in the south rises Monte Amiata. South of Livorno lies the coastal **plain** of the Maremma. Tuscany has more **woodland** than any other Italian region.

• Tourism is an important contributor to the region's **economy**, as are agriculture (especially beef, wine and olive oil) and textile production, which is concentrated in the Arno valley and Prato.

Umbria

• **Umbria** is the only landlocked region of the Italian peninsula. Of its 900,000 **population**, 150,000 live in Perugia, the capital.

• The **terrain** is gentler than Tuscany, but the Apennines run along the eastern border, where, in the Sibillini mountains, Monte Vettore reaches 2476m just over the border in Marche. Some 30 percent of Umbria is woodland.

• Perugia manufactures food and clothing, and factories dot the Vale of Spoleto, but the major **industries** (steel, chemicals, textiles, paper and food) are in the south, around Terni. Traditional **crafts** are also significant, especially pottery.

Food and drink

Simplicity remains the defining characteristic of the cuisine of Tuscany and Umbria. Complicated sauces play no part in the classic recipes of these regions: here it's all about top-quality local produce, brought to the table with a minimum of intervention. A swift grilling, a drizzle of olive oil, a light garnish of herbs – that's all the enhancement deemed necessary for a cut of prime Tuscan beef or Umbrian pork. Vegetables tend to feature as side dishes and starters (the thick bean soup called ribollita is a signature Tuscan creation), and spinach and artichokes are staples of most menus, as are Umbrian truffles in the autumn. As for wine, you're spoiled for choice: Chianti is the best-known abroad, but the vineyards of Montalcino, Montelpuciano, Scansano, Montefalco and Orvieto – to name only the most obvious – all regularly produce outstanding vintages.

If Florence tends to take the limelight today, rivalry between the towns of both provinces – an important factor in a region whose inhabitants feel a strong loyalty to their particular locality – ensured that pictures and palaces were sponsored by everyone who could afford them. Exquisite Renaissance works adorn almost every place of any size from the Tuscan coast to the Apennine slopes of eastern Umbria, while the largest towns can boast artistic projects every bit as ambitious as those to be seen in Florence: the Piero della Francesca frescoes in **Arezzo**, for example, or those by Luca Signorelli in **Orvieto** or Giotto in **Assisi**.

Moreover, the art of the Renaissance did not spring out of thin air: Tuscany and Umbria both can boast a cultural lineage that stretches back unbroken to the time of Charlemagne and even beyond. **Lucca** is one of the handsomest Romanesque cities in Europe, and **Pisa** – whose Campo dei Miracoli, with its Leaning Tower, is one of Europe's most brilliant monumental ensembles – is another city whose heyday came in the Middle Ages. **Siena**'s red-brick medieval cityscape, arranged around its fabulous scallop-shaped Campo, makes a refreshing contrast with the darker tones of Florence, while a tour through Umbria can seem like a procession of magnificent ancient hill-towns. The attractions of **Assisi** (birthplace of St Francis), **Spoleto** and the busy provincial capital of **Perugia** are hardly secrets, but other Umbrian towns remain more obscure – such as **Gubbio** and the backwater delights of **Bevagna** and **Todi**. Many of the Umbrian towns retain a fair showing of their ancient past, too, with Etruscan and Roman walls and tombs to be seen on sites left undisturbed for centuries.

The variety of **landscape** within this comparatively small area is astounding. A short distance from central Florence spread the thickly wooded uplands of the **Mugello** and the **Casentino**, much of the latter still maintained by the monasteries to which the forests were entrusted hundreds of years ago. Lucca is a springboard for the **Alpi Apuane**, whose mountain quarries have supplied Europe's masons with pure white marble for centuries. Along the Tuscan shoreline the resorts are interspersed by some of Italy's best-kept wildlife reserves, including the fabulous **Monti dell'Uccellina**, the last stretch of virgin coast in the whole country. Out in the **Tuscan archipelago**, the island of **Giglio** is relatively unspoilt by the sort of tourist development that has infiltrated – though certainly not ruined – nearby **Elba**. The pastoral archetype is perhaps most strikingly subverted in the deep south of the province, where the agricultural hinterland of Siena soon gives way to the bleak **crete** and the sulphurous pools of **Saturnia**.

Landlocked Umbria may not be as varied as its neighbour, but the wild heights of the **Valnerina**, the **Piano Grande**'s prairie-like expanse and the savage peaks of the **Monti Sibillini** all contrast with the tranquil, soft-contoured hills with which the region is most often associated. In **Lago Trasimeno** the province has the largest body of water on the Italian peninsula, while in the south there's the **Cascate delle Marmore**, a spectacular if sporadic waterfall.

▲ Val d'Orcia, near Pienza

When to go

Midsummer in central Italy is not as pleasant an experience as you might imagine: the heat can be stifling, and from May to September you'll require luck to find accommodation in all but the most out-of-the-way spots. If at all possible, the month to **avoid** is **August**, when the great majority of Italians take their holidays. As a result many town restaurants and some hotels are closed for the entire month and the beaches are jammed solid. As the standard Italian idea of an enjoyable summer break is to spend a few weeks towel-to-towel on the sand, Umbria escapes the worst of the rush, but the problem of limited opening remains.

Florence throughout the summer is such a log jam of tour groups that the major attractions become a purgatorial experience: a two-hour queue for the Uffizi is not unusual. To enjoy a visit fully, go there shortly **before Easter** or in the **late autumn** – times of the year that are the best for Tuscany and Umbria as a whole, as the towns are quieter and the countryside is blossoming or taking on the tones of the harvest season. The Umbrian climate is slightly more extreme than Tuscany's, chiefly because of its distance from the sea; temperatures in summer are fractionally higher, while the hill-top locales of many towns can make them surprisingly windy and cool at other times. Winter is often quite rainy, but the absence of crowds makes this a good option for the cities on the major art trails. Bear in mind, however, that the high altitude of much of the region means many roads are impassable in midwinter, and in places like the upper Casentino or the Sibillini the snow might not melt until March or even April.

▼ Washing hanging from shuttered windows, Piazza Anfiteatro, Lucca

Renaissance art

Tuscany was the powerhouse of what has come to be known as the Renaissance, and the city of Florence is the supreme monument to European civilization's great evolutionary leap into modernity. Buildings by the likes of Brunelleschi and Alberti, the architects who reinvented the style of ancient Rome, still adorn the fabric of the city, while within its churches you can admire paintings and sculptures by artists who put the study of humanity back at the centre of western art: Donatello, Masaccio, Botticelli, Uccello, Ghirlandaio, Michelangelo, and the greatest

of their forerunners, Cimabue and Giotto. The city's museums contain an astounding abundance of masterpieces, with the galleries of the Uffizi constituting the world's richest showcase of Renaissance art. But almost every sizeable town in central Italy commissioned works during this period that have proved to be of durable fascination – as in the stunning fresco cycles in Arezzo (Piero della Francesca), Orvieto (Luca Signorelli), Siena (Pinturicchio), San Gimignano (Benozzo Gozzoli), Montefalco (Gozzoli again), Perugia (Perugino) and Prato (Fra Filippo Lippi), to name only a few.

It's always worth checking when each town has its **festivals** or pilgrimages. Accommodation is always tricky during these mini peak seasons, but some of the festivities are enjoyable enough to merit planning a trip around. Many have been crucial to their town's image for centuries – the most celebrated of these being the Siena **Palio**, a hell-for-leather horse race round the central square. The frenzy of Gubbio's semi-pagan **Corsa dei Ceri** almost matches it, as does the passionate commitment of Florence's **Calcio Storico**, a football match in medieval attire with no holds barred. Costumed **jousts** and other martial displays are a feature of several festive calendars, notable examples being the jousts in Pistoia and Arezzo, and the twice-yearly **crossbow competitions** between Gubbio and Sansepolcro. **Holy days** and **saints' days** bring in the crowds in equal numbers, with Assisi leading the way as the most venerated site.

Among the innumerable **arts festivals**, the highest profiles are achieved by the contemporary arts extravaganza in Spoleto, the *Umbria Jazz* festival

Saints

Florence has St Peter Martyr and the more obscure St Giovanni Gualberto; Siena has St Catherine, joint patron of Italy, and St Bernardino, patron saint of advertising... but Tuscany's roll-call of the holy is meagre compared to that of its neighbour, the so-called *terra dei santi* ("land of the saints"). Umbria's towns and villages are littered with shrines to holy men and women, none more peculiar than those of Montefalco, where a trio of mummified bodies are the object of veneration. St Francis of Assisi lies in the greatest of Umbria's pilgrimage churches, a short distance from the resting-place of his devout companion, St Clare. The founder of western monasticism, St Benedict, hailed from Norcia, not far from the hometown of St Rita, patron saint of the impossible. And just outside Terni, there's a pilgrimage site dedicated to St Valentine, who is said to have been born there. The one Umbrian saint who could be said to rival the fame of Francis, Valentine differs from him in one crucial respect: in all likelihood, he didn't exist.

in Perugia and the *Maggio Musicale* in more conservative Florence – but as with the more folkloric events, even the smallest towns have their cultural *stagione*. Finally, there's scarcely a hamlet in Tuscany or Umbria that doesn't have a **food** or **wine** festival, the region seeming to find an excuse to celebrate almost everything that breathes or grows. Appealing mainly to the local population and often lasting for just a day, these events place less stress on the hotels, though it might be a good idea to book a room if you're dropping by; fountains running with wine and other such excesses are pretty common.

Climate of Tuscany and Umbria

The table shows average daytime temperatures and average monthly rainfall.

	January	April	July	October
Florence				
°C	6	13	25	16
°F	42	55	77	60
mm	62	70	23	96
inches	2.5	3	1	4
Livorno				
°C	9	15	24	15
°F	47	59	75	59
mm	70	62	6	110
inches	3	2.5	0	4
Siena				
°C	5	12	25	15
°F	40	54	77	59
mm	70	62	20	110
inches	3	2.5	1	4
Perugia				
°C	5	11	24	13
°F	40	52	75	55
mm	70	70	30	115
inches	3	3	1	4.5

▶ Pitigliano

things not to miss

It's not possible to see everything that Tuscany and Umbria have to offer in one trip — and we don't suggest you try. What follows is a selective taste of the regions' highlights: great places to visit, outstanding buildings, spectacular scenery and unforgettable events. They're arranged in five colour-coded categories, which you can browse through to find the very best things to see and experience. All entries have a page reference to take you straight into the guide, where you can find out more.

01 **San Gimignano** Page **422** • San Gimignano is one of the best-preserved medieval towns in Italy. Fifteen of the original 72 towers built in the Middle Ages survive.

02 **The Uffizi** Page **115** • Gentile da Fabriano's *Adoration of the Magi* is but one masterpiece amid dozens in the galleries of the Uffizi.

ACTIVITIES | CONSUME | EVENTS | NATURE | SIGHTS

04 **Spoleto** Page **648** • The facade of Spoleto's cathedral owes its charm to the restrained combination of Romanesque and Renaissance elements.

03 **Duomo, Siena** Page **386** • The dome and bell-tower of Siena's cathedral rise above the city's medieval rooftops.

05 Santa Croce, Florence
Page **161** • With an extraordinary array of paintings and sculptures, and one of Florence's finest examples of Renaissance architecture, Santa Croce is another amazing monument.

06 Pienza
Page **472** • The Duomo and Piazza Pio II form the centrepiece of Pienza, designed as a Utopian Renaissance city in the fifteenth century.

07 Barga, Alpi Apuane
Page **290** • The village of Barga, known for its sublime cathedral and summer music festival, is set in the shadow of the Orrecchiella and Alpi Apuane mountains.

08 **Santa Maria Novella, Florence** Page 131 • Frescoes by Andrea di Firenze, Uccello, Masaccio, Ghirlandaio, Filippino Lippi and others make Santa Maria Novella one of Florence's essential sights.

09 **San Lorenzo, Florence** Page 137 • Attached to the parish church of the Medici, Michelangelo's Sagrestia Nuova is one of his most spectacular creations.

10 Piazza del Duomo Page **93** • Florence's cathedral square is a stupendous ensemble of religious architecture.

11 Gubbio Page **582** • Vaulted medieval alleys such as this one below the Palazzo dei Consoli in Gubbio are typical of Umbrian hill-towns.

12 Pisa Page **301** • The Leaning Tower is far from being Pisa's only first-rank attraction.

13 **Ice cream** Page 52 • Until you've sampled *gelato*, you don't know just how good ice cream can be.

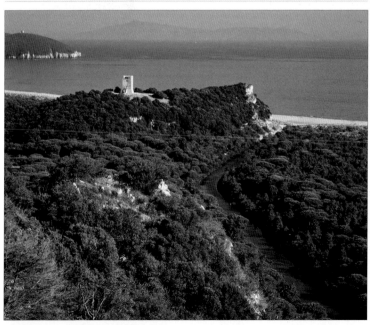

14 **Monti dell'Uccellina** Page 352 • The protected environment of the Monti dell'Uccellina in the Maremma is one of the last pristine stretches of coastline in Italy.

15

Volterra Balze Page **436** • Etruscan and Roman remains, as well as old alabaster mines, dot the eroded and soft-stoned cliffs known as Le Balze close to the ancient city of Volterra.

17 **Piano Grande** Page **677** • The Piano Grande, an extraordinary upland above Norcia, is the most striking feature of the Sibillini mountains, part of the Apennine chain in eastern Umbria.

16 **Orvieto** Page **716** • The monumental facade of Orvieto cathedral is the most spectacular in Italy. It was begun in 1290, but the finishing touches – the bronze doors – were only added in 1965.

18 **Lucca** Page **264** • From the thirteenth-century facade of San Michele in Foro the archangel Michael gazes over the centre of the graceful small city of Lucca.

19 **Cortona** Page **531** • With barely a single level street in the *centro storico*, Cortona is the hilliest of hill-towns.

20 **The Casentino** Page **526** • Leave the crowds behind in the lush wooded hills of the Casentino.

21 **The Crete** Page **453** • The almost bare, clay hills of the Crete south of Siena make up one of Tuscany's most beautiful and distinctive landscapes. In summer the fields blaze with poppies, sunflowers and ripening wheat.

22 **Perugia** Page **545** • Looking towards Assisi over the rooftops of Perugia, whose lofty hill-top position has been inhabited since at least Etruscan times.

23
Tuscan wine Page **55** • Some of Italy's finest vintages can be sampled in the wine bars of Tuscany and Umbria.

24 **Sant'Antimo** Page **466** • Splendid and serene, Sant'Antimo is one of several working abbeys set in the glorious countryside south of Siena.

25 **Corsa dei Ceri** Page **587** • Processions, pageants and a race between three teams bearing the *ceri*, or candles, mark the Corsa dei Ceri, held in the Umbrian town of Gubbio each year on May 15.

26 **San Francesco, Arezzo** Page **516** • Be sure to book in advance for a visit to Piero della Francesca's sublime fresco cycle.

27 **Assisi** Page **600** •Morning mist settles in the Vale of Spoleto below Assisi, birthplace of St Francis and one of the most beautiful of Umbria's many hill-towns.

Basics

Basics

Getting there

The easiest way to get to Tuscany or Umbria is to fly. The main airports are at Pisa, Rome and Bologna, though the smaller ones at Florence, Perugia and Ancona are served by an increasing number of flights. From the UK and Ireland, competitive prices for charter or scheduled flights outweigh the inconvenience of the long rail or bus journey. The two-day drive is a viable, though expensive, option. Flights from North America and Australasia come into Rome (or, less conveniently, Milan), from where you can move on by plane or overland; from down under, you may find it cheaper to fly to London and get a budget onward flight from there.

For Tuscany, flying into **Pisa** (PSA; see p.303) is the best bet, with an easy rail or bus trip from the airport to the centre of Florence. The small airport at **Florence** (FLR) has fewer international flights, although travel links are straightforward (see p.80). **Bologna** airport (BLQ) is a shuttle-bus ride from Bologna main train station, from where Florence is an hour away.

For much of Umbria, flying into **Rome** is simplest, with an onward journey by road or rail of around two hours to Perugia or Spoleto, three hours to Florence. **Fiumicino** (FCO), the common name for Rome's main Leonardo da Vinci airport, is about 30km west of the city centre, from where a half-hourly express train takes thirty minutes to reach Stazione Termini, Rome's principal station. Many charter flights and no-frills airlines use Rome's smaller **Ciampino** airport (CIA), southeast of the city, which is linked by half-hourly buses to Ciampino train station, from where trains run every fifteen minutes to Stazione Termini. The tiny airport at **Perugia** (PEG) has few flights, but easy travel links (see pp.550 & 596) to the city and the region. The east-coast port of **Ancona** (AOI) is another possibility, with a shuttle bus from the airport to the main train station for onward travel into Umbria.

Airfares usually depend on the **season**, with the highest being around Easter and from June to August when the weather is best; fares drop during the "shoulder" seasons – September to October and April to May – and you'll get the best prices during the November to March low season (excluding Christmas and New Year). Note also that it is generally more expensive to fly at weekends; price ranges quoted below assume midweek travel. You can often cut costs by going through a **discount flight agent** who may also offer special student and youth fares and a range of other travel-related services such as travel insurance, rail passes, car rentals, tours and the like. Some agents specialize in **charter flights**, which may be cheaper than anything available on a scheduled flight, but departure dates are fixed and withdrawal penalties are high. Some agents offer "**open-jaw**" deals, whereby you can fly into one Italian city and back from another – a good idea if you want to make your way across the country and generally no more expensive than a standard charter return. You may even find it cheaper to pick up a **package deal** that takes care of flights and accommodation for an all-in price. Many airlines and discount travel websites offer you the opportunity to **book tickets online**, cutting out the costs of agents and middlemen. Good deals can often be found through discount or auction sites, as well as through the airlines' own websites.

Online booking agents

ⓦ **www.flyaow.com** Online air travel info and reservations site.

ⓦ **travel.yahoo.co.uk** Good information and destination coverage.

ⓦ **www.cheaptickets.com** Discount flight specialists from the US only.

ⓦ **www.cheapflights.com** A "shop-window" site, linking to various agents and airlines. Bookings from the UK and Ireland only.

Ⓦ **www.cheapestflights.co.uk** Good source of budget flights from UK.

Ⓦ **www.expedia.co.uk** Discount airfares and accommodation. Go to expedia.com for deals from North America.

Ⓦ **www.flights4less.co.uk** Does just what it says on the tin.

Ⓦ **www.flynow.com** Simple-to-use independent travel site offering good-value fares.

Ⓦ **www.hotwire.com** Bookings from the US only. Last-minute savings of up to forty percent on regular published fares.

Ⓦ **www.lastminute.com** Bookings from the UK only. Offers good last-minute holiday package and flight-only deals.

Ⓦ **www.skyauction.com** Bookings from the US only. Auctions tickets and travel packages using a "second bid" scheme.

Ⓦ **www.skyscanner.net** This site performs a very efficient search of budget and charter flights from the UK.

Ⓦ **www.travelocity.co.uk** Destination guides, hot web fares and best deals for car rental, accommodation and lodging as well as fares.

Ⓦ **www.travelshop.com.au** Australian website offering discounted flights, packages, insurance and online bookings.

Packages and organized tours

Tuscany and Umbria are prime destinations in most "specialist" Italian programmes, and – a definite plus – most of these holidays are sold by small, independently run travel companies. Holidays on the market mostly fall into one of the following categories (sample prices in British pounds and US dollars):

• **Flight-plus-hotel**. These deals can be excellent value, usually featuring a good three-star hotel. All-in prices for a week's bed and breakfast in Florence, for example, start at around £500/$900 per person per week, rising by about £50/$90 in high season.

• **Villas and farmhouses**. Numerous companies offer villa or farmhouse accommodation in rural Tuscany and Umbria; charter flights, ferry crossings or fly-drives are usually available as part of a package deal, but it's generally possible to book just the house if you prefer. This is one of the boom markets for Italian tourism, so you need to book well in advance for the summer season. Properties vary enormously, from small, simple farmhouses sleeping four to eight people

right up to castles fitted out to accommodate groups of 25 or more; reckon on paying at least £100/$175 per person per week for the simplest places (and considerably more than that in July and August). Rental prices usually include insurance, water and electricity, and sometimes linen, cooking and maid service in the smarter places. Check carefully what is and isn't included. Italian villa companies are notorious for their "added extras", so read all printed information diligently. The term "villa" is a loose one: your dream medieval retreat may turn out to be a concrete monstrosity. Villas and farmhouses often form part of complexes, with apartments and wings rented out to various groups, so privacy can become an issue (it's common, too, for the owner to live on or near the property). Check that the swimming pool attached to the villa is for your sole use: the "shared pool" is very common.

• **Specialist holidays**. An increasing number of operators offer walking tours, riding holidays, cycling trips, art and archeology holidays, and food and wine jaunts. Many are group tours and most don't come cheap: accommodation, food, local transport and the services of a guide are nearly always included, and a week's half-board holiday can cost £1200/$2175 or more per person. As a result, there's a growing trend for smaller packaged and self-guided activity trips for individuals or groups of friends, particularly among walking and cycling companies. Such trips may be half the price of escorted trips: transparent pricing policies should enable you to see just how much you're spending and where your money's going.

• **Short-break deals**. Florence is a standby in major holiday companies' "Italian City Break" programmes; reckon on spending about £350–500/$620–900 per person for three nights in a two- or three-star hotel, depending on season, though you should bear in mind that last-minute bargains can often be found. Always check precisely where your hotel is located: cheaper places may be some way from the city centre. Some companies have city breaks to Siena, Lucca and Pisa.

• **Fly-drive deals**. If you want to rent a car in Italy, it's well worth checking with tour operators before you leave: most fly-drive deals work out a lot cheaper than renting on the spot.

From the UK and Ireland

No-frills airlines in the UK include Ryanair, which has regular flights from London Stansted, Glasgow and Liverpool to Pisa, Bologna (Forlì), Rome Ciampino and Ancona, with departures often linked to flight arrivals at Stansted from Dublin, Shannon and Prestwick. EasyJet also flies from Bristol to Pisa and from Stansted to Ciampino, with connections coming into Stansted from Edinburgh, Glasgow, Newcastle and Belfast. In summer Jet2 flies from Manchester and Leeds to Pisa and Rome, and Thomson from Bournemouth, Coventry and Doncaster to Pisa. If you book well in advance you can sometimes find tickets for as little as £25 return for mid-week off-peak flights, though these rock-bottom prices tend to apply only to early-morning or late-evening flights. For more reasonable flight times from these budget airlines, you're looking at something in the region of £100–150 return in summer, as long as you make your reservation well in advance: prices can rise so much for last-minute bookings on no-frills airlines (ie within two weeks of departure date) that they become more expensive than their full-service rivals. You may also find that a **charter flight** is a better bargain in high season: it's worth checking with a specialist agent or scouring the classified section of the weekend newspapers for last-minute deals.

Of the **full-service airlines in the UK** British Airways serves **Pisa** several times daily out of London Gatwick and Manchester, and Alitalia flies there via Milan or Rome. A return flight with Alitalia or BA from London to Pisa in low season can cost from around £80, with prices at £150 and upwards (to around £300) in high season. Again, it pays to book as far in advance as possible, and to keep your eyes open for special offers, which have become more numerous in the wake of the competition from the no-frills outfits. Meridiana is currently the only airline with non-stop flights from Gatwick to **Florence Perètola**; their tickets tend to be more expensive – from £150 off-peak. Meridiana operates a connecting flight from Perètola to

Perugia, which is also served by Alitalia, via Milan or Rome.

For flights to **Rome Fiumicino**, British Airways and Alitalia operate daily from London Heathrow and Gatwick, while BA flies daily from Manchester and five or six times a week from Birmingham and Edinburgh. Prices are much the same as for Pisa.

There are also regular British Airways flights from London Gatwick to **Bologna** Marconi airport. This is generally a cheaper option than flying to Pisa or Rome, and because Bologna is a less popular destination you can often find seats when the Pisa and Rome flights are sold out. Bologna airport is a shuttle-bus ride from Bologna main train station, from where Florence is an hour's rail journey away. (Forlì airport, which Ryanair sells as Bologna, is a good deal further away and will add an extra hour on to your journey.)

From Ireland, the cheapest tickets are on the Ryanair daily service from Dublin to Pisa; special offers can bring the fare down as low as €50, but at peak periods you might find yourself paying five or six times that much, if you don't book well in advance. For those willing to pay a premium for comfort, Aer Lingus has three flights a week to Bologna (Marconi), and three daily flights from Dublin direct to Rome Fiumicino; Alitalia covers the same route three to five times a week. You can find return deals for around €270 if you book early, but prices are usually significantly higher (€345–400).

Airlines in the UK and Ireland

Aer Lingus UK ☎0845/084 4444, Ireland ☎0818/365 000, ⓦwww.aerlingus.ie.
Alitalia UK ☎0870/544 8259, Ireland ☎01/677 5171, ⓦwww.alitalia.com.
British Airways UK ☎0870/850 9850, Ireland ☎1800/626 747, ⓦwww.ba.com.
easyJet UK ☎0905/821 0905 (calls charged at premium rate), ⓦwww.easyjet.com.
Jet2 UK ☎0871/226 1737, Ireland ☎0818/20001, ⓦwww.jet2.com.
Meridiana UK ☎020/7839 2222, ⓦwww.meridiana.it.
Ryanair UK ☎0906/270 5656, Ireland ☎0818/303 030, ⓦwww.ryanair.com.
Thomson UK ☎0870/1900 737, Ireland ☎01/247 7723, ⓦwww.thomsonfly.com.

Flight and travel agents in the UK and Ireland

Aran Travel International Galway ☎091/562 595, ⊛homepages.iol.ie/~arantvl/aranmain.htm. Good-value flights to all parts of the world.

CIE Tours International Dublin ☎01/703 1888, ⊛www.cietours.ie. General flight and tour agent.

Co-op Travel Care UK ☎0870/112 0085, ⊛www.travelcareonline.com. Flights and holidays.

Flightbookers UK ☎0870/010 7000, ⊛www.ebookers.com, Ireland ☎01/241 5689, ⊛www.ebookers.ie. Low fares on an extensive selection of scheduled flights.

Joe Walsh Tours Dublin ☎01/676 0991, ⊛www.joewalshtours.ie. General budget fares agent.

McCarthy's Travel Cork ☎021/427 0127, ⊛www.mccarthystravel.ie. General flight agent.

Neenan Travel Dublin ☎01/607 9900, ⊛www.neenantrav.ie. Specialists in European city breaks.

North South Travel UK ☎01245/608 291, ⊛www.northsouthtravel.co.uk. Friendly, competitive travel agency, offering discounted fares worldwide. Profits are used to support projects in the developing world, especially the promotion of sustainable tourism.

Premier Travel Derry ☎028/7126 3333, ⊛www.premiertravel.uk.com. Discount flight specialists.

STA Travel UK ☎0870/160 0599, ⊛www.statravel.co.uk. Worldwide specialists in low-cost flights and tours for students and under-26s, though other customers welcome.

Top Deck UK ☎020/8879 6789, ⊛www.topdecktravel.co.uk. Long-established agent dealing in discount flights.

Trailfinders UK ☎0845/0585 858, ⊛www.trailfinders.co.uk; Dublin ☎01/677 7888, ⊛www.trailfinders.ie. One of the best-informed and most efficient agents for independent travellers.

General package operators in the UK

Citalia ☎020/8686 0677, ⊛www.citalia.co.uk. Mid-range three-star and smarter four-star hotel and villa packages from a major and long-established company.

Crystal Premier Italy ☎0870/888 0222, ⊛www.crystalitaly.co.uk. Well priced hotel and villa holidays in many Tuscan and Umbrian destinations, plus city breaks to Florence and Siena.

Italian Expressions ☎020/7435 2525, ⊛www.expressionsholidays.co.uk. Good choice of top-end accommodation, some in tucked-away corners of the region.

Kirker Holidays ☎0870/112 3333, ⊛www.kirkerholidays.com. Independent operator renowned for their excellent city and short-break deals to Tuscany.

Magic of Italy ☎0870/027 0480, ⊛www.magicofitaly.co.uk. With Citalia this is the frontrunner among the plethora of multi-service Italian operators. Hotel and villa packages, individual properties, "City Break" deals, tailor-made itineraries and a booking service for opera, events, train and other tickets.

Solo's Holidays ☎08704/998 800, ⊛www.soloholidays.co.uk. Holidays in Tuscany for singles aged 25 and upwards.

Sunvil Holidays ☎020/8758 4722, ⊛www.sunvil.co.uk. City breaks and tailor-made hotel and villa packages.

Villas, farmhouses and apartments

For companies offering villa & farmhouse accommodation but not flights, see p.47.

Carefree Italy ☎01293/552 277, ⊛www.carefree-italy.com. Farmhouses and villas, often in shared complexes, in Tuscany and Umbria: also has a range of small hotels and city apartments.

Cottages to Castles ☎01622/726 883, ⊛www.cottagestocastles.com. Over 100 properties, cottages, villas and apartments in Tuscany alone, plus a more limited selection in Umbria.

CV Travel ☎020/7384 5850, ⊛www.cvtravel.co.uk. Villas and farmhouses at the top of the market, usually with private pool.

Italian Chapters ☎020/7722 9560, ⊛www.villa-rentals.com. This subdivision of the very upmarket Abercrombie & Kent company has some spectacular villas on its books.

Italian Life ☎0870/444 8811, ⊛www.italianlife.co.uk. Has a huge database of properties in Tuscany and Umbria, with a comprehensive online search facility to find just the right one.

Meon Villas ☎0870/909 7550, ⊛www.meonvillas.co.uk. Small selection of villas (all with pools) in all the more popular Tuscan spots.

Simply Travel ☎0870/166 4979, ⊛www.simplytravel.co.uk. Mostly small, stylish apartments, generally sleeping two to six, plus a few villas and small family-run rural hotels.

Specialist tour operators in the UK

Art and culture holidays

ACE Study Tours ☎01223/835 055, ⊛www.study-tours.org. A variety of mainly art and architectural tours under the guidance of genuine experts.

Bellini ☎020/7602 7602, ⊛www.bellinitravel.com. Tailor-made tours by a company specializing in Italy that can arrange private access to art collections and palazzi.

Inscape ℡01993/891 726, ⓦwww.inscapetours
.co.uk. Tuscan and Umbrian towns sometimes feature
on the study courses offered by this well-established
company.
JMB Travel ℡01905/830099, ⓦwww.jmb-travel
.co.uk. Specialists in opera holidays, with packages
to Florence's major opera events and the Maggio
Musicale.
Light and Land ℡01432/839111, ⓦwww
.lightandland.co.uk. Week-long photographic holidays
in Tuscany and Umbria for camera enthusiasts of
all standards. Well-scouted locations, plus time for
sightseeing and relaxation.
Martin Randall ℡020/8742 3355, ⓦwww
.martinrandall.com. One of the best operators in the
sector: imaginative art, music and cultural tours ranging
from three to twelve nights, including Piero della
Francesca, Medici Villas & Gardens, Florence & Siena,
San Gimignano & Tuscan Hill Towns and Florence
Revisited (lesser-known sights and private palaces).

Walking, cycling and riding

ATG ℡01865/315678, ⓦwww.atg-oxford.co.uk.
The best all-inclusive escorted walking holidays in
Tuscany and Umbria. They also run cheaper self-
guided walking and cycling trips: hotel bookings are
made for you and luggage is transported.
Equitour ℡01865/511 642, ⓦwww.ridingtours
.com. Group riding holidays on trails around Siena.
Explore Worldwide ℡0870/333 4001, ⓦwww
.explore.co.uk. Offers a fortnight's camping and
walking between Florence, Siena and Volterra, and a
one-week Chianti excursion.
Headwater ℡01606/720033, ⓦwww.headwater
.com. A variety of guided and independent walking
and cycling holidays in Tuscany and Umbria.
HF ℡020/8905 9558, ⓦwww.hfholidays.co.uk. A
choice of one- and two-week walking holidays from a
long-established company using bases in Tuscany at
Norcia, Albiano and San Quirico d'Orcia.
Inntravel ℡01653/617 788, ⓦwww.inntravel
.co.uk. Self-guided walks around the Tuscan and
Umbrian hills, plus more demanding hikes such as an
Apennine trail from Florence to Bologna.
Naturetrek ℡01962/733051, ⓦwww.naturetrek
.co.uk. Acknowledged leaders in birdwatching,
botanical and natural history holidays, offering small-
group tours of the Umbrian and Tuscan countryside.
Sherpa ℡020/8577 2717, ⓦwww
.sherpa-walking-holidays.co.uk. Offers a selection
of self-guided walks and cycling tours in Tuscany and
Umbria.
Waymark ℡01753/516 477, ⓦwww
.waymarkholidays.co.uk. One of the longer-
established companies, with walks across Italy,
including Tuscany.

Wine and cookery holidays

Arblaster & Clarke ℡01730/893 344, ⓦwww
.arblasterandclarke.com. Upmarket wine tours in
Tuscany and Umbria, staying at four- and five-star
hotels and with tastings at the premier estates.
ATG ℡01865/315678, ⓦwww.atg-oxford.co.uk.
Truffle-hunts in Umbria, plus language, cookery and
painting courses based at a delightful nineteenth-
century house in the countryside outside Colle di Val
d'Elsa.
Italian Cookery Weeks ℡020/8208 0112,
ⓦwww.italian-cookery-weeks.co.uk. Seven-night
cookery courses run by Susanna Gelmetti – the
venues change each year, but Umbria or Tuscany
often feature.
Tasting Places ℡020/8964 5333, ⓦwww
.tastingplaces.com. The best of several companies
offering cooking courses in the region. Leading chefs
such as Alistair Little and Sophie Braimbridge lead
one-week residential courses at country houses and
hotels in Tuscany and Umbria.
Winetrails ℡01306/712 111, ⓦwww.winetrails
.co.uk. Exercise and indulgence combined: tours link
vineyard visits with guided walks and good food. An
independent programme is also available.

By train

Travelling **by train** to Italy won't save much
money. The beauty of train travel and ticketing, however, is that you can break your
journey en route. The eighteen-hour journey
to Florence costs around £210, but special
offers are always worth checking. Bear in
mind that going via Paris on Eurostar you will
have to lug your bags from the Gare du Nord
to the Gare de Lyon. Discounts for under-
26s and special offers are sometimes available and advance booking is essential. An
alternative route is to use the cross-Channel
ferry and catch slower trains through France
and Italy but this won't cut costs significantly
and the connecting trains from Calais to
Paris are notoriously badly timetabled: many
arrive too late for the evening train to Florence, meaning an overnight stay in Paris. If
you're planning to include Italy as part of a
longer European trip you could invest in a
rail pass: the Inter-Rail and Eurail passes
offer a month's unlimited rail travel throughout Europe but they must be bought before
leaving home. See "Getting around" p.42 for
details of all rail passes, including those for
use solely on the Italian rail network.

Train information

Eurostar ☎ 0870/160 6600, ⊛ www.eurostar.com.
Rail Europe UK ☎ 0870/584 8848, ⊛ www
.raileurope.co.uk. First stop for information on
everything to do with international train travel,
including purchase of tickets and passes.
Trainseurope UK ☎ 020/8699 3654, ⊛ www
.trainseurope.co.uk.

By car from the UK

There's no one fixed route to Italy if you're
travelling with **your own vehicle**. The best
cross-Channel options for most drivers will
either be the standard ferry links Dover-Cal-
ais, Dover-Ostend and Newhaven-Dieppe,
or the Channel Tunnel route with Eurotunnel. Any travel agent can provide up-to-
date cross-Channel schedules and make
advance bookings – which are essential in
high season. As regards **routes** from northern France, the Alpine route via Germany
and Switzerland is probably the quickest
and can **save you money** as German
motorways – unlike their French equivalents
– are generally toll-free. Otherwise you could
head straight across France to Chamonix
and the Mont Blanc tunnel, which brings
you out near Turin in northwest Italy. The
AA and RAC provide comprehensive route-
planning services and general advice on
all aspects of driving to Italy, plus details of
useful organizations to contact when you're
there.

Cross-channel operators

Eurotunnel UK ☎ 0870/535 3535, ⊛ www
.eurotunnel.com. Shuttle train via the Channel Tunnel
for vehicles, running continuously between Folkestone
and Coquelles, near Calais (up to 4 per hr; takes
35–45min). Arrive at least 30min before departure. You
can turn up and buy your ticket at the toll booths, though
at busy times booking is advisable. Rates depend on
the season, time of day and length of stay; it's cheaper
to travel between 10pm and 6am. Highest fares are for
weekend departures and travel in July and August.
P&O Ferries UK ☎ 0870/600 0600, ⊛ www
.poferries.com. Dover to Calais.
Sea France ☎ 0870/571 1711, ⊛ www.seafrance
.com. Dover to Calais.
Transmanche Ferries ☎ 0800/917 1201,
⊛ www.transmancheferries.com. Newhaven to
Dieppe.

From North America

There are no direct flights **from the US or
Canada** to Pisa or Florence but it's easy to fly
to Rome or Milan Malpensa (MXP) and pick
up an onward flight or train from there. Alitalia
and Delta fly the widest choice of direct routes
between the US and Italy, with daily flights to
Milan from New York, Miami, Chicago and
Boston, and to Rome from New York. Other
options to Rome include American Airlines
from Chicago, and Alitalia and Air Canada
from Toronto. Many European carriers fly from
most major US and Canadian cities (via their
capitals) to Rome, Florence and Pisa. The
cheapest **round-trip fares** to Rome, travelling
midweek in low season, start at around $550
from New York or C$950 from Toronto, rising
to $950/C$1300 during the summer. Add
another $100–250 for a connecting flight from
Rome or Milan to Florence or Pisa – or there
are plenty of fast rail connections.

Airlines in North America

Air Canada ☎ 1-888/247-2262, ⊛ www
.aircanada.com.
Air France US ☎ 1-800/237-2747, Canada ☎ 1-
800/667-2747, ⊛ www.airfrance.com.
Alitalia US ☎ 1-800/223-5730, Canada ☎ 1-
800/361-8336, ⊛ www.alitalia.com.
American Airlines ☎ 1-800/433-7300, ⊛ www
.aa.com.
Austrian ☎ 1-800/843-0002, ⊛ www.aua.com.
British Airways ☎ 1-800/247-9297, ⊛ www
.ba.com.
Continental ☎ 1-800/231-0856, ⊛ www
.continental.com.
Delta ☎ 1-800/241-4141, ⊛ www.delta.com.
Iberia ☎ 1-800/772-4642, ⊛ www.iberia.com.
KLM/Northwest ☎ 1-800/447-4747, ⊛ www
.klm.com.
Lufthansa US ☎ 1-800/645-3880, Canada ☎ 1-
800/563-5954, ⊛ www.lufthansa.com.
Swiss ☎ 1-877/359-7947, ⊛ www.swiss.com.
United ☎ 1-800/538-2929, ⊛ www.united.com.
US Airways ☎ 1-800/622-1015, ⊛ www.usair.com.
Virgin Atlantic ☎ 1-800/862-8621, ⊛ www
.virgin-atlantic.com.

Flight and travel agents in North America

Airtech ☎ 1-877-247-8324 or 212/219-7000,
⊛ www.airtech.com. Standby seat broker; also deals
in consolidator fares and courier flights.

Educational Travel Center ☎1-800/747-5551 or 608/256-5551, ⓦwww.edtrav.com. Student/youth discount agent.

STA Travel US ☎1-800/329-9537, Canada ☎1-888/427-5639, ⓦwww.sta-travel.com. Worldwide specialists in independent travel; also student IDs, travel insurance, car rental, rail passes, and more.

Student Flights ☎1-800/255-8000 or 480/951-1177, ⓦwww.isecard.com. Student/youth fares, student IDs.

TFI Tours International ☎1-800/745-8000 or 212/736-1140, ⓦwww.lowestairprice.com. Consolidator.

Travelers Advantage ☎1-877/259-2691, ⓦwww.travelersadvantage.com. Discount travel club; annual membership fee required (currently $1 for 3 months' trial).

Worldtek Travel ☎1-800/243-1723, ⓦwww.worldtek.com. Discount travel agency for worldwide travel.

Tour operators in North America

Abercrombie & Kent ☎1-800/323-7308, ⓦwww.abercrombiekent.com. Deluxe village-to-village hiking and biking tours, as well as rail journeys.

Classic Journeys ☎1-800/200-3887, ⓦwww.classicjourneys.com. Hiking and cooking tours.

Cross-Culture ☎1-800/491-1148 or 413/256-6303, ⓦwww.crosscultureinc.com. Small-group cultural tours to Florence and the Tuscan hill-towns.

Delta Vacations ☎1-800/654-6559, ⓦwww.deltavacations.com. City breaks to Florence.

Journeys International ☎1-800/255-8735, ⓦwww.journeys-intl.com. Seven-day walking tours.

New Frontiers ☎1-800/677-0720 or 310/670-7318, ⓦwww.newfrontiers.com. City breaks and independent packages.

Travel Bound ☎1-800/456-8656, ⓦwww.booktravelbound.com. Numerous packages to Florence, including a five-night stay with tickets booked to the Uffizi and Accademia.

From Australia and New Zealand

There are no direct flights to Italy **from Australia or New Zealand**, but plenty of airlines fly to Rome via Asian hubs. Round-trip fares from Sydney with the major airlines (Alitalia, Qantas, Japan, Singapore or Malaysian) are A$1500–1850 in low season, A$1700–2500 in high season. With the same carriers from New Zealand you can expect to pay NZ$2000 in low season, NZ$3400 in high season.

Airlines in Australia and NZ

Alitalia Australia ☎02/9244 2445, NZ ☎09/308 3357, ⓦwww.alitalia.com.

British Airways Australia ☎1300/767 177, NZ ☎09/966 9777, ⓦwww.ba.com.

Cathay Pacific Australia ☎13 17 47, NZ ☎09/379 0861, ⓦwww.cathaypacific.com.

China Airlines Australia ☎02/9244 2121, NZ ☎09/308 3364, ⓦwww.china-airlines.com.

Garuda Australia ☎1300/365 330 or 02/9334 9944, NZ ☎09/366 1862, ⓦwww.garuda-indonesia.com.

Japan Australia ☎02/9272 1111, NZ ☎09/379 9906, ⓦwww.japanair.com.

Malaysian Australia ☎13 26 27, NZ ☎0800/777 747 or 649/379 3743, ⓦwww.malaysiaairlines.com.

Qantas Australia ☎13 13 13, NZ ☎09/357 8900 or 0800/808 767, ⓦwww.qantas.com.

Singapore Australia ☎13 10 11, NZ ☎09/379 3209, ⓦwww.singaporeair.com.

Sri Lankan Australia ☎02/9244 2234, NZ ☎09/308 3353, ⓦwww.srilankan.aero.

Thai Australia ☎1300/651 960, NZ ☎09/377 3886, ⓦwww.thaiair.com.

Flight and travel agents in Australia and NZ

Australian Pacific Touring Australia ☎1800/675 222 or 03/9277 8555, NZ ☎09/279 6077, ⓦwww.aptours.com. Long-established, award-winning operator running package tours and independent travel.

Budget Travel NZ ☎09/366 0061 or 0800/808 040, ⓦwww.budgettravel.co.nz.

CIT Australia ☎02/9267 1255, ⓦwww.cittravel.com.au. Italian specialists, with packages to Florence and elsewhere.

Flight Centre Australia ☎13 31 33, ⓦwww.flightcentre.com.au, NZ ☎0800/243 544, ⓦwww.flightcentre.co.nz. Specializes in discount airfares and holiday packages.

Northern Gateway Australia ☎1800/174 800, ⓦwww.northerngateway.com.au.

Silke's Travel Australia ☎1800 807 860, ⓦwww.silkes.com.au. Gay and lesbian specialist travel agent.

STA Travel Australia ☎1300/733 035, ⓦwww.statravel.com.au, NZ ☎0508/782 872, ⓦwww.statravel.co.nz.

Student Uni Travel Australia ☎02/9232 8444. Great deals for students.

Trailfinders Australia ☎02/9247 7666, ⓦwww.trailfinders.com.au. One of the best-informed and most efficient agents for independent travellers.

Travel.com Australia ☏ 1300/130 482, ⓦ www .travel.com.au, NZ ☏ 0800/468 332, ⓦ www.travel .co.nz. Comprehensive online travel company, with discounted fares.

Tour operators in Australia and NZ

Abercrombie and Kent Australia ☏ 02/9241 3213, NZ ☏ 0800/441 638, ⓦ www .abercrombiekent.com.au. Upmarket tours.

Contiki Holidays Australia ☏ 02/9511 2200, NZ ☏ 09/309 8824, ⓦ www.contiki.com. Frenetic tours for 18–35 year-old party animals.
Viatour Australia ☏ 02/8219 5400. Bookings for hundreds of travel suppliers.
Walkabout Gourmet Adventures Australia ☏ 03/5159 6556, ⓦ www.walkaboutgourmet.com. Classy food, wine and walking tours in Tuscany.

Red tape and visas

All EU citizens can enter Italy, and stay as long as they like, simply on production of a valid passport. Citizens of the United States, Canada, Australia and New Zealand need only a valid passport, but are limited to stays of ninety days. All other nationals should consult the relevant embassies about visa requirements.

Legally, you're required to **register with the police** within three days of entering Italy, though if you're staying at a hotel this will be done for you. Some policemen are more punctilious about this than ever, though others would be astonished by any attempt to register yourself at the local police station while on holiday.

Italian embassies and consulates abroad

Australia Embassy: 12 Grey St, Deakin, Canberra, ACT 2600 ☏ 02/6273 3333, ⓦ www.ambitalia.org. au. Consulates in Melbourne ☏ 03/9867 5744 and Sydney ☏ 02/9392 7900.
Canada Embassy: 275 Slater St, Ottawa, ON, K1P 5H9 ☏ 613/232-2401, ⓦ www.italyincanada. com. Consulates in Montréal ☏ 514/849-8351 and Toronto ☏ 416/977-1566.
Ireland Embassy: 63–65 Northumberland Rd, 6365 Dublin 4 ☏ 01/660 1744.
New Zealand Embassy: 34–38 Grant Rd, PO Box 463, Thorndon, Wellington ☏ 04/473 5339, ⓦ www. italy-embassy.org.nz.
UK Embassy: 14 Three King's Yard, London W1Y 2EH ☏ 020/7312 2200, ⓦ www.embitaly.org.uk.

Consulates in Edinburgh ☏ 0131/226 3695 and Manchester ☏ 0161/236 9024.
US Embassy: 3000 Whitehaven St NW, Washington DC 20008 ☏ 202/612-4400, ⓦ www.italyemb.org. Consulates in Chicago ☏ 312/467-1550, New York ☏ 212/737-9100 and San Francisco ☏ 415/292-9210.

Embassies and consulates in Italy

Australia Embassy: Via Alessandria 215, 00198 Rome ☏ 06.852.721, ⓦ www.australian-embassy. it.
Canada Embassy: Via GB de Rossi 27, 00161 Rome ☏ 06.445.981, ⓦ www.canada.it.
Ireland Embassy: Piazza di Campitelli 3, 00186 Rome ☏ 06.697.9121.
New Zealand Embassy: Via Zara 28, 00198 Rome ☏ 06.441.7171.
UK Embassy: Via XX Settembre 80a, 00187 Rome ☏ 06.4220.0001, ⓦ www.britain.it. Consulate in Florence: Lungarno Corsini 2 ☏ 055.284.133.
US Embassy: Via V Veneto 119/a, 00187 Rome ☏ 06.46.741, ⓦ www.usembassy.it. Consulate in Florence: Lungarno Vespucci 38 ☏ 055.239.8276, ⓦ www.usis.it/florence.

Information, websites and maps

Before you leave home, you might want to contact the Italian State Tourist Office (ENIT) for a selection of maps and accommodation listings – though you can usually pick up much the same information from tourist offices in Italy.

Most Italian towns, major train stations and airports have a **tourist office**, variously signed as "APT" (Azienda Promozione Turistica). Some are more useful and helpful than others, but all should be able to provide at least a town plan and local listings guide. In smaller villages there is sometimes a "Pro Loco" office that has much the same kind of information, but with staff who are less likely to speak English. **Opening hours** also vary: larger city and resort offices are likely to be open Mon–Sat 9am–7pm, often closing for an hour at lunch, and they're sometimes open for a short period on Sunday mornings; smaller offices may open weekdays only, while times for Pro Loco offices are notoriously erratic – some open for only a couple of hours a day, even in summer.

ENIT offices

Worldwide listing at ⓦ www.enit.it.
Australia Level 26, 44 Market St, Sydney, NSW 2000 ☎ 02/9962 1666, ⓔ enitour@ihug.com.au.
Canada 175 Bloor St East #907, South Tower, Toronto, ON, M4W 3R8 ☎ 416/925 4882, ⓦ www.italiantourism.com.
Ireland 63 Northumberland Rd, Dublin ☎ 01/660 1744.
New Zealand 34 Grant Rd, Thorndon, Wellington ☎ 04/473 5339.
UK 1 Princes St, London W1B 2AY ☎ 020/7408 1254, ⓦ www.italiantouristboard.co.uk.
US 630 5th Ave #1565, New York NY 10111 ☎ 212/245 4822; 500 N Michigan Ave #2240, Chicago, IL 60611 ☎ 312/644 0996; 12400 Wilshire Blvd #550, Los Angeles, CA 90025 ☎ 310/820 1898, ⓦ www.italiantourism.com.

Websites

Virtually every town council in Tuscany and Umbria, large or small, has its own **website**; the most useful of these are listed in this guide, but others can be found simply by typing the name of the town plus the word "comune" into your search engine. Sites are usually up to date, include useful information such as opening times and details of festivals, and offer links to more specialized sites. What follows is a list of sources for more general information.

ⓦ **www.enit.it** Italian State Tourist Board.
ⓦ **www.turismo.toscana.it** Official website of the Tuscan tourist board.
ⓦ **www.turismo.umbria.it** The same for Umbria.
ⓦ **www.itwg.com** Italy's reliable and comprehensive tourist web guide, with up-to-date travel information.
ⓦ **www.zoomata.com** E-zine with loads of information about Italy today.
ⓦ **www.terraditoscana.com** Well designed, informative site covering every aspect of Tuscany from walking and sleeping to wild flowers and local cuisine.
ⓦ **www.parks.it** Details of all the national and regional parks in Tuscany and Umbria.
ⓦ **www.camping.it** Details of virtually every campsite in Italy.
ⓦ **www.museionline.it** Links to museums and exhibition sites.
ⓦ **www.tuscanydirect.it** Hundreds of links to Tuscany web pages, plus general tourist information.
ⓦ **www.umbriatravel.com** Detailed travel guide to Umbria.
ⓦ **www.firenze.net** Up-to-date information on everything that's going on in Florence: events, concerts, cinema, nightlife, restaurants.
ⓦ **www.perugiaonline.it** Perugia's official website.
ⓦ **www.assisionline.it** Detailed information for visitors to Assisi.
ⓦ **www.internettrain.it** Chain of cybercafés, present in major cities.
ⓦ **www.lega-calcio.it** Up-to-date news on Italian league football.
ⓦ **www.meteo.it** Italian weather forecast.
ⓦ **www.paginegialle.it** Italian yellow pages.

Maps

Our **maps** should be fine for most purposes; most tourist offices hand out maps of their local area as well. More detailed maps are produced by a multitude of companies, notably Italy's leading street plan publisher LAC (Litografia Artistica Cartografica), and the TCI (Touring Club Italiano), which also produces the country's best road maps: it has excellent 1:200,000 indexed maps for both Tuscany (*Toscana*) and Umbria (*Umbria e Marche*). A less detailed alternative on one sheet is Freytag & Berndt's 1:300,000 *Tuscany*, which also includes the whole of Umbria.

For **hiking** maps, go for the ever-expanding Kompass 1:50,000 series. The company produces several Tuscany maps (including *Florence-Chianti, Siena-Colline Senesi, Maremma-Argentario, Val di Chiana-Chianciano* and *Isola d'Elba*) plus some Umbrian ones (including *Perugia-Deruta, Assisi-Camerino, Gubbio-Fabriano* and *Monti Sibillini*). All the major walking areas of Tuscany and Umbria are covered by the excellent 1:25,000 Multigraphic-Wanderkarte series that you can find at most bookshops and newsstands along with other local maps: these include the 1:16,000 sheet published by the caving, climbing and walking club at Costacciaro in Umbria (northeast of Gubbio), and the 1:25,000 Universo map for the area around Norcia and the Sibillini. Italy's own state-produced maps, the IGM 1:25,000 series, are incredibly detailed but almost impossible to find; most also haven't been updated for decades.

Map outlets

UK and Ireland

Stanfords 12–14 Long Acre, London WC2E 9LP ⊤020/7836 1321, ⊛www.stanfords.co.uk.
Blackwell's Map and Travel Shop 50 Broad St, Oxford OX1 3BQ ⊤01865/793 550, ⊛maps.blackwell.co.uk, see website for branches all over the UK.
Easons 40 Lower O'Connell St, Dublin 1 ⊤01/858 3881, ⊛www.eason.ie.
Map Shop 30a Belvoir St, Leicester LE1 6QH ⊤0116/247 1400, ⊛www.mapshopleicester.co.uk.

North America

Elliot Bay Book Company 101 S Main St, Seattle, WA 98104 ⊤1-800/962-5311, ⊛www.elliotbaybook.com.
Globe Corner 28 Church St, Cambridge, MA 02138 ⊤1-800/358-6013, ⊛www.globecorner.com.
Map Link 30 S La Patera Lane, Unit 5, Santa Barbara, CA 93117 ⊤805/692-6777 or 1-800/962-1394, ⊛www.maplink.com.
Rand McNally US ⊤1-800/333-0136, ⊛www.randmcnally.com.
World of Maps 1235 Wellington St, Ottawa, ON, K1Y 3A3 ⊤1-800/214-8524, ⊛www.worldofmaps.com.

Australia and NZ

Map Shop 6–10 Peel St, Adelaide, SA 5000 ⊤08/8231 2033, ⊛www.mapshop.net.au.
Map World (Australia) 371 Pitt St, Sydney ⊤02/9261 3601, ⊛www.mapworld.net.au. Also at 900 Hay St, Perth ⊤08/9322 5733, Jolimont Centre, Canberra ⊤02/6230 4097 and 1981 Logan Road, Brisbane ⊤07/3349 6633.
Map World (New Zealand) 173 Gloucester St, Christchurch ⊤0800/627 967, ⊛www.mapworld.co.nz.
Mapland 372 Little Bourke St, Melbourne, VIC 3000 ⊤03/9670 4383, ⊛www.mapland.com.au.
Perth Map Centre 1/884 Hay St, Perth, WA 6000 ⊤08/9322 5733, ⊛www.perthmap.com.au.
Specialty Maps 46 Albert St, Auckland 1001 ⊤09/307 2217, ⊛www.ubdonline.co.nz/maps.

Insurance and health

Even though EU health care privileges apply in Italy, you'd do well to take out an insurance policy before travelling to cover against theft, loss and illness or injury.

Before paying for a new policy, however, it's worth checking whether you're already covered: some all-risks home insurance policies may cover your possessions when overseas, and many private medical schemes include cover when abroad. In Canada, provincial health plans usually provide partial cover for medical mishaps overseas, while holders of official student/teacher/youth cards in Canada and the US are entitled to meagre accident coverage and hospital in-patient benefits. Students will often find that their student health coverage extends during the vacations and for one term beyond the date of last enrollment.

After exhausting the possibilities above, you might want to contact a specialist **travel insurance** company, or consider Rough Guides' own travel insurance deal (see box). A typical travel insurance policy usually provides cover for the loss of baggage, tickets and – up to a certain limit – cash or cheques, as well as cancellation or curtailment of your journey. Most exclude so-called dangerous sports unless an extra premium is paid: in Italy this can mean scuba-diving, windsurfing

or trekking. If you do take medical coverage, ascertain whether benefits will be paid as treatment proceeds or only after you return home, and whether there is a 24-hour medical emergency number. When securing baggage cover, make sure that the per-article limit – typically under £500 – will cover your most valuable possession. If you need to make a claim, you should keep receipts for medicines and medical treatment, and in the event you have anything stolen, you must obtain an official statement from the police (either *polizia* or *carabinieri*).

Health

If you're arriving in Italy from elsewhere in Europe, North America or Australasia, you don't need any jabs. Citizens of all EU countries are entitled to emergency medical care under the same terms as the residents of the country. For British citizens, this used to mean presenting a stamped E111 form, but in late 2005 this was phased out and replaced by the new **European Health Insurance Card (EHIC)**, valid for five years. As with the E111, this can be applied for,

---

Rough Guides travel insurance

Rough Guides has teamed up with Columbus Direct to offer you travel insurance that can be tailored to suit your needs.

Readers can choose from many different travel insurance products, including a low-cost backpacker option for long stays; a short-break option for city getaways; a typical holiday package option; and many others. There are also annual multi-trip policies for those who travel regularly, with variable levels of cover available. Different sports and activities (trekking, skiing, etc) can be covered if required on most policies.

Rough Guides travel insurance is available to the residents of 36 different countries with different language options to choose from via our website – Ⓦwww .roughguidesinsurance.com – where you can also purchase the insurance.

Alternatively, UK residents should call ☎0800 083 9507, US citizens ☎1-800 749-4922 and Australians ☎1 300 669 999. All other nationalities should call ☎+44 870 890 2843.

free of charge, at UK post offices. The latest information is available online at Ⓦwww.doh.gov.uk/traveladvice. Note, however, that the EHIC won't cover the full cost of major treatment, and the high charges for medical treatment make travel insurance essential.

You normally have to pay the full cost of emergency treatment upfront – which never comes cheap – and claim it back when you get home (minus a small excess); make very sure you hang onto full doctors' reports, signed prescription details and all receipts to back up your claim.

An Italian **pharmacist** (*farmacia*) is well qualified to give advice on minor ailments and to dispense prescriptions; there's generally one open all night in the bigger towns and cities. They work on a rota system, and the address of the one currently open is posted on any *farmacia* door. If you require a **doctor** (*médico*), ask for help in the first instance at your hotel or the local tourist office. Alternatively look in the Yellow Pages (*Pagine Gialle*): some larger towns have English-speaking doctors specifically earmarked to help visitors. Follow a similar procedure if you have dental problems. Keep all receipts for treatment or medicines for later insurance claims.

If you are taken **seriously ill** or involved in an **accident**, go to the *Pronto Soccorso* (Casualty/A&E) section of the nearest hospital; in a real emergency, phone ☏113 and ask for *ospedale* or *ambulanza*. Major train stations and airports often have first-aid facilities with qualified doctors on hand.

As for potential **health risks**, should you be walking through long grass or rummaging around in old farm buildings, keep an eye out for **vipers** (*viperi*), the only snakes in Italy with a potentially fatal bite. If you're bitten you must get to a *Pronto Soccorso* as quickly as possible: pharmacies do not usually stock the serum. **Mosquitoes** (*zanzare*) can be a nuisance between June and September, especially in low-lying areas on or near the coast; most supermarkets and pharmacies sell sprays, mosquito coils and after-bite cream.

Costs, money and banks

The days are long gone when Italy was a relatively inexpensive country to visit: the glut of visitors and rounding-up effect of the introduction of the euro have conspired to increase prices. Accommodation rates in particular have soared.

Italy is one of twelve European Union countries whose currency is the **euro** (€), composed of 100 cents. There are **notes** of €500, €200, €100, €50, €20, €10 and €5, each a different colour, and **coins** of €2, €1, 50c, 20c, 10c, 5c, 2c and 1c. Coins in the eurozone (Austria, Belgium, Finland, France, Germany, Greece, Ireland, Italy, Luxembourg, the Netherlands, Portugal and Spain) have a common design on one face, but different country-specific designs on the other; regardless of the design, all are legal tender throughout.

An increasing number of tourist centres have automatic money-changing machines (notes only). Otherwise the place to change money or travellers' cheques is at a **bank**, though the process can sometimes be excruciatingly slow. There are a few banking chains that you'll find nationwide – Banca Nazionale del Lavoro, Banca d'Italia and Cassa di Risparmio – as well as regional chains like the Monte dei Paschi di Siena. **Banking hours** are normally Mon–Fri 8.30am–1pm plus an hour in the afternoon (usually 2.30–3.30pm), though there are local variations. Otherwise you can change money at larger hotels or any bureau de change (*cambio*).

Travellers' cheques, credit and debit cards

Although it's a good idea to have some cash when you first arrive (and be sure to shop around for the best exchange deal on cash – rates can vary by as much as 5 percent), it's safer to bring your money in the form of **travellers' cheques**, available from any bank or post office in the UK, and from most banks elsewhere, in various brands: American Express ⓦwww.americanexpress .com, Thomas Cook ⓦwww.thomascook .com or Visa ⓦwww.visa.com. The usual fee for travellers' cheque sales is one or two percent, though this fee may be waived if you buy the cheques through a bank where you have an account. It pays to get a selection of denominations. Make sure you keep the purchase agreement and a record of cheque serial numbers safe and separate from the cheques themselves. In the event that cheques are lost or stolen, the issuing company will expect you to report the loss forthwith to their office in Italy; most companies claim to replace lost or stolen cheques within 24 hours. You'll usually pay a small commission when you **exchange** sterling or dollar travellers' cheques – again around 1 percent of the amount changed, although some banks will make a standard charge per cheque regardless of its denomination. You shouldn't have to pay this commission in Italy if you are using euro travellers' cheques.

Credit and debit cards can be used either in an ATM (*bancomat*) or over the counter. Mastercard, Visa and American Express are accepted in most larger city stores, hotels and restaurants, but some petrol stations and smaller establishments may be reluctant to accept plastic: cash still reigns supreme in parts of Italy, so check first before embarking on a big meal out. ATMs are found even in small towns, and most accept all major cards. Be aware, however, that nearly all banks make substantial charges for cash withdrawals from ATMs abroad – you could find yourself paying a fee as high as 5.5 percent of the amount taken out.

Visa TravelMoney (see ⓦwww.visa .com) combines the security of travellers' cheques with the convenience of plastic. It's a disposable debit card, charged up before you leave home with whatever amount you like, separate from your normal banking or credit accounts. You can then access these dedicated travel funds from any ATM that accepts Visa worldwide, with a PIN that you select yourself. Citicorp and Thomas Cook/Interpayment outlets sell the card worldwide (see the website). When your money runs out, you just throw the card away. Since you can buy up to nine cards to access the same funds – useful for families travelling together – it's recommended that you buy at least one extra card as a back up in case your first is lost or stolen. The 24-hour Visa customer service line from Italy is ☏800.819.014.

Average costs

Most **basics** are inexpensive: delicious picnic meals can be put together for under £5/$9, and a pizza or plate of pasta in a cheap pizzeria or trattoria will come to around £7/$12 on average. However, in most restaurants in Florence and Siena you'll be lucky to pay less than €30 a head for a three-course meal with wine, and prices are rarely much lower in smaller towns. **Public transport** is good value: the train journey from Florence to Siena (97km) costs around £7/$12 for a second-class return. Wine is cheap, but other **drinks** are not, epsecially beer, which can cost as much as £4/$7 per pint. Accommodation in Florence and Siena is expensive, with **room rates** starting at around £50/$90 for a double room in a one-star hotel.

Overall, if you're really watching your budget – camping, hitching a little, buying food from shops and markets – you could get by on around £25/$45 per person per day; a more realistic average minimum daily budget for a couple staying in one-star hotels and eating one modest-priced meal out a day, would be in the region of £60/$110 per person. If you want to allow yourself the occasional extravagance or an intensive bout of museum-visiting, then you'll need £70/$120 per day – and in view of the disproportionate cost of single hotel rooms, a person travelling alone can expect this figure to increase by about twenty-five percent. In July and August, prices escalate along the coast and on the islands, so bear in mind that even camping can become an expensive option in high season.

Youth/student ID cards soon pay for themselves in savings, principally on international air, rail and bus fares, local transport, accommodation, entertainment, admission to larger museums and attractions, and some food outlets and courses in Florence, Siena and Perugia. Full-time students are eligible for the International Student ID Card (ISIC); anybody aged 26 or less qualifies for the **International Youth Travel Card**; and teachers qualify for the **International Teach-**er **Card** – all carrying the same benefits. Check Ⓦ www.isic.org for details of outlets selling the cards. Reductions and discounts for under-18s and over-65s are also usually available in major towns, as well as for entry into state museums.

Getting around

Use of a car is a major advantage if you want to travel extensively around Tuscany and Umbria. You can still get to all the major places by public transport but away from main routes services can be slow and sporadic. In general, trains are more convenient for longer journeys, buses for local routes. Throughout the guide, "Travel details", at the end of each chapter, lists local bus and train information.

By train

The **train** service offered by Italian State Railways (*Trenitalia*, but still often referred to as *Ferrovie dello Stato*, or FS) between major towns and cities is relatively inexpensive, reasonably comprehensive and – despite its reputation – fairly efficient. For extensive train travel in Tuscany and Umbria, however, it's worth bearing in mind that although cities such as Florence and Pisa have centrally located stations, many towns do not; usually, stations are inconveniently situated a good bus ride away from town centres, even at important, heavily visited places such as Siena and Montepulciano. To add insult to injury, you'll often find the vagaries of time-tables and routings forcing you to change trains in otherwise dull little towns such as Terontola or Orte. Perhaps most importantly, plenty of quite important places (Gubbio, the Chianti district, and whole swathes of southern Tuscany and eastern Umbria) are inaccessible by train.

Eurocity trains (EC) connect major cities across Europe, perhaps stopping at only two or three places in each country; **Cisalpino** (CIS) operates tilting Pendolino trains on trans-Alpine routes between Switzerland, Germany and Italy; **Eurostar Italia** (ES) runs between major cities and is faster and more efficient than **Intercity** (IC) trains. You need to reserve for all these services, and pay a supplement of about thirty percent of the ordinary fare. There are no supplements for the **Espresso** (EX), medium-fast trains that stop at major towns and cities, **Interregionali** (IR), similar to the Espresso, but usually with more stops, or **Regionali** (Reg), slow trains that generally stop at every station.

At train stations, separate posters are used for departures (*partenze* – usually yellow) and arrivals (*arrivi* – usually white); be careful not to confuse the two. Florence's main station has a large information centre. If you're planning to travel extensively by train it's worth buying a copy of the twice-yearly *In Treno In Tutt'Italia* timetable (€4.50), which covers the main routes and is normally on sale at train-station newsstands; make sure the booklet is valid during the period in which you want to travel. Pay attention to the **timetable notes**, which may specify the dates between which some services run ("*si effetua dal... al...*"), or whether a service is seasonal (*periodico*). The term *giornaliero* means the service runs daily, *feriale* from Monday to Saturday, *festivi* on Sundays and holidays only.

In addition to the routes operated by FS, there are a number of privately run lines, often using separate stations though charging similar fares; in cases where a private line uses an FS station (such as at Arezzo or Terni), there may often be a separate ticket counter.

The invaluable red-covered **Thomas Cook European Timetables** (ⓦwww.thomascook publishing.com) details schedules of over 50,000 trains in Europe, as well as timings of over 200 ferry routes and rail-connecting bus services. It's updated and issued every month; main changes occur in the June and October editions, which have details of the summer and winter timetables respectively.

Train services in Tuscany and Umbria

Florence is the centre of the Tuscan rail network. Two lines run westwards from the city, one of them passing through **Prato**, **Pistoia**, **Montecatini** and **Lucca** on its way to the coast at **Viareggio**, the other going through **Empoli** and **Pisa** before reaching the sea at **Livorno**. From Lucca, a picturesque line runs through the Garfagnana to **Aulla**, providing access to the Lunigiana region and connections to La Spezia and Milan. To the east, a line rises through the **Mugello** district and then loops out of Tuscany towards Faenza, roughly parallel to the route through the mountains to Bologna.

South of Florence, mainline trains follow the River Arno to **Arezzo**, then south past **Cortona** to **Chiusi**, **Orvieto** and Rome. From Arezzo, a private line branches up into the Casentino region. Just beyond Cortona, **Terontola** marks the junction for the branch line east to **Perugia**, the fulcrum of Umbria's network; several trains a day run directly from Florence to Perugia and on to **Foligno** and **Spoleto**. Trains also run directly from Florence to **Siena** – sometimes with a change at Empoli – although the direct bus journey is quicker and easier. From Siena, train routes continue southeast to Chiusi, and southwest to **Grosseto**.

Mainline trains from Rome to Genoa run along – or just inland from – the Tuscan coast, on a route linking **Orbetello**, Grosseto, Livorno, Pisa, Viareggio and the resorts of the Versilia coast, principally **Massa** and **Carrara**. At **Cecina**, near Livorno, there's a spur inland to within a few kilometres of **Volterra**, where the line abruptly ends.

All Umbria's major towns, with the exception of Gubbio, are easily accessible by train. In the west, the **Rome–Florence** route is the main artery, with branch-line connections throughout the region. Most of the high-speed services between the two cities stop at no Umbrian stations other than **Orvieto**; you'll probably have to change onto a slower train in order to reach the junction towns of Orte (for Narni and Spoleto), Chiusi (for Siena) or Terontola (for Perugia and Assisi).

From **Orte** just over the Lazio border in the south, trains run through the heart of Umbria via **Narni**, **Terni** (terminus of the FCU line; see below), **Spoleto**, **Foligno** and **Gualdo Tadino** on their way to Ancona on the coast. From Terontola on the Rome–Florence line, trains head east along the northern shore of Lago Trasimeno to **Perugia**, and on to **Assisi** and **Spello**, meeting the Rome–Ancona route at Foligno. Perugia lies midway along the **Ferrovia Centrale Umbra** (FCU), a private railway that fills some crucial gaps left by the state network, linking the city with **Terni** and **Todi** in the south, and **Città di Castello** and **Sansepolcro** in the north. Services are frequent, though trains are often replaced by buses over certain sections. A couple of trains a day also run from both Rome and Florence direct to Perugia.

Train companies

Ferrovia Centrale Umbra (FCU)
ⓣ075.572.9121, ⓦwww.fcu.it. Umbrian private line from Terni to Sansepolcro via Todi, Perugia and Città di Castello.

La Ferrovia Italiana (LFI) ⓣ0575.39.881, ⓦwww.lfi.it. Private line in eastern Tuscany, from Arezzo to Stia via Bibbiena and Poppi.

Trenitalia/Ferrovie dello Stato (FS)
ⓣ848.888.088, ⓦwww.trenitalia.it. The state-owned national network.

Tickets and fares

Fares are calculated by the kilometre: a return fare (*andata e ritorno*) is exactly twice

Ticket machines

All stations have small yellow machines at the end of the platforms or in ticket halls in which you must **stamp your ticket** immediately before getting on the train; however, don't stamp the return portion of your ticket until you embark on the return journey. If you don't validate your ticket, you become liable for an on-the-spot fine.

that of a single (*andata*). A ticket (*un biglietto*) can be bought from a station ticket office (*la biglietteria*), from some travel agents, and – to avoid long queues – from many station news kiosks or bars (for short trips). In Florence, the queues for tickets can be extremely long, so you'd be well advised to either buy a ticket the day before or allow plenty of time before your train departs. All tickets must be **validated** just before travel (see box overleaf): once validated, return tickets are valid for two months, but as a return costs the same as two singles it's hardly worth bothering with returns. Make sure you pay any **supplement** when you buy your ticket: it will cost you more if you pay on board. Children aged 4–12 pay half price; under-4s travel free.

A **reservation** (*una prenotazione*) is obligatory on Eurostar Italia trains, and worthwhile for InterCity trains in the summer. **Sleepers** (*cuccetta*) are available on most long-distance services; prices vary according to length of journey and whether or not you're sharing.

Rail passes

A rail pass is worth considering if you plan to travel extensively around Italy or are visiting the country as part of a wider tour of Europe.

The **Inter-Rail pass** (W www.inter-rail.co.uk) – available to European residents – comes in versions for over-26s, under-26s and children, and covers 26 European countries (plus Turkey and Morocco) grouped together in zones: Italy falls in Zone G, along with Greece, Turkey and Slovenia. The pass is available for 16 days (one zone only; €299, or €260 for under-26s), 22 days (two zones; €409/289) or a month (three or more zones; €559/399). The pass doesn't grant free travel between Britain and the continent, although it does give discounted travel on trains within the UK (including London–Paris by Eurostar) and cross-Channel ferries, and gives free travel on the Brindisi–Patras ferry between Italy and Greece. In Italy, Inter-Rail passengers have to pay supplements to use faster trains, but these charges are pretty low.

A **Eurail pass** (W www.raileurope.com) – for non-EU residents only – is not likely to pay for itself if you're just travelling within Italy. The pass, which you must buy before you arrive in Europe, allows unlimited first-

class train travel in Italy and sixteen other countries; it's available for fifteen days, 21 days, one month, two months or three months. There are numerous small-group, youth and saver versions, which are detailed on W www.raileurope.com.

A **Eurodomino** pass – available to anyone who has lived in the EU for at least six months – is valid for three days' (€173, or e130 for under-26s), five days' (€213/160) or eight days' (€253/190) travel within a one-month period in a specific named country.

If you're travelling exclusively in Italy by train you might consider buying a domestic **Trenitalia** pass, though you'd have to cover a lot of ground to make the price worth it. There are different passes for EU citizens not resident in Italy and non-EU citizens, and they can be bought for first- or second-class travel for between four and ten days' travel in a two-month period, with fifty percent discount for children aged 4 to 12, and 28 percent discount for 12 to 26s. The cheapest ticket, for four days of second-class travel, costs €174 ($190 for non-EU passengers). For info on Italian rail passes, visit W www.trenitalia.it.

Train information

UK

Rail Europe T 08708/371 371, W www .raileurope.co.uk. Main agents for Inter-Rail, Eurostar and Eurodomino.

North America

CIT Rail US T 1-800/CIT-RAIL, Canada T 1-800/387-0711, W www.cit-rail.com. Eurail, Europass and Italian passes.
DER Travel US T 1-888/337-7350, W www.der .com. Eurail and many individual country passes.
Europrail International T 1-888/667-9734, W www.europrail.net. Eurail and many individual country passes.
Rail Europe US T 1-877/257-2887, Canada T 1-800/361-7245, W www.raileurope.com. Official Eurail agent; also sells multinational passes and most single-country passes.

Australia and New Zealand

CIT World Travel T 02/9267 1255 or 03/9650 5510, W www.cittravel.com.au. Eurail and Italian rail passes.

Rail Europe @ www.raileurope.com. Click on "other countries" for a list of agents in Australia and NZ.
Rail Plus ☎ 1300/555 003, @ www.railplus.com .au. Sells Eurail passes.
Trailfinders ☎ 02/9247 7666, @ www.trailfinders .com.au. All Europe passes.

By bus

If you're limited to public transport and want to get to know Tuscany and Umbria thoroughly, sooner or later you'll have to use regional **buses** (*autobus* or *pullman*). Unlike the state-owned train network, there are dozens of different bus companies, known by an alphabet soup of initials, all of which are under joint public and private ownership. Some of the companies operate solely on local routes, others run nationwide between major cities; almost everywhere has some kind of bus service, but schedules can be sketchy, and are drastically reduced – sometimes nonexistent – at weekends, a fact that the timetable doesn't always make clear. Bear in mind also that in rural areas schedules are often designed with the working and/or school day in mind, meaning a frighteningly early start if you want to catch the sole bus out of town and perhaps no buses at all during school holidays.

In larger towns, the **bus terminal** (*autostazione*), where you can buy tickets and pick up timetables, is often beside the train station; in smaller towns and villages, most buses pull in at the central piazza, which may have a newsstand selling bus tickets (if not, you can buy tickets on the bus). On most routes it's usually possible to flag a bus down; the convention is to get on at the back, and get off at the front. "Can I get off?" is *"Posso scendere?"*; "the next stop" is *"la prossima fermata"*.

City buses are always cheap, usually a flat €1. In some places each ticket is valid for a single journey, in others it may be valid for any number of journeys within a set period (typically 40–60 minutes). You must always buy a ticket before getting on the bus, from local *tabacchi* or the kiosks at bus terminals and stops; you must also always validate them in the machine inside the bus. In most cities there are regular ticket checks, with hefty spot-fines issued to offenders.

Major bus companies in Tuscany and Umbria

Nationwide

Lazzi Piazza della Stazione 1, Florence ☎ 055.351.061, @ www.lazzi.it.
SITA Via Santa Caterina da Siena 15, Florence. Regional services ☎ 800.373.760, inter-regional services ☎ 055.294.955, @ www.sita-on-line.it.

Tuscany

Ataf Piazza Stazione, Florence ☎ 800.424.500, @ www.ataf.net. Florence city buses.
CAP Largo F.lli Alinari 9, Florence ☎ 055.214.637, @ www.capautolinee.it. Northern Tuscany.
CAT Via Fiume 2, Florence ☎ 055.283.400. Central and southern Tuscany.
CLAP Piazzale Giuseppe Verdi, Lucca ☎ 0583.587.897. Lucca and northern Tuscany.
COPIT Piazza Santa Maria Novella 22, Florence ☎ 055.215.451. Northern Tuscany.
Nardini Via Roma 7, Barga ☎ 0583.73.050. Barga and the Garfagnana.
RAMA Via Topazio 12, Grosseto ☎ 0564.456.745. Grosseto and the Maremma.
TRA-IN Piazza Gramsci, Siena ☎ 0577.204.246. Siena province.

Umbria

APM Pian di Massiano, Perugia ☎ 075.506.781, @ www.apmonline.com. Perugia, Gubbio, Assisi and northern Umbria.
ATC Piazzale della Rivoluzione Francese, Terni ☎ 0744.492.711. Southern Umbria, Orvieto and the Valnerina.
ASP Pian di Massiano, Perugia ☎ 075.751.145. Perugia, Assisi, Todi and northern Umbria.
SIT Via Flaminia Km127, Spoleto ☎ 0743.212.211. Spoleto and the Valnerina.
SULGA Strada dei Cappuccinelli 41/d, Perugia ☎ 0500.9641, @ www.sulga.it. Perugia to Florence and Rome.

By car

Travelling **by car** in Italy is relatively painless. The roads are good, the motorway (*autostrada*) network comprehensive, and Italian drivers rather less erratic than their reputation suggests. The secret, while driving, is to make it very clear what you're about to do, use your horn as much as possible, and then do it with conviction. Drive on the right.

Most motorways are **toll-roads**. Take a ticket as you join and pay as you exit; the amount due is flashed up on a screen in front of you. Rates aren't especially high but they can mount up on a long journey. **Speed limits** are 50kph in built-up areas, 110kph on main roads (dual carriageways) and 130kph on motorways. If you **break down**, dial ☏116 at the nearest phone and tell the operator where you are, the type of car and your number plate; the Automobile Club d'Italia (ACI) will send someone out to fix your car – at a price. Never leave anything visible in the car when parked, including the radio, and always push your aerial down or you might find it snapped off. Most cities and ports have paid garages where you can park safely.

Bringing your own vehicle, you need a valid full driving licence (with paper counterpart if you have a photocard licence) and an international driving permit if you are a non-EU licence holder. It's compulsory to carry your car documents and passport while you're driving: you may be required to present them if stopped by the police – not an uncommon occurrence.

Car rental is pricey, with a Fiat Panda or Renault Twingo (standard "subcompact" models) costing more than £200/$360 per week with unlimited mileage. Italian firms might be a bit cheaper than the multinationals; there are plenty of companies with desks at Pisa airport, but it usually works out cheapest to book before leaving, either by arranging a fly-drive package through a travel agent or by going direct to the rental agency. Most firms will only rent to drivers over 21 who have held a licence for a year.

Car rental agencies

Avis UK ☏0870/606 0100, ⒲www.avis.co.uk, US ☏1-800/331-1084, Canada ☏1-800/272-5871, ⒲www.avis.com, Republic of Ireland ☏01/605 7500, ⒲www.avis.ie, Australia ☏13 63 33, ⒲www.avis.com.au, NZ ☏09/526 2847, ⒲www.avis.co.nz.
Budget UK ☏0800/181 181, ⒲www.budget.co.uk, Republic of Ireland ☏0903/27711, ⒲www.budget.ie, US ☏1-800/527-0700, ⒲www.budget.com, Australia ☏1300/362 848, ⒲www.budget.com.au, NZ ☏09/976 2222, ⒲www.budget.co.nz.
Europcar UK ☏0870/607 5000, Republic of Ireland ☏01/614 2800, US & Canada ☏1-877/940

6900, Australia ☏1300 131 390, ⒲www.europcar.com.
Hertz UK ☏0870/848 4848, ⒲www.hertz.co.uk, Republic of Ireland ☏01/676 7476, ⒲www.hertz.ie, US ☏1-800/654-3001, Canada ☏1-800/263-0600, ⒲www.hertz.com, Australia ☏13 30 39, ⒲www.hertz.com.au, NZ ☏0800/654 321, ⒲www.hertz.co.nz.
Holiday Autos UK ☏0870/400 0099, Republic of Ireland ☏01/872 9366, US ☏1-800/422-7737, Australia ☏1300/554 432, New Zealand ☏0800/144 040, ⒲www.holidayautos.com.
National UK ☏0870/536 5365, ⒲www.nationalcar.co.uk, US ☏1-800/227-7368, ⒲www.nationalcar.com, Australia ☏13 10 45, ⒲www.nationalcar.com.au, NZ ☏0800/800 115, ⒲www.nationalcar.co.nz.
Thrifty UK ☏01494/751 600, ⒲www.thrifty.co.uk, Republic of Ireland ☏1800/515 800, ⒲www.thrifty.ie, US ☏1-800/367-2277, ⒲www.thrifty.com, Australia ☏1300/367 227, ⒲www.thrifty.com.au, NZ ☏09/309 0111, ⒲www.thrifty.co.nz.

Motoring organizations

Australia AAA ☏02/6247 7311, ⒲www.aaa.asn.au.
Canada CAA ☏613/247-0117, ⒲www.caa.ca.
Ireland AA ☏01/617 9988, ⒲www.aaireland.ie.
Italy TCI ☏02.852.6304, ⒲www.touringclub.it.
New Zealand AA ☏09/377 4660, ⒲www.nzaa.co.nz.
UK AA ☏0800/444 500, ⒲www.theaa.co.uk; RAC ☏0800/550 055, ⒲www.rac.co.uk.
US AAA ☏1-800/222-4357, ⒲www.aaa.com.

By bike or motorbike

Cycling is seen as more of a sport than a way of getting around: on a Sunday you'll see plenty of people out for a spin on their Campagnolo-equipped machines, but you'll not come across many luggage-laden tourers. Only in major towns will you find a shop stocking spares for non-racing bikes, so make sure you take a supply of inner tubes, spokes and any other bits you think might be handy. On the islands, in major resorts and in the larger cities it's usually possible to **rent a bike**, but rental facilities elsewhere are few and far between.

An alternative is to tour by **motorbike**, though again there are relatively few places to rent one. **Mopeds** and **scooters**, on the other hand, are easier to find: many people in Italy, from kids to grandmas, ride them, and although they're not built for long-distance travel, they're ideal for shooting around towns and islands. Expect to pay around €40–50 a day rental. Wearing crash helmets is compulsory.

Hitching

Getting around exclusively by **hitchhiking** (*autostop*) could be a frustrating experience, but it's feasible enough for the odd short hop along a quiet country road, as well as for long hauls between major towns. It's illegal to hitch on motorways, and to do so would be to risk a spot fine; stand on a slip-road or at one of the service stations. Also, be aware that few women hitch alone in Italy, and not too many in two-women pairs; if you do it, always ask where the car is headed (*"Dovè diretto?"*) before you commit yourself. If you want to get out, say, *"Mi fa scendere?"*

By ferry

In Tuscany there are three ports with ferry services: broadly, **Livorno** has services to Bastia (on Corsica) and the Tuscan island of Capraia; **Piombino** is the main point of departure for Elba (Portoferraio and smaller ports on the island), and also has some ferries to Corsica; and **Porto Santo Stefano** serves the islands of Giglio and Giannutri. Summer sailings from all ports are heavily subscribed, especially those to Elba, and booking is essential if you want to take a car across. Out of season, services are drastically reduced, and some stop altogether.

You can book tickets online via the Italian ferry website ⓦ www.traghetti.com. In Britain, sole agents for the Elba ferries out of Piombino (both Moby Lines and Toremar routings) are SMS Travel ☎ 020/7244 8422.

Ferry companies

Corsica Ferries Livorno ☎ 0586.881.380, ⓦ www.corsicaferries.com. Livorno to Corsica (Bastia).
Corsica Marittima Livorno ☎ 0586.210.507, ⓦ www.sncm.fr. Livorno to Corsica (Bastia and Porto Vecchio).
Grandi Navi Veloci (Grimaldi) Livorno ☎ 010.589.331, ⓦ www.grimaldi.it. Livorno to Sicily (Palermo).
Mareggiglio Porto Santo Stefano ☎ 0564.812.920, ⓦ www.mareggiglio.it. Porto Santo Stefano to Giglio and Giannutri.
Moby Lines Livorno ☎ 0586.826.823, Piombino ☎ 0565.225.211, ⓦ www.mobylines.it. Livorno to Sardinia (Olbia) and Corsica (Bastia); Piombino to Elba.
Sardinia Ferries Livorno ☎ 0586.881.380, ⓦ www.sardiniaferries.com. Livorno to Sardinia (Golfo Aranci).
TO.RE.MAR Livorno ☎ 0586.896.113, Piombino ☎ 0565.311.100, Porto Santo Stefano ☎ 0564.810.803, ⓦ www.toremar.it. Livorno to Capraia and Gorgona; Piombino to Elba; Porto Santo Stefano to Giglio.

Accommodation

Accommodation is a major cost in Tuscany and Umbria. The hotels are more upmarket than in most Italian regions, with a preponderance of two- and three-star places, with few really inexpensive hotels and only a scattering of hostels. Prices of hotels in all categories tend to rise annually, as there's effectively an infinite demand. Even campsites are fairly pricey. On the plus side, however, both regions have plenty of villas for rent, while two rapidly expanding sectors are bed and breakfast and *agriturismo* – farmhouse rents, similar to the French *gîtes*.

Accommodation in Italy is strictly regulated. All hotels are **star-rated** from one to five; prices are set by law for each room – rates can vary within a hotel – and must be posted at the hotel reception and in individual rooms (usually on the back of the door). Ask to see

Accommodation price codes

Throughout this guide, all accommodation prices have been graded with the codes below, indicating the cost of the least expensive double room in high season. For hostels, the rate per person for Hostelling International (HI) members has been quoted.

- ① up to €60
- ② €60–80
- ③ €80–100
- ④ €100–130
- ⑤ €130–160
- ⑥ €160–200
- ⑦ €200–250
- ⑧ €250–300
- ⑨ over €300

a variety of rooms if the first you're shown is too expensive or not up to scratch; there may be cheaper rooms available, perhaps without a private bathroom. Most tourist offices carry full **lists of hotels** and other accommodation such as private rooms and *agriturismo* options. They may be able to help you find a room at short notice, but few have dedicated accommodation services.

In popular resorts and cities it is essential to **book rooms in advance**, especially for high summer and around Easter and Christmas. In Florence the high season lasts most of the year, with a relative lull only in November, January and February – though some hotels reduce their prices in August, the month when most Italians decamp to the coast or the lakes. To secure a room in Siena for any time between Easter and October requires booking six months in advance.

Always establish the full price of your room – including or excluding breakfast and other extras (tax and service charges are usually included) – before you accept it. You may find that hoteliers in small towns and resorts are open to bargaining in the low season. If you book in advance, you should also always call a day or so before arrival to **confirm your room**. If you're going to be arriving late in the evening, it's even worth another call that morning to reconfirm: it's not uncommon for cheaper places to let your room go if you haven't checked in by lunchtime.

Hotels

Hotels in Italy are known by a variety of names. Most are simply tagged **hotel** or **albergo**. Others may be called a **locanda**, traditionally the cheapest sort of inn, but now sometimes rather self-consciously applied to smart new hotels. A **pensione** was also traditionally a cheap place to stay, though the name now lacks any official status: anywhere still describing itself as a "pensione" is probably a hotel in the one-star class.

The star system is the best way to get an idea of what you can expect from a hotel, though it's essential to realize the system is based on an often eccentric set of criteria relating to facilities (say, the presence of a restaurant or an in-room TV) rather than notions about comfort, character or location. A three-star, for example, must have a phone in every room: if it hasn't, it remains a two-star, no matter how magnificent the rest of the hotel. Equally, a two-star hotel may have phones, but lack some other facility that might have taken it up a rating.

One-star hotels in Tuscany and Umbria start on average at about €40 for a double room without private bath; **two-star** hotels cost upwards of €60 for an en-suite double; **three-star** places – with a phone and a TV – tend to be around €80. **Four-star** hotels are a marked step up: everything has more polish, and in rural four-stars you'll probably get a swimming pool; prices start at around €100, but €150 is far more common (and in some establishments you can pay twice that amount). **Five-star** hotels are rare outside the major tourist centres; expect to pay more than €250 a night. Prices in Florence and Siena are much higher than anywhere else in the region: one-stars start at about €75 for a double room without private bath, two-stars are in the region of €100–150, three-stars charge around €200, four-stars start at around €250–300, and for five-star hotels you should expect to pay more than €300 a night.

In the more popular cities, especially Florence, it's not unusual for hotels to impose a **minimum stay** of three nights. Many proprietors will add the price of **breakfast** to your bill whether you want it or not; try to resist this – you can always eat more cheaply in a bar. Supplements for showers are also common in cheaper places. You can cut costs slightly by cramming three into a double room, but most hotels will charge you an extra 35 percent for this. Note also that people **travelling alone** may be hit for the price of a double room even when taking a single, although kindlier hoteliers – if they have no singles available – may offer you a double room at the single rate.

Self-catering

High hotel prices in this region, especially in Florence and Siena, are making **self-catering** an increasingly attractive proposition: for the price of a week's stay in high summer in a three-star double hotel room in central Florence you should be able to find a two-bedroomed apartment in an equally good location, or an entire villa out in the countryside. Many package company firms offer self-catering as an alternative to hotel accommodation (see p.30), but better selections of apartments and villas are provided by specialist agents such as the companies listed below and on p.30.

Bridgewater ☎0161/787 8587, ⓦwww .bridgewater-travel.co.uk. A company with over 25 years' experience of apartments in Florence, Pisa and Lucca, *agriturismo* and country hotels in Umbria, farmhouses and villas: especially strong on mostly modern houses on the Tuscan coast.

Hello Italy ☎01483/284011, ⓦwww.helloit.co.uk. Wide selection in some out-of-the-way corners of Tuscany and Umbria.

Holiday Rentals ⓦwww.holiday-rentals.co.uk. This site features some 700 properties in Tuscany and Umbria, and puts you in touch directly with the owners.

Ilios Travel ☎01444/880 350, ⓦwww.iliostravel .com. High-quality selection of country mansions and villas, one of their best being a grand palazzo in Todi.

Interhome ☎020/8891 1294, ⓦwww.interhome .com. Large international villa- and apartment-rental firm with plenty of choice in all corners of Tuscany and Umbria.

Invitation to Tuscany ☎020/7603 7111, ⓦwww.invitationtotuscany.com. Villas with pools, apartments in villa, farm and historic property complexes, plus the chance to rent these complexes (sleeping up to 25) in their entirety.

Italian Breaks ☎020/8660 0082, ⓦwww .italianbreaks.com. An excellent range of houses and apartments.

Italian Connection ☎01424/728900, ⓦwww. italian-connection.co.uk. Major upmarket operator with an array of villas and smart apartments throughout the region.

Owners' Syndicate ☎020/7801 9807, ⓦwww .ownerssyndicate.co.uk. More than 200 properties around Tuscany and Umbria.

Traditional Tuscany ☎01553/810 003, ⓦwww .traditionaltuscany.co.uk. Offers B&B in Florentine palaces and on working farms and vineyards, plus a selection of some 25 villas and converted farms at competitive prices.

Tuscan Holidays ☎015394/31120, ⓦwww .tuscanholidays.co.uk. A small company with carefully selected homes in central Tuscany, most with pools in working vineyards.

Tuscany Now ☎020/7272 5469, ⓦwww .tuscanynow.com. This company's villas are among the most luxurious in either region; also has high-quality apartments in town centres and rural locations.

Veronica Tomasso Cotgrove ☎020/7267 2423, ⓦwww.vtcitaly.com. Carefully chosen villas and apartments in both regions, including some very exclusive properties.

Private rooms and B&B

With the summer demand for accommodation, "**rooms for rent**" (*affitacamere*) signs are an increasingly common sight: wandering around towns, or driving through the countryside, you'll see signs in English or German (*Zimmer*) as well as Italian (*camere*). Local tourist offices usually have lists of rooms on offer in their area. Most rooms are in private houses and can often be rented – at a discount – by the week. They generally cost around the same price as you'd pay for a one- or two-star hotel. Many, notably in San Gimignano, are available with kitchenettes, a potentially useful way of keeping down costs.

Bed and breakfast options were introduced in 2000 to deal with the anticipated influx of visitors for Italy's millennium celebrations. The country's normally rigid and prohibitive regulations were relaxed, and the result was a new breed of accommodation in people's homes along the lines of similar establishments in the UK and elsewhere. Prices are usually comparable to private rooms, though one unexpected consequence of the changes has been the emergence of upscale and rather grand bed-and-breakfast options in castles, palaces and large private homes. Tourist offices or local commune and other websites often carry lists of B&Bs, the availability of which, like private rooms, tends to change considerably from year to year.

Hostels and student accommodation

When the extras are factored in, **hostels** don't always represent a saving for two people travelling together – especially when you take into account that some are inconveniently located and require bus journeys from the towns they serve. However, if you're travelling alone, hostels are certainly sociable and can work out very economically; many have facilities such as self-catering kitchens and bargain-basement restaurants that enable you to cut costs further. Most charge about €15 a night for a dormitory bed; you may have to add a couple of euros for breakfast and a shower. Some also offer good all-in deals (around €35 for full board).

Most hostels belong to the **Hostelling International (HI)** network (⦿www.iyhf.org), and strictly speaking you need to be an HI member to stay at them. Many, however, allow you to join on the spot, or simply charge you a small supplement. Whether or not you're an HI member, you'll need to **book ahead** in the summer months, at least two weeks to stay in major cities like Florence. The most efficient way to book – at main city hostels only – is using HI's own International Booking Network (⦿www.hostelbooking.com); for more out-of-the-way locations, you should contact the hostel direct, sending a thirty-percent deposit (or more) with your booking.

HI hostel associations

Australia ☏02/9261 1111, ⦿www.yha.org.au.
Canada ☏1-800/663-5777, ⦿www.hihostels.ca.
England & Wales ☏0870/770 8868, ⦿www.yha.org.uk.
Italy ☏06.487.1152, ⦿www.ostellionline.org.
New Zealand ☏03/379 9970, ⦿www.yha.org.nz.
Northern Ireland ☏028/9032 4733, ⦿www.hini.org.uk.
Republic of Ireland ☏01/830 4555, ⦿www.irelandyha.org.
Scotland ☏0870/155 3255, ⦿www.syha.org.uk.
USA ☏202/783-6161, ⦿www.hiayh.org.

Religious organizations

Religious organizations across Tuscany and Umbria offer cheap accommodation; big centres such as Florence and San Gimignano have them, as do the very smallest villages, such as Spello and Bevagna in rural Umbria. Often the lodgings are annexed to **convents** or **monasteries**, or pilgrim hostels, and in most cases amount to simple hotels. Most have rooms with and without bathrooms; only a few have dorm rooms with bunks. Some accept women only, others familes only or single travellers of either sex. Most have a curfew, but few, contrary to expectations, pay much heed to your coming and going. Virtually none offers meals; the notable exception to this is Assisi, where dozens of places offer food and lodgings to the vast pilgrim market. Elsewhere you may have to root convents out: they are often buried in the accommodation listings issued by tourist offices, but for this reason remain relatively unknown to the majority of travellers.

Camping

There are surprisingly few campsites in rural Tuscany and Umbria, but camping is popular along the Tuscan coast, where the sites are mostly on the upmarket side – well-equipped and expensive. Prices in high season start at around €12 per person, plus €10/15 per tent/caravan, and around €3 for each vehicle. If you're camping extensively, it's worth checking Italy's very informative camping website, ⦿www.camping.it, for details of each site and booking facilities. Camping gas for small portable stoves is easy enough to buy, either from a hardware store (*ferramenta*) or camping/sports shops.

Villas and agriturismo

Travelling with a group of people, or even just in a pair, it's worth considering renting a **villa** or **farmhouse** for a week or two. These are not too expensive if you can split costs between, say, four people, are of a consistently high standard, and often enjoy marvellous locations. British-based operators renting villas, either alone or as part of a package, are detailed on p.30.

If you want a similar experience but on a cheaper daily basis, your best bet is an **agriturismo** property, a scheme whereby farmers rent out converted barns and farm buildings. Usually these comprise a self-contained flat or building, though a few places just rent rooms on a bed-and-breakfast basis. This market has boomed over the last few years, and while some rooms are still annexed to working farms or vineyards, many are smart self-contained rural vacation properties; attractions may include home-grown food, swimming pools and a range of activities from walking and riding to archery and mountain biking. Most *agriturismi* have a minimum-stay requirement of one week in busy periods.

Tourist offices keep lists of local properties, and the Umbria regional tourist authority produces a detailed booklet (*Agriturismo Umbria Ospitalità*) containing all the region's options, available from larger tourist offices. Alternatively, you can search one of the growing number of *agriturismo* websites – there are hundreds of properties at ⓦwww.agriturismo.com, ⓦwww.agriturismo.net, ⓦwww.agriitalia.it and ⓦwww.agriturist.it.

Mountain refuges

If you're planning on hiking or climbing, or even if you're just touring by car or bike, you may want to make use of **rifugi** (mountain and highland refuges). Most huts are owned by the Club Alpino Italiano, which allows non-members to stay for €17–25 a night; a few are privately operated and may charge up to double this. Not all are away from roads: in the Sibillini in Umbria, for example, you can drive or cycle to superbly situated refuges at Forca di Presta and elsewhere, using them as a base for walking.

Rifugi in general are fairly spartan, with bunks in unheated dorms, but their locations can be magnificent, and usually leave you well placed to continue your hike the next day. You do not have to stay the night: most make their basic living selling snacks and hot meals to people coming in off the slopes. All CAI *rifugi* are obliged to take you if you turn up in person, though this may mean you end up sleeping on the floor or in the chicken shed, so it's always best to **book in advance**, either through the local tourist office, Club Alpino Italiano direct (ⓦwww.cai.it), or – best and easiest of all – direct with the *rifugi*. Addresses and phone numbers are given in the guide.

Food and drink

The traditional dishes of Tuscany are Italy's most influential cuisine: the ingredients and culinary techniques of the region have made their mark not just on the menus of the rest of Italy but also abroad. Umbrian cooking may not be accorded quite the same degree of reverence, but its produce is of equally high quality, with its truffles and ham being especially prized. And wine has always been central to the area's economy and way of life, familiar names such as Chianti and Orvieto representing just a portion of the enormous output from Tuscan and Umbrian vineyards.

Tuscan cuisine

The most important ingredient of Tuscan cooking is **olive oil**, which comes into almost every dish – as a dressing for salads, a medium for frying, or simply drizzled over vegetables and into soups and stews just

before serving. Olive-picking begins around November, before the olives are fully ripe; the oil produced from the first pressing is termed *extra virgine*, the purest and most alkaline, with less than one-percent acidity. The quality of the oil declines with subsequent pressings.

There's a detailed **menu reader** of Italian terms on p.785.

The biggest influences on Tuscan cooking are the simple rustic dishes of **Florence**, the most famous of which is *bistecca alla fiorentina*, a thick T-bone steak grilled over charcoal, usually served rare. The meat for true Florentine *bistecca* comes from the Valdichiana area south of Arezzo, from an animal no more than two and a half years old. The Florentines are also fond of the unpretentious *arista*, roast pork loin stuffed with rosemary and garlic, and of *pollo alla diavola*, a flattened chicken marinated with olive oil and lemon juice or white wine, then dressed with herbs before grilling. Wild hare features on many menus, as *lepre in dolce e forte* (cooked in wine and tomatoes with raisins, pine nuts, candied orange peel and herbs), or as *pappardelle con lepre* (noodles topped with hare, fried bacon and tomatoes). These are basically peasant meals that have become staples of the regional cuisine, as have dishes such as *trippa e zampa* – tripe with calf's feet, onions, tomatoes, white wine, garlic and nutmeg.

Each major Tuscan town has its culinary specialities, a vestige of the days when the region was divided into city states. **Pisa's** treats include black cabbage soup, newborn eels (*cieche*) fried with garlic and sage, and *torta coi bischeri*, a cake filled with rice, candied fruit, chocolate, raisins and pine nuts, and flavoured with nutmeg and liqueur. Many of the specialities of **Siena** date back to the medieval period, including *salsicce secche* (dried sausages) and *panforte di Siena*, a celebrated spicy cake of nuts and candied fruit. **Arezzo** has *acquacotta*, a soup of fried onion, tomato and bread, mixed with egg and cheese, while **Livorno** offers *cacciucco*, a mixture of fish with bread, tomatoes, garlic and white wine, and *brodatino*, a red bean and black cabbage soup.

Everywhere in the province, **soups** are central to the cuisine, the most famous being *ribollita*, a thick vegetable concoction traditionally including left-over beans (hence "reboiled"). *Pappa al pomodoro* is a popular broth with bread, tomatoes and basil

cooked to a sustaining stodge. As *secondi*, you'll find a lot of "**hunters' dishes**" (*cacciatore*), most commonly *cinghiale* (wild boar) or *pollo* (chicken). White *cannellini* **beans** are the favourite vegetables, boiled with rosemary and doused with olive oil, or cooked with tomatoes (*all'uccelletto*). Broad beans, peas, artichokes and asparagus are other much-used vegetables, but none is as typically Tuscan as **spinach**, which is served as a side vegetable, in combination with omelettes, poached eggs or fish, mixed with ricotta to make *gnocchi*, or as a filling for *crespoline* (pancakes). Spinach and green beans are often eaten cold, usually with a squeeze of lemon.

Despite some crop reductions caused by outbreaks of tree disease, **wild chestnuts** remain another staple of Tuscan cooking: there's a long tradition of specialities based on dried chestnuts and chestnut flour, such as the delicious *castagnaccio* (chestnut cake), made with pine nuts, raisins and rosemary. Sheep's milk *pecorino* is the most widespread Tuscan **cheese**, but the most famous is the oval *marzolino* from the Chianti region, which is eaten either fresh or ripened, and is often grated over meat dishes.

Dessert menus will often include *cantuccini*, hard biscuits which are dipped in a glass of Vinsanto, or *zuccotto*, a brandy-soaked sponge cake filled with cream mixed with chocolate powder, almonds and hazelnuts – like *tiramisù* elsewhere in Italy.

Umbrian cuisine

Umbria's cooking also relies heavily on rustic staples – pastas and roast meats – and tends to be simple. Umbria is, however, the only region in Italy apart from Piemonte to offer **truffles** in any abundance (see box p.672). Traditionally the white truffle is the most highly prized on account of its aroma, but locals swear by the Umbrian grey-white (*bianchetto*) variety and the black truffle that's most common to the area around Spoleto and Norcia. You're most likely to come across them with *tagliolini* (a super-fine thread of pasta that enables you to taste the truffle), as a modest sprinkling over a dish of *tagliatelle* or meat, or on *crostini* – at a price that prohibits overindulgence. Producing truffles in controlled conditions remains the

Vegetarian dishes

You can generally manage fine, travelling in Tuscany and Umbria as a **vegetarian**. If you eat fish and seafood you'll have no problem at all, but even if you don't, you'll find several pasta sauces and pizza varieties without meat, as well as good, filling salads. Beware vegetable soups, which may be made with meat stock. The only real problem is one of comprehension: many Italians don't really understand someone not eating meat, and stating the obvious doesn't always get the point across.

Saying you're a vegetarian (*"Sono vegetariano"* – or *"vegetariana"* if you're female) and asking if a dish has meat in (*"c'è carne dentro?"*) might still turn up a poultry or *prosciutto* dish. Better is to ask what a dish is made with before you order (*"com'è fatto?"*), so that you can spot the ingredients.

culinary Holy Grail, and until there's success in this field they will remain a treasured commodity.

Meat, and in particular **pork**, is the staple of the Umbrian main course, usually grilled or roasted. The region's small, free-range black pigs are famous, and have lately been joined by wild boar (*cinghiale*) – apparently *emigrés* from Tuscany, now reproducing at a prodigious rate. **Norcia** is the heart of pig country, with a superb selection of all things porcine, though other towns boast their own specialities. **Città di Castello** produces a *salame* made with spices and fennel seed; **Cascia** and **Preci** are known for their *mortadella*; **Foligno** has a distinctive dry *salame*; and **Gualdo Tadino** does a special sausage, the *soppressata*. Also look out for the extraordinary fruit-and-nut-flavoured *salame mezzafegato*. Endemic to the region is *porchetta*, a whole roast suckling pig stuffed with herbs and spices and eaten sliced in crusty white rolls. It's an Umbrian concoction that has spread through most of central Italy, widely available as a snack from markets and roadside stalls. The region's minor specialities are the tiny lentils of **Castelluccio**, the beans of **Trasimeno**, the peas from **Bettona**, and the celery and cardoons from around **Trevi**. Umbrian **olive oil**, though not hyped quite as much as the Tuscan oils, has a high reputation, especially that from around Trevi and Spoleto.

Game may crop up on some menus, most often as pigeon, pheasant or guinea fowl. It's not unknown to be offered *tordo* (thrush), usually as a paté, so if this offends your sensibilities, watch out; other songbirds are hunted, often illegally, but they're unlikely

to find their way into a restaurant. Despite Umbria's lack of a coast, some restaurants make the effort to bring in fresh **fish**, and there's a reasonably wide selection of freshwater specimens available close to lakes and mountain rivers. Trout are pulled out of the Nera, Clitunno and Sordo rivers, while lakes Piediluco and Trasimeno yield eels, pike, tench and grey mullet. **Cheeses** follow the standard variations, with the only genuine one-offs to be found in the mountains around Norcia and Gubbio.

Umbria offers the standard Italian selection of exotically named **desserts**, most of them glorified sponges or tarts. *Perugino* chocolate is outstanding, but it's available throughout Italy. One genuine novelty are the white **figs** of Amelia, mixed in a tooth-rotting combination of almonds and chocolate.

Breakfast and snacks

Most Italians start their day in a bar, their **breakfast** (*prima colazione*) consisting of a coffee and the ubiquitous *cornetto* or *brioche* – a jam-, custard- or chocolate-filled croissant, which you usually take yourself from the counter. Unfilled croissants can be hard to find; ask for *un cornetto vuoto* or *normale*. Breakfast in a hotel will often be a limp affair, usually worth avoiding, although some upper-bracket places present good breakfast buffets.

At other times of the day, **sandwiches** (*panini*) can be pretty substantial, a filled breadstick or roll for two or three euros. Specialized sandwich bars (*paninoteche*) can be found in many larger towns; grocers' shops (*alimentari*), who'll make sandwiches to order, are another standard source. Bars may also offer *tramezzini*, ready-made sliced white bread with mixed fillings – tasty and slightly cheaper than the average *panino*. Toasted sandwiches (*toast*) are common too: in a *paninoteca* you can get whatever you want toasted; in ordinary bars it's more likely to be a variation on cheese or ham with tomato.

There are a number of options for **takeaway food**. It's possible to find slices of pizza (*pizza a taglio* or *pizza rustica*) pretty much everywhere – buy it by weight (an *etto* is 100g) – while you can get pasta, chips and even hot meals in a **tavola calda**, a sort of snack bar that's at its best in the morning when everything is fresh. Some are self-service with limited seating, found mostly in the bigger towns and inside larger train stations. They are, however, a dying breed, as is the **rosticceria**, where the speciality is usually spit-roasted chicken alongside fast foods such as pizza slices, chips and hamburgers.

Other sources of quick snacks are **markets**, some of which sell take-away food from stalls, including *focacce*, oven-baked pastries topped with cheese or tomato or filled with spinach, fried offal or meat; and *arancini* or *suppli*, deep-fried balls of rice filled with meat (*rosso*) or butter and cheese (*bianco*). **Supermarkets**, also, are an obvious stop for a picnic lunch: Co-op, Conad, Standa and PuntoSma are the most common chains in Tuscany and Umbria.

Pizza

All across Italy, **pizza** comes thin and flat, not deep-pan, and the choice of toppings is fairly limited – none of the pineapple and sweetcorn variations common in Britain and America. Most are cooked in the traditional way, in wood-fired ovens (*forno a legna*): they arrive blasted and bubbling on the surface, and with a distinctive charcoal taste. **Pizzerie** range from a stand-up counter selling slices (*a taglio*) to a fully-fledged sit-down restaurant, and on the whole they don't sell much else besides pizza and drinks, though in large towns you'll come across some that also do simple pasta dishes. Some straight restaurants often have pizza on the menu too. A basic cheese-and-tomato pizza (*margherita*) costs around €3.70, a fancier variety anything up to €7; it's quite acceptable to

cut it into slices and eat it with your fingers. Check the menu reader on p.785 for a list of varieties.

Ice cream

Italian **ice cream** (*gelato*) is justifiably famous: a cone (*un cono*) or better-value "cup" (*una coppa*) are indispensable accessories to the evening *passeggiata*. Most bars have a fairly good selection, but for real choice go to a **gelateria**, where the range is a tribute to the Italian imagination and flair for display. You'll sometimes have to go by appearance rather than attempting to decipher their exotic names, many of which don't mean much even to Italians; often the basics – chocolate, strawberry, vanilla – are best. There's no problem locating the finest *gelateria* in town: it's the one that draws the crowds. The procedure is to ask for a *cono* or *coppa*, indicating the size you want.

Restaurants

Traditionally, Tuscan and Umbrian **restaurant** meals (lunch is *pranzo*, dinner is *cena*) are long and pretty solid affairs, starting with an *antipasto*, followed by a risotto or a pasta dish, leading on to a fish or meat course, cheese, and finished with fresh fruit and coffee. Even everyday meals are a miniaturized version of this. Modern minimalism has made inroads into the more expensive restaurants, but the staple fare at the majority of places is exactly what it might have been a century ago. Vegetarianism is a concept that's also been slow to catch on: within Florence, vegetarian places are pretty scarce, and outside the city you're unlikely to find many at all.

Restaurants are most commonly called either **trattorie** or **ristoranti**. Traditionally, a trattoria is a cheaper and more basic purveyor of home-style cooking (*cucina casalinga*), while a ristorante is more upmarket, with aproned waiters and tablecloths. These days, however, there's a fine line between the two, as it's become rather chic for an expensive restaurant to call itself a trattoria. It's in the rural areas that you're most likely to come across an old-style trattoria, the sort of place where there's no written menu (the waiter will simply reel off a list of what's available) and no bottled wine (it comes straight from the vats of the local farm). A true ristorante will always have a written menu and a reasonable choice of wines, though even in smart places it's standard to choose the ordinary house wine. In popular tourist towns, notably Florence, you may well find restaurants unwilling to serve anything less than a full meal: no lunchtime restraint of a pasta and salad allowed.

Increasingly, too, you'll come across **osterie**. These used to be old-fashioned places specializing in home cooking, though recently they have had quite a vogue and the *osteria* tag more often signifies a youngish ownership and clientele, and adventurous foods. Other types of restaurant include **spaghetterie** and **birrerie**, restaurant-bars that serve basic pasta dishes, or beer and snacks, and are again often youngish hangouts.

The menu and the bill

The cheapest – though not the most rewarding way – to eat in bigger city restaurants is to opt for a set price **menù turistico**. This will give you a first course (pasta or soup), main course, dessert (usually a piece of fruit), half a litre of water and a quarter litre of wine per person. Beware the increasingly common *prezzo fisso* menu, which excludes cover, service, dessert and beverages.

Working your way through an Italian menu (*la lista*, or sometimes *il menù*) is pretty straightforward. **Antipasto** (literally "before the meal") is a course generally consisting of various cold cuts of meat, seafood and various cold vegetable dishes. *Prosciutto* is a common *antipasto* dish, ham either cooked (*cotto*) or just cured and hung (*crudo*), served alone or with melon, figs or mozzarella cheese. Also very common are *crostini*, canapés of minced chicken liver and other toppings.

The next course, **il primo**, consists of soup or a risotto, polenta or pasta dish. This is followed by **il secondo** – the meat or fish course, usually served alone, except for perhaps a wedge of lemon or tomato. Watch out when ordering fish or Florence's famous *bistecca alla fiorentina*, which will usually be served by weight: 250g is usually plenty for one person, or ask to have a look at the fish before it's cooked. Anything

marked *S.Q.* or *hg* means you are paying by weight: *hg* stands for a hectogram (*etto* in Italian) – 100g, or around 4oz. Vegetables (**il contorno**) and salads (**insalata**) are ordered and served separately, and often there won't be much choice, if any: most common are beans (*fagioli*), potatoes (*patate*), and salads either green (*verde*) or mixed (*mista*).

For afters, you nearly always get a choice of fresh fruit (*frutta*) and a selection of desserts (**dolci**) often focused on ice cream or usually dull homemade flans (*torta della casa*).

At the end of the meal, ask for the bill/check (**il conto**). In many *trattorie* this amounts to no more than an illegible scrap of paper, and if you want to be sure you're not being ripped off, ask to have a receipt (*ricevuta*), something all bars and restaurants are legally bound to provide anyway. Bear in mind that almost everywhere you'll pay a **cover charge** (*pane e coperto* or just *coperto*) on top of your food of €1–1.50 a head. Legally backed efforts to do away with this, on the grounds that it amounts to charging extra for what should be incorporated in a restaurant's margins, have not yet succeeded. As well as the *coperto*, **service** (*servizio*) will often be added, generally about ten percent; if it isn't, you should perhaps **tip** about the same amount, though *trattorie* outside the large cities won't necessarily expect tips.

Drinking

Drinking is essentially an accompaniment to food: there's little emphasis on drinking for its own sake. Locals sitting around in bars or cafés – whatever their age – will spend hours chatting over one drink. And even in bars, most people you see imbibing one of the delicious Italian grappas or brandies will take just one, then be on their way. The snag is that, since Italians drink so little, prices can be high.

Bars are often very functional, brightly lit places, with a chrome counter, a Gaggia coffee machine and a picture of the local football team on the wall. There are no set licensing hours and children are always allowed in; bars often have a public phone and sell snacks and ice creams as well as drinks. People come to bars for ordinary drinking – a coffee in the morning, a quick beer, or a cup of tea – but don't generally idle away the day or evening in them. In some more rural places it's difficult to find a bar open much after 9pm. It's nearly always cheapest to drink **standing** at the counter (there's often nowhere to sit anyway), in which case you often pay first at the cash desk (*la cassa*), present your receipt (*scontrino*) to the barperson and give your order; sometimes you simply order your drink and pay as you leave. There's always a list of prices (*listino prezzi*) behind the bar. If there's waiter service, you can **sit** where you like, though bear in mind that to do this means your drink will cost perhaps twice as much, especially if you **sit outside** on the terrace. These different prices for the same drinks are shown on the price list as *bar*, *tavola* and *terrazza*.

Coffee, tea and soft drinks

One of the most distinctive smells in an Italian street is that of fresh **coffee**, usually wafting out of a bar. The basic choice is either small and black (*espresso*, or just *caffè*), or white and frothy (*cappuccino*). If you want a longer *espresso* ask for a *caffè lungo* or *americano*; a double *espresso* is *una doppia*, while a short, extra-strong *espresso* is a *ristretto*. A coffee topped with un-frothed milk is a *caffè latte*; with a drop of milk it's *caffè macchiato*; with a shot of alcohol it's *caffè corretto*. Although most places let you help yourself to sugar, a few add it routinely; if you don't want it, you can make sure by asking for *caffè senza zucchero*. Many places also now sell decaffeinated coffee (ask for the brand-name *Hag*, even when it isn't). In summer you might want to have your coffee cold (*caffè freddo*); for a real treat, ask for *caffè granita*, cold coffee with crushed ice, usually topped with cream. Hot **tea** (*tè caldo*) comes with lemon (*con limone*) as standard, unless you ask for milk (*con latte*); in summer you can drink it cold (*tè freddo*). **Milk** itself is drunk hot as often as cold, or you can get it with a dash of coffee (*latte macchiato*) and sometimes as a milkshake (*frappé*).

There are numerous **soft drinks** (*analcoliche*). A **spremuta** is a fruit juice, usually orange (*…d'arancia*), lemon (*…di limone*) or grapefruit (*…di pompelmo*), fresh-squeezed at the bar, with optional added sugar. A *succo di frutta* is a bottled fruit juice, widely drunk at breakfast. There are also crushed-ice **granite** in several flavours, and the usual range of fizzy drinks and concentrated juices: the home-grown Italian cola, Chinotto, is less sweet than Coke – good with a slice of lemon. An excellent thirst-quencher is Lemon Soda (the brand name), a widely available bitter lemon drink; Orange Soda is not as good.

Tap water (*acqua normale* or *acqua dal rubinetto*) is quite drinkable, and free in bars. **Mineral water** (*acqua minerale*) is a more common choice, either still (*senza gas, liscia, non gassata* or *naturale*) or sparkling (*con gas, gassata* or *frizzante*).

Beer and spirits

Beer (*birra*) is nearly always a lager-type brew that comes in bottles or on tap (*alla spina*) – standard measures are a third of a litre (*piccola*) and two-thirds of a litre (*media*). Commonest and cheapest are the Italian brands Peroni, Moretti and Dreher, all of which are very drinkable; to order these, either state the brand name or ask for *birra nazionale* – otherwise you may be given a more expensive imported beer. You may also come across darker beers (*birra scura* or *birra rossa*), which have a sweeter, maltier taste and resemble stout or bitter.

All the usual **spirits** are on sale and known mostly by their generic names. There are also Italian brands of the main varieties: the best local brandies are Stock and Vecchia Romagna. A generous shot of these costs about €2, much more for imported stuff or in smart city bars. The home-grown Italian firewater is **grappa**, originally from Bassano di Grappa in the Veneto but now produced just about everywhere. Grappas are made from the leftovers of the winemaking process (skins, stalks and the like) and drunk as *digestivi* after a meal. The best Tuscan varieties are from Montalcino (Brunello) and Montepulciano.

You'll also find **fortified wines** like Martini, Cinzano and Campari. For the real thing, order *un Campari bitter*; ask for a "Camparisoda" and you'll get a ready-mixed version from a little bottle. Lemon Soda (see above) and Campari bitter makes a delicious and dangerously drinkable combination. The non-alcoholic Crodino, easily recognizable by its lurid orange colour, is also a popular *aperitivo*. You might also try Cynar, an artichoke-based sherry-type liquid often drunk as an aperitif.

There's a daunting selection of **liqueurs**. Amaro is a bitter after-dinner drink, and probably the most popular way among Italians to round off a meal. The top brands, in rising order of bitterness, are Montenegro, Ramazotti, Averna and Fernet-Branca. Amaretto is a much sweeter concoction with a strong taste of marzipan. Sambuca is a sticky-sweet aniseed brew, often served with a coffee bean in it and set on fire. Strega is another drink you'll see in every bar – the yellow stuff in elongated bottles: it's as sweet as it looks but not unpleasant. Also popular, though considered slightly naff in Italy, is *limoncello*, a bitter-sweet lemon spirit that's becoming increasingly trendy abroad.

Wine

Pursuit of **wine** is as good a reason as any for a visit to Tuscany. The province constitutes the heartland of Italian wine production, with sales of Chianti accounting for much of the country's wine exports, and the towns of Montalcino and Montepulciano producing two of the very finest Italian vintages (Brunello and Vino Nobile respectively). Umbria, by contrast, is low-key, except for the white Orvieto – a long-established wine developed by the Etruscans – but is increasingly producing top-quality though as yet little-known wines.

Until recently, most Tuscan wines – including Chianti – were criticized by wine buffs for methods geared principally to high yields, low prices, and never mind the quality. However, nudged along by the **DOC** laws (see box) standards have steadily risen. Besides the finer tuning of established names, there's a

Denominazione d'Origine

The **Denominazione d'Origine** system is the key to understanding what to look for in Italian wine, but it shouldn't be seen as any sort of guarantee. The denomination is a certification of origin, not of quality, and while it may mean a wine will be drinkable, stick to it too rigidly and you could miss out.

Denomination zones are set by government decree. They specify where a certain named wine may be made, what grape varieties may be used, the maximum yield of grapes per hectare and for how long the wine should be aged. **Denominazione d'Origine Controllata** (DOC) guarantees the origin of the wine and that it has been made to the specification of the rules for the zone in which it's produced. *Vino da tavola* (table wine) is simply wine that does not conform to the DOC laws, although that doesn't necessarily mean it's bad. Currently, 309 wines are classed as DOC. **Denominazione d'Origine Controllata e Garantita (DOCG)** is the only designation that has any real meaning. Established in 1980, and awarded to only a handful of wines – notably Brunello di Montalcino, Vino Nobile di Montepulciano, Chianti, Barolo and Barbaresco – this classification now extends to 24 wines, which not only have to conform to DOC laws, but are also quality tested by government-appointed inspectors.

Though it's undoubtedly true that the DOC system has helped raise standards, the laws have come under fire from both growers and critics for their rigidity, which can throw up misleading anomalies: depending on the vintage, Chianti, for instance, can denote a wine of pedigree to be treated with reverence, a quaffable lunchtime drink, or a simply appalling plonk – yet all qualify for a DOC label regardless. Some claim, too, that the restrictions of the DOCG are undermining credibility: the requirement for ageing can mean that all the fruitiness of important reds such as Barolo is destroyed, while the elevation of Albana di Romagna, a somewhat ordinary white, to DOCG status has caused consternation. Increasingly, producers in Tuscany (and elsewhere) who are eager to experiment are disregarding the rules; the sometimes expensive new wines they produce qualify as among Italy's best, and have been nicknamed "Super-Tuscans", despite still officially being labelled *vino da tavola*.

A wine checklist

Tuscany

Bianco di Pitigliano Delicate dry white from southern Tuscany.

Bianco Vergine della Valdichiana Soft dry white from the area south of Arezzo.

Brunello di Montalcino Full-bodied red from south of Siena; one of Italy's finest wines.

Carmignano A dry red produced in the region west of Florence; this area also produces Vin Ruspo, a fresh rosé.

Chianti Produced in seven distinct central Tuscan districts. Ranges from the roughest table wine to some of Italy's most elegant reds. More details on p.225.

Colline Lucchesi A soft and lively DOC red from the hills east of Lucca.

Galestro Light, dry summer white – a recent development, motivated partly by the need to find some use for the surplus of low-grade white wine produced in Chianti.

Grattamacco Produced southeast of Livorno, this non-DOC wine comes as a fruity white and a full, dry red.

Montecarlo A full and dry white – one of Tuscany's finest – from east of Lucca.

Montecucco New DOC red from Cinigiano and Civitella Paganico near Grosseto.

Monteregio di Massa Marittima Another newish DOC red from the Alta Maremma region.

Morellino di Scansano A fairly dry, robust, up-and-coming DOC red, made southeast of Grosseto.

Pomino New DOC from near Rúfina; red, white and Vinsanto.

Rosso di Montalcino A full-bodied DOC from the Montalcino area, aged less than the great Brunello di Montalcino.

Rosso di Montepulciano Excellent-value red table wine.

Sammarco Big Cabernet wine from the Chianti region.

Sassicaia Full ruby wine, best left a few years; from near Livorno.

Solaia Another Cabernet Sauvignon from the Antinori estate.

Spumante Sparkling wines are a relatively new departure in Tuscany, but vineyards all over the province are now using the *champenoise* or *charmat* method to produce quality vintages.

---

good deal of experimentation going on, with French grape varieties such as Chardonnay, Sauvignon and the Pinots being added to the blends of Tuscan wines, and producers using the French technique of *barriques*, 225-litre oak casks, for ageing reds and whites.

The snobbery associated with "serious" wine drinking remains for the most part mercifully absent. Light reds, such as those made from the *dolcetto* grape, are refrigerated in hot weather, while some full-bodied whites are drunk at or near room temperature. Wine is also **very inexpensive**: in some bars you can get a glass of good local produce for as little as €0.50, and table wine in restaurants – often decanted from the barrel – rarely costs more than €6 per litre. Major-name bottles are pricier but still very good value; expect to pay from around €10 a bottle in a restaurant, less than half that from a shop or supermarket.

Tuscan wine

The wines of **Tuscany** are predominantly based on the local Sangiovese grape, the foundation of heavyweights such as Chianti, Brunello di Montalcino and Vino Nobile di Montepulciano. Traditionally, the best Tuscan wines are reds, but new techniques have boosted the quality of many whites.

Chianti, the archetypal Italian wine, is the most difficult to characterize, as the vintages produced by the seven Chianti districts (see box p.225) vary from the lightest swillable stuff to deep-toned masterpieces aged in the cellars of ancient castles. The core of Chianti country is the Chianti Classico region between Florence and Siena, and even within this well-defined zone there are so many variables of climate and terrain that the character of the wine bottled in one estate might be entirely distinct from the neighbouring product. This

Tavernelle California-style red from western Chianti.

Tignanello Traditional Sangiovese Chianti, again from Antinori.

Vernaccia di San Gimignano Subtle dry white DOC from the hills of San Gimignano.

Vino Nobile di Montepulciano A full, classy red DOCG from around Montepulciano, south of Siena.

Vinsanto Toscano Aromatic wine, made from semi-dried grapes and sealed in casks for at least three years. Produced all over Tuscany (and Umbria too), it ranges from dry to sweet, and is often served at dessert.

Umbria

Cabernet Sauvignon di Miralduolo Purplish dry red from Torgiano.

Cervaro della Sala A new white wine, aged in French oak.

Chardonnay di Miralduolo Flowery, dry white from Torgiano, also aged in wood.

Colli Altotiberini A promising new Tiber valley DOC, best drunk young.

Colli Amerini Another new DOC, best known for its reds.

Colli Perugini Umbria's newest DOC – red, white and rosé.

Colli del Trasimeno Huge area producing reds and whites of ever-rising standard.

Decugnano dei Barbi Rosso Fruity red from near Lago di Corbara.

Montefalco From the hills close to Foligno: Montefalco Rosso, a soft, dry red, and the more robust Sagrantino di Montefalco, plus Sagrantino Passito, a superb red dessert wine (see p.637).

Orvieto Umbria's most famous DOC wine, a dry, light white, or a lightly sweet dessert wine (*abboccato*).

San Giorgio A bold, full-bodied red, made in Torgiano.

Solleone Dry, sherry-like aperitif.

Torgiano DOC region southeast of Perugia, producing both red and white wines; look out for the dry, fruity white Torre di Giano, the wood-aged white Torre di Giano Riserva, and the opulent Rubesco Riserva, one of Italy's finest reds.

---

makes it as difficult to get a full grasp of the subject of Chianti wine as it is to master the intricacies of Bordeaux, but it does make a tasting tour a highly rewarding experience.

The greatest Tuscan red, **Brunello di Montalcino**, is produced just outside the Chianti region, around the hill-town of Montalcino south of Siena. First created a little over a century ago, it's a powerful, complex and long-lasting wine, whose finest vintages sell at stratospheric prices. More accessible is the youthful **Rosso di Montalcino**, offering a cut-price glimpse of Brunello's majesty. The mighty, if inconsistent, **Vino Nobile di Montepulciano** completes the upper tier of the Tuscan wine hierarchy, and, similarly, Montepulciano has a good regular red produced by less complex methods.

Highly regarded **Carmignano**, from near Florence, traces its pedigree back to 1716, while **Pomino**, from the Mugello region, is equally ancient and consistently good, available as an excellent red and as a white made from Chardonnay and Pinot grapes. A rapidly improving alternative red DOC is **Morellino di Scansano**, from the coastal Maremma vineyards.

Non-DOC wines include some of the most fashionable Tuscan products. **Sassicaia**, produced near Livorno from Cabernet Sauvignon grapes, was described by Hugh Johnson as "perhaps Italy's best red wine". The Chianti-based Antinori estate, a pillar of the Tuscan wine establishment, joined the experimental wave in merging Sangiovese and Cabernet Sauvignon to make the top-rated **Tignanello**. Cabernet-based wines have tended to steal the limelight from other innovations in recent years, with Castello dei Rampolli's **Sammarco**, Antinori's **Solaia**, and **Tavernelle** from the Villa Banfi doing especially well in blind tastings. However, Merlot and Pinot

Noir grapes have begun to thrive in Tuscany, while **white-wine** producers are achieving excellent results with Chardonnay, Sauvignon Blanc, the Pinot varieties, and even Riesling and Gewurztraminer, usually considered to be best suited to cooler zones. Two top white wines are **Vernaccia di San Gimignano** and **Bianco di Montecarlo**, though the former is of variable quality.

Umbrian wine

Umbria has only a handful of DOC regions, many producing cheap, serviceable wine that rarely finds its way outside the region. Most are made from similar grapes and in similar ways to the workaday reds of Tuscany; however, innovation is producing ever more interesting high-quality vintages, and there's a trove of little-known wines that repay searching out.

The region's most famous liquid export, **Orvieto**, has in recent times been reduced to a shadow of its former self, as local producers realized that the world market was turning to dry, crisp wines. In response they transformed the venerable vintage of antiquity – traditionally a semi-sweet *abboccato* – into a mass-produced plonk for the supermarket shelf. More ambitious producers, however, are returning to the old wine, and with patience you'll find samples of the revamped product in and around the town. Orvieto's pre-eminence in Umbria itself has been taken over by **Grechetto**, a cheap and almost unfailingly reliable white made by countless producers across the region from the eponymous grape.

Amongst the most famous of the region's new names is Giorgio **Lungarotti** at Torgiano near Perugia, who employs new grape varieties and innovative techniques to produce some of Italy's finest wines. Anything with his name on the label should be good, and in some cases – for instance, the *Rubesco Riserva* – of almost unparalleled excellence. Other key names include **Antinori**, the big Tuscan producers, who in Umbria make wine at Sala to the north of Orvieto: look out for their *Cervaro della Sala*.

Other exponents of Umbria's quest for quality are concentrated in the new **Montefalco** DOC region, a tiny area whose wines are at last becoming obtainable outside its environs; the reds are excellent, the key producer being Adanti. Similar progress is being made in the Upper Tiber above Perugia, where much is expected of the **Colli Altotiberini** DOC. The region around Assisi and Amelia (**Colli Amerini**) is also producing ever-improving wines; again, most of the vintages are reliable, and few of them available anywhere but Umbria. The **Colli Perugini** and **Colli del Trasimeno** wines are the region's most humble; the latter include offerings from the Lamborghini vineyard – he of sports-car fame.

Communications

Post

Opening hours of main **post offices** are usually Mon–Sat 8.30am–7.30pm, although smaller offices are open mornings only (Mon–Fri 8.30am–1pm, Sat 8.30am–noon). You can also buy **stamps** (*francobolli*) in *tabacchi*, and in some giftshops in the tourist resorts. The Italian postal system is one of the slowest in Europe so if your letter is urgent make sure you send it *posta prioritaria*, which has varying rates according to weight and destination. Letters can be sent **poste restante** (general delivery) to any Italian post office by addressing them "Fermo Posta" followed by the name of the town; your surname should be double-underlined for easier identification, as filing is often diabolical: when picking items up take your passport, and – in case of difficulty – make sure they also check under your middle names and initials.

Phones

Public **phones**, run by Telecom Italia, come in various forms, usually with clear instructions in English; if you can't find a phone box, bars will often have a phone you can use – look for the yellow or red phone symbol. Some public phones accept coins, but many do not (and others have a tendency to swallow the cash before announcing that they are out of order), so you'll almost certainly have to buy a **phonecard** (*carta* or *scheda telefonica*), available from *tabacchi* and newsstands. There are two types of *carta telefonica*: one is a rigid plastic card which has a microchip in it (on some of these you have to snap off a corner of the card before inserting it into the phone box); the other is a more fragile piece of plastic that functions as a sort of credit card. With the latter type it's necessary to call a free operator number (given on the back of the card) when you use it for the first time, and to key in a PIN number for subsequent calls – a complicated process that has a high failure rate, so you're best advised to stick to the microchip variety. **Tariffs** are among the most expensive in Europe. For national calls, the off-peak period runs Mon–Fri 6.30pm–8am, then Sat 1pm until Mon 8am.

Phone numbers change with amazing frequency in Italy; if in doubt, consult the local directory – there's a copy in most bars, hotels and phone offices. Area codes are now an integral part of the number and must always be dialled, regardless of where you're calling from. Numbers beginning ☏800 are free, an English-speaking operator is on ☏170, and international directory enquiries is on ☏176.

To use your **mobile phone**, check with your provider whether it will work in Italy and what the charges will be. Technology in Italy is GSM (🌐www.gsmworld.com). Unless you have a triband phone, it's unlikely that a mobile bought for use in North America will work elsewhere. Most mobiles in Australia and New Zealand are GSM, but it pays to check before you leave home.

Phoning home from Italy

You can call abroad from nearly all public phones with an international phone card (*carta* or *scheda telefonica internazionale*). These are on sale at many newspaper kiosks and *tabacchi* and start at €5 – though you will need more than that for anything but the briefest of chats. Alternatively, you might consider a **phone charge card** from your phone company back home; most providers in Europe, North America, Australia and New Zealand have their own versions. Using a PIN number, they let you make calls from most hotel, public and private phones – via a toll-free Italian number – that are charged to your home account. Most are free to obtain, but bear in mind that rates aren't necessarily cheaper than calling from a public phone.

Without these cards, you can make **reverse-charge** or **collect calls** (*chiamata con addebito destinatario*) by dialling ☏170 and following the recorded instructions. Dialling **direct**, the off-peak period for international calls is Mon–Sat 10pm–8am and all day Sun.

To the UK ☏0044 + area code without the zero + number.
To Ireland ☏00353 + area code without the zero + number.
To the US or Canada ☏001 + area code + number.
To Australia ☏0061 + area code without the zero + number.
To New Zealand ☏0064 + area code without the zero + number.

Calling Italy from abroad

First dial your **international access code** (00 from the UK, Ireland and New Zealand; 011 from the US and Canada; 0011 from Australia), followed by **39** for Italy, followed by the full Italian number **including the leading zero**.

Email

An easy way to keep in touch while travelling is to sign up for a free internet **email** address that can be accessed from anywhere via the World Wide Web; YahooMail (🌐www.yahoo.com) and Hotmail (🌐www.hotmail.com) are the two most popular, but there are thousands of others. Once you've set up an account, you can use the company's website to pick up and send mail from any Internet café, or hotel with Internet access.

Internet points are now widespread in larger towns, tourist resorts and are even present in some of the smaller centres, though they're not always well advertised: often you'll find them hidden within a newsagent or computer shop. Reckon on paying around €4 for half an hour online, less if you're a student.

ⓦ www.kropla.com is a useful website giving details of how to plug your laptop in when abroad, phone codes around the world, and information about electrical systems in different countries.

The media

Local and national newspapers are readily available and form an essential accompaniment to bar culture: in small towns, folk are drawn to a bar for a read, not a drink. However, television plays a central role in Italian life: it's a rare household that doesn't have the TV switched on from morning to night, regardless of the poor quality of Italy's numerous local and heavily censored national channels.

Newspapers

Tuscany's major **newspaper** is the Florence-based *La Nazione* (ⓦ www.lanazione.it). This is technically a national paper but its sales are concentrated in the central provinces of Italy. It produces local editions, with supplements, including informative entertainments listings, for virtually every major Tuscan town. Umbria's intensely provincial and very widely read tabloid-format paper is the *Corriere dell'Umbria* (ⓦ www.corr.it). Of the other nationals, the centre-left *La Repubblica* and authoritative right-slanted *Corriere della Sera* are the two most widely read and available. *L'Unità*, the Democratic Left (DS) organ, has experienced hard times, even in the party's Tuscan strongholds. The most avidly read papers of all are the pink *Gazzetta dello Sport* and *Corriere dello Sport*; essential reading for the serious Italian sports fan, they devote as much attention to players' ankle problems as most papers would give to the resignation of a government. News magazines are also widely read in Italy, from the similar *L'Espresso* and *Panorama* to the lighter offerings of *Gente*, *Oggi* and *Novella 2000*.

English and **US newspapers** can be found for around twice the normal price in all the larger towns and established resorts, usually on the day of issue in bigger cities like Florence and Siena. Pan-European editions of Britain's *Guardian* and *Financial Times* and the Rome editions of the *International Herald Tribune* and *USA Today* are also usually available on the day of publication.

TV and radio

Italy's three main national **TV** channels are RAI 1, 2 and 3. Silvio Berlusconi's Fininvest runs three additional nationwide channels: Canale 5, TG4 and Italia 1. Although all six are blatantly pro-Berlusconi, the degree of sycophancy displayed on the TG4 news has reached such ludicrous heights (newscaster Emilio Fede is variously overcome by tears of joy or despair, depending on the fortunes of Berlusconi) that most Italians now tune in solely for a giggle. The other main channel is Telemontecarlo, currently reaching seventy percent of the country. Although the stories of Italian TV's stripping housewives are overplayed, the output is pretty bland across the board, with the accent on quiz shows, soaps and plenty of American imports. The RAI channels carry less advertising and try to mix the dross with above-average documentaries and news coverage. Numerous other channels concentrate on sport; if you want to see the weekend's Italian League football action, settle into a bar from 5pm on a Sunday.

While there are always exceptions, you shouldn't expect too much from a hotel TV: if satellite channels are available at all, English-language options are generally restricted to BBC World, CNN and little else.

Radio is highly deregulated in Italy, with FM so crowded that you continually pick up new stations whether you want to or not.

There are some good small-scale stations if you search hard enough, but on the whole the RAI stations are the most professional – though even with them daytime listening is virtually undiluted dance music. The **BBC World Service** (⩍www.bbc.co.uk) is in English on 648kHz medium wave most of the day; they also broadcast continuously online, as do Voice of America (⩍www.voa.gov), Radio Canada (⩍www.rcinet.ca) and others.

Opening hours, holidays and festivals

Tuscany and Umbria have no shortage of religious, traditional and cultural festivals throughout the year. Travelling through at Christmas, Easter or during the summer months you're likely to stumble across local festivals celebrating an historic event, a patron saint's day, a town's local produce or just a village knees-up.

Opening hours

Italian **opening hours** are becoming more flexible. Most shops and businesses in Tuscany and Umbria open Mon–Sat from 8 or 9am until around 1pm, and again from about 4pm until 7 or 8pm, though in the biggest towns major shops and offices increasingly work to a more standard 9am to 5pm (or later). Virtually everything except bars and restaurants – including non-motorway service stations – is **closed on Sunday**, though you might find *pasticcerie* or bakers open until Sunday lunchtime, and in bigger tourist centres all-day opening on Sunday is now common. Many non-food shops are closed on Monday mornings. Numerous businesses (restaurants included) take their annual holidays in August.

Opening hours for museums, galleries, churches and archeological sites are more than usually varied and prone to change; we've detailed them wherever possible throughout the guide.

National holidays

Whenever you visit, you may well find your travel plans disrupted by **national holidays** and local saints' days. Local religious holidays don't generally close down shops and businesses, but they do mean that accommodation space may be tight. However, everything, except some bars and restaurants, closes on Italy's official national holidays, which are:

Jan 1
Jan 6 (Epiphany)
Easter Monday
April 25 (Liberation Day)
May 1 (Labour Day)
Aug 15 (*Ferragosto*; Assumption)
Nov 1 (*Ognissanti*; All Saints)
Dec 8 (Immaculate Conception)
Dec 25
Dec 26

Festivals

Both Tuscany and Umbria have a plethora of **local festivals**, with saints' days being the most common excuse for some kind of binge. All cities, small towns and villages have their home-produced saint, whose mortal remains or image are generally paraded through the streets amid much noise and

Tuscany and Umbria festival calendar

January
Foligno *Festa di San Feliciano* (Jan 24) – traditional fair.
Trevi *Festa di Sant'Emiliano* (Jan 27) – torchlit procession.

February
Norcia Truffle and sausage festival (Feb).
Spello Olive and *bruschetta* (garlic toast) festival (Feb 5).
Viareggio and **San Gimignano** *Carnevale* (early/mid Feb).
Terni St Valentine's Day fair (Feb 14).
Assisi Holy Week celebrations.
Grassina (near Florence), **Gubbio** and **Bevagna** (near Perugia). Good Friday processions.
Florence *Scioppio del Carro* (Easter Sun) – fireworks in Piazza del Duomo.
San Miniato National kite-flying championships (1st Sun after Easter).

March
Norcia Crossbow competition (March 20–24).

April
Montecatini Terme *Fettunta* festival (April 16) – an oil and garlic speciality.
Lucca Sacred music festival (April–June).
Florence *Maggio Musicale* music festival (April–June).

May
Terni *Canta Maggio* (May 1) – parade of illuminated floats.
Assisi *Calendimaggio* (early May) – spring festival.
Gubbio *Corsa dei Ceri* (May 15) – candle race.
Foligno *Giostro della Quintana* (May 15) – medieval joust.
Massa Maríttima *Balestro del Girifalco* (1st Sun after May 19) – crossbow competition.
Cascia *Celebrazioni Ritiane* (May 21/22) – procession in honour of St Rita.
Gubbio Crossbow matches against team from Sansepolcro (last Sun).
Montespertoli Wine festival (last Sun).

June
Orvieto and **Spello** *Corpus Domini* procession (early June).
Pisa *Luminaria* torchlit procession precedes *Regatta di San Ranieri* boat race (June 16 & 17).
Spoleto *Festival dei Due Mondi* – internationally renowned month-long event; a mixture of classical concerts, films, ballet, street theatre and performance art, staged in the ancient walled town (June & July).
Pisa *Gioco del Ponte* (3rd Sun) – costumed mock battle.
Narni Experimental theatre season (June 20–30).
Florence *Festa di San Giovanni* marked by fireworks and the *Gioco di Calcio Storico* football game (week beginning June 24).
Fiesole *Estate Fiesolana* (mid-June to Aug) – music, cinema, ballet and theatre.
San Gimignano Summer festival of music and film (late June to Oct).
Bevagna *Mercato delle Gaite* (last week) – medieval crafts fair.
Campello di Clitunno Trout festival (end of June).
Piediluco *Sagra del Pesce* (end of June).

July
Siena *Palio* horse races (July 2), preceded by trial races on June 29 & 30 and July 1.
Torre del Lago *Festival Pucciniano* (July & Aug).

Perugia *Umbria Jazz* (July & Aug) – major jazz event.
Fivizzano Archery contest (2nd Sun).
Siena *Settimana Musicale* (mid-July).
Gubbio *Spettacoli Classici* (mid-July to mid-Aug) – long-established series of classical plays staged in the town's Roman amphitheatre.
Barga (near Lucca) Opera and theatre festival (second half of July).
Lucca *Festa di San Paolino* (3rd Sun) – torchlit parade and crossbow contest.
Pistoia *Giostro dell'Orso* (July 25) – jousting.
Le Ghiaie (Elba) Wine festival (last week of July).

August
Massa Maríttima Second leg of the crossbow competition (2nd Sun).
Montepulciano Food and wine festival (2nd Sun).
Città della Pieve *Festa della Fontana* (mid-Aug) – flooding of the town fountain with wine.
Lucca *Luminaria di Santa Croce* (Aug 14) – torchlit processions.
Montepulciano *Il Bruscello* (Aug 14–16) – folkloric song festival.
Cortona *Festa della Bistecca* (Aug 15) – excessive consumption of local beef.
Florence *Festa del Grillo* (Aug 15) – fair in the Cascine park.
Orvieto *Festa della Palombella* (Aug 15) – horse race.
Porto Santo Stefano *Palio Marinaro* (Aug 15) – parade and rowing race.
Siena *Palio* horse races (Aug 16), preceded by trial races on Aug 14 & 15.
Livorno *Palio Marinaro* (Aug 17) – boat races.
Città di Castello Chamber music festival (mid-Aug to early Sept).
Arezzo International choral festival (last two weeks).
Città di Castello *Festival delle Nazioni di Musica da Camera* (last week) – highly respected festival of chamber music.
Montepulciano *Bravio delle Botti* (last Sun) – barrel race through the town.

September
Todi Arts festival (ten days in Sept).
Arezzo *Giostro del Saraceno* (1st Sun) – jousting by knights in armour.
Cerreto Guidi near Empoli (1st Sun) – Renaissance processions.
Florence *Festa delle Rificolone* (Sept 7) – torchlit procession.
Prato *Festa degli Omaggi* (Sept 8) – costumed procession.
Sansepolcro Return crossbow matches against Gubbio (2nd Sun).
Greve Chianti Classico wine festival (2nd Sun).
Foligno *Torneo della Quintana* (2nd weekend) – jousting by 600 medieval knights.
Lucca *Festa della Santa Croce* (Sept 14) – procession of sacred image.
Perugia *Sagra Musicale Umbra* (last week) – classical music festival, established in 1937 and now one of the region's most prestigious cultural events.

October
Trevi *Palio dei Terzieri* (Oct 1) – cart race.
Assisi *Festa di San Francesco* (Oct 3–4) – major religious festival.
Piediluco Wine and chestnut fair (mid-Oct).
Umbértide *Sagra della Castagna* – chestnut fair (mid-Oct).

November
Perugia *Festa dei Ognissanti* (Nov 1–5) – All Saints Fair.

December
Siena *Festa di Santa Lucia* (Dec 13) – pottery fair.
Prato Display of Holy Girdle (Dec 25 & 26).

spectacle. There are plenty of other occasions for a **festa** – either to commemorate a local miracle or historic event, or to show off the local products or artistic talent. Many happen at Easter, in May or September, or around *Ferragosto* (Aug 15); local dates are detailed below.

Tickets for some cultural festivals – such as the Maggio Musicale in Florence or Spoleto's Festival dei Due Mondi – can be difficult to obtain. If you have no luck with a festival's box office, it may be worth trying **Liaisons Abroad** (Ⓦwww.liaisonsabroad.com), an agency for tickets to major Italian opera and musical events, timed museum tickets, Siena's Palio, Serie A football matches, and more.

Religious and traditional festivals

Many of the local **religious processions** have strong pagan roots, marking important dates on the calendar subsequently adopted and sanctified by the Church. **Good Friday** is also a popular time for processions, with images of Christ on the cross paraded through towns accompanied by white-robed, hooded figures singing penitential hymns. The separate motivations to make some money, have a good time and pay your spiritual dues all merge in the celebrations for a town's **saint's day**, where it's not unusual to find a communist mayor and local bishop officiating side by side.

Umbria has the edge over Tuscany in religious festivities. **Assisi** – with its Franciscan associations – has a disproportionate number of events, the biggest being the *Festa di San Francesco* (Oct 3–4), a celebration of the saint's canonization that draws religious leaders and pilgrims from all over Italy. Holy Week in Assisi attracts one of the world's biggest concentrations of nuns, monks and lesser religious fanatics, and *Calendimaggio*, celebrating Francis's more worldly youth, is also huge, lasting for a week from the first Tuesday in May. In **Cascia**, another of the region's foremost saints, Rita (as popular in some parts of Italy as the Virgin), attracts many thousands of devotees – mainly women – to the torchlight *Celebrazioni Ritiane* (May 21–22). Also heavily patronized are *Corpus Domini* in **Orvieto**, celebrated with a costumed procession and

a panoply of associated events, and **Gubbio**'s *Corsa dei Ceri* (see p.587).

In Tuscany, the best traditional festivals are of a more secular nature. Top honours go to the Palio horse races in **Siena**, which see jockeys careering around the central square in a fiercely contested spectacle. Other towns put on medieval-origin contests, too, though they are somewhat phoney, having been revived recently for commercial ends. Among the most enjoyable are the Gioco di Calcio Storico, a rough-and-tumble football game played between the four quarters of **Florence** in June, and the crossbow competitions between teams from **Gubbio** and **Sansepolcro**, held during May and September.

There's also been a revival of **carnival** (*carnevale*), the last fling before Lent, although the anarchic fun that was enjoyed in the past has generally been replaced by elegant, self-conscious affairs, with ingenious costumes and handmade masks – at their most extravagant at the coastal resort of **Viareggio**. Carnival usually lasts for the five days before Ash Wednesday; because it's connected with Easter the dates change from year to year.

Food, wine and arts festivals

Food- and **wine**-inspired festivals are more low-key affairs than the religious and traditional events, but no less enjoyable for that. They generally celebrate the edible speciality of the region to the accompaniment of dancing, music from a local brass band and noisy fireworks at the end of the evening. At Easter and through the summer and autumn there are literally hundreds of such events, most of them catering to locals rather than tourists; for details, ask at tourist offices or check the local newspapers (where you'll find them listed as *sagre*).

The ancient inter-town rivalries across Tuscany and Umbria – encapsulated neatly by the term *campanilismo*, implying that the only things that matter are those that take place within the sound of your village's church bells – find a highly positive expression in the willingness of local councils to put money into promoting their own **arts festivals**. For the size of the towns involved, the events are often almost ludicrously rich, celebrating the work of a native composer or artist by inviting major international names to perform or direct. Many festivals are given an added enjoyment by their location: in sum-mer, open-air performances are often staged in restored ancient amphitheatres, churches or town squares.

Outdoor activities

The hills, mountains, lakes and rivers of Tuscany and Umbria offer a wide range of outdoor activities. Some, such as hiking, are potentially outstanding, despite a relative lack of marked paths and good maps in many areas – though some parts of Umbria, southern Tuscany and the Alpi Apuane are well covered. Other activities, notably skiing, fail to provide the range of opportunities found in the Alpine and Abruzzese resorts to the north and the south. Cycling and riding are also first rate, and there are good – but limited – opportunities for climbing, caving, fishing, canoeing and diving.

Walking

Tuscany and Umbria offer a plethora of **walking** opportunities. The gentle pastoral landscapes of both regions are perfect for easygoing strolls, while the high-mountain terrains of areas such as the Alpi Apuane in Tuscany and Monte Cucco and the Monti Sibillini in Umbria provide the chance for longer and more challenging hikes. Spring is by far the best time to visit, with glorious wildflowers and verdant countryside from mid-April in the lowlands and late May to early June in the mountains. Temperatures are equally kind in September – midsummer is too hot for comfortable hiking – and the weather a touch more reliable, with less chance of rain than in spring, but the landscapes can be sun-scorched.

Hiking in this part of Italy, unlike the Dolomites or western Alps, is still in its infancy. You'll find very few marked **trails** or recognized footpaths, and even fewer **maps** (see p.36) of sufficient detail to let you navigate with confidence. One option is to trust the practicalities to one of the growing number of UK- and US-based walking companies offering guided or self-guided walks – with luggage transported between hotels – in both regions (see p.31).

Certain areas do have marked trails, generally the work of local enthusiasts or the **Club Alpino Italiano** (CAI). Most towns have a CAI office, but these are typically open only for a few hours one day a week: you're better off visiting a local tourist office for details of local marked trails. Such paths exist in the Alpi Apuane, Orecchiella, Monte Cucco and parts of the Monti Sibillini, as well as in other areas with an active local CAI branch, such as the Val d'Orcia south of Montalcino, parts of Elba, the Casentino, areas around Spoleto and on Monte Subasio above Assisi. Shorter trails can be found in protected parks such as the Monti dell'Uccellina in the Maremma. All CAI paths are indicated by **red and white markers**, and may be numbered, but – crucially – are often not of sufficient quality to let you follow a route confidently or safely without the backup of a map. This is especially true in the mountains, and on the long-distance routes, where marking is not as good or as coherent as in France, Switzerland or the UK.

CAI has also played a part in establishing several **long-distance paths**. These are "Garfagnana Trekking" (a 10-stage walk in the Alpi Apuani and Orecchiella from Castelnuovo del Garfagnana), "Apuane Trekking" (4–8 days from Carrara) and "Piglione

Trekking" (3 days from Metato in the southern Alpi Apuane). Another major route, the 25-day Grande Escursione Appennica, runs along the crest of the Apennines, part of a much longer, multi-regional route designed to follow the Apennines' crest from north to south.

Access is rarely a problem: as long as there is a path, marked or otherwise, and you cause no damage, you can generally roam at will. Locals are on the whole happy for you to tramp the paths and centuries-old muletracks that criss-cross their land, but have very little understanding of why you would want to walk anywhere when you could drive. Hikers are likely to be met by landowners with amused curiosity rather than hostility.

Other activities

Many of the companies that offer walking tours also offer **cycling** tours, though this is an activity where you can easily strike out alone. Unlike walking, it's also an activity that is extremely popular among Italians, and on Sunday mornings in particular you'll find a lot of fellow enthusiasts on the road.

It's as well to remember that much of Tuscany and Umbria is hilly and that summer temperatures, especially in the afternoon, are off-puttingly high. Also bear in mind that celebrated areas such as Chianti are largely wooded and so not as scenically tempting as the more open reaches of southern Tuscany or the backroads of Umbria. Many minor country roads are gravel-surfaced *strade bianche* ("white roads") and so not ideal for cycling long distances.

Riding is another activity to which both Tuscany and Umbria are well suited. Many foreign companies offer riding holidays, usually in Chianti or the Maremma (see p.31), but virtually every rural town and village has at least one stable (*un maneggio* or *club ippico*) where you can take a horse out by the hour, the day or longer. Tourist offices carry full lists of these, and of *agriturismo* accommodation options (see p.48), many of which also offer riding.

Climbing is possible in the Alpi Apuane, where the limestone and marble offer some of the best rock on the Italian peninsula. The finest climbs are on the Procinto, Pizzo

d'Uccello, Monte Nona and Pania della Croce, and in winter you can make ice climbs on Pania della Croce and the crests of Pisanino. CAI publish books on climbs in the region, available from larger bookshops in Lucca, Pisa or Florence, and you can pick up local information from CAI offices or the park office in Castelnuovo di Garfagnana (see p.292). In Umbria, there are climbs on Le Lecce and Fossa Secca around Monte Cucco, while the crags around Ferentillo (see p.695) have become one of Italy's leading free-climbing centres.

The karst formations of much of the region offers Italy's best **caving**, especially around Monte Cucco (see p.594), which has some of the world's deepest cave systems and at least twenty pots open to speleologists (some for experts only). There are almost equally good opportunities in the Alpi Apuane, including the Grotta del Vento (see p.291), which is also accessible to non-specialists. CAI offices are the best sources of information.

Italy's best **hang- and para-gliding** is also found on and around Monte Cucco, notably the Val di Ranco (see p.594), and in the Sibillini above the Piano Grande, where the thermals and steep and treeless slopes provide ideal conditions for both activities.

Fishing and watersports

You can charter boats with guides for saltwater **fishing** from any number of ports on the Tuscan coast. The region's best freshwater fishing (for trout) is on the Nera in the Valnerina (see p.664): the river is well stocked and heavily fished, but comes with a raft of regulations and licence requirements, details of which can be had from the tourist office in Terni, or from the Federazione Italiana Pesca Sportiva (FIPS), which has branches in many major towns. Fishing is also possible on lakes Trasimeno and Piediluco.

Canoeing is also practised on the Nera, though there are no organized rental possibilities. This is not the case with **sailing** and **windsurfing** up and down the Tuscan coast, where all the larger resorts have watersport rental outlets for sailboards, catamarans, Zodiacs and the like. You can also rent scuba **diving** and **snorkelling** equipment, or take guided day or night dives, especially around the key diving destinations of Monte Argentario, Elba and smaller islands such as Giannutri.

Winter sports

Downhill skiers are unlikely to make special trips to the regions' limited number of modest skiing centres. Snow is never as good or as reliable this far south as it is in the Alps or in the higher, bleaker heartlands of the Abruzzo. There's a handful of ragged runs in the Alpi Apuane and Orecchiella, and a scat-tering of lifts above Abetone on the Tuscan border with Emilia-Romagna. Umbria has a tiny, one-hotel resort at Forca Canapine in the Sibillini.

Where the regions score more highly is in **cross-country skiing**. The woodland trails of the Orecchiella, the Piano Grande below Forca Canapine, and the magnificent empty scenery of Monte Cucco are excellent and virtually untapped areas for the more adventurous cross-country skier. Recommended trails are indicated on the relevant Kompass maps.

Trouble and the police

In Tuscany and Umbria, the only trouble you're likely to come across are gangs of *scippatori* ("snatchers"), often kids, who operate in crowded streets or markets, train stations and packed tourist sights. As well as handbags, *scippatori* grab wallets, tear off any visible jewellery and, if they're really adroit, unstrap watches.

You can **minimize the risk** of this happening by being discreet: wear money in a belt or pouch; don't put anything down on café or restaurant tables; don't flash anything of value; keep a firm hand on your camera; and carry shoulder bags slung across your body, as Italian women do. It's a good idea, too, to entrust money and credit cards to hotel managers. Never leave anything valuable in your **car** and park in car parks or well-lit, well-used streets.

Italy's reputation for **sexual harassment** of women is based largely on experiences in the south of the country. However, even in the "civilized north", travelling on your own, or with another woman, you can expect to be tooted and hissed at from time to time and may attract occasional unwelcome attention in bars, restaurants or on the beach. This pestering is not usually made with any kind of violent intent, but it's still annoying and frustrating. There are a few things you can do to ward it off. Indifference is often the most effective policy, as is looking as confident as possible, walking with a purposeful stride and maintaining a directed gaze. Sitting around in **parks** – especially Florence's Cascine – it's best to pick a spot close to other people.

The police

In Italy there are several different branches of the **police**, ostensibly to prevent any single branch seizing power. You're not likely to have much contact with the Guardia di Finanza, who investigate smuggling, tax evasion and other finance-related felonies. Drivers may well come up against the **Polizia Urbana**, or town police, who are mainly concerned with traffic and parking offences,

Emergency phone numbers

Police *(Carabinieri)* ☎112
Any emergency service *(Soccorso Pubblico di Emergenza)* ☎113
Fire service *(Vigili del Fuoco)* ☎115
Roadside assistance *(Soccorso Stradale)* ☎116

and also the **Polizia Stradale**, who patrol motorways.

If you're unlucky, you may have dealings with the **Carabinieri**, dressed in military-style uniforms and white shoulder belts (they're part of the army), who deal with general crime, public order and drugs control. These are the ones Italians are most rude about, but a lot of this stems from the usual north–south divide. Eighty percent of the *Carabinieri* are from southern Italy, where joining the police is seen as one way to escape the poverty trap.

The **Polizia Statale**, the other general crime-fighting branch, enjoy a fierce rivalry with the *Carabinieri*, and are the ones to whom thefts should be reported at their base, the **Questura** (police station) – you'll find *Questura* addresses throughout the guide, and in the local phonebook. They'll issue you with a *denuncia*, an impressively stamped report form which you'll need for any insurance claims after you get home. The *Questura* is also where you should go to obtain a a visa extension or a *permesso di soggiorno*.

In any brush with the authorities, your experience will depend on the individuals you're dealing with. It's not unheard of – and is perfectly legal – to be stopped and searched simply for being young and carrying a rucksack. These are usually just routine spot checks, but don't expect easy treatment if you're picked up for any offence, especially if it's **drugs**-related. Any distinction between "hard" and "soft" drugs is blurred: everything is illegal above the possession of a small amount of marijuana "for personal use", though there's no proper definition of what this means.

Travellers with disabilities

With their steep hills, narrow cobbled streets and medieval buildings, Tuscan and Umbrian hill-towns are by no means accommodating to travellers with disabilities.

As part of the European *Turismo per Tutti* (Tourism for All) project – administered in Italy by the national disabled support organization CO.IN – museum, transport and accommodation facilities are slowly improving in Florence and some larger towns, but there's still a considerable way to go elsewhere. While stairs and steps present the most obvious difficulties – restaurants tend to have their bathrooms downstairs, for instance – other problems arise from oblivious traffic, cars parked on pavements and the sheer distances of car parks from old-town centres. Public transport is becoming more attuned, though you still need to give 24 hours' notice for porter service or special help at any train station. Away from Florence, targeted tourist information is limited, but if independent travel in the region seems too daunting then you could consider joining an organized custom-designed tour (see below).

Contacts for travellers with disabilities

UK and Ireland

Holiday Care ☎0845/124-9971, Minicom: ☎0845/124 9976, ⓦwww.holidaycare.org.uk. Provides free lists of accessible accommodation abroad.

Irish Wheelchair Association ☎01/818 6400, ⓦwww.iwa.ie. Useful information about travelling abroad with a wheelchair.

Tripscope The Vassall Centre, Gill Ave, Bristol BS16 2QQ, ☎0845/7 58 56 41 ⓦwww.tripscope .org.uk. This registered charity provides a national telephone information service offering free advice on

UK and international transport for those with a mobility problem.

North America

Access-Able www.access-able.com. Online resource for travellers with disabilities.
Directions Unlimited ☏1-800/533-5343 or 914/241-1700. Tour operator specializing in custom tours for people with disabilities.
Mobility International USA Voice and TDD ☏541/343-1284, www.miusa.org. Information and referral services, access guides, tours and exchange programmes. Annual membership $35 (includes quarterly newsletter).
Society for the Advancement of Travelers with Handicaps (SATH) ☏212/447-7284, www.sath.org. Non-profit educational organization actively representing travellers with disabilities.
Wheels Up! ☏1-888/389-4335, www

.wheelsup.com. Discounted airfares and tours for disabled travellers, plus information on financial help for holidays.

Australia and New Zealand

ACROD (Australian Council for Rehabilitation of the Disabled) ☏02/6282 4333 & 02/9554 3666. Provides lists of travel agencies and tour operators for people with disabilities.
Disabled Persons Assembly ☏04/801 9100. Resource centre with lists of travel agencies and tour operators.

Italy

Accessible Italy ☏0549.875.392, www .accessibleitaly.com. Group or individual tours to Florence and Chianti.
CO.IN ☏06.2326.9231, www.coinsociale.it. National disabled support organization.

Gay and lesbian travellers

In larger towns and cities across Tuscany and Umbria, attitudes towards homosexuality are generally tolerant. The age of consent is 16.

Florence has a thriving gay scene, matched only by the Versilia coast in the summer: **Torre del Lago** and **Viareggio** are popular resorts with plenty of gay bars, clubs and beaches. The scene in Umbria is less overt than in Tuscany but there are a couple of gay clubs in **Perugia** and **Terni**.

The national gay organization ARCI-Gay (☏051.649.3055, www.arcigay.it) has branches in most big towns; *Babilonia* (www.babiloniaweb.it) is the national gay magazine, published monthly (€5.16); and www.gay.it (in association with www .gay.com) has a wealth of information for gays and lesbians in Italy.

Contacts for gay and lesbian travellers

UK

Gay Travel www.gaytravel.co.uk. Online travel agent, offering good deals on all types of holiday. Also

lists gay- and lesbian-friendly hotels around the world.
Madison Travel ☏01273/202 532, www .madisontravel.co.uk. Established travel agents specializing in packages to gay- and lesbian-friendly mainstream destinations, and also to gay/lesbian destinations.

US and Canada

Damron Company ☏1-800/462-6654 or 415/255-0404, www.damron.com. Publisher of the *Men's Travel Guide*, a pocket-sized yearbook full of listings of hotels, bars, clubs and resources for gay men; the *Women's Traveler*, which provides similar listings for lesbians; and *Damron Accommodations*, which provides detailed listings of over 1000 accommodations for gays and lesbians worldwide.

Australia and New Zealand

Parkside Travel ☏08/8274 1222, @parkside@herveyworld.com.au. Gay travel agent associated with local branch of Hervey World Travel; all aspects of gay and lesbian travel worldwide.

Silke's Travel ☎ 1800/807 860 or 02/8347 2000, ⓦ www.silkes.com.au. Long-established gay and lesbian specialist, with the emphasis on women's travel.

Directory

Addresses These are usually written as the street name followed by the number: Via Roma 69. *Interno* refers to the flat-number, eg interno 5 (often abbreviated as int.). Confusingly, some towns (notably Florence) have two parallel systems for numbering properties, one for shops and restaurants and another for businesses and private residences; sometimes a shop or restaurant is suffixed by the letter "r", meaning that Via Garibaldi 15r might be in an entirely different place from Via Garibaldi 15. Addresses with "s/n" (*senza numero*) have no building number.

Bargaining Not really done in shops and restaurants, though you'll find you can get a "special price" for some private rooms and cheap hotels if you're staying a few days. Things like boat or bike rental and guided tours (especially out of season) are negotiable. In markets, you can in theory haggle for everything except food.

Beaches You'll have to pay for access to some of the better beaches (referred to as *lido*), plus an extra couple of euros to rent a sunbed and shade, and to use the showers all day. During winter most beaches look like rubbish dumps: nobody bothers to clean them until the season starts at Easter.

Children Kids are adored in Italy and will be made a fuss of in the street, and welcomed and catered for in bars and restaurants. Two recent laws have improved the situation for parents even further: the ban on smoking in restaurants and bars has transformed the air and made them far more family-friendly, while the law on disabled access makes it far easier to take a pushchair (*passeggino*) into museums and churches. Hotels normally charge around thirty percent extra to put a bed or cot in your room. The only hazards in summer are the heat and sun; sunblock can be bought in any pharmacy, and bonnets or straw hats in most markets. Take advantage of the less intense periods – mornings and evenings – for travelling, and use the quiet of siesta-time to recover flagging energy. The rhythms of the southern climate soon modify established patterns, and you'll find it quite natural carrying on later into the night, past normal bedtimes. In summer, it's not unusual to see Italian children out at midnight, and not looking much the worse for it.

You can buy **baby** equipment – nappies, creams and foods – in chemists. See the website ⓦ www .travelforkids.com for more information on child-friendly sights and activities in Florence and Siena.

Electricity The supply is 220V, though anything requiring 240V will work. Most plugs are two round pins: UK equipment will need an adaptor, US equipment a 220-to-110 transformer as well.

Football Tuscany's premier soccer team is Florence's Fiorentina, but at the time of going to press Livorno were also performing well in the top-flight Serie A, along with Siena and Empoli. Umbria has no teams in Serie A.

Language courses An excellent way of learning Italian is to take a package, combining accommodation with tuition. There are a great many places where you can do this, usually offering courses of varying levels of intensity for between a fortnight and three months. Reckon on paying around £490/$870 for a two-week course, including accommodation, which will normally be with an Italian family. For details, contact the long-established British Institute of Florence ⓦ www §.britishinstitute.it or the Università Italiana per Stranieri in Siena ⓦ www.unistrasi .it. Euro-Academy ⓦ www.euroacademy.co.uk and CESA Languages Abroad ⓦ www.cesalanguages. com in the UK, and Languages Abroad ⓦ www .languagesabroad.com in the US, run Italian courses in Florence.

Laundries Coin-operated laundrettes are available only in larger towns.

Public toilets Almost unheard of outside train and bus stations; usually your only option is to dive into a bar. In stations and some smarter establishments, there might be an attendant who guards the facilities, dispenses paper (*carta*) – and expects a tip of a few cents. Standards seem to be improving, although it is worth carrying your own paper supply.

Tax If you are thinking of splashing out on a designer outfit or some other expensive item, bear in mind that visitors from outside the EU are entitled to an IVA (purchase tax) rebate on single items valued at over €155. The procedure is to get a full receipt from the shop, describing the purchase in detail. This receipt must be presented to customs on your return home, and then sent back to the shop within ninety days of the date of the receipt; the shop will then refund the IVA component of the price, a saving of eighteen percent.

Time Italy is on Central European Time (CET): 1hr ahead of London, 6hr ahead of New York and 8hr behind Sydney.

Guide

Guide

1

Florence

CHAPTER 1 # Highlights

✳ **The Duomo** Climb Brunelleschi's dome, the city's signature building. **See p.94**

✳ **The Uffizi** The world's greatest collection of Italian Renaissance paintings. **See p.115**

✳ **The Bargello** Magnificent sculpture and applied arts collection. **See p.156**

✳ **Santa Maria Novella** Amazing frescoes by Masaccio, Ghirlandaio, Uccello and others. **See p.131**

✳ **San Lorenzo** Crowds flock to see *David* at the Accademia, but the Michelangelos at San Lorenzo are just as remarkable. **See p.137**

✳ **San Marco** Showcase for the devotional art of Fra' Angelico. **See p.145**

✳ **Santa Croce** Giotto's frescoes and Brunelleschi's superb Pazzi chapel. **See p.161**

✳ **Palazzo Pitti** Another top-flight art gallery, and Florence's finest garden. **See p.174**

✳ **Cappella Brancacci** Epoch-defining art in the church of Santa Maria del Carmine. **See p.181**

△ Ponte Vecchio from the west

Florence

Since the early nineteenth century, **FLORENCE** (**Firenze** in Italian) has been celebrated as the epitome of everything that is beautiful in Italian civilization: Stendhal staggered around its medieval streets in a stupor of delight, the Brownings sighed over its idyllic charms, and E.M. Forster's *A Room with a View* portrayed it as the great antidote to the bloodless sterility of Anglo-Saxon life. And for most modern visitors the first, resounding impressions of the city tend to confirm the myth. The stupendous dome of the cathedral is visible over the rooftops the moment you step out of the train station, and when you reach the Piazza del Duomo the close-up view is even more breathtaking, with the multicoloured **Duomo** rising behind the marble-clad **Baptistery**. Wander from there down towards the River Arno and the attraction still holds: beyond the **Piazza della Signoria**, site of the immense **Palazzo Vecchio**, the water is spanned by the shop-laden medieval **Ponte Vecchio**, with gorgeous **San Miniato al Monte** glistening on the hill behind it.

It has to be said, however, that intensive exploration of the city is not always a stress-free business. The wonders of Florence are known to the whole world, which means that in high season the sheer number of tourists at the major sights is overwhelming – the Uffizi, for instance, is all but impossible to get into unless you've pre-booked your tickets many days in advance. And yet, such is the wealth of monuments and artistic treasures here, it's impossible not to find the experience an enriching one. Tuscany was the powerhouse of what has come to be known as the Renaissance, and Florence – the region's dominant political and cultural centre – is the continent's supreme monument to European civilization's major evolutionary shift into modernity. The development of this new sensibility can be plotted stage by stage in the vast picture collection of the **Uffizi**, and charted in the sculpture of the **Bargello**, the **Museo dell'Opera del Duomo** and the guild church of **Orsanmichele**. Equally revelatory are the fabulously decorated chapels of **Santa Croce** and **Santa Maria Novella**, forerunners of such astonishing creations as Masaccio's frescoes at **Santa Maria del Carmine**, Fra' Angelico's serene paintings at **San Marco**, and Andrea del Sarto's work at **Santissima Annunziata**, to name just a few. During the fifteenth century, the likes of Brunelleschi and Alberti began to transform the cityscape of Florence, raising buildings that were to provide generations of architects with examples from which to take a lead, and still adorn the fabric of the city today. The Renaissance emphasis on harmony and rational design is expressed with unrivalled eloquence in Brunelleschi's interiors of **San Lorenzo**, **Santo Spirito** and the **Cappella dei Pazzi**, and in Alberti's work at Santa Maria Novella and the Palazzo Rucellai. The bizarre architecture

FLORENCE

HOTELS

Annalena	22
Antica Dimora	7
Ausonia e Rimini	12
Benvenuti	3
Cimabue	5
Genzianella	3
Giovanna	14
J & J	17
Kursaal	12
Marcella	11
Nazionale	15
Nella	14
Orto de' Medici	9
Panorama	8
Residenza JohannaDue	2
Residenza JohannaUno	4
Residenza JohleaDue	6
Residenza JohleaUno	6
Silla	21
Sorelle Bandini	19
Via Faenza 56	13

HOSTELS

Ostello Archi Rossi	10
Ostello Villa Camerata	1
Pio X – Artigianelli	20
Santa Monaca	18
Suore Oblate dell'Assunzione	16

Stadio Comunale ▲

Stazione Campo di Marte

Cimitero degli Inglesi

Innocenti

▲ Fiesole

▲ Museo Stibbert

River Mugnone

Museo Botanico

Giardino dei Semplici

Museo Archeologico

SS. Annunziata

Spedale degli Innocenti

Accademia

Scalzo

Museo di San Marco

Sant'Apollonia

Cenacolo di Foligno

Palazzo delle Mostre

Fortezza da Basso

Stazione Santa Maria Novella

Bus Station

See 'Central Florence' map for detail

Giardino della Gherardesca

▲ Prato & Pistoia

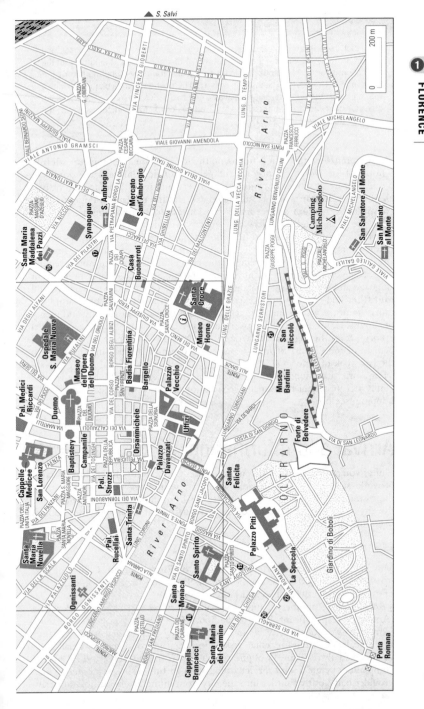

Santa Maria Maddalena dei Pazzi

Synagogue

S. Ambrogio

Mercato Sant'Ambrogio

Santa Maria Novella

Ognissanti

Pal. Rucellai

Santa Trinita

Pal. Strozzi

Cappelle Medicee

San Lorenzo

Pal. Medici Riccardi

Ospedale S. Maria Nuova

Museo dell'Opera del Duomo

Duomo

Baptistery

Campanile

Orsanmichele

Pal. Davanzati

Badia Fiorentina

Bargello

Palazzo Vecchio

Uffizi

Palazzo Davanzati

Casa Buonarroti

Santa Croce

Museo Horne

San Niccolò

Museo Bardini

Santa Felicita

Santo Spirito

Santa Monaca

Cappella Brancacci

Santa Maria del Carmine

La Specola

Palazzo Pitti

Giardino di Boboli

Forte di Belvedere

OLTRARNO

Camping Michelangiolo

San Salvatore al Monte

San Miniato al Monte

Porta Romana

River Arno

River Arno

200 m

Florentine addresses

Note that there is a double **address** system in Florence, one for businesses and one for all other properties – that, at least, is the theory behind it, though in fact the distinction is far from rigorous. Business addresses are followed by the letter **r** (for *rosso*) and are marked on the building with a red number on a white plate, sometimes with an r after the numeral, but not always. The two series are independent of each other, which means that no. 5 may be followed by no. 18r, for example, while no. 120 might be a long way from no. 120r.

of San Lorenzo's **Sagrestia Nuova** and the marble statuary of the **Accademia** – home of the *David* – display the full genius of **Michelangelo**, the dominant creative figure of sixteenth-century Italy. Every quarter of Florence can boast a church or collection worth an extended call, and the enormous **Palazzo Pitti** constitutes a museum district on its own: half a dozen museums are gathered here, one of them an art gallery that any city would envy.

So there are sights enough to fill a month, but to enjoy a visit fully it's best to ration yourself to a couple each day, and spend the rest of your time strolling and involving yourself in the life of the city. Though Florence might seem a little sedate on the surface, its university – and the presence of large numbers of language and art schools – guarantees a fair range of term-time diversions and **nightlife**. The city has some excellent **restaurants** and **café-bars** amid the tourist joints, as well as the biggest and liveliest **markets** in Tuscany, and plenty of browsable, high-quality **shops**. And there's certainly no shortage of special events – from the high-art festivities of the **Maggio Musicale** to the licensed bedlam of the **Calcio Storico**, a series of costumed football matches held in the last week of June.

For a brief introduction to the history of Florence, see p.737; for the Medici family tree (essential for dispelling confusion in the first few days of church-hopping) see p.744.

Arrival and information

Unless you're driving into the city, your point of arrival will be **Santa Maria Novella station**, which is located within a few minutes' walk of the heart of the historic centre: rail and bus connections from the three airports that serve the city all terminate at the station, as do international trains and buses from all over Tuscany and Umbria.

By air

Most scheduled and charter flights fly to **Pisa**'s Galileo Galilei airport (☎050.849.300, ⓦwww.pisa-airport.com), 95km west of Florence. For details of connections between Pisa and Florence, see p.303.

An increasing number of international air services use Florence's **Perètola** (Amerigo Vespucci) airport (☎055.306.1300, ⓦwww.aeroporto.firenze.it), 5km northwest of the city centre. There's a tiny arrivals hall with exchange machine, half a dozen car rental desks, a lost baggage counter and a small tourist office (daily 7.30am–11.30pm; ☎055.315.874). The SITA and ATAF bus companies operate a joint service called **Vola in bus** (ⓦwww.ataf.net), which provides half-hourly shuttles into the city from immediately outside the arrivals area. The first bus into the city is 6am (last 11.30pm), the first out to the airport at 5.30am (last 11pm). Tickets (€4) can be bought on board or from machines at the airport and bus station, and the journey takes around thirty minutes. Most buses arrive at and depart from the main SITA bus terminal on Via di Santa Caterina da Siena, off Piazza della Stazione, a few steps west of Santa Maria Novella train station; after 9pm, however, the buses depart from outside *Bar Cristallo* in Largo Alinari, off the eastern side of Piazza della Stazione. A **taxi** from Perètola into central Florence should cost about €15–20, and take around twenty minutes.

A few airlines use **Bologna** (ⓌWwww.bologna-airport.it) – about the same distance from Florence as Pisa – as a gateway airport for Florence. Aerobus shuttles depart every twenty minutes (7.30am–11.45pm) from outside the airport's Terminal A (Arrivi) to Bologna's main train station (about 25min), from where regular trains run to Florence's Santa Maria Novella station in about an hour. Note, however, that Ryanair services to Bologna in fact fly to Forlì airport, which is more than 60km southeast of Bologna, and very inconvenient for Florence.

By train and bus

Most **trains** arrive at Florence's main central station **Santa Maria Novella**, called "**Firenze SMN**" on the timetables. It's located just north of the church and square of Santa Maria Novella, a couple of blocks west of the Duomo. In the station you'll find left-luggage facilities (see p.211) and a 24-hour pharmacy. While in and around the station, you should keep a close eye on your bags at all times: it's a prime hunting-ground for thieves and pickpockets. Also avoid the concourse's various taxi and hotel touts, however friendly they may appear.

If you're planning to move on from Florence by train, be sure to leave yourself plenty of time to buy your ticket: the **queues** at the ticket offices and ticket machines are notorious, and you could find yourself waiting in line for half an hour.

Half a dozen **bus** companies run to Florence from various parts of Tuscany. The main operator is SITA, which has a terminal right opposite the train station at Via Santa Caterina da Siena, although all the other companies are based nearby. For addresses and routes, see p.43.

By car

Only residents are allowed to park on the streets in the centre, so you have to leave your **car** in one of the city's main car parks. North of the Arno, the car parks nearest the centre are: underneath the train station; Fortezza da Basso (usually the one with most space); Mercato Centrale; and along the Arno at Lungarno Amerigo Vespucci, Lungarno delle Grazie and Lungarno della Zecca Vecchia. South of the river the best options are Piazza del Carmine, Piazza Cestello or around Porta San Frediano (there's a cluster of car parks here). You can also find parking spaces alongside the city's main ring roads (the *Viali*). The lowest tariff you'll find is around €1 per hour; a more typical rate is €5 for two hours.

If you want to leave your car for a prolonged period, try Piazzale Michelangelo, the nearest substantial **free parking** area to the centre. It's about twenty minutes' walk to the Piazza della Signoria from here, or a short ride into the centre of town on bus #12 or #13. Watch out for a scam in which bogus car-park attendants direct you into a parking space, thus implying there's a charge: there isn't.

Florence on the Internet

Tourist information ⓦ www.firenze.turismo.it. The chief official tourist office site, with an English-language option. Useful for information on forthcoming exhibitions and hotel listings.

Firenze Online ⓦ www.fionline.it/turismo. Classy if commercially oriented site from one of Florence's main service providers, with information on art, music, theatre, cinema, shopping – and even finding a job.

Firenze.net ⓦ www.firenze.net. Smart, stylish website, packed with city info and links.

Uffizi Gallery ⓦ www.uffizi.firenze.it. The official website of the Uffizi, with images of the paintings, historical notes, news, virtual reality tours of some rooms and an index of artists.

Your Way to Florence ⓦ www.arca.net/florence.htm. The most comprehensive site, with news plus information on transport, accommodation and opening hours.

Information

For information about Florence's sights and events, the main **tourist office** is at Via Cavour 1r, five minutes' walk north of the Duomo (Mon–Sat 8.30am–6.30pm, Sun 8.30am–1.30pm; ☎055.290.832 or 055.290.833). A quieter office, run by the town council, is just off Piazza Santa Croce at Borgo Santa Croce 29r (Mon–Sat 9am–7pm, Sun 9am–2pm; ☎055.234.0444). There's also a convenient office close to the train station, to the right of the back of Santa Maria Novella church, on the far side of the large Piazza della Stazione (Mon–Sat 8.30am–7pm, Sun 8.30am–2pm; ☎055.212.245).

All three provide an adequate **map** and various leaflets, including a sheet with updated opening hours and entrance charges. The office at Via Cavour also handles information on the whole of Florence province. None of these offices will book accommodation, but can give you the names of private booking agencies. They also hand out the free information booklets *Informacittà* and *Vivifirenze*. One of the best sources of information on events is *Firenze Spettacolo* (€1.60), a monthly, partly bilingual listings magazine available from bookshops and larger newsstands.

City transport

Finding your way around central Florence is straightforward – it's just ten minutes' **walk** from Santa Maria Novella to the central Piazza del Duomo, along Via de' Panzani and Via de' Cerretani. You can't really miss these roads: stand with your back to the train station and they form the main thoroughfare sweeping away in front of you and to the left. The great majority of the major sights are within a few minutes of the Duomo.

Within the historic centre, walking is generally the most efficient way of getting around, and the imposition of the **zona a traffico limitato** (ZTL) – which limits traffic in the centre to residents' cars, delivery vehicles and public transport – has reduced the once unbearable pollution and noise. On the other hand, the ZTL has increased the average speed of the traffic, so you should be especially careful before stepping off the narrow pavements.

Buses

If you want to cross town in a hurry, or visit some of the peripheral sights, your best option is to use one of the frequent and speedy orange ATAF **buses**. Tickets are valid for unlimited travel within one hour (€1), three hours (€1.80), 24 hours (€4.50), two days (€7.60), three days (€9.60) and seven days (€16). A *Biglietto Multiplo* gives four sixty-minute tickets for €3.90. You can buy tickets from the main ATAF **information office** in the bays to the east of Santa Maria Novella train station (daily 7am–8pm; Ⓦ www.ataf.net), from any shops and stalls displaying the ATAF sign and from automatic machines all over Florence; tickets cannot be bought on buses. Once you're on board, you must stamp your ticket in the machine to begin its period of validity. There's a hefty on-the-spot **fine** for any passenger without a validated ticket.

Most of the routes that are useful to tourists stop by the station, notably #7 (for Fiesole), and #12/13: #13 goes clockwise through Piazzale Michelangelo, San Miniato and Porta Romana (all on the south side of the river), while #12 goes anti-clockwise round the same route). In addition to these, small **electric buses** run along four very convenient central city routes. Bus #A runs from the station right through the historic centre, passing close by the Duomo and Signoria, then heading east just north of Santa Croce; #B follows the north bank of the Arno; while #C descends from Piazza San Marco, heading south past Santa Croce and across the Ponte delle Grazie on its way to Via Bardi. These three buses follow similar routes on their return journeys. Bus #D leaves the station and crosses the river at Ponte Vespucci; from here it becomes a handy Oltrarno bus, running right along the south bank of the river and, on the return journey, jinking up past Palazzo Pitti, Santo Spirito and the Carmine church on its way back to the Ponte Vespucci.

Taxis

Taxis are white with yellow trim. It's difficult to flag down a cab on the street but there are plenty of central ranks: key locations include the station, Piazza della Repubblica, Piazza del Duomo, Piazza Santa Maria Novella, Piazza San Marco, Piazza Santa Croce and Piazza Santa Trìnita. You can also call a "radio taxi" on ☎055.4242, ☎055.4798 or ☎055.4390. If you do, you'll be given the car's code name – usually a town, city or country – and its number, both of which are emblazoned on the cab, together with the phone number of the company. Italians tend not to order cabs far in advance; simply call up a few minutes beforehand.

All rides are metered; expect to pay €5–8 for a short hop within the centre. Supplements on the metered fare are payable between 10pm and 6am (€2.80), all day on Sunday and public holidays (€1.65), for journeys outside the city limits (to Fiesole, for example) and for each piece of luggage placed in the boot (€0.60). If you call a cab it will arrive with a small sum on the meter, which the driver switches on when he begins the journey to pick you up.

Accommodation

Accommodation in Florence can be a problem: hotels may be plentiful but prices are high and standards often not. Worse still, the tourist invasion has very few slack spots: "low season" is defined by most hotels as meaning mid-July to the end of August (the weeks during which nearly all Italians head for the beaches or the mountains), and from mid-November to mid-March, except for the Christmas and New Year period. Between March and October you'll need to book your room well in advance or reconcile yourself to staying some way from the centre. If you're considering a package deal, check the location of your hotel carefully.

If you haven't reserved ahead, the main tourist office can give you the numbers of various private booking agencies, but there is no longer an official accommodation booking service in Florence. Be wary of resorting to touts, who hang around the queues for this office and around the station in general: some of their hotels are genuine but are likely to be expensive or far from the centre, while others are unlicensed private houses whose safety standards may be dubious.

Florence's hostels and campsites are detailed on pp.91–92. Accommodation in central Florence is marked on the **map** on pp.86–87, while more outlying places are shown on the map on pp.78–79.

Hotels

Hotels in Italy are graded on a scale running from one-star to five-star (see p.46), but bear in mind that prices in Florence are higher than anywhere else in the country except Venice: one-star establishments in this city cost as much as two-star – even three-star – places elsewhere in Tuscany. The main concentration of lowish-cost hotels is to the east of the station, centred on Via Faenza and Via Nazionale, an area that has a sizeable night-time population of assorted low-life, with pimps and prostitutes on every corner. Note that some of the places in this zone are unlicensed; if you're at all doubtful about a hotel, give it a miss. At the other end of the scale, the great majority of the top-bracket hotels are to be found within a brief stroll of Piazza della Signoria and Piazza del Duomo.

Our **price codes** (see p.46) indicate the price of each establishment's cheapest double room in high season; you will often find lower rates between mid-November and mid-March, as well in July and August. Smaller hotels may regard the whole year as peak period, but it is always worth asking, since most places will drop their prices to fill rooms. Watch out for the hidden extra cost of breakfast: some hotels include it in the room price, but many don't (it's always cheaper and often nicer to eat in a bar or café if you have the option). Prices for rooms may also vary within the same hotel, so if the first price you're quoted seems high, ask if there's anything cheaper – rooms without a private bathroom always cost less. As ever in big cities, **single rooms** are at a premium: you'll do well to get away with less than two-thirds the cost of a double. The maximum cost of a room, plus any charge for breakfast, should be posted on the back of the door; if it isn't, or if you have any other complaints, contact the tourist office. Note that many hotels require a **deposit** to secure booking, which will involve sending credit card details; if a hotel demands a cash deposit, go elsewhere.

Piazza del Duomo and Piazza della Signoria
Up to €100

Maria Luisa de' Medici Via del Corso 1 ☎055.280.048. Slightly rundown quirky one-star, on the first floor (no lift), with painting-by-numbers portraits of the Medici in the rooms. But it is comfortable, central, small (nine rooms, two with private bathroom) and quiet. No credit cards. Booking by phone only. Curfew 11.30pm. ❸

Maxim entrances at Via dei Calzaiuoli 11 (lift) and Via de' Medici 4 (stairs) ☎055.217.474, ℻055.283.729, 🌐www.hotelmaximfirenze.it. Few one-star hotels offer a better location than this friendly 26-room place just a minute from the Duomo. The clean air-conditioned double rooms are all good value; the quietest look onto a central courtyard. ❸

€100–200

Aldini Via dei Calzaiuoli 13 ☏ 055.214.752, ℻ 055.291.621, ⓦ www.hotelaldini.it. A two-star at a very convenient address on the corner of Piazza Duomo. Of its fourteen rooms, all the doubles have private bathrooms; the singles come with and without. ❺

Costantini Via dei Calzaiuoli 13 ☏ 055.213.995, ℻ 055.215.128, ⓦ www.hotelcostantini.it. This fourteen-room two-star shares a great location with the *Aldini*, on the city's main pedestrian street, close to the Duomo and Piazza della Signoria. ❺

Firenze Piazza dei Donati 4 ☏ 055.214.203, ℻ 055.212.370, ⓦ www.albergofirenze.net. Clean and central no-frills one-star hotel. It has 57 rooms, so there's a better chance of finding space here than in some of the smaller places. All rooms have private bathrooms; those on top floors enjoy a touch more daylight. No credit cards. ❹

Over €200

Benivieni Via delle Oche 5 ☏ 055.238.2133, ℻ 055.239.8248, ⓦ www.hotelbenivieni.it. This small, friendly and family-run three-star is situated between the Duomo and Piazza della Signoria, tucked away on a quiet backstreet. Fifteen smallish rooms are ranged around two floors of a former synagogue; the rooms on the upper floor are brighter but all are simple, modern and in perfect condition. As they should be: the place only opened in 2001. Doubles at around €225 – but they sometimes have rooms going at almost half that price, so it's always worth asking. ❼

Brunelleschi Piazza Santa Elisabetta 3 ☏ 055.27.370, ℻ 055.219.653, ⓦ www .hotelbrunelleschi.it. Designed by leading architect Italo Gamberini, this four-star hotel is built around a Byzantine chapel and fifth-century tower. A small in-house museum displays Roman and other fragments found during building work. Decor is simple and stylish, with the original brick and stone offset by lots of wood; the 95 rooms are spacious – the best, on the fourth floor, have views of the Duomo and Campanile. The rack rate for a double is upwards of €370, but there are often special deals to be had. ❾

Gallery Hotel Art Vicolo dell'Oro 5 ☏ 055.27.263, ⓦ www.lungarnohotels.com/gallery. This immensely stylish four-star is unlike any other hotel in central Florence. A member of the Design Hotels group, it has a sleek, minimalist and hyper-modern look – lots of dark wood and neutral colours – and tasteful contemporary art displayed in the reception and all 74 rooms. There is a small but smart bar, a sushi restaurant and an attractive lounge with art-filled bookshelves and comfortable sofas. The location is perfect, in a small, quiet square ten seconds' walk from the Ponte Vecchio. Doubles from €385 and (way) up. ❾

🏃 **Hermitage** Vicolo Marzio 1/Piazza del Pesce ☏ 055.287.216, ℻ 055.212.208, ⓦ www.hermitagehotel.com. Pre-booking is essential to secure one of the 28 rooms in this superbly located three-star hotel right next to the Ponte Vecchio, with unbeatable views from some rooms as well as from the flower-filled roof garden. The service is friendly, and rooms are cosy, decorated with the odd antique flourish; bathrooms are small but nicely done. Double-glazing has eliminated the noise problems once suffered by the front rooms, and you'll need to book many months in advance to secure one of these. ❽

Savoy Piazza della Repubblica 7 ☏ 055.27.351, ⓦ www.roccofortehotels.com. The *Savoy* had become something of a doddery old dowager before being taken in hand by the Rocco Forte group. Now it's once again one of the city's very best hotels, having been refurbished in discreetly luxurious modern style, with plenty of bare wood, stone-coloured fabrics and peat-coloured marble. And the location could not be more central. Costs vary according to the time of year and whether there are special offers, but you can expect to pay from €485 for a double, and more than €2000 for the Repubblica suite. Prices do not include breakfast. ❾

West of the centre

Up to €100

🏃 **Elite** Via della Scala 12 ☏ 055.215.395, ℻ 055.213.832. A tiny two-star run by one of the most pleasant managers in town. Five double rooms have private bathrooms; one cheaper room has a shower but shares a toilet with two single rooms. Quieter rooms are at the back. ❸

Ottaviani Piazza degli Ottaviani 1 ☏ 055.239.6223, ℻ 055.293.355, ⓔ pensioneot taviani@hotmail.com. The best of this one-star's nineteen rooms (only two with private bathrooms) overlook Piazza Santa Maria Novella; others aren't so good, but are still better than many in this category. No credit cards. ❷

€100–200

🏃 **Alessandra** Borgo Santi Apostoli 17 ☏ 055.283.438, ⓦ www.hotelalessandra .com. One of the best and friendliest of the central two-stars, with 27 rooms (20 with bathroom) occupying a sixteenth-century palazzo and furnished in a mixture of antique and modern styles. Used by the fashion-show crowd, so booking is essential in September. Discreetly signed on the street, so easy to miss. ❻

HOTELS

Aldini	**N**	Bellettini	**I**	Casci	**F**	Desirée	**A**	Gallery Hotel Art	**ee**	J.K. Place	**L**
Alessandra	**dd**	Benivieni	**Q**	Concordia	**H**	Elite	**K**	Globus	**G**	La Scaletta	**hh**
Bavaria	**W**	Bretagna	**bb**	Costantini	**N**	Erina	**B**	Helvetia & Bristol	**S**	Loggiato	
Beacci Tornabuoni	**Z**	Brunelleschi	**U**	Dali	**P**	Firenze	**O**	Hermitage	**ff**	dei Servili	**C**

▲ San Marco

CENTRAL FLORENCE

VIA GUELFA
VIA FADOLA
VIA S ROSINA
VIA DE GINORI
VIA DELLA STUFA
Accademia
SS Annunziata
Opificio delle Pietre Dure
PIAZZA SANTISSIMA ANNUNZIATA **C**
VIA DELLA COLONNA
VIA LAURA **D**

F
i
Pal. Gerini
Spedale degli Innocenti
Museo Archeologico

DE NELLI
VIA CAVOUR
Pal. Medici Riccardi
VIA RICASOLI
VIA DEI SERVI
VIA DEGLI ALFANI
S. Maria d. Angeli
PIAZZA F. BRUNELLESCHI
VIA N. DEI CACCINI
N

PIAZZA SAN LORENZO
VIA DE GORI
Pal. Niccolini
VIA DEL CASTELLACCIO
VICOLO DI PERGOLA
VIA DELLA PERGOLA

BORGO S. LORENZO
VIA MARTELLI
VIA DEI BIFO
Pal. Pucci
VIA BUFALINI
Ospedale Santa Maria Nuova
VIA DELLA PERGOLA

Palazzo Niccolini
PIAZZA S.M. NUOVA
VIA DELLA PERGOLA
BORGO PINTI
VIA FIESOLANA

PIAZZA S. GIOVANNI
Duomo
Museo dell'Opera del Duomo
Teatro della Pergola

Baptistery
PIAZZA DEL DUOMO
Museo di Firenze com'era
VIA SANT'EGIDIO

Campanile
VIA DEI CASTELLANI
Pal. dei Canonici **O**
S. Maria in Campo
VIA DELL'ORIUOLO

VIA ROMA
Loggia d. Bigallo **N**
VIA DELLA CANONICA
Museo dell'Antropologia **P**
TOSINGHI
VIA DELL' OCHE
Pal. Salviati
Pal. Altoviti
Pal. Albizi

R
VIA DE MEDICI
PIAZZA SANT' ELISABETTA **U**
BORGO DEGLI ALBIZI
Pal. Alessandri **X** PIAZZA G. SALVEMINI

T
VIA D. SPEZIALI
VIA DEL CORSO
Casa di Dante
V
Pal. Pazzi **W**
VIA DELL'ULIVO

CALIMALA
VIA DEI CALZAIUOLI
VIA TAVOLINI
VIA DANTE ALIGHIERI
VIA DEI PANDOLFINI
VIA PALMIERI

VIA ORSANMICHELE
Orsanmichele
S. Martino
Casino Borghese
VIA G. GIUSEPPE
VIA DELL'AGNOLO

DE'LAMBERTI
VIA DEI CIMATORI
Badia
VIA GHIBELLINA
VIA DEI PEPI

Mercato Nuovo
VIA DELLA CONDOTTA
Bargello
VIA DELLA VIGNA VECCHIA
Teatro Verdi
Casa Buonarroti

CALIMARUZZA
PIAZZA SAN FIRENZE
VIA D. BURELLA
VIA G. DA VERRAZZANO
VIA DEL FICO

VIA VACCHERECCIA
PIAZZA DELLA SIGNORIA
Pal. Gondi
San Firenze
VIA DELL'ANGUILLARA
VIA TORTA
S.Simone
VIA DI S. CRISTOFANO

Loggia della Signoria
VIA GONDI
BORGO DEI GRECI
PIAZZA SANTA CROCE
BORGO ALLEGRI

LAMBERTESCA
Uffizi
Palazzo Vecchio
VIA DELLA NINNA
PIAZZA DE' PERUZZI
Casa dell'Antella
VIA DI SAN GIUSEPPE

VIA DEI GIROLAMI
PIAZZA DEL GRANO
VIA DEI NERI
Pal. Rasponi **i**
Santa Croce

ARCHIBUSIERI
Pal. Vita
VIA DEI NERI
BORGO S. CROCE
VIA A. MAGLIABECHI

Museo di Storia della Scienza
VIA DEI SAPONAI
VIA DE' VAGELLAI
Museo dell'Opera di Santa Croce

PIAZZA DE GIUDICI
Borsa
PIAZZA MENTANA
VIA V. MALENCHINI
Museo Horne
CORSO DEI TINTORI
Biblioteca Nazionale

LUNGARNO GENERALE DIAZ

0   100 m

N

								HOSTELS	
Maria Luisa de' Medici	**V**	Ottaviani	**M**	Scoti	**Y**	Istituto Gould		**gg**	
Maxim	**R**	Porta Rossa	**aa**	Torre Guelfa	**cc**	Suore Oblate dello Spirito Santo		**E**	
Morandi alla Crocetta	**D**	Residenza Castiglioni	**J**						
Orchidea	**X**	Savoy	**T**						

Bretagna Lungarno Corsini 6
℡055.289.618, ℻055.289.619, ⓦwww
.hotelbretagna.net. This one-star riverfront hotel
has a superb location and rococo-style breakfast
and living rooms. The new management is increasing to six the number of rooms overlooking the
Arno, and by 2006 all 24 rooms should have en-
suite bathrooms and air-conditioning. ❹

Porta Rossa Via Porta Rossa 19 ℡055.287.551,
℻055.282.179, ⓦwww.hotelportarossa.it. Florence has smarter three-star hotels, but none as
venerable as the 78-room *Porta Rossa*, which has
been a hotel since the fourteenth century and
hosted, among others, Byron and Stendhal. You
come here for character and nineteenth-century
ambience, rather than luxurious modern touches.
Doubles (five have baths, the rest have showers)
cost from €150, or for €100 more you can splash
out on one of the two fabulous tower rooms. ❻

Scoti Via de' Tornabuoni 7 ℡ & ℻055.292.128,
ⓦwww.hotelscoti.com. The best budget option
on this notoriously expensive street. Just eleven
rooms, most with bathrooms, but all more than
decent. ❹

Torre Guelfa Borgo SS Apostoli 8
℡055.239.6338, ⓦwww.hoteltorreguelfa
.com. Twenty tastefully furnished rooms are
crammed on to the third floor of this ancient tower,
the tallest private building in the city. Guests can
enjoy the marvellous views all over the city from
the tower's small roof garden. There are also six
cheaper doubles on the first floor (no TV and more
noise from the road). Very charismatic, and very
popular. ❺

Over €200

Beacci Tornabuoni Via de' Tornabuoni 3
℡055.212.645, ℻055.283.594, ⓦwww
.tornabuonihotels.com. With 28 rooms occupying
the top two floors of a fifteenth-century palazzo,
this is a beguilingly antiques-stuffed three-star
hotel, perfectly placed on Florence's poshest shopping street. The roof garden is superb, especially
in spring, when the jasmine is blossoming. Special
offers are often available on the website. ❽

Helvetia & Bristol Via dei Pescioni 2
℡055.26.651, ⓦwww.royaldemeure.com.
In business since 1894 and favoured by such luminaries as Pirandello, Stravinsky and Gary Cooper.
Following a refit in the 1990s, this is now undoubtedly Florence's finest small-scale five-star hotel.
The public spaces and 67 bedrooms and suites
(each unique) are faultlessly designed and fitted,
mixing antique furnishings and modern facilities
– such as jacuzzis in many bathrooms – to create
a style that evokes the Belle Epoque without being

suffocatingly nostalgic or twee. If you're going to
treat yourself, this is a leading contender. Rooms
start at around €440 without breakfast. ❾

J.K. Place Piazza Santa Maria Novella 7
℡055.264.5181, ⓦwww.jkplace.com. One of the
newest and most appealing of Florence's designer
hotels occupies a fine eighteenth-century building
on Piazza Santa Maria Novella. *J.K. Place*'s big
idea is to create a homely rather than a hotel-like
atmosphere, with a hostess rather than a recep-
tionist, a bar from which you help yourself, and a
communal breakfast table where you can chat with
fellow guests. The twenty rooms bear designer
Michele Bönan's exotic-elegant stamp, and have
DVD players and flat-screen TVs. Doubles from
€325. ❾

North of the centre
Up to €100

Benvenuti and **Genzianella** Via Cavour 112
℡055.572.141, ✉bensecc@iol.it. Two dependable, if unthrilling, hotels sharing the same reception, with 27 rooms in all, virtually on the Piazza
della Libertà, which means a bus or long walk to
the sights. ❸

Giovanna Via Faenza 69 ℡ &
℻055.238.1353, ⓦwww.albergogiovanna
.it. Third-floor hotel (no lift) that's small, tidy
and as cheap as any on Via Faenza. It has just
seven rooms from around €70, a handful with
private bathrooms. The *Nella* on the second floor
(℡055.265.4346, ⓦwww.hotelnella.net) has
rooms from €90, for which you also get air-conditioning and en-suite bathrooms. ❷–❸

Marcella Via Faenza 58 ℡ & ℻055.213.232.
Seven good-sized rooms in this third-floor one-star,
one with private bathroom. No credit cards. ❷

Nazionale Via Nazionale 22 ℡055.238.2203,
ⓦwww.nazionalehotel.it. An average but serviceable family-run one-star place with nine rooms,
five with private bathroom (planned renovations
will give all rooms en-suite bathrooms), equidistant
from the train station and the San Lorenzo market.
Has doubles with and without bathrooms, and
remarkably cheap singles. ❸

Via Faenza 56 Several budget hotels are
crammed into this address near the station – note
there is no lift. Best of the one-stars is the *Paola*
(℡055.213.682, ⓦwww.albergopaola.com), up
on the top floor, with seven rooms (from €70)
all painted in bright colours and all with shower
cubicles in the corner of the rooms. Toilets are
on the corridor. On the same floor is the *Merlini*
(℡055.212.848, ⓦwww.hotelmerlini.it), which
has ten rooms, six with private bathrooms. You'll
pay from €95 for a double here (€15 less for

one without a bathroom), but you have to be in by the 1am curfew. On the second floor there's the twelve-room *Marini* (℡055.284.824; €75), which is comfortable but bland, as is the seven-room *Armonia* (℡055.211.146), one floor down again, where rooms go for around €65. On the ground and first floor you'll also find the slightly pricier, two-star *Azzi* (℡055.213.806, ⓦwww.hotelazzi .it), which has friendly staff and garden views from some of its sixteen rooms. Doubles here go from €115 with bathroom, and €20 less without. ❷–❸

€100–200

Ausonia e Rimini and **Kursaal** Via Nazionale 24 ℡055.496.547 & ℡055.496.324, ⓦwww .kursonia.com. Two co-managed and nicely refurbished hotels near the station: the two-star *Kursaal* is on the second floor and the one-star *Ausonia* on the third. Altogether they have thirty rooms: superior doubles with air-conditioning and en-suite bathrooms, and some standard rooms without bathrooms, costing around €30 less. They also offer Internet access and a laundry service. ❺

Bellettini Via dei Conti 7 ℡055.213.561, ⓦwww.hotelbellettini.com. The warm welcome of owner Signora Gina counts for much in this 27-room two-star, close to San Lorenzo; so, too, do her copious breakfasts. Most of the simple rooms have private bathrooms, all have TVs and air-conditioning. ❻

Casci Via Cavour 13 ℡055.211.686, ⓦwww.hotelcasci.com. It would be hard to find a better two-star hotel in central Florence than this 26-room hotel. Only two (sound-proofed) rooms face the busy street: the rest are quiet, clean and well fitted-out, plus they're well-priced. The welcome is warm and the owners are unfailingly helpful and courteous. The big buffet breakfast in the vaulted and frescoed reception area is a major plus, as is free Internet access. ❻

Cimabue Via Bonifacio Lupi 7 ℡055.471.989, ⓕ055.463.0906, ⓦwww.hotelcimabue.it. This sixteen-room hotel offers more than the usual two-star establishment, though its location is a touch remote. Some of the double and triple rooms have frescoed ceilings, and all are kitted out with antiques and pleasant fabrics. All rooms have (mostly small) private bathrooms; the family atmosphere is welcoming and the breakfasts more than generous. ❹

Concordia Via dell'Amorino 14 ℡055.213.233, wwww.albergoconcordia.it. An extremely convenient first-floor hotel (no lift), located at the back of San Lorenzo church. There are sixteen rooms, all with private bathrooms, and they have been given a warm, tastefully coloured look, as part of an upgrade to two-star status. ❹

Desirée Via Fiume 20 ℡055.238.2382, ⓦwww. desireehotel.com. Completely overhauled two-star featuring stained-glass windows, simulated antique furniture and a bath in each of the eighteen rooms. Located one block east of the station, so there are better-situated hotels at this price, but it's nonetheless a reasonable choice. ❺

Erina Via Fiume 17 ℡055.288.294, ⓕ055.284.343. A two-star hotel located on the third floor of an old palazzo, very close to the station. Has fourteen double rooms, one without en-suite. ❹

Globus Via Sant'Antonino 24 ℡055.211.062, ⓦwww.hotelglobus.com. Tastefully renovated three-star close to San Lorenzo. The 23 air-conditioned rooms are furnished simply, in modern style, and are excellent value. ❹

Panorama Via Cavour 60 ℡055.238.2043, ⓕ055.264.404. A 31-room two-star that's a favourite with school groups, in the university area just north of San Marco on the city's main north-running road. ❹

Residenza JohannaUno Via Bonifacio Lupi 14 ℡055.481.896, ⓦwww.johanna.it. Genteel place that feels very much a "residence" rather than a hotel, hidden away in the same apartment building as the Swedish Consulate in a very quiet, leafy corner of the city, five minutes' walk north of San Marco; ring the bell on the brass plaque by the wrought-iron gates and go in the door on the right-hand side. Rooms are cosy and well kept, and the two *signore* who run the place are as friendly and helpful as you could hope for. The very similar *Residenza JohannaDue* (℡055.473.377) is located a bit further from the main sights, at Via Cinque Giornate 12, to the north of the Fortezza da Basso, and has parking spaces. You need to check in before 7pm on the first day to pick up your key. No credit cards. ❹

Residenza JohleaUno Via San Gallo 80 ℡055.463.3292, ⓦwww.johanna.it. Another venture from the people who created the nearby *Residenza Johanna* (see above), offering the same low-cost, high-comfort package, with the same level of hospitality, but slightly plusher, more spacious and more expensive – though it's still outstanding value by Florentine standards. At neighbouring Via San Gallo 76 you'll find *JohleaDue* (℡055.461.185), which in design, atmosphere and cost is indistinguishable from *Uno*. Some rooms have showers, some baths. As with *Johanna*, you must check in by 7pm. Further down at no.72 is yet another, rather smarter, establishment run by the same team, the *Antica Dimora* (℡055.462.7296, ⓦwww.anticadimorafirenze.it; ❺). No credit cards. ❹

Over €200

Loggiato dei Serviti Piazza Santissima Annunziata 3 ☎055.289.592,
℉055.289.595, ⓦwww.loggiatodeiservitihotel
.it. This elegant, extremely tasteful and well-priced
three-star hotel is situated on one of Florence's
most celebrated squares. Its 39 rooms (five in the
new annexe nearby) have been stylishly incorporated into a structure designed in the sixteenth
century in imitation of the Brunelleschi hospital
across the square, to accommodate the Servite
priests who worked there and provide lodgings for
itinerant Servites. Their relative plainness reflects
something of the building's history, but all are
decorated with fine fabrics and antiques, and look
out either onto the piazza or peaceful gardens to
the rear: top-floor rooms have glimpses of the
Duomo. ❼

Morandi alla Crocetta Via Laura 50
☎055.234.4747, ⓦwww.hotelmorandi
.it. An intimate three-star gem, whose small size
and friendly welcome ensure a home-from-home
atmosphere. Rooms are tastefully decorated with
antiques and old prints, and vivid carpets laid on
parquet floors. Two rooms have balconies opening
onto a modest garden: the best room – with fresco
fragments and medieval nooks and crannies – was
converted from the site's former convent chapel. ❼
Orto de' Medici Via San Gallo 30 ☎055.483.427,
ⓦwww.ortodeimedici.it. A 31-room frescoed and
antique-furnished three-star, occupying a quiet palazzo in the university area. Via San Gallo is not the
most attractive street in Florence, but the hotel has
been very recently and impressively refurbished,
and there is a breakfast terrace. See its website for
excellent offers. ❼
Residenza Castiglioni Via del Giglio 8
☎055.239.6013, ℉055.264.7251, ⓦwww
.residenzacastiglioni.com. Run by the same team
as runs the *Torre Guelfa*, this is a discreet and
hugely stylish hideaway that does not feel like a
hotel at all. Just half a dozen spacious en-suite
double rooms (three of them frescoed) on the
second floor of a palazzo very close to San Lorenzo
church. All credit cards except Amex accepted. ❼

East of the centre
Up to €100

Bavaria Borgo degli Albizi 26 ☎ &
℉055.234.0313, ⓦwww.eidinet.com
/hotelbavaria. A simple and decent one-star near
the city centre (second floor, no lift) with just nine
rooms, including some palatial chambers on the
upper floor, and a couple of inexpensive rooms
with shared bathroom. The hotel occupies part
of a sixteenth-century palazzo built for a follower

of Eleonora di Toledo. Be sure to book, especially
in summer, when it's popular with student tour
groups. ❸
Dalì Via dell' Oriuolo 17 ☎ & ℉055.234.0706,
ⓦwww.hoteldali.com. One of the least expensive
one-star options close to the centre. The nine
rooms (three with bath, are plain and rather basic,
but the location – on the top floor of a palazzo built
in 1492 – helps, as does the view from the back
rooms of the giant magnolia in the garden below.
The friendly young owners speak good English. ❷
Orchidea Borgo degli Albizi 11 ☎055.248.0346,
ⓦwww.hotelorchideaflorence.it. On the first floor
of a lovely twelfth-century building, with seven big
rooms, including three doubles, one with a shower
in the room. ❸

Over €200

J & J Via di Mezzo 20 ☎055.263.121, ⓦwww
.cavalierehotels.com. The bland exterior of this
former fifteenth-century convent, located very close
to Piazza Sant'Ambrogio, conceals a romantic nineteen-room four-star hotel. Some rooms are vast
split-level affairs – but all have charm and are furnished with modern fittings, attractive fabrics and
a few antiques. Common areas are decked with
flowers and retain frescoes and vaulted ceilings
from the original building. In summer breakfast is
served in the convent's lovely old cloister. Doubles
from around €300. ❾

Oltrarno
€100–200

Annalena Via Romana 34 ☎055.222.402,
ⓦwww.hotelannalena.it. Situated a short
way beyond Palazzo Pitti (and right by an entrance
to the Bóboli gardens), this twenty-room three-star,
once owned by the Medici, passed to a young
Florentine noblewoman (Annalena) who retired
from the world after a disastrous love affair and
bequeathed the building to the Dominicans. The
best rooms open onto a gallery with garden views,
and a sprinkling of antiques lend a hint of old-
world charm. ❻
La Scaletta Via Guicciardini 13 ☎055.283.028,
ⓦwww.lascaletta.com. A two-star hotel under new
management, offering eleven air conditioned rooms
with tiled floors, three of them with views across
to the Bóboli gardens. Drinks are served on the
rooftop terrace, where you look across the Bóboli in
one direction and the city in the other. ❺
Silla Via de' Renai 5 ☎055.234.2888, ⓔhotel
.silla@tin.it. A three-star place occupying a fifteenth-century palazzo building that has been
somewhat masked by a 1980s refit, but the 35
rooms are in good shape and reasonably sized

– and nine have a view over a small park and road to the river. Breakfast is served on the terrace in summer. ⑥

Sorelle Bandini Piazza Santo Spirito 9 ☎055.215.308, ⒻF055.282.761. Some of the twelve rooms in this one-star *pensione* are vast

and have marble fireplaces, but other rooms are grim – so make sure you inspect before paying. Location is a plus: the hotel is on Piazza Santa Spirito, one of the city's more happening squares, and the hotel's loggia, which runs round two sides of the building, gives you a grandstand view. ④

Hostels

Florence has only a handful of **hostels** and the best of these is some distance from the centre. To help matters a little, there are a number of places run by religious bodies, plus student institutions which provide beds for non-natives at the city universities. Out of term time (June–Oct) some of these places are open to young tourists, and a few even have accommodation throughout the year. In addition to the houses listed below, there are also a number of *Case dello Studente*, which are run by the university authorities and occasionally made available to visitors; for latest information on these, ask at the tourist office.

Istituto Gould Via dei Serragli 49 ☎055.212.576, ⓦwww.istitutogould.it. Occupies part of a former seventeenth-century palazzo (the doorbell is easily missed). Its 97 beds are extremely popular, so it's wise to book in advance, especially during the academic year. Street-front rooms can be noisy (rear rooms are better) but the old courtyard, terracotta floors and stone staircases provide atmosphere throughout. Open for check-in Mon–Fri 8.45am–1pm & 3–7.30pm, Sat 9am–1.30pm & 2–6pm– but closed Sun. Singles (with/without private bathroom) €41/36; doubles (per person) €29/25; triples €24/21; quads €23/21. No curfew.

Ostello Archi Rossi Via Faenza 94r ☎055.290.804, ⓦwww.hostelarchirossi.com. A five-minute walk from the train station, this privately owned hostel is spotlessly clean and decorated with guests' wall-paintings and graffiti. It's popular – the 96 places fill up quickly – and has a pleasant garden and terrace. Evening meals are available at extra cost; spacious dining room with satellite TV and films shown on request. Single rooms around €30. Dorm beds €20–25, depending on size of dorm (4–9 beds) and whether or not there's an internal bathroom; all prices include breakfast and thirty minutes' Internet time. Disabled access rooms available. Curfew at 2am for dorms.

Ostello Villa Camerata Viale Augusto Righi 2–4 ☎055.601.451, ⒻF055.610.300, ⓦwww.ostellionline.org. An HI hostel tucked away in a beautiful park to the northeast of the city. This is one of Europe's most attractive hostels, a sixteenth-century house with frescoed ceilings, fronted by lemon trees in terracotta pots. Doors open at 2pm; if you're going to arrive later, call ahead to make sure there's space – bookings by email or fax only. Midnight curfew. There are 322 dorm places, and a few

family rooms. Breakfast and sheets are included, but there are no kitchen facilities; optional supper costs about €9. Films in English are shown every night. Dorm beds €17; two-/three-bed rooms €23/19 per person. Take bus #17b from the train station (takes about 30min).

Pio X – Artigianelli Via dei Serragli 106 ☎ & ⒻF055.225.044. One of the cheapest options in town, often booked up by school groups. Don't be put off by the huge picture of Pope Pius X at the top of the steps; the management is friendly and the atmosphere relaxed. Get there by 9am, as the 64 beds are quickly taken. Showers are free. Beds in doubles, triples, quads and quins cost around €17, or €19 with en-suite bathrooms; minimum stay two nights, maximum five. Open all day throughout the year; midnight curfew; no reservations by phone.

Santa Monaca Via Santa Monaca 6 ☎055.268.338, ⓦwww.ostello.it. Privately owned hostel in Oltrarno, close to Santa Maria del Carmine. Has 114 beds, arranged in a dozen dorms with between four and twenty beds. Kitchen facilities (no utensils), washing machines, free hot showers and a useful noticeboard with information on lifts and onward travel. It's a fifteen-minute walk from the station, or take bus #11, #36 or #37 to the second stop after the bridge. Credit cards accepted. Open for check-in 9.30am–1pm and 2pm–12.30am. Dorm beds €17. Curfew 1am.

Suore Oblate dell'Assunzione Via Borgo Pinti 15 ☎055.248.0583, ⒻF055.234.6291. Not far from the Duomo, this convent-run hostel is open to both men and women, as long as rooms are not required by the nuns or their visitors. There's no breakfast. Singles €38, doubles €37 per person, both with private bathrooms. Triples and quads also available.

Suore Oblate dello Spirito Santo Via Nazionale 8 ☎ 055.239.8202, ☏ 055.239.8129. Also run by nuns, this clean and pleasant hostel, a few steps from the station, is open to women, families and married couples only, and is closed to the public during school terms. Doubles, triples and quads all have private bathroom. Breakfast included, and there's a minimum stay of two nights. Doubles and triples cost €27 per person.

Campsites

The situation for **camping** isn't very good: in summer, you're almost certain to find that the only available spaces are at the *Area di Sosta*, an emergency accommodation area sometimes set aside by the city authorities which usually amounts to a patch of ground sheltered by a rudimentary roof, with a shower block attached. Contact the tourist offices for details, if any, of the current location.

Camping Michelangiolo Viale Michelangelo 80 ☎ 055.681.1977, ⊛ www.ecvacanze.it. A 240-pitch site that's always crowded, owing to its superb hillside location in an olive grove. Kitchen facilities and well-stocked, if expensive, shop nearby. Take #13 bus from the station. April–Oct.
Camping Panoramico Via Peramondo 1, Fiesole ☎ 055.559.069, ⊛ www.florencecamping.com.

Located in Fiesole, a fifteen-minute ride on bus #7 from Florence train station, this 120-pitch site has a bar, restaurant, pool and small supermarket.
Villa Camerata Viale Augusto Righi 2–4 ☎ 055.601.451, ⊛ www.ostellionline.org. Basic 55-pitch site in the grounds of the *Villa Camerata* HI hostel.

The City

Greater Florence now spreads several kilometres down the Arno valley and up onto the hills north and south of the city, but the major sights are contained within an area that can be crossed on foot in little over half an hour. A short walk from the train station brings you to the **Baptistery**, **Duomo** and the Museo dell'Opera del Duomo; the area south from here to **Piazza della Signoria** – site of the **Palazzo Vecchio** and the **Uffizi** gallery – is the inner core, into which most of the tourists are packed. A square drawn so that the Duomo and Uffizi stood in the centre of opposite sides would cover many of the best-preserved of Florence's medieval streets and the majority of its fashionable streets.

Immediately north of the Duomo is the **San Lorenzo** quarter, where market stalls surround one of the city's first-rank churches, in effect the chapel of the Medici dynasty. Within a short radius of here are the monastery of **San Marco**, with its paintings by Fra' Angelico, the **Accademia**, residence of Michelangelo's *David*, and **Piazza Santissima Annunziata**, Florence's most attractive square.

The Uffizi backs onto the Arno River, across which lies the district known as the **Oltrarno**, where the **Palazzo Pitti** and Masaccio's church of **Santa Maria del Carmine** exert the strongest pull, followed by the churches of **Santo Spirito** and the colourful **San Miniato al Monte**.

Florence museum admission

All of Florence's state-run museums belong to an association called **Firenze Musei** (ⓦ www.firenzemusei.it), which sets aside a daily quota of tickets that can be **reserved in advance**. The Uffizi, the Accademia and the Bargello belong to this group, as do the Palazzo Pitti museums, the Bóboli garden, the Medici chapels in San Lorenzo, the archeological museum and the San Marco museum. For the first trio you should certainly consider making use of this facility, because in high season the queues for tickets on the door can be enormous.

For the Uffizi you can reserve tickets at the reception area, or use the **telephone booking line**, which currently is the only outlet for reserved tickets for the other museums in the Firenze Musei scheme. You call ⓣ055.294.883 (Mon–Fri 8.30am–6.30pm, Sat 8.30am–12.30pm) and an English-speaking operator allocates you a ticket (with a €3 booking fee) for a specific hour; the ticket is collected at the museum, again at a specific time, shortly before entry. That's the theory, but in reality the phone line tends to be engaged for long periods at a stretch, so perseverance is nearly always required. And if you're going to pre-book a visit, you should do it as soon as possible, because the allocation of reservable tickets is often sold out many days ahead. (For more details on the Uffizi, see p.116.)

Note that on-the-door admission to all state-run museums is free for EU citizens under 18 and over 65, on presentation of a passport, and that nearly all of Florence's major museums are routinely **closed on Monday**, though some are open for a couple of Mondays each month. In the majority of cases, museum ticket offices close thirty minutes before the museum itself. At the Palazzo Vecchio and Museo Stibbert however, it's one hour before, while at the Uffizi, Bargello, Museo dell'Opera del Duomo, the dome of the Duomo, the Campanile and Pitti museums it's 45 minutes.

Close to the eastern side of Piazza del Duomo stands the **Bargello**, the main museum of sculpture; farther east, the area around the Franciscan church of **Santa Croce** forms a nucleus of activity. On the western side of the city, directly opposite the train station, the unmissable attraction is **Santa Maria Novella**, Florentine base of the rival Dominican order.

Piazza del Duomo

From the train station, all first-time visitors gravitate towards **Piazza del Duomo**, beckoned by the pinnacle of Brunelleschi's dome, which lords it over the cityscape with an authority unmatched by any architectural creation in any other Italian city. Yet even though the magnitude of the **Duomo** is apparent from a distance, first sight of the church and the adjacent **Baptistery** still comes as a jolt, their colourful patterned exteriors making a startling contrast with the dun-toned buildings around. Each of these great buildings is as remarkable inside as out, and an ascent of the cathedral's **dome** will give you astounding views over the city to the hazy Tuscan hills beyond.

After exploring the cathedral, you can escape the crowds by climbing the **Campanile**, the Duomo's detached bell-tower, or visit the **Museo dell'Opera del Duomo**, a repository for works of art removed over the centuries from the Duomo, Baptistery and Campanile. With pieces by Donatello, Michelangelo and many others, it's the city's second-ranking sculpture collection after the Bargello.

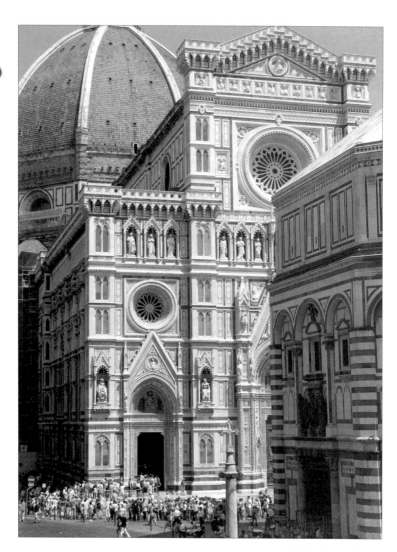

△ The Baptistery and Duomo

The Duomo

Some time in the seventh century the seat of the Bishop of Florence was transferred from San Lorenzo to Santa Reparata, a sixth-century church which stood on the site of the present-day **Duomo**, or **Santa Maria del Fiore** (Mon–Wed & Fri 10am–5pm, Thurs closes 3.30pm, Sat 10am–4.45pm, Sun 1.30–4.45pm; on 1st Sat of month closes 3.30pm; free). Later generations modified this older church until 1294, when Florence's ruling priorate was stung into action by the magnificence of newly commissioned cathedrals in Pisa and Siena. Their own

THE DUOMO

0   15 m

Entrance to the dome

Campanile

Remains of former cathedral

N

1   Stained glass: St Stephen (left), Assumption (centre) and
    St Lawrence (right), Lorenzo Ghiberti
2   Tomb of Antonio d'Orso, bishop of Florence (1323),
    Tino da Camaino
3   Mosaic: Coronation of the Virgin (1300), attributed to
    Gaddo Gaddi
4   Clock (1443) – decoration, Paolo Uccello
5   Stained glass: St Lawrence and Angels, Lorenzo Ghiberti
6   Tondo: Bust of Brunelleschi (1447), Andrea Cavalcanti
7   Bust: Giotto at Work (1490), Benedetto da Maiano
8   Gothic water stoup (1380), attributed to Urbano da
    Cortona
9   Entrance and steps to Santa Reparata
10 Porta del Campanile
11 Painting: St Bartholomew Enthroned (1408), Rossello
    di Jacopo Franchi
12 Painted sepulchral monument: Fra Luigi Marsili (1439),
    Bicci di Lorenzo
13 Statue: Isaiah (1427), Bernardo Ciuffagni
14 Painted sepulchral monument: Archbishop Pietro
    Corsino of Florence (1422), Bicci di Lorenzo
15 Stained glass: Six Saints (1395), Agnolo Gaddi
16 Bust: Marsilio Ficino (1521), philosopher friend of
    Cosimo I, holding a copy of Plato's works
17 Porta dei Canoncini: sculpture (1395–99),
    Lorenzo d'Ambrogio
18 Eight statues of the Apostles (1547–72) against the
    pillars of the octagon
19 Tribune: each tribune has five chapels; each chapel has
    two levels of stained glass, most by Lorenzo Ghiberti
20 Frescoes below windows of west and east tribunes:
    Saints (1440), attributed to Bicci di Lorenzo
21 Altar, attributed to Michelozzo

22 Fresco fragment: Madonna del Popolo (13th century),
    attributed to Giotto
23 Dome fresco cycle: The Last Judgement (1572–79),
    Giorgio Vasari and Federico Zuccari
24 Enamelled terracotta (above door): Ascension (1450),
    Luca della Robbia
25 Sagrestia Vecchia (Old Sacristy)
26 Bronze reliquary (1432–42) of St Zenobius (below altar),
    Lorenzo Ghiberti
27 Candle-holders: Two Angels (1450), Luca della Robbia
28 Enamelled terracotta: Resurrection (1444), Luca della
    Robbia
29 Bronze doors (1446–67), Luca della Robbia and
    Michelozzo
30 Sagrestia Nuova (New Sacristy): intarsia
    (1436–45), Benedetto and Giuliano da Maiano
31 Former site of Michelangelo's Pietà, currently in the
    Museo dell'Opera
32 Entrance and stairs to the dome
33 Porta della Mandorla: sculpture, Nanni di Banco and
    Donatello
34 Painting: Dante with the Divine Comedy (1465),
    Domenico di Michelino
35 Fresco: SS Cosmas and Damian (1429), Bicci di Lorenzo;
    two windows by Agnolo Gaddi
36 Statue (in recess) designed for old cathedral facade:
    King David (1434), Bernardo Ciuffagni
37 Equestrian portrait: Sir John Hawkwood (1436),
    Paolo Uccello
38 Equestrian portrait: Niccolò da Tolentino (1456),
    Andrea del Castagno
39 Bust: Antonio Squarcialupi (former cathedral organist,
    1490), Benedetto da Maiano
40 The Prophet Joshua (1415), Nanni di Bartolo; the head
    is by Donatello

The Pazzi Conspiracy

The **Pazzi Conspiracy**, perhaps the most compelling of all Florence's murkier acts of treachery, had its roots in the election in 1472 of **Sixtus IV**, a pope who distributed money and favours with a largesse remarkable even by papal standards. Six of his nephews were made cardinals, one of them, the uncouth **Girolamo Riario**, coming in for particularly preferential treatment, probably because he was Sixtus's son. Sixtus's plan was that Riario should take over the town of Imola as a base for papal expansion, and accordingly he approached Lorenzo de' Medici for the necessary loan. Aware that Imola was too close to Milan and Bologna to be allowed to fall into papal hands, Lorenzo rebuffed the pope, despite the importance of the Vatican account with the Medici bank, and the family's role as agents for the papacy's alum mines in Tuscany (alum a vital part of the dyeing industry, and therefore essential to Florence's textile trade). Enraged by the snub, and by Lorenzo's refusal to recognize **Francesco Salviati** as archbishop of Pisa (Sixtus had ignored an agreement by which appointments within the Florentine domain could only be made by mutual agreement), Sixtus turned to the Pazzi, the Medici's leading Florentine rivals as bankers in Rome.

Three co-conspirators met in Rome in the early months of 1477: Riario, now in possession of Imola but eager for greater spoils; Salviati, incandescent at Lorenzo's veto and desperate to become archbishop of Florence; and **Francesco de' Pazzi**, head of the Pazzis' Rome operation and determined to usurp Medici power in Florence. Any plot, however, required military muscle, and the man chosen to provide it, a plain-speaking mercenary called **Montesecco**, proved intensely wary of the whole enterprise: "Beware of what you do," he counselled, "Florence is a big affair." In the end he made his co-operation conditional on papal blessing, a benediction that was readily obtained. "I do not wish the death of anyone on any account," was Sixtus's mealy-mouthed observation, "since it does not accord with our office to consent to such a thing" – yet he knew full well Lorenzo's death was essential if the plot was to succeed. "Go, and do what you wish," he added, "provided there be no killing." **Jacopo de' Pazzi**, the Pazzis' wizened godfather, was also won over by Sixtus's disingenuous support, despite being on good terms with the Medici – indeed, one of his nephews was married to Lorenzo's sister.

cathedral, they lamented, was too "crudely built and too small for such a city".

A suitably immodest plan to remedy this shortcoming was ordered from Arnolfo di Cambio, who drafted a scheme to create the largest church in the Roman Catholic world and "surpass anything of its kind produced by the Greeks and Romans in the times of their greatest power". Progress on the project faltered after Arnolfo's death in 1302, but by 1380 Francesco Talenti and a string of mostly jobbing architects had brought the nave to completion. By 1418 the tribunes (apses) and the dome's supporting drum were also completed. Only the dome itself – no small matter – remained unfinished (see p.99).

The exterior

Parts of the Duomo's **exterior** date back to Arnolfo's era, but most of the overblown and pernickety main **facade** is a nineteenth-century simulacrum of a Gothic front. The original facade, which was never more than quarter-finished, was pulled down in 1587 on the orders of Ferdinand I. A competition to produce a new front proved fruitless, and for three centuries the cathedral remained faceless. After Florence became capital of the newly unified Italy in 1865, however, no fewer than 92 plans were submitted. The winning entry, by the otherwise obscure Emilio de Fabris, was completed in 1887. To its credit, the new frontage at least retained the original colour scheme and materials,

After numerous false starts, it was decided to **murder** Lorenzo and Giuliano whilst they attended Mass in the cathedral. The date set was Sunday, April 26, 1478. Montesecco, however, now refused "to add sacrilege to murder", so Lorenzo's murder was delegated to two embittered priests, Maffei and Bagnone, whereas Giuliano was to be dispatched by Francesco de' Pazzi and **Bernardo Baroncelli**, a violent Pazzi sidekick deeply in debt to the family. Salviati, meanwhile, accompanied by an armed troop, was to seize control of the Palazzo della Signoria.

It all went horribly wrong. Giuliano was killed in a crazed frenzy, his skull shattered and his body rent with nineteen stab wounds, but Lorenzo managed to escape, fleeing wounded to the Duomo's new sacristy, where he and his supporters barricaded themselves behind its heavy bronze doors. Across the city, Salviati was separated from his troops, thanks to newly installed secret doors and locks in the Palazzo della Signoria, and arrested by the *Gonfaloniere*, Cesare Petrucci.

Apprised of the plot, a furious mob dispensed summary justice to several of the conspirators: Salviati's troops were massacred to a man, whilst Salviati and Francesco de' Pazzi were hanged from a window of the Palazzo della Signoria. Of the latter execution, Poliziano, the eminent humanist, noted that "as the archbishop rolled and struggled at the end of his rope, his eyes goggling in his head, he fixed his teeth into Francesco de' Pazzi's naked body". Maffei and Bagnone, the bungling priests, were castrated and hanged. Baroncelli escaped to Constantinople but was extradited and executed. Montesecco was tortured, but given a soldier's execution in the Bargello. Jacopo's end was the most sordid. Having escaped Florence, he was recaptured, tortured, stripped naked, and hanged alongside the decomposing Salviati. He was then buried in Santa Croce, but exhumed by the mob, who blamed heavy rains on his evil spirit. His corpse was dragged through the streets, tipped in a ditch, and finally propped up outside the Pazzi palace, where his rotting head was used as door knocker. Eventually the putrefying body was thrown in the Arno, fished out, flogged and hanged again by a gang of children, and finally cast back into the river.

with marble quarried from three different sources: white from Carrara, red from the Maremma and green from Prato.

The cathedral's south (right) side is the oldest part of the exterior – both its side portals deserve a glance – but the most attractive adornment is the **Porta della Mandorla** (number 33 on our plan), on the other side. This takes its name from the almond-shaped frame (or *mandorla*) that contains the grime-streaked relief of *The Assumption of the Virgin* (1414–21), sculpted by Nanni di Banco; the lunette features a mosaic of the *Annunciation* (1491) to a design by Ghirlandaio. The two heads in profile either side of the gable may be early works by Donatello.

The interior

The Duomo's **interior** is the converse of the exterior – a vast, uncluttered enclosure of bare masonry. Its ambience is more that of a great assembly hall than a devotional building, and yet its apparently barren walls hold a far greater accumulation of treasures than at first appears.

The most conspicuous decorations are a pair of memorials to *condottieri* (mercenary commanders). Paolo Uccello's monument to **Sir John Hawkwood** (37), created in 1436, is often cited as the epitome of Florentine mean-spiritedness; according to local folklore – unsupported by any evidence – the mercenary captain of Florence's army was promised a proper equestrian statue as his memorial, then was posthumously fobbed off with this trompe l'oeil version. Perhaps the slight was deserved. Before being employed by Florence, Hawkwood and his White Company had marauded their way through Tuscany, holding entire cities to ransom under threat of ransack. Look back at the entrance wall and you'll see another Uccello contribution to the interior – a **clock** (4) adorned with four rather abstracted Evangelists. It uses the old *hora italica*, common in Italy until the eighteenth century, when the 24th hour of the day ended at sunset.

Andrea del Castagno's monument to **Niccolò da Tolentino** (38), created twenty years later, is clearly derived from Uccello's fresco, but has an aggressive edge that's typical of this artist. Just beyond the horsemen, Domenico di Michelino's 1465 work *Dante Explaining the Divine Comedy* (34) gives Brunelleschi's dome – then only nearing completion – a place scarcely less prominent than the mountain of Purgatory. Dante stands outside the walls, a symbol of his exile from Florence.

Judged by mere size, the major work of art in the Duomo is the 1572–79 fresco of **The Last Judgement** (23), which fills much of the interior of the dome. At the time of its execution, however, a substantial body of opinion thought Vasari and Zuccari's combined effort did nothing but deface Brunelleschi's masterpiece, and quite a few people today are of the same opinion.

Barriers usually prevent you from getting close to the high altar, so you might not be able to look into the **Sagrestia Nuova** (30), where the lavish panelling is inlaid with beautiful intarsia work (1436–45) by Benedetto and Giuliano Maiano, notably a delicate *Annunciation* in the centre of the wall facing the door. The relief of the *Resurrection* (1442) above the entrance is by Luca della Robbia, his first important commission in the enamelled terracotta for which he became famous. The stunning **sacristy door** (1445–69), created in conjunction with Michelozzo, was his only work in bronze. It was in this sacristy that Lorenzo de' Medici took refuge in 1478 after his brother Giuliano had been mortally stabbed on the altar steps by the Pazzi conspirators (see p.96): the bulk of della Robbia's recently installed doors protected him from his would-be assassins. Small portraits on the handles commemorate the brothers.

Across the way, della Robbia's *Ascension* (1450) can be seen above the door of the **Sagrestia Vecchia** (25); it was once accompanied by Donatello's sublime *cantoria*, or choir-loft, now in the Museo dell'Opera. Luca della Robbia's equally mesmeric *cantoria*, in the same museum, occupied a matching position above the Sagrestia Nuova.

Santa Reparata

In the 1960s, remnants of the Duomo's predecessor, **Santa Reparata** (9), were uncovered underneath the west end of the nave, where a flight of steps leads down into the excavation. The remains (admission €3) are extensive, as the nave of the Duomo was built, on the same alignment, several feet above that of the old church, which was thus not fully demolished. Subsequent excavations have revealed a complicated jigsaw of Roman, Paleochristian and Romanesque remains, plus fragments of mosaic and fourteenth-century frescoes. The explanatory diagrams tend to intensify the confusion: to make sense of it all, you'll have to keep referring to the colour-coded model in the farthest recess of the crypt. In 1972, further digging revealed **Brunelleschi's tomb**, an unassuming marble slab so simple that it had lain forgotten under the south aisle. The tombstone's present position is hardly any more glorious (it can be seen,

Brunelleschi's dome

Since Arnolfo di Cambio's scale model of the Duomo collapsed under its own weight some time in the fourteenth century, nobody has been sure quite how he intended to crown his achievement. In 1367 Neri di Fioraventi proposed the construction of a magnificent **cupola** (dome) that was to span nearly 43m, broader than the dome of Rome's Pantheon, which had remained the world's largest for 1300 years, and rise from a base some 55m above the floor of the nave – taller than the highest vaulting of any Gothic cathedral. Just as radical was Fioraventi's decision to dispense with flying buttresses, regarded as ugly vestiges of the Gothic barbarism of enemy states such as France and Milan.

There was just one problem: nobody had worked out how to build the thing. Medieval arches were usually built on wooden "centring", a network of timbers that held the stone in place until the mortar was set. In the case of the Duomo, the weight of the stone would have been too great for the timber (the entire dome is thought to weigh some 33,000 tonnes), and the space to be spanned was too great for the measuring cords that would be needed to guide the masons – any cord strung across the church would sag and stretch too much for accuracy. A committee of the masons' guild was set up to solve the dilemma. One idea was to build the dome from pumice. Another, according to Vasari, was to support the dome on a vast mound of earth that would be seeded with thousands of coins; when the dome was finished, the mound would be cleared by inviting Florence's citizens to excavate the money.

After years of bickering the project was thrown open to competition. A goldsmith and clockmaker called **Filippo Brunelleschi** presented the winning scheme, defeating Ghiberti in the process – revenge of sorts for Ghiberti's triumph seventeen years earlier in the competition to design the Baptistery doors (see p.101). Doom-mongers, Ghiberti among them, criticized Brunelleschi at every turn, eventually forcing the authorities to employ both rivals. An exasperated Brunelleschi feigned illness and resigned. Ghiberti, left to his own devices, found himself baffled, and in 1423 Brunelleschi was invited to become the dome's sole "inventor and chief director".

The key to Brunelleschi's success lay in the construction of the dome as two masonry shells, each built as a stack of ever-diminishing rings. Secured with hidden stone beams and enormous iron chains, these concentric circles formed a lattice that was filled with lightweight bricks laid in a herringbone pattern that prevented the higher sections from falling inward. Brunelleschi's relentless inventiveness extended to a new hoist with a reverse gear, a new type of crane, and even a boat for transporting marble that was so ungainly it was nicknamed *Il Badalone* (the Monster).

The dome's completion was marked by the **consecration** of the cathedral on March 25, 1436 – Annunciation Day, and the Florentine New Year – in a ceremony conducted by the pope. Even then, the topmost piece, the lantern, remained unfinished, with many people convinced the dome could support no further weight. But once again Brunelleschi won the day, beginning work on the dome's final stage in 1446, just a few months before his death. The whole thing was finally completed in the late 1460s, when the cross and gilded ball, both cast by Verrocchio, were hoisted into place.

Today it is still the largest masonry dome in the world. Only the gallery around the base remains incomplete – abandoned with just one face finished after Michelangelo compared it to "cages for crickets". This criticism aside, Michelangelo was awestruck: gazing on the cupola he is supposed to have said: *Come te non voglio, meglio di te non posso* ("Similar to you I will not, better than you I cannot").

without paying, through a grille to the left at the foot of the steps), but the architect does at least have the honour of being one of the very few Florentines to be buried in the Duomo itself.

The dome

Climbing the **dome** (Mon–Fri 8.30am–7pm, Sat 8.30am–5.40pm; 1st Sat of month closes 4pm; €6) is an amazing experience, both for the views from the top and for the insights it offers into Brunelleschi's engineering genius (see box overleaf). Be prepared for the queue that usually stretches from the entrance, on the north flank of the nave; it does, however, move fairly briskly. Also be ready for the 463 lung-busting steps. Claustrophobics should note that the climb involves some very confined spaces.

After an initial ascent, you emerge onto a narrow gallery that runs around the interior of the dome, with a dizzying view down onto the maze-patterned pavement of the nave. It's also the best vantage point from which to inspect the seven **stained-glass roundels**, designed by Uccello, Ghiberti, Castagno and Donatello, below Vasari's *Last Judgement* fresco. Beyond the gallery, you enter the more cramped confines of the dome itself. As you clamber up between the inner and outer shells, you can observe many ingenious features of Brunelleschi's construction: the ribs and arches, the herringbone brickwork, the wooden struts that support the outer shell – even the hooks and holes left for future generations of repairers. From the base of the white marble lantern that crowns the dome, the views across the city are breathtaking.

The Campanile

The **Campanile** (daily 8.30am–7.30pm; €6) – the cathedral's bell-tower – was begun in 1334 by Giotto during his period as official city architect and *capo maestro* (head of works) in charge of the Duomo. By the time of his death three years later, the base, the first of five eventual levels, had been completed. Andrea Pisano, fresh from creating the Baptistery's south doors, continued construction of the second storey (1337–42), probably in accordance with Giotto's plans. Work was rounded off by Francesco Talenti, who rectified deficiencies in Giotto's original calculations in the process: the base's original walls teetered on the brink of collapse until he doubled their thickness. When completed, the bell-tower reached 84.7m, well over the limit set by the city in 1324 for civic towers, the building of which had long been a means of expressing aristocratic or mercantile power.

These days a climb to the summit is one of the highlights of any Florentine trip, though it's worth first taking in the tower's decorative **sculptures and reliefs** (most are now copies, the originals being in the Museo dell'Opera del Duomo). As it moved up the tower, the decoration was intended to mirror humanity's progress from original sin to a state of divine grace, a progress facilitated by manual labour, the arts and the sacraments, and guided by the influence of the planets and the cardinal and theological virtues. Thus the first storey is studded with two rows of bas-reliefs; the lower register, in hexagonal frames – some designed by Giotto, but all executed by Pisano and pupils – illustrates the *Creation, Art and Works of Man*, while in the diamond-shaped panels of the upper register are allegories of the *Seven Planets, Seven Sacraments* and *Seven Virtues*. A century or so later Luca della Robbia added the *Five Liberal Arts* (Grammar, Philosophy, Music, Arithmetic and Astrology) on the north face. Further works in the second-storey niches by Pisano were eventually replaced by Donatello and Nanni di Bartolo's figures of the *Prophets, Sibyls, Patriarchs* and *Kings* (1415–36).

The parapet at the top of the tower is a less lofty but in many ways more satisfying viewpoint than the cathedral dome, if only because the view takes in the Duomo itself. Be warned, though, that there are 414 steps to the summit – and no lift.

The Baptistery

Florence's **Baptistery** (Mon–Sat noon–7pm, Sun 8.30am–2pm; €3) stands immediately west of the Duomo, whose geometrically patterned marble cladding mirrors that of the smaller, older building. Generally thought to date from the sixth or seventh century, the Baptistery is the oldest building in Florence, first documented in 897, when it was recorded as the city's cathedral before Santa Reparata. Though its origins lie buried in the Dark Ages, no building better illustrates the special relationship between Florence and the Roman world.

The Florentines were always conscious of their **Roman** ancestry, and for centuries believed that the Baptistery was a converted Roman temple to Mars, originally built to celebrate the defeat of Fiesole and the city's foundation. This belief was bolstered by the interior's ancient granite columns, probably taken from the city's old Roman Capitol (other columns from this site found their way to San Miniato). Further proof was apparently provided by traces of an ancient pavement mosaic, remains now thought to belong to an old Roman bakery. But if the building itself is not Roman, its exterior marble cladding – applied in a Romanesque reworking between about 1059 and 1128 – is clearly classical in inspiration, while its most famous embellishments, the gilded **bronze doors**, mark the emergence of a more scholarly, self-conscious interest in the art of the ancient world.

The south doors

Responsibility for the Baptistery's improvement and upkeep lay with the *Arte di Calimala*, the most powerful of Florence's guilds. It was they who initiated the building's eleventh-century revamp, and they who in the 1320s turned their attention to the exterior, and in particular to the question of a suitably majestic entrance. In this they were stung into action by arch-rival Pisa, whose cathedral was not only famous for its bronze portals, but whose craftsmen had recently completed some celebrated bronze doors for the great cathedral at Monreale in Sicily.

The arrival of Andrea Pisano in Florence in 1330 offered the chance of similar glories. Within three months the Pisan sculptor had created wax models for what would become the Baptistery's **south doors**. (They were originally placed in the east portal, but were displaced when Ghiberti's "Gates of Paradise" – see overleaf – were finished.) Over the next eight years the models were cast in bronze, probably with the assistance of Venetian bell-makers, then Italy's most accomplished bronzesmiths. Twenty of the doors' 28 panels, installed in 1339, form a narrative on the life of St John the Baptist, patron saint of Florence and the Baptistery's dedicatee; the lowest eight reliefs depict Humility and the Cardinal and Theological Virtues. The figures above the portal – the Baptist, Salome and executioner – are copies of late-sixteenth-century additions; the originals are in the Museo dell'Opera del Duomo.

The north doors

Some sixty years of financial and political turmoil, and the ravages of the Black Death, prevented further work on the Baptistery's other entrances until 1401. That year a competition was held to design a new set of doors, each of the six main entrants being asked to create a panel showing the Sacrifice of Isaac. The doors were to be a votive offering, a gift to God to celebrate the passing of another plague epidemic.

The judges found themselves equally impressed by the work of two young goldsmiths, Brunelleschi and **Lorenzo Ghiberti** (both winning entries are displayed in the Bargello). Unable to choose between the pair, it appears that the judges suggested that the two work in tandem. Brunelleschi replied that if he couldn't do the job alone he wasn't interested – whereupon the contract was handed to Ghiberti, leaving his rival to stomp off to study architecture in Rome. Ghiberti, barely 20 years old, was to devote much of the next 25 years to this one project, albeit in the company of distinguished assistants such as Masolino, Donatello and Paolo Uccello. His fame rests almost entirely on the extraordinary result.

His **north doors** (1403–24) show a new naturalism and classicized sense of composition, copying Pisano's 28-panel arrangement while transcending its traditional Gothic approach: the upper twenty panels depict Scenes from the New Testament, while the eight lower panels describe the Four Evangelists and Four Doctors of the Church.

The east doors

The north doors, while extraordinary, are as nothing to the sublime **east doors** (1425–52), ordered from Ghiberti as soon as the first set was finished. The artist would spend some 27 years on the new project, work which he pursued, in his

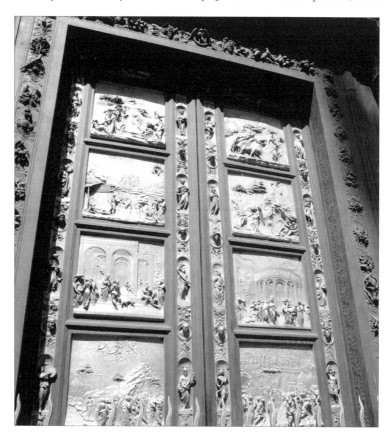

△ The east doors of the Baptistery

own words, "with the greatest diligence and greatest love". These doors have long been known as the "Gates of Paradise", supposedly because Michelangelo once remarked that they were so beautiful they deserved to be the portals of heaven. However, it's more likely that the name came about because these doors face the cathedral – the space between a cathedral and its baptistery was known as the *Paradiso*, because the sacrament of baptism put its recipient on the threshold of paradise.

The doors have just ten panels, a departure from both previous sets of doors, while their enclosing squares abandon the Gothic diamond or quatrefoil frame. Unprecedented in the subtlety of their casting, the **Old Testament scenes** – the Creation, the Ten Commandments, the Sacrifice of Isaac, and so on – are a primer of early Renaissance art, using rigorous perspective, gesture and sophisticated groupings to intensify the drama of each scene. Ghiberti's power of compression and detail is such that several narratives are often woven into a single scene. The sculptor has also included an understandably self-satisfied self-portrait in the frame of the left-hand door: his is the fourth head from the top of the right-hand band – the bald chap with the smirk. The gorgeous golden doors now in place are reproductions, as the original panels have been restored and exhibited, to great effect, in the Museo dell'Opera del Duomo.

The pair of pitted **marble columns** to the side of the east doors were presented by the city of Pisa in the twelfth century, and would have been slotted into the walls had they not turned out to be too weak to bear any substantial weight. Another marble column, just north of the Baptistery, is decorated with bronze branches and leaves to commemorate a miracle of January 429 AD, brought about by the body of St Zenobius, Florence's first bishop; as the corpse was being carried from San Lorenzo into Santa Reparata it brushed against a barren elm here, which thereupon sprang into leaf.

The interior

The Baptistery **interior** is stunning, with its black and white marble cladding and miscellany of ancient columns below a blazing **mosaic ceiling**. Mosaics were not a Florentine speciality – in the centuries to come they would give way to fresco, but in the thirteenth century they were the predominant decorative medium. Encouraged by the interest surrounding the restoration of mosaics then taking place in the early Christian basilicas of Rome and Ravenna, the city was keen to match its rivals, principally Venice.

The earliest mosaics (1225) lie above the square apse, and depict the Virgin and John the Baptist. Above them, a wheel of prophets encircles the Lamb of God. The main vault is dominated by a vast figure of Christ in Judgement, flanked by depictions of Paradise and Hell. Just to the left of the monstrous, man-eating Lucifer, the poet Virgil (in a white cloak) can be seen leading Dante (in black) through the Inferno. These figures were a later insertion, added after the poet's death during something of a frenzy of recognition. The other five sections of the octagonal ceiling depict Biblical scenes, beginning above the north doors with the Creation, and proceeding through the stories of Joseph and John the Baptist towards the Crucifixion and Resurrection, seen above the south doors.

The interior's semi-abstract **mosaic pavement** also dates from the thirteenth century. The empty octagon at its centre marks the spot once occupied by the huge font in which every child born in the city during the previous twelve months would be baptized on March 25 (New Year's Day in the old Florentine calendar). When a child was born, a coloured bean was dropped into an urn in the Baptistery: black for a boy, white for a girl – a system which allowed the birth rate to be calculated.

To the right of the altar lies the **tomb of Baldassare Cossa**, the schismatic Pope John XXIII, who was deposed in 1415 and died in Florence in 1419. At the time of his death he was a guest of his financial adviser and close friend, Giovanni di Bicci de' Medici, the man who established the Medici at the political forefront of Florence. It was through Pope John that Giovanni became chief banker to the Papal Curia, a deal that laid the foundations of the Medici fortune: for years over half the Medici's profits would come from just two Rome-based banks. The monument, draped by an illusionistic marble canopy, is the work of Donatello and his pupil Michelozzo.

The Museo dell'Opera del Duomo

In 1296 a body called the Opera del Duomo, literally the "Work of the Duomo", was created to oversee the maintenance of the Duomo. Since the early fifteenth century its home has been the building behind the east end of the cathedral at Piazza del Duomo 9, which now also houses the **Museo dell'Opera del Duomo** (Mon–Sat 9am–7.30pm, Sun 9am–1.40pm; €6), a repository of the most precious and fragile works of art from the Duomo, Baptistery and Campanile. As an overview of the sculpture of Florence the museum is second only to the Bargello. (Incidentally, you can see the stonemasons of the present-day Opera at work in their studio at Via dello Studio 23a, on the south side of the Duomo.)

The ground floor

Beyond the ticket office, rooms devoted to sculpture from the Baptistery (mostly works by Tino da Camaino) and the Duomo's lateral doors precede the museum's **courtyard**, a site thick with historical associations despite its ultra-modern makeover: it was here that much of Michelangelo's *David* was sculpted. Now glazed over, the courtyard is home of all eight of Ghiberti's panels from the "Doors of Paradise" (see p.103), finally brought together following restoration, and now sharing the space with the graceful *Baptism of Christ* (1502–25), by Andrea Sansovino and assistants.

The largest room on this floor is a large hall devoted to the original sculptures of the cathedral's west front, foremost among which are works by the cathedral's first architect, **Arnolfo di Cambio** (and his workshop), including an eerily glass-eyed *Madonna and Child*; all were rescued from Arnolfo's quarter-finished cathedral facade which was pulled down by Ferdinand I in 1587. Equally striking is the sculptor's vase-carrying figure of *St Reparata*, one of Florence's patron saints, a work long thought to be of Greek or Roman origin. Also noteworthy is the ramrod straight statue of Boniface VIII, one of the most unpleasant of all medieval popes. Along the entrance wall are four seated figures of the Evangelists, also wrenched from the facade: Nanni di Banco's St Luke and **Donatello**'s St John are particularly fine.

The room off the far end of the hall features a sequence of **marble reliefs** (1547–72), by Bacio Bandinelli and Giovanni Bandini, part of an unfinished sequence of 300 panels proposed for the choir of the cathedral. Also here is a collection of paintings from a series of altars in the cathedral, all torn from their original home in 1838 as they were considered an affront to the purity of the building. The adjoining modern **octagonal chapel** features an assembly of reliquaries which contain, among other saintly remains, the jaw of Saint Jerome and an index finger of John the Baptist. It's easy to miss the room off to the right of the **Lapidarium** (a collection of modest works in stone), which contains items removed from the cathedral's Porta della Mandorla, including a lovely terracotta *Creation of Eve* (1410) attributed to Donatello.

The upper floor

Up the stairs on the mezzanine level stands **Michelangelo**'s anguished **Pietà** (1550–53), moved from the cathedral as recently as 1981 while restoration of the dome was in progress, but probably fated to stay here. This is one of the sculptor's last works, carved when he was almost 80, and was intended for his own tomb; Vasari records that the face of Nicodemus is a self-portrait. Dissatisfied with the quality of the marble, Michelangelo mutilated the group by hammering off the left leg and arm of Christ; his pupil Tiberio Calcagni restored the arm, then finished off the figure of Mary Magdalene, turning her into a whey-faced supporting player.

Although he's represented on the lower floor, it's upstairs that **Donatello**, the greatest of Michelangelo's precursors, really comes to the fore. The first room at the top of the stairs features his magnificent **Cantoria**, or choir-loft (1433–9), with its playground of boisterous *putti*. Facing it is another splendid *cantoria* (1431–8), the first-known major commission of the young **Luca della Robbia** (the originals are underneath, with casts replacing them in the *cantoria* itself); the earnest musicians embody the text from Psalm 33 which is inscribed on the frame: "Praise the Lord with harp. Sing unto Him with the psaltery and instrument of ten strings." Both lofts were dismantled and removed from their position above the cathedral's sacristies in 1688 on the occasion of the ill-fated marriage of Violante Beatrice of Bavaria to Ferdinand de' Medici, the hopelessly ineffectual heir of Cosimo III. The ceremony gave the cathedral authorities the excuse to decorate the cathedral in a more fitting "modern" style. The ensuing clear-out left the *cantorie* languishing in dusty storage for some two centuries.

Around the room are arrayed the life-size figures that Donatello carved for the Campanile, perhaps the most powerful of which is the prophet Habbakuk, the intensity of whose gaze is said to have prompted the sculptor to seize it and yell "Speak, speak!" Donatello was apparently also responsible for the statue's nickname *Lo Zuccone* (the Pumpkin) – after its bald head. Keeping company with Donatello's work are four Prophets (1348–50) and two Sybils (1342–8) attributed to Andrea Pisano, and *The Sacrifice of Isaac* (1421), a collaboration between Nanni di Bartolo and Donatello.

Donatello's later style is exemplified by the gaunt wooden figure of Mary Magdalene (1453–5), which confronts you on entering the room off the *cantorie* room. The *Magdalene* came from the Baptistery, as did the silver altar-front at the far end of the room, a dazzling summary of the life of St John the Baptist. Begun in 1366, the piece was completed in 1480, the culmination of a century of labour by, among others, Michelozzo (responsible for the central figure of *John the Baptist*), Verrocchio (the *Decapitation* to the right) and Antonio del Pollaiuolo (the *Birth of Jesus* on the left side), who was the chief creator of the silver cross atop the altar. Ranged around the walls are more reliquaries, fabrics, copes and other religious vestments, including 27 sublimely worked **needlework panels** – former vestments and altar panels from the Baptistery – produced between 1466 and 1487 by French, Flemish and Florentine artists, including members of the Arte di Calimala (one of the key textile guilds) working to designs by Pollaiuolo. Not surprisingly, given their provenance, they portray scenes from the life of the Baptist, one of Florence's patrons and the Baptistery's dedicatee.

In the room on the other side of the *cantorie* room you'll find the **bas-reliefs** that once adorned the Campanile. Though darkened with age, their allegorical panels remain both striking and intelligible, depicting the spiritual refinement of humanity through labour, the arts and, ultimately, the virtues and sacraments. The display reproduces the reliefs' original arrangement, the key panels being the hexagonal reliefs of the lower tier, all of which – save for the last five, by

FLORENCE | Piazza del Duomo

Luca della Robbia (1437–9) – were the work of Andrea Pisano and his son Nino (c.1348–50), probably to designs by Giotto.

A corridor at the end of Room II leads past a mock-up of Brunelleschi's building site, complete with broken bricks, wooden scaffolding and some of the tools that were used to build the dome, many invented specifically for the purpose by the architect himself. More arresting is Brunelleschi's **death mask**, which almost – but not quite – looks out of the window at the dome just across the way.

The sequence of rooms beyond displays various proposals for completing the balcony of the drum below the cupola and the Duomo's west front, including models created by Michelangelo, Giuliano da Maiano, Giambologna, Antonio da Sangallo, Andrea Sansovino and other leading architects. The wooden model of the **cathedral lantern** is presumed to have been made by Brunelleschi as part of his winning proposal for the design of the lantern in 1436. The final room, just off the main staircase, shows plans submitted to the three competitions held in the 1860s, when Florence was briefly capital of Italy and the question of the facade standing "ignominious in faded stucco", as George Eliot put it, once more became pressing. They mostly provoke relief that none came to fruition, while Emilio de Fabris's winning design of 1876 is mostly remarkable for how little it differs from the other nineteenth-century Gothic pastiches.

The Museo del Bigallo

On the other side of Piazza del Duomo, at the top of Via de' Calzaiuoli, stands the **Loggia del Bigallo**, which was built in the 1350s for the Compagnia della Misericordia, a charitable organization founded by St Peter Martyr in 1244, to give aid to the sick and to bury the dead. (The Misericordia still exists: their headquarters is just across the way, with their ambulances parked outside.) By the time the loggia was built, the Misericordia was also functioning as an orphanage – the building was commissioned as a place to display abandoned babies, in the hope that they might be recognized before being given to foster parents. For most of the fifteenth century the Misericordia was united with another orphanage, Compagnia del Bigallo (from the village in which it began), hence the loggia's name. Nowadays it houses the three-room **Museo del Bigallo** (daily except Tues 10am–6pm; €2), which contains a tiny collection of religious paintings commissioned by the two companies. As you might expect, the Madonna and Child is a dominant theme, and St Peter Martyr is present as well, but the two highlights are a remnant of a fresco painted on the outside of the loggia in 1386, showing the transfer of infants to their adoptive parents, and the *Madonna of the Misericordia*, painted by a follower of Bernardo Daddi in 1342, which features the oldest known panorama of Florence.

The Museo di Firenze com'era

The top of Via del Proconsolo, just a few yards from the Museo dell'Opera del Duomo, forms a major junction with Via dell'Oriuolo, home to the **Museo di Firenze com'era** (daily except Thurs 9am–2pm; €2.70). This "Museum of Florence as it used to be" is one of the city's unsung museums, but its contents and setting – in a pleasant garden-fronted palazzo – are delightful. There are plans to move the museum to the Palazzo Vecchio, but the transfer does not appear to be imminent.

The story begins with a collection of models, plans and photographs of the excavation of the Piazza della Signoria that took place in the 1980s. As one would expect, a number of discoveries were made, but for want of any better ideas the piazza was simply paved over once the dig was complete. A large, somewhat speculative model of the **Roman city** stands at the far end of the room, with coloured sections showing the buildings whose locations the archeologists are sure of.

The long, vaulted main gallery stands on the other side of the entrance corridor. Maps, prints, photos and topographical paintings chart the growth of Florence from the fifteenth century to the present, and while none of the exhibits is a masterpiece, most of them are at least informative. Perhaps the most impressive item comes right at the start: a meticulous 1887 reproduction of a colossal 1472 aerial view of Florence called the *Pianta della Catena* (Chain Map), the original of which was destroyed in Berlin during World War II. It's the oldest accurate representation of the city's layout.

Almost as appealing are the twelve lunette pictures (1555) of the **Medici villas**, reproductions of which you'll see on postcards and posters across the city. They're the work of Flemish painter Justus Utens and were painted for the Medici's Villa dell'Artimino. A poignant wooden model portrays the labyrinthine jumble of the **Mercato Vecchio**, the city's ancient heart, which was demolished to make space for the Piazza della Repubblica at the end of the nineteenth century. Elsewhere, a graphic picture portrays Savonarola's execution (see p.146), and eighteenth-century Florence is celebrated in the elegiac engravings of Giuseppe Zocchi.

Piazza della Signoria and the Uffizi

Whereas the Piazza del Duomo provides the focus for the city's religious life, the **Piazza della Signoria** – site of the magnificent **Palazzo Vecchio** and forecourt to the **Uffizi** – has always been the centre of its secular existence. Ever busy, it's at its liveliest for political rallies and other civic events, when speakers address the crowds from the terrace in front of the Palazzo Vecchio. (The terrace is called the *arringhiera*, from the same root as the English word "harangue.") Tempers can get frayed at these gatherings, but things used to be a lot wilder: in 1343, for example, one inflammatory meeting ended with a man being eaten by a mob. Most famously, it was here that Savonarola held his "Bonfires of the Vanities" (see p.146) – on the very spot where, on May 23, 1498, he was to be executed for heresy. A plaque near the fountain marks the place.

For so important a square, the history of the Piazza della Signoria is one of oddly haphazard and piecemeal development. Originally the area belonged to the Uberti family, leading members of the city's Ghibelline faction. When the Ghibellines were defeated in 1268, the land and buildings on it were confiscated and allowed to fall into ruin, supposedly as a lasting memorial to Ghibelline treachery. In time, part of the area was paved, a further act of humiliation designed to prevent the Uberti – exiled from the city – from ever raising another building within its precincts. The alleged reluctance of the city authorities to encroach on this "tainted" land partly explains the asymmetrical shape of the square and the Palazzo Vecchio.

The square took on a public role in 1307, when a small area was laid out to provide a setting for the Palazzo Vecchio, then known as the Palazzo dei Priori. By 1385 the piazza was completely paved, and wheeled traffic was banned from the area (as it still is). Further restructuring occurred during Cosimo I's reordering of the Uffizi around 1560, and more alterations followed in 1871, when the medieval Loggia dei Pisani was demolished, opening up much of the square's present-day westward sweep. By this time, some of the piazza's most salient features – its statues – were already firmly in place.

The Florentine Republic

Dante compared Florence's constant political struggles to a sick man forever shifting his position in bed, and indeed its medieval history often appears a catalogue of incessant civic unrest. Yet between 1293 and 1534 – bar the odd ruction – the city maintained a **republican** constitution that was embodied in well-defined institutions. The nucleus of this structure was formed by the city's merchants and guilds, who covertly controlled Florence as early as the twelfth century and formalized their influence during the so-called **Primo Popolo** (1248–59), a quasi-democratic regime whose ten-year rule, claimed Dante, was the only period of civic peace in Florence's history. During the **Secondo Popolo** (1284), the leading guilds, the *Arti Maggiori*, introduced the **Ordinamenti della Giustizia** (1293), a written constitution that entrenched mercantile power still further and was to be the basis of Florence's government for the next two hundred and fifty years.

The rulers of this much vaunted republic were drawn exclusively from the ranks of guild members over the age of 30, and were chosen in a public ceremony held every two months, the short tenure being designed to prevent individuals or cliques assuming too much power. At this ceremony, the names of selected guild members were placed in eight leather bags (*borse*) kept in the sacristy of Santa Croce; the ones picked from the bags duly became the **Priori** (or *Signori*), forming a government called the **Signoria**, usually comprising nine men, most of them from the *Arti Maggiori*. Once elected, the *Priori* moved into the Palazzo della Signoria, where they were expected to stay, virtually incommunicado, for their period of office – though they were waited on hand and foot, and enjoyed the services of a professional joke-teller, the *Buffone*.

Headed by the **Gonfaloniere** (literally the "Standard-Bearer"), the *Signoria* consulted two elected councils or **Collegi** – the **Dodici Buonomini** (Twelve Citizens) and **Sedici Gonfalonieri** (Sixteen Standard Bearers) – as well as committees introduced to deal with specific crises (the Ten of War, the Eight of Security, the Six of Commerce...). Permanent officials included the Chancellor (a post once held by Machiavelli) and the **Podestà**, a chief magistrate brought in from a neighbouring city as an independent arbitrator, and housed in the Bargello. In times of extreme crisis, such as the Pazzi Conspiracy (see p.96), all male citizens over the age of 14 were summoned to a **Parlamento** in Piazza della Signoria by the tolling of the Palazzo Vecchio's famous bell, known as the *Vacca* (Cow), after its deep, bovine tone. When a two-thirds quorum was reached, the people were asked to approve a **Balìa**, a committee delegated to deal with the situation as it saw fit.

All this looked good on paper but in practice the set-up was far from democratic. The lowliest workers, the **Popolo Minuto**, were totally excluded, as were the **Grandi**, or nobles. And despite the *Signoria's* apparently random selection process, political cliques had few problems ensuring that only the names of likely supporters found their way into the *borse*. If a rogue candidate slipped through the net, or things went awry, then a *Parlamento* was summoned, a *Balìa* formed, and the offending person replaced by a more pliable candidate. It was by such means that the great mercantile dynasties of Florence – the Peruzzi, the Albizzi, the Strozzi, and of course the Medici – retained their power even when not technically in office.

The Piazza's statues

Florence's political volatility is encapsulated by the Piazza della Signoria's peculiar array of **statues**, most of which were arranged in the sixteenth century to accentuate the axis of the Uffizi. From left to right, the line-up starts with Giambologna's equestrian statue of **Cosimo I** (1587–94). An echo of the famous Marcus Aurelius statue in Rome, it was designed to draw parallels between the power of medieval Florence (and thus Cosimo) and the glory of imperial Rome. Three bas-reliefs at the base portray key events in Cosimo's career: becoming duke of Florence (1537); the conquest of Siena (1555); and acquiring the title Grand Duke of Tuscany (1569) from Pius V.

Next comes Ammannati's fatuous **Neptune Fountain** (1565–75), a tribute to Cosimo's prowess as a naval commander; Neptune himself is a lumpen lout of a figure, who provoked Michelangelo to coin the rhyming put-down *Ammannato, Ammannato, che bel marmo hai rovinato* (". . . what a fine piece of marble you've ruined"). After a copy of Donatello's **Marzocco** (1418–20), the original of which is in the Bargello, comes a copy of the same sculptor's **Judith and Holofernes** (1456–60), which freezes the action at the moment Judith's arm begins its scything stroke – a dramatic conception that no other sculptor of the period would have attempted. Commissioned by Cosimo de' Medici, this statue doubled as a fountain in the Palazzo Medici but was removed to the Piazza della Signoria after the expulsion of the family in 1495, to be displayed as an emblem of vanquished tyranny; a new inscription on the base reinforced the message for those too obtuse to get it. The original is in the Palazzo Vecchio.

Michelangelo's **David**, at first intended for the Duomo, was also installed here as a declaration of civic solidarity by the Florentine Republic (see opposite); the original is now cooped up in the Accademia. Conceived as partner piece to the *David*, Bandinelli's **Hercules and Cacus** (1534) was designed as a personal emblem of Cosimo I and a symbol of Florentine fortitude. Benvenuto Cellini described the musclebound figure as looking like "a sackful of melons", and it's a sobering thought that the marble might well have ended up as something more inspiring. In the late 1520s, when the Florentines were once again busy tearing the Medici emblem from every building on which it had been stuck, Michelangelo offered to carve a monumental figure of Samson to celebrate the Republic's latest victory over tyranny; other demands on the artist's time put paid to this project, and the stone passed to Bandinelli, who duly vented his mediocrity on it.

The Loggia della Signoria

The square's grace note, the **Loggia della Signoria**, was begun in 1376, prompted by that year's heavy rains, which had washed out Florence's entire calendar of public ceremonies. It was completed in 1382, serv-

△ The Neptune Fountain

ing as a dais for city dignitaries, a forum for meeting foreign emissaries, and a platform for the swearing-in of public officials. Its alternative name, the Loggia dei Lanzi, comes from Cosimo I's bodyguard of Swiss lancers, who were garrisoned nearby.

Although Donatello's *Judith and Holofernes* was placed here as early as 1506, it was only in the late eighteenth century that the loggia became exclusively a showcase for sculpture. In the corner nearest the Palazzo Vecchio stands a figure that has become one of the iconic images of the Renaissance, Benvenuto Cellini's **Perseus** (1545), now back in its rightful place after a painstaking restoration. (The base is a copy, however; the original is on display in the Bargello – see p.157.) Made for Cosimo I, the statue symbolizes the triumph of firm Grand Ducal rule over the monstrous indiscipline of all other forms of government. The traumatic process of the statue's creation is vividly described in Cellini's rip-roaring autobiography: seeing the molten bronze beginning to solidify too early, the ever-resourceful hero saved the day by flinging all his pewter plates into the mix. When the bronze cooled the figure emerged from the mould missing only three toes, which were added later.

Equally attention-seeking is Giambologna's last work, to the right, **The Rape of the Sabine** (1583), conjured from the largest piece of sculptural marble ever seen in Florence, and the epitome of the Mannerist obsession with spiralling forms. The sculptor supposedly intended the piece merely as a study of old age, male strength and female beauty: the present name was coined later. The figures along the back wall are Roman works, traditionally believed to portray Roman empresses, while of the three central statues only one – Giambologna's **Hercules Slaying the Centaur** (1599) – deserves its place. The seven figures in the spandrels between the arches above depict the Virtues (1384–89), all carved to designs by Agnolo Gaddi save the head of *Faith*, which was replaced by Donatello when the original crashed to the ground.

The Palazzo Vecchio

Probably designed by Arnolfo di Cambio, Florence's fortress-like town hall, the **Palazzo Vecchio** (daily 9am–7pm; Thurs closes 2pm; €6 – or joint ticket with the Cappella Brancacci €8), was begun as the Palazzo dei Priori in the last year of the thirteenth century, to provide premises for the Priori or Signoria, the highest tier of the city's republican government. Changes in the Florentine constitution over the years entailed alterations to the layout of the palace, the most radical coming in 1540, when Cosimo I moved his retinue here from the Palazzo Medici and grafted a huge extension onto the rear. The Medici remained in residence for only nine years before moving to the Palazzo Pitti; the "old" (*vecchio*) palace, which they left to their son, Francesco, then acquired its present name. Between 1865 and 1870, during Florence's brief tenure as capital of a newly united Italy, the palace housed the country's parliament and foreign ministry.

As for the sights, much of the palace's decoration comprises a relentless eulogy to Cosimo and his relations, propaganda that's made tolerable by some of the palace's examples of Mannerist art – among the finest pieces produced by that ultra-sophisticated and self-conscious movement. There are also frescoes by Domenico Ghirlandaio and some outstanding sculptures, not least works by Michelangelo and Donatello. It's also possible to visit hidden parts of the palace on hour-long guided tours known as **Percorsi Segreti**, while for the youngsters there's the innovative **Emozioni da Museo** programme (see box on p.114).

PALAZZO VECCHIO
FIRST FLOOR

VIA DEI LEONI

VIA DEI GONDI

QUARTIERE DI LEONE X

Udienza   Salone dei Cinquecento

VIA DELLA NINNA

Sala dei Dugento

PIAZZA DELLA SIGNORIA

1 Monumental staircase (1561–71), Vasari
2 Virtue Overcoming Vice (1565), Giambologna
3 The Labours of Hercules (1562–84), Vincenzo de' Rossi
4 Victory (1533–4), Michelangelo
5 Studiolo di Francesco I (1570–75)
6 Tesoretto (1559–61)

A Stairs from ground floor
B Stairs to second floor

The courtyard and first floor

Work on the palace's beautiful inner **courtyard** was begun by Michelozzo in 1453. The decoration was largely added by Vasari, court architect from 1555 until his death in 1574, on the occasion of Francesco de' Medici's marriage to Johanna of Austria in 1565. The bride's origin explains the otherwise puzzling presence of cities belonging to the Habsburg Empire amid the wall's painted townscapes. Vasari also designed the central fountain, though the winsome putto and dolphin (1476) at its crown are the work of Verrocchio (the present statues are copies; the originals are on the Terrazzo di Giunone on the palace's second floor). Vasari was also let loose on the **monumental staircase** (marked 1 on our plan), a far more satisfying affair which leads to the palace's first floor (though visitors are sometimes directed to take a different route upstairs).

Vasari was given fuller rein in the huge **Salone dei Cinquecento** at the top of the stairs, where tickets are checked. It was originally built in 1495 as the meeting hall for the Consiglio Maggiore (Great Council), the ruling assembly of the penultimate republic. The chamber might have had one of Italy's most remarkable decorative schemes: Leonardo da Vinci and Michelangelo were employed to paint frescoes on opposite sides of the room, but Leonardo's work, *The Battle of Anghiari*, was abandoned (or destroyed) after his experimental technique went wrong, while Michelangelo's *The Battle of Cascina* had got no further than a fragmentary cartoon when he was summoned to Rome by Pope Julius II in 1506. Instead, the hall received six drearily bombastic murals (1563–65) – painted either by Vasari or under his direction – illustrating Florentine military triumphs over Pisa (1496–1509) and Siena (1554–55). It has generally been assumed that Vasari obliterated whatever remained of Leonardo's fresco before beginning his work, but the discovery of a cavity behind *The Battle of Marciano* has raised the possibility that Vasari instead contructed a false wall for his fresco, to preserve his great predecessor's painting. Investigations are proceeding.

The **ceiling**'s 39 panels, again by Vasari, celebrate the *Apotheosis of Cosimo I* (centre), a scene surrounded by the crests of the city's guilds and further paeans to the prowess of Florence and the Medici. (One of the Percorsi Segreti takes you into the attic above the roof, an extraordinary space where it's possible to see how Vasari pulled off the trick of suspending such a large ceiling without visible supports.) The **sculptural** highlight is

Percorsi Segreti

The Palazzo Vecchio's various so-called **Percorsi Segreti** ("Secret Passageways") allow access – on guided tours only – to parts of the building that are normally off limits. Most visually impressive is the trip up through the palace and into the **Attic of the Salone del Cinquecento**. From the vantage point of a balcony high above the hall, the guide describes the complex way in which Vasari created such a huge space within the medieval structure, and explains the allegorical meaning of the paintings. You are then led up into the vast attic itself, where two sets of trusses support the roof above and the ceiling below. Some of the beams are over 20m long.

Less magnificent, but still worth it for the guides' commentary, is the route leading from the street outside up through the secret **Stairway of the Duke of Athens**. The doorway was knocked through the exterior wall of the Palazzo in 1342 as an emergency escape route for the duke, who briefly took up the reins of power here. He never in fact used the staircase, but only because his fall from grace came rather sooner than he had imagined.

Another Percorso Segreto allows you inside the **Studiolo di Francesco I**, then through one of the hidden doors and up a secret little staircase to the *studiolino* or **Tesoretto** (6), Cosimo's tiny private study, which was built ten years before the *studiolo*.

All three tours (each costs €7 and includes admission to Palazzo Vecchio) last roughly an hour; further tours cost €2. These are not accessible for visitors in wheelchairs. Tours go every day in Italian, French and/or English, but exactly what language they are conducted in depends on demand, so it is worth asking about tours in English either at the desk by the ticket office or by phone (☎055.276.8224). Guides usually take one party on each Percorso Segreto from Monday to Friday at 9.30am and 11am, on Saturday at 3.30pm, 4.30pm and 5.30pm, and on Sunday at 10am, 11am and noon (though times change frequently); as a rule, there's at least one English-language party for each Percorso every day. Further *percorsi* are planned, depending on the success of the present tours.

Michelangelo's *Victory* (4), almost opposite the entrance door. Carved for the tomb of Pope Julius II, the statue was donated to the Medici by the artist's nephew, then installed here by Vasari in 1565 to celebrate Cosimo's defeat of the Sienese ten years earlier. Directly opposite, on the entrance wall, is the original plaster model of a companion piece for the Victory, Giambologna's **Virtue Overcoming Vice (2)**, another artistic metaphor for Florentine military might – this time Florence's victory over Pisa. The remaining statues, the masterpiece of sixteenth-century artist Vincenzo de' Rossi, portray the **Labours of Hercules (3)** and are yet another example of Florentine heroic propaganda: the innocuously classical Hercules is also one of Florence's many civic symbols.

From the Salone del Cinquecento, a roped-off door allows a glimpse of the strangest room in the building, the **Studiolo di Francesco I (5)**. Designed by Vasari towards the end of his career and decorated by no fewer than thirty Mannerist artists (1570–74), this windowless cell was created as a retreat for the introverted son of Cosimo and Eleanor. Each of the miniature bronzes and nearly all the paintings reflect Francesco's interest in the sciences and alchemy: the entrance wall pictures illustrate the theme of Earth, while the others, reading clockwise, signify Water, Air and Fire. The outstanding paintings are the two that don't fit the scheme: Bronzino's portraits of the occupant's parents, facing each other across the room. The oval paintings on the panels at the base hinted at the presence of Francesco's most treasured knick-

PALAZZO VECCHIO
SECOND FLOOR

VIA DEI LEONI

VIA DEI GONDI

Cancelleria

Sala delle Carte

QUARTIERE DEGLI ELEMENTI

VIA DELLA NINNA

QUARTIERE DI ELEONORA

Sala dei Gigli

Sala dell'Udienza

PIAZZA DELLA SIGNORIA

1 Sala degli Elementi
2 Terrazza di Saturno
3 Sala di Ercole
4 Terrazza di Giunone
5 Sala di Giove
6 Sala di Opi
7 Gallery
8 Cappella di Eleonora
9 Camera Verde
10 Camera delle Sabine
11 Sala di Ester
12 Camera di Penelope
13 Camera di Gualdrada
14 Cappella della Signoria

knacks, which were once concealed in the compartments behind; the wooden structure is actually a nineteenth-century re-creation, though the paintings are original.

Much of the rest of this floor is still used by council officials, though if the seven rooms of the **Quartiere di Leone X** and **Sala dei Dugento** are open (they rarely are), don't miss the opportunity. The latter, in particular, is outstanding: Benedetto and Giuliano da Maiano, excellent sculptors both, were responsible for the design (1472–77) and for the fine wooden ceiling; the tapestries (1546–53) were created to designs by Bronzino, Pontormo and others.

The second floor

Steps lead from the Salone to the **second floor**, passing an intriguing fireworks fresco (1558) showing Piazza della Signoria during the celebrations for the feast of St John the Baptist. Turn left at the top of the stairs and you enter the **Quartiere degli Elementi**, one of the floor's three distinct suites of rooms. All five salons here are slavishly devoted to a different member of the Medici clan. Persevere, though, if only to enjoy the city **views** from the Terrazza di Saturno and Verrocchio's original Putto and Dolphin statue on the Terrazzo di Giunone.

Return to the stairs and head straight on and you cross a gallery with views down into the Salone. Immediately afterwards come the six rooms of the **Quartiere di Eleonora di Toledo**, the private apartments of Cosimo I's wife. The first room, the **Camera Verde (9)**, has some charming wildlife on its ceiling, but the star turn is the tiny and exquisite **Cappella di Eleonora (8)**, vividly decorated by Bronzino in the 1540s. The wall paintings show scenes from the Life of Moses, episodes probably intended to draw parallels with the life of Cosimo. In the *Annunciation* that flanks the *Deposition* on the back wall, Bronzino is said to have used Cosimo and Eleanora's eldest daughter as the model for the Virgin.

Those who find all this Mannerist stuff unhealthily airless can take refuge in the more summery rooms which follow. The **Sala dell'Udienza**, originally the audience chamber of the Republic, boasts a stunning gilt-coffered ceiling by Giuliano da Maiano. The Mannerists reassert themselves with a vast fresco sequence (1545–48) by Cecchino Salviati, a cycle widely considered to be this artist's most accomplished work.

Giuliano was also responsible, with his brother Benedetto, for the intarsia work on the doors and the lovely doorway that leads into the **Sala dei Gigli**, a room that takes its name from the lilies (*gigli*) that adorn most of its surfaces

For the kids: Emozioni da Museo and Encounters

Emozioni da Museo (from €6) is anything but a traditional museum experience, though there's a whiff of the classroom about the "interactive workshops" held in rooms dotted around the palace. These are aimed more at local *ragazzi* than visitors' kids, but some classes are held in English, usually at weekends.

Most satisfying is perhaps "**Clothing and the Body**". Guides lead the group through a secret door in the Sala delle Carte and down to a vaulted space dominated by a four-poster bed in which an actress playing Eleonora di Toledo lies sleeping. Her maid enters and gets her mistress washed, combed, primped and ready for the day: Eleonora ends up dressed exactly as in Bronzino's portrait in the Uffizi. Meanwhile, their gossipy conversation, joined by Duke Cosimo and his servant, leads into a discussion that compares clothing and attitudes to the body now and in the Renaissance. Even when the actresses are speaking Italian, English-speaking guides are on hand to translate.

In "**Architecture of the Palazzo**" the children create, walk upon and, inevitably, destroy a load-bearing arch made from special bricks, and reconstruct a model of the Palazzo Vecchio in order to see how it was built. "**The Magic of Lenses**" allows the kids to play with various lenses, learn about optical effects and then put together a basic telescope. From the basement classroom it's up to the balcony of the palace to test out designs perfected by Galileo, among others. More scientific still is "**Horror Vacui?**" – ("[Nature] abhors a vacuum?") – which reproduces the experiments of the Florentine mathematician Torricelli, who proved the existence of atmospheric pressure.

Organized by the Associazone Museo dei Ragazzi di Firenze, **Encounters** are guided tours led by costumed actors that are aimed at both children and adults, but probably will appeal most to the youngsters. Vasari himself leads a tour of the Palazzo Vecchio, Galileo explains his radical inventions in the Museo di Storia della Scienza, and Suleiman the Magnificent takes a group of captured Christians round his armoury in the Museo Stibbert. During the school holidays, at least one tour a day is normally given in English; call ☎055.276.8224 to book.

– the lily is the emblem of Saint Zenobius and of the Virgin, both patron saints of Florence. The room has another splendid ceiling by the Maiano brothers, and a wall frescoed by Domenico Ghirlandaio with *SS Zenobius, Stephen and Lorenzo* (1481–85) and lunettes portraying *Six Heroes of Ancient Rome*. The undoubted highlight here, however, is Donatello's original *Judith and Holofernes* (1455–60), removed from Piazza della Signoria.

Two small rooms are attached to the Sala dei Gigli: the **Cancelleria**, once Machiavelli's office and now containing a bust and portrait of the oft-maligned political thinker, and the lovely **Sala delle Carte**, formerly the Guardaroba (Wardrobe), the repository of Cosimo's state finery. Now it is decorated with 57 maps painted in 1563 by the court astronomer Fra' Ignazio Danti, depicting what was then the entire known world. One of the maps, in the far right-hand corner, conceals a door to a hidden staircase.

A door leads out from the second floor onto the broad balcony of the Palazzo Vecchio's **tower**. The views are superb, if not as good as those enjoyed from the cell in the body of the tower above, which was known ironically as the Alberghinetto (Little Hotel); such troublemakers as Cosimo de' Medici and Savonarola were once imprisoned here. The final section of the museum, just before the exit, is something of an afterthought, and is devoted to second-rate pictures once owned by the American collector Loeser.

The Uffizi

Florence can prompt an over-eagerness to reach for superlatives; in the case of the **Galleria degli Uffizi**, the superlatives are simply the bare truth: this is the finest picture gallery in Italy. So many masterpieces are collected here that it's not even possible to skate over the surface in a single visit. Though you may not want to emulate Edward Gibbon, who visited the Uffizi fourteen times on a single trip to Florence, it makes sense to limit your initial tour to the first fifteen rooms, where the Florentine Renaissance works are concentrated, and to explore the rest another time.

The gallery is housed in what were once government offices (*uffizi*) built by Vasari for Cosimo I in 1560. After Vasari's death, work on the elongated U-shaped building was continued by Buontalenti, who was asked by Francesco I to glaze the upper storey so that it could house his art collection. Each of the succeeding Medici added to the family's trove of art treasures. The accumulated collection was preserved for public inspection by the last member of the family, Anna Maria Lodovica, whose will specified that it should be left to the people of Florence and never be allowed to leave the city. In the nineteenth century a large proportion of the statuary was transferred to the Bargello, while most of the antiquities went to the Museo Archeologico, leaving the Uffizi as essentially a gallery of paintings supplemented with some classical sculptures.

Rooms 1 to 8

On the ground floor, in rooms that once formed part of the eleventh-century church of San Pier Scheraggio, are shown **Andrea del Castagno**'s frescoes of celebrated Florentines; the imaginary portraits include Dante and Boccaccio, both of whom spoke in debates at the church. Close to a Botticelli *Annunciation*, a lift goes up to the galleries; if you take the staircase instead, you'll pass the

△ The courtyard of the Uffizi

Uffizi practicalities

The Uffizi is open Tues–Sun 8.15am–6.50pm; in high summer and at festive periods it sometimes stays open until 10pm. This is the busiest single building in the country, with over one and a half million visitors a year, so during peak season you've almost no chance of getting in without paying the €3 surcharge for booking a ticket **in advance**. For next-day tickets, there's a reservations desk that opens at 8.15am at Door 2, and has an allocation of just 200. For reservations further in advance, go to Door 3, or call the Firenze Musei line on ☎055.294.883 (see p.93 for more information). If you've booked by phone, make sure you arrive well before the allocated admission time, as there's often a substantial queue just to collect tickets. Full admission costs €6.50 but EU citizens aged 18–25 pay half price and entry is free to under-18s and over-65s. You should be aware that it's very rare for the whole Uffizi to be open; a board by the entrance tells you which sections are closed. In 2004 it was announced that over the next few years the Uffizi would be doubling the number of rooms open to the public, in order to show some 800 works that have usually been kept in storage; work on the exhibition spaces should soon be starting, which will inevitably mean that some pictures will not be on show precisely where they appear in the following account.

entrance to the prints and drawings collection, the bulk of which is reserved for scholarly scrutiny, though samples are often on public show.

Upstairs, all the rooms lead off the statue-lined monumental corridor that runs round the building. **Room 1**, housing an assembly of antique sculptures, many of which were used as a kind of source book by Renaissance artists, is often shut. The beginnings of the stylistic evolution of that period can be traced in the three altarpieces of the *Maestà* (Madonna Enthroned) that dominate **Room 2**: the *Madonna Rucellai*, *Maestà di Santa Trìnita* and *Madonna d'Ognissanti*, by **Duccio**, **Cimabue** and **Giotto** respectively. These great works, which dwarf everything around them, show the softening of the hieratic Byzantine style into a more tactile form of representation.

Painters from fourteenth-century Siena fill **Room 3**, with several pieces by Ambrogio and Pietro Lorenzetti and **Simone Martini**'s glorious *Annunciation*, the Virgin cowering from the angel amid a field of pure gold.

Other trecento artists follow in **Rooms 5 and 6**, among them Florence's first-rank Gothic painters, **Orcagna** and **Lorenzo Monaco**, whose majestic *Coronation of the Virgin* catches the eye first. The *Adoration of the Magi* by **Gentile da Fabriano** is the summit of the precious style known as International Gothic, spangled with gold so thick in places that the crowns of the kings, for instance, are like low-relief jewellery. The right-hand panel of the predella, below, was stolen by Napoleon and replaced with a copy which, unlike the rest of the painting, is not painted directly onto gold – hence the relative matt dullness of its surface. Nearby is the *Thebaid*, a beguiling little narrative that depicts monastic life in the Egyptian desert as a sort of holy fairytale; though sometimes assigned to the young Fra Angelico, it's more generally thought to be by the now-obscure Gherardo di Jacopo Starnina.

Gothic golds are left behind in **Room 7**, which reveals the sheer diversity of early Renaissance painting. **Paolo Uccello**'s *The Battle of San Romano* once hung in Lorenzo the Magnificent's bedchamber, in company with its two companion pieces now in the Louvre and London's National Gallery. Warfare is the ostensible subject, but this is really a semi-abstract compendium of perspectival effects – a toppling knight, a horse and rider keeled onto their sides, the foreshortened legs of a kicking steed, a thicket of lances – creating a fight scene with no real sense of violence. *The Madonna and Child with SS Francis, John the Baptist, Zenobius and Lucy* is one of only twelve extant paintings by **Domenico Veneziano**, who spent much of his life in Venice but died destitute in Florence.

Veneziano's greatest pupil, **Piero della Francesca**, is represented in **Room 8** by the paired portraits of *Federico da Montefeltro and Battista Sforza*, the duke and duchess of Urbino. These panels were painted two years after Battista's death; in the background of her portrait is the town of Gubbio, where she died giving birth to her ninth child and only son, Guidobaldo. Most space in Room 8 is given over to **Filippo Lippi**, whose *Madonna and Child with Two Angels* supplies one of the gallery's most popular faces, and one of its least otherworldly devotional images: the model was Lucrezia Buti, a convent novice who became the mother of the aptly named **Filippino** "Little Philip" **Lippi**, whose lustrous *Madonna degli Otto* shows the later influence of Leonardo.

Rooms 9 to 17

Lippi's pupil, Botticelli, steals some of the thunder in **Room 9**, where the artists centre-stage are **Piero** and **Antonio del Pollaiuolo**; their sinewy *SS Vincent, James and Eustace*, one of their best works, is chiefly the work of Antonio. This room also contains the *Portrait of Young Man in a Red Hat*, sometimes referred to as a self-portrait by Filippino, but now widely believed to be an eighteenth-century fraud.

It's in the merged **Rooms 10–14** that the greatest of **Botticelli**'s productions are gathered. A century ago most people walked past his pictures without breaking stride; nowadays – despite their elusiveness – the *Primavera* and the *Birth of Venus* stop all visitors in their tracks. The identities of the characters in the **Primavera** are not contentious: on the right Zephyrus, god of the west wind, chases the nymph Cloris, who is then transfigured into Flora, the pregnant goddess of spring; Venus stands in the centre, to the side of the three Graces, who are targeted by Cupid; on the left Mercury wards off the clouds of winter. What this all means, however, has occupied scholars for decades. Some see it as an allegory of the four seasons, but the consensus now seems to be that it shows the triumph of Venus, with the Graces as the physical embodiment of her beauty and Flora the symbol of her fruitfulness – an interpretation supported by the fact that the picture was placed outside the wedding suite of Lorenzo di Pierfrancesco de' Medici.

Botticelli's most winsome painting, the **Birth of Venus**, probably takes as its source the myth that the goddess emerged from the sea after it had been impregnated by the castration of Uranus, an allegory for the creation of beauty through the mingling of the spirit (Uranus) and the physical world. The supporting players are the nymph, Cloris, and Zephyrus, god of the west wind. Zephyrus blows the risen Venus to the shore where the goddess is clothed by Hora, daughter and attendant of Aurora, goddess of dawn. A third allegory hangs close by: *Pallas and the Centaur*, perhaps symbolizing the ambivalent triumph of reason over instinct. (Incidentally, the *Birth of Venus* was one of the first large-scale works to be painted onto canvas.)

Botticelli's devotional paintings are generally less perplexing. The *Adoration of the Magi* is traditionally thought to contain a gallery of Medici portraits: Cosimo il Vecchio as the first king, his sons Giovanni and Piero as the other two kings, Lorenzo the Magnificent on the far left, and his brother Giuliano as the black-haired young man in profile on the right. Only the identification of Cosimo is reasonably certain, along with that of Botticelli himself, on the right in the yellow robe. In later life, influenced by Savonarola's teaching, Botticelli confined himself to devotional pictures and moral fables, and his style became increasingly severe and didactic. The transformation is clear when comparing the easy grace of the *Madonna of the Magnificat* and the *Madonna of the Pomegranate* with the more rigidly composed *Pala di Sant'Ambrogio* or the angular and agitated *Calumny*. Even the *Annunciation* (1489), painted just as Savonarola's preaching began to grip Florence, reveals a new intensity in the expression of the angel and in the twisting treatment of the body of the Virgin, who appears almost blown back by the force of the message.

Not quite every masterpiece in this room is by Botticelli. Set away from the walls is the *Adoration of the Shepherds* by his Flemish contemporary **Hugo van der Goes**. Brought to Florence in 1483 by Tommaso Portinari, the Medici agent in Bruges, it provided the city's artists with their first large-scale demonstration of the realism of northern European oil painting, and had a great influence on the way the medium was exploited here.

Works in **Room 15** trace the formative years of **Leonardo da Vinci**, whose distinctive touch appears first in the *Baptism of Christ* (in room 14) by his master Verrocchio. Vasari claimed that only the wistful angel in profile was by the 18-year-old apprentice, and the misty landscape in the background, but recent X-rays have revealed that Leonardo also worked heavily on the figure of Christ. A similar terrain of soft-focus mountains and water occupies the far distance in Leonardo's slightly later *Annunciation*, in which a diffused light falls on a scene where everything is observed with a scientist's precision: the petals of the flowers on which the angel alights, the fall of the Virgin's drapery, the carving on the lectern at which she reads. In restless contrast to the aristocratic poise of the *Annunciation*, the sketch of *The Adoration of the Magi* – abandoned when Leonardo left Florence for Milan in early 1482 – presents the infant Christ as the eye of a vortex of figures, all drawn into his presence by a force as irresistible as a whirlpool.

Most of the rest of the room is given over to Raphael's teacher, **Perugino**, who is represented by a typically contemplative *Madonna and Child with Saints* (1493), and a meditative *Pietà* (1494–5). It also contains a bizarre *Incarnation* by **Piero di Cosimo**, the wild man of the Florentine Renaissance. Shunning civilized company, Piero did everything he could to bring his life close to a state of uncompromised nature, living in a house that was never cleaned, in the midst of a garden he refused to tend, and eating nothing but hard-boiled eggs. His wildness is most obviously realized in the nightmarish *Perseus Freeing Andromeda*, where even the rocks and the sea seem to twist and boil monstrously.

Rooms 18 to 23

Room 18, the octagonal **Tribuna**, now houses the most important of the Medici's collection of classical sculptures, chief among which is the *Medici Venus*, a first-century BC copy of the Praxitelean *Aphrodite of Cnidos*. She was kept in the Villa Medici in Rome until Cosimo III began to fret that she was having a detrimental effect on the morals of the city's art students, and ordered her removal to Florence. The move clearly didn't affect the statue's sexual charisma, however: it became traditional for eighteenth-century visitors to Florence to caress her buttocks. Around the walls are hung some fascinating portraits by **Bronzino**: Cosimo de' Medici, Eleanora of Toledo, Bartolomeo Panciatichi and his wife Lucrezia Panciatichi, all painted as figures of porcelain, placed in a bloodless, sunless world. More vital is Andrea del Sarto's flirtatious *Ritratto d'Ignota (Portrait of a Young Woman)*, and there's a deceptive naturalism to Vasari's portrait of Lorenzo the Magnificent and Pontormo's of Cosimo il Vecchio, both painted long after the death of their subjects.

The last section of this wing throws together Renaissance paintings from outside Florence, with some notable Venetian and Flemish works. **Signorelli** and **Perugino** – with some photo-sharp portraits – are the principal artists in **Room 19**, and after them comes a room largely devoted to **Cranach** and **Dürer**. Each has an *Adam and Eve* here, Dürer taking the opportunity to show off his proficiency as a painter of wildlife. Dürer's power as a portraitist is displayed in the *Portrait of the Artist's Father*, his earliest authenticated painting, and Cranach has a couple of acute pictures of Luther on display, one of them a double with his wife.

A taste of the Uffizi's remarkable collection of Venetian painting follows, with an impenetrable *Sacred Allegory* by **Giovanni Bellini**, and three rare works by **Giorgione** (if you accept the attribution of the mesmerizing portrait of a young soldier traditionally known as the *Gattemelata*). A clutch of northern European paintings is chiefly notable for **Holbein**'s *Portrait of Sir Richard Southwell*, while a crystalline triptych by **Mantegna** in Room 23 is not in fact a real triptych, but rather a trio of small paintings shackled together. To the side are a couple of other pictures by Mantegna – a swarthy portrait of Carlo de' Medici and the tiny *Madonna of the Stonecutters*, set against a mountain that looks like a gigantic fir cone.

Rooms 24 to 28

Beyond the stockpile of statues in the short corridor overlooking the Arno, the main attraction in **Room 25** is **Michelangelo**'s *Doni Tondo*, the only easel painting he came close to completing. Nobody has yet explained the precise significance of every aspect of this picture, but plausible explanations for parts of it have been put forward. The five naked figures behind the Holy Family seem to be standing in a half-moon-shaped cistern or font, which would relate to the infant Baptist to the right, who – in the words of St Paul – prefigures the coming of Christ just as the new moon is "a shadow of things to come". In the same epistle, Paul goes on to commend the virtues of mercy, benignity, humility, modesty and patience, which are perhaps what the five youths represent.

Room 26 contains **Andrea del Sarto**'s sultry *Madonna of the Harpies* and a number of compositions by **Raphael**, including the lovely *Madonna of the Goldfinch* and the late *Pope Leo X with Cardinals Giulio de' Medici and Luigi de' Rossi* – as shifty a group of ecclesiastics as was ever gathered in one frame. The Michelangelo tondo's contorted gestures, hermetic meaning and virulent colours were greatly influential on the Mannerist painters of the sixteenth century, as can be gauged from *Moses Defending the Daughters of Jethro* by **Rosso Fioren-**

tino, one of the seminal figures of the period, whose works hang in **Room 27**, along with two major religious works by Bronzino and his adoptive father, Pontormo – one of the very few painters not seen at his best in the Uffizi.

Room 28 is entirely given over to another of the titanic figures of sixteenth-century art, **Titian**, with nine paintings on show. His *Flora* and *A Knight of Malta* are stunning, but most eyes tend to swivel towards the *Urbino Venus*, the most fleshy and provocative of all Renaissance nudes, described by Mark Twain as "the foulest, the vilest, the obscenest picture the world possesses".

A brief diversion through the painters of the sixteenth-century Emilian school follows, centred on **Parmigianino**, whose *Madonna of the Long Neck* is one of the pivotal Mannerist creations. Parmigianino was a febrile and introverted character who abandoned painting for alchemy towards the end of his short life, and many of his works are marked by a sort of morbid refinement, none more so than this one. The Madonna's tunic clings to every contour, an angel advances a perfectly turned leg, the infant Christ drapes himself languorously on his mother's lap – prefiguring the dead Christ of the Pietà – while in the background an emaciated figure unrolls a scroll of parchment by a colonnade so severely foreshortened that it looks like a single column.

Rooms 31 to 45

Rooms 31 to 34 feature artists from Venice and the Veneto, with outstanding paintings such as **Moroni**'s *Portrait of Count Pietro Secco Suardi*, **Paolo Veronese**'s *Annunciation* and *Holy Family with St Barbara*, and **Tintoretto**'s *Leda*. Sebastiano del Piombo's *Death of Adonis* was reduced to little more than postage-stamp tatters by the bomb that wrecked part of the Uffizi in 1993; the restoration is little short of miraculous.

Room 41, entered off the main corridor, is dominated by **Rubens** and **Van Dyck**. The former's *Portrait of Isabella Brandt* makes its point more quietly than most of the stuff around it. Rubens lets rip in *Henry IV at the Battle of Ivry* and *The Triumphal Entry of Henry IV into Paris* – Henry's marriage to Marie de' Medici is the connection with Florence. Rubens's equally histrionic contemporary, **Caravaggio**, has a cluster of pieces in **Room 43**, including a screaming severed head of *Medusa*, a smug little *Bacchus*, and a throat-grabbing *Sacrifice of Isaac*.

Alongside, **Room 44** is in effect a showcase for the portraiture of **Rembrandt**. His sorrow-laden *Self-Portrait as an Old Man*, painted five years or so before his death, makes a poignant contrast with the self-confident self-portrait of thirty years earlier. Although there are some good pieces from **Tiepolo**, portraits again command the attention in the following room of eighteenth-century works, especially the two of Maria Theresa painted by **Goya**, and **Chardin**'s demure children at play.

On the way out, in the hall at the top of the exit stairs squats one of the city's talismans, the *Wild Boar*, a Roman copy of a third-century BC Hellenistic sculpture; it was the model for the *Porcellino* fountain in the Mercato Nuovo.

The Corridoio Vasariano

A door on the west corridor, between rooms 25 and 34, opens onto the **Corridoio Vasariano**, a passageway built by Vasari in 1565 to link the Palazzo Vecchio to the Palazzo Pitti through the Uffizi. Winding its way down to the river, over the Ponte Vecchio, through the church of Santa Felìcita and into the Giardino di Bóboli, it gives a fascinating series of clandestine views of the city. As if that weren't pleasure enough, the corridor is completely lined with paintings, the larger portion of which comprises a gallery of **self-portraits**. Once

Michelangelo

Michelangelo spent much of his life in Rome, and two of
his greatest masterpieces – the Sistine Chapel frescoes and
the Pietà in St Peter's – are to be seen in that city, yet Florence
is the place where you can best appreciate the extraordinary
scope of his achievement, because the city possesses creations
from every phase of his life and in every genre in which he excelled
– painting, sculpture and architecture (and he was also a fine poet).
Moreover, though stone-carving was perceived by many of Michelangelo's
contemporaries (including his father) as the least dignified of the arts,
Michelangelo always regarded himself primarily as a sculptor, and Florence has
the world's finest collection of his sculptural work.

Early years

Michelangelo Buonarroti was born on March 16, 1475 in Caprese, in eastern Tuscany, the second son of Francesca di Neri (who was to die just six years later) and Lodovico di Leonardo Buonarroti Simoni, the town's *podestà* (chief magistrate). One month later, the family moved to Florence, where, in 1488, Michelangelo was apprenticed to the painters Davide and Domenico Ghirlandaio. Little is known about how Michelangelo learned to carve: Vasari writes that he trained as a sculptor with Bertaldo di Giovanni (a pupil of Donatello and a protégé of the Medici),

Battle of the Lapiths and Centaurs

but Michelangelo always insisted that he was self-taught. What's certain is that his first stone reliefs were made for Lorenzo de' Medici, to whom he was introduced by the Ghirlandaio brothers and in whose household he lived from 1490 to 1492. In the Casa Buonarroti you can see two pieces from this period: the *Battle of the Lapiths and Centaurs*, which depicts a subject proposed by Poliziano (one of the neo-Platonist scholars of the Medici entourage); and the *Madonna of the Stairs*, which shows the influence of Donatello's methods of relief carving.

The flight to Rome – and return to Florence

In October 1494, as the French invaded Italy, Michelangelo fled Florence – a month before the expulsion of the Medici. His journey took him to Bologna, Venice, back to Bologna and thence briefly back to Florence, before arriving in Rome in 1496. There he carved the *Bacchus* that's now in the Bargello, a pseudo-antique statue of such brilliance that it was taken by some to be a genuine relic of ancient Rome. By the spring of 1499 he had completed the *Pietà* for St Peter's, a work that definitively secured his reputation as the pre-eminent sculptor of his day.

Meanwhile, the Florentine republic had become more peaceable after the overthrow of Savonarola, and in 1501 Michelangelo went back to his home city, where he was promptly commissioned to create the *David*, and then a sequence of Apostles for the Duomo, of which only the *St Matthew* (now in the Accademia, with *David*) was started. The latter, in which the

Doni Tondo

figure seems to be twisting itself free from the stone, has been interpreted as marking the emergence of a new heroic expressivity in Michelangelo's art (some would have you see it as a metaphor for the imprisonment of the soul in the body), but interpretation of this unfinished work, as with his other unfinished works, is highly problematic. Similarly, the precise meaning of every feature of the *Doni Tondo* (1503–04) – one of his very few forays into what he regarded as the menial art of easel painting – is elusive, but the picture exemplifies many characteristics unique to this painter: the complex and psychologically charged relationship between the figures; the vivid and crisp colouration; and the enigmatic male nudes in the background.

Other commissions from this period include the *Pitti Tondo* (now in the Bargello), and a fresco of the *Battle of Cáscina*, for the Palazzo Vecchio. Only the cartoon for the fresco was finished, but this became the single most influential work of art in the city, with its emphasis on the nude male form (no previous painter had made the naked male body so central to his art) and its use of figures in torsion, a recurrent motif in later Mannerist art.

One of the Slaves from the Accademia

1505–16: Rome

Work on the *Battle of Cáscina* was suspended in 1505 when Michelangelo was called to Rome by Pope Julius II, who wanted him to create his monumental tomb. The project was never finished, like so many of Michelangelo's schemes, and cost him decades of intermittent labour. When completed in 1545, the tomb bore little resemblance to what had been originally planned: it was built not in St Peter's but in San Pietro in Vincoli, and instead of having forty statues it had just seven, only three of them by Michelangelo: Moses, Leah and Rachel. The Leah and Rachel (both 1542) were the last sculptures that Michelangelo finished; the unfinished *Slaves* in the Accademia were made for another version of the tomb. His relationship with the fiery Julius was always fractious (in 1506 he ran back to Florence for a while, where he resumed work on the cartoon), but in 1508 he was summoned back to the Vatican to commence the most superhuman of all his undertakings – the decoration of the Sistine Chapel ceiling.

Final return to Florence

In 1516, with the Sistine ceiling finished, Michelangelo returned to Florence, where his plans for the facade of San Lorenzo church – sponsored by the Medici pope, Leo X – eventually came to nothing. In 1521, however, Leo contracted him to design a new sacristy for San Lorenzo, as a Medici mausoleum. Work on this, Michelangelo's first architectural project, was interrupted frequently, and building really only began in 1523, when he was also asked to build a library alongside the church, the Biblioteca

Tomb of Giuliano de' Medici

Laurenziana. In the San Lorenzo project Michelangelo created a vocabulary that was to provide the basis of Mannerist design, employing paradoxical details such as brackets that support nothing, and emphasizing the building as a dynamic rather than a static ensemble (eg columns that shrink into the wall rather than stand out from it). The sacristy contains a remarkable group of sculptures by Michelangelo, but again what one sees is but a portion of what was planned.

The Medici were again expelled from Florence in 1527, and Michelangelo stayed in the city to supervise the defences when it was besieged in 1530 by Emperor Charles V, who planned to install the despotic and malign Alessandro de'Medici as his puppet ruler. Once Alessandro was in place, Michelangelo's life in the city was far from easy. In 1534 he left Florence for the last time.

1534–64: Rome

He was to spend his last thirty years in Rome, where he was soon appointed architect to St Peter's, which Bramante had begun to rebuild in 1506. The colossal dome was Michelangelo's most spectacular addition to the architecture of the Vatican; he made a similarly profound

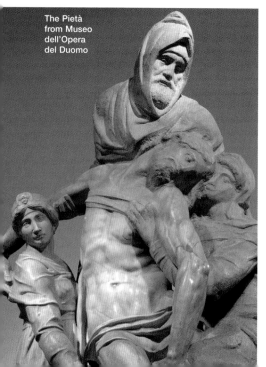
The Pietà from Museo dell'Opera del Duomo

alteration to the civic fabric of the city, when he remodelled the Campidoglio (the Capitol) in the 1540s. In the earlier part of this final period he also produced the tumultuous *Last Judgement* in the Sistine Chapel (1536–41), and two frescoes for Pope Paul III in the Cappella Paolina: the *Crucifixion of St Peter* and the *Conversion of St Paul*, scenes of tortured intensity that are a very long way from the contemplative serenity of the early *Pietà*. Some time around 1540 he carved his last secular work, the *Brutus* (now in the Bargello), but the greatest sculptures of his last years are versions of the *Pietà*. One of these – an ensemble that exemplifies the quality that contemporaries termed *terribilità* ("awesome powerfulness" is an approximation) – was intended for his own tomb, and is now in Florence's Museo dell'Opera del Duomo. Michelangelo died in Rome on February 18, 1564; his body was transported to Florence, where it was carried in torchlit procession to a tomb in Santa Croce.

you're past the portrait of Vasari, the series proceeds chronologically, littered with illustrious names: Raphael, Andrea del Sarto, Bronzino, Bernini, Rubens, Rembrandt, Velázquez, David, Delacroix and Ingres.

Because of staff shortages and strict limits on numbers allowed into the corridor (there is no fire escape), access is somewhat problematic. At the time of going to press, **tours** are being conducted by Uffizi staff on some mornings, usually on Wednesday and Friday, but there is no definite schedule, so for the latest situation you should ask at the gallery's ticket office, or ring ℡055.294.883. If you don't mind paying a premium for the privilege, you could contact Florence Art (🅦www.FlorenceArt.it), a private company that can sometimes arrange guided tours of the corridor.

West of the centre: from Via dei Calzaiuoli to the Cascine

The main catwalk of the Florentine *passeggiata* is **Via dei Calzaiuoli**, the broad pedestrianized avenue that links Piazza della Signoria with Piazza del Duomo. Shop-lined for most of its length, it boasts one stupendous monument, the church of **Orsanmichele**. Despite the urban improvement schemes of the nineteenth century and the bombings of World War II, several streets south of here retain their medieval character: an amble through streets such as Via Porta Rossa, Via delle Terme and Borgo Santi Apostoli will give you some idea of the feel of Florence in the Middle Ages, when every important house was an urban fortress. Best of these medieval redoubts is the **Palazzo Davanzati**, whose interior looks little different from the way it did six hundred years ago but has been undergoing a very lengthy restoration. Nearby, the fine church of **Santa Trìnita** is home to an outstanding fresco cycle by Domenico Ghirlandaio, while beyond the glitzy **Via de' Tornabuoni** – Florence's prime shopping street – you'll find a marvellous chapel designed by Alberti and a museum devoted to the work of Marino Marini. A few minutes' walk away, there's yet more Ghirlandaio, and work by Botticelli, in the church of **Ognissanti**. And if all this art is beginning to take its toll, you could take a break in the tree-lined avenues of the **Cascine** park, right on the western edge of the city centre.

Piazza della Repubblica and Orsanmichele

Halfway along Via dei Calzaiuoli, Via dei Speziali connects with the vacant expanse of **Piazza della Repubblica**. Impressive solely for its size, this square was planned in the late 1860s, when it was decided to demolish the central marketplace (Mercato Vecchio) and the tenements of the Jewish quarter in order to give Florence a public space befitting the capital of the recently formed Italian nation. The clearance had not even begun when, in 1870, the capital was transferred to Rome, and it wasn't until 1885 that the Mercato Vecchio and its disease-ridden slums were finally swept away. On the west side a vast **arch** bears the triumphant inscription: "The ancient city centre restored to new life from the squalor of centuries." The free-standing **column** is the solitary trace of the piazza's history. Once surrounded by stalls, it used to be topped by Donatello's statue of Abundance, and a bell that was rung to signal the start and close of trading.

Nowadays, Piazza della Repubblica is best known for the three large and expensive **cafés** that stand on the perimeter: the *Gilli*, founded way back in

ORSANMICHELE

VIA DEI CALZAIUOLI

VIA ORSANMICHELE

VIA DE' LAMBERTI

Entrance

1 John the Baptist (1412–16), Lorenzo Ghiberti (copy) for the Arte di Calimala (Textiles Guild); niche, Albizzo di Piero to a design by Ghiberti
2 The Incredulity of St Thomas (1473–83), Verrocchio (copy) for the Mercatanzia (Merchants' Tribunal); niche (1423–5), Donatello and Michelozzo
3 St Luke (1610), Giambologna for the Giudici e Notai (judges and notaries); niche, Niccolò di Pietro Lamberti (1404–6)
4 St Peter (1408–13), attrib. Brunelleschi (copy) for the Beccai (butchers)
5 St Philip (1412–15), Nanni di Banco (copy) for the Conciapelli (tanners)
6 Quattro Coronati (1409–17), Nanni di Banco for the Maestri di Pietre e Legname (masons and carpenters)
7 St George (1416–7) and relief of St George and Dragon, Donatello (copies) for the Corazzai (armourers)
8 St Matthew (1419–22), Lorenzo Ghiberti for the Cambio (bankers); tabernacle to a design by Ghiberti
9 St Stephen (1425–8), Lorenzo Ghiberti for the Arte della Lana (wool)
10 St Eligius (1417–21), Nanni di Banco (copy) for the Maniscalchi (smiths)
11 St Mark (1411–13), Donatello (copy) for the Linaiuoli (linen-drapers); niche (1411), Perfetto di Giovanni and Albizo di Piero
12 St James (1420) and bas relief of the Martyrdom of St James, attrib. Niccolò di Pietro Lamberti (copy) for the Pellicciai (furriers)
13 Madonna della Rosa (1400), attrib. Simone Talenti (copy) for the Medici e Speziali (doctors and pharmacists); Madonna Enthroned (above), Luca della Robbia (1465)
14 St John the Evangelist (1515), Baccio da Montelupo for the Setaiuoli (silk)

1733 (albeit on a different site – it moved here in 1910), and the most attractive of the trio; the *Giubbe Rosse*, once the intellectuals' café of choice (the Futurist manifesto was launched here in 1909); and the *Paszkowski*, which began business as a beer hall in the 1840s, is now a listed historic monument, and bears the suffix "Caffè Concerto", betokening the smarmy music with which it beguiles the piazza most evenings.

Orsanmichele

Standing like a truncated military tower towards the southern end of Via dei Calzaiuoli, **Orsanmichele** (closed for restoration at time of going to press; usual hours Mon–Fri 9am–noon & 4–6pm, Sat & Sun 9am–1pm & 4–6pm; closed 1st & last Mon of month) is the oddest-looking church in Florence, and one of the most impressive. Not only is the building itself a major monument, but its exterior was once the most remarkable outdoor sculpture gallery in the city. Several of the pieces have been or are being restored, however, after which most of them will be displayed in the Orsanmichele museum, with replicas in their places outside the church. Copies or not, this church is one of the city's great sights.

The first building here was a small oratory secreted in the orchard or vegetable garden (*orto*) of a now-vanished Benedictine monastery. A larger church stood on the site from the ninth century: San Michele ad Hortum, later San Michele in Orte – hence the compacted form of Orsanmichele. Even after the church was replaced by a **grain market** in the thirteenth century, the place retained its religious associations. In 1300, the chronicler Giovanni Villani claimed "the lame walked and the possessed were liberated" after visiting a miraculous image of the Virgin painted on one of the market pillars.

After a fire in 1304, the building was eventually replaced by a **loggia** designed by Francesco Talenti to serve as a trade hall for the *Arti Maggiori*, the Great Guilds which governed the city. Between 1367 and 1380 the loggia was walled in, after which the site was again dedicated almost exclusively to religious functions, while leaving two upper storeys for use as emergency grain stores.

As far back as 1339, plans had been made to adorn each pillar of the building with a patron statue, each assigned to a different guild. In the event, only one statue was produced in sixty years – a St Stephen commissioned by the *Arte della Lana*. In 1408, weary of the delay, the city elders set a ten-year deadline, warning that the niches would be allocated to rival guilds if commissions remained unfulfilled. The delay was to posterity's benefit, for the statues that were eventually produced spanned the emergent years of the Renaissance: sixty years earlier, lesser talents than Donatello, Ghiberti, Verrocchio and Luca della Robbia would have been put to work on the project.

The exterior

Beginning on the far left of Orsanmichele's Via dei Calzaiuoli flank, the first tabernacle is occupied by a replica of Ghiberti's **John the Baptist** (number 1 on plan), the earliest life-size bronze statue of the Renaissance. It was made for the *Calimala*, the guild of wholesale cloth importers. The adjacent niche is occupied by a replica of *The Incredulity of St Thomas* by Verrocchio, which replaced an earlier gilded statue by Donatello, *St Louis of Toulouse*, now in the Museo dell'Opera del Duomo; Giambologna's *St Luke* similarly replaced an earlier statue by Lamberti now in the Bargello.

Round the corner, Brunelleschi's *St Peter* is followed by two works from Nanni di Banco: *St Philip* and the so-called **Quattro Coronati**. These four Christian stonemasons executed by Diocletian for refusing to carve a pagan idol were patron saints of the masons' guild, sponsors of this niche. Their name comes from the manner of their execution: they were killed by having an iron crown (*corona*) driven onto their heads. A copy of Donatello's *St George* occupies the next niche – the original is in the Bargello, as is the original accompanying bas-relief of *St George and the Dragon*.

On the church's west side stand *St Matthew* and *St Stephen*, both by Ghiberti, and *St Eligius* by Nanni di Banco; the *St Matthew*, posed and clad like a Roman orator, makes a telling comparison with the same artist's *St John*, cast just ten years before but still semi-Gothic in its sharp-edged drapery and arching lines. Earlier than either is Donatello's **St Mark**, made in 1411 when the artist was 25; the work is often considered one of the first statues of the Renaissance, a title based on the naturalism of

△ St George, Orsanmichele

St Mark's stance and the brooding intensity of his gaze. A replica of Pietro Lamberti's *St James* precedes the benign **Madonna della Rosa**, probably by Simone Talenti; the weakest of the sculptures, Baccio da Montelupo's *John the Evangelist*, brings up the rear.

The interior

Orsanmichele's interior centrepiece is a pavilion-sized glass and marble **tabernacle** by Orcagna, the only significant sculptural work by the artist. Decorated with lapis lazuli and gold, it cost 86,000 florins in 1355, and frames a *Madonna* painted in 1347 by Bernardo Daddi as a replacement for the miraculous image of the Virgin destroyed by the 1304 fire. The brotherhood that administered Orsanmichele paid for the tabernacle from thanksgiving donations in the aftermath of the Black Death; so many people attributed their survival to the Madonna's intervention that the money received in 1348 alone was greater than the annual tax income of the city coffers. Other paintings can be seen on the pillars: devotional images of the guilds' patron saints, they can be regarded as the low-cost ancestors of the Orsanmichele statues.

The original lines of the bricked-up loggia are still clear, while the vaulted halls of the upper granary – one of the city's most imposing medieval interiors – also survive. The halls now house the **Museo di Orsanmichele** (tours daily 9am, 10am & 11am; closed 1st and last Mon of month; free), entered via the footbridge from the Palazzo dell'Arte della Lana, the building opposite the church entrance. In practice, opening times can be affected by the use of the space for temporary exhibitions. If you get the chance, be sure to visit, not only for the fine interior, but also for the chance to see several of the most important original exterior statues. As restoration work is completed, it is planned that all the statues will eventually be exhibited here, though no one expects to wrest the most famous of all, Donatello's *St George*, from the clutches of the Bargello.

From the Mercato Nuovo to Santi Apostoli

One block west of the southern end of Via dei Calzaiuoli lies the **Mercato Nuovo**, or Mercato del Porcellino (mid-Feb to mid-Nov daily 9am–7pm; mid-Nov to mid-Feb Tues–Sat 9am–5pm), where there's been a market since the eleventh century, though the present loggia dates from the sixteenth. Having forked out their euros at the souvenir stalls, most people join the small group that's invariably gathered round the bronze boar known as *Il Porcellino*: you're supposed to earn yourself some good luck by getting a coin to fall from the animal's mouth through the grille below his head. This superstition has a social function, as the coins go to an organization that runs homes for abandoned children.

Palazzo Davanzati

Perhaps the most imposing exterior in this district is to be seen just to the south of the market – the thirteenth-century Palazzo di Parte Guelfa, financed from the confiscated property of the Ghibelline faction and later expanded by Brunelleschi. However, for a more complete re-creation of medieval Florence you should visit the fourteenth-century **Palazzo Davanzati** in Via Porta Rossa. In the nineteenth century the palazzo was divided into flats, but at the beginning of the twentieth it was restored to something very close to the modified appearance of the 1500s, when a loggia replaced the battlements on the roof, and the Davanzati stuck their coat of arms on the front. (The immense amount of metalwork on the exterior was used variously for tying up animals, draping wool and wet washing, suspending bird cages or fixing banners, carpets and other hangings on the occasion of festivities and processions.) Apart from those haute-bourgeois emendations, the place now looks much as it did when first inhabited. Virtually every room is furnished and decorated in predominantly medieval style, using genuine artefacts gathered from a variety of sources.

Nowadays the palazzo is maintained as the **Museo della Casa Fiorentina Antica**. The building was closed in 1995 for major structural repairs, and currently just a section of the building is open to the public (Tues–Sat 8.15am–1.30pm, open 1st, 3rd & 5th Sun of month, and 2nd & 4th Mon; free). No full opening date has been fixed; the description that follows gives you an idea of the interior of the museum before its closure.

The interior

The owners of this house were obviously well prepared for the adversities of urban living, as can be seen in the siege-resistant doors, the huge storerooms for the hoarding of provisions, and the private water supply. The courtyard's **well** was something of a luxury at a time when much of Florence was still dependent on public fountains: a complex series of ropes and pulleys allowed it to serve the entire house. Similarly, the palace's **toilets** were state-of-the art affairs by the standards of 1330.

An ancient staircase – the only one of its kind to survive in the city – leads to the **first floor** and the Sala Grande or **Sala Madornale**. This room, used for family gatherings, underlines the dual nature of the house: furnished in the best style of the day, it also has four wood-covered hatches in the floor to allow the bombarding of a besieging enemy. Merchants' houses in the fourteenth century would typically have had elaborately painted walls in the main rooms, and the Palazzo Davanzati preserves some fine examples of such decor, especially in the dining room or **Sala dei Pappagalli**, where the imitation wall hangings of the lower walls are patterned with a parrot (*pappagallo*) motif, while the upper walls depict a garden terrace.

Before the development of systems of credit, wealth had to be sunk into tangible assets such as the tapestries, ceramics, sculpture and lacework that alleviate the austerity of many of these rooms; any surplus cash would have been locked away in a strongbox like the extraordinary example in the **Sala Piccola**, whose locking mechanism looks like the innards of a primitive clock. There's also a fine collection of *cassoni*, the painted chests in which the wife's dowry would be stored.

Plushest of the rooms is the first-floor **bedroom**, or Sala dei Pavoni – complete with en-suite bathroom. It takes its name from the beautiful frescoed frieze of trees, peacocks (*pavoni*) and other exotic birds: the coats of arms woven into the decoration are the crests of families related to the Davizzi. The rare Sicilian linen bed cover is decorated with scenes from the story of Tristan.

The arrangements of the rooms on the upper two floors, together with their beautiful array of furniture and decoration, mirror that of the first floor. For all the splendour of the lower rooms, the spot where the palace's occupants would have been likeliest to linger is the third-floor **kitchen**. Located on the uppermost floor to minimize damage if a fire broke out, it would have been the warmest room in the house. A fascinating array of utensils are on show here: the *girapolenta*, the polenta-stirrer, is extraordinary. The leaded glass – like the toilets – was considered a marvel at a time when many windows were covered with turpentine-soaked rags stretched across frames to repel rainwater.

Santi Apostoli

Between Via Porta Rossa and the Arno, on Piazza del Limbo (the former burial ground of unbaptized children), stands the ancient church of **Santi Apostoli** (Mon–Sat 10am–noon & 4–5.30pm, Sun 4–5.30pm). Legend has it that this was founded by Charlemagne, but it's not quite that ancient – the eleventh century seems the likeliest date of origin. Santi Apostoli possesses some peculiar relics, in the form of stone fragments allegedly brought from the Holy Sepulchre in Jerusalem by a crusading Florentine; on Holy Saturday sparks struck from these stones are used to light the flame that ignites the "dove" that in turn sets off the fireworks in front of the Duomo (see p.204). Orderly and graceful, the interior of grey *pietra serena* against white walls looks like an anticipation of the architecture of Brunelleschi.

Piazza and Ponte Santa Trìnita

West of the Palazzo Davanzati, Via Porta Rossa runs into **Piazza Santa Trìnita** – not really a square, just a widening of the city's most expensive street, Via de' Tornabuoni. The centrepiece of the piazza is the Colonna della Giustizia (Column of Justice), which Pope Pius IV uprooted from the Baths of Caracalla and sent to Cosimo I, who in 1565 raised it on the spot where, in August 1537, he had heard of the defeat of the anti-Medici faction at Montemurlo. The column stands on the axis of the sleek **Ponte Santa Trìnita**, construction of which was begun in 1567 on Cosimo's orders, ten years after its predecessor was demolished in a flood – and ten years after Siena had finally become part of Florentine territory, a subjugation which the bridge was intended to commemorate. The roads on both sides of the river were raised and widened to accentuate the dramatic potential of the new link between the city centre and the Oltrarno, but what makes this the classiest bridge in Florence is the sensuous curve of its arches, a curve so shallow that engineers have been baffled as to how the bridge bears up under the strain. Ostensibly the design was conjured up by Ammannati, one of the Medici's favourite artists, but the curves so closely resemble the arc of Michelangelo's Medici tombs that it's likely the credit belongs to him.

In 1944 the Nazis blew the bridge to smithereens and a seven-year argument ensued before it was agreed to rebuild it using as much of the original material as could be dredged from the Arno. To ensure maximum authenticity in the reconstruction, all the new stone that was needed was quarried from the Bóboli gardens – where the stone for Ammannati's bridge had been cut – and hand tools were used to trim it, as electric blades would have given the blocks too harsh a finish. Twelve years after the war, the reconstructed bridge was opened, lacking only the head from the statue of *Spring*, which had not been found despite the incentive of a hefty reward. At last, in 1961, the missing head was fished from the riverbed; having lain in state for a few days on a scarlet cushion in the Palazzo Vecchio, it was returned to its home.

Santa Trìnita church

The antiquity of the church of **Santa Trìnita** (Mon–Sat 8am–noon & 4–6pm, Sun 4–6pm) is manifest in the Latinate pronunciation of its name: modern Italian stresses the last, not the first syllable. The church was founded in 1092 by a Florentine nobleman called **Giovanni Gualberto**, scenes from whose life are illustrated in the frescoes in the alcove at the top of the left aisle. One Good Friday, so the story goes, Gualberto set off intent on avenging the murder of his brother. On finding the murderer he decided to spare his life – it was Good Friday – and proceeded to San Miniato (see p.184), where a crucifix is said to have bowed its head to honour his act of mercy. Giovanni went on to become a Benedictine monk and found the reforming Vallombrosan order and – notwithstanding the mayhem created on Florence's streets by his militant supporters – was eventually canonized.

The church was rebuilt between about 1300 and 1330, work being interrupted by the plague of 1348. Further rebuilding took place between 1365 and 1405, while the facade – by Buontalenti – was added in 1594. Piecemeal additions over the years have lent the church a pleasantly hybrid air: the largely Gothic interior contrasts with the Mannerist facade, itself at odds with the Romanesque interior facade. Santa Trìnita's architecture is softened by a number of works of art, the best of which are Ghirlandaio's frescoes. Resist the temptation to head straight for these, however, and work round the church, beginning at the **Cappella Cialli-Sernigi**, which contains a damaged fresco and detached *sinopia* depicting the *Mystical Marriage of St Catherine* (1389) by Spinello Aretino, recently discovered below the frescoes in the adjoining chapel.

The next chapel, the **Cappella Bartolini-Salimbeni**, is one of only a handful in the city whose decorative scheme has remained uncorrupted by subsequent additions and changes. The frescoes (1420–25) of episodes from the **Life of the Virgin** are by Lorenzo Monaco, who also painted its *Annunciation* altarpiece. The lunette and right wall of the next chapel, the **Cappella Ardinghelli**, features Giovanni Toscani's contemporaneous frescoes of the *Pietà* (1424–25) and an unfinished altar tabernacle by Benedetto da Rovezzano (1505–13). In the sacristy, if it's open, you'll find the tomb of Onofrio Strozzi, scion of a major banking dynasty: long thought to be the work of Donatello, the tomb is now cautiously attributed to Michelozzo.

Next comes the church's highlight, the **Cappella Sassetti**, famous for its cycle of frescoes of scenes from the *Life of St Francis* (1483–86) by **Domenico Ghirlandaio**. Commissioned by Francesco Sassetti, a friend of Lorenzo the Magnificent, they were intended, in part, to rival the frescoes of Sassetti's rival, Giovanni Tornabuoni, in Santa Maria Novella, also by Ghirlandaio (see p.133). These frescoes are concerned as much with a portrayal of fifteenth-century Florence as with the narrative of their religious themes. St Francis, floating in the sky, is shown bringing a child back to life in Piazza Santa Trìnita: the church of Santa Trìnita is in the background, painted as it then appeared. (Opposite the church you can see the child plummeting to his temporary death.) Above this scene, *St Francis Receiving the Rule* sets the action in Piazza della Signoria – note the Loggia della Signoria – and features (right foreground) a portrait of Sassetti between his son, Federigo, and Lorenzo the Magnificent (Sassetti was general manager of the Medici bank). On the steps below them are the humanist Poliziano and three of his pupils, Lorenzo's sons; the blonde-haired boy, at the back of the line, is Giovanni, the future Pope Leo X.

Ghirlandaio has depicted himself in the lower scene, with his hand on his hip, and is also present in the chapel's altarpiece, the *Adoration of the Shepherds* (1485) – he's the shepherd pointing to the Child and, by way of self-identification, to the garland (*ghirlanda*). A persuasive Renaissance fusion of Classical and Christian iconography, the painting sets its protagonists amid Classical columns, a Roman sarcophagus (used as the manger) and a triumphal arch transplanted from the Roman forum. The figures of the donors – Sassetti and his wife, Nera Corsi – kneel to either side; they are buried in Giuliano da Sangallo's black tombs under the side arches.

Displayed in the neighbouring **Cappella Doni** is the miraculous crucifix, formerly in San Miniato, said to have bowed its head to Gualberto (see p.133). The last of the church's major works, a powerful composition by Luca della

Robbia – the **tomb of Benozzo Federighi, bishop of Fiesole** – occupies the left wall of the Cappella Scali; moulded and carved for the church of San Pancrazio, it was transported here in 1896. The fine wooden **statue of Mary Magdalene**, which owes much to Donatello's Magdalene in the Museo dell'Opera del Duomo, was begun by Desiderio da Settignano and completed, according to Vasari, by Benedetto da Maiano.

Via de' Tornabuoni to the Cascine

The shops of **Via de' Tornabuoni** are effectively out of bounds to those who don't travel first class. Versace, Ferragamo, Prada, Cavalli, Gucci and Armani have their outlets here: indeed, in recent years they have come to monopolize the street (and nearby Piazza Strozzi), to the dismay of many, who see further evidence of the loss of Florentine identity in the eviction of local institutions such as the Seeber bookshop, the Farmacia Inglese and the *Giacosa* café. The last of this trio – famed as the birthplace of the Negroni cocktail – now exists in name only, as an adjunct to the huge Roberto Cavalli shop. Conspicuous wealth is nothing new on Via de' Tornabuoni. Looming above everything is the vast **Palazzo Strozzi**, the most intimidating of all Florentine Renaissance palaces, with windows as big as gateways and embossed with lumps of stone the size of boulders. It was begun by the banker Filippo Strozzi, a figure so powerful that he was once described as "the first man of Italy", and whose family provided the ringleaders of the anti-Medici faction in Florence. He bought and demolished a dozen town houses to make space for Giuliano da Sangallo's inhabitable strongbox, and the construction of it lasted from 1489 to 1536. The interior of the palazzo is open only for special exhibitions.

The Palazzo Rucellai

Some of Florence's other plutocrats made an impression with a touch more subtlety than the Strozzi. In the 1440s Giovanni Rucellai, one of the richest businessmen in the city (and an esteemed scholar too), decided to commission a new house from Leon Battista Alberti, whose accomplishments as architect, mathematician, linguist and theorist of the arts prompted a contemporary to exclaim, "Where shall I put Battista Alberti: in what category of learned men shall I place him?" The resultant **Palazzo Rucellai**, two minutes' walk from the Strozzi house at Via della Vigna Nuova 18, was the first palace in Florence to follow the rules of classical architecture; its tiers of pilasters, incised into smooth blocks of stone, evoke the exterior wall of the Colosseum. Alberti later produced another, equally elegant design for the same patron – the front of the church of Santa Maria Novella. In contrast to the feud between the Medici and the Strozzi, the Rucellai were on the closest terms with the city's de facto royal family: the **Loggia dei Rucellai**, across the street (now a shop), was in all likelihood built for the wedding of Giovanni's son to the granddaughter of Cosimo il Vecchio, and the frieze on the Palazzo Rucellai features the heraldic devices of the two families, the Medici emblem alongside the Rucellai sail.

The Museo Marino Marini and the Cappella di San Sepolcro

Round the corner from the Palazzo Rucellai stands the ex-church of San Pancrazio, deconsecrated by Napoleon, then successively the offices of the state lottery, the magistrates' court, a tobacco factory and an arsenal. It is now the swish **Museo Marino Marini** (10am–5pm; closed Tues & Sun, plus Sat in June & July and all Aug; €4), where the attire and demeanour of the attendants might make you think you'd strayed into a fashion house. Holding some two hundred works left to the city in Marini's will, the museum itself is perhaps the most intriguing artefact and it's debatable whether Marini's pieces can stand up to the reverential atmosphere imposed by the display techniques. Variations on the sculptor's trademark horse-and-rider theme – familiar from civic environments all over Europe – make up much of the show.

Once part of the church but now entirely separate from the museum, the **Cappella Rucellai**, which was redesigned by Alberti, houses the **Cappella di San Sepolcro**, the most exquisite of his creations (June–Sept hours vary but usually Mon–Fri 10am–noon; Oct–May Mon–Sat 10am–noon & 5–5.30pm; free). Designed as the funerary monument to Giovanni Rucellai, it takes the form of a diminutive reconstruction of Jerusalem's Church of the Holy Sepulchre.

Ognissanti

In medieval times one of the main areas of cloth production – the mainstay of the Florentine economy – was in the western part of the city. **Ognissanti** (daily 7.30am–12.30pm & 3.30–7.30pm), or All Saints, the main church of this quarter, stands on a piazza that might be taken as a symbol of the state of the present-day Florentine economy, dominated as it is by the five-star *Grand* and *Excelsior* hotels.

The church was founded in 1256 by the Umiliati, a Benedictine order from Lombardy whose speciality was the weaving of woollen cloth. In 1561 the Franciscans took over the church, the new tenure being marked by a Baroque overhaul which spared only the medieval campanile. The facade (1637) of the church is of historical interest as one of the earliest eruptions of the Baroque in Florence – it was abhorred by many Florentines at the time as an affront to the city's Renaissance traditions. The building within, however, is made appealing by earlier features – **frescoes** by Domenico Ghirlandaio and Sandro Botticelli.

The young face squeezed between the Madonna and the dark-cloaked man in Ghirlandaio's *Madonna della Misericordia* (1473), the higher of the two works over the second altar on the right, is said to be that of Amerigo Vespucci, an agent for the Medici in Seville, whose two voyages in 1499 and 1501 would lend his name to a continent. The altar was paid for by the Vespucci, a family of silk merchants from the surrounding district, which is why other members of the clan appear beneath the Madonna's protective cloak. Among them is Simonetta Vespucci (at the Virgin's left hand), the mistress of Giuliano de' Medici and reputedly the most beautiful woman of her age – she is said to have been the model for Botticelli's *Venus*, now in the Uffizi.

The idea may not be so far-fetched, for Botticelli also lived locally, and the Vespucci and Filipepi families were on good terms. Botticelli is buried in the church, beneath a round tomb slab in the south transept, and his painting of *St Augustine's Vision of St Jerome* (1480) lies on the same wall as the Madonna, between the third and fourth altars. Facing it is Ghirlandaio's more earthbound *St Jerome*, also painted in 1480. In the same year Ghirlandaio painted the *Last Supper* that covers one wall of the **refectory**, reached through the cloister entered to the left of the church (Mon, Tues & Sat 9am–noon; free).

The Cascine

Florence's public park, the **Cascine**, begins close to the Ponte della Vittoria (bus #17e from the Duomo or station) and dwindles away 3km downstream, at the confluence of the Arno and the Mugnone. Once the Medici dairy farm (*cascina*), then a hunting reserve, this narrow strip of green mutated into a high-society venue in the eighteenth century: if there was nothing happening at the opera, all of Florence's beau monde turned out to promenade under the trees of the Cascine. A fountain in the park bears a dedication to Shelley, who was inspired to write his *Ode to the West Wind* while strolling here on a blustery day in 1819.

Thousands of people come out here on Tuesday mornings for the colossal market beyond the former train station (which now houses a new arts centre, the Stazione Leopolda), and on any day of the week the Cascine swarms with joggers, cyclists and roller-bladers. Parents bring their kids out here too, to play on the grass (a rare commodity in Florence) or visit the small zoo. However, the Cascine also has a reputation as a haunt for the city's junkies, and it's emphatically not a place for a nocturnal stroll, as it has long been a hunting ground for the city's pimps.

The Santa Maria Novella district

Scurrying from the train station in search of a room, or fretting in the queues for a rail ticket, most people barely give a glance to **Santa Maria Novella train station**, but this is a building that deserves as much attention as many of the city's conventional monuments. Its principal architect, Giovanni Michelucci – who died in January 1991 just two days short of his hundredth birthday – was one of the leading figures of the Modernist movement, which in Mussolini's Italy was marginalized by the officially approved pomposities of the Neoclassical tendency. Accordingly, there was some astonishment when, in 1933, Michelucci

St Peter Martyr and the Paterenes

In the twelfth century Florence became the crucible of one of the reforming religious movements that periodically cropped up in medieval Italy. The **Paterenes**, who were so numerous that they had their own clerical hierarchy in parallel with that of the mainstream Church, were convinced that everything worldly was touched by the Devil. Accordingly they despised the papacy for its claims to temporal power and spurned the adoration of all relics and images. Furthermore, they rejected all forms of prayer and all contracts – including marriage vows – and were staunch pacifists.

Inevitably their campaign against the financial and moral corruption of the Catholic Church brought them into conflict with Rome; the displeasure of the Vatican eventually found its means of expression in the equally zealous but decidedly non-pacific figure of the Dominican known as **St Peter Martyr**. Operating from the monastery of Santa Maria Novella, this papal inquisitor headed a couple of anti-Paterene fraternities, the Crocesegnati and the Compagnia della Fede, which were in effect his private army. In 1244 he led them into battle across the Piazza Santa Maria Novella, where they proceeded to massacre hundreds of the theological enemy. The epicentre of the carnage is marked by the Croce del Trebbio in Via delle Belle Donne, off the eastern side of the piazza.

After this, the Dominicans turned to less militant work, founding the charitable organization called the Misericordia, which is still in existence today (see p.106). In 1252 Peter was knifed to death by a pair of assassins in the pay of a couple of Venetians whose property he'd confiscated, which is why he's usually depicted with a blade embedded in his skull. The official version, however, identifies the assassins as Paterene heretics, and relates that the dying man managed to write out the Credo with his own blood before expiring – an incident depicted in the frescoes in Santa Maria Novella's Cappellone degli Spagnoli. Within the year he'd been made a saint.

and his colleagues won the open competition to design the main rail terminal for one of the country's showpiece cities. It's an example of impeccably rational planning, so perfectly designed for its function that no major alterations have been necessary in the half-century since its completion.

Cross the road from the front of the train station, and you're on the edge of a zone free from the hazards of speeding traffic and petrol fumes. On the other side of the church of Santa Maria Novella – whose back directly faces the station – lies **Piazza Santa Maria Novella**, a square with a distinctly squalid undertone, though the development of an upmarket hotel complex on the eastern side (formerly something of a backpackers' den), and the long-awaited opening of the Alinari photography museum in the Loggia di San Paolo, will doubtless be followed by more stringent policing of the area.

The church of Santa Maria Novella

Santa Maria Novella (Mon–Thurs & Sat 9am–5pm, Fri & Sun 1–5pm; €2.50) stands on the site of the more humble Santa Maria delle Vigne, which in 1221 was handed to the Dominicans, who then set about altering the place to their taste. By 1360 the interior was finished, but only the Romanesque lower part of the **facade** had been completed. This state of affairs lasted until 1456, when Giovanni Rucellai paid for Alberti to design an elegantly classicized upper storey that would blend with the older section while improving the facade's proportions. The sponsor's name is picked out across the facade in Roman capitals (IOHANES·ORICELLARIVS...), while the Rucellai family emblem, the billowing sail of Fortune, runs as a motif through the central frieze. One other external feature is worth noting: the route into the church takes you through the cemetery, which – uniquely – is ringed by an arcade of *avelli*, the collective burial vaults of upper-class families.

△ Santa Maria Novella

SANTA MARIA NOVELLA

0   25 m

PIAZZA DELLA STAZIONE

VIA DEGLI AVELLI

Refectory

Entrance to Church
PIAZZA SANTA MARIA NOVELLA
Entrance to Museum

1 Annunciation, anon. 14th-century Florentine painter
2 Nativity (lunette above door), attrib. Botticelli
3 Annunciation (1602), Santi di Tito
4 Tomb of Beata Villana delle Botti (d. 1361), a Dominican nun,
  by Bernardo Rossellini (1451) and Desiderio da Settignano
5 Pulpit (1443), Brunelleschi
6 Trinity (1427), Masaccio
7 Crucifix, Giotto (c. 1288–90)
8 Tomb of the Patriarch of Constantinople (d.1440)
9 Cappella Rucellai (1303–52): Madonna and Child (1348),
  Mino da Fiesole; tombplate of Leonardo Dati (1425–6), Ghiberti
10 Cappella Bardi: 14th-century frescoes
11 Cappella di Filippo Strozzi: frescoes (1489–1502), Filippino Lippi;
   tomb of Filippo Strozzi (1491–5), Benedetto da Maiano
12 Chancel: fresco cycle (1485–90), Domenico Ghirlandaio
13 Cappella Gondi: crucifix (1410–14), attrib. Brunelleschi
14 Cappella Strozzi: frescoes (1350–7), Narno di Cione;
   altarpiece (1357), Orcagna
15 Chiostro Verde
16 The Flood (1425–30), Paolo Uccello
17 Cappellone degli Spagnoli
18 Chiostrino dei Morti
19 Chiostro Grande

Santa Maria Novella's **interior** – which was designed specifically to enable preachers to address their sermons to as large a congregation as possible – is filled with masterworks, not least a ground-breaking painting by Masaccio, a crucifix by Giotto and no fewer than three major **fresco cycles**.

The nave

Entwined around the second nave pillar on the left is a **pulpit**, designed by Brunelleschi and notorious as the spot from which the Dominicans first denounced Galileo for espousing the Copernican theory of the heavens. The actual carving was completed by Buggiano, Brunelleschi's adopted son, who may well have advised Masaccio on the Renaissance architectural details present in the background of his extraordinary 1427 fresco of the **Trinity**, which is painted on the wall nearby. This was one of the earliest works in which the rules of perspective and classical proportion were rigorously employed, and Florentines queued to view the illusion on its unveiling, stunned by a painting which appeared to create three-dimensional space on a solid wall. Amazingly, the picture was concealed behind an altar in 1570 and rediscovered only in 1861. Surmounting a stark image of the state to which all flesh is reduced, the main scene is a dramatized diagram of the mechanics of Christian redemption, with the lines of the painting leading from the picture's donors, through the Virgin and the Baptist, to the crucified Christ and the stern figure of God the Father at the pinnacle.

Giotto's Crucifix, a radically naturalistic and probably very early work (c.1288–90), now hangs in what is thought to be its intended position, poised dramatically over the centre of the nave. Hitherto, it had been hidden away in the sacristy, veiled by a layer of dirt so thick that many scholars refused to recognize it as the work of the great master; the attribution is still disputed, a common complaint being that Christ's body is depicted in an unusually heavy way. But as seen from below, suspended in an eerily life-like manner, the weight of flesh seems only to contribute to its painful realism.

The Cappella di Filippo Strozzi

In 1486 the chapel to the right of the chancel was bought by Filippo **Strozzi**, a wealthy banker, who then commissioned Filippino Lippi to paint a much-interrupted fresco cycle (1489–1502) on the life of his namesake, St Philip the Apostle, a saint rarely portrayed in Italian art. The paintings, a departure from anything seen in Florence at the time, were completed well after Strozzi's death in 1491. Before starting the project Filippino spent some time in Rome, and the work he carried out on his return displays an archeologist's obsession with ancient Roman culture. The right wall depicts Philip's *Crucifixion* and his *Miracle before the Temple of Mars*. In the latter, the Apostle uses the cross to banish a dragon which had been an object of pagan worship in a Temple of Mars. The enraged temple priests then capture and crucify the saint. The figures swooning from the dragon's stench are almost overwhelmed by an architectural fantasy derived from Rome's recently excavated Golden House of Nero. Look carefully in the top right-hand corner and you'll see a minuscule figure of Christ, about the same size as one of the vases behind the figure of Mars.

SANTA MARIA NOVELLA CHANCEL FRESCOES

A	Joachim chased from the Temple
B	The Birth of the Virgin
C	Presentation in the Temple
D	The Marriage of the Virgin
E	The Adoration of the Magi
F	The Massacre of the Innocents
G	The Death of the Virgin and Assumption
H	Giovanni Tornabuoni (donor) at prayer
J	Francesca Pitti, wife of Giovanni Tornabuoni
K	The Annunciation
L	St John in the Wilderness
M	St Dominic burning heretical books
N	St Peter Martyr
P	The Coronation of the Virgin
Q	The Visitation
R	The angel appears to Zachariah
S	Zachariah writes down the name of his son
T	The birth of St John Baptist
U	The baptism of Christ
V	St John the Baptist preaching
W	The Feast of Herod

The left wall depicts *The Raising of Drusiana* and the *Attempted Martyrdom of St John*: the latter scene alludes to the persecutions of the emperor Domitian, during which John was dipped in boiling oil in an attempt to kill him – but the Apostle emerged miraculously rejuvenated by the experience. The vaults portray Adam, Noah, Jacob and Abraham and, like the chapel's stained glass and impressive trompe l'oeil decoration, were also the work of Lippi. Behind the altar of this chapel is **Strozzi's tomb** (1491–95), beautifully carved by Benedetto da Maiano.

The chancel (Cappella Tornabuoni)

As a chronicle of fifteenth-century life in Florence, no series of frescoes is more fascinating than **Domenico Ghirlandaio**'s pictures around the **chancel** and high altar. Ostensibly depicting scenes from the life of the Virgin (left wall) and episodes from the life of St John the Baptist, the paintings were commissioned by **Giovanni Tornabuoni**, a banker and uncle of Lorenzo de' Medici (Lorenzo the Magnificent), which explains why they are liberally sprinkled with contemporary portraits and narrative details – such as certain illustrious ladies of the Tornabuoni family being present at the births of both John the Baptist and the Virgin. Such self-glorification made the frescoes the object of special ire after they were completed, drawing the vitriol of Savonarola during his hellfire and brimstone sermons (see p.146).

In truth, there are few frescoes in the city with such immediate charm, and none which are so self-conscious a celebration of Florence at its zenith – it's no accident that one of the frescoes on the right-hand wall includes a prominent Latin inscription (on an arch to the right) which reads: "The year 1490, when the most beautiful city renowned for abundance, victories, arts and noble buildings profoundly enjoyed salubrity and peace." Having found the inscription, you might then want to identify some of the portraits scattered around the paintings. Ghirlandaio features as a self-portrait in the scene (left wall) in which Joachim, the Virgin's father, is chased from the temple because he has been unable to have children – the painter is the figure in the right-hand group with hand on hip. In the neighbouring fresco, the young woman in the white and gold dress leading the group of women is Ludovica, Tornabuoni's only daughter, who died in childbirth aged 15: it's doubtless no accident that the scene painted in the fresco depicts the birth of the Virgin. Across the chancel, on the right wall, the **Visitation** features Giovanna degli Albizi, Tornabuoni's daughter-in-law, who also died in childbirth – she's the first of the trio of women to the right of the Virgin. The **Birth of St John the Baptist** features Tornabuoni's sister, Lucrezia, better known as the mother of Lorenzo de' Medici (the Magnificent): she's the woman in front of the servant carrying the fruit on her head.

The Cappella Strozzi

The next chapel beyond the chancel is the **Cappella Gondi**, which houses Brunelleschi's crucifix, supposedly carved as a riposte to the uncouthness of Donatello's cross in Santa Croce. It is the artist's only surviving sculpture in wood. Legend claims that Donatello was so struck on seeing his rival's work that he dropped a basket of eggs.

Even more startling, however, is the great fresco cycle in the next chapel but one, the **Cappella Strozzi**, which lies above the level of the rest of the church at the end of the north (left) transept. Its frescoes (1350–57) were commissioned as an expiation of the sin of usury by Tommaso Strozzi, an ancestor of Filippo Strozzi, patron of the chapel across the church. The pictures are the masterpiece of Nardo di Cione, brother of the better-known Orcagna (Andrea di Cione), with whom Nardo collaborated to design the chapel's stained glass.

Orcagna alone painted the chapel's magnificent high altarpiece, *Christ Presenting the Keys to St Peter and the Book of Wisdom to Thomas Aquinas* (1357). A propaganda exercise on behalf of the Dominicans, the picture shows Christ bestowing favour on both St Peter and St Thomas Aquinas, the latter a figure second only to St Dominic in the order's hierarchy. Behind the altar, the central fresco depicts the *Last Judgement*, with Dante featured as one of the saved (in white, third from the left, second row from the top). So, too, are Tommaso Strozzi and his wife, shown being led by St Michael into paradise, with an angel helping the righteous up through a trapdoor; on the right of the altar, a devil forks the damned down into hell. The theme of judgement is continued in the bleached fresco of Dante's *Inferno* on the right wall, faced by a thronged *Paradiso* on the left.

The Museo di Santa Maria Novella

Further remarkable paintings are to be found in the spacious Romanesque conventual buildings to the left of the church of Santa Maria Novella, home to the **Museo di Santa Maria Novella** (Mon–Thurs & Sat 9am–5pm, Sun 9am–2pm; €2.70). The first set of cloisters beyond the entrance, the **Chiostro Verde**, dating from 1332 to 1350, features damaged but nonetheless remarkable frescoes of *Stories from Genesis* (1425–30) executed by Paolo Uccello and his workshop. The cloister takes its name from the green base *terra verde* pigment they used, and which now gives the paintings a spectral undertone.

The windswept image of **The Flood**, the best-preserved of the cloister's frescoes, is rendered almost unintelligible by the telescoping perspective and

Paolo Uccello

Some of the most curious and haunting images to come out of the Florentine Renaissance are the products of **Paolo Uccello**'s obsession with the problems of perspective and foreshortening. Born in 1396, he trained in Ghiberti's workshop before moving to Venice, where he was employed on mosaics for the Basilica di San Marco. He worked periodically in Florence, returning for an extended period in 1431. Five years later he was contracted to paint the commemorative portrait of Sir John Hawkwood in the Duomo (see p.97), the trompe l'oeil painting which gives the first evidence of his interest in foreshortening.

After an interlude in Padua, Uccello completed the frescoes for the cloister of Santa Maria Novella, in which his systematic but non-naturalistic use of perspective is seen at its most extreme. In the following decade he painted the three-scene sequence of the **Battle of San Romano** (Louvre, London National Gallery and Uffizi) for the Medici – his most ambitious non-fresco paintings, and similarly notable for their unsettling multiple perspectives and strange use of foreshortening.

Uccello was driven halfway round the bend by the study of **perspective**, locking himself away for weeks at a time when he'd got his teeth into a particularly thorny problem. Chronically incapable of looking after his more mundane concerns, he was destitute by the time of his death in 1475: "I am old and without means of livelihood. My wife is sick and I am unable to work any more." Yet he left behind some of the most arresting paintings of the Renaissance, in which his preoccupation with mathematical precision coexists with a fundamentally Gothic sense of pageantry.

the double appearance of the ark (before and after the flood), whose flanks form a receding corridor in the centre of the picture: on the left, the ark is rising on the deluge, on the right it has come to rest as the waters subside. In the foreground, two men fight each other in their desperation to stay alive; the chequered lifebelt that one of these men is wearing around his neck is a favourite Uccello device for demonstrating a mastery of perspective – it's a *mazzocchio*, a 72-faceted wicker ring round which a turbanned headdress was wrapped. Another man grabs the ankles of the visionary figure in the foreground – presumably Noah, though he is a much younger Noah than the hirsute patriarch leaning out of the ark on the right to receive the dove's olive branch. In the right foreground there's a preview of the universal devastation, with tiny corpses laid out on the deck, and a crow gobbling an eyeball from one of the drowned.

The Cappellone degli Spagnoli

Off the cloister opens what was once the chapterhouse of the immensely rich convent of Santa Maria, the **Cappellone degli Spagnoli**, or Spanish Chapel, which for a time was the headquarters of the Inquisition. It received its present name after Eleonora di Toledo, wife of Cosimo I, reserved it for the use of her Spanish entourage. Presumably she derived much inspiration from its majestic fresco cycle (1367–69) by Andrea di Firenze, an extended depiction of the triumph of the Catholic Church that was described by Ruskin as "the most noble piece of pictorial philosophy in Italy".

Virtually every patch of the walls is covered with frescoes, whose theme is the role of the Dominicans in the battle against heresy and in the salvation of Christian souls. The **left wall** as you enter depicts *The Triumph of Divine Wisdom*, a triumph exemplified by Thomas Aquinas, who is portrayed enthroned below the Virgin and Apostles amidst the winged Virtues and the "wise men" of the Old and New Testaments. The more spectacular **right wall** depicts *The Triumph of the Church*, or more specifically, the "Mission, Work and Triumph of the Dominican Order". At the bottom is a building supposed to be Florence's cathedral, a pinky-purple creation imagined one hundred years before the structure was completed. Before it stand the pope and Holy Roman Emperor, society's ultimate spiritual and temporal rulers. In front of them stand ranks of figures representing religious orders, among which the Dominicans are naturally pre-eminent. In particular, note St Dominic, the order's founder, unleashing the "hounds of the lord", or *Domini Canes*, a pun on the Dominicans' name: heretics, the dogs' victims, are shown as wolves.

Among the group of pilgrims (in the centre, just below the Duomo) are several portraits, real or imagined: Cimabue (standing in a large brown cloak); Giotto (beside him in profile, wearing a green cloak); Boccaccio (further right, in purple, holding a closed book); Petrarch (above, with a cloak and white ermine hood); and Dante (alongside Petrarch in profile, with a white cap). Above and to the right, are scenes of young people dancing, hawking, playing music and engaging in other pleasures of the sort that the Dominicans so heartily condemned.

Those able to resist such abominations – the saved – are shown being marshalled by a nearby friar who hears their confession before dispatching them towards St Peter and the Gate of Paradise. Once through the gate, the blessed are shown in adoration of God and the angels with the Virgin at their midst. Foremost among those confessing is the chapel's donor, one Buonamico Guidalotti (shown kneeling), who paid for the chapel in honour of his wife, who died during the 1348 plague. The far wall shows scenes connected with the Crucifixion, with some very unhappy devils in the bottom right-hand corner, while the near (entrance) wall, which is excluded from the frescoes' unified theme, contains episodes from the life of St Peter Martyr, one of the Dominicans' leading lights.

The contemporaneous decoration of the **Chiostrino dei Morti**, the oldest part of the complex, has not aged so robustly; it was closed for restoration at the time of writing. The **Chiostro Grande**, to the west, is also out of bounds, but for the more unusual reason that it is a practice parade ground for aspiring *carabinieri* (Italy's semi-military police force). The small museum adjoining the Chiostro Grande is notable chiefly for some peculiarly glamorous fourteenth- and fifteenth-century reliquary busts, containing remnants of St Ursula and Mary Magdalene, among others.

North of the centre: the San Lorenzo, San Marco and Annunziata districts

A few blocks from the train station and the Duomo lies the San Lorenzo district, the city's main market area, with scores of stalls encircling a vast and wonderful food hall. The racks of T-shirts, leather jackets and belts almost engulf the church of **San Lorenzo**, a building of major importance that's often overlooked in the rush to the Duomo and the Uffizi. Attached to the church is another of the city's major draws, the **Cappelle Medicee** (Medici Chapels). While various of the Medici's most important members are buried in the main part of San Lorenzo, dozens of lesser lights are interred in these chapels, with two of the most venal being celebrated by some of **Michelangelo**'s finest funerary sculpture. The Medici also account for the area's other major sight, the **Palazzo Medici-Riccardi**, with its exquisite fresco-covered chapel, while the most celebrated of all Michelangelo's works in stone – the *David* – can be admired in the nearby galleries of the **Accademia**. The devotional art of Fra' Angelico fills the nearby **Museo di San Marco**, which in turn is but a stroll away from **Piazza Santissima Annunziata**, one of Florence's most photogenic locales, thanks to Brunelleschi's **Spedale degli Innocenti** and the church of **Santissima Annunziata**.

San Lorenzo

Founded in 393, **San Lorenzo** (Mon–Sat 10am–5pm; €2.50) has a claim to be the oldest church in Florence. For some three hundred years it was the city's cathedral, before renouncing its title to Santa Reparata, the precursor of the Duomo. By 1060 a sizeable Romanesque church had been built on the site, a building which in time became the Medici's parish church, benefiting greatly over the years from the family's munificence.

The family was in a particularly generous mood in 1419, when a committee of eight parishioners headed by Giovanni di Bicci de' Medici, founder of the Medici fortune, offered to finance a new church. **Brunelleschi** was commissioned to begin the project, starting work on the Sagrestia Vecchia (Old Sacristy) before being given the go-ahead two years later to rebuild the entire church. Construction lapsed over the next twenty years, hampered by financial problems, political upheavals and Brunelleschi's simultaneous work on the cathedral dome. Giovanni's son, Cosimo de' Medici, eventually gave the work fresh impetus with a grant of 40,000 *fiorini* (florins) – at a time when 150 florins would support a Florentine family for a year. Cosimo's largesse saved the day, but was still not sufficient to provide the church with a facade. No less a figure than Michelangelo laboured to remedy the omission, one of many to devote time to a scheme to provide a suitable front-

SAN LORENZO

PIAZZA MADONNA DEGLI ALDOBRANDINI

CANTO DE' NELLI

PIAZZA SAN LORENZO

1 Marriage of the Virgin (1523), Rosso Fiorentino
2 Bronze pulpits (1455–66), Donatello
3 Pala del Sacramento (1458–61), Desiderio da Settignano
4 Sarcophagus, fresco and crucifix (1470), Antonio da Pollaiuolo
5 Tomb of Cosimo de' Medici (Cosimo il Vecchio)
6 Tomb of Giovanni and Piero de' Medici (Cosimo's sons)
7 Tomb of Giovanni and Piccarda de' Medici (Cosimo's parents)
8 Funerary memorial to Donatello
9 Annunciation (1440), Filippo Lippi
10 Martyrdom of St Lawrence (1565–9), Bronzino
11 Stairs to Ricetto and Biblioteca

A Entrance to the Cappelle Medicee
B Cappella dei Principi
C Sagrestia Nuova
D Sagrestia Vecchia
E Ricetto (vestibule), Michelangelo
F Biblioteca Medicea-Laurenziana

age. None of the efforts was to any avail: to this day the exterior's bare brick has never been clad.

The interior

When you step inside the church, what strikes you first is the cool rationality of Brunelleschi's design, an instantly calming contrast to the hubbub outside. San Lorenzo was the earlier of Brunelleschi's great Florentine churches (the other is Santo Spirito) but already displays his mastery of Classical decorative motifs and mathematically planned proportions.

The first work of art to catch your attention, in the second chapel on the right, is Rosso Fiorentino's **Marriage of the Virgin**, with its uniquely golden-haired and youthful Joseph. There's another arresting painting at the top of the left aisle – Bronzino's enormous fresco of *The Martyrdom of St Lawrence* – but it seems a shallow piece of work alongside the nearby bronze pulpits by **Donatello**. Clad with reliefs depicting scenes preceding and following the Crucifixion, these are the artist's last works (begun c.1460), and were completed by his pupils as increasing paralysis limited their master's ability to model in wax. Jagged and discomforting, charged with more energy than the space can contain, these panels are more like brutal sketches in bronze than conventional reliefs. Donatello is buried in the nave of the church, next to his patron, Cosimo de' Medici, and commemorated by a **memorial** on the right wall of the chapel in the north transept, close to Filippo Lippi's 1440 altarpiece of the *Annunciation*. In the centre of the church, the **tomb of Cosimo de' Medici** bears the inscription "Pater Patriae" (Father of the Fatherland) – a title once borne by Roman emperors.

The Sagrestia Vecchia

Four more leading Medici members lie buried in the **Sagrestia Vecchia** or Old Sacristy, one of Brunelleschi's earliest projects (1421–26), and the only one completed in his lifetime. Brunelleschi's biographer, Manetti, wrote that "it astounded all men both of the city and foreigners . . . for its new and beautiful manner. And so many people came continuously that they greatly bothered those who worked there."

The space was commissioned by Giovanni Bicci de' Medici, the principal founder of the Medici fortune, as a private chapel. On his death, Giovanni, along with his wife Piccarda, was buried beneath the massive marble slab at the centre of the chapel. Another tomb, easily missed, lies immediately on the left as you enter: the last resting place of Giovanni's grandsons, Giovanni and Piero de' Medici, it was commissioned from Verrocchio in 1472 by Lorenzo de' Medici. To the modern eye the tomb looks relatively plain, but a Florentine of the day would have been abundantly aware that it was made from the three most precious materials of antiquity – marble, porphyry and bronze.

More arresting than either of the tombs, however, is the chapel's ornamentation. Here Brunelleschi's genius was complemented by the decorative acumen of Donatello, who worked in the sacristy between 1434 and 1443, some twenty years before sculpting the pulpits in the main body of the church. He was responsible for both the cherub-filled frieze and the eight extraordinary tondos above it. The tondos' subjects are the four Evangelists and a quartet of scenes from the life of St John the Evangelist.

Two large **reliefs**, also probably by Donatello, adorn the space above the two doors on the end wall: one shows SS Lawrence and Stephen, twin protectors of Florence, the other SS Cosmas and Damian. These last two, twins and early Christian martyrs, were the patron saints of doctors (*medici*) and thus of the

Medici, who were probably descended from doctors or apothecaries. By happy coincidence, Cosimo de' Medici, the church's chief patron, was born on the saints' feast day (27 September), so the two are often seen in paintings or buildings commissioned or connected with him.

Donatello was also responsible for the two bronze doors below with their combative martyrs to the left, and the Apostles and Fathers of the Church to the right. The chapel beyond the left door has a sublime little marble *lavabo*, probably by Verrocchio: many of its fantastic creatures have Medici connections – the falcon and lamb, for example, are the heraldic symbols of Piero de' Medici, who commissioned the work.

Lastly, the **stellar fresco** on the dome above the recessed altar inevitably draws your eye: opinion differs as to whether the position of the painted stars is synonymous with the state of the heavens on July 16, 1416, the birthday of Piero de' Medici, or on July 6, 1439, the date on which the union of the Eastern and Western churches was celebrated at the Council of Florence.

The Biblioteca Medicea-Laurenziana

A gateway to the left of the church facade leads through a pleasant cloister and through a doorway up to the **Biblioteca Medicea-Laurenziana** (Mon–Sat 8.30am–1.30pm; free, except during special exhibitions). Wishing to create a suitably grandiose home for the precious manuscripts assembled by Cosimo and Lorenzo de' Medici, Pope Clement VII – Lorenzo's nephew – asked Michelangelo to design a new Medici library in 1524. The **Ricetto**, or vestibule (1559–71), of the building he eventually came up with is a revolutionary showpiece of Mannerist architecture, delighting in paradoxical display: brackets that support nothing, columns that sink into the walls rather than stand out from them, and a flight of steps so large that it almost fills the room, spilling down like a solidified lava flow.

From this eccentric space, you're sometimes allowed into the tranquil **reading room**; here, too, almost everything is the work of Michelangelo, even the inlaid desks. Exhibitions in the connecting rooms draw on the 15,000-piece Medici collection, which includes manuscripts as diverse as a fifth-century copy of Virgil – the collection's oldest item – and a treatise on architecture by Leonardo. Note how the coffered ceiling and terracotta floor mirror each other's designs.

The Cappelle Medicee

Michelangelo's most celebrated contribution to the San Lorenzo complex forms part of the **Cappelle Medicee** (Tues–Sat 8.15am–4.50pm; 1st, 3rd & 5th Sun of month and 2nd & 4th Mon of month same hours; €6), entered from Piazza Madonna degli Aldobrandini, at the back of the church. These chapels divide into three sections: the crypt, burial place of many minor Medici; the **Cappella dei Principi**, housing the tombs of six of the more major Medici; and the **Sagrestia Nuova**, home to three major groups of Michelangelo sculpture.

Hardly any of the Medici, however humble, suffered the indignity of a modest grave. Some might have expected more, though, than the low-vaulted **crypt** of the Cappelle Medicee, home to the brass-railed tombs of many of the family's lesser lights. Most were placed here in 1791 by Ferdinand III with what appears to have been scant regard for his ancestors: one contemporary recorded how the duke had the corpses thrown "together pell-mell . . . caring scarcely to distinguish one from the other".

After filing through the crypt, you climb steps at its rear into the larger of the chapels, the **Cappella dei Principi** (Chapel of the Princes), a morbid and dowdy marble-plated hall built as a mausoleum for Cosimo I and the grand dukes who succeeded him. The octagonal chapel took as its inspiration the floorplan of no less a building than the Baptistery, and the extent of Medici conceit was underlined by the chapel's intended centrepiece – the Holy Sepulchre of Christ, a prize that had to be forfeited when the pasha refused to sell it and an expedition sent to Jerusalem to steal it returned empty-handed. Dismissed by Byron as a "fine frippery in great slabs of various expensive stones, to commemorate rotten and forgotten carcasses", this was the most expensive building project ever financed by the Medici, and the family were still paying for it in 1743 when the last of the line, Anna Maria Ludovica, joined her forebears in the basement. Scaffolding, suitably rich in gold and black, has adorned the walls since a section of cornice fell off in January 2000, revealing major structural faults.

The Sagrestia Nuova

Begun in 1520, the **Sagrestia Nuova** was designed by Michelangelo as a tribute to, and re-invention of, Brunelleschi's Sagrestia Vecchia in the main body of San Lorenzo. Architectural experts go into raptures over the sophistication of the architecture, notably the empty niches above the doors, which play complex games with the vocabulary of classical architecture, but the lay person will be drawn to the three fabulous **Medici tombs** (1520–34), two wholly and one partly by Michelangelo. The sculptor was awarded the commissions by Pope Leo X – a Medici – and the pope's cousin, Cardinal Giulio de' Medici, later to become Pope Clement VII.

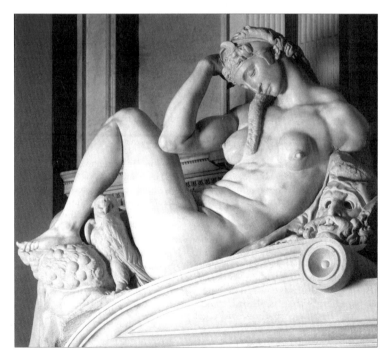

△ *Night*, from Giuliano de' Medici's tomb

With your back to the entrance door, the tomb on the left belongs to **Lorenzo, duke of Urbino**, the grandson of Lorenzo the Magnificent. Michelangelo depicts him as a man of thought, and his sarcophagus bears figures of *Dawn* and *Dusk*, the times of day whose ambiguities appeal to the contemplative mind. Opposite stands the tomb of Lorenzo de' Medici's youngest son, **Giuliano, duke of Nemours**; as a man of action, his character is symbolized by the clear antithesis of *Day* and *Night*. A contemporary writer recorded that the sculptor gave his subjects "a greatness, a proportion, a dignity . . . which seemed to him would have brought them more praise, saying that a thousand years hence no one would be able to know that they were otherwise." The protagonists were very much otherwise: Giuliano was in fact an easygoing but feckless individual, while Lorenzo combined ineffectuality with unbearable arrogance. Both died young and unlamented of tuberculosis, combined in Lorenzo's case with syphilis.

The two principal effigies were intended to face the equally grand tombs of Lorenzo de' Medici and his brother Giuliano, two Medici who had genuine claims to fame. The only part of the project completed by Michelangelo is the **Madonna and Child**, the last image of the Madonna he ever sculpted. The figures to either side are Cosmas and Damian, which were completed to Michelangelo's original design. Wax and clay models exist in the Casa Buonarroti (see p.169) and British Museum of other figures Michelangelo planned for the tomb, including allegorical figures of Heaven and Earth and statues of river gods representing the Tiber and Arno. Sketches relating to this scheme are visible behind the altar (visitors are allowed to see them, under supervision, every thirty minutes), but the chapel was never completed as Michelangelo intended: in 1534, four years after the Medici had returned to Florence in the wretched form of Alessandro, Michelangelo decamped to Rome, where he stayed for the rest of his life.

The Palazzo Medici-Riccardi

On the edge of the square in front of San Lorenzo stands the **Palazzo Medici-Riccardi** (daily except Wed 9am–7pm; €4), built for Cosimo de' Medici by Michelozzo between 1444 and 1462, possibly to a plan by Brunelleschi. Another story has it that Cosimo did indeed ask Brunelleschi to design the new palace, but the result was so grandiose that Cosimo rejected it on political grounds, saying "envy is a plant one should never water". Brunelleschi, who was renowned for his temper, is said to have smashed the splendid model in rage. With its heavily rusticated exterior, this palace was the prototype for several major Florentine buildings, most notably the Palazzo Pitti and Palazzo Strozzi, and it remained the family home and Medici business headquarters until Cosimo I moved to the Palazzo Vecchio in 1540. After 1659 the palace was greatly altered by its new owners, the Riccardi, and it now houses the offices of the provincial government. The chief attraction for tourists is the cycle of Gozzoli **frescoes** in the chapel, which a maximum of seven people may view at any one time. To avoid the queues, book tickets in advance at the ticket office, at Via Cavour 3, or call ☏055.276.0340.

The Gozzoli frescoes

Today all that survives of the interior of the original palace is Michelozzo's deep, colonnaded courtyard, which closely follows the new style established by Brunelleschi in the foundling hospital (see p.152), and a tiny **chapel**, reached by stairs leading directly from the court. The walls of the chapel are covered

The Medici balls

You come across the **Medici emblem** – a cluster of red balls (*palle*) on a gold background – all over Florence, yet its origins are shrouded in mystery. Legend claims the family was descended from a Carolingian knight named Averardo, who fought and killed a giant in the Mugello, north of Florence. During the encounter his shield received six massive blows from the giant's mace, so Charlemagne, as a reward for his bravery, allowed Averardo to represent the dents as red balls on his coat of arms.

Rival families claimed that the balls had less exalted origins, that they were medicinal pills or cupping glasses, recalling the family's origins as apothecaries or doctors (*medici*). Others claim they are *bezants*, Byzantine coins, inspired by the arms of the *Arte del Cambio*, the money-changers' guild to which the Medici belonged. In a similar vein, some say the balls are coins, the traditional symbols of pawnbrokers.

Whatever the origin, the number of *palle* was never constant. In the thirteenth century, for example, there were twelve. By Cosimo de' Medici's time the number had dropped to seven, though San Lorenzo's Old Sacristy, a Cosimo commission, strangely has eight, while Verrocchio's roundel in the same church's chancel has six and Grand Duke Cosimo I's tomb, in the Cappella dei Principi, has five. Cosimo Il Vecchio was said to be so fond of displaying the *palle* on the buildings he had funded that a rival alleged that even the monks' privies in San Marco were adorned with Medici balls.

by some of the city's most charming frescoes: **Benozzo Gozzoli**'s sequence depicting *The Journey of the Magi*, painted around 1460 and recently restored to magnificent effect. The landscape scenes to either side of the altar are by the same artist.

Despite the frescoes' ostensible subject, the cycle probably portrays the pageant of the Compagnia dei Magi, the most patrician of the city's religious confraternities, whose annual procession took place at Epiphany. Several of the Medici, inevitably, were prominent members, including Piero de' Medici (Piero il Gottoso – the Gouty), who may have commissioned the pictures. It's known that several of the Medici household are featured in the procession, but putting names to these prettified faces is a problem. The man leading the cavalcade on a white horse is almost certainly Piero, while the figure behind him, in the black cloak, is probably his father, Cosimo il Vecchio. Piero's older son, the future Lorenzo il Magnifico, 11 years old at the time the fresco was painted, is probably the gold-clad young king in the foreground, riding the grey horse detached from the rest of the procession, while his brother, Giuliano, is probably the one preceded by the black bowman, to the left of Cosimo il Vecchio. The artist himself is in the crowd at the rear of the procession, his red beret signed with the words "Opus Benotii" in gold. Finally, the bearded characters among the throng might be portraits of the retinue of the Byzantine emperor John Paleologus III, who had attended the Council of Florence twenty years before the fresco was painted.

The first floor

Another set of stairs leads from the passageway beside the courtyard up to the **first floor**, where a display case in the lobby of the main gallery contains a *Madonna and Child* by **Filippo Lippi**, one of Cosimo de' Medici's more troublesome protégés. Cosimo set up a workshop for him in the Medici palace, from which he often absented himself to go chasing women. On one occasion Cosimo actually locked the artist in the studio, but Filippo escaped down a rope of bed sheets; having cajoled him into returning, Cosimo declared that he would in future manage the painter with "affection and kindness", a policy that seems to have worked more successfully.

The ceiling of the grandiloquent **gallery** glows with Luca Giordano's fresco of *The Apotheosis of the Medici*, from which one can only deduce that Giordano had no sense of shame. Perhaps he had no time to consider the commission – he was known as Luca Fa-presto (Luca Does-It-Quickly). Accompanying Cosimo III on his flight into the ether is his son, the last male Medici, Gian Gastone (d. 1737), who grew to be a man so dissolute and inert that he could rarely summon the energy to get out of bed in the morning.

Even more sumptuous interior decoration can be seen in the **Biblioteca Riccardiana–Moreniana**, on the opposite side of the palace (entered from Via Ginori; Mon–Sat 9am–1pm; free), one of the Riccardi's more successful remodellings. It is still a working library, but brief, silent visits can be made to see the array of gilded eighteenth-century shelves, overlooked by Luca Giordano's allegory of *Intellect Liberated from the Bonds of Ignorance* (1685).

From the Mercato Centrale to the Fortezza da Basso

The **Mercato Centrale** is Europe's largest covered food hall, built in stone, iron and glass by Giuseppe Mengoni, architect of Milan's famous Galleria. Opened in 1874, it received a major overhaul a century later, reopening in 1980 with a new first floor. Butchers, *alimentari*, tripe-sellers, greengrocers, pasta stalls – they're all gathered under the one roof, and all charging prices lower than you'll readily find elsewhere in the city. Get there close to the end of the working day at 2pm and you'll get some good reductions.

Each day from 8am to 7pm the streets around the Mercato Centrale are thronged with **stalls** selling bags, belts, shoes, trousers – some of it of doubtful quality. This is the busiest of Florence's daily street markets, and a half-hour's immersion in the haggling mass of customers provides as good a break as any from a pursuit of the city's art.

The Cenacolo di Foligno

One of Florence's more obscure *cenacoli* (Last Suppers), the **Cenacolo di Foligno**, is to be found a short distance from the market at Via Faenza 42, in the ex-convent of the Franciscans of Foligno (Mon, Tues & Sat 9am–noon; free). It was once thought to be by Raphael but is now reckoned to have been painted in the 1490s by Perugino. Certainly it shows many of Perugino's stylistic idiosyncrasies – the figures arranged in flat ranks, their gestures compiled from a repertoire of poses that can be seen in many of his other works.

The Fortezza da Basso

Beyond Via Faenza, the **Fortezza da Basso** was built to intimidate the people of Florence by the vile Alessandro de' Medici, who ordained himself duke of Florence after a ten-month siege by the army of Charles V and Pope Clement VII (possibly Alessandro's father) had forcibly restored the Medici. Michelangelo, the most talented Florentine architect of the day, had played a major role in the defence of the city during the siege; the job of designing the fortress fell to the more pliant Antonio da Sangallo.

Within a few years the cruelties of Alessandro had become intolerable; a petition to Charles V spoke of the Fortezza da Basso as "a prison and a slaughterhouse for the unhappy citizens". Charles's response to the catalogue of Alessandro's atrocities was to marry his daughter to the tyrant. In the end, another Medici came to the rescue: in 1537 the distantly related **Lorenzaccio de' Medici** stabbed the duke to death as he waited for an amorous assignation in Lorenzaccio's house. The reasons for the murder have never been clear but it seems that Lorenzaccio's mental health was little better than Alessandro's: in his earlier years he and Alessandro had regularly launched lecherous sorties on the city's convents, and he had been expelled from Rome after lopping the heads off statues on the Arch of Constantine. The assassination, however, had favourable consequences for the city: as Alessandro died heirless, the council proposed that the leadership of the Florentine republic should be offered to **Cosimo de' Medici**, the great-grandson of Lorenzo il Magnifico. Subsequent Medici dukes had no need of a citizen-proof fort, and the Fortezza da Basso fell into dereliction after use as a gaol and barracks.

Since 1978 there's been a vast modern shed in the centre of the complex, used for trade fairs and shows such as the *Pitti Moda* fashion jamborees in January and July. The public gardens by the walls are fairly pleasant, if you want an open-air spot to relax before catching a train.

The Accademia

Florence's first academy of drawing, the Accademia del Disegno, was founded in 1563 by Bronzino, Ammannati and Vasari. Initially based in Santissima Annunziata, it moved in 1764 to Via Ricasoli, and soon afterwards was transformed into a general arts academy, the Accademia di Belle Arti. Twenty years later the Grand Duke Pietro Leopoldo I founded the nearby **Galleria dell'Accademia** (Tues–Sun 8.15am–6.50pm; €6.50), filling its rooms with paintings for the edification of the students. Later augmented with pieces from suppressed religious foundations and other sources, the Accademia has an extensive collection of paintings, especially of Florentine work of the fourteenth and fifteenth centuries.

The **picture galleries** which flank the main sculpture hall are quite small and generally unexciting, with copious examples of the work of "Unknown Florentine" and "Follower of . . . ". The pieces likeliest to make an impact are Pontormo's *Venus and Cupid* (1532), painted to a cartoon by Michelangelo; a *Madonna of the Sea* (1470) attributed to Botticelli; and the painted fifteenth-century *Adimari Chest*, showing a Florentine wedding ceremony in the Piazza del Duomo. A cluster of rooms near the exit house gilded religious works from the thirteenth and fourteenth centuries, including an altarpiece of the Pentecost by Andrea Orcagna (c.1365).

Michelangelo's David

Commissioned by the Opera del Duomo in 1501, the **David** was conceived to invoke parallels with Florence's freedom from outside domination (despite the superior force of its enemies), and its recent liberation from Savonarola and the Medici. It's an incomparable show of technical bravura, all the more impressive given the difficulties posed by the marble from which it was carved. The four-metre block of stone – thin, shallow and riddled with cracks – had been quarried from Carrara forty years earlier. Several artists had already attempted to work with it, notably Agostino di Duccio, Andrea Sansovino and Leonardo da Vinci. Michelangelo succeeded where others had failed, completing the work in 1504 when he was still just 29.

Four days and a team of forty men were then required to move the statue from the Opera del Duomo to the site that was eventually chosen for it, in the Piazza della Signoria; another three weeks were needed to raise it onto its plinth. During the move the statue required protection day and night to prevent it being stoned by Medici supporters all too aware of its symbolism. Damage was done a few years later, in 1527, when the Medici were again expelled from the city: a bench, flung from a window of the Palazzo Vecchio by anti-Medici rioters, struck and smashed the left arm, but the pieces were gathered up and reassembled. The statue remained in its outdoor setting, exposed to the elements, until it was sent to the Accademia in 1873, by which time it had lost its gilded hair and the gilded band across its chest. Also missing these days is a skirt of copper leaves added to spare the blushes of Florence's more sensitive citizens.

Thoroughly cleaned in 2002, *David* now occupies a specially built alcove, protected by a glass barrier that was erected in 1991, after one of its toes was cracked by a hammer-wielding artist. With its massive head and gangling arms, the *David* looks to some people like a monstrous adolescent, but its proportions would not have appeared so graceless in the setting for which it was conceived: the statue was commisioned as a piece of monumental sculpture for the Duomo, where it would have been placed at rather higher altitude, and at a greater distance from the public, than the position it occupies in the Accademia's chapel-like space.

The Slaves

Michelangelo once described the process of carving as being the liberation of the form from within the stone, a notion that seems to be embodied by the remarkable unfinished **Slaves** (or Prisoners). His procedure, clearly demonstrated here, was to cut the figure as if it were a deep relief, and then to free the three-dimensional figure; often his assistants would perform the initial operation, working from the master's pencil marks, so it's possible that Michelangelo's own chisel never actually touched these stones.

Probably carved in the late 1520s, the statues were originally destined for the tomb of Julius II, intended perhaps to symbolize the liberal arts left "enslaved" by Julius's demise. The tomb underwent innumerable permutations before its eventual abandonment, however, and in 1564 the artist's nephew gave the carvings to the Medici, who installed them in the grotto of the Bóboli garden. Four of the original six statues came to the Accademia in 1909. Two others found their way to the Louvre in Paris.

Close by is another unfinished work, *St Matthew* (1505–6), started soon after completion of the *David* as a commission from the Opera del Duomo; they actually requested a full series of the Apostles from Michelangelo, but this is the only one he ever began. It languished half-forgotten in the cathedral vaults until 1831.

San Marco

A whole side of Piazza San Marco is taken up by the Dominican convent and church of San Marco, the former building now the home of the **Museo di San Marco** (Tues–Fri 8.15am–1.50pm, Sat 8.15am–6.50pm; also 1st, 3rd & 5th Mon of month 8.15am–1.50pm, and 2nd & 4th Sun of month 8.15am–6.50pm; €4). The Dominicans acquired the site in 1436, after being forced to move from their former home in Fiesole, and the complex promptly became the recipient of Cosimo's most lavish patronage. In the 1430s he financed Michelozzo's enlargement of the conventual buildings (1437–52), and went on to establish a vast library here. Abashed by the wealth he was transferring to them, the friars of San Marco suggested to Cosimo that he need not continue to support them on such a scale, to which he replied, "Never shall I be able to give God enough to set him down as my debtor." Ironically, the convent became the centre of resistance to the Medici later in the century: Girolamo **Savonarola**, leader of the government of Florence after the expulsion of the Medici in 1494, was the prior of San Marco. In 1537 Duke Cosimo expelled the Dominicans once more, reminding them that it was another Cosimo who had established the building's magnificence in the first place.

As Michelozzo was altering and expanding San Marco, the convent's walls were being decorated by one of its friars and a future prior, **Fra' Angelico**, a Tuscan painter in whom a medieval simplicity of faith was uniquely allied to a Renaissance sophistication of manner. He was born in Vicchio di Mugello (see p.233), son of a wealthy landowner, some time between the late 1380s and 1400. He entered the Dominican monastery of nearby Fiesole aged around 20, where he was known as Fra' Giovanni da Fiesole. Already recognized as an accomplished artist, he flourished when he came to San Marco.

Here he was encouraged by the theologian Antonino Pierozzi – the future St Antonine – the convent's first prior and later archbishop of Florence. By the time Fra' Giovanni succeeded Pierozzi as prior, the pictures he had created for the monastery over the course of a decade and others for numerous churches in Florence and elsewhere – principally Orvieto cathedral and the Vatican

Savonarola

Girolamo **Savonarola** was born in 1452, the son of the physician to the Ferrara court. He grew up to be an abstemious and melancholic youth, sleeping on a bare straw mattress and spending much of his time reading the Bible and writing dirges. At the age of 23 he absconded to a Dominican monastery in Bologna, informing his father by letter that he was "unable to endure the evil conduct of the heedless people of Italy".

Within a few years, the Dominicans had dispatched him to preach all over northern Italy, an enterprise which got off to an unpromising start. Not the most attractive of men – he was frail, with a beak of a nose and a blubbery mouth – Savonarola was further hampered by an uningratiating voice and a particularly inelegant way of gesturing. Nonetheless, the intensity of his manner and his message attracted a committed following when he settled permanently in the monastery of **San Marco** in 1489.

By 1491, Savonarola's sermons had become so popular that he was asked to deliver his Lent address in the Duomo. Proclaiming that God was speaking through him, he berated the city for its decadence, for its paintings that made the Virgin "look like a whore", and for the tyranny of its Medici-led government. Following the death of Lorenzo il Magnifico, the rhetoric became even more apocalyptic. "Wait no longer, for there may be no more time for repentance," he told the Duomo congregation, summoning images of plagues, invasions and destruction.

When Charles VIII of France marched into Italy in September 1494 to press his claim to the throne of Naples, Savonarola presented him as the instrument of God's vengeance. Violating Piero de' Medici's declaration of Tuscan neutrality, the French army massacred the garrison at Fivizzano, and Florence prepared for the onslaught, as Savonarola declaimed, "The Sword has descended; the scourge has fallen." With support for resistance ebbing, Piero capitulated to Charles; within days the Medici had fled and their palace had been plundered. Hailed by Savonarola as "the Minister of God, the Minister of Justice", Charles and his vast army passed peacefully through Florence on their way to Rome.

The political vacuum in Florence was filled by the declaration of a **republican constitution**, but Savonarola was now in effect the ruler of the city. Continual decrees were issued from San Marco: profane carnivals were to be outlawed, fasting was to

– had earned him the title "the angelic painter", the name by which he's been known ever since. In 1982 he was beatified (a halfway house to sainthood), thus formalizing the name by which he had long been known, Beato Angelico, or the Blessed Angelico.

The ground floor

Immediately beyond the **entrance** lies the **Chiostro di Sant'Antonino** (2), designed by Michelozzo and now dominated by a vast cedar of Lebanon. Most of the cloister's faded frescoes are sixteenth-century depictions of episodes from the life of Antonino Pierozzi, Angelico's mentor and the convent's first prior. Angelico himself painted the frescoes in its four corners, of which the most striking is the lunette of *St Dominic at the Foot of the Cross* (3).

This weather-bleached work pales alongside the twenty or so paintings by the artist gathered in the **Ospizio dei Pellegrini** (5), or Pilgrims' Hospice, which lies between the cloister and the piazza. Many of the works – including several of Angelico's most famous – were brought here from churches and galleries around Florence; all display the artist's brilliant colouring and spatial clarity, and an air of imperturbable piety. On the right wall as you enter is a *Deposition* (4), 1432–35, originally hung in the church of Santa Trìnita.

be observed more frequently, children were to act as the agents of the righteous, informing the authorities whenever their parents transgressed the Eternal Law. Irreligious books and paintings, expensive clothes, cosmetics, mirrors, board games, trivialities and luxuries of all types were destroyed, a ritual purging that reached a crescendo with a colossal "**Bonfire of the Vanities**" on the Piazza della Signoria.

Meanwhile, Charles VIII was installed in Naples and a formidable alliance was being assembled to overthrow him: the papacy, Milan, Venice, Ferdinand of Aragon and the emperor Maximilian. In July 1495 the army of this Holy League confronted the French and was badly defeated. Charles's army continued northwards back to France, and Savonarola was summoned to the Vatican to explain why he had been unable to join the campaign against the intruder. He declined to attend, claiming that it was not God's will that he should make the journey, and thus set off a chain of exchanges that ended with his **excommunication** in June 1497. Defying Pope Alexander's order, Savonarola celebrated Mass in the Duomo on Christmas Day, which prompted a final threat from Rome: send Savonarola to the Vatican or imprison him in Florence, otherwise the whole city would join him in excommunication.

Despite Savonarola's insistence that the Borgia pope was already consigned to hell, the people of Florence began to desert him. The region's crops had failed, plague had broken out again, and the city was at war with Pisa, which Charles had handed over to its citizens rather than return to Florence's control, as he had promised. The Franciscans of Florence, sceptical of the Dominican monk's claim to divine approval, now issued a terrible challenge. One of their community and one of Savonarola's would walk through an avenue of fire in the Piazza della Signoria: if the Dominican died, then Savonarola would be banished; if the Franciscan died, then Savonarola's main critic, Fra' Francesco da Puglia, would be expelled.

A thunderstorm prevented the trial from taking place, but the mood in the city had anyway turned irrevocably. The following day, Palm Sunday 1498, a siege of the monastery of San Marco ended with Savonarola's **arrest**. Accused of heresy, he was tortured to the point of death, then **burned at the stake** in front of the Palazzo Vecchio, with two of his supporters. When the flames had finally been extinguished, the ashes were thrown into the river, to prevent anyone from gathering them as relics.

MUSEO DI SAN MARCO
GROUND FLOOR

15

14

13
12   10   9

3   11
                 7
2
                 8

4   5   6

1

1 Museum entrance
2 Chiostro di Sant'Antonino
3 St Dominic at the Foot
   of the Cross
4 Deposition (1432–5)
5 Ospizio dei Pellegrini
6 Madonna dei Linaiuoli
   (1433).
7 Sala del Lavabo
8 Refettorio Grande
9 Sala di Fra' Bartolomeo
10 Sala di Alesso Baldovinetti
11 Convent bell (Il Piagnone)
12 Sala Capitolare
   (Chapter House)
13 Crucifixion
14 Refettorio Piccolo
15 Foresteria

Commissioned by the Strozzi family, the painting was begun by Lorenzo Monaco, who died after completing the upper trio of triangular pinnacles, and continued by Fra Angelico. At the opposite end of the room hangs the *Madonna dei Linaiuoli* (6), Angelico's first major public painting (1433), commissioned by the *linaiuoli* or flax-workers' guild, for their headquarters. Halfway down the room, on the inner wall, the so-called *Pala di San Marco* (1440), though badly damaged by the passage of time and a disastrous restoration, demonstrates Fra' Angelico's familiarity with the latest developments in artistic theory. Its figures are arranged in lines that taper towards a central vanishing point, in accordance with the principles laid out in Alberti's *Della Pittura* (*On Painting*), published in Italian just two years before the picture was executed. The work was commissioned by the Medici as an altarpiece for the church of San Marco, hence the presence of the family's patron saints Cosmas and Damian, who can be seen at work as doctors in the small panel immediately to the right.

Back in the cloister, a doorway in its top right-hand corner opens into the **Sala del Lavabo** (7), where the monks washed before eating. Its entrance wall has a *Crucifixion with Saints* by Angelico, and its right wall two panels with a pair of saints, also by Angelico. The left wall contains a damaged lunette fresco of the *Madonna and Child* by Paolo Uccello, plus part of a predella by the same artist. The impressive room to the right, the **Refettorio Grande** (8), or Large Refectory, is dominated by a large fresco of the *Crucifixion* by the sixteenth-century painter Giovanni Sogliani. Of more artistic interest are the rooms devoted to paintings by **Fra' Bartolomeo** (9) and **Alesso Baldovinetti** (10). Note in particular Fra' Bartolomeo's suitably intense portrait of Savonarola, and his unfinished *Pala della Signoria* (1512), originally destined for the Salone dei Cinquecento in the Palazzo Vecchio.

Further round the cloister lies the **Sala Capitolare** (12), or Chapter House, which now houses a large conventual bell, the Piagnone (11), which was rung to summon help on Savonarola's arrest on the eve of April 8, 1498: it became a symbol of anti-Medici sentiment ever after. Here, too, is a powerful fresco of the *Crucifixion* (13), painted by Angelico and assistants in 1441. At the rear of this room, entered via a passageway alongside the Chapter House, lies the **Refettorio Piccolo** (14), or Small Refectory, with a lustrous *Last Supper* (1480) by Ghirlandaio. This forms an anteroom to the **Foresteria** (15), home to the convent's former guest rooms, which is cluttered with architectural bits and pieces salvaged during nineteenth-century urban improvement schemes.

The first floor

Stairs off the cloister by the entrance to the Foresteria lead up to the first floor, where almost immediately you're confronted with one of the most sublime paintings in Italy. For the drama of its setting and the lucidity of its composition, nothing in San Marco matches Angelico's **Annunciation** (A). The pallid, submissive Virgin is one of the most touching images in Renaissance art, and the courteous angel, with his scintillating unfurled wings, is as convincing a heavenly messenger as any ever painted. An inscription on this fresco reminds the passing monks to say a Hail Mary as they venerate the image.

Angelico and his assistants also painted the simple and piously restrained pictures in each of the 44 **dormitory cells** on this floor, into which the brothers would withdraw for solitary contemplation and sleep. The outer cells of the corridor on the left (1–11) almost all have works by Angelico himself – don't miss the *Noli Me Tangere* (1), the *Annunciation* (3), the outstanding *Transfiguration* (6) and the *Coronation of the Virgin* (9). The marvellous **Madonna delle Ombre** (B), or Madonna of the Shadows, on the wall facing these cells, is probably also by Angelico. Several of the scenes include one or

MUSEO DI SAN MARCO
FIRST FLOOR

A Annunciation
B Madonna delle Ombre
C Library
D Sala Greca

1 Noli Me Tangere
2 The Body of Christ
3 Annunciation
4 Crucifixion
5 Nativity
6 Transfiguration
7 Mockery of Christ
8 The Marys at the Sepulchre
9 Coronation of the Virgin
10 Presentation in the Temple
11 Madonna and Child with Saints
12–14 Savonarola's cells
22 Crucifixion with the Virgin
23 Crucifixion with the Virgin and St Dominic
24 Baptism of Christ
25 Crucifixion with the Virgin, Magdalen and St Dominic

26 Pietà with St Dominic or St Thomas
27 Christ at the Column with the Virgin and St Dominic
28 Christ Carrying the Cross
29 Crucifixion with the Virgin and St Dominic
30 Crucifixion with the Virgin and St Dominic
31 Christ in Limbo
32 Sermon on the Mount
33 Arrest of Christ
34 Agony in the Garden
35 Institution of the Eucharist
36 Crucifixion
37 Crucifixion
38 Adoration of the Magi
39 Crucifixion with SS. Cosmas and Damian
40 Crucifixion
41 Crucifixion
42 Crucifixion with SS. Mark, Dominic, Mary and Martha

both of a pair of monastic onlookers, serving as intermediaries between the occupant of the cell and the personages in the pictures: the one with the star above his head is St Dominic; the one with the split skull is St Peter Martyr (see p.130).

At the end of the far corridor is a knot of rooms (12–14) once occupied by Savonarola. These now contain various relics – a belt, a cape, a torn vest – questionably authenticated as worn by the man himself; most dubious of all is the piece of wood from his funeral pyre, which is depicted in a couple of paintings here. If you turn right at the main *Annunciation* and continue to the end of the corridor you'll come to the cells that were the personal domain of Cosimo de' Medici. The fresco of the *Adoration of the Magi* (39) may well be the work of Angelico's star pupil Benozzo Gozzoli. Its subject may have been suggested by Cosimo himself, who liked to think of himself as a latter-day wise man, or at least as a gift-giving king.

On the way to these VIP cells you'll pass the entrance to **Michelozzo's Library** (C), built in 1441–44 to a design that exudes an atmosphere of calm study, though – as the plaque by the doorway tells you – it was here that Savonarola was finally cornered and arrested in 1498. Cosimo's agents roamed as far as the Near East garnering precious manuscripts and books; in turn, Cosimo handed all the religious items over to the monastery, stipulating that they should be accessible to all, making it Europe's first public library. At the far end, a door leads through to the **Sala Greca** (D; usually open for guided visits on the hour), which was added to house a growing collection of Greek codices.

San Marco church

Greatly altered since Michelozzo's intervention, the church of **San Marco** (Mon–Sat 9.30am–noon & 4–5.30pm) is worth a quick call for two works on the second and third altars on the right: a *Madonna and Saints* painted in 1509 by Fra' Bartolomeo, and an eighth-century mosaic of *The Madonna in Prayer* (surrounded by later additions), brought here from the Constantine basilica in Rome. This had to be cut in half in transit, and you can still see the break across the Virgin's midriff.

West and north of Piazza San Marco

Within a couple of minutes' stroll west and north of **Piazza San Marco** are two little-visited art attractions, one of the city's obscurer parks, and a cluster of specialist museums. None would feature in a rushed itinerary, but the first pair in particular are worth the diversion on any high-culture point-to-point.

The Cenacolo di Sant'Apollonia

Running off the west side of Piazza San Marco, Via degli Arazzieri soon becomes Via XXVII Aprile, where the former Benedictine convent of **Sant'Apollonia** stands at no. 1 (Tues–Sat 8.15am–1.50pm; 2nd & 4th Sun of month and 1st, 3rd & 5th Mon of month same hours; free). Most of the complex has now been turned into apartments, but one entire wall of the former refectory houses Andrea del Castagno's *Last Supper*, one of the most disturbing versions of the event painted in the Renaissance. Blood-red is the dominant tone, and the most commanding figure is the diabolic, black-bearded Judas, who sits on the near side of the table. The seething patterns in the marbled panels behind the Apostles seem to mimic the turmoil in the mind of each, as he hears Christ's announcement of the betrayal.

The Chiostro dello Scalzo

To the north of San Marco, at Via Cavour 69, is **Lo Scalzo**, the home of the Brotherhood of St John, whose vows of poverty entailed walking around barefoot (*scalzo*). The order was suppressed in 1785 and their monastery sold off, except for the **cloister** (Mon, Thurs & Sat 8.15am–1.50pm; free). This was the training ground for Andrea del Sarto, an artist venerated in the nineteenth century as a painter with no imperfections, but now regarded with slightly less enthusiasm on account of this very smoothness. His monochrome paintings of the *Cardinal Virtues* and *Scenes from the Life of the Baptist* occupied him off and on for a decade from 1511, beginning with the *Baptism*, finishing with the *Birth of St John*. A couple of the sixteen scenes – *John in the Wilderness* and *John meeting Christ* – were executed by his pupil Franciabigio in 1518, when del Sarto was away in Paris.

The Giardino dei Semplici and natural history museums

The **Giardino dei Semplici** or **Orto Botanico** (April–Oct Tues 9am–1pm & 3–6pm, Wed–Fri 9am–1pm; Nov–March Mon–Fri 9am–1pm; €4), northeast of San Marco, was set up in 1545 for Cosimo I as a medicinal garden, following the examples of Padua and Pisa. Entered from Via La Pira, it now covers five acres, most of the area being taken up by the original flowerbeds and avenues. It's the nearest equivalent to the Bóboli garden on the north side of the city, but unfortunately it closes at exactly the time you could use it for a midday break.

The garden entrance at Via Micheli 3 also gives access to a number of **museums** administered by the university. The **Museo Botanico** (currently open only to scholars; ☎055.275.7462), set up for Leopoldo II of Lorraine, contains over four million botanical specimens, supplemented by plaster mushrooms and wax models of plants. Masses of rocks are on show in the **Museo di Mineralogia e Litologia** (June–Sept Wed & Fri 9am–1pm; Oct–May Tues 9am–1pm & 2–5pm, Wed–Sat 9am–1pm; €6 joint ticket with the next museum), including a 150-kilo topaz from Brazil and a load of worked stones from the Medici collection – snuff boxes, little vases, a quartz boat. The **Museo di Geologia e Paleontologia** (same hours and ticket as above) is one of Italy's biggest fossil shows, featuring such delights as prehistoric elephant skeletons from the upper Valdarno and a skeleton from Grosseto once touted as the missing link between monkeys and *Homo sapiens*.

Piazza Santissima Annunziata

Nineteenth-century urban renewal schemes spoiled many of the squares of central Florence, which makes the pedestrianized **Piazza Santissima Annunziata**, with its distinctive arcades, all the more attractive a public space. It has a special importance for the city, too. Until the end of the eighteenth century the Florentine year used to begin on March 25, the Festival of the Annunciation – hence the Florentine predilection for paintings of the Annunciation, and the fashionableness of the Annunziata church, which has long been the place for society weddings. The festival is still marked by a huge fair in the piazza and the streets leading off it; later in the year, on the first weekend in September, the square is used for Tuscany's largest crafts fair.

Brunelleschi began the piazza in the 1420s, with additions made later by Ammannati and Antonio da Sangallo. The equestrian **statue** of Grand Duke Ferdinand I (1608) at its centre was Giambologna's final work, and was cast by his pupil Pietro Tacca from cannons captured at the Battle of Lepanto. Tacca was also the creator of the grotesque **fountains** (1629), on each of which a pair of aquatic monkeys spit water at two whiskered sea slugs.

The Spedale degli Innocenti

Piazza Santissima Annunziata's tone is set by the **Spedale degli Innocenti**, or Ospedale (Mon, Tues & Thurs–Sun 8.30am–2pm; €4). Commissioned in 1419 by the Arte della Seta, the silk-weavers' guild, it opened in 1445 as the first foundlings' hospital in Europe, and is still an orphanage today. It was largely designed by Brunelleschi (whose activity as a goldsmith, strangely, allowed him membership of the guild), and his nine-arched loggia was one of Europe's earliest examples of the new classically influenced style.

Andrea della Robbia's blue-backed ceramic tondi (1487) of well-swaddled babies advertise the building's function, but their

△ Grand Duke Ferdinand I, Piazza SS Annunziata

gaiety belies the misery associated with it. Slavery was part of the Florentine economy as late as the fifteenth century (it's probable that Leonardo da Vinci's mother was a slave), and many of the infants given over to the care of the Innocenti were born to domestic slaves. From 1660 children could be abandoned anonymously in the *rota*, a small revolving door whose bricked-up remains are still visible at the extreme left of the facade; it remained in use until 1875.

The building within centres on two beautiful cloisters, Brunelleschi's central **Chiostro degli Uomini** (Men's Cloister) and the narrow, graceful **Chiostro delle Donne** (Women's Cloister) to the right. Stairs from the left-hand corner of the former lead up to the **museum**, a miscellany of Florentine Renaissance art that includes one of Luca della Robbia's most beguiling Madonnas and an *Adoration of the Magi* (1488) by Domenico Ghirlandaio. The latter, commissioned as the altarpiece of the building's church, features a background depicting the *Massacre of the Innocents*. The parallel of the slaughter of Bethlehem's first-born with the orphanage's foundlings, or *innocenti*, was deliberately made.

Santissima Annunziata

Santissima Annunziata (daily 7am–12.30pm & 4–6.30pm) is the mother church of the Servites, or Servi di Maria (Servants of Mary), a religious order founded by Filippo Benizzi and six Florentine aristocrats in 1234. From humble beginnings, the order blossomed after 1252, when a painting of the Virgin begun by one of the monks – abandoned in despair because of his inability to create a truly beautiful image – was completed by an angel while he slept. So many people came to venerate the image that by 1444 a new church, financed by the Medici, was commissioned from Michelozzo (who happened to be the brother of the Servites' head prior). The project, completed by Leon Battista Alberti in 1481, involved laying out the present-day Via dei Servi, designed to link Santissima Annunziata and the cathedral, thus uniting the city's two most important churches dedicated to the Madonna.

The Chiostrino dei Voti

As the number of pilgrims to the church increased, so it became a custom to leave wax votive offerings (*voti*) in honour of its miraculous Madonna. In the early days these were placed around the walls. Later they were hung from the nave ceiling. Eventually they became so numerous that in 1447 a special atrium, the **Chiostrino dei Voti**, was built onto the church. In time this came to house some six hundred statues, some of them life-sized depictions of the donor, with full-size wax horse in close attendance. The collection was one of the city's great tourist attractions until 1786, when the whole lot was melted down to make candles.

More lasting alterations to the cloister's appearance, in the shape of a major **fresco cycle**, were made in the 1510s, following the canonization of Filippo Benizzi, the Servites' founding father. Three leading artists of the day, Andrea del Sarto, Jacopo Pontormo and Rosso Fiorentino, were involved, together with several lesser painters. Some of the panels are in a poor state – all were removed from the walls and restored after the 1966 flood – but their overall effect is superb.

There are two sequences here, one depicting scenes from the *Life of the Virgin* (an obvious theme given the church's Marian dedication), the other portraying scenes from the *Life of St Filippo Benizzi*. If you start to the right of the entrance to the cloister, the sequence works backwards from the Virgin's death, beginning with an **Assumption** by Rosso Fiorentino, one of his first works, painted when he was aged around 19. Alongside lies Pontormo's **Visitation**, which was said to have taken some eighteen months to paint. It's followed by Franciabigio's **Marriage of the Virgin**, in which the painter is said to have taken a hammer to the Virgin's face: apparently he was angry at the monks for having secretly looked at the work before its completion, and after the artist's tantrum no one had the courage to repair the damage.

Before the next lunette comes a fine marble bas-relief of the *Madonna and Child* attributed to Michelozzo, followed by the cloister's masterpiece, Andrea del Sarto's **Birth of the Virgin**. To the right of the large church door is the same artist's **Journey of the Magi**, which includes a self-portrait in the right-hand corner. Left of the door lies Alesso Baldovinetti's **Nativity**, its faded appearance the result of poor initial preparation on the part of the artist. The sequence devoted to Filippo Benizzi begins on the next wall with Cosimo Rosselli's **Vocation and Investiture of the Saint**; the five remaining damaged panels are all the work of Andrea del Sarto.

The interior

Few Florentine interiors are as striking at first sight as Santissima Annunziata, but in order to be sure of seeing it you should visit in the afternoon: this church commands the devotion of a large congregation, and there are Masses every hour all morning. Beyond the startling first impression made by the gilt and stucco gloss that was applied in the seventeenth and eighteenth centuries, the church contains few genuine treasures. One notable exception is the ornate **tabernacle** (1448–61) immediately on your left as you enter, designed by Michelozzo to house the miraculous image of the Madonna. Michelozzo's patron, Piero di Cosimo de' Medici, made sure that nobody remained unaware of the money he sank into the shrine: an inscription reads *Costò fior. 4 mila el marmo solo* ("The marble alone cost 4000 florins"). The painting encased in the marble has been repainted into illegibility, and is usually kept covered anyway.

To the tabernacle's right lies a chapel (1453–63) originally created as an oratory for the Medici, adorned with five panels of inlaid stone depicting the Virgin's principal symbols (sun, moon, star, lily and rose) and a small picture of the *Redeemer* (1515) by Andrea del Sarto. Piero de' Medici loaned out the space to visiting dignitaries to allow them a privileged view of the Madonna.

The **Cappella Feroni**, next door, features a restrained fresco by Andrea del Castagno of *Christ and St Julian* (1455–56). The adjacent chapel contains a more striking fresco by the same artist, the *Holy Trinity and St Jerome* (1454). Now restored, both frescoes were obliterated after Vasari spread the rumour that Castagno had poisoned his erstwhile friend, Domenico Veneziano, motivated by envy of the other's skill with oil paint. Castagno was saddled with this crime until the nineteenth century, when an archivist discovered that the alleged murderer in fact predeceased his victim by four years.

Separated from the nave by a triumphal arch is the unusual **tribune**, begun by Michelozzo but completed to designs by Alberti; you get into it along a corridor from the north transept. The chapel at the farthest point was altered by Giambologna into a monument to himself, complete with bronze reliefs and a crucifix by the sculptor. The chapel to its left contains a sizeable *Resurrection* (1550) by Bronzino.

The spacious **Chiostro dei Morti** is worth visiting for Andrea del Sarto's intimate *Madonna del Sacco* (1525), over the door that opens from the north transept (if you can't find the sacristan to open it, you may be able to enter the cloister from the street – the entrance is to the left of the main entrance); depicting the *Rest during the Flight into Egypt*, the picture takes its curious name from the sack on which St Joseph is leaning.

The Museo Archeologico

On the other side of Via della Colonna from the side wall of Santissima Annunziata, the **Museo Archeologico** (Mon 2–7pm, Tues & Thurs 8.30am–7pm, Wed & Fri–Sun 8.30am–2pm; €4) houses the most important collection of its kind in northern Italy. Its special strength is its **Etruscan** finds, many of them part of the Medici bequest. On the ground floor there's a comprehensive display of Etruscan funerary figures, but even more arresting than these is the *François Vase*, an Attic krater (bowl) from the sixth century BC, discovered in an Etruscan tomb at Chiusi. Pride of place in the first-floor **Egyptian collection**, where the rooms are handsomely decorated in mock-Egyptian funerary style, goes to a Hittite chariot made of bone and wood and dating from the fourteenth century BC. The grisly exposed mummies may be popular with kids.

The rest of this floor and much of the floor above are given over to the **Etruscan, Greek and Roman collections**, arranged with variable clarity. Of the Roman pieces the outstanding item is the *Idolino*, probably a copy of a fifth-century BC Greek original. Nearby is a massive Hellenistic horse's head, which once adorned the garden of the Palazzo Medici, where it was studied by Donatello and Verrocchio. In the long gallery you'll find the best of the Etruscan pieces: the *Arringatore* (Orator), the only known Etruscan large bronze from the Hellenistic period; and the *Chimera*, a triple-headed monster of the fifth century BC. A symbol of the three-season pre-Christian Mediterranean year, the *Chimera* was much admired by Cosimo I's retinue of Mannerist artists and many subsequent connoisseurs of the offbeat.

The Museo Stibbert

About 1500m north of San Marco, at Via Stibbert 26 (bus #4 from the station), is the loopiest of Florence's museums, the **Museo Stibbert** (Mon–Wed 10am–2pm, Fri–Sun 10am–6pm; compulsory guided tour €5). This rambling, murky mansion was the home of the half-Scottish half-Italian Frederick Stibbert, who in his twenties made a name for himself in Garibaldi's army. Later he inherited a fourteenth-century house from his mother, then bought the neighbouring mansion and joined the two together, thus creating a place big enough to accommodate the fruits of his compulsive collecting. The 64 rooms contain over fifty thousand items, ranging from snuff boxes to paintings by Carlo Crivelli and a possible Botticelli.

Militaria were Frederick's chief enthusiasm, and the Stibbert **armour** collection is reckoned one of the world's best. It includes Roman, Etruscan and Japanese examples (the highlight of the whole museum), as well as a fifteenth-century condottiere's outfit and the armour worn by the great Medici commander Giovanni delle Bande Nere, retrieved from his grave in San Lorenzo in 1857. The big production number comes in the great hall, between the two houses, where a platoon of mannequins is clad in full sixteenth-century gear. Also on show is the regalia in which Napoleon was crowned king of Italy.

East of the centre: from the Bargello to Campo di Marte

The dense network of streets northeast of the Piazza della Signoria is dominated by the campanile of the **Badìa Fiorentina**, the most important of several buildings in the area that have the strongest associations with Florence's – indeed Italy's – foremost poet, Dante Alighieri. Immediately opposite the church stands the forbidding bulk of the **Bargello**, once the city's prison, now home to a superb assemblage of sculpture, plus excellent collections of enamels, ivories, glassware, silverware and other *objets d'art*. To get a full idea of the achievement of the Florentine Renaissance, a visit to the Bargello is as important as a day in the Uffizi, and as a corrective to the notion that Florence's contribution to European civilization has been limited to the arts, you should call in at the fascinating **Museo di Storia della Scienza** at the back of the Uffizi. Further east rises the vast Franciscan church of **Santa Croce**, whose architecture and frescoes make it one of the most compelling sights in Florence. The church is the centrepiece of a district which was one of Florence's more densely populated districts before November 4th, 1966, when the Arno burst its banks and the low-lying Santa Croce area, packed with tenements and small workshops, was very badly damaged. Many residents moved out permanently in the following years, but now the more traditional shops, bars and restaurants that survived the flood have been joined by a growing number of new and often extremely good bars and restaurants, a transformation that's particularly noticeable around the **Sant'Ambrogio** market. In addition to the great church and its museum, the other main cultural attractions in this part of the city are the **Museo Horne**, a modest but pleasing collection of art treasures, and the **Casa Buonarroti**, a less than entirely satisfying homage to Michelangelo.

The Museo di Storia della Scienza

Long after Florence had declined from its artistic apogee, the intellectual reputation of the city was maintained by its scientists, many of them directly encouraged by the ruling Medici-Lorraine dynasty. Two of the latter, Grand Duke Ferdinando II and his brother Leopoldo, both of whom studied with Galileo, founded a scientific academy at the Pitti in 1657. Called the Accademia del Cimento (Academy of Experiment), its motto was "Try and try again." The instruments made and acquired by this academy are the core of the **Museo di Storia della Scienza** (Mon & Wed–Fri 9.30am–5pm, Tues & Sat 9.30am–1pm; Oct–May open Sat till 5pm and 2nd Sun of month 10am–1pm; €6.50).

The first eleven exhibition rooms feature **measuring instruments**, notably a selection of beautiful Arab astrolabes. There's also a massive armillary sphere made for Ferdinando I to provide a visual demonstration of the supposed veracity of the earth-centred Ptolemaic system and the fallacy of Copernicus's heliocentric universe. Galileo's original instruments are on show here, such as the lens with which he discovered the four moons of Jupiter (which he tactfully named the Medicean planets). On this floor you'll also find the museum's equivalent of a religious relic – a bone from one of Galileo's fingers – but the most impressive of several fascinating rooms is Room 7, filled with dozens of gorgeous globes and old maps.

On the floor above there are all kinds of **scientific and mechanical equipment**, some – such as a perpetual motion machine – from the quasi-magical realms of scientific endeavour. Room 12 sets the tone, with dozens of old clocks and timepieces. There are also a couple of remarkable outsized exhibits: the huge lens made for Cosimo III, with which Faraday and Davy managed to ignite a diamond by focusing the rays of the sun, and the enormous lodestone given by Galileo to Ferdinando II. Other rooms feature pharmaceutical and chemical apparatus.

The best is saved for last: a **medical section** full of alarming surgical instruments and anatomical wax models for teaching obstetrics. Room 19 concludes with the contents of a medieval pharmacy, displaying such unlikely cure-alls as Sangue del Drago (Dragon's Blood) and Confetti di Seme Santo (Confections of Blessed Seed).

The Bargello

The Renaissance sculpture collection of the **Museo Nazionale del Bargello** (Tues–Sat 8.15am–1.50pm; 2nd & 4th Sun of month and 1st, 3rd & 5th Mon of month same hours; €4), at Via del Proconsolo 4, is the richest in Italy, but the museum also devotes a vast amount of space to the decorative arts: carpets, enamels, ivories, glassware, tapestries, silverware and other *objets d'art* of the highest quality. Although they receive scant attention from most visitors, it would be as easy to spend as much time on the dozen or more rooms filled with these treasures as the four rooms devoted to sculpture.

The Bargello's home, the daunting Palazzo del Bargello, was built in 1255 immediately after the overthrow of the aristocratic regime. The first of the city's public palaces, it soon became the seat of the *Podestà*, the city's chief magistrate, and the site of the main law court. Numerous malefactors were tortured, tried, sentenced and executed here, the elegant courtyard having been the site of the city's gallows and block. The building acquired its present name after 1574, when the Medici abolished the post of *Podestà*, the building becoming home to the chief of police – the *Bargello*. Torture and capital punishment were banned in 1786 (the first such abolition in Europe), though the building remained a prison until 1859.

The ground floor

You've no time to catch your breath in the Bargello: the first room to the right of the ticket office is crammed with treasures, chief of which are the work of **Michelangelo**, in whose shadow every Florentine sculptor laboured from the sixteenth century onwards. The tipsy, soft-bellied figure of *Bacchus* (1496–97) was his first major sculpture, carved at the age of 22, a year or so before his great *Pietà* in Rome. Michelangelo's style soon evolved into something less ostentatiously virtuosic, as is shown by the tender *Tondo Pitti* (1503–05), while the rugged expressivity of his late manner is exemplified by the square-jawed *Bust of Brutus* (c.1540), the artist's sole work of this kind. A powerful portrait sketch in stone, it's a coded celebration of anti-Medicean republicanism, carved soon after the murder of the nightmarish Duke Alessandro de' Medici (see p.143).

Works by Michelangelo's followers and contemporaries are ranged in the immediate vicinity; some of them would command prolonged attention in less exalted company. **Benvenuto Cellini**'s huge *Bust of Cosimo I* (1545–47), his first work in bronze, was a sort of technical trial for the casting of the *Perseus*, his most famous work. Alongside the two preparatory models for the *Perseus* in wax and bronze are displayed the original marble base and four statuettes that comprise the statue's pedestal; Perseus himself still stands in his intended spot, in the Loggia della Signoria (see p.110).

Close by, **Giambologna**'s voluptuous *Florence Defeating Pisa* (1575) – a disingenuous pretext for a glamour display if ever there were one – takes up a lot of space, but is eclipsed by his best-known creation, the wonderful *Mercury* (1564), a nimble figure with no bad angles. Comic relief is provided by the reliably inept Bandinelli, whose coiffured *Adam and Eve* look like a grandee and his wife taking an *au naturel* stroll through their country estate. The powerfully erotic *Leda and the Swan* by **Ammannati** (1540–50) was inspired by a painting of the subject by Michelangelo that was later destroyed.

Part two of the ground floor's collection lies across the Gothic **courtyard**, which is plastered with the coats of arms of the *Podestà*. Against the far wall stand six allegorical figures by Ammannati from the fountain of the Palazzo Pitti courtyard. Of the two rooms across the yard, the one to the left features largely fourteenth-century works, notably pieces by Arnolfo di Cambio and Tino da Camaino; temporary exhibitions are often held in the room to the right.

The first floor

At the top of Giuliano da Sangallo's courtyard **staircase** (1502), the first-floor loggia has been turned into a menagerie for Giambologna's quaint bronze animals and birds, imported from the Medici villa at Castello, just outside Florence. The nearer doorway to the right opens into the tall, Gothic **Salone del Consiglio Generale**, the museum's second key room. Here again the number of masterpieces is breathtaking, though this time the presiding genius is **Donatello**, the fountainhead of Renaissance sculpture.

Vestiges of the sinuous Gothic manner are evident in the drapery of his marble *David* (1408), but there's nothing antiquated in the **St George** (1416), carved for the tabernacle of the armourers' guild at Orsanmichele and installed in a replica of its original niche at the far end of the room. If any one sculpture could be said to embody the shift of sensibility that occurred in quattrocento Florence, this is it: whereas Saint George had previously been little more than a symbol of valour, this alert, tensed figure represents not the act of heroism but the volition behind it. The slaying of the dragon is depicted in the small, badly eroded marble panel underneath, a piece as revolutionary as the figure of the saint, with its seamless interweaving of foreground and background.

Also here is the sexually ambivalent bronze **David**, the first freestanding nude figure created since classical times (1430–40). A decade later the sculptor produced the strange prancing figure known as *Amor-Atys*, which was mistaken for a genuine statue from classical antiquity – the highest compliment the artist could have wished for. Donatello was just as comfortable with portraiture as with Christian or pagan imagery, as his breathtakingly vivid terracotta *Bust of Niccolò da Uzzano* demonstrates; it may be the earliest Renaissance portrait bust. When the occasion demanded, Donatello could also produce a straightforwardly monumental piece like the nearby *Marzocco* (1418–20), Florence's heraldic lion.

Donatello's master, **Ghiberti**, is represented by his relief of *Abraham's Sacrifice*, his entry in the competition to design the Baptistery doors in 1401, easily missed on the right-hand wall; the treatment of the theme submitted by Brunelleschi, effectively the runner-up, is hung alongside. Set around the walls of the room, **Luca della Robbia**'s simple sweet-natured humanism is embodied in a sequence of glazed terracotta Madonnas.

The rest of this floor is occupied by a superb collection of European and Islamic applied art, with dazzling specimens of work in enamel, glass, silver, majolica and ivory: among the ivory pieces from Byzantium and medieval France you'll find combs, boxes, chess pieces, and devotional panels featuring scores of figures crammed into a space the size of a paperback. Room 9, the **Cappella di Santa Maria Maddalena**, is decorated with frescoes discovered in 1841 when the room was converted from a prison cell; long attributed to Giotto, they're now thought to be by followers.

The second floor

Sculpture resumes upstairs, with a room largely devoted to the della Robbia family, a prelude to the **Sala dei Bronzetti**, Italy's best assembly of small Renaissance bronzes. Giambologna's spiralling designs predominate, a testament to his popularity in late sixteenth-century Florence: look out for the Hercules series (Ercole, in Italian), showing the hero variously wrestling and clubbing his opponents into submission. An interesting contrast is provided by **Antonio del Pollaiuolo**'s earlier and much more violent *Hercules and Antaeus* (c.1478), which stands on a pillar nearby. Like Leonardo, Pollaiuolo unravelled the complexities of human musculature by dissecting corpses.

Also on this floor there's another roomful of della Robbias and a splendid display of bronze medals, featuring specimens from the great pioneer of this form of portable art, Pisanello, among whose coin-sized portraits you'll see Leonello d'Este (the lord of Ferrara), Sigismondo Malatesta (the lord of Rimini) and John Paleologus III (the penultimate emperor of Byzantium). Lastly, there's a room devoted mainly to **Renaissance portrait busts**, where the centrepiece is Verrocchio's *David*, clearly influenced by the Donatello figure downstairs. Around the walls you'll find Mino da Fiesole's busts of Giovanni de' Medici and Piero il Gottoso (the sons of Cosimo de' Medici), Antonio del Pollaiuolo's *Young Cavalier* (which is probably another Medici portrait), and a bust labelled *Ritratto d'Ignoto* (Portrait of an Unknown Man) – beside Verrocchio's *Madonna and Child* – which may in fact depict Macchiavelli. Also outstanding are Francesco Laurana's *Battista Sforza* (an interesting comparison with the Piero della Francesca portrait in the Uffizi), the *Woman Holding Flowers* by Verrocchio (the first such portrait bust to show the subject's hands), and the fraught marble relief in which Verrocchio portrays the death of Francesca Tornabuoni-Pitti, from whose tomb this panel was taken.

The Badìa Fiorentina and around

Directly opposite the Bargello lies the **Badìa Fiorentina**, now approaching the end of many years of restoration. Tourist visits are allowed on Monday afternoons (3–6pm); at other times the church is open for prayer only, following the monastic rules of the Fraternity of Jerusalem, whose church this is.

The dark interior and fresco-covered cloister are well worth a few minutes. The Badìa (Abbey) is also a place of reverence for admirers of Dante, for this was the parish church of Beatrice Portinari, for whom he conceived a lifelong love as he watched her at Mass here (see p.160). Furthermore, it was here that Boccaccio delivered his celebrated lectures on Dante's theological epic.

Founded in 978 by Willa, widow of the Margrave of Tuscany, in honour of her husband, the Badìa was one of the focal buildings in medieval Florence: the city's sick were treated in a hospital founded here in 1031, while the main bell marked the divisions of the working day. The hospital also owed much to Willa's son, Ugo, who further endowed his mother's foundation after a vision of the hellish torments which awaited him by "reason of his worldly life, unless he should repent". The 1280s saw the church overhauled along Cistercian Gothic lines, probably under the direction of Arnolfo di Cambio, architect of the Duomo and Palazzo Vecchio. Later Baroque additions smothered much of the old church in 1627, though the narrow **campanile** – Romanesque at its base, Gothic towards its apex – escaped unharmed. Completed between 1310 and 1330, it remains a prominent feature of the Florentine skyline.

On the left, as you enter from Via Dante Alighieri, hangs **Filippino Lippi**'s superb *Apparition of the Virgin to St Bernard*; set back to the right is the church's second highlight, the **tomb monument** to Ugo, sculpted by Mino da Fiesole between 1469 and 1481. Mino was also responsible for the nearby tomb of Bernardo Giugni and an altar frontal of the *Madonna and Child with SS Leonard and Lawrence*. Giugni was a lawyer and diplomat, hence the figures of Justice and Faith accompanying his effigy.

A staircase leads from the choir – take the door immediately right of the high altar – to the upper storey of the **Chiostro degli Aranci** (Cloister of the Oranges), named after the fruit trees that used to be grown here. Two of its flanks are graced with an anonymous but highly distinctive fresco cycle (1436–39) on the life of St Benedict. A later panel – showing the saint throwing himself into bushes to resist temptation – is by the young Bronzino (1526–28). The cloister itself (1432–38) is the work of Bernardo Rossellino, one of the leading lights of early Renaissance architecture.

The Dante district

After visiting the Badìa Fiorentina, you might want to explore the city's knot of buildings with **Dante** associations – some of them admittedly spurious – that cluster together in the grid of minor streets behind the Badìa, between Piazza del Duomo and Piazza della Signoria. Start your peregrinations at the Baptistery, one of only three Florentine churches mentioned by the poet. Nearby, south of the Duomo, search out the so-called **Sasso di Dante** (Dante's Stone), set between Via dello Studio and Via del Proconsolo. Dante is supposed to have sat here and watched the construction of the cathedral. Walk down Via dello Studio, and at its junction with Via del Corso lies the **Palazzo Salviati**, site of Beatrice's former home. The courtyard still contains the so-called Nicchia di Dante (Dante's Niche), from which the young Dante is said to have watched his *inamorata*.

Cross Via del Corso from the Palazzo Salviati then head down Via Santa Margherita and you come to a small piazza fronting the **Casa di Dante** (Tues–Sat

Dante Alighieri

Dante signed himself "Dante Alighieri, a Florentine by birth but not by character", a bitter allusion to the city he served as a politician but which later cast him into exile and was to inspire some of the most vitriolic passages in his great epic poem, *La Divina Commedia* (The Divine Comedy).

The poet was born in 1265 into a minor and impoverished noble family. He was educated at Bologna and later at Padua, where he studied philosophy and astronomy. The defining moment in his life came in 1274 when he met the 8-year-old **Beatrice Portinari**, a young girl whom Boccaccio described as possessed of "habits and language more serious and modest than her age warranted". Her features were "so delicate and so beautifully formed," he went on, "and full, besides mere beauty, of so much candid loveliness that many thought her almost an angel."

Dante – just 9 at the time of the meeting – later described his own feeling following the encounter: "Love ruled my soul," he wrote, "and began to hold such sway over me... that it was necessary for me to do completely all his pleasure. He commanded me often that I should endeavour to see this so youthful angel, and I saw in her such noble and praiseworthy deportment that truly of her might be said these words of the poet Homer – *She appeared to be born not of mortal man but of God.*"

Unhappily, Beatrice's family had decided their daughter was to marry someone else – Simone de' Bardi. The ceremony took place when she was 17; seven years later she was dead. Dante, for his part, had been promised – aged 12 – to Gemma Donati. The wedding took place in 1295, when the poet was 30.

His romantic hopes dashed, Dante settled down to a military and political career. In 1289 he fought for Florence against Arezzo and helped in a campaign against Pisa. Later he joined the Apothecaries' Guild, serving on a variety of minor civic committees. In 1300 he was dispatched to San Gimignano, where he was entrusted with the job of coaxing the town into an alliance against Pope Boniface VIII, who had designs on Tuscany. In June of the same year he sought to settle the widening breach between the **Black** (anti-imperial) and **White** (more conciliatory) factions of Florence's ruling Guelph party. The dispute had its roots in money: the Whites contained leading bankers to the imperial powers (the Cerchi, Mozzi, Davanzati and Frescobaldi), while the Blacks counted the Pazzi, Bardi and Donati amongst their number, all prominent papal bankers. Boniface, not surprisingly, sided with the Blacks, who eventually emerged triumphant.

Dante's White sympathies sealed his fate. In 1302, following trumped-up charges of corruption, he was sentenced with other Whites to two years' exile. While many of the deportees subsequently returned, Dante rejected his city of "self-made men and fast-got gain". He wandered instead between Forlì, Verona, Padua, Luni and Venice, writing much of *The Divine Comedy* as he went, before finally settling in Ravenna, where he died in 1321.

plus 1st Sun of month 10am–5pm, other Sundays 10am–1pm, but closed last Sun of month; €4). Somewhat fraudulently marketed as Dante's house, the building is actually a medieval pastiche dating from 1910. The modest museum upstairs is a homage to the poet rather than a shrine: it contains nothing directly related to his life, and in all likelihood Dante was born not on the house's site but somewhere in the street that bears his name.

As contentious as the Casa di Dante's claims is the story that Dante married Gemma Donati in **Santa Margherita de' Cerchi** (Mon–Sat 10am–noon & 3–6pm, Sun 10am–noon), the ancient little church up the street from the Casa di Dante on the right. Documented as early as 1032, the building does, however, contain several tombs belonging to the Portinari, Beatrice's family name; the porch also features the Donati family crest, as this was also their local parish church.

Over Via Dante Alighieri from the poet's house, on Piazza San Martino, lies the tiny **San Martino del Vescovo** (Mon–Thurs & Sat 10am–noon & 3–5pm, Fri 10am–noon), built on the site of a small oratory founded in 986 that served as the Alighieri's parish church. Rebuilt in 1479, it later became the headquarters of the Compagnia di Buonomini, a charitable body dedicated to aiding impoverished better-class citizens for whom begging was too demeaning a prospect. The Buonomini commissioned from Ghirlandaio's workshop a sequence of frescoes showing various altruistic acts and scenes from the life of St Martin, and the result is as absorbing a record of daily life in Renaissance Florence as the Ghirlandaio frescoes in Santa Maria Novella (see p.133).

Opposite San Martino soars the thirteenth-century **Torre della Castagna**, meeting place of the city's *priori* before they decamped to the Palazzo Vecchio. This is one of the most striking remnants of Florence's medieval townscape, when over 150 such towers rose between the river and the Duomo, many of them over two hundred feet high.

Santa Croce

The focal point of the eastern quarter of the city centre is **Piazza Santa Croce**, one of Florence's largest squares and traditionally one of the city's main arenas for ceremonials and festivities. Thus when Lorenzo the Magnificent was married to the Roman heiress Clarice Orsini, the wedding was celebrated on this square, with a tournament that was more a fashion event than a contest of skill: Lorenzo's knightly outfit, for instance, was adorned with pearls, diamonds and rubies. It's still used as the pitch for the Gioco di Calcio Storico, a mad football tournament between the city's four *quartieri* (see p.204).

The church of **Santa Croce** (Mon–Sat 9.30am–5.30pm, Sun 1–5.30pm; €4) is the Franciscans' principal church in Florence – a rival to the Dominicans' Santa Maria Novella – and is often said to have been founded by St Francis himself. In truth it was probably begun seventy or so years after Francis's death, in 1294, possibly by the architect of the Duomo, Arnolfo di Cambio. It replaced a smaller church on the site, a building that had become too small for the vast congregations gathering to hear the Franciscans' homilies on poverty, chastity and obedience in what was then one of the city's poorest areas. Ironically, it was Florence's richest families who funded the construction of Santa Croce, to atone for the sin of usury on which their fortunes were based. Plutocrats such as the Bardi, Peruzzi and Baroncelli sponsored the extraordinary **fresco cycles** that were lavished on the chapels over the years, particularly during the fourteenth century, when artists of the stature of Giotto and the Gaddi family worked here. In further contradiction of the Franciscan ideal of humility, Santa Croce has long served as the national pantheon: the walls and nave floor are lined with the **monuments** to more than 270 illustrious Italians, many of them Tuscan, including Michelangelo, Galileo, Machiavelli, Alberti, Dante and the great physicist Enrico Fermi (though the last two are not buried here).

Of all the events that have happened at Santa Croce, none was more momentous than the **Council of Florence**, held in 1439 in an attempt to reconcile the differences between the Roman and Eastern churches. Attended by the pope, the Byzantine emperor and the Patriarch of Constantinople, the council arrived at a compromise that lasted only until the Byzantine delegation returned home. Its more enduring effect was that it brought scores of classical scholars to the city, some of whom stayed on to give an important impetus to the Florentine Renaissance.

Florence's floods

The calamity of the November 1966 flood had plenty of precedents. Great areas of the city were destroyed by a flood in **1178**, a disaster exacerbated by plague and famine. In **1269** the Carraia and Trìnita bridges were carried away on a torrent so heavy that "a great part of the city of Florence became a lake". The flood of **1333** was preceded by a four-day storm, with thunder and rain so violent that all the city's bells were tolled to drive away the evil spirits thought to be behind the tempest: bridges were demolished and the original Marzocco – a figure of Mars rather than the leonine figure that inherited its name – was carried away by the raging Arno. Cosimo I instituted an urban beautification scheme after a deluge put nearly twenty feet of muddy water over parts of the city in **1557**; on that occasion the Trìnita bridge was hit so suddenly that everyone on it was drowned, except for two children who were left stranded on a pillar in midstream, where for two days they were fed by means of a rope slung over from the bank.

It rained continuously for forty days prior to **November 4, 1966**, with nearly half a metre of rain falling in the preceding two days. When the water pressure in an upstream reservoir threatened to break the dam, it was decided to open the sluices. The only people to be warned about the rapidly rising level of the river were the jewellers of the Ponte Vecchio, whose private nightwatchman phoned them in the small hours of the morning with news that the bridge was starting to shake. Police watching the shopkeepers clearing their displays were asked why they weren't spreading the alarm. They replied, "We have received no orders." When the banks of the Arno finally broke down, a flash flood dumped around 500,000 tonnes of water and mud on the streets, moving with such speed that people were drowned in the underpass of Santa Maria Novella train station. In all, 35 Florentines were killed, 6000 shops put out of business, more than 10,000 homes made uninhabitable, some 15,000 cars wrecked, and thousands of works of art damaged, many of them ruined by heating oil flushed out of basements.

Within hours an impromptu army of rescue workers had been formed – many of them students – to haul pictures out of slime-filled churches and gather fragments of paint in plastic bags. Donations came in from all over the world, but the task was so immense that the restoration of many pieces is still unaccomplished. Some rooms in the archeological museum, for example, have remained closed since the flood, and many possessions of the National Library are still in the laboratories. In total around two-thirds of the 3000 paintings damaged in the flood are now on view again, and two massive laboratories – one for paintings and one for stonework – are operating full time in Florence, developing restoration techniques that are often taken up by galleries all over the world. Today, throughout the city, you can see small marble plaques with a red line showing the level the floodwaters reached on that dreadful day in 1966.

The interior

The church's **facade** is a neo-Gothic sham which dates from as recently as 1863. The church had languished for centuries without a suitable frontage, a situation remedied when someone claimed to have discovered long-lost plans for the "original" facade; in truth the scheme was no more than a giant-sized pastiche of Orcagna's tabernacle in Orsanmichele. The vast interior is infinitely more satisfying.

Hurry towards the high altar and the Giotto-painted chapels to its right if all you want to see are the church's most famous works of art. Otherwise, take a more measured walk down the **south aisle**. Against the first pillar stands the tomb of Francesco Nori, one of the victims of the Pazzi Conspiracy (see p.96), surmounted by Antonio Rossellino's lovely relief of the *Madonna del Latte*.

Nearby is Vasari's **tomb of Michelangelo**; the sculptor's body was brought back from Rome to Florence in July 1574, ten years after his death, and his tomb is said to have been positioned close to the church's entrance at his own request, so that when the graves fly open on the Day of Judgement, the first thing to catch his eye will be Brunelleschi's cathedral dome.

The Neoclassical **monument to Dante** is a cenotaph rather than a tomb, as the exiled poet is buried in Ravenna, where he died in 1321. Three centuries

SANTA CROCE

Primo Chiostro

1 Madonna del Latte (1478), Antonio Rossellino
2 Tomb of Michelangelo (1570), Giorgio Vasari
3 Cenotaph to Dante (1829), Stefano Ricci
4 Pulpit (1472–6), Benedetto da Maiano
5 Monument to Vittorio Alfieri (1810), Antonio Canova
6 Tomb of Niccolò Machiavelli (1787), Innocenzo Spinazzi
7 Annunciation (1435), Donatello
8 Tomb of Leonardo Bruni (1446–7), Bernardo Rossellino
9 Tomb of Giacchino Rossini (1900), Giuseppe Cassioli
10 Cappella Castellani: frescoes (1385), Agnolo Gaddi
11 Cappella Baroncelli: frescoes (1332–8), Taddeo Gaddi
12 Cappella Medici (1434), designed by Michelozzo
13 Madonna and Child altarpiece (1480), Andrea della Robbia
14 Church shop
15 Sacristy
16 Cappella Rinuccini: frescoes (1365), Giovanni da Milano
17 Cappella Velluti: altarpiece, Giovanni di Biondo
18 Cappella Peruzzi: Lives of St John the Evangelist and St John the Baptist (1326–30), Giotto
19 Cappella Bardi: Life of St Francis (1315–20), Giotto
20 Chancel: Frescoes and stained glass (1380), Agnolo Gaddi
21 Cappella Pulci-Beradi: Martyrdom of SS Lorenzo and Stefano (1330) frescoes, Bernardo Daddi
22 Cappella Bardi di Vernio: Scenes from the Life of San Silvestro (1340) frescoes, Maso di Banco
23 Cappella Bardi: wooden crucifix (1412), Donatello
24 Monument to Leon Battista Alberti (d. 1472), Lorenzo Bartolini (early 19th-century)
25 Tomb of Carlo Marsuppini (1453), Desiderio da Settignano
26 Pietà (1560), Agnolo Bronzino
27 Tomb of Lorenzo Ghiberti and his son Vittorio (pavement slab)
28 Tomb of Galileo (1737), Giulio Foggini
29 Cappella dei Pazzi
30 Refectory and museum
31 Inner Cloister

before Dante finally received this bland nineteenth-century tribute, Michelangelo had offered to carve the poet's tomb – a tantalizing thought. Against the third pillar there's a marvellous **pulpit** by Benedetto da Maiano, adorned with niche statuettes of the virtues and scenes from the life of St Francis.

Canova's **monument to Alfieri** commemorates an eighteenth-century Italian poet and dramatist as famous for his amatory liaisons as his literary endeavours. The tomb was paid for by his mistress, the so-called Countess of Albany, erstwhile wife of Charles Edward Stuart (aka Bonnie Prince Charlie). She modelled for the tomb's main figure, an allegory of Italy bereaved by Alfieri's death. The nearby **tomb of Machiavelli**, carved 260 years after his death, is unexceptional save for its famous inscription: *Tanto nomini nullum par elogium* ("No praise can be high enough for so great a name"). The side door at the end of the aisle is flanked by Donatello's gilded stone relief of the *Annunciation*.

Beyond the door is Bernardo Rossellino's much-imitated **tomb of Leonardo Bruni**, chancellor of the Republic, humanist scholar and author of the first history of the city – his effigy is holding a copy. Bruni, who died in 1444, was the first man of any great eminence to be buried in the church, which is a little surprising given his predominantly humanist rather than Christian beliefs. The tomb, one of the most influential of the Renaissance, makes the point: for the first time the human figure dominates, with the Madonna and Child banished to a peripheral position high in the lunette.

The Castellani, Baroncelli and Medici chapels, and the sacristy

The **Cappella Castellani**, at the end of the south aisle, is strikingly, if patchily, covered in frescoes by Agnolo Gaddi and his pupils. To the right are depicted the stories of St John the Baptist and St Nicholas of Bari: the latter, the patron saint of children (he's the St Nicholas of Santa Claus fame), is shown saving three girls from prostitution and reviving three murdered boys. The left wall features episodes from the lives of St John and St Antony Abbot; the latter gave away his wealth, making him a favourite of the poverty-inspired Franciscans. Also note the chapel's fine tabernacle, the work of Mino da Fiesole, and its funerary monuments, including that of the Countess of Albany.

The adjoining **Cappella Baroncelli** was decorated by Agnolo's father, Taddeo, a long-time assistant to Giotto. Taddeo's cycle, largely devoted to the life of the Virgin, features one of the first night scenes in Western painting, *The Annunciation to the Shepherds*, in which the angel appears amid a blaze of light that's believed to be a representation of Halley's Comet. The main altar painting, the *Coronation of the Virgin*, may also be by Taddeo, though an increasing number of critics now attribute it to his master, Giotto.

The corridor to the right ends at the **Cappella Medici**, usually open only for those taking Mass. It's notable for the large terracotta altarpiece by Andrea della Robbia and a nineteenth-century forged Donatello; the chapel, like the corridor, was designed by Michelozzo, the Medici's pet architect. Finely carved wooden doors lead off the corridor into the beautifully panelled **Sacristy**, where the highlight is a marvellous *Crucifixion* by Taddeo. The tiny **Cappella Rinuccini**, separated from the sacristy by a grille, is impressively covered with frescoes on the life of the Virgin (on the left) and St Mary Magdalene (on the right): the Lombard artist responsible, Giovanni da Milano, was one of Giotto's most accomplished followers.

The east chapels: Giotto's frescoes

Both the **Cappella Peruzzi** and the **Cappella Bardi** – the two chapels on the right of the chancel – are entirely covered with frescoes by Giotto, with some assistance in the latter. Their deterioration was partly caused by Giotto's having painted some of the pictures onto dry plaster, rather than the wet plaster employed in true fresco technique, but the vandalism of later generations was far more destructive. In the eighteenth century they were covered in whitewash, then they were heavily retouched in the nineteenth; restoration in the 1950s returned them to as close to their original state as was possible.

Scenes from the lives of St John the Evangelist and St John the Baptist cover the Peruzzi chapel, while a better-preserved cycle of the life of St Francis fills the Bardi. Despite the areas of paint destroyed when a tomb was attached to the wall, the *Funeral of St Francis* is still a composition of extraordinary impact, the grief-stricken mourners suggesting an affinity with the lamentation over the body of Christ – one of them even probes the wound in Francis's side, echoing the gesture of Doubting Thomas. The *Ordeal by Fire*, showing Francis about to demonstrate his faith to the sultan by walking through fire, shows Giotto's mastery of understated drama, with the sultan's entourage skulking off to the left in anticipation of the monk's triumph. On the wall above the chapel's entrance arch is the most powerful scene of all, *St Francis Receiving the Stigmata*, in which the power of Christ's apparition seems to force the chosen one to his knees.

Agnolo Gaddi was responsible for the design of the **stained glass** in the lancet windows round the high altar, and for all the chancel **frescoes**, which depict the legend of the True Cross – a complicated tale tracing the wood of the Cross from its origins as the Tree of Paradise (see p.517). The vast polyptych on the high altar is a composite of panels by several artists.

The **Cappella Bardi di Vernio** was painted by Maso di Banco, perhaps the most inventive of Giotto's followers. Following tradition, the frescoes, showing scenes from the life of Saint Sylvester, portray the saint baptizing Emperor Constantine, notwithstanding the fact that Sylvester died some time before the emperor's baptism. The second **Cappella Bardi** houses a wooden crucifix by Donatello, supposedly criticized by Brunelleschi as resembling a "peasant on the Cross". According to Vasari, Brunelleschi went off and created his own crucifix for Santa Maria Novella to show Donatello how it should be done (see p.134).

The north aisle

As you walk back towards the entrance along the north aisle, the first pillar you pass features a ghastly nineteenth-century **monument to Leon Battista Alberti**, the Renaissance architect and artistic theorist whose writings did much to influence Rossellino in his carving of the Bruni tomb across the nave. The Bruni tomb in turn influenced the outstanding **tomb of Carlo Marsuppini** by Desiderio da Settignano. Marsuppini's lack of Christian qualifications for so prominent a church burial is even more striking than Bruni's: he's said to have died without taking confession or communion. The tomb inscription opens with the words, "Stay and see the marbles which enshrine a great sage, one for whose mind there was not world enough."

A *Pietà* by the young Bronzino, a future Mannerist star, briefly disturbs the parade of tombs that follows. A surprisingly modest pavement slab marks the **tomb of Lorenzo Ghiberti** – the artist responsible for the Baptistery's marvellous doors – and his son Vittorio. The **tomb of Galileo** is more ostentatious, though it was some ninety years after his death in 1642 that the "heretic" scientist was deemed worthy of a Christian burial in Florence's pantheon.

The Cappella dei Pazzi

The door in the south (right) aisle leads through into the church's Primo Chiostro (First Cloister), site of Brunelleschi's **Cappella dei Pazzi**, the epitome

What is the Renaissance?

In the middle of the sixteenth century Giorgio Vasari coined the term **Rinascenza** (rebirth) to designate an epoch that stretched from around 1300 (the lifetime of Giotto) to the era of Michelangelo. It was in the latter half of the nineteenth century, however, that the term "**Renaissance**" entered general usage, in the wake of the writings of the French historian Jules Michelet, and – above all – Jacob Burckhardt, whose book *The Civilization of the Renaissance* in Italy (published in German in 1860, and in English translation in 1878) is perhaps the most influential single study of the subject. To historians of this period, the Renaissance was seen as a singular and all-pervasive phenomenon, in which the rediscovery of ancient classical culture gave impetus to a wholesale regeneration of European civilization after the intellectual impoverishment of the Middle Ages. This epoch was characterized above all by its focus on humanity, and the epicentre of this explosion of humanist art and scholarship was Florence.

Whilst nobody doubts that many of the artists, writers and patrons of Renaissance Italy believed themselves to be participants in the creation of a new society, it's highly debatable that "Renaissance values" reached deeply into the lives of everyone. For the general populace, life continued to be "medieval" long after their masters had taken to reading Plato: the belief in witches, for example, survived for centuries beyond the supposed triumph of humanism. And the material circumstances of existence were little changed for most people. Agriculture was still a precarious business, and there can have been few more dangerous periods in Italian history than the so-called "High Renaissance" – from 1494 to 1559 the peninsula was an almost continuous battleground for the major powers of Europe, and at the end of this period, with Habsburgs as the dominant force, most of the Italian city-states reduced to the ranks of bit-players.

The notion of uniqueness of the Renaissance has many critics too. Where earlier writers tended to use the terms "Renaissance" and "Italian Renaissance" interchangeably, historians now speak of a variety of "Renaissances". Charlemagne is seen as having presided over a "Carolingian Renaissance", for example, just as the court of the Emperor Frederick II (1194–1250) is seen by some as the centre of another episode of European cultural realignment.

The problem of beginnings

And, to focus purely on the Italian Renaissance, this itself becomes problematic when one tries to identify its beginnings. **Giotto** (1267–1337) is often taken as a starting point, and when we compare his paintings to the art of the "Gothic" era, it does seem as if he introduced a new realism and drama to European art. His great contemporary Dante (1265–1321), who presents Giotto as an innovator in the *Divina Commedia*, appears modern in his use of vernacular Tuscan rather than Latin. On the other hand, the stern theology of Dante's masterpiece strikes us as belonging to a distinctly pre-modern world.

It's true that Dante's immediate successors, **Petrarch** (1304–1374) and **Boccaccio** (1313–75) – both of them Tuscans – feel closer to us than he does. Petrarch's love poetry, his collecting of classical manuscripts and his appreciation of landscape for itself (in his celebrated description of his ascent of Mont Ventoux) might be described as manifestations of the Renaissance spirit, just as his coronation as poet laureate (in Rome in 1341) can be taken as an instance of the Renaissance celebration of creative genius. Similarly, Boccaccio's *Decameron* has a claim to be the first example of modern prose fiction. And yet in the visual arts there's no parallel to Boccaccio's bawdy secularism: indeed, it can seem that painting barely advanced in the century after Giotto – certainly not enough to support the idea that his work initiated a process of unstoppable momentum. A partial explanation of this hiatus is that outbreaks of the plague – reaching a peak with the Black Death, which struck Tuscany with particular vehemence – cut short the lives of many artists, and rendered many communities too poor to commission new work. It wasn't until Masaccio's frescoes in the Brancacci chapel – painted a hundred years after Giotto's in Santa Croce – that Italian art could be said to have taken its next leap forward.

The case of Florence

If it's impossible to locate where the Renaissance begins, it's incontestably the case that the high culture of Florence (and most of Italy) in 1500 was radically different from that of 1300. Furthermore, it's incontrovertible that Florence in the fifteenth century nurtured more of these "avant garde" figures than any other city in Italy. A highly selective roll-call of artists and architects suffices to make the point: **Masaccio, Filippo and Filippino Lippi, Donatello, Brunelleschi, Ghiberti, Alberti, Michelozzo, Piero di Cosimo, Luca della Robbia, Uccello, Verrocchio, Fra' Angelico, Michelangelo, Leonardo da Vinci** and **Botticelli**. But what were the circumstances that made Florence the pre-eminent centre of creativity?

A primary factor was of course the city's wealth. Buoyed by revenues from banking and manufacture, the Florentine upper classes had plenty of surplus cash with which to fund the accumulation of libraries and art collections, and to employ the most "advanced" artists as a means of advertising the prosperity not just of their individual families, but of a city which, by the start of the fifteenth century, was established as the prevailing power in Tuscany. Competing against each other in displays of educated taste, clans such as the **Strozzi**, the **Medici**, the **Rucellai** and the **Tornabuoni** were furthering a Florentine self-image that can be traced back at least as far as Giovanni Villani (1275–1348), author of a twelve-volume history of the city (written in Tuscan), in which he wrote that Florence, "the daughter and offspring of Rome, is on the increase and destined to do great things".

Even before Villani, Florence had something of a humanist tradition. Dante's teacher, **Brunetto Latini** (c.1210–94), for instance, studied Aristotle and Cicero, wrote in the vernacular (both Italian and French) and with his *Livre du trésor* produced what might be called the first encyclopedia. A century later, it was the chancellor of Florence's university that invited **Manuel Chrysoloras** (c.1350–1415) to travel from Constantinople to teach Greek – the first time for seven hundred years that the language had been taught in Italy. Chrysoloras translated Plato and Homer, wrote about the monuments of Rome and Byzantium, and numbered among his pupils **Leonardo Bruni** – author of the *History of the Florentine People* and books on Dante, Petrarch and Boccaccio, translator of Plato and Aristotle, and the first scholar to define his work as *studia humanitatis*. From 1427 to 1444 Bruni was chancellor of the Florentine Republic, a post in which he was succeeded by **Carlo Marsuppini**, a similarly learned man, who in one lecture managed to quote from every Greek and Latin writer then known.

In 1439 the **Council of Florence** – convened to forge a reconciliation between the Roman and Eastern churches – brought a host of classical scholars to the city, some of whom remained in Florence, to be joined after 1453 by others who fled from Constantinople following its conquest by the Turks. These refugees further enriched an environment in which developed so many great artists and such prodigious philosopher scholars as **Marsilio Ficino**, **Poliziano** and **Pico della Mirandola** (author of the famous *Oration on the Dignity of Man*), all of whom were members of the Medici court.

But again, on the subject of the revolutionary nature of the Florentine Renaissance, a note of caution is needed. Whereas Botticelli's *Birth of Venus* or Michelangelo's *David* unarguably mark the arrival of something new, contemporaneous philosophy is essentially an elaboration of the work of ancient thinkers – of Plato in particular. For all their learning, Ficino and the rest produced nothing to equal the originality of medieval philosophers such as Thomas Aquinas or Duns Scotus.

Finally, as a corrective to the idea of a uniform Renaissance culture, a couple of dates. In the Uffizi you can see Gentile da Fabriano's *Adoration of the Magi*, an exquisite example of International Gothic – it was painted in 1423, just a year before Masaccio began work on the Brancacci chapel. And **Niccolo Macchiavelli**, a distinctly modern thinker, began his political career in 1494, the year that Florence fell under the sway of Savonarola, a man whose world-view was neo-medieval.

of the learned, harmonious spirit of early Renaissance architecture. Begun in 1429 as a chapter house for Santa Croce, it was commissioned by Andrea de' Pazzi, a member of a banking dynasty that played a prominent role in the Pazzi Conspiracy (see p.96). Its exterior remained unfinished at the time of the plot, however, and it seems none of the family was ever buried here.

Brunelleschi worked on the chapel between 1442 and his death in 1446, though financial problems meant that work was only completed in the 1470s. Geometrically perfect without seeming pedantic, the chapel is exemplary in its proportion and in the way its decorative detail harmonizes with the design. The polychrome lining of the portico's shallow cupola is by Luca della Robbia, as is the garland of fruit which surrounds the Pazzi family crest. The frieze of angels' heads is by Desiderio da Settignano, though Luca was responsible for the tondo of *St Andrew* (1461) over the door. The portico itself may be the work of Giuliano da Maiano, while the majestic wooden doors (1472) are the product of a collaboration between the brothers Maiano, Giuliano and Benedetto. Inside, the twelve blue and white tondi of the *Apostles* are by Luca della Robbia, while the four vividly coloured tondi of the *Evangelists* in the upper roundels were produced in the della Robbia workshop, possibly to designs by Donatello and Brunelleschi.

The Museo dell'Opera di Santa Croce and the inner cloister

The **Museo dell'Opera di Santa Croce**, which flanks the first cloister, houses a miscellany of works of art, the best of which are gathered in the Refettorio (refectory). Foremost of these is Cimabue's famous *Crucifixion*, very badly damaged in 1966 and now the emblem of the havoc caused by the flood. Other highlights include a detached fresco of the *Last Supper* (1333), considered the finest work by Taddeo Gaddi (end wall), and the earliest surviving example of the many Last Suppers (*Cenacoli*) dotted around the city. This theme was of obvious relevance given its position, which – as here – was invariably the refectory where monks gathered to eat. Equally compelling is Donatello's enormous gilded *St Louis of Toulouse* (1424), six fresco fragments by Orcagna (on the side walls) and Domenico Veneziano's *SS John and Francis*.

A series of rooms sparsely filled with various damaged fragments leads you towards the spacious **Inner Cloister**, another late project by Brunelleschi. Completed in 1453, after the architect's death, it is the most peaceful spot in the centre of Florence, achieving its atmosphere by the slow rhythm of the narrow, widely spaced columns.

The Museo Horne

On the south side of Santa Croce, down by the river at Via dei Benci 6, stands one of Florence's more recondite museums, the **Museo della Fondazione Horne** (Mon–Sat 9am–1pm; €5). Its collection was left to the state by the English art historian Herbert Percy Horne (1864–1916), who was instrumental in rescuing Botticelli from neglect with a pioneering biography. The half-a-dozen or so rooms of paintings, sculptures, pottery, furniture and other domestic objects contain no real masterpieces, but are diverting enough if you've already done the major collections. With winning eccentricity, the exhibits are labelled with numbers only and you have to carry round a key in the form of a long list, available from the ticket office. The museum building, the Palazzo Corsi-Alberti (1489), is worth more than a glance even if you're not going into the museum. Commissioned by the Corsi family, it's a typical merchant's house of the period, with huge cellars in which wool would have been dyed, and an open gallery above the courtyard for drying the finished cloth.

The pride of Horne's collection was its drawings, which are now salted away in the Uffizi, though a small, usually captivating display is maintained in the room on the right of the **ground floor**. Of what's left, the pick in the left-hand downstairs room is a bas-relief of the Madonna and Child attributed to Jacopo Sansovino. On the **first floor**, the highlights of Room 1 are a worn crucifix by Filippino Lippi; part of a predella with a tiny age-bowed panel of *St Julian* by Masaccio; a dark *Deposition* by Gozzoli, his last documented work; and a group of saints by Pietro Lorenzetti. The next room contains the collection's big draw, Giotto's *St Stephen* (a fragment from a polyptych), followed in Room 3 by Beccafumi's *Holy Family*, shown in its original frame. The wooden figure of *St Jerome* nearby is by Verrocchio. One of the main exhibits on the **second floor** is a piece of little artistic merit but great historical interest: a copy of part of Leonardo's *Battle of Anghiari*, once frescoed on a wall of the Palazzo Vecchio (see p.111). Here, too, are further works by such big names as Filippo and Filippino Lippi, Simone Martini and Beccafumi, as well as some lovely pieces of furniture.

Casa Buonarroti and the Sant'Ambrogio district

The enticing name of the **Casa Buonarroti**, located north of Santa Croce at Via Ghibellina 70 (daily except Tues 9.30am–2pm; €6.50), is somewhat misleading. Michelangelo Buonarroti certainly owned three houses here in 1508, and probably lived on the site intermittently between 1516 and 1525, but thereafter the properties' associations with the artist become increasingly tenuous. On Michelangelo's death, for example, they passed to his nephew, Leonardo, whose son converted them into a single palazzo, leaving little trace of the earlier houses (though he built a gallery dedicated to his great-uncle). Michelangelo's last descendant, Cosimo, left the building to the city on his death in 1858. Today the house contains a smart but low-key museum, but among the jumble of works only a handful are by Michelangelo: most were created simply in homage to the great man.

Etruscan and Roman fragments have been wrested back from the archeological museum to languish on the ground floor once more, but the two main treasures are to be found in the room on the left at the top of the stairs. The **Madonna della Scala** (c.1490–92) is Michelangelo's earliest known work, a delicate relief carved when he was no older than 16. The similarly unfinished *Battle of the Centaurs* was created shortly afterwards, when the boy was living in the Medici household. In the adjacent room you'll find the artist's wooden model (1517) for the facade of San Lorenzo. Close by is the largest of all the sculptural models on display, the torso of a **River God** (1524), a work in wood and wax probably intended for the Medici chapel in San Lorenzo. Other rooms contain small and fragmentary pieces, possibly by the master, possibly copies of works by him.

Sant'Ambrogio: the markets and the church

Two of Florence's markets lie within a few minutes' stroll of the Casa Buonarroti. To the north, the Piazza dei Ciompi is the venue for the **Mercato delle Pulci** or Flea Market (summer Mon–Sat 10am–1pm & 4–7pm; winter Mon–Sat 9am–1pm & 3–7pm; also open same hours on last Sun of month). Much of the junk maintains the city's reputation for inflated prices, though you can find a few interesting items at modest cost – old postcards, posters and so on. Vasari's Loggia del Pesce (1567) gives the square a touch of style; built for the fishmongers of the Mercato Vecchio in what is now Piazza della Repubblica, it was dismantled when that square was laid out, and rebuilt here in 1951.

A short distance to the east, out of the orbit of nearly all tourists, is the **Mercato di Sant'Ambrogio** (Mon–Sat 7am–2pm), a smaller, tattier but even more enjoyable version of the San Lorenzo food hall. The *tavola calda* (snacks and meals stall) here is one of Florence's lunchtime bargains, and – as at San Lorenzo – the stalls bring their prices down in the last hour of trading.

Nearby **Sant'Ambrogio** (daily 8am–12.30pm & 4–7pm) is one of Florence's older churches, having been documented in 988, though rebuilding over the centuries means that it is now somewhat bland in appearance. Inside, the most compelling feature is the Cappella del Miracolo, the chapel to the left of the high altar, and its tabernacle (1481–83) by Mino da Fiesole, an accomplished sculptor whose name crops up time and again across Tuscany. This was one of Mino's last works – he died in 1484 – making it fitting that he should be buried close by, in a tomb marked by a pavement slab at the chapel entrance. (Another great artist, the multi-talented Verrocchio, who died in 1488, is buried in the fourth chapel.) The narrative **fresco** (1486) alongside Mino's tabernacle alludes to the miracle that gave the Cappella del Miracolo its name. The work of Cosimo Rosselli, it describes the discovery and display of a chalice full of blood in 1230. The Florentines believed the chalice saved them from, among other things, the effects of a plague outbreak in 1340. The painting is full of portraits of Rosselli's contemporaries, making it another of Florence's vivid pieces of Renaissance social reportage: Rosselli himself is the figure in the black beret at the extreme left of the picture.

The synagogue, Santa Maria Maddalena dei Pazzi and the English Cemetery

The enormous domed building rising to the north of Sant'Ambrogio church is the **Synagogue**; the ghetto established in this district by Cosimo I was not demolished until the mid-nineteenth century, which is when the present Moorish-style synagogue was built. It contains a small **museum** that charts the history of Florence's Jewish population (April–Oct Sun–Thurs 10am–5/6pm, Fri 10am–2pm; Nov–March Sun–Thurs 10am–3pm, Fri 10am–2pm; €4).

West of the synagogue, on Borgo Pinti, stands the church of **Santa Maria Maddalena dei Pazzi** (Mon–Sat 9–11.50am & 5–5.20pm & 6.10–6.50pm, Sun 9–10.45am & 5–6.50pm), named after a Florentine nun who was famed for her religious ecstasies: when possessed by the holy spirit she would spew words at such a rate that a team of eight novices was needed to transcribe her inspired dictation. She was also prone to pouring boiling wax over her arms, and was fond of reclining naked on a bed of thorns. This unflinching piety was much honoured in Counter-Reformation Florence: when Maria de' Medici went off to marry Henry IV of France, Maria Maddalena transmitted the news that the Virgin expected her to re-admit the Jesuits to France and exterminate the Huguenots, which she duly did.

Founded in the thirteenth century but kitted out in Baroque style, the church is not itself much of an attraction, but its chapterhouse – reached by a tortuous subterranean passageway that's accessed from the top of the right aisle – is decorated with a radiant **Perugino** fresco of the *Crucifixion* (€1). As always with Perugino, there is nothing troubling here, the Crucifixion being depicted not as an agonizing death but rather as the necessary prelude to the Resurrection.

North of the Pazzi church, at the end of Borgo Pinti, is the **English Cem-**

etery at Piazza Donatello (daily 9am–noon & 3–6pm). Now a funerary traffic island, this patch of garden is the resting place of Elizabeth Barrett Browning and a number of contemporaneous artistic Brits, among them Walter Savage Landor and Arthur Hugh Clough.

San Salvi and Campo di Marte

Twenty minutes' walk beyond Piazza Beccaria, east of Sant'Ambrogio (or bus #10 from the station, or #6 from Piazza San Marco), is the ex-convent of **San Salvi**, which was reopened in 1982 after the restoration of its most precious possession, the *Last Supper* by Andrea del Sarto (Tues–Sun 8.15am–1.50pm; free). As a prelude to this picture, there's a gallery of big but otherwise unremarkable Renaissance altarpieces, a gathering of pictures by various del Sarto acolytes, and the beautiful reliefs from the tomb of Giovanni Gualberto, founder

Crisis and revival at Campo di Marte

In recent years there have been some tough times for **Fiorentina** football club – known as the *Viola*, after the distinctive violet colour of their shirts. Fans still shudder at the memory of 1990, when the great **Roberto Baggio** was transferred – for what was then a world record fee – to Juventus, amid scenes of fervent protest. In 1996, with Argentinian striker Gabriel Batistuta (aka **"Batigol"**) attracting the sort of morbid affection that Baggio once commanded, Fiorentina won the Italian cup, and they came close to a league championship in 1999, finishing third. But then Batigol was lured to Roma, sparking demonstrations of such violence that the club's owner, TV and film magnate Vittorio Cecchi-Gori, required police protection. Roma promptly rubbed salt into the wound by becoming champions of Serie A (Italy's top division), but far worse was to come in 2002, when Fiorentina became the most spectacular casualty of the financial crisis that engulfed what used to be the world's wealthiest league. For many years the clubs in Serie A had been paying insupportable salaries on the basis of projected TV revenue, while consistently failing in the lucrative pan-European Champions' League. By 2002 the aggregrate debts of the Serie A teams had passed the equivalent of $750 million, and for Fiorentina the situation was almost terminal: declared **bankrupt**, they were kicked out of Serie A and demoted to Serie C2B – in effect, the bottom of the heap.

The once-great club was reformed under the new ownership of footwear millionaire Diego della Valle. Though the star players promptly departed in the wake of the bankruptcy, the team quickly fought its way back up the leagues, returning to Serie A for the 2004/2005 season, and the support at the Stadio Franchi – stoked by the fans' longstanding sense of themselves as the unloved outsiders of Italian football – has remained as intense as ever, so **tickets** can be hard to obtain. (They cost from around €20 and can be bought at the ground itself, or three or four days in advance from the *Toto* booth on the west side of Piazza della Repubblica. For information on availability, call ☎055.292.363.)

Though the club is now solvent and successful once more, the whiff of scandal is still in the air: a public prosecutor is currently investigating the premature deaths of three ex-Fiorentina players between 1987 and 2004, and other cases of severe ill-health (including heart and kidney disease, and cancer) among men who appeared for the club in the 1970s. The suspicion is that players might have been doped with strength-building drugs, administered in the form of a coffee-like drink. Nello Saltutti, who played for the *Viola* from 1972 to 1975 and died of a heart attack in 2003, spoke to an investigator in 1997, after his first cardiac arrest, and told him: "That 'coffee' was very good for us. We all played very well and played twice as fast as usual. The day after, however, we were all destroyed."

of the Vallombrosan order to whom this monastery belonged. The tomb was smashed up by Charles V's troops in 1530 but they refused to damage the *Last Supper*, which is still in the refectory for which it was painted, accompanied by three del Sarto frescoes brought here from other churches in Florence.

The Stadio Comunale

As befits this monument-stuffed city, Florence's football team play in a stadium that's listed as a building of cultural significance, the **Stadio Comunale** (or **Stadio Artemio Franchi**) at **Campo di Marte** (bus #17 from the train station). It was designed by Pier Luigi Nervi in 1930, as a consequence of two decisions: to create a new football club for Florence and to stage the 1934 World Cup in Italy.

The stadium was the first major sports venue to exploit the shape-making potential of reinforced concrete, and its spiral ramps, cantilevered roof and slim central tower still make most other arenas look dreary. From the spectator's point of view, however, it's far from perfect: for instance, the peculiar D-shape of the stands – necessitated by the straight 200-metre sprint track – means that visibility from some parts of the ground is awful. But the architectural importance of Nervi's work meant that when Florence was chosen as one of the hosts for the 1990 World Cup there could be no question of simply building a replacement (as was done brilliantly at Bari), nor of radically altering the existing one (as happened at most grounds). Much of the seventy billion lire spent on the refurbishment of the Stadio Comunale was thus spent ensuring that the improvements did not ruin the clean modernistic lines, and most of the extra space in the all-seater stadium was created by lowering the pitch a couple of metres below its previous level, in order to insert another layer of seats where the track had been.

Oltrarno

Visitors to Florence might perceive the River Arno as a simple interruption in the urban fabric, but some Florentines still talk as though a ravine runs through their city. North of the river is known as *Arno di quà* ("over here"), while the other side, hemmed in by a ridge of hills that rises a short distance from the river, is *Arno di là* ("over there"). More formally, it's known as the **Oltrarno** – literally "beyond the Arno" – a terminology which has its roots in medieval times, when the district was not as accessible as the numerous bridges now make it.

Traditionally an artisans' quarter, the Oltrarno has nonetheless always contained more prosperous enclaves: many of Florence's ruling families chose to settle in this area, and nowadays some of the city's plushest shops line the streets parallel to the river's southern bank. Further in, the area around **Santo Spirito** and **Piazza del Carmine** is a good place to come in the evening, as it's here you'll find some of Florence's best bars and restaurants. Window-shopping, eating and drinking are not the area's sole pleasures, however, as the district also contains several of the city's key sights, most notably the **Palazzo Pitti** and the frescoes of **Santa Maria del Carmine**. In the eastern part of Oltrarno, as on the opposite bank of the river, blocks of historic buildings were destroyed by mines left behind by the Nazis in 1944. Some characterful parts remain, however, in particular the medieval Via de' Bardi and its continuation, Via San Niccolò, which leads you towards **San Miniato al Monte**, one of the most beautiful churches in Tuscany.

The Ponte Vecchio

The direct route from the city centre to the heart of the Oltrarno crosses the Arno via the **Ponte Vecchio**, the last in a line of bridges at the river's narrowest point that stretches back to Etruscan and Roman times. Until 1218 the crossing here was the city's only bridge, though the version you see today dates from 1345, built to replace a wooden bridge swept away by floods twelve years earlier. The name (Old Bridge) was coined to distinguish it from the Ponte alla Carraia, the bridge raised in 1218. Over its arcades runs Vasari's concealed passageway (see p.120), commissioned by the Medici in 1565 to allow them to pass unobserved from the Palazzo Vecchio to the Palazzo Pitti. Much later in its history the Ponte Vecchio was the only bridge not mined by the Nazis in 1944 as they retreated before the advancing American Fifth Army; Field Marshal Kesselring is said to have spared it on Hitler's express orders. Much of the rest of the city, including medieval quarters at either end of the bridge, was not so lucky: the Nazis reneged on a promise to spare the city, blowing up swathes of old buildings to hamper the Allied advance.

The bridge's present-day **shops** and **hawkers** can come as a shock, but the Ponte Vecchio has always been loaded with stores like those now propped over the water. Their earliest inhabitants were butchers and fishmongers, attracted to the site by the proximity of the river, which provided a convenient dumping ground for their waste. Next came the tanners, who used the river to soak their hides before tanning them with horses' urine. The current plethora of jewellers dates from 1593, when Ferdinando I evicted the butchers' stalls and other practitioners of what he called "vile arts". In their place he installed eight jewellers and 41 **goldsmiths**, also taking the opportunity to double the rents. Florence had long revered the art of the goldsmith, and several of its major artists were skilled in the craft: Ghiberti, Donatello and Cellini, for example. The third of this trio is celebrated by a bust in the centre of the bridge, the night-time meeting point for Florence's unreconstructed hippies and local lads on the pull.

Santa Felicita

Santa Felicita (Mon–Sat 9.30am–12.30pm & 3–6.30pm) might be the oldest church in Florence, having possibly been founded in the second century by Greek or Syrian merchants, pioneers of Christianity in the city. It's known for certain that a church existed on the site by the fifth century, by which time it had been dedicated to St Felicity, an early Roman martyr who is often shown in Renaissance paintings with her seven sons, each of whom was executed in front of her for refusing to renounce his faith (the saint herself was either beheaded or thrown into boiling oil). New churches were built on the site in the eleventh and fourteenth centuries, while in 1565 Vasari added an elaborate portico to accommodate the *corridoio* linking the Uffizi and Palazzo Pitti; a window from the corridor looks directly into the church. All but the facade was extensively remodelled between 1736 and 1739.

The interior demands a visit for the amazing Pontormo paintings in the **Cappella Capponi**, which lies to the right of the main door, surrounded by irritating railings. Under the cupola are four tondi of the *Evangelists* (painted with help from his adoptive son, Bronzino), while on opposite sides of the window on the right wall are the Virgin and the angel of Pontormo's delightfully simple *Annunciation*, the arrangement alluding to the Incarnation as the means by which the Light came into the world. The low level of light admitted by this window was a determining factor in the startling colour scheme of

Born near Empoli, Jacopo Carrucci (1494–1556) – better known as **Pontormo** after his native village – was successively a pupil of Leonardo da Vinci, Piero di Cosimo and Andrea del Sarto. It was through del Sarto that he received one of his earliest independent commissions, for *The Visitation* in the atrium of Santissima Annunziata in Florence, where del Sarto had already completed several frescoes. Begun when Pontormo was only 20, *The Visitation* displays an eccentric quality – notably in the foreground figure of the sunbathing boy – that was always to be characteristic of him, and evidently appealed to many: in the early 1520s he was hired by the Medici to decorate part of their villa at Poggio a Caiano, then executed a *Passion* cycle for the Certosa, to the south of the city, after which he painted what is generally regarded as his masterpiece: the *Deposition* in Santa Felicita. The major project of his later years, a fresco cycle of the Last Judgement, painted in the chancel of San Lorenzo, has been totally destroyed, but other paintings by him can be seen in the Uffizi, at Carmignano and at Sansepolcro.

A crucial figure in the evolution of the hyper-refined Mannerist style, Pontormo was always a strangely intense artist: the *Deposition* is said to have taken him three years to complete, during which time the chapel was walled up, so that nobody could observe him at work. In later life he seems to have become even crankier. A chronic hypochondriac – his diary is a tally of the state of his kidneys, bowel disorders and other assorted ailments – he came to find the company of others almost intolerable, spending much of his time in a top-floor room that could be reached only by a ladder, which he drew up behind him. One contemporary writer attributed to him an all-consuming terror of death and called his room a "beast's lair", while another insisted that he kept corpses in a tub as models for a *Deluge* that he was painting – an antisocial research project that allegedly brought protests from the neighbours.

Pontormo's weirdly erotic **Deposition** (1525–28), one of the masterworks of Florentine Mannerism. Nothing in this picture is conventional: the figure of Mary is on a different scale from her attendants; the figures bearing Christ's body are androgynous figures clad in billows of acidic sky-blue, puce green and candy-floss pink drapery; and there's no sign of the cross, the thieves, soldiers or any of the other scene-setting devices usual in paintings of this subject; the sole background detail is a solitary ghostly cloud. The bearded brown-cloaked figure on the extreme right is believed to be a self-portrait of the artist.

The Palazzo Pitti

Beyond Santa Felìcita, the street opens out at Piazza Pitti, forecourt of the largest palace in Florence, the **Palazzo Pitti**. Banker and merchant Luca Pitti commissioned the palace to outdo his rivals, the Medici. Work started around 1457, possibly using a design by Brunelleschi which had been rejected by Cosimo de' Medici for being too grand. No sooner was the palace completed, however, than the Pitti's fortunes began to decline, and by 1549 they were forced to sell out to the Medici. The Pitti subsequently became the Medici's base in Florence, growing in bulk until the seventeenth century, when it achieved its present gargantuan dimensions. Later, during Florence's brief tenure as the Italian capital between 1865 and 1870, it housed the Italian kings.

Today the Palazzo Pitti and the pavilions of the Giardino di Bóboli (see p.177) contain eight museums, of which the foremost is the **Galleria Palatina**, a painting collection second in importance only to the Uffizi. Separate tickets are required for the Galleria and **Museo degli Argenti**, the most compelling of the palace's other collections, and for the **Galleria d'Arte Moderna** – these tickets, however, cover entry into other museums in the complex.

The Galleria Palatina and Appartamenti Reali

Many of the paintings gathered by the Medici in the seventeenth century are now arranged in the **Galleria Palatina** (Tues–Sun 8.15am–6.50pm; €6.50, includes admission to the Appartamenti Reali), a suite of 29 rooms on the first floor of one wing of the palace. The ticket office and the grand staircase leading up to the gallery both lie off the main courtyard to the rear of the palace. Beyond the huge chandelier at the head of the stairs, the first two rooms – which have wonderful views – lead into two parallel suites of six rooms. If you want to head for the meat of the collection, walk straight to the end of the first section, then turn left and back down the parallel row of state rooms. It's here that you'll find the gallery's eleven paintings by **Raphael**, as well as the fourteen **Titians**. The pictures are not arranged in the sort of didactic order observed by most galleries, but are instead hung as they would have been in the days of their acquisition, three deep in places, with the aim of making each room pleasurably varied. The best thing to do is wander at random until a picture takes your fancy. The big names just keep on coming, and the highlights are many, so you'll need several hours to see the collection properly.

The current itinerary takes you straight through into the suite containing mostly less famous works, though some individual paintings are well worth seeking out, notably: **Fra' Bartolomeo**'s *Deposition*; a tondo of the *Madonna and Child with Scenes from the Life of St Anne* (1452) by **Filippo Lippi**; his son Filippino's *Death of Lucrezia*; a *Sleeping Cupid* (1608) by **Caravaggio**; and Cristofano Allori's sexy **Judith and Holofernes**, for which Allori himself, his mother and his mistress provided the models for the principal characters. Also in this section are the Corridoio del Volterrano, which houses mainly Florentine works of the seventeenth century, and the Corridoio della Colonna, which has a Flemish theme.

In the second, more captivating part of the gallery, **Andrea del Sarto** is represented in strength, his seventeen works including a beautifully grave *Annunciation*. Even more remarkable is the Pitti's collection of paintings by his great contemporary, **Raphael**. When Raphael settled in Florence in 1505, he was besieged with commissions from patrons delighted to find an artist for whom the creative process involved so little agonizing. In the next three years he painted scores of pictures for such people as Angelo Doni, the man who commissioned Michelangelo's *Doni Tondo*, now in the Uffizi. Raphael's portraits of Doni and his wife, Maddalena (1506–7), display an unhesitating facility and perfect poise; if the Maddalena's pose looks familiar, incidentally, it's because it's copied directly from Leonardo's *Mona Lisa*. Similar poise illuminates Raphael's splendidly framed 1515 *Madonna della Seggiola*, or Madonna of the Chair, which for centuries was Italy's most popular image of the Virgin: nineteenth-century copyists had to join a five-year waiting list to study the picture. According to Vasari, the model for the famous *Donna Velata* (Veiled Woman), in the Sala di Giove, was the painter's mistress, a Roman baker's daughter known to posterity as La Fornarina.

The assembly of paintings by the Venetian artist **Titian** includes a number of his most trenchant portraits. The lecherous and scurrilous Pietro Aretino – journalist, critic, poet and one of Titian's closest friends – was so thrilled by his 1545 portrait that he gave it to Cosimo I; Titian painted him on several other occasions, sometimes using him as the model for Pontius Pilate. Also here are likenesses of Philip II of Spain and the young Cardinal Ippolito de' Medici

(1532) – who fought in the defence of Vienna against the Ottomans only to be poisoned at the age of 24 – and the so-called *Portrait of an Englishman* (1540), who scrutinizes the viewer with unflinching sea-grey eyes. To his left, by way of contrast, is the same artist's sensuous and much-copied *Mary Magdalene* (1531), the first of a series on this theme produced for the duke of Urbino. In the same room, look out for Rosso Fiorentino's recently restored *Madonna Enthroned with Saints* (1522), and the gallery's outstanding sculpture, Canova's *Venus Italica*, commissioned by Napoleon as a replacement for the Venus de' Medici, which he had whisked off to Paris.

Much of the rest of the Pitti's first floor comprises the **Appartamenti Reali**, the Pitti's state rooms. They were renovated by the dukes of Lorraine in the eighteenth century, and then by Vittorio Emanuele when Florence became the country's capital, so the rooms display three distinct decorative phases. The gallery leads straight through into the apartments, and after Raphael and Titian it can be difficult to sustain a great deal of enthusiasm for such ducal elegance, notwithstanding the sumptuousness of the furnishings.

The other Pitti museums

On the floor above the Palatina is the **Galleria d'Arte Moderna** (Tues–Sat 8.15am–1.50pm; also 1st, 3rd & 5th Sun of month and 2nd & 4th Mon of month same hours; joint ticket with Galleria del Costume €5), a chronological survey of primarily Tuscan art from the mid-eighteenth century to 1945. Most rewarding are the products of the *Macchiaioli*, the Italian division of the Impressionist movement; most startling, however, are the sculptures, featuring sublime kitsch such as Antonio Ciseri's *Pregnant Nun*.

The **Museo degli Argenti** (Jan, Feb, Nov & Dec 8.15am–4.30pm; closes 1hr later in March, 2hr later in April, May, Sept & Oct, 3hr later June–Aug; closed 1st & last Mon of month; joint ticket with Museo delle Porcellane and Giardino di Bóboli €4), entered from the main palace courtyard, is a museum not just of silverware but of luxury artefacts in general. The lavishly frescoed reception rooms themselves fall into this category: the first hall, the Sala di Giovanni da San Giovanni, shows Lorenzo de' Medici giving refuge to the Muses; the other three ceremonial rooms have trompe l'oeil paintings by seventeenth-century Bolognese artists. As for the exhibits, the least ambivalent response is likely to be aroused by Lorenzo the Magnificent's trove of antique vases, all of them marked with their owner's name. The later the date of the pieces, though, the greater the discrepancy between the skill of the craftsman and the taste by which it was governed; by the time you reach the end of the jewellery show on the first floor, you'll have lost all capacity to be surprised or revolted by seashell figurines, cups made from ostrich eggs, portraits in stone inlay, and the like. One-off exhibitions are sometimes held here, which can affect the ticket price and opening hours.

Visitors without a specialist interest are unlikely to be riveted by the other Pitti museums that are currently open. In the Palazzina della Meridiana, the eighteenth-century southern wing of the Pitti, the **Galleria del Costume** (same hours & ticket as Galleria d'Arte Moderna) provides the opportunity to see the dress that Eleonora di Toledo wore in Bronzino's famous portrait of her (in the Palazzo Vecchio). The well presented if esoteric collection of porcelain, the **Museo delle Porcellane**, is located on the other side of the Bóboli garden (same hours and ticket as Museo degli Argenti), while the **Museo delle Carrozze** (Carriage Museum) has been closed for years and, despite what the Pitti handouts tell you, will almost certainly remain so for the foreseeable future, to the chagrin of very few.

The Giardino di Bóboli

The delightful formal gardens of the Palazzo Pitti, the **Giardino di Bóboli** (same hours and ticket as Museo degli Argenti), takes its name from the Bóboli family, erstwhile owners of much of this area, which was once a quarry; the bedrock here is one of the sources of the yellow sandstone known as *pietra forte* (strong stone) that gives much of Florence its dominant hue. Carefully shaped into a rough, boulder-like texture, this stone was also used to "rusticate" the Palazzo Pitti's great facade. When the Medici acquired the house in 1549 they set to work transforming their back yard into an enormous 111-acre garden, its every statue, view and grotto designed to elevate nature by the judicious application of art.

Work continued into the early seventeenth century, by which stage this steep hillside had been turned into a maze of statue-strewn avenues and well-trimmed vegetation. Opened to the public in 1766, it is the only really extensive area of accessible greenery in the centre of the city, and can be one of the most pleasant spots for a midday picnic or coffee. (There's a café, the *Kaffeehaus*, with a panoramic view in the garden.) It's no place to seek solitude, however: some five million visitors annually, more than at any other Italian garden, take time out here. (If the queues at the main entrance are too daunting, walk about three hundred metres further along the main road, the Via Romana, where you'll find another, invariably quieter, entrance.)

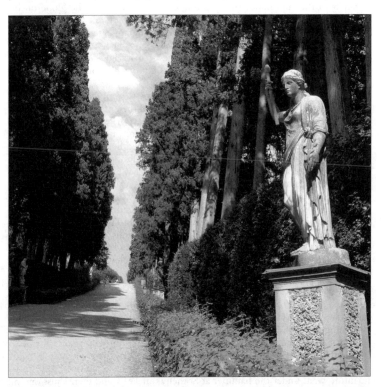

△ Giardino di Bóboli

The birth of opera

The Medici pageants in the gardens of the Pitti were the last word in extravagance, and the palace has a claim to be the birthplace of the most extravagant modern performing art, **opera**. The roots of the genre are convoluted, but its ancestry certainly owes much to the singing and dancing tableaux called *intermedii*, with which high-society Florentine weddings were padded out. Influenced by these shows, the academy known as the Camerata Fiorentina began, at the end of the sixteenth century, to blend the principles of Greek drama with a semi-musical style of declamation. The first composition recognizable as an opera is *Dafne*, written by two members of the Camerata, Jacopo Peri and Ottavio Rinucci, and performed in 1597; the earliest opera whose music has survived in its entirety is the same duo's *Euridice*, premiered in the Pitti palace on the occasion of the proxy marriage of Maria de' Medici to Henry IV.

Aligned with the central block of the palazzo, the garden's **amphitheatre** was designed in the early seventeenth century as an arena for Medici entertainments. The site had previously been laid out by Ammannati in 1599 over an earlier stone quarry as a garden in the shape of a Roman circus. For the wedding of Cosimo III and Princess Marguerite-Louise, cousin of Louis XIV, twenty thousand guests were packed onto the stone benches to watch a production that began with the appearance of a gigantic effigy of Atlas with the globe on his back; the show got under way when the planet split apart, releasing a cascade of earth that transformed the giant into the Atlas mountain. Such frivolities did little to reconcile Marguerite-Louise to either Florence or her husband, and after several acrimonious years this miserable dynastic marriage came to an effective end with her return to Paris, where she professed to care about little "as long as I never have to set eyes on the grand duke again".

Of all the garden's Mannerist embellishments, the most celebrated is the **Grotta del Buontalenti** (1583–88), to the left of the entrance, beyond Giambologna's much-reproduced statue of Cosimo I's favourite dwarf astride a giant tortoise. Embedded in the grotto's faked stalactites and encrustations are replicas of Michelangelo's *Slaves* – the originals were lodged here until 1908. Lurking in the deepest recesses of the cave (which is usually opened on the hour), is Giambologna's *Venus Emerging from her Bath*, leered at by attendant imps.

Another spectacular set piece is the fountain island called the **Isolotto**, which is the focal point of the far end of the garden; from within the Bóboli the most dramatic approach is along the central cypress avenue known as the **Viottolone**, many of whose statues are Roman originals. These lower parts of the garden are its most pleasant – and least visited – sections. You come upon them quickly if you enter the Bóboli by the little-used Porta Romana entrance or by the gate that's a short distance past La Specola (see below).

Casa Guidi and La Specola

Within a stone's throw of the Pitti, on the opposite side of the road, on the junction of Via Maggio and Via Romana, you'll find the home of Robert Browning and Elizabeth Barrett Browning, the **Casa Guidi** (April–Nov Mon, Wed & Fri 3–6pm; free, but donations welcome). It's something of a shrine to Elizabeth, who wrote much of her most popular verse here (including, naturally enough, *Casa Guidi Windows*) and died here. Virtually all the Casa Guidi's furniture went under the hammer at Sotheby's in 1913, and there's just one oil painting left, but two of the three rooms still manage to conjure up something of the spirit. It makes a spectacular place to stay – you can rent it through the Landmark Trust but it is booked months ahead and is far from cheap (Ⓦwww .landmarktrust.org.uk)

There's more to enjoy on the third floor of the university buildings at Via Romana 17, in what can reasonably claim to be the strangest museum in the city. Taking its name from the telescope (*specola*) on its roof, **La Specola** (Mon, Tues & Thurs, Fri, Sun 9am–1pm, Sat 9am–5pm; €4; Ⓦwww.specola.unifi .it/cere) is a tripartite museum of zoology. One section, comprising the country's largest collection of skeletons, is open to the public only on Saturday mornings. Of the other parts, the first is conventional enough, with ranks of shells, insects and crustaceans, followed by a veritable ark of animals stuffed, pickled and desic-cated, including a hippo given to Grand Duke Pietro Leopardo which used to reside in the Bóboli garden. Beyond some rather frayed-looking sharks lie the exhibits everyone comes to see, the **Cere Anatomiche** (Anatomical Waxworks). Wax arms, legs and internal organs cover the walls, arrayed around satin beds on which wax cadavers recline in progressive stages of deconstruction, each muscle fibre and nerve cluster moulded and dyed with scarcely believable precision. Most of the six hundred models – and nearly all of the amazing full-body man-nequins – were made between 1775 and 1791 by one Clemente Susini and his team of assistants, and were intended as teaching aids, in an age when medical ethics and refrigeration techniques were not what they are today.

In a separate room towards the end, after the obstetrics display and a few zoo-logical models, you'll find the grisliest section of La Specola, a trio of tableaux that were moulded in the late seventeenth century by **Gaetano Zumbo**, a cleric from Sicily who was one of the pioneers of the art of anatomical wax-works. Whereas Susini's masterpieces were created to educate, these were made to horrify, and to horrify one man in particular: the hypochondriacal Cosimo III, a Jesuit-indoctrinated bigot who regarded all genuine scientific enquiry with suspicion. Enclosed in tasteful display cabinets, they depict Florence during the plague: rats teasing the intestines from green-fleshed corpses, mushrooms growing from the mulch of fleshly debris, and the pink bodies of the freshly dead heaped on the suppurating semi-decomposed. A fourth tableau, illustrating the horrors of syphilis, was damaged in the 1966 flood, and now consists of a loose gathering of the deceased and diseased. In the centre of the room lies a dissected waxwork head, built on the foundation of a real skull; it's as fastidious as any of Susini's creations, but Zumbo couldn't resist giving the skin a tint of putrefaction, before applying a dribble of blood to the mouth and nose.

Santo Spirito

Designed in 1434 as a replacement for a thirteenth-century church, **Santo Spirito** (Mon–Sat 10am–noon & 4–5.30pm, closed Wed pm, and open only for Mass on Sun) was one of Brunelleschi's last projects, a swansong later described by Bernini as "the most beautiful church in the world". The church is so perfectly proportioned that nothing could seem more artless, yet the plan is extremely sophisticated: a Latin cross with a continuous chain of 38 chapels round the outside and a line of 35 columns running without a break round the nave, transepts and chancel. The exterior wall was originally designed to follow the curves of the chapels' walls, creating a flowing, corrugated effect. As built, however, the exterior is a plain, straight wall, and even the main facade remained incomplete, disguised today by a simple plastering job. Inside the church, only the Baroque baldachin, about as nicely integrated as a jukebox in a Greek tem-ple, disrupts the harmony.

A fire in 1471 destroyed most of Santo Spirito's medieval works, including famed frescoes by Cimabue and the Gaddi family, but as a result, the altar paintings in the many chapels comprise an unusually unified collection of religious works, most having been commissioned in the aftermath of the fire. For the first time, single painted panels replaced the previously preferred genre of the polyptych, and there was a new emphasis on the so-called *Sacra Conversazione*, representing the Madonna and child surrounded by saints, each apparently lost in private meditation. Most prolific among the artists is the so-called **Maestro di Santo Spirito**, but some of the best paintings are found in the transepts.

In the south transept is Filippino Lippi's so-called **Nerli Altarpiece**, an age-darkened Madonna and Child with saints (second chapel from the left of the four chapels on the transept's south wall). The Nerli were the family who commissioned the chapel and the painting, the donors Tanai and Nanna dei Nerli being portrayed amidst the latter's saints; their Florentine home, the Palazzo dei Nerli near Porta San Frediano, is depicted in the background.

Across the church, in the north transept, is an unusual **St Monica and Augustinian Nuns** (1460–70), probably by Verrocchio or Francesco Botticini, that's virtually a study in monochrome, with black-clad nuns flocking round their black-clad paragon; it's in the second chapel on the right wall as you stand with your back to the high altar.

A door in the north aisle leads through to Giuliano da Sangallo's stunning vestibule and **sacristy** (1489–93), the latter designed in imitation of Brunelleschi's Pazzi chapel. The meticulously planned proportions and soft grey and white tones create an atmosphere of extraordinary calm that is only disrupted by the exuberantly botanical carvings of the capitals, some of which were designed by Sansovino. Hanging above the altar is a wooden crucifix, attributed to **Michelangelo**. With its distinctive, tenderly feminized body, its existence had long been documented, but it was feared lost until discovered in Santo Spirito in 1963.

The Chiostro dei Morti and the Cenacolo di Santo Spirito

A glass door at the far end of the vestibule, usually locked, gives out onto the **Chiostro dei Morti**, the only cloister in the complex that is still part of the Augustinian monastery. The 1471 fire destroyed much of the rest of the monastery, with the exception of its refectory (entered to the left of the main church, at Piazza Santo Spirito 29), which is now the home of the **Cenacolo di Santo Spirito** (Tues–Sun: April–Nov 9am–2pm; Dec–March 10.30am–1.30pm; €2.20), a one-room collection comprising an assortment of carvings, many of them Romanesque, and a huge fresco of *The Crucifixion* (1365) by Orcagna and his workshop.

Santa Maria del Carmine

Nowhere in Florence is there a more startling contrast between exterior and interior than in **Santa Maria del Carmine**, a couple of blocks west of Santo Spirito in Piazza del Carmine. Outside it's a drab box of shabby brick; inside – in the dazzlingly restored frescoes of the **Cappella Brancacci** (Mon & Wed–Sat 10am–5pm, Sun 1–5pm; €4 or €8 joint ticket with Palazzo Vecchio) – it provides one of Italy's supreme artistic experiences. The chapel is barricaded off from the rest of the Carmine, and visits are restricted to a maximum of thirty people at a time, for just fifteen minutes. The time limit is strictly enforced in high season, but tends to become more flexible as the crowds ebb away. (You can either book a slot on ☎055.276.8224 or pay at the ticket office; if you choose the latter option, bear in mind that tickets are timed, so you may have to come back some time after buying them.)

The Cappella Brancacci

The **Cappella Brancacci** frescoes were commissioned in 1424 by Felice Brancacci, a silk merchant and leading patrician figure, shortly after his return from a stint in Egypt as the Florentine ambassador. The decoration of the chapel was begun in the same year by **Masolino** (1383–1447), fresh from working as an assistant to Lorenzo Ghiberti on the Baptistery doors. Alongside Masolino was Tommaso di Ser Giovanni di Mone Cassai – known ever since as **Masaccio** (1401–28), a nickname meaning "Mad Tom". The former was aged 41, the latter just 22.

Two years into the project Masolino was recalled to Budapest, where he was official painter to the Hungarian court. Left to his own devices Masaccio began to blossom. When Masolino returned in 1427 the teacher was soon taking lessons from the supposed pupil, whose grasp of the texture of the real world, of the principles of perspective and of the dramatic potential of the biblical texts they were illustrating far exceeded that of his precursors. In 1428 Masolino was called away to Rome, where he was followed by Masaccio a few months later. Neither would return to the chapel.

Masaccio died the same year, aged just 27, but, in the words of Vasari, "all the most celebrated sculptors and painters since Masaccio's day have become excellent and illustrious by studying their art in this chapel." (Michelangelo used to come here to make drawings of Masaccio's scenes, and had his nose broken on the chapel steps by a young sculptor whom he enraged with his condescension.) Some fifty years later the paintings were completed by **Filippino Lippi**, whose copying skills were such that his work was only recognized as distinct from that of his predecessors in 1838.

The small scene on the left of the entrance arch is the quintessence of Masaccio's art. Plenty of artists had depicted **The Expulsion of Adam and Eve** before, but none had captured the desolation of the sinners so graphically: Adam presses his hands to his face in bottomless despair, Eve raises her head and screams. The monumentalism of these stark naked figures – whose modesty was preserved by strategically placed sprigs of foliage prior to the restoration – reveals the influence of Donatello, who may have been involved in the

CAPPELLA BRANCACCI

1 The Expulsion, Masaccio
2 The Tribute Money, Masaccio
3 St Peter Preaching, Masolino
4 The Baptism of the Neophytes, Masaccio
5 The Healing of the Cripple and the Raising of Tabitha, Masolino–Masaccio
6 The Temptation, Masolino
7 St Paul Visits St Peter in Prison, Filippino Lippi
8 The Raising of the Son of Theophilus and St Peter Enthroned, Masaccio–Lippi
9 St Peter Healing the Sick with his Shadow, Masaccio
10 The Distribution of Alms and the Death of Ananias, Masaccio
11 The Disputation, Filippino Lippi
12 St Peter Freed from Prison, Filippino Lippi

planning of the chapel. In contrast to the emotional charge and sculptural presence of Masaccio's couple, Masolino's almost dainty **Adam and Eve** on the opposite arch, pose as if to have their portraits painted.

St Peter is chief protagonist of all the remaining scenes. It's possible that the cycle was intended as propaganda on behalf of the embattled papacy, which had only recently resolved the long and bitter Great Schism, during which one pope held court in Rome and another in Avignon. By celebrating the primacy of St Peter, the rock upon whom the Church is built, the frescoes by implication extol the apostolic succession from which the pope derives his authority.

Three scenes by Masaccio are especially compelling. First off is the **Tribute Money**, most widely praised of the paintings and the Renaissance's first monumental fresco. The narrative is complex, with no fewer than three separate events portrayed within a single frame. The central episode shows Christ outside the gates of Capernaum being asked to pay a tribute owing to the city. To the left, St Peter fetches coins from the mouth of a fish in order to pay the tribute, Christ in the central panel having pointed to where the money will be found. The third scene, to the right, depicts Peter handing over the money to the tax official.

Masaccio's second great panel is **St Peter Healing the Sick** with his Shadow, in which the shadow of the stern and self-possessed saint (followed by St John) cures the infirm as it passes over them, a miracle invested with the aura of a solemn ceremonial. The third panel is **The Distribution of Alms and Death of Ananias**, in which St Peter instructs the people to give up their possessions to the poor. One individual, Ananias, retains some of his wealth with the knowledge of his wife, Sapphira. Rebuked by Peter, Ananias dies on the spot, closely followed by a similarly castigated Sapphira.

Filippino Lippi's work included the completion of Masaccio's **Raising of Theophilus' Son and St Peter Enthroned**, which depicts St Peter raising the son of Theophilus, the Prefect of Antioch (apparently after he'd been dead for fourteen years). The people of Antioch, suitably impressed by the miracle, build a throne from which St Peter can preach, shown as a separate episode to the right. The three figures to the right of the throne are thought to be portraits of Masaccio, Alberti and Brunelleschi, who made a trip to Rome together. Masaccio originally painted himself touching Peter's robe, a reference to the enthroned statue of Peter in Rome, which pilgrims touch for good luck. Lippi considered the contact of the artist and saint to be improper and painted out the arm; at the moment, his fastidious over-painting has been allowed to remain, but you can clearly see where the arm used to be.

Lippi left another portrait in the combined scene of **SS Peter and Paul in Disputation with Simon Magus before Nero** and the **Crucifixion of St Peter**: the central figure looking out from the painting in the trio right of the crucifixion is Botticelli, the painter's teacher, while Filippino himself can be seen at the far right.

The Museo Bardini

The best way to reach the Bardini museum from the Ponte Vecchio and elsewhere in the Oltrarno is to take Via de' Bardi, known in the Middle Ages as the Borgo Pitiglioso – the "miserable" or "flea-bitten" street. Part way down the street on the left, beyond the small Piazza di Santa Maria Soprarno, you'll pass the tiny church of **Santa Lucia dei Magnoli**, founded in 1078. Pop inside if you're lucky enough to find it open: the first altar on the left has a panel of *St Lucy* by the Sienese master Pietro Lorenzetti.

The **Museo Bardini** (closed for restoration at the time of writing – as it has been for some time), which stands at the end of the street at Piazza de' Mozzi 1, is like the Museo Horne just across the Arno (see p.168), in that it was built around the bequest of a private collector. Whereas Horne was a moderately well-off connoisseur, however, his contemporary Sergio Bardini (1836–1922) was once the largest art dealer in Italy. His tireless activity, at a time when Renaissance art was relatively cheap, laid the cornerstone of many important modern-day European and North American collections. Determined that no visitor to his native city should remain unaware of his success, he ripped down a church that stood on the site and built a vast home, studding it with fragments of old buildings. Doorways, ceiling panels and other orphaned pieces are strewn all over the place: the first-floor windows, for instance, are actually altars from a church in Pistoia. The more portable items are equally wide-ranging: musical instruments, carvings, ceramics, armour, furniture, carpets, pictures – if it was vaguely arty and had a price tag, Bardini snapped it up. His artistic pot-pourri was bequeathed to the city on his death. The museum may lack genuine mas-terpieces, but it's crammed with a sufficiently wide variety of beautiful objects to appeal to most tastes. Displays are spread over a couple of floors and some twenty rooms, though only the more precious exhibits are fully labelled.

On the **ground floor**, beyond the open-plan spread of rooms in the vestibule, Tino da Camaino's *Charity* (Room 7) stands out. In Room 10, upstairs, there's a room of funerary monuments arranged as if in a crypt, with an enamelled ter-racotta altarpiece attributed to Andrea della Robbia. On the **first floor**, beyond several rooms of weapons, three pieces in Room 14 also grab the attention: a polychrome terracotta of the *Madonna and Child* by Donatello; an extraordinarily modern-looking stucco, mosaic and glass relief of the *Madonna dei Cordai* (1443), also probably by Donatello; and a terracotta *Madonna and Child with San Giovan-nino* by Benedetto da Maiano. Room 16 has some lovely *cassoni*, or medieval chests, and several of the museum's many depictions of the Madonna and Child, a subject with which Bardini appears to have been obsessed. Other highlights of the final rooms include some gorgeous carpets and Domenico Beccafumi's *Hercules at the Crossroads between Vice and Virtue* (Room 15); Michele Giambono's *St John the Baptist* (Room 16); a painted relief in terracotta from the workshop of Jacopo della Quercia (Room 17); a *St Michael* by Antonio del Pollaiuolo and a beautiful terracotta *Virgin Annunciate*, an anonymous piece from fifteenth-century Siena (Room 18).

From San Niccolò to San Miniato

Beyond the Museo Bardini, Via San Niccolò swings past **San Niccolò sopr'Arno** (daily 10am–noon), another of this quarter's interesting little churches. Restoration work after the 1966 flood uncovered several frescoes underneath the altars, but none is as appealing as the fifteenth-century fresco in the sacristy; known as *The Madonna of the Girdle*, it was probably painted by Baldovinetti. In medieval times the church was close to the edge of the city, and two of Florence's fourteenth-century gates still stand in the vicinity: the diminu-tive **Porta San Miniato**, set in a portion of the walls, and the huge **Porta San Niccolò**, overlooking the Arno. From either of these gates you can begin the climb up to San Miniato: the path from Porta San Niccolò weaves up through **Piazzale Michelangelo**, with its replica *David* and bumper-to-bumper tour coaches; the more direct path from Porta San Miniato offers a choice between the steep Via del Monte alle Croci or the stepped Via di San Salvatore al Monte, both of which emerge a short distance uphill from Piazzale Michelangelo.

San Miniato al Monte

One of the finest Romanesque structures in Tuscany, **San Miniato al Monte** (daily: summer 8am–7.30pm; winter 8am–noon & 3–6pm) is also the oldest surviving church building in Florence after the Baptistery. Its brilliant multicoloured facade lures troops of visitors up the hill from Oltrarno, and the church and its magnificent interior and works of art more than fulfil the promise of its distant appearance. The **walk** up to San Miniato has some steep sections; if you don't fancy the climb, take **bus** #12 or #13 as far as Piazzale Michelangelo and then continue on foot.

The church's dedicatee, **St Minias**, was Florence's first home-grown martyr. Possibly a Greek merchant or the son of an Armenian king, he originally left home to make a pilgrimage to Rome. Around 250 he moved to Florence, where he became caught up in the anti-Christian persecutions of the emperor Decius. Legend has it that after martyrdom by decapitation – close to the site of Piazza della Signoria – the saintly corpse was seen to carry his severed head over the river and up the hill to this spot, an area where he'd previously lived as a hermit: a shrine was subsequently erected on the slope. The hill, known as **Mons Fiorentinus**, was already the site of several pagan temples and a secret oratory dedicated to Peter the Apostle. A chapel to Miniato is documented on the site in the eighth century, though construction of the present building began in 1013. Initially run as a Benedictine foundation, the building passed to the Cluniacs until 1373, and then to the **Olivetans**, a Benedictine offshoot,

△ San Miniato al Monte

who reside here to this day, and sell their famous liquors, honeys and tisanes from the shop next to the church.

The exterior

San Miniato's gorgeous marble **facade** alludes to the Baptistery in its geometrical patterning, and, like its model, the church was often mistaken for a structure of classical provenance during the later Middle Ages. The lower part of the facade is possibly eleventh-century, while the angular upper levels date from the twelfth century onwards, and were financed in part by the Arte di Calimala (cloth merchants' guild), the body responsible for the church's upkeep from 1288: their trademark, an eagle clutching a bale of cloth, perches on the roof. The mosaic of *Christ between the Virgin and St Minias* dates from 1260. The original **bell-tower** collapsed in 1499 and was replaced in the 1520s by the present campanile, still unfinished. During the 1530 siege of Florence it was used as an artillery post, thus attracting the attention of enemy gunners. Michelangelo, then advising on the city's defences, had it wrapped in woollen mattresses to protect it from cannon balls.

The interior

With its choir raised on a platform above the large crypt, the sublime **interior** of San Miniato is like no other in the city, and its general appearance has changed little since the mid-eleventh century. The main additions and decorations in no way spoil its serenity, though the nineteenth-century recoating of the marble columns is a little lurid: the columns' capitals, however, are Roman and Byzantine originals removed from older buildings. The intricately patterned panels of the **pavement** are dated 1207; some claim the zodiac and strange beast motifs were inspired by Sicilian fabrics, others that they are of Byzantine origin, introduced into Italy through trade and the Crusades.

The lovely tabernacle, or **Cappella del Crocefisso**, which dominates the middle of the nave, was designed in 1448 by Michelozzo, and is one of the few works commissioned by Piero de' Medici, or Piero il Gottoso (the Gouty), during his brief tenure as head of the Medici dynasty. The marble medallion to the rear and other parts of the work are adorned with Piero's motto (*Semper*) and several Medici symbols – the eagle holding three feathers and a diamond ring, the latter a symbol of durability and toughness. The chapel originally housed the miraculous crucifix associated with St Giovanni Gualberto (see p.126), which was moved to Santa Trìnita in 1671. Today it contains painted **panels** by Agnolo Gaddi depicting the *Annunciation, Stories of the Passion* and *SS Giovanni Gualberto and Miniato* (1394–96). Maso di Bartolomeo crafted the twin eagles (1449), symbols of the Calimala, to stress that while Piero was the work's sponsor, the guild was responsible for overseeing all stages of its construction. The terracotta in the barrel vault is by Luca della Robbia.

Steps either side of the cappella lead down to the **crypt**, the oldest part of the church, where the original high altar still contains the bones of St Minias. The vaults, supported by 36 wonderfully mismatched pillars, contain gilt-backed frescoes (1341) of the saints, martyrs, prophets, virgins and Evangelists by Taddeo Gaddi.

Back in the main body of the church, steps beside the Cappella del Crocefisso lead to the raised **choir** and **presbytery**, where there's a magnificent Romanesque **pulpit** and screen dating from 1207. The odd totem-like figures supporting the lectern may represent three of the four Evangelists or, possibly, humanity placed in a middle state between the animal world (the lion) and the divine (the eagle). The great **mosaic** in the apse was created in 1297, probably by the same artist who created the facade mosaic, as their subjects are identical – *Christ Pantocrator* enthroned between the Virgin and Saint Minias. Off the presbytery lies the **sacristy**, whose walls are almost completely covered in a superlative fresco cycle by Spinello Aretino (1387), the first such complete cycle in Tuscany devoted to the life of St Benedict.

Back in the lower body of the church, off the left-hand side of the nave, the **Cappella del Cardinale del Portogallo**, dating from a few years after the Cappella del Crocefisso, is one of the masterpieces of Renaissance chapel design and a marvellous example of artistic collaboration. Completed in 1473, it was built as a memorial to Cardinal James of Lusitania, who died in Florence in 1459, aged just 25. Aside from that of Minias himself, this is – remarkably – the church's only tomb.

The chapel's basic design was the work of Antonio di Manetto (or Manetti), a pupil and biographer of Brunelleschi, who borrowed heavily from his master's work in San Lorenzo's Sagrestia Vecchia (see p.137). The **tomb** itself was carved by Antonio and Bernardo Rossellino; their elder brother Giovanni oversaw the chapel's construction after Manetto's death. Antonio Rossellino's tondo of the *Madonna and Child* keeps watch over the deceased. The chapel's architectural and sculptural work was followed in 1466 by carefully integrated frescoes and **paintings**: an *Annunciation* (to the left) and the *Evangelists* and *Doctors of the Church* by Alesso Baldovinetti (lunettes and beside the arches). Antonio and Piero del Pollaiuolo produced the **altarpiece** depicting the cardinal's patron saint, St James, with SS Vincent and Eustace: the present picture is a copy, the original being in the Uffizi. The ceiling's tiled decoration and four glazed terracotta medallions, perhaps the finest such work in the city, were provided by Luca della Robbia. All the decorative details were carefully designed to complement one another and create a unified artistic whole. Thus Rossellino's tondo of the *Madonna and Child*, for example, echoes the round windows of the walls; the colours in Baldovinetti's *Annunciation* deliberately echo the tones of the surrounding porphyry and serpentine inlays; and the curtain held aside by angels on the cardinal's tomb is repeated in a similar curtain half-shielding the altar.

From the Forte di Belvedere to San Leonardo in Arcetri

The **Forte di Belvedere**, standing on the crest of the hill above the Bóboli garden, was built by Buontalenti on the orders of Ferdinando I between 1590 and 1595, ostensibly to protect the city, but in fact to intimidate the grand duke's subjects. The urban panorama from here is superb, and ambitious exhibitions are often held in and around the shed-like palace in the centre of the fortress, as are occasional summer evening film screenings. The city's new Museo delle Arme (Arms and Armour Museum) is also due to open here soon.

In the past it has sometimes been possible to get up to the fort from the Bóboli gardens, but if you want to be certain of getting in, approach the fort from the **Costa di San Giorgio**, a lane which you can reach by backtracking slightly from the Museo Bardini, or pick up directly from the rear of Santa Felìcita. Look out for the villa at no. 19, home to Galileo between 1610 and 1631.

East from the Belvedere stretches the best preserved section of Florence's fortified **walls**, paralleled by Via di Belvedere. South of the Belvedere, Via San Leonardo leads past olive groves to the rarely open church of **San Leonardo in Arcetri** (daily 10am–noon), site of a beautiful thirteenth-century pulpit brought here from a church now incorporated into the Uffizi. Dante and Boccaccio are both said to have preached from the spot.

Eating, drinking, nightlife and shopping

For a small city, Florence has plenty of big-city attractions: scores of **cafés** and **restaurants**, a full calendar of **cultural events** and a lot of very chic **shops** to give focus to the evening *passeggiata*. The main problem is one of identity, in a city whose inhabitants are heavily outnumbered by outsiders from March to October. Restaurant standards are often patchy and prices pitched at whatever level the tourists can bear, while many of the locals swear there's scarcely a single genuine Tuscan place left in the Tuscan capital – an exaggeration, of course, but a reflection of a general feeling that too much has been lost to tourism. Yet the situation is nowhere near as bad as some reports would have it, and if anything it's been improving in recent years, with the appearance of several stylish and good-value restaurants, alongside some superb wine bars. As for **nightlife**, the university and the influx of language students keep things lively, and **seasonal events** such as the *Maggio Musicale* maintain Florence's standing as the hub of cultural life in Tuscany.

Restaurants

In gastronomic circles, Florentine cuisine is accorded as much reverence as Florentine art, a reverence encapsulated in the myth that French eating habits acquired their sophistication in the wake of Catherine de' Medici's marriage to

---

Snacks and food shops

If you want to put together a picnic, an obvious place to shop is the Mercato Centrale by San Lorenzo church (Mon–Sat 7am–2pm, plus Sat 4–8pm in winter), where everything you could possibly need can be bought under one roof: bread, ham, cheese, fruit, wine, ready-made sandwiches. Also comprehensive is the Mercato Sant' Ambrogio over by Santa Croce (Mon–Fri 7am–2pm). Every district has its *alimentari*, which in addition to selling the choicest Tuscan produce often provide sandwiches. *Vera*, at the southern end of Ponte Santa Trìnita, Piazza Frescobaldi 3r, is a fine example of a Florentine deli; other excellent central *alimentari* include *Tassini*, Borgo Santi Apostoli 24r, *Pegna*, near the Duomo at Via dello Studio 26r (closed Wed afternoons), and *Alessi Paride*, Via delle Oche 27–29r. For a hearty sit-down lunchtime snack, each of the two markets has an excellent *tavola calda*, serving meatballs, pasta, stews, soups and sandwiches: *Nerbone* (Mon–Sat 7am–2pm) in the Mercato Centrale, and *Tavola Calda da Rocco* (Mon–Sat noon–2.30pm), in the Mercato di Sant'Ambrogio. If you really want to go native, you could join the throng of office workers around *L'Antico Trippaio*, a tripe stall in Piazza dei Cimatori (Mon–Fri 8.30am–8.30pm). Its speciality is the local delicacy called *lampredotto*: hot tripe served in a bun with a spicy sauce. The stall also sells wine, so you can wash the taste away should you realize you've made a horrible mistake. There's a similar operation – *Da Sergio e Pierpaolo* – near the Sant'Ambrogio market, in Via de' Macci (Mon–Sat 7.15am–3pm), and another tripe stall next to the Mercato Nuovo (Mon–Fri 8.30am–8.30pm).

RESTAURANTS		Belle Donne	17	Francescano	47	Marione		Oliandolo	20	Palle d'Oro	7	BARS & CAFÉS	
Acqua al Due	35	Benvenuto	54	Il Contadino	10	Natalino	26	Oliviero	39	Quattro		All'Antico Vinaio	52
Alle Murate	27	Borgo Antico	62	Il Latini	25	Nuti	9	Osteria dei		Leoni	59	Art Bar	28
Antico Fattore	51	Da Ganino	31	L'Antico Noè	19	Osteria Caffè		Cento Poveri	13	Zà-Zà	2	Astor Caffè	12
Baldovino	48	Dante	43	La Casalinga	63	Italiano	36	Osteria				Baldoria	50
Beccofino	45	Enoteca Pinchiorri	40	La Lampara	1	Osteria de'Benci	56	Santo Spirito	61			Beccofino	45

▲ San Marco

SS Annunziata

Accademia

CENTRAL FLORENCE
RESTAURANTS, BARS & CAFÉS

Opificio delle Pietre Dure

PIAZZA SANTISSIMA ANNUNZIATA

Pal. Gerini

Spedale degli Innocenti

Museo Archeologico

Pal. Medici Riccardi

S. Maria d. Angeli

PIAZZA SAN LORENZO

Pal. Niccolini

PIAZZA F. BRUNELLESCHI

Pal. Pucci

Ospedale Santa Maria Nuova

Palazzo Niccolini

Duomo

Museo dell'Opera del Duomo

Baptistery

PIAZZA DEL DUOMO

Campanile

Teatro della Pergola

Loggia del Bigallo

Pal. dei Canonici

Museo di Firenze com'era

S. Maria in Campo

Pal. Salviati

Museo dell' Antropologia

Pal. Altoviti

Pal. Albizi

PIAZZA G. SALVEMINI

Casa di Dante

BORGO DEGLI ALBIZI

Pal. Pazzi

Pal. Alessandri

S. Martino

Casino Borghese

Orsanmichele

Bargello

VIA DELLA VIGNA VECCHIA

Teatro Verdi

Casa Buonarroti

Mercato Nuovo

Badia

PIAZZA DELLA SIGNORIA

Pal. Gondi

San Firenze

S. Simone

Loggia della Signoria

Palazzo Vecchio

Uffizi

BORGO DEI GRECI

PIAZZA DE' PERUZZI

Casa dell'Antella

PIAZZA SANTA CROCE

Santa Croce

Pal. Rasponi

PIAZZA DEL GRANO

Pal. Vita

Museo di Storia della Scienza

Borsa

Pal. Corsini

Museo dell'Opera di Santa Croce

PIAZZA DE' GIUDICI

Museo Horne

Biblioteca Nazionale

PIAZZA DI SANTA MARIA SOPRARNO

PONTE ALLE GRAZIE

LUNGARNO DELLA ZECCA VECCHIA

▲ Sant'Ambrogio

0   100 m

Boccadama	49	Caffè I Ricchi	64	Caracol	3	Mariano	33	Rivoire	42
Cabiria	60	Caffè Italiano	34	Casa del Vino		I Fratellini	32	Moyo	53	Robin Hood's
Caffè Amerini	30	Caffèlatte	8	Chiaroscuro	22	I Visacci	23	Nannini	Tavern	16
Caffè degli Artigiani	57	Cantinetta dei		Fiaschetteria Nuvoli	14	Il Santo Bevitore	44	Coffee Shop	11	Slowly	37
Caffè di Paci	55	Verrazzano	29	Fiddler's Elbow	15	L'Antico Noè	19	Procacci	21	Zanobini	4
Caffè Gilli	18	Capocaccia	41	Gustavino	38	Le Volpi e L'Uva	58	Quasigratis	46	
						Lion's Fountain	24			

the future Henry II of France. In fact, Florentine food has always been characterized by modest raw materials and simple technique: beefsteak (*bistecca*), tripe (*trippa*) and liver (*fegato*) are typical ingredients, while grilling (*alla Fiorentina*) is a favoured method of preparation. In addition, white beans (*fagioli*) will feature on most menus, either on their own, garnished with liberal quantities of local olive oil, or as the basis of such dishes as *ribollita*.

There aren't many restaurants where you can get away with spending less than €30 per person for three courses plus wine, although Florence has some decent low-budget places serving food that at least give some idea of the region's characteristic dishes, and even the simplest trattoria should offer *bistecca alla Fiorentina* – though you should bear in mind that this dish is priced per hundred grams, so your bill will be considerably higher than the figure written on the menu. And, of course, if the budget is tight, there's always the option of a pizzeria: Florence has several very good ones, usually charging in the region of €7–8.

The restaurants below are organized by area. Very roughly, the cheapest places tend to be near the station and San Lorenzo market, while the main concentrations of mid-range and top-class restaurants are around Santa Croce and Sant'Ambrogio and over in the Oltrarno. You can of course keep costs down even in more expensive places by having just two courses (pasta and main), and retiring to a bar for ice cream or coffee and digestif. Remember, too, that you often needn't buy a whole bottle of wine: ask for a half-bottle or quarter-bottle or jug of house wine (*mezza bottiglia* or *un quartino*). Another useful tip is that any place displaying the Slow Food sign is likely to be good; founded in 1986, the Slow Food movement promotes the use of fresh local food and well-executed cooking.

Many restaurants are closed on Sunday, so if you want to be sure of a table it's a good idea to make a reservation for that night. And bear in mind that meals – not just snacks – are served in many Florentine bars and cafés, so if you're exploring a particular area of the city and fancy a quick bite to eat rather than a full-blown restaurant meal, take a look at the relevant section in the "Cafés and bars" and "Wine bars" listings below.

Piazza della Signoria

Antico Fattore Via Lambertesca 1–3r ☎055.288.975. Simple Tuscan dishes dominate the menu, and the soups are particularly good; close to the Piazza della Signoria, but not as expensive as the locale might suggest. Service can be grim, though. Mains cost around €10–14. Closed Sun, plus Sat in summer, Mon in winter, & Aug.

Da Ganino Piazza dei Cimatori 4r, off Via Dante Alighieri ☎055.214.125. One of only a handful of recommendable places close to the Signoria. Produces good homemade pastas and desserts, though the prices reflect the locale as much as the quality of the kitchen – mains from €10. In summer, when tables are moved out onto the tiny square, it's essential to book. Mon–Sat 7pm–1am.

West of the centre

Belle Donne Via delle Belle Donne 16r. A tiny, convivial, faux-rustic trattoria, where you sit elbow-to-elbow on bare benches and stools, under swags of foliage, drinking your wine from a tumbler. Not a place to linger over your meal, but it's honest food, cheerfully presented at honest prices – main courses €7–12 – and serves up seasonal specialities such as *baccelli* (raw broad beans in their pods) with pecorino. Open every day, except for August, when it's shut for the annual holiday.

Il Contadino Via Palazzuolo 71r. Small, popular place with simple black-and-white interior and fascinating large photos of old Florence on the walls. Fast, friendly service, shared tables (no booking), very cheap but good fare. Fixed price for three-course lunch and dinner (around €10, plus a small extra charge for a *quartino* of wine). No written menu: the four or so choices for each course are recited rapidly. Daily noon–2.30pm & 6–9.30pm.

Il Latini Via dei Palchetti 6r ☎055.210.916. Once a trattoria of the old school, the quasi-legendary *Latini* is now something of a caricature of itself. It still looks the part – hams hanging from the ceiling, family photos on the wall, simple tables and old rush chairs. Food quality, though, is average (the *bistecca* is an honourable exception), and prices well above those of most trattorias (mains from

€10). Old regulars still eat here, but you'll find the queues in the evenings (booking is difficult) are full of foreigners. 11am–midnight; closed Mon & lunch Tues.

Marione Via della Spada 27r ☎055.214.756, ⓦwww.marione.firenze.net. Simple, good-value Tuscan cooking, at prices that are a pleasant surprise for this location, a stone's throw from Via Tornabuoni. Expect to pay €30–35 per person. Daily noon–3pm & 7–11.30pm. Closed first two weeks of Aug.

🏃 **Oliviero** Via delle Terme 51r ☎055.240.618. Currently enjoys a reputation for some of Florence's best food. It has a welcoming and old-fashioned feel – something like an Italian restaurant of the 1960s. The innovative food is predominantly Tuscan, but includes other Italian dishes; desserts, for once, are excellent. The menu includes fresh fish when available, something of a rarity in Florence. Expect to pay upwards of €50, without wine. Mon–Sat 11am–3pm & 7pm–1am. Closed Aug.

Osteria dei Cento Poveri Via Palazzuolo 31r ☎055.218.846. A small and busy restaurant (you won't be the only tourist here) with a strong Pugliese accent and offering more fish than is customary in this city. The lobster gnocchi (€17) is an interesting novelty – the pasta is made across the road – and there's always a fish of the day. Fairly expensive, with main courses at around €18. May–Sept Tues–Sun 7pm–midnight, Sun 12.30am–2.30pm; Oct–April also open for lunch Tues–Sat.

North of the centre

La Lampara Via Nazionale 36r ☎055.215.164. The narrow entrance is deceptive: this is a huge place that goes back and back and has a terrace, too, at the rear. Don't be put off by the multilingual menus: the food is very good, the prices moderate (mains €9–13) and the waiters attentive. Packed with locals at lunchtime and evening, so try to book a table. Daily noon–midnight.

Nuti Borgo San Lorenzo 39r ☎055.210.410. This massive place, with a restaurant on one side of the street and a pizzeria on the other, claims to be the oldest pizzeria in town; the menu isn't limited to pizzas, and prices are reasonable (pizzas from €6.50, two-course menus from €12) – though the service sometimes isn't. Open 11.30pm–1am. Closed Sun in winter.

Oliandolo Via Ricasoli 38–40r ☎055.211.296. A small, fast and very cheap spot (dishes from €4) that's very popular with locals at lunchtime – you'll probably have to queue if you come after 12.30pm. Good roast pork and beans and excellent baked cheesecake. Mon–Sat 8am–7pm.

Palle d'Oro Via Sant'Antonino 43r ☎055.288.383. Close to San Lorenzo market, this is the plainest possible type of trattoria, serving very good fare – such as chicken in a green peppercorn sauce for €7. Packed at lunchtime. Besides full meals, they do sandwiches to take away. Mon–Sat noon–2.30pm & 6.30–9.45pm.

🏃 **Zà-Zà** Piazza del Mercato Centrale 26r ☎055.210.756, ⓦwww.trattoriazaza.it. In business for more than twenty years, and perhaps the best of several trattorias close to the Mercato Centrale. In recent years it has raised its profile to the extent that booking is virtually obligatory in summer. The interior is dark, stone-walled and brick-arched, with a handful of tables – though in summer there are more tables on the outside terraces. There's usually a set-price menu for less than €15 which offers a choice of three or four pastas and main courses; otherwise you'll pay around €25–30 per head. The omelette with a creamy truffle sauce is exquisite (€8.50) and the mixed antipasti are generous and tasty. Daily 11am–11pm; closed Aug.

East of the centre

🏃 **Acqua al Due** Via dell'Acqua 2r/Via della Vigna Vecchia 40r ☎055.284.170. Always packed (often with foreigners but with Italians too), chiefly on account of its offbeat decor, lively atmosphere and *assaggio di primi* – a succession of pasta dishes shared by everyone at the table. Evenings only; main courses from around €12.

Alle Murate Via Proconsolo 16r ☎055.240.618. A highly regarded and very slick operation, recently relocated to a magnificent frescoed old building that boasts the earliest known portrait of Dante. It offers a couple of tempting set menus (but only if all the people at the table order them), and the wine vault is famously well stocked. You pay for the quality: starters cost €18 and main courses are €22–24. Tues–Sun 7.30pm–1am.

🏃 **Baldovino** Via San Giuseppe 22r ☎055.241.773, ⓦwww.baldovino.com. Run by an enterprising Scottish couple, *Baldovino* is renowned above all for its pizzas (made in a wood-fired oven according to Neapolitan principles), but the main menu (which changes monthly) is full of excellent Tuscan and Italian dishes, with mains around €12–17 – although you pay the usual premium for the succulent *bistecca alla Fiorentina*. It's very much on the tourist map now, but standards remain high, and portions very generous. Tues–Sun 11am–3pm & 7pm–1am.

Benvenuto Via della Mosca 15r, corner Via de' Neri. Just a couple of minutes' walk from Piazza della Signoria, this place has been around for years and maintains its reputation for low prices. What it lacks in atmosphere it makes up for with reliable cooking. Mains from €9. Closed Wed & Sun.

Cibrèo Via de' Macci 118r ☏055.234.1100. The *Cibrèo* restaurant – which has now spawned a café, trattoria and shop – is the first Florentine port-of-call for many foodies, having achieved fame well beyond the city. The recipe for success is simple: superb food with a creative take on Tuscan classics, in a tasteful dining room with friendly and professional service. You'll need to book days in advance for a table in the main part of the restaurant, but next door there's a small, somewhat spartan and sometimes overly busy trattoria section (called *Cibreino*) where the food is virtually the same, no bookings are taken and the prices are much lower: around €15 for the main course, as opposed to €30+ in the restaurant. 12.30am–2.30pm & 7–11.15pm. Closed Sun, Mon & all Aug.

Enoteca Pinchiorri Via Ghibellina 87 ☏055.242.777, ⦿www.enotecapinchiorri.com. No one seriously disputes the *Pinchiorri*'s claim to be Florence's best restaurant, certainly not Michelin, who've given it three of their coveted rosettes. The food is as magnificent as you'd expect, given the plaudits, but the ceremony that surrounds its presentation strikes many as excessive. Choose from 80,000 different wines, including some of the rarest and most expensive vintages on the planet. None of this comes cheap – you could easily spend in excess of €200 per person, excluding wine – but there's nowhere better for the never-to-be repeated Florentine treat. Just make sure you've packed your best outfit. Closed Mon & Wed lunch, all day Sun & Aug.

Francescano Largo Bargellini 16 ☏055.241.605. *Francescano* began life as a sibling of *Baldovino*, and though it is now independently owned, still offers similarly good food in a friendly, clean-cut setting. The menu is simpler, smaller and a little less expensive than at *Baldovino*. Noon–2.30pm & 7–11pm. Oct–May closed Tues.

Il Pizzaiuolo Via de' Macci 113r ☏055.241.171. Many Florentines reckon the pizzas here are the best in the city. Wines and other menu items have a Neapolitan touch, as does the atmosphere, which is friendly and high-spirited. Booking's a good idea, at least in the evening. The kitchen stays open until a little after midnight. 12.30–3pm & 7pm–1am. Closed Sun & Aug.

L'Antico Noè Volta di San Piero 6r ☏055.234.0838. Situated next door to the *vinaio* of the same name, this tiny trattoria has a very insalubrious setting (you'll doubtless pass a drunk or two on your way to the door), but the food is

fine and the prices low – mains from €9. Mon–Sat noon–3pm & 7–11pm.

La Pentola dell'Oro Via di Mezzo 24r ☏055.241.821. Run by Giuseppe Alessi, the owner of a fine upmarket restaurant in Fiesole, *La Pentola* has one of the more imaginative menus in Florence, mingling the innovative with the profoundly traditional (some recipes date back to the sixteenth century). The main basement restaurant isn't the cosiest of dining rooms, but the quality is difficult to match for the price. Expect to pay upwards of €35, or a little less in the more informal ground-floor section, which focuses on traditional rather than aristocratic cuisine. Mon–Sat noon–3.30pm & 9pm–midnight.

Natalino Borgo degli Albizi 17r ☏055.289.404. Slighly pricier than your average trattoria but excellent food, untouristy for the location and has outside tables. The truffled courgettes with pecorino are astounding. Tues–Sun noon–3pm & 7–11pm.

Osteria Caffè Italiano Via Isola delle Stinche 11–13r ☏055.289.368. The high vaulted ceilings lend a medieval touch to this café, wine bar and restaurant, but the clientele are à la mode Florentine – smart but relaxed. The cuisine is typically Tuscan – lots of beef, veal and wild boar – and first-rate, even the cakes; expect to pay upwards of €35 per head. Tues–Sun 10am–1am.

Osteria de' Benci Via de' Benci 13r ☏055.234.4923. A modern, busy and reasonably priced osteria, with a bar next door. The interior is pretty and pleasant, and is augmented by outside tables when it's warm enough – in summer it attracts big crowds. The tables have paper tablecloths and you eat off chunky ceramic plates. The moderately priced menu offers well-prepared standards plus innovative Tuscan cuisine. The strawberry risotto is an unexpected and delicious starter (€9) and the *goloso* and *piccante* steaks are very good. Staff are young, and the atmosphere friendly. Restaurant open Mon–Sat 1–2.45pm & 7.30–10.45pm; bar open 8am–midnight.

Ruth's Via Luigi Carlo Farini 2a ☏055.248.0888. Next to the synagogue, this is one of the few kosher places in Florence, and is getting a reputation as a good vegetarian restaurant. Mains €9–16. Open 12.30–3.30pm & 8–10.30pm; closed Fri eve & Sat lunchtime.

Oltrarno

All'Antico Ristoro di Cambi Via Sant'Onofrio 1r ☏055.217.134, ⦿www.anticoristorodicambi.it. Run by the same family since the 1940s, this rough and ready trattoria is particularly good for meaty Florentine standards such as wild boar and steak, and has a very good wine list. It's vast, but none-

FLORENCE
RESTAURANTS,
BARS & CAFÉS

0   250 m

See 'Central Florence' map for detail

N

RESTAURANTS				BARS & CAFÉS					
All'Antico		Cibrèo	4	La Pentola		Caffè Cibrèo	7	Enoteca		Mamma	3
Ristoro di Cambi	9	Del Carmine	10	dell'Oro	2	Caffè La Torre	20	Le Barrique	14	Pitti Gola
Alla Vecchia		I Tarocchi	18	Pane e Vino	8	Caffè Pitti	27	Fuori Porta	22	e Cantina	16
Bettola	15	Il Guscio	11	Ruth's	1	Dolce Vita	13	Hemingway	12	Zoe	19
		Il Pizzaiuolo	5	Sabatino	6			Il Rifrullo	21	

theless gets packed on a Saturday night, when even the large terrace fills up. Main dishes from €10. Mon–Sat 12.30am–2.30pm & 7.30–11pm.
Alla Vecchia Bettola Viale Lodovico Ariosto 32–34r ☎055.224.158. Located on a major traffic intersection a couple of minutes' walk from the Carmine, this place – with its long tables – has something of the atmosphere of a drinking den, which is what it once was; the menu boasts a good repertoire of Tuscan meat dishes, with main courses reasonably priced from €10. Noon–2.30pm & 7.30–10.30pm. Closed Sun & Mon.
Beccofino Piazza degli Scarlatti 1r ☎055.290.076, ⓦwww.beccofino.com. The most upmarket venture from David Gardner, the Scottish boss of *Baldovino* (see p.191) – indeed, some might find its cooking and expensively austere decor a bit too self-consciously cutting edge. Prices are above average – €18–22 for *secondi* – but so is the quality. If you'd like to test the waters first,

have a drink at the attached wine bar. Tues–Sun 7–11pm, plus Sun lunch.
Borgo Antico Piazza di Santo Spirito 6r ☎055.210.437. The spartan chic of *Borgo Antico*'s white tile and pink plaster decor reflects the increasingly trendy character of this once notoriously sleazy Oltrarno piazza, and there's no Oltrarno restaurant trendier than this place. It's usually very crowded and noisy (the soundtrack can be a bit relentless), though in summer the tables outside offer relative quiet. Choose from a menu of pizzas or a range of Tuscan standards at reasonable prices (€13–18). Salads here are good, and there's often a selection of fresh fish and seafood pastas. Servings – on the restaurant's famous huge plates – are generous to a fault. Open daily noon–midnight.
Dante Piazza Nazario Sauro 10r ☎055.219.219. *Dante* is another Oltrarno institution, popular mainly for its pizzas (€7), though it also offers a menu of

FLORENCE | Restaurants

193

pasta, fish and meat dishes (from €10 for mains). Closed Wed & last 2 weeks of Aug.

Del Carmine Piazza del Carmine 18r
☎055.218.601. Years ago this was an unsung local trattoria; now the tourists have taken over, but it hasn't altogether lost its soul. Uncomplicated Florentine cooking, with a frequently changing menu. Mon–Sat noon–3pm & 6.30–10.30pm.

I Tarocchi Via dei Renai 12r ☎055.234.3912. There are a few simple dishes on the menu, but this is essentially an inexpensive pizzeria – and one of the best in the city. Tues–Fri 12.30–2.30pm & 7–10pm, Sat & Sun 7–10pm only. Closed Mon.

Il Guscio Via dell'Orto 49 ☎055.224.421. A long-established upper-range Oltrano favourite: high-quality Tuscan meat dishes, home made pasta and superb desserts, plus a wide-ranging wine list. Evenings only; closed Sat & Aug.

🏃 **La Casalinga** Via del Michelozzo 9r
☎055.218.624. Located in a side-street off Piazza di Santa Spirito, this long-established family-run trattoria serves up some of the best low-cost Tuscan dishes in town (€10 for a *secondo*). No frills – paper tablecloths, so-so house wine by the flask and brisk service – but most nights it's filled with regulars and a good few outsiders. Closed Sun & last 3 weeks of Aug.

Osteria Santo Spirito Piazza di Santo Spirito 16r/Via Sant' Agostino ☎055.238.2383. Run by the owners of the *Borgo Antico* (see above), this osteria is part of the new wave of Florentine restaurants. Informal and modern, its walls are painted deep red and blue, and the lighting is bright over hearty Tuscan dishes presented with contemporary flair.

Tables are on two floors, and in summer you can eat outdoors on the piazza. Pasta dishes €6–12, mains €12–20. Open daily until midnight.

🏃 **Pane e Vino** Piazza di Cestello 3r
☎055.247.6956. *Pane e Vino* began life as a bar (over by San Niccolò), so it's no surprise that the wine list is excellent and well priced, with bottles from €13. In its new home, the ambience is stylish yet relaxed and the menu small (*primi* around €10, *secondi* €15), featuring a very enticing *menu degustazione* (€30). Small TV screens in the dining area show the chefs beavering away in the kitchen, producing some of the best food in town – the ravioli with asparagus in a lemon cream melts in your mouth. Mon–Sat 8pm–1am.

Quattro Leoni Via dei Vellutini 1r/Piazza della Passera ☎055.218.562, ⊕www.4leoni.com. Occupying a three-roomed medieval interior, this is a young, relaxed place with wooden beams and splashy modern paintings strung across the rough stone walls. In summer you can also eat alfresco under vast canvas umbrellas in the tiny Piazza della Passera – one of the most appealing outdoor eating venues in the city. It's popular with visiting stars – Dustin Hofmann and Sting feature on the walls, and Anthony Hopkins ate here while filming *Hannibal*. For everyone else booking is essential. You can eat very well for around €30 a head. Noon–2.30pm & 7–11pm; closed Wed lunch.

Sabatino Via Pisana 2r ☎055.225.955. Situated right by Porta San Frediano, this old-fashioned, no-frills, long-running family trattoria is not a gourmet venue, but it's excellent value and the atmosphere is always terrific. Closed Sat, Sun & Aug.

Cafés and bars

Virtually every street in central Florence has a café or bar of some sort; what follows is a guide to the best and the most popular. Predictably enough, there's a heavy concentration on and around the big tourist streets and squares: Piazza della Repubblica, Piazza del Duomo, Via dei Calzaiuoli and so on. Many of these are expensive and characterless, but some – as listed below – are expensive and very good, especially when it comes to cakes and other sweet delicacies. To find places where prices are lower and non-Florentine faces fewer, only a little effort is needed: a short walk east from the Signoria gets you into the burgeoning Santa Croce area, and it's just as easy to get over into the Oltrarno, the most authentic quarter of the historic centre.

As elsewhere in Italy, the distinction between bars and cafés is tricky to the point of impossibility, as almost every café serves alcohol and almost every bar serves coffee. It's really just a question of degrees of emphasis: in some cafés, most of the custom comes first thing in the morning, as people on their way to work stop off for a dash of caffeine and a brioche or *cornetto* (croissant); in others, the tables are busiest late at night, when people drop by after an evening out, to relax over a Campari or a glass of wine. As a further complication, many bars and cafés offer a small range of meals, which blurs the distinction between them and restaurants.

There's one category of bar that's quite distinct from cafés, and that's the *enoteca*, where the enjoyment of wine is the chief point of the exercise – though in this case the complicating factor is that almost all *enoteche* serve food, which in some instances makes them almost indistinguishable from restaurants. You'll find *enoteche* and more humble wine dens reviewed in the "Wine bars" section (see p.197). Bars where music – live or recorded – is the main attraction are reviewed in "Nightlife" (see p.200).

Piazza del Duomo

Astor Caffè Piazza del Duomo 20r. From its modest street-front opposite the northeast corner of the Duomo you wouldn't guess that this was the hottest spot on the piazza, but inside you'll find a glitzy and spacious three-storey set-up. Food is served in the upstairs restaurant, in the basement you get DJs playing anything from hip-hop to Brazilian music most nights, and in the ground-floor bar you sip cocktails with the city's gilded youth. Mon–Sat 10am–3am.

Chiaroscuro Via del Corso 36r. Nice cakes, but caffeine's the main draw, as you might guess from the coffee-related paraphernalia in the window. Also a good place for a quick cheap lunch – choose food at the bar and take it to tables at the back. Mon–Sat 8am–9.30pm, Sun 3–8.30pm.

Piazza della Signoria

Caffè Italiano Via della Condotta 56r. Located one block north of the piazza, this is a combination of old-fashioned stand-up bar and smart café, with lots of dark wood, silver teapots and superb cakes, coffees and teas. Lunch is inexpensive and excellent, as you'd expect from a place owned by Umberto Montano, boss of the outstanding *Osteria Caffè Italiano* (see p.192). 8am–8.30pm; June–Sept closed Sun.

Rivoire Piazza della Signoria 5r. If you want to people-watch on Florence's main square, this is the place to do so, and the outside tables are invariably packed. Founded in 1872, the café started life specializing in hot chocolate, still its main claim to fame. Ice creams are also fairly good, but the sandwiches and snacks are overpriced and poor: this is a place for one pricey beer or cappuccino, just to say you've done it. Closed Mon.

West of the centre

Art Bar Via del Moro 4r. A fine little bar near Piazza di Carlo Goldoni. The interior looks like an antique shop, while the club-like atmosphere attracts a rather smart crowd. Especially busy at happy hour (7–9pm), when the low-priced cocktails are in heavy demand. The after-hours ambience is also ideal for a laid-back nightcap. Mon–Sat 7pm–1am.

Caffè Amerini Via della Vigna Nuova 63r. The intimate interior's medieval brick arching contrasts with modern furniture and a couple of Art Deco mirrors. Sandwiches, salads and snacks are particularly good – point at what you want from the bar and then sit down to be served: there's only a small premium for sitting down. Mon–Sat 8am–8pm.

Caffè Gilli Piazza della Repubblica 36–39r. Founded in 1733, this most appealing of the square's expensive cafés moved to its present site in 1910. The staggering Belle Epoque interior is a sight in itself, but most people choose to sit on the big outdoor terrace. On a cold afternoon try the famous hot chocolate – it comes in five blended flavours: almond, orange, coffee, gianduia and cocoa. 8am–1am; closed Tues.

Capocaccia Lungarno Corsini 12–14r, Ⓦ www.capocaccia.com. The well-designed interior is roomy and has plenty of tables and stools; there's a DJ every night; and you'll be mixing almost entirely with fashionable locals, especially later on – it's been voted the Florentines' favourite night-time rendezvous several times. If you have neither youth nor beauty on your side, however, you'd best stay away. Sushi aperitifs on Tuesdays – you pay €1–2 on top of the drink price to get access to the substantial snacks. Sunday brunch 12.30–3.30pm. Open daily noon–4pm & 6pm–1am.

Mariano Via Parione 19r. It just says *Alimentari* above the door, but this is a smartish local café-bar just behind the Santa Trìnita church that does brisk lunchtime business with its freshly prepared sandwiches and snacks, including *pannini tartufati*. 8am–3pm & 5–7.30pm; closed Sat afternoon.

Procacci Via de' Tornabuoni 64r. Famous café that doesn't serve coffee, just wine and cold drinks. Its reputation comes from the extraordinary *tartufati*, or truffle-butter rolls (€1.60), which are delicious, if not exactly filling. Mon–Sat 10.30am–8pm; closed Aug.

Slowly Via Porta Rossa 63. This extremely trendy bar attracts a showy, beautifully dressed young crowd, chatting over pricey cocktails and high-end bar snacks. Time will tell whether its appearance in all the designer magazines will lead to style tourists edging out the Florentines. Mon–Sat 7pm–2.30am; closed July & Aug.

North of the centre

Caffèlatte Via degli Alfani 39r ☎055.247.8878. *Caffèlatte* began life in the 1920s, when a milk and coffee supplier opened here. Nowadays, it's expanded its operation to include an organic bakery, which produces delicious breads and cakes, served in the one-room café. The speciality drink, as you'd expect, is caffè latte, served in huge bowls. Laid-back music and temporary exhibitions of paintings and photographs enhance the vaguely "alternative" mood. Mon–Sat 8am–8pm, Sun 10am–4pm.

Caracol Via Ginori 10r. Florence has a few pseudo-Latin American dives, of which this is by far the best. A big wooden bar and ranks of tequila bottles create the right look and feel, while a multi-ethnic crowd provides the noise and energy levels. Happy hour (6–8.30pm) is the best and busiest time to show up: cocktails are cheap, and there are snacks and tortillas to help them down. Tues–Sun 6pm–2am; closed June–Sept.

Nannini Coffee Shop Via Borgo San Lorenzo 7r. The Florentine outpost of Siena's *Nannini* operation, famed for its superb coffee and tooth-wrecking *panforte*, an extremely dense and delicious cake. Daily 7.30am–8pm.

East of the centre

Caffè Cibrèo Via Andrea del Verrocchio 5r. Possibly the prettiest café in Florence, with a chi-chi clientele to match. Opened in 1989, but the wood-panelled interior looks at least two hundred years older. Cakes and desserts are great, and the light meals bear the culinary stamp of the *Cibrèo* restaurant kitchens opposite. Tues–Sat 8am–1am.

Caffè di Paci Via dei Neri 37r. Friendly, small bar with tables at the back, serving a range of delicious truffle-flavoured dishes plus homemade pasta and a few other Florentine staples. Mon–Sat 7am–midnight.

I Visacci Borgo degli Albizi 82r. A bright, stylish and popular small bar, serving crostini and a few more substantial dishes. Tues–Sat 10am–2.30am (May–Aug closes earlier) & Sun–Mon 10am–10pm.

Moyo Via de' Benci 23r. A young crowd flocks to this bar every evening – the food's pretty good, the free wireless Internet access is a plus (it was the first place in Florence to offer it), but it's the buzz that really brings them in. With *Osteria de' Benci* just down the road (see p.192), this is one of the

city's sparkiest corners. Open daily noon–4pm & 8pm–2am (3am Fri & Sat).

Oltrarno

Cabiria Piazza di Santo Spirito 4r. Trendy in look, feel and clientele, but still rather cosy. The main seating area is in the room to the rear, but plenty of punters (some locals and lots of foreigners) sit out on the piazza, or crowd into the bar area at the front. There's a DJ-run soundtrack most nights from around 9pm – drinks are cheaper until then. Open 8am–1.30am; closed Tues & 10 days in mid-Aug.

Caffè degli Artigiani Via dello Sprone 16r. Slightly ramshackle and very welcoming café on a delightful small square near the Ponte Vecchio, much used by local students. Serves salads and sandwiches. Mon 7am–7pm, Tues–Sat 7am–1am.

Caffè Pitti Piazza Pitti 9r. Sit outside or in the old-style interior, which is nicely done out with wooden floors and subdued gold-yellow walls. Panini and other snacks are available at lunch, with a full dinner menu later – a *menu degustazione* for €30, and mains €15–19. Daily 10am–2am; June & July closed Mon.

Caffè I Ricchi Piazza di Santo Spirito 9r. The most relaxed of the cafés on this square, with a more than acceptable restaurant attached. Summer Mon–Sat 7am–1am; winter closes 8pm.

Caffè La Torre Lungarno Cellini 65r. This bar changes its decor every year, which is one reason it has managed to remain one of the most fashionable bars in Florence. The other is its superb location, in the shadow of the tower of the Porta San Niccolò, close to the Arno, with lots of outdoor seating. Excellent, imaginative cocktails complete the picture. Daily 10.30am–3am.

Dolce Vita Piazza del Carmine. A smart, modern-looking and extremely popular bar that's been going for more than a decade and has stayed ahead of the game through constant updating; aluminium bar stools, sleek black-and-white photos on the walls and the chance to preen with Florence's beautiful things, who like to drop in here for a cocktail on their way to a club. Daily 5pm–2am.

Hemingway Piazza Piattellina 9r, off Piazza del Carmine. Self-consciously trendy, but don't let that put you off – there's nothing else like it in Florence. Choose from one of countless speciality teas, sample over twenty coffees, or knock back one of the "tea cocktails". Owners Paul de Bondt and Andrea Slitti are members of the Compagnia del Cioccolato, a chocolate appreciation society – and it shows: the handmade chocolates are sublime. Tues–Sun 4.30pm–1am.

Il Rifrullo Via San Niccolò 53–57r. New owners have smartened and expanded this bar, which is still a nice place to unwind after the hike up to San Miniato, or for a nightcap. Lying to the east of the Ponte Vecchio–Pitti Palace route, it attracts fewer tourists than many Oltrarno cafés. Has pleasant garden terrace, too. Serves tapas in the early evening, larger dishes after that, and offers brunch (€18) on Sat & Sun. Mon–Sat 7am–1am, Sun 7am–7pm.

Mamma Lungarno Santa Rosa. Delightful venue for summer nights, occupying a small park in the shadow of the high city walls behind the Porta San Frediano. Romantic at dusk, when candles are set out, it becomes hugely busy later on – more than a thousand people have been known to come

out here on fine nights. DJs two or three nights a week keep the fashionable, cocktail-drinking and almost entirely Italian crowd happy. Occasional live gigs; antipasti available from the bistro. April–Oct Mon–Thurs & Sun 11am–2am, Fri & Sat till 3am.

Zoe Via dei Renai 13. Just set back from the Arno, on the south side of the grassy Piazza Demidoff, *Zoe* and neighbouring bar *Negroni* are perennially popular for summer evening drinks. *Zoe* is a little louder, a little trendier and a little younger in spirit. Both bars specialize in the *aperitivo*, with a free buffet laid out between 7.30 and 10.30pm, and attract lots of young Florentines right through into the small hours. Mon–Sat 8am–2.30am, Sun 4pm–2am.

Wine bars

As you'd expect in a city that lies close to some of the best vineyards in the country, Florence has plenty of bars dedicated to the **wines** of Chianti and other Tuscan producers. At one end of the scale there's the endangered species known as the *vinaio* (see box), which consists of little more than a niche with a few shelves of generally workaday wines, plus a counter of snacks. At the opposite pole there's the *enoteca*, which is in effect a restaurant devoted to wine: all of them have kitchens (cooking excellent food in many cases), but the wine menu will be far more extensive, often running to hundreds of different vintages. Increasingly popular among younger Florentines, the city's *enoteche* are becoming more numerous with every passing year, and their quality is consistently high.

Piazza del Duomo

Fiaschetteria Nuvoli Piazza dell'Olio 15. It's something of a surprise to find such a traditional place so close to the Duomo. The tiny, dark, bottled-lined shop is dominated by a counter laden with cold meats, crostini and other snacks, plus a few opened wine bottles. There's room inside to eat sitting down, but most of the customers are content with a quick glass at the bar. Mon–Sat 8am–8pm.

Piazza della Signoria

🏃 Cantinetta dei Verrazzano Via dei Tavolini 18–20r. Owned by Castello dei Verrazzano, a major Chianti vineyard, this wood-panelled place near Orsanmichele is part-bar, part-café and part-bakery, making its own excellent pizza, focaccia and cakes. A perfect spot for a light lunch or an early evening drink. July & Aug Mon–Sat 8am–4pm; Sept–June Mon–Sat 8am–9pm.

Gustavino Via della Condotta 37r ⓦ www.gustavino.it. A minute's walk from Piazza della Signoria, this *enoteca con cucina* is the antithesis

of the faux-rustic Tuscan wine bar, with its steel chairs and glass-topped tables. Some might find it a bit too businesslike, but it has a more than adequate selection of wines, and the kitchen turns out some interesting dishes – such as black tagliolini with sea urchin and zucchini-flower pesto (€12). The *cucina* itself is on full view, both from the tables and from the street. Its wine shop next door has a cosier feel (noon–midnight daily), serving snacks. Tues–Sun noon–3pm & 7.30pm–midnight.

North of the centre

🏃 Casa del Vino Via dell'Ariento 16r. Located just west of the Mercato Centrale, and passed by hordes of tourists daily – yet probably visited by only a handful. Patrons are mostly Florentines, who pitch up for a drink, a chat with owner Gianni Migliorini and an assault on various panini, crostini and saltless Tuscan bread and salami. Mon–Fri 9.30am–7pm.

🏃 Zanobini Via Sant'Antonino 47r. Like the *Casa del Vino*, its rival just around the corner, this is an authentic Florentine place, whose

Vinaii

The *vinaio* was once a real Florentine institution. These tiny places with no seating would typically see customers lingering for no more than a couple of minutes – long enough to down a tumbler of basic red wine and exchange a few words with the proprietor. The number of *vinaii* has declined markedly in recent years; the following are the notable survivors.

All'Antico Vinaio Via dei Neri 65r. Though recently revamped, this place – located between the Uffizi and Santa Croce – preserves much of the rough-and-ready atmosphere that's made it one of Florence's most popular wine bars for the last hundred years. Also serves coffee, rolls and plates of pasta. Mon–Sat 8am–10pm; closed 3 weeks in late July & early Aug.

I Fratellini Via dei Cimatori 38r. This minuscule dirt-cheap wine bar is somehow clinging on in the immediate vicinity of the high-rent Via dei Calzaiuoli. Serves decent panini and local wines. Mid-June to Aug Mon–Fri 8am–5pm; Sept to mid-June daily 8am–8pm.

L'Antico Noè Volta di San Piero 6r. A long-established stand-up wine bar, tucked into an uninviting little alley to the north of Santa Croce, at the eastern end of Borgo degli Albizi. Mon–Sat noon–3pm & 7pm–midnight.

Quasigratis Piazza del Grano 10 (formerly known as Via dei Castellani). Little more than a window in a wall at the back of the Uffizi, and it doesn't say Quasigratis ("Almost free") anywhere – just "Vini". Rolls, nibbles and wine – in tiny glasses called *rasini* – are consumed standing up. Daily 10am–11pm; closed Jan & Feb.

feel owes much to the presence of locals and traders from the nearby Mercato Centrale. Offers acceptable snacks, but most people are simply here for a chat over a glass of wine. Mon–Sat 8am–2pm & 3.30–8pm.

East of the centre

Baldoria Via San Giuseppe 18r. An offshoot of the excellent *Baldovino* restaurant across the road, this is a stylish place to sample gastronomic snacks (and pizzas) or drink top-quality wine, either at the bar or one of the tables to the rear. Summer daily noon–midnight; winter Tues–Sun noon–4pm & 6pm–midnight.

Boccadama Piazza Santa Croce 25–26r. A smart and well-stocked wine bar, offering vintages from all over the country and a good menu of snacks and simple meals. Tues–Sun 3.30–11pm; also March–Oct Mon 3.30–11pm.

Caffè Italiano Via Isola delle Stinche 11–13r. As well as serving a superb range of mainly Tuscan wines, the wine bar section of *Caffè Italiano* (see p.192) has an excellent kitchen – but only three tables and little standing room, so the queues outside can be long. No credit cards. Tues–Sun 7.30–1am.

Oltrarno

Beccofino Piazza degli Scarlatti 1r. Like the restaurant to which it's attached, this wine bar is a sophisticatedly stylish establishment – the

selection of wines is terrific, and there's a menu of innovative dishes from the restaurant's kitchen, at somewhat lower prices. Tues–Sun 7pm–midnight.

Enoteca Le Barrique Via del Leone 40r. A fine small wine bar, a short distance west of Santa Maria del Carmine, with a wide-ranging list of vintages and a modest menu of full meals. Tues–Fri & Sun 4.30pm–1am.

Fuori Porta Via del Monte alle Croci 10r ℡055.234.2483, ⊛ www.fuoriporta.it. If you're climbing up to San Miniato you could take a breather at this superb and justly famous wine bar-osteria. There are over four hundred wines to choose from by the bottle, and an ever-changing selection of wines by the glass, as well as a wide selection of grappas and malt whiskies. Bread, cheese, hams and salamis are available, together with a choice of pasta dishes and tasty salads, all very elegantly presented. Has a summertime terrace and large dining area, but it's still wise to book if you're coming here to eat. Mon–Sat 12.30–3.30pm & 7pm–12.30am; closed 2 weeks in mid-Aug.

Il Santo Bevitore Via Santo Spirito 64–66r ℡055.211.264. The Holy Drinker is an airy and stylish "gastronomic enoteca" with a small but classy food menu (around €20 for a meal without drinks) to complement its enticing menu of wines. Good range of salads at lunchtime, with a more extensive evening menu. Mon–Sat 12.30–2.30pm & 7.30–11.30pm.

Le Volpi e L'Uva Piazza dei Rossi 1r, off Piazza di Santa Felicita ⓦ www.levolpieluva .com. This discreet, friendly little place, just over the Ponte Vecchio, does good business by concentrating on the wines of small producers and providing tasty cold meats and snacks to help them down (the selection of cheeses in particular is tremendous). At any one time you can choose from at least two dozen different wines by the glass. Mon–Sat 10am–8pm.

Pitti Gola e Cantina Piazza Pitti 16. A small and friendly wine bar, very handily placed for a glass of Chianti after a slog around the Pitti museums. Tues–Sun 10am–11.30pm. Closed 2 weeks in mid-Aug.

Gelaterie

Devotees of Italian ice cream will find that Florence offers plenty of opportunities to indulge: the city has some superb *gelaterie*, and some would claim that *Vivoli* is the best purveyor in the country. The procedure is the same wherever you buy. First decide whether you want a cone (*un cono*) or a cup (*una coppa*). Then decide how much you want to pay: cone and cup sizes tend to start around €2, going up in €1 increments. Unless you plump for the smallest size you'll usually be able to choose a combination of two or three flavours. Finally, you may be asked if you want a squirt of cream (*panna*) on top – it's usually free.

Bondi (also known as **Il Triangolo delle Ber-mude**) Via Nazionale 61r. The Bondi family make some of the most unusual concoctions in town, such as cinnamon, oreo (made from the American biscuit) and Mars bar. Closed Mon.

Café delle Carizze Piazza Pesce 3r. Good outlet right by the Ponte Vecchio. Daily except Wed 11am–8pm.

Caffè I Ricchi Piazza di Santo Spirito 9r. Excellent ice creams at a popular location – flavours include English trifle.

Carabe Via Ricasoli 60r. Wonderful Sicilian ice cream made with Sicilian ingredients as only they know how. Also serves a variety of cakes. May–Oct daily 10am–midnight; Nov, March & April daily noon–7.30pm; first half of Dec & last half of Jan Tues–Sun noon–7.30pm; closed mid-Dec to mid-Jan.

Pubs

Every Italian town of any size now has at least one pub, generally with an Irish theme, in which the clientele tends to be a mix of local lads and students sipping slowly at their half-pints, and English-speaking tourists showing them how it's really done. Florence has an increasing number of such places, of which the following trio are more convincing than most of the rest.

Fiddler's Elbow Piazza di Santa Maria Novella 7r. Part of an Italy-wide chain, with just one smoky, dark and wood-panelled room, invariably heaving with homesick foreigners – fortunately there's also seating out on the piazza. Women travellers are likely to find themselves the object of concerted attention from packs of Guinness-sozzled Italians. Daily noon–2am.

Lion's Fountain Borgo degli Albizi 34r. Background music isn't traditional, but it's inoffensive; the decor is pseudo-Irish, and the bar staff and atmosphere are generally friendly. Food is simple and good – lots of salads and sandwiches – and you can catch big sporting events on the TVs. Drinks are reasonably priced, and include a good range of cocktails as well as the ubiquitous Guinness. Daily 6pm–2am.

Robin Hood's Tavern Via dell'Oriuolo 58r. One of the biggest and most successful of several places that try to affect the look of an English pub – probably because it was started by a former biker from Birmingham. Happy hour 5–9pm. Open daily 2pm–3am.

Festival del Gelato Via del Corso 75r. Around seventy varieties of ice cream, with some very exotic combinations. Tues–Sun 10am–midnight.

Frilli Via San Miniato 5r. Tiny family operation just inside the San Miniato gate in the San Niccolò district: recommended are the orange and lemon mousse. Tues–Sun 10am–8pm, but open till midnight on summer weekends.

Gelateria dei Neri Via dei Neri 20–22r. Small place in contention for the best ice creams in town. Close to the Uffizi but away from the crowds. The range of flavours is fantastic – fig and walnut, Mexican chocolate (very spicy), rice – and

they also have some non-dairy ice creams. Daily 11am–midnight.

Perchè No! Via de' Tavolini 19r. Superb *gelateria*, in business since the 1930s; go for the rum-laced tiramisù, the chocolate or the gorgeous pistachio. Daily 11am–midnight, except Tues 11am–7.30pm; closed Nov.

Vivoli Via Isola delle Stinche 7r. Operating from deceptively unprepossessing premises in a side street close to Santa Croce, this has long been rated the best ice-cream-maker in Florence – and some say in Italy. Tues–Sun 7.30am–1am; closed Aug.

Nightlife and cultural events

Florence has a reputation for catering primarily to the middle-aged and affluent, but like every university town it has its pockets of **nightlife** activity, not to mention the added nocturnal buzz generated by thousands of summer visitors.

Full details of the city's dependable club and live music venues are given below, but for up-to-the-minute **information** about what's on, call in at the tourist office in Via Cavour (see p.82) or at Box Office, which has outlets at Via Almanni 39 (☎055.210.804 Mon 3.30–7.30pm, Tues–Sat 10am–7.30pm) and Via Porta Rossa 82r, near the corner with Via de' Tornabuoni (☎055.219.402 Mon 1–8pm, Tues–Sat 9am–8pm). Tickets for most events are available at Box Office; otherwise, keep your eyes peeled for advertising posters, or pick up monthly magazines such as *Firenze Spettacolo* (€1.60), which has an English section ("Florenscope") as well as a map of places open after midnight.

Clubs

Put together balmy summer evenings, a big student population and Florence's huge summer surge of young travellers, and you have a recipe for a massive **club** scene. Unfortunately, those same ingredients don't necessarily add up to produce the most sophisticated of venues, and in any case, clubs in Italy don't resemble their equivalents in London or other big cities. For one thing, most Florentines aren't in clubs to dance or drink; they're there to see and be seen, and dress up to the nines. Foreigners are a different matter, and one or two – mostly central – clubs have a slightly more sweaty and familiar atmosphere as a result.

Faced with a low income from the bar, most clubs charge a fairly stiff **admission**: reckon on €15 and up for the bigger and better-known places. This is not quite as bad as it sounds, for the admission often includes a drink. Prices at the bar after that are usually pretty steep. Other more insidious admission

The streets of central Florence are generally safe at night, but women should be wary of strolling through the red-light districts alone: the area around the **station** and **Piazza Ognissanti** have a particularly dodgy reputation, and kerb-crawling is not unknown. Unaccompanied tourists of either sex should stay well clear of the **Cascine park** at night: if you're going to one of the clubs located there, get a taxi there and back.

Gay and lesbian Florence

Florence's history is scattered with the names of some of history's greatest gay and bisexual artists, including Michelangelo, Leonardo and Botticelli: *Florenzer* was, during the seventeenth century at least, German slang for gay. The city remains, for the most part, tolerant towards gay and lesbian visitors. The leading gay bar is **Crisco**, a short distance east of the Duomo at Via Sant'Egidio 43r (℡055.248.0580, ⓦwww .crisco.it; Mon & Wed–Sun 10/11pm till late), but the ambience can be a bit heavy for some tastes. **Il Piccolo Caffè**, Borgo Santa Croce 23r (℡055.241.704; daily 5pm till late), has a more chilled-out atmosphere, while **Y.A.G. B@r**, also near Santa Croce at Via de' Macci 8r (℡055.246.9022, ⓦwww.yagbar.com), is stylish and draws a trendy, mixed crowd. The key bar-club is the pioneering **Tabasco**, which has been going for more than thirty years at Piazza Santa Cecilia 3r (℡055.213.000, ⓦwww.tabascogay .it; daily 10pm–6am, with music Thurs–Sun). For more information and contacts, check out ⓦwww.gay.it/pinklily. For lesbian contacts, check the noticeboard at the women's bookshop Libreria delle Donne, Via Fiesolana 2b (Mon 3.30–7.30pm, Tues–Sat 9am–1pm & 3.30–7.30pm).

procedures include a card system, where you're given a card on (usually free) entry that gets stamped every time you spend money at the bar. By the end of the night you have to have spent a minimum sum; if not, you have to pay the difference before the bouncers will let you out. And of course everyone loses their card. Alternatively, the card may be used just to keep tabs on your drinks, with the bill settled at the end of the evening. Payment always has to be in cash: credit cards are not accepted.

Opening and closing times for clubs are rarely set, though the weekly closing day, if there is one, doesn't usually vary. Clubs are also prone to closure, or to closing then opening up under a different name.

West of the centre

Central Park Via di Fosso Macinante 2, Parco delle Cascine. One of the city's biggest and most commercial clubs, with adventurous, wide-ranging and up-to-the-minute music on several dance floors from DJs who know what they're doing and have access to a superb sound system. A card system operates for drinks, and the first drink is included in the admission – around €20 after midnight, usually free before. It's unsafe to wander around the park outside, especially for women. Summer Tues–Sat 11pm–4am; winter Fri & Sat same hours.

Loonees Via Porta Rossa 15r. Run by a former biker from Birmingham, this is a relaxed bar in the centre of town, with live music Wed–Sat. Daily 9pm–2am.

Meccanò Viale degli Olmi 1/Piazzale delle Cascine ℡055.331.371. People flock here for a night out from across half of Tuscany. The place is labyrinthine, with a trio of lounge and bar areas, and a huge and invariably packed dance floor playing mostly house. In summer, when the action spills out of doors, you can cool off in the gardens bordering the Cascine. The €15 admission (usually less during the week) includes your first drink. Summer Wed–Sat 8.30pm–4am; winter

Thurs–Sat same hours; closed Nov & two weeks in Aug.

Space Electronic Via Palazzuolo 37 ℡055.293.082, ⓦwww.spaceelectronic.net. You'll find all the disco clichés of a big Continental club here – glass dance floors and mirrored walls – and one or two less familiar features, such as the piranha tank in the downstairs bar, near the karaoke area. Cooler-than-thou clubbers might be sniffy about its popularity with youthful tourist coach parties and local lads on the pull, but it's fine if all you want to do is dance, and the music can be surprisingly good. Admission €14 with one free drink; drinks are reasonably priced. Mon–Fri & Sun 10pm–2.30am, Sat 10pm–3am; winter closed Mon.

Yab Via Sassetti 5r ℡055.215.160, ⓦwww.yab .it. Long-established place crammed into a basement and currently enjoying something of a vogue, especially on a Thurs night. On other nights it doesn't have the most up-to-the-minute playlist in the world, but still offers probably the most relaxed and reliable night's clubbing in central Florence. You're given a card and pay on leaving if you've spent less than €15 at the bar. Aug–April Mon & Wed–Sun 9pm–4am; May–July Mon 11pm–4am.

East of the centre

Blob Club Via Vinegia 21r ☏ 055.211.209. A favourite with Florentine students, possibly on account of its free admission and the 6–10pm happy hour. Seating upstairs, bar and tiny dance floor downstairs, but don't expect to do much dancing – later on, especially on weekend nights, *Blob* gets packed full with a very happy and very drunken crowd. Quieter in the summer months. Daily 6pm–3am.

Full-Up Via della Vigna Vecchia 25r ☏ 055.293.006. Situated close to the Bargello, this club has been going so long it's become something of an institution, but new management is trying to move it upmarket. Admission €13. Reckon on around €7 for most drinks. Tues–Sat 11pm–4am. Closed June–Sept.

🏃 **Rex** Via Fiesolana 25r ⓦ www.rexcafe.it. One of the city's big night-time fixtures, a friendly bar-club with a varied and loyal clientele. Vast curving lights droop over the central bar, which is studded with turquoise stone and broken mirror mosaics. Big arched spaces to either side mean there's plenty of room, the cocktails are good and the snacks excellent. DJs provide the sounds at weekends. Daily 5pm–3am. Closed June–Aug.

Oltrarno

🏃 **Universale** Via Pisana 77r ☏ 055.221.122, ⓦ www.universalefirenze.it. Located beyond the city gates, this is perhaps the most stylish night venue in Florence, with a restaurant and various club zones installed in a beautiful converted 1950s cinema. Snobby and nouveau, maybe, but definitely glamorous. The music is predominantly house. Tues–Sun 8.30pm–3am; closed Mon & May–Sept.

Perètola

Tenax Via Pratese 46 ☏ 055.632.958, ⓦ www .tenax.org. Florence's big-hitting club, pulling in the odd big-name DJ. Given its location in the north-west of town, near the airport (take a taxi), you'll escape the hordes of *internazionalisti* in the more central clubs. With two large floors, it's a major venue for concerts, as well. Admission varies from around €10 to around €20. Thurs–Sat 10.30pm– 4am; closed mid-May to mid-Sept.

Live music

Florence's **live music** scene isn't the hottest in Italy, but there's a smattering of venues for small-time local outfits, and a couple of big stages for visiting stars. In addition to the recommendations below, a few of the places reviewed under "Cafés and bars" and "Clubs" lay on live bands from time to time: check listings magazines for one-off events.

Piazza della Signoria

Caruso Jazz Café Via Lambertesca 14/16r ☏ 055.281.940. Regular live jazz at this small venue. e8 for admission and first drink. Closed Sun.

North of the centre

Be Bop Via dei Servi 28r. A nice and rather classy rock, jazz and blues bar with bow-tied bar staff and faux Art Nouveau decor. Located close to the university district, and often full of students as a result. No dance floor as such; this is more a place to sit and chill out to the music. Daily 6pm–1am.

🏃 **Girasol** Via del Romito 1 ☏ 055.474.948. Florence's liveliest Latin bar, located on a minor road due north of the Fortezza da Basso, is hugely popular. Rather than relying solely on salsa classes, cocktails and the usual vinyl suspects – although it does all these – the place draws in some surprisingly good live acts, with different countries' sounds each day of the week, from Brazilian bossa nova to Cuban son; Friday is party night. Daily 7pm–2.30am.

East of the centre

Jazz Club Via Nuova de' Caccini 3 ☏ 055.247.9700. Florence's foremost jazz venue has been a fixture for years. The €6 "membership" fee gets you down into the medieval brick-vaulted basement, where the atmosphere's informal and there's live music most nights (and an open jam session on Tuesdays). Cocktails are good, and you can also snack on bar nibbles and focaccia. Tues–Fri 9.30pm–1.30am, Sat 9.30pm–2.30am; closed June–Aug.

Nelson Mandela Forum Viale Pasquale Paoli ☏ 055.210.804. Along with *Tenax* (see below), this place – located a long way east of the centre, at Campo di Marte – is the city's main venue for big-draw mainstream acts, such as Mark Knopfler and Lenny Kravitz.

Il Poggetto

Auditorium Flog Via Michele Mercati 24b ☏ 055.490.437, ⓦ www.flog.it. One of the city's best-known mid-sized venues, and a perennial student favourite – with a suitably downbeat studenty look and feel – for all forms of live music (and DJs), but particularly local indie-type bands. It's usually packed, despite a position way out in the northern suburbs at Il Poggetto; to get there take buses #8, #14, #20 or #28.

Perètola
Tenax Via Pratese 46 ☏ 055.308.160, ⓦ www

.dada.it/tenax. The city's longest-running venue for new and established bands, as well as big-name international acts. Keep an eye open for posters around town or call at the tourist office for upcoming gigs. The place is enormous but easy-going, and doubles as a club after hours (p.202). There are ranks of bars, pool tables, computer games and plenty of seating.

Classical music

The **Maggio Musicale**, Italy's oldest and most prestigious music festival, is the most conspicuous sign of the health of the city's classical music scene, though it should be said that the fare tends towards the conservative. In addition to the major festivals listed below, the city has numerous organizations that put on concerts at various times of the year. The **Amici della Musica** hosts a season of chamber concerts with top-name international performers from October to April, mostly in the Teatro della Pergola, occasionally in the Teatro Goldoni. Events are held throughout the year by the **Associazione Giovanile Musicale**: two of their best are the *Concerti di Pasqua*, a series of Easter concerts usually held in the church of Orsanmichele, and the *Festival Estate*, a festival held in July in the courtyard of the Palazzo Pitti.

The **Orchestra da Camera Fiorentina** (Florence Chamber Orchestra ⓦ www.orcafi.it) plays from March to October, often in Orsanmichele or the Badía Fiorentina, while from April to September concerts and dances in period dress are staged in the Oratorio di San Bernardino by the **Orchestra Historica di Firenze**. The main concert season of the Filarmonica di Firenze G. Rossini is in January and February, but in June it also performs a series of concerts in Piazza della Signoria, and Tuscany's major orchestra, the **Orchestra Regionale Toscana** (ⓦ www.orchestradellatoscana.it), plays one or two concerts a month in the city between November and May in the Teatro Verdi as well as a couple of concerts in the Bóboli Gardens. The Lutheran church on Lungarno Torrigiani regularly holds free chamber music and organ recitals.

Teatro Comunale Corso Italia 16 ☏ 055.213.535. Florence's main municipal theatre, out to the west of Santa Maria Novella, which hosts many of the city's major classical music, dance and theatre events. It has its own orchestra, chorus and dance company, attracting top-name international guest performers. The main season (concerts, opera and ballet) runs Jan–April and Sept–Dec, with concerts usually held on Friday, Saturday and Sunday evenings.
Teatro Goldoni Via Santa Maria 15 ☏ 055.210.804. This exquisite little eighteenth-century theatre, located a little way past the Pal-

azzo Pitti, is occasionally used for chamber music and opera performances, but lately it has hosted more dance productions than anything else.
Teatro della Pergola Via della Pergola 18 ☏ 055.226.4316, ⓦ www.pergola.firenze.it. The beautiful little Pergola was built in 1656 and is Italy's oldest surviving theatre – Verdi's *Macbeth* was first performed here. It plays host to chamber concerts, small-scale operas, and some of the best-known Italian theatre companies.
Teatro Verdi Via Ghibellina 99–101 ☏ 055.212.320, ⓦ www.teatroverdifirenze.it. Another of the city's premier music venues.

Music festivals

Maggio Musicale Fiorentino ⓦ www .maggiofiorentino.com. The highlight of Florence's cultural calendar and one of Europe's leading festivals of opera and classical music; confusingly, it isn't restricted to May (*Maggio*), but

lasts for a couple of months from late April or early May. The festival has its own orchestra, chorus and ballet company, plus guest appearances from foreign ensembles. Events are staged at the Teatro Comunale (or its Teatro Piccolo), the Teatro della

Florence's main cultural festivals are covered in the "Classical Music" section; what follows is a rundown on its more folkloric events.

Scoppio del Carro

The first major folk festival of the year is Easter Sunday's **Scoppio del Carro** (Explosion of the Cart), when a cartload of fireworks is hauled by six white oxen from the Porta a Prato to the Duomo; there, during the Gloria of the midday Mass, the whole lot is set off by a "dove" that whizzes down a wire from the high altar. The origins of this incendiary descent of the Holy Spirit lie with one Pazzino de' Pazzi, leader of the Florentine contingent on the First Crusade. On getting back to Florence he was entrusted with the care of the flame of Holy Saturday, an honorary office which he turned into something more festive by rigging up a ceremonial wagon to transport the flame round the city. His descendants continued to manage the festival until the Pazzi conspiracy of 1478, which of course lost them the office. Since then, the city authorities have taken care of business.

Festa del Grillo

On the first Sunday after Ascension Day (forty days after Easter), the **Festa del Grillo** (Festival of the Cricket) is held in the Cascine park. In amongst the stalls and the picnickers you'll find people selling tiny wooden cages containing crickets, which are then released onto the grass – a ritual that may hark back to the days when farmers had to scour their land for locusts, or to the tradition of men placing a cricket on the door of their lovers to serenade them.

St John's Day and the Calcio Storico

The saint's day of **John the Baptist**, Florence's patron, is June 24 – the occasion for a massive fireworks display up on Piazzale Michelangelo, and for the first game of the **Calcio Storico**. Played in sixteenth-century costume to perpetuate the memory of a game played during the siege of 1530, this uniquely Florentine mayhem is a three-match series staged in this last week of June, with fixtures usually held in Piazza Santa Croce (scene of that first match) and Piazza della Signoria. Each of the four historic quarters fields a team, Santa Croce playing in green, San Giovanni in red, Santa Maria Novella in blue and Santo Spirito in grossly impractical white. The prize for the winning side is a calf, which gets roasted in a street party after the tournament and shared among the four teams and the inhabitants of the winning quarter.

Festa delle Rificolone

The **Festa delle Rificolone** (Festival of the Lanterns) takes place on the Virgin's birthday, September 7, with a procession of children to Piazza Santissima Annunziata. Each child carries a coloured paper lantern with a candle inside it – a throwback to the days when people from the surrounding countryside would troop by lantern light into the city for the Feast of the Virgin. The procession is followed by a parade of floats and street parties.

Festa dell'Unità

October's **Festa dell'Unità** is part of a nationwide celebration run by the Italian communists. Florence's is the biggest event after Bologna's, with loads of political stalls and restaurant-marquees. Box Office will have details of venues, while news about the *Feste* and other political events in Florence can be found in *Anteprima*, a local supplement published with Friday's edition of the communist daily *L'Unità*.

Pergola, the Palazzo dei Congressi, the Teatro Verdi and occasionally in the Bóboli gardens. Informa- : tion and tickets can be obtained from the Teatro Comunale.

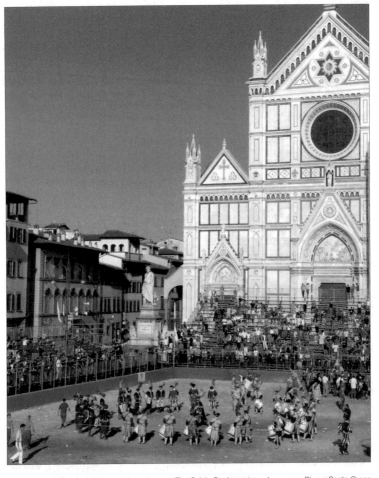

△ The Calcio Storico gets under way on Piazza Santa Croce

Estate Fiesolana ⓦ www.estatefiesolana.it.
Slightly less exclusive than the Maggio Musicale,
concentrating more on chamber and symphonic
music. It's held in Fiesole every summer, usually

from June to late August. Films and theatre are
also featured, and most events are held in the
open-air Teatro Romano.

Theatre

Should your Italian be up to a performance of plays by Machiavelli or Pirandello in the original, Florence's **theatres** offer year-round entertainment.
In addition to the places listed below, various halls and disused churches are
enlisted for one-off performances.

Stazione Leopolda Viale Fratelli Rosselli 5
ⓉⓉ055.212.622, ⓦ www.stazione-leopolda.com.
New contemporary arts centre in Florence's first

railway station, 1km west of Santa Maria Novella.
Built in 1848 and closed down in 1861, the old
station is a fine Neoclassical space for dance, arts

events and occasional concerts.

Teatro Comunale Corso Italia 16 ☎055.213.535. Florence's principal performance space hosts theatre productions, as well as dance and classical music concerts; offerings here are usually mainstream.

Teatro Le Laudi Via Leonardo da Vinci 2r ☎055.572.831. Located northeast of the centre, a few minutes' walk from San Marco; stages a fair amount of modern work.

Teatro della Pergola Via della Pergola 18 ☎055.226.4350, ⊕www.pergola.firenze.it. Fine old theatre, staging productions that are usually Italian, or foreign classics in translation. The season runs from October to April.

Teatro Verdi Via Ghibellina 99–101 ☎055.212.320, ⊕www.teatroverdifirenze.it. Productions at the Teatro Verdi are more or less similar to the mainstream fare of the Teatro Comunale, though you may also catch the odd musical.

Cinema

Florence has a large number of **cinemas**, but very few show subtitled films. The vast majority of English-language films are dubbed, though a couple of cinemas do regularly have undubbed screenings (*versione originale*). See *Firenze Spettacolo* or the listings pages of *La Nazione* for locations and latest screenings.

Florence has two major **film festivals**: Under Florence (first two weeks of Dec), which shows Italian independent films and videos, and the more earnest Festival dei Popoli (2 weeks in Nov or Dec), run by an academic institution concerned with documentary film. For information on both events contact the Cinema Alfieri Atelier, Via dell'Ulivo 6 (☎055.240.720).

Cinema Goldoni Via dei Serragli 109 ☎055.222.437. Florence's best cinema. Most weeks it has an English-language night, usually Wed. The shows are popular, however, so turn up early to be sure of a seat. Closed June & July.

Odeon Original Sound Via de' Sassetti 1 ☎055.214.068. Films are screened in their original language at this air-conditioned cinema once a week, generally on Mon, for most of the year, plus Tues and Thurs in summer.

Shopping

If you're after high-quality **clothes** and accessories, paintings, prints and marbled paper, or any number of other beautiful or luxury objects, then you'll find them in Florence – though this is not a city for the bargain-hunter. Its best-known area of manufacturing expertise is leather goods, with top-quality shoes, bags and gloves sold across the city. The main concentration of outlets is around **Via de' Tornabuoni** – the city's premier shopping thoroughfare – and the tributaries of Via degli Strozzi and Via della Vigna Nuova, also home to the shops of Italy's top fashion designers. If their prices are too steep, passable imitations (and outright fakes) can be unearthed at the various **street markets**, of which San Lorenzo is the most central. It's also worth having a look in the area of Via Matteo Palmieri and Borgo degli Albizi (a couple of minutes' walk east and north of the Bargello, respectively) for cheaper trendy clothes and jewellery.

If you want everything under one roof, there's also a handful of **department stores**. Marbled paper is another Florentine speciality, and, as you'd expect in this arty city, Florence is also one of the best places in the country to pick up **books** on Italian art, architecture and culture. The whole Ponte Vecchio is crammed with **jewellers'** shops, most of them catering strictly to the financial stratosphere. Those of more limited means could either take a chance on the counterfeits and low-cost originals peddled by the street vendors on and around the bridge, or check out our recommendations below. For delicatessens and **food** stores see the box on p.187, and for **wine** shops see the *enoteche* on p.197.

Markets

Cascine Parco del Cascine. The biggest of all Florence's markets happens Tuesday morning at the Cascine park near the banks of the Arno (bus #1, 9, 12 or 17c), where hundreds of stallholders set up an alfresco budget-class department store. Fewer tourists make it out here than to San Lorenzo, so prices are keener. Clothes (some secondhand) and shoes are the best bargains, though for cheaper still, you should check out the weekday morning stalls at Piazza delle Cure, just beyond Piazza della Libertà (bus #1 or #7; Tues 8am–1pm).

San Lorenzo Piazza di San Lorenzo. Another open-air warehouse of cheap clothing. San Lorenzo is as well organized as a shopping mall: huge waterproof awnings ensure that the weather can't stop the trading, and some of the stallholders even accept credit cards. You'll find plenty of leather jackets, T-shirts and other cheap clothes: it may be what you're looking for, but it may not be that much of a bargain. For anything pricey, try to haggle. Daily 8am–7pm.

Mercato Centrale Piazza del Mercato Centrale. Europe's largest indoor food hall is situated at the heart of the stall-filled streets around San Lorenzo, and is well worth a sightseeing and people-watching visit whether you intend to buy anything or not. Its popularity as a tourist sight has pushed prices up, but it's still unbeatable for picnic supplies. Mon–Sat 7am–2pm, plus Sat 4–8pm in winter.

Mercato Nuovo Loggia del Mercato Nuovo. Just to the west of Piazza della Signoria (and also known as the Mercato del Porcellino), this is the main emporium for straw hats, plastic *David*s and the like. Mid-Feb to mid-Nov daily 9am–7pm; mid-Nov to mid-Feb Tues–Sat 9am–5pm.

Mercato delle Pulci Piazza dei Ciompi. A flea market stacked with antiques and bric-a-brac, pitched every day near the Sant'Ambrogio food market. Summer Mon–Sat 10am–1pm & 4–7pm; winter Mon–Sat 9am–1pm & 3–7pm; also open same hours on last Sun of month. More serious antique dealers swell the ranks on the last Sunday of each month (same hours).

Mercato San Ambrogio Piazza Ghiberti. Big, cheap market just beyond Santa Croce, with food stalls in the central hall, as well as cheap clothes and leather. Mon–Sat 7am–2pm.

Books and maps

BM Borgo Ognissanti 4r ☎055.294.575. English-language bookshop selling a wide selection of guidebooks and general titles, with particular emphasis on Italian literature in translation, as well as books on Italian art, cookery and travel in Italy. Mon–Sat 9.30am–7.30pm; April–Dec also Sun 10.30am–1pm & 3.30–7pm.

Edison Piazza della Repubblica 27r ☎055.213.110. This US-style operation is arranged on four floors (with English-language books on the top), the stock is impressive and the opening hours unique. Mon–Sat 9am–midnight, Sun 10am–midnight.

Feltrinelli Via de' Cerretani 30r ☎055.238.2652, ⓦ www.feltrinelli.it. This branch of the Feltrinelli chain, a short distance west of the Duomo, is best for Italian titles, maps and guides. Mon–Fri 9am–7.30pm, Sat 10am–8pm, Sun 10.30am–1.30pm & 3.30–7.30pm.

Feltrinelli International Via Cavour 12–20r ☎055.219.524. Bright and well staffed, this is the first port of call for English or other foreign-language books, newspapers and videos, as well as posters, cards and magazines. Mon–Sat 9am–7.30pm.

Libreria EPT Via Condotta 42r ☎055.240.489. City maps and walking maps (1:25,000) of surrounding area. Mon 3.30–7.30pm, Tues–Sat 9.30am–1pm & 7.30pm.

McRae Via de' Neri 32r ☎055.238.2456, ⓦ www.mcraebooks.com/shop. Run by a former staff member of Seeber (see below), this bookshop, not far from the Uffizi, has one of the finest collections of English-language books in town: guides, cookery books, literature and art all covered. Daily 9am–7.30pm.

Paperback Exchange Via delle Oche 4r ☎055.293.460, ⓦ www.papex.it. A bit remote – north of Santa Croce – but always has a good stock of English and American books, with the

emphasis on Italian-related titles and secondhand stuff; also exchanges secondhand books and has informative and friendly staff. Mon–Fri 9am–7.30pm, Sat 10am–1pm & 3.30–7.30pm.
Seeber Via de' Cerretani 54r ☎ 055.215.697, ⓦ www.melbookstore.it. Displaced from its famous old HQ on Via de' Tornabuoni, the venerable Seeber now occupies a former cinema, and has been thoroughly "modernized" by its new owners. It's lost its soul in the process, but the stock is still impressive. Mon–Sat 9.30am–7.30pm.

Clothing

Armani Via de' Tornabuoni 44–50r ☎ 055.219.041, ⓦ www.armani.com. Gorgeous clothes from the most famous designer in Italy, at prices that make you think you must have misread the tag. Mon 10am–2pm & 3–7pm, Tues–Fri 10am–7pm, Sat 10.30am–7.30pm.
Compai Via Matteo Palmieri 6r ☎ 055.234.0606, ⓦ ww.compai.com. Whacky recycled vintage clothes by young designers. Mon 3.30–8pm, Tues–Sat noon–8pm.
Dolce e Gabbana Via della Vigna Nuova 27 ☎ 055.281.003. The Venetian-Sicilian double act are now in the same big league as Armani and Versace, but their extravagant – often camp – aesthetic hasn't been tamed by success. Mon 3–7pm, Tues–Sat 10am–7pm.
Emporio Armani Piazza Strozzi 14–17r ☎ 055.284.315, ⓦ www.emporioarmani.com. The lowest-priced wing of the Armani empire, this is the place to go if you're desperate to get the Armani label on your back. Mon 3.30–7.30pm, Tues–Sat 10am–1pm & 3.30–7.30pm.
Ferragamo Via de' Tornabuoni 14r t055.292.123. Salvatore Ferragamo emigrated to the US at the age of 14 and became the most famous shoemaker in the world, producing everything from pearl-studded numbers for Gloria Swanson to gladiators' sandals for Cecil B. de Mille. Managed by his widow and children, Ferragamo now produces ready-to-wear outfits, but the company's reputation still rests on its beautiful shoes. The shop, occupying virtually the entire ground floor of a colossal palazzo on Piazza Santa Trinita, is unbelievably grandiose. Mon–Sat 10am–7.30pm.
Gucci Via de' Tornabuoni 73r and 81r ☎ 055.264.011. The Gucci empire was founded at no. 73, which remains the flagship showroom, though the creative head of the company is no longer a member of the Gucci clan – Texan designer Tom Ford masterminded the reinvention of the label as one of the coolest around, before moving on in 2004. Mon 3–7pm, Tues–Sat 10am–7pm.
Luisa at Via Roma Via Roma 19–21r ☎ 055.217.826. A longstanding fixture at this address, gathering together a host of different labels every season, but with a tendency to play it safe. Mon–Sat 10am–7.30pm, Sun 11am–7pm.
Poncif Borgo Albizi 35r. Elegant contemporary women's fashion outlet, stocking a range of labels. Mon 3.30–7.30pm, Tues–Thurs 10am–1.30pm & 3.30–7.30pm, Fri & Sat 10am–7.30pm.
Prada Via de' Tornabuoni 51–55r & 67r ☎ 055.283.439, ⓦ www.prada.it. During the 1990s the severe style of Milanese designer Miuccia Prada became supremely trendy, and she's still riding high. Mon–Sat 10am–7.30pm, last Sun of the month 10am–7pm.
Pucci Via de' Tornabuoni 20–22r ☎ 055.294.028. The Pucci family was one of the city's mercantile dynasties, until Marchese Emilio Pucci gatecrashed the fashion world of the 1950s with his vivid, swirling-patterned silks, which remain the Pucci signature. Mon–Sat 10am–7pm Sun 2–7pm.
Raspini Via Por Santa Maria 70r & Via Roma 25r ☎ 055.213.077, ⓦ www.raspini.com. Florence's biggest multi-label clothes shop, with a good stock of diffusion lines. These are the two main branches, and there's a third one at Via de' Martelli 5–7r. Mon 3.30–7.30pm, Tues–Sat 10.30am–7.30pm.

Department stores

Coin Via dei Calzaiuoli 56r, but with entrances on all four sides of the block, ☎ 055.280.531, ⓦ www.coin.it. Clothes-dominated chain store in an excellent central position. Quality is generally high, though styles are fairly conservative except for one or two youth-oriented franchises on the ground floor. Also a good place for linen and other household goods. Mon–Sat 10am–8pm, Sun 11am–8pm.

Rinascente Piazza della Repubblica 1 ☎ 055.239.8544, ⓦ www.rinascente.it. Like Coin, Rinascente is part of a countrywide chain, though this store, opened in 1996, is a touch more upmarket than its nearby rival. Sells clothing, linen, cosmetics, household goods and other staples. Mon–Sat 9am–9pm, Sun 10.30am–8pm.

Jewellery

Alessandro Dari Via San Nicolò 115r ☎ 055.244.747, ⊛ www.alessandrodari.com. This goldsmith's workshop, in eastern Oltrarno, produces intricate rings with musical and architectural motifs. You can walk around the display of Alessandro's work to loud classical music as the master works away. Mon–Sat 9.30am–1.30pm & 4–7.30pm.

Dettagli per donzelle, comari e sognatori Borgo degli Albizi 40r ☎ 055.234.0333. Funky, brightly coloured handmade jewellery and accessories at reasonable prices. Mon 3.30–7.30pm, Tues–Sat 10am–7.30pm.

Gatto Bianco Borgo SS Apostoli 12r ☎ 055.282.989. Strange combinations of precious and everyday materials are the signature of this outlet, one of the city's more adventurous jewellery workshops. Mon 3.30–7.30pm, Tues–Sat 9.30am–1pm & 3.30–7.30pm.

Moltissimo Via Matteo Palmieri 27r ☎ 055.242.038. Remodelled vintage jewellery – strong on 50s style – and accessories, as well as pleasingly simple designs of retro hand-painted china. Mon–Sat 10.30am–7.30pm.

Torrini Piazza del Duomo 10r ☎ 055.230.2401. Torrini registered its trademark – a distinctive half-clover leaf with spur – as early as 1369. Seven centuries later this store remains one of the premier places to buy Florentine jewellery: gold predominates, but all manner of classic and modern pieces are available, at a price. Mon 3–7pm, Tues–Sat 10am–1.30pm & 2.30–7pm.

Music

Alberti Via de' Pucci 16r & Borgo San Lorenzo 45–49r ☎ 055.284.346. Founded in 1873, this is the city's leading supplier of domestic hi-fi, videos, records and CDs. The Borgo San Lorenzo store is good for opera, classical and jazz, while the Via de' Pucci shop (a couple of blocks to the east) concentrates on contemporary music (dance, rock etc). June–Sept Mon 3.30–7.30pm, Tues–Sat 9am–7.30pm; Oct–May Mon–Fri 9am–7.30pm, Sat 9am–1pm.

Data Records 93 Via de' Neri 15r ☎ 055.287.592. Huge collection of new and secondhand albums covering rock, pop, reggae, jazz, punk, heavy metal etc, not far from the Uffizi.

Fenice Via Santa Reparata 8b ☎ 055.238.1880. Small record shop in the back streets beyond San Lorenzo, with a fantastic stock of classical music and helpful staff. They also have a smaller selection of jazz and other music. Mon–Sat 9am–1pm & 3.30–7.30pm.

Ricordi Media Store Via Brunelleschi 8–10r ☎ 055.214.104. The city's biggest general CD store, just off Piazza della Repubblica. Mon–Sat 9am–7.30pm, plus Sept–June last Sun of month 3.30–7.30pm.

Paper and stationery

Giulio Giannini e Figlio Piazza Pitti 36r ☎ 055.212.621, ⊛ www.giuliogiannini.it. Established in 1856, this paper-making and book-binding firm has been honoured with exhibitions dedicated to its work. Once the only place in Florence to make its own marbled papers, it now offers a wide variety of diaries, address books and so forth as well. Mon–Sat 10am–7.30pm, Sun 10.30am–6.30pm.

Il Papiro Via Cavour 55r ☎ 055.215.262, ⊛ www.ilpapirofirenze.it. Huge range of marbled paper and gifts in seven outlets around the city, including Via de' Tavolini 13r and Piazza del Duomo 24r. Mon–Sat 10am–1pm, 2–7.30pm.

Pineider Piazza della Signoria 13r & Via de' Tornabuoni 76r ☎ 055.284.655. Pineider sells briefcases, picture frames and other accessories for home and office, but their reputation rests on their colour co-ordinated calling cards, handmade papers and envelopes – as used by Napoleon, Stendhal, Byron and Shelley, to name just a few past customers. Mon 3–7pm, Tues–Fri 10am–1.30pm & 2.30–7pm, plus Sat 2.30–7pm in July & Aug; closed 2nd week of Aug.

Il Torchio Via de' Bardi 17 ☎ 055.234.2862. A marbled paper workshop using manufacturing techniques known only to the owner. Desk accessories, diaries, albums and other items in paper and leather are also available. Mon–Fri 9am–7.30pm, Sat 9.30am–1pm.

Perfume and toiletries

Farmacia Santa Maria Novella Via della Scala 16 ☎ 055.216.276, ⊛ www.smnovella.it. Occupying the pharmacy of the Santa Maria Novella monastery, this sixteenth-century shop was founded by Dominican monks as an outlet for their potions, ointments and herbal remedies. Many of these are still available, including distillations of flowers and herbs, together with face-creams, shampoos, and other, more esoteric products. The shop's as famous for its wonderful interior as for its products, which are sold worldwide. Mon–Sat 9.30am–7.30pm, Sun 10.30am–6.30pm.

Prints and photos

Alinari Largo Alinari 15 ☎ 055.239.51, ⊛ www.alinari.com. Founded in 1852, this is the world's oldest photographic business. Owners of the best archive of old photographs in Italy – 400,000 glass plates and 700,000 negatives – they will print any image you choose from their huge catalogue. They also publish books, calendars, posters and cards. Tues–Fri 9am–1pm & 2.30–6.30pm, Sat 9am–1pm 3–7pm; closed two weeks in mid-Aug.

Shoes, bags, gloves and hats

Borsalino Via Porta Rossa 40r ☎ 055.218.275. Fine trad hat shop for men, with some genuine fold-away Panamas. Another branch at Via della Vigna Nuova 60r sells women's hats and younger styles.

Cellerini Via del Sole 37r ☎ 055.282.533. Bags, bags and more bags. Everything here is made on the premises under the supervision of the firm's founders, the city's premier exponents of the craft; bags don't come more elegant, durable – or costly. Summer Mon–Fri 9am–1pm & 3–7pm, Sat 9am–1pm; winter Mon 3–7pm, Tues–Sat 9am–1pm & 3–7pm.

Cristina e i suoi Colori Piazza N. Sauro 8r ☎ 055.268.605. Located at the southern end of Ponte alla Carraia, *Cristina and her Colours* is as the name suggests – it's overflowing with dramatic, colourful handmade hats, bags, jewellery and lovely flower-shaped lamps. Mon 4–8pm, Tues–Sat 10.30am–1.30pm & 4–8pm.

Spezieria Erborista Palazzo Vecchio Via Vaccherccia 9r ☎ 055.239.6055. A celebrated old shop, selling its own natural remedies and a range of unique perfumes, such as Acqua di Caterina de' Medici. July & Aug Mon–Fri 9am–7.30pm, Sat 9am–5pm; Sept–June Mon–Sat 9.30am–7.30pm, 1st and last Sun of month 1.30–7pm.

Giovanni Baccani Via della Vigna Nuova 75r ☎ 055.214.467. You'll see prints and engravings in shops across Florence, but nowhere is the selection as mouthwatering as in Baccani, a beautiful old shop (established in 1903) that's crammed with all manner of prints, frames and paintings. Prices range from a few euros into the realms of credit card madness. Mon 3.30–7.30pm, Tues–Sat 9am–1pm & 3.30–7.30pm; July closed Sat afternoons; closed first three weeks of Aug.

Francesco da Firenze Via Santo Spirito 62r ☎ 055.212.428. Handmade shoes for men and women at very reasonable prices. Classical footwear combined with striking designs. Mon–Sat 9am–1pm & 3.30–7.30pm; Aug closed Sat afternoon.

Madova Via Guicciardini 1r ☎ 055.239.6526. The last word in gloves – every colour, every size, every style. Prices range from around €35 to €90. Mon–Sat 9.30am–7.30pm.

Mannina Via Guicciardini 16r ☎ 055.282.895. This famed Oltrarno shoemaker has been going for donkey's years, producing beautifully made and sensible footwear at prices that are far from extravagant. Mon–Sat 9.30am–7.30pm, Sun 10.30am–1pm & 2–6pm.

Stefano Bemer Borgo San Frediano 143r ☎ 055.211.356, ⊛ www.bemers.it. If you're in the market for made-to-measure Italian shoes, there's no better place than this. Mon–Sat 9am–1pm & 3.30–7.30pm.

Listings

Banks and exchange Florence's main bank branches are on or around Piazza della Repubblica, but exchange booths (*cambio*) and ATM cash card machines (*bancomat*) for Visa and Mastercard advances can be found across the city. Banks generally open Mon–Fri 8.20am–1.20pm and 2.35–3.35pm, though some are open longer hours. A useful Travelex branch is at Lungarno Acciaiuoli

6r (Mon–Sat 9am–6pm, Sun 9.30am–5pm; ☎ 055.289.781); American Express is at Via Dante Alighieri 22r (Mon–Fri 9am–5.30pm, Sat 9am–12.30pm; ☎ 055.50.981).

Bike, scooter & moped rental Alinari, Via Guelfa 85r ☎ 055.280.500, ⊛ www.alinarirental .com; Florence by Bike, Via San Zanobi 120–122r ☎ 055.488.992, ⊛ www.florencebybike.it (they also do repairs); or Geordie Chopin at Via Fiesolana 10r ☎055.245.013 (Mon–Sat 9am–1pm & 3–7.30pm; for rental or repair of bicycles only). There are more scooter rental places on Borgo Ognissanti.

Bus information City buses are run by ATAF ☎800.424.500, ⓦwww.ataf.net. For details of buses to Siena, see p.212.

Car rental Avis, Borgo Ognissanti 128r ☎055.239.8826; Europcar, Borgo Ognissanti 53r ☎055.290.437/8; Excelsior, Via Lulli 76 ☎055.321.5397; Hertz, Via Maso Finiguerra 33r ☎055.282.260; Italy by Car/Thrifty, Borgo Ognissanti 134r ☎055.287.161; Maggiore, Via Maso Finiguerra 31r ☎055.210.238; Program, Borgo Ognissanti 135r ☎055.282.916.

Consulates UK, Lungarno Corsini 2 ☎055.284.133, Ⓔconsular.florence@fco.gov.uk; US, Lungarno Amerigo Vespucci 38 ☎055.266.951.

Doctors The Tourist Medical Service is a private service used to dealing with foreigners; they have doctors on call 24 hours a day on ☎055.475.411 (ⓦwww.medicalservice.firenze.it), or you can visit their clinic at Via Lorenzo il Magnifico 59 (Mon–Fri 11am–noon & 5–6pm, Sat 11am–noon). Note that you'll need insurance cover to recoup the cost of a consultation, which will be at least e50. Florence's central hospital is on Piazza Santa Maria Nuova.

Emergencies Police ☎112 or t113; Fire ☎115; car breakdown ☎116; first aid ☎118. If your passport is lost or stolen, report it to the police and contact your consulate.

Flight information Aeroporto Galileo Galilei, Pisa ☎050.849.300, ⓦwww.pisa-airport.com; information also from the check-in desk at Santa Maria Novella train station, platform 5 (daily 7am–8pm). Aeroporto Florence-Perètola (Amerigo Vespucci), Via del Termine 11 ☎055.306.1300, ⓦwww .safnet.it – for recorded information on international flights call ☎055.306.1702, on domestic flights ☎055.306.1700. Aeroporto G. Marconi, Bologna, ⓦwww. bologna-airport.it, ☎051. 647.9615.

Internet cafés D@dov@go, Via dei Seragli 80r; *Internet Train* (ⓦwww.internettrain.it) – more than a dozen outlets, including Via de Benci 36r (open till 1am), Via Guelfa 54/56r and Piazza Stazione 1; *La Ch@t*, Via Ghibellina 98r (open till midnight); *meridiaNet*, Borgo San Frediano 5r (Mon–Fri 11am–10.30pm, Sat & Sun 2–9pm); *Net Village*, Via San Egidio 10r (daily 9am–midnight); *Webpuccino*, Via dei Conti 22r (Mon–Sat 10am–10pm, Sun noon–9pm); *WWW village*, Via degli Alfini 11/13. Most charge around €4.50 an hour; the tourist office has a full list.

Laundry Florence has plenty of self-service *lavanderie* costing around €3–4 for a complete wash, with the main concentration being near the one-star hotels of the station and San Lorenzo districts. Ask at your hotel for the nearest, or head for one of the following: Guelfa, Via Guelfa 106r; Onda Blu, Via degli Alfani 24r; Self Service, Via Faenza 26r; Wash & Dry, which has eleven sites in the city open till 10pm, including Via dei Servi 105r, Via della Scala 52r, Via del Sole 29r, Via Ghibellina 143r, Via dei Serragli 87r and Via Nazionale 129r.

Left luggage Santa Maria Novella station by platform 16 (daily 6am–midnight); €3.80 per piece for 5hr, then €0.60 per hour. You'll need to produce some form of identification.

Lost property Lost property handed into the city or railway police ends up at Via Circondaria 17b (Sept–July Mon, Wed, Fri & Sat 9am–noon, Tues & Thurs 9am–noon & 2.30–4.30pm; Aug Mon–Fri 9am–noon; ☎055.367.943; take bus #23 to Viale Corsica). There's also a lost property office at Santa Maria Novella station, on platform 16 next to left luggage (daily 7am–noon; ☎055.235.2190).

Pharmacies The Farmacia Comunale, on the train station concourse, is open 24hr, as is All' Insegna del Moro, Piazza San Giovanni 20r, on the north side of the Baptistery, and Farmacia Molteni, Via dei Calzaiuoli 7r. Normal opening hours for pharmacies are Mon–Sat 8.30am–1pm & 4–8pm. All pharmacies display a late-night roster in their window; otherwise ring ☎182 for information.

Police Emergency ☎112 or 113. The Questura, where you should report a lost passport or a theft, is at Via Zara 2 (daily 8am–8pm; translator on hand 8am–2pm; ☎055.49.771). If you do report a theft or other crime, you will have to fill out a form (*una denuncia*): this may be time-consuming, but it's essential if you want to make a claim on your travel insurance on returning home.

Post office The main central post office is near Piazza della Repubblica at Via Pellicceria 8 (Mon–Sat 8.15am–7pm); the poste restante section is through the door immediately on the left as you enter. If you're having mail sent to you poste restante, make sure it's marked for Via Pellicceria, otherwise it will go to Florence's biggest post office, at Via Pietrapiana 53–55 (Mon–Fri 8.15am–7pm, Sat 8.15am–12.30pm). If all you want is stamps (*francobolli*), then it's easier to buy them at a tobacconist's (*tabaccaio*), which are marked by a sign outside with a white "T" on a blue background.

Toilets Public toilets are usually open 10am–6pm daily and cost €0.60. They are marked on a map given out by the tourist office. Locations include the top of Via Filippina behind the Bargello; at the tourist office on Borgo Santa Croce; in the subway at Santa Maria Novella station; and Via della Stuffa 25, near the Mercato Centrale.

Travel details

Trains

Florence to: Ancona (hourly; 2hr 30min–4hr); Arezzo (hourly; 1hr); Assisi (11 daily; 2hr 35min); Bari (12 daily; 8hr 15min–9hr); Bologna (every 30min; 1hr 5min–1hr 40min); Bolzano (14 daily; 4hr 10min–5hr 50min); Borgo San Lorenzo (hourly; 70min); Empoli (every 20min; 25min); Foligno (11 daily; 2hr 55min); Genoa (hourly; 3hr 10min–4hr 30min); Lecce (7 daily; 10hr 25min–12hr); Livorno (12 daily; 1hr 30min); Lucca (hourly; 1hr 5min–1hr 50min); Milan (18 daily; 2hr 50min–4hr 50min); Naples (2 daily; 4hr); Perugia (12 daily; 2hr 10min); Pisa airport (7 daily; 70–90min); Pisa central (hourly; 55min); Pistoia (hourly; 30–45min); Prato (every 30min; 20min); Reggio Calabria (from Campo di Marte station: 4 daily; 11hr; from Santa Maria Novella station: 7 daily, change at Rome; 11hr); Rimini (hourly; 3hr 30min–6hr); Rome (hourly; 2hr 15min–3hr 30min); Siena (via hourly connection at Empoli; 1hr 20min); Trieste (9 daily, usually changing at Venice-Mestre; 5hr–6hr 15min); Udine (10 daily; 5hr 20min–6hr); Venice central (hourly; 3hr 25min–4hr 10min); Venice-Mestre (10 daily; 2hr 45min–3hr 20min); Verona (14 daily; 2hr 40min–3hr 40min); Viareggio (hourly; 1hr 30min–2hr 25min).

Buses

Most buses to destinations outside the city depart from the bus station at Via Santa Caterina da Siena 17, immediately west of the train station. Of the companies operating intertown buses from Florence, only SITA publishes a reliable timetable.

CAP Largo Fratelli Alinari 9 ☎ 055.214.637. Buses to Borgo San Lorenzo, Impruneta, Montepiano and Prato.

CAT Via Fiume 2 ☎ 055.283.400. Buses to Anghiari, Arezzo, Caprese, Città di Castello, Figline Valdarno, Incisa Valdarno and Sansepolcro.

CLAP Piazza Stazione 15 ☎ 055.283.734. Buses to Lucca and Lucca province.

COPIT Piazza Santa Maria Novella ☎ 055.215.451. Buses to Abetone, Pistoia, Poggio a Caiano and Vinci.

Lazzi Piazza Stazione 1 ☎ 166.845.010. Buses to Abetone, Calenzano, Cerreto Guidi, Empoli, Forte dei Marmi, Incisa Valdarno, Livorno, Lucca, Marina di Carrara, Marina di Massa, Montecatini Terme, Montevarchi, Pescia, Pisa, Pistoia, Pontassieve, Pontedera, Prato, Signa, Tirrenia, Torre del Lago and Viareggio.

SITA Via Santa Caterina di Siena 15 (Tuscany routes ☎ 055.483.651, national routes ☎ 055.214.721). Buses to: Barberino di Mugello (17 daily; 40min); Bibbiena (8 daily; 2hr 15min); Castellina in Chianti (1 daily; 1hr 35min); Certaldo (4 daily; 1hr 40min); Gaiole (2 daily Mon–Fri; 2hr); Greve (around 30 daily; 1hr 5min); Poggibonsi (10 daily; 1hr 20min); Pontassieve (12 daily; 50min); Poppi (9 daily; 2hr 5min); Radda in Chianti (1 daily Mon–Sat; 1hr 40min); San Casciano (14 daily; 40min); Siena (12 expresses daily; 1hr 15min; also 9 stopping services); Volterra (6 daily; 2hr 25min).

2

Around Florence

CHAPTER 2   Highlights

* **Medici villas** Explore the country houses of Florence's pre-eminent family. See p.218

* **Chianti** The country's most famous vineyards. See p.222

* **Prato** A handsome medieval centre lurks within Prato's palisade of factories. See p.236

* **Pistoia** Off the tourist trail, but well worth a day's investigation for some remarkable sculptures. See p.241

* **Certaldo** The quintessential hill-town: tiny and perfectly preserved. See p.255

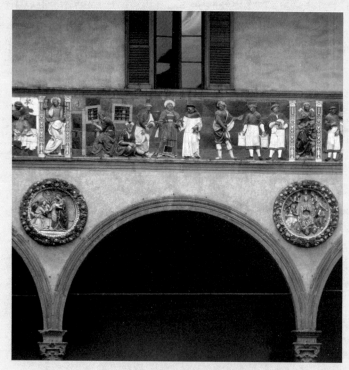

△ Ospedale del Ceppo, Pistoia

Around Florence

H aving paid their respects to the sights of Florence, most people doing a Tuscan tour set off for another of the big-league towns, such as Siena or Pisa, leapfrogging the city's immediate surroundings. Yet there's a lot to be gained by lingering a few days in this area, either using Florence as a base, or staying at a couple of the smaller places within the city's orbit.

Inside the boundaries of Greater Florence, city buses run to the village of **Fiesole**, once Florence's keenest rival, and to many of the **Medici villas**, countryside retreats now all but engulfed by the suburbs. Farther afield but readily accessible by train, the busy commercial centre of **Prato** and quiet provincial capital of **Pistoia** each make fine day-trips, with their medieval buildings and Florentine-inspired Renaissance art – and either could be used as a springboard for exploring some of the more obscure corners of Tuscany.

West of Florence, an industrialized stretch of the Arno valley leads to **Empoli**, the point of access for a number of upland attractions: **Vinci** (Leonardo da Vinci's village), the imperial settlement of **San Miniato** and the hill-towns of **Castelfiorentino** and **Certaldo**. To the north and south of Florence lie two rural regions that require independent transport for proper investigation: the **Mugello**, the lush agricultural area around the upper valley of the Sieve river; and **Chianti**, Italy's premier wine region and expatriate settlement.

The places covered in this chapter lie on or very near several of the principal routes through Tuscany, and can easily be visited on a journey between major centres. Three of these routes radiate from Florence: to Pisa (via Empoli); to Lucca (via Prato and Pistoia); and to Siena (via Chianti). The first two can be done by train or bus, the third by bus only. The fourth route – from Empoli to Siena via Castelfiorentino and Certaldo – is again possible by train or bus, though if you intend stopping off at San Gimignano, which is really the point of this trip, only the bus will do.

Fiesole

The hill-town of **FIESOLE**, which spreads over a cluster of hills above the Mugnone and Arno valleys some 8km northeast of Florence, is conventionally described as a pleasant retreat from the crowds and heat of summertime Florence. Unfortunately, its tranquillity has been so well advertised that in high season it's now hardly less busy than Florence itself; you'd probably also need paranormal sensitivity to detect much climatic difference between the two on an airless August afternoon.

AROUND FLORENCE

That said, Fiesole offers a grandstand view of the city, has something of the feel of a country village, and bears many traces of its history – which is actually lengthier than that of Florence. First settled in the Bronze Age, then later by the Etruscans, and then absorbed by the Romans, it rivalled its neighbour until the early twelfth century, when the Florentines overran the town. From that time it became a satellite, favoured as a semi-rural second home for wealthier citizens such as the ubiquitous Medici.

Fiesole is one of the easiest short trips from Florence: ATAF city **bus** #7 runs from Santa Maria Novella train station to Fiesole's central Piazza Mino da Fiesole (every 15–20min; takes 20min; €0.80). Fiesole's **tourist office** is nearby at Via Portigiani 3/5, next to the entrance to the archeological site (March–Oct Mon–Sat 9am–6pm, Sun 10am–1pm, 2–6pm; Nov–Feb Mon–Sat 9am–5pm, Sun 10am–4pm; ☎055.598.720, ⓦwww.comune.fiesole.fi.it).

The Town

When the Florentines wrecked Fiesole in 1125, the only major building they spared was the **Duomo**, on the edge of Piazza Mino. Subsequently, nineteenth-century restorers managed to ruin the exterior, which is now notable only for its lofty campanile. The most interesting part of the bare interior is the raised choir: the altarpiece is a polyptych, painted in the 1440s by Bicci di Lorenzo, and the Cappella Salutati, to the right, contains two fine pieces carved around the same time by Mino da Fiesole: an altar frontal of the Madonna and Saints and the tomb of Bishop Salutati. Fiesole's patron saint, St Romulus, is buried underneath the choir in the ancient crypt. Behind the Duomo at Via Dupré 1, the **Museo Bandini** (summer daily 10am–7pm; winter 10am–5pm, closed Tues; joint ticket valid all day covering admission to all Fiesole's museums €6.50; Ⓦ www.fiesolemusei.it) possesses a collection of glazed terracotta in the style of the della Robbias, the odd piece of Byzantine ivory work and a few thirteenth- and fourteenth-century Tuscan pictures, none of them inspiring.

Across the road from the museum are the town's other museums: the **Teatro Romano**, and the **Museo Archeologico** (same times and ticket as Museo Bandini). Built in the first century BC, the 3000-seat theatre was excavated towards the end of the nineteenth century and is in such good repair that it's used for performances during the Estate Fiesolana festival in July and August (see p.62). Parts of the site may be closed as excavation work continues. Most of the exhibits in the site's small **museum** were excavated in this area, and encompass pieces from the Bronze Age to Roman occupation.

Fiesole's other major churches, Sant'Alessandro and San Francesco, are at the top of the steep Via San Francesco, which runs past the **Oratorio di San Jacopo** (Sat & Sun 10am–7pm; same ticket as the museums), a little chapel containing a fifteenth-century fresco and some ecclesiastical treasures. A little further up, a terrace offers a knockout view of Florence. **Sant'Alessandro** was founded in the sixth century on the site of Etruscan and Roman temples; repairs have rendered the outside a whitewashed nonentity, but the beautiful *marmorino cipollino* (onion marble) columns of the basilical interior make it the most atmospheric building in Fiesole. Again, restoration has not improved the Gothic **San Francesco**, which occupies the site of the acropolis: the interior is a twentieth-century renovation, but the tiny cloisters are genuine. The church itself contains an *Immaculate Conception* by Piero di Cosimo (second altar on right), and below the church is a small museum featuring material gathered mainly by missions to the Far East, much of it from China, as well as a piece of Etruscan wall. From the front of San Francesco a gate opens into a wooded public park, the most pleasant descent back to Piazza Mino.

If you want to wring every last drop of historical significance from Fiesole, you could follow the signposts from here up the hill to the east of the Teatro, to the ruins of a couple of **Etruscan tombs** from the third century BC.

To San Domenico

The most enjoyable excursion from Fiesole is a wander down the narrow Via Vecchia Fiesolana, which passes the **Villa Medici** – built for Cosimo il Vecchio by Michelozzo – on its way to the hamlet of **SAN DOMENICO**. Fra' Angelico was once prior of the Dominican **monastery** at this village and the church retains a *Madonna and Angels* by him, in the first chapel on the left; the chapterhouse also has a Fra' Angelico fresco of *The Crucifixion* (ring at no. 4).

Five minutes' walk northwest from San Domenico stands the **Badia Fiesolana** (Mon–Fri 8.30am–6.30pm), Fiesole's cathedral from the ninth century to the eleventh. Cosimo il Vecchio had the church altered in the 1460s, a project which kept the magnificent Romanesque facade intact while transforming the interior into a superb Renaissance building.

Practicalities

Fiesole's **tourist office** is at Piazza Mino da Fiesole 37 (Mon–Sat 8.30am–1.30pm; ☎055.598.720, ⊛www.comune.fiesole.fi.it). Fiesole itself is small enough to be explored in a morning, but the country lanes of its surroundings invite a more leisurely tour, and might even tempt you to stay.

Accommodation on a tight budget is a problem. The charming one-star *Villa Sorriso*, Via Gramsci 21 (☎055.59.027; ✉s.benigni@inwind.it; ❷), is the cheapest close to the centre; 2km farther out, *Villa Baccano*, Via Bosconi 4 (☎055.59.341, ⊛www.villabaccano.it; ❷), is fractionally more expensive. At the other end of the scale, Fiesole boasts one of Tuscany's most sybaritic hotels, the astronomically expensive *Villa San Michele*, Via Doccia 4 (☎055.567.8200, ⊛www.villasanmichele.orient-express.com; ❾ – doubles from around €800), occupying a former monastery that was designed in part by Michelangelo, surrounded by gorgeous parkland, offering terrific views of Florence, and boasting a great restaurant: a once-in-a-lifetime kind of place. For more modest meals, you can't do better than the *San Domenico* trattoria-pizzeria, at Piazza San Domenico 11, which draws a lot of customers from the nearby European University. Details of Fiesole's **campsite**, *Camping Panoramico*, are on p.92.

The Medici villas

The finest country houses of the Florentine hinterland are, predictably enough, those built for the **Medici**. The earliest of these were primarily intended as fortified refuges to which the family could withdraw when the political temperature in the city became a little too hot. In time, as the family grew more secure, the houses became somewhere to show off the humanistic culture of the Medici. In the sixteenth and seventeenth centuries, with the Medici established as unchallenged rulers of Florence, the villas became more ostentatious, as if to express the might of the dynasty through their sheer luxuriousness. The land they were built on later became a valuable asset: when Florence's importance as a manufacturing centre was diminished, the Medici were able to divert some resources into agriculture.

Not every Medici villa is covered in this section, just the ones that are easily accessible on a day-trip from Florence and whose interior or grounds are open to the public. The villas of Trebbio and Cafaggiolo are described later in this chapter (see p.235), while the Villa Medici at Cerreto Guidi, closer to Empoli than to Florence, is dealt with on p.251.

This section also includes a few sights which can be visited on an excursion to one of the houses – the church at **Carmignano**, for example, with its remarkable Pontormo altarpiece.

Villa Medicea La Petraia

The **Villa La Petraia** was adapted from a medieval castle in the 1570s and 1580s by Buontalenti, working to a commission from the future Grand Duke Ferdinando I (bus # 28 from Santa Maria Novella train station – ask the driver to set you down near the villa). Only the watchtower of the fortress was retained, to serve as a high-rise belvedere above the simple two-storey house. The **interior** (daily: June–Aug 8.15am–8pm; April, May & Sept closes 7pm; March & Oct closes 6pm; Nov–Feb closes 5pm; closed 1st & 3rd Mon of month; €2, includes gardens of Villa di Castello) was altered in turn by Vittorio Emanuele II, who glassed over the interior courtyard to convert it into a ballroom. Its walls are covered by a seventeenth-century fresco cycle glorifying the Medici and the Knights of St Stephen, a pseudo-chivalric order founded by Cosimo I to rid the Tuscan coast of pirates. The suffocating style of the House of Savoy tends to prevail in the villa's apartments, though this is offset by the occasional sixteenth-century tapestry or painting. There is also Giambologna's bronze statue of *Venus*, now transplanted indoors from the fountain on the upper terrace of the garden.

Laid out in geometrical order, in half-hearted imitation of the Castello estate, the garden isn't much to get excited about, but the **park** behind the villa to the east is glorious, with its ancient cypress trees (grounds close 1hr later than the villa).

Villa Medicea di Castello

From Villa La Petraia, follow Via della Petraia past Villa Bel Riposo (where Carlo Lorenzini wrote *Pinocchio*) to the Baroque Villa Corsini, from where Via di Castello leads to the **Villa di Castello**. This house was bought in 1477 by Lorenzo and Giovanni de' Medici, second cousins of Lorenzo il Magnifico, and the principal patrons of Botticelli; the *Birth of Venus* and the *Primavera* both used to hang here. Wrecked after the expulsion of the Medici, it was rebuilt for Cosimo I, and is now the headquarters of the Accademia della Crusca, the society charged with maintaining the purity of the Italian language.

The society doesn't allow visitors into the house, but that's no great hardship, as its Pontormo and Bronzino frescoes perished a long time back, and the villa's fame rests entirely on its **gardens** (same hours & ticket as Villa La Petraia), which were laid out by Tribolo for Cosimo and continued by Buontalenti, who also redesigned the house. Had the full scheme been carried out, over fifty sculptural tableaux would have represented the seasons, the virtues, the landscapes of Tuscany and, of course, the triumphs of the Medici. Even in a state of semi-completion, Castello's gardens were astonishing (delighted by their labyrinths, sculptures, fountains and myriad water tricks, Montaigne judged them to be the best in Europe). Of the surviving eccentricities, the outstanding set pieces are Ammannati's colossal shivering figure of *January*, the triple-bowled fountain topped by the same sculptor's *Hercules and Antaeus*, and the *Grotto degli*

Animali by Giambologna and his school – a man-made cave against the walls of which are stacked a menagerie of plaster birds and animals (the bronze originals of some of these are on show in the Bargello in Florence).

Villa Medicea di Careggi

Originally a fortified farmhouse, the **Villa di Careggi**, 5km northwest of central Florence, came into the possession of the Medici in 1417 and was altered by Michelozzo for Cosimo il Vecchio in the 1430s. It was the old man's favourite home: he brought his private library out here and hung the walls with paintings by his protégés. Cosimo died here, too, as did his son Piero and grandson Lorenzo il Magnifico, with whom the house is particularly associated, as it was here that his academy of Platonic scholars used to meet. Bus #14C runs from Florence train station to the villa, or you can follow the signposts and walk from Villa La Petraia.

Low-slung and blank-faced, Careggi is not a gracious building, its one amusing touch being a fresco in one of the garden loggias: it depicts a man being thrown down a well, demonstrating the fate of the doctor whose incompetence was (apparently unjustly) alleged to have resulted in the death of Lorenzo. The villa is now a nurses' home, and the interior can be viewed only by appointment (℡055.427.7981; visits Mon–Fri 9am–6pm, Sat 9am–noon), although the extensive surrounding gardens and woodland can be explored freely.

Poggio a Caiano and around

For the most complete picture of what life was like in the Medici villas in the family's heyday, you should make the trip to the **Villa Medici di Poggio a Caiano** (same hours as La Petraia; €2), 18km northwest of Florence, on the crest of the main road through the village of **POGGIO A CAIANO**. A COPIT bus heads to the village from Florence train station (every 30min; takes 30min), or you could take the CAP bus #M from Prato.

Lorenzo il Magnifico bought a farmhouse on this site in 1480 and commissioned Giuliano da Sangallo to rebuild it as a classical rural palace – the only architectural project instigated by Lorenzo that has survived, and the first Italian house to be built specifically as a place of country leisure. Raised on a kind of arcaded podium, it is the most elegant of the Medici villas and its impact is enhanced by later additions: the entrance loggia, for instance, was commissioned by Lorenzo's son Giovanni, the future Pope Leo X, and the curving double stairway was added in the eighteenth century. The house was often used to accommodate guests of state before they made ceremonial entrance into Florence: Charles V stayed here, and it was at Poggio a Caiano that Eleanor of Toledo was introduced to her future husband, Cosimo I.

You enter the villa through the basement, where the plush **games room** and private **theatre** hint at the splendour to come. Upstairs, the focal point is the double-height **salone** which Sangallo created out of the courtyard between the two main blocks, and which Vasari pronounced the most beautiful room in the world. Its sixteenth-century frescoes include del Sarto's *Caesar Receiving Egyptian Tribute* (the giraffe shown in the background was a gift to Lorenzo from the Sultan of Egypt), Franciabigio's *Triumph of Cicero* (a reference to Cosimo il Vecchio's return from exile) and, best of the lot, Pontormo's gorgeous *Vertumnus and Pomona*, the perfect evocation of a sun-stunned Tuscan afternoon. Also on this floor is a reconstruction of the salon from the Villa Topaia built by Cosimo III at Castello and since destroyed. This was set among orchards, and the literal-minded Cosimo duly ordered scores of horticultural **paintings** to fill the house;

the Dutch still-lifes are like ideal fruit stalls, each variety of grape, peach and apple assiduously numbered and labelled. Other such painted images from La Topaia are scattered throughout the main floor.

Many of the rooms were redecorated in the nineteenth century, but one that escaped was the **apartment of Bianca Cappello**, wife of Francesco I and inspiration of many a romantic tale. Born into an upper-class Venetian family, she fled her native city with a young man, whom she quickly dumped to become Francesco's mistress. Banned from the city by Francesco's first wife, she remained an outcast even after she had become his second, being blacklisted by many of Florence's elite. In October 1587 both she and her husband died here on the same day – perhaps poisoned, perhaps victims of a particularly virulent virus.

In Lorenzo's time the grounds of Poggio a Caiano were far more extensive than they are today, and included a farm and a hunting estate; in the eighteenth century the **gardens** (same hours) were converted into an English-style landscape, now containing some magnificent old trees.

Carmignano

Some 5km west of Poggio a Caiano, the church of San Michele in the village of **CARMIGNANO** contains one of Pontormo's greatest paintings, the *Visitation*. Created in 1530, it's as unusual an interpretation of a common theme as his *Deposition* in Florence: clad in bright pink, green and orange, the women seem to be clutching each other in an almost static dance. There's a fairly regular CAP bus service to Carmignano from Poggio (taking 10–20min, depending on whether they go via Comeana; see below). Should you want to stay, the place to pick is the two-star **hotel** *Montalbano* (☎ & ⓕ055.879.9008; ❶), at Via Madonna della Valicarda 1 in the outlying district of Pianali.

Villa del'Artimino

Some of the buses from Poggio a Caiano to Carmignano take a circuitous route via Comeana, 3km south, where a couple of large **Etruscan tombs** dating from the seventh century BC have been excavated (Thurs–Sat 9am–1pm; free). A few of these bus services then loop through the walled village of **ARTIMINO**, another 3km on.

Villa del'Artimino is known as *La Ferdinanda* after Grand Duke Ferdinando I, for whom Buontalenti designed the house as a hunting lodge, with no intervening garden to smooth the transition from civilization to nature. Unlike most of the other Medici villas it's still in the countryside, with superb views towards Florence in one direction and west along the Arno in the other. A white rectangular block with details picked out in grey *pietra serena*, the house has the appearance of a rather dandified fortress, and its most distinctive external feature has earned it the nickname "the villa of the hundred chimneys". Half of the **interior** is open by appointment only (Tues 9.30am–12.30pm; free; ☎055.875.1427), but the paintings of the various Medici villas that once hung here are now on show in Florence's Museo di Firenze com'era. In the basement is a dreary museum of Etruscan finds from the Comeana tombs (Feb–Oct Mon, Tues & Thurs–Sat 9.30am–12.30pm, Sun 10am–noon; €4).

While you're here, take a look at the village church of **San Leonardo**, which was put together in the twelfth century from stones recovered from an Etruscan necropolis. Hang around until the evening and you could sample the menu at the excellent and well-priced village **restaurant**, *Da Delfina* (☎055.871.8074; closed Sun eve & Mon, also Aug & 1st two weeks of Jan).

Pratolino and Monte Senario

Nothing remains of Francesco I's favourite villa at **Pratolino**, 12km north of Florence (bus #25), except for its huge park (April–Sept Thurs–Sun 10am–7.30pm; March & Oct Sun 10am–6pm; €3, free on Thurs & Fri, and in March & Oct) – and even this is but a shadow of its former self. The mechanical toys, trick fountains and other practical jokes that Buontalenti installed here were the most ingenious ever seen, and required so much maintenance that there was a house in the grounds just for the court plumbers. The only surviving pieces are a couple of fountains, a little temple by Buontalenti, and Giambologna's immense *Appennino*, a shaggy man-mountain who gushes water. Nonetheless, the park – known as the **Parco Demidoff**, after the nineteenth-century owners of the estate – is still one of the most pleasant green spaces within easy reach of Florence.

If you're travelling under your own steam, you could take an eight-kilometre diversion northeast off the main road into the Mugello to **Monte Senario**, a monastery established by the seven founder members of the Servite order in 1233. The complex is impressive, with gilded Rococo basilica and hermitages scattered up the hill, but the architecture is less rewarding than the views of Mugello from the terrace.

Poggio Imperiale

South of central Florence, Viale del Poggio Imperiale rises from the Porta Romana to the **Villa di Poggio Imperiale** (bus #11 from the Duomo), built by the Salviati family but confiscated by Cosimo I. The Medici did little to improve the place when they enlarged it; nor did the post-Medici rulers of the city, who glued a Neoclassical facade onto the house. The goverment department that now occupies most of the villa allows prearranged visits (Wed 10am–noon; closed Aug; free; ☎055.220.151), but it's a tour for the committed Medicean only.

Chianti

Ask a sample of northern Europeans to define their idea of paradise and the odds are that several will come up with something that sounds much like **Chianti**, the territory of vineyards and hill-towns that stretches between Florence and Siena (who contested ownership of much of this region until Siena's final capitulation in 1557). Every aspect of life in Chianti seems in perfect balance: the landscape is the sort of harmoniously varied terrain beloved of painters evoking any mythical Golden Age; the climate for most of the year is balmy, rarely too grim even in the pit of winter; and on top of all this there's the **wine**, the one Italian vintage that's familiar to just about everyone.

The British, and others from similarly ill-favoured zones, were long ago alerted to Chianti's charms, and the rate of immigration has been so rapid since the 1960s that the region is now popularly known as "Chiantishire" or even "Surrey in the Sun" (happily, however, foreign residents still account for only five percent of Chianti's 45,000 inhabitants). With up to a million visitors a year, tourism has overtaken wine to become the region's most important cash crop, and has helped push property prices beyond the reach of the local population – thus altering the tone of certain parts irreparably. Tourist handouts might talk of the charm of Chianti's medieval hamlets, but many of them are places where history has become just another commodity and where the abiding impressions are of newly varnished shutters and locks the size of letter boxes. There is, nonetheless, much to enjoy in Chianti – quiet back roads, hundreds of acres of woodland, and of course the vineyards.

Buses from Florence and Siena connect with the main Chianti towns, but the best way to really get to know the region is **by car**. Your own transport allows you to roam the quieter recesses of the hills, and visit any of the eight hundred wine producers to sample the local product: every village mentioned below has wine tastings on offer within a few hundred metres of the main street. There's basically a choice of two main roads to follow through Chianti: the old Florence to Siena road (**N2**) along the western edge of the region, or the so-called **Chiantigiana** road (**SS222**), through the Chianti heartland.

If you get hold of a detailed survey map of the region, you can also pick out some of the innumerable miniature **lakes**, which offer the quietest swimming you'll find anywhere in Tuscany in the summer. Hotels in Chianti are rarely inexpensive (the only truly low-budget options are two hostels and a few campsites), but this is prime **agriturismo** territory, with scores of farms offering rooms or apartments (or even self-contained mini-villas), generally for a minimum period of one week, which for an extended stay can provide a good-value alternative to hotel accommodation. There are already far too many *agriturismi* in Chianti to list here, and with every passing month a new operation starts up, but you can find a good choice of properties at: ⓦwww.agriturismo .net; ⓦwww.agriturismo.it/ChiantiFiorentino.htm; and ⓦwww.chiantishire .org/agriturismi.htm. The Chiantishire website, despite its dreadful name, is a good source of topical information on the area.

Western Chianti

A stretch of *superstrada* connects Florence to Siena along the western edge of Chianti, but to get some sense of the character of the land it's better to opt for the older **N2** road, which takes in a few of the major Chianti towns en route. Apart from being a far more diverting drive, it's actually not that much slower: even with a few stops on the way (to explore the **Certosa di Galluzzo** or visit a wine house), you could reach San Gimignano or Siena comfortably in a half-day drive from Florence.

The Certosa di Galluzzo

On the city side of the Autostrada del Sole, beyond Poggio Imperiale, the N2 sweeps by the Carthusian monastery of the **Certosa di Galluzzo** (Tues–Sat 9am–noon & 3–6pm, Sun 3–6pm; winter closes 5pm; free), founded in the fourteenth century by the Florentine banker Niccolò Acciaioli. Bus #37 runs here from Florence train station, so it can easily be included as an excursion from the city.

The Certosa (or charterhouse) is now occupied by Cistercian monks, one of whose number shows visitors round the enormous complex. Its main architectural attraction is the **Chiostro Grande**, with its tondi of prophets and saints by Andrea and Giovanni della Robbia and their workshop. One of the eighteen monks' cells adjoining this cloister is open – a typical Carthusian arrangement, with three rooms and its own patch of garden. Beyond, the tour reaches the **Palazzo degli Studi**, now a picture gallery, though built as a study centre by the well-educated Acciaioli, who counted Boccaccio and Petrarch among his friends. The Certosa was once so rich that it owned over five hundred works of art, most of which were carried off by Napoleon; the best of those that remain are the five scenes of the Passion, painted for the Chiostro Grande by Pontormo in 1522, while he and his pupil Bronzino were taking refuge from a plague outbreak in the city. In the **church** itself, down in the crypt of the lay brothers' choir, are the tombs of the monastery's founder and his descendants, including a beautiful slab originally thought to have been by Donatello, now attributed to Francesco da Sangallo.

Sant'Andrea and San Casciano Val di Pesa

South of the Certosa, the N2 passes to the east of **Sant'Andrea in Percussina**, where Machiavelli alleviated the boredom of exile by writing *The Prince*, the manual of statecraft that he hoped, in vain, would seal his rehabilitation. A house has been identified as his residence but it is not open to visitors.

SAN CASCIANO VAL DI PESA, 17km south of Florence, is the first real town on the N2 road. In fact, with a population of around 15,000, it is the only place in Chianti that is really more than an extended village. It is also home to one of the slickest commercial operations in Tuscany, the six-hundred-year-old **Antinori wine house**, as well as one of Chianti's most interesting churches, **Santa Maria del Prato**, which stands by the one surviving gateway in the town walls. The church was built in the fourteenth century and contains some beautiful works of art from the same period: a Crucifix by an anonymous follower of Giotto, an altarpiece of the Madonna and Child, and a pulpit by a pupil of Andrea Pisano.

Chianti wines

Chianti became the world's first officially defined wine-producing area in 1716, the year Cosimo III drew the boundaries within which vineyards could use the region's name on their product. Modern Chianti dates from the 1860s when Bettino Ricasoli, the second prime minister of unified Italy, established the classic formula for the wine at his estate at Brolio, based on **Sangiovese** – central Italy's predominant red grape.

White grapes used to be an important part of the mix, as were red grapes imported from southern Italy. This, combined with the huge area of production that extends well beyond the geographical area known as Chianti, meant that the quality and style of the wine varied dramatically – at its worst symbolized by the straw-covered bottle known as a *fiasco*. Following a crisis of confidence, many of the better producers put their efforts into making smart, expensive wines sold as simple *vini da tavola*. The situation improved with Chianti becoming a **DOCG** in 1984 and total output is now about 90 million litres per annum, making it Italy's highest-volume DOCG by far.

The wine-growing area is split into seven classified **regions**, of which the most highly regarded are Chianti Classico and Chianti Rúfina. The better Chiantis mature in around four to seven years, and the best recent vintages to look out for are 1995, 1997, 1998, 1999, 2001 and 2004, but one to avoid is 2002 – the worst Chianti summer in living memory, with torrential rain that rotted the vines all over the region. A *riserva* is a *cru* version aged for a minimum of two and a half years before bottling.

The Chianti districts

• **Chianti Classico** – the original delineated district (see map on p.223), accounting for a third of the Chianti produced. In 1924 Chianti Classico was institutionalized, taking as its trademark the black cock (*Gallo Nero*) that was once the heraldic symbol of the baronial alliance called the Lega di Chianti.

• **Chianti Colli Aretini** – from the hills on the east side of the Arno valley, to the north of Arezzo. Tends to be lighter than Classico and best drunk young.

• **Chianti Colli Fiorentini** – from the area immediately south and east of Florence, and along the Arno and Pesa valleys. Good quaffing wine and staple *Rosso* of many a restaurant in Florence.

• **Chianti Colli Senesi** – the largest Chianti zone, split into three distinct districts: around Montalcino, around Montepulciano, and south of the Classico region east of San Gimignano. Variable quality, with the name of the producer all-important.

• **Chianti Colline Pisane** – the lightest Chianti comes from this region, southeast of Pisa around Casciana Terme.

• **Chianti Montalbano** – from the hills west of Florence and south of Pistoia, the wines usually soft and scented.

• **Chianti Rúfina** – from the lower Sieve valley, northeast of Florence, producing some of the most refined and longest-living Chiantis. Not to be confused with the big Chianti producer Ruffino.

For **accommodation**, San Casciano town offers the well-appointed three-star *Antica Posta*, Piazza Zannoni 1 (☎055.822.313; ❹); a meal in the attached **restaurant** (closed Tues) should cost around €35 – booking is essential. You can also get a fine meal at *Da Nello*, Via IV Novembre 64, a family-run establishment that's been in operation for more than half a century now (closed Wed evening & Thurs). The best place to stay in the vicinity, however, is the spectacular ✈ *Villa Il Poggiale*, set amid a cypress grove about 3km west of San Casciano at Via Empolese 69 (☎055.828.311, ⓦwww.villailpoggiale.it; closed Feb; ❺); rebuilt in the sixteenth century and discreetly decorated in the style of the early nineteenth century, the villa is a beautiful and spacious building, and has a restaurant and outdoor pool.

Mercatale and around

The road east from San Casciano passes the Chianti-producing **Villa Le Corti** – one of many Florentine gentry residences in this part of the region – before reaching the once-major market town of **MERCATALE**, 5km from San Casciano. Mercatale has the tiny one-star *Paradise* hotel, right in the centre at Piazza Vittorio Veneto 28 (☎055.821.327, ⓔhotelparad@ftbcc.it; ❷). There's also an outstanding **restaurant**: *Il Salotto del Chianti*, at Via Sonnino 92 (☎055.821.8016; closed Wed), where you'll spend around €40 per person.

A couple of kilometres farther east, on the road towards Greve (see opposite), stands the eleventh-century **Castello di Gabbiano**, built by the Bardi, the wealthiest Florentine banking dynasty before the coming of the Medici. As with Le Corti, it produces wine – and olive oil, another great Chianti speciality.

Bargino and southwards

Back on the N2 south of San Casciano, you pass the castle of **Bibbione** – home of the Buondelmonte family, who triggered the Guelph versus Ghibelline battles – before coming into **BARGINO**, which has low-cost rooms at the one-star *Bargino*, Via Cassia 122 (☎055.824.9055, ⓕ055.824.9045; ❶). From here it's a short diversion east to the fortified village of **Montefiridolfi**, whose castle once belonged to the sons of Ridolfo Buondelmonte (*figli di Ridolfo*).

South of Bargino, the N2 rolls into **TAVARNELLE VAL DI PESA**, which expanded as an agricultural centre in the nineteenth century. There's a reasonable **restaurant** here, *La Fattoria* at Via del Cerro 11 (closed Mon lunch & all Tues), and, 300m from the bus-stop, one of two **hostels** in Chianti, the HI *Ostello del Chianti*, Via Roma 137 (☎055.805.0265, ⓦwww.ostellionline.org; March 15–Oct 31), which has 82 beds, from around €14 per night.

About 2km beyond lies the more ancient **BARBERINO VAL D'ELSA**, site of one of the rare **campsites** in Chianti, *Semifonte*, Via Ugo Foscolo 4 (☎055.807.5454, ⓦwww.semifonte.it). The beautiful Romanesque **Pieve di Sant'Appiano**, parts of which date back to the tenth century, is a few kilometres southwest of the village (well signposted); due south, on the main road, is the major town of Poggibonsi (see p.422), hub for buses to San Gimignano and Siena.

The Chianti heartland

There's no better way to experience the village life of Chianti than to drive along the **Chiantigiana** road (**SS222**), which cuts right across the hills from Florence to Siena, connecting with a tangle of minor roads that traverse the most unspoilt parts of the region. If you put your foot down, its twists and turns can be negotiated in only a little longer than the major N2 road to the west, but this is more of a route to dawdle along, taking turnings on a whim and dropping by at any vineyard that takes your fancy. If you want to see the best of Chianti in a single day, devise an itinerary that takes in **Greve** and **Radda**, two of the region's most alluring little towns.

Santa Caterina d'Antella and Impruneta

As you leave Florence on the SS22, the access road for the *Chiantigiana*, a short detour just before the autostrada brings you to the village of **PONTE A EMA** and, 1km beyond, the church of **Santa Caterina d'Antella**. This has a fine cycle of scenes from the life of St Catherine of Siena, painted by Spinello Aretino in 1387. Executed immediately prior to his work at San Miniato al Monte (see p.186), they make an interesting comparison with Agnolo Gaddi's less monumental fresco cycle in Florence's church of Santa Croce, painted at the same time.

Another rewarding detour, this time just south of the autostrada, presents itself at **Grássina**. Take a right turn here and, after 9km of winding road, you arrive at **IMPRUNETA**. The **Collegiata** here, restored after heavy bomb damage in 1944, was founded in the eleventh century to house a miraculous icon of the Madonna and Child dug up in a nearby field and said to have been painted – as these things often are – by St Luke. It's housed in one of a pair of matching chapels by Michelozzo, the second of which contains a fragment of the True Cross; both have lovely enamelled terracotta decoration by Luca della Robbia. Impruneta has long been a centre of the terracotta industry, and holds a big fair in October on the main square. In nearby **Bottai**, at Via San Cristofano, there's the *Camping Internazionale Firenze* **campsite** 2 (☎055.237.4704, ⓦwww .florencecamping.com; open all year), and you'll find a good two-star **hotel**, the *Scopeti*, at Via Cassia 183 (☎ & ⓕ055.202.2008; ❷).

Grássina to Strada

Go east rather than west at Grássina and you'll come to **Santo Stefano a Tizzano**, with its Romanesque church and contemporaneous Castello di Tizzano, a producer of good wines but best known for its *extra vergine* olive oil. About 2km further is **San Polo in Chianti**, where a major iris festival, the *Festa del Giaggiolo*, held in mid-May, celebrates the village crop of Florence's floral emblem. A good place for a coffee is the *Antica Toscana*.

From San Polo a minor road reconnects with the *Chiantigiana* near **STRADA IN CHIANTI**. The turnoff southeast from Strada to Dudda is overlooked by the mighty Castello di Mugnana, which once protected this stretch of road down into the Arno valley and is now the headquarters of a massive wine estate.

Greve and around

For casual oenophiles, perhaps the best target is **GREVE**, 10km south on the *Chiantigiana* from Strada. The venue for Chianti's biggest **wine fair** (the Rassegna del Chianti Classico, usually held during the second weekend in Sept), this is a town with wine for sale on every street: the best outlets are the *Enoteca di Gallo Nero*, Piazzetta Santa Croce 8, the *Cantinetta di Checucci*, Via Vittorio Veneto, and the *Cantina di Greve in Chianti*, at Piazza delle Cantine 6, which claims to have the biggest selection of Chianti Classico wines in the whole region. Though razed to the ground in 1325 by Castruccio Castracani (the ruler of Lucca), by the fifteenth century Greve had re-established itself as a thriving mercantile town, focused on the funnel-shaped **Piazza Matteotti**, where a Saturday morning market is still held today. Its irregular arcades are explained by the fact that various merchants paid for their own stretches of colonnade. The statue in the centre is of Giovanni da Verrazzano, the man who "discovered" New York harbour; he was born in the nearby Castello di Verrazzano. Other than the piazza, the Greve townscape has just one feature that might be classified as a sight: the **Museo d'Arte Sacra di San Francesco**, at Via San Francesco 4 (April–Sept Thurs & Fri 10am–1pm, Sat & Sun 4–8pm; Oct–March Thurs & Fri 10am–1pm, Sat & Sun 3.30–6.30pm; €3), a very minor museum where the chief exhibit is a painted terracotta *Lamentation*, created in the 1530s, and thus one of the last examples of a genre that originated with Luca della Robbia more than a century earlier.

As the chief town of the *Gallo Nero* region, Greve is equipped with an efficient **tourist office**, in the building at the end of the car park that is Piazzale Ferrante Mori (Mon–Fri 9am–1pm & 2.30–6.30pm; ℡055.854.5243, ⓦwww .comune.greve-in-chianti.fi.it), which can also give information on accommodation in local farmhouses and trekking in Chianti. There are a number of interesting **villas** a stone's throw from Greve, including Verrazzano, five minutes' drive north, and Vignamaggio, just south of Greve, where Kenneth Branagh filmed *Much Ado about Nothing.*

A couple of three-star **hotels** on Piazza Matteotti offer comfortable accommodation: the *Del Chianti* at no. 86 (℡055.853.763, ⓦwww.albergodelchianti .it; ❸) and ⚒ *Da Verrazzano* at no. 28 (℡055.853.189, ⓦwww.verrazzano. it; ❹). The latter is slightly more characterful and also has an extremely good **restaurant**, at around €40 for a full meal (closed Mon & mid-Jan to mid-Feb), with a terrace overlooking the piazza. The *Gallo Nero*, just off the piazza at Via Cesare Batisti 6 (closed Thurs), is a perfectly acceptable bar-trattoria-pizzeria, as is *Torre delle Civette*, Via Luca Cini 5 (open daily for lunch & dinner in summer; in winter open for lunch Mon-Fri, for dinner Thurs-Sun).

For travellers on a tight rein, there's the *Villa San Michele*, at Via Casole 42 (℡055.851.034, ⓦwww.villasanmichele.it) in **LUCOLENA**, 9km east of Greve (there's no public transport); in addition to a small dormitory (beds €16 per night), it has hotel-style double rooms (€70), and three apartments for two people (€80 per night), plus a restaurant and bar.

Montefioralle and the Badia a Passignano

Five minutes' drive from Greve, west up a steep zigzagging road, lies the much restored hamlet of **MONTEFIORALLE**, where a single elliptical street – Via di Montefioralle – encompasses a few tower houses and a pair of Romanesque churches. This street has one of the best simple **trattorie** in Chianti, the *Taverna del Guerrino* (℡055.853.106; winter open Thurs–Sun for lunch & dinner; summer open daily for dinner, Thurs–Sun for lunch). A menu of locally produced sausages, beans and vegetables provides a good Tuscan meal for around €35.

Continuing west from Montefioralle, the road passes the vestiges of the castle of Montefili, whose owners were benefactors of the **Badìa a Passignano** (ⓦwww.badia-a-passignano.com), situated a few kilometres on towards the N2. A monastery was founded here towards the end of the ninth century, then in 1049 was re-dedicated to the Vallombrosan order, whose founder, St Giovanni Gualberto, died here in 1073 and is buried in the abbey church of San Michele. It became one of the wealthiest religious houses in Tuscany, but is now occupied by just a handful of Vallombrosan monks, who on Sunday afternoons (usually at 3pm) allow visitors to explore the site. A painting by Alessandro Allori and a bust of Giovanni Gualberto are on display, but the highlight is the refectory fresco of the *Last Supper*, painted in 1476 by Davide and Domenico Ghirlandaio.

△ Vineyards near Panzano

Panzano and Castellina

About 8km south of Greve along the *Chiantigiana*, the hill-top town of **PAN-ZANO** overlooks a circle of hills known as the Conca d'Oro (Golden Valley) because of their sun-trap properties; the resultant wines can be sampled at the *Enoteca del Chianti Classico*, Via Giovanni da Verrazzano 8 (closed Mon). Sign-posted down a branch road, the Romanesque **Pieve di San Leolino**, 1km south of the village, is one of the oldest churches in Chianti, and traces its ori-gins to the first Christian settlers; the most notable of its paintings is a *Madonna with SS Peter and Paul*, created in the mid-thirteenth century. The town is also known as the home of the **Antica Macelleria Cecchini,** perhaps the most famous butcher's shop in the country, though it stands in relation to ordinary butcher's shops in the same way as a Ferrari relates to a Fiat van – it even has a downstairs room for wine tastings, art shows and concerts. In existence for 250 years, it's run by Dario Cecchini, a charismatic and eloquent champion of Tuscan carnivorous cuisine and Chianti traditions in general.

The summit of the next main hill, 15km south, is occupied by well-heeled **CASTELLINA IN CHIANTI**, which formerly stood on the front line of the continual wars between Florence and Siena. The walls, fortress and the covered walkway known as the **Via delle Volte** – a kind of gallery looking east from underneath the town (it was originally open, but houses were later built over it) – all bear testimony to an embattled past. Traces of a more distant era can be seen at the **Ipogeo Etrusco di Montecalvario** (open daylight hours; free), a complex of subterranean sixth-century BC Etruscan burial chambers, carved into the summit of a small hill that's five minutes' walk to the south of the village. But neither the Etruscan tombs nor the town's one sizeable church – the neo-Romanesque San Salvatore (notable only for a single fifteenth-century fresco and the mummified remain of the obscure St Fausto) – are what brings in the tourists. Wine is of course Castellina's primary attraction, as is evident from the power-station bulk of the **wine co-operative** on the main road; the local vintages (and olive oil) can be sampled at several places in town, notably *La Castellina*, which occupies much of the ground floor of a huge fifteenth-century palazzo at Via Ferruccio 28, and *Bottega del Vino*, at Via della Rocca 13.

The Castellina **tourist office** is at Via Ferruccio 40 (daily 10am–1pm & 3–6pm). Pick of the **hotels** in town is the three-star ⚒ *Palazzo Squarcialupi*, above the *Castellina enoteca* at Via Ferruccio 22 (☎0577.741.186, ⊛www .palazzosquarcialupi.com; ❹). Another good three-star, the *Hotel Colle Etrusco Salivolpi*, is located at Via Fiorentina 89, a short distance northwest of Castellina on the road to San Donato (☎0577.740.484, ⊛www.hotelsalivolpi .com; ❺); surrounded by a beautiful garden, it has an outdoor pool and large timber-ceilinged bedrooms. In the village of Trégole (4km south), there's nice B&B accommodation at the *Fattoria Trégole* vineyard (☎0577.740.991, ⊛www .fattoria-tregole.com; ❹), which also has a couple of self-contained apartments and a pool. For **eating** in Castellina, look no further than *La Torre*, Piazza del Comune 15 (☎0577.740.236; closed Fri) – it's a fine, unspoilt and well-priced Tuscan trattoria.

Radda and around

The best of Chianti lies east of Castellina and the *Chiantigiana*, in the less domesticated terrain of the **Monti del Chianti** – the stronghold of the Lega di Chianti, whose power bases were Castellina itself and the two principal settlements of this craggy region, Radda and Gaiole. The nearer of these, the ancient Etruscan-founded town of **RADDA IN CHIANTI**, became the league's capital in 1384, and the imprint of the period is perhaps stronger here than anywhere else in Chianti. The street plan of this minuscule but historic centre is focused on Piazza Ferrucci, where the frescoed and shield-studded Palazzo Comunale faces a church raised on a high platform. Neither is an outstanding building on its own, but taken together they form an impressive ancient core that gives Radda its appeal.

The **tourist office** lurks behind the church, on the corner of Piazza del Castello (Mon–Sat 10am–1pm & 3–7pm, Sun 10.30am-12.30pm). Stylish accommodation is on offer at the three-star *Hotel Podere Le Vigne* (⊛www.tuscany.net /vigne; ☎0577.738.640; ❹), a converted farm located a kilometre outside Radda, just off the road between Radda and the hamlet of Villa a Radda; in addition to the rooms at the former farm, *Le Vigne* has some plainer but still very pleasant accommodation in the centre of Radda, and there's a terrific restaurant at the main site, where you'll pay around €40 each. At Via Roma 33 you'll find the *Hotel Palazzo Leopoldo* (☎0577.735.603, ⊛www.palazzoleopoldo.it; ❺), which was founded as a pilgrims' hostel, then converted into a magnificent town house prior to becoming an extremely elegant four-star hotel, with a very good restaurant. At the top of the range lies the *Relais Fattoria La Vignale*, on the edge of the village at Via Pianigiani 9 (ⓦ www.vignale.it; ☎ 0577.738.592; ❼); it has a good wine bar in the cellars, and a restaurant (☎ 0577.738.094; closed Thurs & mid-Jan to mid-March), a touch pricier than *Le Vigne*. There are no low-cost hotels in Radda, but you can eat cheaply and well at the *Da Michele* trattoria-pizzeria (Closed Mon) – it's at the end of the car park below the town walls, and is prominently signposted off the main road.

About 7km north of Radda lies the unspoilt village of **VOLPAIA**, which from the tenth to the sixteenth century was an important military lookout over the valley of the Pesa. The medieval donjon still stands, but the most interesting structure is the deconsecrated Commenda di Sant'Eufrosino, designed by Michelozzo, and now used as a *cantina* and exhibition space by the Castello di Volpaia wine estate (ⓦ www.volpaia.it).

South of Radda

The same distance south of Radda is **AMA**, once a fortification on the southern edge of Florentine territory. Round the village are ranged the vineyards of one of Chianti's first-rank wine estates, **Castello di Ama**, which offers tastings throughout the year (not Aug). A little further south, in **SAN SANO**, you'll find the pleasant *Trattoria Grotta della Rana* and the *Hotel Residenza San Sano* (☎ 0577.746.130; ❻; closed Nov–March). About 5km south of San Sano, at Pievasciata (on the minor road parallel to the N408), you'll come across the **Chianti Sculpture Park**, an intriguing new initiative where artists from a great range of cultures (India, Zimbabwe, Colombia and Japan are all represented) have been commissioned to create site-specific open-air work (April–Oct Tues–Sun 10am–sunset; €7.50).

Badìa a Coltibuono

Heading east from Radda and taking the first turning left after the *Villa Miranda*, you pass the foot of the hill on which stands the **Badìa a Coltibuono**, 6km from Radda. This Vallombrosan abbey (see p.512) was founded on the site of an eighth-century hermitage, and its church of San Lorenzo, built in 1050, is one of Tuscany's finest Romanesque buildings. The monastic complex is now owned by one of the biggest wine estates in the region, whose vintages are served at the famous *Badìa a Coltibuono* **restaurant**, adjoining the abbey (☎ 0577.749.424, ⓦ www.coltibuono.com; Nov–April closed Mon; also closed Jan to early March) – a meal here will cost upwards of €40 per head, but some might say that the standard of cooking doesn't always live up to the reputation. The Badìa is also celebrated for its lavish residential cookery courses, detailed on its website, and since 2005 – when it began marketing itself as Italy's first "wine resort" – has been offering accommodation in ten beautifully converted monastic cells (from €150). There are some good Club Alpino **walks** laid out through the oak and pine woods on the surrounding slopes.

Gaiole and Brolio

Modern times have caught up with the third of the Lega di Chianti triad, **GAIOLE**, 5km south of Coltibuono. Now a brisk market town, it has a **wine co-operative** at Via Mulinaccio 10 which offers splendid tasting opportunities, as does the *Enoteca Montagnani*, Via Bandinelli 13–17, which has a superlative range of Chianti Classico. The most impressive sights in the immediate area are the ruins of the **Castello di Vertine**, occupying the heights 3km west of the village, and the fortified village of **Barbischio**, up a winding little road to the east. Devotees of military ruins could follow the signposted *Strada dei Castelli* from Gaiole, an itinerary of half a dozen fortresses between Spaltena (1km) and Vistarenni (6km). There are a couple of pricey hotels in the Gaiole vicinity, but it's not the pick of the Chianti towns, so it's better to drive on; the same goes for places to eat.

A couple of kilometres south of Gaiole, the twin circular towers of the **Castello di Meleto** peer from behind a screen of cypresses over the road leading to **Castagnoli**, where the houses form a fringe to a thickset fortress. Meleto was founded by the monks of Coltibuono, but by 1269 it was in the hands of the Ricasoli family, who built its massive fortifications in the fifteenth century. The highlights of the guided tour (Mon–Sat at 11.30am, 3pm & 4.30pm, Sun 11.30am, 4.30pm & 5pm) are the delicate eighteenth-century theatre and the visit to the *cantina*, where you can sample the Meleto estate's olive oil, wine or food (the price of the tour varies according to which option you choose). Meleto has accommodation too, ranging from B&B (from around €120 per double to seven-bed *agriturismo* apartments, costing €1700 per week.

The busiest Chianti *cantina* is that of the **Castello di Brolio**, just outside the nearby village of **BROLIO**: from Castagnoli you should take the minor road through San Martino al Vento; or, coming from Gaiole, you could take the turning off the N408 after Meleto. This building passed to the Ricasoli family as far back as the twelfth century, and was the object of frequent tussles between the Florentines and the Sienese. Demolished by the Sienese army, it was rebuilt in the sixteenth century, then converted in the nineteenth century into a colossal mock-medieval country residence by the vinicultural pioneer **Baron Bettino Ricasoli**. The baron's apartments can be visited on a tour of the house (summer 9am–noon & 2–6pm; winter 10am–noon & 3–5pm; €3), but a far more rewarding experience is to buy some Castello di Brolio wine at the estate's enoteca (Mon–Sat 9am–6pm, Sun 11am–7pm), or sample it as an accompaniment to a meal in the excellent *Osteria del Castello* **restaurant**, one of the best places to eat in Chianti (℡0577.747.277; closed Thurs). High-quality food at a lower price is provided by *Il Carlino d'Oro*, alongside the church in the neighbouring village of San Règolo (℡0577.747.136) – expect to pay around €30 a head.

The Mugello

For every hundred tourists who give over a day to the vineyards of Chianti, perhaps one will give a few hours to the **Mugello** (Ⓦwwww.mugellotoscana .it), the lushly fertile region on the Tuscan side of the Apennine ridge separating the province from Emilia-Romagna. Like Chianti, this is a benign, humanized sort of landscape, with nothing that will take your breath away – but it's easier to avoid the crowds here, even though it's a favourite weekend hangout of the Florentine bourgeoisie. Its celebrated olive groves and vineyards are concentrated in the central Mugello basin, formed by the Sieve and its tributary valleys; elsewhere the vegetation is principally oak, pine and chestnut forest, interspersed with small resorts whose customers tend to be short-stay vacationers from the city. The fringes of the eastern part of the Mugello lie inside the Parco Nazionale delle Foreste Casentinesi – for more on this national park, and its visitor centres, see p.527.

As with Chianti, you'll need your own transport to see anything much. Three main roads run from Florence: the Via Bologna (**N65**), which passes Pratolino

The Sistema Museale in Mugello e Valdisieve

Like the Casentino, the Mugello has a network of small museums devoted to the traditional way of life and the culture of the region, most of them open at weekends only. The best of the museums affiliated to this *Sistema Museale in Mugello e Valdisieve* – such as the one in Reggello – are covered in the main part of the guide. Others that you might want to take a look at, should you find yourself close by, are listed below.

Borgo San Lorenzo: Museo della Manifattura Chini (Chini ceramics museum); Museo della Civiltà Contadini (museum of rural traditions)

Firenzuola: Museo della Pietra Serena (stonework museum); Museo del Paesaggio Storico dell'Appennino (Apennine historical landscape museum); Museo Storico-Etnografico (museum of local history)

Palazzuolo: Museo delle Genti di Montagna (mountain people's museum); Museo Archeologico Alto Mugello (archeological museum)

Pelago: Museo d'Arte Sacra (sacred art museum)

Rúfina: Museo della Vite e del Vino (vine and wine museum)

Scarperia: Museo dei Ferri Tagliente (knife museum); Museo di Vita Artigiana e Contadina (museum of rural and artisan life); Raccolta di Arte Sacra (sacred art collection)

on its way to the Passo della Futa; the **N302** direct to Borgo San Lorenzo; and the **N67/551**, which winds up to Borgo San Lorenzo along the Sieve. By public transport, there's a choice between the Sieve valley **train** line to Borgo San Lorenzo (nearly all of these Faenza-bound trains depart from Campo di Marte station rather than Santa Maria Novella), or SITA and CAP **buses** along the same route; buses run from Borgo San Lorenzo to the western and northern parts of Mugello.

Eastern Mugello

The Sieve flows into the Arno at the unprepossessing town of **PON-TASSIEVE**, which makes its money from the **Rúfina wine** district immediately to the north. From here the N70 clambers over the **Passo della Consuma**, then drops south into the Casentino, towards Poppi (see p.528). The N67 trails the valley through the moderately industrialized area up to Rúfina, then on through **Dicomano**, where it veers off towards Forlì (in Emilia-Romagna), passing through the Alpe di San Benedetto. The main settlement in this part of the Mugello is **San Godenzo**, which boasts an eleventh-century abbey and not a lot else.

Hugging the course of the Sieve beyond Dicomano, the N551 runs on through **VICCHIO**, the birthplace of Fra' Angelico. Unsurprisingly, the village makes the most of the Angelico connection, but the **Museo di Arte Sacra e Religiosità Popolare Beato Angelico** (June 16–Sept 14 Thurs, Sat & Sun 10am–noon & 3.30–6.30pm; rest of year Sat & Sun 10am–noon & 3–6pm; €3) is a context-setting exercise rather than a celebration of the man himself, and doesn't contain anything that's likely to excite greatly, though the array of workaday religious artefacts is very well displayed. The best place to stay in Vicchio is the very pleasant parkland-girdled three-star **hotel**, *Villa Campestri*, Via di Campestri 19–22 (☎055.849.0107, ⓦ www.villacampestri.it; ❺), which has a very good restaurant and – in the cellars – Italy's first *oleoteca*, where hotel guests can sample and learn about the region's finest olive oils. There are two good **campsites** in the vicinity: *Vecchio Ponte*, at Via Costoli 16 (☎055.844.8306;

June–Sept), and *Residence Park Valdisieve* in Caldeta, midway between Vicchio and Dicomano (☎055.844.256; June–Sept).

Next stop along the main road is another exalted birthplace, **VESPIG-NANO**, where **Giotto** was born in around 1266. His career started, so the story goes, when Cimabue happened to pass by the spot where the boy was tending his father's flock; Giotto was drawing a picture of one of the sheep on a stone, and Cimabue was so astonished by the shepherd's proficiency that he immediately took him on as an apprentice. The bridge where the crucial encounter is said to have occurred is a few hundred metres out of Vespignano and is well signposted. The farmhouse in which Giotto was actually born – the **Casa di Giotto** (Thurs–Sun: June 16–Sept 14 10am–noon & 3.30–6.30pm; rest of year 10am–noon & 3–6pm; €3) – is 1km off to the north, also well signposted; as with the homes of Leonardo and Michelangelo, this has value only as a pilgrimage site.

Borgo San Lorenzo

With a population of 15,000 or so, **BORGO SAN LORENZO** is the giant of Mugello towns, with industrial plots and tracts of new housing spreading further with each year – improved rail connections with Florence have given an added boost to the town in recent years. Substantially rebuilt after a massive earthquake in 1919, it has just one major building, the **Pieve di San Lorenzo**, an eleventh-century foundation that was renovated in the sixteenth century but still retains its irregularly hexagonal Romanesque tower. This isn't the most photographed sight in town, though – that honour goes to the ghastly statue of *Fido* in Piazza Dante, a memorable example of monumentalized sentimentality. Pick of the **hotels** in town is the tiny three-star *Locanda degli Artisti*, Piazza Romagnoli 2 (☎055.845.5359, ⓦwww.locandaartisti.it; ❹), but better value is offered by the three-star *Tre Fiumi*, a converted post-house in Tre Fiumi, just 2km outside nearby Ronta (☎055.840.3015, ⓦwww.albergotrefiumi.com; ❸), which also has a restaurant. Alternatively, the **tourist office** in the Villa Pecori Giraldi, Via P. Togliatti (Tues–Sun 10am–1pm & 3.30–6.30pm; ☎055.845.6230), which is the main office for the whole Mugello, has details of plentiful *agriturismi*.

If you're travelling by public transport from Florence and want to carry on westwards into Mugello, you'll have to change here for the local **bus** route through San Piero a Sieve and Scarperia to Barberino di Mugello. The **train** line heads north from Borgo San Lorenzo to Faenza, while the road north divides after about 20km, one branch going to the bland resort of Palazzuolo sul Sénio, the other to the similar Marradi. If you're driving that way, you could call at the church of **San Giovanni Maggiore** (open Sun 9am–1pm), 3km north of the town at the end of an avenue of cypress trees. Like San Lorenzo, it too has a fine Romanesque campanile, and inside there's a twelfth-century marble pulpit, plus a lot of slightly incongruous Liberty-style decoration, applied to the church in the 1910s.

San Piero a Sieve and western Mugello

The N551 continues up the Sieve from Borgo San Lorenzo to **SAN PIERO A SIEVE**, crossing the N65 coming up from Florence. The Mugello landscape is at its best here, with ploughed fields foregrounding the slopes of tree-crested conical hills. San Piero's Romanesque church, spoiled by an eighteenth-century facade, houses a beautiful terracotta font, possibly by Luca della Robbia; its other main monument is the Medici fortress overlooking the town, built by Buontalenti in 1571.

San Piero has an uncharismatic **hotel**, the three-star *Ebe*, Via Le Mozzete 1a (☏055.848.019, Ⓦ ebeweb.it; ❹); the hotel **restaurant** is more than acceptable, with a menu that tends to favour dishes from Emilia-Romagna rather than Tuscany. The *Ebe* has ludicrously cheap rooms at its one-star *dipendenza* (annexe), Via di Cafaggio 11 (☏055.849.8333, Ⓕ055.848.567; ❶). There's also an all-year **campsite**, *Mugello Verde* (☏055.848.511, Ⓦwww.florencecamping.com), 2km outside the town at La Fortezza.

Trebbio and Cafaggiolo

The Medici were originally from Mugello, and the environs of San Piero contain two rough-hewn villas which encapsulate something of the flavour of the period when the family secured its political ascendancy.

Near Novoli, an unsurfaced road runs west from the Via Bologna to the Medici castle of **Trebbio**, whose fortified tower peeps over a cordon of cypresses from the top of its hill. This fourteenth-century castle was converted into a country abode by Michelozzo in 1461 and became a particular favourite with Giovanni delle Bande Nere and his branch of the Medici clan: it was from here that Giovanni's son, Cosimo, rode down to Florence to assume power after the assassination of Alessandro de' Medici. The small garden is often open to the public, and the house itself can be visited on overpriced guided tours (Tues–Fri mornings; bookings ☏055.845.6230; €12).

A short distance north, right on the Via Bologna, lies the villa of **Cafaggiolo**, which like Trebbio was a fortress converted for less bellicose use by Michelozzo. When Cosimo il Vecchio set about consolidating the family fortune through land acquisition in their ancestral domain, one of his first ventures was to buy this estate, which comprised the castle and tracts of land for hunting and agriculture. It was at Cafaggiolo that Cosimo's immediate descendants Lorenzo il Magnifico and his brother grew up, and Lorenzo's own children – Piero, Giovanni (Pope Leo X) and Giuliano – were taught here by such luminaries as Ficino, Poliziano and Pico della Mirandola. In those days the house would have had an even less suave appearance than it does now: alterations in the nineteenth century did away with the surrounding walls, the moat, the drawbridge and one of its towers. The interior (now home to a cooking school) can be seen only on group guided tours (summer Wed, Fri & Sat 2.30–6.30pm, plus Sat & Sun 10am–12.30pm; winter Sun 10am–12.30pm & 2.30–6.30pm; €5).

Barberino di Mugello to the Passo della Futa

North of Cafaggiolo the gradient of the road gets pretty savage as it begins the climb to Passo della Futa; if you don't have enough under the bonnet to do the climb comfortably, there's a less strenuous loop that goes through the main market town of western Mugello, **BARBERINO DI MUGELLO**. In the early fourteenth century this became a Florentine border post, and in later years Michelozzo picked up some work here too, giving the main square its loggia – the **Loggie Medicee**, naturally; the neighbouring, much decorated Palazzo Pretorio and the Castello dei Cattani are the only other buildings to catch the eye.

Barberino has a good-value two-star **hotel**, *Il Cavallo*, Viale della Repubblica 7 (☏055.841.8144, Ⓦwww.albergocavallo.it; ❸), with a fine **restaurant** attached. Outside Barberino, at Via Santa Lucia 24/a in Monte di Fo, is the well-equipped all-year *Sergente* **campsite** (☏055.842.3018, Ⓔinfo@campingilsergente.it).

From where the Barberino loop rejoins Via Bologna it's an unrelenting haul up to the **Passo della Futa**, from whose 900-metre vantage all of the Mugello's valleys and ridges are visible. This isn't the highest point on the Mugello's road network – Passo della Raticosa, 13km on, is a few metres higher – but it's easily the best viewpoint.

Bosco ai Frati, Scarperia and beyond

The secluded monastery of **Bosco ai Frati**, reached by taking a left turn off the N503 immediately north of San Piero (it's a rough 4km track), traces its roots back to a community of Greek monks who arrived here in the seventh century. In the early eleventh century the settlement was abandoned, but two centuries later St Francis established his order here. One of the earliest Franciscan saints, Bonaventure, was the prior at Bosco ai Frati; a man of exemplary modesty, he refused to put on the cardinal's attire brought to him by a papal delegation until he'd finished washing up his brothers' pots and pans. The tree where the outfit was hung is still there.

Cosimo il Vecchio sank a lot of money into this monastery, hiring Michelozzo to redesign the complex in the plainest early Renaissance style; in the tiny museum attached to Michelozzo's porticoed **church** (daily 8.30am–7pm) is the most remarkable work of art in the Mugello: a pain-racked *Crucifix*, probably carved by Donatello for the Medici, and certainly donated to the monastery by them.

Beyond the turning for Bosco ai Frati, the N503 continues to **SCARPERIA**, once the biggest producer of cutlery in Tuscany and now a high-quality centre for the industry. Sitting on a platform of rock above a valley 5km from San Piero, it's essentially a one-street town, laid out by the Florentines after they turned it into their chief military base in the region in 1306. The **Palazzo dei Vicari**, built in the same year along the lines of Florence's Palazzo Vecchio, has a rash of coats of arms on the outside, and extensive frescoes on the inside. None of its churches is remarkable, though one of them bears an unusual dedication, to Our Lady of the Earthquakes. Scarperia has a plain little two-star **hotel**, *Cantagallo*, Via Kennedy 17 (☎055.843.0442, ✆hotelcantagallo@libero.it; ❸). If you're perplexed by crowds around the town, they're on their way to the **motor-racing track** on the eastern outskirts; built in the 1970s, it's best known as Italy's grand prix motorbike circuit.

A small road climbs northwest to the tiny village of **SANT'AGATA**, where the Romanesque parish church contains some beautiful inlaid panels from a dismantled twelfth-century pulpit, and a tabernacle by Giovanni della Robbia. The N503 becomes a switchback after this turnoff, swooping through the region known as Mugello's "Little Switzerland" to the hill resort of **FIRENZUOLA**, 22km from Scarperia, rebuilt after a fierce battle in 1944 and with few blandishments.

Prato

Taking its name from the meadow (*prato*) where the ancient settlement's great market used to be held, **PRATO** has long been a commercial success, and is now the second-largest city in Tuscany, after Florence. It's been Italy's chief textile centre since the early Middle Ages, and even though recession has damaged exports, it still produces three-quarters of all the woollen cloth sold from Italy, with some 8000 local companies being involved in the production and marketing of textiles. It might not feature on a list of the most attractive places in the region, but its long-time wealth has left a fair legacy of buildings and art, including an unequalled collection of paintings by **Filippo Lippi**, whose frescoes adorn the beguiling **Duomo**.

A close Florentine connection goes back to 1350, when the self-governing *comune* of Prato was besieged by its neighbour, which by then was becoming alarmed at the economic threat of Prato's cloth mills. The year after, Florence bought the titles to the town from its Neapolitan rulers, thus sealing their union. Thereafter, political events in the capital were mirrored here, a relationship that was to cost Prato dear after Savonarola's example led the Pratese to join him in rejecting the Medici. Under the direction of Leo X, the imperial army sacked Prato in 1512 as a warning to the rebellious Florentines. Two days of slaughter and pillage ensued, recorded by historian Guicciardini: "Nothing would have escaped the avarice, lust and cruelty of the invaders had not the Cardinal de' Medici placed guards at the main church and saved the honour of the women who had taken refuge there. More than two thousand men died, not fighting… but fleeing or crying for mercy." A more pacific relationship was soon established, and Florence limited its bullying to the imposition of quotas on Prato's factories. Today the balance has shifted: while Prato is fairly self-sufficient, Florence struggles to find some alternative to a service-based economy.

The City

The historic centre remains enclosed within its hexagon of grey stone walls, making orientation very straightforward. Buses from Florence run direct to the Piazza del Duomo; if you're coming from the main train station it's basically a question of following your nose – cross the Ponte della Vittoria over the

Bisenzio river, and Viale Vittorio Veneto leads you through the walls at Piazza San Marco.

The Castello area

Walking from the train station, if you veer sharp left at Piazza San Marco (where the traffic swirls around a large Henry Moore sculpture), you'll pass under the **Cassero** – a fortified corridor built in the middle of the fourteenth century to link the castle to the city walls – and soon come to the former Campolmi factory in Via Santa Chiara, a huge nineteenth-century textile mill that has recently been converted into a very impressive home for the **Museo del Tessuto** (Mon & Wed–Fri 10am–6pm, Sat 10am–2pm, Sun 4–7pm; €4, free on Sun). Tracing the city's literal rise from rags to riches, the museum also displays a collection of more than five thousand fabrics from all over the world, ranging right back to the third century. It's a venue for one-off exhibitions on textile- or fashion-related themes, too.

Five minutes' walk away stands the city's signature building, the white-walled **Castello dell'Imperatore** (April–Sept daily 9am–1pm & 4–7pm; Oct–March 9am–1pm, closed Tues; €2.50, or joint ticket with Museo dell'Opera del Duomo & Museo di Pittura Murale €6), built in the 1230s for Emperor Frederick II as a base for his representative in the city and as a way-station for imperial progresses between Germany and his domains in southern Italy and Sicily. The castle is heavily restored and empty except for the rooms used for temporary exhibitions, but you can wander around the ramparts for views over the old city and its industrial suburbs.

Round the back is Prato's major Renaissance monument, Giuliano da Sangallo's church of **Santa Maria delle Carceri** (daily 7am–noon & 4–7pm), built to honour a miraculous talking image of the Virgin that was painted on the walls of the gaol here – hence the name "Mary of the Prisons". With its perfect proportions and uncluttered lines, the church is a rather severe demonstration of the correctness of the Brunelleschian style, though the exterior makes a decorative gesture towards the Romanesque with its half-completed bands of green and white marble. The interior is lightened by Andrea della Robbia's tondi of the Evangelists and ceramic frieze.

Twin-coloured marble cladding also features on the facade of the thirteenth-century church of **San Francesco**, which presents its back to the other side of the square. Inside are a couple of fine monuments: on the left wall of the single aisle you'll find Bernardo Rossellino's worn-down tomb of Gemignano Inghirami, and set into the floor near the high altar is the slab of Francesco di Marco Datini, Prato's most celebrated citizen. The subject of Iris Origo's classic study, *The Merchant of Prato*, Datini became one of Europe's richest men through his dealings in the cloth trade, and played a crucial role in the rationalization of accounting methods: on his death, his offices were found to contain tens of thousands of scrupulously kept ledgers, all inscribed "To God and profit". Off the cloister, the Cappella Migliatori has lovely frescoes of *The Lives of St Anthony Abbot and St Matthew* and *The Crucifixion*, painted in the 1390s by Niccolò di Pietro Gerini.

Datini's house, **Palazzo Datini**, is a couple of minutes from the church, on the junction of Via Rinascelda and Via Ser Lapo Mazzei. Built in the 1390s, this is now home to the city archives and the *Ceppo*, a charity established by Datini himself. The barely legible fresco sketches on the facade show scenes from his life; the interior is heavily frescoed, but is currently accessible to the public only when the building is being used as an exhibition space.

Piazza del Comune and Piazza del Duomo

A short distance north of here, Datini is commemorated with a statue and bronze reliefs at the centre of the trim little **Piazza del Comune**. Inevitably, he crops up again amongst the myriad portraits of local worthies in the **Quadreria Palazzo Comunale** (free by appointment – ring ☎0574.616.220). Across from the Palazzo sits the huge medieval Palazzo Pretorio, whose museum, the **Museo Civico**, has been undergoing restoration for many years; in the meantime, its contents have been transferred to the Museo di Pittura Murale (see overleaf).

The wide and lively Piazza del Duomo, a couple of blocks farther in, forms an effective space for the Pisan-Romanesque facade of the **Duomo** (Mon–Sat 7am–noon & 3.30–7pm, Sun open until 8pm), distinguished by another Andrea della Robbia terracotta over the portal and by Donatello's and Michelozzo's beautiful **Pulpit of the Sacred Girdle**. This unique addition was constructed for the ceremonial display of the girdle of the Madonna, a garment allegedly dropped into the hands of the ever-incredulous apostle Thomas at her Assumption. The girdle (or *Sacro Cingolo*) was supposedly bequeathed by Thomas to a priest, one of whose descendants married a crusader from Prato, who in turn brought it back to his home town in 1141. Replicas have replaced the Donatello reliefs of gambolling children, the originals now being housed in the cathedral museum. The girdle itself is displayed five times a year: on Easter Sunday, May 1, August 15, September 8 and Christmas Day.

The story is detailed in the chapel immediately left of the entrance in Agnolo Gaddi's fresco cycle of *The Legend of the Holy Girdle* (1392–95) – though sadly it's all but invisible behind the grating, as is the *Madonna and Child* carved by Giovanni Pisano. Close by, in the left aisle, is another fine piece of stonework, a chalice-shaped pulpit by Antonio Rossellino and Mino da Fiesole.

Filippo Lippi's famous frescoes, around the high altar, were completed over a period of fourteen years (1452–66) and depict the lives of John the Baptist and St Stephen. These are marvellously sensuous paintings in which even the Baptist's wilderness looks enticing, a whisked-up landscape like a confectioner's fantasy. Especially decadent is the *Feast of Herod*, where the decapitation seems like a

△ Piazza del Duomo, Prato

regrettable incident that needn't ruin the party. There's a scandalous story to the creation of these pictures: during the period of their creation, Lippi – himself a friar, at least in name – became so besotted with a young nun named Lucrezia Buti that he abducted her as she was preparing to attend the ceremony of the girdle. Later to become the mother of Filippino Lippi, Lucrezia is said to have been the model for the dancing Salome. Her lover also depicted himself among those mourning St Stephen: he's third from the right.

For several years the Lippi cycle has been undergoing restoration, but it's possible to view the pictures at close range, from the restorers' scaffolding, if you book a ticket in advance at the Museo dell'Opera del Duomo (see below); the fee is €8 per person, and visits are conducted on Saturdays at 10am, 11am, 4pm and 5pm, plus Sundays at 4pm and 5pm. There's no impediment to a viewing of the scenes from the lives of the Virgin and St Stephen in the chapel to the right of the high altar. Some believe – though studies of the underpainting have cast doubt on the attribution – that these were begun by Paolo Uccello in 1435, a year before he was called away to Florence to paint the Hawkwood monument in the Duomo, having finished just the vault and the lunettes of *The Birth of the Virgin*, *The Birth of St Stephen* and *The Stoning of St Stephen*; the lower part of the chapel is less controversially attributed to Andrea di Giusto Mamzini.

Housed alongside the Duomo, around the cloister of the bishop's palace, the **Museo dell'Opera del Duomo** (Mon & Wed–Sat 9.30am–12.30pm & 3.30–6.30pm, Sun 9.30am–12.30pm; €4, or joint ticket with Castello & Museo Pittura Murale €6) contains the Donatello panels from the great pulpit; they are badly cracked and stained by exhaust fumes but their sculpted putti make a sprightly contrast with the lumbering little lads on Maso di Bartolomeo's tiny silver *Reliquary for the Sacred Girdle*, the museum's other main treasure. Also on show is Filippino Lippi's plucky *St Lucy*, unperturbed by the gigantic sword lodged in her neck, and the magnificent painting that Filippo Lippi produced to demonstrate his suitability for the fresco commission, *The Death of Jerome*. A doorway on the far side of the cloister opens into the Duomo's frescoed **crypt**; beside the altar is the head of one of the city's main wells, which – as the inscription records – was choked with corpses by the invaders of 1512.

The rest of the town

A five-minute walk west of the Duomo, in the ex-monastery adjoining the mainly fourteenth-century church of San Domenico, the **Museo di Pittura Murale** (Mon, Wed, Thurs & Sun 9am–1pm, Fri & Sat 9am–1pm & 3–6pm; €4, or joint ticket with Museo dell'Opera & Castello €6) currently houses one of the town's star attractions – Filippo Lippi's *Madonna del Ceppo*. The painting contains portraits of the five men who financed the picture; Datini coughed up more than the other four, so he's the one depicted large-scale. Among the other Lippi pieces on show is a tender *Nativity with SS George and Vincent Ferrer*: the Madonna and Christ were probably modelled on Lucrezia and Filippino. There are works by Filippino here as well, plus – among a variety of fourteenth-century altarpieces – a predella by Bernardo Daddi narrating the story of the Girdle of the Madonna. The rest of the display features a hotchpotch of minor frescoes, culled mostly from churches in and around Prato.

Practicalities

Prato's **tourist office** (Mon–Fri 9am–1.30pm & 2–6.30pm, Sat closes 6pm; ☏0574.24.112, ⓦwww.comune.prato.it) is opposite the Carceri church in Piazza delle Carceri. Prato has a single one-star **hotel**, *Roma*, outside the southern gate at Via Carradori 1 (☎0574.31.777; ❷), and two two-stars: *Il Giglio*, tucked against the city walls at Piazza San Marco 14 (☎0574.37.049, ✉albergoilgiglio@tin.it; ❷); and *La Toscana*, just outside the walls on the north side, at Piazza Ciardi 3 (☎0574.28.096, 🖷0574.25.163; ❷). The more expensive hotels (and there's quite a leap from two- to three-star prices in Prato) tend to be featureless concrete blocks catering for business visitors; one exception is the recently renovated three-star ✈ *Flora*, Via Cairoli 31 (☎0574.3352, 🌐www. hotelflora.info; ❺), which occupies a handsome nineteenth-century building very close to the Piazza del Comune. Of the rest, the pick is *Giardino*, Via Magnolfi 2–6 (☎0574.606.588, ✉info@giradinohotel.com; ❺), which has the advantage of being just twenty metres from the Duomo.

The expansive Piazza Mercatale has two good **trattorie**: *Lapo*, at no. 141 (☎0574.23.745; closed Sun), and ✈ *Osteria Cibbè* at no. 49 (☎0574.60.759; closed Sun). *Lo Scoglio*, Via Verdi 42 (☎0574.22.760; closed Mon), does pizzas and inexpensive fish dishes, while the considerably pricier *Il Baghino*, Via dell'Accademia 9 (☎0574.27.920; closed Sun eve & Mon lunch), is a longstanding local favourite, serving Prato specialities in a traditional atmosphere. *Enoteca Barni*, near Piazza San Marco at Via Ferrucci 22 (☎0574.607.845; closed lunchtime Sat & Sun), is an excellent family-run restaurant/wine bar, where you'll spend in the region of €30–40 a head.

A Prato speciality is the *Biscotto di Prato*, a very hard yellow biscuit, traditionally eaten over the Christmas period, and made a touch less resistant by dipping in wine or coffee. The best outlet for these and other Prato pastries is *Antonio Mattei*, which has been in existence at Via Ricasoli 22 (very close to Piazza San Francesco) since 1858.

If you're staying, you might want to check out what's on at the magnificent old **Teatro Metastasio** at Via Cairoli 59 (☎0574.608.501, 🌐www.metastasio .net), a world-famous venue for concerts (classical and jazz) and theatre productions. Exhibitions and cultural events are organized year-round by the **Centro per l'Arte Contemporanea L. Pecci** (🌐www.centropecci.it), one of the country's most prestigious contemporary art centres; it's 2km southeast of the centre in Viale della Repubblica, and can be reached by bus from Viale Pieve (close to the Castello).

Pistoia

The provincial capital of **PISTOIA** is one of the least visited cities in Tuscany, an unjustified neglect for this quiet, well-preserved medieval settlement at the base of the Apennines. Just 35 minutes or so by train from Florence (about the same by bus), it is an easy and enjoyable day-trip – and also forms an attractive approach to Lucca and Pisa, with both of which it has strong architectural links. In terms of art attractions, its appeal lies in a sequence of Romanesque churches and medieval sculptures, and one of the masterpieces of the della Robbia workshop.

The town's **Roman** forerunner, Pistoria, was where Catiline and his fellow conspirators against the republic were finally run to ground; the town went on to earn itself a reputation as a lair of malcontents. It was a Ghibelline city until its conquest by the Guelph city of Florence in 1254, whereupon it allegedly brought about the **division** of the Guelphs into the Black and White factions. According to the folkloric version, one Pistoiese child injured another while playing with a sword; the miscreant's father sent him to apolo-

RESTAURANTS
La BotteGaia **2**
Lo Storno **1**
San Jacopo **3**

ACCOMMODATION
Autisti **D**
Firenze **A**
Leon Bianco **B**
Patria **C**

PISTOIA

0   200 m

▼ *Florence*

▶ *Prato*

gize, whereupon the father of the injured party chopped the offender's hand off, telling him, "Iron, not words, is the remedy for sword wounds." The city promptly polarized into the Neri and the Bianchi camps (taking the names from ancestors of the two parties), and by some osmotic process these battle names were taken up in Florence. Such was Pistoia's reputation for mayhem, Dante found it entirely appropriate that this should have been the home of Vanni Fucci, a thuggish factional leader whose exploits included stealing the silver from the cathedral; he's encountered in the *Inferno*, enmeshed in a knot of snakes and cursing God.

Except for a brief spell at the start of the fourteenth century, when Castruccio Castracani held the city for Lucca, Pistoia remained a **Florentine** fief, yet for centuries the mythology of murderous Pistoia endured, and Michelangelo spoke for many when he referred to the Pistoiese as the "enemies of heaven". It's fitting that, according to one school of thought, the word **pistol** should be derived from this violent town; meaning "from Pistoia", a *pistole* was originally a dagger, but the name was transferred to the first firearms made here in the sixteenth century. These days, Pistoia maintains its industrial tradition with a large rail plant, but is better known for the acres of garden nurseries on the slopes around.

The liveliest time to be in Pistoia is July, for the **Luglio Pistoiese**, a month-long programme of concerts and events (including the Pistoia Blues music festival featuring major international jazz and blues artists), and culminating in the *Giostra dell'Orso* (see box p.245).

The City

Arriving by train or by bus from Florence you're left just a couple of minutes' walk south of the historic centre: Viale XX Settembre points the way through the **city walls**, which were raised in the fourteenth century and reinforced by the Medici. The interesting part of the city begins one block north of Largo Treviso, at the junction with the centre's widest avenues, Corso Gramsci and Corso Fedi.

Around Piazza Garibaldi

Turn right here for Piazza Garibaldi, where you'll find the thirteenth-century church of **San Domenico** (daily 7.30am–noon & 4.30–6pm, Sun closes 8pm), rebuilt in the 1970s after terrible damage during the war. Scraps of medieval frescoes remain inside, but the most arresting feature is the Rossellino brothers' tomb of the teacher Filippo Lazzari, on the right near the door. In the cloister (entered from the aisle) there are remnants of a fresco of *The Journey of the Magi* by Benozzo Gozzoli, who died of the plague in Pistoia and is buried here.

Opposite San Domenico, the **Cappella del Tau** (Mon–Sat 9am–1pm; free), or Sant'Antonio Abate, preserves a chaos of mainly fourteenth-century frescoes depicting the Creation (in the vault), the life of St Anthony Abbot, and the story of the Sacred Girdle (see p.239). Next door, in the Palazzo del Tau, is the **Museo Marino Marini** (Mon–Sat 10am–6pm; €3.50; joint ticket with Museo Civico and Museo Rospigliosi €6.50), showing a selection of work by Pistoia's most famous modern son. Marini found an early influence in the realism of Etruscan sarcophagi, expressed in the sculptures of horses and riders that he churned out throughout his life; in the 1940s he diversified into portraiture – subjects here include Thomas Mann, Henry Miller and Marc Chagall.

On the same side of the Cappella del Tau, a couple of minutes' walk east, looms the late thirteenth-century facade of **San Paolo**; the front of greenish stone with dark green and white inlays is topped by a statue of St James, possibly by Orcagna.

San Giovanni Fuorcivitas and Madonna dell'Umiltà

All streets north from Piazza Garibaldi link with Via Cavour, now the main street of the city's inner core but once the settlement's outer limit – as the name of the majestic **San Giovanni Fuorcivitas** ("outside the walls") proclaims. The church (daily 7.30am–noon & 5–6.30pm) was founded in the eighth century, but rebuilt between the twelfth and fourteenth centuries, when it received the dazzling green and white flank that serves as its **facade**. Rather than being the focal point of the wall, the doorway is just a brief interruption in the infinitely repeatable pattern of the triple arcade and bands of contrasting marble, a colour scheme echoed in the oratory across the alleyway (now a shop). The **interior** is just as remarkable, as this is one of three Pistoia churches distinguished by pulpits that rank among the finest examples of the sophistication of Tuscan sculpture in the thirteenth century. The **pulpit** was carved in 1270 by a pupil of Nicola Pisano, whose son, Giovanni, executed the cardinal and theological virtues on the holy water stoup. On the opposite side of the church is a life-size terracotta *Visitation*, probably by Luca della Robbia.

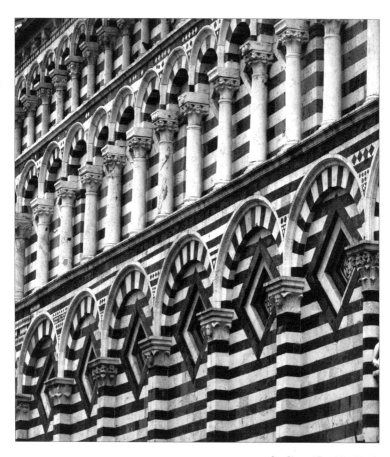

△ San Giovanni Fuorcivitas, Pistoia

From here, a turn up Via Roma is the quickest way into the central square, but if you want to make sure you don't miss any of Pistoia's architectural sights, follow the westward arc of Via Cavour into Via Buozzi until you come to **Madonna dell'Umiltà** (daily 7.45am–noon & 4–7pm). This handsome colossus was designed by a pupil of Bramante and finished off by Vasari with a dome so heavy that the walls had to be reinforced to prevent the church from collapsing.

Piazza del Duomo

The direct path from Via Cavour to Piazza del Duomo crosses the market square, Piazza della Sala. A marginally more long-winded alternative is to walk through the minuscule Piazza San Leone, a few blocks east; this was the centre of the ancient Lombard settlement, and its stocky tower was later the bolt hole of Vanni Fucci.

The medieval complex of the **Piazza del Duomo** is a superb and slightly eccentric ensemble, reversing the normal priorities of the Italian central square: the ornate baptistery lurks in a recess off one corner and the Duomo faces it,

The Giostra dell'Orso

The earliest forerunner of the **Giostra dell'Orso** was a peculiar ritual mentioned in a chronicle of 1300. On March 10 of that year, the feast day of San Francesca Romana, a dozen knights fought a ceremonial battle against a bear dressed in the town's coat of arms. The precise form of this joust changed many times over the following centuries but some version of it was fought every year until 1666, when it seems suddenly to have been abandoned. In 1947 it was revived in more humane form and now takes place on July 25, feast of the city's patron, St James. It forms the centrepiece of the festival season known as the *Luglio Pistoiese* (Pistoia July).

The fun begins with a procession of around three hundred standard bearers, trumpeters, knights, halberdiers and assorted costumed extras from the Porta Lucchese to the Piazza del Duomo. These characters represent the villages around Pistoia, the city's crafts and trades, and the four districts of the historic centre. Each of these four districts is represented in the joust by three knights, their regalia bearing the heraldic emblems of the Lion, the Stag, the Griffon and the Dragon. Having led the procession into the arena laid out on the piazza, the knights are separated into pairs, who then ride against each other around the track, scoring points by hitting the two highly stylized "bears" set on bales on opposite sides of the circuit. Points are awarded according to which parts of the target are hit with the lance, and at the end of the day two prizes are awarded – to the highest-scoring district and the highest-scoring knight.

The *giostra* is always a sell-out; to be sure of tickets, you should contact the regional tourist office at least a month in advance (℡0573.21.622).

turning its sparsely adorned side to the open space and leaving the huge campanile and monolithic civic buildings to take the limelight. There's something odd about the expanse of the piazza too, as if it were conceived for a town considerably larger than present-day Pistoia. Once a year, though, the square is packed to capacity for the **Giostra dell'Orso** (see box above), Pistoia's answer to the medieval shenanigans of Siena's Palio.

The Duomo

If you've come from Pisa or Lucca, the style of Pistoia's **Duomo**, the Cattedrale di San Zeno (daily 8am–12.30pm & 3.30–7pm), will be immediately familiar, with its tiered arcades and distinctive Pisan-Romanesque decoration of striped black and white marble. Set into this soberly refined front is a tunnel-vault portico of bright terracotta tiles by Andrea della Robbia, creator also of the *Madonna and Child* above the door.

The **interior** has an outstanding array of sculptural pieces, one of which is part of the entrance wall – a marvellous font designed by Benedetto da Maiano, showing incidents from the life of the Baptist. Close by, on the wall of the right aisle, is the monument to Dante's friend, the diplomat, teacher and poet Cino da Pistoia; it is said that Boccaccio is one of the pupils to whom he's shown lecturing in the bottom panel.

Just beyond this monument is the **Cappella di San Jacopo** (€3.60), now incorporated into the cathedral museum, which boasts one of the richest pieces of silverwork to be seen in Italy, the **Altarpiece of St James**. Weighing almost a ton and populated with 628 figures, it was begun in 1287 and completed in the fifteenth century, when Brunelleschi cast the two half-figures of prophets on the left-hand side. The length of time taken on the work is clear if you compare the scenes on the front with the bolder figures in the scenes from the life of St James on the left-hand flank, where an extra suppleness and vitality is evident. The artist responsible for these latter panels was a certain Leonardo di Ser Giovanni, who immediately after completing them was given the commission to begin another remarkable piece of silverwork – the altarpiece now in Florence's Museo dell'Opera del Duomo.

In the chapel to the left of the high altar is Antonio Rossellino's bust of Bishop Donato de' Medici, and the so-called *Madonna di Piazza*, begun by Verrocchio and finished by Lorenzo di Credi (often kept under wraps); Verrocchio, with his workshop, was also responsible for the flurried tomb of Cardinal Forteguerri, in the left aisle by the door.

The Duomo's adjacent **Campanile** was originally a Lombard watchtower, then was spruced up with Romanesque arcades in the twelfth century and a Gothic turret in the sixteenth; the swallowtail crenellations near the summit give away the town's old Ghibelline loyalties.

Around Piazza del Duomo

Similarly you have to book at the tourist office in order to see inside the partly clad Palazzo dei Vescovi, now home of the small **Museo di San Zeno** (guided tours Tues, Thurs & Fri 10am–1pm & 3–5pm; €3.60), where the chief exhibit is Ghiberti's reliquary of St James. The basement has an even more modest archeological collection, with relics from the Roman settlement.

Opposite is the dapper Gothic **Baptistery** (Tues–Sun 10am–6pm), designed by Giovanni Pisano and completed in the mid-fourteenth century by Cellino di Nese, creator of the Duomo's monument to Cino da Pistoia. Commercial art shows sometimes fill the space around the font.

Though its interior is closed to the public, you can take a look at the courtyard of the **Palazzo del Podestà** (or Palazzo Pretorio), the law-court building to the side of the baptistery. From the stone benches half-sheltered by the portico the Pistoian judges used to pronounce sentences notorious for their severity; a grimly humorous speciality was to sentence the guilty to be elevated to the ranks of the nobility – thus depriving them of any civic rights under the town's republican constitution.

On the far side of the square, the flaking pale limestone facade of the **Palazzo Comunale** bears a small basalt head that may be a portrait of the Moorish king of Mallorca whom the Pistoiese defeated in the twelfth century; local folklore prefers to interpret it as the image of a man who betrayed the city to the army of Castruccio Castracani in 1315, which is about the time the head was mounted here (though in all likelihood it went up several years before the city fell). The building contains the **Museo Civico** (Tues–Sat 10am–6pm, Sun 9.30am–12.30pm; €3.50; joint ticket with Museo Marini and Museo Rospigliosi €6.50), where the customary welter of run-of-the-mill medieval and Renaissance pieces is counterweighted by an impressive showing of Baroque hyperactivity – including a couple of hideous battle scenes by the evidently disturbed Ciccio Napoletano. Adjoining the museum is a display (same hours & ticket) devoted to Pistoia-born architect Giovanni Michelucci.

The Palazzo Rospigliosi, in Ripa del Sale (down the right-hand side of the Palazzo Comunale), houses the combined **Museo Diocesano** and **Museo Rospigliosi** (Tues–Sat 10am–1pm & 3–6pm, plus same hours on 2nd Sun of month; €3.50; joint ticket with Museo Civico and Museo Marini €6.50), where much of the space is occupied by chalices, censers and crosses, mediocre paintings and miscellaneous pieces of furniture, many of them bequeathed by Pope Clement IX.

The northern quarters

At the back of the Palazzo Comunale, Via Pacini is the obvious route to take to explore the northern part of the town. Across this road, on Piazza San Bartolomeo, is the **Abbazia di San Bartolomeo in Pantano** ("St Bartholomew in the Swamp"), named after the marshy ground on which it was raised in the eighth century. The semi-complete facade is as appealing as any of the city's more polished fronts, and inside (daily 8.30am–noon & 4–6pm) there's the earliest of Pistoia's trio of remarkable pulpits. Executed in 1250 by Guido da Como, and reconstructed from its dismantled parts, it's far less sophisticated than the other two, comprising a rectangular box whose principal scenes are filled with figures arrayed in level ranks like a crowd in a stadium.

The most publicized episode of the Pistoia townscape is not a church but a hospital in a square at the end of Via Pacini – the **Ospedale del Ceppo**, which takes its name from the hollowed-out tree stump (*ceppo*) in which alms were traditionally collected. Established in the thirteenth century, it was embellished in the fifteenth with a portico like the one Brunelleschi designed for the Innocenti in Florence. Emblazoned along its length is the feature that makes it famous, Giovanni della Robbia's painted terracotta **frieze** of the *Theological Virtues* and the *Seven Works of Mercy*. Completed in the early sixteenth century, it is a startlingly colourful panoply of Renaissance types and costume: pilgrims, prisoners, the sick, the dead.

A couple of minutes' walk over to the west, the twelfth-century **Sant'Andrea** (daily 8am–12.30pm & 3–6.30pm) has a typically Pisan facade with a pair of Romanesque lions and a panel of *The Journey of the Magi* stuck onto it. The murky and corridor-slim aisle contains the third and greatest of the pulpits; carved in 1297 by Giovanni Pisano, it is based on his father's design for the Pisa baptistery pulpit and only marginally less elaborate than his own slightly later work in Pisa cathedral. It shows scenes from the life of Christ and the Last Judgement, the figures carved in such deep relief that they seem to be surging out of a limitless depth. Giovanni was the first to appreciate the glory of his achievement; Nicola Pisano had boasted of being the greatest living sculptor, and Giovanni's inscription brags that he has now surpassed his father. The church also has a second piece by Giovanni – the Crucifix mounted on the wall of the right aisle.

The plainest of the city's churches, the Franciscans' **San Francesco al Prato** (daily 7.30am–noon & 4–6.30pm), is a little farther to the west, on the edge of one of the main bus terminals. Tattered fourteenth-century frescoes are preserved in the single nave, and some healthier specimens adorn the chapels at the east end, where there's a fine *Triumph of Augustine* in the chapel to the left of the high altar. To the side of the church there's an unusual memorial to Aldo Moro, the Italian prime minister killed by the Red Brigades on May 7, 1978; the bronze plaques are imprinted with the newspaper headlines from the day his body was found.

Fattoria di Celle

Some 4km east of Pistoia at Santomato, the **Fattoria di Celle** holds a remarkable private art collection, established in 1982 to give Italy an international forum for contemporary art comparable to such centres as the Kröller-Müller in the Netherlands. Everything here, in the rooms and park of the Villa Celle, could be described as environmental art: the large-scale outdoor pieces are conceived as interactions with the natural world, while the smaller installations inside take their cue from the enclosing space of the rooms.

Artists from all over Europe and the United States have contributed to the **sculpture park**, devising a variety of responses to its woodlands and grassy slopes, and to the wider cultural environment of Tuscany. Alice Aycock's steel constructions recall such Renaissance mechanisms as the astrolabe, but are built on a scale to echo the curves and angles of the landscape. A labyrinth of polished green and white marble by Robert Morris recalls the Romanesque churches of the region, and is so perfectly placed on the gradient of the hill that it seems to be a single mass of stone until you come to the entrance. An artificial stream and grotto laid out in the nineteenth century has been used by Anne and Patrick Poirier to evoke the epic struggle between Zeus and the Titans, with steel lightning flashes and fragments of huge marble heads littering the water course. In hi-tech contrast, Dennis Oppenheim's massive contraption of steel towers, immovable pulleys and functionless wires looks like a visual pun on the ski-lifts of the winter resorts north of Pistoia. Most of the installations date from the inaugural year, but new pieces are being commissioned all the time, maintaining the Fattoria di Celle's status as one of the most vital art centres in the country.

The centre is open from April to September and visitors must first write for an appointment, to Fattoria di Celle, 51030 Santomato di Pistoia (Ⓕ0573.479.486). The entrance gate is not signposted, but rather signalled by a huge spherical metal ribcage construction by Alberto Burri.

Practicalities

Pistoia's central **tourist office** is at Piazza del Duomo 4 (Tues–Sun 9am–1pm & 3–6pm; Ⓣ0573.21.622, Ⓦwww.comune.pistoia.it). The city's low tourist profile means a dearth of **accommodation** – so if you plan to stay, phone ahead. There's a single one-star hotel, the clean and friendly *Albergo Autisti*, Viale Pacinotti 89 (Ⓣ0573.21.771; **❶**), and there's only one two-star within the walls, the *Albergo Firenze*, Via Curtatone e Montanara 42 (Ⓣ & Ⓕ573.231.141, Ⓦwww .hotel-firenze.it; **❷**). Central alternatives are the three-star *Leon Bianco*, Via Panciatichi 2 (Ⓣ0573.26.675, Ⓦwww.hotelleonbianco.it; **❹**), or the *Patria*, Via Crispi 6–8 (Ⓣ0573.25.187, Ⓦwww.patriahotel.com; **❹**). If you have your own transport, you could stay at the extremely welcoming and well-priced ⚘ *Villa Vannini* (Ⓣ0573.420.31, Ⓦwww.volpe-uva.it; **❸**), 6km to the north of Pistoia, in the village of Villa di Piteccio; it's a tranquil family-run country house, with an outstanding restaurant.

In the centre of town, there's an excellent **osteria** in Via del Lastrone, off Piazza della Sala: *La BotteGaia*, at no. 4 (closed Sun lunch & Mon), which has a fine range of *crostini* and *bruschette* plus a few more substantial offerings (the *menù degustiazione* is very good value), and a terrific wine list. Very close by, at no. 8, ⚘ *Lo Storno* (Ⓣ0573.26.193; open for lunch every day, plus Wed–Sat evenings) serves robust and good-value local dishes, and is so popular that reservations are advisable. There's also a straightforward, inexpensive and good-quality Tuscan menu at *San Jacopo*, Via Crispi 15 (closed Mon eve & Tues).

Leaving Pistoia, Lazzi **buses** for Florence and Prato run from the train station; COPIT buses bound for Empoli, where you can also change for Vinci, leave from Piazza San Francesco. The route to Vinci goes over beautiful Monte Albano and allows a loop to Florence or Pisa if you set out early in the day.

Montecatini and Monsummano

Known as the **Valdinievole** (Valley of Mists), the area to the west of Pistoia is a region of subterranean streams and springs that now harbours one of Italy's main concentrations of **spa towns**. As with the German spas, such resorts as a rule don't have the same aura of social exclusivity as they do in Britain, but the two big centres of the Valdinievole, **Montecatini Terme** and **Monsummano Terme**, are nonetheless unlikely to tempt you to linger overnight, though you might want to stop for a couple of hours just to sample the peculiar Belle Epoque ambience. As long as you're not passing through some time between November and Easter, that is, because in winter these places are comatose. Florence-to-Viareggio trains stop at Montecatini, but Monsummano is only really worth a call if you're driving.

Montecatini Terme

No spa in Italy has a glossier reputation than **MONTECATINI TERME**, as can be gauged from the fact that the likes of Gucci and Gianfranco Ferre find it profitable to maintain outlets here – and it was in Montecatini that Fellini filmed the spa scenes in *8½*. A leafy grid of indistinguishable apartment blocks and villas, where it seems to be eternally siesta time, surround the central **Parco delle Terme** (a ten-minute walk from the train station), where each of the nine sulphate springs is encased in its own separate building. Fronting the piazza at the edge of the park is the pompous **Terme Leopoldine**, a shrine to the healing properties of mud baths. North of this is the **Tettuccio**, discovered in the fourteenth century but not exploited to the full until Grand Duke Leopoldo I gave it the works in the eighteenth. Inside, Art Nouveau paintings and ceramics create a suitably sybaritic environment in which to compose your letters in the spa café or imbibe the acrid water. Across the way, the Palladian home of the **Regina** spring suggests more astringent regimes, while at the back of the park, the mock-medieval **Torretta** embodies the straightforwardly escapist element of all spa resorts. All these spas are open from May to October; there's one establishment, the hybrid Neo-Renaissance-modernist **Excelsior**, that's open all year. Details of the treatments at offer at the *Excelsior* and its siblings are available at the tourist office (see below).

The non-thermal delights of Montecatini can all be sampled by following Viale Diaz, which curves round the north side of the park. Here, across the road from the Regina spa, you'll find the **Accademia d'Arte** (Mon–Sat 3–6pm; free), a mishmash of gifts from illustrious guests such as Verdi, who composed *Otello* while staying in Montecatini, refining the score on the piano that's kept here. Ten minutes' walk beyond is the relatively unkempt verdure of **Le Panteraie**, a wooded park with a swimming pool and deer reserve.

Halfway between the gallery and the woods is the only inexpensive way of having fun in Montecatini, the **funicular** to Montecatini Alto, a few hundred metres above the spa (April–Oct daily every 30min; €5 return); if you drive, it's a five-kilometre haul. The original Montecatini settlement here offers excellent views, especially of Monsummano, and in summer the tiny Piazza Giusti becomes a pleasant outdoor extension of its cafés and *pizzerie*. If you want to get out of the sun for a while, there's the stalactite-heavy **Grotta Maona** (April–Oct daily 9am–noon & 2–6pm; €4.50), a couple of kilometres below Montecatini Alto; it's the only cave in Italy that contains two separate springs.

Practicalities

The **tourist office**, Viale Verdi 66 (Mon–Sat 9am–12.30pm & 3–6pm; summer also Sun 9am–noon; ☏0572.772.244, ⊛www.termemontecatini.it), has full details of Montecatini's plentiful **accommodation**; there are around three hundred places to stay, predominantly top-bracket, but with about thirty one-star hotels. Most of Montecatini's **restaurants** are attached to the posh hotels; of the independent places, the best are *Enoteca da Giovanni*, Via Garibaldi 25 (closed Mon & Aug), and *La Rughetta* in Piazza Giusti, Montecatini Alto (closed Tues), both of which will set you back around €40 a head. Nearly as good, and appreciably less expensive, is the *Bolognese* restaurant-pizzeria, Corso Matteotti 90 (closed Mon).

Monsummano Terme

Montecatini's sister spa, **MONSUMMANO TERME**, a few kilometres southeast, has its own speciality act: the steam cave. The family of the poet Giuseppe Giusti – who was born here in 1809 – set the business in motion when they discovered a flooded cave filled with mineral-saturated steam. Divided into chambers tagged *Inferno*, *Purgatorio* and *Paradiso*, the **Grotta Giusti** (April–Oct), on the eastern outskirts, is still the town's big draw – half luxury hotel, half medical centre. Competition is provided by the artificial **Grotta Parlanti** (May–Oct) to the north, whose vapours are allegedly even more efficacious. The old town of **Monsummano Alto**, 3km from the centre up a relentlessly steep and narrow road, is now little more than a twelfth-century church and a few very ruined castle ruins; the panorama is spectacular though, with the massed glasshouses of Pescia catching the sun like a lake.

Empoli and around

The N67, tracking the Arno west of Florence, is as dispiriting as the road that follows the river to the east. Busy and slow, it's strung with drab towns, industrial sites, megastores and warehouses, and – apart from a handful of attractions in **Empoli** – is only worth bothering with for the diversions to be found off it. The most popular of these, by far, are to be found in **Vinci**, birthplace of Leonardo, but the diminutive hill-town of **San Miniato** is a more substantial attraction.

Empoli

The manufacturing town of **EMPOLI**, purveyor of glass and raincoats to the nation, is a major junction of road and rail routes between Florence, Pisa, the coast and Siena, and thus might well be a place you'll find yourself passing through. Most people limit their exploration to a change of platforms at the train station, or a confused tour of the one-way road system.

If you want to spare time for a quick look around, head for the central **Piazza Farinata degli Uberti**, named after the commander of the Ghibelline army of Siena which defeated the Florentine Guelphs at Montaperti in 1260; he's revered not for his military prowess, but for his advocacy at the "parliament of Empoli", when he dissuaded his followers from wrecking Florence. The green and white **Collegiata**, on the square, was founded as far back as the fifth century; its lower portion is the most westerly example of Florentine Romanesque architecture, the top a postwar reconstruction of a nineteenth-century imitation.

Adjacent is the **Museo Collegiata**, entered from Piazzetta della Propositora (Tues–Sun 9am–noon & 4–7pm; €3; joint ticket with the Museo Leonardiano in Vinci and the ceramics museum in nearby Montelupo €6). Highlights of the collection of sculpture and painting are a couple of triptychs by Lorenzo Monaco, a small *Maestà* attributed to Filippo Lippi, a superb Masolino *Pietà*, sculptures by Bernardo Rossellino and Mino da Fiesole, and Lorenzo di Bicci's *St Nicholas of Tolentino Saving Empoli from the Plague*, featuring a view of the town in the 1440s. The museum also possesses an item relating to one of Tuscany's stranger Easter rituals, a winged mechanical donkey that used to perform a version of Florence's incendiary dove ceremony, the donkey being propelled from the Collegiata tower down to Piazza Farinata degli Uberti, where it would ignite a pile of fireworks. (Nowadays a papier-mâché beast performs the role.) The museum ticket also gives you access to the adjacent church of **Santo Stefano** (Tues–Fri 9am–noon), where you can see the remnants of frescoes by Masolino and a marble *Annunciation* by Bernardo Rossellino.

Close by, at Piazza della Vittorio 15, stands the birthplace of Empoli's most famous native of recent times, the great composer-pianist Ferruccio Busoni (1866–1924). The town commemorates him with a series of concerts from October to May (details on ⓦwww.comune.empoli.fi.it). The Busoni house contains a small museum, but it's not open to casual visitors.

If you're keen on Pontormo's paintings, you might want to drive out to the hamlet of **PONTORME**, on the outskirts of Empoli on the road to Florence. This was the birthplace of the artist baptized as Jacopo Carrucci, and the parish church of San Michele retains a couple of pictures by him, a *St John the Evangelist* and a *St Michael*.

Cerreto Guidi

From the time of Cosimo I to the end of the dynasty, the Medici administered their estates in this northern part of Tuscany from the villa at **CERRETO GUIDI** (daily 9am–7pm, closed 2nd & 3rd Mon of month; €2), 8km northwest of Empoli and served by COPIT bus. Having converted this former castle into something more domestic, and having got Buontalenti to build the huge approach ramps that remain the villa's most distinctive feature, the clan set about making it the focus of rural life in the Empoli district: they instituted a weekly fair here, with compulsory attendance for the local peasants. The **villa** is a plain box of a house and the church that Cosimo built next door is no more exciting – though there's a good view from the top of the ramps, with Frederick II's tower at San Miniato (see p.252) standing out in the middle distance. Unless you're a bloodsports enthusiast, in which case the Cerreto Guidi hunting museum may be of interest, the main point of visiting the **interior** is to see the gallery of Medici portraits, and even these are less than scintillating. One section is entitled "Unhappy marriages among the descendants of Cosimo I", and includes a likeness of Cosimo's daughter Isabella, murdered here by her husband in 1576 for her infidelity; the Medici hitmen caught up with her alleged lover in Paris the following year.

Vinci

Sitting on the southern slopes of Monte Albano, 11km north of Empoli, **VINCI** is set amid a rolling swathe of vineyards and olive groves. The landscape is not what draws people along the road between Empoli and Pistoia, however – it's the village's association with **Leonardo da Vinci**, who in April 1452 was born in the nearby hamlet of Archiano and baptized in Vinci's church of Santa Croce.

Vinci itself is a torpid place but preserves a mighty thirteenth-century castle, the Castello dei Conti Guidi, which houses the main part of the **Museo Leonardiano** (daily 9.30am–7pm; winter closes 6pm; €5; joint ticket with the Museo Collegiata in Empoli and the Montelupo ceramics museum €6) – the ticket office is in the Palazzina Uzielli, in Via Rossi. Opened on the five-hundredth anniversary of Leonardo's birth, the museum is dedicated to Leonardo the inventor and engineer rather than Leonardo the artist, with a large and fairly imaginative display of models – tanks, water cannon, flying machines, looms and gear mechanisms – all reconstructed from his notebook drawings, which are reproduced alongside the relevant contraptions. Too much space is devoted to Leonardo's more whimsical jottings – half a room is given over, for example, to a mock-up of his skis for walking on water – but high production values prevail throughout. Avoid the museum on a Sunday, when it can feel as if half the population of Tuscany has turned up. If you want a bite to eat before heading back, drop in at *Il Ristoro del Museo*, at the back of the museum at Via Montalbano 9 (closed Fri evening & Sat lunch).

Leonardo's **birthplace** (same hours; free) is in **ANCHIANO**, some 2km farther north into the hills, a pleasant walk past fields of poppies. The house was owned by his father, a Florentine clerk called Ser Piero; Leonardo's mother is generally believed to have been a *contadina* (peasant girl), but the only things that are known for certain is that her name was Caterina and she didn't marry his father, possibly because Ser Piero was already betrothed – within eight months of his son's birth he had married the sixteen-year-old daughter of a Florentine notary, and soon afterwards Caterina was married to a man who went by the name of Accattabriga, who may have been a soldier. (Meaning something like "trouble-maker", Accattabriga was a common nickname among mercenaries.) Placard-size captions and a couple of reproduction drawings are pretty well all there is to see inside the house.

San Miniato

The strategic hill-top site of **SAN MINIATO**, more or less equidistant between Pisa and Florence, has been exploited since the era of Augustus, when the Roman settlement of Quarto was founded here. A Lombard town succeeded it, and at the end of the tenth century Otto I made this an outpost of the Holy Roman Empire. A later emperor, Frederick II, gave the town its landmark fortress, and the imperial connection led to the nickname *San Miniato dei Tedeschi* ("of the Germans"). Today it's a brusque little agricultural town, good for a couple of hours' break of journey, but unlikely to tempt you to give it longer.

The train station and main, predominantly modern, part of town – **San Miniato Basso** – are sited down in the valley. From here it's a steep four-kilometre climb to **San Miniato Alto**, the old quarter. A mini orange bus does the run to San Miniato Alto from the train station (daily, about every 30min 6.30–10.30am & 3.45–7.30pm). It deposits you just below the walls in Piazzale Dante Alighieri, which is also the place to park.

Beyond the town gate, a right turn leads to **Piazza del Popolo**, where a plan of the town is displayed outside the tourist office. At the top end of the square is the much rebuilt church of **San Domenico**, which contains the fine tomb of a Florentine doctor named Giovanni Chellini. Carved by one Pagno di Lapo Portigiani, it's modelled on the tomb of Leonardo Bruni in Florence's Santa Croce.

From here Via Conti rises to the **Piazza della Repubblica**, jazzed up by seventeenth-century *graffiti* on the long facade of the seminary, part of whose ground floor is a row of restored fourteenth-century shops, a rare survival. Opposite the seminary, a flight of steps rises to the **Prato del Duomo**, where a tower of the imperial fortress now houses a hotel. Next door, the **Palazzo dei Vicari dell'Imperatore** is a relic of the time when San Miniato was the seat of the vicars of the Holy Roman Empire: Countess Matilda of Tuscia, daughter of one of these vicars, was born here.

The red-brick **Duomo**, dedicated to St Genesius, the patron saint of actors, is hacked-about Romanesque, with an interior of Baroque gilding and marbling.

△ Piazza della Repubblica, San Miniato

Next door, the tiny **museum** (April–Nov Tues–Sun 10am–1pm & 3–7pm; Dec–March Sat & Sun same hours; €2) has a *Crucifixion* by Filippo Lippi and a terracotta bust of Christ by Verrocchio. At the back of the Duomo, the ponderous Santuario del Crocifisso was built to house a Crucifix that was thought to have played a part in saving the town from the plague of 1637; the Crucifix is still there, but the sanctuary is rarely open.

From the Prato del Duomo it's a short walk up to the tower of the **Rocca** (daily 10am–7pm), which was rebuilt by Frederick II and restored brick by brick after damage in World War II; the main point of the climb is the stupendous panoramic view (on a clear day) of the surrounding countryside. Dante's *Inferno* perpetuates the memory of Pier della Vigna, Frederick's treasurer, who was imprisoned and blinded here, a fate that drove him to suicide by jumping from the tower – as the inscription at its foot records.

Below the tower, on the opposite side from the Duomo, stands the church of **San Francesco**, occupying the site where the Lombards dedicated the chapel to San Miniato that gave the town its name. The church was altered by the Franciscans, who were given the property after Francis himself had visited the town, and traces of their Romanesque building can still just about be discerned through the later Gothic.

Practicalities

The **tourist office** is in Piazza del Popolo (summer daily 9am–1pm & 4–7.30pm; winter Mon–Sat 10am–1pm & 3–6.30pm; ☎0571.418.739, ⓦwww .comune.san-miniato.pi.it). The tower of the Prato del Duomo is now occupied by the three-star *Miravalle* **hotel** (☎0571.418.075; ❸), San Miniato's best place to stay, with marvellous views and a good restaurant in the palazzo next door. Other recommendable **restaurants** are *Da Canapone* in Piazza Buonaparte (closed Mon), serving local food at reasonable prices, and the *L'Antro di Bacco* (closed Wed), in Via IV Novembre.

San Miniato boasts a rich cultural calendar between the months of May and October, with a good choice of **concerts** and **exhibitions**, both in the village itself and in outlying areas. There's a monthly **antiques market** in the Loggiata di San Domenico (1st Sun of month). On the first Sunday after Easter, this zone around the Rocca is packed with competitors in the national **kite-flying championships,** which competes with a flower festival held the same day.

South of Empoli

The **N429** road and Empoli–Siena **train** line, which head south between Empoli and San Miniato, provide an easy and direct approach to San Gimignano and Siena. Along the way are two interesting, if modest, hill-town attractions: **Castelfiorentino,** home to a couple of delightful Gozzoli fresco cycles, and **Certaldo,** where Boccaccio spent his last years.

Castelfiorentino

A fief of the bishops of Florence from the twelfth century onwards, **CASTEL-FIORENTINO** remained in the city's orbit through most of its uneventful history. Today it's a fairly large urban centre, with light industry and block housing spreading out in the modern, lower quarter of town, across the river Elsa. It's not a particularly pretty stop and, for once in Tuscany, you may well find yourself the only visitor in the place.

From the **train station** – where you'll find the tourist office at Via Ridolfi 1 (9.30am–12.30pm & 3.30–6.30pm, Fri–Sun closes 7pm; ⓦwww.comune .castelfiorentino.fi.it) – you can see the expansive Piazza Gramsci straight ahead. It's flanked by cafés, bars and the only central **hotel,** the three-star *Hotel-Ristorante Lami* at no. 82–83 (☏0571.64.076, ⓦwww.albergolami.it; ❷). Best of a dozen or so **restaurants,** most grouped in the area around Piazza Gramsci, is *La Magona,* Via Ridolfi 10 (closed Sun & Aug), to your right out of the station.

The Town

To look around the **Castello** – the old, upper town – head up the stairs at the corner of Piazza Gramsci, by the Teatro del Popolo, and you'll reach a patch of garden square, to either side of which runs **Via dei Tilli.**

Turn left and you come to the **Biblioteca Comunale** (summer Tues, Thurs & Sat 4–7pm, Sun 10am–noon & 4–7pm; winter Tues, Thurs & Sat 3–6pm, Sun 10am–noon & 3–6pm; €2.60), where frescoes by Gozzoli are displayed on the top floor, having been detached from a pair of local sanctuary chapels. To the left of the gallery entrance is a complete reconstruction of the *Madonna della Tosse* chapel, including a frescoed "altarpiece" and side-wall scenes of the death and assumption of the Virgin, their landscapes studded with cypress trees and rolling Tuscan hills. More fragmentary but more interesting are the flood-damaged frescoes and *sinopie* from the *Sanctuary of the Visitation.* These again depict episodes from the life of the Virgin, and of her parents, Joachim (Gioacchino) and Anne, the best of them full of genre detail of everyday fifteenth-century life. Both sets of frescoes were completed in the 1480s, late in Gozzoli's career, possibly during periods when the plague had hit Florence.

Turn right from the garden square along Via dei Tilli, and you come to the main **Piazza del Popolo,** flanked by the Collegiata di San Lorenzo – built on Lombard foundations – and a nineteenth-century Municipio. The stepped street above the piazza leads to the summit of the town, marked by the Romanesque **Pieve di San Ippolito e Biagio** (currently closed for restoration). It was here in 1197 that the rectors of the Tuscan League, which was formed to defend the cities against "any emperor, king, or prince", were sworn in – Castelfiorentino's only real episode in the limelight.

Down in the **lower town**, east of Piazza Gramsci (left as you face the station and river), a small park gives onto the Baroque church of **Santa Verdiana**, adjacent to which there's a museum (Sat 4–7pm, Sun 10am–noon & 4–7pm; €3) displaying paintings from churches in the town and region, including works by Duccio, Taddeo Gaddi and Gozzoli. Many of these panels came from nearby **San Francesco**, which has two fragmentary fresco cycles of the *Life of St Francis*; the finer, by Cenno di Cenni, is in the nave. As so often in these parts, the church claims foundation by St Francis himself. St Verdiana – the local patron saint – was his contemporary and ordained by him into the order; she is generally depicted with a couple of serpents whose lives she saved, in a pause between other miracles.

San Vivaldo

If you're driving and feel like a rambling, fourteen-kilometre cross-country route down to San Gimignano, follow the road southwest of Castelfiorentino through either Montaione, a quiet little hill-town with a less-than-essential paleontology museum, or through the minor spa of Gambassi Terme – with the lovely Romanesque **Pieve a Chianni** on its outskirts – to the village of **SAN VIVALDO**. Here, amid the woods, a fourteenth-century Franciscan hermit founded the monastery of **Sacro Monte**, which between 1500 and 1515 was endowed with 34 chapels, representing the Stations of the Cross and other scenes from the life of Christ. The surviving fifteen chapels are not quite the "Jerusalem in Tuscany" the local tourist literature promotes; clustered together by the entrance gate to the monastery, they look more like a miniature cemetery and hardly a credible alternative to a pilgrimage to the Holy Land. However, each of the chapels is endowed with a large-scale painted terracotta tableau, completed with impressive animation by artists of the della Robbia school.

Certaldo

Even without its Boccaccio connection, **CERTALDO** would justify a visit. A tiny but very striking hill-town – all red-brick towers, battlements and mansions – it is visible for miles along the Elsa valley, and itself has views out to San Gimignano. For a spell in the twelfth century, its rulers, the Alberti dukes of Prato, controlled a domain stretching north to the Arno, but subsequent domination by Florence and incursions by Siena led to its assuming a largely provincial role. Nowadays its lower town, built along the N429, is a prosperous place, making its money from wine and agriculture, as well as glass, brick and pasta factories. In late July or early August the town (Ⓦ www.comune.certaldo.fi.it) holds the atmospheric **Mercantia** festival, which features various medieval-themed events, all illuminated by torches and candles. There's also a **cultural festival** in September, the first Sunday of which is the feast of Santa Giulia della Rena, signal for a reunion of all the town's emigrants.

You're not allowed to drive into the old town – **Certaldo Alto** – unless you're staying overnight up there. Arriving by bus or train, you'll find yourself close to the central Piazza Boccaccio in the **lower town**, from where you can either walk up the steep Vicolo Signorini or take the funicular (daily: summer 7am–midnight; winter 7am–10pm; every 15min; €1.20 return).

Certaldo Alto

Certaldo's upper town is little more than a single street, predictably dubbed **Via Boccaccio**, which stretches from the western side (where the funicular arrives) to the archetypally Tuscan town hall, or Palazzo Vicariale.

Halfway along the street stands the **Casa del Boccaccio** (summer Mon & Wed–Sun 10am–7pm, Tues 10am–4.30pm; winter Mon & Wed–Sun 10.30am–4.30pm, Tues closed; €3.10; joint ticket with Palazzo Vicariale & Museo d'Arte Sacra €6). This is as likely a candidate for the home of the poet as any of the town's mansions, though scholars continue to dispute quite which towered house Boccaccio specified in his will. If indeed it is his home, then he spent the last twelve years of his life here – despite a considerable reputation – in very modest circumstances. Given the uncertainty over its attribution, the house contains no direct links with Boccaccio: indeed it contains nothing of any great antiquity, other than a case of medieval shoes. Instead, all you get are photos of portraits of the writer, illustrations of scenes from the *Decameron* and various editions of his masterpiece, in the original and in translation.

More interesting is the church of **SS Michele e Jacopo**, a short distance farther up the street, which Boccaccio attended and where he was buried. A simple marble diamond on the floor of the nave marks his grave, above a mock-medieval funerary slab, which replaces the tomb destroyed in 1783: the burghers of Certaldo – having concluded, as the author did, that the *Decameron* was an ungodly work – ripped up the tombstone and scattered his ashes. Byron, who came to pay his respects a few years later, was scandalized:

> ...even his tomb
> Uptorn must bear the hyena bigot's wrong;
> No more amidst the meaner dead find room.

Byron's verses had an effect, prompting the Marquise Lenzoni – a straggler from the Medici family – to buy up and restore the Boccaccio house and arrange the **monument** on the left-hand wall of the church, which comprises a sixteenth-century bust and a slab bearing the lines the poet wrote as his own epitaph. The church's other notable features are a trio of pieces from the workshop of Andrea della Robbia, a fourteenth-century Sienese fresco of the Madonna and Child, and the tomb of Certaldo's patron saint, Giulia della Rena, who spent thirty years in a walled-up cell beside the sacristy, and at whose death in 1367 all the bells of Certaldo are said to have spontaneously begun to ring. The small **Museo d'Arte Sacra**, off the church's cloister (summer daily 10am–7pm; winter Sat & Sun 10.30am–4.30pm; €2.60; joint ticket with Palazzo Vicariale & Casa di Boccaccio €6), is a typical small-town collection of humdrum paintings and ecclesiastical applied art.

As you'll see from a long way off, the **Palazzo Vicariale** (summer daily 10am–7pm; winter Tues–Sun 10.30am–4.30pm; €3; joint ticket with Casa di Boccaccio & Museo d'Arte Sacra €6) is blazoned with coats of arms (including further examples from the della Robbia workshop) that attest to its use as the governor's residence, after the demise of its original owners, the Alberti. Inside, the arcaded courtyard displays further coats of arms and a fragmentary array of frescoes, many either painted or repainted at the end of the fifteenth century. To the right as you enter, the room in which the law court convened is dominated by a fresco of Doubting Thomas, attributed to Gozzoli. Cells for minor felons adjoin this room; serious offenders were dispatched to the grim, almost windowless dungeons at the rear of the courtyard, next to the women's prison. Among the graffiti etched by the prisoners you'll find a diagram of the

Boccaccio

Giovanni Boccaccio was born, according to the account he gave his friend Petrarch, in Paris, probably in 1313. The son of a banker from Certaldo, he returned fairly early in his childhood to Tuscany. As a youth he rejected the banking career planned by his family, instead going to study in Naples, where he fell in love with Fiammetta, an illegitimate princess and the inspiration for numerous of his sonnets. He returned to Florence reluctantly, after the collapse of his father's business, and there – as well as in Milan and Avignon, where he worked as a diplomat – wrote his major works, including the **Decameron**. Aged around 50, he met a monk who so impressed him with a vision of his death that he decided to reject his worldly excesses of old and retire to Certaldo. The rest of the years here were spent producing learned volumes on geography, the vanity of human affairs, and mythology, and preparing lectures on Dante. He died on December 21, 1375.

sun, each beam signifying a day spent confined. Upstairs lie the more spacious chambers of the governor and his servants, again with the odd faded fresco. These rooms are used on and off for special exhibitions, often with a Boccaccian theme.

Back downstairs, a door from the magistrates' hall opens onto a walled garden that gives you a wonderful view from its parapet. On the far side of the garden is the entrance to the deconsecrated church of **San Tommaso e Prospero**, which was used as a storeroom from the eighteenth century, then restored after World War II. It contains a miscellany of frescoes and *sinopie*, the most notable being the *Deposition* that forms the focus of Gozzoli's *Tabernacle of the Condemned*, which was moved here from the local chapel for which it was created.

Practicalities

There are two **hotel–restaurants** up in Certaldo Alto. The two-star *Il Castello*, Via della Rena 6 (T0571.668.250, Wwww.albergoilcastello.it; ❹), occupies an appealingly dowdy old mansion at the western end of Via Boccaccio; it has a splendid garden, overlooking the lower town, and offers good-value if rather basic food (restaurant closed Tues; around €35). The food at the ⚵ *Osteria del Vicario*, Via Rivellino 3 (T0571.668.228, Wwww.osteriadelvicario.it; ❹), just beyond the Palazzo Vicariale, is somewhat more expensive (around €45; restaurant closed Wed) and correspondingly more refined; the rooms are a touch pricier and cosier too – five of them are in the same thirteenth-century monastic building as the restaurant, four are in a neighbouring house (these have splendid views) and a further six are located in a third building, 100m away. The excellent **campsite** *Toscana Colliverdi*, Via Marcialla 349 (T0571.669.334; April–Sept), is a short distance south in the village of Marcialla, on the very edge of the Chianti hills.

Travel details

Trains

Empoli to: Castelfiorentino (hourly; 20min); Certaldo (hourly; 30min); Florence (every 30min; 25min); Pisa (every 30min; 25min); Poggibonsi (hourly; 40min); Siena (hourly; 1hr).

Florence to: Borgo San Lorenzo (every 2hr; 1hr); Empoli (every 30min; 30min); Lucca (hourly; 1hr 20min); Montecatini (hourly; 50min); Pistoia (hourly; 35min); Prato (every 30min; 20min); Viareggio (hourly; 1hr 40min).

Pistoia to: Florence (hourly; 30–45min); Lucca

(hourly; 45min); Montecatini (hourly; 15min); Viareggio (hourly; 1hr 15min).

Prato to: Florence (every 30min; 20min); Lucca (hourly; 1hr); Montecatini (hourly; 30min); Pistoia (hourly; 15min); Viareggio (hourly; 1hr 30min).

Buses

Borgo San Lorenzo to: (SITA) San Piero a Sieve, Scarperia, Barberino di Mugello and other villages in the Mugello.

Castelfiorentino to: (SITA) Empoli, Florence, Certaldo and Volterra.

Empoli to: Cerreto Guidi and Vinci (from outside train station), Castelfiorentino and Certaldo (from Piazza della Vittoria).

Florence to: (ATAF) La Petraia, Careggi, Pratolino and Fiesole; (SITA) Castellina in Chianti, Greve, Radda in Chianti, Gaiole, Barberino di Mugello, Certaldo, Pontassieve, Borgo San Lorenzo and San Casciano; (Lazzi) Cerreto Guidi, Empoli, Incisa Valdarno, Montecatini Terme, Prato, Pistoia and Pontassieve; (CAP) Borgo San Lorenzo, Impruneta and Prato; (COPIT) Pistoia and Poggio a Caiano.

Montecatini Terme to: (Lazzi) Monsummano, Pescia, Collodi, Pistoia, Prato, Florence, Pisa and Livorno.

Pistoia to: (Lazzi) Montecatini, Prato, Florence, Lucca, Pisa and Viareggio; (COPIT) Montecatini, Poggio a Caiano, Empoli and Vinci.

Prato to: (Lazzi) Montecatini, Pistoia, Florence, Lucca, Pisa and Viareggio; (CAP) Florence, Siena, Barberino and Mugello.

3

Lucca and northern Tuscany

CHAPTER 3 # Highlights

* **Lucca** An amazing array of Pisan-Romanesque churches in this most urbane of Tuscan towns. **See p.264**

* **Villa Reale** The best of several villas and gardens around Lucca. **See p.276**

* **Walking in the Alpi Apuane** Long and short walks in these dramatic mountains that rise just behind the Riviera della Versilia. **See p.282**

* **Carrara** Fascinating centre of Tuscany's marble-mining region. **See p.285**

* **The Garfagnana** A verdant patchwork of valleys and mountains, with excellent hiking in the Orecchiella. **See p.288**

△ The Alpi Apuane

3

Lucca and northern Tuscany

Northern Tuscany is one of the province's least-known regions. Very few non-Italians holiday on its resort-lined coast, the so-called Riviera della Versilia, and fewer still penetrate inland to the mountains of the Alpi Apuane or the remote hills and valleys of the Garfagnana and Lunigiana. The one city on the Tuscan sightseeing trail is Lucca – and even there tourism, strangely, is very much a secondary consideration.

Lucca's proximity to Pisa – half an hour by road or rail – makes it an excellent first or last Tuscan stop if you're flying in or out of that city's airport. Even if you're not, Lucca is well worth an overnight stay or a day-trip from Florence (the train takes around an hour). Contained within vast, park-lined walls, it's an urbane, affluent place, with as rewarding an ensemble of Romanesque churches as any you'll find in Italy.

For a quick break by the sea, the sands of the **Riviera della Versilia** are pleasant enough, and easily reached from Lucca. Though there is often little to distinguish the resorts, where the beaches are usually staked out by private operators, the towns of **Viareggio** and **Forte dei Marmi** have their moments – Viareggio at carnival time, when it mounts Italy's most amazing procession of floats, and in high summer, when it's the first-choice resort for many Florentines having a day out by the sea. And from this coast it is a simple matter to explore the jagged peaks of the **Alpi Apuane**, which run parallel to the sea for some 40km. The mountains are best known for the **marble quarries** around **Carrara**, but head beyond these and you will find yourself amid steep forested valleys, threaded by a network of clearly marked **footpaths**. Many of these can be trekked in a day from their village trailheads, though there are longer trails and accommodation refuges if you fancy something more strenuous. More important still, the area is well mapped, not always the case in Italy.

Equally easy to visit from Lucca is the **Garfagnana**, a lovely rural enclave that focuses on the **Serchio valley** and is flanked by the eastern slopes of the Apuane on one side and the more rounded mountains of the **Orecchiella** on the other. Plenty of trails strike off into these upland regions, each of which is protected by a regional nature reserve. **Castelnuovo di Garfagnana** is the only town of any size, a good base for excursions to the hills or a visit to nearby **Barga**, the one outstanding medieval centre. North of the Serchio is one of the

most marginalized areas of Tuscany, the **Lunigiana**, a wild and unspoilt region of rocky, forested landscape peppered with castles and tiny hamlets.

By virtue of their microclimates and a position that puts them at a meeting point of Alpine and Mediterranean vegetation zones, the Apuane and Orecchiella constitute one of the finest **floral** zones in the country: two-thirds of

Italy's known species grow here, and in late spring the upland meadows are carpeted with flowers. Besides these and a wide variety of fungi, the reserves here abound in often spectacular **wildlife** such as wolves, red deer and golden eagles. At least 165 bird species have been reported, some 85 of them breeding here, including kestrels, buzzards and sparrowhawks.

Lucca

LUCCA is the most graceful of Tuscany's provincial capitals, set inside a ring of Renaissance walls fronted by gardens and huge bastions. It's quiet without being dull, absorbs its tourists with ease, has a peaceful, self-contained historic centre and offers a range of good restaurants. Henry James's eulogy – "a place overflowing with everything that makes for ease, for plenty, for beauty, for interest and good example" – still holds true. Lucca is a delightful town simply to wander at random: it's one of the few places in Tuscany where many locals ride bikes, and as a result much of the old centre is refreshingly free of traffic. The city is reputed to have once had seventy churches, and even today you can

ACCOMMODATION

Alla Corte degli Angeli	C
A Palazzo Busdraghi	B
Bernadino	H
Diana	G
La Romea	E
Locanda L'Elisa	N
Melecchi	I
Moderno	L
Ostello San Frediano	A
Piccolo Hotel Puccini	D
Rex	K
Stipino	J
Universo	F
Villa La Principessa	M

◄ Viareggio

▼ **L**, **M**, **N** & Pisa

hardly walk for five minutes without coming upon a small piazza and marble-fronted church facade. Most were built obliquely to the grid of streets, so you rarely confront a church head on, but rather as a sudden apparition as you enter a square.

Lucca lies at the heart of one of Italy's richest agricultural regions ("half-smothered in oil and wine and corn and all the fruits of the earth," James wrote) and has prospered since the Romans, whose gridiron orthodoxy is still obvious in the layout of the streets. Under the **Lombards** it was the capital of Tuscia (Tuscany), though its heyday was between the eleventh and fourteenth centuries, when banking and the silk trade brought wealth and, for a time, political power. In a brief flurry of military activity Lucca lost its independence to Pisa in

RESTAURANTS

Buca di Sant'Antonio	9	La Mora	1
Canuleia	7	Osteria Baralla	5
Da Guido	4	Ristorante Puccini	8
Da Giulio	2	Slim Jones	10
Da Leo	6	Trattoira Buralli	3
Gli Orti di Via Elisa	12	Uffa Baruffa	11

Lucca's festivals

Lucca's festive month is September, with the events of **Settembre Lucchese** (Ⓦwww.settembrelucchese.it) centred on a candlelit procession on the 13th, when the *Volto Santo*, complete with diamond-studded crown and a huge pair of silver slippers, is carried through the streets from San Frediano to the Duomo. The tourist office has details of classical concerts (at the intimate, four-tiered **Teatro Comunale** in Piazza del Giglio), jazz events and art shows during September and at other times. Another key event is July's **Summer Festival** (Ⓦwww.summer-festival.com), when big-name bands stage concerts in Piazza Anfiteatro and Piazza Napoleone.

1314, but regained it under the command of a remarkable adventurer, **Castruccio Castracani**, who went on to forge an empire covering much of western Tuscany. Pisa and Pistoia both fell to the Lucchesi, and but for Castracani's untimely death from malaria, Florence might have followed. In subsequent centuries the city remained largely independent – if fairly inconsequential – until passing to **Napoleon** (and rule by his sister, Elisa Baciocchi), the Bourbons, and, just short of Italian unification, to the Grand Duchy of Tuscany.

Today the city is reckoned among the wealthiest in Tuscany, a prosperity gained largely through **silk** that was produced here by scores of small family businesses, and on the region's high-quality **olive oil** and other produce. There is, too, a tradition of decorum, traceable to eighteenth- and nineteenth-century court life; up until the turn of the twentieth century, smart Italian families sent their daughters to Lucca to pick up the better manners presumed to prevail here.

Arrival, information and accommodation

The **train station**, with foreign exchange facilities, is on Piazza Ricasoli, a short way outside the walls to the south: from there, walk up to the main road and turn left, and after about 200m cross the street right and follow the road ahead through the walls. **Buses** arrive just inside the western stretch of walls, in Piazzale Giuseppe Verdi, while **city buses** leave from the same piazza and Corso Garibaldi.

The main **tourist office** is Piazza Santa Maria in the north of the town (daily: April–Oct 9am–8pm; Nov–March 9am–6.30pm; ☎0583.919.931, Ⓦwww.luccaturismo.it). Other tourist information points are at Piazzale Verdi (daily 9am–7pm; Nov–March closes 6pm; ☎0583.583.150) – a swish affair with public toilets downstairs – and Viale Luporini (daily: March–Oct 9am–6pm; Nov–Feb 9.30am–5.30pm; ☎0583.583.462).

Though Lucca isn't a major stop on the tourist trail, its limited **accommodation** always seems in demand: it's wise to book ahead at any time of year. There are very few hotels within the city walls so you might consider staying in a more centrally located private room or B&B, or the hostel.

Hotels

A Palazzo Busdraghi Via Fillungo 170 ☎0583.950.856, Ⓦwww.apalazzobusdraghi .it. A new, intimate and central four-star hotel, with only seven rooms, all furnished with fine antiques; one of the rooms even boasts a wardrobe owned by Puccini. ❼

Alla Corte Degli Angeli Via degli Angeli 23 ☎0583.469.204, Ⓦwww.allacortedegliangeli.com. A bright, airy and colourful hotel situated inside the medieval walls. The decor of each room is inspired by the colours of different flowers. ❸–❹

Bernardino Via di Tiglio 109 ☎0583.953.356, Ⓦwww.hotelbernadino.it. A two-star whose thirty rooms all have private bathrooms; marginally the most expensive and closest to the centre of the three hotels on this street. ❸

Diana Via del Molinetto 11 ☎0583.492.202, Ⓦwww.albergodiana.com. A two-star hotel located within the walls a block west of the Duomo and only 500m from the train station. **①**–**②**

La Romea Vicolo delle Ventaglie 2
☎0583.464.175, ⓦwww.laromea.com. A welcoming three-star hotel, 30m from the Guinigi Tower, with only five rooms. It's run by a young couple and is on the first floor of a fourteenth-century building. **⑤**

🏋 **Locanda L'Elisa** SS 12bis del Brennero 1952, Massa Pisana ☎0583.379.737, ⓦwww.locandalelisa.it. A luxury five-star and one of Tuscany's top hotels, 3km south on the road to Pisa. The €390-a-night price tag buys you one of ten beautiful suites and all the pampering and elegance you'd expect for this sort of money. Closed Jan & Feb. **⑨**

Melecchi Via Romana 37 ☎0583.950.234, ⓦwww.dormireintoscana.it/melecchi. A decent two-star with ten en-suite rooms and private parking, situated a couple of blocks outside the walls. **②**

Moderno Via V. Civitali 38 ☎0583.55.840, ⓦwww.albergomoderno.com. A twelve-room two-star outside the city walls, southwest of the train station on the wrong (south) side of the tracks. All rooms have private bathrooms. **②**

Piccolo Hotel Puccini Via di Poggio 9 ☎0583.55.421, ⓦwww.hotelpuccini.com. Friendly, central three-star with fourteen rooms. It's located almost beside San Michele, so is an obvious first choice – and thus definitely needs booking. Private parking for an extra €15. **③**

Rex Piazza Ricasoli 19 ☎0583.955.443, ⓦwww.hotelrexlucca.com. A modern, characterless but comfortable three-star hotel with 25 rooms just east of the train station. **④**

Stipino Via Romana 95 ☎0583.495.077, ⓕ0583.490.309. Adequate two-star hotel with 21 rooms, some with private bathrooms. **①**–**②**

Universo Piazza del Giglio 1 ☎0583.954.854, ⓦwww.universolucca.com. Lucca's not-so-grand grand old hotel: a three-star with sixty rooms that lacks atmosphere, made up for by its location bang on the central Piazza Napoleone. **⑤**

Villa La Principessa Via Nuova per Pisa 1616, Massa Pisana ☎0583.370.037, ⓦwww.hotelprinc-

ipessa.com. Experience Lucca in style by staying 3.5km south of the city in this beautifully appointed 41-room nineteenth-century four-star villa set in lovely grounds, with a pool. **⑦**

Private rooms

Casa Alba Via Fillungo 142, second floor ☎0583.495.361, ⓦwww.casa-alba.com. Five clean, pleasant rooms (doubles and singles) with or without private bathroom on Lucca's main street, just north of Piazza Anfiteatro. **②**

Centro Storico Corte Portici 16 ☎0583.490.748, ⓦwww.affittacamerecentrostorico.com. Six convenient rooms, four with bathroom, located on a courtyard off Via Calderia just northwest of Piazza San Michele. **②**–**④**

L'Arancio 1 Via Romano 57 ☎0583.496.517, ⓦwww.arancioaffittacamere.com. 26 rooms outside the walls, four of them spacious, wood-beamed doubles with private bath. **②**

La Torre Via del Carmine 11 ☎0583.957.044. Five nice double rooms with or without bathroom; located off Piazza del Carmine south of Piazza Anfiteatro. **③**–**⑤**

Sainte Joustine Via San Giustina 30 ☎0583.587.96. Seven rooms, four with private bathroom, on the street that runs to the Palazzo Mansi. **②**

San Frediano Via degli Angeli ☎0583.469.630, ⓦwww.sanfrediano.com. Six rooms, including singles and doubles with a choice of private and shared bathrooms. Situated on a street between Via Fillungo and Via C. Battisti just southeast of San Frediano. **③**

Villa Romantica Via N. Barbantini 246 ☎0583.496.872, ⓦwww.villaromantica.it. Six rooms near Piazza del Carmine, four double and two suites, all with private bathrooms. There's also a pool, garden and solarium. **③**–**④**

Hostel

Ostello San Frediano Via della Cavallerizza 12 ☎0583.469.957, ⓦwww.ostellionline.org. Conveniently located HI hostel just within the walls, with a midnight curfew. Dorm beds €16.50.

The City

Confined within its walls, Lucca is an easy place to get your bearings. The centre of town is ostensibly **Piazza Napoleone**, a huge expanse carved out by the Bourbons to house their administration. From here the main **Via Fillungo** – the "long thread" – heads north through the heart of the medieval city. You're most likely to gravitate to **Piazza San Michele**, home to the church of San Michele, the apotheosis of the Pisan–Romanesque style. From here, you might want to potter around the streets to the west, or push straight on to the **Duomo**, another Romanesque gem, with one of Italy's most sublime funerary sculptures. Further east, the Fosso ("ditch") cuts off the quarter around **San Francesco**, while to the north is **Piazza Anfiteatro**, built over the old Roman arena, and **San Frediano**, the third of the city's trio of outstanding churches. A trip to Lucca is not complete without strolling part of the panoramic and tree-lined promenade atop the **walls**, accessed from almost any part of the city.

San Michele

Head to the long-time historical heart of Lucca and you come to the site of the Roman forum, now the square surrounding **San Michele in Foro** (daily: summer 7.40am–noon & 3–6pm; winter 9am–noon & 3pm–6pm; closed dur-

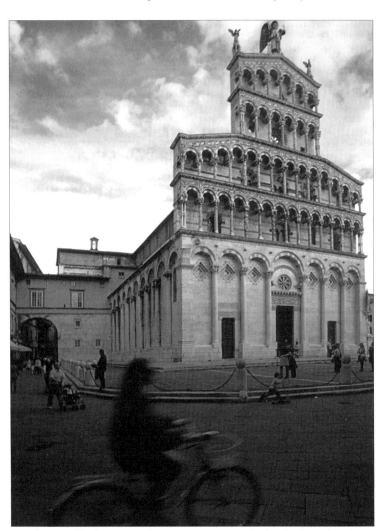

△ San Michele

ing services), a church with one of Tuscany's most exquisite facades. The church is first mentioned in 795, but most of the present structure dates from between 1070 and the middle of the twelfth century (you can see the date 1143 marked on a pillar on the left side of the main portal's triumphal arch). The building is unfinished, however, money having been diverted to the **facade**, begun in the thirteenth century; funds ran out before the body of the church could be raised to the standard of the facade. The effect is wonderful, the upper loggias and the windows fronting air, like the figure of the archangel at their summit. Its Pisan-inspired intricacy is a triumph of eccentricity, mirrored in many of Lucca's churches. Each of its myriad columns is different – some twisted, others sculpted or candy-striped. The impressive twelfth-century **campanile** is the city's tallest.

It would be hard to match the facade's bravura architectural display, and the **interior** barely tries. On the rear wall is a statue of the *Madonna and Child* by local sculptor Matteo Civitali, previously on the facade. Italians flock for spiritual regeneration to the second altar on the left, the so-called *Rifugio dei Peccatori* (Refuge of Sinners). On the opposite altar is a modest terracotta *Madonna and Child* by Andrea della Robbia; the best work of art is a beautifully framed painting of *SS Jerome, Sebastian, Roch and Helena* by **Filippino Lippi**, at the end of the right-hand nave. Look out also for the organ, marvellously painted with intricate fleurs-de-lys.

The western quarter

The birthplace and family home of Giacomo Puccini, the **Casa di Puccini** (Tues–Sun: June–Sept 10am–6pm; Oct–May 10am–1pm & 3–6pm; €3; Ⓦwww.puccini.it), is in Corte San Lorenzo 9, off Via di Poggio, very close to San Michele – where the composer's father and grandfather both played the organ. Today the house is a school of music, and maintains a small museum containing the Steinway on which he wrote *Turandot*, scores, photographs, even his overcoat.

A short way west of San Michele is **San Paolino**, where Puccini cut his teeth as organist. A dull Baroque church, begun in 1522, it was built over a vast Roman edifice, possibly a temple, and founded in honour of Lucca's first bishop and patron saint, St Paulinus, whose remains are kept behind the high altar. Some third-rate eighteenth-century frescoes are his only memorial. South of San Paolino, tucked behind the Palazzo Ducale, is **San Romano**, a big, blunt Romanesque hall, probably founded in the eighth century and adapted and enlarged after 1281 in a bizarre hotchpotch of styles; it would be one of the city's more interesting churches if the restoration started in 1987 had actually shown any real progress. At the moment the whole place is sadly dilapidated.

North of San Paolino is the **Museo Nazionale di Palazzo Mansi**, Via Galli Tassi 43 (Tues–Sat 8.30am–7.30pm, Sun 8.30am–1.30pm; €4; joint ticket with Museo Guinigi €6.50). This seventeenth-century building is worth seeing for its magnificently over-the-top Rococo decor; from a vast, frescoed Music Salon, you pass through three drawing-rooms hung with seventeenth-century Flemish tapestries to a spectacularly gilded bridal suite. Rooms 11–14 in the far wing house the **Pinacoteca Nazionale**, an eclectic grouping of pictures whose real highlights are a Pontormo portrait – possibly of Alessandro de' Medici (see p.746 for the dirt on this sensitive youth); Bronzino's portrait of Cosimo I (the artist painted several versions of this portrait); two male portraits by Tintoretto; and works by the Sienese Mannerists Beccafumi and Rutilio Manetti. Also worth seeing is the section of the museum that traces the development of Lucca's important **textile** industry, in particular its silks and damasks.

Duomo di San Martino

It needs a double-take before you realize why the **Duomo di San Martino** (Mon–Fri 9.30am–5.45; winter closes 6.45pm) looks odd. The building is fronted by a severely asymmetric facade, its right-hand arch and loggias squeezed by the bell tower, which was already in place from an earlier building. Nonetheless, the building sets the tone for Lucca's other Romanesque churches, and little detracts from its overall grandeur, created by the repetition of tiny columns and loggias and by the stunning **atrium**, whose bas-reliefs are some of the finest sculptures in the city.

It's worth looking closely at these carvings, some dated as early as the fifth century, which were executed by a variety of mainly Lombard artists, most of them unknown. Part of the sculpture is attributed to **Nicola Pisano**, and may well be his first work after arriving in Tuscany from Apulia. His are probably the offerings around the left-hand door: the *Deposition* (in the lunette), *Annunciation*, *Nativity* and *Adoration of the Magi*. Other panels display a compendium of subjects: a symbolic labyrinth, a Tree of Life (with Adam and Eve at the bottom and Christ at the top), dragons, bears, a bestiary of grotesques, and the months of the year with their associated activities – December has a particularly graphic pig-sticking. The panels of the *Life of St Martin* (1204–10), between the doors, are the masterpiece of the architect, **Guidetto da Como**, responsible for the upper facade's three tiers of arcades. Walk along the flanks of the building to take in the ornate apse and transepts, as well as the extraordinary patterns of arches and marbles in the bricked-up side walls. One of the greatest of the exterior sculptures, a group depicting *St Martin on Horseback with the Beggar* by an unknown early fourteenth-century Lombard sculptor, has been removed inside the church, and stands at the rear right against the west wall.

The interior

The Duomo's **interior** is best known for the contribution of **Matteo Civitali** (1435–1501), who only gave up his job as a barber to become a sculptor in his mid-thirties. He's represented here by a couple of water stoups near the entrance, the pulpits and several tombs and altars – notably the tomb of Pietro da Noceto, secretary to Pope Niccolo V (right wall of the south transept); the tomb of Domenico Bertini, to the left of the preceding tomb on the transept's adjoining wall; and the altar of San Regolo, on the chancel wall immediately right of the apse.

Civitali's most famous work is the **Tempietto**, the gilt and marble octagon encountered halfway down the church. Some fanatically intense acts of devotion are performed in front of it, directed at the **Volto Santo** (Holy Face), Lucca's most famous relic. A cedarwood Crucifix with bulging eyes, it's said to be a true effigy of Christ carved by Nicodemus, an eyewitness to the Crucifixion, but is probably a thirteenth-century copy of an eleventh-century copy of an eighth-century original. Legend has it that the *Volto Santo* came to Lucca of its own volition in 782, first journeying by boat from the Holy Land, and then brought by oxen guided by divine will – a story similar to the ecclesiastical sham of St James's bones at Santiago di Compostela in Spain. As at Santiago, the icon brought considerable power to the local church: it may be no coincidence that it appeared during the bishopric of Anselmo di Baggio, who was later elevated to the papacy. The effigy attracted pilgrims from all over Europe and inspired devotion in all who heard of it: King William Rufus of England used to swear by it ("Per sanctum vultum de Lucca!"), London merchants kept a copy of it, and in France a certain St Vaudeluc was conjured into existence from a corruption of *saint vault de Lucques*, the French name for the icon.

Elsewhere in the church the works of art are of less disputed origin. The finest of them is the **Tomb of Ilaria del Carretto** (1407–10), housed in the **sacristy** entered midway down the south nave (April–Oct Mon–Fri 9.30am–5.45pm, Sat 9.30am–6.45pm, Sun 9am–5.45pm; Nov–March Mon–Fri 9.30am–4.45pm, Sat 9.30am–6.45pm, Sun 11.30am–4.45pm; €2; joint ticket with Museo della Cattedrale and San Giovanni €5.50). Considered the masterpiece of Sienese sculptor Jacopo della Quercia, it consists of a dais and the sculpted body of Ilaria, second wife of Paolo Guinigi, one of Lucca's medieval big shots. In a touching, almost sentimental gesture, the artist has carved the family dog at Ilaria's feet, a symbol of fidelity. Restoration of the work in the mid-1990s led to accusations by Professor James Beck, the world's leading authority on Jacopo della Quercia, that the restorer's cleaning techniques were overenthusiastic, and had robbed the stone of its variegated textures. Also within the sacristy is a superb *Madonna Enthroned with Saints* by **Domenico Ghirlandaio**.

Other pictorial highlights of the cathedral include a *Madonna and Child* in the enclosed chapel to the left of the high altar in the north transept, painted in 1509 by **Fra Bartolommeo**. In the main part of the Duomo, the first chapel on the left has a *Presentation of the Virgin* by Alessandro Allori (1598), and the third altar on the right a *Last Supper* (1592) by **Tintoretto**.

Around the Duomo

Occupying a converted twelfth-century building across Via Arcivescovato from the cathedral is the **Museo della Cattedrale** (April–Oct 10am–6pm; Nov–March Mon–Fri 10am–2pm, Sat & Sun 10am–5pm; €4; joint ticket with the cathedral sacristy and San Giovanni €5.50). The museum's four floors are home to a collection of ecclesiastical and other ephemera interspersed with the occasional artistic gem. Room I has a collection of illustrated miniatures, while Room II on the floor above houses a reliquary from Limoges decorated with stories from the Life of St Thomas à Becket; an ivory diptych from Constantinople dated 506; and – one of the highlights – the *Croce dei Pisani*, an ornate crucifix probably commissioned by Paolo Guinigi after 1408. Room VII contains sculpture from the cathedral, most notably a large statue of St John the Evangelist by Jacopo della Quercia.

On the north side of the square stands the large basilica of **SS Giovanni e Reparata** (same hours; €2.50; joint ticket with cathedral sacristy and Museo della Cattedrale or €5.50), Lucca's original cathedral until 715. Rebuilt many times, it preserves a lion-flanked carved Romanesque portal, saved during restructuring of the facade in 1589. Inside, excavations have uncovered a tangle of architectural remains, embracing a wide range of much earlier buildings on the site. Earliest fragments include first-century Roman villa mosaics (columns in the present nave are mostly Roman in origin), parts of the original fourth-century church pavement, an eighth-century baptistery with fine 1393 ceiling, and traces of a ninth-century Carolingian church and crypt of San Pantaleone.

A short distance east is the twelfth-century **Santa Maria Forisportam** ("outside the gate"), signalling the limit of the Roman and medieval city until 1260. Ruskin claimed that it was this church that sparked his interest in medieval architecture. The facade sports just two unfinished tiers and none of its relatives' decorative columns, but it's appealing for all that, with a few carvings above the doors and the usual jutting animals high on the front. The interior has the angular simplicity of the other churches, though no particular works of art.

North of the Duomo, **Via Fillungo** cuts through Lucca's luxury shopping district, a tight huddle of streets and alleys where medieval fragments and bricked-up loggias compete with Liberty-style shop fronts and lunchtime and early-evening throngs. Amid the crowds it's easy to miss the gorgeous facade of **San Cristoforo**, the deconsecrated church at the southern end; inside, the left-hand wall is completely covered in writing – the names of Lucca's dead in the two world wars. Farther on is the **Torre delle Ore**, the city's clock tower since 1471; then at no. 58 there's the famous *Caffè di Simo*, a bar worth the price of a drink just for the early twentieth-century ambience. Beyond, the street branches into a warren of lanes that lead to **Piazza San Frediano**.

San Frediano

The church of **San Frediano** (Mon–Sat 8.30am–noon & 3–5pm, Sun 10.30am–5pm; closed during services; free) is again Pisan-Romanesque, built between 1112 and 1147 on the site of a sixth-century basilica of San Vincenzo but orientated back to front (west-facing), probably because the old entrance would have been blocked by the new set of medieval city walls nearby. In place of the characteristic multiple loggias of Lucca's other great facades is a magnificent thirteenth-century mosaic of *The Ascension* with the apostles gathered below.

The **interior** lives up to the facade's promise – a delicately lit, hall-like basilica, with subtly varied columns and capitals and some fine treasures. Immediately facing the door is one of the best, the **Fonte Lustrale**, a huge twelfth-century piece executed by three different craftsmen. The first, an unknown Lombard, carved the stories of Moses on the outer slabs of the basin, including a superb *Crossing of the Red Sea*, with the Egyptian soldiers depicted as medieval knights. The second, one Maestro Roberto, added the Good Shepherd and six prophets on the other two basin slabs, their enframing arches showing a clear Byzantine influence. To the third sculptor, an unknown Tuscan, is owed the decoration

---

A walk around the walls

Climbing up at any of the bastions, some of which are signposted, you can follow the four-kilometre circuit of the city **walls**, either on bike or on foot. The mid-afternoon shutdown is perhaps the best time to walk their broad promenade, which is lined successively with plane, lime, ilex and chestnut trees.

Construction of the walls started around 1500, prompted by the need to replace medieval ramparts rendered inadequate by advances in weapon technology. By 1650 the work was completed, with eleven bastions to fortify walls that were 30m wide at the base, 12m high and surrounded by moats 35m across. There were originally just three gates. Perhaps the best feature, from the present-day perspective, was the destruction of all trees and buildings within a couple of hundred metres of the walls, creating a green belt of lawns that has shielded the old town from the ugliness that's sprouted on the outside.

Ironically, having produced a perfect set of walls, Lucca was never called on to defend them. The only siege was against the floodwaters of the River Serchio in 1812, when the gates were sealed against the deluge that had flooded the countryside. Napoleon's sister and city governor, Elisa Baciocchi, one of the last people allowed in, had to be winched over the ramparts by crane. Marie Louise of Bourbon, her successor, had the walls transformed to their present garden aspect, arranging them, as the local tourist handout puts it, "with unparalleled good taste and moderation".

of the Apostles and the Months on the cup above the basin and the beautiful fantasy masks from which the water is disgorged. Set behind the font is an *Annunciation* attributed to Matteo della Robbia, festooned with trailing garlands of ceramic fruit.

A figure of St Bartholomew by Andrea della Robbia is to be found lower down to the left, close to the left-hand of the two chapels behind the font, the Cappella Fatinelli, which houses the incorrupt body of **St Zita** (died 1278). A Lucchese maidservant, Zita achieved sainthood from a fortuitous white lie: she used to give bread from her household to the poor and when challenged one day by her boss as to the contents of her apron, replied "only roses and flowers" – into which the bread was duly transformed. She is commemorated on April 27 by a flower market outside the church and by the Lucchesi freeing her of her finery and bringing her out to touch.

Moving to the top of the church, note the wonderful twelfth-century Cosmati marble **pavement** of the presbytery, while on the left are fragments of the original tomb of San Frediano, an Irish monk who is said to have brought Christianity to Lucca in the sixth century. Moving back down the left (north) nave from the high altar, the first chapel, the **Cappella Trenta**, contains a superb carved altarpiece with niche statues of the Madonna, Child and Saints by Jacopo della Quercia; the worn pavement tombs of the chapel's donors, Lorenzo Trenat and his wife, are also by della Quercia.

The best frescoes in the city adorn the Cappella di Sant'Agostino, the next chapel but one: **Amico Aspertini**'s *The Arrival of the Volto Santo* and *The Baptism of St Augustine* on the left wall, and *The Miracle of St Frediano* on the right, the last depicting the River Serchio in flood being diverted by the saint's crib. Dating from the early sixteenth century, the murals are painted in a style that is much influenced by the realism of Flemish and German painters. The large fresco of the Madonna and Child on the right of the entrance door is also by Aspertini, while the nearby statue *Virgin Annunciate* is by Matteo Civitali.

Palazzo Pfanner

Near San Frediano is the **Palazzo Pfanner**, Via degli Asili 33 (March–Nov daily 10am–6pm; €4), whose interesting rear loggia and statued gardens are also visible from the city walls, as is another fine church, **Sant'Agostino**. The palazzo hosts temporary exhibitions.

Piazza Anfiteatro and around

East of San Frediano is the remarkable Piazza Anfiteatro, aerial shots of which feature in just about all of Lucca's tourist literature. A ramshackle circuit of medieval buildings, as yet unprettified, it incorporates elements of the Roman amphitheatre that once stood here. Much of the original stone was carted off in the twelfth century to build the city's churches, while parts of the old structure were used as a medieval prison and salt warehouse, but arches and columns can still be seen embedded in some of the houses, particularly on the north side of the outer walls. Medieval slums used to occupy the centre of the arena, but these were cleared in 1830 on the orders of the Bourbon ruler, Marie Louise.

A couple of blocks east is **San Pietro Somaldi**, its delicate facade dating from 1248, this time stone on the lower levels, topped with two tiers of Pisan marbling and tiny columns. Above the lovely **portal** is a good carved frieze executed by Guido da Como in 1203, *Jesus Giving the Keys to St Peter*, and the customary pair of lions, common symbols for the Resurrection in medieval art – after the belief that cubs, when born, lay dead for three days until a male lion brought them to life by breathing in their faces. The church's interior is whitewashed and blank, save for a sumptuous detached fresco of the *Assumption* on the right wall, and an uncredited fifteenth-century work above the first left-hand altar.

Torre Guinigi

The **Torre Guinigi** (daily: March–Sept 8.30am–7.30pm; Oct 10am–6pm; Nov–Feb 9.30am–4.30pm; €4), south of San Pietro in Via Sant'Andrea, is the strangest sight in Lucca's cityscape. This battlemented tower, attached to the fifteenth-century **Casa Guinigi**, town house of Lucca's leading family, is surmounted by an ancient holm oak whose roots have grown into the room below. You can climb the 44-metre tower, entering on Via Sant'Andrea, for a close-up of the tree and easily the best view over the city. The adjacent fortress, which has some wonderful austere medieval details, fronts a startling number of streets.

The eastern quarter

The city's canal and parallel road, the **Via del Fosso**, mark the entry to Lucca's more lacklustre eastern margins. The most attractive part of this quarter is the **Orto Botanico** (Mon–Fri 9.30am–12.30pm; April–Oct also Sat & Sun 9.30am–12.30pm & 3.30–6.30pm; €3) at the southern end of Via del Fosso, an extensive patch of green laid out in 1820 which neatly complements the ramparts. Green-fingered visitors should enjoy some of the rarer exhibits, especially the medicinal plants, the sequoia, gingko tree, camphor tree and a cedar of Lebanon planted at the garden's opening.

Otherwise, the only significant sights are in the north of this quarter, around the church of **San Francesco**, fronted by a relatively simple facade and adjoining a crumbling brick convent. The inside of the church is a vast empty barn, relieved only by a delicate rose window, some lovely inlaid choir stalls and fine but damaged Florentine fresco fragments to the right of the high altar depicting the Marriage and Presentation of the Virgin.

Across the street from San Francesco is the much-restored **Villa Guinigi**, built to supplement the family's medieval town house. It's now home to Lucca's major museum, the **Museo Nazionale di Villa Guinigi** (Tues–Sat 8.30am–7.30pm, Sun 8.30am–1.30pm; €4; joint ticket with Palazzo Mansi €6.50), an extremely varied collection of painting, sculpture, furniture and applied arts. The lower floor is mainly sculpture and archeological finds, with numerous Romanesque pieces and works by della Quercia and Matteo Civitali. Upstairs, the gallery moves on to paintings, with lots of big sixteenth-century canvases, and more impressive works by early Lucchese and Sienese masters, as well as fine Renaissance offerings from artists such as Fra' Bartolommeo.

Eating and drinking

As a wealthy, gastronomic centre, Lucca has some high-quality **restaurants**. Local specialities often feature *zuppa di farro*, a thick soup of *farro*, an ancient variety of grain grown in the Garfagnana; other dishes include roast mountain goat (*capretto*) and puddings based on chestnut flour, such as *castagnaccio*.

For sixty types of bread, rolls or delicious *focaccia* (freshly baked every two hours) head for Forno Amedeo Giusti, Via Santa Lucia 18–20. La Cacioteca, Via Fillungo 242, sells a wide variety of cheeses, and two places on Piazza San Michele are worth a call: Pizzeria Pellegrini (no. 25), for excellent pizza by the slice, and Pasticceria Taddeucci (no. 34), partly for its cakes (the aniseed and raisin *buccellato* is the traditional favourite), partly for its 1881 wood-panelled and mosaic-tiled interior. Caniparoli in Via San Paolino is a wonderful chocolate shop.

Cafés and bars

Antico Caffè di Simo Via Fillungo 58 ℡0583.496.234. Lucca's famous century-old *locale* with original liberty-style furnishings and delicious cakes and pastries.

L'Enoteca Via Vittoria Emanuele 34. Popular local hangout serving beer, wine and sandwiches. Closed Tues.

Mirò Via del Fosso. Late-night bar with live jazz and blues. Closed Mon.

Restaurants

Buca di Sant'Antonio Via della Cervia 3 ℡0583.55.881. Lucca's finest restaurant has been around for over two hundred years and still retains some of its old-world charm. Excellent service, top quality meat or fish menu and delicious house pasta and desserts such as *semifreddo Buccellato*. Around €30 a head. Closed Sun eve & Mon; booking essential.

Canuleia Via Canuleia 14 ℡0583.467.470. Original dishes with plenty of veggie options, served in a converted medieval workshop, with no more than ten tables. Good value at €30 a head, given the quality. Located close to Piazza Anfiteatro. Closed Sat & Sun.

Da Guido Via Cesare Battisti 28 ℡0583.467.219. A small locals' hangout and more like an extended bar than a restaurant, this is one of the cheapest places in town for basic Lucchese nosh. Closed Sun.

Da Leo Via Tegrimi 1 ℡0583.492.236. Another good-value family-run place near Piazza San Michele which preserves the authentic look and feel of an old-fashioned trattoria. Closed Sun eve.

Gli Orti di Via Elisa Via Elisa 17 ℡0583.491.241. Popular pizzeria/trattoria with wonderful risottos and some vegetarian dishes, open evenings only. Closed Wed.

La Mora Via Sesto di Moriano 1748, Località Ponte Moriano ℡0583.406.402, ⊛www.ristorantelamora .com. The best place locally, 9km north of town along the river. Its sublime regional cooking and extensive wine list enjoy a Michelin star. Set menu €40. Closed Wed.

Locanda Di Bacco 36 via San Giorgio ℡0583.493.136. This restaurant with lovely wood-panelled interior does quality food at good prices. Specialities include salt cod with chickpeas.

Osteria Baralla Via Anfiteatro 5 ℡0583.440.240. Something of an institution in Lucca, this traditional *osteria* serves simple local food at moderate prices. Occasional live music. Closed Sun.

Ristorante Puccini Corte San Lorenzo 1 ℡0583.316.116. Another of Lucca's top-notch restaurants, with a welcoming interior, excellent service and imaginative seafood menu. Closed Wed eve & Tues.

Slim Jones Corte Campagna 3. Modern burger joint also serving huge salads as a main course – a rare find in Tuscany. A good lunch stop. Closed Sun.

Trattoria Buralli Piazza Sant'Agostino 10 ℡0583.950.611. Traditional trattoria with a wide choice of home-style local cooking and a selection of wines from the Lucchesi hills. Closed Tues & Wed.

Uffa Baruffa Corte Campana 3 ℡0583.312.037. Just off the Piazza San Michele, this bright and breezy restaurant, with a summer veranda, specializes in rabbit and lamb and other Tuscan dishes. Reckon on around €30 a head. It's also one of the few places open for a drink late in the evening in winter.

Listings

Banks and exchange At the train station (daily 6am–9pm), most city banks and also Lucca Change, Piazza Napoleone 23 and Money Change, Via San Paolino 105, and in Piazza San Michele.

Bike rental The tourist office in Piazzale Verdi; Barbetti Cicli, Via dell'Anfiteatro 23; Cicli Bizzarri or Biciclette Poli, either side of the tourist office in Piazza Santa Maria; Biciclette crono on Corso Garibaldi.

Buses Vaibus (⊛www.vaibus.it) operates out of Piazzale G. Verdi and runs an extensive network in the region. See "Travel details" at the end of the chapter for route information.

Hospital Campo di Marte, Via dell'Ospedale ℡0583.9701.

Lost property At the *Comune*, Ufficio Economato, Via Cesare Battisti 10 ℡0583.442.388.

Market A vast antiques market takes place on the third weekend of the month in and around Piazza San Martino.

Police Questura, Via Cavour 38 ℡0583.4551.

Post office Via Vallisneri 2 (Mon–Sat 8.15am–5pm).

Taxis Radio taxi ℡0583.333.434.

East of Lucca

As with Florence's hinterland, Lucca's surroundings are dotted with outstanding **villas**, built by wealthy merchants as retreats from the rigours of city life, or simply as an indulgence on the part of aristocratic landowners. Some of these started life as simple country houses, others had grandiose ambitions from the word go; most have been repeatedly altered since their construction. Many involved the leading architects of their day, either in the construction of the villas themselves, or in the design of the magnificent **gardens** that accompanied them.

Three of the villas – **Villa Reale**, **Villa Mansi** and **Villa Torrigiani** (also known as the Villa di Camigliano) – lie within a ten-kilometre radius of Lucca to the northeast; they can all be reached in an hour or so by bike. Slightly farther afield is the **Villa Garzoni** at **Collodi**, which competes for attention with the **Parco di Pinocchio**, an attraction advertised on roadside hoardings all over Tuscany.

Villa Reale

By general consent, the **Villa Reale** at **MARLIA** is the most beautiful of the villas close to Lucca. Access is via the SS445 from Lucca to Barga, turning off to Marlia after 8km; a less direct but better-signposted route takes the SS435 for Montecatini Terme, with a left turn after 7km, also signed for the villa.

The Villa Reale's life as a country house started with the destruction of a fortress on this site in the fourteenth century, its first gardens being laid out a century later. The present Neoclassical look dates from 1806, when Napoleon's sister, Elisa Baciocchi, compelled the Orsetti family to sell up. Having ousted the owners, she and her personal architect, Morel, set about a radical remoulding of the villa and garden, completely refurbishing the interior and planning an English park complete with huge monumental lake. Some of the garden's most important earlier fixtures were respected, though Napoleon's downfall and Elisa's subsequent eviction undoubtedly saved other older components from destruction. Sadly, the vigour of court life at the Villa Reale also vanished with Elisa. The violinist Paganini had been employed as resident composer; he was later known to claim his playing had caused his patroness to swoon with ecstasy.

Only the **garden** is open to the public, and only on guided tours (March–Nov Tues–Sun hourly 10am–7pm; Dec–Feb bookings only ☎0583.30.108; €6). Its most striking aspect is the sweeping lawn that runs from the house down to the lake, a feature of the original layout that was enlarged under the Baciocchi regime. To its left, set deep in the woods, is the **Grotto of Pan**, an elaborate two-storey hideaway with mosaic floor, much trailing greenery and a ceiling of stone plants and flowers. The hidden fountains which once sprayed the unwary are regrettably no longer working. To one side of the lawn, an avenue of ilex trees leads to the heart of the original garden, centred on a trio of **garden rooms**, which become progressively more confined. The first has a collection of lemon trees and a pool on which swans drift; the second features a high-spouting fountain; the third is a tiny and intimate "green theatre", its orchestra pit and seats all made of box and yew hedges, and edged with a variety of exotic flora.

Villa Mansi

Perhaps the least interesting of the villa quartet is the **Villa Mansi** at **SEGROMIGNO**, 5km east of Marlia. Originally a plain sixteenth-century country house, the villa was enlarged in 1635 by Muzio Oddi and expanded many times in subsequent centuries. The harmonious late-Renaissance facade remains, much adorned with statuary, and flanked by two pavilions joining the three-arched portico. The **garden** (Tues–Sun 10am–12.30pm & 3–7pm; winter closes 5pm; villa and garden €7) has suffered more brutal treatment. The few early sections that remain intact are the best: the French-inspired eastern part, with its star-shaped avenues and irregular arrangement of fountains and basins; and the western part, laid out between 1725 and 1732 by the Sicilian architect Filippo Juvarra – the man who refashioned Turin. At the beginning of the nineteenth century much of Juvarra's geometric work was replaced by haphazard borrowings from English garden design. Innovations by the present owners have continued the garden's dubious development.

Villa Torrigiani

At **CAMIGLIANO**, 2km from the Villa Mansi, the **Villa Torrigiani**, or Villa di Camigliano (March to early Sept Mon & Wed–Sun 10am–12.30pm & 3pm–6.30pm, ☏0583.928.041; garden and villa €8, garden only €6) was built for the Buonvisi family in the sixteenth century, and transformed almost entirely by Alfonso Torrigiani in the eighteenth century to conform with the prevailing taste for villas and gardens in the English manner. Though little from the original survives, the present ensemble is a fine example of less formal garden design. From Lucca, take the SS435 for Montecatini Terme, and fork left at Borgonuovo (11km). The villa is clearly signed from Camigliano.

A magnificent avenue of cypresses leads to the villa's stately Baroque facade, adorned with a similar surfeit of statuary to the Villa Mansi's; Oddi was probably the architect here, too. The **interior** has been slightly diminished by a spate of thefts, but there's still a wealth of furniture and some odd points of passing interest. The extravagantly decorated central hall and the elliptical staircase are outstanding, both products of the eighteenth-century modifications.

The **gardens**, and larger park alongside, are complex and beautiful affairs, noted above all for their *giochi d'acqua* (water games). Intended to drench unsuspecting visitors with hidden sprays and fountains activated by the owner, or by the pressure of footsteps on levered flagstones, these tricks were especially popular with Mannerist gardeners, but in fact were first used in Roman times. The devices here, initiated by the fun-loving Marquis Niccolò Santini – Lucca's ambassador to the court of Louis XIV – are among the finest examples still functioning. They're all contained in the **Garden of Flora**, a sunken garden to the east of the villa – all that has survived the garden's eighteenth-century anglicization. The Marquis would first herd his guests into the garden from an upper terrace, whereupon they would find their path blocked by a wall of spray. Attempting to retreat back down the beautiful pebble-mosaic path, they would discover that this too was now awash with water. Seeking sanctuary on the roof of the Temple of Flora, a small cupola-topped grotto, they would blunder into the biggest soaking of all, as water gushed from the domed roof, from the four statues set in the walls (representing the four winds), and, as if this weren't enough, shot up from the floor as well. In 1985, frosts damaged some of the underground piping, but the gardeners occasionally provide impromptu demonstrations of the temple's aquatic surprises.

Collodi and around

When, in 1881, Carlo Lorenzini published the first instalment of the children's book that was to make him famous, he used the pen-name Carlo Collodi, in honour of his mother's birthplace, a small town 15km east of Lucca. And so, whereas other Tuscan towns are devoted to a patron saint, **COLLODI** has dedicated itself to a living puppet with an erectile nose – **Pinocchio**. To English-speakers reared on the Disney version, it's difficult to appreciate the reverence accorded Pinocchio in his homeland, where the tale's moral simplicity and exemplary Tuscan prose ensures it a massive following. It's indicative of *Pinocchio*'s standing that an Italian national newspaper poll once shortlisted the book as a contender for the title of "Greatest Novel of All Time", and that actor-director Robert Benigni lavished so much attention on his 2002 film version that it ended up being the most expensive film ever made in Italy.

Created in the 1950s, the **Parco di Pinocchio** (daily 8.30am–sunset; Ⓦwww .pinocchio.it; €7, under-14s €5) honours the famous book with statues of its characters, a sequence of mosaics depicting moments from Pinocchio's life, and various tableaux scattered around the paths that wind through the park. The monsters and mazes are fun without any background knowledge, but you'll need to have read the book in order to get the most from the park – and to field questions should you be visiting with infatuated children. Pinocchio's importance to the nation can be gauged from the fact that Michelucci – architect of Florence's train station and several prestigious churches – was commissioned to design the **restaurant** and **museum** near the entrance. There's also a very inviting toy shop ready to hook the kids as you leave.

Overshadowing the Pinocchio park, the vast **Villa Garzoni** evolved from a castle that stood here in the days before Lucca surrendered this region to Florence. The house took on its present form in the second half of the seventeenth century, but it was towards the end of the following century that it acquired the magnificent formal **garden** (daily 9am–sunset; Nov–March closed noon–2pm; €5.20) that makes this one of Italy's finest villas. Access is usually through a gate on the main road, but the garden was designed to be entered through the wood adjoining the villa, so that the visitor would emerge from the wilderness into this precisely orchestrated landscape. Maximizing the theatrical possibilities of the steep slope, it deploys the full resources of the Baroque garden: circular fountains, topiary animals, patterns of flowers and coloured stones, a water staircase, a zigzagging cascade of steps and terraces, and terracotta figures in every corner.

One of the most dramatically sited Romanesque churches in Tuscany is a short distance north of Collodi at **VILLA BASILICA**, a tiny village clinging to a ridge below Monte Pietra Pertusa; follow the main road for 3km, then keep an eye out for a sharp left turn. It's a sternly unadorned building, made attractive by the backdrop of woods and terraces.

Pescia and Castelvecchio

The medium-sized town of **PESCIA**, 8km west of Montecatini Terme (see p.249), is Italy's top producer of cut flowers, boxing around three million lilies, carnations, gladioli and other blooms per day at the height of the season. Each September of even-numbered years it hosts the technicolour **Biennale del Fiore** (Ⓦwww.biennaledelfiore.it; €6.50) held in the gargantuan market hall on the outskirts.

Split by the Pescia river, the town has two distinct zones: the left bank forms the ecclesiastical quarter, the right is the secular and commercial district. The **Duomo**, rebuilt Baroque but with a fourteenth-century campanile, takes second slot to **San Francesco** in Via Battisti – reached by walking towards the river from the cathedral and turning right before the bridge. Here Bonaventura Berlinghieri's panel *Six Scenes from the Life of St Francis* (third altar on the right), painted nine years after Francis's death, provides what's publicized as the most accurate surviving portrait of the saint, but is in truth a routinely stylized image. On the other side of the nave, the Cappella Cardini was added to the Gothic church by the architect known simply as Buggiano, employing the style of his adoptive father, Brunelleschi. The nearby oratory of **Sant'Antonio Abbate** has a *Deposition* that's an outstanding specimen of thirteenth-century woodcarving. Over on the right bank, at one end of the elongated Piazza Mazzini, the church of **Madonna di Piè di Piazza** is another worthy creation by Buggiano. At the other end of the square stands the bemedalled **Palazzo dei Vicari**, Romanesque home of the local council. The Museo Civico on Piazza Santo Stefano was closed for restoration at the time of writing. The only reason to hang around in Pescia is to sample the town's edible specialities – asparagus and a questionable stew known as *cioncia*, made from ox's muzzle; *Cecco*, Via Forti 84 (☎0572.477.955; closed Mon) is an excellent, moderately priced **restaurant**.

About 13km upstream from Pescia – past the paper mills that keep the town's second industry going – stands the strange **Pieve San Tommaso** in the village of **CASTELVECCHIO**. Founded in the eleventh century, it bears a frieze of ghoulish faces on the facade and apse, suggesting a strong pagan undertow to the Christian piety of this area. Inside are some wonderfully carved capitals and a gloomy crypt that intensifies the threatening aura of the grimacing heads.

The Riviera della Versilia

The northern coast of Tuscany is known, somewhat hyperbolically, as the **Riviera della Versilia**. The beach resorts that run unbroken between **Viareggio** and **Forte dei Marmi** offer Italian beach culture in all its glory. Much of the sand is leased to the virtually indistinguishable *stabilimenti*, who in turn charge admission to their strips and rent out chairs and umbrellas; there are free public beaches (*spiaggia pubblica*), too, at regular intervals. For a swim and some sun in cheerfully crowded conditions, this coast is not as bad as it's usually painted: the water may be cleaner elsewhere but it's not filthy, and the sand is immaculately groomed. Bus and train links to all points are excellent, especially in the summer, when you can move up and down the coast with more ease than anywhere else in Tuscany.

Viareggio

The best town on the coast, **VIAREGGIO** is also Tuscany's biggest seaside resort, with an air of elegance lent mainly by the long avenue of palms that runs the length of its seafront promenade. A modest collection of Liberty-style frontages – designed by the father of Italian Art Nouveau, Galileo Chini – adds

---

Carnevale at Viareggio

The only time Viareggio hits national headlines is during its three-week **Carnevale** (mid-Feb/early March), one of the liveliest in Italy. Each Sunday there's a parade of colossal floats, or *carri*, carrying lavishly designed papier-mâché models of politicians and celebrities. The recently inaugurated "Cittadella del Carnevale" to the north of Viareggio has been designed as a home for the vast hangars in which the artists construct their imaginative creations and also boasts a theatre and multimedia museum. You can visit all year round; contact the Fondazione Carnevale, Piazza Mazzini 22 (☎0584.962.568, ⊛www.viareggio.ilcarnevale.com) for further details.

to the sense of refinement, though for the most part the buildings are old-style seaside hotels. In the early part of last century, the town's reputation for exclusivity was well deserved; these days all that's left is the high prices. The excellent **beaches** are all private, charging €18 and upwards for admission – except for the free stretch between Viareggio and Torre del Lago – and in summer the few hotels that aren't full usually hold out for *pensiona completa*. You may prefer to join the majority and cram into the train for a day-trip: this is what many Florentines do – in summer, special early-morning trains from the city are packed with raucous *ragazzi*.

Viareggio's main focus is its promenade, the **Passeggiata Margherita**, a broad thoroughfare that runs along the seafront for 3km. Most of the Art Nouveau fronts are crowded together around the town's best-known spot, the *Gran Caffè Margherita*, seemingly inspired by a pastry chef rather than an architect, close to the start of the Passeggiata near the marina. Across the marina and distinct from the town, the **Viale dei Tigli** is a beautiful avenue of lime trees that stretches 6km south, giving access to various beaches and most of the town's campsites.

Practicalities

Viareggio's **train station**, ten minutes' walk back from the seafront, has a summer-only **tourist office** (April–Sept Mon–Sat 9am–1pm & 3.30–7pm; ☏0584.46.382), supplementing the main tourist office in town, Viale Carducci 10 (Mon–Sat 9am–2pm & 3–7.30pm, Sun 9am–1pm; ☏0584.962.233, ⓦwww.versilia.turismo.toscana.it). **Buses** stop near the centre at Piazza d'Azeglio and Piazza Mazzini. Vaibus have an office in Piazza d'Azeglio for tickets and information (☏0584.30.996). A series of kiosks at the Pineta di Ponente (see map) have **bikes for rent**.

The town has over a hundred one-star **hotels**, many near the tourist office on Viale Carducci, and along Via Vespucci and Via Leonardo da Vinci. More upmarket options are equally numerous. Among the cheaper options are *Villa Amadei*, Via F. Gioia 23 (☏0584.45.517, ⓔamadei@caen.it; ❶; April–Sept); the central two-star *Ely*, Via Carrara 16 (☏0584.50.758, ⓔelyhotel@iol.it; ❷; April–Sept); and the two-star *Bella Riviera*, Viale Manin, 34 (☏0584.962.182, ⓦwww.hotelbellariviera.it; ❷). There are several **campsites** off Viale dei Tigli on the edge of the Parco Regionale (see below); the first is the *Viareggio*, Via Comparini 1 (☏0584.391.012, ⓔcampingviareggio@tin.it; April–Sept), after about 1km, followed by the larger *Paradiso* (☏0584.392.005, ⓦwww.campeggioparadiso.com; April–Sept).

Restaurant prices are considerably over the odds – especially on the seafront. For sublime fish and seafood cooking, make for the Michelin-starred *Romano*, Via Mazzini 120 (☎0584.31.382; closed Mon). Also good for seafood and pizza is *Piccola Tito*, Lungomolo del Greco 1 (☎0584.962.016). Lower down the ladder try the moderately priced *La Darsena*, Via Virgilio 150 (☎0584.392.785; closed Sun). On a tighter budget you can get cheap plates of pasta or good pizza from *Da Dino*, Via Cesare Battisti 35–37 (☎0584.962.053; closed Thurs); otherwise you're more likely to depend on pizzas or takeaway food from the Piazza Cavour **market**.

Torre del Lago and around

The journey south from Viareggio along Viale dei Tigli is worth it just for the lime trees; whether you press on to the hamlet of **TORRE DEL LAGO** (served by half-hourly buses #2 & #4 from Viareggio's Piazza d'Azeglio) depends on how much you value Puccini, who spent the later part of his life in a villa on the edge of the adjacent **Lago di Massaciuccoli**.

In Torre del Lago, it's easy to miss the **Villa Puccini**, set back from the shore and surrounded by bars, trees and high iron railings. Visits are in guided groups of no more than eighteen people (every 30min; Tues–Sun 10am–12.30pm & 3–6pm; closed Nov; €7; ⓦwww.giacomopuccini.it); the rooms feature original furnishings, mementos and the piano on which Puccini bashed out many of his operas. In late July and August the **Festival Pucciniano** (ⓦwww.puccinifestival .it) presents the master's works in Torre del Lago's outdoor theatre and various other venues. It's an extremely popular show, as are the international regattas held on the lake through the summer.

The Lago di Massaciuccoli, no more than 2m deep, yet covering an area the size of Pisa, is one of the few Tuscan lagoons not lost to land reclamation. Once it supported virtually all Italy's species of aquatic bird, but many have been wiped out by pollution and hunters; Puccini himself came here to practise "my second favourite instrument, my rifle". Now the lake forms part of the **Parco Regionale di Migliarino-San Rossore** (☎050.525.500, ⓦwww.parks.it), and is also a protected bird sanctuary; as a result there are some 80 breeding and another 65 occasional species on the lake. You can take a **boat trip** for an hour's tour around the lake (☎0584.350.252; €5) or arrange a **birdwatching** trip with the bird-protection charity LIPU (☎0584.975.567): a boat costs €35 for a two-hour outing with an English guide and you'll need to pre-book.

Torre del Lago has six **campsites**, including *Bosco Verde*, Viale Kennedy 5 (☎0584.359.343, ⓦwww.boscoverde.com; April–Sept) and the popular *Burlamacco*, Viale Marconi (☎0584.359.544, ⓦwww.campingburlamacco.com; April–Sept). Of its **hotels**, most are on the main Viale Marconi, except for *Butterfly*, Belvedere Puccini 24 (☎ & ℻0584.341.024; ❶), right by the lake, and the three-star *Turandot*, Viale Kennedy 27 (☎0584.341.025, ⓦwww.hotelturandot .com; ❸), on the way to the sea. Along the *lungomare* there are plenty of good restaurants and *pizzerie*, and a couple of **clubs** that draw crowds from as far afield as Florence.

North of Viareggio

The Versilia's ribbon development continues **north of Viareggio**, distinguishable only by a gradual shift downmarket. The town of **PIETRASANTA**, 2km back from the Marina di Pietrasanta beach, is no more than a busy marble centre with one or two old buildings; it is, though, a good base from which to head up into the Alpi Apuane. Buses into the mountains leave from the terminal outside the train station, with hourly services to Seravezza (where you can change for connections to Levigliani and Stazzema), and three daily to Castelnuovo di Garfagnana. There is little reason to stay – unless you are planning some local hikes in the foothills – but there are several **hotels** including the two-star *Stipino*, Via Provinciale 50 (✆0584.71.448, ✉stipino@tiscalinet.it; **❷**), and three-star *Palagi*, Piazza Carducci 23 (✆0584.70.249, ✆0584.71.198; **❺**). The town's **tourist office** occupies a small kiosk at Piazza Statuto (Mon–Wed, Fri & Sat 9.30am–12.30pm; April–Sept also 5–7pm; ✆0584.284.877). Another inland town, **CAMAIORE**, has a couple of Romanesque churches and the eighth-century **Badia dei Santi Benedetti**, but it's an ugly, semi-industrial spot, worth passing through only if you're taking the minor road back to Lucca.

Forte dei Marmi

As these places go, **FORTE DEI MARMI** is a pleasant resort, with lush, tree-lined streets and a good beach. It's a place for a swim and stroll, but there's nothing here to justify its reputation as the trendiest spot on the coast, nor the high prices in its top hotels and restaurants. Once a major port for marble from the Apuane, it's now one of the second-home capitals of Tuscany, and a retreat for writers and artists who hole up in its more isolated, tree-surrounded villas. For a few hundred metres north of the town there's a stretch of **dunes** with no development at all; it looks a tempting camping option, but local police will shift you within minutes if you try to pitch a tent. Beyond the dunes, nondescript Cinquale and Ronchi resume the corridor of beach-front commercialism.

Like Pietrasanta, though, Forte dei Marmi is a good point of access to the mountains, with **buses** to Seravezza, Levigliani, Stazzema and Farnocchia. There are services to the interior and to Lucca, Viareggio and Pietrasanta from the Forte dei Marmi-Seravezza-Querceto **train station**, located 3km inland at Querceta, and also from Via Matteotti in the town. Buses also run from nearby Via Pascoli to La Spezia, Pisa, Lucca and Florence. The **tourist office**, Via Achille Franceschi 8b (April–Sept Mon–Sat 9am–1pm & 3pm–6pm, plus July & Aug Sun 9am–1pm; Oct–March Mon–Sat 9am–1pm, Fri & Sat also 3pm–7pm; ✆0584.80.091, ⊛www.comune.fortedeimarmi.lu.it), can provide full lists of the hundred-odd hotels. **Restaurants** largely cater to the well-heeled, though there are the usual seafront *pizzerie*. For about €80-plus you can have one of the region's finest culinary experiences at the Michelin-starred *Lorenzo*, Via Carducci 61 (✆0584.874.030; Tues–Sun eves). Fish at its freshest is the choice: "A fish has 24 virtues," says owner Lorenzo Viani, "but loses one with each hour that passes."

The Alpi Apuane

Tuscany's Versilia coast is dominated by the mountains of the **Alpi Apuane**, a forty-kilometre spread of genuinely Alpine spectacle. Now a protected Parco Regionale, they are crisscrossed by well-marked footpaths, and offer huge rewards for the walker and naturalist. If you want to do more than admire the jagged knife-edge ridge of the mountains from afar, there are numerous marked trails starting from roadheads deep in the mountains; the biggest concentration of these tracks is in the peaks east of Forte dei Marmi and Pietrasanta, centred on **Pania della Croce** (1859m) and **Monte Forato** (1223m). The main towns are **Massa** and **Carrara**, known above all else as the marble capitals of Italy, characterized by huge blocks of stone littering the roadsides, fine white dust everywhere and mine-scarred rockfaces.

Thanks to their position and height, the Apuane are a perfect combination of different ecological habitats, from tundra through Alpine meadow to Mediterranean grassland. An extraordinary variety of **wild flowers** makes this one of the country's richest botanic enclaves, but the most noticeable vegetation is the immense **forests** of chestnut and beech which cover virtually all the lower slopes. These shelter some of the mountains' three hundred species of **birds**, including the golden eagle, which has recently returned to nest here; sadly, protection came too late to preserve many larger **mammals** from hunters, though you may see marmots – rare in the Apennines – on the higher, sunnier slopes.

Walks in the Apuane

For information on the Parco Regionale contact the **tourist office** and park **visitor centre**, at Via Corrado del Greco 11 in **SERAVEZZA** (Mon–Sat 9.30am–12.30pm, plus Tues & Thurs 3.30–5.30pm; Ⓣ0584.75.821, Ⓦwww .parks.it, Ⓦwww.parcapuane.it); during the summer they organize full-day guided walks, free of charge, that you should book in advance. The detailed *Multigraphic* 1:25,000 map (widely available locally for €5.50) marks all the main walking trails and refuges.

The main approach to the northern group of peaks, round **Pania della Croce**, is from **LEVIGLIANI**, reached by bus from Forte dei Marmi and Pietrasanta; it has a couple of two-star hotels: *Vallechiara*, Via Lambora 12 (Ⓣ & Ⓕ0584.778.054; ❷), and *Raffaello*, Via Nord 11 (Ⓣ & Ⓕ0584.778.063; ❶). A mining road runs from Levigliani towards Monte Corchia (1677m), about half of which has been removed by quarrying. You can sometimes get lifts up this far from mining lorries, although travelling on the road on the mine's working days is officially prohibited. From the top of the road, you can pick up trail #9 to the 31-bed *Rifugio Giuseppe del Freo* (2hr 30min walk from Levigliani; mid-June to mid-Sept open daily; rest of year open Sat & Sun only; Ⓣ0584.778.007; ❶). From here, the best walk leads up Pania della Croce (trail #126; 2hr 30min from the refuge).

Behind **COLONNATA** village (site of many quarries, 8km inland from Carrara; see p.285), the CAI trail #38 leads to a dense web of paths around Monte Rasore (1422m) and Monte Grondice (1805m). **CAMPO CECINA**, 18km north of Carrara on the SS446, has the all-year *Rifugio Carrara* (1320m; Ⓣ0585.841.972; €20) and a rather more gentle selection of paths.

For the southern peaks, round **Monte Forato**, the best access point is **STAZZEMA**, a lovely village in its own right, with the one-star hotel *Procinto*, Via IV Novembre 21 (Ⓣ0584.777.004; ❶). The bus from Forte dei Marmi and

Caving in the Apuane

The Apuane has the best in Italian **speleology**, riddled with some of the greatest challenges in European caving. An estimated 400km of galleries run through the mountains, the largest of which – the *Antro del Corchia* – extends for over 50km and reaches depths of more than 1200m.

Caves open to the public include the *Antro del Corchia* at Levigliani – a two-hour guided tour costs €12 (Ⓣ0584.778.405, Ⓦwww.antrocorchia.it), the *Grotta del Vento* at Fornovolasco (Ⓣ0583.722.024, Ⓦwww.grottadelvento.com) and the *Grotta di Equi Terme* at Fivizzano (Ⓣ0585.97.544).

For more serious cavers there is an opportunity to explore the less "touristy" caves in the company of a professional guide – the daily rate starts at around €120 plus an extra ten percent for hiring equipment. Contact the park centre at Seravezza for further information and a list of guides.

Pietrasanta to Stazzema goes via Farnocchia, itself the starting point for some easy paths through the trees. The classic walk from Stazzema (trail #5) is a gentle climb through chestnut woods to the **Procinto**, a huge table-top crag mentioned by Dante. Below it, at 865m, is the 45-bed *Rifugio Forte dei Marmi* (early June to early Sept daily; rest of year open Sat & Sun only; ☎0584.777.051; bed only €12). This makes a comfortable day's outing, with time to walk up to Monte Nona (1279m), drop back to the refuge for a snack, and then return to Stazzema by trails #121/126. The refuge is also a perfect base for walks along the main ridge – for example, to the *Rifugio Giuseppe del Freo* (see p.283; 2hr).

Massa and around

It might have a castle and cathedral, but the character of busy, modern **MASSA** is encapsulated more by its bland broad streets and Fascist civic architecture. The town's most distinctive sight is on the main street, a **fountain** consisting of a big marble ball and fat babies – easily seen from a passing bus or car. The **Castello Malaspina** (Sat 9.30am–noon, Sun 3–6pm; €5), with its loggia and spread of Renaissance rooms, is worth an hour of your time. Otherwise there's only the two-tiered **Duomo** – in local marble, of course – and the Piazza degli Aranci, hub of what remains of the old town.

Behind Massa, a road climbs up into the Alpi Apuane towards Castelnuovo di Garfagnana (see p.292), a scrappy ride, with new villas and ramshackle *pizzerie* taking the edge off the views. About 2km above the village of **ANTONA**, just beyond the council-owned *Rifugio-Albergo di Massa* (mid-April to Sept), are Club Alpino Italiano trails #41/188 leading up to Monte Altissimo (1589m) and a couple of low ridge walks. Just before the refuge, at Pian della Fioba, is the small **Pietro Pellegrini' botanical garden** of wild flowers (mid-May to mid-Sept daily 9–10am & 3–6pm; free).

Practicalities

Buses come and go from Massa's **train station**: to get to the beaches, take the bus to **MARINA DI MASSA**, and then transfer to one of the services that stop every few hundred metres up and down the coast (every 2hr; more frequent in July & Aug). Most of the **hotels** are in Marina di Massa. Recommended is *Hotel Luna*, Via Tornaboni 17, located 300m from the sea (☎0585.241.472, ⓦwww.lunahotel.net; ❺). A list of other hotels is available from the **tourist office**, Viale Vespucci 24, Marina di Massa (May–Sept Mon–Sat 9am–1pm & 3–7pm, Sun 9.30am–12.30pm; rest of the year Mon–Sat 9am–1pm & 3–5pm; ☎0585.240.063, ⓦwww.aptmassacarrara.it). The **hostel**, *Ostello Apuano*, Via delle Pinete 237, Partaccia (☎0585.780.034, ⓦwww.ostellionline.org; mid-March to Sept; curfew 11.30pm; €11) is on the seafront north of Marina di Massa; buses go north along the coast, as well as direct from Carrara train station. There's a free beach nearby, but the sand's poor; you're better off heading south.

Marina di Massa's best-known **restaurant** is the moderately priced *Da Riccà*, Via Casola 1 (☎0585.241.070; closed Mon). For something different try *La Peniche*, at Via Lungobrugiano 3 (☎0585.240.117, ⓦwww.lapeniche.com), a country-style restaurant built on stilts, with good, inventive cooking from around €20 a head. A cheap option is *Trattoria Baria*, Via San Leonardo (☎0585.240.278; closed Tues), while snack and pizza outlets abound. In Massa itself, the best bet is the wonderfully old-fashioned and moderately priced *Il Passeggero*, run by the same family for over fifty years, just off the main Piazza degli Aranci at Via Alberica 1 (☎0585.489.651; closed Mon–Thurs eves & all day Sun). For a choice of exotic **picnic** supplies in Massa, visit Gli Svizzeri, Via Cairoli 53 – a shop that's been around since the 1850s.

Carrara

You can't get away from marble in **CARRARA**, a town whose very name is said to derive from *kar*, the Indo-European word for stone. However, the town itself is a surprisingly attractive place, once you get away from the sprawling factories around the station. Set in the hills above this mess, central Carrara has a rural hill-town feel, with peeling pastel stucco on its houses, elegant side streets lined with rows of green shutters, and a couple of piazzas and a **Duomo** that would do credit to any Tuscan town. By contrast, the town's "resort", **Marina di Carrara**, is grim – more a container port than a beach. If you want the sea, it's best to drive inland to Massa, and then drop down to the coast there.

Carrara feels like a self-sufficient town, and its people have always had a reputation as a breed apart – something they preserved even under the long-term domination of the Malaspina nobles, the local medieval big shots. Before their rule, the town had developed as a trading centre poised between Tuscany, the

△ Carrara with its marble quarries

mountains and the Ligurian coast. Roman exploitation of marble made trade with the nearby colony of Luni, over the Ligurian border, particularly brisk; something of its scale can be seen in the ruins of the colony currently being excavated there.

The town and quarries

Today, more than two hundred working concerns extract 700,000 tonnes of stone annually, making this area still the world's single largest producer of marble. Huge wire saws slice into the mountains at a rate of about 8cm an hour, their twenty-four-hour whine the bane of local residents. Environmentalists oppose the speed of extraction, and the industry is threatened by government plans to give Parco Nazionale status to the Apuane, but the quarry owners will fight all the way to preserve the two thousand jobs that remain, in an industry which employed as many as 14,000 men barely a century ago. With an estimated one thousand jobs directly dependent on each job in the quarries, the Carrara employers have no lack of supporters elsewhere in Italy.

Carrara's old town centres on **Piazza Alberica**, a gracious square whose beauty owes much to the hills which come down on two sides, and to the elegant colours and tone more often associated with Liguria than Tuscany. Stray blocks of marble sit at its centre, a legacy of the biennial Scolpire all'Aperto, a festival in which sculptors from around the world are invited to the town, given a block of marble, and left to work in the middle of the square. If you're here between late July and early October, you may get to watch them chipping away.

A short walk brings you to the eleventh-century **Duomo**, rather squashed into its piazza, but graced with a huge tower and a lovely facade built to the inevitable Pisan-Romanesque pattern. Only the intricate rose window, a superb fourteenth-century addition, departs from the norm. The interior has a severe simplicity but contains some beautiful works – a fifteenth-century **pulpit** and five appealing statues by the fourteenth-century sculptor Bergamini. The piazza's fountain, known locally as *Il Gigante* (The Giant), is an incomplete work by the lacklustre Florentine Bandinelli. Also in the square is the house where Michelangelo put up while checking out his marble supplies; nearby in Via Santa Maria are Petrarch's digs, Casa Repetti. The impressive castle on Piazza Gramsci was once a Malaspina fortress and is now the **Accademia delle Belle Arti**, with a few Roman fragments and plaster casts in its courtyard.

In Via XX Settembre, 2km southwest of town on Marina di Carrara road (and served by a bus from Via Don Minzoni), is the **Museo Civico di Marmo** (July & Aug daily 10am–8pm; May, June & Sept daily 10am–6pm; Oct–April Mon–Sat 9am–5pm; €4.50). Run as a promotional exercise by the local Chamber of Commerce, it's an impressive display that looks at the history and production of the stone – lots of photographs, examples of different types of marble, and a room devoted to rather dubious examples of marble art.

Any short trip into the interior brings you across the huge scars of the marble **quarries**, some of the most startling sights in Tuscany. A particularly accessible

Carrara marble

Ever-present on the Versilia coast, whether as blocks waiting shipment or as huge snow-like scars on the mountains, **marble** has been the lifeblood of the region for over two thousand years. Marble is a metamorphic form of limestone, hardened by colossal heat and pressure. Though it takes many forms, **Carrara stone** is usually white-grey and is prized for its flawless lustre. The many other types you'll see are mostly blocks which have been imported – from as far away as Russia – to be worked by the highly rated local factories.

The **Romans** were the first to extract this stone commercially, driving pegs of fig-wood into natural faults and then soaking them until the swollen wood split the stone. In time they used scored lines and iron chisels to produce uniform blocks about two metres square – still the basic measure.

Practices remained little changed until the Renaissance, when **Michelangelo** began to visit the area. His wet nurse was from this part of Tuscany, and he claimed he became a sculptor by ingesting the marble dust in her milk; he also claimed to have introduced the art of quarrying to Carrara, a process he considered as important as sculpting itself. The *David* is sculpted from Carrara marble, and local folklore is full of Michelangelo's pilgrimages to distant corners of the mountains in search of perfect stone.

site is at **COLONNATA** (taking its name from a column of Roman slaves brought in to work the mines), 8km from Carrara and served in summer by eight daily CAT **buses** from Carrara's main bus terminus at Via Don Minzoni. Don't go all the way to Colonnata village, but get off at the *Visita Cave* signs by the mine; if you're driving, follow the yellow *Cava di Marmo* signs from the town up the twisting road. You'll see a huge, blindingly white marble basin, its floor and sides perfectly squared by the enormous wire saws used to cut the blocks that litter the surroundings. There are even bigger quarries farther south, notably at Monte Corchia.

Practicalities

Carrara's **train station** is close to the sea, and has a regular bus service to the old town. Bus connections for La Spezia and Florence leave from Piazza Menconi in Marina di Carrara. The nearest **tourist office** is also at Marina di Carrara (June–Sept Mon–Sat 9am–1pm & 4–6.30pm; ☏0585.632.519), but you'd do better at the main office in Marina di Massa (see p.284).

Accommodation in the old town is limited to the potentially noisy two-star *Da Roberto*, Via Apuana 3 (☏0585.70.634; ❶) and the more salubrious three-star *Michelangelo*, Corso Carlo Rosselli 3 (☏0585.777.161, ✉hm.carrara@tin.it; ❸). There's a **hostel** near Marina di Carrara (see p.284), or the one-star *Maurin*, near the station at Via Fiorino 2 (☏0585.859.385; ❶).

Restaurants are numerous, few of them tourist-oriented. For a moderate price you can eat at the *Osteria della Contrada*, Via Ulivi 2 (☏0585.776.961; closed Mon); the *Roma*, Piazza Cesare Battisti 1 (☏0585.70.632; closed Tues); or for fresh fish try the family-owned *Petite Cusine*, Via Verdi 4 (☏0585.70.226; closed Sun & in Aug). An excellent little spot for a drink is the *Bar Fuori Porta*, Piazza Battisti 1 (closed Sun), which also serves inexpensive *antipasti* and *primi*; for something more sophisticated try the expensive *Enoteca Ninan*, Via Bartolini 3 (☏0585.74.741; closed Sun). For **picnic** supplies, aim for Ricci, Via Rosselli 1 (closed Wed afternoon & Sun), which preserves a wonderful Art Nouveau interior. For a treat, head out to **Colonnata**, where the *Venanzio*, Piazza Palestro 3 (☏0585.750.062; closed Sun eve & Thurs; booking essential) has attracted even the president of Italy: reckon on around €40 for what should be a sensational meal.

The Garfagnana

The **Garfagnana** is the general name for the area encompassing the Serchio valley north of Lucca, one of Tuscany's least-explored yet most spectacular corners. The paucity of visitors is accounted for by the lack of any great sights – medieval **Barga** and the spa town of Bagni di Lucca are the only historic towns – but for anyone with an interest in hiking or fine scenery, there are rewards aplenty. Much of the Garfagnana is protected as a regional **nature reserve**, whose excellent on-the-ground organization has mapped and signposted a good range of walks. The best of these are on the east of the Serchio valley, up in the mountainous **Orecchiella** range. The Serchio's western flanks comprise the equally spectacular mountains of the Alpi Apuane, best reached from the coastal side (see p.282).

If you don't have your own transport, the best way to see the Garfagnana is on the **train** line which runs the entire length of the Serchio, past Barga and the region's rather lacklustre hub, **Castelnuovo di Garfagnana** – the handiest place to stay as a base for exploring. The line then cuts through the head of the valley to Aulla, centre of the Lunigiana, from where you can drop down by train to La Spezia (in Liguria), and complete a loop back to Lucca via Massa and Viareggio. Since Bagni di Lucca's train station is about 4km out of town, it's best to travel there by **bus** from Lucca. Other buses from Lucca run up and down the valley, with stops in Barga, Castelnuovo di Garfagnana and elsewhere.

The Lower Serchio valley

Although the road north up the **Serchio valley** soon leaves Lucca behind, there's something laborious about the first part of the journey, with dusty hills and patches of light industry dotting the way to Barga, 50km north. A possible detour is the **Pieve di Brancoli**, a twelfth-century abbey reached by a twisting hillside road on the east bank of the valley, 10km out of Lucca. More easily visited, with its own rail stop, is **DIECIMO**, over on the west bank. Its Latin name is explained by a past as a Roman outpost, positioned ten Roman miles (17km) from Lucca. No more than a hamlet, it is dominated by a large, white Romanesque campanile, clearly visible from the river.

Some 4km on, road and rail line bypass **BORGO A MOZZANO**, which comprises a single cobbled street of medieval houses and the famous **Ponte della Maddalena** (or Ponte del Diavolo). Narrow, steep and elegant, this strange five-arched bridge was constructed in the eleventh century. According to legend it was built by the Devil in exchange for the soul of the first person to cross it; as in every European village where a version of this tale survives, the villagers outfoxed Satan by sending across an unsuspecting animal – in this case a dog. **Accommodation** includes *Pensione Gallo d'Oro*, Via del Brennero 3 (☎0583.88.380; ❶), whose seven rooms share a single bathroom, and two-star *Il Pescatore*, Via Primo Maggio 8 (☎0583.88.071; ❶), with eight en-suite doubles.

Bagni di Lucca and around

Though it had been a spa for centuries, **BAGNI DI LUCCA**, 25km north of Lucca, hit the social big time only in the early nineteenth century, when the patronage of Elisa Baciocchi brought in Europe's fashionable elite. The town boasted one of Europe's first official casinos – roulette was invented here – and was graced by the presence of such luminaries as Byron, Shelley, Browning and Heine.

Today, Bagni di Lucca retains its elegance and pretty surroundings; the atmosphere is fairly subdued. A dozen reasonably priced **hotels**, spread out along the valley, cater to those who've come to soak in the salty or sulphurous waters. For some old-world charm, try the two-star *Svizzero*, Via C. Casalini 30 (☎ & ℉0583.805.315; ❶; April–Sept); the one-star *Roma*, Via Umberto I 110 (☎ & ℉0583.87.278; ❶; March–Oct); or the three-star *Bridge*, 2km away in the square at Ponte a Serraglio (☎ & ℉0583.805.324, ⓦwww.bridge-hotel.it; ❷). The best **place to eat** is the *Circolo Dei Forestieri*, Piazza Varraud 10 (☎0583.86.038; closed Mon & Tues lunch), which serves food both exquisite and inexpensive, in a beautiful building with a columned terrace. The busy pizzeria *Da Vinicio* lies a block downstream from the bridge (closed Mon).

The Lima valley

East of Bagni, the **Lima valley**, a tributary of the Serchio, rises towards the border with Emilia-Romagna. Two **buses** daily (morning and afternoon) make the run over the hills to San Marcello Pistoiese, the afternoon service continuing to the skiing and walking centre of Abetone.

In the valley itself, there are several possible rough road diversions to villages with ancient churches and spectacular mountain surroundings. **Pieve di Controne**, 3km northeast of Bagni, has a strange old church in red stone, fronted by a facade covered with odd diagonal motifs. **San Cassiano**, 7km further, has a twelfth-century church with a wonderful carved facade, three tiers of very shallow arches, and a much older and dirtier tower that cuts off half the marble-faced front. Just south of the valley, **Lucchio**, cascading down the mountainside 18km from Bagni, is crowned by a castle ruin.

Past Lucchio, you enter the province of Pistoia near **SAN MARCELLO PISTOIESE**, the business centre of these mountains. The main road north of here – a continuation of the N66 from Pistoia – leads 18km to **ABETONE**, the nearest winter-sports resort to Florence. Its six chair-lifts can cope with an hourly capacity of 14,000 people and at the height of the skiing season the system is tested to the fullest; even in summer there's often not too much space in the town's thirty-odd hotels, as thousands come up from the sweltering lowlands to revive themselves in the mountain air. As a package-tour destination Abetone isn't too bad, but it's not a place to go out of your way to see. With your own transport, you could make a more exciting approach to Abetone by taking the high mountain road from Bagni di Lucca to Montefegatesi, and then over the main ridge of the Orecchiella (impassable in bad weather and potentially dangerous at any time of year – consult the tourist office before setting out) to the dramatic **Orrido di Botri** gorge before climbing up to the pass of **Foce a Giovo** (1674m).

Barga and around

The ancient hill-town of **BARGA** – poised 3.5km east of its train station on the Serchio – marks the start of the Garfagnana's best scenery, dominated by hills and incredibly lush vegetation. A couple of tempting minor roads lead into the wild country of the Orecchiella, offering stunning views over steep wooded slopes and across to the jagged profiles of the Alpi Apuane.

The old village is quiet and pretty, with a long tradition of independence and a strong economic base founded on silk and, later, wool: felt hats became a speciality in the nineteenth century. It grew up originally around a Lombard castle, and was besieged by Lucca and Pisa before falling to Florence, under whose influence it remained until 1859. Where it differed from other Lucchesi strongholds was in its rule by elected council, a system it retained even under the Florentines.

The Town

Barga's **Duomo**, San Cristofano, was founded in the ninth century and expanded over the next four hundred years, with remedial work in 1920 after a severe earthquake. It stands at the village's highest point, fronted by a terrace that provides a huge panorama of rooftops, mountains and villa-spotted hills. Built in a honey-blonde stone known as *alberese di Barga*, the **facade**, probably adapted from part of the earliest church, is decorated in a shallow pattern of Lombard Romanesque-influenced reliefs and tiny arches, a delicate contrast to the **campanile**, which seems to have erupted from the tiled roof. Left of the door is a wonderful little relief of an obviously convivial feast, sculpted in 1200; on the architrave is an equally rustic harvest scene and twin lions.

Inside, the **naves** are beautifully divided by low walls of inlaid marble and overlooked by a superlative and idiosyncratic **pulpit**, widely considered one of the finest such creations prior to the pulpits of Nicola and Giovanni

Pisano in Pisa, Siena and elsewhere. Probably created by the thirteenth-century sculptor Guido Bigarelli da Como (or a pupil), it consists of a huge rectangular stand, lavishly carved with scenes from the Scriptures and supported by four red marble pillars, the front pair of which are propped up by another pair of lions: one, with an inane smirk, surmounts a dragon (a symbol of evil), while the other stands on a man (a symbol of heresy) who is simultaneously stroking and stabbing the animal. The rear left pillar is supported by a grotesque dwarf, snub-nosed symbol of the pagan world. The church's other unmissable artefact is a tenth- or twelfth-century **statue** of St Christopher, looking rather like a huge wooden puppet; continuing the building's eccentric streak, the saint carries a child on one shoulder and a club the size of a small tree on the other. Around the church, you'll spot a cluster of della Robbia **terracottas** in the right chapel, **frescoes** on several pillars, a carved choir screen

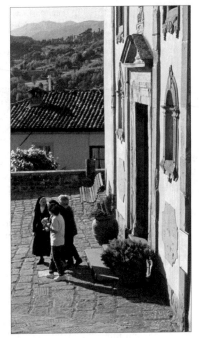

△ Barga

and two Giottesque **Crucifixes** – the overpoweringly framed example above the altar is particularly good.

Just below the Duomo to the left, the *centro storico* signs point the way to the Baroque chapel of **Santissimo Crocifisso dei Bianchi**, an oddly attractive extravagance, with a blue-gilt altar and four diversely excessive side chapels. Also worth a quick look up by the cathedral is the **Museo Civico del Territorio di Barga**, Palazzo Pretorio, Arringo del Duomo (April–Oct hours vary: call ⓣ0583.711.100; €3.50), a collection of geological and paleological exhibits tracing the area's prehistoric background.

Grotta del Vento

From Gallicano, across the river from Barga train station, you can drive west for 9km, following the bottom of the Turrite valley, to what is rated as Tuscany's best cave, the rather commercialized **Grotta del Vento** in **FORNOVO LASSO**; arrive early to miss the crowds. The guides put on three different tours daily (April–Oct) through the caverns and lakes of this bizarre subterranean landscape, lasting either one hour (on the hour 10am–noon & 2–6pm; €7.50), two hours (11am, 3pm, 4pm & 5pm; €12), or three hours (10am & 2pm; €17). In winter (Nov–March), all three tours run on Sundays and public holidays, while only the one-hour visit is available from Monday to Saturday.

Practicalities

It's a long haul up from Barga's **train** station to the town; coming from Lucca it's easier to use the regular **bus** (1hr 15min). All buses depart from the Porta

Reale, alongside the big car park where the road stops outside the walls. Barga's **tourist office** is at Via di Mezzo 45 (Mon–Fri 8am–2pm, Sat & Sun 10am–noon & 2.30–5pm; ☎0583.724.743, ⓦwww.barganews.com); check their website for details of the town's two small, high-quality summer **music festivals**, Barga Jazz and Opera Barga.

Several **hotels** and **restaurants** are ranged along the road north down to the Serchio at **Albiano**, a rather scrappy neighbourhood, but with good views. Aim for the three-star *Villa Libano*, Via del Sasso 6 (☎0583.723.059, ⓦwww.hotelvillalibano .com; ❷), next to the town park and linked to a nice restaurant with a garden terrace (open to guests only). The three-star *Alpino* is at Via Pascoli 41 (☎0583.723.336, ⓦwww.bargaholiday.com; ❷; closed Nov). Just south of Barga, in Fornaci di Barga, near the train station, is the two-star *Gorizia*, Viale Cesare Battisti (☎ & ⓕ0583.75.074; ❶), with a garden and lunch-only restaurant.

Castelnuovo di Garfagnana

Garfagnana's main town, **CASTELNUOVO DI GARFAGNANA**, is a disappointment, despite its mountain-ringed location. A rather featureless sprawl, it has a daytime market bustle to its centre but virtually no life after 5pm except on balmy summer evenings. However, Castelnuovo is the obvious base if you intend to explore the Orecchiella. Some of the mountain roads that radiate east and west offer astounding views for drivers, and the villages around are highly attractive. For serious hiking, it's also worth stopping in order to pick up maps and information. The only thing to see is the fourteenth-century **Rocca**, built by the Este dukes of Ferrara and best known for its former commander, the poet Ariosto, author of *Orlando Furioso*. By all accounts he didn't much enjoy his tour of duty in the 1520s, and mournful evocations of the area's landscape were to colour much of his later poetry. The rest of the town was badly damaged by bombing in World War II, though a lovely **terracotta** of *St Joseph and the Angels*, attributed to Verrocchio or the della Robbia, survived on the Duomo's north wall.

Practicalities

There are two **tourist offices** in Piazza delle Erbe, just beyond the arch of the town's main square, Piazza Umberto I. The more helpful is the **park visitor centre** (daily 9am–1pm & 3.30–5.30pm; ☎0583.65.169) which offers a wealth of information on trekking, local produce and rural tourism in the Garfagnana, as well as an accommodation booking service with a wide range of hotels, *agriturismi* and *rifugi*. The **Pro Loco** across the square (summer daily 9.30am–1.00pm & 3.30–7pm; winter Mon–Sat 10am–1pm, 3.30–6.30pm; ☎0583.641.007) is mainly concerned with the town itself and Lucca. For specialized **climbing** information contact the Club Alpino office (☎0583.655.77, ⓦwww.garfagnanacai.it), below the car park in Via Vittorio Emanuele.

Most people **stay** in the three-star *Da Carlino*, Via Garibaldi 15 (☎0583.644.270, ⓕ0583.65.575; ❷), up the steep street out of Piazza Umberto I, a fairly modern place with a moderately priced **restaurant**. For good homemade food and local produce try the excellent *Vecchio Mulino*, Via Vittorio Emanuele 12 (7.30am–8.30pm; closed Mon; ☎0583.62.192, ⓦwww.ilvecchiomulino.com), a century-old *enoteca* with inexpensive snacks (including great *panini*) and simple meals: it also sells a good range of wines by the bottle or glass. *Caffè Ariosto* (closed Sun pm), Piazza Umberto I 2, does wicked cocktails, including some fruit-based concoctions of barman Walter Borelli's own invention. Out of town in **Le Monarche** is the three-star *La Laterna* (☎ & ⓕ0583.62.272; ❷), with good views and a moderately priced restaurant.

Walks in the Orecchiella

If you're going in for serious **walking** in the Orecchiella, you should pick up one of the widely available *Multigraphic* 1:25,000 maps, which show all the marked trails in the area.

There are three marked circular walks pioneered by *Airone*, the leading Italian natural history magazine, which you can tackle without too much planning. There's a board-plan at the park centre near Corfino, or staff can help you make sense of the routes. **Walk 1** (5hr) takes in the summit of the craggy limestone Cima Pania (1602m) and the nature reserve of the Pania di Corfino, the most important of the three special reserves in the park and a noted area for nesting birds of prey, including peregrine falcons. **Walk 2** (4hr) passes through oak and beech forest and a stretch of grassy meadow. **Walk 3** needs two days, with a choice of overnight stops: *Rifugio C. Battisti*, or, in an emergency, *Rifugio La Bargetana* or *Rifugio di Monte Prado*. In addition to these, there are seven **Club Alpino paths** (2–3hr) in the area.

For a real challenge, there's a long-distance marked path known as **Garfagnana Trekking**, which starts and finishes at Castelnuovo and is designed to take about ten days. As well as taking in the best of the Orecchiella, five stages of this walk lead you through the Alpi Apuane. For details, contact the Comunità Montana della Garfagnana at the park visitor centre in Castelnuovo.

An even more ambitious long-distance route, the linear **Grande Escursione Appenninica (GEA)**, runs through the Orecchiella on its 24-stage trail from Sansepolcro across the roof of Tuscany to the Passo dei due Santi above La Spezia. Contact the Club Alpino for details (ⓦ www.cai.it).

There's a **campsite**, *Parco di Piella* (☎0583.62.916; caravans all year, tents April–Oct), in a wooded setting close to the train station at **Piella**, ten minutes from the centre. To get there from the station turn right and first left up Viale della Rimembranza. Aside from this site, the only official camping area in the Garfagnana is *Monte Argegna* (☎0583.611.182; June–Sept), near **Giuncugnano** (876m) in the north of the valley above Piazza al Serchio.

The Orecchiella

Though higher than the spectacular Apuane opposite, the **Orecchiella** mountains are generally tamer – but no less beautiful: rounded and thickly wooded, with steep lateral valleys and gentle grassy slopes above the treeline. The one monument of note is the monastery at **San Pellegrino**, now home to a museum of Garfagnana traditions. If you have transport, and whether you intend to hike or not, it's well worth following some of the minor roads into the mountains for a glimpse of one of the prettiest and least known of Tuscany's scenic enclaves.

Reached from Castelnuovo by a beautiful road past meadows, thatched barns and views, **CORFINO** is a small hill village (850m) which provides walkers with a choice of three **hotels**: the *Panoramico*, Via Fondo la Terra 9 (☎0583.660.161, ⓕ0583.660.159; ❷; March–Dec) and *California*, Via Bagno 1 (☎0583.660.173; ❶), both three-stars, and the similarly priced two-star, *La Baita*, Via Prato all'Aia (☎0583.660.084; June–Sept; ❶). The last is definitely the best: it's run by a pleasant family, with *mamma* in inspired charge of the kitchen.

It's worth heading north through the wild countryside for 7km to visit the excellent chalet-style **park centre** (July & Aug daily 9am–7pm; June & Sept Sat & Sun 10am–5pm; ☎0583.619.002). It has a restaurant, bar, phones, an information and exhibition centre, a lake with nicely sited picnic spots, and a fine botanical garden. The nearby *Rifugio Isera* (☎0583.660.203; April–Oct; €13) has rooms and a camping area.

San Pellegrino in Alpe

From Castelnuovo, the drive 16km up a minor road northeast to **SAN PEL-LEGRINO IN ALPE** (1524m) offers stunning views over the steep valleys and ridges of the Orecchiella. Two daily summer **buses** from Castelnuovo take the parallel and almost equally impressive major road via Castiglione.

San Pellegrino's magnificently sited monastery is partly given over to an excellent **Museo Etnografico Provinciale**, Via del Voltone 14 (Tues–Sat: April & May 10am–1pm & 2–4.30pm; June–Sept 10am–1pm & 2–6.30pm; Oct–March 9.30am–1pm; plus Sun in July & Aug; €2.50). This unusually fascinating display of the Garfagnana's peasant traditions covers four floors, ranging over every aspect of country life.

The adjacent hamlet has a bar, a couple of run-down *pensioni*, and shops where you can buy local honey, oil, mushrooms, grappa and sweet chestnut flour, once the area's staple diet. You can find other **accommodation** on the Foce delle Radici pass at the top of the road, where there's a bleak and isolated hotel, the two-star *Lunardi*, Passo delle Radici (☎0583.649.071, ℉0583.649.079; ❶). Down the parallel road towards Castiglione stands the three-star *Il Casone* (☎0583.649.028, ⓦwww.hotelilcasone.com; ❷), perched at 1300m in a great location about 6km from the pass (ask the bus driver to drop you off).

The eastern Apuane

North of Castelnuovo di Garfagnana, the Serchio valley floor is itself not very memorable but if you have transport – or can fit in with very sparse bus services – there are several possible diversions into the **Alpi Apuane** to the west.

The most obvious is the road which climbs over the main ridge to Massa, a route covered by a morning and afternoon bus from Castelnuovo. The road is not quite the scenic backwater it appears on the map, but the early stretch, up the **Turrite valley**, is verdant and tree-lined, with good views of the vast crags of the Pania della Croce (1859m). Much of the road was widened following the opening of the hydroelectric station at Torrite, but it degenerates immediately beyond a tunnel into Massa province.

The one hamlet of consequence is **ISOLA SANTA**, with two inexpensive **restaurants**: the rustic *Da Giacco*, especially good during the mushroom season (Sept & Oct), overlooking the river and a small lake, and *La Ceragetta* at nearby Capanne di Careggine (☎0583.667.065; closed Mon). A section of the long-distance *Garfagnana Trekking* (GT; see box opposite) passes 100m west of the hamlet, and you can follow it north towards Lago di Vagli (about 5hr walking) or south for a couple of hours to the above-average bar and accommodation of *Rifugio Freo*. The best circular walk from Isola Santa is north on the GT.CAI-marked trail #145 to Monte Sumbra (1764m), and back the same way: a stiff climb but only about 8km in total.

Lago di Vagli

North of Castelnuovo, the best diversion comes at Poggio (8km), where there's a choice of two roads. One runs to the high village of **CAREGGINE** (882m), notable for little except its views. The other leads to **Lago di Vagli**, an artificial creation that submerged the village of Fabbriche, but left three others intact – Roggio, Vagli di Sotto and Vagli di Sopra. Every ten years the lake is drained and the ghost village slowly revealed – next due in 2014.

ROGGIO is immersed in chestnut trees; it boasts the biggest single specimen in Italy, 10m round and 26m high. It has a small one-star hotel, *La Guardia*, Piazza La Guardia (☎0583.649.121; ❶), or you may be able to rent one of four en-suite rooms at *Coletti Pietro*, Via del Fiore (☎0583.649.179; ❶). Equally

Vagli di Sotto provides the starting point for a couple of excellent **walks** onto the highest ridges of the Alpi Apuane – for which the widely available *Multigraphic* map is invaluable.

The **first path** follows the road southwest up the Tambura valley, before linking with the CAI-marked trail #31; you can then follow this west to **Monte Focoletta** (1620m), or, more interestingly, east to CAI #144, which takes you to the top of **Monte Sumbra** (1764m) and then in a wide circle via the Tassetora valley back to Vagli di Sotto – a fantastic and varied day's walk (16km).

The **second path**, CAI #177, climbs to the Passo della Focolaccia (1650m), a meeting point of several other trails. The pass offers excellent views to the Apuane's highest point, **Monte Pisanino** (1947m), just to the north, and gives access to a superb ridge (trail #179) that takes you to the top of **Monte Grondilice** (1805m). From the summit you can carry on to Carrara, or north (on the GT) to the 22-bed *Rifugio Serenaia* (☎0583.610.085, ©diamanti.diamanti@libero.it; April–Oct; around €35 half-board), the starting point for many more trails. The refuge is also accessible by road from the Serchio valley to the north, via Piazza al Serchio and Gramolazzo.

enticing, **VAGLI DI SOTTO** sits on an arm of the lake, offering boat rental and a range of worthwhile walks (see box). It has a popular three-star **hotel**, *Le Alpi*, Via Vandelli 8 (☎ & ℱ0583.664.057; ❷; April–Sept), offering somewhat average evening meals; and four recently renovated rooms at *Ristorante Il Pescatore*, Via Europa 1 (☎0583.664.052; ❶). **VAGLI DI SOPRA**, above the lake, has a few rooms for rent. All of these villages have *trattorie* which, though small, offer excellent cooking.

The Lunigiana

Few people make it to Tuscany's northernmost tip, the **Lunigiana**. A land of rocky, forested landscape, with just two sizeable towns – **Aulla** and **Pontrémoli** – this is one of the most insular regions in Tuscany. Its isolation was ensured over centuries by its mountainous approaches, only breached in the nineteenth century by the carving out of a rail tunnel and twisting mountain road at Piazza al Serchio.

The Lunigiana's name derives from the **Luni**, an ancient tribe who proved a tough nut for the Romans to crack and were equally impervious for some centuries to Christianity. Later, numerous would-be rulers built castles to exact tolls from anyone passing through the valley – hence the tourist-board name for the area, "Land of the Hundred Castles". Many of these castles are now in private hands and many others were left in ruins after World War II, but the region still repays a visit for its scenery and self-contained atmosphere. **Train** connections are frequent, and Aulla is the hub of an extensive **bus** network.

Equi Terme, Fosdinovo and Fivizzano

The train from the Garfagnana emerges from its long tunnel at **EQUI TERME**, which advertises itself for guided tours of **La Buca**, a cave once inhabited by lions, leopards and Neolithic people (closed at time of writing). The tiny village enjoys a superb scenic backdrop of crags and knife-edge peaks, sitting at the foot of the towering Il Solco canyon, and boasts a large outdoor swimming pool (June–Oct daily 9.30–6.30pm; €4.50, half-day €2.50). The central *La Posta*

hotel, Via Provinciale 15 (℡0585.97.937; ❶; closed Jan), has an inexpensive **restaurant** and garden; or you could try the three-star *Hotel Terme*, Via Noceverde (℡0585.97.830, ℻0585.97.831, 🌐www.hoteltermeequi.it; ❷).

Heading towards the coast from here by road, the most interesting route is via **FOSDINOVO**, a beautifully situated village that sits along a spur overlooking steep, wooded valleys. Host to Dante in 1306, the Castello della Malaspina here is certainly the best of the region's fortresses although it is now closed to the public. If you want to break for a **meal**, head for the long-established and family-run *Il Cucco*, Via Cucco 26 (℡0187.68.907).

FIVIZZANO – to the north, on the N63 road into Emilia – is a more substantial place, with its medieval Piazza Medicea, dominated by a Medici fountain and a retinue of Florentine palazzi. The village also has a fine thirteenth-century church, SS Jacopo e Antonio, with a handful of Renaissance paintings. If you want a **room** or **meal**, the obvious choice is the central two-star *Hotel-Ristorante Giardinetto* in Via Roma 151 (℡0585.92.060; ❶; restaurant closed Mon). You might pass this way heading for the **Passo di Cerreto** (1261m), a walking and skiing centre on the Emilia-Romagna border. En route, 6km out of Fivizzano, look for the hamlet of Vendaso on the right, home to the Romanesque church of **San Paolo**.

Aulla and around

AULLA, squeezed onto a green strip at the confluence of two rivers, was almost totally destroyed in the last war and has virtually nothing of note except for the **Fortezza della Brunella**, a sixteenth-century Genoese castle that testifies to the town's early strategic importance and contains a small natural history museum (Tues–Sat 9am–noon & 3–6pm; €3.50). With time on your hands, you might look into the parish church, built within the ruins of the eighth-century **San Caprasio**, an abbey that long dominated the hinterland.

Your best bet for really getting to grips with the Lunigiana is to head for some of the surrounding villages, most of which were fortified by the Malaspina nobles. Try Licciana Nardi, named after an early freedom fighter shot in 1844 while leading an uprising in southern Italy (his remains are in the big sarcophagus in the village's Piazza del Municipio), Caprigliola (6km south on the border with Liguria), Bibola or Ponzanello.

A more well-defined target is **VILLAFRANCA IN LUNIGIANA**, halfway from Aulla to Pontrémoli, again with the ruins of a Malaspina castle, but of more interest for its **Museo Ethnografico** (summer Tues–Sat 9am–noon & 4–7pm; winter same days 9am–noon, plus 3–6pm Fri–Sun; €3). Occupying an old mill in Via Borgo, this documents the area's rural traditions, with a special nod to the omnipresent sweet chestnut. From **BAGNONE**, 5km east, there are opportunities for walks into the remote chestnut-covered ridges of Monte Sillara (1867m) and Monte Marmagna (1851m).

Pontrémoli

PONTRÉMOLI is the Lunigiana's biggest centre, and the northernmost town in Tuscany. Part is still evocatively medieval, especially the area rambling north of the **Torre del Campanone**. The tower, now the Duomo's campanile, originally formed part of a fortress built by Lucca's Castruccio Castracani in 1322 to keep the town's warring factions apart: hence its nickname, *Cacciaguerra* – "chaser-away-of-war". The **Duomo** itself is an extraordinary Baroque affair.

The most captivating things in the town, however, are the twenty or so prehistoric stele housed in the **Museo del Comune** (Tues–Sun: summer 9am–noon & 3-6pm; winter 9am–noon & 2–5pm; €3.10), whose home is the Castello del

Piagnaro, a bleak fourteenth-century castle. These highly stylized statues fall into three groups. The oldest date from 3000–2000 BC, and are crude rectangular blocks with just a "U" for a face, and only the suggestion of arms and trunk. The second group (2000–800 BC) have more angular heads and more detail; the last pieces (700–200 BC) are more sophisticated still, and usually have a weapon in each hand. Most stele were funerary headstones, but here it's thought they represented a pagan communion between heaven (the head), earth (the arms and their weapons) and the underworld (the buried bottom third). Those with heads missing perhaps suffered at the hands of Christians intent on doing away with idolatry.

Fifteen minutes' walk south of the town, the small church of **Santissima Annunziata** was built to celebrate an appearance of the Virgin in 1471; it contains a trio of treasures, the most important an octagonal marble tempietto by Jacopo Sansovino, the others a fifteenth-century *Annunciation* and a Florentine altarpiece by an unknown artist.

Pontrémoli has the only **tourist office** in the Lunigiana (☎0187.831.180, ⓦwww.lunigiana.net), in the central Piazza Municipio off Piazza Repubblica. Enquire here about the plentiful **accommodation** possibilities, or call at the three-star *Napoleon*, Piazza Italia 2 (☎0187.830.544; ❷), which has its own inexpensive **restaurant**. The local culinary speciality is a type of large pancake-like pasta, *testaroli*, available in any one of the town's top *trattorie*: *Da Bussè*, Piazza Duomo 32 (☎0187.831.371; closed Fri & eves on Mon–Thurs), is best, a lovely, snug place that's been in the same family for generations. Another traditional, inexpensive place is the *Trattoria del Giardino da Bacciottini*, Via Ricci Armani 13 (☎0187.830.120; closed weekdays in Jan & Feb), which serves homemade local food throughout the day and specializes in Lunigiana cakes and puddings. For drinks and more wonderful cakes, head for the historic *Caffè degli Svizzeri* at Piazza della Repubblica 21 (closed Mon).

Travel details

Trains

Aulla to: Castelnuovo di Garfagnana (10 daily; 1hr); Equi Terme (10 daily; 25min); Fivizzano (10 daily; 10min); Lucca (10 daily; 2hr); Pontrémoli (hourly; 25min); Villafranca in Lunigiana (hourly; 15min).
Lucca to: Aulla (10 daily; 2hr); Bagni di Lucca (10 daily; 30min); Barga (10 daily; 40min); Castelnuovo di Garfagnana (10 daily; 1hr); Equi Terme (10 daily; 1hr 30min); Fivizzano (10 daily; 1hr 50min); Florence (hourly; 1–2hr); Montecatini (hourly; 25min); Pescia (hourly; 15min); Piazza al Serchio (10 daily; 1hr 20min); Pisa airport (4 daily; 45min); Pisa Centrale (hourly; 30min); Pistoia (hourly; 40min); Prato (hourly; 1hr); Viareggio (hourly; 20min).
Massa to: Livorno (6 daily; 40min); Pisa (6 daily; 30min); Viareggio (6 daily; 15min).

Buses

Aulla to: Equi Terme (6 daily; 1hr); Pontrémoli (9 daily; 20min).

Barga to: Bagni di Lucca (4 daily; 40min); Castelnuovo di Garfagnana (8 daily; 30min); Lucca (8 daily; 1hr 15min).
Castelnuovo di Garfagnana to: Barga (8 daily; 45min); Lucca (9 daily; 1hr 30min); Pietrasanta (3 daily; 1hr 45min); Vagli di Sotto (6 daily; 30min).
Lucca to: Bagni di Lucca, via Borgo a Mozzano (8 daily; 55min); Barga (11 daily; 1hr 15min); Camaiore (6 daily; 1hr); Castelnuovo di Garfagnana (9 daily; 1hr 30min); Florence (22 daily; 1hr 15min); Forte dei Marmi (9 daily; 1hr 20min); La Spezia (2 daily; 2hr 50min); Marina di Carrara (8 daily; 1hr 40min); Marina di Massa (8 daily; 1hr 30min); Massa (5 daily; 1hr 50min); Pescia (12 daily; 1hr 15min); Pietrasanta (10 daily; 1hr – change at Viareggio); Pisa (hourly; 50min); Viareggio (at least hourly; 45min).
Pontrémoli to: Aulla (9 daily; 20min); Villafranca in Lunigiana (10 daily; 10min).
Viareggio to: Florence (hourly; 1hr 30min); Forte dei Marmi (hourly; 30min); Marina di Massa (hourly; 50min); Torre del Lago (every 30min; 15min).

Pisa, the central coast and Elba

CHAPTER 4 # Highlights

* **The Leaning Tower, Pisa** Thanks to high-tech intervention, the most famous building in Tuscany is safe for the next few centuries at least. See p.306

* **The Duomo, Pisa** One of the finest Romanesque churches in all of Italy. See p.308

* **The Baptistery, Pisa** Italy's largest baptistery, famed for its sculptures and amazing acoustics. See p.309

* **The Camposanto, Pisa** A tranquil, grassy cloister and beautiful frescoes make this one of the world's most impressive burial grounds. See p.309

* **Elba** If you need a break from all the art, head for the beaches of Elba. See p.326

* **Capraia** And if the crowds of Elba are too much, you can always take refuge here. See p.338

△The Campo dei Miracoli, Pisa

Pisa, the central coast and Elba

Flying into Tuscany you'll most likely arrive at **Pisa**, a city which – thanks to its leaning tower – is known, at least in name, to almost every visitor to Italy. Like Lucca, a little way to the north, Pisa bears the architectural stamp of the Middle Ages, the tower being just one element of its **Campo dei Miracoli**, or Field of Miracles, Italy's most refined ensemble of medieval architecture. Since before the time of Galileo, Pisa has had one of Italy's major universities, and student life remains an important aspect of the city's strong sense of identity. It's an underrated place, seen by most outsiders on a whistle-stop trip – which means that finding accommodation is often less troublesome than in Tuscany's more overtly enticing towns. Furthermore, its excellent road and rail connections to Florence and to the north and south make it a good base for wider exploration.

The chief city of the central Tuscan coast is the no-nonsense port of **Livorno** – worth a call more for its food than for its sights. To the south, the so-called **Costa degli Etruschi**, or Etruscan Riviera, is one of the least attractive areas of Tuscany, with its dingy resorts and drab hinterland of low hills and reclaimed swampland, known often as the Pisan Maremma. When this coastal strip becomes clogged with the huge numbers of Italian holidaymakers who spend their summers here, the temptation to press on south can be overwhelming. However, it is not all bad: there are pockets of unspoilt sand around **Baratti**, and some beautiful areas of pine woodland (*pineta*) have been preserved at an important nature reserve at **Bólgheri**.

Close to Baratti, at the southern tip of the flatlands, **Piombino** provides the main point of embarkation for the biggest island of the Tuscan archipelago, **Elba**. Though peak-season crowds fill every hotel room on the island, Elba can be a seductive place in spring or early autumn, when it almost rivals the charm of outlying **Capraia**, a spot still remarkably little touched by tourism.

Pisa

Since the beginning of the age of the tourist brochure, **PISA** has been known for just one thing – the **Leaning Tower**, the favourite shorthand image for

PISA, THE CENTRAL COAST & ELBA

invoking Italy. It is indeed a freakishly beautiful building, a sight whose impact no amount of prior knowledge can blunt. Yet it's just a single component of the **Campo dei Miracoli**, the city's amazing religious core, where the Duomo, Baptistery and Camposanto complete an unrivalled quartet of medieval masterpieces. These, and a dozen or so churches and palazzi scattered about the town, belong to Pisa's golden age, from the eleventh to the thirteenth century, when the city, then still a port, was one of the maritime powers of the Mediterranean. The **Pisan-Romanesque architecture** of this period, distinguished by its white and black marble facades, is complemented by some of the finest late-medieval sculpture in Italy, much of it from the workshops of Nicola and Giovanni Pisano.

The city's political zenith came in the second half of the eleventh century with a series of victories over the Saracens, whom the Pisans drove out from Corsica, Sardinia and the Balearic islands, and harassed even in Sicily. Decline set in early, however, with defeat at sea by the Genoese in 1284 followed by the silting up of the harbour. From 1406 the city was governed by Florence, whose Medici rulers re-established the University of Pisa, one of the intellectual forcing houses of the Renaissance; **Galileo**, Pisa's most famous native, was one of the teachers there. Subsequent centuries saw the city fade into provinciality – its state when the Shelleys and Byron took palazzi here, forging what Shelley termed their "paradise of exiles". The modern city has been revitalized by its airport and industrial suburbs and, of course, money from tourism.

Arrival, information and accommodation

Trains arrive at Pisa Centrale station, on Piazza della Stazione about 1km south of the Arno. **Buses** come into the nearby Piazza San Antonio. From either, the Campo dei Miracoli is about twenty minutes' walk north (up the pedestrianized Corso Italia and across the Ponte di Mezzo), or a five-minute ride on bus #1 from outside the train station; local bus tickets are sold at a kiosk to the right out of the station. There's an official, signposted **car park** outside the Porta Nuova, just west of the Campo dei Miracoli, and a free long-term car park at the airport.

To pick up a map and full hotel lists for the city and province look in at one of the **tourist offices**: close to the stations, on Piazza Vittorio Emanuele (summer

Transport from Pisa airport

Pisa's **Galileo Galilei airport** (☎050.849.300, ⓦwww.pisa-airport.com), most visitors' point of entry to Tuscany, lies about 3km south of the city centre. It has an impressive turnout of **car-rental** firms, though on-the-spot deals are more expensive than those arranged in advance. All require a deposit to cover a full tank of fuel: usually you just leave your credit card details. When you return the car, you'd do well to refuel before getting to the airport, since petrol is pricier here than elsewhere. The **drive** to Florence is straightforward (an airport slip road takes you directly onto the motorway), but the road into Pisa is so confusing that, without directions from the car-rental desk, you may well end up getting lost.

If you've arrived on one of the budget airlines, you can use the shuttle **buses** that leave roughly every hour from in front of the terminal and arrive at Florence's Santa Maria Novella station seventy minutes later. You can buy tickets (€7.50 single) at the stand right in front of you as you come out into the airport concourse. Otherwise you'll have to take a train, which is cheaper (€5), if often slower (70–100min in total, depending on connections at Pisa Centrale); there are only seven direct trains daily (6.40am–10.20pm; no service between 12.40pm and 6pm), but every thirty minutes a shuttle train runs from the airport to Pisa Centrale (6min), where you can change to one of the hourly trains to Florence (journey time 1hr). Trains depart from a platform at the end of the airport concourse, to the left as you emerge from Arrivals. Tickets can be bought from the office at the opposite end of the concourse from the station. Remember to validate your ticket in the platform machines before boarding the train. If you're arriving late, you'll have to take the five-minute bus (€1; every 20min), train or taxi ride to Pisa Centrale, from where trains to Florence start running from around 4am. Returning from Florence to Pisa Aeroporto, shuttle buses run from 5.50am to 7.30pm. After that, there is a direct train at 8.37pm, but otherwise you'll have to take the train to Pisa Centrale and then get a bus, train or taxi.

PISA

▲ ● & Viareggio

San Rossore

Lucca

CAMPO DEI MIRACOLI

Camposanto

Duomo ⓘ

Leaning Tower

Baptistery

Porta Nuova

Museo delle Sinopie

Museo del Duomo

Palazzo Arcivescovile

Santa Caterina

Orto Botanico

Palazzo dei Cavalieri

PIAZZA DEI CAVALIERI

Santo Stefano

San Francesco

San Frediano

Museo di Storia Naturale

Università

Santo Stefano

San Michele in Borgo

Teatro Verdi

San Nicola

Palazzo Reale

Arsenale

Santa Maria della Spina

Palazzo Lanfranchi

Museo Nazionale di San Matteo

Fortezza Vecchia

River Arno

Palazzo Gambacorti

Logge di Banchi

River Arno

San Paolo a Ripa d'Arno

Santa Maria del Carmine

San Martino

Palazzo Scotti

Bastione Sangallo

Train Station

0   200 m

Airport   Florence

Mon–Sat 9am–7pm, Sun 9.30am–3.30pm; winter Mon–Fri 9am–7pm, Sat 9.30am–1.30pm; ℡050.42.291); or behind the Leaning Tower at the northern end of the Campo dei Miracoli (summer Mon–Sat 9am–7pm, Sun 10.30am–4.30pm; winter Mon–Sat 9am–5.30pm; ℡050.560.464). For online information, go to ⓦ www.comune.pisa.it.

Among **regular events**, look out for concerts at the Teatro Comunale Verdi in Via Palestro, and for more offbeat and contemporary shows (even the odd rock concert) held in a former church at the end of Via San Zeno. The city also has an adventurous **art-house cinema**, Cinema Nuovo, in Piazza della Stazione.

Most people cover Pisa as a day-trip, or stay just one night, so **accommodation** is usually not too hard to find. In summer, however, it's still best to phone ahead or arrive early in the day. Prospects for budget travellers are good, with two hostels (one women-only) and a fairly central campsite.

Hotels

Alessandro della Spina Via Alessandro della Spina 5–9 ☏ 050.502.777, ⓦ www.hoteldellaspina .it. This three-star hotel is not the best located place in central Pisa (it's in a quiet side street to the east of the station), and the building isn't terribly characterful, but it's spacious, smart and well-run. ❺

Amalfitana Via Roma 44 ☏ 050.29.000, ⓕ 050.25.218. Pleasant if unexceptional two-star, a couple of minutes south of the Campo dei Miracoli. ❷

Bologna Via Mazzini 57 ☏ 050.502.120, ⓦ www .albergobologna.com. Large three-star on the station side of the river with choice of shared or private bathroom. ❹

Clio Via San Lorenzino 3 ☏ 050.28.446. Clean and welcoming one-star place at the river end of Corso Italia. ❶

Di Stefano Via Sant'Apollonia 35 ☏ 050.553.559, ⓦ www.hoteldistefano.pisa.it. Tidy if characterless three-star hotel, in a quiet street just off the north-east side of Piazza dei Cavalieri. ❹

Galileo Via Santa Maria 12 ☏ & ⓕ 050.40.621. Nine big, nicely decorated one-star rooms, with and without private bathrooms; not the quietest hotel in town, but central and good value. ❶

Giardino Piazza Manin 1 ☏ 050.562.101, ⓔ giardino@csinfo.it. Modern sixteen-room three-star hotel; its main attraction is that it's very near the Campo dei Miracoli. ❹

Helvetia Via Don G. Boschi 31 ☏ 050.553.084. Spotless and friendly one-star off Piazza Arcives-covado offering doubles with or without private bathroom. ❶

Milano Via Mascagni 14 ☏ 050.23.162, ⓦ www .pisaonline.it/hotelmilano. Situated in a side street leading into Piazza della Stazione, this two-star is one of the better hotels in the station area. ❷

Rinascente Via del Castelletto 28 ☏ & ⓕ 050.580.460. This very popular one-star occu-pies an old palazzo south of Piazza dei Cavalieri. Shared or private bathrooms. ❷

Royal Victoria Lungarno Pacinotti 12 ☏ 050.940.111, ⓦ www.royalvictoria.it. Run by the same family since its foundation in 1837, this old-fashioned, good-looking and in places rather frayed three-star is the most welcoming and characterful of central Pisa's hotels. Rooms on the riverfront side can be noisy, though the views more than compensate. Copious buffet breakfast, too. ❻

Serena Via D. Cavalca 45 ☏ 050.580.809, ⓔ ser-ena.pisa@pisaonline.it. A cheap one-star, and a favourite with students. Thirteen rooms with just three bathrooms. ❶

Hostels

Casa della Giovane Via Corridoni 29 ☏ 050.43.061. Church-run women's hostel, five minutes' walk from the station. Single room €27, double €31.

Ostello della Gioventù Via Pietrasantina 15, Madonna dell'Acqua ☏ & ⓕ 050.890.622, ⓦ www.pisaonline.it/AlbergoDellaGioventu. This non-HI hostel is 1km from Campo dei Miracoli: If you don't want to walk, take bus #3 from the sta-tion or the airport. Make sure you have mosquito repellent in summer, as the hostel is right by a swamp, although it benefits from a nearby super-market, pizzeria and burger joint. Reception opens 6pm. Dorm bed €15.

Campsites

Campeggio Torre Pendente Viale delle Cascine 86 ☏ 050.561.704, ⓕ 050.561.734. Large, well-maintained site, with a laundry, bar, pool, restau-rant and shop; 1km west of the Campo dei Miracoli (signposted from Piazza Manin). April to mid-Oct.

Internazionale Via Litoranea 7, Marina di Pisa ☏ & ⓕ 050.35.211. Large-ish beach site, 10km west of central Pisa. May–Sept.

Mare e Sole Viale del Tirreno, Pisa Calambrone ☏ 050.32.757, ⓕ 050.30.488. Another beach campsite, 15km from Pisa; take bus marked "Tir-renia-Calambrone". April–Sept.

The Campo dei Miracoli

Since it was first laid out, Pisa's ecclesiastical centre has been known as the **Campo dei Miracoli**, or Field of Miracles, and the sight of it is as stunning today as it must have been to medieval travellers. Nowhere else in Italy are the key buildings of a city – the cathedral, baptistery and bell-tower – arrayed with such precision, and nowhere else is there so beautiful a contrast of stonework and surrounding meadow. Underneath the pavements and the turf lies a mix of sand and silt, whose instability accounts for the crazy tilt of the Leaning Tower, and of its companions. Take a close look at the Baptistery and you'll see that it's inclined some way out of the vertical, while the facade of the Duomo is a few degrees out of true as well. The weird angles aren't the only oddity: the tapering domes of the Baptistery and Duomo, with the precarious top storey of the Leaning Tower behind them, comprise the strangest skyline in Tuscany.

The souvenir stalls around the edge of the Campo are in themselves quite a sight, offering an inexhaustible range of kitsch delights, such as a silver-plated plastic replica of the Leaning Tower with a mermaid wrapped round its base – presumably an arcane reference to Pisa's maritime history.

The Leaning Tower

Perhaps the strangest fact about the **Leaning Tower** (Torre Pendente) is that it has always tilted. Begun in 1173, it started to subside when it had reached just three of its eight storeys, but it leaned in the opposite direction to the present one. Odd-shaped stones were inserted to correct this deficiency, whereupon the tower lurched the other way. Over the next 180 years a succession of architects continued to extend the thing upwards, each one endeavouring to compensate for the angle, the end result being that the main part of the tower is slightly banana-shaped. Around 1350, Tommaso di Andrea da Pontedera completed the magnificent stack of marble and granite arcades by crowning it with a bellchamber, set closer to the perpendicular than the storeys below it, so that it looks like a hat set at a rakish angle.

Tickets for the Campo dei Miracoli sights

The **ticket office** for the **Campo dei Miracoli** is next to the Campo's tourist office. The five museums and monuments of the Campo dei Miracoli – the Duomo, Baptistery, Museo dell'Opera, Camposanto and Museo delle Sinopie – share a complicated system of **ticketing**. Admission to the Duomo costs €2, except from November 1 to March 1, when it's free. Single admission to the other sights costs €5. Admission to any two sights costs €6, and combined admission to the Baptistery, Museo dell'Opera, Camposanto and Museo delle Sinopie costs €8.50.

Between March and October you can also buy a €13 ticket which gives you one visit to all the Camposanto sights, plus the Museo Nazionale di Palazzo Reale, the Museo Nazionale di San Matteo, the church of Santa Maria della Spina, and the Torre Guelfa della Cittadella Vecchia.

There's a separate ticket (€15) for thirty-minute guided tours of the **Leaning Tower**, which depart every 35min; expect long queues in high season. For an extra €2 you can pre-book your visit online at ⓦwww.opapisa.it, as long as you're making your reservation at least sixteen days in advance. Children under the age of 8 are not allowed into the tower.

Finally, there is also a joint €6.50 ticket for the Museo Nazionale di San Matteo and the Museo di Palazzo Reale, and a €2.50 ticket for the Torre Guelfa della Cittadella Vecchia and Santa Maria della Spina – though it's worth pointing out that Pisa's multiple tickets are notoriously changeable.

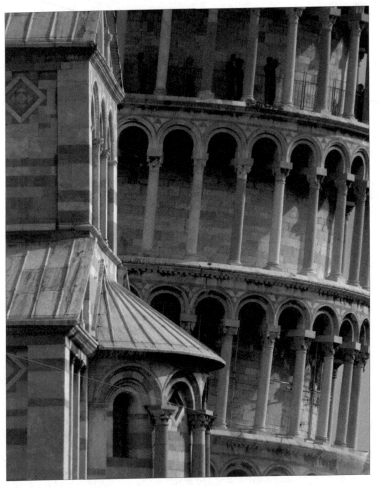

△ The Leaning Tower

By the end of the twentieth century, the tower was leaning 4.5m from the upright and nearing its limits. The collapse of a church tower in Pavia, killing four people, concentrated minds on the dangers of procrastination, and in 1990 the Leaning Tower was shut to the public. Soon after the closure, ten steel bands were wrapped round the lowest section of the tower to prevent the base from buckling under the weight of the 15,000 tonnes of marble above. Various schemes aimed at arresting the effects of gravity were discussed, and in the end it was decided to place more than 900 tonnes of lead ingots at its base to counterbalance the force of the leaning stonework. In 1998, when it was clear that the weights had stabilized the structure, the project entered its second phase with a delicate drilling operation – supervised by Professor John Burland of London's Imperial College – to remove water and silt from beneath the tower's northern foundations. The resulting subsidence corrected the building's southwards tilt by ten percent, bringing it back to its 1838 position, and to ensure that it stayed that way for the foreseeable future (300 years, according to Professor Burland), the foundations were strengthened and steel reinforcement bars were inserted into the walls of the tower. After eleven years and $30 million, the tower was officially reopened to the public in November 2001.

The thirty-minute guided **tour** of the tower leads you to the bellchamber up a dark and narrow spiral staircase of 294 steps, at a fairly disorientating five-degree angle. It's not for the claustrophobic or acrophobic, but you might think the steep admission fee is worth it for the privilege of getting inside one of the world's most famous and perilous buildings. The opening hours are extremely complicated, but the briefest opening period is from November to February, when tours begin at 9.30am and finish around 4.20pm; for most of the summer (April–Sept) they run from 8.30am to 7.50pm, but from June 16 to September 5 the last tour departs at around 10.20pm. Tours are given in English between April and September at 11.20am, 3.20pm and 5.20pm. For details on how to book tickets, see p.306.

The Duomo

The **Duomo** (March 9am–6pm; April–Sept Mon–Sat 10am–8pm; Oct 10am–7pm; Nov–Feb 10am–1pm & 3–5pm; Sun all year, no admittance to tourists before 1pm) was begun a century before its campanile, in 1064. With its four levels of variegated colonnades and its subtle interplay of dark grey marble and white stone, it's the archetype of the Pisan-Romanesque style, a model often imitated but never surpassed. Squares and discs of coloured marble are set into the magnificent facade, but the soberly graceful effect of the primary grey and white is such that you notice these strong tones only when you look closely.

Entrance to the Duomo is usually by the **Portale di San Ranieri**, opposite the Leaning Tower, but while they are being restored you may be directed to either the door on the north side, or the west door. This original bronze door-way of the main facade shows scenes from the life of Christ, cast around 1180 by Bonanno Pisano, first architect of the Leaning Tower, that are powerfully diagrammatic; the Massacre of the Innocents, for example, is represented by the smallest possible cast – Herod, one mother and one soldier. The Portale's place on the main facade opposite the Baptistery has been taken by massive doors from the workshop of Giambologna, a panoply of high-Renaissance detail.

Inside the Duomo, the impact of the crisp black and white marble of the long arcades – recalling the Moorish architecture of Córdoba – is slightly diminished by the incongruous gilded ceiling, the fresco in the squashed circle of the dome, and the massive air vents bunged through the upper arches. Much of the interior was redecorated, and some of the chapels remodelled, after a fire in 1595, so most of the paintings and sculpture are Renaissance or later.

The magnificent apse mosaic of *Christ in Majesty* is one of the survivors of the blaze. It was completed by Cimabue in 1302, the year in which **Giovanni Pisano** began to sculpt the cathedral's extraordinary **pulpit**. This was packed away after the fire, sixteenth-century Pisans evidently no longer concurring with the Latin inscription around the base, which records that Giovanni had "the art of pure sculpture… and would not know how to carve ugly or base things, even if he wished to". Only in 1926 was it rediscovered and reassembled in the nave. The last of the great series of pulpits created in Tuscany by Giovanni and his father Nicola (the others are in Siena and Pistoia), it is a work of amazing virtuosity, the whole surface animated with figures almost wholly freed from the block. Its narrative density rewards close attention: the story of the Passion, from Judas's betrayal to the scourging of Christ, for instance, is condensed into a single panel. Unfortunately, a column prevents you from properly viewing the most tumultuous panel of all, the *Last Judgement*.

In the right transept are the mummified body of Pisa's patron saint, **Ranieri**, and (set into the east wall) the tomb of the Holy Roman Emperor **Henry VII**, who died near Siena, allegedly from eating a poisoned wafer at Mass. After laying Siena to waste, the pro-imperial Ghibelline Pisans bore the body of their hero back to the Camposanto, where Tino da Camaino carved the effigy in 1315. In photographs the sculpture looks wonderful, but it's now mounted so high on the wall that you can see little more than its delicate profile.

A final item of interest is the huge bronze incense lamp, which is used to fumigate the central aisle – it's said that a forerunner provided the inspiration for Galileo's theory of the movement of the pendulum.

The Baptistery

The third building of the Miracoli ensemble, the circular **Baptistery** (daily: March 9am–6pm; April–Sept 8am–8pm; Oct 9am–7pm; Nov–Feb 10am–5pm), is a slightly bizarre mix, with three storeys of Romanesque arcades peaking in a crest of Gothic pinnacles and a dome shaped like the stalk end of a lemon. It was begun in the mid-twelfth century by a certain Deotisalvi ("God save you"), who left his name on the column to the left of the door. Lack of money – caused mainly by Genoa's incursions into the Pisan trade network – prevented its completion in the style in which it had been started. In the second half of the thirteenth century the Gothic top storeys and attendant flourishes were applied by Nicola and Giovanni Pisano, who rounded off the job with a glorious gallery of statues – the originals of which are now displayed in the Museo dell'Opera del Duomo (see p.310).

This is the largest baptistery in Italy, and the plainness of the vast interior is immediately striking, with its unadorned arcades and bare dome. The acoustics are astonishing too, as demonstrated at intervals by the custodian. At the centre, continuing the exotic strain of Pisan-Romanesque, is a mosaic-inlaid **font** by Guido da Como (1246), raised on stone steps for ease of immersion.

Overlooking it is Nicola Pisano's splendid **pulpit**, sculpted in 1260, half a century before his son's work in the cathedral. This was the sculptor's first major commission and manifests a classical spirit in part attributable to the influence of the court of Emperor Frederick II, whose Italian power base was in Nicola's native Apulia. Thus the seated Virgin in the *Adoration of the Magi* is almost a literal copy of a figure of Phaedra on a Roman sarcophagus now housed in the Museo dell'Opera del Duomo, while the nude figure of Daniel (underneath the *Adoration*) is evidently Hercules under an alias. The complexity of the cultural make-up of fourteenth-century Pisa is shown by the Gothic sharp-angled drapery and by the architectural elements of the pulpit, the decoration of the arches and the foliage of the capitals recalling the stonework of French Gothic cathedrals. For good views out over the Campo dei Miracoli, climb the **stairs** to the upper gallery and from there up inside the dome.

The Camposanto

The screen of sepulchral white marble running along the north edge of the Campo dei Miracoli is the perimeter wall of what has been called the most beautiful cemetery in the world, the **Camposanto** (same hours as Baptistery). According to Pisan legend, at the end of the twelfth century the city's archbishop brought back from the Crusades a cargo of soil from Golgotha, in order that eminent Pisans might be buried in holy earth. The building enclosing this sanctified site was completed almost a century later.

The Camposanto takes the form of an enormous Gothic cloister, each of whose long sides is as big as a cathedral nave. A few tombs are set into the rectangle of lawn at its centre, but most are housed under the shelter of the **arcades**. Some of the memorials, such as the Egyptian examples, are installed here as museum pieces, but most are for people who were actually buried in the Camposanto. Together they constitute a virtual encyclopedia of the ways in which death has been accommodated, from the terse classical style – recording the occupant's name, status and nothing else – to the opposite extreme, where the focus of interest is not on the deceased but on those left behind, as in the romantic tomb surmounted by a woman identified as "The Inconsolable".

However, when Ruskin described the Camposanto as one of the three most precious buildings in Italy (along with the Sistine Chapel and the Scuola di San Rocco in Venice), it was not its tombs but rather its **frescoes** that he was praising. Paintings once covered over two thousand square metres of cloister wall, now mostly bare brickwork. Incendiary bombs dropped by Allied planes on July 27, 1944 set the roofing on fire and drenched the frescoes in a river of molten lead; the masterpieces of **Benozzo Gozzoli** were all but destroyed – just a few patches of his Old Testament scenes remain, and recent restoration work (the first stage of a planned restoration of all the Camposanto frescoes) has sparked a fierce dispute over a cleaning technique which, experts say, has bleached and permanently ruined the painting. Close by is another picture that came through the bombing: a fascinating fourteenth-century **Theological Cosmograph**, showing the concentric spheres of the universe and the tripartite division of the Earth into Europe, Asia and Africa.

The most important surviving frescoes are the remarkable fourteenth-century cycle by **Buonamico Buffalmacco**, otherwise known as the *Maestro del Trionfo della Morte*, the "Master of the Triumph of Death". These have been detached from the wall and put on show in a room opposite the entrance, beyond a photographic display of the Camposanto before the bombing. Painted within a few months of the Black Death of 1348 – a pestilence which hit Tuscany so badly that it was known throughout Europe as the Florentine Plague – the *Triumph* shows a trio of aristocratic huntsmen stopped in their tracks by a trio of coffins, the contents of which are so putrescent that one of the riders has to pinch his nose. Over to the right, squadrons of angels and demons bear away the souls of the dead, whose final resting place is determined in the terrifying *Last Judgement* at the far end of the room; there's no more ruthless catalogue of horrors than this in Western art.

The Museo dell'Opera del Duomo

A vast array of statuary from the Duomo and Baptistery, plus ecclesiastical finery, paintings and other miscellaneous pieces are displayed in the **Museo dell'Opera del Duomo** (same hours as Baptistery), at the southeast corner of the Campo.

The collection kicks off with pieces dating from the period of the Duomo's construction, showing how Islamic influences, filtered through the intermediary of Byzantium, came to be expressed in the city's art – notably in the marble inlays from the Duomo facade. A large bronze griffon is a more direct borrowing from Islam, having been thieved from the Middle East by a Pisan war party in the eleventh century. The other main cultural input shown here is from Burgundy, source of the strange painted wooden Crucifix, a gigantic figure with a tiny head and mantis-thin arms.

Sculptures by the various Pisanos are the high points of the museum, but the first pieces you encounter – Nicola and Giovanni's figures from the Baptistery

– are too eroded and pitted to give much of an idea of their power. Room 5, which is given over to works by **Giovanni Pisano**, contains the most affecting statue in Pisa, the *Madonna del Colloquio*, so called because of the intensity of the gazes exchanged by the Madonna and Child. Giovanni's great contemporary, **Tino da Camaino**, monopolizes the next room, where fragments from the tomb of Emperor Henry VII are assembled; the magnificent figures of the emperor and his counsellors may have come from the tomb as well.

Nino Pisano – no relation to Nicola and Giovanni – is the subject of room 7, where his creamy marble monuments to archbishops Giovanni Scherlatti and Francesco Moricotti show the increasing suavity of Pisan sculpture in the late fourteenth century. Giovanni Pisano returns in the **treasury**, his ivory *Madonna and Child* showing a remarkable ingenuity in the way it exploits the natural curve of the tusk from which it's carved. The other priceless object here is the *Pisan Cross*, which was carried by the Pisan contingent on the First Crusade.

Upstairs, big and witless altarpiece paintings take up a lot of room, as do cases of ecclesiastical clothing and lavish examples of intarsia, the art of inlaid wood, much practised here in the fifteenth and sixteenth centuries. The strangest objects on view are the two ancient parchment rolls known as **Exultets**, from the opening word of the chant on the eve of Holy Saturday. It was during this service that the cantor would unfurl these scrolls from the pulpit, so that the congregation could follow his words through the pictures painted on them.

A fine collection of engravings by **Carlo Lasinio** comes near the end of the museum; it was mainly thanks to his efforts that the Camposanto was rescued from ruin at the beginning of the nineteenth century, and his fastidious record of the cloister frescoes is one of the most poignant items on show. The museum has a large collection of **Roman and Etruscan** pieces, many of which were slotted into odd corners of Pisa's churches to brighten them up; the most famous image is a thin-lipped bust of Julius Caesar, featured on a dozen editions of his writings.

The Museo delle Sinopie and the city walls

On the south side of the Campo, the only gap in the souvenir stalls is the entrance to the **Museo delle Sinopie** (same hours as Baptistery). After the catastrophic damage wreaked on the Camposanto by the bombers, the building's restorers removed its *sinopie* (monochrome sketches for the frescoes). These great plates of plaster are now hung from the walls of this high-tech museum, where gantries and galleries give you the chance to inspect the painters' preliminary ideas at close range, but it's a rather scholastic enterprise.

You may get more reward from **walking on the city walls**: access is at the northwest corner of the lawns (June–Aug 11am–2pm & 3–6pm; €2), where you can climb up inside the medieval **Torre di Santa Maria** to look down into the Camposanto.

The rest of the city

Away from the Campo dei Miracoli, Pisa takes on a very different character. Few tourists penetrate far into its squares and arcaded streets, with their Romanesque churches and – especially along the banks of the Arno – ranks of fine palazzi. With the large student population it can be quite a lively place, particularly during the summer festivals and the monthly market, when the main streets on each side of the river become one continuous bazaar.

Piazza dei Cavalieri and the eastern districts

The **Piazza dei Cavalieri** is an obvious first stop from the Campo, a large square that opens unexpectedly from the narrow backstreets. Perhaps the site of the Roman forum, it was the central civic square of medieval Pisa, before being remodelled by Vasari as the headquarters of the Knights of St Stephen. This order was established by Cosimo I, ostensibly for crusading, though in reality they amounted to nothing more than a gang of licensed pirates, given state sanction to plunder Turkish shipping. Their palace, the curving **Palazzo dei Cavalieri** (now a school), covered in *sgraffiti* and topped with busts of the Medici, faces a statue of Cosimo and adjoins the order's church of **Santo Stefano** (summer daily 10am–7pm; winter Mon–Sat 11am–4.30pm, Sun 11.30am–5.30pm; €1.50), designed by Vasari and housing banners captured from the Turks.

On the other side of the square is the Renaissance-adapted **Palazzo dell'Orologio**, with its archway and clock tower. This was a medieval palace, in whose tower the military leader Ugolino della Gherardesca was starved to death in 1208, along with his sons and grandsons, as punishment for his alleged duplicity with the Genoese enemy – an episode described in Dante's *Inferno* and Shelley's *Tower of Famine*.

Northeast from here, across the wide Piazza dei Martiri della Libertà, stands the Dominican church of **Santa Caterina**, whose Romanesque lower facade dates from the year of its foundation, 1251. Inside, there's an *Annunciation* and a tomb by Nicola Pisano, and a fourteenth-century painting of the *Triumph of Thomas Aquinas*, the ideological figurehead of the Dominicans. Nearby, in front of the **Porta Lucca** – the main northern gate of medieval Pisa – you can see the unimpressive remnants of the city's Roman baths, while tucked into the northeast corner of the city walls is the church of **San Zeno**, parts of which go back to the fifth century.

From Via San Zeno, Via Buonarroti runs south to the plain Gothic **San Francesco**, whose well-preserved frescoes include work by Taddeo Gaddi and Niccolò di Pietro Gerini. Count Ugolino and his offspring are buried in the second chapel on the right. If you continue down Via di Simone from the back of the church, you'll come out at the Museo Nazionale di San Matteo.

Borgo Stretto and the Museo Nazionale di San Matteo

Heading from Piazza dei Cavalieri towards the Arno, Via Dini swings into the arcaded **Borgo Stretto**. Recently pedestrianized to create a traffic-free route that extends across the river and down Corso Italia, this is Pisa's smartest street, and its windows full of Laura Biagiotti jewellery, Dolce e Gabbana shades and other desirables seem slightly out of tune with the city's unshowy style. More typically Pisan is the **market** just off Via Dini (Mon–Fri mornings & Sat all day), its fruit, vegetable, fish, meat and clothing stalls spilling onto the lanes around Piazza Vettovaglie.

Past the Romanesque-Gothic facade of **San Michele** – built on the site of the Roman temple to Mars – the Borgo meets the river at the traffic-knotted Piazza Garibaldi and **Ponte di Mezzo**, the city's central bridge. A left turn along Lungarno Mediceo takes you past the **Palazzo Toscanelli** (now the city archives), which was rented by Byron in 1821–22 after his expulsion from Ravenna for seditious activities. The poet's lunatic reputation, already well-established thanks to his menagerie of horses, cats and dogs, was given a further boost when he got into a scrap with a bunch of Pisan soldiers, a contretemps that brought his brothers in exile – Shelley, Leigh Hunt and Walter Savage Landor – out onto the streets. This display of hot-blooded solidarity prompted the writer Guerrazzi to muse that he at last understood "why the English are a great people, and the Italians a clump of rags in the shop of a second-hand dealer".

A couple of doors farther along the *lungarno* is the **Museo Nazionale di San Matteo** (Tues–Sat 9am–7pm, Sun 9am–2pm; €4), where most of the major works of art from Pisa's churches are now gathered. Fourteenth-century religious paintings make up the meat of the collection, with a Simone Martini polyptych and work by Antonio Veneziano outstanding in the early sections. Later on, there's a stash of Middle Eastern ceramics pilfered by Pisan adventurers, a panel of *St Paul* by Masaccio, Gozzoli's strangely festive *Crucifixion* and Donatello's reliquary bust of the introspective *St Rossore*. Also housed in the museum are the antique armour and wooden shields used in the annual *Gioco del Ponte* pageant (see p.314).

West of Ponte di Mezzo

The faculty buildings of Pisa's university – still one of the most important in Italy – are scattered all over the city, but the main concentration is to the west of the Ponte di Mezzo, around lively **Piazza Dante**. The general tone of the streets – especially the *osterie* and bars – is the attraction of this quarter, though it does have a couple of sights worth singling out.

Immediately north of Piazza Dante, the bare stone nave of the eleventh-century **San Frediano** preserves some capitals from that period. West of here, off the main **Via Santa Maria**, lies the university's **Orto Botanico** (Mon–Sat 8.30am–1pm; free); founded in 1591, this is the oldest botanical garden in the world. At the southern end of Via Santa Maria rises Pisa's second leaning tower, the thirteenth-century campanile of **San Nicola**. Cylindrical at its base, mutating into an octagon then a hexagon, it contains a majestic spiral staircase that was Bramante's inspiration for his grand Belvedere staircase in the Vatican. Inside the church, the Crucifix in the first chapel on the left is attributed to Giovanni Pisano, while Nino Pisano is credited with the wooden *Madonna and Child* in the fourth chapel on this side. In the chapels on the other side of the nave, there's a *Madonna* by Francesco Traini and a painting showing Pisa around 1400, being protected from the plague by St Nicholas of Tolentino.

Alongside San Nicola, fronting the Arno at Lungarno Pacinotti 46, is the **Museo Nazionale di Palazzo Reale** (Mon–Sat 9am–2pm; €3), displaying artefacts that once belonged to the Medici, Lorraine and Savoy rulers of the city, who successively occupied the house. Lavish sixteenth-century Flemish tapestries share space with antique weaponry, ivory miniatures, porcelain and a largely undistinguished picture collection, featuring a copy of Bronzino's famous portrait of Cosimo I's wife, Eleanora di Toledo. Just as memorable is the lovely river view from the balcony.

Further along the river, on the Lungarno Simonelli, lies the **Arsenale Mediceo**, built by Cosimo I. Just west of the arsenal rises the **Torre Guelfa della Cittadella Vecchia**, or **Fortezza Vecchia** (Jan, Feb, Nov & Dec Sat & Sun 2–5pm, plus 10am–1pm on 2nd Sun of month; rest of year Fri–Sun 3–7pm; €2). This ancient fortress, originally built in the thirteenth century, once stood guard over Pisa's harbour but now punctuates an otherwise little-explored district; the **view** from the tower is spectacular.

South of the river

The more down-at-heel districts south of the Arno are popularly known as the *mezzogiorno*, the name more widely used in Italy to refer to the under-developed south of the country. On the second Sunday and the preceding Saturday of each month both banks are linked by a big **street market**, with

Gioco del Ponte

Pisa's big traditional event is the **Gioco del Ponte**, held on the last Sunday of June, when twelve teams from the north and south banks of the city stage a series of "push-of-war" battles, shoving a seven-tonne carriage over the Ponte di Mezzo. The event has taken place since Medici times and continues in Renaissance costume. Other celebrations – concerts, regattas, art events – are held around the same time, and the city has a festive feel for most of June, with banners and pavement drawings brightening the streets. Most spectacular of the ancillary shows is the **Luminara di San Ranieri**, when buildings along both river banks are lit by 70,000 fairy lights in honour of Pisa's patron saint.

hippie earrings, candles and other craft stuff filling the lower reaches of Borgo Stretto, and furniture and general bric-a-brac around the south-bank **Logge di Banchi**. Formerly the city's silk and wool market, this vast and usually deserted loggia stands at the top of the main shopping street of the *mezzogiorno*, the pedestrianized Corso Italia, which starts off classy and gets progressively shabbier as it nears the train station.

East along the Lungarno Galilei, the only real sight is the octagonal **San Sepolcro**, built for the Knights Templar by Diotisalvi, first architect of the Baptistery. A short way past here is the ruined **Palazzo Scotti**, Shelley's home during the period when Byron was in residence on the other side of the river.

Along the *lungarni* to the west of the Ponte di Mezzo, the rather monotonous line of palazzi – mirroring those on the facing bank – is suddenly enlivened by the spry turreted oratory of **Santa Maria della Spina** (Jan, Feb, Nov & Dec Tues–Sun 10am–2pm, except 2nd Sun of month 10am–1pm & 2.30–5pm; March–Oct Tues–Fri 10am–1.30pm & 2.30–6pm, Sat & Sun 10am–7pm; €1.50). Rebuilt in 1323 by a merchant who had acquired one of the thorns (*spine*) of Christ's crown, it's the finest flourish of Pisan-Gothic. Originally built closer to the river, it was moved here for fear of floods in 1871. The tiny single-naved interior has mullioned windows on the river side, but has lost most of its furnishings.

Farther west again, **San Paolo a Ripa d'Arno** probably occupies the site of Pisa's very first cathedral. The arcaded facade was built in imitation of the present cathedral in the twelfth century; the interior, badly damaged in World War II, has a handsome Roman sarcophagus and a finely carved capital (second on left). Behind the church is the octagonal **Cappella di Sant'Agata**, also built in the twelfth century.

San Michele dei Scalzi

Some 2km east of the centre, secreted in a residential area, stands Pisa's third leaning tower, the campanile of **San Michele dei Scalzi** – you get to it by walking along the riverbank upstream from Ponte di Mezzo. Everything in this building is severely askew: the columns in the nave lurch this way and that, the windows in the apse are all over the place, and the walls set up a drunken counterpoint to the tilt of the tower.

Eating and drinking

Pisa's proximity to the coast means that seafood is the staple of its **restaurant** menus, notably *baccalà alla Pisana* (dried cod). Those in the environs of the Leaning Tower are generally not good value, though any of the numerous *pizzerie* down Via Santa Maria will do for a quick refuel. Head a few blocks south, to the areas around Piazza dei Cavalieri and Piazza Dante, and you'll find predominantly local places. The university is as strong an influence as the tourist trade, supporting places that cater for a regular clientele of impecunious students at one end of the range, and for their teachers at the other. There's the usual scattering of city centre **bars**, but at night Pisa can be an eerily quiet place, as the majority of its students are Pisan natives who still live at home. In term time, though, there's usually a fair number of one-off events going on – Piazza Dante is the place to look for posters.

Al Ristoro dei Vecchi Macelli Via Volturno 49 ☎050.20.424. Acclaimed as Pisa's best restaurant, with a wide range of sophisticated, innovative takes on Tuscany's gourmet traditions – choose from meat or fish set menus for upwards of €45. Closed Sun lunch & Wed.

Bruno Via L. Bianchi 12 ☎050.560.818. Simple Pisan dishes such as the local *baccalà* have kept this place well-regarded for years. Closed Mon eve & Tues.

Cassio Piazza Cavallotti 14. Just off Via Santa Maria, this excellent *tavola calda* and pizzeria is the place to come for a midday pit-stop. Closed Sat & Sun.

Da Cucciolo Vicolo Rosselmini 9 ☎050.26.086. *Da Cucciolo* is always reliable, offering unfussy, delicious traditional meals (with an emphasis on organically produced food) from around €30. Closed Sun eve & Mon.

Il Campano Via Domenico Cavalca 44 ☎050.580.585. Homemade pasta and local seafood are the big things at this first-rate trattoria – sit on the narrow terrace and you'll be assailed by the aromas of the nearby fishmongers. Extremely good selection of wines, too. Closed Wed.

Il Vecchio Dado Lungarno Pacinotti 21 ☎050.580.900. Next to the *Royal Victoria Hotel* on the waterfront; classy pizzas, excellent fish and a lively atmosphere. Closed all Wed & Thurs lunch.

La Cereria Via Pietro Gori 33 ☎050.20.336. Popular, unpretentious restaurant tucked away north of Via Benedetto Croce. Excellent seafood and pasta dishes, superb pizzas (the best in the city, some reckon) and a pleasant garden. Closed Tues.

La Mescita Via Domenico Cavalca 2 ☎050.544.294. This wine bar/restaurant has established a good reputation with its ever-changing Tuscan menu and excellent cellar. Closed Mon & 3 weeks in Aug.

Ombono Piazza Sant'Ombono 6 ☎050.540.847. This city-centre trattoria serves terrific authentic Pisan home cooking, featuring dishes such as *brachette alla renaiaola* – pasta in a purée of greens and smoked fish. Closed Sun & 2 weeks in Aug.

Osteria dei Cavalieri Via San Frediano 16 ☎050.580.858. Outstanding quality, with English-speaking staff and a calm, fresh atmosphere. The fish is exquisite, Tuscan meat and game dishes are expertly prepared, and their vegetarian options are excellent. Eat à la carte or choose from set menus starting around €20. Closed Sat lunch & Sun.

Osteria dei Mille Via dei Mille 32 ☎050.556.263. Smart and very popular *osteria* with excellent fresh pasta *primi* and meat or fish *secondi* – the place to come for a *tagliata* (finely sliced steak served with rocket and parmesan). Closed Fri.

Spaghetteria alle Bandierine Via Mercanti 4 ☎050.500.000. Popular place for a bowl of pasta with large choice of original sauces. Closed Sun & Mon.

Taverna Kostas Via del Borghetto 39. Entrenched local favourite, offering a mix of Greek and Mediterranean cooking as well as Pisan seafood. Closed Sun lunch, Mon & Aug.

Around Pisa

The most obvious destinations moving on from Pisa are Lucca, half-an-hour by train or bus, and Florence, an hour by train. East along the Arno, the most interesting diversions are beyond San Miniato (see p.252); on the Pisan side, the only compelling detour is to the **Certosa di Pisa**, a marvellous Baroque charterhouse, which you could take in on a brief loop from the main road.

Heading south for Siena, take a train for Florence and change at Empoli. With your own transport, though, you could roam through the Pisan hills to

Volterra (see p.436), via **Casciana Terme**, or follow the coast, turning inland at Cécina.

West of Pisa, **Marina di Pisa** and **Tirrenia** are the city's local resorts. Neither is very inspiring, but the area just inland has the **Parco Regionale di San Rossore** and the ancient church of San Piero a Grado.

The Certosa di Pisa

Of the thirty Carthusian monasteries left intact in Italy, none makes a more diverting excursion than the fourteenth-century **Certosa di Pisa**, set at the foot of the forested Monte Pisano near the village of **CALCI**, 10km east of Pisa. A regular CPT **bus** service runs to the village from Pisa's Piazza San Antonio; if you're driving, just get to the amazing Medici aqueduct – immediately visible on the eastern outskirts of the city – and follow it all the way. The monastery's **guided tour** (hourly: Tues–Sat 9am–6pm, Sun 9am–noon; €4) gives a remarkable sense of how the building related to the lives of this order.

The size of the Certosa is startling. From the frescoed central **church**, where a freestanding marble angel does service as a lectern, the tour passes through eleven other **chapels** in which Sunday Mass was apparently conducted simultaneously. Looking as fresh as the day they were decorated (they have not been restored), these are strangely sybaritic interiors – all powder blue, baby pink, pale violet and pallid green, with stucco details and trompe l'oeil pillars and balustrades to perk things up. Floors are covered with tiles that are only paint-deep, and there's a rectangular chapel tricked out to look like an oval room with a dome.

This ballroom decor contrasts with the more conventional monasticism of the **cloister** and its cells. Each of the monks had a suite of three sparse rooms – a bedroom, a study and a workroom. Attached to every suite is a self-contained garden, walled so that the monks could maintain their soul-redeeming isolation. Their meals were served through hatches, positioned to minimize the possibility of coming face to face – except on Sundays, when conversation was permitted and all the monks ate together. From the cloister the tour progresses

△ The Certosa di Pisa

to the **refectory**, where frescoes of seminal moments in the history of the monastery are interspersed with images of the months and their associated crops as a reminder of the order's agricultural self-sufficiency. Nearby are the luxuriously appointed **guest rooms**, where high-born VIPs – various Medici among them – would stay for a bout of not-too-rigorous scourging of the spirit. Their private cloister features yet more trompe l'oeil, its windows "opening" onto the dining room and monks' cloister.

The visit is made especially absorbing by little details pointed out by the guide – like the panel with sliding wooden paddles to designate the day's duties (eg head-shaving), or, at the end of the tour, the measuring machines in the **pharmacy**. Above the gate as you leave, an inscription reads *Egredere sed non omnis* ("Leave, but not entirely"), once addressed to any monk who had to go out on some mission in the wider world.

Parts of the Certosa complex are owned by the University of Pisa, who have installed their **natural history** collections here (mid-June to mid-Sept Tues–Fri 10am–7pm, Sat & Sun 4pm–midnight; rest of year Tues–Sat 9am–6pm, Sun 9am–7pm; €5).

Monte Serra

If you're driving, you could make a loop down to the Arno from the Certosa by following the scenic mountain pass over **Monte Serra** – where the *Rosa dei Venti* bar-restaurant provides an opportunity for a quick bite. Beyond the summit, the road meanders down to the village of **BUTI**, its Gothic-windowed castle looking down over the Arno valley. The descent has flattened out by the time you get to **VICOPISANO** (Ⓦ www.viconet.it). Built on a plump little hummock, the core of the village retains four towers of its fortifications, two of which were built or rebuilt by Brunelleschi after the Florentines had conquered Pisa (guided tours April–July & Sept–Nov Sat 3.30–5.30pm, Sun 10am–12.30pm & 3–5.30pm). In the lower part of the village is a handsome Romanesque church, fronted by a grassy piazza and backed by the Monte Pisano foothills.

Along the Arno and into the Pisan hills

A couple of kilometres south of Vicopisano, the Arno valley commences with a glum stretch of unrelievedly industrialized development. **CÁSCINA**, about 15km east of Pisa – a town that, but for the road signs, you wouldn't realize you'd entered – might have been well known had Michelangelo's ill-fated fresco for Florence's Palazzo Vecchio survived: this was the site of the battle depicted in it. A clutch of **churches** within Cáscina's medieval walls might justify a stop – the frescoed San Giovanni Evangelista, built by the Knights of St John, and the Romanesque San Casciano and San Benedetto a Settimo, the latter with a fourteenth-century alabaster altarpiece carved in Ireland. There's even less to be said for **PONTEDERA**, 4km east – it's home of the Piaggio factory that produces the ubiquitous Vespa scooter, and that's about all you need to know. San Miniato (see p.252) is a short drive further east.

South to Casciana Terme

From Cáscina or Pontedera, the N439 road south to Volterra (see p.436) goes through **Ponsacco** and then past a less-than-scintillating Medici villa (closed to the public) at **Camugliano**, built by Alessandro de' Medici and continued by his successor, Cosimo I. There's a fine thirteenth-century church east of the road at **PALÁIA**, though only devout admirers of the Romanesque will want to drive the 10km from Capánnoli to see it. South of Capánnoli you're into a humdrum procession of hills, the Alta Valdera (Ⓦwww.valdera.org), until Volterra's cliffs rear up ahead.

West of the N439, **CASCIANA TERME** is a pleasant, workaday spa town, 6km north of the attractive little medieval hamlet of **Rivalto**. The main road to the south of Casciana (through Castellina Maríttima) takes in the best-looking of the Pisan hills, though with little to warrant prolonged exploration. It emerges on the N68 a short distance east of Cécina.

West of Pisa

Some 6km west of Pisa, on the road to the coast, is the monastic complex of **San Piero a Grado**, allegedly founded by St Peter himself, on his way to Rome and martyrdom. The site is now in ruins except for the glorious eleventh-century basilica, a double-apsed church built from lustrous local yellow sandstone. St Peter's story is detailed in a sequence of pale fourteenth-century frescoes inside the basilica (daily 9am–noon & 3–6pm), where the whiff of the sea conjures a uniquely evocative atmosphere. At one end of the basilica a section of a fourth-century oratory has been excavated, the most ancient Christian site in this part of Tuscany.

MARINA DI PISA at the end of the road is an unobjectionable little town cursed with water made grubby by industrial waste. The view out to sea is impaired by a long breakwater parallel to the shore, a sight frequently worsened by passing tankers. These factors, combined with the usual private beach strips, don't exactly entice. **TIRRENIA**, 5km south, is a better bet – with finer sand, separated from the road by pines and parkland. It has a good spread of hotels and a couple of campsites. **Buses** do the half-hour run from Pisa to both resorts (summer every 15min, winter every 30min); they are best avoided on Sundays, when hundreds of locals nip down to the sea.

The Parco Regionale di San Rossore

The **Parco Regionale di San Rossore** (Ⓦwww.parks.it/parco.migliarino .san.rossore) spreads over much of the coastal hinterland between Viareggio and Livorno. Its pine woods are among the densest in Tuscany, supporting populations of deer, goats and wild boar, and until World War II were also home to a herd of dromedaries, descendants of the animals placed here by Grand Duke Ferdinando II in the 1620s. Two visitor centres offer **guided tours** on foot, bike or horseback (Ⓣ050.530.101, Ⓔvisitesr@tin.it, or Ⓔturismo@sanrossore .it for horse riding reservations), while the San Rossore archeological site – where in 1998 a fleet of Roman ships, almost perfectly preserved in mud for two millennia, were discovered in the ancient port – can be visited by prior appointment. Eight vessels have so far been recovered, including what experts believe could be the oldest Roman warship ever found.

At the park's centre lies the village of **GOMBO**, scene of the 1822 cremation of Percy Bysshe Shelley, drowned while sailing from Livorno, and here reduced to ashes in front of his friends Edward Trelawny and Lord Byron. Trelawny recorded that "the brains literally seethed, bubbled and boiled as in a cauldron… What surprised us all was that the heart remained entire. In snatching this relic from the fiery furnace, my hand was severely burnt; and had anyone seen me do the act I should have been put into quarantine."

Livorno

As Tuscany's third-largest city (after Florence and Prato) and Italy's second-biggest port (after Genoa), **LIVORNO** should really have more going for it than it does. Unfortunately, its docks invited blanket bombing in World War II, and the rebuilt commercial centre is not pretty. Henry James's observation still largely holds true: "It has neither a church worth one's attention, nor a municipal palace, nor a museum, and it may claim the distinction, unique in Italy, of being the city of no pictures." Livorno's principal appeal, apart from its ferry connections, is the excellent **seafood**.

Livorno's origins go back to Roman times, though the port was only developed under Cosimo I as an alternative to Pisa, whose harbour was silting up. Later Medici dukes declared it a **free port** and instituted a liberal constitution, an extraordinarily enlightened move which prompted an influx of Jews, Greeks, Spanish Muslims, English Catholics and a cosmopolitan throng of other refugees. As one of the few Italian harbours safe from the Spanish, it flourished on the back of trade with England and Holland, and attracted a community of British expatriates (such as Shelley), whose anglicization of the city's name to **Leghorn** is still used in some tourist brochures. Greater freedom of European trade brought some decline, though the city retained a reputation for enterprise that was especially manifest after World War II, when it was amongst the first to realize the importance of container traffic – the basis of its current prosperity.

The City

Livorno **train station** is 2km east of the centre; city buses #1 and #2 run from here to **Piazza Grande**, the heart of what's left of the old town. Most intertown **buses** also stop on Piazza Grande, although buses from Florence, Pisa and Lucca use Piazza Manin, a short distance to the south.

The **Porto Mediceo** – the canal-enclosed area in which Piazza Grande stands – is the town's most picturesque corner, and still conforms to the pentagonal plan devised for the Medici by Buontalenti in 1557. The focal point of the piazza is the **Duomo**, a postwar reconstruction of interest mainly for its doorway by Inigo Jones, whose subsequent plan for London's Covent Garden was a direct

---

Ferries from Livorno

There are dozens of ferry sailings from Livorno, to **Corsica** (Bastia or Porto Vecchio), **Sardinia** (Olbia, Golfo Aranci or Cagliari), **Sicily** (Palermo), and the Tuscan islands of **Capraia** and **Gorgona**. Nearly all ferries to Corsica and Sardinia leave from alongside the Stazione Marittima, west of the centre, although some (and boats to Sicily) depart from Varco Galvani, a long way north of town. Ferries to Elba and Capraia leave from the central Porto Mediceo.

Check with the tourist office and with the ferry companies themselves for times and prices, and reserve well ahead in summer.

Corsica Ferries ☎019.215.511, ⓦwww.corsicaferries.com. To Bastia (Corsica).

Corsica Marittima ☎0586.210.507, ⓦwww.sncm.fr. To Bastia and Porto Vecchio (Corsica).

Moby Lines ☎199.303.040, ⓦwww.mobylines.it. To Olbia (Sardinia) and Bastia (Corsica).

Sardinia Ferries ☎019.215.511, ⓦwww.sardiniaferries.com. To Golfo Aranci (Sardinia).

Toremar ☎0586.896.113, ⓦwww.toremar.it. To Capraia and Gorgona.

LIVORNO

Train Station

▲ Pisa, Genoa & Florence

▶ Museo Civico & Montenero

San Giuseppe

San Andrea

Fortezza Nuova

Santa Caterina

Mercatino Americano

Santa Maria del Soccorso

Mercato Centrale

Duomo

Bus Terminal

Monumento ai Quattro Mori

Fortezza Vecchia

Zoo & Gardens

Ferry Terminal

Ferry Terminal

Porto Mediceo

Bacino Cappellini

Bacino Firenze

MOLO MEDICEO

CANTIERE ANSALDO

N

500 m

0

copy of the square. From here Via Grande leads down to the sea, where San-gallo's **Fortezza Vecchia** guards the bustling harbour and its tributary canals, about 100m north of central Livorno's only artwork of note, the **Quattro Mori** statue (1623) by the Carraran sculptor Pietro Tacca. Though Ferdinando I is the centrepiece, the key figures are the four Moors, alternatively considered to be slaves or memorials to the success of Tuscan raids against North African shipping.

To the east of the Duomo, on Via Buontalenti, the ochre **Mercato Centrale** stands at the heart of a boisterous street market. Follow the canal northeast from here and you'll come to Piazza XX Settembre, home of the **Mercato Americano** (Mon 2–7pm, Tues–Sat 9am–8pm; Ⓦwww.ilmercatinoamericano .it), so-called because of the amount of GI surplus on sale here after the war; it still deals in military gear (there's a big US naval base near Livorno) and the usual flea-market paraphernalia.

North of here lies the Venezia district, where crumbling old tenement build-ings overlook the bulky **Fortezza Nuova** (daily 8am–7pm; free), a moated, semi-derelict recreation area ringed around by quiet canals. At the end of July and beginning of August the area comes alive with the *Effetto Venezia* (Ⓦwww .effettovenezia.com), a free street festival with concerts, street performers and fireworks.

Modigliani and Livorno

There's a nice irony to the fact that the most famous son of the sensible mercantile city of Livorno was an archetypal bohemian – hard-drinking, womanizing **Amedeo Modigliani**. By the time Modigliani reached his mid-twenties he was renowned as the most dissolute figure in Montparnasse, but his family background in Livorno could not have been more respectable. His mother, Eugenia Garsin, was from a prosper-ous and highly intellectual family, brought up speaking French, Italian, English and Hebrew. His father's ancestors, also Sephardic Jews, were equally grand: Amedeo's great-grandfather had been an adviser to Napoleon.

Modigliani was born in Via Roma in 1884, the year that his father's wood and coal company was declared bankrupt. The family was obliged to move from their villa to a more humble property in Via delle Ville, where Amedeo was still living when he began his studies at the Livorno art school. By 1900, aged 16, he had become bored with the academic nature of his training, and soon embarked on a travelling apprentice-ship that was to take him to Naples, Florence and Venice. In 1906 he arrived in **Paris**, where he was to spend most of the rest of his life. He returned to Livorno briefly in 1909 for a vacation by the sea, and came back again four years later, antagonizing most people he met with his arrogance and wild behaviour. A friend tried to persuade him to take a studio near the Carrara marble quarries, but he missed the big city too much, and left after a few months. He lived for just one more decade. "I am going to drink myself dead," he declared, and in effect he did, dying of meningitis at the age of 35 – leaving the latest of his innumerable mistresses nine months pregnant. She committed suicide on the afternoon of his death.

Before leaving Livorno for the last time, he had asked some students at his former art school if they knew of somewhere he could store a group of sculptures he had carved. "Throw them in the canal," they are alleged to have replied. In 1984 the city authorities decided to follow up the lead by dredging the canal round the old town – and duly discovered three stone heads. They turned out to be fakes, the three schoolboys responsible for the hoax appearing on TV to demonstrate how they used power tools to create the sculptures that nearly sold for millions.

If you've time to kill in Livorno, you could visit the **Museo Civico Giovanni Fattori** (Tues–Sun 10am–1pm & 4–7pm; €6.50), which is devoted to Fattori and the late-nineteenth-century Macchiaioli movement, Italy's version of Impressionism; it's housed in the Villa Mimbelli, 1km south of the centre at Via San Jacopo in Acquaviva 65 (bus #1 goes there). Alternatively, hop on bus #2 from the station or Piazza Grande for the ride up to the hilltop **Santuario di Montenero**, 6km south, which has been a pilgrimage site since an apparition of the Virgin in the fourteenth century, long before the marshes below were populated. A clutch of stalls and cafés surrounds the eighteenth-century church, and you'll find quiet footpaths and plenty of vantage points for views over Livorno and the hillside villas which were once home to expatriates such as Byron, Shelley and Napoleon III.

Practicalities

The main **tourist office** is just off Via Cairoli, at Piazza Cavour 6 (Mon–Fri 9am–1pm & 3–5pm, Sat 9am–1pm; ℡0586.204.611, Ⓦwww.livorno.turismo.toscana.it); in summer there's also a small booth at the Calata Carrara ferry dock. Hour-long boat trips on the town's canals are available for much of the year; contact the tourist office for information.

Livorno's best **hotel** is the eighteenth-century villa *La Vedetta*, on the Montenero hill, at Via della Lecceta 5 (℡0586.579.957, Ⓦwww.hotellavedetta.it; ❹–❺), with modern rooms and panoramic views. Being a port town, Livorno has a rash of basic hotels, some of which – around the harbour and station – are truly grim; to find a reasonable room it's best to head for the centre of the old town. One of the best one-star choices is *Milano*, Via degli Asili 48 (℡0586.219.155, Ⓕ0586.219.118; ❶), which offers quiet, clean rooms and a garden. Pricier options include the two-star *Giardino*, Piazza Mazzini 85 (℡0586.806.330, Ⓔhotel-garden@hotmail.com; ❷); *Ariston*, Piazza della Repubblica 13 (℡0586.880.149, Ⓦwww.hotelaristonlivorno.com; ❷); and *Europa*, Via dell'Angiolo 23 (℡0586.888.581, Ⓦwww.hoteleuropalivorno.it; ❸). Livorno's **youth hostel**, the *Villa Morazzana*, is up in the hills, at Via di Collinet 68 and also has some hotel rooms from €30 (℡0586.500.076, Ⓦwww.villamorazzana.it; €16); take bus #1 from the train station to Piazza Grande and then bus #3. The nearest **campsite** is the *Miramare* (℡0586.580.402, Ⓦwww.campingmiramare.com; mid-April to Sept), a short way south of town on the Via Aurelia past Antignano; there's another, the *Collina 1*, on the road to Castellaccio, Via di Quercianella 269 (℡0586.579.573, Ⓦwww.collina1.it).

For **eating**, the great temptation is seafood. The local speciality is *cacciucco*, a spicy fish and seafood stew, traditionally made from scraps the boats couldn't sell, served with garlic toast. A choice restaurant, if you can spare €45 a head, is *Le Chiave*, Scali delle Cantine 52/54 (℡0586.829.865; closed Wed). Two other recommended restaurants specializing in typical fish dishes are the *Vecchia Livorno*, Scali delle Cantine 34 (℡0586.884.048; closed Tues), and the *Osteria del Mare*, Borgo dei Cappuccini 5 (℡0586.881.027; closed Thurs & Sept). There are dozens of good trattorie, including the moderately priced *Aragosta*, Piazza Arsenale 6 (closed all day Tues & Sun eve), *Le Volte*, Via Calafati 4 (closed Sun), *Galileo*, Via della Campana 20 (closed Wed & Sun eve) and the big, busy *La Barcarola*, Viale Carducci 39 (℡0586.402.367; closed Sun). On Venezia's canalsides you'll find the attractive couscous house *Mediterraneo*, Scali Ponte di Marmo 14 (℡0586.829.799; closed Tues), which often has **live music** at the weekends. *Café d'Etoile*, Via Indipendenza 13 (closed Sun), is a breezy **café** off Piazza Cavour serving fresh salads and snacks.

The Costa degli Etruschi

There's little to distinguish the resorts that cling to the road south from Livorno along the so-called **Costa degli Etruschi** (Etruscan Coast). Most are remorselessly developed and edged with stony or scrubby beaches, and have an appeal only if you want to share the Italian cheek-by-jowl seaside experience. All points on the coast as far south as Follónica can be reached by bus or train from Livorno; faster Pisa–Rome expresses often stop only at Cécina, which has connections inland to Volterra.

Quercianella to Vada

About 13km south of Livorno, **QUERCIANELLA** is a relatively small resort that has clung onto a hinterland of scrub-covered hills and rocky headlands. The beach is pebbly, but nevertheless popular and well developed. If you want to **stay**, the one-star *Pensione Sottocosta*, Via G. Pascoli 32 (T & F 0586.491.027, W www.sottocosta.com; ❶), overlooking the sea, is a reasonable bet.

    CASTIGLIONCELLO, the biggest of the resorts, sprawls over several small bays, some with sand, most with pebbles, and all crammed with boats and beach huts. The best beach is the fee-charging Quercetano; the bay at Caletta is one to avoid, as is Rosignano (1km south), graced as it is with a vast chemical works with outlets into the sea. Smaller **VADA**, 5km south of Rosignano, has a featureless modern centre but is preferable to Castiglioncello, with a good beach and a long flat stretch of sand and pines to the south that shade a couple of large **campsites**, the better being the *Tripesce*, Via Cavallaggeri 88 (T 0586.788.017, W www.campingtripesce.com; April to mid-Oct).

Cécina

The town of **CÉCINA**, 3km inland, marks the start of the Maremma's coastal plains, and has **buses** and **trains** heading inland to Saline di Volterra (see p.437). The cheapest **hotel** in town is *Il Ponte*, Largo 1 Maggio 3 (T 0586.680.795, W www.hotelilponte.com; ❶). There are fair sections of beach at **MARINA DI CÉCINA**, most freely accessible save for a patch cordoned off by the local military academy. A summer-only **tourist office** in Viale Galliano (T 0586.622.844) has information on the back-to-back **festivals**: antiques in July, arts and music in September and a miscellaneous "October Fair". Among the **hotels** on Viale della Vittoria is two-star *Azzurra* (T & F 0586.620.595; ❶). To the north are some huge **campsites**. For inexpensive food, there's the good *rosticceria Peccati di Gola*, Viale Galliano 5 (April–Sept).

The Bólgheri reserve and Bibbona

South of Cécina the main road pulls back from the coast, leaving a few tracts relatively unspoilt. If you take any of the minor turnings to the sea you'll find pine forest and beaches only slightly touched by development, but the best stretch is the exquisite **Rifugio Faunistico di Bólgheri**, a nature reserve run by the World Wide Fund for Nature (visits, only available with a guide, need to be pre-booked 24hr in advance with the WWF in Piombino; T 0565.224.361; Fri & Sat 9am–2pm; €5, children €3). The entrance is off the main SS1, just south of the glorious avenue of trees that runs to Bólgheri village; take the lane that runs over the rail tracks to the sea.

    Founded in 1962, this was the first private nature reserve in Italy, and is now recognized as a wildlife centre of international importance. The reserve is a microcosm of the various habitats associated with the ancient Maremma:

seashore, dunes (full of rare plants), marsh and lakeland, pine groves, tracts of juniper and mixed scrub forest, *macchia*, grassland and some of the oldest stands of cypress in Italy. Such is the tranquillity of the area that even in daylight you can expect to see **boar**, **roe-buck**, **martens**, black and white **porcupines**, even **otters** – an extremely rare species in Italy. Thousands of **birds** also settle here: it's the southern limit of the lapwing and a spot for rarities like bluethroats, Blyth reed warblers (their first sighting in Italy), grey herons, cranes, black storks and hunters such as the osprey and lesser-spotted eagle.

The nearby resort of **MARINA DI BIBBONA** has an immensely broad stretch of sand running for miles south from the village along a pinewood backdrop: to find privacy, just walk beyond the beach umbrellas. For a reasonable **beach hotel** with a garden, bear left on the approach road to Forte di Bibbona to the two-star *Paradiso Verde*, Via del Forte 1 (T0565.600.022, Wwww .hotelparadisoverde.com; **2**).

San Vincenzo

SAN VINCENZO, about 20km south, is the fast-growing resort of the moment, though it has a good beach with plenty of quieter spots out on the fringes. There's a **tourist office** on Via B. Alliata 2 (Mon–Sat 9am–1pm, also 3–7pm Mon, Wed & Fri; T0565.701.533). Summer **accommodation** is at a premium; without a booking, you may have to settle for the only **campsite**, *Park Albatros*, 2km from the sea at Pineta di Torre Nuova (Wwww.ecvacanze.it).

Inland – Castagneto Carducci to Campiglia

If you're driving south from Pisa, you could take time out from the plain-induced monotony of the Via Aurelia by turning off at **Donaratico**, 8km before San Vincenzo, for a 35-kilometre loop into the hills of the Monte Calvi nature reserve via a handful of scarcely visited medieval villages. This area is home to the Montescudaio, Bolgheri and Val di Cornia DOC wines – worth seeking out by following the **Strada del Vino degli Etruschi** wine road (Wwww.lastradadelvino.com) that's signposted everywhere.

CASTAGNETO CARDUCCI, 6km east of Donaratico, is renowned for two things: it was the birthplace of the poet Carducci, winner of the Nobel Prize in 1906; and it produces what is widely considered the best **olive oil** in Italy. The village is riddled with little alleyways and has a parish church filled with faded frescoes and painted terracotta saints.

Beyond, the road is a rollercoaster of sea views and woods, with a single **hotel-restaurant**, the two-star *La Selva*, Via delle Fornaci 32 (T0565.794.239, Ehotelselva@tiscalinet.it; **2**), just before the road touches the little village of **SASSETTA**, a car-free maze of minute streets, home to a good restaurant, *Osteria C'era Una Volta* (T0565.794.102), Piazza del Plebiscito, with tables outside. For the first three Sundays of October, the alleys are filled with tables laden with seasonal dishes and chestnuts for the annual *Festa della Tordata*, a gastronomic festival celebrating the thrush. The road then twists down to **SUVERETO**, whose thin shield of modern outskirts hides another old centre, with its thirteenth-century Palazzo Comunale and the Pisan-Romanesque church of San Giusto. The village's December festival addresses itself to the local wild boar.

A slight detour on the return to the coast takes in **CAMPIGLIA MARÍTTIMA**, another little gem, partly spoilt by new houses and holiday homes, but with a perfect central piazza, composed of civic palazzi and a fine Romanesque church. The inexpensive trattoria opposite the train station is popular, and for

△ Bottles of Ornellaia, Bólgheri

excellent fish you could try the moderately priced *Il Canovaccio*, Via Vecchio Asilo 1 (☎0565.838.449; closed Tues in winter). Near the train station you'll find a reasonable two-star hotel, *Il Piave*, Piazza Niccolini 2 (☎0565.226.050; **❶**).

Populonia and the Golfo di Baratti

Perched on a high, rocky headland 5km off the coast road, **POPULONIA** was once a centre of Etruscan and Roman iron production, using ore from Elba. Now it's a tiny place looking down on the broad, half-moon bay of the **Golfo di Baratti**, with some of the best beaches for miles around. There's an impressive-looking fortress at the edge of the village, disappointing inside except for the fine views across the hills. The enterprising inhabitants of Via S. Giovanni di Sotto 8 (off the main street) have opened a small private **museum** of Etruscan odds and ends (March–Nov daily 9am–7pm; Dec–Feb on request; small admission fee). The same street has a moderately priced **restaurant**, the *Populonia*.

On the bay below, once Populonia's port, there's a cluster of houses glorified with the name of **BARATTI**, a colourful base for fishing boats, whose Etruscan roots are celebrated in an eighty-hectare archeological park (June–Sept Mon–Sat 10am–7pm; rest of year hours and days vary; €9 includes access to one tomb; €12 for both; ⓦwww.parchivaldicornia.it). A multimedia presentation provides background detail, followed by tours of the caves and a necropolis or two – allow a good three hours for the whole tour. There's scope for some freelance **camping** locally, or try the campsite *Sant'Albinia*, Via della Principessa (☎0565.29.389; May to mid-Sept). The nicest low-cost **hotel** is the seafront *Alba* (☎0565.29.521; **❷**), which has a pleasant garden.

PIOMBINO, the main port of departure to Elba, is not a place to linger, since it's dominated by a massive steelworks that was rebuilt after wartime bombing and is likely to be shut down sometime soon. The only point in passing through is to take a ferry to Elba, in which case, if you're travelling by train, you should change at **Campiglia Maríttima** (see above), from where connecting trains run through Piombino to Piombino Maríttima. Should ferry timings oblige you to stay overnight, go for the two-star *Roma*, Via San Francesco 43 (☎0565.34.341; ❶), or the *Piave* in Campiglia. The main **tourist office** is on Via Ferruccio (Mon–Sat 8am–1pm ☎0565.63.269).

Elba

Nearly 30km long and 20km across, **ELBA** is the third-largest Italian island (after Sicily and Sardinia), yet until thirty years ago it was known only for its mineral resources and as Napoleon's place of exile. Now, however, it's suffering the fate of many a Mediterranean idyll, devoured by tourism in the summer and all-but-deserted in the long off-season. If you come here in August, when an estimated one million visitors flood onto Elba, you'll have trouble finding a room or even space to camp. To get the most out of the island, visit in spring or late summer.

Elba has been inhabited since about 3000 BC owing to its **mineral** wealth. The Greeks named it *Aethalia* ("Sparks") after its many forges, and Roman swords were made of Elban iron. The last iron ore mine closed in 1984, but it's still a geologist's dream, with an estimated thousand different minerals, from andalusite to zircon.

The island's enduring appeal comes from its exceptionally clear water, fine white beaches and a mountainous interior ideally suited to easy summer strolls. Development is spread over a series of fairly restrained resorts and the towns and villages retain their distinct characters. **Portoferraio** is very much the capital, and centre of the good road and transport network; **Marina di Campo**, on the south coast, has the best beach. The least visited and loveliest part of the island centres on **Monte Capanne** (1018m) and the western coast from Marciana to Fetovaia. **Poggio** and the central interior villages are sheltered by lush woods and give access to hikes in the hills. In the island's eastern segment – the old mining district – **Porto Azzurro**, and the more pleasant **Capoliveri**, give access to a string of smaller but much-visited villages.

Ferries to Elba

At Piombino port you'll find plenty of ticket outlets for all **ferry** companies sailing to Elba. Ferries run to Portoferraio every day of the year, the first around 6am, the last around 9pm (earlier and later in high summer); a one-way ticket costs from €8.50, plus around €30 per car depending on the day and the season.

Moby Lines ☎0565.225.211, ⓦwww.mobylines.it. Daily ferries to Portoferraio (1hr).

Toremar ☎0565.311.100, ⓦwww.toremar.it. Daily ferries to Portoferraio (1hr), Rio Marina (1hr) and Porto Azzurro (1hr 30min). Also a four-daily hydrofoil (*aliscafo*) to Portoferraio via Cavo (25–35min) – half the journey time of the ferry, but almost double the price.

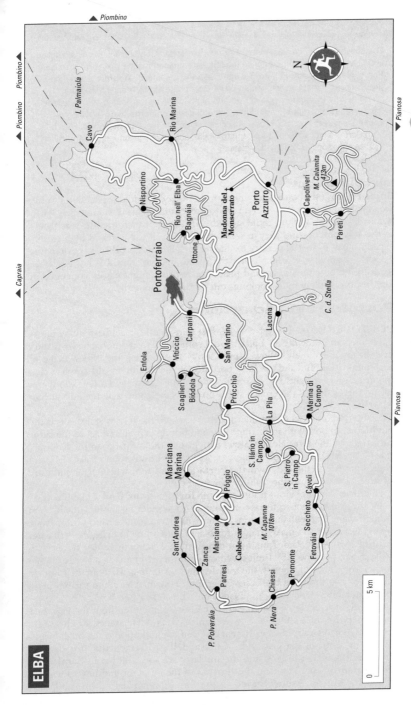

ELBA

0   5 km

Piombino
◀ Piombino
◀ Piombino

I. Palmaiola

Cavo

Rio Marina

Nisportino

Rio nell' Elba
Bagnáia

Ottone

Madonna del Monserrato

Porto Azzurro

Capoliveri

M. Calamita 413m

Pareti

▶ Pianosa

Portoferraio

Carpani
Viticcio

Enfola

Scaglieri
Biódola

San Martino

Prócchio

La Pila

Lacona

C. d. Stella

Marina di Campo

Marciana Marina

Póggio

S. Ilário in Campo

S. Pietro in Campo

Cávoli

▶ Pianosa

Sant'Andrea

Zanca

Marciana

Cable-car

M. Capanne 1018m

Seccheto

Fetováia

Patresi

Chiessi

Pomonte

P. Polveráia

P. Nera

◀ Capraia

Parco Nazionale Arcipelago Toscano

The seven Tuscan islands – Elba, Capraia, Gorgona, Montecristo, Pianosa, Giglio and Giannutri – together comprise the largest protected marine park in Europe, the **Parco Nazionale Arcipelago Toscano** (@www.islepark.it). **Capraia** was once a prison island, a function still performed by **Gorgona**, the tiny island to the north. The jail on nearby **Pianosa** is now closed and although access is limited, an occasional ferry shuttles day-trippers from Elba. The rocky islet of **Montecristo** – poking 645m above the waves south of Elba – is accessible only to research scientists. Reached from Porto Santo Stefano further south, **Giglio**, and its tiny neighbour **Giannutri**, are increasingly popular holiday destinations.

Island transport

Buses run to just about everywhere on the island (limited service after 8pm); the key services from Portoferraio are to Procchio, Marina di Campo and Porto Azzurro; other routes are more sporadic. **Boats** are much used to reach out-of-the-way beaches and they're well advertised at all the ports; in high season, expect to pay €70–100 per day, excluding fuel. Renting a **bike** or **scooter** (see p.330) is a good way of exploring the island, but **car rental** is less advisable: roads to the beaches and around the major resorts can get nastily congested in high season, while winter bookings can be hard to come by.

Portoferraio and around

PORTOFERRAIO is most people's first port of call, and unless you're interested solely in beach life it's a place you'll come back to: it's probably the island's liveliest town – closely followed by Capoliveri – and has the widest range of accommodation. Beyond the busy port area, it also retains an **old town** which might be low on sights but has more than a little charm, and a few kilometres inland there's one of the crucial sights on the Napoleonic trail, the villa at **San Martino**.

Portoferraio consists of a modern sector – where the ferries arrive – and the old Medicean port with its fortifications and fishing harbour. To get to the latter, turn right off the ferry along Calata Italia, past all the car parks, to the harbour-side Calata Mazzini, the town's *passeggiata* parade. Midway round Calata Mazzini is the entrance to the old town, the **Porta a Mare**, from where an ampitheatre of streets rises towards the walls on the high cliffs.

The town's most obvious features are the **fortifications**, built – like Livorno's – by the Medici; you can pass an hour or so wandering around them, even though many of the main bastions are now in private hands. Most visitors walk up Via Garibaldi and make straight for Napoleon's home in exile, the **Villa dei Mulini** (Mon–Sat 9am–7pm, Sun 9am–1pm; €3; joint three-day ticket with Villa di San Martino €5). Built specifically for the ex-emperor on a site chosen for its fine views of the bay, the villa features a stunning Baroque bedroom, a library of two thousand books sent over from Fontainebleau, and various items of memorabilia – including the Napoleonic Elban flag (see box).

A small, rock-enclosed **beach** called Le Viste is signposted from the Palazzina, but otherwise there's little else to see, unless you're determined to check out every Napoleon-related scrap. In that case you could drop into the small Napoleonic museum in Via Garibaldi's **Chiesa della Misericordia** (for opening hours call ☎0565.914.009) and the similar place lower down in **Santissimo Sacramento** – both contain death masks of the emperor and not a lot more. There's a **Museo Archeologico** in the fort (summer daily 9am–1.30pm &

Napoleon and Elba

Elba is indissolubly linked with **Napoleon**, even though he was exiled here for little more than nine months – from May 4, 1814 to February 26, 1815. According to island tradition, after renouncing the thrones of France and Italy by the Treaty of Fontainebleau, Napoleon chose Elba as his place of exile for the "gentleness of its climates and its inhabitants". In fact, he had no choice: the allies packed him off here, sweetening the pill by ordaining that Elba would be "a separate principality for his lifetime, held by him in complete sovereignty". The dethroned emperor spent the journey south doodling a new flag for his pocket-sized domain: a red diagonal on a white background – echoing the Medici banner – plus the bees of his own imperial emblem.

After a confusing episode in which his ship was shelled from Portoferraio, Napoleon came ashore to a rousing welcome, and soon set about reorganizing the island's economy and infrastructure. Some of this work might have been motivated by altruism or an inability to forgo politics, but much of what he achieved was for his own ends. The iron ore mines were revamped to supplement his income, his promised salary from Louis XVII having never materialized; the public works were to occupy and pay for the five-hundred-strong Napoleonic Guard that stuck by him. Portoferraio was given drains because the stench offended the imperial nostrils.

Some of the longer-term planning, however, undoubtedly paid dividends to the islanders: education and the legal system were overhauled, roads were built, agriculture was modernized, land was cleared, defences were repaired. These multifarious schemes suggested that Napoleon had resigned himself to his life sentence, but intrigue, rumour and unrest in France persuaded him to have another go. The day after Sir Neil Campbell, his British keeper, left for Livorno, he returned to France and the "Hundred Days" that were to culminate in his defeat at Waterloo.

3–7pm; €2), which houses mainly Roman remains found in the sea around Elba and pieces from pre-Roman sites on the island.

Villa di San Martino

Napoleon's sister Elisa bought the **Villa di San Martino** (Tues–Sat 9am–7pm, Sun 9am–1pm; €3; joint three-day ticket with Villa dei Mulini €5), in the hills 5km southwest of Portoferraio, as a summer residence just before the emperor – who'd built it as a retreat – left the island for good. From Portoferraio, bus #1 goes to the gates.

Engulfed by a vast car park and trolleys flogging Napoleonic souvenirs, the villa is a rather chilly affair, but its drab Neoclassical facade is at least sprinkled with exuberant "N" motifs. The monograms were the idea of Prince Demidoff, husband of Napoleon's niece – and it was he who bought up the villa to create a Napoleonic museum. By all accounts, the great man himself hardly spent any time here, and the permanent exhibits are no great shakes, though special annual exhibitions are held on a Napoleonic theme. Highlight of the house is the **Sala Egizio**, with friezes outlining Napoleon's Egyptian campaign, one of his more successful. At the back of the palazzo is Napoleon's own modest summer retreat – in some respects he had simple tastes – which was home to the famous graffito "Ubicunque felix Napoleon" (Napoleon is happy anywhere) until 1993, when it was discovered to be a fake and consequently removed.

On the way to or from San Martino, the bus passes the **Open Air Museum Italo Bolano** (June–Sept Mon–Sat 10am–noon & 4–7.30pm; free; ⓦ www.italobolano.com), where the artist has landscaped huge walls of ceramic tiles into the countryside.

Practicalities

Portoferraio's **tourist office** is housed in the tallest building in town, an unmissable eyesore rising ten storeys above the quay, Calata Italia 26 (Mon–Sat: summer 8am–8pm; winter 8am–2pm & 3–6pm; ℡0565.914.671, Ⓦwww.aptelba.it). A newsagent opposite the bus station sells hiking **maps** such as the Kompass *Isola d'Elba* and the green *Carta Turistica e Sentieri*. For information about Elba's wildlife, contact the national park headquarters, Via Guerrazzi 1 (℡0565.919.411, Ⓦwww.islepark.it).

If you're stuck for accommodation, the **Associazione Albergatori**, Calata Italia 20 (Mon–Fri 9am–1pm & 3.30–7pm, Sat 9.30am–12.30pm; ℡0565.914.754, Ⓦwww.albergatorielbani.it), will phone around to find a room, or book you an apartment (most with two doubles plus cooking facilities – available July & Aug by the week, rest of year by the day). If these fail to turn up something – as is all too likely in August – tour the bars and ask about **private rooms**.

Accommodation

Portoferraio's best **hotel**, thanks to its sense of exclusive isolation and impeccable service, is the *Park-Hotel Napoleon*, a nineteenth-century mansion beside the emperor's villa at San Martino (℡0565.918.502, Ⓦwww.parkhotelnapoleone.it; ❻). Other good upmarket choices are the *Villa Ombrosa*, Via de Gasperi 9 (℡0565.914.363, Ⓦwww.villaombrosa.it; ❻), or the plush *Crystal*, Via Cairoli (℡0565.917.971, Ⓦwww.hotelcrystal.it; ❻), both on or near the beach at Le Ghiaie.

In town, the best options are *L'Ape Elbana*, just off Piazza della Repubblica at Salita Cosimo de' Medici 9 (℡0565.914.245, Ⓔapeelbana@elba2000.it; ❸), and nicely located *Il Touring* at Via Roma 13 (℡0565.915.851; ❸). If you're stuck for a bed, *Massimo*, Calata Italia 23 (℡0565.914.766, Ⓦwww.elbahotelmassimo.it; ❺), with 69 rooms, should have some chance of space. The nearest **campsites** are *La Sorgente* (℡0565.917.139, Ⓦwww.campinglasorgente.it; April–Oct), *Acquaviva* (℡0565.915.592, Ⓦwww.campingacquaviva.it) and *La Enfola* (℡0565.939.001, Ⓦwww.campingenfola.it), all 5–6km along the road west to Viticcio, and accessible by bus.

Eating and drinking

Portoferraio's **restaurants** are expensive and few have food to merit the prices. The well-patronized *Pizzeria Il Castagnacciaio* in Via del Mercato Vecchio (parallel to Piazza della Repubblica) sells the cheapest – and smallest – pizzas, or try the inexpensive *Pane e Pomodoro* next door. *L'Ape Elbana* hotel-restaurant (see above) has a choice of six inexpensive tourist menus. Best known of the more upmarket choices are *La Ferrigna*, Piazza della Repubblica (℡0565.914.129; closed Tues in winter), and *Trattoria La Barca*, Via Guerazzi 60 (℡0565.918.036; closed Wed in winter). For a treat, book ahead at the expensive terrace restaurant of the *Park-Hotel Napoleon* at San Martino (see above); the classic Tuscan cuisine is exquisite, and the multilingual service is something special. For **bars**, pick from any of the places around Piazza della Repubblica in the heart of the old town, or Piazza Cavour – particularly *Bar Roma*, which is the most popular bar with locals, with music in the summer and upmarket prices; or try *Bar Kursaal* in the same square.

Listings

Bike and moped rental Both are available from TWN, by the bus station, Viale Elba 32 ℡0565.914.666, Ⓦwww.twn-rent.it; mountain bikes and mopeds cost around €25 a day.
Car rental In the port area try Rent Chiappi, Calata Italia 30 ℡0565.930.681, Ⓦwww.rentchiappi

.it, or nearby Tesi Viaggi ℡ 0565.930.222. In town, try Happy Rent, Viale Elba ℡ 0565.914.665, or Rent Mondo, Via Renato Fucini 6 ℡ 0565.917.276. Reckon on €40–60/day.

Ferry information Return ferries to Piombino are often packed, and you should book your return as far in advance as possible; shop around on both price and convenience. Toremar are at Calata Italia 23 ℡ 0565.918.080, Ⓦ www.toremar-elba.it; Moby Lines at Via Ninci 1 ℡ 0565.918.101, Ⓦ www .mobylines.it.

Left luggage At the bus terminal, Viale Elba 20.

Post office Piazza Hutre, off Piazza della Repub-blica.

Eastern Elba

Eastern Elba is a distinct geographical area, comprising two tongues of land, each dominated by mountain ridges. Away from the main seaside centres of **Rio Marina** and **Porto Azzurro** the beaches are comparatively quiet, but much of the southern isthmus – Monte Calamita – was the heart of the mining industry, and is still owned by the quarrying companies. Close by, on the southern coast, **Lacona** boasts one of the island's main concentrations of campsites; **Barbaros-sa** is another popular camping spot, with some particularly fine beaches.

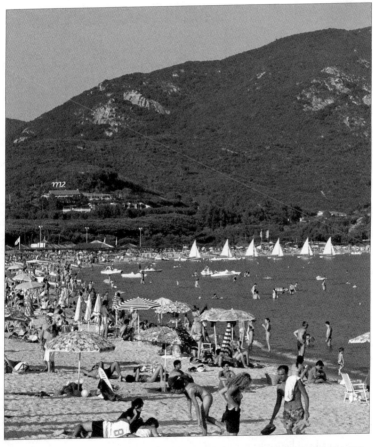

△ Beach on the island of Elba

Heading out of Portoferraio the main road south divides, one spur going west, the other east towards Porto Azzurro. Along the latter, first stop is the spa of **SAN GIOVANNI**, where visitors pay through the nose for the privilege of wallowing in sulphurous marine mud. A few kilometres on at **LE GROTTE** are the ruins of a **Roman villa**, little more than a few stones and mosaic fragments among the gorse, but worth a stop for a great view over the sea, into which most of the building has tumbled.

Soon after comes a left turn for Rio nell'Elba and **MAGAZINI**, a little place with a sand and shingle beach and a couple of hotels: the three-star *Mare* (℡0565.933.069, ⓦwww.hotelmare.org; ❹; April–Oct) and two-star *Tirrena* (℡0565.933.002, ⓔanselmis@elbalink.it; ❷). Just beyond at **OTTONE** is the one-star *Villa Gaia* (℡0565.933.160; ❷), and the *Rosselba le Palme* **campsite** (℡0565.933.101, ⓦwww.rosselbalepalme.it; mid-April to Sept), rated by many the island's best. West-facing **BAGNAIA**, a little further, is famous for its sunsets. There are two hotels here, the *Punta Pina* (℡0565.961.077, ⓔluk@elba2000.it; ❸) and *La Feluca* (℡0565.961.084, ⓦwww.hotellafeluca .it; ❸), plus a minimarket and the *Kikuty* bar. The route from Magazini to Rio nell'Elba passes the old castle at **Volterraio**, once the strongest in Elba and now a silent and evocative ruin, with a great view over its desolate surroundings. It's a stiff climb from the road.

Following the twisting coast road north of Bagnaia, you'll come to the tiny twin hamlets of **NISPORTO** and **NISPORTINO**, marking the beginning of the most unspoilt beaches and coastline on Elba's north shore. You can walk into the hills behind, or take boats out to the beaches beyond the end of the road. The only accommodation here is *Camping-Villaggio Sole e Mare* at Nisporto (℡0565.934.907, ⓦwww.soleemare.it) or the neighbouring campsite *Cala di Nisportino* (℡0565.934.908; May–Sept).

From Nisporto the narrow scenic road to Rio nell'Elba climbs through **LA GINESTRA**, 2km from the sea, where you'll find the three-star *La Ginestra* (℡0565.943.181; ❸). **RIO NELL'ELBA** itself is a graceless place, though old enough in parts and rare in having apparently resisted Elba's tourist boom. From its high vantage it surveys a wild and beautiful countryside with good sea views. The town was once the capital of Elba and centre of the mining district, evidence of which can be found in the tiny **Museo dei Minerali Elbani** (summer 10am–1pm & 4–7pm; €2). There's nowhere to stay, but a couple of inexpensive places to **eat**: *Da Cipolla* in Piazza del Popolo and *Ristorante Carpe Diem* in Via S. Galletti.

Halfway between Rio nell'Elba and Cavo is the Eremo di Santa Caterina and the **Orto dei Semplici Elbano** (Tues–Sun 1–7pm), a botanical garden of wild flowers from all over the Tuscan archipelago.

Cavo and Rio Marina

CAVO, on the northern extremity of Elba, is a small beach resort with little on offer bar a hydrofoil link with Portoferraio. There are several **hotels**, including the waterfront *Maristella* (℡0565.949.859; ❸), and the pleasant, mid-priced **restaurant** *La Scogliera*, with tables overlooking the beach.

The main town on Elba's east coast is **RIO MARINA**, 9km south of Cavo, a ferry terminal for connections to Piombino, Portoferraio and Porto Azzurro. Tourism and a busy harbour have replaced iron ore as the source of revenue, but this isn't one of the better Elban towns. There's just one **hotel**, the *Rio* at Via Palestro 31 (℡0565.924.225, ⓦwww.hotelriomarina.it; ❺; April–Oct), next to the small public gardens overlooking the port. Close by is one of the island's best **restaurants**, *La Canocchia*, Via Palestro 3 (closed Mon in winter). Other options in the lower port include a moderately priced fish restaurant and pizzeria, *Da Oreste la Strega*, in Piazza V. Emanuele (closed Tues in winter).

South of here, the hamlet of **ORTANO** is dominated by a big tourist complex, but has a public beach too, with the **campsite** *Canapai* (☎0564.939.165; May–Sept) and **hotel** *Easytime*, Via Pan Porticciolo (☎0565.962.531, ⓔeasytime@tiscalinet.it; ➍).

Porto Azzurro

The resort of **PORTO AZZURRO** was heavily fortified by Philip III of Spain in 1603 as protection against continual raids by the French and the Austrians; today his fortress is the island's prison but you can walk around the walls and admire the inmates' artwork at a small craft shop. The town's small, pretty, old quarter, closed to traffic, centres on **Via d'Alarcon**, a bustle of bars, shops and restaurants, with traditional open-front shops and balconied houses in the cobbled area near Piazza Matteotti. The best place to swim is from the rocks east of the harbour. **Boat trips** (around €20 for 3hr) run south along the coast twice daily in summer. Hobby Motor, Viale Italia 25, and TWN, at the ferry terminal, **rents mopeds** and **bikes**.

Accommodation is limited and lacklustre: go for the *Belmare*, Banchina IV Novembre 25 (☎0565.95.012, ⓔbelmare@elbalink.it; ➌), *Arrighi*, Via V. Veneto 18 (☎0565.95.315; ➋; closed Feb), or *Villa Italia*, Viale Italia 41 (☎0565.95.119, ⓔvillaitalia@infoelba.it; ➋). Best of the **campsites** are at the small nearby resort of **BARBAROSSA** – *Da Mario* (☎0565.958.032; mid-April to mid-Oct) and *Arrighi* (☎0565.95.568; April–Nov). Both give straight onto the beach, near the one-star hotel *Barbarossa* (☎0565.95.087; ➊). For **food** there are plenty of identikit joints on Porto Azzurro's waterfront; better-value options in the back streets include *Il Sottoscala*, Via Ricasoli 11, *Taverna Lo Scoglio*, Via Cavour 15, and *Osteria dei Quattro Gatti*, Piazza del Mercato 4 – all with inexpensive to moderately priced menus.

Off the Rio Marina road to the north, at **TERRANERE**, there's a bizarre sulphurous pond, its half-stagnant waters a violent yellow contrast to the sea; the beach here is scattered with mine debris. Nearby, up an unsignposted left turn off the same road, is the **Santuario della Madonna di Monserrato**, about 1km beyond the so-called Piccolo Miniera, a tourist-trap mine reconstruction. The short walk at the end of the road brings you to the church whose chief claim to fame is its replica of the Black Madonna of Montserrat; chapel and Madonna were both commissioned in 1606 by the island's Spanish governor, who claimed this site reminded him of the holy mountain outside his native Barcelona.

Naregno

East of the road between Porto Azzurro and Capoliveri, **NAREGNO** is a small resort with a good beach, though not as good as the less accessible sand to the south at Côte Piane, Liscolino and Buzzancone. None can match the village's **accommodation** possibilities, however, which include the seafront *Villa Rodriguez* (☎0565.968.423, ⓦwww.villarodriguez.it; ➍), the 53-room *Frank's Hotel* (☎0565.968.144, ⓦwww.frankshotel.com; ➍) and *La Voce del Mare* (☎0565.968.455, ⓕ0565.935.924; ➋).

Capoliveri and south

CAPOLIVERI, 3.5km south of Porto Azzurro, is the best of the towns in eastern Elba, a prosperous centre whose close-knit streets have made few concessions to tourism. Occupying a naturally fortified spot, it's amongst the oldest settlements on the island: in Roman times its name was Caput Liberi. Its hinterland remains undeveloped, as the mining companies have not yet sold their disused plots to the hoteliers – though much of the area is thus out of bounds.

There's nothing specific to see, but **old streets** such as Via Roma, Via Cavour and Vicolo Lungo are pleasant places to roam, and there are numerous half-hidden bars in the alleyways, as well as a sprawl of outside tables in the central piazza. The town is at its busiest on Thursdays, when locals and tourists flood in for the weekly **street market**; it is also very lively in the evenings, with a reputation for being the place to go for a night out.

Capoliveri makes an ideal base for visits to the fine **beaches** at Naregno, Morcone and Innamorata. However, it's practically impossible to stay cheaply: it only has expensive **apartments** rented out by numerous private agencies, such as *Agenzia della Lucia* (@www.agenziacapoliveri.com), Via Melline 9 (Mon–Sat 9am–12.30pm & 3–7pm). Moderate-to-expensive **restaurants** include *Il Chiasso*, Vicolo Sauro 9 (T0565.968.709; closed Tues), specializing in seafood; *Osteria Summertime*, Via Roma 56 (T0565.935.180); and *Porto Franco* in Via da Brescia, off the main piazza. To sample local **wines** make for *Enoteca Fandango,* Via Cardenti 1, or *Da Graziano*, Via Pietra Gori 33; and for delicious homemade ice cream drop in at *Patelli Gelateria*, Via Roma 38. Capoliveri brims with **nightlife** well into the small hours: *Ophir* disco, 2km away at La Trappola, is the prime dancing spot, with *Sugar-Reef* (@www.sugar-reef.com), a friendly late-night jazz bar, just below it.

South of Capoliveri

The much touted local church at **Madonna delle Grazie** – another place of pilgrimage – has a school-of-Raphael altarpiece but is otherwise more or less a waste of time, as is the overbuilt area around. It's better to continue to the trio of resorts at **MORCONE**, **PARETI** and **INNAMORATA**. The last is the quietest and has a fine sand and shingle beach; the other hamlets have large beaches, Morcone's being more regimented than its neighbour. Parking is difficult, as is **accommodation**. Morcone has no hotels, though there are some rooms to rent and *Residence la Scogliera* will put people up on a nightly basis in mini-apartments (T0565.968.424; ❸). Pareti has the *Pensione Villa Miramare* (T0565.968.673, @www.hotelvillamiramare.it; ❷), *Dino* (T0565.939.103, @www.hoteldino.com; ❹) and *Stella Maris* (T0565.968.425, @www.albergostellamaris.com; ❺). There's nowhere to stay in Innamorata except a tourist village, but it's worth visiting for its two **restaurants**, *Conte Domingo* and *Spaghetteria/Pizzeria Innamorata*, with terraces overlooking the sea – perfect for sunsets.

Roads continue south into the hills of **Monte Calámita**, and to the stretch of unspoilt coast known as the **Costa dei Gabbiani**, both areas with mine-restricted access. The area's name ("Calamity") is a pun referring to the magnetic properties of the rocks, which allegedly attract boats towards them: *calamita*, without the accent, means "magnet".

Lacona

LACONA, well round the coast west of Porto Azzurro, is one of the island's main camping centres, and its flat foreshore is crowded with **bars** and **clubs** designed to cater to the beach crowd once the sun's gone down. The **campsites** to head for are *Il Lacona* (T0565.964.161) or the nearby *Lacona Pineta* (T0565.964.322, @www.campinglaconapineta.com), both set in the pine woods on the eastern arm of the Golfo di Lacona. *Stella Mare* (T0565.964.007, @www.stellamare.it), which offers free bike rental, as well as windsurfing lessons, is on the beach a bit farther out along the headland, also amidst plenty of greenery. The best-value **hotel** is *Pensione Giardino* (℡ 0565.964.059, ⓔ hotelgiardino@elbalink.it; ❷).

Western Elba

Western Elba's road system allows for a circular tour of the area, but many people make immediately for specific targets – usually **Marina di Campo**, with its huge beach and many hotels. Upmarket alternatives are offered by the north-coast resorts of **Procchio** and **Marciana Marina**, while backpackers favour the relatively less commercialized **Énfola** area.

Fewer visitors venture inland to **Marciana**, one of Elba's most attractive villages, or explore the long sweep of the **western coast**, whose hamlets and beaches are amongst the island's most tranquil. Though the western zone tends to be rockier than the east, it's better for **walking**, the highlights being **Monte Capanne** and its surrounding ridges.

Énfola, Viticcio, Scaglieri and Biodola

For a spread of beach and a choice of campsites near Portoferraio, follow the scenic road below Monte Poppe to the headland at **Capo d'Énfola**. You pass through the hamlets of Sorgente and Punta Acquaviva (each with a campsite) before reaching **ÉNFOLA**, where the land narrows to a 75-metre-wide isthmus with beaches on both sides. The road ends at a small car park next to the *Bar Emanuel* (closed winter), where you can get down to either strip of pebbly beach. The one daily bus from Portoferraio will drop you off at Bivio Enfola – 1km from the bar – and continue to **VITICCIO**, another spot with a dead-end road, parking area, and sand and shingle beach. Pick of the numerous **hotels** in the area are the three-star *Paradiso* at Viticcio (℡ 0565.939.034, ⓔ paradiso@elbaturistica.it; ❺), all the rooms of which have sea views; and the two-star *Scoglio Bianco* (℡ 0565.939.036, ⓦ www.scogliobianci.it; ❸). Énfola has a shady **campsite**, *Énfola Camping* (℡ 0565.939.001, ⓦ www.campingenfola.it; April to mid-Oct). The popular Sansone **beach** is off the main road from Portoferraio on the right: take the track 50m before *Ristorante Tre Colonne* or ask the bus driver to stop.

From Viticcio, a footpath runs 2km round the coast to Scaglieri and Biodola, otherwise reached by a side road from the main highway out of Portoferraio. **BIODOLA** consists simply of a road, two big hotels and a superb **beach**, which inevitably gets a summer blitz of visitors. Parking is difficult, but there are no buses. Biodola's two **hotels** are very expensive, though there's a beautifully situated place two minutes from the beach, the *Casa Rosa* (℡ 0565.969.931, ⓔ casarosa@elbalink.it; ❻). **SCAGLIERI** is similar but a touch livelier and more picturesque, fronted by a shop, two bars and a couple of moderately priced places to **eat**: *I due Pini* is the better of the two. You can **stay** at the *Albergo-Ristorante Danila* (℡ 0565.969.915, ⓦ www.hoteldanila.it; ❹) or the **campsite** *Scaglieri* (℡ 0565.969.940, ⓦ www.campingscaglieri.it; April to mid-Oct), on the hillside.

Procchio

PROCCHIO suffers from being at a junction of main roads, the greenery of its surroundings offset by an incessant stream of summer traffic. With its shops and bars it's not a place to get away from it all, but the sea is good and the white beach excellent; access to much of the sand is free and it's large enough not to seem overcrowded. Pick of the **hotels** are *Da Renzo* (℡ 0565.907.505;

❷), _Hotel di Procchio_ (☎0565.907.477, ☎0565.907.350; ❷), and _Monna Lisa_ (☎0565.907.519, ⓦwww.hotelmonnalisa.it; ❷), along with _Fontalleccio_ (☎0565.907.431, ⓔfontalleccio@elbalink.it; ❹) and _Edera_ (☎0565.907.525, ⓔhedera@elbalink.it; ❺). **Restaurants** along the roadside strip are much of a muchness; the _Orso Bianco_ does good ice cream. You can **rent bikes** and **mopeds** from Rent Procchio, Via Provinciale (☎0565.907.783, ⓦwww.rentprocchio.it).

Marciana Marina

Farther round the north coast, **MARCIANA MARINA** has the minor distinction of being the smallest _comune_ in Tuscany, a status it's proud of, allowing only a few hotels and aiming to preserve an air of residential order away from the seafront. The traffic-filled promenade of bars, restaurants and trinket shops does nothing to lure you into staying. Even the beach, overlooked by a Pisan watchtower, is shingly and forgettable. Accommodation is largely restricted to private houses and apartments.

Poggio

Situated 5km inland from Marciana Marina, **POGGIO** is renowned for its _Fonte di Napoleone_ mineral water and a tight medieval centre whose decorated doorways and patchwork of cheerful gardens make it an attractive place to stay. The best **hotel** is _Albergo-Ristorante Monte Capanne_, Via Pini 1 (☎ & ☎0565.99.083; ❶), in a lovely, peaceful setting. **Food** here is good, and the village claims one of the island's leading restaurants, _Publius_, Via XX Settembre 13 (☎0565.99.208) – great views and classic Elban cooking including _cacciucco_ and wild boar with mushrooms.

Marciana

The high and isolated village of **MARCIANA**, the oldest settlement on Elba, is perfectly placed between great beaches (Promonte and Sant'Andrea), mountainous interior (Monte Capanne) and a modern centre for supplies (Procchio). Its **old quarter** is a delight, too, its narrow alleys, arches, belvederes and stone stairs festooned with flowers and climbing plants. There's virtually no traffic or commercial development, and with the skeletal outline of its old fortifications it feels very distinct from the rest of the island's towns.

Marciana's history is encapsulated in the small **Museo Archeologico** in Via del Pretorio (closed for restoration), just below the **Fortezza Pisana**, which is closed to the public but worth the steep climb through the village for its spectacular views.

Outside the village there's a trio of interesting **churches**, the oldest of which is the twelfth-century Pisan-influenced **San Lorenzo**; now largely in ruins, it's on a track off the road to Poggio. More intriguing is the **Santuario della Madonna del Monte**, about half an hour's walk along the road curving uphill west of the village. Though it dates from the eleventh century – and was probably a pagan temple well before that – its appearance is largely sixteenth-century, the Renaissance church serving to house a stone painted by a heavenly hand with the image of the Virgin. The island's most important shrine, it's also featured on the Napoleonic trail, as the ex-emperor came here to seek spiritual solace from the monks; by all accounts he received solace of a different kind when he was joined by his Polish mistress, Maria Walewska.

The third church, the **Santuario di San Cerbone**, is passed on the **walk** to Monte Capanne (trail #1; 3hr). The track starts from the southern tip of the village, the church appearing after an hour at the junction with trail #6. San Cerbone was buried here, during a miraculous cloudburst that hid the ceremony from Lombards who had the saint's valuable remains in their sights.

If you don't want to walk up Monte Capanne, there's a popular **cable car** 1km south of the town which takes you to the top (June–Sept 10am–12.15pm & 2.30–6.30pm; Oct–May 10am–12.15pm & 2.30–5.30pm; €12 return); most people choose to walk down either to Marciana or Poggio, though if you're trekking with your gear you could drop down to the coast via one of the numerous marked trails.

Marciana's only drawback is its shortage of **accommodation**, restricted to rented rooms and apartments available through the *Birreria La Porta*, Piazza Fuor di Porta (℡0565.901.275; closed Wed), which serves good sandwiches and salads; other decent places to eat are the reasonably priced *Osteria del Noce*, Via della Madonna 14 (℡0565.901.284; lunch only), or the *Enoteca Manilli* at the fortress, which serves sandwiches, pizza and a selection of wines until 2am.

Sant'Andrea and around

The dispersed village of **SANT'ANDREA**, 6km west of Marciana, just off the coast road, is one of Elba's more fashionable retreats, with villas and hotels creeping farther into the wooded hinterland each year. It's popular with divers, drawn here by what is reputedly some of the clearest sea water around Elba. **Accommodation** is at a premium, but it's not necessarily expensive, and most is discreetly set amid almost tropical vegetation. On the beach itself there's the small *Bambu* (℡0565.908.012; ❶); the pleasant *La Cernia* (℡0565.908.210, Ⓦwww.hotelcernia.it; ❸) lies midway between the coast and the main road; or try *L'Oleandro* (℡0565.908.088; ❷), *Piccola Pineta* (℡0565.908.022, Ⓔpiccolapineta@elbalink.it; ❸) or *Bella Vista* (℡0565.908.015, Ⓦwww.hotel-bellavista.it; ❷). There are plenty of rental apartments.

Immediately south are the linked hamlets of **PATRESI**, **MORTAIO** and **LA GUARDIA**, rated as having the island's finest seas and still fairly unspoilt into the bargain. Cliffs drop to the sea, as they do all round this section of coast, with plenty of rock pillars and stacks for underwater enthusiasts. Most local **accommodation** is in apartments, though there are two **hotels**, the eleven-room *Villa Rita* (℡0565.908.095, Ⓔvilla.rita@elbasun.com; ❸) and two-star *Belmare* (℡0565.908.067, Ⓦwww.hotelbelmare.it; ❷), at Patresi. For inexpensive pizza and full **meals**, try *Il Faro*, on the road near Patresi, with a veranda and sea view.

The southwest coast: Chiessi to Cavoli

Further round the coast road, **CHIESSI** and **POMONTE** each have a small stony beach, beautifully clear water, rocky hinterland and little commercialism. By the time you reach **FETOVAIA** you're back to beach development, but the sand is superb. Fetovaia has lots of apartment accommodation and several top-whack hotels; try the central *Lo Scirocco* (℡0565.988.033, Ⓔscirocco@fetovaia.it; ❹), the *Pensione Montemerlo* out of town on the hill (℡ & ℻0565.988.051; ❸), *Anna* (℡0565.988.032, Ⓔanna@fetovaia.it; ❹) or *Da Alma* (℡0565.988.040, ℻0565.988.074; ❷).

Further on, **SECCHETO** is good for a swim from the rocks at the western end of town, or for tanning on the largely nudist stretch beyond – *le piscine* – where the water forms deep pools in the hollows of a Roman granite mine. Two **hotels** are *La Stella* (℡0565.987.013, Ⓔla.stella@elbalink.it; ❹), at the end of the road to the sea, and the nearby *Da Fine* (℡0565.987.017, Ⓦwww.hoteldafine.it; ❸). A cheaper option away from the coast is *Locanda dell'Amicizia* (℡0565.987.051, ℻0565.987.277; ❷), set in a peaceful spot at **Vallebuia**, in the little valley north of Seccheto. The **bar** on the main road, which can sometimes direct you to available apartments, is popular, fairly cheap and does excellent pizzas.

Nearby **CAVOLI** is more upmarket, though the beach is good if crowded. It has two similar beachside *pensioni*: the *Lorenza* (℡0565.987.054, ©lorenz@tin .it; ❸) and *Conchiglia* (℡0565.987.010, ℗0565.987.257; ❸).

Marina di Campo

Set in one of the island's few areas of plain, **MARINA DI CAMPO** was the first and is now the largest resort on Elba. The huge white **beach** is what makes the place popular: the water's clean, and there's space on land if you walk to the east end or out to the rockier west. There's also all the tourist frippery and nightlife you'd expect in any major seaside centre.

Pick of the numerous **hotels** are *Lido*, Via Mascagni 29 (℡0565.976.040, ©hotellido@tin.it; ❸), *Pensione Elba*, Via Mascagni 51 (℡0565.976.224, ⓦwww.hotel-elba.it; ❷), *Santa Caterina*, Viale Elba (℡0565.976.452, ©santacaterina@elbalink.it; ❹), *Barracuda*, Viale Elba 78 (℡0565.976.893, ©barracuda@elbalink.it; ❹), and *Thomas*, Via Giannutri (℡0565.977.732, ©elbathomashotel@infinito.it; ❷). If you arrive early in the day you might find space at one of the three **campsites**. There are plenty of places to **eat**: the *Rosticceria Mazzarri*, Via Roma 19, has inexpensive meals and cheap snacks; for a full-blown fish meal try the moderately priced *Aragosta* or *Ristorante Il Cacciucco* in Piazza Cavour. You can **rent bikes** and **boats** from Bikos, Via Donizetti 27 (℡0565.976.194). For a break from the crowds you might take a bus trip out to two smaller hill-villages close by – the very pretty **SANT'ILARIO IN CAMPO** and **SAN PIERO IN CAMPO**, whose parish church has a hotch-potch of frescoes.

Capraia

The island of **CAPRAIA**, 30km northwest of Elba, is unspoilt, with just a couple of hotels and one road that links the small port to the old town on the hill. Its former use as a penal colony ensured that the terrain remained largely untouched, and now – despite considerable pressure from potential hoteliers – the local council have held back on commercial development, instead promoting the island's status as a *Parco Nazionale* to protect the natural heritage. This makes it difficult to visit, and the two hotels and single campsite come close to saturation point in summer: it's best to come slightly out of season. A **ferry** runs daily from Livorno throughout the year (summer Thurs & Sat twice daily).

Capraia Isola

From the tiny harbour to the town of **CAPRAIA ISOLA** – the only inhabited part of the island except the port – is a gentle walk of about 1km (there's a regular bus in summer). The island's long periods of desolation, mainly because of pirate raids, have done little for its monuments. Capraia Isola's Baroque church and convent of **Sant'Antonio** is largely ruined, and the big castle, the privately owned **Fortezza di San Giorgio**, has seen better days.

For information on wildlife, walking, accommodation and boat trips, contact the **Cooperativa Parco** (℡0586.905.071, ©agparco@tin.it) or the **tourist office** (April–Sept 10am–6pm; ℡0586.905.138), both on the harbourfront Via Assunzione.

Hotels include the three-star *Da Beppone*, Via Assunzione 78 (℡ & ℱ0586.905.001; ❷), and, in the upper part of town, four-star *Il Saracino*, Via L. Cibo 30 (℡0586.905.018, ℱ0586.905.062; ❻); you'll probably have to pay at least half-board in peak periods. There are numerous private **rooms** and **apartments**; the tourist office will call round for you, or you can just wander through town and look for the signs. There's a single **campsite**, *Le Sughere* (℡0586.905.066; May–Sept), behind the small church of the Assumption.

One of the best **restaurants** is *La Garitta*, Via Genova 14 (℡0586.905.230), up near the castle; run as a bar during the day, it's an informal place, dedicated to simple, moderately priced seafood. There are a couple of other inexpensive places down on the harbour, best of which is *Da Beppone*.

The interior and the beaches

The scrubby, almost treeless island has a knobbly spine of 400m hills, with the eastern slope shallow and riven with valleys, and the western coast featuring cliffs rising almost sheer from the sea. From Capraia Isola you can easily strike off into the uninhabited interior: tracks crisscross the whole island, but there are four distinct and fairly obvious **walks**: to the **Torre dello Zenobito**, a Genoese watchtower on the island's southernmost tip; to **Il Piano** and the Pisan church of **Santo Stefano**, using the rough road south of the town; to the lighthouse on the west coast, farther down the same track; and to the **Laghetto**, a tarn in the hills.

Isolation has favoured the development of various indigenous animal and vegetable species, several of them similar to species otherwise confined to Corsica and Sardinia. These include subspecies of buzzard, sparrow, large finch and La Marmora's warbler amongst the birds, and campion, toadflax and blue button amongst the plants. Birds are the main natural interest, with numerous itinerant visitors, and forty resident species including peregrines, shearwaters and up to a hundred pairs of the rare Corsican gull.

Winter storms in 1998 stripped the island's only real beach, the Cala della Mortola, of all its sand. However, there are plenty of rocky coves and the water's clean and clear everywhere. There's a range of small **boats** available for rent, from canoes (around €10/hr) to powered rubber dinghies (around €100/day). Both the Cooperativa Parco and Agenzia Della Rosa (℡0586.905.266) run trips round the entire island (twice daily in season). There's a couple of **subaqua** clubs based in the port; contact the Capraia Diving Club (℡0586.905.137, ⓦwww.capraiadiving.it) for help and equipment rental.

Travel details

Trains

Campiglia Maríttima to: Piombino Maríttima (hourly; 30min).

Livorno to: Campiglia Maríttima (every 30min; 1hr); Castagneto Carducci (every 30min; 45min); Castiglioncello (every 30min; 25min); Cecina (every 30min; 35min); Florence (12 daily; 1hr 30min); Quercianella (every 30min; 15min); Rome (hourly; 3–4hr); San Vincenzo (every 30min; 55min).

Pisa to: Cascina (hourly; 15 min); Empoli (hourly;

35min; change for Volterra and Siena); Florence (hourly; 1hr); Livorno (every 20min; 15min); Lucca (hourly; 20min); Pisa Airport (hourly 8am–6.15pm; 6min); Pontedera (every 30min; 15min); San Rossore (every 30min; 5min).

Buses

Cécina to: Bibbona (10 daily; 20–35min); Castagneto Carducci (1 daily; 25min); Livorno (every 30min; 1hr); Saline di Volterra (6 daily; 30min).
Livorno to: Castiglioncello (every 30min; 35min);

Cecina (every 30min; 1hr); Piombino (2 daily; 1hr 30min); Pisa (hourly; 40min).

Piombino to: Campiglia Maríttima (11 daily; 30min); Donoratico (3 daily; 35min); Populonia (2 daily; 15min); San Vincenzo (3 daily; 25min); Sassetta (2 daily; 1hr 15min); Suvereto (7 daily; 50min).

Pisa to: Florence (hourly via Lucca and Monte-catini; 2hr 30min); Livorno (hourly; 40min); Lucca (hourly; 50min); Viareggio (hourly; 50min).

Populonia to: Baratti (4 daily; 5min).

Portoferraio to: Capoliveri (7 daily; 30min); Marciana Alta (8 daily; 1hr); Marciana Marina (8 daily; 35min); Marina di Campo (10 daily; 30min); Porto Azzurro (10 daily; 30min); Rio nell'Elba/Rio Marina (7 daily; 50min).

5

The Maremma

CHAPTER 5   # Highlights

✳ **Massa Maríttima** Fine hill-town with a glorious Romanesque cathedral. See p.345

✳ **Rusellae and Vetulonia** Two of Tuscany's most tempting Etruscan sites. See p.351

✳ **Monti dell'Uccellina** Italy's most pristine stretch of coastal scenery. See p.352

✳ **Marina di Alberese** The trees come right down to this unspoilt sandy beach, which has gently shelving water and views across to the Argentario. See p.355

✳ **Monte Argentario** Spectacular headland with chic coastal resorts. See p.359

✳ **Giglio** Pleasant, if popular, little island an hour offshore. See p.360

△ Massa Maríttima

The Maremma

he **Maremma** – the coastal plain that runs south from the Piombino headland – was the northern heartland of the **Etruscans**, whose drainage and irrigation canals turned it into an area of huge agricultural potential. Their good work, however, was largely lost under the Romans, who abandoned much of the land and left it to revert to marsh, a decline that continued through the Middle Ages, when war and further dereliction turned the region into a malarial swamp. For years, virtually the only inhabitants were migrant charcoal burners and shepherds (who in summer abandoned the infested lowlands for the hill-villages of Amiata), and the famous *butteri*, cowboys who tend the region's oxen and horses.

Modern attempts to revive the Maremma were started in 1828 by Grand Duke Leopoldo of Tuscany, who instigated new drainage schemes and introduced a crude health service with free quinine for malaria sufferers, but even at the turn of the last century, Grosseto's regional council still had to move its offices annually to the healthier surroundings of Scansano. Real progress only began under Mussolini; the malarial mosquito was finally banished in 1950, but something of the Maremma's grim legacy lives on in its common Italian nickname, *La Miseria*.

Drainage has returned a measure of prosperity to the Maremma, though it remains very much an agricultural area with few urban centres away from **Grosseto**, the provincial capital. Inland Maremma is now highly regarded for its DOC wines and olive oil and the last few years have seen a significant rise in

The butteri

The **butteri**, the Maremma's cowboys, have for centuries taken care of the region's half-feral horses and celebrated white cattle, a special breed imported from Asia for their resilience to the rigours of the Maremma climate and terrain. For most of the year, the *butteri* ride with the herds on the Maremma's grasslands, the key event of the year being the so-called *merca* in April, when the one-year-old calves and foals are rounded up, counted and branded.

You stand most chance of seeing the *butteri* on the Ombrone estuary, particularly on the road to Marina di Alberese, although from time to time they make an appearance in local festivals and special events. Such performances are nothing new: in 1911 Buffalo Bill brought a travelling troupe of cowboys to Rome, where they were trounced by the *butteri* in a series of rodeo events in the Piazza del Popolo. Today the best known of their tourist shows is the August **rodeo** in Alberese, and they also prove their skills in perhaps the most demanding equestrian arena in the world – as riders in the Siena Palio.

Volterra ▲   ▲ Colle di Val d'Elsa & Siena   ▲ Siena

Monterotondo
Marittimo

S. Galgano

River Ombrone

Buonconvento

Piombino & Pisa

Massa Marittima

Montalcino

S. Quirico

Castiglione
d'Orcia

Roccastrada

River Orcia

Follónica

Pagánico

Montepescali

Montorsáio

Castel di Piano

Monte
Amiata ▲

Vetulónia

Necrópoli
Etrusca

Batignnano

Roselle

Arcidosso

S. Fiora

Punta
Ala

Roccalbegna

Le
Rocchette

Grosseto

Murci

Castiglione
della
Pescáia

Marina di
Grosseto

Alberese

Scansano

Satúrnia

Pitigliano

N

Marina di
Alberese

PARCO NATURALE
DELLA MAREMMA

MONTI DELL'UCCELLINA

SS1

Magliano in Toscana

S. Bruzio

Manciano

Talamone

Tombolo di Giannella
Laguna di Orbetello

Albína

Capalbio

Péscia
Fiorentina

Porto Santo
Stefano

Orbetello

Giardino
dei Tarocchi

LAZIO

Il Telegrafo
635m ▲

SS1

Ansedónia

Chiarone
Scalo

Giglio Campese

Giglio Porto

Port'
Ercole

Lago di
Burano

Giglio   Giglio
        Castello

Tombolo
di Feniglia

Rome

0   10 km

Giannutri

THE MAREMMA

agriturismo holidays based on wine estates and smaller farms. A few efforts have been made to preserve the natural world, mainly in the **Monti dell'Uccellina** but also in the nature reserves at **Burano** and **Orbetello**, two of the finest birdwatching spots in the country. You'll also stand a chance of seeing wild boar: the hoary-skinned sub-species *Sus scropha majori* have developed in isolated, swamp-encircled habitats.

There are plenty of seaside diversions here as well, with glorious beaches at **Marina di Alberese** and in the Uccellina, and moderately upmarket resorts at **Punta Ala** and around **Monte Argentario**. Increasingly well known are the idyllic island of **Giglio**, visited from the Argentario, and the area around the Lazio border – both are undergoing slow colonization by Rome's bourgeoisie. **Massa Maríttima** is the area's most historically interesting town, its medieval centre a fine example of Romanesque architecture.

The coast is served by the main Rome–Pisa **rail line** and the old Roman road, the Via Aurelia (SS1). To cut across country, there's a rail link from Grosseto to Siena, and a few **buses** that run inland from Grosseto, Orbetello and Massa Maríttima.

Massa Maríttima

Once the second city of the Sienese Republic and still graced with some of Siena's civic style, **MASSA MARÍTTIMA** is the finest historic town of the Maremma. Named "Massa" by the Romans – their word for a large country estate – it gained its maritime suffix in the Middle Ages, when it became the pre-eminent town of this coastal region. The sea has receded since that time, and is now 20km distant across a silt-filled plain, scarcely visible from the town's hilltop.

Massa, like Volterra to the north, has long been a **mining** town, its silver, copper and other mineral reserves generating wealth since Neolithic times. Designation as a bishopric in the ninth century – in place of declining Populonia – gave it additional impetus, leading to the formation of an independent republic in 1225. In 1310 it produced Europe's first charter for the protection of miners, the *Codice Mineraio*. Sadly for Massa, its mineral riches attracted the

345

rival attentions of Pisa and Siena, the latter finally absorbing the town in 1335. Those hundred years of glory, however, funded the building of its monuments – notably the exquisite **Duomo** – and saw the doubling of the population (a trend reversed after absorption into the Grand Duchy of Tuscany in 1555). Subsequent visitations of plague and malaria, together with a downturn in mining activity, left Massa a virtual ghost town by 1737, its population reduced to just 537. Like other Maremma towns, its recovery only began with the reopening of mines and the draining of coastal marshes in the 1830s.

Massa's oldest sporting event, the **Balestro dei Girifalco** – a medieval crossbow competition between the town's three *contrade* – takes place on the fourth Sunday in March and the second Sunday in August. Through July and August, the **Toscana Foto Festival** has hundreds of award-winning photos exhibited in different venues around the town (Ⓦ www.toscanafotofestival.it).

The Town

A small industrial estate mars the approach to Massa, and blocks of new buildings do little to improve the effect. All this is overshadowed, however, by the medieval splendour of Piazza Garibaldi in the lower, mainly Romanesque, **Città Vecchia**; it's a small, eccentric but exquisite example of Tuscan town planning, with the thirteenth-century Duomo set on broad steps at a dramatically oblique angle to the square.

The upper town, **Città Nuova**, is more Gothic in appearance and was built largely as a residential centre. An immensely steep and picturesque lane, **Via Moncini**, connects the two; for most of the Middle Ages, the lower town was inhabited by a Pisan clan, the Todini, the upper by their Sienese rivals, the Pannochieschi.

The Duomo

The **Duomo** (daily 8am–noon & 3–7pm) is essentially Pisan Romanesque, with a few later additions blending harmoniously with the blind arches and tiny columns (most notably the extraordinary Gothic **campanile**, added in about 1400). The cathedral's dedication is to St Cerbone, the Bishop of Populonia in the sixth century. Although famous for persuading a flock of geese to follow him when he was summoned to Rome on heresy charges, Cerbone is usually depicted with a bear licking his feet, a reference to the beast he tamed when Totila the Hun threw him into a pit full of wild animals. Bas-reliefs in the architrave of the main door show scenes from the saint's life.

Inside, the bare stone walls set off some superb carvings and works of art. The most admired carvings are the thirteenth-century ones by Giraldo da Como, on the huge **baptistery** and also the quadrangular **font**. Almost as arresting are the fifteenth-century tabernacle (under the marble canopy of the baptistery), and some eleventh-century Romanesque carvings close to the entrance featuring powerful and primitive grinning faces, that are in dramatic contrast with the severe, polished Roman sarcophagus to their right. Over the altar is a large Giovanni Pisano altarpiece, and behind it the *Arca di San Cerbone*, an arch of bas-reliefs depicting the life of the saint, carved by Gori di Gregorio in 1324. Take a look, too, at the *Madonna delle Grazie* at the end of the left transept, a damaged but gorgeous Sienese work attributed to Duccio or Simone Martini. Finally, the fine little crypt has a single fresco featuring St Cerbone and St Bernardino.

The Museo Archeologico

The smaller of the two palaces on Piazza Garibaldi, the Palazzo del Podestà, contains the **Museo Archeologico** (Tues–Sun: April–Oct 10am–12.30pm &

3.30–7pm; Nov–March 10am–12.30pm & 3–5pm; €3), where the chief exhibit is one of the finest altarpieces in Tuscany, a *Maestà* painted in 1335 by Ambrogio Lorenzetti. Vivid pink, green and tangerine illuminate the figures of Faith, Hope and Charity below the Madonna, while Cerbone and his geese lurk in the right-hand corner. The museum otherwise houses only a handful of minor paintings and some local archeological finds.

Città Nuova

The town council has organized what it calls a "tourist itinerary", a signposted route that takes you to some very dull spots. The best thing to do is wander up to the **Città Nuova** by Via Moncini, whose tributary alleyways reveal small gardens and good views. At the end of the street, you emerge beneath an impressive but militarily useless arch, the **Arco dei Senesi**, into **Piazza Matteotti**, flanked by a segment of the town wall, and the **Torre del Candeliere** with panoramic views from the top (April–Oct Tues–Sun 10am–1pm & 3–6pm; Nov–March Tues–Sun 11am–1pm & 2.30–4.30pm; €2.50). There's also a small park, ideal for a picnic or siesta. Across the piazza stands the **Museo di Arte e Storia delle Miniere** (April–Oct Tues–Sun 3–5.30pm; €1.50), which houses a puny collection of fossils, mining equipment and archive photographs of local history. Otherwise, the only things to see up here are the church of **Sant'Agostino**, graced with simple cloisters, and the **Antico Frantoio**, Massa's oldest oil mill, in Via Populonia (April–Oct Tues–Sun 11.30am–1pm & 3.30–5.30pm; €1.50).

The Museo della Miniera

Inevitably, given its mining heritage, Massa boasts a **Museo della Miniera** (Mining Museum), housed in an underground air-raid shelter five minutes from Piazza Garibaldi off Via Corridoni (guided tours only; €5; ☎0566.902.289). The mock-up mine has 700m of galleries, and a chronological display of the area's mining methods and equipment.

Practicalities

Intertown **buses** from Siena, Grosseto and Larderello (for Volterra), as well as hourly buses from the Massa–Follonica **train station**, 19km west on the main Pisa–Rome line, stop on Via Corridoni close to Piazza Garibaldi: get off when you see the campanile of the Duomo. The **tourist office** is at Via Todini 3 (Mon–Sat 9.30am–12.30 & 3–6pm; also open Sun April–Sept 10am–1pm, plus 4–7pm June–Sept; ☎0566.902.756, ⊛www.altamaremmaturismo.it) and has plenty of information about *agriturismi* in the area, Massa's Monteregio **DOC wine** and the local **Strada del Vino**.

Despite Massa's popularity, there are surprisingly few **places to stay**. The two central hotels are the three-star *Il Sole*, Via della Libertà 43 (☎0566.901.971, ⊛www.ilsolehotel.it; ❸; closed 10 Jan–10 Feb), and the three-star *La Fenice*, Corso Diaz 63 (☎0566.903.941, ⊛www.lafeniceparkhotel.it; ❷). Two modern hotels lie on the approaches to Massa: the pleasant three-star *Duca del Mare*, Piazza Dante Alighieri 1–2 (☎0566.902.284, ⊛www.ducadelmare.it; ❸; closed mid-Jan to Feb), and the two-star *Girifalco*, Via Massetana Nord 25 (☎0566.902.177, ⊛www.ilgirifalco.com; ❸; closed mid-Nov to mid-April).

Piazza Garibaldi has some pleasant **bars**, though its restaurants are geared towards the tourist trade. **Restaurant** options include the inexpensive and excellent-value *Taverna del Vecchio Borgo*, Via Parenti 12 (☎0566.903.950; closed Mon & Sun eve); the *Trattoria dei Cavalieri* (☎0566.902.093; closed Thurs), with moderate prices, Tuscan cuisine and a garden; *Le Catene*, Piazza Garibaldi 4 (T0566.902.164), which offers a wonderful view of the Duomo; and the highly recommended *Osteria da Tronca*, Vicolo Porte 5 (T0566.901.991; closed Wed), offering inexpensive *osteria*-style fare in an atmospheric stone-wall and vaulted-ceiling setting. *Barbablu* (closed Wed), up on Piazza Matteotti, has excellent *pizza gialla* (a pizza base sprinkled with saffron, scamorza and parmesan cheeses and rocket), and outside tables.

Roccatederighi

Situated 15km east of Massa, **ROCCATEDERIGHI** is difficult to fit into any logical itinerary, but with transport is well worth the twenty-minute journey. Perched on a needle of rock, the village has been literally carved from stone, and offers one of the finest views of the Maremma. Gird yourself for the haul up one of the impossibly steep alleys, to the rock pillars that command the area.

Follónica and southwards

The popular, downmarket resort of **FOLLÓNICA**, which has the nearest train station to Massa Maríttima, marks something of a watershed on the Maremma coast. To the north, the flatlands drag up towards Cécina, but to the south lies a tract of relatively unspoilt, hilly countryside, a landscape similar to that of the Tuscan heartland. Pick of the mixed bag of small resorts along this stretch is **Castiglione della Pescaia**, beyond which lies a magnificent belt of classic Maremma pine forest.

Follónica itself is a large and scruffy town, its untidy beach spoilt by high-rise buildings and, at the far southern end, by factory-outlet pipes. It's very much a family resort, packed out in summer; the big, colourful Friday **market** is about the only real attraction. The **train station** is at the top of Via Matteotti, which leads straight down to the sea. If you're passing through and want an hour's sun and sea, aim for the best part of the **beach** along the stands of pines to the south, before the pipes: follow the main road for about 1km from the centre, then strike off through the trees at the garage on the left; you'll spot cars parked on the roadside.

The **tourist office** is at Via Roma 51 (T0566.52.012, Wwww.grosseto .turismo.toscana.it). Of the numerous **hotels** – most on or near the sea-front – good choices are the two-star *Miramare*, Lungomare Italia 84 (T & F0566.41.521; ❷; April–Oct), and *Orchidea*, Via Italia 41 (T0566.40.334; ❷). There are two seafront **campsites**: *Tahiti*, Viale Italia 320 (T0566.260.255, Wwww.campeggiotahiti.it; mid-May to Sept), is not as nicely situated as *Pineta del Golfo*, Via delle Collachie 2 (T & F0566.53.369; end April to mid-Sept), at the southern edge of town off the main SS322. There are plenty of modest **restaurants**; Follónica's finest gastronomic experience is at the expensive *Leonardo Capelli*, Piazza XXV Aprile 33 (T0566.57.360; closed Mon).

Scarlino and Tirli

SCARLINO is invitingly situated on a steep, wooded hillside 9km east of Follónica, beyond a huge, red-striped chimney that does its best to wreck the view. The medieval village is attractive, if unexceptional, while the hills behind are dotted with fragments of castles and monasteries. It has a very friendly restaurant-pizzeria, *La Vecchia Locanda*, Piazza Garibaldi 7 (T0566.372.99, Wwww .vecchialocanda.it; closed Wed), specializing in mushrooms and truffles.

Farther south by minor roads through the hills is **TIRLI**, where – as in other local villages – they venerate the hermit St Guglielmo, renowned for slaying a dragon, a "rib" of which is held in the village church. There are walks into the woods behind the village, one to the ruins of **Malavalle** monastery – scene of the slaying – and to the miraculous spring of **Sant' Anna**, a point of pilgrimage on July 24. Guglielmo's feast day is the first Sunday in May, an excuse for a *festa* which involves the saint's old drum and some "miracle herbs".

Punta Ala and Le Rocchette

Unless you're feeling particularly flush, there's not a lot of point in making the detour to **PUNTA ALA**, a ritzy, purpose-built resort on the southern spur of the Gulf of Follónica. Beautifully situated below a castle-topped headland, it's dominated by its millionaires' marina. All but a couple of the **hotels** are four-star, as are the **campsites**, most of which are at Capo Civinini, north of the resort where the lane from the main road meets the coast. The cheapest place to stay is the three-star *Punta Ala*, Via del Pozzino 5 (T & F 0564.922.636; ❹): prices drop considerably out of season. The most acclaimed (and expensive) restaurant is in the plush four-star *Gallia Palace Hotel*, Via delle Sughere (T 0564.922.022, W www.galliapalace.it; ❾).

The minor road marked on the TCI road map, between Punta Ala and **LE ROCCHETTE** to the south, is little more than a footpath: car access is from the main SS322. There's a handful of bars close to a good beach, whose tiny approach lane is chaotic in high summer. With transport, it could be a convenient point to camp, though the **campsites** have little free space in August. Try the 300-pitch *Rocchette* (T 0564.941.213, W www.rocchette.com; March–Oct), the smaller *Baia Azzurra* (T 0564.941.092, W www.baiaazzurra.it; April–Oct) or the 350-pitch *Santa Pomata* (T 0564.941.037, W www.campingsantapomata.it; April–Oct).

Castiglione della Pescaia

Set among low, wooded hills that are a welcome break from the flat around Grosseto, **CASTIGLIONE DELLA PESCAIA** still affects the air of a fishing village. It does admittedly have a marina and tourist centre, but lacks Punta Ala's exclusivity, and of all the Maremma resorts, this is where you're most likely to have a good time. The bars are fun, the beach is okay, and the walled **old town** on the hill – believed to have been an Etruscan port – is a charming spot to wander, with great views from the castle. The harbourfront fish **market**, in the morning and late afternoon, is worth checking out if you're self-catering.

There's a **tourist office** in Piazza Garibaldi (Mon–Fri 9am–1pm & 2–6pm, Sat 9am–5pm; T 0564.933.678, W www.lamaremma.info). The best-sited **hotels** are on the main road north, an area still blessed with stands of umbrella pines. The modern three-star *Miramare*, Via Vittorio Veneto 35, overlooks the sea (T 0564.933.524, E miramare@tin.it; ❸); two-star *Rossella,* Via Fratelli Bandiera 18 (T 0564.933.832, W www.albergorossella.it; €75 half-board), also has sea views. The best of the seven local **campsites** are on the road towards Grosseto, the pick being *Etruria* (T 0564.933.483, W www.campeggioetruria .net; May–Sept), about 1km south. There are a lot of cheap **restaurants** and pizzerias: the *Miramare* is renowned for its innovative but expensive fish restaurant, or try the excellent and moderately priced *Il Corallo*, Via Nazario Sauro 1 (T 0564.933.668; closed Tues).

About 2km east of Castiglione, at the entrance to the Diaccia Botrona nature reserve, is the **Museo Multimediale della Casa Rossa Xiemenes** (Tues–Sun

4–10pm; €5). Built in 1765, this "Red House" has been restored and converted into a high-tech observation point over the reserve, which is one of the most important wetland areas in Italy. The idea is that visitors can observe the flora and fauna via three strategically positioned webcams, without disturbing the ecosystem.

South to Marina di Grosseto

The road south from Castiglione runs through a stunning woodland of **umbrella pines** (*pineta*), a small section of which is administered as a nature reserve by the World Wide Fund for Nature and has restricted access. The rest of the woodland – about twelve square kilometres in all – is accessible on foot, and the thing to do is to leave your car on the roadside, and walk down to the superb beaches via one of the many tracks through the trees. A **bus** service between Grosseto and Castiglione stops en route.

At first glance **MARINA DI GROSSETO** looks a dreadful place, with its gridiron streets and scattering of big, brand-new houses. As Maremma resorts go, however, it's surprisingly upbeat, and the clean, broad **beach** is backed by low-key bars and restaurants. Trees shade the open-plan residential district, giving it a touch of style.

You could get a bus out here from Grosseto for the day, though with a car or bike you'd be better off heading to the superior beaches at Marina di Alberese. The **tourist office** is on Via Grossetana (summer daily 9am–12.30pm & 4–7.30pm; winter Mon–Fri 9am–12.30pm; ☎0564.34.449, ⓦwww.prolocomarinadigrosseto .it). There is at least no shortage of **accommodation** in Marina's purpose-built modern hotels, ranging from the *Tre Stelle*, Via dei Platani 15 (☎0564.34.538, ⓦwww.marinadigrosseto.it/trestelle; ❸), to the three-star *Lola Piccolo*, Via XXIV 39 Maggio (☎0564.34.402, ℉0564.34.011; ❸). **Campsites** are plentiful; the more enticing are strung out on the main road north through the *pineta*. Most convenient is the three-star *Rosmarina*, Via delle Colonie 37 (☎0564.36.319, ⓦwww.campingrosmarina.it; May–Sept), 1km north; it also has hotel accommodation (☎0564.34.408, ⓦwww.rosmarina.it; ❹). About 2km south at Principina a Mare is the huge campsite *Principina*, Via del Dentice 10 (☎0564.31.424, ℉0564.31.414; April–Oct).

Grosseto

Travelling by train, the chances are that you'll pass the provincial capital, **GROSSETO**, with no more than a glance, but by bus or car you'll be forced into the heart of its unappealing centre. Ringed by a factory-ridden plain, and composed mainly of characterless condominiums, this commercial metropolis was raised from the ruins of heavy bombing and now serves principally as a functional and administrative centre. Most **trains** on the main Rome–Pisa line stop at Grosseto, where you can change for Siena, or for *locale* connections to Orbetello, Cécina (for Volterra) and Follónica (for Massa Maríttima). Timetabling often leaves about an hour or so between connections – which is about all the time you need for the **old centre**, contained within a largely intact hexagon of walls commissioned by Cosimo I, after the Florentines wrested control of the city from the Sienese.

In August, Grosseto hosts one of the largest environmental festivals in Europe, the **Festambiente** (ⓦwww.festambiente.it), which draws crowds from all over Italy for three weeks of concerts, cinema, eco-markets, seminars and organic food. Also in August (on the 10th) is the **Festa di San Lorenzo**, which features a group of *butteri* leading an ox-drawn cart bearing a statue of St Lawrence, patron saint of Grosseto.

The Town

To reach the old centre, walk up from the station to join Via Roma, a road interrupted by an over-the-top post office and bleak piazza, both monuments to Fascist architectural endeavour. The best of what survives in Grosseto is on **Piazza Dante**, where a quirky statue shows Leopoldo II protecting Mother Maremma and crushing the serpent malaria under his foot. The **Duomo** was started in 1294, but there's virtually nothing left to suggest antiquity: the white and pink marble facade is a product of the nineteenth century, while the interior has suffered repeated and ill-advised modifications.

The best pieces from the Duomo have been transferred to the **Museo Archeologico** at nearby Piazza Baccarini (March & April Tues–Sun 9am–1pm & 4–6pm; May–Oct Tues–Sun 10am–1pm & 5–8pm; Nov–Feb Tues–Fri 9am–1pm, Sat & Sun 9am–1pm & 4–6pm; free). The upper-floor **Pinacoteca** has a handful of good Sienese paintings, notably Sassetta's *Madonna of the Cherries*, and a *Madonna and Child* attributed to Simone Martini. Most of the archeological finds are from the Etruscan settlements at Vetulonia and Rusellae, neatly arranged and well-labelled, but not likely to set the pulse racing.

The town's only other significant work is an early Crucifix by Duccio in **San Francesco**, just north of the museum, also home to a few patches of fresco. Look out for the cloisters alongside the church, distinguished by a well called the *Pozzo della Bufala* (Well of the Buffalo). From San Francesco you can walk round the **walls** (40min), one of the more rewarding things Grosseto has to offer. Public gardens fill the spaces in the corner turrets, apart from one, which retains some Florentine fortifications.

Practicalities

Grosseto's **tourist office** is inconveniently far from the town centre; head north from the station, turn left at Via Abruzzi then right onto Via Monterosa 206, and it's within the concrete building on the left-hand side at no. 206 (Mon–Fri 8.30am–12.30pm & 3–6pm, Sat 8.30am–12.30pm; ☎0564.462.611). The **market** is on Thursday and draws people from all over the province.

There's little reason to stay overnight, but in emergencies there are plenty of reasonable **hotels**. Central options include the one-star *Appennino*, Viale Mameli 1 (☎0564.23.009, ℗0564.23.292; ❶), and the three-star *Mulinacci*, Via Mazzini 78 (☎ & ℗0564.28.419, ℮pmulinacci@libero.it; ❸). There are several reputable **restaurants** to choose from, including the moderately priced *Buca di San Lorenzo*, Via Manetti 1 (☎0564.25.142; closed Sun & Mon), and *Il Canto del Gallo*, Via Mazzini 29 (☎0564.414.589; open eves daily, lunchtimes vary). For an inexpensive plate of cheese and cold meats try the *Vineria da Romolo*, Via Vinzaglio 3 (☎0564.27.551; closed Tues).

Rusellae and Vetulonia

Etruscan enthusiasts might want to visit **Rusellae** and **Vetulonia**, two ancient sites north of Grosseto. To reach either, you really need your own transport. For **RUSELLAE**, the nearer of the sites, take the SS223 Siena road for 10km and watch for the signpost to the ruins on the plateau above – *don't* take the turn for modern **Roselle** about 1km earlier. The track leads to a small car park, with the site about five minutes away on foot (daily 9am–dusk; €4). One of the twelve towns of the Etruscan federation, Rusellae rose above the lake and marshy ground now occupied by Grosseto, and survived the arrival of the Romans. By the fifth century, however, it had all but been abandoned, eclipsed by the rise of Grosseto. Most of the finds are in Grosseto's museum, and all that's visible are the foundations of some buildings, scattered necropolises, and the outlines of a Roman amphitheatre. The tombs are perhaps more interesting than those at Vetulonia, but unfortunately are closed.

About 20km north of Grosseto off the SS1 Follónica road, **VETULONIA** is a more rewarding destination. This ancient city was another member of the Etruscan federation and survived through to the Middle Ages, though Massa Maríttima had long taken over its pivotal function. It was probably destroyed during a revolt against the Pisans in the fourteenth century; blocks from its buildings are now incorporated into the village above the ruins, which stand at the road junction for Buriano to the south. Little of genuine Etruscan vintage remains apart from a couple of big **tombs**, the Tomba della Pietrera and the Tomba del Diavolino (daily 8am–dusk; free), though scholars claim to have unearthed an Etruscan brothel, complete with lewd graffiti apparently left by the women who staffed it. Many of the finds can be seen in the **Museo Civico Archeologico "Isidoro Falchi"**, Piazza Vetluna 1 (daily: summer 10am–2pm & 4–8pm; winter 10am–4pm; €4). Perhaps the best reason for a visit to the area, though, is the fine, inexpensive **restaurant**, *Taverna Etrusca*, Via Piazza Stefani 12 (℡0564.949.601, ⓦwww.tavernaetrusca.it; closed Mon), in the main square of modern Vetulonia, with a handful of rooms next door (℡0564.949.802; ❷).

Monti dell'Uccellina

The hills and coastline of the **MONTI DELL'UCCELLINA** are protected as the **Parco Naturale Regionale della Maremma**, set to be upgraded to a Parco Nazionale, recognition for an area claimed to be the last virgin coastal landscape on the Italian peninsula. The "Mountains of the Little Bird" take their name from the number of birds that use these hills as a stepping-stone between Europe and North Africa.

The heart of the park is a hump of hills that rises suddenly from the plain, about 12km south of Grosseto. A breathtaking piece of countryside that combines cliffs, coastal marsh, *macchia*, forest-covered hills, pristine beaches and some of the most beautiful stands of **umbrella pines** in the country, it is a microcosm of all that's best in the Maremma – devoid of the bars, marinas, hotels, roads and half-finished houses that have destroyed much of the Italian littoral. Kept remote for centuries by malaria and impassable swamp, it's now preserved through the determination of its owners to keep the region sacrosanct. The result is an area that rewards the casual walker, birdwatcher, botanist, or anyone simply in search of a stretch of unspoilt sand.

Park practicalities

There is no public road access into the park (daily: July–Sept 7.30am–dusk; rest of year 9am–dusk): all drivers should park near the reserve headquarters in the main square at **ALBERESE**. Hourly **buses** (#15, #16 & #17) run there from Grosseto station, and there's one daily **train** (in the morning) to Alberese station, 4km from the village.

△ Umbrella pines lining the road to Alberese

Alberese's park headquarters and **visitors' centre**, in Via del Fante (April–Sept daily 8am–3.30pm; ☎0564.407.098, ⓦwww.parks.it), has details of **walks** – both guided and self-guided – and can take bookings for a three-hour night walking tour. We've detailed the pick of the marked trails below. The centre can also provide information on renting bikes and canoes.

Admission to the park secures you a basic map and a place on an hourly bus (€1), which runs 10km into the hills, drops you at the trailhead **Pratini** (really just a field) and leaves you to your own devices. It's about a twenty-minute stroll from Pratini to the beach. Energetic types might walk all the way from Alberese; if you want to see the wildlife at dusk (the best time) you'll have to walk back anyway, as the last bus back from Pratini departs at 5.30pm in summer, earlier in winter. You can buy bus tickets for the return journey from Alberese to Grosseto at *Bar Il Parco*, just behind the visitors' centre.

Walks in the Uccellina

Once off the bus from Alberese at Pratini, most people rush headlong along the *Strada degli Olivi* for the **beach**, an idyllic curving bay backed by cliffs and wooded hills; the obvious stretch is to the left, though you can trudge the beach for miles to the right, round the huge *pineta* towards the mouth of the Ombrone, Tuscany's second-longest river. Alternatively, you could choose one of the **marked trails** that crisscross each other within the park; there are more starting from Talamone (see p.355), and also several shorter trails, if you're just looking for a quick stroll.

The best of the marked routes is the circular **Trail A1** (*San Rabano*; 6km; 5hr; guided walks in summer at 8am), which starts from Pratini. The track climbs quickly to the Uccellina's main ridge (417m), with views to the coast and to Monte Amiata in the interior, reaching the abbey of San Rabano after about

Flora and fauna in the Uccellina

Even if you're not looking out for it, you'd have to be unlucky not to see any interesting wildlife in the protected environment of the Uccellina. An extraordinary range of species thrive here, in what is effectively a compendium of Mediterranean coastal **habitats** – wooded hills, olive groves, pastures, marshland, *pineta*, primary and secondary *macchia*, dunes, retro-dunal areas, estuary and mudflats.

The Ombrone estuary is the key target of serious **birdwatchers** during the spring and autumn migratory cycles, when a varied assortment of waders, ducks, herons and egrets can be seen. Rarities like ospreys, bee-eaters, flamingoes and even falcons and short-toed eagles can be spotted in the rockier hinterland, and you're almost guaranteed the sight of herons wheeling away from the canals, perhaps with hoopoes, shrikes, kingfishers, and the rare, brightly coloured black-winged stilt.

Other species are most likely to be encountered towards dusk, with **roe-deer** prevalent in the hills. The famous **wild boar** is an often audible inhabitant of the scrub and pine forest; an indigenous Maremma breed, it's a smaller specimen than other Italian boar, most of which are descended from bulky, Eastern European stock. The crested **porcupine**, introduced by the Romans, is also fairly common (Italy is the only place it's found outside Africa), as are badgers and foxes; it is hoped that the increasingly rare **otter** will flourish here too. In the cultivated land to the north and on the flat fringes of the estuary you'll see the semi-wild **horses** for which the Maremma is famous.

Tracking down **flora** is more a job for the specialist, though the pines and cork oaks are unmissable, as are the huge banks of rosemary bushes, purple with flowers in the late summer. The dwarf pine, Italy's only indigenous pine, has its northernmost natural limit in the park, and numerous floral rarities pepper the park's dunes, *macchia* and marshes.

ninety minutes. Built in the eleventh century and abandoned five hundred years later, the church is now an ivy-covered ruin, with stone carvings littering the grass. The path then drops right, returning below the ridge to the *Strada degli Olivi* through evergreen woods.

Trail A2 (*Le Torri*; 5km; 3hr; guided walks in summer at 9am & 4pm; tours in English every Fri 4.30pm) starts nearer the beach and connects some of the medieval watchtowers built by the Spanish, who, with the Sienese, were the only people to bother with the area, using it as a source of cork and charcoal. Taking in several coastal habitats, it offers an extraordinary view over the umbrella pines (*Pinus pinea*) on the sand bar and dunes below. These are the park's crowning glory and one of the most memorable natural sights in Tuscany – a vast canopy of emerald green that stretches almost as far as the eye can see. It's well worth dropping down from the tower to explore the woods, where you could roam for hours, restricted only by the areas of marsh at their fringes. Many of these pines were planted (the domestic variety to be harvested for their pine nuts, the maritime ones to consolidate the dunes on the estuary).

The level **Trail A3** (*Le Grotte*; 8km; 4hr) takes in a long stretch of the woods and the canals that divide the park; although it's one of the less rewarding walks, it is quite remote and offers good chances to see wildlife. It starts near no. 2 and its ultimate destination is a group of caves, one of which (*La Grotta della Fabbrica*) has yielded some of the oldest human remains found in Italy.

Trail A4 (*Cala di Forno*; 12km; 6hr) is the longest, most varied, and least used of the trails, taking in hill, coast and cliff scenery, and reaching the large Cala di Forno headland that dominates the bay to the south. The return takes you along the dunes and a superb stretch of beach at Portovecchio.

Marina di Alberese

Although located within the park, entry restrictions do not apply to **MARINA DI ALBERESE**, whose **beach** – though not as superb as that in the park proper – rates as one of the best in Tuscany. It's open all year, but there's a barrier at Spergolaia, which is closed when pressure of numbers becomes too great. You need to buy a **ticket** in advance at Piazza del Combattente in Alberese (full day €4.20, half-day €2.60). Campers, caravans and trailers are excluded, but in practice no one seems to take much notice. There's nowhere to stay and camping is prohibited.

The arrow-straight access road is a pleasure in itself, shaded by an avenue of pines, and flanked by hills, corrals of horses and fields of white oxen. Towards the sea it enters a dense *pineta*, and ends with a car park. Except for a mobile bar and pleasant picnic area, there's no other development. The pines come right down to the beach, and in places into the sea itself, their smooth, bleached trunks creating the feel of a tropical island. The Italians, gregarious as ever, stick to the area at the end of the road, so you don't have to walk far to find solitude. The sand is clean, the sea shallow and perfect for swimming – and it's all rounded off by beautiful views to the Argentario, Giglio and the tree-covered backdrop of the Uccellina.

Talamone

At the southern tip of the Uccellina, and just outside the park's confines, **TALAMONE** is a fishing village and discreet summer resort. Save for a yacht-filled marina, most of its old charm remains intact. The Sienese – who never had a proper outlet to the sea – once planned to turn its hole-in-the-wall harbour into a port to rival Pisa's, but clogging weed doomed the project to failure (in the *Inferno*, Dante used this as a metaphor for pointless enterprise). The town's greatest moment came in 1860, when Garibaldi and the Thousand stopped here for three days on their way to Sicily. Talamone's sixteenth-century Spanish castle is closed to the public.

Two **walking trails** (closed 1–4pm) lead off into the hills from Talamone, making this a good base for exploring the southern edge of the park. To reach the trailhead at Caprarecce, turn right just before Talamone and continue up a dirt track for about 1km; here you'll also find a **visitors' centre** (April–Sept daily 8am–1pm). Admission to tackle these self-guided walks is the standard €6. **Trail T1** (2.5km; 1hr 30min) is simply a shorter version of **trail T2** (4km; 3hr); both start from Podere Caprarecce and head up through Mediterranean scrub to the Punta del Corvo, from where you can admire spectacular views of the park's southernmost coastline and the Monte Argentario beyond. The trails loop back to the starting-point through holm-oak woodland.

Talamone's summer-only **tourist office** at Piazzale del Porto (May–Sept Mon–Sat 9am–1pm & 3–7pm; ☎0564.887.410) can point you in the direction of the badly signposted **Acquario della Laguna di Orbetello** (July & Aug daily 5.30–11.30pm; April–June & Sept Tues–Sun 9.30am–12.30pm & 4–7pm; Oct–March Tues–Sun 9am–12.30pm & 3–5.30pm; €2.55). You can **rent boats** from the port area for around €50 per day, excluding fuel.

Talamone has three **hotels**: the central *Telamonio*, Piazza Garibaldi 4 (☎0564.887.008, ⓦwww.hoteliltelamonio.com; ❹); the three-star *Capo d'Uomo*, Via Cala di Forno 7 (☎0564.887.077, ⓦwww.hotelcapoduomo.com; ❹), with sea views; and *Baia di Talamone*, Via della Marina 23 (☎0564.887.310, ⓔhotelbaia@tiscalinet.it; ❹). There's also a **campsite**, *Talamone International Camping* (☎0564.887.026, ⓕ0564.887.170; April–Sept). Among the **res-**

taurants, try the central, popular and moderately priced *La Buca*, Via Porta Garibaldi (☎0564.887.067; closed Mon), or the expensive *Da Flavia*, Piazza IV Novembre (☎0564.887.091; closed Tues), known for its fish and seafood.

Scansano and Magliano

The settlements of **Magliano** and **Scansano** offer one of the Maremma's many rewarding inland diversions. If you're spending any time in the region, Scansano is worth considering as an alternative base to Grosseto, and even if you're just passing through, the enclosing walls of Magliano are a sight not to be missed. The landscape here is more inviting than most of the coast, with vineyards and woods of sweet chestnut reminiscent of Chianti – as well as excellent vistas of the Uccellina. Both villages are somewhat off the beaten track, with limited bus service from Grosseto; a car is thus a distinct advantage, allowing you to visit both on a cross-country route towards Monte Amiata.

Scansano

About 25km southeast of Grosseto on the SS322, **SCANSANO** is a cramped little hill-village with fine, clear views to the ridges of the Uccellina. It is sited 500m above sea level, on a spur that pushes into an impressive wooded gorge; the end of the spur is capped in picturesque style by the bulk of the parish church. The main road climbs into **Piazza Garibaldi**, occupied by a stern statue of the eponymous hero, several tiny *trattorie* and the one-star **hotel**, *La Posta*, Piazza Garibaldi (☎0564.507.189; ❶). There's quieter but more upmarket accommodation in the **old town**, entered through the arch off Piazza Garibaldi, and little more than a single street that runs the length of the spur. The mid-price option here is the two-star *Magini*, Via XX Settembre 64 (☎ & ℱ0564.507.181; ❷). Alternatively, 3km out of town at Castagneta, on the SS322 to Manciano, there's the *Antico Casale* (☎0564.507.219, ⓦwww .anticocasalediscansano.com; ❸), but if you're planning to stay longer in the area you might consider one of the many *agriturismo* options (☎0564.23.680, ⓦwww .agriturismoinmaremma.com), for which you'll need to book in advance.

The Scansano area produces a fine DOC wine, **Morellino di Scansano** (ⓦwww.cantinadelmorellino.it) which, like the better-known Brunello di Montalcino, is made entirely from Sangiovese grapes. You can find out more about the Morellino grape and its wine at the **Museo della Vite e del Vino**, Piazza Pretorio 4 (April–Oct Tues–Sun 10am–1pm & 4–7pm; Nov–March Fri–Sun 10am–1pm & 3–6pm; free), which doubles as the town's **Museo Archeologico**. To combine wine-tasting with a **meal**, try the excellent *Ristorante/Enoteca la Cantina*, Via della Botte 1 (☎0564.507.605; closed Tues). This is also one of the very few restaurants in Tuscany that offers a selection of **olive oils** to taste with your food. For excellent-value Tuscan cuisine head for the friendly *Il Rifrullo*, Piazza Garibaldi (☎0564.507.183; closed Thurs), with outdoor tables in summer.

Magliano in Toscana

South of Scansano the road passes through the hamlet of Pereta – where a single huge tower crowns a fortified *borgo* and a couple of streets – before reaching **MAGLIANO IN TOSCANA**, descendant of the Etruscan town of Heba. The place today is essentially a village, its most remarkable feature an almost completely intact circle of **walls**, those on the south side dating from the thirteenth century, the rest a fifteenth-century legacy of the Sienese. The bastions are so impressive from a distance that they draw you towards the town, through the ugly estate that suddenly appears round a bend in the road. Close up, the village is a strange, crumbling mixture of old and new, with concrete houses squeezed in alongside medieval dwellings. The main **church**, in Corso Garibaldi, is a Baroque mess, but retains some well-preserved frescoes from the original building. Close by are the tiny Piazza del Popolo and the abandoned **Palazzo dei Priori**, built by the Sienese. The ghost-town atmosphere doesn't invite further exploration, but you should carry on to the end of the main street, where an arch in the walls frames a view over classic Tuscan countryside.

A short hike away are the ruins of **San Bruzio**, 2km south on the road to Marsiliana. A single, bleached white stump of a tower is all that remains of this twelfth-century abbey, but it's a pleasant place, set in a large olive grove. Local legend suggests it was built on the site of a pagan temple and, more salaciously, that it was connected by a tunnel to the now-vanished nunnery of Sant'Anna.

Magliano has a single one-star **hotel**, *I Butteri*,Via Provinciale 8 (☎0564.589.824; ❶), and also a bed-and-breakfast establishment, *Locanda delle Mura*, Piazza Marconi, 5 (☎0564.593.057, ⓦwww.locandadellemura.it; ❹), with only five rooms, a lovely garden and a small cosy restaurant. There are several moderately priced **restaurants**, including *Sandra,* Corso Garibaldi 20 (☎0564.592.196; closed Mon), *Antica Aurora*, Chiasso Lavagnini 12 (☎0564.592.030; closed Wed) and *Ristorante Da Guido*,Via Roma 18 (☎0564.592.447; closed Tues).

Orbetello and its lagoon

In the southwest corner of Tuscany, some 35km south of Grosseto and just before the Lazio border, **ORBETELLO** is principally distinguished by its strange location on a narrow isthmus in the middle of the **Laguna di Orbetello**. Little in the place excites real attention, but it has become something of a resort, thanks to its being the gateway to the dramatic rocky outcrop of **Monte Argentario**; on summer weekends, it becomes a bottleneck, as cars full of tourists pile in to Porto Ercole and Porto San Stefano, the Argentario's supposedly chic resorts. As well as seafront attractions, the Orbetello area offers much to naturalists, its lagoon boasting a **nature reserve** superb for birdwatching.

Long ago, Monte Argentario was an island. Over several thousand years, inshore currents built up two narrow sand spits, or **tomboli**, between the mountains and the mainland, creating a lagoon between them. The ancient settlement of Orbetello occupied a peninsula sticking out into the lagoon; then the Romans built a causeway to link Orbetello to the Argentario, forming a third spit of land and dividing the lagoon in two.

The Town
Orbetello is a pleasant, unassuming place, graced with palm trees, the pastel-coloured remnants of its Spanish walls, and a main street – the **Corso Italia** – thronged each evening with a particularly vigorous *passeggiata*. It was probably Etruria's leading port, though little evidence of its ancient past remains except for a few blocks of Etruscan wall underwater near the causeway. The Byzantines took advantage of its easily defended position, holding out longer here than anywhere else on the Tyrrhenian coast. Thereafter the papacy gained control, and did not relinquish it until 1559, when the Spanish established a military *Presidio* with Orbetello as its capital. The town's last claim to fame was as the

△ Orbetello

headquarters of Mussolini's seaplane squadrons; the surviving aircraft hangar is one of Tuscany's more bizarre architectural attractions.

The Spanish **fortifications** are the town's conspicuous feature, and a fine example of military architecture. The elegant arsenal, **Polveriera de Guzman**, houses a small archeological museum. Nearby, the **Duomo** in Piazza della Repubblica appears promising with its lovely Gothic facade, only to disappoint with a grim Baroque interior. Orbetello's lively **street market** is held on Saturdays.

The Laguna di Orbetello

Orbetello's **lagoon** offers exceptional **birdwatching**, with confirmed sightings of 200 of Italy's estimated 450 species. One reason for the variety is the relative lack of avian refuge on Italy's west coast. Another is the lagoon's modest depth (only 1m), which means an accessible mulch of fish and assorted food; there's also a variety of marsh, *macchia*, dune and reed habitats for nest-building. Even rare species are frequently sighted, and many of them are known to breed in the area. Notable are the stone curlew, osprey, black-winged stilt, bee-eater, Montagu's harrier, and – most importantly – the black-winged stilt, otherwise known only to breed in Sardinia and the Po delta. Little egrets, terns, storks and herons arrive in large numbers, glossy ibis and cranes are regular visitors, and it's not unknown for pink flamingoes to stay for the summer. Evening is the best time around the lagoon: not only is the wildlife most visible then, but the sunsets over the water and the mountains of the Argentario are fabulous.

It's possible to see wildlife from almost any point on the lagoon. In the northernmost corner, near the town of **Albinia**, the World Wide Fund for Nature has established a small **nature reserve**, L'Oasi di Protezione della Laguna di Orbetello (guided tours in Italian Sept–April Sun & Thurs 10am & 2.30pm; €5). The entrance to the reserve is off the main road 2km south of Albinia, marked by a small panda sign; the warden can sometimes be contacted at the building at the end of the track, or contact the tourist office in Orbetello for further information.

If time is tight, exploring the southern **Tombolo di Feniglia** is a good substitute for a tour of the reserve (the northern Tombolo di Giannella is less appealing, with its campsites and driveable road). Tombolo di Feniglia has one of Italy's most beautiful *pinete*, a long sandy dune covered in parasol pines, and is also protected by a small nature reserve, where you can often see roe deer. The road along it is off-limits for cars, though you can walk its whole course, dropping down to the lagoon side for great views, or to the other side for a fine beach. If you continue the walk through Ansedonia, and then along the beach south for about an hour, you'll reach the Lago di Burano.

Practicalities

The **train station** is 4km east at Orbetello Scalo, on the mainland edge of the lagoon, a prominent stop for trains on the Rome–Pisa line. There are connections for Siena, and slow trains to smaller stations to the north and south. Connecting buses run from the station to Orbetello's **bus terminal** just off Piazza della Repubblica; from here there are regular services to Grosseto, Porto Ercole and Porto San Stefano, as well as daily buses to Capálbio and Pitigliano.

The **tourist office** in Piazza della Repubblica (daily 9am–noon & 4–7pm; ☎0564.860.447, ⓦwww.proloco-orbetello.it) is a useful source of information on accommodation in Orbetello and the mainland hamlets of Albinia and Ansedonia (both served by local buses). Orbetello is the nicest option, and has two one-star **hotels**, the central *Piccolo Parigi*, Corso Italia 169 (☎0564.867.233, ⓕ0564.867.211; ❷), and *La Perla*, Via Etruria 2 (☎0564.863.546, ⓕ0564.865.210; ❷). Most of the area's fourteen **campsites** are on and around the lagoon and along the main SS1 Via Aurelia. The most attractive is the all-year *Feniglia* (☎0564.831.090, ⓕ348.304.0100), the only site on the Tombolo di Feniglia. Two more are to be found out on the Tombolo di Giannella: the three-star *Il Veliero* (☎0564.820.201, ⓕ0564.821.198; all year) and the two-star *Comunale Giannella* (☎0564.820.049, ⓦwww.giannellacosta.com; all year), which is the friendlier, if not the smarter, of the two. Albinia also has a couple of sites, and there are four more within 6km, on the SS1 to the west. *Campo Regio* (☎0564.870.163, ⓕ0564.871.572), 4km west, is situated around 200m from the beach and is the only one of these open all year.

Orbetello's best budget **restaurant** is the inexpensive *Pizzeria Gennaro* at Corso Italia 104 (closed Mon). For a moderately priced fish meal try the *Osteria Nochino* just off Piazza della Repubblica in Via Furio Lenzi (☎0564.860.329; eves only).

Monte Argentario

The high, rocky terrain of **Monte Argentario** is as close to wilderness as southern Tuscany comes. The interior is mountainous, reaching 635m at its highest point, **Il Telegrafo**, and the coast is sectioned dramatically into headlands, bays and shingle beaches. Away from the villas of rich Romans, much of the area is still uninhabited scrub and woodland, badly prone to forest fires but still superb walking country. The main centres of **Porto Santo Stefano** and **Porto Ercole** once had a reputation for exclusivity, but these days they're too well known to pander solely to the top end of the market. Prices are manageable, as are the crowds, though you'll probably need to book ahead for peak periods. With your own transport you could follow the touted *gita panoramica* (**scenic drive**) around half the mountain; the other half is currently impassable.

Porto Santo Stefano

PORTO SANTO STEFANO is the more developed of the Argentario resorts, and also the more fashionable – which in Italy is a lot worse than just being popular. Something of the charm which first brought people here still shines through, however, despite the hotels and villas that have all but obliterated the original village. A few fishing boats still cluster in the town's smaller harbour, having relinquished the main port to the marina and its mega-yachts. You'll probably stay only as long as it takes to get a **ferry** to the island of Giglio. Buses run to the port from the train station at Orbetello Scalo, so you can avoid almost any contact with the place at all.

The **tourist office**, Piazzale Sant'Andrea 1 (Mon–Sat: Jan–March 9am–1pm & 2–4pm; April–Dec 9am–1pm & 3–5pm; ☏0564.814.208, ⓦwww.lamaremma .info), has information on affordable accommodation – mainly in private rooms. You'll need to book well ahead for either of the town's cheaper **hotels**: the central *Alfiero*, Via Cuniberti 14 (☏0564.814.067, ⓦwww.hotelalfiero.com; ❷), or the less convenient *Week End*, Via Martiri d'Ungheria 3 (☏0564.812.580, ⓦwww.pensioneweekend.it; ❷). Santo Stefano's finest is the three-star *Belvedere* (☏0564.812.634; ❹), near the beaches at Poggio Calvella, a short way west.

Restaurants are generally swanky and overpriced; back-street *pizzerie* and bar snacks are the best options. If you're going for a blowout, *Da Siro*, Corso Umberto I 102 (☏0564.812.538; closed Mon), has quite a reputation. For a moderately priced meal *La Bussola*, Piazzale Facchinetti (☏0564.814.225; closed Mon), is good for fish, or try *La Formica* (☏0564.814.205), one of the more popular and reasonable fish restaurants at Pozzerella, 1500m east.

Porto Ercole

On the south side of the Argentario, **PORTO ERCOLE** is more intimate than Santo Stefano, with an attractive old quarter and a fishing-village atmosphere. Though founded by the Romans, its chief historical monuments are two Spanish **fortresses** facing each other on opposing sides of the harbour, and a third one above the new town. At the entrance to the old town, a plaque on the stone gate commemorates the painter **Caravaggio**, who in 1610 keeled over with sunstroke on a beach nearby (taken to a local tavern, he soon died of a fever, and was buried in the parish church of Sant'Erasmo).

A couple of good **walks** suggest themselves from the village, the most obvious being along the Tombolo di Feniglia (see p.359). The other is to the top of **Il Telegrafo**, accessible either by road and track from the ridge that runs up from the lighthouse to the south, or on a rough road that leaves the port to the north and then runs west under the main ridge. The way is fairly open, and superb views make the haul worthwhile.

Reasonably priced **hotels** are limited to the one-star *Conchiglia* in Via della Marina (☏0564.833.134; ❷), and the *Marina* in Lungomare A. Doria (☏0564.833.055, ⓦwww.hotelmarina.it; ❹). For private **rooms**, try *Villa Azzurra*, Via Caravaggio 93 (☏0564.833.037, ⓔvillaazzurracamere@libero.it; ❷). The moderately priced waterfront **restaurant** *Gambero Rosso* (☏0564.832.650; closed Wed) serves excellent fish.

Giglio and Giannutri

The largest of the Tuscan islands after Elba, **Giglio**, 15km west of Monte Argentario, is visited by an ever-increasing number of foreign tourists and is so

Ferries to Giglio

The embarkation point for Giglio is **Porto Santo Stefano** (see p.360), served by regular buses direct from the train station at Orbetello Scalo and also from Orbetello town. Both Toremar (℡0564.810.803, ⓦwww.toremar.it) and Maregiglio (℡0564.812.920, ⓦwww.maregiglio.it) operate **ferries** to Giglio Porto (summer almost hourly, winter 3–5 daily; takes 1hr; €7 one-way). It's usually no problem to buy your ticket from a quayside kiosk and board immediately. You should leave your **car** on the mainland; it's expensive to take it onto the island at any time of year, and in summer you need a permit. There are plenty of trustworthy parking companies on the Porto Santo Stefano waterfront that charge roughly €10 per day; parking on the street is both unsafe and lays you open to hefty fines.

popular with holidaying Romans that in high season you may find that there's standing-room only on the ferries. Yet it's well worth making the effort to stay on this fabulous island: the rush is fairly short-lived, most visitors are day-trippers, and few of them explore the tracks across the unspoilt interior, a mix of barren rock and reforested upland. The island is rich in fauna such as peregrine falcons, mouflon, kestrels and buzzards, and in wild flowers too: this is the only place outside North Africa to shelter wild mustard, and the sole spot in Tuscany to support the yellow flowers of artemisia.

The island derives its name not from *giglio* (lily), but from the Roman colony Aegilium, in its day a resort for the rich and famous, a function it continued to fulfil throughout most of the Middle Ages. Granite quarries kept the economy buoyant, and Giglio stone was used to construct many medieval churches. Later, pirate incursions took the edge off its appeal, despite the miraculous defensive power of St Mamiliano's right arm, a relic hacked from a sixth-century Sicilian bishop exiled on the island of Montecristo. The limb proved effective when waved at Tunisian pirates in 1799, but less so on other occasions – notably in 1534, when Barbarossa carried off most of the island's population.

Boats dock at the main town **Giglio Porto**, from where there's an excellent bus service to the island's two other main villages, **Giglio Castello** and **Giglio Campese**. You can rent bikes or mopeds inexpensively from Giglio Porto to explore at your own pace. Giglio and the neighbouring islet of **Giannutri** are the southernmost islands of the Parco Nazionale Arcipelago Toscano (see p.328).

Giglio Porto

Small, rock-girdled **GIGLIO PORTO** is the place you're most likely to stay on Giglio, as it boasts eight of the island's thirteen hotels. It has no particular sights, but the view from the ferry is wonderful as the town draws closer, its pale-coloured houses offset by a backdrop of terraced vineyards and framed between two lighthouses – one red, one green. The narrow harbourfront is crammed with a mix of touristy restaurants and boat mechanics, but behind the **Torre del Saraceno**, built by Ferdinand I in 1596, you'll find a tranquil, barely visited little inlet, with the wall of a Roman eel farm visible below the waterline.

As much of the land around rises sheer from the sea, the **beaches** are modest: you'll find one to the north of the port at Punta Aranella, and a couple to the south at Cala delle Canelle and Cala delle Caldane. You can **rent boats** from Giglio Yachting Marine on the port, Via Thaon de Revel 9 (℡0564.809.610). The Blue Scuba Diving Club (ⓦwww.bluescubadiving.com) organizes **scuba** courses and **diving** around Giglio and Giannutri.

There's a **tourist office** on Via Provinciale (☎0564.809.400, ⓦwww
.isoladelgigliouffcioturistico.com), which can provide details of accommodation options – including a fair number of houses around the port that have
rooms to let. In high season, the **hotels** generally offer only full board, and
most are also open only from June to September. The one to go for is the small
three-star *Pardini's Hermitage* in the Cala degli Alberi cove, accessible by boat
or on foot (☎0564.809.034, ⓦwww.finalserv.it/hermitage; ❺; April–Sept).
More modest choices include *La Pergola* in the port's Via Thaon de Revel (☎
& ⒻΦ0564.809.051; ❸), *Demo's*, at the end of the harbour, with lovely top-floor
rooms offering a sea view (☎0564.809.235, ⓦwww.hoteldemos.com; ❺), and
two-star *Da Ruggero*, Via del Saraceno 86 (☎ & ⒻΦ0564.809.121; ❷). The most
visited quayside **restaurants** are *Doria* and *Margherita*, both offering standard
fishy specials; the food at *Demo's* hotel is better and comes with beach views.

The port's big day is August 10, when locals vie with one another to retrieve
a flag tied to the end of a greasy pole over the harbour (the Cuccagna a Mare).
Further frolics ensue later in the day during the Palio Marinaro, a competition
at sea between the port's three districts.

Giglio Castello

GIGLIO CASTELLO, perched at the highest point of the hills, up 6km of
hairpins from the port, was for a long time the island's only settlement and the
sole spot safe from pirate attack. Surprisingly well preserved, its maze of arches
and medieval alleyways is still surrounded by thick walls. Buses stop near a vine-
covered patio **bar** in the large Piazza Gloriosa, also the entrance to the granite
fortress and medieval quarter. The **castle** was begun by the Pisans and completed by the Grand Duchy of Tuscany; rough paths around the walls enable you
to clamber over the rocks for superb views over the island and ruins far below.
For a look at St Mamiliano's miraculous arm, check out the Baroque **church**.
Accommodation is limited to private rooms; *Affittacamere Mario Landini*, Via
Contrada Santa Maria, is one possibility (☎0564.806.074, ⓦwww.camerealgiglio
.vze.com; ❷; open in summer only). *Da Maria* in Via Casamatta is one of the
island's best moderately priced **restaurants** (☎0564.806.062; closed Wed);
Santi, Via Marconi 20 (closed Mon in winter), is another option.

To explore Giglio's interior, follow a minor road that winds from Castello
9km south all along the spine of the ridge to **Punta del Capel Rosso**, the
southernmost tip of the island – a wild and lonely bike-ride or three-hour
hike. Walking from Castello down to either Campese or Porto takes less than
an hour.

Giglio Campese

At the western end of the island road is the growing resort of **GIGLIO
CAMPESE**. It has the island's best **beach**, a fine stretch of sand overlooked by
a Medici tower and curving for 2km from a huge phallic rock which the tourist brochures are too modest to photograph. Around the base of the tower is a
modern, turreted apartment complex with a couple of restaurants, tennis courts
and all manner of watersports facilities – including dive shops with lessons and
gear to rent. The resort has four **hotels**, cheapest of which are *La Lampara*, Via
Provinciale 66 (☎ & ⒻΦ0564.804.022; ❷), and *Giardino delle Palme*, Via della
Torre (☎0564.804.037, ⒺΦlepalme@interfree.it; ❸). Otherwise try the *Da Giovanni*, Via di Mezzo Franco 10 (☎0564.804.010, ⒺΦpinipaola@tiscalinet.it; ❸);
while top of the range with private beach is the three-star *Campese*, Via della
Torre 18 (☎0564.804.003, ⒻΦ0564.804.093; ❹; open only in summer). There's
also a **campsite**, *Baia del Sole* (☎0564.804.036, ⒺΦbaia.delsole@flashnet.it).

Giannutri

The southernmost Tuscan island, **GIANNUTRI**, a rocky half-moon islet 15km south of Giglio, is privately owned, and overnight stays are impossible unless you're a friend of the inhabitants. The few people who come over for the day do so to dive, or to visit the ruins of a **Roman villa** at Cala Maestra. Given the island's physical make-up – flat, and walkable end-to-end in two hours – it's a place for island obsessives only. **Day-trips** (€15) are run by Maregiglio (see box, p.361), with departures from Giglio Porto and, in summer, direct from Porto Santo Stefano.

South of Orbetello

South of Orbetello, most of the terrain is a drab foretaste of the expanses of Lazio, but there are several worthwhile diversions. At **Ansedonia** you can inspect one of Tuscany's few ancient Roman sites, before moving on to the important nature reserve at **Lago di Burano**. Inland **Capálbio** rates as one of the area's loveliest villages, while near **Chiarone**, which has fine beaches, is the **Giardino dei Tarocchi**, a small park of monumental sculptures that's quickly becoming both a tourist attraction and artistic talking point.

Ansedonia and Lago di Burano

ANSEDONIA crouches under a rocky crag at the end of the Tombolo di Feniglia. Peppered with holiday villas, it has a long beach and, on the hilltop above, the remains of **Cosa**, founded by the Romans in 273 BC as a frontier post against the Etruscans. It was one of their most important commercial centres in the area until its population – according to the historian Rutilius – was driven out by an army of mice. Most of the old *municipium* was devastated by the Visigoths in the fourth century, and what survived was sacked by the Sienese in 1330. Recent excavations have exposed enough of the Roman colony to suggest some idea of its former layout.

To reach the **site** (daily 9am–7pm; Oct–April closes 1pm; free), leave Ansedonia on the road east, passing a couple of medieval towers (converted into houses) and the **Tagliata Etrusca**, a series of cuts into the rock believed to have been part of a system to drain the marshland. After about 1km, where the road bends sharp right, there's a signed track to Cosa off to the left. You'll find a ring of **walls** 8m high in places, the remains of a defensive cordon of eighteen towers. There's also the outline of the gridiron street plan, a **forum** (with basilica and senate discernible nearby), two **temples** and some **mosaics** and wall paintings. It's worth climbing to the top of the hill, not only to see the remains of the **acropolis**, but also for fine views across to Giannutri and Monte Argentario. Halfway up the hill is a small **Museo Archeologico** (same hours; €2), housing some of the site's finds. Near the Tagliata Etrusca stands the two-star **hotel** *Vinicio*, Via delle Mimose 86 (℡0564.881.220, ⓔvinicio@ouverture.it; ❷).

Lago di Burano

You can walk to the **Lago di Burano** along the beach from Ansedonia, or catch a slow train from Orbetello to Capálbio Scalo, less than 100m from the water. Technically a lagoon rather than a lake, Burano is a placid stretch of water, shielded from the sea by vegetation-covered dunes. Completing the scenic picture – which is captivating at dusk, with the sun behind Monte Argentario – is a superb and mysterious-looking tower, the **Torre di Burinaccio**.

Though you can walk onto the enclosing beach, access to the lagoon itself is restricted, as Burano is a protected **nature reserve**. Recognized as a wetland habitat of international significance, this and the Orbetello lagoon (see p.358) are together rated as the most important area for birds on Italy's west coast. The lagoon shares many of the species found in Orbetello, and for similar reasons (the lagoon here is also only 1m deep). Notable species include the bluethroat, great spotted cuckoo, great white heron and velvet scoter. The **entrance** to the reserve is on the perimeter road 500m east of the station. **Guided walks** (Sept–April Thurs & Sun 10am & 2.30pm; €5; ☎0564.898.829) follow the nature trail that takes in the dune, woodland and scrub habitats around the lake, stopping at the observation points en route. The *Agrialbergo Capalbio*, Strada della Sugherella 3 (☎0564.898.472, ℻0564.898.763; ❷), is a one-star **hotel** near Capálbio Scalo station; camping is prohibited.

Chiarone and inland

CHIARONE is nothing more than a station and a couple of bars, though its **beaches** – fifteen minutes' walk away – are some of the best and quietest on this part of the coast. The virgin coastal stretch is commonly regarded as enjoying the first unpolluted water north of Rome: 15km of unbroken sand stretch away towards Monte Argentario, with plenty of opportunities for **camping** in the dunes. Things get grubby on-shore as the summer wears on, but the gentle, shelving seabed makes for good swimming, and all it takes for solitude on the sand is a few minutes' walk.

A handful of **trains** to and from Grosseto stop at Chiarone station. There's one **hotel**, *La Palma*, Via del Chiarone 5 (☎0564.890.341, ⓦwww.albergolapalma .com; ❸). At the end of the road to the dunes is the beach **bar**, **restaurant** and **campsite**, *Il Campeggio di Capalbio*, Via Graticciaia (☎0564.890.101, ⓦwww .campingcapalbio.it; mid-April to Sept).

The Giardino dei Tarocchi

By car from Chiarone it's possible to visit one of Italy's oddest and increasingly well-known works of modern art: **Il Giardino dei Tarocchi** (The Tarot Garden; May to mid-Oct daily 2.30–7.30pm; €10.50; ☎0564.895.122, ⓦwww .nikidesaintphalle.com), a huge set of sculptures by Niki de Saint Phalle, who died in 2002 and is most famous for the *Fontaine Stravinsky*, created with her husband Jean Tinguely outside the Pompidou Centre in Paris. The brightly coloured pieces are clearly visible from the Via Aurelia: to reach them it's a five-kilometre drive on the road from Chiarone to Pescia Fiorentina.

Using land donated by friends, the work took almost seventeen years to complete (1979–1996) and the result is a truly staggering sight – a whimsical mix of Gaudí, arcane symbolism and sheer fun that children love, and which inspires bewildered admiration in adults. Each piece represents one of the Tarot's twenty-two major arcana. Plants and fountains form an integral part of the scheme.

Capálbio

Stranded in empty country, the hill-village of **CAPÁLBIO** is virtually unknown to outsiders, though not to Rome's cultural and political elite, many of whom have homes in the locality. Most are attracted by the almost perfectly medieval interior, which at night is a deathly quiet maze of streets straight out of the Middle Ages. Views are superb, and though there's little to see apart from a few frescoes and the Aldobrandeschi fortifications, it definitely warrants a look if you're touring by car; there are also three buses daily from Orbetello. There are several **restaurants** to choose from, including the superb, moderately priced *Trattoria la Torre da Carla*, Via V. Emmanuele 33 (℡0564.896.070; closed Thurs), in the heart of the old town. The two-star **hotel** *La Mimosa* is on Via Torino (℡ & ℱ0564.890.220; ❸), several kilometres out of Capálbio towards the Via Aurelia, while the hotel/residence *Valle del Buttero*, Via Silone 21 (℡0564.896.097, ⓦwww.valledelbuttero.it; ❸) is more central.

Travel details

Trains

Grosseto to: Capálbio (hourly; 35min); Follónica (hourly; 35min; change for Massa Maríttima); Florence (8 daily via Siena; 3–4hr); Orbetello (hourly; 30min); Rome (hourly; 1hr 30min–2hr 30min); Siena (8 daily; 1hr 20min).

Buses

Follónica to: Castiglione (5 daily; 30min); Punta Ala (6 daily; 35min); Scarlino (7 daily; 30min).

Grosseto to: Castiglione della Pescaia (hourly; 45min); Florence (8 daily; 2hr 30min); Massa Maríttima (2 daily; 1hr 15min); Orbetello (3 daily; 1hr); Roccatederighi (2 daily; 1hr 10min); Scansano (4 daily; 1hr 20min); Siena (10 daily; 1hr 35min).
Massa Maríttima to: Follónica (every 45min; 10min); Grosseto (1 daily; 1hr 20min); Piombino (2 daily; 25min); Siena (2 daily; 1hr 40min).
Orbetello to: Capálbio (3 daily; 45min); Grosseto (3 daily; 1hr); Porto Ercole (14 daily; 20min); Porto Santo Stefano (6 daily; 15min).

6

Siena

* **The Campo** Soak up the atmosphere in Siena's scallop-shaped main square. **See p.376**

* **The Palio** Siena's historic, chaotic horse race, run over three frenetic laps of the Campo. **See second colour insert**

* **Museo Civico** Frescoes by Simone Martini, Ambrogio Lorenzetti and many others adorn the medieval salons of the Campo's Palazzo Pubblico. **See p.381**

* **The Duomo** The dazzling, art-filled cathedral features a superb fresco cycle by Pinturicchio in the Libreria Piccolomini. **See p.386**

* **Ospedale di Santa Maria della Scala** Once the city hospital, now a remarkable medieval monument, with frescoed halls and chapels. **See p.391**

* **Museo dell'Opera del Duomo** A treasure-chest of religious art that also gives access to Tuscany's giddiest viewpoint, atop the walls of the Duomo's abandoned new nave. **See p.396**

△ Overview of the Campo, Siena

6

Siena

SIENA is the perfect counterpoint to Florence. Self-contained and still partly rural behind its medieval walls, its attraction lies in its cityscape: a majestic Gothic whole that could be enjoyed without venturing into a single museum. In its great scallop-shaped piazza, **Il Campo**, it has the loveliest of all Italian public squares; in its zebra-striped **Duomo**, a religious focus to match; and the city's whole construction, on three ridges, presents a succession of beautiful vistas over medieval cityscapes to the bucolic Tuscan countryside on all sides. It is also a place of immediate charm: airy, easy-going and pedestrianized – where Florence is cramped, busy and traffic-ridden – and it is startlingly untouristed away from the few centres of day-trip sightseeing. Perhaps most important of all, the city is host to the undisputed giant of Italian festivals, the **Palio**, a bareback horse race around the Campo, whose sheer excitement and unique importance to the life of the community is reason enough to plan your holiday around one of the two race dates – July 2 and August 16.

The contrasts with Florence are extended in Siena's monumental and artistic highlights. The city's Duomo and **Palazzo Pubblico** are two of the purest examples of Italian Gothic, and the finest of the city's paintings – of which many are collected in the Palazzo's **Museo Civico** and the separate **Pinacoteca Nazionale** – are in the same tradition. Other outstanding Sienese painting remained stamped with Byzantine, Romanesque and Gothic influences long after classical humanism had transformed Florence. It is a style characterized by brilliance of colour and decorative detail and an almost exclusive devotion to religious subjects – principally the city's patroness, the Virgin. Its traditions were shaped by a group of artists working in the last half of the thirteenth century and the first half of the fourteenth: Duccio di Buoninsegna, Simone Martini and the brothers Ambrogio and Pietro Lorenzetti. Arguably the greatest of all Siena's paintings belongs to the first of these, a magnificent *Maestà* housed in another of Siena's outstanding galleries, the **Museo dell'Opera del Duomo**. Another supreme work, the fresco cycle of Domenico di Bartolo, an artist working on the cusp of the Renaissance, fills part of **Santa Maria della Scala**, the city's hospital for some eight hundred years, now one of its premier exhibition spaces.

In its sculpture, Siena drew mainly on foreign artists: the Florentines Donatello and Ghiberti worked on the font in the **Baptistery**, while Michelangelo and Nicola and Giovanni Pisano left their mark on the Duomo.

As a provincial capital, Siena has good transport links with some of the finest sights and countryside of Tuscany. The city makes a good base for much of the territory covered in the following two chapters, while to the north, the wine heartland of Chianti (see p.222), extends to Florence, which lies 78km north.

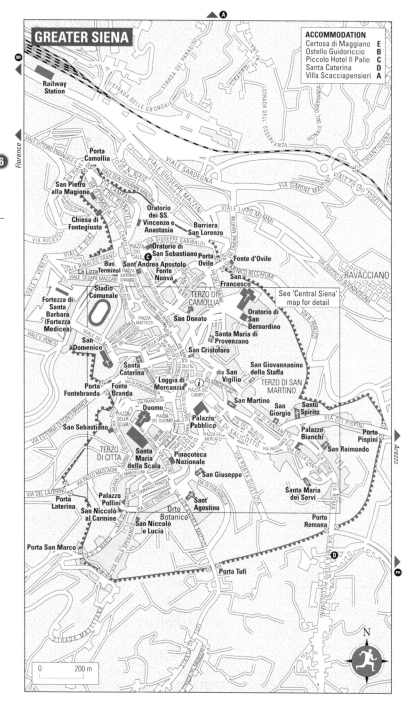

Some history

Though myth attributes its origins to Senius and Acius, sons of Remus (hence the she-wolf emblem of the city), **Siena** was in fact founded by the Etruscans and refounded as a Roman colony – Saena Julia – by Augustus. Over the course of the next millennium it grew to be an independent republic, and in the thirteenth and fourteenth centuries was one of the major cities of Europe. It was almost the size of Paris, controlled most of southern Tuscany and its flourishing wool industry, dominated the trade routes from France to Rome, and maintained Italy's richest banks. The city also developed a highly sophisticated civic life, with its own written constitution and a quasi-democratic council – the *comune*. It was in this great period that the city was shaped, and in which most of its art and monuments are rooted.

This golden era, when the Republic of Siena controlled a great area of central and southern Tuscany, reached an apotheosis with the defeat of a much superior Florentine army at the **Battle of Montaperti** in 1260. Although the result was reversed nine years later, shifting the fulcrum of political power towards Florence, Siena's merchants and middle classes – the so-called *Popolo Grasso* – embarked on an unrivalled urban development; from 1287 to 1355, under the rule of the **Council of Nine**, the city underwrote first the completion of the **Duomo** and then the extraordinary **Campo**, with its exuberant **Palazzo Pubblico**. Sienese bankers, meanwhile, had spread their operations throughout Europe, and with Duccio, Martini and the Lorenzettis, the city was at the forefront of Italian art.

Prosperity and innovation came to an abrupt halt with the **Black Death**, which reached Siena in May 1348. By October, when the disease had run its course, the population had dropped from 100,000 to 30,000. The city was never fully to recover (the population today is around 60,000) and its politics, always factional, moved into a period of intrigue and chaos. Its art, too, became highly conservative, as patrons looked back to the old hierarchical religious images. The chief figures in these war-ridden and anarchic years were the city's two nationally renowned saints, **Caterina** (1347–80) and **Bernardino** (1380–1444), who both exercised enormous influence, amid two further outbreaks of the plague.

As the sixteenth century opened, a period of autocratic rule under the tyrannical Pandolfo Petrucci (the self-styled Il Magnifico) brought a further military victory over Florence, but ended with the city embroiled in ever-expanding intrigues involving the Borgias, the Florentines, the papacy, the French and the empire of **Charles V**. The last proved too big to handle for the Sienese; imperial troops imposed a fortress and garrison, and then, after the Sienese had turned to the French for help to expel them, the imperials laid siege to the city and the surrounding countryside. The effects of the siege (1554–55) proved more terrible even than the Black Death, with the population plummeting from 40,000 to as few as 8000. The republic was over, although a band of loyalists – comprising around 700 families – took refuge at Montalcino and prolonged it there for a while, at least in name.

Two years after the siege, Philip II, Charles's successor, gave up Siena to **Cosimo I**, Florence's Medici overlord, in payment for war services, the city subsequently becoming part of Cosimo's Grand Duchy of Tuscany. This was the death knell. For sixty years the Sienese were forbidden even to operate banks, while control of what was by now an increasingly minor provincial town reverted, under Medici patronage, to the nobles.

Siena's swift decline from republican capital to little more than a market centre explains the city's astonishing state of medieval preservation. Little was built and still less demolished, while allotments and vineyards occupied the spaces

Within the fabric of the medieval city, Siena preserves its ancient division into wards, or **contrade**. These are integral to the competition of the Palio (see second colour insert) and sustain a unique neighbourhood identity, clearly visible as you wander around the streets. Each of the seventeen *contrade* has its own church, social centre and museum, as well as a flag and heraldic **animal motif**, after which most of them take their names. The animals – giraffe, snail, goose, porcupine, and others – can be seen all around the city on wall plaques and are represented in a series of modern fountains near the *contrada* churches or headquarters, in each of the city's three *terzi*:

Aquila – Eagle (Città). Casato di Sotto ☏0577.288.086, ⓦwww.contradadellaquila.it.

Bruco – Caterpillar (Camollia). Via del Comune 44 ☏0577.44.842.

Chiocciola – Snail (Città). Via San Marco 37 ☏0577.45.455, ⓦwww.chiocciola.org.

Civetta – Owl (San Martino). Piazzetta del Castellare ☏0577.285.505.

Drago – Dragon (Camollia). Piazza Matteotti 19 ☏0577.40.575, ⓦwww.contradadeldrago.it.

Giraffa – Giraffe (Camollia). Via delle Vergini 18 ☏0577.287.091, ⓦwww.comune.siena.it/giraffa.

Istrice – Porcupine (Camollia). Via Camollia 87 ☏0577.48.495, ⓦwww.istrice.org.

Leocorno – Unicorn (San Martino). Via di Follonico 15 ☏0577.288.549.

Lupa – She-Wolf (Camollia). Via di Vallerozzi 71/73 ☏0577.270.777.

Nicchio – Shell (San Martino). Via dei Pispini 68 ☏0577.49.600, ⓦwww.nobilecontradadelnicchio.it.

Oca – Goose (Camollia). Vicolo del Tiratoio 11 ☏0577.285.413, ⓦwww.contradadelloca.it.

Onda – Wave (Città). Via Giovanni Dupré 111 ☏0577.48.384, ⓦwww.contradacapitanadellonda.it.

Pantera – Panther (Città). Via San Quirico ☏0577.48.468.

Selva – Forest (Città). Piazzetta della Selva ☏0577.45.093, ⓦwww.contradadellaselva.it.

Tartuca – Turtle (Città). Via Tommaso Pendola 21 ☏0577.49.448, ⓦwww.tartuca.it.

Torre – Tower (San Martino). Via Salicotto 76 ☏0577.222.181, ⓦwww.contradadellatorre.it.

Valdimontone – Ram (San Martino). Via di Valdimonte 6 ☏0577.222.590, ⓦwww.valdimonte.it.

There were once social distinctions between the *contrade*, and although today these are blurred to the point of extinction, allegiance to one's *contrada* – conferred by birth – remains a strong element of social life. After a conventional church baptism, anyone born in a ward division is baptized for a second time in their *contrada* fountain. Subsequently, the *contrada* plays a central role in activities: for kids in the flag-twirling and drumming for the Palio and local *contrada* festivals, for adults in the social clubs – a mix of bar and dining club – and in the attendance of a herald at marriages and funerals. *Contrade* also dispense social assistance to needy members. The respect accorded to the institution of *contrade* is said to have a significant effect on the city's social cohesion. Certainly, for a city of its size, Siena has remarkably low levels of crime and drug usage. Indeed, the only violence tolerated is during the Palio, when *contrada* members may get into fights with their ancient rivals.

For an insight into the workings of the *contrade*, it is worth paying a visit to one of their **museums**, each of which gives pride of place to its displays of Palio trophies. All the museums are open to visitors during the build-up to the Palio and at other times by appointment; ask the tourist office to phone. Each *contrada* also has its own **annual celebration**, accompanied by parades and feasts. And at almost any time of year, you'll see groups practising flag-waving and drum-rolling in the streets.

between the ancient quarters, as they do today. This near-pristine state also reflects its escaping war damage in 1944 and 1945 (unlike nearby Poggibonsi and other Tuscan towns); Siena was taken, unopposed, by the French Expeditionary Force on July 3, 1944.

Since the last war, however, Siena has again become prosperous, partly due to **tourism**, partly to the resurgence of the **Monte dei Paschi di Siena**. This bank, founded in Siena in 1472, is one of the major players in Italian finance and in its home base is one of the city's largest employers.

The Monte dei Paschi coexists, apparently easily enough, with one of Italy's strongest **left-wing councils**. Though this quiet, rather bourgeois provincial capital may not look like a red city, some 35,000 of the 250,000 population of Siena province are card-carrying PDS or Communist Party members – a loyalty partly won by the communists' role in the resistance during the last war.

Arrival and information

Most **intercity buses** arrive in the city centre on Viale Federico Tozzi, the road running alongside Piazza Gramsci, or at La Lizza nearby, but note that some stop near the church of San Domenico, while others avoid the centre altogether and terminate at the train station instead. Ticket offices beneath Piazza Gramsci have information on all routes. The bus company serving Siena and its hinterland is called TRA-IN (℡0577.204.246, ⓦwww.trainspa.it), which confusingly has nothing to do with trains.

Siena's **train station** is inconveniently sited at Piazza Fratelli Rosselli, down in the valley 2km northeast of town. Its foyer has a small train information office, exchange facilities, basic tourist information and a counter selling city bus tickets. To get into town, take just about any city bus heading left: #3, #9 to Tozzi; #4, #7, #8, #14, #17, #77 to Garibaldi/Sale; #10 to Gramsci. All these drop at various points on or near Piazza Matteotti or Piazza Gramsci on the northern edge of the centre. If in doubt, ask at the information desk. Local **city taxis** are to be found at ranks by the train station (℡0577.44.504) and on Piazza Matteotti (℡0577.289.350), or can be called elsewhere between 7am and 9pm by phone (℡0577.49.222). Note, however, that in Siena it's virtually impossible to book taxis in advance and you should allow plenty of time for cabs to reach you through the city's labyrinthine one-way system.

Parking in Siena can be a problem. Parking **garages** (ⓦwww.sienaparcheggi .com) are clearly signposted, secure and affordable, but the two biggest are misleadingly named: "Parcheggio Il Campo" is a long way from the Campo, just inside the Porta Tufi, and "Parcheggio Il Duomo" is just within Porta San Marco, nowhere near the Duomo. **Street-parking** outside the city walls is free; inside the walls, it can be expensive and hard to find. Follow signs to the *centro* and try to find a parking space at one of the following: around Piazza Gramsci or the large triangle of La Lizza; opposite San Domenico in the car park alongside the stadium; off the Viale Manzoni, which loops around the northeast wall of the city; or around the Porta Romana. Viale Manzoni is free parking; at the others a machine or an attendant issues tickets, usually by the hour: rates are reasonable. If you know you'll be driving in, you'd do well to arrange parking with your hotel in advance. You can drive through the old town alleys only in order to load or unload baggage at your hotel. Note that you cannot park around La Lizza on Wednesday mornings (8am–2pm), when the market takes place; offending cars are towed away.

Transport from Florence

From Florence, hourly or more frequent TRA-IN **buses** bound for Siena depart from the bus station on Via di Caterina da Siena just west of the main train station; be sure to jump on a *Corse Rapide* or *Rapido* (about 1hr 15min; €6.50 bought in advance, €8 on board), as some buses (misleadingly called *Corse Dirette* or *Diretta*) are much slower and run via Colle di Val d'Elsa and Poggibonsi (1hr 35min; €4.50 in advance, €6 on board). Both services arrive at La Lizza-Piazza Gramsci. Some **trains** run direct to Siena (fastest journey 1hr 27min), but many involve changing at Empoli (about 1hr 40min). By **car**, the two cities are linked by a fast four-lane highway that starts from the Firenze Certosa junction on the A1 autostrada, 6km south of Florence; from central Florence, head through the Oltrarno to the Porta Romana and follow "Certosa" signs.

Information

Siena's main **tourist office** is at Piazza del Campo 56 (Mon–Sat 9am–7pm; ℡0577.280.551, ⓦwww.terresiena.it). It provides hotel lists, a town map and a range of information booklets. "Ecco Siena" **guided walks** (in English) start from the Campo (April–Oct Mon–Fri 3pm; €15 per person); book with the tourist office, Siena Hotels Promotion (℡0577.288.084, ⓦwww.hotelsiena .com), or visit ⓦwww.guidesiena.it.

Accommodation

Securing a hotel room in Siena for any time between Easter and October requires booking six months in advance. If you arrive without a booking, and find that all the establishments listed below are full, make your way to the **Siena Hotels Promotion** booth (Mon–Sat 9am–8pm; winter closes 7pm; ℡0577.288.084, ⓦwww.hotelsiena.com), opposite the church of San Domenico on Piazza Madre Teresa di Calcutta. The staff here are generally very helpful and can book rooms in any of the city's hotels. The city's second specialist agency, **Vacanze Senesi**, is situated in the tourist office at Piazza del Campo 56 (Mon–Fri 9am–7pm; ℡0577.45.900, ⓦwww.vacanzesenesi.it). **Il Casato Booking Service** is another option, just off the Campo at Via del Casato di Sotto 12 (Mon–Sat 10.30am–6.30pm; ℡0577.46.091, ⓦwww.sienaholiday .com), where you can also buy bus tickets and rent bikes.

All accommodation reviewed in this section is located on a map: central places on pp.378–379, outlying options on p.370.

Hotels

Antica Residenza Cicogna Via dei Termini ℡0577.285.613, ⓦwww.anticaresidenzaci-cogna.it. A little-known bed-and-breakfast option in a perfect, if tucked-away location near the *Osteria del Ficomezzo*. The owner, Elisa Trefoloni, is charming, and there are five rooms, all frescoed, delightfully appointed and recently restored – the "Liberty" and "Leoni" rooms are especially nice. All have private bathroom. Breakfast is taken in an extraordinary, high-ceilinged room with colossal beams. Rooms, with breakfast for two, are a bargain at €78. ❷

Antica Torre Via Fieravecchia 7 ℡ & ℉0577.222.255, ⓦwww.anticatorresiena.it. By far the nicest and most intimate of the three-star places: just eight smallish rooms squeezed into an old medieval tower. Top rooms have views. ❹

Bernini Via della Sapienza 15 ℡ & ℉0577.289.047, ⓦwww.albergobernini.com. Nine inexpensive but rather pokey one-star rooms, most en suite. ❸

Cannon d'Oro Via Montanini 28 ℡0577.44.321, ⓦwww.cannondoro.com. A stylish thirty-room two-star hotel tucked down an alleyway just beyond where Banchi di Sopra becomes Via Montanini. Friendly and well maintained, this is the best choice among the central mid-price hotels. ❸

Centrale Via Cecco Angiolieri 26 ☏ 0577.280.379, ℻ 0577.42.152, ✉ hotelcentrale.siean@libero.it. Just seven large rooms on an upper floor in a quiet street as central as the name suggests, a block north of the Campo. ❷

🏃 **Certosa di Maggiano** Via Certosa 82 ☏ 0577.288.180, ⓦ www.certosadimaggiano.com. A former monastery in the countryside 1km southeast of Siena that offers luxurious comfort in its few, tasteful rooms (€594 plus per night) and an alluring retreat from worldly affairs in its library cloister and tranquil terrace. ❾

Chiusarelli Viale Curtatone 15 ☏ 0577.280.562, ⓦ www.chiusarelli.com. A nice old three-star villa hotel with 49 rooms and a garden at the back, but it's on a busy street near the bus stops – ask for one of the back rooms, several of which are very large and comfortable. Also has some private parking. ❹

Duomo Via Stalloreggi 34 ☏ 0577.289.088, ⓦ www.hotelduomo.it. Rooms are reliable but unexceptional – apart from those with views of the Duomo – but this is nonetheless the best located of the city's three-star hotels. ❺

🏃 **Grand Hotel Continental** Via Banchi di Sopra 85 ☏ 0577.56.011, ⓦ www .royaldemeure.com. For years Siena had no luxury five-star hotel – until the hugely expensive restoration of this former palace in a perfect location. The public spaces, especially the grand salon, are astounding, with frescoes and a large covered courtyard. The best rooms and suites are also exceptional – vast, entirely frescoed, and with stunning views of the Duomo. Other rooms are still excellent and superbly appointed, but mostly lack the fabulous period details you'll see in the brochures or on the website. The evening

piano bar is a dubious afterthought, horribly out of keeping with the hotel's sense of taste and style. Otherwise this is first choice for a treat or if money is no object: be prepared to say goodbye to around €900 nightly, less for upper rooms under the eaves, or if you go through a tour operator. ❾

La Perla Via delle Terme 25 ☏ 0577.47.144, ✉ info@albergolaperla.it. Regular one-star with thirteen rooms (all with bathroom), in a very central location, two blocks north of the Campo. Curfew 1am. ❷

La Toscana Via Cecco Angiolieri 12 ☏ 0577.46.097, ℻ 0577.270.634. Big, well-priced 41-room three-star in an atmospheric and central location, on an alley behind Piazza Tolomei. Rooms with and without bathrooms – unusual in this category. ❸

Locanda Garibaldi Via Giovanni Dupré 18 ☏ 0577.284.204. A good, no-nonsense seven-room two-star (four shared bathrooms), sited above one of the city's better low-cost restaurants, just south of the Campo. Midnight curfew. ❷

🏃 **Palazzo Ravizza** Pian dei Mantellini 34 ☏ 0577.280.462, ⓦ www.palazzoravizza.it. This elegant 35-room three-star, located in a pleasant area near San Niccolò al Carmine, has been run by the same family since opening for business in the 1920s, and has recently been renovated in a way that has freshened the place without sacrificing its period charm. The rooms are sparingly and tastefully furnished with antiques, and paved with terracotta or parquet tiles, with ceiling frescoes in several of them. In high season, reservations are accepted on a half-board basis only; at other times of the year they have doubles from around €120 and beautiful suites (with Jacuzzis) from around €260. The little garden at the back is a charming place for afternoon tea. ❽

Piccolo Hotel Etruria Via Donzelle 3 ☏ 0577.288.088, ⓦ www.hoteletruria.com. A very

---

Long-stay accommodation

For long-stay budget accommodation, call in at the tourist office, which has lists of **rooms** (*affittacamere*) available in private houses. These are offered mainly to students, either at the university or on the numerous language and art courses held in the city, but some are willing to offer shorter lets. They're certainly worth a try if you're staying for a week or more; rates are around €25 per person per night, usually for a shared room (less for long-term lets).

Another option is to arrange a let through one of the local *agriturismo* agencies; most rent out **villas** and **farmhouses**, as well as rooms or flats on **farms**, in the nearby countryside. Siena-based companies include Agriturist Provinciale, Strada Massetana Romana 52 (☏ 0577.47.669, ⓦ www.agriturist.it) and Casa Club, Via Veneto 41 (☏ 0577.44.041, ⓦ www.casa-club.it). The accommodation booklet issued by the tourist office also has full lists of the *agriturismo* options in the area.

neat two-star, and deservedly popular: advance booking for high season is a must to secure one of its thirteen rooms. ❷

Piccolo Hotel Il Palio Piazza del Sale 19 ⊤0577.281.131, ⓦpiccolohotelilpalio.it. Perfectly located for bus arrivals, right near all the bus stops, 200m north of the centre. Clean, good-sized rooms and friendly, helpful staff. ❷

Santa Caterina Via Piccolomini 7 ⊤0577.221.105, ⓦwww.hscsiena.it. A nineteen-room three-star ten minutes' walk from the Campo, on the street that leads out of town from Porta Romana. Has the advantages of air-conditioning and parking. ❺

Tre Donzelle Via Donzelle 5 ⊤0577.280.358, ⓕ0577.223.933. Excellent one-star option right in the heart of town, just off Banchi di Sotto, north of the Campo. Good, clean rooms, some with private bath, but has a curfew of 12.30am and its 27 rooms are often booked solid. ❷

Villa Scacciapensieri Via di Scacciapensieri 10 ⊤0577.41.441, ⓦwww.villascacciapensieri.it. Four-star country villa 3km north of Siena, with every luxury including a pool. ❼

Hostels

Alma Domus Via Camporegio 31 ⊤0577.44.177. An old pilgrim hostel behind San Domenico, with doubles from €60, all with private bathrooms. Triple and quad rooms are also available. Curfew 11.30pm. Bookings taken only Mon–Sat 1–3pm.

Ostello della Gioventù "Guidoriccio" Via Fiorentina 89, Lo Stellino ⊤0577.52.212, ⓦwww .ostellionline.org. Rather sterile and uninspiring HI hostel with 111 beds, located 4km northwest of the centre. Take bus #15 from Piazza Gramsci, or, if you're coming from Florence, ask to be let off at "Lo Stellino", just after the Siena city sign. Has several double rooms, a restaurant (meals €9) and bar. Curfew 11.30pm. Dorm beds €13.75, including breakfast. Doubles are €27.50.

Campsite

Campeggio Siena Colleverde Strada di Scacciapensieri 47 ⊤0577.280.044, ⓕ0577.333.298. Secure, well-maintained campsite, 2km north; take bus #8 from Piazza del Sale or #3 from Piazza Gramsci. Shop, bar and pool. Mid-March to mid-Nov. Places cost €7.75 per person.

The City

The centre of Siena is its great square, the **Campo**, built at the intersection of a Y-shaped configuration of hills and the convergence of the city's principal roads, the **Banchi di Sopra**, **Banchi di Sotto** and **Via di Città**. Each of these roads leads out across a ridge, straddled by one of the city's three medieval districts, or *terzi* (literally "thirds"): the **Terzo di Città** to the southwest, the **Terzo di San Martino** to the southeast, and the **Terzo di Camollia** to the north.

This central core – almost entirely medieval in plan and appearance – is initially a little disorientating, though with the Campo as a point of reference you won't go far wrong. Movement around is also made easier by the fact that the city centre has been effectively pedestrianized since the 1960s. Everywhere of use or interest in the city is within easy walking distance, with the exception of St Bernardino's monastic retreat, L'Osservanza, the Guidoriccio hostel and the campsite.

The Campo

The Campo is the centre of Siena in every sense: the main streets lead into it, the Palio takes place around its perimeter, and in the evenings it is the natural place to gravitate towards, for visitors and residents alike. Four hundred years ago, Montaigne described it as the most beautiful square in the w... assessment that still seems pretty fair.

With its amphitheatre curve, the Campo appears an almost organic pie... city planning. In fact, when the Council of Nine began buying up land in 12... they were adopting the only possible site – the old marketplace, which lay at th... convergence of the city quarters but was a part of none (the old Roman forum probably also occupied the site). To build on it, it was necessary to construct an enormous buttress beneath the lower half of the square, where the Palazzo Pubblico was to be raised. The piazza itself was completed in 1349, when the council laid its nine segments of paving to commemorate their highly civic rule and pay homage to the Virgin, the folds of whose cloak it was intended to symbolize.

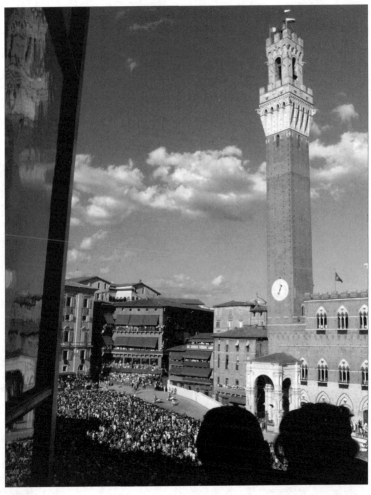

△ A balcony view of the Campo, full of people watching the Palio

▲ Porta Ovile

San Francesco
PIAZZA S. FRANCESCO
Oratorio di San Bernardino

VIA DI ORTA FONTANELLA
VIA DEL COMUNE
ORBACCI

San Pietro a Ovile
VIA PROV. SALICOTTO
V. PROVENZANO
VIA DEL BARONCELLI
VIA DELLE VERGINI

1

Santa Maria di Provenzano
PIAZZA PROVENZANO SALVANI
VIA DEL FOSSO

GIRAFFA

VALLICHIALI

CIVETTA

VIA SALLUSTIO BANDINI
VIA VIGILIO
VIA S.
ANGIOLIERI

San Vigilio

San Giovannino della Staffa

Palazzo Piccolomini
RINALDINI
BANCHI DI SOTTO
PIAZZA GRASSI
VIA DI LOLLI ONICA

LEOCORNO

5

Loggia del Papa

VIA DI PANTANETO

Torre del Mangia
✡

VIA DEL PORRIONE
VIA DI SALICOTTO
V. D. FORTUNA
VIA DEL RIALTO
VIA D. LUPARELLO

San Martino

6

VIA MAGAGNOTTI

Santo Spirito

San Gaetano

VIA DEI PISPINI
VIA DELL'OLIVIERA
▶ Porta Pispini

PIAZZA DEL MERCATO
VIA D. MALCONTENTI
VIA D. MANNA
VIA DI SALICOTTO
VIA DI S. ROSA
V. D. CONTRADINO

San Giorgio

VIA DEL PANTANETO
VIC. DEL SASSO
VIA FIERA VECCHIA
VIA ROMA
VIC. DEL REFUGIO

L

VIA NUOVA

San Raimondo al Refugio

San Giacomo

VIA DEL SOLE
VIA DI PORTA GIUSTIZIA
VIA S. MARTINO
VIA DELL'ORO
VINCENZO DEGLI AZZARINI
V. D. SCALELLE
VIA PAGLIARESI
VIA SAN GIROLAMO
VIA SAN

10

San Girolamo

Società Esecutori di Pie Disposizioni
VIA DELLE CANTINE
VIA DEI SERVI
VIC. D. SAN CLEMENTE

▶ Porta Romana

Oratorio della SS. Trinità

VALDIMONTONE
VIA VALDIMONTONE

Santa Maria dei Servi

VIA DI FONTANELLA

Convento Tolomei

VIA BALDASSARRE PERUZZI

N

0   100 m

Siena museum admission

Rather than paying admission at each attraction, it's a good idea to pick up a **pass** or **joint ticket** (*biglietto cumulativo*) covering entry to several sites. Siena has an array of these, though they have a tendency to change from year to year. Usually they are available at any of the participating museums. All, though, permit only a single entry to each attraction.

The **cathedral authorities** have an "Opera" pass which gives entry to the Museo dell'Opera, the Baptistery and San Bernardino for €10 and is valid for three days. The **civic museum authorities** have their own two-day pass, which gives entry to the Museo Civico (but *not* the Torre del Mangia), Santa Maria della Scala and the Palazzo delle Papesse, for €10. A joint ticket covering only the Museo Civico and Torre del Mangia costs €10.

Finally, there are seasonal versions of an all-encompassing seven-day "Art Itinerary" pass – the **SIA Inverno**, or **Itinerario d'Arte Inverno** (Winter Art Itinerary; available Nov to mid-March), covering entry to the Museo dell'Opera, the Baptistery, Libreria Piccolomini, Museo Civico, Santa Maria della Scala and Palazzo delle Papesse for €13; or the **SIA Estate**, or **Itinerario d'Arte Estate** (Summer Art Itinerary; available mid-March to Oct), valid for all these plus the Oratorio San Bernardino, Museo Diocesano and the church of Sant'Agostino, for €16. Note that the Pinacoteca Nazionale is administered by a separate body from all the above, and so is not included on any of the passes.

From the start, the stage-like Campo was a focus of city life. As well as its continuing role as the city's marketplace – for livestock as well as produce – it was the scene of executions, bullfights, communal boxing matches, and, of course, the Palio. St Bernardino preached here, too, holding before him the monogram of Christ's name in Greek ("IHS"), which he urged the nobles to adopt in place of their own vainglorious coats of arms. A few did so (the monogram is to be seen on various palazzi), and it was adopted by the council on the facade of the **Palazzo Pubblico**, alongside the city's she-wolf symbol, which is itself a reference to Siena's legendary foundation by the sons of Remus.

At the highest point of the Campo is the Renaissance **Fonte Gaia** ("Gay Fountain"), designed and carved by Jacopo della Quercia in the early fifteenth century. Its panels are poor, nineteenth-century reproductions – some of the original marble pieces are currently being restored in the *Fienile* section of Santa Maria della Scala – but they give an idea of what was considered one of the city's masterpieces. Its conception – the Virgin at the centre, flanked by the Virtues – was a conscious emulation of the Lorenzetti frescoes on *Good and Bad Government* in the Palazzo Pubblico (see p.384). The fountain's name comes from festivities celebrating its inauguration in 1419, the climax of a long process that began in the 1340s, when masons managed to channel water into the square.

The Palazzo Pubblico

Making no bones about its expression of civic pride, the **Palazzo Pubblico**, bristling with crenellations and glorious medieval detail, occupies virtually the entire south side of the Campo, loomed over by its giant bell-tower, the **Torre del Mangia**. Built largely in the first decade of the fourteenth century, the palace's lower level of arcading is characteristic of Sienese Gothic, as are the columns separating the windows. The council were so pleased with this aspect of the design that they ordered its emulation on all other buildings on the square – and it was indeed gracefully adapted on the twelfth-century Palazzo Sansedoni on the north side.

The other main exterior feature of the Palazzo Pubblico is the **Cappella di Piazza**, a stone loggia set at the base of the tower, which the council vowed to build at the end of the Black Death in 1348. Funds were slow to materialize, however, and by 1376, when the chief mason at the cathedral turned his hand to its design, new Florentine ideas were already making their influence felt. The final stage of construction, a century later, when the chapel was heightened and a canopy added, was wholly Renaissance in concept.

The Museo Civico

In the days of the *comune*, the lower floors of the Palazzo Pubblico housed the city accounts, and the upper storeys, as today, the council. Nowadays, its principal rooms have been converted into the **Museo Civico** (daily: Jan 7–Feb 15 & Nov 26–Dec 22 10am–5.30pm; Feb 16–March 15, Nov 1–25 & Dec 23–Jan 6 10am–6.30pm; March 16–Oct 31 10am–7pm; €7, or €10 with Torre del Mangia; for other joint tickets see opposite; €6 with reservations made at Ⓦ www.comune.siena.it/museocivico), entered through the courtyard to the right of the Cappella di Piazza.

The museum starts on the first floor of the palazzo. At the top of the stairs you're directed through a disappointing, miscellaneous five-room picture collection, whose nineteenth-century hunting scenes are enough to put you off eating *cinghiale* (wild boar) for the rest of your visit. You then wind round into the **Sala del Risorgimento** (1878–90), painted with scenes commemorating Vittorio Emanuele, first king of Italy. These depict various battle campaigns, the king's coronation and his earlier meeting with Garibaldi and his army on the road to Capua, where he refused Garibaldi governorship of the Neapolitan provinces, instead inflicting a decade of martial rule.

Sala di Balia

The first of the rooms of any real interest is the **Sala di Balia** (or Sala dei Priori), frescoed by Spinello Aretino and his son, Parri, in 1407 with episodes from the life of Siena-born Pope Alexander III – in particular his conflict with Frederick Barbarossa, the German Holy Roman Emperor. The story is a complex one. The pope and emperor came into dispute following Barbarossa's destruction of Milan in 1162, an event that caused the formation of a Lombard League of Italian states, supported by the Vatican and the Venetians. Barbarossa entered Rome in 1166, whereupon the pope fled to Venice (where he is depicted, disguised as a monk, but recognized by a French pilgrim). The scenes include a superbly realized naval conflict – in which the Venetians are shown capturing the emperor's son and the Germans desperately trying to rescue him – and the pope's eventual reconciliation with Barbarossa, in a procession led by the doge of Venice.

Anticamera and Sala del Concistoro

Beyond is the **Anticamera del Concistoro** (or Sala dei Cardinali). A detached fresco, *Three Saints and Donor*, attributed to Ambrogio Lorenzetti, graces the wall by the entrance door. It was transferred here in the nineteenth century and was probably once part of a much larger work depicting the *Madonna and Child*: in such pictures the donor – the individual responsible for commissioning the picture – would have been shown kneeling at the feet of the Madonna. In the centre of the left wall is a beautiful *Madonna and Child* attributed to Matteo di Giovanni, whose Madonna has the unquiet look typical of this painter: his propensity for the unsettling found expression in several grisly depictions of the *Massacre of the Innocents*, one of which is on display in another room of the museum (see p.385).

The next room is the **Sala del Concistoro**, entered via an ornate marble doorway (1448) by Bernardo Rossellino, the sculptor and architect responsible for redesigning much of the southern Tuscan town of Pienza (see p.472) for Pope Pius II. The room's vault was superbly frescoed by the Mannerist star, Domenico Beccafumi, between 1529 and 1535. The panels are either allegories or describe events from Greek and Roman history, but, like virtually every painting in the palazzo, deliberately evoke parallels with the civic virtues or historical achievements of Siena itself.

Vestibolo, Anticappella and Cappella

Doors from the Anticamera behind you lead on into the **Vestibolo**, which contains a damaged fresco of the *Madonna and Child* (1340) by Ambrogio Lorenzetti and a gilded bronze of the *She-Wolf Suckling Romulus and Remus* (1429), an allusion to the city's mythical foundation by Senius, son of Remus. On the left is the more interesting **Anticappella**, decorated between 1407 and 1414 by Taddeo di Bartolo, the last major exponent of Siena's conservative Gothic style, with a vast *St Christopher* and frescoes – like those in the Sala del Concistoro – whose Greek and Roman themes reflect Siena's own civic concerns. Taddeo also frescoed the **Cappella** alongside with episodes from the *Life of the Virgin* (1407–08), work overshadowed by Sodoma's altarpiece, the vast wrought-iron screen (1435–45) – attributed to Jacopo della Quercia – and the exceptional set of inlaid choir stalls (1415–28).

Sala del Mappamondo

All these works, though, are little more than a warm-up for the **Sala del Mappamondo**, one of the great set pieces of Italian art. Taking its name from its now scarcely visible ceiling fresco of a map of the cosmos, executed by Ambrogio Lorenzetti, the room was used for several centuries as the city's law court and contains one of the greatest of all Italian frescoes, **Simone Martini**'s fabulous and recently restored *Maestà*, a painting of almost translucent colour, which was the *comune*'s first major commission for the palace. Its political dimension is apparent in the depiction of the Christ Child holding a parchment inscribed with the city's motto of justice, and the inscription of two stanzas from Dante on the steps below the throne, warning that the Virgin will not intercede for those who betray her or oppress the poor. It is one of Martini's earliest known works, painted in 1315 at the age of 30; before this extraordinary debut not a thing is known of him. He touched up parts of the picture, following damage from damp, six years later. The richly decorative style is archetypal Sienese Gothic and its arrangement makes a fascinating comparison with the *Maestà* by Duccio (with whom Martini perhaps trained) in the Museo dell'Opera del Duomo. Martini's great innovation was the use of a canopy and a frieze of medallions which frame and organize the figures – a sense of space and hint of perspective that suggest a knowledge of Giotto's work. Martini was to experiment further in this direction, in his great cycle of the *Life of St Martin* in Assisi, painted a couple of years later.

The fresco on the opposite wall, the marvellous **Equestrian Portrait of Guidoriccio da Fogliano**, is a motif for medieval chivalric Siena, and was, until recently, also credited to Martini. Depicting the knight setting forth from his battle camp to besiege a walled hill town (thought to be Montemassi, a village southwest of Siena near Roccastrada), it would, if it were by Martini, be accounted one of the earliest Italian portrait paintings. Art historians, however, have long puzzled over the apparently anachronistic castles: according to some, they are of a much later architectural style than the painting's supposed date of 1328. The work would also seem to be part-painted over a fresco to the right by Lippo Vanni, which is dated 1364. In the mid-1980s the waters were further

△ Equestrian Portrait of Guidoriccio da Fogliano

muddied when, during restoration, another apparently anachronistic fresco was found – the painting now beneath the equestrian portrait showing two men in front of a castle, believed to be the one at Arcidosso in southern Tuscany; it has been variously attributed to Martini, Duccio, Pietro Lorenzetti and Memmi di Filippuccio.

The current state of the debate is confused, with a number of historians – led by the American Gordon Moran (whom the council for a while banned from the Palazzo Pubblico and accused of belonging to the CIA) – interpreting the *Guidoriccio* as a sixteenth-century fake, and others – including an Italian commission of experts – maintaining that it is a genuine Martini overpainted by subsequent restorers. Things reached such a pitch that a neutral referee – an Englishman, Professor Andrew Martindale – was called in to arbitrate; his findings, however, proved inconclusive. Tempers recently boiled over when the Americans accused the Sienese of deliberately destroying evidence that would support their case during a "routine" restoration. Much rests on a scrupulous analysis of Siena's vast archives in the Palazzo Piccolomini: details contained in the records of payments for various paintings of the period may well help solve the mystery. The only other option – often suggested but not yet countenanced – is to strip away all the frescoes concerned to study exactly what overlays what.

At least there's no problem with the coffered figures to the right and left of the uncovered fresco beneath the equestrian portrait; these are a pair of saints by Sodoma dating from 1529. The other large frescoes in the room also depict Sienese military victories, namely the *Victory at the Val di Chiana* (1364) by Lippo Vanni (on the long wall) and the *Victory at Poggio Imperiale* (1480) by Christoforo Ghini and Francesco d'Andrea. Don't miss the figures on the pilasters below the latter, which from left to right depict Sodoma's *Blessed Tolomei* (1533), founder of the abbey at Monte Oliveto Maggiore; *St Bernardino* (1450) by Sano di Pietro; and *St Catherine of Siena* (1461) by Vecchietta.

Sala dei Nove (Sala della Pace)

The Palazzo Pubblico's most important and interesting frescoes adorn the **Sala dei Nove** (or **Sala della Pace**) next door; these are Ambrogio Lorenzetti's **Allegories of Good and Bad Government**, commissioned in 1338 to remind the councillors of the effects of their duties, and widely considered one of Europe's most important surviving cycles of secular paintings. The walled city they depict is clearly Siena, along with its countryside and domains, and the paintings are full of details of medieval life: agriculture, craftwork, trade and building, even hawking and dancing. They form the first-known panorama in Western art and show an innovative approach to the human figure – the beautiful, reclining Peace (Pax) in the *Good Government* hierarchy is based on a Roman sarcophagus still on display in the Palazzo Pubblico. An odd detail is that the "dancing maidens" in *Good Government* are probably young men: women dancing in public, according to the historian Jane Bridgeman, would have been too shocking in medieval Siena, and the figures' short hair and slit skirts were characteristic of professional male entertainers.

The moral theme of the frescoes is expressed in a complex iconography of allegorical virtues and figures. *Good Government*, painted on the more brightly lit walls and better preserved, is dominated by a throned figure representing the *comune* (he is dressed in Siena's colours), flanked by the Virtues (Peace – from which the room takes its name – is the nonchalantly reclining figure in white) and with Faith, Hope and Charity buzzing about his head. To the left, on a throne, Justice (with Wisdom in the air above) dispenses rewards and punishments, while below her throne Concordia advises the republic's councillors on their duties. All hold ropes, symbol of agreement. *Bad Government* is ruled by the figure of Fear (or the Devil), whose scroll reads: "Because he looks for his own good in the world, he places justice beneath tyranny. So nobody walks this road without Fear: robbery thrives inside and outside the city gates." Fear is surrounded by figures symbolizing the Vices.

Ironically, within a decade of the frescoes' completion, Siena was engulfed by the Black Death – in which Lorenzetti and his family were among the victims – and the city was under tyrannical government. However, the paintings retained an impact on the citizenry: St Bernardino preached sermons on their themes.

Sala dei Pilastri and loggia

The room adjoining the Sala della Pace, the **Sala dei Pilastri** (or delle Colonne), displays panel paintings from the thirteenth to the fifteenth century, whose conservatism and strict formulaic composition points up the scale of Lorenzetti's achievement. Notable among them is one of the earliest Sienese masterpieces, Guido da Siena's gripping *Maestà* (1221/1260), for which Duccio repainted the Virgin's face; a fascinating picture of *St Bernardino Preaching in the Campo* by Neroccio di Bartolomeo (note how the men and women in the crowd are separated by a white cloth); and a graphically violent *Massacre of the Innocents* removed from Sant'Agostino, painted by Matteo di Giovanni – one of four he completed in the city. The stained-glass figure of St Michael in one of the windows is attributed to Ambrogio Lorenzetti.

Backtracking through the museum, it is worth climbing the stairs between the Sala del Risorgimento and Sala di Balia to the rear **loggia**, where you can enjoy a view over the Piazza del Mercato, now mainly a car park with a belvedere-like platform and a pleasant café-pizzeria and restaurant. It is here you realize how abruptly the town ends: buildings rise to the right and left for a few hundred metres along the ridges of the Terzo di San Martino and Terzo di Città, but in the centre the land drops away to a rural valley.

The Torre del Mangia

Within the Palazzo Pubblico's courtyard, opposite the entrance to the Museo Civico, is separate access to the 97-metre **Torre del Mangia** (daily 10am–6.15/7pm; Nov to mid-March closes 4pm; €6 or €10 with the Museo Civico). Climb the 388 steps and you have fabulous, vertigo-inducing views across the town and countryside. Built between 1338 and 1348 – the cresting was designed by Lippo Memmi – the tower takes its name from its first watchman, a spendthrift (*mangiaguadagni*) named Giovanni di Balduccio, who is commemorated by a statue in the courtyard. It was the last great project of the *comune* before the Black Death and exercised a highly civic function: its bell was rung to order the opening of the city gates at dawn, the break for lunch, the end of work at sunset and the closing of the city gates three hours later.

Piazza del Duomo

Dominating the hill on which it stands, visible from many parts of the city, Siena's mighty **Duomo** is the focus of an ensemble of art and architecture arrayed around the **Piazza del Duomo**. The southwest side of the square is occupied by the medieval complex of **Santa Maria della Scala**, Siena's main hospital for over eight hundred years and now a museum and arts complex displaying some staggering medieval frescoes. Two floors below it is the **Museo Archeologico**, a modest but well-presented collection, and part of a scheme that will see the former hospital turned into Siena's principal exhibition space. The other sides of the square continue the history of Sienese power, with the Palazzo dei Vescovi (Archbishop's Palace), the Palazzo del Magnifico built for Petrucci in 1508, and the Palazzo Granducale, erected later the same century for the Medici. More interesting than any of these, though, is the **Museo dell'Opera del Duomo**, home to Siena's single greatest work of art – Duccio's *Maestà* – and a range of other significant sculptures and paintings.

The Duomo

Few buildings reveal so much of a city's history and aspirations as Siena's **Duomo** (March to late Aug Mon–Sat 10.30am–7.30pm, Sun 1.30–7.30pm; rest of year closes an hour earlier, except late Aug to late Oct 9.30am–7.30pm for the showing of the pavement; €3, including entry to Libreria Piccolomini; €6 late Aug to late Oct). Completed to virtually its present size around 1215, the Duomo was subjected to constant plans for expansion throughout the city's years of medieval prosperity. A project at the beginning of the fourteenth century attempted to double its extent by building a baptistery on the slope below and using this as a foundation for a rebuilt nave, but the work ground to a halt as the walls gaped under the pressure. For a while, the chapter pondered knocking down the whole building and starting from scratch to the principles of the day, but eventually they hit on a new scheme to re-orientate the cathedral instead, using the existing nave as a transept and building a **new nave** out towards the Campo. Again cracks appeared, and then in 1348 came the Black Death. With the population halved and funds suddenly cut off, the plan was abandoned once and for all. The part-built extension still stands at the north end of the square, a vast structure that – had it been completed – would have created the largest church in Italy outside Rome.

Despite all the grand abandoned plans, the Duomo is still a delight. Its style is an amazing conglomeration of Romanesque and Gothic, delineated by bands of black and white marble, an idea adapted from Pisa and Lucca – though here with much bolder and more extravagant effect. The lower part of the **facade** was designed by the Pisan sculptor Giovanni Pisano, who from 1284 to 1296 created, with his workshop, much of its statuary – the philosophers, patriarchs and prophets, now removed to the Museo dell'Opera and replaced by copies.

In the next century the **Campanile** was added, its windows multiplying at each level, as was the Gothic **rose window** above the doors. Thereafter work came to a complete halt, with the **mosaics** designed for the gables having to wait until the nineteenth century, when money was found to employ Venetian artists. Immediately above the central door, note St Bernardino's bronze monogram of Christ's name.

The pavement

The facade's use of black and white decoration is echoed by the Duomo's great marble **pavement**, or floor, which begins with geometric patterns and a few scenes outside the church and takes off into a startling sequence of 56 figurative panels within. These were completed between 1349 and 1547, with virtually every artist who worked in the city trying his hand on a design. The earliest employed a simple *sgraffito* technique, which involved chiselling holes and lines in the marble and then filling them in with pitch; later tableaux are considerably more ambitious, worked in multicoloured marble. Unfortunately,

SIENA: THE DUOMO

0   25 m

Baptistery

Sacristy

Pecci Tomb

Pulpit

PIAZZA DEL
DUOMO

▼ Santa Maria della Scala

DUOMO PAVEMENT

A She-Wolf Suckling Romulus and Remus
B Sibyl (1483). Benvenuto di Giovanni.
C Sibyl (1483). Matteo di Giovanni.
D Allegory of The Hill of Wisdom (1505). Pinturicchio.
E Wheel of Fortune (restored in nineteenth century). Attributed to Domenico dei Cori.
F Akab is mortally wounded. Domenico Beccafumi.
G The pact between Akab and Elijah. Domenico Beccafumi.
H The Sacrifice of Elijah. Domenico Beccafumi.
I Death of the Prophets. Domenico Beccafumi.
J Sacrifice of the Priests. Domenico Beccafumi.
K Massacre of the Innocents (1482). Matteo di Giovanni.
L Judith and Holofernes (restored 1790). Francesco di Giorgio Martini.
M Moses Striking Water from the Rock (1524). Domenico Beccafumi.
N Adoration of the Golden Calf (1531). Domenico Beccafumi.
O The Sacrifice of Isaac (1547). Domenico Beccafumi.

SIENA DUOMO

1 Altare Piccolomini (1491). Andrea Bregno. Sculptures by Michelangelo.
2 Libreria Piccolomini. Frescoes on the life of Pope Pius II (1505–07) by Pinturicchio.
3 Flagpole from the Battle of Montaperti.
4 Cappella di San Giovanni Battista. Frescoes (1501–04) by Pinturicchio; bronze by Donatello of St John the Baptist (1457).
5 Pulpit. Nicola Pisano and assistants (1268).
6 Tomb of Bishop Pecci of Grosseto (1426–7). Donatello.
7 Tomb of Cardinal Riccardo Petroni (1314–18). Tino da Camaino.
8 Bronze candleholders (1548–50). Domenico Beccafumi.
9 Bronze candleholders (1497–99). Francesco di Giorgio Martini.
10 High altar (1532). Baldassarre Peruzzi.
11 Ciborio (1467–72). Vecchietta.
12 Stained glass (1288). To a design by Duccio.
13 Cappella del Sacramento. Bas-reliefs (1425) by Domenico dei Cori.
14 Cappella Chigi (1659–62). To a design by Gian Lorenzo Bernini.
15 Tomb of Tommaso Piccolomini (1484–5). Neroccio di Bartolomeo Landi. Below: bas-reliefs of Episodes from the Life of the Virgin (1451) by Urbano da Cortona.

---

the whole effect can only be seen for about a month in August (dates vary); the rest of the year, most of the panels are rather unimaginatively protected by underfoot boarding.

The subjects chosen for the panels are a strange mix, incorporating biblical themes, secular commemorations and allegories. The most ordered part of the scheme are the ten Sibyls – mythic prophetesses who foretold the coming of Christ – on either side of the main aisle. Fashioned towards the end of the fifteenth century, when Sienese painters were still imprinting gold around their conventional Madonnas, they are totally Renaissance in spirit. Between them,

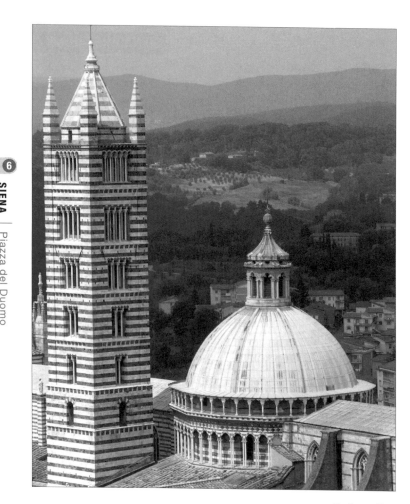

△ The Duomo, Siena

in the central nave, are the much earlier *Sienese she-wolf enclosed by the republic's twelve cities* (marked as A on our plan) and the *Wheel of Fortune* (E), along with Pinturicchio's *Allegory of Virtue* (D), a rocky island of serpents with a nude posed between a boat and the land. Moving down the nave, the central hexagon is dominated by Domenico Beccafumi's *Stories from the Life of Elijah* (F–I). Beccafumi worked intermittently on the pavement from 1518 to 1547, also designing the vast friezes of *Moses Striking Water from a Rock and on Mount Sinai* (M) and *The Sacrifice of Isaac* (O). To the left of the hexagon is a *Massacre of the Innocents* (K), almost inevitably the chosen subject of Matteo di Giovanni.

It's interesting also to note the **choir stalls**, in the context of the pavement. These use intarsia techniques of a superb standard and again were made between the mid-fourteenth and mid-sixteenth centuries.

The pulpit, sculptures and chapels

The rest of the cathedral interior is equally arresting, with its zebra-stripe bands of marble, and the line of popes' heads – including several Sienese – set above the pillars. These stucco busts were added through the fifteenth and sixteenth centuries and many seem sculpted with an apparent eye to their perversity: the same hollow-cheeked scowls crop up repeatedly.

The greatest individual artistic treasure is the **pulpit**. This was completed by Nicola Pisano in 1268, soon after his pulpit for the Baptistery at Pisa, with help from his son Giovanni and Arnolfo di Cambio. The design of the panels duplicates those in Pisa, though they are executed with much greater detail and high relief. The carving's distance from the Byzantine world is perhaps best displayed by the statuette of the *Madonna*, whose breast is visible beneath the cloak for the first time in Italy, and by the *Last Judgement*, with its mastery of the human figure and organization of space. Come equipped with plenty of coins for lighting.

Almost all the sculpture is of an exceptional standard. Near the pulpit in the north transept are Tino di Camaino's *Tomb of Cardinal Petroni* (1318), a prototype for Italian tomb architecture over the next century, and, in front, **Donatello**'s bronze pavement *Tomb of Bishop Pecci* (1426). The Renaissance high altar is flanked by superb candelabra-carrying angels by Beccafumi. In the **Piccolomini Altarpiece**, the young **Michelangelo** also makes an appearance. He was commissioned to carve the whole series of fifteen statues here, but after completing saints Peter, Paul, Pius and Gregory in the lower niches he left for a more tempting contract in Florence – the *David*.

There are further Renaissance sculptural highlights in the two circular transept chapels. The **Cappella di San Giovanni Battista**, on the left, focuses on a bronze statue of the *Baptist* by Donatello, cast in 1457, a couple of years after his expressionist *Mary Magdalene* in Florence, whom the Baptist's stretched and emaciated face recalls. The frescoes in this chapel, with their delightful landscape detailing, are by Pinturicchio.

The **Cappella Chigi**, or Cappella del Voto, was the last major addition to the Duomo, built at the behest of Pope Alexander VII, another local boy, in 1659. It was designed by Bernini as a new setting for the *Madonna del Voto*, a thirteenth-century painting that commemorated the Sienese dedication of their city to the Virgin on the eve of the Battle of Montaperti. The style of the chapel is pure Roman Baroque, most notably seen in the four niche statues, two of which are by Bernini himself – wild, semi-clad figures of Mary Magdalene and St Jerome, the latter holding a cross in ecstasy like some 1970s rock guitarist. Outside the chapel, the walls are covered in a mass of devotional objects – silver limbs and hearts, *contrada* scarves, even the odd Palio costume and crash helmet.

Libreria Piccolomini

Midway along the nave, on the left, Pinturicchio's brilliantly coloured fresco of the *Coronation of Pius II* marks the entrance to the **Libreria Piccolomini**, well worth a visit for the beautiful fresco cycle within. The frescoes and library were commissioned by Francesco Piccolomini (who for ten days was Pope Pius III) to house the books of his uncle, Aeneas Sylvius Piccolomini (Pius II). They do justice to the man whom Jacob Burckhardt adopted almost as a hero in his classic *The Civilization of the Renaissance in Italy*. Pius, born at nearby Pienza in 1405, was the archetypal Renaissance man, writing poetry, a geography and the *Commentaries*, a deeply humanist work in which he enthuses over landscape, antiquity and architecture and describes the languages, customs and industries encountered on his travels.

Pinturicchio's frescoes, painted with an equal love of nature and classical decor as well as a keen sense of drama, commemorate the whole gamut of Pius's career. The cycle begins to the right of the window, with Aeneas's secular career as a diplomat: attending the Council of Basle as secretary to an Italian bishop (panel 1); presenting himself as an envoy to James II of Scotland (panel 2); being crowned poet laureate by the Holy Roman Emperor, Frederick III (panel 3); and then representing Frederick on a visit to Pope Eugenius IV (panel 4). Aeneas subsequently returned to Italy and took orders, becoming first Bishop of Trieste and then of Siena, in which role he is depicted presiding over the meeting of Frederick III and his bride-to-be, Eleonora of Portugal, outside the city's Porta Camollia (panel 5).

In 1456 Aeneas was made a cardinal (panel 6) and just two years later was elected pope (panel 7), taking the title Pius II. In political terms, his eight-year rule was not a great papacy, despite his undoubted humanism and diplomatic skill, with much of the time wasted in crushing the barons of Romagna and the Marche. The crusade he called in 1456 at Mantua (panel 8) to regain Constantinople from the Turks – who took the city in 1453 – came to nothing, and the last picture of the series (panel 10) shows his death at Ancona, where he had gone to encourage the troops. It was said that his death was brought on by grief for the failure to get the crusade off the ground, or possibly by poisoning by the troops, eager to terminate their pledge. Between these two panels is the event for which Siena most remembers him – the canonization of St Catherine.

In art history terms, Pinturicchio stands as a relatively minor figure. Originally from Perugia, he worked with Perugino in the Sistine Chapel before beginning this, his acknowledged masterpiece, in 1502. His skills lie in the brilliant colouring, the naturalistic detail – the storm scene in Aeneas's departure for Basle is one of the first in Western art – and in an easy disposition of crowds, ideal for the pageants here, and enhanced by their illusionistic placing within a series of loggias.

The library is now used to display the cathedral's **choirbooks**, illuminated by Sano di Pietro and other Sienese Gothics. At the centre of the room is displayed a Roman statue of the **Three Graces**, supposedly copied from a lost Greek work by Praxiteles. It was bought by the Piccolomini nephew and was used as a model by Pinturicchio and Raphael.

The Baptistery

The cathedral **Baptistery** (daily: March–May & Sept 9.30am–7.30pm; June–Aug hours vary, but usually 9am–7.30pm; Oct 9am–6pm; rest of year 10am–1pm & 2–5pm; €3 or €10 with joint ticket – see p.380) contains one of the city's great Renaissance works – a hexagonal font with scenes illustrating the Baptist's life. It's unusual in being placed beneath the main body of the church: to reach it, turn left out of the Duomo, follow the walls left and then take the flight of steps leading down behind the cathedral.

The cathedral chapter responsible for the **font** (1417–30) must have had a good sense of what was happening in Florence at the time, for they managed to commission panels by **Ghiberti** (*Baptism of Christ* and *John in Prison*) and **Donatello** (*Herod's Feast*), as well as by the local sculptor **Jacopo della Quercia** (*The Angel Announcing the Baptist's Birth*). Jacopo also executed the marble tabernacle above, and the summit statue of *John the Baptist* and five niche statues of the Prophets. Of the main panels, Donatello's scene, in particular, is a superb piece of drama, with Herod and his cronies recoiling at the appearance of the Baptist's head. Donatello was also responsible for two of the corner angels

A history of Santa Maria della Scala

According to legend, the hospital of Santa Maria della Scala was founded by **Beato Sorore**, a ninth-century cobbler-turned-monk who worked among orphans, a story given credence by the reputed discovery of his "tomb" in 1492. Sorore was almost certainly mythical, his name a corruption of *suore*, or nuns, who for centuries tended the sick as a part of their vocation. The hospital was probably founded by the cathedral's canons, the first written record of its existence appearing in 1090. Its development was prompted by the proximity of the **Via Francigena**, a vital trade and pilgrimage route between Rome and northern Europe, which in the early Middle Ages replaced the deteriorating Roman consular roads used previously. Its route passed below Siena's walls, giving rise to the growth of numerous rest-places (*ospedali*) where travellers and pilgrims could seek shelter and succour. Some forty of these grew up in Sienese territory alone, the most important of which was Santa Maria della Scala. Initially pilgrims were the main concern: hospital work, in the modern sense, came later: "hospitality rather than hospitalization" was the credo.

The foundation was one of the first European examples of the **Xenodochium**, literally an "abode", a hospital that not only looked after the sick but could also be used as a refuge and food kitchen for an entire town in times of famine and plague. This role made it a vital part of the city's social fabric, its importance leading to a long-running and ill-mannered tussle between lay and secular authorities. In time it passed from the cathedral canons into the hands of hospital friars, and in 1404, after an intense dispute, into the care of the *comune*, who appointed its rectors and governing body. Alms and bequests of money over the centuries kept it richly endowed, the Sienese taking to heart St Paul's stricture that charity was the most important of the three Cardinal Virtues.

Some of the donated funds were diverted away from humanitarian concerns, and into artistic and architectural commissions: as early as 1252, Siena's bishop gave permission for Santa Maria's abbot to build a **church**, the precursor of the present Santissima Annunziata. In 1335 the hospital commissioned Simone Martini and Pietro and Ambrogio Lorenzetti, the city's three leading painters, to fresco the building's exterior facade (works that have since been lost to the elements). In 1359 it paid an exorbitant sum to acquire from Constantinople a nail used during the Passion, a piece of the True Cross, and a part of the Virgin's girdle, along with a miscellany of **saints' relics**. In 1378 it financed the setting of a stone bench along the length of the hospital's exterior, its original purpose being to provide the hospital's dignitaries with somewhere to sit during the city's interminable religious and civic ceremonies – and still much used today as a shady spot from which to view the facade of the Duomo.

(*Faith* and *Hope*) and (with Giovanni di Turino) for the miniature angels on the tabernacle above.

The lavishly frescoed **walls** almost overshadow the font, their nineteenth-century overpainting having been removed after a vigorous assault by the restorers. With your back to the entrance, the best include (on the left arched vault lunette) a fresco of scenes from the life of St Anthony (1460) by Benvenuto di Giovanni, a pupil of Vecchietta; scenes from the life of Christ by Vecchietta himself (inside left wall of the central stepped chapel); and the same artist's *Prophets*, *Sibyls* and *Articles of the Creed* (the main vaults), the last a repeat of a theme he would use in the Ospedale di Santa Maria della Scala (see p.395).

Santa Maria della Scala

The complex of **Santa Maria della Scala** (daily: mid-March to Oct 10am–6.30pm; rest of year 10.30am–4.30pm; €6; for joint tickets see p.380; ⓦ www

.santamaria.comune.siena.it), opposite the Duomo, served as the city's hospital for over eight hundred years, listing among its charitable workers St Catherine and St Bernardino. Its closure in 1995 aroused mixed feelings, for the functioning building gave a sense of purpose to the cathedral square, which won't be matched by its intended use as Siena's principal cultural and museum space. At the same time, the *comune*'s grandiose plans for the enormous building – which include a new home for the Pinacoteca Nazionale – mean that some extraordinary works, long hidden from all but the most determined visitors, are now on public view for the first time in centuries.

While some of the complex still remains off-limits, the last few years have seen the restoration and opening of the church of **Santissima Annunziata**; the **Cappella del Sacro Chiodo** with its highly acclaimed fresco cycle by Vecchietta; a beautiful Beccafumi fresco in the **Cappella del Manto**; the **Oratorio di Santa Caterina della Notte**, a finely decorated subterranean chapel used by, among others, St Catherine; and, adjacent to this, Jacopo della Quercia's original marble panels from the Fonte Gaia in the **Fienile**. Best of all, in the **Sala del Pellegrinaio**, is a vast secular fresco cycle by Domenico di Bartolo, a work now talked of as third only to the frescoes in the Duomo and Palazzo Pubblico in Siena's artistic pantheon. Siena's **Museo Archeologico** occupies the converted basement of the building.

Santissima Annunziata and the Cappella del Manto

To the left of the ticket desk, and also with its own door onto Piazza del Duomo, is the church of **Santissima Annunziata**, wholly within the complex of Santa Maria della Scala. Remodelled in the fifteenth century, the church is disappointingly bland, but worth a look for the high altar's marvellous bronze statue of the *Risen Christ* by Vecchietta, its features so gaunt the veins show through the skin. Vecchietta clearly understood and absorbed the new approach of Donatello, and several art historians consider this the finest Renaissance sculpture in the city. Before the church's remodelling, frescoes by Vecchietta had entirely covered its walls, a loss as tantalizing as the missing Martini and Lorenzetti frescoes on the hospital's exterior.

The other way from the ticket office leads into a small vestibule known as the **Cappella del Manto**, which contains an arresting and beautifully restored fresco of *St Anne and St Joachim* (1512), the earliest major work in Siena by the Mannerist Domenico Beccafumi. The protagonists depicted are the parents of the Virgin, whose story – popular in Tuscan painting – is told in the apocryphal gospels, biblical adjuncts reintroduced to the medieval world in the *Golden Legend* by Jacopo da Voragine. Having failed to conceive during twenty years of marriage, the pair are each told by an angel to meet at Jerusalem's Golden Gate. Here they kiss (the scene depicted in the fresco), a moment which symbolizes the Immaculate Conception of their daughter.

Sala del Pellegrinaio

Uplifted by contemplation of this event, you turn left from the Cappella del Manto into a vast hall, a majestic whitewashed space typical of the "longitudinal" architectural elements introduced into Italy by French Cistercians travelling the Via Francigena, and now partly used as a bookshop. Turning immediately left (rooms off to the right are used for temporary exhibitions) brings you into another similarly elongated space, the **Sala del Pellegrinaio**, its walls completely covered in a fresco cycle of episodes from the history of Santa Maria della Scala by Domenico di Bartolo and Vecchietta. Incredibly, this astounding space was used as a hospital ward until relatively recently.

△ Detail from the Sala del Pellegrinaio

The ward was built around 1380 and the frescoes begun in 1440, their aim being to not only record scenes from the hospital's history, but also to promote the notion of charity towards the sick and – in particular – the orphaned, whose care had been a large part of the hospital's early function. Their almost entirely **secular** content was extraordinary at the time they were painted, still some years short of the period when Renaissance ideas would allow for other than religious narratives. It's well worth taking the trouble to study the eight major panels in detail – each is full of insights into the Sienese daily life of the time – along with the two paintings on the end wall by the window. The cycle starts at the left end of the left wall and moves clockwise.

The left wall

The **first panel**, *The Dream of the Mother of Beato Sorore*, is by Vecchietta, his only contribution to the cycle. It depicts in part a dream in which the mother of Sorore, the hospital's mythical founder, foresees her son's destiny. Her vision focuses on the abandoned children of the hospital, the *gettatelli* (from *gettare*, to throw away), who are shown ascending to Paradise and the waiting arms of the Madonna. Sorore is shown twice: on the right of the painting with upraised hand receiving the first *gettatello*, and kneeling at the foot of the child-filled ladder. This ladder (*scala*) is the key to the Santa Maria della Scala, which may take its name from this part of the legend. Another version of the story suggests that a three-runged ladder, a symbol of the Trinity, was found during the hospital's construction – although the more likely explanation is that the hospital was simply built opposite the steps, or *scala*, of the Duomo. Whatever the origins, a three-runged ladder surmounted by a cross is the symbol you now see plastered all over the museum's literature and displays.

The **second panel**, *The Building of the Hospital*, depicts a mounted bishop of Siena at the head of a procession passing the hospital, which is in the process of being built, and almost running down a stonemason in the process. Note the buildings, a strange mixture of Gothic and Renaissance that bear little relation to anything in Siena, and the rector of the hospital, portrayed behind the ladder on the right doffing his hat to the visiting dignitaries. The **third panel**, the weakest of the cycle, is by Priamo della Quercia, brother of the more famous Jacopo, and shows the *Investiture of the Hospital Rector by the Blessed Agostino Novello*, the latter traditionally, but erroneously, credited as being the author of the hospital's first statute. The decorous figure on the left is thought to be a portrait of Emperor Sigismondo (who passed through Siena in 1432), or, more probably, a representation of the Byzantine emperor Paleologus III, who took part in the Council of Florence in 1439. The **fourth panel** shows one of Santa Maria's defining moments, when in 1193 Pope Celestine III gave the hospital the right to elect its own rector, thus transferring power from the religious to lay authorities. For the rest, the fresco is an excuse to portray day-to-day life in Siena – note, for example, the preponderance of oriental merchants.

The end wall

The paintings on either side of the **end wall** are late sixteenth-century works, but illustrate two fascinating aspects of the hospital's work. The vast number of orphans taken in meant that an equally large number of wet nurses, or *baliatici*, were needed to feed the infants. At one time their numbers were such that feeding took place in the vast hall now occupied by the bookshop. The pictures here show the nurses in action, and the payment for their services: in grain (on the left wall) and hard cash (on the right).

The right wall

On the long right wall, the **fifth panel**, the most famous in the cycle, shows *The Tending of the Sick*, a picture crammed with incident, notably the close scrutiny being given to a urine sample by two doctors on the left, the youth with a leg wound being washed, and the rather ominous scene on the right of a monk confessing a patient prior to surgery.

The **sixth panel** shows *The Distribution of Charity*, one of the hospital's main tasks, an event that takes place in the old hospital church (now replaced by Santissima Annunziata) with the central door of the Duomo just visible in the background. Bread is distributed to beggars, pilgrims and children (one of whom passes it on to his mother); at the centre an orphan puts on clothes that it has been given. In one strange vignette a child is shown trying to express milk from its mother's breast. On the left, meanwhile, the hospital's rector is shown doffing his hat, possibly to Sigismondo.

The **seventh panel** illustrates further work of the hospital, underlining the vital part it played in maintaining the social fabric of the city. It shows the reception, education and marriage of one of the female orphans, who were provided with a small grant designed to enable them to marry, stay on in the hospital or join a convent. Also included are details that suggest how the hospital not only took in children, but committed itself to caring for them over a long period. Thus the wet nurses are shown in action on the table to the left, along with scenes to suggest weaning, education and play. Bartolo also shows off his Renaissance credentials by including a wealth of extraneous detail, as well as his arcane knowledge of exotic lands, notably in the carpet under the feet of the married couple, whose dragon and phoenix symbols belong to the period of the Ming dynasty.

The final **eighth panel**, which details the feeding of the poor and the elderly, is less engaging than the rest, partly because of the awkwardly sited window, reputedly built by a nineteenth-century superintendent so that he could survey the sick from his upper-floor office without the bother of having to go down into the ward.

The Cappella del Sacro Chiodo

Some idea of what was lost in the remodelling of Santissima Annunziata can be grasped in Vecchietta's fresco cycle (1446–49) in the **Cappella del Sacro Chiodo**, so named because it once housed the nail (*chiodo*) from the Passion and other holy relics; it's also known as the **Sagrestia Vecchia**, reached through the small Cappella della Madonna beside the Sala del Pellegrinaio. Some art critics pay these frescoes more attention than the Bartolo cycle in the Sala del Pellegrinaio, but for the casual viewer they are less easy to interpret, principally because the subject matter – an illustration of the *Articles of the Creed* – requires some theological knowledge. If you can manage the Italian, however, the various panels and vaults are well described. Each lunette illustrates one or more articles, the figure of one of the Apostles to the right holding the text of the article in question, the scenes below or to the left depicting an episode from the Old Testament which embodies the article's meaning.

The frescoes are extremely unusual, partly in that they illustrate a written text – something that remained rare until much later in the Renaissance – and partly in that they revolve around the figure of Christ (depicted twice in the main vaults). The latter was a strange choice in a city dedicated to the Madonna, where virtually every work of note either eulogizes Siena itself or includes Christ only as an adjunct to the Virgin. It's thought that the choice was suggested by the "nail from the Cross" contained in the chapel, a relic with obvious relevance to the story of Christ.

Domenico di Bartolo's **high altarpiece**, the *Madonna della Misericordia* (1444), is more intelligible than much of the cycle, and shows the Madonna casting a protective cloak over various of Siena's inhabitants. This theme, a common one in Sienese and other central Italian works, derives from a vision of the Madonna experienced by a ninth-century Cistercian monk. At first painters depicted only members of the religious orders beneath the protective cloak, monks to one side, nuns to the other. At the beginning of the twelfth century members of religious confraternities were allowed protection, and a few decades later the privilege was extended to all inhabitants of a town or city. Men and women usually remained segregated, however, which makes this version – in which they're mixed – unusual. The fresco once graced the Cappella del Manto (see above), the Virgin's cloak (*manto*) having given the chapel its name. It was detached and fixed here in 1610, its side parts torn away to fit the dimensions of the new altar; in 1969, however, the discarded fragments were found and reattached.

The rest of Santa Maria della Scala

Stairs lead down to the **Fienile**, the hospital's old hayloft, now housing Jacopo della Quercia's original marble panels from the Fonte Gaia (1409–19), transferred here from the Palazzo Pubblico. With their serious state of erosion it was hard to appreciate that Jacopo della Quercia was rated by Vasari on a par with Donatello and Ghiberti, with whom he competed for the commission of Florence's Baptistery doors. Michelangelo, too, was an admirer, struck perhaps by the physicality evident in the *Expulsion of Adam and Eve*.

Adjacent is the **Oratorio di Santa Caterina della Notte**, which belonged to one of a number of the medieval confraternities who maintained oratories in the basement vaults of the hospital. It's a dark and strangely spooky place, despite the wealth of decoration; you can easily imagine St Catherine passing nocturnal vigils down here. Even if you prove immune to the atmosphere, it's worth coming down here for Taddeo di Bartolo's sumptuous triptych of the *Madonna and Child with SS Andrew and John the Baptist* (1400).

Stairs lead down again to the lavishly decorated **Compagnia della Madonna sotto le Volte**, the oratory and meeting-room of the Società di Esecutori di Pie Disposizioni, the oldest of the lay confraternities, where you'll find a wooden crucifix said to be the one that inspired St Bernardino to become a monk.

From the small columned courtyard (**Corticella**) back on the Fienile level you enter the medieval storerooms – now used for temporary exhibitions – from where stairs lead down into the spacious labyrinth of the **Museo Archeologico**, which houses private collections from the late nineteenth century and plenty of local finds from excavation work in and around Siena, Chianti, the upper Val d'Elsa and Etruscan Murlo.

The Museo dell'Opera del Duomo

Tucked into a corner of the proposed – and abandoned – new nave of the Duomo is the impressive **Museo dell'Opera del Duomo** (daily: mid-March to Sept 9am–7.30pm; Oct 9am–6pm; rest of year 9am–1.30pm; €6; joint tickets see p.380; ⓦ www.operaduomo.it), which offers the bonus of some fine views over Siena.

On the ground floor, in the **Galleria delle Statue**, the statuary by Giovanni Pisano (1250–1314) seems a little bizarre when displayed at eye level: the huge, elongated, twisting figures are obviously adjusted to take account of the original viewing position, which was ranged across the Duomo's facade. They are totally Gothic in conception, and for all their subject matter – philosophers from antiquity are represented alongside Old Testament prophets and other characters – show little of his father Nicola's experiment with classical forms on the cathedral pulpit. In marked contrast is Donatello's ochre-coloured *Madonna and Child*, a delicate piece in the centre of the room (removed from the door of the Duomo's south transept), alongside a bas-relief by Jacopo della Quercia of *St Anthony Abbot and Cardinal Antonio Casini*.

Upstairs, a curator admits you to the **Sala di Duccio**, curtained and carefully lit to display the artist's vast and justly celebrated **Maestà**. Originally painted on both sides, it depicts the *Madonna and Child Enthroned* (or *Maestà*) and the *Story of the Passion*. The four saints in the front rank of the main painting, the *Maestà*, are Siena's patron saints at the time, Ansano, Savino, Crescenzio and Vittore, while the ten smaller figures at the rear of the massed ranks represent ten of the Apostles. (Peter and Paul are in the second rank, accompanied by John the Baptist and other saints.) On its completion in 1311 the work was, as far as scholars can ascertain, the most expensive painting ever commissioned, and had occupied Duccio for almost four years. It was taken in a ceremonial procession from Duccio's studio around the Campo and then to a special Mass in the Duomo; everything in the city was closed and virtually the entire population attended. It then remained on the Duomo's high altar until 1505. This is one of the superlative works of Sienese art – its iconic, Byzantine spirituality accentuated by Duccio's flowing composition and a new attention to narrative detail in the panels of the predella and the reverse of the altarpiece, both now displayed to its side.

The *Maestà* – the Virgin as Queen of Heaven surrounded by her "court" of saints – was a Sienese invention, designed as a "sacrifice" to the Virgin, the city's patron (the consecration took place in 1260), a quality emphasized by the lavish use of gold. Duccio's rendering of the theme was essentially the prototype for the next three centuries of Sienese painters; his achievement, as Bernard Berenson put it, was to add "the drama of light to that of movement and expression" and a realization of the space in which action takes place.

This quality is best observed in the narrative panels, most of which have been gathered here, after the altarpiece's dismemberment in 1771 and its removal to the museum in 1887. Only a handful of panels are missing and – to quite understandable local disgust – will not be released by their owners to the city: two are in Washington, three in London's National Gallery and three in the Frick and Rockefeller collections in New York. One of the most effective of the surviving panels is the *Betrayal of Judas*, where trees relieve the main group of figures – Christ is "pointed" by the central tree – and rows of lances break the golden sky. The *Descent from the Cross*, too, is a marvellously composed image.

Also in the room is a *Madonna di Crevole*, an early work by Duccio, and Pietro Lorenzetti's triptych of the *Nativity of the Virgin*, the latter remarkable for breaking with the tradition of triptych painting by running a single scene across two of the painting's three panels. The gilded statues in the room off to the right of the *Madonna and Child with Four Saints* are attributed to Jacopo della Quercia, as is the separate statue of *St John the Baptist*. In the room behind the Sala is a fascinating nineteenth-century drawing of the cathedral pavement, providing a unified view impossible on the spot.

For the art that followed Duccio, and some that preceded him you need to make your way upstairs again. Here you enter the **Sala di Tesoro**, featuring amid its reliquaries the head of St Galgano and a startling *Christ on the Cross* (1280), an important early work in wood by Giovanni Pisano in which Christ is shown on a Y-shaped tree growing out of the skull of Adam. The latter symbolizes the Tree of Life, or Tree of Knowledge, which grew from a sprig planted in the dead Adam's mouth and would – in the apocryphal story – eventually yield the wood used to crucify Christ (Piero della Francesca tells this story in Arezzo's fresco cycle depicting the *Story of the True Cross*; for the full story see p.518).

Beyond the Sala di Tesoro you reach the **Sala della Madonna dagli Occhi Grossi**. The work that gives its name to this room is the cathedral's original, pre-Duccio altarpiece – a stark, haunting Byzantine icon (literally the "Madonna of the Big Eyes") in the centre of the room. It occupies a special place in Sienese history, for it was before this painting that Siena's entire population came to pray before their famous victory over the Florentines at Montaperti in 1260. It was also a promise made in front of the painting prior to the battle that saw Siena dedicated to the Madonna in the aftermath of victory. Around it are grouped a fine array of panels, including works by Simone Martini, Pietro Lorenzetti and Sano di Pietro. Note the panels flanking Sano's *Madonna and Child*: one shows St Bernardino preaching in the Campo and Piazza San Francesco (the latter now home to the saint's oratory; see p.408); the other shows St Apollonia, patron saint of dentists, martyred in Alexandria in the fourth century for refusing to make sacrifices to pagan gods.

Don't miss the tiny entrance to the so-called **Panorama dal Facciatone**: this leads to steep spiral stairs that climb out of the building, up within the walls of the abandoned nave. The sensational view from the top over the city and surrounding hills is definitely worth the two-stage climb, but beware that the topmost walkway – teetering along the very summit of the abandoned nave walls – is narrow and scarily exposed.

Terzo di San Martino

Banchi di Sotto, the main thoroughfare through the **Terzo di San Martino**, leads southeast from the Campo past the imposing Renaissance buildings of **Palazzo Piccolomini** and the **Loggia del Papa** towards the medieval Servite order's huge monastic base, **Santa Maria dei Servi**. Students outnumber tourists in this university-dominated area that ends at the south gate of the city, **Porta Romana**, but there is plenty of scope for aimless wandering through the quiet backstreets off Via Pantaneto with a loop back to the centre via the church of **San Martino**.

Loggia di Mercanzia

Marking the start of Banchi di Sotto, the main thoroughfare through Terzo di San Martino, is the **Loggia di Mercanzia** (or Loggia dei Mercanti), designed as a tribune house for merchants to do their deals. The structure was the result of extraordinary architectural indecision by the city authorities, the chronicles recording that "on one day they build in a certain way and on the following destroy and rebuild in a different manner." It was completed in 1421 in accordingly hesitant style, with Gothic niches for the saints carved by Vecchietta and Antonio Federighi, two of the city's leading Renaissance sculptors.

Palazzo Piccolomini

Following Banchi di Sotto from the loggia, you pass the more committed Renaissance buildings of the **Palazzo Piccolomini** (at Banchi di Sotto 52) and **Loggia del Papa**, commissioned in the 1460s by Pope Pius II, the Pienza-born Aeneas Sylvius Piccolomini. Pius was the city's great Renaissance patron and an indefatigable builder. The loggia was built in 1462 by Federighi. The palace – one of three the pope built for his family in the city – was designed by Bernardo Rossellino, architect of Piccolomini's famous "new town" of Pienza (see p.472); note the half-moon symbols, Pius's coat of arms, insinuated across much of the façade.

The Palazzo Piccolomini now houses the **Archivio di Stato**, the city's archives (guided visits Mon–Fri at 9.30am, 10.30am & 11.30am; free, no booking required), an unmissable detour, but one made by probably one visitor in five hundred to the city. You're taken through corridors of archives – great bundles of vellum and leather-bound documents for each of the towns and villages in Siena's domain, each one labelled in ancient medieval script with the year in question: 1351, 1352, 1353 – a quite overwhelming amount of information for any potential historian, and most of it still unread. If you're lucky you'll also be able to pop out onto the palace's terrace, which offers a rarely seen view of the Campo.

Eventually you come to the **Museo delle Tavolette di Biccherna**, containing the city's account books, tax records (the *Gabelle*) and hallowed manuscripts dating back to the earliest days of Siena's recorded history. The chief exhibits, though, are the *Tavolette*, fascinating painted wooden panels designed as covers for civic records and accounts: what makes them more interesting still is the fact that the *comune* commissioned some of the leading painters of the day to execute the beautifully detailed vignettes. Among those employed were Sano di Pietro and Ambrogio Lorenzetti, who painted the 1344 *Gabella* with a version of his *Good Government* fresco in the Palazzo Pubblico. The paintings began with religious themes, but soon moved towards secular images of city life, providing a record of six centuries of Sienese history. Later panels were designed to be hung as pictures in the council offices, rather than mounted on the books. The city is depicted frequently in the background, protected by the Virgin and mushrooming with towers – much like San Gimignano today. Early panels include several pictures of the *camerlingo* (a duty always filled by a Cistercian monk from San Galgano) doing the audits. Later ones move into specific events: victories over the Florentines; Pius's coronation as pope (1458); entrusting the city keys to the Virgin in the Duomo (1483); the demolition of the Spanish fortress (1552); the fall of Montalcino, the Sienese Republic's last stand (1559), and the entry into Siena of Cosimo I (1560); war with the Turks (1570); and subsequent Medicean events.

San Martino

From the Palazzo Piccolomini and the Loggia, Via di Pantaneto, Via del Porrione or Via di Salicotto take you quickly away from the bustle around the Campo towards the Porta Romana. Before setting off, however, Mannerist fans should spend a couple of minutes in the church of **San Martino**, founded in the eighth century or earlier, but now a pale Baroque shadow of its former self. The third altar on the left (north) wall features an outstanding *Nativity* (1522–24) by Domenico Beccafumi, a work painted at the same time as the artist was working on the Duomo's pavement, and one which encapsulates his passion for bizarre structures and peculiar light effects. The Virgin's strange gesture, in which she covers the Infant Jesus with a veil, prefigures the Crucifixion, at which she also covers Christ's naked body.

In **Via di Salicotto** – which runs directly behind the Torre del Mangia, a couple of blocks from the Loggia del Papa – you find yourself in the territory of the Torre (tower) *contrada*. They maintain a museum at no. 76 (closed for restoration; ☎0577.222.181, Ⓦwww.capitanodellatorre.it) and a fountain-square a few houses beyond. A famous sign on this street, posted in 1641, informs the citizens that the Florentine governor forbids prostitutes to practise in the neighbourhood.

Santa Maria dei Servi

Via di Salicotto or Via San Martino bring you southeast into the Valdimontone *contrada*, whose museum (☎0577.222.590, Ⓦwww.valdimontone.it), fountain and parish church are in Via di Valdimontone, alongside the massive brick church and campanile of **Santa Maria dei Servi**, the Servites' monastic base. The church (closed 12.30–3pm), which is well worth the walk, is set in a quiet piazza, approached by a row of cypresses and shaded by a couple of spreading trees – good for a midday picnic or siesta. It also offers tremendous views across the city.

The Renaissance-remodelled **interior** is remarkable for a variety of top-notch paintings. The first, above the first main altar on the right (south) wall, is the so-called *Madonna di Bordone* (1261) by **Coppo di Marcovaldo**, a Florentine artist captured by the Sienese at the Battle of Montaperti and forced to paint this picture as part of his ransom for release. The next altar to the left features the *Nativity of the Virgin* (1625) by Rutilio Manetti, Siena's leading follower of Caravaggio. Two altars down, in the last altar of the left aisle, is Matteo di Giovanni's *Massacre of the Innocents* (1491), one of two versions of this episode in the church, and one of four in the city by the infanticide-obsessed Matteo. The popularity of this subject in the late fifteenth century may have been due to the much-publicized massacre of Christian children by the Saracens

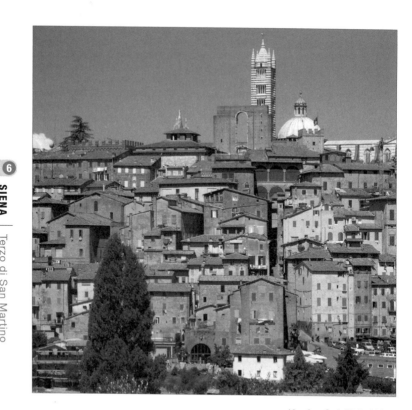

△ View from Santa Maria dei Servi

at Otranto in 1480. Matteo's rendition is a touch less blood-crazed than his Sant'Agostino version (moved to the Palazzo Pubblico since its restoration), but only just – certain features are common to both, including the powerful sense of claustrophobia and several unnecessarily perverse details, of which the most disturbing are the woman scratching the face of the soldier about to dispatch her child and the two smiling children watching the massacre from the balcony on the right.

Cheek-by-jowl violence also characterizes Pietro Lorenzetti's much earlier version of the *Massacre*, which is found on the right wall of the second chapel to the right of the high altar. (Note Herod watching the carnage from a balcony on the left.) The serene *Madonna and Child* to the right is by Segna di Bonaventura, nephew of the great Duccio. Lorenzetti is further represented by damaged frescoes of the *Banquet of Herod* and the *Death of John the Baptist*, located on the right wall of the second chapel to the left of the high altar. A fine *Adoration of the Shepherds* (1404) by one of Lorenzetti's followers, Taddeo di Bartolo, hangs in the same chapel.

Moving to the **left transept** involves a progression along a line of Sienese art history, for it contains a *Madonna della Misericordia* or *Madonna del Manto* (1436) by one of Taddeo's pupils, Giovanni di Paolo. The painting shows the Virgin sheltering a group of nuns on one side and a group of monks on the other, the latter led by Filippo Benizzi (1235–85), a Florentine general of the

Servite order. Down the north aisle towards the entrance, the last altar before the rear wall contains the small but eye-catching *Madonna del Belvedere* (1363), one of only a handful of works attributed to Jacopo di Mino, a pupil of Lippo Memmi.

Porta Romana

From Santa Maria dei Servi, you're just 100m from the **Porta Romana**, the massively bastioned south gate of the city. Its outer arch has a fragmentary fresco of the *Coronation of the Virgin*, begun by Taddeo di Bartolo and completed by Sano di Pietro. If you leave the city here, and turn left along Via Girolamo Gigli, you could follow the walls north to the **Porta Pispini**, another impressive example of defensive architecture and again flanked by a fresco of the Virgin, this time a Renaissance effort by Sodoma.

Just within the Porta Romana, opposite the huge ex-convent of San Niccolò (which now houses a psychiatric hospital), is the little church of **Santuccio**, worth looking into for its seventeenth-century frescoes depicting the life of St Galgano (see p.451). In the adjacent sacristy, at Via Roma 71, are the premises of the **Società Esecutori di Pie Disposizioni** (the Society of Benevolent Works, formerly the Society of Flagellants). This medieval order, suppressed in the eighteenth century, and later refounded along more secular lines, maintains a small collection of art works (Mon, Wed & Fri 9am–noon, Tues & Thurs 3–5pm; open on request; free), including a triptych of the *Crucifixion, Flagellation and Burial of Christ* attributed to Duccio, and a semicircular tablet, with wonderful Renaissance landscape, of *St Catherine of Siena Leading the Pope Back to Rome*.

Terzo di Città

Via di Città, one of Siena's key streets, cuts across the top of the Campo through the city's oldest quarter, the **Terzo di Città**, the area around the cathedral. The street and its continuation, Via di San Pietro, are fronted by some of Siena's finest private palazzi, including the Buonsignori, home to the **Pinacoteca Nazionale**, Siena's main picture gallery. The district is also worth exploring for its own sake, with a variety of options taking you in loops past churches such as **Sant'Agostino** and some of the city's tucked-away corners.

Palazzo Chigi-Saracini and Palazzo delle Papesse

Walking to the Pinacoteca, you pass the **Palazzo Chigi-Saracini** at Via di Città 82, a Gothic beauty, with its curved facade and back courtyard. Although the palace is closed to the public, it houses the **Accademia Chigiana** (Ⓦwww .chigiana.it), which sponsors music programmes throughout the year and maintains a small art collection, including exceptional works by Sassetta, Botticelli and Donatello. It was from this palace that the Sienese victory over the Florentines at Montaperti was announced, the town herald having watched the battle from the tower.

Almost opposite, at Via di Città 126, is a second Palazzo Piccolomini, this one built in 1460 by Bernardo Rossellino as a residence for Pius II's sister, Caterina. Known as the **Palazzo delle Papesse**, it now houses Siena's museum of contemporary art (Tues–Sun noon–7pm; €5; joint tickets see p.380; Ⓦwww

.papesse.org). Its four airy floors house excellent temporary exhibits covering anything from architecture to video art, displayed in rooms, some with nine-teenth-century frescoes, that still conserve many of their original Renaissance structural and decorative features.

Pinacoteca Nazionale

Via di Città continues to a small piazza, from where Via San Pietro leads left (south) to the fourteenth-century Palazzo Buonsignori, now the home of the superb **Pinacoteca Nazionale** (Mon 8.30am–1.30pm, Tues–Sat 8.15am–7.15pm, Sun 8.30–1.15pm; €4). Its collection is a roll of honour of Sienese Gothic painting, and if your interest has been spurred by the works by Martini in the Palazzo Pubblico or Duccio in the cathedral museum, a visit is the obvious next step. The collection offers an unrivalled chance to assess the development of art in the city from the twelfth century through to late Renaissance Mannerism.

The main rooms are arranged in chronological order, starting on the second floor. Room 1 begins with the earliest known Sienese work, an altar frontal dated 1215 of *Christ Flanked by Angels*, with side panels depicting the discovery of the True Cross (see p.517 for this story). The figures are clearly Roman-esque; the gold background – intricately patterned – was to be a standard motif of Sienese art over the next two centuries. The first identified Sienese painter, Guido da Siena, makes an appearance in this room and covers the same subject in **room 2**, though the influences on his work – dated around 1280 – are distinctively Byzantine rather than Romanesque, incorporating studded jewels amid the gold. In some of his narrative panels – *Christ Entering Jerusalem,*

△ Madonna and Child by Ambrogio Lorenzetti

The Life of St Peter and *St Clare Repelling a Saracen Attack* – his hand seems rather freer, though the colouring is limited to a few delicate shades.

Duccio di Buoninsegna (1260–1319), the dominant figure in early Sienese art, is represented along with his school in **rooms 3 and 4**. Bernard Berenson considered Duccio the last great painter of antiquity, in contrast to Giotto, the first of the moderns. The painter's advances in composition are best assessed in his *Maestà*, in the Museo dell'Opera del Duomo. Here Duccio simply shows that he "fulfilled all that the medieval mind demanded of a painter", in the words of Berenson: his dual purpose being to demon-strate Christianity to an illiterate audience and make an offering (the painting) to God. A rather more Gothic and expressive char-acter is suggested by Ugolino di Nerio's *Crucifixion* and *Madonna* in room 4.

Sienese art over the next century has its departures from Duccio – Lorenzetti's mastery of landscape and life in the *Good and Bad Government* in the Palazzo Pubblico, for example – but the patrons responsible for commissioning works generally wanted more of the same: decorative paintings, whose gold backgrounds made their subjects stand out in the gloom of medieval chapels. As well as specifying the required materials and composition, the Sienese patrons – bankers, guilds, religious orders – would often nominate a particular painting as the model for the style they wanted.

Even within the conventions required by patrons, however, there were painters whose invention and finesse set them apart. One such was Simone Martini. Though his innovations – the attention to framing and the introduction of a political dimension – are perhaps best seen in the Palazzo Pubblico, there are several great works on show here, mainly in room 5, housing one of his masterpieces, the *Blessed Agostino Novello and Four of his Miracles*. Perhaps more rewarding, however, are the works by the Lorenzetti brothers, Pietro and Ambrogio, in **rooms 7 and 8**. Pietro's include a marvellous *Risen Christ*, which could almost hold company with Masaccio, and the *Carmine Altarpiece*, whose predella has five skilful narrative scenes of the founding of the Carmelite order. Attributed to Ambrogio, or, more likely, to Sassetta, are two tiny panels in room 12, *City by the Sea* and *Castles by a Lake*, which the art historian Enzo Carli claims are the first ever "pure landscapes", without any religious purpose. They are thought to have been painted on a door, one above the other.

Moving through the fourteenth century, in **rooms 9 to 11** you come to the major Sienese artists Bartolo di Fredi (1353–1410) and his pupil Taddeo di Bartolo (1362–1422). Bartolo is best known for the New Testament frescoes in San Gimignano, whose mastery of narrative is reflected in his *Adoration of the Magi*. Taddeo, painter of the chapel in the Palazzo Pubblico, has archaic elements – notably the huge areas of gold around a sketch of landscape – but makes strides in portraiture and renders one of the first pieces of dynamic action in the museum in his *Stoning of SS. Cosmas and Damian*.

These advances are taken a stage further in Sassetta's *St Anthony Beaten by Devils* (no. 166), where Siena seems at last to be entering the mainstream of European Gothic art, and taking note of Florentine perspective. The influence of the patrons, however, is still prevalent in the mass of stereotyped images – gold again very much to the fore – by Giovanni di Paolo (1403–82), which fill most of **rooms 12 and 13**, and the exquisite Madonnas by Sano di Pietro (1406–81) and Matteo di Giovanni (1435–95) in **rooms 14 to 18**. It is astonishing to think that their Florentine contemporaries included Uccello and Leonardo. Subsequent rooms include some sublime paintings by Beccafumi, Siena's leading Mannerist artist, and works by Antonio Bazzi (better known as Sodoma) and Bernardino Mei, the last an increasingly studied and admired seventeenth-century artist.

The **third floor** of the museum – not always open – presents the self-contained **Collezione Spannocchi**, a miscellany of Italian, German and Flemish works, including a Dürer, a fine Lorenzo Lotto *Nativity*, Paris Bordone's perfect Renaissance *Annunciation*, and Sofonisba Anguissola's *Bernardo Campi Painting Sofonisba's Portrait* – the only painting in the museum by a woman artist. Anguissola, who is mentioned by Vasari as a child prodigy, painted at the height of Mannerism; this work is a neat little joke, the artist excelling in her portrait of Campi, but depicting his portrait of her as a flat, stereotyped image.

Sant'Agostino and a loop to the Duomo

South of the Pinacoteca is the church of **Sant'Agostino**, open some years, closed others, where – if you are lucky – you can admire a *Crucifixion* (1506) by Perugino (second altar of the south aisle), an *Adoration of the Magi* (1518) by Sodoma and a lunette fresco of the *Madonna and Child with Saints* by Ambrogio Lorenzetti (both in the Cappella Piccolomini), and two monochrome lunette medallions by Luca Signorelli (Cappella Bichi, south transept). The church **piazza** is quite a pleasant space, with a kids' playground and usually a few football games in progress. Along with the Campo, this square was the site of violent medieval football matches – *ballone*, as they called it – which were eventually displaced in the festival calendar by the Palio.

At no. 5 in the church piazza is the **Accademia dei Fisiocritici** (Mon–Wed & Fri 9am–1pm & 3–6pm, Thurs 9am–1pm; Ⓦwww.accademiafisiocritici .it; free), housing museums of zoology, geology and mineralogy – all a bit pedestrian, though with a few oddities – like terracotta models of *funghi* – to entertain botanists. Continuing the theme, you could make your way across the piazza to the **Orto Botanico** (Mon–Fri 9am–12.30 & 2.30–5.30pm, Sat 8am–noon; free), Via Pier Andrea Mattioli 4, whose herbarium is stocked with every Tuscan species.

An interesting walk from Sant'Agostino is to loop along the **Via della Cerchia**, a route that takes you past some good neighbourhood restaurants (see p.409) to the Carmelite convent and church of **San Niccolò al Carmine** (or Santa Maria del Carmine) in a predominantly student-populated section of the town. The church, a Renaissance rebuilding, contains a sensational *St Michael* by Domenico Beccafumi (midway down the south wall), painted following the monks' rejection of his more intense Mannerist version of the subject in the Pinacoteca (deemed to contain too many nudes for comfort). An hermaphrodite St Michael is shown at the centre of the crowded painting, looked down on by God, who has ordered the saint to earth to dispatch the Devil; the Devil's extraordinary face can be seen at the base of the picture. To the painting's left is a fragment of an *Annunciation* attributed to Ambrogio Lorenzetti.

If you follow the **Via del Fosso di San Ansano**, north of the Carmine square, you find yourself on a country lane, above terraced vineyards and allotments, before emerging at the Selva (wood) *contrada*'s square and **museum** (☎0577.45.093, Ⓦwww.contradadellaselva.it) and church of **San Sebastiano**. Climb up the stepped Vicolo di San Girolamo from here and you come out at the Duomo. Alternatively from Sant'Agostino, you could cut back to the Campo along **Via Giovanni Duprè**, where the *Onda* (wave or dolphin) *contrada* has its base at no. 111; to visit the **museum** you need to make an appointment at least a week in advance (☎0577.48.384, Ⓦwww.contradacapitanadellonda.it). The *Onda* church is San Giuseppe, at the Sant'Agostino end of the street.

Terzo di Camollia

The northern **Terzo di Camollia** is flanked, to west and east, by the churches of the most important medieval orders, the **Dominicans** and **Franciscans**, vast brick piles which rear above the city's outer ridges. Each has an important association with Siena's major saints, the former with **Catherine**, the latter with **Bernardino**. Bernardino's pilgrim trail also leads out of the city to the north, to the **Osservanza** monastery, his principal retreat.

The central part of the Camollia takes in the main thoroughfare of **Banchi di Sopra**, the base of the **Monte dei Paschi** – long the city's financial power. North from here, you move into a quiet residential quarter, all the more pleasant for its lack of specific sights or visitors. To the west, interestingly detached from the old city, is the **Fortezza di Santa Barbara**.

San Domenico

The Dominicans founded their monastery in the city in 1125. Its church, **San Domenico** (daily: April–Oct 7am–1pm & 3–6.30pm; Nov–March 9am–1pm & 3–6pm), begun in 1226, is a vast, largely Gothic building, typical of the austerity of this militaristic order. The Catherine association is immediately asserted. On the right of the entrance is a kind of raised chapel, the **Cappella delle Volte**, with a contemporary portrait of her by her friend and disciple Andrea Vanni, who according to tradition captured her likeness from life during one of her ecstasies in 1414; below are steps and a niche, where she received the stigmata, took on the Dominican habit, and performed several of her miracles. The saint's own chapel, the **Cappella di Santa Caterina** (erected in 1488), is located midway down the right (south) side of the church. Its entrance arch has images of saints Luke and Jerome by Sodoma, while the marble tabernacle on the high altar (1466) encloses a reliquary containing Catherine's head (other parts of her body lie dotted across Italy). The church's highlights, however – frescoes by Sodoma (1526) – occupy the walls to the left and right of the altar and, respectively, depict her swooning and in ecstasy. Just to the left of the chapel, above the steps to the crypt, is a detached fresco of the *Madonna and Child, John the Baptist and Knight* by Pietro Lorenzetti.

Other notable paintings are found in some of the other chapels, especially the first to the right of the high altar, which contains a Matteo di Giovanni triptych of the *Madonna and Child with SS. Jerome and John the Baptist* and fragments of detached frescoes by Lippo Memmi and Andrea Vanni. The high altar boasts a fine marble tabernacle and two sculpted angels (1465) by the sculptor and architect Benedetto da Maiano, best known for the Palazzo Strozzi in Florence and several fine works in San Gimignano (see p.422). The second chapel to the left of the high altar houses *St Barbara, Angels and SS. Catherine and Mary Magdalene* surmounted by an *Epiphany*, considered the masterpiece of Matteo di Giovanni, though its effect is somewhat undermined by the odd eighteenth-century frescoes around it. The more appealing *Madonna and Child with Saints* (1483) opposite is by the Florentine-influenced Benvenuto di Giovanni.

St Catherine of Siena

Born Caterina Benincasa, the daughter of a dyer, on March 25, 1347 – Annunciation Day – **St Catherine** had her first visions aged 5 and took the veil at age 8 (16 in some versions), against strong family opposition. She spent three years in silent contemplation, before experiencing a mystical "Night Obscure". Thereafter she went out into the turbulent, post-Black Death city, devoting herself to the poor and sick, and finally turning her hand to politics. She prevented Siena and Pisa joining Florence in rising against Pope Urban V (then absent in Avignon), and proceeded to bring him back to Rome. It was a fulfilment of the ultimate Dominican ideal – a union of the practical and mystical life. Catherine returned to Siena to a life of contemplation, visions and stigmata, retaining a political role in her attempts to reconcile the later schism between the popes and anti-popes. She died in Rome in 1380 and was canonized by Pius II (as depicted in the cathedral) in 1460. She joined St Francis as a patron saint of Italy in 1939. John Paul II declared her co-patron of Europe in 1999.

Casa di Santa Caterina

St Catherine's family home, where she lived as a Dominican tertiary – of the order but not resident – is just south of San Domenico, down the hill on Via Santa Caterina. Known as the **Casa e Santuario di Santa Caterina** (daily 9am–12.30pm & 3–6pm; free), the building has been much adapted, with a Renaissance loggia and a series of oratories – one on the site of her cell. The paintings here are mostly unexceptional Baroque canvases but it is the life that is important: an extraordinary career that made her Italy's patron saint and among the earliest women to be canonized (see box overleaf).

Near the Santuario are the church of **Santa Caterina**, home of the Oca (goose) *contrada* (℡0577.285.413, ⓦwww.contradadelloca.it) – known as *gli infami* ("the infamous ones") after their record number of Palio victories – and, down in the valley, the best-preserved of Siena's several fountains, the **Fonte Branda**. Aided by the fountain's reliable water supply, this part of the city was an area for tanneries into the twentieth century. The fountain also features in Sienese folklore as the haunt of werewolves, who would throw themselves into the water at dawn to return to human form.

Monte dei Paschi di Siena and north

Between the two monastic churches lies the heart of business Siena, the **Piazza Salimbeni**, whose three interlocking palazzi have formed, since the fifteenth century, the head office of the **Monte dei Paschi di Siena**. Banking was at the heart of medieval Sienese wealth, the town capitalizing on its position on the Via Francigena, the "French road" between Rome and northwest Europe, and the main road between Rome and Florence and Bologna. Sienese banking families go back to the twelfth century and by the end of the thirteenth they were trading widely in France, Germany, Flanders, England and along the Danube, where they maintained networks of corresponding dealers. Activity declined after the Black Death but in the fifteenth century the Republic set up the Monte dei Paschi di Siena as a lending and charitable institution, to combat the abuses of usury. It consolidated its role under Medici rule and slowly moved into more strictly banking activities. In the twentieth century it merged with other Tuscan and Umbrian banks to become one of the key financial institutions in Italy.

There is some historical interest in the exteriors of the bank's palazzi: the **Spannocchi**, on the right, was the first great Renaissance palace built in Siena (1473) and the prototype for the Palazzo Strozzi in Florence, while the **Salimbeni**, in the centre, was a last flourish of Gothicism. However, to appreciate the role of the *Monte* in Siena you need to tour the building. In 1972, Pierluigi Spadolino undertook a **radical restructuring**, encasing the building's interior medieval and Renaissance features within an ultra-modern and hi-tech framework. This is a sight in itself, but it also provides a wonderful showcase for the bank's **art collection** – the bulk of which is housed in the deconsecrated church of San Donato, linked by an underground passage with the main palazzi. The paintings here include some of the finest Gothic works in Siena, among them an exquisitely coloured *Madonna* by Giovanni di Paolo, a *Deposition* by Sano di Pietro and a *Crucifixion* by Pietro Lorenzetti. Also displayed are a series of paintings depicting the Palio and its sixteenth-century bullfighting precursor in the Campo.

The bank sometimes exhibits its art collections during banking hours and occasionally by **appointment** only (details from the tourist office). With any luck, you will be shown the archives and major halls of the bank, as well as the paintings, and the visit ends with a trip up to the tower for a view over the Campo.

To Porta Camollia and the Fortezza

Heading north from the Piazza Salimbeni, Banchi di Sopra changes name to **Via Montanini** and then **Via di Camollia**, which run through the less monumental parts of the Terzo di Camollia, good for regular shopping and largely untouristed bars and restaurants.

Two churches are worth a brief look on this street, though both are only rarely open. **Santa Maria delle Nevi** contains a famous altarpiece – *Our Lady of the Snows* (1477) – by Matteo di Giovanni, while **San Bartolomeo** fronts one of the nicest *contrada* squares in the city, home of the Istrici (porcupine); the *contrada* has its museum at Via Camollia 87 (visits to be booked a week in advance: ☎0577.48.495, ⓦ www.istrice.org). At the end of the street is the Renaissance **Porta Camollia**, inscribed on its outer arch "Siena opens her heart to you wider than this gate." It was here that a vastly superior Florentine force was put to flight in 1526, following the traditional Sienese appeal to the Virgin.

A short distance east of Banchi di Sopra – reached by a circuitous network of alleys – is another of the city's fountains, the **Fonte Nuova**. A further, highly picturesque fountain, the **Fonte Ovile**, is to be seen outside the Porta Ovile, a hundred metres or so beyond. Both were built at the end of the twelfth century. Near Fonte Nuova, in Via Vallerozzi, is the church of **San Rocco**, home of the Lupa (she-wolf) *contrada*; its museum is at nos. 71–73 (visits by appointment; ☎0577.270.777).

Away to the west, behind the church of Santo Stefano, the gardens of **La Lizza** – taken over on Wednesdays by the town's large market – lead up to the walls of the **Forte di Santa Barbara** (free access). The fortress was built initially by Charles V after the siege of 1554–55, but subsequently torn down by the people, and had to be rebuilt by Cosimo I, who then moved his troops into the garrison. Its Medicean walls resemble the walls of Lucca, designed by the same architect. Occasional summer concerts are held within the fort, which is also a permanent home to the wine collections and bar of the *Enoteca Italiana* (see p.410).

San Francesco

St Bernardino, born in the year of Catherine's death, began his preaching life at the chill monastic church of **San Francesco**, across the city to the east. A huge, hall-like structure, like that of the Dominicans, it has been heavily restored after damage by fire in 1655 and subsequent use as a barracks. Its remaining art works include fragmentary frescoes by Pietro and Ambrogio Lorenzetti: a *Crucifixion* (1331) by Pietro in the first chapel to the left of the high altar and two collaborative frescoes in the third chapel to the left of the high altar (the latter depicting *St Louis of Toulouse becoming a Franciscan* and the graphic *Martyrdom of Six Franciscans at Ceuta in Morocco*). There is also a glittering polyptych by Lippo Vanni of the *Madonna and Child with Four Saints* (1370) in the sacristy (entered from the right of the south transept). It's also worth hunting down the detached fresco right of the entrance door, its choir of angels part of a *Coronation of the Virgin* (1447) by Sassetta that once decorated the city's original Porta Romana. It was completed by Sano di Pietro, a pupil of Sassetta, after the master contracted a fatal chill while working outdoors on the fresco.

If you walk to the end of the right (south) aisle, you'll find the fourteenth-century **Tomba dei Tolomei**, the best of the church's many funerary monuments. It houses various scions of the Tolomei, one of Siena's grandest medieval families. The clan provided numerous of the city's bankers, as well as some of its leading churchmen, among them Bernardo Tolomei, founder of the abbey at Monte Oliveto Maggiore (see p.454). Also buried here is Pia de' Tolomei, first wife of Baldo Tolomei who came to live in Siena after his marriage to his second wife. Pia died, consumed with jealousy, in a castle in the Maremma, prompting Dante's famous reference to her in the *Purgatorio*: *Siena me fè, disfecemi Maremma* ("Siena made me, the Maremma unmade me").

Oratorio di San Bernardino and Museo Diocesano

In the piazza to the right of San Francesco as you face the church, adjoining the cloisters, is the **Oratorio di San Bernardino** (mid-March to Oct Mon–Sat 10.30am–1.30pm & 3–5.30pm; €3; joint tickets see p.380). The best art works here are in the beautifully wood-panelled upper chapel: fourteen large frescoes by Sodoma, Beccafumi and Girolamo del Pacchia on the *Life of the Virgin*, painted between 1496 and 1518 when the former pair were Siena's leading painters. In the lower chapel are seventeenth-century scenes of the saint's life, which was taken up by incessant travel throughout Italy, preaching against usury, denouncing the political strife between the Italian city states and urging his audience to look for inspiration to the monogram of Christ. Sermons in the Campo, it is said, frequently went on for the best part of a day. Bernadino's actual political influence was fairly marginal but he was canonized within six years of his death in 1444, and remains one of the most famous of all Italian preachers. His dictum on rhetoric – "make it clear, short and to the point" – was rewarded in the 1980s with his adoption as the patron saint of advertising.

Attached to the Oratorio is the **Museo Diocesano** (same hours and tickets), which contains an array of devotional art from the thirteenth to the seventeenth century; the pieces are beautifully displayed, but as a collection it ranks well below the Museo dell'Opera del Duomo.

L'Osservanza

If your interest in Bernardino extends to a short pilgrimage, take bus #12 from Piazza Matteotti to Madonnina Rossa (10–15min), from where it's a short walk uphill to the monastery of **L'Osservanza** (daily 9am–1pm & 4–7pm). This was founded by Bernardino in 1423 in an attempt to restore the original Franciscan rule, by then corrupted in the cities. Much rebuilt since, the monastery has a small museum and a largely Renaissance church, whose features include an Andrea della Robbia *Annunciation* and a triptych by Sano di Pietro.

Eating and drinking

Siena feels distinctly provincial after Florence. The main action of an evening is the *passeggiata* from Piazza Matteotti along Banchi di Sopra to the Campo – and there's not much in the way of nightlife to follow. For most visitors, though, an evening in one of the city's **restaurants** provides diversion enough, while the presence of the university ensures a bit of life in the **bars**, as well as a cluster of cheaper *trattorie* alongside the restaurants.

The
Siena Palio

"The Palio helps Siena to survive in its own mind. It is a metaphor for the continuity of the life of the people."

Roberto Barzanti, former Siena MEP and mayor

The Siena Palio is the most exciting and spectacular festival event in Italy, a twice-yearly bareback horse race around the Campo, supported by days of preparation, pageantry and intrigue. It has been held since at least the thirteenth century, in honour – like almost everything in Siena – of the Virgin, and it remains a living tradition, felt and performed with an intensity that comes as a shock in these days of cosily preserved folklore. For days around the festivals the air of rivalry is palpable, quite often breaking into violence amid the bragging celebration of victory by one or other of the *contrade*.

Except at times of war, the Palio has virtually always taken place. In 1798, for example, when the city was in chaos after an earthquake, the July Palio was cancelled but the August race took place. The following year, however, the Palio was again cancelled, owing to political unrest: Sienese counter-revolutionaries took the opportunity to rise against the French-held fortress and sacked the ghetto area of the city. In 1919, when half of Italy was in the throes of strikes and rioting, Siena's factions of the left and right agreed to defer such politics until after the Palio.

The drawing of lots

Even before the race, fortune plays the pre-eminent part: since there's only room for ten riders, each year the seventeen *contrade* have to **draw lots** to take part. The participants also draw lots both for the horses and for starting positions in the race itself. The **jockeys** are professional outsiders, traditionally the *butteri*, or cowboys, of the Maremma (see p.343), employed according to an unreliable and shifting combination of loyalties reinforced by large cash payments and bonuses – and sometimes the threat of violence if they are treacherous. During the run-up to the races they live under the suspicions of their own *contrada* and in fear of the threats of

The build-up

Originally the Palio followed a circuit through the town, but since the sixteenth century it has consisted of **three laps** of the Campo, around a track covered with sand and padded with mattresses in an attempt to minimize injury to horses and riders. Despite all probabilities, no jockey has ever been killed.

There are two annual Palios, held on July 2 (formerly the Feast of the Visitation) and August 16 (the day after the Feast of the Assumption), each of which is preceded by a fascinating sequence of events.

June 29/August 13: the year's horses are presented in the morning at the town hall and drawn by lot. At 7.15pm the first trial race is held in the Campo.

June 30/August 14: further trial races at 9am and 7.45pm. The evening race is usually followed by a concert in the Campo.

July 1/August 15: two more trial races at 9am and 7.45pm, followed by a street banquet and late-night revelry in each of the *contrade*. Restaurants also move their tables outside for these Palio nights.

July 2/August 16: the day of the Palio begins with a final trial race at 9am. In the early afternoon, each of the ten chosen *contrade* takes its horse to be blessed in its church: "Go, little horse, and return a winner" are the priest's words. It's worth trying

to see one of these horse blessings, which are often preceded by an extraordinary struggle to get the animal up or down the entrance steps. It's taken as a good omen if the horse defecates in church. At around 5pm the town hall bell begins to ring and the **corteo storico**, a pageant of horses, riders and medieval-costumed officials, processes through the city to the Campo. The *corteo* includes *comparse* – symbolic groups of equerries, ensigns, pages and drummers – from each of the *contrade*, who perform various *sbandierata* (flag-twirling) and athletic feats in the square. They are preceded by officials of the *comune* of Siena and representatives from all the ancient towns and villages of the Sienese Republic, led by the standard-bearer of Montalcino, which offered refuge to the last republicans.

rival *contrade*. They may be bribed to throw the race, or to whip a rival or his horse; *contrade* have been known to drug horses, and even to mount an ambush on a jockey making his way to the race.

The result of all this is that in any one year perhaps three or four *contrade* go to the start-line with any chance of victory; for those *contrade* disadvantaged by poor horses or jockeys, and the seven *contrade* who aren't even taking part, the race becomes a vehicle for schemes, plots and general mayhem. Each *contrada* has its traditional rival, and ensuring that one's rival loses is as important as winning for oneself. The only rule of the race is that the jockeys cannot interfere with the others' reins; everything else is accepted and practised. And it's the **horse** that wins – it doesn't matter if the jockey has been thrown en route to victory.

Celebratory meal after the Palio

The race

The **race** itself begins on July 2 at 7.45pm, on August 16 at 7pm, and lasts for little more than ninety seconds. There's no PA system to tell you what's going on. At the start (in the northwest corner of the Campo) all the horses except one are penned between two ropes; the free one charges the group from behind, when his rivals least expect it,

Galloping towards the finish

and the race is on. It's a hectic, violent and bizarre spectacle, and the jockeys don't even stop at the finish line but gallop at top speed out of the Campo, followed by a frenzied mass of supporters. Losers can be in danger of assault, especially if there are rumours about the race being fixed.

The **palio** – a silk banner – is subsequently presented to the winning *contrada*, who then make their way to the church of Provenanzo (in July) or the Duomo (in August) to give thanks. The younger *contrada* members spend the rest of the night and much of the subsequent week swaggering around the town celebrating their victory, even handing out celebratory sonnets. In the evening all members of the *contrada* hold a jubilant street banquet.

Inevitably, hotel rooms are extremely difficult to find at Palio time, and if you haven't booked, either reckon on staying up all night, or travelling in from a neighbouring town. The races are shown live on national TV and repeated endlessly all evening. All year round, Cinema Moderno on Piazza Tolomei screens a twenty-minute film explaining the history and drama of the race, dubbed into English.

Prime viewing point over the Campo

Palio practicalities

It's not hard to get a view of any of the practice races or ceremonies, but for the Palio proper you need to plan ahead a little. **Tickets** for grandstand or balcony seats, ranged around the Campo, cost from €150 to €300 or more, and are sold out months before the race. To nab a seat for next year's event, contact Palio Viaggi, Piazza Gramsci 7 (T0577.280.828, F0577.289.114, no website). In the UK, contact Liaisons Abroad (T020/7376 4020, Wwww.liaisonsabroad.com).

Most ordinary spectators crowd for free into the centre of the Campo. For the **best view** you need to have found a position by 2pm on the inner rail (ideally at the start/finish line), and to keep it for the next six hours. If you're not installed here, there's really no rush, as you'll be able to see a certain amount from anywhere within the throng. Be prepared to stand your ground: people keep pouring in right up until a few minutes before the race, and the swell of the crowd can be overwhelming. Be aware that you won't be able to leave the Campo for at least two hours after the race. Toilets, shade and refreshment facilities are minimal (which is perhaps why so little drinking goes on). If you arrive late in the day, you might try making your way to Via Giovanni Dupré, behind the Palazzo Pubblico, from where the police usually allow people into the centre of the square an hour or so before the race.

Every last vantage point is commandeered for a view of the action

Restaurants

Siena used to have a poor reputation for **restaurants** but over the last few years things have improved, with a range of imaginative *osterie* opening up and a general hike in standards. The only place you need surrender gastronomic ideals is for a meal out in the Campo: the posh restaurant here, *Il Campo*, isn't worth the money – though it's the one to go for if you want to eat in style in the square – which leaves a choice of routine but reasonably priced *pizzerie*. For cheaper meals, you'll generally do best walking out a little from the centre, west towards San Niccolò al Carmine, or north towards the Porta Camollia.

Local specialities include *pici* (noodle-like pasta with toasted breadcrumbs), *salsicce secche* (dried sausages), *finocchiona* (minced pork flavoured with fennel), *capolocci* (spiced loin of pork), *pappa col pomodoro* (bread and tomato soup), *tortino di carciofi* (artichoke omelette) and *fagioli all'uccelletto* (bean and sausage stew). The city is also famous for a whole range of **cakes and biscuits**, including the ubiquitous *panforte*, a dense and delicious wedge of nuts, fruit and honey that originated with pilgrimage journeys, *cavallucci* (aniseed, nut and spice biscuits), *copate* (nougat wafers) and rich, almond *ricciarelli* biscuits.

All these restaurants are located on the map on pp.378–379.

Al Marsili Via del Castoro 3 ☎0577.47.154, ⓦwww.ristorantealmarsili.it. A large, elegant and upmarket restaurant with good local dishes (including some choice for vegetarians) and attentive service. The *risotto al limone* is worth dallying over, plus they have plenty of more exotic dishes such as guinea fowl with prunes, pine nuts and almonds. €40 buys a memorable meal.

Antica Osteria Da Divo Via Franciosa 29 ☎0577.286.054. A close second behind *Osteria Le Logge* for ambience, thanks to its extraordinary subterranean cellar dining rooms. Upstairs is pretty, too, and the food is well above average, with starters at around €8–12 and mains at €14–22. Closed Tues.

Cane e Gatto Via Pagliaresi 6 ☎0577.220.751. Don't be put off by the un-Sienese art nouveau-style decor: this friendly restaurant serves superb Tuscan *cucina nuova*, featuring seven courses on its *menù degustazione*: this will cost you around €50, with a selection of wines included. Located southeast of the Campo, off Via di Pantaneto. Closed Thurs and lunch daily.

Da Trombicche Via delle Terme 66 ☎0577.288.089. A tiny, youthful no-nonsense trattoria with a limited menu of glorified snacks – soup, cheese, salami and meat stews – accompanied by rough wine served straight from the barrel. Closed Sun.

Gallo Nero Via del Porrione ☎0577.284.356, ⓦwww.gallonero.it. Quirky, vaulted place, offering a Tuscan menu for around €16, or a six-course medieval menu for half as much again, boasting dishes such as bittersweet duck with cheese ravioli and chicken in sweet wine with fruit. Daily except Mon from Nov to Feb.

La Cina Casato di Sotto 56 ☎0577.283.061. Quiet, affordable Chinese restaurant 150m from the Campo. The food is adequate, and makes a change from Tuscan cooking.

La Taverna del Capitano Via del Capitano 8 ☎0577.288.094. A stone's throw from the Duomo, this is a serene dining room with medieval vaulted ceiling and straight-down-the-line Tuscan cooking: *panzanella* (bread salad), *pici*, *pappardelle*, *bistecche* and the like. Closed Tues.

Le Campane Via delle Campane 6 ☎0577.284.035. High-quality and innovative Sienese cuisine, with an emphasis on fish and seafood, at a small, formal restaurant just below the Duomo. Set menus – *di terra* or *di mare* – cost around €40. Closed Mon.

Osteria Boccone del Prete Via di San Pietro 17 ☎0577.280.388. One of Siena's newer restaurants, near the Pinacoteca Nazionale, serving delicious crostini, salads and pasta dishes in a stylish setting. Closed Sun.

Osteria Castelvecchio Via di Castelvecchio 65 ☎0577.49.586. Adventurous, first-rate and nicely informal *osteria* – a good bet for vegetarians (plus plenty of meat dishes and homemade pasta too). Menus change daily. Sited off Via San Pietro, near the Pinacoteca Nazionale. Closed Tues & July. Moderate.

Osteria del Ficomezzo Via dei Termini 71 ☎0577.222.384. A small, simple *osteria* a touch off the tourist track with a cool, pastel interior: good value set-price menus at lunch, with innovative Tuscan food (menus change weekly), and pricier à la carte in the evening. Closed Sun.

Carroccio Via del Casato di Sotto 32
1.165. Just 50m from the Campo, and
tables – room for forty inside and twenty
serves fine Tuscan food in a welcom-
...rmal atmosphere. Menus change weekly.
Closed Wed.
Osteria Il Grattacielo Via Pontani 8
℡0577.289.326. A very local *vinaio* serving wine
and snacks, this minuscule cafe-*osteria* – ironically
named "The Skyscraper" – makes a popular lunch
stop for its marinated anchovies, Tuscan beans
and salami.

 Osteria Le Logge Via del Porrione 33
℡0577.48.013. The best-looking restaurant

in central Siena, occupying a fine old cabinet-lined
farmacia off the Campo by the Loggia del Papa.
Good pasta and some unusual *secondi*, but the
quality of food – once exceptional – is these days
merely above average. Closed Sun.
Trattoria Garibaldi Via Giovanni Dupré 18. A
cheap and basic trattoria sited below a *locanda*,
just south of the Campo. Closed Sat.

 Tullio ai Tre Cristi Vicolo Provenzano 1
℡0577.280.608. A Sienese institution since
1830, this is the neighbourhood restaurant of the
Giraffa *contrada* and is draped with heraldic banners.
Serves an ambitious, predominantly fish and seafood
menu. Terrace tables in summer. Closed Wed.

Bars, clubs and events

There are pleasant neighbourhood **bars** in most *contrade* and plenty of neon-
lit modern establishments scattered around the city for quick refreshment.
The *Enoteca Italiana* (Mon noon–8pm, Tues–Sat noon–1am; ℡0577.288.497,
Ⓦwww.enoteca-italiana.it; free), inside the Fortezza di Santa Barbara, is Italy's
largest national **wine** collection. Its cellar stocks and exhibits every single Italian
wine (almost a thousand of them), and there's a bar where you can order a glass
of any of the cheaper wines, or buy any bottle. You need to head to the *Dublin
Post*, uninspiringly situated on Piazza Gramsci, or *Barone Rosso*, Via dei Termini
9, for a pint of beer, the latter open in the evenings only with live music until
late. Of the terrace cafés ringing the Campo, the small *Liberamente* at the corner
of Casato dei Barbieri has more charm than most.

Club life is fairly limited in Siena but for a glimpse of the smart Sienese
on the dance floor try *Al Cambio*, Via di Pantaneto 48 – a dark, moody place
with conventional dance music and a steep entrance fee; somewhat livelier is

Picnics, snacks and ice cream

It's an easy matter to put together your own **picnic**, allowing a very cheap meal in the
Campo or other squares; Piazza Santa Maria dei Servi is a nice spot. You can buy
pizza by weight from many small hole-in-the wall places around the city, or phone an
order ahead for fresh-baked pizza (whole or by the slice) from *Mister Pizza*, Via delle
Terme 94 (℡0577.221.746; closed Sun). Browse gourmet supplies at the sensational
and extravagantly stocked **food stores** such as Manganelli 1879, Via di Città 71.
The **covered market** south of the Campo in Piazza del Mercato is also good for
picnic provisions, while Wednesday mornings see a full-scale open-air **market** – with
food and clothing stalls – sprawl across La Lizza. A good place for local **wines** is
the *Enoteca San Domenico*, Via del Paradiso 56 (Ⓦwww.enotecasandomenico.it).
Panforte is best bought fresh by the *etto* (hectogram; 100g) from any of the bakeries or
pasticcerie along Banchi di Sopra; the gift-packaged slabs aren't so good. La Nuova
Pasticceria, Via Giovanni Dupré 37, is one option, but the best place to start is Nannini, Banchi di Sopra 22–24. This is also among the best **bars** for snacks, with locals
constantly dropping in to choose from the wide range of sweet and savoury nibbles.
Most Sienese buy **ice cream** at one end or the other of the *passeggiata* – either at
the *Nannini Gelateria*, at the northern end of Banchi di Sopra, or *Brividio*, just off the
Campo where Via di Città meets Via dei Pellegrini.

the pub/disco *Barone Rosso* (see above), the local haunt of foreign students and Sienese army boys, with a fair selection of beers and a range of dance music. The *Walkabout Pub*, Via di Pantaneto 90, is a predictable "Aussie" pub with Sky TV for big sports events and Australian and British beers.

City events and **festivals** are advertised on posters around Piazza Matteotti and in the Campo back streets; the website Ⓦ www.terresiena.it is also a good source of information. Classical music tastes are the most likely to be rewarded, as the Monte dei Paschi and Accademia Chigiana (℡ 0577.22.091, Ⓦ www.chigiana .it) sponsor impressive concerts throughout the year. The Siena supplement of *La Nazione* newspaper has a what's on section. The most prestigious classical music festival – often featuring a major opera production – is July and August's **Estate Musicale Chigiana** (Ⓦ www.chigiana.it). Other cultural events include **Siena Jazz** (℡ 0577.271.401, Ⓦ www.sienajazz.it) in late July and August (concerts are held in venues around the city and local towns and villages) and the modest but increasingly popular Siena Film Festival (℡ 0577.222.999, Ⓦ www .sienafilmfestival.it) in September.

Listings

Banks and exchange Banks are concentrated along Banchi di Sopra, north of the Campo, and there's an automatic exchange machine in the window of the Monte dei Paschi at no. 92. The train station ticket office will also change cash and travellers' cheques, but the most central option is Exact in Via di Città, which charges a hefty commission but is open daily 8.30am–11pm.

Bike and scooter rental Rent bikes at DF Bike, Via Massetana Romana 54 ℡ 0577.271.905; scooters and bikes at DF Moto, Via dei Gazzani 16–18 ℡ 0577.288.387, or Automotocicli Perozzi, Via del Romitorio 5 ℡ 0577.223.157.

Books and newspapers English-language books – novels plus a fair selection of books on Siena and Tuscany – are at the Libreria Senese, Via di Città 94, two branches of Feltrinelli, Banchi di Sopra 66, and Bassi, Via di Città 6–8. Tempo Libero, Casato di Sotto 20 (closed Mon) is a smaller and friendlier local bookshop with an English selection.

Bus information Ticket offices beneath Piazza Gramsci have information on all routes. The bus company serving Siena and its hinterland is called TRA-IN (℡ 0577.204.246, Ⓦ www.trainspa.it).

Language courses Scuola Leonardo da Vinci, Via del Paradiso 16 ℡ 0577.249.097, Ⓦ www.scuola-leonardo.com; Saena Iulia, Via Monna Agnese 20 ℡ 0577.44.155; Università per Stranieri, Via Pantaneto 45 ℡ 0577.280.695.

Left luggage 24hr locker service at the train station; staffed facility at bus station in Piazza Gramsci (daily 7am–7.45pm; €3.50 per bag per day).

Lost property *Comune di Siena*, Casato di Sotto 23 (Mon–Sat 9am–12.30pm, Tues also 3–5pm).

Market Siena's market takes place at La Lizza (Wed 8am–1pm).

Police *Questura* is on Via del Castoro; *Ufficio Stranieri* (Foreigners' Office), Piazza Jacopo della Quercia (Mon & Tues 8.30am–10.30am, Wed 8.30am–10.30am & 3.30–5.30pm).

Post office Piazza Matteotti (Mon–Fri 8.15am–7pm, Sat 8.15am–noon).

Travel details

Trains

Siena to: Asciano (12 daily; 35min); Buonconvento (6 daily; 25min); Chiusi (12 daily; 1hr 35min); Empoli (hourly; 50min–1hr 20min; change for Pisa and Florence); Florence (9 daily; 1hr 40min); Grosseto (6 daily; 1hr 20min).

Buses

Siena to: Arezzo (8 daily; 1hr 30min); Asciano (3 daily; 1hr); Buonconvento (7 daily; 50min); Castellina in Chianti (7 daily; 35min); Castiglione della Pescaia (2 daily in summer; 1hr 55min); Chianciano (2 daily; 1hr 40min); Colle di Val d'Elsa (hourly;

30min); Florence (hourly; 1hr 15min); Gaiole in Chianti (5 daily; 50min); Grosseto (hourly; 1hr 25min); Monticiano (4 daily; 1hr 5min); Montalcino (7 daily; 1hr 15min); Montepulciano (5 daily; 1hr 25min); Monteriggioni (hourly; 25min); Pienza (6 daily; 1hr 15min); Poggibonsi (hourly; 45min); Radda in Chianti (5 daily; 55min); San Gimignano (10 daily; 1hr 15min); Sinalunga (2 daily; 50min).

7

The Sienese hill-towns

CHAPTER 7

Highlights

✳ **Monteriggioni** Dante alluded to the towers of this fortified citadel, and they still lord it over the countryside today. **See p.417**

✳ **Colle di Val d'Elsa** Intimate town with a medley of tiny churches and museums. **See p.418**

✳ **San Gimignano** Italy's best-known village,

famous for its towers, its crowds and the stunning Collegiata, one of the most comprehensively frescoed churches in Tuscany. **See p.422**

✳ **Volterra** Moody hill-town with its roots in the Etruscan era, now celebrated for its alabaster workshops. **See p.436**

△ Piazza della Cisterna, San Gimignano

The Sienese hill-towns

J ust as Siena provides a perfect antidote to Florence, so the rural **hill-towns** that cluster around the old capital of the Sienese Republic provide an intimate counterpoint to the larger towns that crowd in on the Tuscan capital. Most of Siena's satellites are more appealing than their Florentine equivalents, and benefit from surroundings that exemplify the timeless pastoral quality for which the region is renowned. **San Gimignano** is the pick of the bunch, thanks mainly to its famous towers, a vision of medieval perfection now badly compromised in summer by the huge numbers of day-trippers who crowd its warren of streets. That said, the fresco-lined Collegiata and a clutch of minor churches, not to mention an excellent civic museum, are all unmissable attractions, and well worth building an overnight stay around. **Monteriggioni**, a less well-known and thus less spoilt medieval village is another must-see, and can easily be incorporated into a visit to **Colle di Val d'Elsa**, another centuries-old enclave but one that is often overlooked by visitors who are deterred by its unlovely outskirts. You should also try to fit **Volterra** into your itinerary; slightly cut off from the other Sienese hill-towns, it's a dramatically situated, brooding sort of town whose Etruscan origins are never far from the surface. Known primarily for its archeological museum, it also has a fascinating art gallery and a captivating cathedral square.

From Siena to San Gimignano

Heading west from Siena, most people have San Gimignano firmly in their sights. If you have time, the best route to follow is the N2 as far as the turreted fortress-hamlet of **Monteriggioni**, then turn west to **Colle di Val d'Elsa**, whose striking medieval upper town extends along a narrow ridge. From Colle, a scenic and minor road, which walkers might try paralleling across country, runs on via Bibbiano to San Gimignano.

On **public transport**, you can stop easily enough at Colle, before catching another bus to the industrial town of Poggibonsi – and a connection from there to San Gimignano; for Monteriggioni, you can catch a bus to the turning up to

THE SIENESE HILL-TOWNS

▲ Monte San Savino & Arezzo

Radda in Chianti

Corsignano

Montaperti

Siena

C H I A N T I

Poggibonsi

Colle di Val d'Elsa

Monteriggioni

Gracciano d'Elsa

M O N T E   M A G G I O

San Gimignano

Borgatello

Castel San Gimignano

San Donato

Castelvecchio

Casole d'Elsa

Mensano

Monteguidi

Radicondoli

M. Voltraio
458m

Pignano

Volterra

Saline di Volterra

Pomarance

M E T A L L I F E R E

Rocco
di Sillano

Larderello

C O L L I N E

Montecatini
Val di Cecina

0   5 km

◀ Florence

◀ Certaldo & Empoli

◀ Certaldo & Empoli

▲ Cécina, Pisa & Piombino

◀ Pontedera & Pisa

▲ Massa Marittima

San Galgano & Grosseto ▶

Petriolo & Grosseto ▶

Buonconvento ▶

N

the village (and hail another one on from there to Colle or back to Siena). Most buses from Siena to San Gimignano involve a Poggibonsi connection, though there's a direct TRA-IN service in summer.

Note that the route north from Poggibonsi to Empoli – via Certaldo and Castelfiorentino – is covered from p.254 onwards.

Monteriggioni

The perfectly preserved walls of **MONTERIGGIONI** declare their presence for miles ahead from the N2 and the Siena–Florence autostrada. The citadel, begun by the Sienese in 1213, was a strategic target for any troops marching on Siena from the north and is immortalized in Dante's *Inferno*, in which he compares the fourteen towers – added during reconstruction in 1260 after the Sienese victory at Montaperti – to giants in an abyss. The verse greets you on the wall of the gate as you enter the village, which consists of a couple of dozen houses, gardens, two restaurants, the odd bar and several overpriced tourist outlets. The houses give way to gardens as they near the ramparts, and an athlete could probably run the main street, from south to north gates, in about ten seconds. All of which, of course, accounts for the charm of the place, though like San Gimignano, it's severely compromised in summer by the legions of day-trippers.

The walls apart, there are virtually no sights bar a pretty Romanesque church and a small museum, the **Museo Multimediale**, Piazza Roma 23 (daily: mid-March to mid-Nov 9.30am–7.30pm; rest of the year 11am–5pm; closed mid-Jan to mid-Feb; €2), which exhibits archeological fragments from sites in and around the village.

You don't necessarily need a car or bike to reach Monteriggioni: the **train station** is 2km north at Castellina Scalo, about twenty minutes' walk away. There's a small **tourist office**, Largo Fontebranda 5 (May–Oct daily 9.30am–5.30pm; Nov–April Tues–Sun 1.30–7pm; ☎0577.304.810). Of the two moderately priced

△ Monteriggioni's medieval walls

restaurants, *Il Pozzo* (☎0577.304.127; closed Sun eve & Mon) in Piazza Roma, the main square, is perhaps the better known, but *Il Piccolo Castello* opposite (☎0577.304.370) is equally good. Both specialize in game and add liberal sprinklings of truffles and *porcini* to many dishes. Also on the main street is the Fattoria Castello di Monteriggioni wine shop, which sells a fine local Chianti, Vinsanto and grappa. The village also boasts a classy and very pleasant four-star **hotel** *Monteriggioni*, Via I Maggio 4 (☎0577.305.009, ⓦwww.hotelmonteriggioni .net; ❼), whose twelve rooms – despite steep prices – are quickly snapped up. There are also **private rooms** in the village; the tourist office has details.

A good three-star **hotel**, *La Casalta* (☎0577.301.002; ⒠casalta@chiantiturismo .it), lies 4km west at the hamlet of **Strove** – worth the trip just for its excellent and moderately priced **restaurant**. Midway to Strove are the outstanding Romanesque church and monastic remains of **Abbadia a Isola**, originally (as the name suggests) an abbey set on an island amid marshes. If the church is closed ask for the key from the caretaker in the house to the left of the church or at the bar across the road.

Colle di Val d'Elsa

COLLE DI VAL D'ELSA, despite plentiful bus connections to Siena and San Gimignano, is not much explored. Perhaps **Colle Bassa**, the lower town, puts visitors off: paper-making, and then nail factories, have long made it a prosperous place, and today it's a sprawl of light industry and housing developments. However, the walled upper town, **Colle Alta**, is a beauty, stretching along a ridge with its one long street lined with medieval palazzi.

Of pre-Roman foundation, the town occupies a noted place in the annals of Florentine and Sienese rivalry, for it was at the **Battle of Colle** in 1269 that the Florentines bloodily avenged their defeat by the Sienese at the Battle of Montaperti nine years earlier. The town then vacillated between the two powers, but also retained a measure of independence, its free *comune* instigating the office of *Capitano del Popolo* in 1286, just a few years after Florence and Siena. It remained racked by factional disputes, and in 1333 voluntarily put itself under the protection of Florence. The ensuing period of relative peace enabled the town to develop its wool and paper industries, both of which made use of the abundant supplies of local water, which was channelled through the area in a series of specially built canals. Glass and paper are still local specialities.

Colle Bassa

Colle Bassa's main square, **Piazza Arnolfo**, is named after Arnolfo di Cambio, who was the architect of the Duomo and Palazzo Vecchio in Florence, and was born here in around 1232. A block north is the town's major piece of modern architecture, a regional headquarters of the Monte dei Paschi bank, designed by Giovanni Michelucci; mixing Portakabin-like offices with open girders, it's not one of his most captivating efforts.

Just south of the piazza at Via dei Fossi 8a is the **Museo del Cristallo** (Tues–Sun 10.30am–noon & 4–7.30pm; ⓦwww.cristallo.org; €3). Built on the site of an eighteenth-century glass furnace, the museum outlines the transition from Colle's traditional glass-making industry from pre-industrial pieces to 1820, the year of the first furnace, and from 1820 to the beginning of crystal production in 1963; today, Colle produces 95 percent of Italy's, and fifteen percent of the world's crystal. Virtually next door to the museum is Colle Bassa's only other worthwhile sight, the thirteenth-century church of **Sant'Agostino**, largely rebuilt by Antonio da Sangallo the Elder in 1521, three years after embarking on his masterpiece, the church of San Biagio in Montepulciano (see p.485). The second altar on the right contains a glorious *Madonna and Child with Saints* by Taddeo di Bartolo, probably a surviving panel of a triptych. The eye-catching marble tabernacle in the north aisle, the *Madonna del Piano*, is attributed to Baccio da Montelupo (1469–1535).

Colle Alta

From Piazza Arnolfo, it's a pretty steep ten-minute climb up to **Colle Alta**: follow Via San Sebastiano and then the brick-paved *costa*, which brings you out at the eastern tip of the town. If you drive or take a bus up, you're directed around a circuitous route to the west end of the ridge, by the Porta Nuova.

At the top of the *costa*, you've little choice but to follow **Via del Castello**, the centre of a three-street grid, past a scattering of tower houses; Arnolfo di Cambio was born at no. 63, in the so-called Torre di Arnolfo. Just a little farther down is the small Romanesque church of **Santa Maria in Canonica**, built in the twelfth or thirteenth century, but thought to have far older origins. Its interior is notable for a stupendous late fourteenth-century tabernacle of the *Madonna and Child with Saints* by Pier Francesco Fiorentino; the frame, almost as impressive as the painting, is original.

Midway along Via del Castello, the **Piazza del Duomo** opens out, flanked by the cathedral and three museums. The **Duomo**, its Romanesque origins all but obliterated by later remodelling (1603–1815), features a marble pulpit (1465) by Giuliano da Maiano, who used four pillars and capitals from a much older work to frame his bas-reliefs. His brother Benedetto was responsible for the font (1468), the two having worked together during the same period in San Gimignano. The fourth chapel on the right has a famous *Nativity* (1635), the masterpiece of Rutilio Manetti, the leading Sienese follower of Caravaggio. In the depths of the right transept stands the Cappella del Santo Chiodo, commissioned by the Piccolomini pope, Pius II, to house a nail (*chiodo*) from the Cross, the relic providing the inspiration for the beautiful tabernacle attributed to Mino da Fiesole. The nearby bronze lectern, palm branch and eagle are by Pietro Tacca, a pupil of Giambologna, whose eccentric work will be familiar if you've seen his strange fountains in Florence's Piazza Santissima Annunziata. Tacca also probably cast the impressive bronze Crucifix above the high altar, the work having been designed by Giambologna.

In the Palazzo Pretorio (1335) beside the Duomo, at Via del Castello-Piazza del Duomo 42, is the **Museo Archeologico "Ranuccio Bianchi Bandinelli"** (May–Oct Tues–Sun 10.30am–12.30 & 4.30–7.30pm; Nov–April Tues–Fri 3.30–5.30pm, Sat & Sun 10am–noon & 3.30–6.30pm; €3). It's only of passing interest, save for the finds from the local *Tomba dei Calisna Sepu*, one of Tuscany's most important Etruscan tombs: key treasures from it are scattered in museums as far afield as Berlin. Just out of the piazza, the attractive three-room **Museo Civico e d'Arte Sacra** housed in the Palazzo dei Priori, the old bishop's palace at Via del Castello 31 (Tues–Sun 10.30am–12.30 & 4.30–7.30pm; €3) is more interesting, retaining frescoes of hunting scenes by Bartolo di Fredi. It has a fair collection of Sienese paintings gathered from local churches, with more works due to be installed here. The most interesting canvas is a *Maestà* from Abbadia Isola, once attributed to Duccio, but now given to the anonymous Maestro di Badia a Isola.

About 100m beyond Piazza del Duomo stands the covetable **Palazzo Campana**, a Mannerist *tour de force* built in 1539 by Baccio d'Agnolo, the architect responsible for the rather less amenable Palazzo Bartolini in Florence. From here, a bridge connects the town's medieval core to its fifteenth- and sixteenth-century expansions. Off to the north stands an imposing Franciscan monastery, whose church, **San Francesco**, claims a high altarpiece (occasionally removed) of the *Madonna and Child with Four Saints* (1479) by Sano di Pietro, a painting that's more than worth the walk (ring the bell of the seminary if the church is shut). It's worth paying particular attention to the scenes in the predella, which illustrate episodes from the lives of the saints depicted in the main painting (Benedict, Cyrinus, Donatus and Justina). The second panel from the left shows Cyrinus, a Croatian saint, preaching to the crowd that has come to watch his martyrdom: he's shown miraculously floating on the stone that had been tied round his neck in an attempt to drown him. Donatus, patron saint of Arezzo (his birthplace), was martyred in the fourth century, and is remembered primarily for frightening off a dragon which had been poisoning local wells: Sano shows him with his mule, bravely marching to meet the dragon emerging from its cave. The right-hand scene shows the third-century Justina, a royal princess, patron of Padua but much venerated in Pisa, being martyred on the orders of her father.

Sticking with the main road through this quarter you come to *Hotel Arnolfo* in Piazza Santa Caterina. Off this square is the alleyway **Vicolo della Fontanella**, with a glass workshop – Colle makes much of its money from glass factories in the lower town – and the *Enoteca della Fortuna*, a wine shop with a tiny upstairs restaurant. At the end of the main road stands the hugely bastioned **Porta Nuova**, attributed to Giuliano da Sangallo.

Practicalities

Inter-town **buses** from Florence, Siena, Volterra and elsewhere stop in Colle Bassa's Piazza Arnolfo. The **tourist office** is in Colle Alta at Via Francesco Campana 43 (April–Oct Mon–Sat 10am–1pm & 2.30–7pm, Sun 10am–1pm & 3–6pm; Nov–Jan & March Mon–Sat 10am–1pm & 2.30–5pm; closed Feb; ☎0577.922.791, ⓦwww.collevaldelsa.net). Piazza Arnolfo in Colle Bassa is home to the **police station** (☎0577.920.003; lost property ☎0577.920.831). You can rent bikes and scooters from Mario Antichi, Via Livini 1 (☎0577.923.366). There's a **taxi** rank in Piazza Arnolfo, or you can call ☎0577.923.610 or 0577.921.379. Colle's busy Friday **market** spreads out from Piazza Arnolfo.

The only budget **hotel** is the 24-room, two-star *Hotel Il Nazionale*, in Colle Bassa just west of Piazza Arnolfo, Via Garibaldi 20 (☎0577.920.039, ☎0577.920.168; ❷). More upmarket is *La Vecchia Cartiera*, a 38-room three-star in Bassa, just off the piazza at Via Oberdan 5–9 (☎0577.921.107, ⓦwww.chiantiturismo .it; ❺). The only hotel in Colle Alta is the 32-room, very central three-star *Arnolfo*, Via Francesco Campana 8 (☎0577.922.020, ⓦwww.hotelarnolfo.it; ❷) – although it can be noisy. Two kilometres out of town, the three-star *Hotel Villa Belvedere* (☎0577.920.966, ⓦwww.villabelvedere.com; ❺), occupies an eighteenth-century villa on the Monteriggioni road, with fifteen rooms, fine grounds, tennis courts and a pool. The views over the town from the thirty-room four-star *Relais della Rovere,* Via Piemonte 10 (☎0577.924.696, ⓦwww .chiantiturismoit; ❾), are good – but perhaps not good enough to justify the high prices charged. The outdoor pool is a boon in summer, and the fine hotel restaurant, *Il Cardinale* (☎0577.923.707, ⓦwww.ilcardinale.net; closed Wed and periods between Jan & Feb and Nov & Dec), open to non-patrons, occupies three atmospheric rooms of a former fifteenth-century papal wine cellar.

If the town's artistic attractions seem on the slight side, **food** provides a major spur to a couple of hours' exploration. In Alta, the *Enoteca della Fortuna*, Vicolo della Fontanella (☎0577.923.102), is a great little Tuscan restaurant with moderate prices. Otherwise, investigate the highly recommended and Michelin-starred ♣ *Arnolfo*, Via XX Settembre 50–52a (℡ 0577.920.549, ⊛ www.arnolfo .com; closed Tues & Wed), worth the expense (starters around €25, mains €35) for a wonderful meal. In Bassa, try the large and beautifully converted twelfth-century mill, the *Molino il Moro* at Via della Ruota 2 (℡ 0577.920.862; closed Mon & at lunchtime on Tues), for good, moderately priced local food and wine. To round things off, call in at the main café in Piazza Arnolfo for an **ice cream**, reckoned by not a few Tuscans as the finest in the province. **Nightlife** is restricted to several late bars in Colle Bassa.

Casole d'Elsa

The roads south of Colle di Val d'Elsa lead into the **Colline Metallífere** (Metal Hills), dotted with geo thermal energy plants (the largest are out towards Larderello; see p.443) and their snaking pipelines. Other sights are few, though the countryside, as ever, is liberally sprinkled with Romanesque churches and inspiringly placed farmhouses and cypress groves.

One very pretty rural route leads through **CASOLE D'ELSA**, a village which looks inviting from a distance but yields relatively little of substantial interest. TRA-IN buses also pass this way from Colle. Council offices now occupy Casole's fortress, the village's most imposing sight. An Etruscan tomb discovered nearby, reputedly one of the richest ever found, contributed some of the treasures in the attractively presented **Museo Civico e della Collegiata**, Piazza della Libertà 1 (Jan–March Tues–Fri 10am–noon, Sat & Sun 4–7pm; April–Oct Tues–Sun 10am–noon & 4–7pm; Nov & Dec Tues–Fri 4–7pm, Sat & Sun 10am–noon & 4–7pm; closed Mon except on public holidays; €3), which has three first-floor rooms devoted to these and other archeological finds, and five rooms given over to painting and the decorative arts. Highlights of the latter rooms are a *Maestà* by a follower of Duccio, several works by Alessandro Casolani, a local sixteenth-century artist, and a bust of Bishop Tommaso Andrei (see below) by Gano di Fazio. The museum stands alongside the fifteenth-century Gothic **Collegiata** church (restored after war bomb damage), highlights of which are an important *Madonna and Child* and *Massacre of the Innocents* by Andrea di Niccolò, and a *Madonna and Child* attributed to Segna di Buonaventura. The church is also worth a look for Gano da Siena's tomb of Bishop Tommaso Andrei, a local cleric who died in 1303.

Casole's **tourist office** is at Piazza della Libertà 1 (same hours as Museo Archeologico; ℡ 0577.948.705 or 0577.949.737). Markets are held in the piazza on the first and third Mondays of the month. The stunning *Relais La Suvera* (℡ 0577.960.300, ⊛ www.lasuvera.com; ❾) is a four-star **hotel** located in the nearby hamlet of **Pievescola**. Originally a Sienese castle, it was converted into a villa by Baldassare Peruzzi during the Renaissance. The hotel incorporates the villa along with a converted church and mill: with its loggia, extensive grounds, stepped terraces, antique furniture, priceless works of art, ritzy suites and beautiful rooms, it's ranked by many as Tuscany's finest hotel of its type. It should be – double rooms in various annexes start at around €335; stay in the Villa proper and you'll drop a cool €500 a night. Off-season and web deals, however, can bring these prices down.

At a more realistic level, both the Casole area and **Radicóndoli**, another pretty though insubstantial village 15km to the south, have useful run-of-the-mill hotels: the big four-star *Gemini* with swimming pool, at Strada Provinciale 4, 15km from Casole (℡ 0577.948.622, ℻ 0577.948.241, ⊛ www .gemini-lapergola.it; ❺), and the smaller three-star *Verde Oasis*, Via Guido Rossa

18 in Radicóndoli (☎0577.790.760, 🌐www.verdeoasis.it; ❷). Both towns also have plenty of *agriturismo* rooms to let. For a moderately priced **meal** try the excellent *Osteria del Caffè Casolani* (☎0577.948.733; closed Thurs) in Casole's main street. Since 2004 Radicóndoli has had a small museum at Via Tiberio Gazzei 2, the **Museo dell'Energia** (July to mid-Oct Wed–Mon 10am–1pm & 3–6pm; mid-Oct to April Mon, Wed, Fri, Sat & Sun 10am–1pm; May–July Mon, Fri, Sat & Sun 10am–1pm, plus Wed & Thurs 8.30am–2.30pm; €2), devoted to the region's geothermal power. It is best seen in conjunction with the similar museum and strange geothermal region around Larderello (see p.443).

Poggibonsi

POGGIBONSI, 8km east of San Gimignano, has little more than its transport links and its politics to recommend it. A serious industrial town, conspicuously ugly alongside its Tuscan neighbours, it is home to what is reputed to be Italy's reddest council. Prior to World War II, it might have looked more like Colle, but bombing left little trace of its past other than the **Castello della Magione**, a little Romanesque complex, possibly with Templar origins, consisting of a chapel and pilgrim hospice. The unfinished Medici fort at the top of the town isn't worth the slog, although the superb four-star **hotel** up here is: the ⚓ *Villa San Lucchese*, Località San Lucchese 5 (☎0577.937.119, 🌐www.villasanlucchese .com; ❻), is a lovely villa hotel with pool, tennis courts and a rural setting that seems a world away from the tatty town down in the valley.

On a **bus** journey from Siena to San Gimignano, you're likely to have to call in at Poggibonsi to switch buses. Poggibonsi also has a **train station** on the Siena–Empoli–Florence line; walk the length of platform 1, exit the gates and cross the road to reach the bus bays. Should transport connections not be working in your favour, there are bars and cafés to pass the time, and the **restaurant** *Piero*, Via della Libertà 62 (☎0577.938.871; closed Wed), for inexpensive thin-crust pizzas and reliable pastas. If you get stranded, head for the two-star **hotel** *Italia*, Via Trento 36 (☎0577.936.142, 🌐www.albergo-italia.it; ❷).

San Gimignano

SAN GIMIGNANO – "delle Belle Torri" – is perhaps the best-known village in Italy, 27km northwest of Siena. Its stunning skyline of towers, built in aristocratic rivalry by the feuding nobles of the twelfth and thirteenth centuries, evokes the appearance of medieval Tuscany more than any other sight. And its image as a "Medieval Manhattan" has for decades caught the tourist imagination, helped along by its convenience as a day-trip from Florence or Siena.

The town is all that it's cracked up to be: quietly monumental, very well preserved, enticingly rural and with a fine array of religious and secular frescoes. However, from Easter until October, San Gimignano has very little life of its own – and a lot of day-trippers, who don't always respect the place: antisocial behaviour and litter are starting to become a problem. If you want to get any feel for the town, beyond the level of art treasures or quaintness, you really need to come well out of season. If you can't, then aim to spend the night here: in the evenings San Gimignano takes on a very different pace and atmosphere.

Some history

San Gimignano was probably founded by the **Etruscans** – tombs in the surrounding countryside bear witness to their presence – and later inhabited by the **Romans**. It reputedly took its name in 450 from St Gimignano, a bishop of Modena, whose intervention is supposed to have saved the settlement from the attacks of Attila the Hun. During the tenth century a feudal castle was built on the site, a stronghold that was soon surrounded by a cluster of houses, and which, by the twelfth century, had become a free *comune*. A second (surviving) set of walls was added in the middle of the thirteenth century, about the time

SAN GIMIGNANO

Certaldo, Pontedera, **A** & **B**

VIA CEPARELLI

VIA N. CANNICCI

VIALE GARIBALDI

VIA GHIACCIAIA

P

VIA BAGNAIA

Sant'Agostino

San Iacopo

Porta
San Iacopo

PIAZZA
S. AGOSTINO

San
Pietro

Museo
Archeologico

V. CELLOLESE

V. SAN MARTINO

VIA FOLGORE DA S. GIMIGNANO

Porta
San Matteo

1

V. VENTI SETTEMBRE

Hospital

VIALE GARIBALDI

VIA MANGINI

2 **3**

D

VIA DIACCETO

4

Palazzo
Tinacci

VIA DELLA VERGINA

VIA CAPASSI

VIA SAN MATTEO

VIA DELLE FONTI

Casa
Pesciolini

VIA DELLE ROMITE

Porta delle
Fonti

Fonti

San Bartolo

Palazzo della Cancelleria

Torri Salvucci

VIALE DEI FOSSI

P

Rocca

Collegiata

Museo
d'Arte
Sacra

PIAZZA DEL
DUOMO

Pal. del Podestà

i

Pal. d.
Popolo

E

PIAZZA
CISTERNA

VIA D. CASTELLO

Museo
della
Tortura

5

VIA S.

San Lorenzo
in Ponte

VIA PRUNELLO

F

Arco dei
Becci

VIA D. QUERCECCHIO

VIA D. INNOCENTI

VIA D. PALESTRO

G

VIA S. STEFANO

Porta
Quercecchio

Museo
Ornitologico

Palazzo
Pratellesi

VIA PIANDORNELLA

N

VIALE DEI FOSSI

VIA BERIGNANO

VIA S. GIOVANNI

VIA DI RONDA

San Francesco

H

P

STRADA DI RACCIANO

Porta
San Giovanni

PIAZZALE
DEI MARTIRI
DI MONTE
MAGGIO

VIA VECCHIA

P

VIA ROMA

▼ C , J , G , Poggibonsi, Volterra & Siena

ACCOMMODATION
L'Antico Pozzo	D
Bel Soggiorno	H
Casolare Le Terre Rosse	J
La Cisterna	F
La Collegiata	B
Foresteria del Monastero San Girolamo	C
Leon Bianco	E
Pescille	A
Relais Santa Chiara	I
Le Vecchie Mura	G

RESTAURANTS
Birreria Pietrafitta	6
La Mangiatoia	3
Osteria del Carcere	5
Osteria delle Catene	2
Ristorante Il Pino	1
Ristorante La Stella	4
Le Vecchie Mura	G

0   200 m

that the town's predominantly wooden houses began to be replaced by stone structures and the first of the famous **towers**.

Wealth increased during the Middle Ages, and San Gimignano's population of 15,000 (twice the present number) prospered as a result of agricultural holdings and a position close to the Via Francigena, the ancient trade and pilgrimage route between Rome and northern Europe. At its heyday, in the fourteenth century, the town's walls enclosed five monasteries, four hospitals, public baths and a brothel. A force to be reckoned with, the town was mostly controlled by two great families, the Ardinghelli and the Salvucci – heads of the **Guelph** and **Ghibelline** factions respectively. Inter-family feuds, however, had long wreaked havoc. The first conflict erupted in 1246, and for the following century there were few years of peace; whenever the town itself was united there were wars with Volterra, Poggibonsi and other nearby towns. The vendettas came to a halt only after the Black Death of 1348, which had a devastating effect both on the population and – as the pilgrim trade collapsed – on the economy. The Ardinghelli family, despite opposition from the Salvucci, applied to Florence for the town to become a part of that city's *comune*; the request was approved by only one vote, in a reflection of San Gimignano's fractious reputation.

Subjection to Florence in 1353 broke the power of the nobles, leaving San Gimignano unaffected by the struggles between aristocracy and local council that racked other Tuscan towns. The tower houses, symbolic of real control elsewhere, posed little threat and so were not torn down; today, fifteen (of an original 72) survive. The town itself, further hit by plague in 1464 and 1631, passed into a rural backwater existence. At the turn of the nineteenth century, travellers spoke of San Gimignano as "miserably poor"; it was hardly romanticized by E.M. Forster, who took the place (under the name Monteriano) as the setting for his novel *Where Angels Fear to Tread*. San Gimignano's postwar history has been one of ever-increasing affluence, through **tourism** and the production of an old-established, but recently rejuvenated, white **wine**, *Vernaccia di San Gimignano*.

Arrival, information and accommodation

Most people visit San Gimignano as a day-trip from Siena. Using public transport you'll need to take a bus from Siena or a train or bus to Poggibonsi (40min) and then pick up one of the roughly hourly buses from the station for the twenty-minute journey to San Gimignano. There's also a fairly regular bus service from Colle Val d'Elsa.

Arriving by **bus**, you can get out either at Piazzale Martiri di Monte Maggio, just outside Porta San Giovanni, the south gate, or by the northern gate, Porta San Matteo. You can buy bus tickets and pick up timetables at the tourist office. The road that runs around the walls has three pay **car parks** – the simplest option for a short stay. Free parking is possible on the outskirts of town, close to Piazzale Martiri di Monte Maggio, but this is only worthwhile if you need a space for several days. To drive within the walls – not necessary unless you're dropping off luggage at your hotel – you need to be issued with a permit from one of the hotels; the way in is through Porta San Jacopo at the northeast corner.

The helpful **tourist office** (daily 9am–1pm & 3–7pm; ☎0577.940.008, ⓦwww.sangimignano.com) is on the south side of Piazza del Duomo, supplying lists of hotels, rooms and apartments. It also has transport information and does foreign exchange, though San Gimignano is full of *cambio* kiosks and cash/exchange machines. Book at the tourist office for "Strada del Vino" **wine-tasting** sessions and **walking tours** of local cellars.

San Gimignano Festival

San Gimignano's first **festival** was held at the end of the 1920s, and except for a break during World War II has run just about every year since in July and August, with a series of classical concerts, plus theatre and open-air films. Some of the great (and many of the not-so-great) names of Italian opera have passed through over the years, including Galliano Masini, Mario Del Monaco, Gino Bechi, Giovacchino Forzano and Iris Adami Corradetti – not that this has given the town false airs. Where else could you find *Tosca* on the same bill as Enrico Morricone's soundtrack for *A Fistful of Dollars*? Not to mention a series of Italian popular songs – offered by the Filarmonica "G. Puccini" no less – which includes such novelties as *La Canzone del Grappa*, a paean to Italian hooch.

These days the festival's quiet provincial air is increasingly compromised by snooty outsiders, particularly at the highlights of the event – the outdoor opera performances in Piazza del Duomo. The atmosphere remains cheerfully informal, however, with the steps of the Collegiata set aside as terracing for the town's kids. Even the official blurb exhorts you to *mettere il vestito della festa* and *cantare con la compagnia* ("put on your party clothes and sing along"). Details and tickets are available from the tourist office (@www.sangimignano.com).

Accommodation

A crucial factor to enjoying the town is to get a room inside the walls – which from Easter to October means booking ahead and/or arriving early in the day. The town's four main **hotels** are all expensive three-star establishments, but **private rooms**, scattered around a dozen or so houses within the walls, offer a budget alternative: charges start at around €35 for a double, a little less for a single; most have shared bathrooms. It's also possible to rent **apartments** with cooking facilities by the day, but be sure to reserve ahead.

Accommodation is bookable for free through the very helpful **booking agency** Siena Hotels Promotion, located just inside the southern gate at Via San Giovanni 125 (Mon–Sat: summer 9.30–7pm; winter 9.30am–12.30pm & 3–6pm; ☎0577.940.809, @www.sangimignano.com), which arranges rooms in hotels and private houses, apartments and *agriturismo* lets. The tourist office website (@www.sangimignano.com) provides an updated list of private rooms for rent (options tend to change from year to year), together with links and details of the accommodation offered.

Hotels

Bel Soggiorno Via San Giovanni 91
☎0577.940.375, @www.hotelbelsoggiorno.it.
Similar to the *Leon Bianco* (see below) in quality, price and facilities, though beware of having to take full board in summer. The hotel restaurant rates quite highly, but you pay extra for breakfast, unlike the *Cisterna* and *Leon Bianco*. The 22 rooms are smallish but beautifully done; eight have air-conditioning. ❺

Casolare Le Terre Rosse Località San Donato ☎0577.9021, @www.hotelterrerosse
.it. A great choice out of town, in the hamlet of San Donato 4km to the southwest on the road to Castel San Gimignano. The three-star hotel has 42 rooms in a classic Tuscan country house and a lovely rural setting; the big pool is a summer draw. Closed Nov–Feb. ❹

L'Antico Pozzo Via San Matteo 87
☎0577.942.014, @www.anticopozzo.com. An upmarket, medium-sized three-star hotel occupying a fifteenth-century town house. Very swanky decor, which is reflected in the price. ❺

La Cisterna Piazza della Cisterna 24
☎0577.940.328, @www.hotelcisterna.it. Elegant town hotel, established in 1919 and built into a medieval ensemble at the base of some of the piazza's fourteenth-century towers. It's worth paying more for a room with either a (potentially noisy) piazza outlook, or (more restful) countryside view. ❹

La Collegiata Località Strada 27 ☎0577.943.201, @www.lacollegiata.it. Sixteenth-century Franciscan convent, converted into one of Tuscany's new breed of super-expensive hotels, for honeymoons

and very special occasions. Double rooms come in at around €520. Located 2km north of town off the Certaldo road. ❾
Le Vecchie Mura Via Piandornella 15 ☏0577.940.270, ✉vecchiemura@tin.it. A couple of double rooms above a restaurant, but more appealing than it sounds, with welcoming owners and superb views. ❶
Leon Bianco Piazza della Cisterna 13 ☏0577.941.294, ⓦwww.leonbianco.com. Tasteful, air-conditioned three-star hotel with seventeen rooms, occupying a fourteenth-century mansion in the main square. Like the *Cisterna*, the better rooms, which have medieval features such as vaulted ceilings, look out over the square or the Val d'Elsa. The roof terrace for breakfast, drinks or lounging is a bonus. ❺
Pescille Località Pescille, Strada Castel San Gimignano ☏0577.940.186, ⓦwww.pescille.it. A large three-star hotel ringed by vineyards and olive groves 4km north of town, with a pool and tennis courts. Rooms are restrained and suitably rustic: the best is the panoramic and eyrie-like

Tower Room. Breakfast is available, but there's no restaurant. ❹
Relais Santa Chiara Via G. Matteotti 1 ☏0577.940.701, ⓦwww.rsc.it. A smart four-star hotel with 41 rooms, a pool and spacious grounds in a panoramic position on the Poggibonsi road 500m east of town. Breakfast and lunch are served, but there's no restaurant. ❼

Convent
Foresteria del Monastero San Girolamo ☏0577.940.573, ⒻRead0577.940.573. Nine rooms available in a convent run by Benedictine nuns just behind Porta San Jacopo. €25 per person including breakfast; half price for children. ❶

Campsite
Il Boschetto di Piemma Santa Lucia ☏0577.940.352, ✉bpiemma@tiscalinet.it. The nearest campsite to town, with a bar, restaurant and pool. Located 3km downhill from Piazzale Martiri di Monte Maggio, off the Volterra road.

The Town

San Gimignano is not much more than a village: you could walk from one end to the other in fifteen minutes, or around the walls in an hour. It deserves at least a day, however, both for the frescoes in the churches and museums, and for the surrounding countryside – some of the loveliest in Tuscany. From the fine south gate, **Porta San Giovanni** (1262) – the best place to start a tour – the palazzo-lined **Via San Giovanni** leads to the town's interlocking main squares, the Piazza della Cisterna and Piazza del Duomo. On the right of the street, about a hundred metres up, is the former church of **San Francesco** – a Pisan-style Romanesque building converted now, like many of the palazzi, to a shop selling *Vernaccia* and other local wines. Ignore the scrum around the tasting table and walk through to the lovely garden at the rear, where before tackling the town you can enjoy an incomparable view across the Tuscan hills.

You enter the **Piazza della Cisterna** through another majestic gateway, the **Arco dei Becci**, part of the original fortifications built before the town expanded and acquired its second set of thirteenth-century walls. The square is flanked by an anarchic cluster of towers and palazzi, and is named after the public cistern (1273) – still functioning – at its centre. The well was extended in 1346 on the orders of the then *Podestà*, Guccio de' Malvoli, whose coat of arms adorns one of the faces: note the rope-cut grooves, witness to centuries of use. It was in this square, and in other streets within the older inner walls, that most of the leading families had their houses.

San Gimignano museum admission

The most economical way to see the town's sights is to buy the combined **museum ticket** that covers admission to the Museo Civico, Pinacoteca, Torre Grossa, Museo Archeologico, Spezieria dello Spedale di Santa Fina, Galleria di Arte Moderna and Museo Ornitologico. The cost is €7.50.

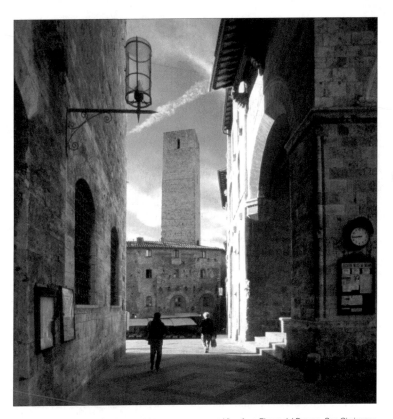

△ View from Piazza del Duomo, San Gimignano

To the left (northwest) of the square, beside an arch leading through to the Piazza del Duomo, are the twin Ardinghelli towers and palace; a Salvucci rival rears up close by. The tower on the square's northeast flank, topping the Palazzo Cortesi, is known as the Torre del Diavolo, so named, according to legend, because its owner returned after a long journey convinced that it had grown taller, the only explanation for the phenomenon, he alleged, being that a DIY-inclined devil had been busy during his absence. At its foot lies the little **Vicolo dell'Oro**, so named because it probably once housed the workshops of the town's goldsmiths (*orefici*).

The more austere **Piazza del Duomo**, off to the left of Piazza della Cisterna, introduces further towers and civic palazzi. Facing the Duomo (more properly the **Collegiata**, as San Gimignano no longer has a bishop), the crenellated **Palazzo del Popolo** (or Palazzo Comunale), the town hall and home to the Museo Civico, stands to your left, the older **Palazzo del Podestà** (1239) behind you.

The Palazzo del Popolo was begun in 1270, probably to a plan by Arnolfo di Cambio, born in nearby Colle di Val d'Elsa, also responsible for Florence's Duomo and Palazzo Vecchio. Oddly, the lower, older half, shows a Sienese influence, while the upper sections have a decidedly more Florentine flavour. The palace's Torre Grossa (see p.430) was completed in 1311, some time after a 1255 ordinance in which the *comune* decided that the town's tower-building frenzy had run its course. The Torre della Rognosa of the Palazzo del Podestà, which survives, was set as the maximum height (54m) for any subsequent private tower, the idea being that none should exceed the towers of the civic authorities. Looking around the skyline, it would seem that the rule was not much respected. The Salvucci clan, for example, responded at one point by building two towers in Via San Matteo, the Torri Salvucci, each shorter than the maximum, but arranged so close together as to make it clear that their combined height would be higher than anything conjured up by the *comune*.

The Collegiata

❼ The first church on the site of the **Collegiata** (April–Oct Mon–Fri 9.30am–7.10pm, Sat 9.30am–5.30pm, Sun 12.30–5.30pm; March & Nov to Jan Mon–Sat 9.30am–4.30pm, Sun 12.30–4.40pm; Feb religious services only; €3.50) was begun in the tenth century. Work on the present building, which is orientated back to front in respect of the earlier structure, began in the early twelfth century. The church was consecrated by Pope Eugenius III in 1148 and enlarged and altered by Giuliano da Maiano between 1466 and 1468. The plain facade (1239) could hardly provide a greater contrast with the **interior**, whose frescoes fill just about every available space, their brilliant colours set off by Pisan-Romanesque arcades of black and white striped marble. The entrance is from a courtyard to the left of the church, accessed under an arch surmounted by a statue of St Gimignano (1342).

The three principal **fresco cycles** fill the right and left walls, plus two short side walls which protrude from the inside wall of the facade. Beginning on this rear wall you'll find a large central fresco of *St Sebastian* (1465) by Benozzo Gozzoli, painted five or six years after the artist's sumptuous fresco cycle in the Palazzo Medici-Riccardi in Florence (see p.141). Sebastian was often invoked during plague epidemics – one had struck San Gimignano in 1464, which was the reason for Gozzoli's commission – thanks largely to his powers of recovery: he actually survived an assault with arrows – though rather oddly remains the patron saint of archers – and was eventually martyred by being pummelled to death. The inscription below the heavily arrowed saint, who appears blithely unaffected by the casual and courtly display of archery, reads "in praise of the most glorious athlete, Sebastian".

Either side of Sebastian, on pedestals, are two wooden **statues** of the *Archangel Gabriel* and the *Madonna Annunciate*, carved by the Sienese sculptor Jacopo della Quercia in 1421 and given their slightly garish painted finish by Martino di Bartolomeo five years later. In front of each statue are pillars painted with frescoes by Gozzoli of the *Annunciation* and saints Anthony, Augustine and Bernardino. These pillars anchor the side walls containing the first of the church's fresco cycles, Taddeo di Bartolo's *Last Judgement* (1410), with *Paradiso* depicted to the right, *L'Inferno* to the left. One of the most gruesome depictions of a customarily lurid subject, the latter offers a no-holds-barred illustration of the Seven Deadly Sins, including Bosch-like fantasies on lust and gluttony, each wonderfully grisly detail now bright and clear after a recent restoration.

The church's other cycles depict scenes from the Old Testament (two tiers on the left wall) and the New Testament (two tiers on the right); in the lunettes above, scenes of the Creation above the Old Testament episodes are paralleled across the church by episodes from the Nativity. Somewhat surprisingly, the **Old Testament** and **Creation** scenes (26 in all), whose vision seems entirely medieval, were painted later, between 1356 and 1367. Created by Bartolo di

Fredi, they reflect the influence of Lorenzetti's *Good and Bad Government* in Siena in their delight in genre detail, forming an essentially human narrative: *Abraham and Lot leading their flock towards Canaan*, for example, is a Tuscan farming scene, with appropriate landscape. They are also quirkily naturalistic – there are few odder frescoes than that of the *Drunkenness of Noah*, exposing a prominent penis in his stupor: Noah is traditionally considered to have been the first to promote agriculture and viticulture, and – more to the point – the first to have abused the products of the vine.

The cycle (which is read left to right, top to bottom) follows the story of the *Flood* with those of *Abraham and Lot* (their trip to Canaan), *Joseph* (his dream; being let down the well; having his brothers arrested and being recognized by them), *Moses* (changing a stick into a serpent before the Pharoah; the Red Sea; Mount Sinai) and *Job* (temptation; the devil killing his herds and destroying his house; thanking God; and being consoled by friends). Above, note the fresco, perhaps the most beautiful of the entire cycle, depicting the *Creation of Eve* (fourth lunette from the left), in which Eve emerges from the rib of the sleeping Adam.

The authorship of the **New Testament** scenes (begun 1333) is disputed, with some historians now attributing them to Lippo Memmi, collaborator and brother-in-law of Simone Martini, or to a member of Memmi's workshop. Traditionally, the attribution is to Barna di Siena, another follower of Martini, possibly a pupil, who is supposed to have died in a fall from the scaffolding while at work here in the 1350s. Whatever, the scenes of Christ's Life and the Passion mark a distinct departure from Martini's style, with their interest in emotional expression. In *The Kiss of Judas* the focus of eyes is startlingly immediate, as is the absorption of all the figures in the action – St Peter thrusting into the foreground with his assault on the Roman soldier, while the other disciples gather their cloaks and flee. The same dramatic vision comes through in *Christ Carrying the Cross* and the dark dealings of *Judas Accepting the Pieces of Silver*. One of the most dramatic scenes of all is the *Resurrection of Lazarus*, in which a dumbstruck crowd witnesses the removal of a door to reveal the living Lazarus in the winding bandages of burial.

Cappella di Santa Fina

Many of the chapels of the cathedral were remodelled between 1468 and 1475 as part of Giuliano da Maiano's renovation of the church, work which brought San Gimignano more fully into the Florentine Renaissance orbit. The **Cappella di San Gimignano**, to the left of the high altar, features an altar by Giuliano's brother, Benedetto da Maiano, partly constructed from fragments of an earlier work. The ciborium atop the high altar is also by Benedetto, though both brothers reserved their best work for the **Cappella di Santa Fina**, a Renaissance masterpiece located at the top of the right (south) aisle. Giuliano designed the chapel (1468–75), while Benedetto designed its altar, marble shrine and bas-reliefs (1475), though the most eye-catching part of the ensemble, which is dedicated to San Gimignano's patron saint, is a pair of frescoes in opposing lunettes by Domenico Ghirlandaio (1475).

St Fina, the subject of the frescoes and the frieze of the shrine, was born in San Gimignano in 1238 and struck by a dreadful and incurable disease at the age of 10. She gave herself immediately to God, repented her sins (the worst seems to have been accepting an orange from a boy), and insisted on spending the agonized five years until her death lying on a plank on the floor (the idea being that she would be brought closer to Christ through increased suffering). As a result of her position, and her complete paralysis during her final days, she was tormented, among other things, by mice, which she was unable to scare away. The board, on her death, was found to be covered in flowers.

Both details appear in the fresco of the right lunette, which depicts the *Announcement of Death*, the time of Fina's demise having been vouchsafed to her by St Gregory in a vision (notice the flower-covered board and the wonderfully ugly mouse in the semi-darkness to the rear of the composition). The fresco in the opposite (left) lunette, the *Funeral of St Fina*, is more accomplished – it is said to have greatly impressed Raphael – and shows the saint on her deathbed with the towers of San Gimignano in the background. Also depicted are three miracles associated with Fina: the restoration of a blind choirboy's sight; the curing of her nurse's paralysed hand; and the ringing of San Gimignano's bells by angels on the saint's death.

Ghirlandaio left a self-portrait (in the figure behind the bishop saying Mass), as well as portraits (in the figures to either side) of Davide, his brother, and Sebastiano Mainardi, his brother-in-law. Both probably assisted Ghirlandaio with the frescoes, as they did with his masterpiece, the fresco cycle in the sanctuary of Santa Maria Novella in Florence (see p.133). The fresco's composition, with the dead saint surrounded by onlookers, owes much to Benozzo Gozzoli's almost identical scene painted ten years earlier in Sant'Agostino (see p.433), which in turn was influenced by Giotto's iconoclastic treatment of the *Funeral of St Francis* in Santa Croce in Florence (see p.165).

The Baptistery and Museo d'Arte Sacra

Accessed by a loggia in the same courtyard as the entrance to the Collegiata is the **Baptistery**, frescoed with an *Annunciation* by Ghirlandaio and Sebastiano Mainardi (1482). The **Museo d'Arte Sacra** (daily 9.30am–7.30pm; Nov–March closes 5pm; closed Jan; €3) is housed in the old Rector's Palace off to the left of the court in Piazza Pecori, which is a favourite for busking musicians in summer. Its highlights include a *Madonna and Child* by Bartolo di Fredi, a superb wooden Crucifix, perhaps from as early as the eleventh century, several glorious illuminated choir books, and a marble bust of *Onofrio di Pietro* (1493) by Benedetto da Maiano, a work commissioned by San Gimignano's *comune* to honour Di Pietro, an eminent local scholar.

The Museo Civico and Pinacoteca

The Palazzo del Popolo, the other key component of the Piazza del Duomo, is partly given over to council offices, but most of the building is devoted to the **Museo Civico**, home to an outstanding miscellany of paintings and to the **Torre Grossa**, the only one of San Gimignano's towers which you can climb (both daily: March–Oct 9.30am–7.20pm; Nov–Feb 10am–5.30pm; €5; joint ticket see p.426).

On entering the palazzo from the square you find yourself within a courtyard, built in 1323 during extension work on the palace. Its well (1360) incorporates fragments removed from local Etruscan tombs, while the stone crests around the walls represent the coats of arms of various medieval magistrates. A loggia opens on the right, from which justice and public decrees were occasionally proclaimed, hence the subject matter of its three frescoes, all of which make an allusion to justice: the left wall features an allegory (1513) by Sodoma depicting a throned magistrate flanked by the figures of Dishonesty, Prudence and Truth; in front is a *Madonna and Child* by Taddeo di Bartolo (the artist responsible for the Collegiata's *Last Judgement*) in which the Madonna is flanked by saints Gimignano and Gregory – the Child meanwhile holds a biblical inscription recommending sagacity in the administration of justice; the right wall features a chiaroscuro by Sodoma depicting St Ivo, a Breton lawyer whose *pro bono* legal work among the poor, widowed and orphaned saw him canonized in 1366 and made patron saint of lawyers, jurists and magistrates.

From the courtyard, stairs lead to a picturesque little balcony and the cramped ticket office. The first of the museum's rooms and the palazzo's public chambers, frescoed with hunting and tournament scenes, is known as the **Sala del Consiglio**, or Sala di Dante – the poet visited as Florence's ambassador to the town in 1300, making a plea here for Guelph unity. Most of the paintings displayed are fourteenth-century works, Sienese in origin or inspiration, and executed in the years before San Gimignano passed under Florentine control and influence. The room's highlight is Lippo Memmi's *Maestà* (1317), his finest work, closely modelled on Simone Martini's painting on an identical theme, completed two years previously, in Siena's Palazzo Pubblico (see p.383). San Gimignano's *Podestà* at the time, Mino de' Tolomei, is shown kneeling at the Madonna's feet, looked down on by a multitude of saints arranged in distinct rows. The fresco was enlarged at a later date, Benozzo Gozzoli having added the two saints at the extreme right and left in 1466. The fresco on the end wall shows San Gimignano's population swearing allegiance to Charles of Anjou.

Four smaller rooms on this floor are often given over to temporary exhibitions, usually easily ignored in favour of the main **Pinacoteca**, or art gallery, on the next floor. Arranged in four rooms, the **finest pictures** are in the large salon immediately on the right at the top of the stairs. On the wall on the right as you enter is a superb painted Crucifix (1260–65) by Coppo di Marcovaldo, a Florentine artist – believed to have been the teacher of Cimabue – captured by the Sienese at the Battle of Montaperti in 1260. This work, reckoned one of the masterpieces of early Tuscan painting, was probably also painted while the artist was in "captivity". It's a far more complex painting than it first appears, its apex being crowned by panels of the *Assumption of the Virgin* and *Christ Pantocrator*. (The similar – but eight-metre high – *Christ* on Florence's baptistery ceiling is attributed to Marcovaldo.) Panels next to each of Christ's hands depict the Madonna and St John, and the three Marys. Christ's body is flanked by six scenes from the Passion: the *Kiss of Judas*, *Flagellation*, *Crucifixion*, *Christ and Pilate*, the *Crown of Thorns* and the *Deposition*.

Other outstanding pictures in the room include two early tondi of the *Annunciation* (1482–83) by Filippino Lippi on the opposite end wall, with the Madonna portrayed separately in one, the Archangel Gabriel in the other; both are beautifully offset by their vast original frames. Between them is Pinturicchio's *Madonna Enthroned with SS Gregory and Benedict* (1512), commissioned by the abbey of Monte Oliveto Maggiore (see p.454), one of the last works and masterpieces of this artist. Equally arresting are two contrasting paintings of the *Madonna and Child with Saints* by Benozzo Gozzoli, both painted in 1466. The more interesting of the two shows the Madonna with John the Baptist, Mary Magdalene, St Augustine and St Martha, the last (the sister of Lazarus) being particularly venerated in Tuscany, as she is the patron saint of builders and – even more significantly – of cooks.

The larger of the two rooms off to the right contains lesser but no less interesting paintings. Look out in particular for the triptych by Taddeo di Bartolo depicting *Scenes from the Life of St Gimignano* (1393), the first of three panel paintings in this and the adjoining room devoted to the lives of the saints. It was painted when Taddeo was working on the *Last Judgement* frescoes in the Collegiata, where the painting was originally installed above the high altar. The large central panel, which shows the saint with San Gimignano on his lap, is flanked on each side with vignettes from his life. The most extraordinary is one of the four scenes on the right, in which the saint is disturbed while praying by what is euphemistically described as an urgent "*bisogno*" or need – in other words, a desperate call of nature. In answering the call he finds himself met by the Devil, whom he causes to vanish by making the sign of the Cross. The other panels on the right, which describe the saint's exorcism of the Byzantine emperor's daughter, show Gimignano being borne to Constantinople, his calming of a storm during the voyage and the eventual exorcism of the princess. The four panels on the left depict St Severus officiating at Gimignano's burial; saving San Gimignano from Attila the Hun (the saint is seen remonstrating vigorously with Attila); and preventing a downpour of rain soaking his followers in a leaky church.

Also of interest are *Scenes from the Life of St Bartholomew* (1401) by Lorenzo di Niccolò, whose panels include the attempt to martyr the saint by flaying him alive (top right) – the operation is shown in graphic detail – and his subsequent beheading, in which bloody strips of skin hanging from the saint's body hamper the work of the exasperated executioners. The same artist was responsible for the double-sided **reliquary tabernacle** showing *St Fina* and *St Gregory* and *Eight Scenes from the Life of St Fina* (1402), San Gimignano's patron saint (see p.429). Fina is shown holding San Gimignano in one hand, and a bunch of violets – a symbol of humility – in the other. The scenes on one face show the mother of St Fina looking after her daughter (with a relative desperately trying to beat off hordes of mice) and the Devil casting Fina's mother down some stairs (to no ill effect); San Gimignano's citizens in procession paying homage to the dead saint (note Fina's flower-covered board); and the funeral procession during which Fina's nurse, Beldia, miraculously recovered the use of her paralysed hand. The panels on the other face show Fina miraculously extinguishing a fire; saving a boat in a storm; saving a builder falling from a building; and exorcising a man possessed by the Devil.

Perhaps the gallery's most fascinating and enjoyable paintings, though, are the **frescoes of wedding scenes** hidden away in a small room off the stairs (straight ahead on exiting the main salon). Unique in their subject matter, they show a tournament where the wife rides on her husband's back, followed by the lovers taking a shared bath and climbing into bed: the man, remarkably, manages to keep on the same red hat through all three operations. Some commentators, however, have seen the pictures in a less jolly light, describing them as allegorical scenes designed to warn men of the wiles of women. They were completed in the 1320s by Memmo di Filippuccio, the father of Lippo Memmi, who since 1303 had been working as a more or less official painter for the *comune*.

The Rocca

Just behind the Piazza del Duomo, a signposted lane leads to the **Rocca**, the old fortress, with its one surviving tower. It was built in 1353, to Florentine orders but at local expense, "in order to remove every cause of evil thinking from the inhabitants". A couple of centuries later, its purpose presumably fulfilled, it was dismantled by Cosimo I. Nowadays its 283-metre perimeter encloses an orchard-like public garden, with figs, olives and a well in the middle. From the ramparts, there are superb views over the countryside.

A block south of the Rocca in Via Quercecchio, a **Museo Ornitologico** (April–Sept 11am–6pm; €1.50 or with combined ticket) has been created from the stuffed bird collections of some local worthy in the deconsecrated church near the Porta Quercecchio.

San Gimignano's position, with the best of Tuscan countryside spread below, may well inspire the idea of **walking**. If you plan anything more than a ramble, it's worth calling in at the *Ufficio Tecnico* in the town hall to buy copies of the local IGM contour maps.

A good **circular walk**, which would take most of the day, is to strike directly west into the hills to Poggio Attendi, follow the ridge south to San Donato, and loop back to San Gimignano via Montauto and Santa Lucia. Another possibility is to walk to **Colle di Val d'Elsa** (about 5hr): follow the Volterra road out of town, turn immediately left to Monteoliveto and Santa Lucia, and then make for the villages of Monti and Borgatello. With an early start, you could also walk to **Volterra** (6–7hr): make initially for San Donato, then cut across country past Castelvécchio (now a farm), the villa of Pignano and Monte Voltráio.

To San Lorenzo in Ponte

Heading away from the central squares and Via San Giovanni, the crowds quickly thin away. Just east of Piazza della Cisterna on Via di Castello is the highly publicized **Museo della Tortura** (daily 10am–midnight; €8), a shocking collection of original medieval torture instruments. Farther down Via di Castello is the Romanesque **San Lorenzo in Ponte** (1240; closed to the public at time of writing), whose brick-built interior is almost completely covered with dramatic frescoes (1413) by the little-known but accomplished Florentine Cenni di Francesco. The dramatic fragments include a *Last Judgement* on the left wall and (in the presbytery) the figures of the *Apostles*, *Christ and the Virgin with Angels*, and *Scenes from the Life of St Benedict*. Cenni was also responsible for the restored frescoes in the adjoining oratory, notably the entrance wall's *St Lawrence and Saints* and *Madonna and Child with Angels*, in which the Madonna's head – an earlier work – has been attributed to Simone Martini.

At the end of the street a rural lane winds down to the walls, a public well-house – the **Fonti** – and open countryside. The little Pisan-Romanesque church here, **San Iacopo**, has a painting of *St James* by Pier Francesco Fiorentino.

Via San Matteo leads north from Piazza del Duomo, one of the town's grandest and best-preserved streets, with quiet little alleyways branching off down to the walls. Passing a couple of mighty tower houses, the street ends at the **Porta San Matteo**, just inside which, in a corner of the walls, is the Convento di Sant'Agostino.

Sant'Agostino

After the Collegiata, **Sant'Agostino** (daily: April–Oct 7am–noon & 3–7pm; Nov–March 7am–noon & 3–6pm) is the most important church in San Gimignano, a large, hall-like thirteenth-century structure with several fine paintings, an impressive Renaissance altar, and an outstanding restored fresco cycle by Benozzo Gozzoli on the *Life of St Augustine*.

On the rear wall, immediately on the left as you enter by the church's side door, is the **Cappella di San Bartolo**. Framed by a draped marble curtain, it houses the remains of St Bartolo (1228–1300), yet another of San Gimignano's patron saints. Born near Pisa, he became a lay Franciscan, but at 52 contracted leprosy and was forced to retire to a leper colony, where he died twenty years later. According to legend, while he was in the colony several of his leprous toes came off in the hands of a nun who was washing his feet. Mortified with embarrassment, he took the loose toes and miraculously reattached them to his foot. This is one of three miracles depicted in the predella reliefs on the magnificent altar by Benedetto da Maiano (1495). The three figures above are the *Theological Virtues*, while the frescoes to the left, by Sebastiano Mainardi depict saints Lucy, Nicholas of Bari and Gimignano, who holds the town of San Gimignano in his arms.

On the right (south) wall are several striking frescoes, among them a *Madonna and Child with Eight Saints* (1494) by Pier Francesco Fiorentino and a figure of *Christ with the Symbols of the Passion* by Bartolo di Fredi (author of the Collegiata's Old Testament cycle), who was also responsible for the frescoes on the *Life of the Virgin* (1356) on the side walls of the chapel to the right of the high altar. The chapel's striking altarpiece, the *Nativity of the Virgin* (1523), is by Vincenzo Tamengi (1492–1530), an otherwise little-known local artist.

All paintings in the church, however, pale beside those on the walls around the high altar, a seventeen-panel fresco cycle on the **Life of St Augustine** (1463–67) by Benozzo Gozzoli, pictures which provide a superb record of life in Renaissance Italy, particularly the city life of Florence, which forms a backdrop to many of the scenes. Read from low down on the left, the first panels depict the saint – who was born in 354 in what is now Tunisia – being taken to school by his parents and flogged by his teacher, studying grammar at Carthage university and crossing the sea to Italy. The next recount his academic career: teaching philosophy and rhetoric in Rome and Milan – Gozzoli depicts the journey between the cities as a marvellously rich procession – and being received by the Emperor Theodosius. Then comes the turning point in his life, when he listens to the preaching of St Ambrose, and then, while reading St Paul's Epistle to the Romans, hears a child's voice extolling him "*Tolle, lege*" (take and read). After this, Augustine was baptized, returned to Tunisia to form a monastic community and was subsequently made bishop of Hippo. He was one of the fathers of the early Christian Church, producing two of its fundamental great theological works – the *Commentaries* and the *City of God*. Gozzoli depicts just a few crucial scenes: Augustine meeting the child whose voice he had heard (and who now rebuked him for trying to penetrate the mysteries of the Trinity); the death of his mother, St Monica; blessing the people, as bishop; confuting a heretic; having a vision of St Jerome in Paradise; and his death, a scene which almost exactly prefigures Ghirlandaio's depiction of the death of St Fina in the Collegiata.

Gozzoli started out with considerable promise, working as assistant to Fra' Angelico at the Vatican, then landing the contract for the Palazzo Medici chapel in Florence. These frescoes were painted late in life, after a frustrating career spent on minor commissions around the Tuscan countryside. The wonderful narrative freshness of the cycle prompted Bernard Berenson to characterize him as "a Fra' Angelico who had forgotten heaven and become enamoured of the earth and the spring time".

Given the richness of the cycle, it's remarkable that the high altar's *Coronation of the Virgin* (1483) manages to hold its own. It's by Piero del Pollaiuolo, brother and collaborator of the more famous Antonio del Pollaiuolo. Moving back down the left (north) wall you come to a door leading to the **sacristy** and Renaissance **cloister** and another fresco by Sebastiano Mainardi of *San Gimignano Blessing Three Dignitaries* (1487). The effigy above is of *Fra Domenico Strambi*, the patron who commissioned the Gozzoli frescoes and Pollaiuolo altarpiece. The marble reliefs (1318) beyond, showing four half-figures of bishops, are believed to be part of the original shrine to St Bartolo and are attributed to Tino da Camaino. The fresco fragment beyond, a *Madonna* by Lippo Memmi, is overshadowed by a large fresco of *St Sebastian*, painted by Gozzoli in 1464, the year in which plague ravaged San Gimignano.

The Museo Archeologico

Just south of Sant'Agostino is the former convent of Santa Chiara, now home to the interesting **Museo Archeologico** (April–Dec daily 11am–6pm; €3.50; joint ticket see p.426), which boasts a large collection of local finds and details the history of the area from the Etruscans to the eighteenth century. In the same complex is a reproduction of the **Spezieria dello Spedale di Santa Fina**, one of Tuscany's oldest pharmacies, exhibiting all sorts of exotic herbal remedies and other sixteenth-century medicinal concoctions. Upstairs is the **Galleria d'Arte Moderna e Contemporanea** "Raffaele de Grada", showing work by nineteenth- and twentieth-century Tuscan artists and temporary exhibits.

Eating and drinking

San Gimignano isn't especially famous for its **food** – there are too many tourists and too few locals to ensure high standards. However, the tables set out in summer on the car-less streets and squares and the local wines still make for a beguiling evening. At lunchtime, you might prefer to pick up supplies from the bars or delicatessens and head out to the countryside – a matter of walking out from just about any of the gates. As an after-meal treat, drop in on the award-winning *Gelateria di Piazza*, at Piazza della Cisterna 4 – the jovial owner creates some of the best ice cream in Tuscany. At night, San Gimignano is very much on the quiet side, with little entertainment beyond the evening *passeggiata* along Via San Giovanni and Via San Matteo. For a late-night bar and occasional live music head down to the *Birreria Pietrafitta* (see below).

Birreria Pietrafitta 4km east of town on the road to Poggibonsi. This popular pub with its large shady beer garden provides welcome relief from the crowds of San Gimignano. Wide selection of beers, wines and cocktails. Good panini and snacks available all day. Daily 11am–2am.

La Mangiatoia Via Mainardi 2 ☏0577.941.528. Popular restaurant with good Tuscan staples (mains €10–12, pasta €7–9) and a garden open in the summer. Closed Tues.

Le Vecchie Mura Via Piandornella 15 ☏0577.940.270. Housed in an old vaulted stable within the structure of the city walls; follow the sign off Via San Giovanni. Good atmosphere and reasonable value, with starters at €4–8, pasta from €8 and mains €10.50–12.50. Be sure to book. Closed Tues.

Osteria del Carcere Via del Castello 13 ☏0577.941.905. A relatively new and informal *osteria* with young owners, a few steps from Piazza

del Duomo. Excellent hams and salami, plus Tuscan cooking with an innovative edge. Reckon on around €25–30 for three courses. Just thirty covers, so booking is advised. Closed Wed.

Osteria delle Catene Via Mainardi 18 ☏0577.941.966. A thoroughly reliable place for straightforward Tuscan food. The wine list – over a hundred choices – is good, too. A good lunch will cost around €30, dinner €10–15 more. Closed Wed.

Ristorante Il Pino Via San Matteo 102 ☏0577.942.225. San Gimignano's first-choice restaurant, with a lovely interior. Specializes in antipasti and dishes sprinkled with truffle. From €25 upwards. Closed Thurs.

Ristorante La Stella Via San Matteo 75 ☏0577.940.289. Well-reputed restaurant that serves produce from its own farm; often extremely touristy, but still good value, with pasta dishes under €10. Closed Wed.

Listings

Bike rental Bruno Bellini, Via Roma 41 ☏0577.940.201, ⊛www.bellinibruno.com.
Lost property Vigili Urbani, Via Santo Stefano 23 ☏0577.940.346.
Markets The main market, with clothes, crafts and a variety of food – including rolls with *cinghiale* fill-

ing – is in Piazza del Duomo, Piazza delle Erbe and Piazza della Cisterna (Thurs 8am–1pm). There is a much smaller market on Saturdays.
Police Piazza Martiri di Monte Maggio ☏0577.940.313.
Taxis ☏0577.940.499 or ☏0577.941.572.

Volterra

Built on a high plateau enclosed by yellowy-grey volcanic hills, lofty **VOLT-ERRA** has a bleak, isolated appearance – a surprise after the pastoralism of the region around. D.H. Lawrence wrote, accurately, that "it gets all the wind and sees all the world… a sort of inland island, still curiously isolated and grim." However, its small, walled medieval core certainly merits a stop, with its cobbled and austere stone streets, dark stone palazzi and walled gateways. There are great views from the windswept heights, enjoyable walking, and one of the country's most important Etruscan museums.

The town lies at the heart of a mining region that yields **alabaster** (every other shop sells artefacts), as well as a variety of minerals. The mines – and the easily defended site – made it one of the largest **Etruscan** settlements, Velathri, and ensured its survival through the **Roman** era as Volaterrae. During the Dark Ages it became an important Lombard centre, and even sheltered the Lombard kings for a time. In the Middle Ages, however, the mines proved Volterra's downfall as the **Florentines** began to cast a covetous eye over their wealth. Florence took control of the town from 1360, and in 1472 – anxious to secure the town's alum deposits, vital for Florence's dyeing industry – crushed all pretensions to independence with a terrible siege and pillage by Lorenzo de' Medici and the Duke of Urbino, one of the three principal crimes Lorenzo confessed to Savonarola on his deathbed.

Subsequently, Volterra was a Florentine fief, unable to keep pace with changing and expanding patterns of trade and sliding into provincial obscurity. It was to remain part of the Grand Duchy of Tuscany until Italian

▲ Pisa & Florence

VOLTERRA

Etruscan Walls

Camping Le Balze

VIA DI MANDRINGA

San Giusto

VIA PISANA

Etruscan Walls

Porta Menseri

BORGO SAN GIUSTO

VIA PISANA

VIA LECCETTI

Le Balze

Santa Chiara

Santo Stefano

BORGO SANTO STEFANO

VIALE

P

Le Balze

ACCOMMODATION	
Convento Sant'Andrea	A
Etruria	C
La Locanda	B
Nazionale	D
San Lino	E
Sole	G
Villa Nencini	F

RESTAURANTS	
Da Badò	1
Da Beppino	3
Del Duca	5
Etruria	4
Vecchia Osteria dei Poeti	2

unification in 1860. Physically, the town also began to subside, its walls and houses slipping away to the west over the **Balze** (cliffs), which form a dramatic prospect from the Pisa road. Today, Volterra occupies less than a third of its ancient extent.

Arrival, information and accommodation

The nearest **train** station is 9km west at Saline di Volterra, from where CPT #790 buses shuttle into town. **Buses** arrive on the south side of the town at Piazza Martiri della Libertà, including three daily CPT services from Colle di Val d'Elsa (the #770 line). From the piazza it's a two-minute walk to the central Piazza dei Priori, close to the Duomo and **tourist office** at Via Giusto Turazza 2 (daily: April–Oct 9am–1pm & 2–8pm; Nov–March 10am–1pm & 2–6pm; ☎0588.86.159 or 0588.86.150, ⓦwww.provolterra.it), where you can buy bus tickets. **Cars** are best parked outside the north circuit of the walls, by the Porta San Francesco or Porta Fiorentina. Best of all, if you can find a spot, is the signed, underground "Dogana" parking, convenient for the Duomo. A local **taxi** company is Longarini (☎0588.87.517).

The major Volterran **festival** is the Gioco delle Contrade, a medieval tug of war held in the Piazza dei Priori at the beginning of June. The Volterra Teatro (ⓦwww.volterrateatro.it) and Volterra Jazz festivals take place in July and August; the tourist office has details.

Accommodation

Accommodation options include a hostel, campsite and a couple of villas just outside the town. Ask about apartments and *agriturismo* stays at the tourist office, which has a free accommodation service, or at Viaggi ATUV,

△ View over the rooftops of Volterra

Piazza Martiri della Libertà (Mon–Fri 9.30am–12.30pm & 4–7.30pm, Sat 9.30am–noon; ☎0588.86.333, ⓔvolterraviaggi@sirt.pisa.it).

Hotels

Etruria Via Matteotti 32 ☎ & ⓕ0588.87.377. Best value of the hotels proper – and located on the main street, right in the centre – this restored eighteenth-century building has 22 comfortable rooms and a private garden. ❷

La Locanda Via Guarnacci 24–28 ☎0588.81.547, ⓦwww.hotel-lalocanda.com. The *San Lino* (see below) had its own way for years among Volterra's top hotels, but the recently opened four-star *La Locanda*, smartly converted from a former nunnery, has stolen its thunder. It also has the advantage of a slightly more central position, north of Piazza dei Priori near the Porta Fiorentina. ❹

Nazionale Via dei Marchesi 11 ☎0588.86.284, ⓦwww.albergonazionalevolterra.it. In the heart of town, this three-star hotel is the inn D.H. Lawrence stayed at when researching *Etruscan Places* – the medieval palazzo was transformed into a hotel in 1860. Now much modernized, with 36 mostly tiny rooms, all with bathroom. ❷

San Lino Via San Lino 26 ☎0588.85.250, ⓦwww.hotelsanlino.com. Volterra's grandest hotel until the arrival of *La Locanda*, this four-star place with 43 rooms and pool is still a good bet. It's located on the street leading in from Porta San Francesco. ❸

Sole Via dei Cappuccini 10 ☎ & ⓕ0588.84.000. A modern three-star in a quiet location outside the town walls, near the church of San Alessandro. All ten rooms come with bathroom. ❷

Villa Nencini Borgo Santo Stefano 55 ☎0588.86.386, ⓕ0588.80.601. Attractive three-star hotel insinuated into a seventeenth-century building, with a pool and garden, sited just outside Porta San Francesco on the town's northwest edge. ❸

Convent

Convento Sant'Andrea ☎0588.86.028. On the northeast outskirts of the town; follow the road out of Porta Marcoli. There are beautiful views from the old cells, now let as private rooms with old painted brass beds – to both single women and men, and couples. 18 per person in a room with private bathroom; €14 in a room with shared bathroom.

Campsite

Le Balze Via Mandringa ☎0588.87.880. Well-equipped and nicely positioned site 1km west of the centre, outside Borgo San Giusto (follow signs for the *Balze*). Has a pool and tennis courts; riding can also be arranged. April–Sept.

The Town

The **Piazza dei Priori** is the heart of Volterra, enclosed by an almost totally medieval group of buildings. The battlemented town hall, or **Palazzo dei Priori**, is the eyecatcher. Built between 1208 and 1257, and said to be the oldest such palace in Italy, it may have served as the model for Florence's Palazzo Vecchio – though the influences are largely reversed on its facade, which is studded with Florentine medallions. It's worth paying for spectacular views from the top of the tower (Sat & Sun 9am–1pm & 2–6pm; €1). In the main building, you can take a look at the upper-floor **Sala del Consiglio Comunale**, used as the town's council chamber without interruption since 1257. Its end wall is frescoed with a huge *Annunciation* (1383) attributed to Jacopo di Cione.

Opposite the town hall is the **Palazzo Pretorio**, surmounted by the **Torre del Porcellino** (Piglet's Tower), named after the much-worn carved boar on a bracket to the right of the top window; completing the ensemble are the **Palazzo Vescovile**, or Bishop's Palace (formerly the town's granary), and a pair of tower houses, the **Buomparenti**, at the junction of Via Roma and Via Ricciarelli. Modest relatives of those of San Gimignano, the towers are linked by a passageway above the street.

The Bishop's Palace houses the rich little three-room **Museo di Arte Sacra** (daily: mid-March to Oct 9am–1pm & 3–6pm; rest of year 9am–1pm; joint ticket with Pinacoteca e Museo Civico and Museo Etrusco Guarnacci €8) at Via Roma 13. Displays in the first room include an Andrea della Robbia bust of *St Linus*, a Volterran who was St Peter's successor as pope; a silver reliquary bust of *St Ottaviano* by Andrea del Pollaiuolo; a fifteenth-century painted wooden tabernacle by Bartolomeo della Gatta, better known for his work around Arezzo and Cortona; and a clutch of Sienese altarpieces by Neri di Bici, Taddeo di Bartolo and Segna di Bonaventura. The second room has a gilded Crucifix by Giambologna, though the real highlights, especially for fans of Mannerism, reside in room 3, which features Rosso Fiorentino's *Madonna di Villamagna* (1521) and the *Madonna di Ulignano* (1545) by the leading local artist Daniele da Volterra.

The Duomo and its square

Backing directly onto the civic power centre, Volterra's cathedral square seems a touch down-at-heel, with its partial facades and crumbling masonry. The **Duomo**, or Basilica di Santa Maria Assunta (consecrated in 1120), and **Baptistery** (second half of the thirteenth century) are essentially Romanesque, clad in bands of black and white marble – the style popularized in the twelfth century by Pisa. Behind the baptistery, della Robbia plaques of swaddled babies signal a building that was once a foundlings' hospital. On the baptistery's exterior note the main portal, whose rounded arch contains the carved heads of *Christ*, the *Madonna* and the *Apostles* (1283). Inside are a water stoup fashioned from an old Etruscan funerary monument and a fine baptismal font (1502) by Andrea Sansovino.

Inside the Duomo, striped marble Romanesque aisles and a coffered Renaissance ceiling lend the building a rather makeshift appearance. Moving down the right (south) aisle you come to a chapel in the right transept with an outstanding Pisan *Deposition* (1228), its life-size figures disarmingly repainted in their original bright colours. On the right side of the choir lies the Cappella di San Ottaviano, which contains the body of the eponymous saint, a sixth-century hermit whose relics saved Volterra from a plague in 1522 – he is one of the town's patron saints. The high altar, a nineteenth-century travesty, is surmounted by an exquisite tabernacle (1471) by Mino da Fiesole. Mino also carved the two kneeling angels flanking the high altar. In the left (north) aisle the highlights are two fifteenth-century terracotta figures in the oratory near the entrance: they depict the *Nativity* and *Adoration of the Magi*, the former graced with a painted background by Benozzo Gozzoli. Farther down is a thirteenth-century Pisan pulpit, assembled in 1584 from a variety of earlier fragments. On the altar alongside is a beautiful *Annunciation* (1497), generally attributed to Fra' Bartolommeo.

Pinacoteca e Museo Civico and Ecomuseo dell'Alabastro

Paintings and sculpture gathered from Volterra's churches, including one that was swallowed up by the *Balze*, are displayed at the **Pinacoteca e Museo Civico**, installed in the Palazzo Minucci-Solaini, Via dei Sarti 1 (daily 9am–7pm; Nov to mid-March closes 2pm; joint ticket with Museo d'Arte Sacra and Museo Etrusco Guarnacci €8). The mansion is an interesting building in its own right, part frescoed and with a multi-level cloister; its designer may have been Antonio da Sangallo.

The collections are arranged chronologically, and begin with **statuary** from the lost church of San Giusto al Bostro; there's a wonderful Romanesque capital carved from local alabaster, its mix of pagan and Christian emblems including a double-tailed mermaid and Daniel in the lions' den. The **painting** displays begin with largely Sienese works, notably Taddeo di Bartolo's polyptych of the *Madonna and Child with Saints* (1411) and the same artist's *Madonna della Rosa*, part of a dismembered polyptych, and panel of *SS Nicola da Totentino and Peter*. But by the fifteenth century Florence dominated art, as it did politics. Major Renaissance paintings from this period include a *Christ in Glory* (1492) with a marvellous imaginary landscape by Ghirlandaio (room X), and a *Madonna and Saints* (1491) and *Annunciation* by Luca Signorelli, the latter reckoned one of the artist's masterpieces (room XI).

The museum's best work, however, is **Rosso Fiorentino**'s extraordinary *Descent from the Cross*, painted for the church of San Francesco in 1521. This is one of the masterpieces of Mannerism, its figures, without any central focus, creating an agitated, circular tension from sharp lines and blocks of discordant colour. The art historian Frederick Hartt saw in the painting "the dilemma of a lost generation" – it was painted in the decade that culminated in the Sack of Rome – as well as virtual blasphemy in the vision of a smiling Christ and gibbering Joseph of Arimathea.

In the Torre Minucci of the same palace complex is the **Ecomuseo dell'Alabastro** (mid-March to Oct daily 11am–5pm; rest of the year Sat & Sun 9am–1.30pm; €3), opened in 2003 and the main focus of a three-part museum devoted to the local alabaster industry, with other bases in the villages of Santa Luce and Castellina Marittima (12km apart, 40km west of Volterra, on the scenic minor road north from the N68 Cecina road). The museum has details of two driving itineraries taking in these and other points of interest connected with the industry. It also has displays chronicling the industry's development, as well as objects in albaster, including two Etruscan urns and two capitals, the latter virtually the only surviving local items in alabaster from the medieval period.

On the same street as the Pinacoteca e Museo Civico is the **Palazzo Incontri-Viti**, Via dei Sarti 41, a private residence built in about 1500; its forty-metre street frontage is attributed to Bartolomeo Ammannati. A variety of its beautifully frescoed and luxuriously furnished rooms are open to the public

(April–Oct daily 10am–1pm & 2.30–6.30pm; rest of year by appointment only at the tourist office; €4).

The Rocca, Arco Etrusco and archeological remains

South of Piazza dei Priori, Via Marchesi leads to a lush area of grass, trees and shade known as the **Parco Archeologico** (daily 10am–noon & 4–7pm; free). There's not much archeology about the place – a few odd lumps of rock, said to be part of a Roman bathhouse – but it's a beautiful part of the town to lie around for a few hours, and there's a good-value café-bar in one corner. Overlooking the park to the east is the **Rocca**, built by the Medici after their sacking of the town; with its rounded bastions and central tower, it's one of the great examples of Italian military architecture. For the last 150 years it's been a prison for lifers and hard cases. Just north of the castle, at Piazza XX Settembre 5, is the crowd-pleasing **Museo della Tortura**, which, like the similar museum in San Gimignano, is a gratuitous affair.

The first turning left off Via Marchesi, Via Porta dell'Arco, runs downhill to the **Arco Etrusco**, an Etruscan gateway, third-century BC in origin, built in Cyclopean blocks of stone, with Roman and medieval surrounds; the three blackened and eroded lumps on its outer face are probably images of Etruscan gods. The gate was narrowly saved from destruction in World War II during the course of a ten-day battle between the partisans (Volterra was a stronghold) and the Nazis. A memorial commemorates the partisan losses.

If you turn north instead off Via Marchesi, and follow Via Matteotti and its continuation, Via Guarnacci, you reach the Porta Fiorentina. Just to the west of the gate, below the road, is an area of excavations including a **Roman theatre** (now restored for use in the summer theatre festival) and a **bath complex** with mosaic floors. Following the **Via Diana**, straight ahead from the gate, makes for a pleasant walk, leading past the cemetery to remains of the Etruscan Porta Diana. Out beyond here tracks lead through farmland that was once a vast **Etruscan necropolis**; wandering through, you'll spot various unmarked, underground tombs.

The Museo Etrusco Guarnacci

Volterra's Etruscan legacy is represented most importantly at the **Museo Etrusco Guarnacci**, Via Don Minzoni 15 (daily 9am–7pm; Nov to mid-March closes 2pm; joint ticket with Museo d'Arte Sacra and Pinacoteca €8). One of Italy's major archeological museums, it consists entirely of local finds, including some six hundred **funerary urns**.

Made of alabaster, tufa and terracotta, the **urns** date from the fourth to first centuries BC – earlier tombs were lost as the cliffs fell to nothing. On their sides, bas-reliefs depict domestic events (often boar hunting) or Greek myths (usually a trip to the underworld); on the lid are a bust of the subject and symbolic flowers – one for a young person, two for middle-aged, three for elderly.

The vast collection is organized by theme, with informative notes in each room. Most of the best are arranged on the top floor and date from the "golden age" of the third and second centuries BC; past a large Roman mosaic transferred here from the baths complex outside town, is the **Urna degli Sposi**, a disturbing portrait scene of a supposed husband and wife – all piercing eyes and dreadful looks. The star piece, among a number of small bronze sculptures, is the exceptional **Ombra della Sera** ("Evening Shadow"), an elongated nude which provided inspiration for the twentieth-century Swiss sculptor Alberto Giacometti. The farmer who unearthed it displayed rather less reverence: he used it as a poker for a few years.

To the Balze

To reach the *Balze* – Volterra's famous eroded cliffs – follow Via di San Lino northwest from the Piazza dei Priori. This passes the church of **San Francesco**, whose adjoining Cappella della Croce di Giorno, built in 1315, contains fascinating and very early narrative frescoes (1410) of the *Legend of the True Cross* by Cenni di Francesco, an accomplished but little-known local artist. Rosso Fiorentino's famous *Descent from the Cross*, now in the Pinacoteca e Museo Civico, once stood above the high altar. From the nearby **Porta San Francesco**, follow Borgo Santo Stefano and its continuation, Borgo San Giusto, past the Baroque church and former abbey of **San Giusto**, its dilapidated but striking facade framed by an avenue of cypress trees.

At the **Balze** themselves, almost 2km west of Piazza dei Priori, you gain a real sense of the extent of Etruscan Volterra, whose old town walls drop away into the chasms. Gashes in the slopes and the natural erosion of sand and clay are made more dramatic by alabaster mines, ancient and modern. Below are buried great tracts of the Etruscan and Roman city, and landslips continue – as evidenced by the locked and ruined eleventh-century Badia monastery ebbing away over the precipice.

Eating and drinking

As a hunting centre, Volterra's **restaurant** menus are dominated by wild boar (*cinghiale*). You see stuffed heads of the unfortunate beasts throughout town, and the meat is packaged as salamis or hams, as well as roasted in the restaurants, along with hare (*lepre*) and rabbit (*coniglio*).

Restaurants listed below cover the best of a similarly priced bunch. Cheaper options include a few *pizzerie*, such as the central *L'Antica Taverna* at Via dei Sarti 18–22.

Restaurants

Da Badò Borgo San Lazzaro 9 ☎0588.86.477. Excellent local trattoria on the SS68 Florence–Siena road run by two amiable brothers (with mother in the kitchen) which has made a name for itself in national foodie guides. Serves up delicious *crostini* and Volterran game staples such as *pappardelle alla lepre*. Closed Wed & periods in July and Sept.

Da Beppino Via delle Prigioni 13–21 ☎0588.86.051. Reliable, established and family-run restaurant in the heart of the old town, with lots of space (160 covers inside, 20 outside). Serves homemade pasta, pizzas and plenty of hunting dishes, with an emphasis on truffles and mushrooms. Closed Thurs & around mid-Nov to mid-Dec.

Del Duca Via di Castello 2 ☎0588.81.510. On the edge of the old centre, this small restaurant (one dining room and just 35 covers) is currently the best place in town, thanks to its lovely setting (high ceilings and impressive *cantina*), surprisingly fair prices and fine Tuscan food with a creative twist. Closed Tues except July–Sept.

Etruria Piazza dei Priori 6 ☎0588.86.064. Best of the more expensive places: located on the main square in an old palazzo, with period furniture and frescoes. Despite its à la carte prices, it has inexpensive tourist menus. Closed Wed.

Vecchia Osteria dei Poeti Via Matteotti 55–57 ☎0588.86.029. One of the most popular and welcoming restaurants in town – and they don't stint on portions. A central location, with one dining room and a rustic appearance that retains many features of the original medieval building. Closed Thurs.

South of Volterra

Most travellers take in Volterra from the Florence–San Gimignano–Siena route, heading back east, or striking north to Pisa. The road south (N439), over to **Massa Maríttima** (covered by APT buses), is much less explored – a very wild, mountainous route that is given an added surreal quality by the presence of *soffioni*, hot steam geysers from which boric acid is extracted. To the east of the road are the **Colline Metallifere** – the metal hills – mined by the Etruscans and still inhabited by wolves (an odd thought), just fifty miles from Rome.

Pomarance, Larderello and Castelnuovo

Leaving Volterra, you've a highly scenic drive down to **POMARANCE**, a dull and largely modern centre – the area was badly bombed in 1945 – noteworthy only for a handful of paintings in the parish church of **San Giovanni Battista**. Just east is the great ruined bastion of the **Rocca di Silano** – a landmark for almost the whole extent of this route.

Billing itself as the "World Centre of Geothermal Energy", **LARDERELLO** signals the heart of *soffioni* country and takes its name from a nineteenth-century Frenchman, François De Larderel, who introduced the system for harnessing energy from the vapours. ENEL, the electricity company, has set up the **Museo della Geotermia di Larderello** on the subject (mid-March to mid-Sept Mon–Fri 9am–noon & 1.30–5.30pm, Sat & Sun 10am–noon & 1.30–6.30pm; rest of year Mon–Fri 8am–noon & 1.30–4.30pm, Sun 9am–noon & 1.30–5.30pm; free; guided tours to a geothermal power station on request ☎0588.22.111). Modernist buffs might also take a look at the 1950s glass-and-concrete church by **Giovanni Michelucci**, near the centre of town.

All around Larderello huge silver pipes run across the fields, with steam and smoke rising intermittently from chimneys amid the dark foliage. There are fourteen power stations and some sixty kilometres of piping. Settlements are few, presumably owing to the strong whiffs of sulphur, and the only sizeable village past Larderello is **Castelnuovo di Val di Cecina**, a neat little *borgo medioevale*. Beyond here, the road is hemmed in by woods and there's scarcely a farmhouse to be seen until the open plains around Massa Marittima, 30km away. With transport, you could cut east along a tiny, winding road, south of Castelnuovo, through **Montieri** and on to San Galgano (see p.447).

Travel details

Trains

Poggibonsi to: Florence (hourly; 1hr 15min); Siena (hourly; 25min).
Saline di Volterra to: Cécina (8 daily; 35min; connections to Pisa and Rome).

Buses

Colle di Val d'Elsa to: Casole d'Elsa (4 daily; 20min); Florence (hourly; 1hr); Monteriggioni (hourly; 15min); Poggibonsi (hourly; 15min); Radicóndoli (3 daily; 40min); Siena (hourly; 30min); Volterra (3 daily; 45min).

Poggibonsi to: Colle di Val d'Elsa (hourly; 15min); Florence (hourly; 50min); San Gimignano (every 30min; 25min); Siena (hourly; 45min).
San Gimignano to: Poggibonsi (10 daily; 25min); Siena (10 daily; 1hr 15min).
Siena to: Colle di Val d'Elsa (hourly; 30min); Florence (hourly; 1hr 15min); Monteriggioni (hourly; 25min); Poggibonsi (hourly; 45min).
Volterra to: Colle di Val d'Elsa (3 daily; 45min); Larderello (10 daily; 45min); Pisa (1 daily; 1hr 10min); Saline di Volterra (5 daily; 15min).

Southern Tuscany

* **Monte Oliveto Maggiore**
A mighty monastery set amid wonderful upland countryside. See p.454

* **Montalcino** This perfect pocket hill-town produces some of Tuscany's finest wines. See p.459

* **Sant'Antimo** An austerely beautiful abbey in an idyllic pastoral setting. See p.466

* **Bagno Vignoni** Atmospheric village with a sulphur pool instead of a central piazza. See p.470

* **Pienza** Pope Pius II's town-sized monument to himself. See p.472

* **Montepulciano** Is there a more attractive hill-town anywhere in the country? See p.480

* **Pitigliano** A cliff-top hideaway in the deep south of Tuscany. See p.500

△ Tuscan farmhouse with cypress trees, Val d'Órcia

8

Southern Tuscany

T he region **south of Siena** is Tuscany at its best: an infinite gradation of hills, trees and cultivation that encompasses the Crete Senese, the vineyards of Montepulciano and Montalcino, the Monte Amiata uplands and finally a landscape of sulphurous springs and castle-topped outcrops of tufa. The *crete*, especially, is fabulous: a sparsely populated region of pale clay hillsides, dotted with sheep, cypresses and the odd monumental-looking farmhouse.

The towns on the whole live up to this environment. **Montepulciano** is the most elegant and makes a superb base, with its independent hill-town life, acclaimed Vino Nobile wine and backdrop of Renaissance buildings. **Montalcino**, too, has appealing wines (its Brunello is regarded as Tuscany's finest vintage) and classic hill-town looks, while **Pienza** is a unique Renaissance monument, a town created by the great humanist pope, Pius II. In the south of the region, the urban highlights are **Pitigliano**, isolated on an extraordinary crag, and nearby the forgotten, half-abandoned medieval town of **Sovana**.

Monasteries are a major attraction of the area, and feature some of the greatest houses of the medieval Italian orders: Cistercian **San Galgano** and **Abbadia San Salvatore**, Benedictine **Monte Oliveto Maggiore** and **Sant'Antimo**, and Vallombrosan **Torri**. All are tremendous buildings, encompassing the best Romanesque and Gothic church architecture in Tuscany.

Equally memorable are the extraordinary sulphur springs that erupt from the rocks, or are channelled into geothermal energy, punctuating the landscape with pillars of white smoke. Several of the springs have for centuries formed the nucleus of spas. The most interesting is **Bagno Vignoni**, still with its Medicean basin in the village square. Here, and at **Bagni di Petriolo**, **Bagni San Filippo** and – most spectacularly – **Saturnia**, you can immerse yourself in open-air rock pools below warm cascades.

San Galgano and the western crete

If you have transport, the route past the abbeys of **Torri** and **San Galgano**, the sulphur spring of **Petriolo** and the villages of the western *crete* makes one of the best trips out from Siena. It could be done in a day, or alternatively with a night's stop at Buonconvento, Montalcino or one of the Murlo villages. If you're dependent on public transport, it's perhaps best to content yourself with San Galgano, which lies just off the N73 Siena–Massa Maríttima road; in a day, you could return to Siena, continue to Massa Maríttima, or stop at the village of **Palazzetto** near the abbey.

UMBRIA

Lago di Chiusi

**Tomba di
Scimmia**

Chiusi

Castiglione del Lago

▲ Arezzo

Cortona

Castiglion
Fiorentino

▲ Arezzo

Monte
San Savino

Sinalunga

Torrita di
Siena

Montepulciano

Chianciano

Chianciano
Terme

Sarteano

Montefollónico

Petróio

Castelmúzio

Monticchiello

Bagni San Filippo

Trequanda

San Giovanni
d'Asso

Pienza

Campiglia
d'Orcia

Asciano

Chiusure

Val d'Asso

San Quírico
d'Orcia

Castiglione
d'Orcia

N

**Monte
Oliveto
Maggiore**

Buonconvento

Torrenieri

Bagno
Vignoni

Sant'Antimo

River Orcia

LE CRETE

Montalcino

▲ Florence

Siena

Vescovado

Murlo

River Ombrone

Casciano
di Murlo

Bagni di
Petriolo

Torri

Civitella
Maríttima

San Galgano

Palazzetto

Roccastrada

8

0   10 km

Lago di Bolsena

M O N T I   V O L S I N I

Bolsena

Acquapendente

L A Z I O

Valentano

San Casciano dei Bagni

Radicófani

Pancastagnáio

Monte Amiata
1738m ▲

Abbadia
San Salvatore

Santa Fiora

Castell'Azzara

Sorano

San Martino
sul Fiora

Sovana

Pitigliano

Castel del Piano

Arcidosso

Triana

Roccalbegna

Semproniano

Terme di
Satúrnia

Manciano

Satúrnia

Montemerano

Murci

Cingiano

Scansano

River Ombrone

Pagánico

Magliano in
Toscana

Grosseto

M O N T I   D E L L ' U C C E L L I N A

▶ Orbetello

Torri

Driving south from Siena, it's best to follow the N223 Grosseto road as far as the junction signposted to Brenna, Stigliano and Torri. Taking this minor road, you find yourself in the **Rosia valley**, a belt of ancient farmland increasingly marred by the expansion of a huge Bayer chemical factory, and overlooked by a series of cream-stone villages set along the wooded ridge to the south. All these villages are pastoral beauties, approached from the valley floor along cobbled roads and avenues of cypress trees, with farmyards backing onto many of the houses.

To give a point of focus to the trip, come on a Monday or Friday morning, when you can visit the **Monastero dei Santi Trinità e Mustiola** (Mon & Fri 9am–noon) at **TORRI**, the last of the villages, just 2km east of the Siena–Grosseto road. The monastery, founded in the eleventh century, was an important power base for the Vallombrosan order, until difficulties with the papacy led to its suppression by Pius II in 1464. It retains its Romanesque church and a magnificent three-tiered cloister, executed in panels of black and white marble. The capitals of the lower tier, in particular, are outstanding; their style and subject matter (fantastic animals and Old Testament stories) recalling the French-influenced work at Sant'Antimo (see p.466). Abandoned in the sixteenth century, the complex was bought privately in 1966. It is scarcely ever visited; note that outside the opening hours, it's kept firmly locked and nobody local has a key.

Nearby **Brenna** makes an ideal picnic lunch and swim stop on the banks of the River Merse; **Rosia** village has a supermarket and a couple of bars for sandwiches.

San Galgano

The **Abbazia di San Galgano**, midway between Massa and Siena, is among the greatest Gothic buildings in Italy. It is certainly the most romantic – roofless, with a grass field for a nave, patches of fresco amidst the vegetation, and panoramas of the sky, clouds and hills through a rose window. (If you have ever seen Andrei Tarkovsky's film *Nostalgia*, it will be immediately familiar from the finale, in which the director transformed the nave into a Russian landscape complete with a *dacha*.)

In the twelfth and thirteenth centuries, San Galgano – which was one of the **Cistercians**' two largest foundations in Italy – was the leading monastic power in Tuscany. Its abbots ruled over disputes between the cities, and at Siena its monks supervised the building of the Duomo and held posts as *casalinghi* (accountants) for the *comune*. The monks were a mix of Italians and French, and through them the ideas of Gothic building were imported to Italy, along with sophisticated schemes for land drainage and agriculture. As at all Cistercian houses, the monastic population included large numbers of lay brothers, who dedicated themselves to manual labour while the "choir monks" looked after the prayer and study.

The abbey

The Cistercian order built the **church** and **abbey** (daily 8am–8pm; Oct–April closes 6pm; free) between 1218 and 1288, at which time the complex must have looked like a small town, with its numerous workshops, dormitories and guest quarters. However, at the end of the century, during the wars between the Tuscan cities, the English *condottiere* Sir John Hawkwood and his mercenary troops sacked the abbey, and by 1397 the abbot was San Galgano's sole occupant. During the fifteenth century it was repopulated for a while, until the papacy handed its income to a particularly profligate cardinal. The monks left and the building gradually decayed; the campanile actually collapsed during a Mass attended by villagers.

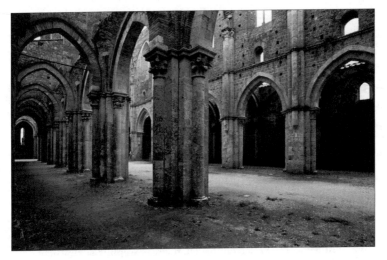

△ Main and side nave of the Abbazia di San Galgano

The vast church, with its seventy-metre nave and shored-up aisles, now encloses little more than a stone altar. Birds hover about the glassless windows and capitals. Outside, there are brief runs of cloister and a few conventual buildings, part-occupied by members of the Communità Incontro who are responsible for the maintenance of the abbey and its surrounds.

The monastery commemorates **St Galgano Guidotti**, a noble from the nearby village of Chiusdino, who spent his youth in the usual saintly apprenticeship of dissipation and battles. Upon having a vision of St Michael, he renounced the life of a knight and embarked on a career as a hermit. His conviction was fortified by a kind of reversed sword-in-the-stone miracle when, during a visit from his family and fellow knights (who tried to persuade him to return to the world), he ran his sword into a rock beside his hut: it stuck fast, forming a crucifix. In 1181, at the age of 33, Galgano died, and within four years had been canonized.

The saint's hermitage was transformed into the circular **Cappella di Monte Siepi** – the building on the hill above the main abbey – between 1182 and 1185, with the **sword in the stone** forming the centrepiece. The chapel was designed as a mausoleum, but Galgano's body has been lost, though his head is preserved in the Siena cathedral museum. In the fourteenth century a Gothic second chapel was added to the original Romanesque chapel, and in the 1700s a rectory was attached, the three forming a rustic, farmhouse-like group. It is well worth the climb up the hill, as much for the views over the abbey as for the chapels themselves. The interior of the rotunda is interesting for its strange striped dome, and the side chapel has patches of frescoes by Ambrogio Lorenzetti, including a just-about-discernible image of Galgano offering the rock-embedded sword to St Michael.

Practicalities

To one side of the abbey, in the old vaulted scriptorium, is a small **tourist office** (daily: summer 10.30am–6pm; winter 10.30am–1.30pm & 3–5pm; ☎0577.756.738, ✉prolocochiusdino@tin.it), which has some useful local information and sells tickets for the occasional Accademia Chigiana and Associ-azione Monfardini concerts held in the abbey. Accommodation is in the village of **Palazzetto**, 4km south on the Massa road, at the *Bar-Albergo Il Palazzetto* (☎ & ℱ0577.751.160; ❶), which also has a good, inexpensive restaurant/pizzeria (closed Wed), as well as bar snacks.

Bagni di Petriolo and into the crete

From San Galgano, you can cut across to the N223 Siena–Grosseto road by means of a minor road that leaves the N73 at the walled village of Monticiano. The road east of Monticiano is attractive if unremarkable, twisting its way through wooded hills before finally emerging on the N223 about 20km south of Siena.

South from here, the N223 follows the River Merse before rearing into the hills by way of various viaducts. To reach the spa of **BAGNI DI PETRIOLO** you need to turn right after about 4km, then follow this road for 9km (no buses) down to a bridge beside the River Farma (a tributary of the Ombrone) and a rough enclosure of huge medieval walls. Here, on the left, is a tiny thermal station offering treatments (April–Nov; ☎0577.757.104, ⓦ www.termesaluteambiente .com). Just below the bridge on the left, the spa's **sulphur springs** continue to flow freely into little rock pools before mixing with the river. If you're going for a soak, you should leave your clothes well away from the sulphur, and wash off afterwards with a dip in the river. You're unlikely to have the place to yourself, but it's a good base from which to walk into the Riserva Naturale del Basso Merse along the river and visit the picturesque village of **Pari** nearby.

At the spa there's a summer-only sandwich bar for snacks and drinks. The **hotel** *L'Imposto* (☎0577.757.094, ℱ0577.757.085; ❷), back up the hill near the main road, has a moderately priced **restaurant**.

The Murlo villages

With transport, you can follow a paved track off the Petriolo road, through the hills to **CASCIANO DI MURLO**; the track runs alongside a formidable estate that is fenced off to protect its woodland and shooting. Scarcely more than a hamlet, Casciano has a 29-room, three-star **hotel**, the *Mirella* (☎0577.817.667, ⓦ www.hotelmirella.com; ❸), a **riding centre** (☎0577.817.779) and a **camp-site**, *Le Soline* (☎0577.817.410, ⓦ www.lesoline.it), open year-round, located at nearby Casafranci. A fine place to break your journey, or base yourself for a few days, Casciano is also easily reached from the N223 (it's 6km from the turning).

East of Casciano, a very high and beautiful road leads into the beginnings of the *crete*, with hills punctuated by the occasional lake and farmhouse on the approach to **VESCOVADO DI MURLO**. There's little reason to stop at Vesco-vado, a largely modern village, but it has a hotel with swimming pool, the three-star *Murlo*, Via Martiri di Rigosecco (☎0577.814.033, ⓦ www.albergodimurlo .com; ❸), roadside signs for which you'll have seen dotted across half of southern Tuscany. There's also *agriturismo* accommodation at *Palazzina* (☎0577.817.776, ⓦ www.lapalazzina.com; ❸–❻ depending on size of apartment), a farmhouse between Casciano and Vescovado.

Just a couple of kilometres south of Vescovado is **MURLO** – a tiny medieval *borgo* whose ring of houses forms defensive walls, enclosing the town hall and church. The oldest settlement in the area, Murlo's Etruscan past is commemo-rated in the **Museo Etrusco**, housed in the Castello di Murlo (April–Sept

Tues–Sun 10am–1pm & 3–7pm; March & Oct Tues–Sun 10am–1pm & 3–5pm; Nov–Feb Tues–Fri 10am–1pm, Sat & Sun 10am–1pm & 3–5pm; ⓦ www .comune.murlo.siena.it; €3.20). Exhibits include sphinx statues, a large terracotta tomb frieze depicting hunting scenes, and some odd bowls, decorated with warriors holding women whose legs form the handles. The museum also doubles as the village's tourist office (same hours as museum; ☎ 0577.814.099). South of Murlo, a track leads to an even smaller *borgo*, the ten-house **LA BEFA**, which has a renowned, moderately-priced **osteria** (closed Wed), set in rich mushroom territory.

At Vescovado or Murlo you're within easy striking distance of Buonconvento, and near enough to Asciano, Montalcino or Siena. The Montalcino route is lovely, as is the superbly scenic Asciano road, taking you into the heart of the *crete* across sparsely populated countryside. Just off the N2, which you need to join for a few kilometres before heading east to Asciano, there are rooms at the *Borgo Antico* (☎ 0577.374.688, ⓦ www.hotelborgoantico.com; ❷) in the medieval hamlet of **Lucignano d'Arbia**.

Monte Oliveto and the central crete

The heartland of the *crete* is the area southeast of Siena, around the Benedictine monastery of **Monte Oliveto Maggiore** – arguably Tuscany's finest. The region is studded with lonely cypresses on sun-baked clay hills, and contains all the other classic Tuscan images. The abbey is reached easily enough by car via **Asciano** or **Buonconvento**, 9km distant to the north and west, respectively; **Montalcino**, too, is only 24km distant to the south and makes an excellent base for the whole district. You can get to Asciano or Buonconvento by train or bus from Siena, though you'll have to hitch (more promising from Buonconvento) or hike (prettier from Asciano) the rest of the way.

Buonconvento

BUONCONVENTO is the most obvious base if you are visiting Monte Oliveto Maggiore and travelling on south. The small town looks unremittingly industrial as you approach, but once through the suburbs you come upon a perfect, walled medieval village. In its day, this was one of Siena's key outer defences, and it was here, in 1313, that Emperor Henry VII of Luxembourg, en route to besiege Siena, famously died of malaria, exhaustion or – in some versions – being fed a poisoned Host during Mass. This was a man whom Dante, among others, had seen as the saviour of Italy (Dante particularly wished the emperor to attack Florence, from which he was then exiled – he rather loquaciously equated the emperor's arrival with that of the "lamb of God, who removes the sins of the world").

The old centre is characteristically Sienese, with its brick bastions, town hall and works of art – most of which have been removed from local churches to the excellent and little-known **Museo d'Arte Sacra della Val d'Arbia**, in the main street of the old quarter at Via Soccini 18 (mid-March to mid-Oct Tues–Sun 10am–1pm & 3–7pm; rest of the year Sat & Sun 10am–1pm & 2.30–6pm; €3.50). Pride of place in the charming museum – which on its own is worth the trouble of pulling into town – goes to a small *Madonna and Child with Angels* by Matteo di Giovanni, whose knowing Mary must surely be a portrait. Other works include a *Madonna and Child* attributed to Duccio; a *Madonna and Saints* (1470–82) and *Coronation of the Virgin* by Sano di Pietro;

a lovely four-panelled *Annunciation* (1397) by Andrea di Bartolo; the curious *Madonna del Latte* by Luca di Tommè showing a breast-feeding *Madonna*; and an *Annunciation* (1490–1500) by Benvenuto di Giovanni, a Florentine-influenced work that strikes an anomalous note among the surrounding Sienese treasures.

An interesting new museum, the **Museo della Mezzadria** (Tues–Sun 10am–6pm; ⓦ www.museomezzadria.it) has opened in Piazzale Garibaldi, with varied displays devoted to the region's rural and social history. The museum occupies a superb brick-vaulted space, a late medieval granary built in and around part of the town's old walls. Numerous original objects and artefacts document an almost-vanished agrarian world, and one that most Tuscan families would have lived virtually unchanged for generations until about fifty years ago. The second floor contains part of a reconstructed "casa colonica", the classic rural Tuscan farmhouse, offering a vivid glimpse into the life and living conditions of Tuscan peasant farmers.

These attractions aside, Buonconvento makes an enjoyable stop. You can get here easily by **train** or **bus** from Siena, Montalcino and elsewhere: there are also a couple of fast through-trains to Florence and Grosseto daily, this being one of the key stations for southern Tuscany.

You can get **tourist information** at Piazzale Garibaldi 2 (Tues–Sun 10am–6pm; ☎0577.807.181) or at the *comune* (council office) at Via Soccini 32 (☎0577.80.971). If you need to stay – and there are worse overnight stops if you're travelling far and don't want to get tangled up in Siena – the town has two **hotels**: the *Roma*, Via Soccini 14 (☎0577.806.021, ⓕ0577.807.284; ❶), with an inexpensive **restaurant** next door that represents a perfect piece of old-fashioned 1950s Italiana, and the three-star *Ghibellino* in Via Dante Alighieri 1 (☎0577.809.112, ⓦwww.hotelghibellino.it; ❸). The lively weekly **market** (Sat 8am–1pm) is held in Piazza Gramsci and there's an antiques fair on the last Sunday of each month.

Alternative **accommodation** near Buonconvento is offered by the *Pieve a Salti* farm (☎0577.807.244, ⓦwww.pieveasalti.it; ❸) at Pieve a Salti (signed from Buonconvento), part of the *agriturismo* scheme. Up in the hills, just 4km east of town, it's comfortable and welcoming, and the beautifully situated swimming pool has views over what seems like half of southern Tuscany. You can rent rooms for the night, or simple self-contained apartments in the rustic houses dotted across the estate. Meals are available in the cosy central house.

Monte Oliveto Maggiore

The **Abbazia di Monte Oliveto Maggiore**, 26km southeast of Siena, is sited in one of the most beautiful tracts of Sienese countryside. Approaching from Buonconvento, you climb through forests of pine, oak and cypress, and then into the olive groves that enclose the monastery. From the east, coming through Asciano or San Giovanni d'Asso, the road passes through perhaps the wildest section of all the *crete*. It all appears much as it would have to Pope Pius II, who in 1459 eulogized the woods and gardens that the monks had created from the chalk hills, and the way the russet-coloured brick buildings merged with their setting. Also preserved here is one of the most absorbing Renaissance fresco cycles that you'll find anywhere, a *Life of St Benedict* painted by Sodoma and Luca Signorelli.

The monastery had been founded a century and a half before Pius's visit by one Giovanni Tolomei. A Sienese noble, Giovanni was a major political force

△ The Abbazia di Monte Oliveto Maggiore

in Siena, who renounced all worldly goods after being struck blind and experiencing visions of the Virgin. Adopting the name Bernardo, he came with two companions to the *crete* and lived the life of a hermit. They soon drew a following in this heyday of monasticism, and within six years the pope recognized them as an order – the **Olivetans**, or White Benedictines. Attempting to recapture the simplicity of the original Benedictine rule, these first Olivetans were a remarkable group, going out in pairs during the Black Death to nurse the sick and minister to the dying in all the Sienese towns. During the Feast of the Assumption in 1348, they all met up in Siena – miraculously with no casualties – after their months of perilous work, though Bernardo died later in the year as did many of the brothers.

The remaining monks rebuilt the order, and over the following two centuries Monte Oliveto Maggiore was transformed into one of the most powerful monasteries in the land. (Pius II had a personal reason to visit, as his relative Ambrogio Piccolomini was one of Bernardo's original companions, and in 1536, Emperor Charles V paid a call, together with a two-thousand-strong army.)

The monastery only really fell from influence with the nineteenth-century suppression of the Italian orders, and after the last war, the Italian government allowed Olivetan monks to repopulate it. They have largely restored the buildings and gardens, which they continue to maintain as a monument, supplementing their state income with a highly advanced workshop in restoring ancient books. They also produce wine, honey, olive oil and a cure-all herb liquor, *Flora di Monte Oliveto*, for sale at the monastery shop.

The monastery

At the gatehouse there is a good, moderately priced **café-restaurant**, *La Torre* (restaurant closed Tues). From the **gateway**, surmounted by a square watchtower and niches containing della Robbia terracottas, an avenue of cypresses leads to the abbey. Off to the right, signs direct you along a walk to the **Blessed Bernardo's grotto** – a chapel built on the site where Tolomei settled as a hermit.

The **abbey** itself (daily 9.15am–noon & 3.15–5.45pm; winter closes 5pm) is a huge complex, though much of it remains off limits to visitors (guided tours take you to the library during the same hours as the abbey, except from November to February, when it is only open at weekends). The entrance leads past the gift shop and Foresteria Monastica or **hostel**, as is the Benedictine custom (☎0577.707.652; closed Nov; ❶), to the **Chiostro Grande**, covered by frescoes of the *Life of St Benedict*, the man traditionally regarded as the founder of Christian monasticism.

Sodoma and Signorelli's Life of St Benedict

The St Benedict fresco cycle was begun by **Luca Signorelli**, a painter from Cortona who trained under Piero della Francesca before working for the papacy on the Sistine Chapel. He worked at Monte Oliveto in 1497, completing nine panels (in the middle of the series) before abandoning the work for a more stimulating commission at Orvieto Cathedral. Like much of his work elsewhere, the scenes show a passionate interest in human anatomy, with figures positioned to show off their muscularity to maximum effect.

A few years after Signorelli's departure, Antonio Bazzi (known as **Il Sodoma**), took over, painting the remaining 27 scenes between 1505 and 1508. Sodoma was from Milan and familiar with Leonardo's work, which he often emulated. How he took his nickname is unclear: Vasari suggests it was apt since "he was always surrounded by young men, in whose company he took great pleasure", though letters by Sodoma himself speak of three wives and thirty children. Whatever, the artist was a colourful figure, keeping an extraordinary menagerie of pets: "Badgers, apes, cat-a-mountains, dwarf asses, horses and barbs to run races, magpies, dwarf chickens, tortoises, Indian doves...".

Sodoma brought a sizeable contingent of these pets to Monte Oliveto, including a raven which imitated his voice, and they make odd appearances throughout his colourful, sensual frescoes – a badger is depicted at his feet in a self-portrait in the third panel. There's a notable eroticism, too, in many of the secular figures: the young men coming to join Benedict as monks, and the "evil women", seen tempting the monks in a panel towards the end of the series – these were originally nudes, before protests from the abbot. If the panels strike you as of differing quality, you might give credence to Vasari's anecdote that Sodoma complained about the money he was being paid, which the abbot subsequently raised on condition that he took more care over the remaining work, the first three historical panels of the sequence.

The **cycle** begins on the east wall, on the right of the door into the church. St Benedict, who was born in Norcia in 480, is depicted in events recorded in Gregory the Great's *Dialogues*. In the early panels he is shown leaving home to study in Rome, before withdrawing to the life of a hermit, where he experiences various tribulations and temptations before agreeing to become abbot to a group of disciples. He was an indefatigable builder of monasteries, and the next panels focus on this activity: the foundation of the twelve houses, which formed the basis of the Benedictine order, as well as depictions of various miracles to help in their construction.

The mid-sequence of the cycle depicts various attempts by an evil priest, Florentius, to disrupt the saint's work: he tries first to poison Benedict and then sends in the temptresses, before God steps in and flattens his house (the first of Signorelli's panels). The following eight scenes painted by Signorelli depict aspects of monastic life, and Benedict's trial by – and reception of – Totila, king of the Goths, before Sodoma takes over again, with the saint foretelling the destruction of Monte Cassino, the chief Benedictine house, by the Lombards.

More scenes of monastic life follow, including the burial of a monk whom the earth would not accept, another monk's attempted escape (Benedict intercepts him with a serpent) and the release of a peasant persecuted by a Goth.

The church, library and refectory

The rest of the monastery is inevitably overshadowed by the frescoes. The main **church** – entered off the Chiostro Grande – was given a Baroque remodelling in the eighteenth century and some superb stained glass in the twentieth. Its main treasure is the **choir stalls**, inlaid by Giovanni di Verona and others, from 1500 to 1520, with architectural, landscape and domestic scenes (including a nod to Sodoma's pets with a depiction of a cat in a window).

Back in the cloister, stairs lead up, past a Sodoma fresco of the Virgin, to the **library**, a fine Renaissance arcade lavished with carvings by Giovanni and associates. Sadly, it has had to be viewed from the door since the theft of sixteen codices in 1975. Also on view is the **refectory**, a vast room frescoed with allegorical and Old Testament figures, which gives some idea of Monte Oliveto's heyday.

Asciano

ASCIANO, 9km north of Monte Oliveto, lies on a tiny branch rail line between Siena and Grosseto that takes you through marvellous *crete* countryside. The railway station (which has no ticket office), Asciano Centro (there is also an Asciano Scalo) is in Via Roma. The road approach, the N438 from Siena, is still more scenic, with scarcely a hamlet amid the hills; this route is covered by one bus a day.

Of Etruscan foundation, Asciano is first mentioned in records in 715. In the ninth century it was ruled by the powerful Scialenghi counts, but in 1169 passed to Siena, which promptly ordered the destruction of the town's fortress. In 1234 it fell briefly to Florence, but was soon recaptured by the Sienese. Its most famous son is Domenico di Bartolo (1400–45), the painter responsible for the fresco cycle in Siena's Santa Maria della Scala (see p.391). The town is partially walled and shelters a glorious provincial museum. In the restored Palazzo Corboli at Corso Matteotti 120 stands the **Museo Civico Archeologico e d'Arte Sacra** (Tues–Sun 10am–1pm & 3–7pm; closes 5.30pm Nov–March; €4), which, like the museum in Buonconvento, contains an unexpected wealth of Sienese paintings and (on the second floor) the contents of the town's former Etruscan museum. It has a dozen or so works by major Sienese painters (among them Ambrogio Lorenzetti, Sano di Pietro, Taddeo di Bartolo and Matteo di Giovanni). At Via Mameli 36, the **Museo Cassioli** (open on request; ☎0577.719.510) displays paintings by local artist Amos Cassioli (1832–91).

For information visit the summer-only **tourist office** at Corso Matteotti 18 (☎0577.719.510). The town has a reasonably priced, three-star **hotel**, *Il Bersagliere*, Via Roma 39–41 (☎0577.718.715, ℗0577.710.028, ⓦwww .hotellapace.net; ❷), and a slightly grander, co-owned sister hotel, the three-star *La Pace* (same details; ❹), about 30m away. Local bars provide basic food, though the best **restaurant** in the vicinity is the moderately priced *La Pievina* with an excellent vegetarian menu (☎0577.718.368; closed Mon & Tues), 5.5km north along the Siena road at the hamlet of the same name.

San Giovanni d'Asso and east to Sinalunga

The next stop on the train line from Asciano – and another possible starting point to hike to Monte Oliveto – is **SAN GIOVANNI D'ASSO**, a quiet, rustic place, whose medieval past is hinted at by the presence of half a dozen churches. Romanesque San Pietro, an eleventh-century gem, is the most interesting, and there's an imposing, if extremely blunt thirteenth-century **castle**. Only ever a Sienese fiefdom, the fortress was inhabited at various times by the Buonsignori, whose Sienese palace now houses the city's Pinacoteca, and by the Salimbeni, whose dynastic seat in the city is now the headquarters of the Monte dei Paschi bank. Later it became a granary, and in time was given to Siena's Santa Maria della Scala (see p.391). The village is in truffle country, and has a recently inaugurated museum devoted to the tuber (the first in Italy), the **Museo del Tartufo** (mid-May to June Sat 2–6pm, Sun 10am–1pm & 2–6pm; July & Aug Sat & Sun 10am–1pm & 5–9pm; Sept to mid-May 10am–1pm & 2–6pm; €3), housed in part of the castle at Piazza Gramsci 1 (you can also obtain tourist information here; ☎0577.803.101). As well as insights into truffles, the museum also offers the chance to admire some of the castle's austere but, in parts, prettily frescoed chambers.

East from San Giovanni, a fine though bus-less road meanders towards Sinalunga. The attraction here is primarily the landscape – classic Tuscan miniatures – though the road is marked out by a series of hill-top villages, most of them endowed with a castle and a smattering of medieval churches. **CASTELMUZIO**, 10km from San Giovanni d'Asso, was a favourite preaching ground for Bernardino of Siena, whose confraternity houses a small **Museo d'Arte Sacra** (open on request; ☎0577.665.077); the saint is also depicted in panels by Giovanni di Paolo, his close friend, and Giovanni's pupil Matteo di Giovanni, in the church of SS Trinità e Bernardino. Close by is one of Tuscany's oldest churches – the eighth-century **Pieve di Santo Stefano** in **CENNANO** – while at neighbouring **PETROIO**, built on a curious circular plan, is the best **castle** in the district, a thirteenth-century brick affair where Siena's magistrates were obliged to live for a period in the thirteenth century. A few kilometres to the northeast is the **Abbadia a Sicille**, built by the Templars as a hospice on the pilgrim road to Rome. **TREQUANDA**, a slightly larger village with a couple of restaurants and bars, also preserves a good section of its castle. In the central square, the simple Romanesque parish church of **SS Pietro e Andrea**, fronted by a brown-and-white chequered stone facade, has a fresco by Sodoma of the *Transfiguration*, and a high altarpiece of the *Madonna and Saints* by Giovanni di Paolo. The inlaid wooden urn contains the body of Bonizella Piccolomini (1235–1300), a mere beatific, who never reached the heights of more illustrious family descendants such as Aeneas Piccolomini (Pope Pius II).

East of Trequanda you reach **SINALUNGA**, a modern, thriving centre with rail connections to Siena, Arezzo and Chiusi. It has one notable painting – an *Annunciation* by Benvenuto di Giovanni – in the church of **San Francesco**, sited beside the Franciscan convent at the top of an avenue of cypresses. The church should have another fine picture – a *Madonna* by Sano di Pietro – but that went missing in 1972 and has been replaced by a sad facsimile. Just out of town in the hamlet-suburb of Pieve is a pleasant **hotel**, the *Santorotto* (☎ & ℱ0577.679.012; ❶). Other good-value **hotels** in these parts are to be found 7km south at the next rail stop, Torrita di Siena: the *Belvedere* (☎0577.686.442; ❶) and *La Stazione* (☎ & ℱ0577.685.158; ❷). There is further accommodation at the **spas** of Rapolano Terme and Terme San Giovanni, north of Sinalunga on the Siena road. Both are modern, upmarket places of little interest to anyone not visiting "to take the cure".

Montalcino

MONTALCINO, 37km south of Siena, is a classic Tuscan hill-town, set within a full circuit of walls and watched over by a castle of almost fairytale perfection. A quiet, immediately likeable place, affluent in an unshowy way, it is scarcely changed in appearance since the sixteenth century. It looks wonderful from below, its walls barely sullied by any modern building, and once up in the town the rolling hills, vineyards, orchards, olive groves and ancient oaks look equally lovely in turn. While there are few specific sights, the town makes an excellent base for much of southern Tuscany, lying within easy striking distance of the

MONTALCINO

Porta Burelli
ex-Ospedale di S. M. della Croce
N

Madonna del Soccorso
PIAZZA CAVOUR
Bus Stop
VIALE ROMA
Bar Il Prato

San Francesco

VIA DEL PINO
VIA MAZZINI
San Lorenzo
VIA MOGLIO
PRATO OSPEDALE

VIALE STROZZI
VIA DELLA LIBERTA
VIA SPAGNI
VIA CALORNI
VIA DELLE SCUOLE
VIA DEL MISTERO
VIA CASTELLANA
Porta Castellana

COSTA SPAGNI
Fonte Castellane

Duomo
Palazzo Vescovile
PIAZZA DEL POPOLO
Loggia
VIA MOGLIO

VIA DELLA LIBERTA
VIA SPAGNI
Sant'Agostino
Palazzo dei Priori
VIA MATTEOTTI

VIALE P. STROZZI
VIA RICASOLI
PIAZZA GARIBALDI

Museo Civico e Diocesano
VIA BOLORINI
Sant' Egidio
Santa Croce
VIA DONNOLI

VIA S. SALONI
Porta Gattoli

PIAZZALE FORTEZZA
V. PANFILO
DELLA TORRE

Porta del Cassero
Rocca

VIA A. MORO
Bus Stop
Stadium
Porta Cerbaia

ACCOMMODATION
Bellaria	E
Castello di Velona	F
Dei Capitani	A
Il Giardino	B
Il Giglio	C
Vecchia Oliviera	D

RESTAURANTS
Enoteca La Fortezza	8
Fiaschetteria	4
Il Giardino d'Alberto	1
Il Moro	2
Il Re di Macchia	7
Pizzeria San Giorgio	6
Taverna Grappolo Blu	3
Trattoria L'Angolo	5

0   100 m

Torrenieri, Buonconvento & Via Cassia

Grosseto ▼   ▼ & Sant'Antimo

abbeys of Monte Oliveto and Sant'Antimo, and close to the towns of Pienza, 20km east, and Montepulciano, 11km farther.

Some history

Montalcino's origins are unknown, though it has probably been inhabited since **Paleolithic** or **Etruscan** times. No one is quite sure where its name comes from, though its coat of arms – a holm oak atop six hills – suggests that it derives from the Latin *Mons Ilcinus* (the Mount of the Holm Oak). The first reference to the town appears in 814, when it is mentioned in a list of territories ceded to the abbey of Sant'Antimo by **Louis the Pious**, the son of Charlemagne (see p.466). It was probably only permanently settled around the year 1000, colonized by fugitives fleeing Saracen attacks on the Maremma coast. The exiles' four family groups – the Borghetto, Pianello, Ruca and Travaglio – defined the four quarters or *contrade* of the town: the rival flags still hang outside the houses and they compete against each other in twice-yearly archery tournaments.

Though independent for much of its early medieval history, the town succumbed to **Sienese** rule in 1260 after the Battle of Montaperti, having previously looked to Florence for protection. Having been forced to change sides, the town eventually took its new rulers to heart. In 1526 it took just two days for its citizens to fight off a besieging army dispatched by Pope Clement VII. In 1553, over a period of four months, it withstood the attack of a combined Spanish and Medici army. The town's finest hour, however, came in 1555, when on April 21 the venerable Sienese Republic was forced, once and for all, to capitulate to the Medici. A group of Sienese exiles, supported by the French, then formed a last bastion of Sienese power in Montalcino, flying the flag of the old Republic for four years in the face of almost constant attack. Surrender was only countenanced following the treaty of Cateau Cambrésis (1559) between France and Spain. This heroic interlude is acknowledged at the Siena Palio, where the Montalcino contingent, under their medieval **banner** proclaiming "The Republic of Siena in Montalcino", still takes place of honour.

In the following centuries, the town declined to a poor, malaria-stricken village. Although the malaria was sorted out in the nineteenth century, in the 1960s Montalcino was still the poorest locality in Siena. Now the second-richest, its change in fortunes is due principally to the revival and marketing of its wines, notably the **Brunello**, which is reckoned by many the finest in Italy. The production of high-quality honey and olive oil and income from tourism also play a part.

Arrival, information and accommodation

Roads up to Montalcino, perched 567m above sea level, wind through bucolic swathes of vineyards and pretty pastoral countryside (note the decorative roses grown at the end of many rows of vines): views to all sides are stupendous. Once up at the town, you find yourself on a road that rings the walls. Buses will stop just below the **Rocca** if you wish, but terminate in **Piazza Cavour** at the northern end of Via Mazzini, the main street: either point is convenient for Piazza del Popolo, the centre of town. If you're driving, aim to park either in the small pay **car park** by the Rocca (take the narrow road which strikes through the arch – the **Porta al Cassero** – in the castle walls) or, alternatively, use the large, free car park below the fortress (take the second turning on the right at the mini-roundabout below the Rocca).

The small – and, it must be said, not terribly helpful – **tourist office** is located just up from Piazza del Popolo at Costa del Municipio 8 (Tues–Sun

10am–1pm & 2–5.40pm; ☎0577.849.331, ⓦwww.prolocomontalcino.it). It offers lists of rooms to rent and **foreign exchange** facilities, as does the Monte dei Paschi bank in Via Mazzini, which has a cash machine next door for Visa and Mastercard withdrawals. For local **guides**, **maps** and a small selection of English-language **books** visit the excellent and friendly bookshop at Via Matteotti 22 (Tues–Sat 8.30am–1pm & 3–8pm, Sun 10am–1pm & 3–8pm). It has a particularly good selection of large-scale local maps, useful for **hiking**, including the 1:25,000 Multigraphic *Val d'Órcia* (€5.50) and the 1:50,000 Kompass *Pienza/Montalcino/Monte Amiata* (€6.95). Montalcino's weekly **market** is held on Fridays (7am–1pm) in Viale della Libertà. If you need a taxi, or a car with a driver, call ☎0577.849.113.

Accommodation

Accommodation is severely limited and it's wise to book ahead at almost any time of year. There is only a handful of hotels, though if you have transport you could try one or two tempting places in the countryside nearby. **Private rooms** are more numerous and less expensive and a far better option than in many other places. Try *Affitacamere Mariuccia*, Piazza del Popolo 28 (☎0577.849.113; ❶), with three double rooms and an apartment; or *Anna Affitacamere* (☎0577.848.666; ❷), which has five comfortable rooms with TV and private bathrooms, plus a four-bed apartment – contact or call at the *Albergo Il Giglio* (see below) for details and directions. There are also numerous private rooms and *agriturismo* rooms in the countryside immediately around town. Details are available from the tourist office.

Albergo Il Giardino Piazza Cavour 4 ☎ & ⒻⒻ0577.848.257. The cheapest hotel option in town is cheap for a reason – its rooms, a mixed bag of ten doubles, are pretty sparse, and those facing onto the piazza are likely to be a little noisy. ❶

Albergo Il Giglio Via Soccorso Saloni 5 ☎0577.848.167, ⓦwww.gigliohotel.com. A long-established hotel in a central, sixteenth-century town house that had seen better days, but has been spruced up and offers pleasant, clean rooms, some with terraces. ❷

Bellaria Via Osticcio 19 ☎0577.848.668, ⓦwww .hotelbellariamontalcino.it. The location about 2km out of town is not ideal, but this modern, 25-room three-star is a good, family-run choice. It is a modern construction, but copies the traditional style and materials of a rural Tuscan house. ❸

Castello di Velona Località Castello di Velona, Castelnuovo dell'Abate ☎0577.800.101, ⓦwww.castellodivelona.it. Until 2001 this twelfth-century "castle" was little more

than a pile of rubble: now it is a superb twenty-room, four-star hotel, isolated in lovely open countryside on its own hill and ringed by cypress. It's close to Castelnuovo dell'Abate and Sant'Antimo, about 10km south of Montalcino. Expensive, but rates drop to €210 in low season and there are often web deals. ❾

Dei Capitani Via Lapini 6 ☎0577.847.227, ⓦwww.deicapitani.it. A good, slick three-star choice, with the bonus of a small swimming pool. The 29 rooms vary, however: some are smallish and have no view; others look out over marvellous countryside. Ask to see a selection. ❹

Vecchia Oliviera Via Landi 1 ☎0577.846.028, ⓦwww.vecchiaoliviera .com. Like *Dei Capitani*, a relatively new three-star hotel, but more expensive and not quite as central as its rival. However, it has a pool, its patio has excellent views, and the eleven fine rooms form part of a well-restored former olive mill close to Porta Cerbaia and the walls. A definite first choice for a treat. ❺

The Town

Wherever you end up, the triangular **Piazza del Popolo** lies only a few minutes' walk away. An odd little square, it is set beneath the elongated medieval tower of the **Palazzo dei Priori**, or Palazzo Comunale (1292), apparently modelled on Siena's Palazzo Pubblico. Crests of long-forgotten dignitaries dot the walls, while the statue (1564) beneath the portico, surprisingly, represents the reviled Medici ruler, Cosimo I – it was sculpted just five years after Montalcino had surrendered to the Florentines. Inside the town hall is the *Consorzio di Brunello*, which has information and an exhibition on the history and making of Montalcino's famous Brunello wine; shops the length and breadth of the town sell the stuff, most at ridiculously elevated prices (see p.463).

Occupying other sides of the square are an elegant Renaissance double **loggia**, almost a reprimand in proportional architecture, and a wonderful nineteenth-century **café**, the *Fiaschetteria Italiana* (closed Thurs Nov–Feb). The café is the heart of town life and the focus, inevitably, of the *passeggiata* along Via Mazzini. On busy summer afternoons, however, service can be slow – not a problem if all you want to do is watch the world go by. If you've worked up a thirst, however, the **bar** to the right of the loggia, *Alle Logge di Piazza* (closed Wed), which also has outside tables, is usually quicker with liquid refreshment.

The Rocca

Following Via Mazzini's continuation, Via Matteotti, or Via Ricasoli, and curving up to the right, you emerge at the south end of town by the **Rocca** (April to last Sun in Oct daily 9am–8pm; Nov–March Tues–Sun 9am–6pm; free). It was begun in 1361 on the orders of the Sienese, but by the end of the fifteenth century the advent of artillery had left the castle all but redundant – not that this discouraged those who defended it during the 1526, 1553 and 1555 sieges. The ramparts were added by Cosimo I in 1571, together with the large Medici crest (a shield with six balls), whose present peripheral position – tucked away at the back above the road junction – is surely no accident.

Impressively intact, the walls enclose a public park and in-house **enoteca** (T0577.849.211, W www.enotecalafortezza.it) – a reasonable place to sample some of the famed Brunello along with bread, cheese and salami (though at times it becomes hectic and uncomfortably clogged with tourists). The enoteca also sells tickets for access to the **ramparts** (€3.50; joint ticket with Museo Civico €6) and a glimpse of the famous banner. The castle view is said to have inspired Leonardo's drawing of a bird's-eye view of the earth; the Val d'Órcia is easily made out on a clear day you can even see Siena.

The Museo Civico e Diocesano

Heading north down Via Ricasoli brings you to the excellent **Museo Civico e Diocesano** (Tues–Sun: April–Oct 10am–5.50pm; Nov–March 10am–1pm & 2–5.40pm; €4.50; joint ticket with ramparts €6), built in the former seminary of Sant'Agostino with a grant of almost £500,000 from the EU and a more modest £100,000 from the *comune*. Here the old civic and diocesan collections are featured under one roof for the first time. Like many galleries in the region, the quality of the paintings on show is out of all proportion to the size of the town. Montalcino's begins with a superb *Crucifixion* dating from the end of the twelfth century – one of the oldest pieces of Sienese art in existence. An anonymous work, it was originally hung in the abbey at Sant'Antimo. It is followed by a more mannered *Madonna and Child with Two Angels*, a lovely anonymous late-thirteenth-century work. Bartolo di Fredi has two works on show: an oddly narrow *Deposition* and a more conventional *Coronation of the Virgin*. There's also a *Madonna and Child* by Bartolo's collaborator, Luca di Tommè.

One of the gallery's most interesting works is the *Madonna dell'Umiltà* (Madonna of Humility) by Sano di Pietro, a comparatively rare subject, in which the Virgin is shown sitting or kneeling on a simple cushion rather than poised on a throne or chair. Its appearance dates from the beginning of the fourteenth century, and coincided with the ideas promulgated by the more radical wing of the Franciscan order, which advocated a return to the more rigorous and humble outlook of the first Franciscans. Two paintings by Girolamo di Benvenuto (1470–1524) also merit a close look: an *Adoration of the Shepherds* (with ugly shepherd and fractious Child) and the more spectacular and unusual *Madonna della Cintola*. The latter concerns the Apostle Thomas, who according to legend cast doubt on the Assumption into Heaven of the Virgin (hence "doubting Thomas"). To assuage his worries he opened her tomb, which he found covered in flowers – beautifully depicted in this painting. Casting his eyes upwards, he then saw the Virgin, who removed her belt, or girdle (*cintola*), and let it fall into the hands of the kneeling Thomas. The subject was particularly popular in Tuscany – Agnolo Gaddi, for example, devoted an entire fresco cycle to the theme in Prato, which claims to have the girdle in question (see p.239).

Among the gallery's **sculptures** and miscellaneous **artefacts**, make a special point of looking for the pair of illuminated twelfth-century Bibles and the rare polychrome wooden statue *St Peter*, one of the few documented works of the sculptor Francesco di Valdambrino: it was commissioned in 1425 and given by Pius III to the town's Confraternity of St Peter. You'll also notice an almost comical *Annunciation*, an early fifteenth-century Umbro-Sienese work, in which the puppet-like Gabriel and the Virgin sport impossibly rosy cheeks and beautifully mannered hairstyles.

Churches

Walking a few paces up Via Ricasoli from the museum brings you to the church of **Sant'Agostino**, a severe Gothic-Romanesque affair begun in 1360. The barn-like single nave is dotted with patches of fresco, the most extensive of which – and with a wide variety of themes – cover the arched presbytery, and are probably the work of Bartolo di Fredi. The most interesting pictures, however, are two anonymous panels of *Scenes from the Passion*. One, on the left wall, also shows St Anthony Abbot sharing bread with a curiously attired St Augustine; the second, to the right of the side entrance, is an extraordinary and almost surreal collection of disembodied heads and symbols. Note the moon and sun, which in paintings of the Passion or Crucifixion serve, among other things, to symbolize the anguish of all creation at the death of Christ.

To the north, Via Spagni takes you past the **Duomo**, or San Salvatore, an eleventh-century Romanesque church, horrendously remodelled in Neoclassical style between 1818 and 1832 by an architect aptly called Fantastici; its interior is unarresting, however, save for an impressive little pyramid of reliefs in the baptistery chapel salvaged from the original church. Via Spagni continues to emerge in front of the distinctive Renaissance **Santuario della Madonna del Soccorso**, a seventeenth-century sanctuary built over an ancient chapel; its chief appeal is the sensational view from the adjoining park. Drop down Viale Roma to Piazza Cavour and pop into **Santa Maria della Croce**, a hospital founded in the thirteenth century, more recently appropriated by the local council. Just inside the main entrance is the former pharmacy, still covered in a pretty little array of original frescoes. Nearby, facing the Porta Castellana, is a medieval washhouse, the **Fonte Castellane**, and beyond it the deconsecrated church of **San Francesco**, graced with pleasant cloisters, della Robbia school terracottas and an annexe that was once a medieval hospital.

Wine, food, festivals and transport

Sampling **Montalcino's wines** is easily done. Apart from the enoteca in the Rocca and the *Fiaschetteria Italiana* – which has a superb *cantina* at the back

△ Brunello di Montalcino grapes

– there are half a dozen cheaper café-bars with good stocks. At Via Matteotti 31 there's the *Bar Mariuccia*, with a breathtaking view from the vast windowed terrace at the back. For bottles to take away, try the *Enoteca Les Barriques* at Via Boldrini 19, which has over 800 Tuscan wines, including the major Brunello and Rosso di Montalcino labels. *Enoteca di Piazza*, Piazza Garibaldi 1, has wines from 140 local producers, all well kept in three air-conditioned rooms. In addition to the classic Brunello and the more briefly barrel-aged Rosso di Montalcino table wine, it's worth trying some of the white Moscadelletto di Montalcino, a dessert wine produced in small quantities and at its best chilled.

Eating

Montalcino is remarkably blessed with good **restaurants**, and you'll be hard-pushed to have a bad meal in any of them. In summer it's worth booking a table at just about any of the following places. If all you want is a slice of pizza to take away, head for *Petto's Pizza*, a tiny place on Piazza Garibaldi (closed Wed).

Il Giardino d'Alberto Piazza Cavour 1 ☎ 0577.849.076. Pleasant interior, with good local cooking: the chef is the owner. Closed Wed.
Il Moro Via Mazzini 44 ☎ 0577.849.384. A consistently reliable and no-nonsense modern trattoria with the best budget meals in town. Closed Thurs.
Il Re di Macchia Via Soccorso Saloni 21 ☎ 0577.846.116. Montalcino's swankiest restaurant. While the food is usually excellent, its sometimes pretentious *cucina nuova* leanings may not be to all tastes. Closed Thurs.
Pizzeria San Giorgio Via S. Saloni 10

☎ 0577.848.507. Far and away the best of the town's clutch of *pizzerie*. Crispy pizzas and full meals from €15 in pleasant beamed and brick-vaulted dining rooms. Closed Wed.
Taverna Grappolo Blu Via Scale di Moglio 1 ☎ 0577.847.150. Located in a little alley off Via Mazzini. The old stone-walled interior is cool and appealing, and the unusual pastas are excellent.
Trattoria L'Angolo Via Ricasoli 9 ☎ 0577.848.017. Informal and vaguely trendy little bar-trattoria just down from the Rocca, serving snack lunches and local pasta dishes. Closed Tues.

Festivals

Festa della Madonna del Soccorso (May 8). A small palio – featuring the same horses that will appear later in the year at Siena – is held on the

sports field below the fort.
Montalcino Jazz & Wine (July) in the Fortezza.
Montalcino Teatro (3rd and 4th weeks of July).

An international theatre festival, presenting works in progress in the churches, Rocca, eighteenth-century *Teatro degli Astrusi*, and sometimes in the *crete* around the town.

Torneo della Apertura della Caccia (2nd Sun in Aug). Tournament marking the start of the hunting season that is said to have fourteenth-century origins – inspiring some of the tales in the *Decameron*. Half the town dresses up in medieval costume for parades and archery competitions (on the

sports field) between the *contrade*. Street banquets complete the day.

Festa dell'Unità (mid-Aug). Ten-day festival organized by the former communist party in the pine wood above the town. Live music most nights, cheap food and wine – and usually a lot of fun.

Sagra del Tordo (last Sun in Oct). Similar events to the *Caccia* festival, but if anything even more widely touted.

Transport

TRA-IN **buses** (℡0577.204.111, ⓦwww.trainspa.it) run more or less hourly from Piazza Cavour and Viale P. Strozzi to Buonconvento and Siena via Torrenieri. At Torrenieri you can pick up one of six daily buses to San Quírico, Pienza and Montepulciano. There are four local buses daily from Montalcino to Sant'Angelo Scalo (ⓦwww.bargagliautolinee.it) and just one during the school term to Abbadia San Salvatore and Piancastagnaio. There's also a daily SIRA bus (℡0641.730.083) to and from Rome (it departs for Rome mid-afternoon from Piazza Cavour), useful as a direct way of getting to Pienza and Montepulciano, which it passes en route to the A1 motorway. Bus tickets are available from tobacconists around town, and from the *Bar Il Prato* on the corner of Viale Roma and Piazza Cavour.

For **rail connections** to Siena or Grosseto, head to Buonconvento, Torrenieri or to Sant'Angelo. Most services are slow, stopping numbers, but buried in the timetable are a couple of fast through trains daily to Florence (via Siena) and Grosseto (for connections to Rome and Pisa).

Vineyards and villages around Montalcino

As Brunello is Italy's premier wine, it seems a shame not to get out to at least one of the **vineyards**. As well as those detailed below, you can visit most others if you ask at the winegrowers' headquarters in Montalcino's Palazzo Comunale; the only period when visitors might not be welcome is at harvest time (Sept–Oct).

Fattoria dei Barbi

The **Fattoria dei Barbi** (℡0577.841.111, ⓦwww.fattoriadeibarbi.it) is 7km southeast of Montalcino, signposted off to the left just after the hamlet of La Croce on the Sant'Antimo road. Its *cantina* (Mon–Fri 10am–1pm & 2.30–6pm, Sat & Sun 2.30–6pm; opens until 7pm in summer) offers tasting facilities and a superb stock of vintages. Attached is a very fine **restaurant**, the ✳ *Taverna dei Barbi* (℡0577.841.200 or 0577.847.117; closed Tues at dinner and Wed except in Aug) with strictly local recipes at moderate prices – lots of *porcini*, *pici*, *papardelle* and delicious grilled pork, the *brasato al Brunello*, washed down, of course, with the Barbi's own wine.

Villa Banfi, Castello di Poggio alle Mura and Sant'Angelo in Colle

With a third of its three thousand hectares devoted to vineyards, the **Villa Banfi** (℡0577.840.111, ⓦwww.castellodibanfi.com) is Montalcino's largest and most modern wine producer. It was taken over in the 1970s by an Italian-American wine-importing family, the Mariani. It has English-speaking guides available to show you round (Mon–Fri 4pm; bookings preferred) and a moderately priced

🍴**restaurant** (dinner only Tues–Sat) serving good-quality local cuisine (booking essential). The villa is located 18km southwest of Montalcino just outside the village of Sant'Angelo Scalo where you can get an inexpensive **pizza** at *Il Marrucheto* (☎0577.808.000) by the station. Five kilometres to the west of the station, inside the Banfi estate, is the **Castello di Poggio alle Mura**, a thirteenth-century castle built for the Salimbeni clan of Siena, though subsequently added to in a mishmash of styles. Recently renovated, it has a small **Museo del Vetro** (daily: summer 10am–6.45pm; winter 10am–5.45pm; €2.50) with Roman and Etruscan artefacts, and a display of traditional implements for wine-making.

At the halfway point on the road from Montalcino to Villa Banfi is the tiny walled village of **SANT'ANGELO IN COLLE**, set on a low hill (it can also be reached on a beautiful but partly gravel-surfaced road from Sant'Antimo). The Sienese used it as a military base against Montalcino in the mid-thirteenth century and as part of their frontier thereafter. It has some interesting frescoes inside the Romanesque church, **San Michele**, on the piazza (check out the lovely views from behind the church) and a couple of **bar-restaurants**. The one just off the piazza, *Il Pozzo* (☎0577.844.015; closed Tues), at Piazza Il Pozzo 2, is recommended for its inexpensive pasta dishes and roasts.

Sant'Antimo

It's a moot point which of Tuscany's many abbeys is the most beautiful, has the most fascinating history, or boasts the loveliest setting, but many would put the **Abbazia di Sant'Antimo** (Mon–Sat 10.15am–12.30pm & 3–6.30pm, Sun 9.15–10.45am & 3–5pm; free; Ⓦwww.antimo.it) near the top of their list. It's a glorious, isolated Benedictine monastery that stands comparison with the nearby foundations of San Galgano, Monte Oliveto and San Salvatore. Located a short distance from the hamlet of Castelnuovo dell'Abate, 10km south of Montalcino, and splendidly isolated in a timeless landscape of fields, olive groves and wooded hills, the abbey stood empty for some five hundred years, and is today maintained by a small group of French monks – a Cistercian offshoot known as the Premonstratensians, who celebrate Mass several times daily in haunting Gregorian chant.

Mythology and history of the abbey

Tradition ascribes the foundation of the abbey to **Charlemagne**, who, while returning with his army from Rome in 781, halted in the nearby Starcia valley. Here he prayed to God, asking for relief from the disease which was crippling his army, and offering to found a church if his prayers were answered. An angel appeared, showing the emperor a herb (called *Carolina* in Italian) which he was instructed to dry and give to his men as a powder with wine. The cure worked as promised, and Charlemagne duly founded Sant'Antimo.

If this story sounds too good to be true, it is known that the abbey existed in 814, when Charlemagne's son, **Louis the Pious**, enriched it with vast tracts of land and privileges in a charter dated December 29 of that year. Other scholars suggest it may have been founded on the site of a Roman villa, or possibly by the last of the area's Lombards in about 760, the date of the foundation of the Abbadia di San Salvatore (see p.491). In fact **St Antimo** (feast day May 11) was probably a bishop martyred in Rome during the persecutions of Diocletian and Maximian (304–5 AD). Certainly it's known that in 781, the year of the abbey's supposed foundation, St Antimo's relics, along with those of St Sebastian, were given to Charlemagne by Pope Hadrian I.

Whatever the truth of Sant'Antimo's origins, the decidedly **pre-Romanesque** style of parts of the primitive church, together with documentary evidence, confirms a late eighth- or early ninth-century foundation. Over the two centuries that followed, the abbey's importance grew, thanks in part to its location close to the intersection of several of central Italy's most important medieval **trade and pilgrimage routes**. Oldest of these was a former Etruscan road linking Chiusi with Rusellae on the coast, a route which passed directly in front of the abbey (traces of the sunken lane can still be seen). This was crossed by the old Roman consular road, Via Clodia, again right in front of the abbey. The most important of the ancient roads, however, was the **Via Francigena**, which for centuries was the most important pilgrimage route between Rome and northern Europe. Countless towns and villages grew up along the route, together with numerous hospices for pilgrims: Siena – whose Santa Maria della Scala was one of the most important of these (see p.391) – and San Gimignano are just two local towns which owe their early medieval prosperity to the Via Francigena.

Sant'Antimo's heyday dates from 1118, when an enormous **bequest** allowed work to begin on the main body of the present church and a complex of monastic buildings (now largely lost). The grant's original deed – a document many hundreds of words long – was engraved in the steps of the altar, where it survives to this day. With new-found funds, the abbey authorities now had access to expertise and ideas from elsewhere in Europe, and looked for inspiration to the great Benedictine mother house at Cluny, in Burgundy, and to **French architects**, whose plans for the new church appear to have been based on the abbey church of Vignory (begun in 1050) in the Haute-Marne.

Over the years funds began to run low – hence the unfinished facade – as religious bequests increasingly found their way to new orders such as the Camaldolese and Cistercians. Worse, the rising power of Siena began to strip away the abbey's privileges and lands; in 1212, following Siena's sacking of Montalcino (then under the abbey's ownership), Sant'Antimo's abbot was forced to cede a quarter of the territory of Montalcino to the Sienese Republic. By 1293 it retained only a fifth of its original possessions, which had once made it the second richest abbey in Tuscany. **Financial problems** were soon followed by moral and spiritual decline. In 1439 Pope Eugenius IV had the abbot imprisoned for "villainy"; then in 1462, Pius II **suppressed the abbey** for good, convinced that it was beyond spiritual or financial salvation.

The abbey soldiered on for a few years under the auspices of the bishops of Siena and the newly created diocese of Montalcino, but after 1492 – when Montalcino's bishops opted to live instead in the town – it was largely **abandoned**, its buildings ransacked for stone for use in Castelnuovo and Montalcino. What remained was bought by the state in 1867.

The church

The monks' quarters aside, little remains of the plundered monastic buildings – a ruined refectory and chapterhouse are now used as barns, and accommodation for recently arrived monks. But the twelfth-century **church** itself is in excellent repair and is one of the most outstanding examples of Italian Romanesque, built in a soft, creamy stone and perfectly proportioned.

The **facade** was the last part of the church to be built, and so suffered most from the shortfall of funds. The traces of arches in the stones, and the pilasters with attached columns, suggest that a portico once provided a grander

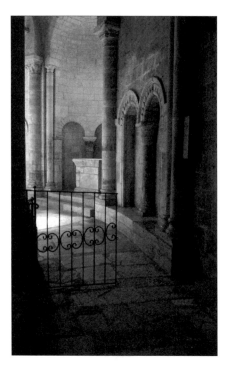
△ Apse, Sant'Antimo

entrance: the lions which supported the portico, and symbolized the power of Satan waiting to devour the faithful, are now inside the abbey. Recent studies suggest the portal on the church of Santa Maria in nearby San Quírico d'Órcia (see p.469) was one of two portals intended for the abbey, and was perhaps given away in the light of the abbey's subsequent decline. The surviving **portal** contains a twelfth-century lintel whose Latin text alludes to one Azzo, a monk who may have been one of the original architects of the church. Otherwise the capitals, frieze and recessed, fluted arch are all lifted directly from French (Languedoc) models. Around the corner, on the left (north) wall, the little filled-in doorway and lintels survive from the earlier ninth-century church.

The interior

The French flavour becomes more marked in the lovely **interior**, whose basilican plan – with an ambulatory, and radiating chapels – is unique in Tuscany, and found elsewhere in Italy in only a handful of churches. Its presence here allowed pilgrims to walk around the apse and pray before the martyrium, the spot under the high altar which contained the relics of the saint being venerated. The **high altar** features a polychrome statue of the crucified Christ, an outstanding Romanesque work dating from the end of the twelfth century. Note the inscription on the altar steps (see p.467).

The **capitals** on the pillars of the ambulatory display some exquisite carving, a feature for which the abbey is particularly celebrated. Many are carved in lustrous alabaster, a stone which features elsewhere in the building, lending a beautifully subtle tone to the walls and sculpture. Here the carving is more Lombard than French, leading to the theory that two separate workshops – one from France (the Auvergne) and one from Lombardy (Pavia) may have worked alongside one another. Equally plausible is the idea that many of the capitals derive from the earlier Carolingian church, built before the French-inspired church of 1118.

The abbey's finest capital sits atop the second column on the right of the nave. It depicts *Daniel in the Lions' Den*, the protagonist – arms raised in prayer – a study of calm while his fellow prisoners are crushed and eaten by rampant beasts. Clearly superior to anything else in the abbey, it is the work of the so-called **Master of Cabestany**, a sculptor of French or Spanish origin whose distinctive hand has been identified in abbeys across France, Catalonia and Italy – he seems always to have worked for the Benedictines. By way of comparison, wander across to study the capital on the second column on the left, which depicts a shepherd and sheep in a far more mundane style.

Increasingly, the rest of the church is often closed to visitors. Areas affected include the **sacristy**, which occupies part of the ninth-century Carolingian church, entered (when open), from a door in the right aisle. It features an array of primitive black-and-white frescoes with such details as a rat looking up attentively at St Benedict, and a pair of copulating pigs. Note the stoup with Pius's Piccolomini crest at each corner. Further frescoes are to be found in some of the rooms built around the **women's gallery**, fitted out in the fifteenth century by the bishops of Montalcino: it's approached from the nave by a circular stairway, though here, too, access is often restricted.

Practicalities

There are occasional **buses** along the Sant'Antimo road, leaving Montalcino from Monday to Friday at 6am and 1.40pm (returning at 7.50am and 3.35pm), and on Saturday at 4.35pm (returning at 4.50pm). Alternatively, it's a pleasant country walk or feasible hitch. Additional rewards are at the moderately priced *Ristorante Bassomondo* (☎0577.835.619; closed Mon) across the road, which does wonderful *crostini*, *ribollita* and *pici*.

The Val d'Órcia and Bagno Vignoni

The **Val d'Órcia** stretches from San Quírico d'Órcia down towards the border with Lazio and the lake of Bolsena. A gorgeous stretch of country, it is marked at intervals by fortresses built from the eighth century on, when the road through the valley, the **Via Francigena**, was a vital corridor north from Rome (see p.467).

The major attraction along the initial section of the valley is the remarkable Medicean sulphur baths of **Bagno Vignoni**. With transport – or enthusiasm for walking – you might strike off south from here to the region's medieval power base, the monastery of San Salvatore (see p.491). **Walkers** might also consider approaching Bagno Vignoni across country from Montalcino (a five-hour hike which would entail staying in Bagno Vignoni), or going on from Bagno Vignoni along the old gravel road to Pienza.

San Quírico d'Órcia

A rambling, part-walled village, **SAN QUÍRICO D'ÓRCIA** stands at a crossroads on the Siena to Bolsena road overlooking the Órcia and Asso valleys. It's quiet and rather decayed – an odd mix of modern and medieval – overlooked by the precarious ruins of a seventeenth-century palazzo, whose Baroque exterior frescoes are fading before your eyes. Its name comes from San Quírico a Osenna, an ancient church on the Via Francigena, though of the eponymous saint little is known except that he was martyred, probably in the fourth century. Hospitals and hospices sprang up here to accommodate pilgrims in the early Middle Ages, as they did in Siena and other settlements along the Via Francigena.

The main – and highly worthwhile – reason for stopping in the town is to look around the exceptionally pretty Romanesque **Collegiata**, with its three portals sculpted with lions and other beasts; the south door may be the work of Giovanni Pisano (or his school), while the main portal is rightly considered the finest piece of Lombard work in the region. The church was built in the

There are plenty of interesting **hikes** around San Quírico and Montalcino, in the **Parco Artístico Naturale e Culturale della Val d'Órcia**. The park information office doubles as San Quírico's tourist office, Via Dante Alighieri 33 (☏0577.897.211 or 0577.898/303, ⓦwww.parcodellavaldorcia.com). Information is also available from the *comune* (council) at Piazza Chigi 2 (☏0577.899.711, ⓦwww.comunesanquirico .it).

A moderately challenging trail runs from Bagno Vignoni out to the castle restaurant at Ripa d'Órcia and back (12km; 4hr). From 100m before the Bagno Vignoni car park, a cart-track rises through vineyards and olive groves to Rocca di Vignoni, the hamlet of Vignoni and on to Podere Bellaria, after which is a junction. One route heads right (north) to San Quírico, the other left (south) through a scenic landscape up to the Ripa d'Órcia castle. Backtracking 500m down the castle hill you'll find a signposted path leading right, down through foliage to a broken bridge over the Órcia river; don't cross, but follow the left-hand riverbank back to Bagno Vignoni.

There's an easier trail from Montalcino to San Quírico, crossing shadeless clay hills and dipping through vineyards (13km; 4hr), good for walking or cycling. From Montalcino's northern Porta Burelli, a track drops down to Gli Angeli and crosses the paved road in front of Podere La Casaccia, heading into an area of hummocks until you reach the provincial highway. Follow the road right for a few hundred metres, coming off at Podere Fiesole and heading east across clay ground to Podere Casello and Poderi Pian dell'Asso. Cross the train track and a couple of streams before climbing to Podere Belladonna and the chapel of Madonna di Riguardo. A rising and falling path covers the last 1500m into San Quírico.

twelfth century, probably on the ruins of a still older church. Inside is a delicate triptych of the *Virgin and Saints* by Sano di Pietro in the north transept, as well as a marvellous set of nine Renaissance choir stalls, whose figures and trompe l'oeil may have been executed to designs by Luca Signorelli. The stalls originally formed part of a larger nineteen-stall set in the Cappella del Battistero in Siena cathedral.

There's a **tourist office** at Via Dante Alighieri 33 (April–Oct daily 10am–1pm & 3.30–6.30pm; ☏0577.897.211), also the headquarters of the **Parco Artístico Naturale e Culturale della Val d'Órcia** (see box above). It provides information about the park and the Treno Natura "tourist" train line that occasionally runs through the Val d'Orcia to Monte Antico (ⓦwww .ferrovieturistiche.it). San Quírico is a regular stop on the Siena–Buoncon-vento–Pienza–Montepulciano TRA-IN **bus** route, as well as a stop on the once-daily SIRA Montalcino–Rome service. It has a small two-star **hotel**, *Il Garibaldi* (☏0577.898.315; ❶) on the Via Cassia, the main road.

If you want an isolated and peaceful place to stay, **Ripa d'Órcia**, about five kilometres southwest of San Quírico at the end of a minor but perfectly passable gravelled road, has an absolutely stunning hotel, *Castello Ripa d'Órcia* (☏0577.897.376, ⓦwww.castelloripadorcia.com; ❹), located in an isolated and ancient castle which is visible for miles around. Views from the castle are sen-sational, and there are lovely strolls and marked trails down to the Órcia valley and Sant'Antimo from right outside the walls.

Bagno Vignoni

Six kilometres south of San Quírico, **BAGNO VIGNONI** is scarcely even a hamlet – just a handful of buildings around a central square. The square, however, is one of Tuscany's most memorable sights, occupied by an arcaded Renaissance *piscina*. This was built by the Medici, who, like St Catherine of Siena, took the sulphur cure here. The hot springs still bubble away in the bath (which formed an amazing set in Tarkovsky's film *Nostalgia*), though they are currently out of bounds for bathing; plans to restore the *piscina* and develop the spa as a resort have so far been thwarted – thankfully – by the Siena council.

You can, however, bathe in the sulphur pools at the foot of the hillside below the village, or use the sulphur pool at the four-star *Posta Marcucci* **hotel** (T0577.887.112, Wwww.hotelpostamarcucci.it; ❻; use of pool for non-residents €10 per day), a fifteenth-century summer house erected by Pius II on the side of the piazza. The village's other hotel, the three-star *Le Terme* (T0577.887.150, Wwww.albergoleterme.it; ❸), which overlooks the *piscina*, has a marginally better restaurant. The best place to **eat**, however, is the moderately priced *Antica Osteria del Leone*, Via dei Mulini 3 (T0577.887.300; closed Mon). Food here is Tuscan with a twist and they have several vegetarian options.

Rocca, Castiglione and Vivo d'Órcia

The **Rocca d'Órcia** (summer 10am–1pm & 3–6pm; winter Sat & Sun 10am–1pm & 2.30–6.30pm; €2), 3km south of Bagno Vignoni, is visible almost the whole way from San Quírico: from the eleventh to the fourteenth century this dramatic pile of a castle belonged, like almost every castle along this stretch of the Via Francigena, to the **Aldobrandeschi** family. Although Santa Fiora (see p.495) was the clan base, this was their most important fortress, a strategic site allowing them to rob or extract tolls from any traffic along the route. After a change of ownership to the Salimbeni family, who built most of the present structure, the castle was only properly incorporated into the Sienese Republic in 1418.

CASTIGLIONE D'ÓRCIA, the village below the *rocca*, is a fine-looking place, built almost entirely of stone, with an elaborately cobbled piazza and a trio of medieval churches. In the Romanesque church of **SS Stefano e Degna** are panels (temporarily removed to the Museo Civico in Montalcino, with some dispute between church and museum as to when they shall be returned) by Pietro Lorenzetti, Vecchietta and one attributed to Simone Martini – a hint of the wealth Castiglione must once have enjoyed. Vecchietta, incidentally, was born in the village in 1412. There is a small summer-only tourist office in Piazza Il Vecchietta (T0577.887.211 or 0577.898.303).

Moving south towards Monte Amiata, the hamlet of **VIVO D'ÓRCIA** is another medieval treat, with beautiful walks along the river and in the woods, where you come upon the Romanesque **Cappella dell'Ermicciolo**, part of a twelfth-century Camaldolese monastery, the Eremo del Vivo, altered in 1536, reputedly by Antonio da Sangallo the Younger. For rooms and *agriturismo* apartments try *I Lecci*, at Località Lecci, 5km from Castiglione (T0577.887.287, Wwww.agriturismoilecci.it; ❷), which also offers inexpensive meals.

Bagni San Filippo and Radicófani

East of Vivo d'Órcia, just a few hundred metres off the N2, is the tiny spa of **BAGNI SAN FILIPPO**. Like Vignoni, this has an outdoor hot sulphur spring cascading from the rocks, as well as an unostentatious modern spa building and pool. There is also a tiny chapel, **La Grotta del Santo**, commemorating the village saint, who took refuge here after being offered the papacy.

On the other side of the N2 from San Filippo, a road veers east into the hills to the majestically situated **Rocca** of **RADICÓFANI** (783m), which vies with the Rocca d'Órcia for the title of most imposing fortress in southern Tuscany. Clamped to a basalt outcrop, it commands the strategic heights between the Paglia and Órcia valleys. The castle is identified with one Ghino di Tacco, a fourteenth-century bandit who features in the writings of both Dante and Boccaccio (the *Decameron* tells of Tacco's imprisoning the abbot of Cluny in this fortress, then curing him of indigestion.) Views from the walls are stunning. Hours vary from year to year: for the latest details contact the small, summer-only tourist office at Via Renato Magi 57 (☎0578.55.684). Below the castle, which was devastated by an explosion in the eighteenth century, is a handsome little village, with an old Capuchin convent, a cluster of churches and the sadly dilapidated **Palazzo La Posta** – the "Great Duke's Inn", where centuries of grand tourists – including Montaigne and Charles Dickens – put up on their way to Rome. The best of the churches, the Romanesque **San Pietro**, features several good glazed terracotta works from the school of Andrea della Robbia, together with a polychrome wooden *Madonna* (second pillar on the left) by Francesco di Valdambrino. A rare sculptor, Valdambrino (1375–1435) often collaborated with the great Sienese sculptor Jacopo della Quercia, having worked with him on the panels for the Fonte Gaia, now displayed in Siena's Palazzo Pubblico. He is best known for his *St Peter* in Montalcino (see p.463).

The village remains a handy place to stay, with a modest **hotel** – *La Torre*, Via Matteotti 7 (☎0578.55.943; ➊) – plus the *Eni*, Via dell'Órcia 16, 14km away in the hamlet of Contignano (☎0578.52.025; ➊).

Pienza

PIENZA, 20km east of Montalcino, is as complete a Renaissance creation as any in Italy, conceived as a Utopian "New Town" by **Pope Pius II**, Aeneas Sylvius Piccolomini (see p.390). The site Pius chose was the village of Corsignano where he was born in 1405, the first of eighteen children of a noble family exiled from Siena in 1385 (the village, at least in part, formed part of the Piccolominis' traditional feudal domain). Archeological evidence suggests it was inhabited as early as the Bronze Age. In Roman times it was a hill-top fort of some renown, and by the thirteenth century it had a reputation as an anarchic border town: Boccaccio spoke of "Corsignan de' Ladri" ("Corsignano of the thieves") in his novel *Cecco di Fotarrigo*. Today there's little to see beyond Pius's central Renaissance piazza – the pope's death marked the end of his beloved project – though few places in Tuscany have as much immediate charm. There are also some extraordinary **views** from the walls, a scattering of good **bars and restaurants**, and a range of **accommodation** – from rooms to a fine historic hotel – if you want to stay.

A brief history – Pius and Rossellino

The **construction** of Pienza began in 1459, less than a year after Pius's election to the papacy in August 1458. History rather harshly suggests the new pope wished to avenge himself on Siena – which had unjustly exiled his family – by building a city that would be both Siena's antithesis and its superior. It's also claimed Pius could not live with the shame of having come from a village as humble as Corsignano. His architect on the project was **Bernardo Rossellino**, who worked on all the major buildings here under the guidance

Landscape

There's plenty to take home from a visit to Tuscany and Umbria, but some of the most enduring memories will probably be of the regions' sublime scenery. In the popular imagination, much of the landscape is pastoral, a patchwork of low hills, vineyards and wooded valleys scattered with crumbling villas and farmhouses. The reality is rather different, for while much of the countryside has been worked for centuries, the variety of landscape is extraordinary.

Classic Tuscan countryside

From high peaks to coastal plains

High mountain scenery is a feature of eastern Umbria, where the Sibillini range tops 2400m, just a little higher than the almost equally dramatic Alpi Apuane and Orrecchiella peaks of northwest Tuscany. In northeast Tuscany, the broad sweep of the Apennines contains the Foreste Casentinesi, a high, wild upland of ancient woodlands, while in the region's opposite corner, close to the coast, the Maremma is a glorious medley of hills, pristine beaches, pine woodlands and a variety of marine habitats. Nearby is the Parco Nazionale Arcipelago Toscano, comprising the islands of Elba, Giglio, Capraia, Gorgona, Pianosa, Giannutri and Montecristo – the largest marine park in Europe.

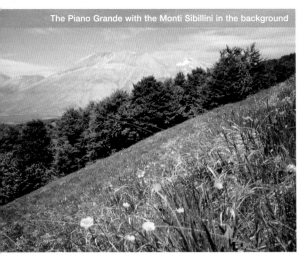
The Piano Grande with the Monti Sibillini in the background

Throughout both regions there are also smaller, anomalous landscapes. In Umbria these include the dulcet Lago Trasimeno, the steep-sided Valnerina valley east of Spoleto, the imposing whaleback mountain of Monte Subasio above Assisi, and the cave-riddled, bare grass slopes of Monte Cucco northeast of Gubbio. In Tuscany the range is even greater, from the small coastal habitats of Bólgheri, Lago di Burano and Laguna di Orbetello to the lonely volcanic peak of Monte Amiata in the south. Most distinctive of all is the *crete* near Siena, a region of bare, clay hills and ridges that make up one of Italy's best-known landscapes.

Many of these landscapes enjoy protected status, including national parks in the Sibillini and Foreste Casentinesi and elsewhere, though protection on the ground is often patchy at best or precarious at worst. Much the same, sadly, goes for smaller state reserves, the Parco Naturale della Maremma a notable exception. Better protection is guaranteed by WWF stewardship, namely at Lago di Burano and other so-called "Oasi" across the region.

Flora

The flora of Tuscany and Umbria is often exceptional, and spring carpets of flowers – particularly on upland meadows – can be breathtaking. The prime times are late April and May (later in the mountains), and the best areas in Tuscany are the Orecchiella and Alpi Apuane, at the meeting point of Alpine and Mediterranean vegetation zones. These contain the vast majority of the species that grow in Italy. In Umbria, the Martani hills, Monte Subasio and the Piano Grande are blanketed in orchids, fritillaries and countless other flowers in May and June. In olive groves and on hillsides – often free of herbicides or pesticides – all manner of common plants thrive: poppies, primroses, violets, grape hyacinth, cyclamen, irises, cistus and many more. Specially adapted marine species can be found in the reserves of the Maremma.

Parasol pines in the Pineta del Tombolo, Maremma

Cypresses and parasol pines are the icons of the Tuscan countryside, while oak forests blanket many of the interior hills, in Chianti in particular. Elsewhere there are

Mammals

Of the larger mammals in the area, the **wild boar** is best known, found through much of Tuscany and now spreading into Umbria. In the Maremma there is an indigenous breed, smaller than the boar of Eastern European origin common elsewhere. Both types are shy, frugal creatures and difficult to spot casually, though you may well see signs of their passage. Porcupines are also common and you often find quills on country walks, though again they are elusive creatures. Roe deer have been reintroduced into the reserves at Bólgheri and the Monti dell'Uccellina, and are readily seen. Elsewhere they've been hunted to extinction, along with the bulk of the larger mammals.

Wolves, however, are making some sort of come-back, drifting into the Valnerina from their heartlands in the Abruzzo mountains to the south. There are at least 150 to 200 specimens in Italy, all protected – in theory. Their largest threat comes from feral dogs – estimated to number 800,000 nationwide – both because they compete for food and because people deal with the dogs by poisoning or shooting them. Wild mountain goats are found on the island of Montecristo, a nature reserve closed to the casual visitor. Elsewhere, you may see **smaller mammals** – hares, rabbits, foxes and weasels – though these too have been much depleted by the hunters' guns. Wilder upland areas are seeing the return of the **wild cat**, but, like the wolf, numbers are tiny, and the chance of seeing them minimal. Snakes, and the viper in particular, are common, particularly around abandoned farmland – of which there's plenty. Small black scorpions are also quite common.

Stand of cypress trees, Val d'Órcia

large tracts of virgin forest, especially in the Casentino around Camáldoli, filled with oak, beech and pines, many of them huge ancient specimens. Sweet chestnut dominates in the Orecchiella and Alpi Apuane, rolling unbroken across mile after mile of the lower hills. On the higher hills, notably in the Sibillini, there are clumps of high beech forest, the predominant tree of the Apennines and of limestone in general. Coastal areas, especially in the Monti dell'Uccellina, have preserved the classic profiles of Mediterranean *macchia*: dwarf trees (usually oak), and a scrub of laurel, broom, lentisk, heather and fragrant plants.

Birds

Tuscany and Umbria host an interesting array of birds. Coastal areas offer the richest pickings, and in particular the reserves set aside to protect them: Lago di Burano, Laguna di Orbetello and the Monti dell'Uccellina. These closely connected areas draw numerous migrant birds, many of them extremely rare. Inland, birdlife is under threat, but you can still see hoopoes, doves, woodpeckers and run-of-the-mill wrens, thrushes and starlings. Birds of prey are comparatively rare, though mountain areas boast a few hawks and buzzards, and perhaps a few pairs of golden eagles.

of Leon Battista Alberti, the great theorist of Renaissance art, building and town planning.

Rossellino's commission was to build a cathedral, papal palace and town hall, but Pius instructed the various cardinals who followed his court to build their own residences too, turning the project into nothing less than a Vatican in miniature (see "Palazzo Vescovile" p.476). Astonishingly, the cathedral, the papal and bishop's palaces, and the core of the town were completed in just three years. Limited though it was, it constituted the first "Ideal City" of the Renaissance to become a reality.

After consecration of the cathedral, Pius issued a papal bull rechristening the "city" Pienza, in his own honour, and stipulating that no detail of the cathedral or palaces should be changed. The wish was fulfilled rather more easily than he could have expected, for he died within two years, and of his successors only Pius III, his nephew, paid Pienza any regard. The city, intended to spread across the hill, never grew beyond a couple of blocks to either side of the main Corso, and its population remained scarcely that of a village. Today, with a population of 2500, it still has an air of emptiness and folly: a natural stage set, which was used by Zeffirelli for his film of *Romeo and Juliet*.

The Town

There is no difficulty finding your way about Pienza. Roads, buses and cars converge on the **Piazza Dante**, just outside the Porta al Murello, main entrance gate to the papal town. From here the **Corso Rossellino** leads to Rossellino's centrepiece, **Piazza Pio II**, enclosed by the Duomo, Palazzo Piccolomini, Palazzo Comunale and Palazzo Vescovile, the last of these built by one of Pius's more ambitious Vatican followers – Cardinal Borgia, the future Pope Alexander VI.

Piazza Pio II

The juxtaposition of civic and religious buildings in the **Piazza Pio II** was deliberate, and aimed to underline the balance between Church and town through architectural harmony. Apart from the Palazzo Comunale, based on the medieval Palazzo Vecchio in Florence, the ensemble is entirely Renaissance in

473

conception. If it all seems a little cramped, it's partly because Rossellino wished to retain the existing east–west axis of Corsignano's main street, and partly because of Pius's insistence that his palace loggia should command a view and that the Duomo should be flooded with light, meaning that the piazza's two key buildings had to be orientated towards the valley to the rear. For the Duomo, in particular, this was to have near-disastrous structural consequences.

The piazza's small well, the **Pozzo dei Cani**, sets the tone, its twin columns and classical frieze a perfect miniature of Renaissance ambitions.

The Duomo

The **Duomo**, or Santa Maria Assunta, has one of the earliest Renaissance **facades** in Tuscany, its three-tiered veneer of Istrian marble surmounted by a vast garland of fruit enclosing Pius's papal coat of arms. The **campanile**, rocked to its foundations by an earthquake in 1545, was virtually rebuilt in 1570.

On Pius's orders, the **interior** took inspiration from Franciscan Gothic churches and the German *Hallenkirchen*, or hall-churches, which he had seen on his pre-papal travels as a member of the Curia. The hall-churches, as here, were distinguished by naves and aisles of equal height. The tall **windows** were also a papal whim, designed to produce a *domus vitrea* (hall of glass), whose flood of light was intended to symbolize the age's humanist enlightenment. Pius's *Commentaries* also talk of the strangely elongated **capitals** of the nave's columns as *felici errori*, or "happy errors". Legend claims the pope found the church's earlier columns too short and insisted that Rossellino find some way of lengthening them. In fact, Rossellino deliberately introduced the capitals, partly to accentuate the nave's soaring Gothic effect, and partly to evoke parallels with similar capitals in Siena's Loggia di Mercanzia, and the Duomo, Loggia dei Lanzi, and church of San Lorenzo in Florence.

To satisfy Pius's whims, and to fit the cramped site, Rossellino had to build on sandstone with a substratum of clay. Before completion a crack appeared, and following an earthquake in the nineteenth century it has required progressively more buttressing and ties. The nave dips crazily towards the back of the church – still shifting at an estimated rate of a millimetre a year – and alarming cracks are still all too obvious, tagged by small glass ties designed to reveal further movement. At last report, however, authorities say there is no imminent danger of collapse and no need for further buttressing.

Several outstanding and contrasting **altarpieces** – the church's highlights – still fill the principal chapels, each commissioned by the pope and his architect from some of the major painters of the age. Pius's choice of artists was deliberate: each was Sienese, as was he (at least by family origin) – Rossellino, it's worth noting, was from Settignano, just outside Florence. This partisan choice, however, rather undermined Pius's Renaissance credentials, for Florentine painters by this time were far ahead of their more backward-looking Sienese counterparts. Pius's choice of each subject – the Madonna, to whom the church was dedicated – was equally considered, as was the choice of saints included in each painting. Thus St Sabina in Giovanni di Paolo's work was featured because Pius was titular head of the Basilica di Santa Sabina in Rome; St Peter appeared because he was the first pope; and saints Catherine and Bernardino achieved prominence through their Sienese connections.

The first painting, midway down the right (south) wall, is Giovanni di Paolo's *Madonna and Child with SS Bernardino, Anthony Abbot, Francis and Sabina* with a *Pietà* above – note the Piccolomini arms at the bottom left and right of the frame. The first apse chapel features Matteo di Giovanni's *Madonna and Child with SS Catherine of Alexandria, Matthew, Bartholomew and Lucy* with the *Flagel-*

lation above: here, too, there's a nod to Pius in the shape of more coats of arms. The next apse contains a travertine tabernacle attributed to Rossellino, behind whose little central door is a **reliquary** containing bones alleged to be from the head of St Andrew, Pienza's patron saint. Another work by Rossellino, a vast **font**, can be seen in the crypt, along with Romanesque fragments recovered from Santa Maria, the former church near the site. The central apse – normally containing the high altar – is empty, Pius having stipulated that nothing should block the light coming from the central windows. Instead he commissioned the choir (1462), the tell-tale papal shield again appearing at the top of the central bishop's throne.

The **fourth chapel** houses a triptych of the *Assumption with SS Agatha, Callistus, Pius I and Catherine of Siena* by **Vecchietta**, born in nearby Castiglione dell'Órcia: it's considered one of his masterpieces and is by far the finest of the church's altarpieces. The fifth chapel features Sano di Pietro's *Madonna and Child with SS Philip, James, Anne and Mary Magdalene.*

Pius, realizing his Sienese painters lagged behind Florentine thinking, made specific requests in an attempt to bring a little Renaissance flavour to what were essentially Gothic works. Thus Sano was asked to replace the niches traditionally used in the predella (panels in the lower part of altarpieces) with a more classical frame of small pillars. The "V" arrangement of the saints around the Virgin was also new – at least in the works of Sano. Vecchietta similarly staked a claim for modernity by enclosing his *Assumption* triptych – very much a Gothic conceit – in a fixed frame that effectively made the painting a single, rather than hinged, tripartite work. Similar efforts towards a more Renaissance effect are found in the last painting, Matteo di Giovanni's *Madonna and Child with SS Nicholas, Martin, Augustine and Jerome*, midway down the north wall. The saints here, for example, are set on different levels – compare the same artist's painting across the nave (where they are on one level) – while the Virgin's upper throne is decorated with heads whose classical inspiration is unmistakable.

Palazzo Piccolomini

Pius's residence, the **Palazzo Piccolomini**, to the right of the Duomo, was modelled on Alberti's Palazzo Rucellai in Florence, and built by Rossellino over the demolished remains of the Piccolomini's former feudal holding in the village. All three main facades are identical, novelty being provided by the imaginative addition of a triple-tiered loggia at the back, making it the first Italian building to be designed specifically to afford views over a swathe of countryside. Its cost was astronomical, Rossellino spending 50,000 gold florins, five times his allotted budget – a charge that he was liable to repay. Pius, however, accepted the expense, delighted at the building and its views. He wrote:

From the three porticoes which face the sun at midday the view extends to Amiata, that towering and densely wooded mountain. Thence the eye travels down into Val d'Órcia, passing over green pasturelands and hills clothed with long grass or rich corn in season, and many vineyards, and so up again to castles and villages set on precipitous rocks, and to the right as far as a place called Bagno di Vignoni, and leftwards to Monte Cetona, which is higher than Radicófani and is the portal of the winter sun.

For this vista, you can walk into the superb courtyard at any time of day and through (on the left) to the original "hanging garden" behind; it has remained unchanged over the centuries and is the perfect embodiment of the Renaissance concept that gardens form an intermediary between nature and architecture. The triple-tiered loggia, with its three orders of Classical columns (Ionic,

Pienza's palaces

Pienza has little to show in the way of the **palaces** Pius envisaged being built by his retinue of cardinals. Twelve houses for the "people" were built, however, and at Pius's own expense, so keen was he to see his perfect city realized. Both carrot and stick were employed to encourage the reluctant hangers-on to comply with papal wishes, most notably in the case of the hapless Francesco Gonzaga, who was informed in no uncertain terms that the promised bishopric of Mantua would not be forthcoming unless a palace appeared in Pienza with his name on it (whether the palace was ever built is still a case for debate). Apart from the Borgia travesty (Palazzo Vescovile; see below), virtually the only palace to see the light of day was the **Palazzo Ammannati** (across the street from the Palazzo Piccolomini), built by the eponymous cardinal, a close friend of Pius; sadly it was still unfinished at the pope's death. To its left is the smaller **Palazzo dei Cardinali**, and to the right the larger **Palazzo Comunale**, the latter probably also designed by Rossellino, despite its appearance, which is more medieval than Renaissance.

Doric and Corinthian), owes a clear debt to the great imperial buildings of ancient Rome.

For a glimpse of the splendour envisaged for Pius, however, you need to climb the steps in the courtyard to the first-floor **papal apartments** (Tues–Sun 10am–12.30pm & 3–6pm; closed mid-Nov to mid-Dec; €3.50), occupied until 1962 by the Piccolomini family. Guided tours conduct you to Pius II's dining room, library and music room, each filled with furniture, books, carpets and manuscripts. The highlights, though, are the papal bedroom – complete with a gloriously vulgar canopied bed – and the cavernous Sala d'Armi, filled with rows of fearsome pikes and other weapons.

Palazzo Vescovile

The **Palazzo Vescovile**, or Palazzo Borgia, to the left of the Duomo, began as a single-storey Gothic palace, but was given to Roderigo Borgia by Pius on condition that he demolish it and rebuild in a more modern manner. Borgia, then a cardinal, would later become the infamous Pope Alexander VI and father four children, among them the notorious Lucrezia and Cesare Borgia. Showing the astuteness, if not the meanness, that would characterize his papacy, Borgia refrained from knocking down the palace, but saved money by altering a few superficial details and adding an extra storey. Thus on the ground floor – clearly of different vintage – you can still see the outlines of the old Gothic windows, bricked in to form tiny square windows more in keeping with Renaissance ideas. Still more visible are the holes that pockmark the upper part of the building, the legacy of a mortar bombardment during **World War II** that also knocked chunks out of the cathedral's apse. The highest marks have an even earlier vintage, having been inflicted by the artillery of Charles V and the Medici during their assault on the Sienese Republic between 1552 and 1559. How much time Borgia spent in the palace is uncertain – though the Borgia arms are clearly visible on the shield on the corner of the building. In any event, it appears he made a gift of the building in 1468, when it became the Palazzo Vescovile, or Bishop's Palace.

Museo Diocesano

Like many small southern Tuscan museums, the **Museo Diocesano**, Corso Rossellino 30 (March–Oct Mon & Wed–Sun 10am–1pm & 3–7pm; Nov–Jan 9

Fri–Sun 10–6; Jan 10 to mid-March Sat & Sun 10am–1pm & 3–6pm; €4.10), deserves more attention than it receives. Its star attraction is a superb thirteenth- or fourteenth-century *piviale*, or **cope**, an English work (signed *Opus Anglicanum*) of fantastically embroidered silk embellished with scenes from the life of the Virgin and St Catherine of Alexandria, together with various saints and apostles (originally the cope would also have been studded with pearls and precious stones). Tradition claims it was given to Pius by Thomas Paleologus, prince of the Peloponnese and brother of the Byzantine emperor. However, it's more likely to derive from a papal wardrobe dating from the papacy's sojourn in Avignon, where it appears in an inventory dated 1369.

The museum also contains superb tapestries, crosiers, miniatures, illuminated manuscripts, choir books with miniatures by Sano di Pietro and others – produced for Orvieto cathedral but bought by Pius – and a whole slew of topnotch **paintings**. Look out in particular for the *Madonna dell'Umiltà and SS Elizabeth of Hungary and John the Baptist*, an anonymous work (by the "Maestro dell'Osservanza"), so-called because its Madonna is shown seated on a simple oriental carpet rather than the more usual ornate throne. Also outstanding are a famous *Madonna della Misericordia* (c.1364) by Bartolo di Fredi, his first signed and dated work; among the figures sheltered by the vermilion-robed Madonna are the Emperor Charles IV (in red cloak and crown on the right), who visited Siena in 1355 en route for Rome, together with the pope (alongside) and Charles's queen (to the left, crowned, in pink). It seems likely Siena's Council of Twelve, then in thrall to the emperor, commissioned the work to commemorate the visit.

More eye-catching still is a magnificent 48-panel painting whose tiny anonymous miniatures depict scenes from the life of Christ. It was one of only a handful of surviving "portable" paintings once used by mendicant monks as a preaching aid during their perambulations around the countryside. The picture was brought here from the castle of Spedaletto in the Val d'Órcia, together with a painting often regarded as the first Renaissance Sienese painting: Vecchietta's seminal polyptych of the *Madonna and Child with SS Blaise, Florian, John the Baptist and Nicholas* (1462). The lunette, clearly Florentine in flavour, depicts the *Annunciation*, whose receding classical columns and three naves of equal height deliberately recall the design of the Duomo. The predella, by contrast, depicts three scenes with a more Sienese touch: the *Crucifixion*, with Siena's bare-hilled *crete* as background; the *Miracles of St Nicholas*; and the *Martyrdom of St Blaise* (for more on Blaise, see p.487).

The rest of the town

A short way down the main street from Piazza Pio II stands the church of **San Francesco**, one of two churches to survive from the original Corsignano, and the only significant medieval building remaining in Pienza. Its walls were once entirely covered in fourteenth-century frescoes, only a few of which (scenes from the life of St Francis) survive in the apse. More remains of the large Crucifix on the right, a fourteenth-century work by a follower of Duccio, and the arresting *Madonna della Misericordia* on the left, attributed to Luca Signorelli.

Be certain to take the alley to the left of the church – or those to either side of the Duomo – to gain access to Pienza's **walls**, rebuilt after being razed to the ground by the armies of the Medici and Charles V of Spain in 1559. You can see why Pius wanted his loggia, for the views from here are some of the finest from any town in Tuscany. Head east past the Duomo and you come to a lovely series of little **lanes** leading back into the village, each with impossibly twee names – notably Via dell'Amore (street of love) and Via del Bacio (street of the kiss): the names were altered from more warlike ones in the nineteenth century so as to be more in keeping with the village's Renaissance idea of itself. In the other direction a more rural lane runs out of Piazza Dante along a level ridge past public gardens.

Not to be missed is the ten-minute downhill walk from Piazza Dante (signed off the south side) to the **Pieve di Corsignano** (or San Vito), the village's original parish church, and the place where Pius was baptized. Extremely ancient, it probably dates from the tenth century, and is one of the best Romanesque churches for miles around. The cylindrical tower – used to shelter the townspeople during bandit raids – is highly unusual, as are the carvings above the main and side doors. You can get the key from the farmhouse just behind the church – leave a small tip.

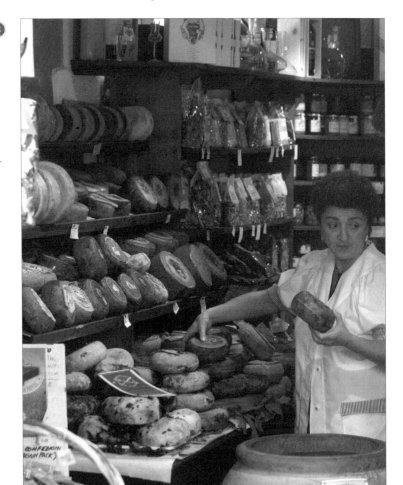

△ Shop selling cheese and other local produce, Pienza

Practicalities

Pienza is a pleasant place to stay, but there's not much life after dark, so it might also be considered as a day-trip from Montepulciano. TRA-IN **buses** cover the routes to Buonconvento and Siena (7 daily) and Montepulciano (9 daily); for details of times, call in at the helpful **tourist office** (Mon–Sat 10am–1pm & 3–7pm; ☎0578.749.071 or 0578.748.252, ⓦwww.comunedipienza.it) inside the Palazzo Comunale on Piazza Pio II. If you're stranded and need a **taxi** ring ☎0335.770.8068. **Bikes** can be rented from Valenti, Via della Madonnina 28 (☎0578.748.465). Among Pienza's **festivals** is the *Incontro con I Maestri dell'Arte* ("Meeting with a Master of Art"), when the work of a contemporary Italian artist is exhibited in the Palazzo Comunale over August and September.

Accommodation is limited: the *Ristorante dal Falco* at Piazza Dante 8 (☎0578.748.551; ❷) has six rooms, each with bathroom, but they're quickly snapped up. Much more expensive is the modern but very pleasant three-star *Hotel Il Corsignano*, Via della Madonnina 11, about 150m west of the piazza on the left (☎0578.748.501, ⓦwww.corsignano.it; ❹): rooms at the back have little terraces and something of a view. If you're doing Tuscany in style, or fancy a treat, the obvious choice is the three-star ⌘ *Il Chiostro di Pienza*, Corso Rossellino 26 (☎0578.748.400, ⓦwww.relaisilchiostrodipienza.com; ❻). The only in-town hotel, it's an extremely chi-chi conversion – complete with frescoes, vaults and other medieval trappings – which has been infiltrated into the old cloister and buildings of a Franciscan monastery.

Among **restaurants**, the best are *Dal Falco* in Piazza Dante (closed Fri), a simple trattoria which offers superb gnocchi and a filling *pecorino alla griglia* (hot cheese wrapped in prosciutto), at around €23 for a full meal; and the excellent, friendly and moderately priced ⌘ *Latte di Luna*, Via San Carlo 2–4 (☎0578.748.606; closed Tues and periods in Nov & Feb), blessed with a small terrace for outdoor eating and an ancient well incorporated into the old interior. Also reasonably good value is *La Buca delle Fate*, Corso Rossellino 38a (☎0578.748.272; closed Mon and periods in Jan & June), housed in part of the fifteenth-century palace of the Gonzagas and with thoroughly Tuscan country food. You can get panini and snacks at the *Enoteca le Crete* in Piazza Martiri, and there's no shortage of picnic food: Pienza is centre of a region producing **pecorino** sheep's cheese, and has gone overboard on *alimentari* and "natural food" shops. The **Fiera del Cacio** (first Sun in Sept) celebrates the local *pecorino* with a medieval market and fair in the main square.

East to Montepulciano: Monticchiello

The area around Pienza is enticing walking country. The track west to Bagno Vignoni is a fine two-hour walk. To the east, it's around 11km along the old road through Monticchiello to Montepulciano.

MONTICCHIELLO, 4km east of Pienza, is a minor attraction in itself: a walled village with a leaning watchtower, lovely views of Pienza and a great **church** (if this is locked, you can collect a key from the house next door), which houses numerous fourteenth-century Sienese frescoes – look out for the gargantuan *St Christopher* – and a *Madonna* by Pietro Lorenzetti. Outside the church, in the corner on the right as you stand with your back to the facade, is a tiny old-fashioned shop selling some of the most beautiful **fabrics** imaginable. They're all made by hand locally, and are exported – quietly – to all corners of the globe. As an added bonus the hamlet has a more-than-decent moderately priced **restaurant**, the *Taverna di Moranda*, Via di Mezzo 17 (☎0578.755.050, ⓦwww.tavernadimoranda.it; closed Mon and periods in Nov, Dec, Jan & Feb), run by an Italo-French couple who offer superb local food and an extensive selection of big-name local wines.

During the last week of July and the first week of August, the village puts on a now-renowned **Teatro Povero** (T0578.755.118 or 0578.755.735, Wwww.teatropovero.it) featuring a play written and performed by the villagers to evoke the local folk and farming traditions – a kind of Tuscan *Archers*. It's a pleasantly informal occasion, enjoyed equally for the food at the *taverna* set up for the duration of the festival. A large exhibition space in a former granary at Piazza Nuova 1 (Tues–Sun: guided yours on the hour 10am–6pm inclusive; free) is given over to props, stage sets and audio-visual displays connected with the play and its history.

Montepulciano

One of the highest of the Tuscan hill-towns, **MONTEPULCIANO** (665m) is built along a narrow tufa ridge, with a long main street and alleys that drop away to the walls. It's a stunningly good-looking town, full of vistas, odd squares and corners, and endowed with dozens of Renaissance palazzi and churches, which embody the state of architecture fifty years after Bernardo Rossellino's pioneering work at Pienza. Largely forgotten in subsequent centuries, the town today makes most of its money from its wine industry, based on the famed **Vino Nobile**, though its tourist profile becomes higher with each passing year. Along with Montalcino it's perhaps the best base in southern Tuscany, with Pienza, Chiusi and Bagno Vignoni all within easy reach by car or public transport.

Some history

Montepulciano's unusually consistent array of Renaissance palazzi and churches is a reflection of its remarkable development after 1511, when, following intermittent alliance with Siena, the town finally threw in its lot with Florence. In that year the Florentines sent **Antonio da Sangallo the Elder** to rebuild the town's gates and walls, which he did so impressively that the council took him on to work on the town hall and a series of churches. The local nobles meanwhile hired him, his nephew, and later the Modena-born architect **Vignola** – a founding figure of Baroque – to work on their own palazzi. The work of this trio, assured in both its conception and execution, makes a fascinating comparison with Rossellino's work at Pienza.

Montepulciano was reputedly founded in the sixth century by a group of **exiles** from Chiusi fleeing the barbarian invasions, the first written allusion to *Mon Politianus* appearing in 715 (hence *poliziani*, the nickname for the town's inhabitants). A constant point of dispute between Florence and Siena, the town chose Florence as its protector in 1202 – on the grounds that it was farther away. Both cities captured and lost the town several times over the next two hundred years, while her citizens suffered several decades of despotic rule during the fifteenth century under the del Pecora clan. In 1511, however, the Florentines again assumed control, this time for good. Famous names from Montepulciano include the great classical scholar Angelo Ambrogini (1454–94), better known by his adopted name of **Poliziano**, which he took in honour of his home town. **Marcellus II** (1501–55), a pope who had the misfortune to die just three weeks after being elected pontiff, was also born here.

Arrival, information and accommodation

Montepulciano is on the main **bus** route between Siena and Chiusi, and is also served by one bus daily from Florence. Its **train station** is on the Siena–Chiusi line too, but you'll need a (not always connecting) bus for the 10km trip into town. Regular buses also link with more frequent main-line trains at Chiusi, not much farther away. The buses stop in town at both the north and south gates,

Cortona, Santa Maria delle Grazie ▲

MONTEPULCIANO

Sant'Agnese

PIAZZA S. AGNESE

Bus Stop ★

Giardino di Poggiofanti

N

VIALE D. SANGALLO

Porta al Prato   San Bernardo

P

VIALE I. MAGGIO

Palazzo Avignonesi
Palazzo Bucelli

Ⓐ

Sant'Agostino

ⓘ   ❶   ❷

VIA GRACCIANO NEL CORSO

RUGA DI MEZZO

Palazzo Cocconi

RUGA DI FUORI

PIAZZA MICHELOZZO

Santa Lucia

VIA PIANA

Ⓑ

❸

Loggia di Mercato

VIA DEGLI ARCHI

PIAZZA DELL'I ERBE

VIA DEL PAOLINO

San Francesco

VIA DEL POGGIO

VIA DEL GIARDINO

VIA DI ORIOLO

❹

Palazzo Cervini

VIA DI PIÉ AL SASSO

VIA VOLTAIA NEL CORSO

Ⓒ

Porta di Grassi   Palazzo Ricci

VIA RICCI

Museo Civico

Ⓓ

Gesù

VIA DI S. BIAGIO

Palazzo Taruggi

PIAZZA GRANDE

Ⓔ   Ⓕ

Palazzo Comunale   Duomo   Palazzo Cantucci

VIA DEL TEATRO

VIA DELL'OPIO NEL CORSO

VIA DI ORIOLO

Ⓖ

VIA DI COLLAZZI

VIA DI S. DONATO

VIA FIORENZUOLA VECCHIA

Porta delle Farine ★

Bus Stop

VIA DI CIRCONVALLAZIONE

San Biagio ▲

Fortezza

Casa di Poliziano

VIA DI S. DONATO

VIA DI VECCHIO CIMITERO

VIA DEL POLIZIANO

Santa Maria dei Servi

VIA DEI FILOSOFI

VIA DEI FILOSOFI

▼ Ⓗ , Pienza, Chianciano & Chiusi

RESTAURANTS
Caffè Poliziano	4
Il Borgo Buio	3
Il Cantuccio	1
Trattoria Diva	2

ACCOMMODATION
Bellavista	C
Il Borghetto	B
Il Cittino	D
Duomo	G
Marzocco	A
Meublè Il Riccio	E
Montorio	H
La Terrazza	F

0   150 m

the **Porta al Prato** and **Porta di Farine**; buses arrive at the latter first – climb the steps above the bus stop to get into town – though Porta al Prato at the lower end of town is the main "bus station". If you're **driving**, follow the road around below the east circuit of walls and look for a parking space; don't be tempted by the area around the Porta al Prato or you'll be ticketed. Up around the **Fortezza** is also a good place to start looking.

The official **tourist office** is towards the lower end of town, close to Sant'Agostino at Via Gracciano nel Corso 59a (April–Oct Mon–Sat 9.30am–12.30pm & 3–7/8pm, Sun 9.30am–12.30pm; Nov–March Mon–Sat 9.30am–12.30pm & 3–6pm, Sun 9.30am–12.30pm; ☎0578.757.341, @www.prolocomontepulciano.it or @www.comune.montepulciano.si.it). Information on local wine and wine tours, and in particular the driving routes around vineyards and producers, is available at Piazza Grande 7 (☎0578.717.484, @www.stradavinonobile.it).

Accommodation

Once again, **accommodation** is sparse and well worth booking ahead. If you can't get into any of our recommendations, try contacting the tourist office to check on the availability of private rooms or *agriturismo* options. Or vist the local hotelers' website, @www.montepulcianohotels.it. Unless you have transport, don't settle for a room or hotel at the outlying station area (Montepulciano–Stazione/Acquaviva), or at Sant'Albino/Terme di Montepulciano (5km southeast). If you're really stuck, it's probably best to get the bus to the bland spa resort of Chianciano Terme, 9km southeast (see p.488).

Bellavista Gabriella Massoni, Via Ricci 25 ☎0578.757.348, @www.cretedisiena.com. Six well situated private rooms, five with private bath. Four have stupendous views. No one lives here, so you must ring first, and the owner will drive up to let you in: there's a public phone in the doorway downstairs. ❶

Duomo Via San Donato 14 ☎ & ℱ0578.757.473, @www.albergoilduomolibero.it. A friendly welcome, thirteen spacious and comfortable rooms, three-star facilities and a nice setting off the Piazza Grande make this the town's best upmarket hotel. ❸

Il Borghetto Via Borgo Buio 7 ☎0578.757.535, @www.ilborghetto.it. Montepulciano's grandest three-star hotel, in a very tastefully refurbished old house off Via Gracciano nel Corso. Just eleven rooms, so be sure to book. ❹

Il Cittino Marcella Trabalzini, Vicolo della Via Nuova 2 ☎0578.757.335. Three decent rooms with a shared bathroom above a restaurant, located midway between the town gates off Via di Voltaia nel Corso. ❶

La Terrazza Via Piè al Sasso 16 ☎0578.757.440, @www.laterrazzadimontepulciano.com. Pleasant two-star rooms in an ancient house near the Duomo. ❸

Marzocco Piazza Giralomo Savonarola 18 ☎0578.757.262, ℱ0578.757.530, @www.albergoilmarzocco.it. Smartest hotel in town, an elegant nineteenth-century inn with a full-size billiard table. Very courteous owners, but loses out to the *Duomo* on position. ❸

Meublè Il Riccio Ivana Migliorucci, Via Talosa 21 ☎ & ℱ0578.757.713, @www.ilriccio.net. Five well-kept private double rooms, each with private bathroom, TV and phone, off Piazza Grande. ❸

Montorio Strada per Pienza 2 ☎0578.717.442, ℱ0578.715.456 @www.montorio.com. A member of the "Abitare la Storia" association, whose hotels occupy historic buildings, in this case a fine country house just outside Montepulciano on the Pienza road, with a lovely garden and terraces covered with cypresses and olive trees. There are five apartments for two or four people, each with kitchen and furnished with antiques. ❺

The Town

The Prato and Farine gates are equally convenient starting points for exploring the town; our account begins at the Porta al Prato. Between the two gates runs the town's main street, the **Corso**, whose name is appended in turn to Via Gracciano, Via di Voltaia and Via dell'Opio. The town's main focus is the **Piazza**

Grande, home to the **Duomo** and an ensemble of palaces. To see the town's other big sight, the Renaissance church of **San Biagio**, requires a pleasant ten-minute stroll (downhill) to the west of town.

The Corso: Porta al Prato to the Fortress

Sangallo's first commission was Montepulciano's main gate, the **Porta al Prato**, at the north end of town. Before embarking on the climb up, you should visit the church of **Sant'Agnese**, named in honour of a local Dominican abbess, Agnese Segni (1268–1317), who was canonized in 1726 and is buried in the church. The first chapel on the right contains the *Madonna di Zoccoli*, attributed to Simone Martini (or his school), while the second altar on the left features a fourteenth-century Sienese fresco of the *Madonna del Latte*. This subject, which shows a breast-feeding Madonna, is a common feature of Sienese (and Tuscan) painting of the period, the Virgin's milk, in Christian iconography, symbolizing the font of Eternal Life (many a Tuscan church in the Middle Ages claimed to have genuine drops of the Madonna's milk). The subject vanished entirely following the Council of Trent, which in a fit of Counter–Reformationary zeal banned any use of "unnecessary" nudity in the portrayal of religious characters.

Inside the Porta al Prato the **Corso** begins, the palazzi immediately making clear the town's allegiance to Florence. In the first square, beside the *Albergo Marzocco*, is the **Colonna del Marzocco**, a stone column bearing the heraldic lion (*marzocco*) of Florence. The original lion, now in the museum (this is an 1856 copy), was fixed to its column in 1511, when it replaced a statue of the she-wolf suckling Romulus and Remus, the symbol of Siena (according to legend the city was founded by Senius, son of Remus). Across the street further lion heads decorate the **Palazzo Avignonesi** (no. 91), probably the work of Vignola. Sangallo makes a second appearance with the **Palazzo Cocconi** (no. 70), virtually opposite the **Palazzo Bucelli** (no. 73), whose base is strikingly inset with Roman and Etruscan reliefs. These were lovingly collected in 1648 by the palace's erstwhile owner, Pietro Bucelli, whose extensive Etruscan collection – an unusual one given the classically obsessed era in which it was amassed – now resides in Florence's Museo Archeologico.

Just beyond this crop of palazzi is the eye-catching church of **Sant'Agostino**, designed around 1427 by the earlier Medici protégé, Michelozzo – who also carved the terracotta relief of the *Madonna and Child* above the door; within are a *Crucifixion* on the third altar on the left wall by Lorenzo di Credi and an equally good *St Bernardino* by Giovanni di Paolo on the right wall. Pride of place goes to a polychrome Crucifix on the high altar attributed to Donatello. Across the street a medieval **tower house**, a rare survival in Montepulciano, is surmounted by a *commedia dell'arte* figure of a clown, the **Pulcinella**, who strikes out the hours on the town clock; most un-Tuscan, it is said to have been put up by an exiled bishop from Naples.

About a hundred metres farther along you reach the Renaissance **Loggia di Mercato** and a fork in the roads: turn right here if you want to make straight for the Piazza Grande (see below). The Corso continues to the left past further palazzi, including the **Palazzo Cervini**, attributed to Sangallo. Begun for the doomed Marcellus II before he became pope, it is now occupied by a bank, and has the grand civic gesture of an external courtyard. Beyond this, you pass the church of **Gesù**, remodelled in Baroque style by Andrea Pozzo (as are many other churches in the town and region), before the road turns the corner and rambles outside the town walls. Just prior to the turn – at no. 5 – is the **Casa di Poliziano**, birthplace of the Renaissance humanist and poet Angelo Ambrogini

(Poliziano), who translated many of the Greek classics under the patronage of Lorenzo de' Medici, as well as teaching the Medici children.

Via di Poliziano loops outside the walls to the Gothic-fronted **Santa Maria dei Servi**, another Baroque interior job by Pozzo. Inside it's visited by devout locals eager to prostrate themselves before the much venerated *Madonna della Santoreggia*, a fifteenth-century fresco (second altar on the left). The only other attention-grabbing work is a *Madonna and Child*, oddly inserted into a larger painting (third altar on the right) by a follower of Duccio. Via di Poliziano then re-enters town by the old **Fortezza**, now partly occupied by houses. At the end of Via di San Donato, the last quiet stretch back into town, you'll find yourself in the cathedral and town hall square, Piazza Grande.

Santa Lucia, Via del Poggio and the Museo Civico

A quicker approach to Piazza Grande at the Loggia di Mercato (see above) would be to head right. A block to the north of here, a beautiful little piazza fronts the church of **Santa Lucia**, built in 1633, which has a fabulous, if damaged, *Madonna* by Luca Signorelli in a chapel on the right, though the church is rarely open. Turning instead to the south, Via del Poggio runs down to the church of **San Francesco**: note the ruined pulpit to the side of the facade, from which St Bernardino of Siena is supposed to have preached. The imposing Via Ricci takes over for the last stretch to the Piazza Grande; it is flanked on one side by the Renaissance **Palazzo Ricci**, and on the other by the Sienese-Gothic **Palazzo Neri-Orselli**.

The latter is home to the town's **Museo Civico** (Tues–Sun 10am–7pm; €4), an extensive collection of small-town Gothic and Renaissance works. The courtyard contains the original Florentine *marzocco* lion removed from the Corso, while the upper-floor room opens with a series of glazed terracottas by Andrea della Robbia. The most important panel is a *St Francis*, painted by the saint's near-contemporary, Margaritone da Arezzo; the most enjoyable is Jacopo de Mino's lush *Coronation of the Virgin*.

The Piazza Grande

The **Piazza Grande**, Montepulciano's theatrical flourish of a main square, is built on the highest point of the ridge, providing the obvious site for the town's Duomo (see below). Its most distinctive building, however, is the **Palazzo Comunale**, a thirteenth-century Gothic palace to which Michelozzo added a tower and rustication in imitation of the Palazzo Vecchio in Florence. The tower is occasionally open, offering views that on the clearest days stretch to Siena, 65km northwest.

Two of the palazzi on the square were designed by Sangallo. The **Palazzo Nobili-Tarugi**, by the lion and griffon fountain, is a highly innovative building, with a public loggia cut through one corner; it originally had an extension on the top floor, though this has been bricked in. More tangible pleasures await at the **Palazzo Cantucci**, one of many buildings scattered about the town that serve as *cantine* for the **wine trade**, offering *degustazione* and sale of the Vino Nobile. The lower part is by Sangallo, the upper by Baldassare Peruzzi, who was Siena's leading sixteenth-century architect.

The Duomo

Sangallo and his contemporaries never got around to building a facade for the **Duomo** (daily 9am–1pm & 3.30–7pm), whose plain brick pales against the neighbouring palazzi. Begun in 1680 by Ippolito Scalzi, the building was raised over an earlier church, of which the ugly fourteenth-century campanile is virtually the only reminder.

The **interior** boasts an elegant Renaissance design, and has several outstanding works of art dotted around its rather foreboding walls. The first of these are fragments of the **tomb of Bartolomeo Aragazzi** (1427–36) by the multi-talented Michelozzo, a monument which was criminally dismembered in the nineteenth century. Aragazzi was born in Montepulciano, and achieved prominence as the secretary to Pope Martin V (pontiff from 1417 to 1431), the first pope to occupy the Holy See in Rome after the Grand Schism (1378–1417) divided the papacy between Rome and Avignon. He is often described as the first "Renaissance" pope, his election coinciding with the competition to design the baptistery doors in Florence. Pope Martin was assisted in his adopted role by Aragazzi, who scoured French and German monasteries for manuscripts and oversaw the publication of classical texts by Vitruvius and others. Bas-reliefs from the tomb can now be seen at the base of the first two columns on either side of the nave (right and left), and the effigy of Aragazzi himself is mounted on the rear (west) wall to the right of the door. At the other end of the church, two of the tomb's statues surmount the high altar – which is also garlanded by putti and festoons from the tomb: two sculpted angels from the piece can be found even farther away, in London's British Museum.

Aragazzi also commissioned a painting that would be a highlight of this or any other church: **Taddeo di Bartolo**'s iridescent high altarpiece of the *Assumption*, perhaps the supreme rendition of a subject that was a favourite among Siena's leading artists. The date of the painting's commission (1401) is noteworthy, for it came at a time when Montepulciano – which oscillated constantly between Florentine and Sienese domination – found itself free of Florentine rule for a brief period (1390–1404); Aragazzi's choice of a Sienese artist, and a subject dear to the Sienese, is thus revealed as an act of political as well as artistic significance. The main panels of the triptych, its predella and its gilt-turreted upper panels are crammed with detail and incident. Note, in particular, the apostles gathered around the Virgin's tomb in the main painting: Doubting Thomas is shown receiving the Madonna's girdle (see p.463), while a grief-stricken St John views her flower-decked sepulchre. Behind the latter to the right is the Apostle Thaddeus, Taddeo's namesake; the face is probably a self-portrait, an extremely unusual feature in a painting executed on the cusp of the Renaissance, when such self-advertisement would later become quite common.

Elsewhere in the church hunt out a work by Vecchietta, best known as a painter but here represented by an excellent piece of sculpture: the marble **ciborium** in the chapel to the right of the high altar. On the left (north) wall of the church, opposite the pillar of the third nave, is a poetic *Madonna del Pilastro* (Madonna of the Pillar) by Sano di Pietro. At the bottom of the north aisle, close to the main remnants of Aragazzi's tomb, the first chapel – the **Baptistery** – contains a wealth of eye-catching big-name art: the font and its six bas-reliefs (1340) are by Giovanni d'Agostino; the riot of glazed terracotta on the wall, the so-called **Altare dei Gigli** (Altar of the Lilies), is by Andrea della Robbia – it frames a relief of the *Madonna and Child* attributed to Benedetto da Maiano; and the niche statues of St Peter and John the Baptist are attributed to Mino da Camaino.

San Biagio

Antonio da Sangallo's greatest commission came in 1518, when he was invited by the town's Ricci nobles to design the pilgrimage church of **San Biagio** (daily 9am–noon & 3–6pm) on the hillside below the town. The model for this was his brother Giuliano's design for the facade of San Lorenzo in Florence,

△ San Biagio

which was never built. The Montepulciano project was more ambitious – the only bigger church project of its time was St Peter's in Rome – and occupied Antonio until his death in 1534. He lived to see its inauguration, however (in 1529), the ceremony performed by the Medici pope Clement VII. To reach the church, follow Via San Biagio out from the Porta di Grassi; it's about fifteen minutes' walk.

The church, built over an earlier chapel to San Biagio, or St Blaise (see box), is one of the most harmonious Renaissance creations in Italy, constructed inside and out from a porous travertine, whose soft honey-coloured stone blends perfectly with its niche in the landscape. A deeply intellectualized building, its major architectural novelty was the use of freestanding towers (only one was completed, in 1545) to flank the facade (note the tower's three orders of Classical columns – Doric, Ionic and Corinthian). Within, it is spoilt a little by extraneous decoration – a Baroque trompe l'oeil covers the barrel vault – but is equally harmonious. It also has superb acoustics.

Nearby, scarcely less perfect a building, is the **Canonica** (rectory), endowed by Sangallo with a graceful portico and double-tiered loggia.

Food, festivals and transport

The town has a fair spread of **restaurants**, all of them offering local wines. For superb homemade pasta try the long-established and moderately priced *Trattoria Diva* (☎0578.716.951; closed Tues), just inside the Porta al Prato on Via Gracciano nel Corso 92, with meals for around €25. For something a bit smarter

San Biagio (St Blaise)

San Biagio (St Blaise in English) was an Armenian doctor who became a bishop before being called by God to abandon his worldly affairs in favour of a contemplative life in the mountains. There he lived in a cave, surrounded by wild animals who brought him food and drink, and in return were healed by him when they became sick; he's often depicted, St Francis-like, talking to the birds. He was eventually imprisoned on a charge of practising magic, and tortured by having his body scraped with a sharp-pronged instrument used to card wool. Paintings of him always show him holding such an instrument. Thus he became the patron saint of carders and textile workers, which is why he appears so frequently in Florentine and Tuscan paintings, the textile industry having been the bedrock of the region's medieval prosperity. In a more domestic vein, he is also invoked by Italians against sore throats, having once saved a child who'd had a fish bone stuck in her throat.

try the moderately priced *Ristorante Il Cantuccio* (℡0578.757.870; closed Mon), Via delle Cantine 1, or *Il Borgo Buio*, Via Borgo Buio 10 (℡0578.717.497, Ⓦwww.borgobuio.it; closed for lunch on Tues & Wed). The *Caffè Poliziano*, Via di Voltaia nel Corso 27–29, has a lovely Art Nouveau interior and a choice of bar, informal restaurant for lunch and evening meals, or more formal restaurant for dinner only.

There's an open-air **market** (with especially good *porchetta*), held in the gardens outside the Porta al Prato on Thursday mornings; this is also the site of the local **youth bar**, with table football and a jukebox through to midnight.

Festivals

Cantiere Internazionale d'Arte (July–Aug; ℡0578.757.089, Ⓦwww.cantiere.toscana.nu). A major international performing arts festival (especially music), founded by composer Hans Werner Henze in the 1970s. The festival makes a point of supporting young musicians, with artists and stagehands alike slumming it in the local co-operative mess rooms.

Bruscello (Aug 14–16). The Festival of Assumption is celebrated with a sequence of masked plays and light opera in the town squares.

Bravìo delle Botti (last Sun in Aug). A barrel race through the streets from Sant'Agnese to the Piazza Grande, between teams from each of the town's eight *contrade*. Costume processions precede the race and a street banquet follows.

Transport

The main **transport** links are with Chiusi. LFI **buses** (℡0578.31.174, Ⓦwww .lfi.it) run more or less every half-hour to Chianciano Terme, Chiusi and Chiusi station (plus one Siena and one to three Florence services daily). To the west, TRA-IN has seven buses daily on the circuit through Pienza, San Quírico d'Órcia, Torrenieri (change for Montalcino) and Buonconvento, with between three and five daily continuing to Siena. All buses leave from outside Porta al Prato and Porta di Farine; buy tickets from bars or shops in town, not on the bus.

If you're making a **train** connection, take a bus to Chiusi; Montepulciano's own station, 10km northeast, is a stop only for slow *regionali* or *inter-regionali* services. Local **car rental** can be arranged through Bernardini (℡0578.716.081) or Paolo Cencini (℡0330.732.723).

East to Chianciano Terme and Chiusi

CHIANCIANO TERME (ⓦwww.termechianciano.it), midway between Montepulciano and Chiusi, is one of Tuscany's major spas, as evidenced by the presence of some two hundred-odd hotels. Its particular specialities are liver and bladder complaints, handy if you've overworked the Vino Nobile, though the clinic-like spa buildings aren't the usual image of a Tuscan holiday.

If you find yourself staying here, with Montepulciano full, you might want to wander up to the old hill-town, **Chianciano Vecchio**, though there's little specific to see, save a Romanesque Collegiata and middling sacred art museum. The local tourist handouts fastidiously trace a series of "Medically Recommended Walks" in its *Chianciano… What a healthy liver!* pamphlet. Perhaps the most compelling is to the huge outdoor **municipal pool**. The only sight to speak of is the **Museo Civico Archeologico delle Acque** at Viale Dante 80 (April–Oct Tues–Sun 10am–1pm & 5–7pm; Nov–March Sat & Sun 10am–7pm; €4), which has good, modern displays devoted to the area's Etruscan and other archeological heritage, with some convincing tomb reconstructions, plus a section at the end that documents the history of the area's thermal springs.

Through Sarteano

If you have transport, a more enjoyable route to Chiusi is the minor road that runs south just before Montepulciano's own little spa at Sant'Albino (ⓣ0578.7911, ⓦwww.termemontepulciano.it; March–May & Nov–mid-Dec Mon-Fri 2–7pm, Sat 8am–12.30pm; June–Oct Mon–Sat 8am–12.30 & 3–7.30pm; closed mid-Dec to Feb; price depends on treatment required). This follows a fine, scarcely populated stretch of the Val d'Órcia down through the estates of Castelluccio and La Foce – the latter the home for many years of the American writer Iris Origo, author of the classic *Merchant of Prato*. It was at La Foce that she hid partisans and Allied troops during the German occupation of Italy after Mussolini's fall in 1943, events recorded in her autobiography *War in Val d'Órcia*. You turn north to reach Chiusi at **SARTEANO**, a pleasant village set below a castle and within patches of Etruscan wall; it has an *Annunciation* by Domenico Beccafumi in the church of San Martino, and an excellent, inexpensive **restaurant**, *La Giara*, at Viale Europa 1 (ⓣ0578.265.511).

Chiusi

CHIUSI, 14km southeast of Montepulciano, is a useful transport hub, with trains and buses west to Siena, south to Orvieto and Rome, and north to Montepulciano, Cortona, Arezzo and the Umbrian lake resort of Castiglione del Lago. As a target in its own right, it is only really worth a special detour for Etruscan enthusiasts: the town – known to the Etruscans as Camars – has a reasonable archeological museum and around half a dozen ancient tombs on its periphery, out towards Lago di Chiusi.

The museum and the Duomo, Chiusi's other worthwhile site, are close by each other on Via Porsenna, a short walk up from the **bus stop** on the Viale Garibaldi. Chiusi's **Museo Archeologico Nazionale e Tombe Etrusche** (daily 9am–7.30pm; €4) ought to be pretty good, for the region is littered with tombs. Many of the best exhibits, however, have been spirited away to Florence and Rome and what remains is a modest collection: numerous sarcophagi, a few terracottas with traces of ancient paint, cabinets of pots (one with erotic dancing scenes), and the odd treasure – notably the *Gualandi Urn*. Many of the tombs in the region are in poor or dangerous condition, and only three are currently open to the public. Two can be seen on request from the museum itself in museum hours and with the museum ticket: the **Tomba della Pellegrina** and **Tomba del Leone** (3km north); a third tomb, the famous, frescoed **Tomba della Scimmia**, is visitable on pre-booked guided tours from the museum (Tues, Thurs & Sat 11am & 4pm in summer, 11am & 2.30pm in winter; ✆0578.20.177; €2).

At the Romanesque **Duomo** there is further evidence of Chiusi's ancient past. The building itself consists almost entirely of Etruscan and Roman blocks (the interior is a mass of what appears at first sight to be mosaic work, but is in reality mock-Byzantine paintwork, created in 1915). The **Museo della Cattedrale** alongside (June to mid-Oct daily 10am–12.45pm & 4–6.30pm; rest of year Mon–Sat 10am–12.45pm, Sun 10am–12.45pm & 3.30–6pm; €2) gives access to the **Labyrinth of Porsenna** (€3 or €4 combined ticket with Museo della Catttedrale), which leads you through the atmospheric tunnels of the Etruscan water-catchment system below the piazza to a huge Roman cistern and then up inside the twelfth-century campanile. At the museum, you can also arrange to meet a guide at the entrance to the **Catacombe di Santa Mustiola**, 2km east of town (tours daily 3pm; April–Sept also 11am; €5), which were used by early Christians in the fourth and fifth centuries. Tickets and bookings must be made at the tourist office in the cathedral square before noon of the day of visit (see "Practicalities" below).

Still more of the ancient underground city can be seen in the **Museo Civico** (May–Oct Tues–Sun tours at 10.15am, 11.30am, 12.45pm, 3.15pm, 6.30pm & 5.45pm; Nov–April tours on Thurs & Fri at 10.10am, 11.10am & 12.10pm, and the same hours on Sat & Sun plus 3.10pm. 4.10pm & 5.10pm; €3), opened in July 2004, and entered on a tiny alley, at Via Seconda Cimina 1, off the north side of Piazza XX Settembre. Atmospheric guided tours lead through 140m of Etruscan tunnel and aqueduct to a lake now some 28m below street level. Also in the tunnels is the Sezione Epigrafica, the only museum display in Italy devoted entirely to funerary inscriptions: over five hundred, mainly Etruscan examples, are on show.

Lago di Chiusi

Chiusi's **lake** lies 5km north of the town, reached along the road past the Etruscan tombs. The route is served only sporadically by bus (4 daily Mon–Fri) but for anyone driving or planning to camp for a few days, it makes a fine detour. The buses run to the **restaurant–bar–campsite** *Pesce d'Oro* (☎0578.21.403), set amid trees by a small quay for rowing boats; the swimming is warm in summer. For food alone, you're best off at the lake's other signposted restaurant, *Da Gino* (☎0578.21.408; closed Wed); they serve good fish meals at moderate prices.

Practicalities

With time to kill in Chiusi, the best thing to do is **eat**. *Il Bucchero* (☎0578.222.092; closed Wed) at Via dei Bonci 32 is an inexpensive restaurant-pizzeria, while the *Ristorante Zaira* (☎0578.20.260; closed Mon), just up the road at Via Arunte, serves "Etruscan dishes" – boar, pigeon and the like at moderate prices.

Chiusi has a helpful **tourist office** at Piazza del Duomo 1 (Mon–Sat 9.30am–12.30pm & 3.30–7pm, Sun 9.30am–12.30pm; ☎0578.227.667, ⓦwww.commune.chiusi.si.it). There's just one **hotel**, *Albergo La Sfinge*, Via Marconi 2 (☎0578.20.157, ⓦwww.albergolasfinge.it; ❷). Less expensive hotels are clustered down at Chiusi Scalo, an unattractive modern suburb that makes its living care of a large slaughterhouse and meat storage plant. An extremely good out-of-town option is the four-star *Villa il Patriarca at Querce al Pino* (☎0578274.407, ⓦwww.ilpatriarca.it; ❻), 4km from Chiusi. Set in fine grounds (with a pool), it is housed in a beautifully restored country villa, and has a superb, if expensive restaurant, *I Salotti* (closed Mon), that is renowned in its own right. Try to peek into the kitchens, which are set in original Etruscan granaries. If you need a **taxi** in town, call ☎0578.20.178.

Monte Amiata

At 1738m, Monte Amiata is the highest point in southern Tuscany, a broad-based mountain whose hazy outline forms the backdrop to many a town and landscape in the region. A circle of towns rings its lower slopes – some historical spots, others more modern, most having been plumped up over the last few years in an attempt to attract tourism to a traditionally impoverished area. None, with one exception, are worth a trip for their own sake, but the effect of all the villages together, plus pretty streets, old castles and plenty of bucolic countryside makes this a good area to tour by car or bike for a day or so. It's also delightful walking country, refreshingly cool in summer – and there's skiing in winter.

MONTE AMIATA

Monte Amiata
Station

Ansidónia

Madonna
d. Querce

Campiglia
d'Órcia

Vivo d'Órcia

Seggiano

Pescina

Bagni
San Filippo

Montegiovi

Castel del Piano

Prato
delle Macináie

▲ Monte Amiata
1385m   1738m

Abbadia
San Salvatore

Radicófani

N

Arcidosso

Bagnolo

Piancastagnáio

Santa Fiora

Saragiolo

0   3 km

The main centre and transport hub is **Abbadia San Salvatore**, worth a visit for its great abbey, whether you intend to venture onto the mountain or not. The town is accessible by bus from Siena (2–3 daily), Buonconvento (5 daily), Chiusi (4 daily), Arcidosso and Santa Fiora (10 daily), and Grosseto (5 daily). Avoid the "Monte Amiata" train station, on the Siena-Asciano-Grosseto line: it's a good 45km north of Abbadia San Salvatore.

Abbadia San Salvatore

There's been a settlement on the site of **ABBADIA SAN SALVATORE**, Monte Amiata's main town, since prehistoric times, though its real significance dates from the eighth century when its great abbey became the controlling centre of the Via Francigena. Its importance only waned with the rise of the Aldobrandeschi in the eleventh century. Thereafter it was contested by Orvieto and Siena, but in 1559 – along with most of southern Tuscany – fell within the orbit of the Medici's Grand Duchy of Tuscany.

Today the town is an initially disorientating modern sprawl that hides a perfect and largely self-contained **medieval quarter**. Buses will drop you on the **Viale Roma**, immediately outside the old walls; if you arrive by car you'll have to negotiate a maze of tree-lined streets. The abbey itself is actually in the modern part of the town, and best reached with Viale Roma as the starting point. From the north end of the street, walk down Via Cavour, passing Via Mentana on the left, and take the next right, Via del Monastero.

The abbey

Church tradition dates the **Abbadia San Salvatore** to 743, making it one of the oldest abbeys in Tuscany, and ascribes its foundation to King Rachis, a Lombard king who is supposed to have converted to Christianity while contemplating a Crucifix now affixed to the abbey's south wall. He was subsequently visited by an apparition of Christ as he went to do battle with the Perugians, a revelation which prompted him to take up a monastic life and found the abbey at the site of the vision. The actual story of the abbey's birth is slightly different. For a start, the Crucifix element is anachronistic, as the work dates from the twelfth century, some four hundred years after Rachis's death. Rachis himself, however, was involved in the foundation, though it appears his withdrawal into monastic isolation was forced on him, principally by leading Lombard nobles who opposed his ever-increasing leanings towards Rome. Forced to abdicate, the king symbolically awarded his crown to the pope and was succeeded by his brother, Astolfo.

The present Romanesque **church**, built in Amiata's distinctive brown trachite, was consecrated in 1036, a rebuilding programme having been instigated a year before when the abbey was at the height of its wealth and power. The present crypt (see below) dates from this period, though other parts of the building were altered during the brief tenure of the Camaldolese and later the Cistercians, who took over the abbey from the Benedictines in 1228.

Among the Cistercian additions was the triform window in the **facade**, though critics are unable to agree on the age of the two distinctive towers (one clearly unfinished), features found in very few other churches in Italy. The narrow frontage, squeezed between the towers, prepares you for a thin and immensely long **interior**, whose Latin-cross plan is generally considered the first of any Romanesque church in Tuscany. The single-naved basilica culminates in a raised chancel, framed by a series of broad and beautifully decorated arches.

Little survives in the way of art, much having been removed to Florence when the abbey was owned by the Medici – a period when it remained monkless for 157 years. The best of what remains is the wooden **Crucifix** involved in the Rachis legend (at the beginning of the right-hand wall), though it's a disquietingly modern-looking piece, and easily passed by. Many of the paintings are by the Nasini clan, a three-generation dynasty of painters born in nearby Castel del Piano (see p.496). The south transept features **frescoes** on the *Legend of King Rachis* by Giuseppe Nasini (1657–1736), the north transept panels on the *Life of the Virgin*; none is terribly accomplished, but they have a faintly ridiculous charm all the same.

The **crypt**, by contrast, is outstanding: one of the most monumental in Tuscany, it is an astounding space of bare, crude stone supported by 35 strange, fluted columns. Atop each pillar is a superbly carved lintel, whose motifs and figures show a Lombard and in some cases Byzantine hand, the latter – distinguished by a more rectangular approach – typical of northern Italian work of the period. Note, too, how each pillar is worked in a wide variety of styles.

If you're lucky enough to get into the **monastery** alongside the abbey (it's rarely open), try to see the **treasury**, which has a minute eighth-century Irish reliquary, a fine reliquary bust of Pope St Mark (1381) and an extremely rare and beautiful red silk Persian cope dating from the eighth century.

Parco Museo Minerario

The **Parco Museo Minerario** (daily mid-June to Oct 9.30–12.30pm & 3.30–6.30pm; rest of the year same hours Sat & Sun; €3) at Piazzale Renato Rossaro 6 is located in part of what was once one of the world's most important mercury mines, the metal having been extracted locally since the end of the nineteenth century. The only other mines of comparable significance were in Spain and Slovenia, but they, like the mines here and elsewhere around Monte Amiata, have been hit by a worldwide decline in the use of mercury. The museum building is a fine piece of industrial architecture in itself, a redoubtable nineteenth-century stone affair with a quaint tower and three rows of arched windows – the effect is more Florentine palazzo than factory. Inside, the museum offers numerous examples of industrial archeology, with old machines and the fittings, fixtures and tools used in the mines. Displays deal with the history of mercury mining, and there are also lots of archive photographs and other documentary material.

Practicalities

Abbadia's **tourist office** is near the cinema, Via Adua 25 (Mon–Sat 9am–1pm & 4–6pm, Sun 9am–1pm; ☏0577.775.811, ⓦ www.amiataturismo.it). As tourism headquarters for the Amiata region, the office is well worth a visit and provides information on **walking**, plus details of some innovative, inexpensive tours that they offer during the summer.

There are numerous **hotels** in the modern town. The cheapest is *Cesaretti*, Via Trento 37 (☏0577.778.198, ℗0577.775.589; ❶). *San Marco*, Via Matteotti 13 (☏ & ℗0577.778.089; ❶), is centrally located, or there's the slightly more upmarket *Italia*, Viale Roma 30 (☏0577.778.007; ❷). The *San Marco* has a moderately priced **restaurant**, and there are any number of cheap, if rather characterless, *pizzerie*.

The **bus terminal** is in front of the *Bar Centrale* in Viale Roma; there's a timetable fixed to the Agenzia VAII, Viale Roma 45, which is also the place to buy **tickets**.

The Monte Amiata summit and slopes

The summit of **Monte Amiata** is accessible by road and in summer is packed out with vehicle-delivered parties, many ill-shod for the last few steps to the highest point. In July and August it has a thrice-daily bus from Abbadia San Salvatore; at other times, hitching should be possible. A number of the tatty bars at the summit rent out mountain bikes to explore the lower slopes.

At the car park is what amounts to an alpine hamlet, with bars, a handful of hotels and a short ski run – all in the shadow of a peculiar Eiffel Tower structure adapted in the form of a cross, erected in 1946 by Pope Pius XII. Alongside are a crop of radio masts, and huts selling some of the trashiest trinkets conceivable. None of this detracts from the **views**, which stretch southeast to Bolsena and west to the sea, with the nearer towns neatly delineated in a circle below. The best viewpoint is from the so-called *Madonna delle Scout*, a statue littered with the pendants of innumerable scout troops.

Amiata walking: the Anello della Montagna

Away from the summit, the woods and pathways of Amiata's **lower slopes** make up one of the region's most beautiful natural enclaves, huge forests of beech and chestnut blanketing the area and providing refuge for deer and wild boar. The mountain's extravagant greenery, so at odds with much of the surrounding countryside, derives from its volcanic origins, eruptions having formed ridges of trachite, which is fertile when broken down and also porous, allowing surface water to filter away. When the water hits the impervious volcanic rock below, it flows out in a series of **springs**, a striking feature of Amiata, whose slopes frequently echo to the sound of running water.

The combination of Amiata's lush vegetation and crisp mountain air makes it superb **walking** territory. Detailed Multigraphic and other maps have made hiking in the region a far more straightforward undertaking, and considerable effort has gone into marking the **Anello della Montagna**, a path which circles the mountain between about 900m and 1300m. With a car you can join the path from virtually any of the roads that climb from the surrounding towns; large boards mark the departure points from the road, and detail the route to either side. It's also possible, however, to walk up from the towns on paths that radiate from the main circuit: the best departure point for this approach is Abbadia San Salvatore.

The Anello's total circuit is 29km, in theory walkable in a day, though the local council has broken it into ten basic sections. It's fairly practical to walk half the route, and then take a **bus** back from Santa Fiora or Arcidosso (each have ten connections daily with Abbadia San Salvatore). The trail markings are clearly indicated on concrete posts in red, yellow and green, though they coincide with the older CAI markings of red and white stripes; either way, it's fairly hard to go wrong. It's also possible to walk at will from the road, though if you venture too far, the chances are you'll wind up lost.

Staying on the mountain

If you want to **stay** on the mountain, the best base is **Prato Macináie** (1385m), a tree-enclosed patch of meadow and the site of one of Amiata's ski lifts (there are fourteen in all, along with twelve pistes). It's not far from the summit, but far enough to be unspoilt and away from the commercialism. The hotel, *Le Macinaie* (☎0564.959.001, ⓦwww.lemacinaie.it; ❷), fills up, so book ahead.

In a similarly pretty setting, the **Prato della Contessa** (1500m), 2km south on the summit road, has the three-star *Hotel Contessa* (☎0564.959.000, ⓕ0564.959.002; ❷), while nearby there's *Lo Scoiattolo* (☎0564.959.003; ❶). All of these hotels have inexpensive to moderately priced **restaurants**. The nearest **campsite** is at Castel del Piano (see p.496).

Villages around Monte Amiata

If you have transport, the ring of towns around Monte Amiata is worth a little exploration. None has outstanding features but all claim a rural setting and more or less medieval centres – usually built around an Aldobrandeschi castle. Most also have a good sprinkling of hotels.

Piancastagnaio

Five kilometres south of Abbadia San Salvatore, **PIANCASTAGNAIO**, at 772m, spreads across the slopes of a mountain plateau, capped by one of the area's most impressive fortresses, a fourteenth-century Aldobrandeschi number. It has a maze of pretty streets, plus a fine Romanesque church – the twelfth-century Santa Maria Assunta. On the road outside the village, left of the main gate, the church of **Santa Maria delle Grazie** has a recently uncovered fifteenth-century fresco cycle by Nanni di Pietro. Another recently discovered cycle resides in **San Bartolomeo**, a humble Franciscan church on the Abbadia road restructured in the eighteenth century. The pictures, which depict the *Life of the Virgin*, are in the chapterhouse, off the cloister.

There is a small, intermittently open Pro Loco office for **information** at Viale Garibaldi 1 (☎0577.784.134), which also has bikes for rent in summer. The village's **hotels** are all grouped along Viale Gramsci and Via Grossetana – the *Del Bosco*, Via Grossetana (☎ & ⓕ0577.786.090; ❷), has pleasant doubles. A rural, and slightly cheaper alternative, is the *Piccolo Mondo* (☎0577.785.100; ❶), 4km east on the minor road to Quaranta.

Davide Lazzeretti of Monte Labbro

Arcidosso-born **Davide Lazzeretti** (1834–78) is the most extraordinary figure that Monte Amiata – a region renowned for its mystics and seers – has thrown up: either a visionary prophet, or a crazed communist born before his time, according to greatly divergent Italian points of view. As young as fourteen, the boy had been marked out for great and strange things by a Franciscan monk; a vision twenty years later prompted Lazzeretti to travel to Rome, to try and interest the pope in his revelation. Scorned, he retired to a contemplative life on Monte Subiaco, in a deliberate imitation of St Benedict, who had retired to the same mountain slopes southeast of Rome 1400 years earlier.

Returning to Amiata between 1870 and 1871, Lazzeretti achieved notoriety as the founder of an ill-defined socio-religious sect, the **Jurisdavidic Church**, which as well as preaching Christianity under the banner "Long live the Republic, God and Liberty" agitated for justice and social reform amongst the peasant community which made up his following. In 1873 he was arrested, the authorities unhappy with his persuasive republican preaching, not to mention his new title: the "Messiah of Monte Amiata". In 1876 he was excommunicated, but continued to preach both in Italy and abroad, calling for a society based on co-operative principles and republican government. In time, his five thousand followers organized themselves into Italy's first **co-operative**, sharing land and animals and building a huge temple to the movement on top of Monte Labbro, south of Arcidosso. In 1877 the Church refused to allow him to continue using the temple, and in 1878 Lazzeretti met a violent end – shot, with the connivance of local landowners, by the *carabinieri* as he led an unauthorized religious procession through Arcidosso.

Repression soon dispersed the movement, which was in any case being undermined by a drift away from the land to Amiata's mercury mines. Nonetheless, Lazzeretti is remembered today as a pre-emptor of socialist and land reform movements still twenty years away at the time of his death. He is commemorated on the night of August 14, the anniversary of his death, with a huge bonfire at the largely ruined temple on Monte Labbro. Whether or not you want to pay your respects, the trip to the summit makes a fine walk or drive: a rough road takes you virtually to the top.

Santa Fiora

SANTA FIORA's craggy position drew an admiring observation from Dante as to its impregnability; its castle – of which only a tower remains – provided the feudal seat of one of the major branches of the **Aldobrandeschi**. This clan, which ruled much of southern Tuscany and the Maremma from the ninth century, had its roots in a Lombard dynasty from Lucca – the family name is an Italian corruption of "Hildebrand", testament to the family's northern German origins. In 1274 the clan divided into two main branches, one of which was installed in Santa Fiora, ruling Monte Amiata and the northern Maremma, the other in nearby Sovana, from where they controlled the coast and the southern Maremma (see p.503). Santa Fiora then passed through the family's female line, and was eventually ceded by marriage to the Sforza Cesarini family, whose **palazzo**, built from the old fortress, lies alongside the Aldobrandeschi **tower**, now a clock tower overlooking a picturesque little square.

The village has a couple of fine churches. The **Pieve di Santa Fiora e Lucilla**, reached on Via Carolina from the square, has its walls, altar and pulpit adorned with a wide variety of topnotch terracottas (1480–90) by Andrea della Robbia and his workshop. The beautiful church, incidentally, was named after two local saints whose relics, brought here in the eleventh century, reside in the nearby priest's house. A steep, partly stepped lane leads to **Sant'Agostino**, which possesses a fine painted wooden image of the Madonna and Child attributed (dubiously) to Jacopo della Quercia, though it's been claimed for the time being by the museum in Pitigliano's Palazzo Orsini (see p.501).

Down the road you come to gardens and the oratory of **Madonna delle Nevi** – the della Robbia figures above the entrance are the local saints Fiora and Lucilla – and then to the village's nicest feature, the **Peschiera** (daily in summer until sunset; in winter, contact Coop Amiata ℡0564.977.571; €1), a spring-fed lake and eighteenth-century garden surrounded by woodland and gurgling brooks. The road beyond passes evidence of Amiata's industrial side, tall chimneys signalling the thermal power plants and mercury mines that have kept the area's economic head above water.

Santa Fiora's **tourist office** is in Piazza Garibaldi (℡0564.977.036) and there are a couple of **hotels**, the three-star *Fiora*, Via Roma 8 (℡0564.977.043, ⓦwww.hotelfiora.it; ❷) and cheaper *Eden*, Via Roma 1 (℡ & ℱ0564.977.033; ❶).

Arcidosso and Castel del Piano

West of the summit, **ARCIDOSSO** is one of the larger Amiata towns, dominated by a blunt Sienese tower, but of little other interest. It was, however, the birthplace of **Davide Lazzeretti** (see box on p.495), and also features in one of the most heated artistic debates ever to embroil Tuscany; it's thought to be Arcidosso's skyline that is depicted in the painting uncovered in Siena's Palazzo Pubblico, a discovery that has thrown into doubt the attribution of Simone Martini's *Guidoriccio da Fogliano* (see p.383 for more on this controversy).

The small **tourist office** is in Piazza Indipendenza (Mon–Sat 10am–1pm & 4.30–7pm; ℡0564.916.025, ⓦwww.arcidosso.galamiata.it) and there are a couple of small **hotels**: *Gatto d'Oro*, Via dei Venti (℡ & ℱ0564.967.074; ❶), and *Toscana*, Via Lazzaretti 47 (℡0564.967.486, ⓦwww.albergotoscana.it; ❸).

More tempting on the horizon is **CASTEL DEL PIANO**, the main commercial town of this area. It doesn't really live up to the promise, though the **old centre** warrants a quick wander, with its covered market, Palazzo Pretorio and Romanesque San Leonardo. Many of its churches are lumbered with the seventeenth-century works of the Nasini, a three-generation dynasty of second-rate painters, all of whom were born in the town: their work is also found in the abbey at Abbadia San Salvatore.

There is a Pro Loco **tourist office** at Via Marconi 9 (℡0564.973.534) and the town is the biggest centre in the region for shopping and provisions.

Seggiano and Pescina

SEGGIANO is an old Etruscan centre, today distinguished principally by its Renaissance church of the **Madonna della Carità**, set in an olive grove just outside the village. The town's inhabitants built it as a votive offering in 1603 as thanks for deliverance from famine. They wouldn't be too impressed to see what's become of their labour of love, for the church has managed to have every one of its altarpieces stolen: grim modern paintings have taken their place. Better-educated thieves might have made for the nicely situated **Oratorio di San Rocco**, also on the village's outskirts, whose *Madonna Enthroned* (1493) by Girolamo di Domenico is by far the best of the paintings in the immediate vicinity. Nearby, also in a beautiful setting, is a tiny fortified hamlet, Potentino.

Just east of the town on the road to Pescina lies the **Giardino di Daniel Spoerri** (Easter–June Sat & Sun 4–8pm; July to mid-Sept Tues–Sun 4–8pm; mid-Sept to Oct Tues–Sun 4–7pm; €7; ⓦwww.danielspoerri.org), a fascinating sixteen-hectare sculpture garden designed by the Swiss artist to incorporate contemporary art (79 installations by forty artists) in a natural setting.

Five very winding kilometres further on is **PESCINA**, which deserves mention for its superlative **restaurant**, 🍴 *Le Silene* (☎0564.950.805; closed Mon). People come from miles around, especially for Sunday lunch, to sample their "modern Tuscan" cuisine and fine Italian wine selection, so booking is strongly advised. The restaurant doubles as a modest hotel (❶). If you don't fancy eating, allow a couple of minutes for the little **parish church**, which has a *Madonna and Child* by Lucca di Tommè, an underrated fourteenth-century Sienese painter with works scattered across southern Tuscany.

South to Saturnia and Manciano

Around 14km from Arcidosso, **TRIANA** stands on the junction of the roads west to Grosseto and south to Saturnia and Pitigliano. A perfect little fortified hamlet, it commands huge views from its castle. If you have a car, a rewarding detour off the road south is to follow the new highway to Grosseto as far as Roccalbegna. Relying on buses, however, this only really makes sense if you're making for Grosseto: two buses cover the route daily.

Roccalbegna

ROCCALBEGNA is one of the finest villages in southern Tuscany: aerial pictures of its perfect medieval streets decorate many local tourist offices, but barely hint at the rugged grandeur of its position, perched 522m up the slopes of Monte Labbro above the Albegna valley. Although the place is not on any obvious route, and visitors are few, the detour here is more than worthwhile, and there's a single **hotel** with moderately priced restaurant if you want to stay – *La Pietra*, Via XXIV Maggio (☎0564.989.019, ⓦwww.locandalapietra.it; ❷).

The **Rocca** of the town's name is obvious from afar, poised on a crag that rises almost to a pyramid above the village. Like so many in the region, it formed a defensive retreat for the Aldobrandeschi, overlords of the Maremma for several centuries. A superb walk to the top starts from the Piazza IV Novembre at the far end of the village: turn left up Salita Sasso (a yellow sign), go past the *Bar-Tabacchi* and it's then ten minutes up the winding lane and a final scramble to the fortifications. The views over the wild and rocky countryside are tremendous, though outdone by the famed vista over the village's grid of streets. The local saying *se il sasso scrocca, addio la Rocca* ("If the rock crumbles, it's goodbye to the village") seems incontrovertible from this point.

In the village, be sure to look in on the Romanesque church of **SS Apostoli Pietro e Paolo**, noted for its medieval interior and patches of fresco, but more for a tremendous triptych of the *Madonna and Child with SS Peter and Paul* (1340) by Ambrogio Lorenzetti. It's astonishing to find a painting here, in the middle of nowhere, by one of Siena's finest – the artist was responsible for the frescoes of *Good and Bad Government* in Siena's Palazzo Pubblico. In a touching detail, Lorenzetti has painted the Madonna affectionately clasping the Child's foot. Note too, the cherries held in the Infant's hands, symbols of Heaven, eternal life and the rewards of a righteous life. Next door to the church, up some steps in Via Campana, is the small **Oratorio del Crocifisso**, now a small museum (open on request). Its high altar contains a fourteenth-century painted Crucifix (1360) by Luca di Tommè, whose presence in Roccalbegna is no accident – Lorenzetti was his main influence.

South to Saturnia

Moving south to Saturnia, there are a couple of minor places of note. **PET-RICCI**, 5km south of Triana, has a two-star **hotel** with moderately priced **restaurant**, *La Cerinella* (☎0564.984.015, ⓦwww.laltramaremma.it; ❶). Another 5km on you reach **SEMPRONIANO**, a crumbling half-forgotten village centred on another Aldobrandeschi castle. Its Romanesque church, SS Vincenzo e Anastasio, has a painting of a dragon supposedly slain nearby and placed in the castle for public edification. By contrast, neighbouring Romanesque Santa Croce has a noted wooden medieval Crucifix. On a minor road 5km to the east is the virtually abandoned hamlet of **ROCCHETTE**, sited below a castle on a spur overlooking the Albegna valley. If you make the detour you'll find one of the prettiest places for miles, along with some cracking views.

Saturnia: Le Cascatelle

Word is spreading about the sulphurous hot springs at **SATURNIA**, 25km south of Triana, as the almost year-round convoys of battered Volkswagen campers and crowds of noisy Italians testify. Nonetheless, they're not that easy to find. If all you want is a dip you should initially ignore the hill-town and follow the road south towards Montemerano. A large **spa complex** (ⓦwww.termedisaturnia .it) – with fierce admission charges, a vast pool and a five-star hotel – is signposted to the left, and about 200m on (as the road takes a sharp curve) a dirt track heads off straight, unsignposted but usually signalled by a cluster of cars and vans. Two minutes' walk from here brings you to the **cascatelle**, sulphur streams and springs which burst from the ground, forming natural rock-pool jacuzzis of warm water, in which you can lie around for hours submerged up to your neck. Entrance is unrestricted and free, and even on cold days there are invariably a few people ready to indulge. The heavy pedestrian traffic means there's a bit of litter, but apart from an inexpensive bar/pizzeria there's surprisingly little commercialism.

The bubbling main pool is a bizarre sight, the water an intense turquoise, and all the more surreal if the weather is overcast and the steam rising overhead. The place also has something of a cult aspect, and it's not unusual for parties to come up at night from Rome. Rumour has it, however, that some of the water here has already been channelled through the resort's treatment centre: not a very nice thought, and perhaps enough to discourage bathing in the April-to-October spa season.

Practicalities

There are three daily **buses** along the road between Semproniano and Manciano: be sure to get out at the springs (*Le Terme*) and not at Saturnia village. Hitching should be reasonably easy, as there's usually someone heading for the springs.

If you intend to **stay** near the springs, you'll need a shower to wash off the sulphur smell, which is not too noticeable when bathing, but can linger for days. The nearest **hotel** is the excellent one-star *Albergo-Ristorante Stellata* (☎0564.602.978; ❸), in an isolated spot 1km down from the falls on the road to Manciano (it's signposted left on a dirt road).

All the other accommodation possibilities are in Saturnia village, a fairly unassuming place. Camper vans are allowed to park overnight in the more modern of the main squares, and there are a couple of **hotels** – the *Saturnia*, Via Mazzini 4 (☎0564.601.007, ⓦwww.laltramaremma.it; ❷), and *Villa Clodia*, Via Italia 43 (☎0564.601.212, ⓦwww.hotelvillaclodia.com; ❸), which is tucked away in one of the village's nicer quarters. When all's said and done, perhaps the best reason to come here is a **restaurant**, the appealing *Bacco e Cerere*, Via Mazzini 4 (℡0564.601.235; closed Wed). The service is friendly, the atmosphere intimate (room for just thirty diners) and the food – puddings especially – worth every one of the €35 it'll cost to do the job properly.

Montemerano

Midway between Saturnia and Manciano lies **MONTEMERANO**, a medieval hill-village (with modern component below) cannily fortified on two levels, its balconies and interlocked alleys decked with a more-than-usual abundance of geraniums and other hanging greenery. A fascinating church and exceptional restaurant are gradually bringing the tourists in, but for the time being it remains a pretty and all-but-undocumented little gem. Come in August and you can partake in the annual tripe festival.

Once you've pottered around the streets – which will take only a few minutes – head for **San Giorgio**, a prettily frescoed little church full of artistic treasures. The first, on the right (south) wall, is a wooden bas-relief of the *Assumption* (1455–65) by Vecchietta, a painter who also successfully turned his hand to sculpture. Beyond it, by the door, is a faded fresco of *St Orsola*. Ahead, at the bottom of the arch beside the high altar, is the winsome and wonderfully titled *Madonna della Gattaiola* ("of the Cat-flap"), painted around 1450 by an anonymous follower of Sassetta known as the "Master of Montemerano". Originally one half of an *Annunciation* (note the Virgin's Bible, a feature of such paintings), the picture probably formed part of an organ or double-doored tabernacle; the archangel Gabriel would have occupied the second panel. It was then used as the door to a granary, probably the point at which it received the hole in the bottom right of the Virgin's cloak which led to its nickname. All this is simply a light-hearted prelude to the church's real highlights, namely a polychrome wooden statue of *St Peter* (1455–60), another work by Vecchietta (left of the high altar steps), and a glorious fifteenth-century polyptych by Sano di Pietro of the *Madonna and Child with SS Peter, George, Lawrence and Anthony of Padua*.

For somewhere to **stay** in or around the village, the smart three-star *Oliveto* (℡0564.602.849, ⓦwww.loliveto.it; ❸) is the upmarket choice, located on the outskirts near the turn-off for Saturnia, although the pastorally situated *Villa Acquaviva* (℡0564.602.890, ⓦwww.laltramaremma.it; ❸), 2km north of Montemerano, is a definite first-choice treat, with rooms in two attractively converted buildings, surrounded by the hotel's own wine estate. The *Laudomia* (℡0564.620.013, ⓕ0564.620.062; ⓦwww.locandalaudomia.com; ❷), for centuries a coaching inn, is at Poderi di Montemerano, midway to Manciano, and has an attractive, moderately priced restaurant attached (℡0564.629.830; closed Tues).

You might be better off, however, saving money on accommodation and splashing out on a meal at the very expensive Michelin-starred **restaurant** ✻ *Da Caino*, Via Canonica 3 (℡0564.602.817; in winter, closed Wed & lunchtime Thurs). The coveted Michelin rosette is not the recommendation in Tuscany it might be elsewhere, but here it reflects absolutely first-class cooking. There are just 22 covers, so booking is essential, and you're looking at around €90 if you're going to stretch the chef. For less than a third of this you can eat at the moderately priced *Osteria Passaparola*, Vicolo delle Mura 21 (℡0564.602.835; closed Thurs), or the *Vecchia Osteria Cacio e Vino*, Via del Bivio 16 (℡0564.602.827), which also has handful of rooms (❶).

Manciano

MANCIANO, though hardly somewhere you'd make a special journey for, is an attractive market town 15km west of Pitigliano, with a medieval quarter grouped around a Sienese fortress, and a plentiful supply of bars in which to soak up its small-town atmosphere.

As well as a supplies stop, Manciano is an important hub of the southern Tuscan **bus** network. RAMA buses leave from the bottom of Via Marsala, the street that leads from the roundabout up to the old town; you can get tickets from the newsagent in Piazza della Pace. Services include five daily to Grosseto, two to Orbetello, two to Scansano and one to Pitigliano via Montemerano and Saturnia. It's unlikely you'll want to stay in the town, but if stranded you'll find a handful of **hotels**, most central of which is the three-star *Rossi*, Via Gramsci 2 (☏0564.629.248, ⓦwww.hotelrossi.it; ❸).

Pitigliano and around

PITIGLIANO, the largest town in Tuscany's deep south, is best approached along the road from Manciano, to the west. As you approach, it soars above on a spectacular outcrop of tufa, with medieval buildings perched above the valley floor, and its quarters linked by the arches of an immense aqueduct. **Etruscan tombs** – some converted to storage cellars for wine – honeycomb the cliffs, a feature repeated all over the surrounding area.

Neolithic remains suggest a settlement on the site from earliest times, though it first rose to prominence as an Etruscan and later Roman town. In the early Middle Ages the town belonged to the ubiquitous **Aldobrandeschi**, who ruled it from nearby Sovana, then one of the clan's two principal southern Tuscan power bases. In 1293 it passed by marriage to the counts of **Orsini**, a major Roman family who produced three popes and countless cardinals, bishops and

△ Pitigliano

minor papal dignitaries. Under the clan the town became more important than Sovana, from which the bishopric was eventually transferred. Its ultimate fate (in 1608), like much of the region, was to become a part of the Grand Duchy of Tuscany.

Pitigliano was also known for its thriving **Jewish community**, which became established during the latter part of the sixteenth century, under the protection of the Orsini. In 1622, however, the Medici confined the Jews of Pitigliano to a **ghetto**, where they remained confined until 1735, when legislation introduced by the last Medici ruler, Gian Gastone, lifted the proscription against Jewish commercial activity and led to the expansion of Jewish businesses on present-day Via Zuccarelli. Before long Pitigliano was being referred to as "Little Jerusalem", and boasted a Jewish university that attracted students from around Europe. By the time of Italian Unification, around 400 of Pitigliano's 2200 residents were Jewish, but in the last decades of the nineteenth century many emigrated to Palestine, a process which accelerated after World War II – though the great majority of Pitigliano's Jews survived the Nazi occupation. Pitigliano's synagogue closed in the late 1950s, and today, in what was formerly one of the centres of Jewish learning in southern Europe, there is just a handful of Jewish residents left.

The town has today a slightly grim, occasionally sinister sort of grandeur, the result partly of its mighty fortress – dividing the upper town from the more modern lower suburb – and partly because of the tall alleys of the ghetto area. Seen on a sunny day, though, it is a gem of small-town Italy, seemingly populated entirely by old women knitting or lacemaking. Together with the villages of **Sorano** and **Sovana** it constitutes one of the most worthwhile and neglected spots in the region.

The Town

The major entry point to the medieval town is through **Piazza Petruccioli** – host to a car park, hotel and the main bus stop, and to a small belvedere that looks along the houses and cliffs on the town's southern edge. Immediately through the gate is the high-walled and rather claustrophobic Piazza Garibaldi, and beyond it the massive **aqueduct** (1543) and **fortress**, contemporary building projects completed in the sixteenth century under Giuliano da Sangallo, along with a complex string of fortifications. Within the fortress is the Renaissance **Palazzo Orsini** and the **Museo del Medioevo e Rinascimento e Fortezza Orsini** (April–Oct Tues–Sun 10am–1pm & 2–7pm; Nov–March Fri–Sun 10am–1pm & 3–7pm; €3), begun in the thirteenth century and extended by Niccolò Orsini two centuries later. The ramp leading to the main entrance arch has a small pillar decorated with a text lauding Gian Francesco Orsini, responsible for instigating the nearby aqueduct. It also has a crest bearing the Orsini's family arms, the head of a lion and a bear (the latter is a pun: *orso* is Italian for bear); the same arms appear on the fine well in the courtyard. Inside, much of the palace has been restored, bringing new lustre to a succession of lovely Tuscan ceilings and interiors. All manner of jewellery, vestments and other ecclesiastical ephemera litter the rooms, with just valuable works of art as distraction: a wooden *Madonna and Child* attributed to Jacopo della Quercia and a painting of the *Madonna Enthroned* (1494) by Guidoccio Cozzarelli. There are also two works by Francesco Zuccarelli (1702–88), who was born in the town but worked mainly in Venice and London. The palace is also home to the five-room **Museo Civico Archeologico della Civiltà Etrusca** (Tues–Sun: April–Oct 10am–1pm & 4–7pm; Nov–March 10am–1pm & 3–6pm; €2.50), which houses an interesting collection of vases, jewellery and trinkets unearthed in the nearby Etruscan site of Poggio Buco.

More absorbing exhibits are on show in the **Museo della Civiltà Giubonnai**, located in a series of cellars beneath the fortress which were discovered by accident during a clean-up. Some of the labyrinth had remained unseen and untouched for three hundred years; other parts had been filled with rubble during Sangallo's work on the foundations. The collection, growing all the time, centres on folk, domestic and agricultural ephemera of the Maremma. At present you need to make an appointment at the Palazzo Orsini, but the hope is to fix regular hours and admission.

The fortress backs onto **Piazza della Repubblica**, the town's elongated and beautiful main square, its symmetry accentuated by a pair of fountains and immaculately pollarded ilex trees. Wander over to the balcony for a panorama taking in the river, trees, waterfalls and the faint outline of Monte Amiata away to the north.

Beyond lies the old town proper, a tight huddle of arches, alleys and medieval streets. It consists of three main streets, merging into one at the end of the town. Take the left fork out of the square and Via Zuccarelli brings you to the former **synagogue**. Via Zuccarelli comes to an end by the Renaissance church of **Santa Maria**, its door flanked by the arms of the Orsini family. To the left of the main door under the tower, note the twelfth-century bas-relief depicting a human figure and two winged dragons. Inside are a few patches of fresco, less interesting than the building's peculiar trapezoidal plan. Nearby, immediately outside the Porto Capisotto and the medieval ramparts, is a stretch of **Etruscan wall**. Heading back to Piazza della Repubblica, Via G. Orsini brings you to Piazza Gregorio VII and the Baroque **Duomo**, with its butter-coloured stucco facade and giant campanile, the latter a surviving portion of a much earlier Romanesque church on the site. The western end of the square features a prominent travertine pillar (1490) with another text praising the Orsini.

The third street of the grid, **Via Roma**, best encapsulates the town's provincial feel, a collection of odd, half-empty shops giving off a smell of mothballs – although some are being converted into smart tourist-orientated boutiques. Here, as elsewhere, the main pleasure is exploring the arches and alleys that lead off on either side.

Practicalities

Pitigliano's helpful **tourist office** is on Piazza Garibaldi (daily 10.20am–1pm & 3–7pm; ℡0564.617.111, ⓦwww.collidimaremma.it). The town doesn't exactly buzz with visitors, though, and with luck you should find room at its single **hotel**, the *Albergo Guastini* on Piazza Petruccioli (℡0564.616.065, ⓦwww.albergoguastini.it; ❸); the hotel is happier doing full-board deals, which is no problem as the rates are reasonable and the food tasty. If the hotel is full, try one of the several rooms for rent around town: the tourist office carries the latest listings. An out-of-town hotel alternative is the *Albergo Corano* (℡0564.616.112, Ⓕ0564.614.191, ⓦwww.hotelcorano.it; ❷), a modern place with a pool; it's located just beyond the village of Madonna delle Grazie on the road to Manciano. Even nicer is the three-star *Valle Orientina* (℡0564.616.611, ⓦwww.valleorientina.it; ❸), at Località Valle Orientina, 3km from Pitigliano. Pleasantly rustic and family run, it is in a rural setting, has a swimming pool, tennis courts, natural mineral spa and offers the opportunity to rent bikes or horses.

The best **restaurants**, if you don't eat at the *Guastini*, are the inexpensive wooden-beamed *Trattoria Del Orso* in Piazza Gregorio VII; the moderately priced *Osteria la Tavernaccia* at Via Roma 92 with *maremmana* specialities; or the award-winning mid-priced ⚘ *Osteria Il Tufo Allegro*, Vicolo della Costituzione 1 (closed Tues). The local **wine**, Bianco di Pitigliano, hard to find elsewhere, is sold at two good-value outlets on Via Santa Chiara (off Piazza Petruccioli) and celebrated in a September **wine festival**.

There's a reasonable **bus** service (pick-up and drop-off in Piazza Petruccioli), with three departures daily to Grosseto via Manciano, five to Orbetello (via Albinia), five to Sorano and one to Semproniano via Sovana.

Sovana

Fine Etruscan tombs and pristine Romanesque architecture would place **SOVANA** firmly on the tour circuit, if only it were closer to Siena or Florence. As it is, you can explore this breathtaking, part-abandoned medieval centre in virtual solitude – save at weekends, when Romans and, increasingly, northern Europeans flock to the place.

The town dates to at least the seventh century BC, when the Etruscans took up residence. It fell to the Romans in the third century BC, later becoming a Lombard fiefdom. The town's principal monuments, though, derive from its time as the capital of the **Aldobrandeschi**, a noble clan whose domain extended over much of southern Tuscany and northern Lazio; they were said to have a castle for every day of the year. Their golden age came with the birth in Sovana in 1020 of a scion, Hildebrand, who in 1073 was to become Pope Gregory VII, a great reformer who also kept a favourable eye on family business. Decline set in during the fourteenth century, when Sovana's low-lying position made it vulnerable both to malaria and Sienese attacks, and its population and power drifted to nearby Pitigliano. Siena took control of the town in 1410, ceding power to the Grand Duchy of Tuscany in 1557. Today, Sovana's residents number just over a hundred.

The village

Sovana's main street, **Via di Mezzo**, is almost the sum of the place, a broad expanse of fishbone-patterned brick paving, laid in 1580 by Ferdinand I de' Medici and recently restored to impressive effect. Guarding its start are the ruins of the Aldobrandeschi castle, built in the eleventh century on Etruscan foundations: it fell into greater disrepair with each of its subsequent owners – the Sienese, Orsini and Medici, who tried to repopulate the place in the seventeenth century by importing 58 families from Albania.

At its end, the street swells slightly to form the **Piazza del Pretorio**, a perfect medieval ensemble dominated on the left by **Santa Maria**, one of the most beautiful churches in southern Tuscany. Built in the thirteenth century to a Romanesque-Gothic plan, it has a simple stone interior dominated by an exquisite **ciborium**, a unique piece of pre-Romanesque paleo-Christian sculpture from the eighth or ninth century. Such canopies disappeared from churches in about the thirteenth century, confirming the work's far earlier provenance. Superbly preserved early frescoes around the walls set the seal on a marvellous building.

Opposite the church is the low-arched **Loggia del Capitano**, whose stone coats of arms proclaim Medici possession, and whose arches conceal a nice bar with a handful of outdoor tables. Next to it is the thirteen-century **Palazzo Pretorio**, home to a small **museum and gallery** (Tues–Sat 10am–1pm & 4–7pm; €3), which traces the area's history, paying particular attention to local Etruscan tombs and discoveries. Particularly illuminating are the reconstructions of how tombs might originally have looked, well worth seeing if you intend to head out and explore the necropolis (see box opposite). The nine stone banners here are those of the town's Sienese and Medici governors. The little pillar to the right of the main door was used to pin up public declarations.

From the square a back lane leads through gardens and olive groves to the huge **Duomo**, or Cattedrale di SS Pietro e Paolo (closed 1–3pm), whose exterior wall and superb portal bear some of the finest Lombard-Romanesque carvings in Tuscany. The church's nucleus went up in the eighth century (the date of many of the carvings) or possibly earlier – it's known the town was a centre of a diocese in the sixth century – and was augmented in the tenth with the addition of an apse and crypt. The bare, triple-naved **interior** features some twelfth-century carved capitals, reminiscent of the Benedictine work in Sant'Antimo; the finest is that on the second pillar in the left aisle, a work which suggests the hand of Lombard masons. There are also traces of fresco, a fine Gothic font and a wonderful **crypt**, divided into five tiny naves by ancient columns, but now, sadly, closed off to the public. The urn in the main church contains the remains of St Mamiliano, a sixth-century saint who evangelized much of the region.

Beyond the Duomo you can walk down to an old town **gateway** and traces of Etruscan wall, or turn back to Piazza Pretorio along the village's modest residential street, which sports little more than a couple of shops.

Practicalities

The **tourist office** (April–Oct daily 10am–1pm & 3–8pm; Nov–March Fri–Sun 10am–1pm & 3–6.30pm; ℡0564.614.074) is at the entrance to the museum in the Palazzo Pretorio.

Sovana presents some genuine medieval charm and has two good **hotels**: opposite Santa Maria is the three-star *Taverna Etrusca* (℡0564.616.183, ℻0564.614.193; ❷), a tiny place worth booking to be sure of one of its twelve room. Its ✻ **restaurant** (closed Wed) is first-rate, a beautifully elegant interior scattered with covetable antique furniture, and fine food at around €35. Just off the piazza is the eight-room, one-star *Hotel Scilla* (℡0564.616.531, ⓦwww

---

Etruscan tombs near Sovana

All round Sovana, but especially on the road to Saturnia, Etruscan tombs riddle the countryside, many approached by original "sunken" Etruscan roads. Why these roads should be sunken still puzzles scholars: some believe the purpose was defensive, in that they would enable people to move unseen from town to town; others posit that they were used for moving livestock, and were cut below ground level to prevent the animals from straying. The larger graves are well marked off the road by yellow signs. The necropolis as a whole, of which the marked tombs form a tiny part, extends for miles and rates in archeological (if not tourist) terms with the graves at Tarquinia and Cerveteri. Most of the tombs date from the seventh century BC and just about every type of Etruscan grave is present, including colombari, small niches cut into the rock to take cinerary urns. What the tombs lack in paintings they often make up for with elaborate carvings.

The key tombs are the Tomba Ildebranda (March–Oct daily 9.30am–dusk; Nov–Feb 10am–dusk; e5.50), considered the best single tomb in Tuscany, and the Tomba della Sirena (same hours and ticket). After the tunnel on the road to Saturnia, however, you'll spot more tombs, all of which can be visited free, including the Poggio Pesca and the Pola, a couple of minutes' uphill scramble from the road.

.scilla-sovana.it; ❸), whose moderately priced restaurant, *Dei Merli* (closed Tues except Aug), also has a beautiful setting, with a pergola draped in flowers and greenery.

Sorano

All the approaches to **SORANO**, 9km northeast of Pitigliano, are extraordinary: from the south the route is lined with caves and tombs cut into the hillside; from the west, the road is cut into walls of tufa. The village, visible for miles on either approach, has a decidedly weird feel, with only a fraction of the old houses still lived in. Parts of the tangled streets suggest a faded grandeur; others are desolate and derelict. Landslips are the main problem, several streets having been declared terminally uninhabitable after one big slide. Attempts to keep Sorano alive have included a policy of sponsoring ceramic workshops and various other arts and crafts businesses. The small **tourist office** on Piazza Busati (April–Oct daily 10am–1pm & 3–8pm; Nov–March Fri–Sun 10am–1pm & 3–6.30pm; ☎0564.633.099) makes a point of promoting these, and will also help if you want guidance around the wealth of Etruscan remnants in the valley.

The village is full of intriguing medieval corners, but has little in the way of specific sights. An old castle dominates the centre, and has been converted into a fine, historic three-star **hotel**, the *Della Fortezza* (☎0564.632.010, ⓦwww .fortezzahotel.it; ❹), entered from Piazza Cairoli. The fifteen rooms are woodbeamed and elegantly furnished with antiques, and the views are superb. Otherwise, nearby Sovana is perhaps a better overnight option, but if you wish to stay locally and pay less, you could go for the one-star *La Botte* at nearby Montorio (☎0564.638.633, ⓕ0564.638.535; ❶).

The other fortress as you enter the town is the **Fortezza Orsini** (April–Oct daily 9am–1pm & 3–7pm; Nov–Feb Fri–Sun 10am–1pm & 3–5pm; €2.50), a blunt and perfectly preserved piece of Renaissance military engineering. Built over an old Aldobrandeschi fort in 1552, it was often besieged but never captured.

San Quírico

From Sorano there are constant views over the wooded gorge of the River Lente, whose rushing waters echo through the streets. Down on the valley floor, tantalizing ancient tracks crisscross the countryside, linking clearly visible rock tombs, Roman wells and old watermill workings. Some 5km east is the hamlet of **SAN QUÍRICO**, to the north of which you can explore the **Rupestre di Vitozza** (April–Oct daily 10am–7pm; Nov–March Fri–Sun 10am–1pm & 3–5.30pm; €2), a series of two hundred tombs, grottoes and paleo-Christian remains, and the remnants of Vitozza, San Quírico's medieval antecedent.

San Quírico has the salubrious two-star **hotel** *Agnelli* (☎0564.619.015, ⓦwww.laltramaremma.it; ❷), whose **restaurant**, *La Vecchia Fonte* (closed Mon), has a great village atmosphere and – in addition to inexpensive pizzas – serves up surprisingly good fish and seafood (bought in fresh daily). Prices are keen (around €20), making it extremely popular with locals.

Travel details

Trains

Buonconvento to: Grosseto (10 daily; 1hr); Siena (10 daily; 30min).
Chiusi-Chianciano Terme to: Asciano (10 daily; 50min); Florence (hourly; 1hr 5min–1hr 40min); Montepulciano (hourly; 15min); Siena (hourly; 1hr 30min); Sinalunga (hourly; 25min).
Siena to: Asciano (hourly; 30min); Buonconvento (10 daily; 30min); Chiusi-Chianciano Terme (hourly; 1hr 30min); Grosseto via Monte Antico (10 daily; 1hr 40min); Montepulciano (hourly; 1hr); Sinalunga (hourly; 50min).

Buses

Abbadia San Salvatore to: Arcidosso (10 daily; 45min); Buonconvento (5 daily; 1hr 10min); Chiusi (4 daily; 1hr 25min); Grosseto (3 daily; 2hr 15min); Piancastagnaio (10 daily; 15min); Santa Fiora (10 daily; 30min); Siena (2–3 daily; 2hr).
Buonconvento to: Abbadia San Salvatore (5 daily; 1hr 10min); Montalcino (9 daily; 20min); Montepulciano (7 daily; 1hr); Pienza (7 daily; 35min); Siena (6 daily; 40min); Torrenieri (6 daily; 25min).
Chiusi to: Chianciano (14 daily; 30min); Montepulciano (14 daily; 45min).
Montalcino to: Buonconvento (9 daily; 30min);

Siena (6 daily; 1hr 10min); Torrenieri (10 daily; 20min).
Montepulciano to: Buonconvento (7 daily; 1hr); Chianciano (every 30min; 25min); Chiusi (every 30min; 50min); Florence (1–3 daily; 2hr); Pienza (7 daily; 20min); San Quírico d'Órcia (7 daily; 40min); Siena (5–6 daily; 90min); Torrenieri (7 daily; 50min).
Pienza to: Buonconvento (7 daily; 35min); Montepulciano (7 daily; 20min); San Quírico (7 daily; 10min); Siena (5 daily; 1hr 30min); Torrenieri (7 daily; 25min).
Pitigliano to: Albinia (6 daily; 1hr); Grosseto via Manciano (3 daily; 1hr 40min); Orbetello (5 daily; 1hr 25min); San Quírico (4 daily; 15min); Semproniano (1 daily; 45min); Sorano (5 daily; 10min); Sovana (3 daily; 10min).
San Quírico d'Órcia to: Montepulciano (7 daily; 30min); Pienza (7 daily; 10min); Siena (5 daily; 1hr 10min); Torrenieri (7 daily; 15min).
Saturnia to: Manciano (3 daily; 25min).
Sovana to: Pitigliano (3 daily; 10min); Sorano (1 daily; 15min).
Torrenieri to: Arcidosso (6 daily; 40min); Buonconvento (6 daily; 25min); Grosseto (2 daily; 1hr 20min); Montalcino (10 daily; 20min); Pienza (7 daily; 25min).

9

Arezzo Province

9

Arezzo Province

Map labels: EMILIA-ROMAGNA, Bologna, Ravenna, ADRIATIC SEA, La Spezia, Massa, Rimini, SAN MARINO, LIGURIA, Pistoia, Lucca, Viareggio, Prato, Empoli, Arno, Florence, LIGURIAN SEA, Pisa, Urbino, Livorno, MARCHE, San Gimignano, TUSCANY, Arezzo, Gubbio, N, Siena, Lago Trasimeno, Montepulciano, Perugia, Assisi, Massa Marittima, UMBRIA, Foligno, Elba, Tiber, Spoleto, Grosseto, Orvieto, Terni, Lago di Bolsena, Montecristo, Giglio, LAZIO, 0 25 km, TYRRHENIAN SEA

CHAPTER 9 **Highlights**

* **Arezzo** The handsome provincial capital is famed for its antiques dealers, goldsmiths and – above all – for Piero della Francesca's sublime fresco cycle. **See p.514**

* **Monterchi** This minuscule village is home to another Piero masterpiece, the *Madonna del Parto*. **See p.522**

* **Sansepolcro** A small walled town that is the third stop on the Piero trail, chiefly for the magnificent *Resurrection*. **See p.524**

* **The Casentino** The upland forests of the Casentino national park offer some of the finest walks in Tuscany. **See p.526**

* **La Verna** St Francis's mountaintop retreat, still a thriving monastery, commands wonderful views of the Apennines. **See p.528**

* **Cortona** The quintessential Tuscan hill-town: ancient, lofty and charismatic, despite the growing influx of tourists. **See p.531**

△ The portico of Santa Maria delle Grazie, Arezzo

9

Arezzo Province

U pstream from Florence, the Arno valley – the **Valdarno** – is a fairly industrialized district, with warehouses and manufacturing plants enclosing many of the small towns strung along the train line. Some of the villages up on the valley sides retain an appealing medieval square or a cluster of attractive buildings but there's no very compelling stop before you reach the provincial capital of the upper Arno region, **Arezzo**, one hour's train ride from Florence. This solidly bourgeois city has its share of architectural delights – including one of the most photogenic squares in central Italy – though the droves of foreign visitors who travel to Arezzo come to see one thing: the fresco cycle by **Piero della Francesca** in the church of San Francesco. These are not the only crowds to fill Arezzo's hotels, for Italians flock here in even greater numbers for antiques, traded each month on the Piazza Grande in quantities scarcely matched anywhere else in the country.

For visitors on the trail of the masterpieces of Tuscan art, there are two essential calls in the vicinity of Arezzo. The first is the modest hill-town of **Monterchi**, where della Francesca painted one of the most powerful images of the Renaissance, the pregnant *Madonna del Parto*. Two other magnificent works by the same artist are to be seen in his birthplace, **Sansepolcro**, almost on the Umbrian border to the east and one of the pleasantest Tuscan backwaters.

Art is far from being this province's sole attraction. In the **Casentino**, the stretch of the Arno valley between Arezzo and the source of the river to the north, small hill-towns such as **Poppi** and **Bibbiena** stand above a terrain of vineyards and pastures, cradled by thickly wooded upland. The secluded peaks of the Casentino also harbour two of Italy's most influential monasteries, **Camaldoli** and the Franciscan sanctuary of **La Verna**, Tuscany's holiest pilgrimage site. The ancient woodlands cradling these sanctuaries have been protected within the new **Parco Nazionale delle Foreste Casentinesi**, an area that extends across the surprisingly high, wild and forested border country of northern Tuscany into Emilia-Romagna.

To the south of Arezzo stretches the agricultural plain of the **Valdichiana**, where the ancient hill-town of **Cortona** is the major attraction – and a nicer overnight stop than Arezzo – its steep streets forming a distinctive urban landscape and giving an unforgettable view over Lago Trasimeno and Valdichiana. It's also home to a pair of fine museums, one of which features major paintings by Fra' Angelico and locally born Luca Signorelli.

Trains on the Florence–Rome rail line run up the Arno valley, through Arezzo and on down the Valdichiana: for Cortona the nearest station on this line is Camucia, though more services stop at the slightly more distant Teróntola. For the Casentino, there's the LFI private rail line which runs to the head of the valley from the main FS station at Arezzo. Otherwise, Arezzo and Cortona are the centres of overlapping **bus** networks, which between them cover most of Arezzo province – including major points on the Piero della Francesca trail. Note that the private FCU railway from Sansepolcro to Perugia by way of Città di Castello gives you another way into Umbria. Generally, though, a **car** is essential if you want to get to some of the region's remoter sights and back on the same day, or to get the most out of the wilder reaches.

From Florence to Arezzo

If you're travelling by public transport from Florence to Arezzo there's no choice of route, as buses and trains all follow the **Valdarno**, just about the most unattractive stretch of waterway in Tuscany. Moving around by car, the obvious choice is between the two major roads that run roughly parallel to the river: the Autostrada del Sole and the SS69. If you want to cover the kilometres quickly, take the former; if you want to see the few sights of Valdarno, go for the latter, but be warned that the tarmac is perpetually clogged with lorries rumbling in and out of the industrial estates that pepper this part of the region. There is a third alternative, in the shape of the road that skirts the upland region known as the **Pratomagno**. It's a fairly tiring drive, with a gear-change required every couple of hundred metres, but at least the passengers have the benefit of the lovely view across to Chianti, and there's the odd Romanesque church along the way, one of them boasting a superb painting by Masaccio.

The Valdarno route

River, rail line and autostrada come together at the bottleneck known as Incisa Valdarno, 25km out of central Florence. Petrarch grew up here and some vestiges of the old town are preserved – but insufficient to make the place appealing. **Figline Valdarno**, 5km south, was the birthplace of another eminent Tuscan, Marsilio Ficino, court scholar-philosopher to Lorenzo il Magnifico. The old quarter around Piazza Ficino has a few handsome buildings and one interesting interior – the frescoed Collegiata di Santa Maria, which contains a fourteenth-century *Madonna* by the so-called Maestro di Figline.

Fashion factory outlets

Tuscany is the powerhouse of the country's textile industry, and the Arno valley – in particular the area between Incisa Val d'Arno and Pontassieve – is the home of many of the factories that manufacture clothes for the top labels. Several of these factories have retail outlets alongside, in which the season's left-overs (sometimes the previous season's) are sold at discounts as high as sixty percent. The best of these shops are listed below. As a shopping environment they may not have the glamour of Florence's Via Tornabuoni, but the bargains attract swarms of Italian cognoscenti and high-spending tourists, especially Japanese. If you want to get the pick of the day's offerings, get there in the first hour of trading.

Dolce e Gabbana Via Pian dell'Isola 49, localita Santa Maria Maddalena, Incisa Val d'Arno ☎055.833.1300. This two-storey shed, a few kilometres north of Incisa Val d'Arno, is packed with clothes, accessories and household items from the main Dolce e Gabbana range, plus cheaper stuff from the D&G diffusion label. Mon–Sat 9am–7pm, Sun 3–7pm.

Fendi, Loewe & Cellini Via Pian dell'Isola 66, Rignano sull'Arno ☎055.834.7155. Situated quite close to Dolce e Gabbana, the Fendi/Loewe/Cellini warehouse is best for bags and other leather accessories. Mon–Sat 10am–7pm, Sun 3–7pm.

The Mall Via Europe 8, Leccio Regello ☎055.865.7775. A short distance east of Fendi and Dolce e Gabbana, and containing separate outlets for Gucci, Bottega Veneta, Sergio Rossi, Loro Piana and Armani. Gucci is the dominant presence, with a huge range of bags, shoes, sunglasses and other accessories. Mon–Sat 10am–7pm, Sun 3–6pm.

Space Levanella, Montevarchi ☎055.91.901. Located just outside Montevarchi, on a small industrial estate in the Levanella district (on the SS69), this unmarked concrete shed is the busiest of all the factory outlets, as it's stacked with clothes from the ineffably stylish Prada label, as well as items from the scarcely less trendy Jil Sander and Helmut Lang, both of which are now subsidiaries of Prada. Also on sale is a good selection from Miu Miu, Prada's mid-priced diffusion range. Mon–Sat 9.30am–7.30pm, Sun 10am–7pm.

SAN GIOVANNI VALDARNO, midway between Florence and Arezzo, is the most heavily industrialized but also the most rewarding town in the valley. The arcaded Palazzo Comunale is yet another design from Arnolfo di Cambio, who in the thirteenth century was put in charge of fortifying this Florentine town against the citizens of Arezzo. At the back of the palazzo, next to the church of Santa Maria della Grazia, the Museo della Basilica di Santa Maria della Grazia (summer Mon, Tues, Fri & Sat 10am–12.30pm & 4–7pm, Sun 4–7pm; winter opens and closes 30min earlier; €3) in Piazza Masaccio houses a Fra' Angelico *Annunciation* painted for the Convento di Montecarlo, plus a beautiful version of the same subject by his more obscure contemporary, Jacopo del Sellaio. Also on show is a *Madonna and Child with Four Saints*, attributed to Masaccio, who was born here in 1401. His house, the Museo Casa Masaccio at Corso Italia 83, is used for exhibitions, often of top-drawer contemporary art (Bruce Nauman and Cornelia Parker have both had shows here). The Gothic church of San Francesco, at right angles to Santa Maria, is blotched with frescoes as well.

In the Pliocene era the Valdarno was a vast lake, its shores patrolled by troops of prehistoric elephants. Fossil remnants of these colossal beasts are the pride of **MONTEVARCHI**, where they are installed at Via Poggio Bracciolini 36–38 in the Museo Paleontologico (Tues–Sat 10am–noon & 4–6pm, Sun 10am–noon; €3); around 1500 other exhibits keep them company. In the centre of town in Via Isidoro del Lungo, the sacristy of the Collegiata di San Lorenzo has been converted into a small Museo di Arte Sacra (Tues, Thurs & Sat 10am–noon; €2), where the main exhibit is a little chapel covered in ceramics by Andrea della Robbia. In the church there's a reliquary containing one of Tuscany's more desperate holy mementos – water from a spring in a cave where the Holy Family are said to have rested on the flight into Egypt.

This might not seem reason enough to stop on the way to Arezzo; beyond Montevarchi, there's no reason at all, unless, that is, you have time to take a meandering diversion off the SS69 into the southeastern corner of the Chianti hills. If you do, you should arm yourself with a large-scale road map and follow the road to **Mercatale**, then take the turning for Bucine; from this road you can reach the fortified hill-top eyrie of **San Leolino**, which gives fabulous views. From there, head to **Cennina**, where the castle ruins stare across the Arno towards the Pratomagno, then strike west for the highlight of this diversion, the completely unspoiled medieval village of **CIVITELLA**, with its magnificent ruined thirteenth-century castle. From here, it's just 8km to the autostrada, to the southwest of Arezzo.

The Pratomagno route

To maximize the pleasure of the wooded road above the east bank of the Arno, drive to Pontassieve and get onto the N70 towards the Passo della Consuma. The first turning to the right rises to **VALLOMBROSA**, whose abbey is the mother foundation of the Vallombrosan order, established in 1038 by the Florentine Giovanni Gualberto (see p.126). After Giovanni was canonized in 1193 this abbey became extremely influential, and by the fifteenth century it was administering wide tracts of Tuscan territory. Much rebuilt since those days, it now resembles a fortified villa with its high perimeter wall and corner towers and impresses mainly by its location, pillowed against the fir-covered hills. Part of the complex is still occupied by monks, part by a forestry school; neither group welcomes visitors.

Milton stayed at Vallombrosa and in *Paradise Lost* he compared the throng of demons in hell to the "autumn leaves that strow the brooks/In Vallombrosa". Though the forests have dwindled in the intervening centuries, they

AREZZO PROVINCE | From Florence to Arezzo

are still extensive, as you'll appreciate if you drive over the Pratomagno ridge to Poppi (see p.528) through **MONTEMIGNAIO**, where the adjoining hamlet of Castello offers accommodation in the shape of two two-star hotel-restaurants: *Il Castello*, Via Roma 56 (☎0575.542.510, @www.ilcastellodimontemignaio.com; open March 15–Oct 31; ❷), and *Da Corrado*, Via Roma 2 (☎0575.542.166, @www.hoteldacorrado.it; ❸). If you'd like a room somewhere even more remote, head up to the nearby **Passo della Consuma**, where you'll find a couple more two-star hotel-restaurants: the *Miramonti*, Via Consuma 61 (☎0575.830.6566, ⓕ0575.830.6469; ❷), and the *Sbaragli*, Via Consuma 3 (☎0575.830.6500; ❷). For a **walk** through the forests, as good a starting point as any is the tiny resort of **Saltino**, the next village after Vallombrosa along the road to Arezzo. From here paths lead up to the peak of Monte Secchieta, a winter ski resort (also accessible by road from the junction 5km east of Vallombrosa on the road to Montemignaio); the view from the summit is amazing.

Beyond Saltino the terrain opens out, with terraces bordering the road as it snakes down to **REGGELLO**, a diffused and characterless place much praised by connoisseurs of Tuscan olive oil. A kilometre to the south, the Romanesque **Pieve of San Pietro a Cascia** is worth a stop for the **Museo di Arte Sacra "Masaccio"** (Tues & Thurs 3–7pm, Sat & Sun 10am–noon & 3–7pm; €3). Opened to mark the six hundredth anniversary of the birth of Masaccio, who was born in nearby San Giovanni Valdarno in 1401, this tiny museum houses the earliest known work by the artist, the *San Giovenale Triptych*, which was painted in 1422. Having disappeared from public view, the painting was rediscovered in 1961, in the minuscule local church of San Giovenale, from where it was removed to the Pieve after restoration. A ground-floor room is devoted to background information on the triptych, while the other rooms are given over to miscellaneous documents, furnishing and minor artworks, including some from Ghirlandaio's pupils, but in essence this is a gallery devoted to one masterpiece.

More Romanesque architecture appears at **PIAN DI SCÒ**, 10km on, where there's an eleventh-century *pieve*. **CASTELFRANCO DI SOPRA**, 2km farther, was yet another town fortified by Arnolfo di Cambio but the street plan and one gate are virtually the only traces of his handiwork; its most attractive feature is a much restored thirteenth-century *badìa* on the main road. There's one hotel, the two-star *Colombo*, Via Europa 5 (☎055.914.9026; ❷). Another 10km brings you to **LORO CIUFFENNA**, where ranks of new apartments form an unflattering prelude to a small medieval quarter down by the Ciuffenna river; a Romanesque tower and bridge form the core.

The most interesting church in this part of the Arno valley comes a couple of kilometres on, in the hamlet of **GRÓPINA**, which is reached by taking a steep and sharp left turn just outside Loro. Here the parish church of **San Pietro** (daily 8am–noon & 4–7pm) has some of the finest Romanesque carving in Tuscany, dating from the early thirteenth century. The capitals depict knights, fighting animals and various standard motifs, but you'll have to travel a long way to find anything quite like the pulpit, with its knotted columns and rows of alarmed-looking figures with upraised arms.

The last place of any interest before Arezzo is **Castiglion Fibocchi**, whose central patch – now enclosed by light industry (clothing and fur factories, mostly) – has changed little in appearance since the Middle Ages, though no one monument in particular stands out.

Arezzo

Maecenas, the wealthy patron of Horace and Virgil, was born in **AREZZO** and it's still a place with the moneyed touch, even though the economy has taken something of a downturn after the prolonged boom of the latter half of the twentieth century. The revenue comes mostly from its jewellers and goldsmiths, a sector whose importance can be gauged from the fact that the city has the world's largest gold manufacturing plant. Topping up the coffers are the proceeds of Arezzo's antiques industry: in the vicinity of the Piazza Grande there are shops filled with the sort of furniture you put in a vault rather than in your house, and every month the **Fiera Antiquaria** (see box, p.516) turns the piazza into a vast showroom.

Occupying a site that controls the major passes of the central Apennines, Arezzo was one of the most important settlements of the Etruscan federation. It maintained its pre-eminence under Roman rule, and was a prosperous independent republic in the Middle Ages until, in 1289, its Ghibelline

ACCOMMODATION				RESTAURANTS				BARS	
Astoria	E	I Portici	F	Antica Osteria		Il Saraceno	3	Bacco e Arrianna	2
Cavaliere Palace	H	Il Patio	D	L'Agania	4	La Buca di		Fiaschetteria	
Cecco	I	La Foresteria	C	I Tre Bicchieri	8	San Francesco	5	de' Redi	6
Chimera	J	La Toscana	B	Il Cantuccio	9	Le Tastevin	7	La Torre di Gnicche	1
Continentale	G	Ostello Villa Severini	A						

allegiances brought about a catastrophic clash with the Guelph Florentines at Campaldino. Arezzo temporarily recovered from this reversal under the leadership of **Bishop Guido Tarlati**, whose bellicosity eventually earned him excommunication. However, subjugation came about in 1384, when Florence paid the ransom demanded of Arezzo by the conquering army of Louis d'Anjou. When the French departed, the city's paymaster was left in power.

Even as a mortgaged political power, Arezzo continued to be a major cultural force – as it had been since Guido d'Arezzo, the first theorist of musical notation, was born here in the tenth century. Petrarch (1304–74) later brought further prestige to the city, and in the sixteenth century Pietro Aretino and Giorgio Vasari, both Aretines, further bolstered its reputation. Yet it was an outsider who gave Arezzo its greatest monument – **Piero della Francesca**, whose frescoes for the church of San Francesco belong in the same company as Masaccio's cycle in Florence and Michelangelo's in Rome.

Arrival, information and accommodation

The main **tourist office** is on the edge of the **train station** forecourt, on the right as you come out of the station (Mon–Sat 9am–1pm & 3–6.30pm, Sun 9am–1pm; ℡0575.377.678, ⓦwww.apt.arezzo.it); the helpful staff speak English and have masses of information on Arezzo and its province. There are car parks by the train station and the archeological museum, but you'll more easily find spaces in the new car park outside the northern stretch of the city walls (near San Domenico), or in the streets to the south of the rail line, or near Santa Maria delle Grazie. The **post office** is at Via Guido Monaco 34.

Accommodation is not plentiful at any time of year in Arezzo, and almost impossible to come by on the first weekend of every month, owing to the antiques fair; in addition the town is booked solid at the end of August and beginning of September, when the *Concorso Polifonico Guido d'Arezzo* and the *Giostra del Saracino* follow in quick succession. Geared primarily to commercial visitors, Arezzo's hotels are generally rather bland and cheerless – but recently, as the city has begun to make more an effort to market itself to tourists, the accommodation situation has improved a little.

Hotels

Astoria Via Guido Monaco 54 ℡ & ℗0575.24.361. A 32-room two-star, close to the busy Piazza Guido Monaco. Looks shabby from the outside, and many of the rooms could do with an overhaul, but it's central and inexpensive – and has some rooms without private baths, at a discount of around fifty percent. ❹

Cavaliere Palace Via della Madonna del Prato 83 ℡0575.26.836, ⓦwww.cavalierehotels.com. Formerly a one-star, now renamed and rebuilt as a 27-room four-star, this is one of the better hotels in central Arezzo. ❺

Cecco Corso Italia 215 ℡0575.20.986, ℮info@hotelcecco.com. Very central 42-room two-star, above a restaurant of the same name; spacious if slightly institutional in feel. Rooms without private baths cost almost €20 less than the rest. ❷

Chimera Via Vittorio Veneto 46 ℡0575.902.494. Located outside the centre, on a busy main road behind the train station; a big (33 rooms), bland and basic one-star. ❶

Continentale Piazza Guido Monaco 7 ℡0575.20.251, ℮info@hotelcontinentale.com. Large old three-star with restaurant right on the hub of the lower town. Excellent views from the roof terrace, but the rooms are generally characterless. ❹

I Portici Via Roma 18 ℡0575.403.132, ⓦwww .hoteliportici.com. This sizeable town house has recently been converted into a very comfortable four-star hotel, though some might find the nostalgic tone a bit stuffy. ❼

Il Patio Via Cavour 23 ℡0575.401.962, ⓦwww.hotelpatio.it. A small (just seven rooms), welcoming and not overly expensive new four-star, just a minute's stroll from San Francesco. As with *I Portici*, the decor reflects Arezzo's love of antiques, but *Il Patio* wears the style more lightly. ❻

La Foresteria Via Bicchieraia 32 ☎ &
🖷 0575.370.474. The only budget accommodation in central Arezzo, *La Foresteria* comprises a dozen nicely decorated rooms in the former convent of the church of San Pier Piccolo. No credit cards. ❷
La Toscana Via M. Perennio 56 ☎ &
🖷 0575.21.692. One-star with thirteen rooms (plus five more in a *dipendenza*, or annexe) on the main road coming in from the west; rooms without private bathroom are €10 cheaper. ❶

Hostel

Ostello Villa Severi Via Francesco Redi 13
☎ 0575.299.047, 🖰 www.peterpan.it/ostello.htm. Arezzo's excellent hostel occupies an old villa some way north of the town – a fifteen-minute walk from the Duomo past the old cemetery, or take bus #4 from Piazza Guido Monaco by the station. 71 beds, in four-, six- and eight-bed rooms. Reception open 8am–2pm & 5pm–midnight. Open June–Sept, plus Easter weekend, Christmas & New Year; €15 (half-board €27, full board €35).

The Town

There are two distinct parts to Arezzo: the **older quarter**, at the top of the hill, and the businesslike **lower town**. Most of the lower town remains hidden from day-trippers, as it spreads behind the train station and the adjacent bus terminal. From the station forecourt, go straight ahead for Via Guido Monaco, the traffic axis between the upper and lower town – a street that nobody walks along except to shop or to call at the main post office. The parallel **Corso Italia**, now pedestrianized, is the route to take up the hill, and the stretch immediately north of Via Francesco Crispi is also the place to hang out in the evenings; the *passeggiata* crowds – and the bars – thin out towards the top of the climb.

San Francesco – Piero della Francesca's church

Off to the left of the Corso, on Via Cavour, not far from its summit, stands the building everyone comes to Arezzo to see: the basilica of **San Francesco** (summer Mon–Fri 9am–7pm, Sat 9am–6pm, Sun 1–6pm; winter closes Mon–Fri

---

Arezzo festivals

Arezzo's premier folkloric event is the **Giostra del Saraceno**, held in the Piazza Grande on the first Sunday in September. The day starts off with various costumed processions; in the afternoon the action switches to the jousting arena in the piazza. The piazza is the junction of the four quarters of the city and the sides of the square are decked with flags to mark their affiliations. Each quarter is represented by a pair of knights on horseback, who do battle with a wooden effigy of a Saracen king. In one hand it holds a shield marked with point scores, a bit like a darts-board; in the other it has a cat-o'-three-tails which swings round when the shield is hit, necessitating nifty evasive action from the rider. A golden lance is awarded to the highest-scoring rider. In recent years this event has become so popular that reduced versions of the show have been staged in the summer; check at the tourist office for the latest information on dates and ticket availability.

The musical tradition that began with Guido d'Arezzo is kept alive chiefly through the international choral competition that bears his name: the **Concorso Polifonico Guido d'Arezzo**, held in the last week of August. The less ambitious **Pomeriggi Musicali** is a season of free concerts held in various churches, museums and libraries; on average there's one concert a week from mid-January to June. In late June and July the **Arezzo Wave** rock festival hits the Fortezza Medicea.

The **Fiera Antiquaria** takes over the Piazza Grande on the Saturday before the first Sunday of each month. The most expensive stuff is laid out by the Vasari loggia, with cheaper pieces lower down the square and in the side streets. The Roman number-plates in the car parks give you a clue as to what league this is; nothing – not even the old postcards – could be described as a bargain.

6pm, Sat & Sun 5.30pm). Built in the 1320s, the shabby brick basilica earned its renown in the early 1450s, when the Bacci family commissioned **Piero della Francesca** to continue the decoration of the choir. The project had been started by Bicci di Lorenzo, who had painted only the *Evangelists* (in the vault) and part of the *Last Judgement* (on the arch outside the chapel) before he died. For the wall paintings, Piero's patrons nominated a subject with rather fewer dramatic possibilities, but which suited the contemplative personality of the artist perfectly: it inspired a work that carries an emotional charge unsurpassed by any other fresco cycle.

The theme chosen was **The Legend of the True Cross**, a story in which the physical material of the Cross forms the link in the cycle of redemption that begins with humanity's original sin. Starting with the right wall, Piero painted the series in narrative sequence, working continuously until about 1457 – the precise chronology isn't known. However, the episodes are not arranged in narrative sequence, as the artist preferred to arrange them according to the precepts of symmetry: thus the two battle scenes face each other across the chapel, rather than coming where the story dictates. As is always the case with this mystical rationalist painter, smaller-scale symmetries are present in every part of the work: the retinue of the Queen of Sheba appears twice, in mirror-image arrangement, and the face of the queen is exactly the same as the face of the Empress Helena. This orderliness, combined with the pale light and the statuesque quality of the figures, create an atmosphere that's unique to Piero, a sense of each incident as a part of a greater plan.

The literary source for the cycle, the *Golden Legend* by Jacopo de Voragine, is a very convoluted story;

THE LEGEND OF THE TRUE CROSS

1a. Adam announces his death and implores Seth, his son, to seek the "oil of mercy" from the Angel of Eden.

1b. Instead the Angel gives Seth a sprig from the Tree of Knowledge, which is planted in the dead Adam's mouth.

2a. Solomon orders a bridge to be built from a beam fashioned from the tree that grew from Adam's grave. The Queen of Sheba, visiting Solomon, kneels in prayer before the bridge, sensing the holiness of the wood.

2b. The Queen of Sheba foresees that the beam will later be used to crucify a man, and that the death will bring disgrace to the Jews; she tells Solomon of her prophecy.

3. Solomon orders the beam to be buried.

4. The Emperor Constantine has a vision of the Cross, hearing a voice that declares "Under this sign shall you be victorious".

5. Constantine defeats the rival emperor Maxentius, and then is baptized. The figure of Constantine – the first emperor to rule Byzantium – may be a portrait of John Paleologus, the penultimate Byzantine emperor, who had been in Florence in 1439 to attend the Council of Florence.

6. The Levite Judas, under torture, reveals to the servants of St Helena – mother of Constantine – the burial place of the three crosses from Golgotha.

7. The crosses are excavated; the true Cross is recognized when it brings about a man's resurrection. Arezzo – serving as Jerusalem – is shown in the background.

8. The Persian king Chosroes, who had stolen the Cross, is defeated by the Emperor Heraclius. On the right he kneels awaiting execution; behind him is visible the throne into which he had incorporated the Cross.

9. Heraclius returns the Cross to Jerusalem.

10. Isaiah.

11. Jeremiah.

12. The Annunciation.

A €12 ticket gives you a single admission to the following monuments and museums in Arezzo: the Museo Archeologico, the Museo Statale d'Arte Medievale e Moderna, the Casa Vasari and the della Francesca frescoes in San Francesco. The ticket can be bought at any of these four locations, but bear in mind that immediate admission to San Francesco may not be possible (see below).

our plan is a basic guide to the events depicted. The images of the *Annunciation* and two prophets on the window wall (Isaiah – painted by one of Piero's assistants – to the left; Jeremiah to the right) have nothing to do with the legend, but of course relate to the theme of the redemptive significance of the Cross, a point underlined by the cruciform plan of the *Annunciation*, which in turns echoes the plan of the *Vision of Constantine* on the other side of the window, where the tent pole and the rim of the tent form an upright cross.

Damp has badly damaged areas of the chapel and some bits have peeled away, partly as a result of Piero's notoriously slow method of working, but most of the rest has emerged in magnificent condition after a decade's restoration work. You can see the frescoes from the nave of the church, but you need to get closer to really appreciate them, and you're not allowed any closer than the altar steps unless you've bought a **ticket** (€6): visits are limited to 25 people at time (same hours as the church), and to thirty minutes per group. You are encouraged to book tickets in advance by phone or online (☎0575.352.727), although outside the peak summer months you can usually make a reservation in person at the ticket office beside the church, and may not have to wait long before getting in (in winter there's rarely any wait at all). If you want to be certain of getting in at your preferred time, however, reserve a ticket as far in advance as possible.

The Pieve di Santa Maria and Piazza Grande

Farther up the Corso from San Francesco stands one of the finest Romanesque structures in Tuscany, the twelfth-century **Pieve di Santa Maria** (daily: summer 8am–1pm & 3–7pm; winter 8am–noon & 3–6pm). Its arcaded facade, elaborate yet severe, belongs to a type associated more with Pisa and western Tuscany, and is doubly unusual in presenting its front to a fairly narrow street rather than to the town's main square. Dating from the 1210s, the carvings of the months over the portal are an especially lively group. The campanile, known locally as "the tower of the hundred holes", was added in the fourteenth century. The oldest section of the chalky grey **interior** is the raised sanctuary, where the altarpiece is Pietro Lorenzetti's *Madonna and Saints* polyptych, painted in 1320. The unfamiliar saint on the far left, accompanying Matthew, the Baptist and John the Evangelist, is St Donatus, the second bishop of Arezzo, who was martyred in 304. His relics are in the crypt, encased in a beautiful gold and silver bust made in 1346 by local goldsmiths known only as Pietro and Paolo.

The **Piazza Grande**, on the other side of the church, is a handsome public square, laid on an interesting gradient. The *passeggiata* runs out of steam before reaching this altitude, and the piazza really comes alive for the *Fiera Antiquaria* and – more raucously – for September's *Giostra del Saraceno*. A diverting assortment of buildings encloses the space, the wooden balconied apartments on the east side facing the apse of Santa Maria, the Baroque Palazzo dei Tribunali and the **Palazzetto della Fraternità dei Laici**, known for its outstanding portal, and in particular for the relief *Madonna della Misericordia* (1434) and its neighbouring niche statues. These are the work of Bernardo Rossellino, and were added to the earlier Gothic work below, which includes a lunette fresco of the *Pietà* by Spinello Aretino. The lovely arched loggia and cornice across the top of the palace are from yet another era – they date from 1460 and are the work of Giuliano da Settignano. The piazza's northern edge is formed by the arcades of the **Loggia di Vasari**, occupied by shops that in some instances still retain their original stone counters.

On the opposite side of the Pieve, occupying the fourteenth-century Palazzo del Capitano del Popolo, the **Casa-Museo Ivan Bruschi** (Tues–Sun: summer 10am–1pm & 3–7pm; winter 10am–1pm & 2–6pm; €3) commemorates the man who started Arezzo's antiques fair. Bruschi's collection of sculptures, armour, books and miscellaneous *objets d'art* are nicely displayed in a simulated jumble, but it's a museum to leave until you've seen the rest of the city's sights.

The Duomo and around

At the highest point of the town rises the large and unfussy **Duomo** (daily 6.30am–12.30pm & 3–6.30pm), whose harmonious appearance belies the protracted process of its construction. Begun in 1278, it was virtually finished by the start of the sixteenth century, but the campanile dates from 1859 and the facade from 1914.

The church's stained-glass windows, a rarity in Italy, were made around 1520 by Guillaume de Marcillat, an Arezzo-based Frenchman who also contributed some frescoes to San Francesco; they let in so little light that his other contributions to the interior – the paintings on the first three bays of the nave – are virtually impossible to see. Off the left aisle, separated from the nave by a huge screen, the Cappella della Madonna del Conforto has terracottas by the della Robbia family, but the best of the building's artworks lie farther down the aisle. Just beyond the organ is the **tomb of Bishop Guido Tarlati** (died 1327), head of the *comune* of Arezzo during its resurgence in the early fourteenth century; the monument, plated with marble reliefs showing scenes from the militaristic bishop's career, was possibly designed by Giotto. The small fresco nestled against the right side of the tomb is **Piero della Francesca**'s *Magdalene*, his only work in Arezzo outside San Francesco. In the chapel closest to the *Magdalene* lies Pope Gregory X, who died in Arezzo in 1276; a plaque on the wall invites you to consider his remarkable life, which overlapped with the lives of many other remarkable individuals, such as St Thomas Aquinas and St Bonaventure (who both taught him in Paris), St Francis, St Dominic, the Emperor Frederick II, Dante and Marco Polo.

The **Museo Diocesano** (open on request Thurs–Sat 10am–noon), alongside the Duomo, won't make anyone's day, as the restricted opening hours seem to concede, but Arezzo's public park, the **Passeggio del Prato**, which extends from the east end of the Duomo to the Fortezza Medicea, is a good place to take a picnic and gaze down over the town or across the vineyards towards the Casentino. Cosimo I's fortress here was demolished in the eighteenth century, leaving only the ramparts.

Just south of the park and the Duomo, at Vicolo dell'Orto 28, stands the putative birthplace of the poet Petrarch (1304–74), the **Casa del Petrarca** (open on request Mon–Fri 10am–noon & 3–5pm, Sat 10am–noon; free; ☏0575.247.00), rebuilt after its destruction during World War II. It's for literary pilgrims only: all that's open to visitors is the library containing a few manuscripts and a letter signed by the poet.

From San Domenico to the Badía

A short distance in the opposite direction from the Duomo you'll come across the church of **San Domenico** (daily 8.30am–7pm), constructed mostly in the late thirteenth century but with a Gothic campanile. Inside there are tatters of fifteenth- and sixteenth-century frescoes on the walls, while above the high altar hangs a dolorous Crucifix by Cimabue (1260), painted when the artist would have been about 20; it was restored in 2002, with beautiful results.

From here signs point the way to the **Casa Vasari** (Mon & Wed–Sat 8.30am–7.30pm, Sun 8.30am–1pm; €2) at Via XX Settembre 55, designed by the biographer-architect-painter. Born in Arezzo in 1511, Giorgio Vasari was taught to paint by his distant relative Luca Signorelli, and went on to become court painter, architect and general artistic supremo to Cosimo I. His major contribution to Western culture, however, is his *Lives of the Most Excellent Italian Architects, Painters and Sculptors*, the first attempt to relate artists' work to their social context, and a primary source for all histories of the Renaissance. Taking greater pleasure from the products of his imagination than later generations have managed to extract, Vasari frescoed much of his house with portraits and mythological characters, a decorative scheme that makes this one of the brashest domestic interiors in Tuscany. Portraits include his wife as the muse of conjugal love (in the "Chamber of Apollo") and Michelangelo and Andrea del Sarto (in the "Chamber of Fame"). Minor paintings are strewn all over the place, proof that Giorgio was far from the most inept painter of his day.

At the foot of the hill, at Via San Lorentino 8, the fifteenth-century Palazzo Bruni-Ciocchi houses the **Museo d'Arte Medioevale e Moderna** (Tues–Sun 8.30am–7.30pm; €4), containing a collection of paintings by local artists and majolica pieces from the thirteenth to the eighteenth centuries, generously spread over three floors. Highlights are the first floor's medieval and Renaissance paintings by the likes of Spinello Aretino, Luca Signorelli and Bartolomeo della Gatta; devotees of ceramics will revel in the five rooms containing works from Deruta, Gubbio, Faenza and other major Italian centres of production.

If you follow Via Cavour from the Museo d'Arte, a huge Baroque tower soon signals the presence of the hulking **Badia di SS Flora e Lucilla** (Mon–Sat 8am–noon & 4–7pm, Sun 7am–12.30pm). The interior was extensively remodelled by Vasari, who also contributed the monstrous main altarpiece, designed as a tomb monument to the Vasari family. The rarely accessible cloister refectory has a similarly heavy-footed example of Giorgio's work.

The Museo Archeologico and Santa Maria delle Grazie

Nearly all the principal sights are in the upper part of Arezzo. One exception is the **Museo Archeologico** (daily 8.30am–7.30pm; €4), which occupies part of an abandoned Olivetan monastery built into a wall of the town's Roman amphitheatre, to the right of the station at Via Margaritone 10. The remains of the amphitheatre (entrance free) amount to little more than the base of the perimeter wall, largely because Cosimo I used the site as a quarry for the fortress up by the Duomo. More impressive are the museum's marvellously coloured coralline vases; produced here in the first century BC, they show why Arezzo's glassblowers achieved their reputation as consummate craftsmen throughout the Roman world. If you're here out of high season you may not be able to see them, though: low demand means that the museum's sometimes shut for days at a time in winter.

Ten minutes' walk away, south of the city centre at the end of Viale Mecenate, stands Arezzo's most exquisite church, **Santa Maria delle Grazie** (daily 8am–7pm). In the sixth century BC the Etruscans held fertility rites here, beside a spring in the midst of the forest that covered this area. At the instigation of St Bernardino the site was purged of its pagan associations by the blocking of the spring and the construction of the church, which still has a Carmelite convent attached to it. Fronted by a neat little pine-ringed meadow that's flanked by a pair of small arcades, the church is entered through a delicate portico built by Benedetto da Maiano in the 1470s. The church is essentially a single room, containing little more than a few seats and an altarpiece by Parri Spinello, painted on the instructions of St Bernardino; the beautiful marble and terracotta altar that encases it was created by Andrea della Robbia.

Eating and drinking

Arezzo's **restaurants** offer menus to suit every budget, at a generally high standard, and there's good food at a number of the city's bars as well. The busiest **cafés** are around piazzas Guido Monaco, Grande and San Francesco, and along Corso Italia. For ice cream, the first choice is *Il Gelato*, off Corso Italia at Via de' Cenci 24, while for picnic provisions you can't do better than Sbarbacipolle, Via Garibaldi 120.

Restaurants

Antica Osteria L'Agania Via Mazzini 10 ☎0575.25.381. A very good and informal trattoria with welcoming atmosphere and local dishes (special emphasis on truffles and mushrooms in season), at around €35 per head; it draws much of its clientele from the antiques dealers. Closed Mon & a period in June.

I Tre Bicchieri Piazzetta Sopra i Ponti 3–5 ☎0575.265.57. A classy and imaginative restaurant, with a notably extensive wine list. You'll pay in the region of €40–50 per head. Closed Wed.

Il Cantuccio Via Madonna del Prato 76 ☎0575.26.830, ⊛www.il-cantuccio.it. Good-value food served in a pleasant vaulted cellar. The homemade pasta dishes are particularly delicious. Expect to pay in the region of €35 per person. Closed Wed.

Il Saraceno Via Mazzini 6 ☎0575.27.644 ⊛www .ilsaraceno.com. Family-run trattoria, founded in 1946, with a good wine cellar and menus of traditional Aretine specialities (notably duck) at around €35 per head; wood-oven pizzas too. Closed Wed & periods in Jan & July.

La Buca di San Francesco Via San Francesco 1 ☎0575.23.271. Tourist-oriented place next to San Francesco, but not at all bad: it's been in business since 1929, and the interior preserves parts of the old Etruscan-Roman pavement and medieval frescoes. Food is reliable and Tuscan in inspiration, at around €45 per head. Closed Mon evening, Tues & two weeks in July.

Le Tastevin Via de' Cenci ☎0575.28.304. Highly recommended for honest Aretine cuisine at about €30. Music in the piano bar might not be to all tastes, but there are outside tables to which you can escape. Closed Mon, plus a period in Aug.

Bars

Bacco e Arrianna Via Cesalpino 10. A terrific enoteca very close to San Francesco, with delicious food too. Closed Mon.

Fiaschetteria de' Redi Via de' Redi 10. Busy little *osteria* with a superb range of vintages and decent simple meals. Closed Mon.

La Torre di Gnicche Piaggia San Martino 8. Located off the northerneastern corner of the Piazza Grande, this place is perfect for a simple and inexpensive meal, washed down with a glass from its huge selection of local Colli Aretini and other Italian wines. Closed Wed, 1 week in Aug & 2 weeks in Jan.

To Sansepolcro: the Piero trail

Arezzo is the springboard for one of Tuscany's most rewarding art itineraries: the Piero della Francesca trail, which extends east of the city to **Monterchi** and **Sansepolcro** (the artist's birthplace), and continues via Perugia, where you'll find a stunning Piero altarpiece in the main art gallery (see p.558). (The trail then reaches beyond the region covered in this guide, going through Urbino and on to Rimini.) There's no train link between Arezzo and Sansepolcro, the sole rail approach to Sansepolcro being the private FCU Terni–Perugia line. The SITA **bus** company runs seventeen services a day from Arezzo to Sansepolcro, nearly all of which continue to Città di Castello (see p.576) for train connections to Perugia; five stop at Monterchi at convenient times for a visit. Otherwise, the nearest regular stop to Monterchi is Le Ville, 2km to the west, from where the buses veer away through **Anghiari** – a pleasant enough place, but best seen by car. If you don't have your own transport, hitching is a viable alternative, as this is a busy stretch of road. And the route will become even busier with the completion of the highly conspicuous and controversial new autostrada from Arezzo, which – if built according to the present plan – will ruin the landscape around Monterchi.

Monterchi – the Madonna del Parto

The farming village of **MONTERCHI** is 25km east of Arezzo, and for the last few kilometres of the journey the roadsides bear signs for the **Madonna del Parto** – surely the only painting in Tuscany to be signposted as if it were a town. The fresco was painted around 1467 for a cemetery chapel that stands on the outskirts of Monterchi, and remained hidden under plaster for centuries before its rediscovery in 1889 – by which time the *St Lucy* and the *Pietà* that Piero also painted here had both been lost. The Madonna was removed to Sansepolcro after an earthquake damaged the chapel in 1917 but at the insistence of the local *comune* it was brought back here within five years. During World War II they became so worried that some misfortune might befall the fresco that a false wall was constructed to protect it, and since then the Madonna has received the attentions of a number of restorers.

In 1993 the fresco was moved from the cemetery chapel to an ex-primary school on **Via della Reglia**, there to undergo major restoration. Security was the reason given for the switch, but local feeling is that it's more to do with the restoration's sponsors, who are well served by the publicity that goes with the painting – publicity which might be unseemly around a cemetery chapel. There are a few **parking spaces** outside the school, but in summer it's best to park below the village just off the main road, and walk up through the village: the school, as undistinguished a building as it's possible to find in Tuscany, lies on the far side, just outside the old village walls. The painting looks likely to remain in its utilitarian box, despite the mutterings of many who feel its former home is more appropriate. It is the focal point of a permanent **exhibition** (Tues–Sun 9am–1pm & 2–7pm; winter closes 6pm; €3) recounting the technical details of the fresco's restoration, and also that of the San Francesco cycle in Arezzo. The picture is still an object of pilgrimage, and the museum is cleared when local pregnant women come to pray to the Virgin.

Despite the restoration, the colours of the *Madonna del Parto* lack the freshness of the Arezzo cycle, but even bleached to black and white this would be an overwhelming picture: two attendant angels draw back the flap of a small pavilion to reveal the pregnant Virgin, who places her hand on the upper curve of her belly, her eyes downcast as if preoccupied with a foreknowledge of the course of the child's life. Images of the pregnant Mary began to appear in Tuscan art in the 1330s (the first major *Madonna del Parto* was painted for the church of San Francsco di Paola in Florence by Taddeo Gaddi, around 1335), a date which has led Renzo Manetti, a Florentine writer and architect, to propose that these pictures should be read as references to a "hidden truth" that was known only to members of the Knights Templar. Proceeding from the facts that the Templars were suppressed in 1312 and that Florence was a major centre for the [...] etti argues that della Francesca's fresco (almost the last *Madonna del P[...]* painted) is perhaps indicative of his Templar sympathies. Others have c[...] his theory as just another exercise in conspiratorial mumbo-jumbo, al[...] lines of the *Da Vinci Code*. Whether this Madonna del Parto is a piece of propaganda or what it plainly appears to be – a meditation on the myst[...] the Incarnation – it's incontestable that few other artists of the Renaissance produced anything comparable to its beautiful gravity.

Anghiari and Caprese Michelangelo

Most buses from Arezzo to Sansepolcro call at **ANGHIARI**, an agricultural and textile-producing hill-town set amid fields of sunflowers and tobacco, with a lucrative side-line in furniture restoration – the town has a renowned training centre for specialists in the craft, and hosts an antiques fair on the third Sunday of each month, as well as a huge annual crafts market in late April. Anghiari's diminutive historic centre of narrow streets, stepped alleyways and tunnels commands a fine view across the upper Tiber towards Sansepolcro. It was on this ground, on June 29, 1440, that the Florentine army defeated the Milanese troops of Filippo Maria Visconti, an engagement that became the subject of perhaps the most famous lost artwork of the Renaissance: Leonardo da Vinci's fresco in Florence's Palazzo Vecchio. There's a small exhibition relating to the battle, in the Palazzo del Marzocco on Piazza Mameli (April–Oct Mon–Sat 9am–1pm & 3–7pm, Sun 9.30–1.30pm & 2.30–7pm; Nov–March Fri–Sun 9am–1pm & 3–6pm; €2). On the same piazza, the imposing Palazzo Taglieschi is home to the **Museo Statale** (Tues–Sat 9am–6.30pm, Sun 9am–12.30pm; €2), a well-displayed collection of mostly unexceptional artworks and domestic items, but with one outstanding piece: a painted wooden *Madonna* by Jacopo della Quercia. The Child that was once perched on her knee has been displayed separately since the sculpture was restored, as the restorers believe it may not have been carved at the same time.

Michelangelo, effectively Leonardo's competitor in the decoration of the Palazzo Vecchio, was born 17km north of Anghiari in the place that now carries the name **CAPRESE MICHELANGELO**; it was just plain Caprese before being renamed in honour of the prodigious son of the town's chief magistrate and his wife. The ancient village is perched high on a cliff overlooking the car park, bus stop (with regular services from Anghiari) and the two-star *Buca di Michelangelo* **hotel-restaurant** (☎0575.793.921, ⓦwww.bucadimichelangelo. it; ❸). A stepped path rises from here through cypresses and allotments to the arched gateway. The castle and Michelangelo's supposed birthplace, the Casa del Podestà, have been converted into a **Museo Michelangiolesco** (daily: summer 9.30am–6.30pm; winter closes 4pm; €3); a few bits of Renaissance furniture and a load of plaster casts create the undernourishing experience that's typical of these shrines to great Tuscan artists.

The best place to eat hereabouts is in nearby Alpe Faggeta, where the *Fonte della Galletta* **restaurant** offers excellent Tuscan food (with the emphasis on local funghi) at around €25 a head (July & Aug open daily; April–June & Sept–Dec closed Tues; Jan–March closed Mon–Thurs). It forms part of the three-star hotel of the same name, which has a lovely hilltop woodland setting (☎0575.793.925, ⓦwww.fontedellagalletta.it; ❸). In the nearby hamlet of Fragaiolo you'll find the *Michelangelo* **hostel** (☎0575.792.092, Ⓕ0575.793.994; €13; June 5–Sept 30).

There are some excellent **walks** in the surrounding hills. The best starts a short distance to the north of Caprese: follow the plunging road to Lama (2km),

Sansepolcro

The SITA bus from Arezzo takes an hour to get to **SANSEPOLCRO**, an unassuming place that makes its way in the world as a manufacturer of lace and, more lucratively, pasta. If the walled *centro storico* within the industrial and commercial belt were a bit more substantial it could make a lot more money out of tourism; as it is, thousands of people come here each year to see **Piero della Francesca**'s *Resurrection*, then leave a couple of hours later. There really isn't much more to the place than these pictures, but it's a relaxing and good-looking small town, and has a couple of fine restaurants to complete the day.

Born here at some time around 1420, Piero spent much of his life in the isolation of what was then the village of Borgo San Sepolcro; a three-year sojourn in Florence was probably his longest continuous absence. Patrons in Ferrara, Rome and Urbino called upon his services, even though his creative process was so painstaking that on one occasion his father had to apologize to a client for Piero's slowness. He returned to Sansepolcro in the 1470s, having abandoned painting as his eyesight failed. Most of his last twenty years were devoted to working on his treatises *On Perspective in Painting* and *On the Five Regular Bodies*, in which he propounded the geometrical rules that determine all accurate representation of the world, and extolled the human form as the exemplar of perfect proportion.

The Museo Civico

The **Museo Civico** is at Via Niccolò Aggiunti 65 (daily: June–Sept 9am–1.30pm & 2.30–7.30pm; Oct–April 9.30am–1pm & 2.30–6pm; €6.20), the road that emerges from the town walls right by the bus station. The museum entrance is on the main square. Minor works include two panels by Matteo di Giovanni that used to flank della Francesca's *Baptism* (now in London's National Gallery), a good *Annunciation* by Santi di Tito and a painted standard by Signorelli, who was one of his pupils.

A couple of minor della Francesca paintings are hung in the vicinity of the **Madonna della Misericordia**, Piero's earliest known painting and the epitome of his graceful solemnity. It was created in the 1440s, soon after he had been made a member of Sansepolcro's governing council, a position he was to hold for the rest of his life. Tiny panels surround the central image of the Madonna, a conventional and antiquated format that was specified by his patrons, the charitable Compagnia della Misericordia. There's no conventional fragility about this Madonna, though: compassionate and all-capable, she protects her worshippers with a cape as solid as a wall. The hooded man at her feet is wearing the uniform of the Misericordia, a sinister garb still worn by members of the modern Misericordia when bearing a body to a funeral.

The **Resurrection**, in the next room, was painted for the adjoining town hall, probably in the early 1450s, and moved here in the sixteenth century. Aldous Huxley once dubbed this "the greatest painting in the world", a piece of hyperbole that may well have saved the painting from obliteration. In 1944 the British Eighth Army was ordered to bombard Sansepolcro, but an officer recalled Huxley's article and delayed the attack in the hope that the Germans would withdraw – which they did. Much of the picture's power comes from its unique emphasis on the Resurrection as a physical event: muscular and implacable, Christ steps onto the edge of the tomb – banner in hand – as if it were the rampart of a conquered city. One of the soldiers in the foreground places his hand on his eyes, a gesture that might be read as simple weariness or the despair of the vanquished heathen. The strange landscape in the background – with leafless trees on one side and reborn foliage on the other – was the starting point for Kenneth Clark's description, which pinpoints a pre-Christian strand to the painting's significance: "This country god, who rises in the grey light while humanity is asleep, has been worshipped ever since man first knew that the seed is not dead in the winter earth, but will force its way upwards through an iron crust."

Everything else here tends to pall alongside the Pieros, but the museum does have a fine double-sided processional banner painted by Luca Signorelli, and it's difficult not to get hooked by Pontormo's sadistic *Martyrdom of St Quentin*, which gives special meaning to the word "fingernails". In the basement the cathedral's treasury is on show, along with a small archeological collection, and on the top floor there's a display of minor frescoes.

The Duomo and San Lorenzo

Other art treasures are to be found round the corner from the Museo Civico in the Romanesque-Gothic **Duomo** (daily 7.30am–noon & 3.30–6.30pm). The main feature of the plain facade is a rose window that's glazed with thin panels of alabaster, as are the other external windows, giving the interior a pleasantly warm gloom. Inside, the chapel to the left of the chancel houses a mighty tenth-century *Volto Santo*, depicting Christ as a robed patriarch. (The crown and gown with which this Crucifix is dressed for November's Feast of the Redeemer are usually on show in the Museo Civico.) Nearby, on the wall of the left aisle, hangs an *Ascension* by Perugino, restored in 1997.

The church of **San Lorenzo** (daily 9am–1pm & 3–7pm; shorter hours in winter), on Via Santa Croce, has as its main altarpiece a *Deposition* by the Mannerist painter Rosso Fiorentino, painted within half a century of della Francesca's last works but seeming to belong to another world.

Practicalities

The last **bus** back to Arezzo leaves at around 7.20pm, the last to Città di Castello (see p.576) at around 9.25pm. If you decide to stay, you should be able to find space in at least one of the town's half-dozen **hotels**. Top recommendation is the three-star ⚜ *Fiorentino*, which has been at Via Luca Pacioli 60 since 1807 (☏0575.740.350, ⓦwww.albergofiorentino.com; ❷); the rooms are small and functional, but the hotel has friendly owners, its prices are low, its central location cannot be beaten (the other three-stars are all outside the walled centre), and it has a very good **restaurant** (closed Fri & 3 weeks in July), in which you can expect to pay around €35. Another excellent place to eat is the family-run ⚜ *Da Ventura*, Via Niccolò Aggiunti 30 (☏0575.742.560, ⓕ0575.759.500; closed Sun eve & Mon, plus Aug & 2 weeks in Jan), which is in the same price range as the *Fiorentino*; the seven two-star rooms above the restaurant are the cheapest in town (❶). *Pizzerie* and bars are clustered in Viale A. Diaz, while the best **food shop** is the Enogastronomia, Via Pacioli 44, a treasure trove of mushrooms, truffles, cheeses and wines.

Just about the only time you'll have difficulty in finding a room is the second Sunday in September, the date of the **Palio della Balestra**, the return leg of the crossbow competition against the archers of Gubbio (see p.582). The shoot-out is preceded by some very flashy flag-hurling, whose practitioners – clad in costumes inspired by Piero's paintings – show off their skills at various other times of the year as well. For details, call in at the **tourist office** on Piazza

Garibaldi (daily: April–Oct 9.30am–noon & 2–7pm; Nov–March 10am–noon & 2–6pm; ☎0575.730.231, ⓦwww.sansepolcro.net), two minutes' walk from the museum.

North of Arezzo: the Casentino

North of Arezzo, beyond the city's textile factories, lies the lush upper valley of the Arno, a thoroughly agricultural area known as the **Casentino**, whose unshowy little towns see few tourists, even though a large part of the area has now been designated a national park, and efforts are being made to direct visitors towards the various museums dedicated to the traditions of the Casentino (see box below). From Bibbiena to Pratovecchio the valley is a broad green dish, ruffled by low hills and bracketed by the peaks of the Pratomagno on one side and on the other by the ridge between the Arno and the Tiber. Thick woodland of oak, beech and pine covers much of the upper slopes, the remnant of the forest that used to coat much of the Casentino. During the Medici centuries the timber from here supplied the shipyards of Pisa, Livorno and Genoa, as well as the building sites of Tuscany.

Florence did not always have territorial rights in this region. From the eleventh century the northern part of the Casentino was ruled by the **Guidi** dynasty of Poppi, who kept control from a string of castles – their ruins still litter the hills. In the Middle Ages Arezzo, landlord of the southern Casentino, brawled constantly with Florence for possession of this lucrative valley. After Florence bested the Aretines at the battle of Campaldino (see p.529), the traditionally Ghibelline Guidi counts recognized the authority of the Guelph victors, and were in return allowed to maintain their power base here, though within a century or so the Florentines had ousted them completely. The seclusion of the higher ground fostered a strong monastic tradition as well, and the communities at **Camáldoli** and at **La Verna** continue to be important centres for their respective orders.

By **public transport**, the best target for a day-trip from Arezzo is **Poppi**; it's connected to the city by bus and by the private LFI **train** line which shares the state FS station in Arezzo. There are fourteen trains daily (five on Sun, when

---

The EcoMuseo del Casentino

The Casentino is littered with tiny museums, which together are referred to as the EcoMuseo del Casentino – the Casentino Environmental Museum. Usually consisting of just a couple of rooms of tools, furniture and photographs, and in several cases open only for a few hours at the weekend (check out ⓦwww.ecomuseo.casentino.toscana.it for full details), none of them is likely to make a rewarding target for a day's excursion, but all are worth at least a look if you happen to be passing by. The list is as follows:

Capolona: Museo dell'Aqua (water museum)
Castel Fococagno: Centro di Documentazione Rurale (centre for rural heritage)
Castel San Niccolò: Museo della Civiltà Castellana (museum of castle heritage)
Cetica: Museo del Carbonaio (charcoal burners' museum)
Chitignano: Museo del Contrabbando e Polvere da Sparo (museum of gunpowder and smuggling)
Stia: Museo dello Sci (skiing) and Museo del Bosco e della Montagna (museum of forests and mountains)
Subbiano: Museo della Civiltà Contadina (museum of rural culture)

services may be replaced by a bus): journey time is 55 minutes. To strike into the hills and to visit the monasteries of La Verna and Camaldoli really requires a car, unless you want to stay overnight; buses do run from Bibbiena train station (see below) to Badia Prataglia and Camáldoli, but they are too infrequent to make a round trip feasible in a day.

Bibbiena

The chief commercial town of the Casentino is **BIBBIENA**, a place swathed in straggling development, much of it connected with tobacco production. In the moderately attractive innermost quarter, the main sight is the church of **San Lorenzo**, a fifteenth-century building that contains a fair quantity of terracotta from the della Robbia workshops. Up the top end of town, close to Piazza Tarlati – its name a sign of its links with Arezzo (see p.514) – the oddly shaped church of **SS Ippolito e Donato** has a fine altarpiece by Bicci di Lorenzo. Once you've seen these, there's no reason to hang around. The town does have a use, however, as a public transport link to the national park. From Monday to Saturday there are eight **buses** daily to Badia Prataglia and four to Camáldoli from outside the train station. Three buses also run to Chiusi Verna, the nearest stop to the monastery of La Verna, half an hour's walk away.

Parco Nazionale delle Foreste Casentinesi

One of Italy's newest national parks, the **Parco Nazionale delle Foreste Casentinesi** (ⓦ www.parks.it/parco.nazionale.for.casentinesi) encompasses a vast area that spans Tuscany and Emilia-Romagna, and has been created to conserve the region's terrain and wildlife, as well as the historic monuments of La Verna and Camáldoli. Much money and effort is being put into promoting the park, so there's plenty of literature, maps and pamphlets available from local tourist offices. Of particular help is the *Servizi Turistico Alberghieri* pamphlet, which lists all accommodation within the park, including many *agriturismo* possibilities.

The tourist office in Arezzo (see p.515) makes a good place to start if you want to plan a trip, but the park **headquarters** is in Pratovecchio, at Via G. Brocchi 7 (Mon–Thurs 8am–1pm & 3–5pm, Fri 8am–1pm; ☏0575.50.301). Within Tuscany there are other **visitor centres**: at Parco Martiri della Libertà 21 (☏0575.532.098) in Chiusi della Verna (near La Verna), at Via del Borgo 12 (☏055.837.5125) in Castagno d'Andrea (7km southeast of San Godenzo, in the Mugello), at Parco del Lago (☏055.835.1202) in Londa (also in the Mugello, 7km southeast of Dicomano) and at Via Nazionale 14a (☏0575.559.477) in Badia Prataglia. The Badia Prataglia centre is open virtually all year, whereas the others are open only in spring and summer.

Though you get good views from the roads between these villages and over the border into Emilia-Romagna, to get to grips with the wilderness you need to **walk**. The forests are criss-crossed by dozens of paths and tracks, most of them marked on the SELCA 1:25,000 map *Carta Escursionistica-Parco Nazionale delle Foreste Casentinesi, Monte Falterona, Campigna*, which is available from the park centres and local bookshops. For less ambitious walkers, there are nine specially marked *Sentieri natura* (nature trails), each of which can comfortably be tackled in a short day. Four of these start in Tuscany: **Trail 3**, *La faggeta*, which begins in Badia Prataglia and follows a pretty valley through an ancient beech wood; **Trail 4**, *Alberi e bosco*, which starts near the Camáldoli monastery and wends through the surrounding woods; **Trail 7**, *Natura, storia e spiritualità sul monte di San Francesco*, which winds around Monte della Verna from Chiusi della Verna; and **Trail 8**, *La civiltà del castagno*, a walk that begins at Castagno d'Andrea and is designed to illuminate the crucial role played by the oak chestnut (*castagno*) in the rural economy of this region.

La Verna

In 1213 a pious member of the Guidi clan, Count Orlando, donated to **St Francis** a plot of land at **LA VERNA** (ⓦ www.santuariodellaverna.com), 23km east of Bibbiena (just inside the modern boundaries of the national park). It was at this hermitage, on September 14, 1224, that Francis received the stigmata from a vision of the crucified Christ, a badge of sanctity never previously bestowed.

Francis's mountain-top sanctuary grew into a monastic village, whose ten chapels are connected by a network of corridors, cloisters, dormitories and stone pathways. Thousands of pilgrims come here annually, some of them staying in the guesthouse adjoining the monks' quarters, most coming to pay an hour's homage at the site of the miracle. A few visitors make the climb chiefly to see the magnificent ceramics by **Andrea della Robbia**, but unlike at the basilica at Assisi, secular sightseers don't obscure the purpose of the place. The sanctuary is open every day from 6am to 8.30pm, though in winter the road is sometimes closed by snow.

Relics of the saint – his walking stick, belt, drinking glass – are displayed in the fifteenth-century **basilica**, where there's a glorious *Ascension* by della Robbia, whose other masterpieces are the focal points of the Chiesa delle Stimmate (built on the spot where Francis received the stigmata) and the Cappella di Santa Maria degli Angeli. Halfway along the corridor leading to the former – a walkway painted with modern scenes of the story of St Francis – a small door opens into a gash in the crag, where Francis used to sleep. (According to Franciscan orthodoxy, the rocks at La Verna split apart at the moment of Christ's death.) The route also passes the marginally more comfortable cell in which St Anthony of Padua stayed in 1230. The Sasso Spicco, reached by a flight of steps near the corridor, was Francis's place of meditation.

A path through the forest above the sanctuary leads to the summit of **La Penna** (1283m), from where there's a panorama of the Casentino meadows in one direction and the savage serrations of the Apennines in the other. The drive from La Verna to Sansepolcro is a fabulous descent into the upper Tiber valley; the valley itself, however, is a mess of light industry and quarries.

Poppi

POPPI, 6km north of Bibbiena and plainly visible from there, is sited high above the bus and train terminals. If you emerge at these, in the modern lower suburb of Ponte a Poppi, follow Via Dante Alighieri, a cobbled short-cut which leads to the upper town in ten minutes' walk.

The old town is not much more than a couple of tiny squares and a narrow arcaded main street (Via Cavour for much of its length), but it is lent a monumental aspect by the Casentino's chief landmark, the **Castello dei Conti Guidi** (March 15–June 30 & Sept 1–Oct 31 daily 10am–6pm; July & Aug daily 10am–7pm; rest of year Thurs–Sun 10am–5pm; €4). Built for the Guidi lords in the 1270s, its design is based closely on Florence's Palazzo Vecchio and it's likely that Arnolfo di Cambio was one of the architects here as well. The deep courtyard, with its wooden landings and beautiful staircases, is the most attractive bit of secular architecture in the Casentino – the stone caryatid at the head of the stairs is a portrait of Count Simone di Battifolle, for whom the castle was built, and whose ghost is said to haunt the place. In the cellars there's a display on warfare and fortifications in the era of the Guidi, featuring a teeming model of the battle of Campaldino (see opposite), plus a dismembered knight under the floorboards for added impact. Upstairs, a fine old library has changing displays

△ Poppi emerging from morning mist

of books and manuscripts, and the top-floor chapel is frescoed with scenes from the life of the Virgin, John the Baptist and John the Evangelist, painted in the 1330s by Taddeo Gaddi. You get a fine view from the windows on this storey, but the best vantage point is the summit of the tower, a 104-step ascent, for which there's an extra €2 charge.

At the upper end of Via Cavour stands the domed **Oratorio del Madonna contro il Morbo**, raised in the sixteenth century to give thanks to Mary for – as the name tells you – delivering the town from plague. At its lower end, the street climaxes at the magnificent twelfth-century **Badia di San Fedele** (daily 10am–noon & 3–7pm), which contains an array of at least competent paintings by some obscure sixteenth-century artists, and the splendid reliquary bust of St Torello, a Vallombrosan monk who was born in Poppi in 1202 and spent the last six decades of his life immured in a cell here.

At Piazza della Repubblica 6, right by the castle, is the town's lone **hotel**, the very pleasant and inexpensive three-star *Casentino* (T 0575.529.090, W www .albergocasentino.it; ❷), with a nice courtyard garden, a bar and a **restaurant** (closed Wed) that's very popular with locals. Should it be full or shut on the night you're in town, you can get a good meal at the nearby *Antica Cantina*, Via Lapucci 2 (closed Mon).

A short distance north of Poppi, where the road splits, is the site of the **Battle of Campaldino**, where on June 11, 1289 the Florentine Guelphs defeated the Arezzo Ghibellines to establish Florence's pre-eminence in the power struggles of Tuscany. Warfare in Italy during this era was chiefly conducted by relatively small companies of hired troops, who would typically hold a town to ransom and then, maybe after a bit of skirmishing, depart with their cash. Pitched battles on the scale of Campaldino were a rarity: some 22,000 men fought here, and nearly 2000 of them were killed. One who survived was Dante, then 24 years old. A column right on the junction marks the battle site.

Badia Prataglia

BADIA PRATAGLIA (ⓦ www.badiaprataglia.com), 12km northeast of Bibbiena and 10km east of Camáldoli, has no great attractions in itself, other than its Romanesque parish church, but it's a good base for walking in the Parco Nazionale (see p.527), as it marks the starting point of several trails, has one of the park's main visitor centres, and has plentiful accommodation (though many hotels here are closed in November and December). The cheapest **hotel** is the one-star *La Quercia*, Via Andria 20 (ⓣ 0575.559.097; ❶); two-stars include the *Giardino*, Via Nazionale 15 (ⓣ 0575.559.016, ⓔ hotelgiardino@tin.it; ❷), the *Bellavista*, Via Nazionale 34 (ⓣ 0575.559.011, ⓔ bellavista@badiaprataglia.com; ❷), and *La Torre*, Via Sassopiano 41 (ⓣ 0575.559.005; ❷). The most comfortable option is the three-star *Bosco Verde*, Via Nazionale 8/10 (ⓣ 0575.559.017, ⓔ hotel.boscoverde@badiaprataglia.it; ❸). There is also a **hostel**, the *Casanova* (ⓣ 0575.559.320; July–Oct).

Camáldoli

One of the best bases for the national park is **CAMÁLDOLI**, just over 15km northeast of Poppi, where in 1012 St Romualdo (aka St Rumbold) founded an especially ascetic order of the Benedictines. Notwithstanding the severity of its order, this sylvan retreat became a favourite with non-monastic penitents, so much so that a second site was opened up to accommodate visitors and to administer the woodlands that Romualdo had been granted. This lower complex has been much rebuilt and the only point of interest is its sixteenth-century pharmacy, which now sells herbal products.

On summer weekends lots of people come out here for a postprandial shop followed by a stroll through the forest up to the **Eremo**, the more fundamentalist wing of the monastery – which is around 3km away, up the mountain. These days both men and women can visit, but no one is allowed near the living quarters. More strenuous walks are possible from the Eremo (the country to the north is very wild), or from Camáldoli village itself – paths worth considering are those to Badia Prataglia (to the east) and Poggio Muschioso (to the west).

There are two one-star **hotels**, the *Camáldoli*, Via Camaldoli 13 (ⓣ 0575.556.019, ⓕ 0575.556.073; ❶), and *La Foresta*, Via Camáldoli 5 (ⓣ & ⓕ 0575.556.015; ❶) – the latter has some even cheaper rooms without private bathroom, and a decent **restaurant** (closed Wed). For more comfort, there's the three-star *Il Rustichello*, Via del Corniolo 14 (ⓣ 0575.556.020, ⓕ 0575.556.046; ❸). In the nearby hamlet of Pucini you'll find the *Parco Pucini* **campsite** (ⓣ 0575.556.006; June–Sept).

Pratovecchio and Stia

PRATOVECCHIO, the birthplace of Paolo Uccello, retains some old arcaded streets, but the major attractions are outside the town, on a narrow little lane to the west of the main road. **Pieve di Romena**, though patched up a few times since its foundation in the twelfth century, is a wonderfully preserved Romanesque church, with splendid capitals and a beehive-shaped sacristy. An inscription on the first column to the right identifies the sculptor as the parish priest, Albericus; on the second pillar on the left another states that was completed during a famine in 1152. Close by are the precarious intimidating ruins of the **Castello di Romena** (closed to the public), but the Guidi counts and once the mightiest castle in the Casentino. Dante was guest here, and in the *Inferno* he mentions one of its former tenants, Adamo da Brescia, whose counterfeit coins wreaked such havoc with the local economy that the enraged Florentines roasted him alive. If you're in town, be certain to drop into *L'Osteria di Giovanni*, Via Roma 57 (closed Tues): Giovanni's speciality, a sandwich made from local ham smoked over a fire of juniper wood, makes a delicious snack.

The LFI rail line finishes 2km on at **STIA**, the nearest town to the source of the Arno, which rises to the north on Monte Falterona. The hills around Stia are dotted with natural springs, and in the town's park – the Parco del Palagio Fiorentino – a modern spa complex has been built around the Fonte di Calcedonia, a long-established source that nowadays provides one of Italy's best-known bottled mineral waters. The porticoed Piazza Tanucci is the heart (and summit) of the medieval town, where the steep roofs give the place an alpine feel. Stia's chief monument, the Romanesque **Santa Maria della Assunta**, houses a *Madonna* by Andrea della Robbia and a triptych by Bicci di Lorenzo. Stia has a couple of reasonably priced **hotels**: the three-star *Falterona*, on Piazza Tanucci (☎0575.550.4569; ✉albergofalternoa@technet.it; ❸), and the two-star *Foresta*, Via Roma 27 (☎0575.550.650; ❸), which has a few doubles without private bathroom, at a discount of around €10. The *Falterona* has a decent restaurant.

At Stia the road divides: to the west of Monte Falterona one branch passes another Guidi fortress and the frescoed church of Santa Maria delle Grazie on its way to the Sieve valley (see p.233); the other, to the east, crosses the Passo la Calla then drops down into Emilia-Romagna.

South of Arezzo: the Valdichiana

Travelling south from Arezzo you enter the **Valdichiana**, prosperous agricultural country that nurtures the Chianina breed of cattle, source of the much prized Florentine *bistecca*. As with the Maremma, this former swampland was first drained by the Etruscans, whose work was allowed to unravel in medieval times, when the encroaching marshes drove the farmers of the region back up to the hill-towns. Only in the nineteenth century, with the reclamation schemes of the Lorraine dukes of Tuscany, did the Valdichiana become fertile again. It's an underwhelming landscape but its flatness does at least mean that the towns on its flanks – of which **Cortona** is the most inspiring – have very long sight-lines.

In contrast to the Casentino, public transport is quite good. Frequent Rome-bound trains from Florence and Arezzo run down the valley, most of them stopping at Camucia or Teróntola (or both), the access points for Cortona. Buses from Arezzo serve the intervening villages, while services from Cortona cover routes across the valley.

Cortona

From the valley floor, a five-kilometre road winds up through terraces of vines and olives to the hill-town of **CORTONA**, whose heights survey a vast domain: the Valdichiana stretching westwards, with Lago Trasimeno visible over the low

RESTAURANTS

Dardano	1
Fufluns	5
Il Falconiere	7
La Grotta	3
Osteria del Teatro	6
Preludio	11
Tonino	2

BARS AND CAFÉS

Caffè degli Artisti	8
Caffè del Teatro	2
Caffè-Enoteca La Saletta	9
Route 66	10
Taverna Pane e Vino	4

Sabrina	B
San Luca	F
San Michele	D
Villa Marsili	G

100 m

Cittá di Cas

Cittá di Cas

Cittá di Castello

▶ S. Maria del Calcinaio, Camucia & Teróntola

▶ S. Maria del Calcinaio & SS71

▶ S. Maria del Calcinaio, Camucia & Teróntola

hills to the south. A scattering of Etruscan tombs aside, it is the medieval period that dominates the steep streets of Cortona: limitations of space have confined almost all later development to the lower suburb of Camucia, which is where the approach road begins. Even without its monuments and art treasures, this would be a good place to rest up, with decent hotels, excellent restaurants and an amazing view at night, with the villages of southern Tuscany twinkling like ships' lights on a dark sea. In recent years Cortona's tourist traffic has increased markedly, in the wake of Frances Mayes' *Under the Tuscan Sun* and *Bella Tuscany*, books that continue to entice coachloads of her (mainly American) readers to the place where Mayes realized the ex-pat dream of the good life in the land of quirky and life-affirming Latins. Accordingly, if you're thinking of visiting any time between Easter and late September, you'd be well advised to book your accommodation in advance.

Folklore has it that Cortona was founded by Dardanus, later to establish the city of Troy and give his name to the Dardanelles. Whatever its precise origins, there was already a sizeable Umbrian settlement here when the **Etruscans** took over in the eighth century BC. About four hundred years later it passed to the **Romans** and remained a significant Roman centre until its destruction by the Goths. By the eleventh century it had become a free *comune*, constantly at loggerheads with Perugia and Arezzo; in 1258 the **Aretines** destroyed Cortona, but the town soon revived under the patronage of Siena. It changed hands yet again at the start of the fifteenth century, when it was appropriated by the Kingdom of Naples and then sold off to the **Florentines**, who never let go.

Arrival, information and accommodation

Cortona is easily visited as a day-trip from Arezzo, but in most ways it's the more pleasant of the two in which to spend the night. There are hourly LFI **buses** between the two towns, and stopping **trains** from Arezzo call at Camucia-Cortona station 6km away, from where a shuttle (roughly every 30min) takes ten minutes to run up to the old town; buy tickets at the station bar. The fast Florence–Rome trains stop at Teróntola, 10km south, which is also served by a shuttle roughly every hour (25 minutes to Cortona's Piazza Garibaldi); Teróntola is the station to get off at if you are approaching from Umbria. The centre is closed to traffic, so if you're driving you should use one of the free car parks on the periphery: in Piazza del Mercato; in Piazza Mazzini by Porta Colonia; on Viale Cesari Battisti; or in front of Santa Margherita below the Fortezza.

The **tourist office** at Via Nazionale 42 (May–Sept Mon–Sat 9am–1pm & 3–7pm, Sun 9am–1pm; Oct–April Mon–Fri 9am–1pm & 3–6pm, Sat 9am–1pm; ☎0575.630.352, ⓦwww.cortonaweb.net) can provide leaflets and help out with accommodation. There's a **hostel** and half-a-dozen **hotels** in the historic centre, as well as some upmarket options out of town.

Hotels

Athens Via S. Antonio 12 ☎0575.630.508, ⓕ0575.604.457. This 22-room one-star is the town's one budget option, other than the hostel (see overleaf). Closed in winter. ❶

Il Falconiere San Martino a Bocena ☎0575.612.679, ⓦwww.ilfalconiere.com. Located 3km away on the SS71 towards Arezzo, this intimate four-star has nineteen rooms, all of them beautifully presented (some frescoed), and two swimming pools: one in the luscious garden, the other amid the hotel's vineyards and olive groves. The restaurant is justly celebrated, and like several other top-rank Tuscan hotel-restaurants, the *Falconiere* offers residential cookery courses. Doubles start at a little under€300 and go up to €420. ❾

Italia Via Ghibellina 5 ☎0575.630.254, ⓦwww .planhotel.com/hitalia. A decent three-star, occupying a rather briskly renovated fifteenth-century house, with 26 rooms and a panoramic terrace. It's not the most attractive hotel in Cortona, but the location – very near Piazza della Repubblica

– makes the price more than reasonable. ❹
Sabrina Via Roma 37 ☎0575.630.397,
✉info@cortonastorica.com. With just eight rooms,
Cortona's other three-star is considerably smaller
than its rival, the nearby *Italia*, and is a shade
cheaper as well. ❸
San Luca Piazza Garibaldi 2 ☎0575.630.460,
ⓦwww.sanlucacortona.com. The four-star *San
Luca* is a charmless sixty-bedroom modern building, but it's next door to a good restaurant and
many of its rooms have lovely views over the Valdichiana. Its prices are low for a four-star too. ❹

🏃 **San Michele** Via Guelfa 15
☎0575.604.348, ⓦwww.hotelsanmichele
.net. The most luxurious in-town choice, this handsome fifty-room four-star has been converted from
a rambling medieval town house. ❺

Villa Marsili Via Cesare Battisti 13
☎0575.605.252, ⓦ www.villamarsili.net. Situated a short distance down the slope from Piazza
Garibaldi, this capacious four-star – occupying an
eighteenth-century villa – looks unexceptional from
the outside, but the rooms are nicely fitted out, and
command a very photogenic view of the valley. ❻

Hostel
Ostello San Marco Via G. Maffei 57
☎0575.601.765, ⓦwww.cortonahostel.com. Clean
and spacious HI hostel situated in the heart of the
town in an old monastery, with fantastic views from
the dormitories and friendly management. Dorm beds
€12; doubles and family rooms available. Open mid-
March to mid-Oct; reception open daily 7–10am &
3.30pm–midnight.

The Town
The bus terminus is in **Piazza Garibaldi**, from where the only horizontal
street in town (and thus the venue for the *passeggiata*), Via Nazionale, leads into
Piazza della Repubblica, where the tall staircase of the squat, castellated Palazzo
del Comune is the grandstand from which the *ragazzi* appraise the world as it
goes by. The Saturday market flows through neighbouring **Piazza Signorelli**
and Piazza del Duomo, on the first of which you'll find the Etruscan museum.
This and Piazza del Duomo's Diocesan museum are essential ports of call before
heading through the **upper town** towards the Fortezza Medicea.

MAEC
One flank of the Palazzo del Comune forms a side of Piazza Signorelli, named
after the artist Luca Signorelli, Cortona's most famous son – as is the decorously
peeling nineteenth-century theatre-cinema. Across the road from the theatre
the hulking Palazzo Casali, its facade like a rockface with windows, is the
home of the town's main big museum, which in late 2005 was reborn as the
Museo dell'Accademia Etrusca e della Città di Cortona – or **MAEC**,
for short (April–Oct daily 10am–7pm; Nov–March Tues–Sun 10am–5pm; €7).
In addition to the snappy acronym, the museum reopened with a considerably
increased entry charge, presumably to cover the costs of the state-of-the-art
subterranean spaces in which MAEC charts the development of Cortona from
the earliest recorded settlements to Roman times – or rather would do, if the
refurbishment had gone according to plan. In the event, work is still far from
finished on one whole floor of the below-ground area, but the parts that have
been completed are certainly impressive, giving a well-presented survey of
Cortona's evolution in the Etruscan and Roman periods.

Some spectacular specimens of Etruscan gold, turquoise and crystal jewellery
catch the eye in the first rooms, along with armour, weaponry and miscellaneous grave goods excavated from tombs in the valley below Cortona. Special
prominence is given to the *Tabula Cortonensis*, a fragmentary bronze plaque
inscribed with a legal text in the Etruscan language. Beyond that, you're into the
Roman section, which is dominated by finds – mainly mosaics and terracotta
– from a large villa 5km south of Cortona.

Founded in 1727 by three brothers from the Venuti family, the Accademia
Etrusca was one of the world's first academies devoted to archeology, and such
was its prestige that Voltaire and Montesquieu were both enrolled as members.

The Accademia is still in existence, and its huge collection of antiquities and art works fills the upper floors of the museum, where – as you'd expect – there's a good deal more Etruscan material on show, most notably an Etruscan bronze lamp from the fourth century BC, which is honoured with a room to itself. This highly complicated object – showing a gorgon's head surrounded by a circle of alternating stayr-like male figures and female sirens – was cast as a single piece, an extraordinary technical achievement. Etruscan and later bronze figurines (none of them labelled) fill an avenue of cabinets in the middle of the main hall, surrounded by some fairly undistinguished pictures, though there's work by Pietro da Cortona, Signorelli and Pinturicchio in amongst the dross.

Another large room is centred on an extraordinary piece of frilly porcelain known as the *Tempio di Ginori*; made in 1737, it's covered with portraits of 76 members of the Medici clan. The bronze medals from which the porcelain images were derived are displayed in a wall case, along with portrait medals by Pisanello, a pioneer of this genre. Also on this floor you'll find a pair of terrestrial and celestial globes made in the 1710s by the eminent astronomer (and Dominican abbot) Silvestro Moroncelli, a clutch of pictures by the Venetian artist Giambattista Piazzetta, a stack of Roman inscriptions from the collection of the Venuti brothers, and – at the end – one of the most alluring items in the whole museum: a Roman painting, on slate, of the Muse Polimnia.

On the top floor you can admire a small array of Egyptian antiquities and the vast old library of the Academy, where the first members held their meetings. Back downstairs, on a mezzanine level, the painter **Gino Severini**, another native of Cortona, gets a room to himself at the end. Once an acolyte of the Futurist firebrand Filippo Marinetti, Severini was nothing if not versatile, as you'll see in this small collection, where jagged quasi-Cubist prints hang alongside some very conventional portraits, including his best-known image, *Maternity* – the sort of thing that Marinetti would have consigned to the flames.

The Duomo and Museo Diocesano

Via Casali links Piazza Signorelli with Piazza del Duomo, where you might not realize that the cathedral is in front of you, as all you see on entering the square is the well-scrubbed arcade along its flank. Though rebuilt in the sixteenth century, the **Duomo** (daily 8.30am–12.30pm & 3–6.30pm) retains elements of its Romanesque precursor in its flaking facade; the interior is rather chilly and grey, but there's a Pietro da Cortona *Nativity* on the third altar on the left, and a possible Andrea del Sarto (an *Assumption*) to the left of the high altar.

The church that used to face the Duomo now forms part of the **Museo Diocesano** (same hours as MAEC; €5), a tiny but high-quality collection of Renaissance art plus a fine Roman sarcophagus, carved with fighting centaurs. Predictably Luca Signorelli features strongly, though only two works – *Lamentation* (1502) and *The Communion of the Apostles* (1512) – are unequivocally his: seven others are attributed to him and his school. Outstanding paintings from Sassetta (a triptych of the *Madonna dell'Umilità with Saints* from 1435), Bartolomeo della Gatta (an *Assumption*) and Pietro Lorenzetti (a *Crucifix* from 1315–20) are also on show, but none of these measures up to Fra' Angelico, represented by a *Madonna, Child and Saints* and an exquisite *Annunciation*. Painted during Fra' Angelico's ten years at Cortona's monastery of San Domenico, the latter has a courtly Adam and Eve being expelled from Eden in the background, the bruised sky contrasting with the dazzle of the angel's wings.

To get the full taste of Cortona take Via Santucci from Piazza della Repubblica and then clamber along Via Berrettini, at the near end of which stands the crusty and ancient church of **San Francesco** – designed by St Francis's disciple Brother Elias, this was the first Franciscan church to be built outside Assisi after the death of Francis himself. It's been *in restauro* for many years, but if you find it open you should see a Byzantine ivory reliquary for a piece of the True Cross on the high altar (behind which Brother Elias is buried), and on the third altar on the left there's an *Annunciation* by the man the street is named after, Pietro Berrettini, otherwise known as Pietro da Cortona. (He was born at no. 33, further up the hill.) This is Pietro's last work, and was left unfinished; the best of his art is in Rome, where he and Bernini were two of the most influential figures in the creation of Roman Baroque. (At the time of writing the picture had been removed to MAEC, but it should return when the builders have finished.)

A further work by Signorelli is to be found in the church of **San Nicolò** (daily 9am–noon & 3–7pm; closes 5pm in winter; €1 minimum offering expected), signposted just beyond Piazza della Pescaia. It's a frail little church with a gravel forecourt, a delicate portico and a fine wooden ceiling that's sagging with age. Signorelli's high altarpiece is a standard which he painted on both sides: a characteristically angular *Entombment* on the front and a *Madonna and Saints* on the back – revealed by a neat hydraulic system that swivels the picture away from the wall, as the sacristan who lets you into the building will demonstrate.

From Piazza della Pescaia, a steep path leads to the neo-Romanesque **Santa Margherita**. Built to honour the town's patron saint, **Saint Margaret of Cortona**, it was begun in 1297, the year of her death, but was remodelled so extensively in the nineteenth century that the only part of the original structure that's left embedded in its replacement is the rose window of the facade. The daughter of a local farmer, Margaret spent her long years of widowhood as a Franciscan nun, helping the poor and sick of Cortona, for whom she founded a hospital that stood close to the site of the church. So intense was her relationship with the Almighty that the townspeople would pack into San Francesco to observe her delirious behaviour at Mass: "She became ashen pale, her pulse ceased, she froze, her throat was so affected by hoarseness that she could scarcely be understood when she returned to her senses," one witness recorded. Her tomb (1362), with marble angels lifting the lid of her sarcophagus, is now mounted on the wall to the left of the chancel; it's unoccupied, as her mummified body lies in a glass coffin at the high altar. The main altarpiece, Signorelli's *Lamentation*, has been removed to the Museo Diocesano, but in the chapel to the right of the chancel you can see a thirteenth-century Crucifix that is said to have spoken to Margaret on a number of occasions, when it was hanging in San Francesco.

The **Fortezza Medicea**, at the summit of the town, is sometimes used as an exhibition space in summer, and the area in front of it is good ground for a picnic, offering superb views over ruined Etruscan and Roman walls towards Trasimeno. You could descend to Piazza Garibaldi by the stepped Via Crucis, where the Stations of the Cross are marked with booths sheltering unsubtle mosaics by Severini.

San Domenico and Santa Maria del Calcinaio

A last church in the centre of town to check out is **San Domenico** (daily 3–6pm), a half-minute's walk from Piazza Garibaldi. Completed in 1438, it has a fine high altarpiece by Lorenzo di Niccolò Gerini (*Coronation of the Virgin*), yet another Signorelli (*Madonna and Child with Saints*) and a dilapidated fresco by Fra' Angelico in the lunette above the main door, but it's almost impossible to see behind its screen of protective glass.

Below the piazza, the middle distance is occupied by the perfectly proportioned though severely eroded Renaissance church of **Santa Maria del Calcinaio** (summer Mon–Sat 4–7pm & Sun 10am–12.30pm; winter Mon–Sat 3–5pm & Sun 10am–12.30pm). The masterpiece of Giorgio di Martini, it was begun in 1484 to enshrine a miraculous image of Mary that a lime burner (*calcinaio*) had unearthed at the tannery here (lime was used in the tanning process). Another Tuscan church of this vintage – Santa Maria delle Carceri in Prato – was built for similar reasons, but the number of pilgrims who flocked to Cortona made it impossible for the architect to employ the fashionable central-plan design used in Prato. Hence this highly refined compromise: classical detailing applied to an old-fashioned cruciform church. Inside, the miraculous Madonna is still displayed on the high altar.

Just past Santa Maria, signs direct you farther down the hill to the **Tanella di Pitagora** – a well-preserved Etruscan chamber tomb that's fancifully identified with the Greek mathematician Pythagoras. In fact it was constructed for a wealthy family by the name of Cuso, who are cited in the *Tabula Cortonensis*.

Eating and drinking
Cortona has numerous **restaurants**, several of which are highly recommendable – as yet, there's no sign of standards dropping as the influx of tourists increases. Nearly all the places to eat and drink are within a very short distance of Piazza della Repubblica.

△ The loggia, Cortona's Piazza della Repubblica

Restaurants

Dardano Via Dardano 24 t0575.601.944. An excellent, unpretentious, inexpensive and very popular trattoria – it's full to bursting most nights. Closed Wed.

Fufluns Via Ghibellina 1–3. If pizza's all you need, this spacious and bustling place is the first choice. Open daily.

Il Falconiere San Martino a Bocena ☎0575.612.679, ⊛www.ilfalconiere.com. The Michelin-awarded restaurant of the *Falconiere* hotel (see p.533) uses ingredients that are produced on the hotel's own land. It's expensive, and worth every euro. Closed 3 weeks in Jan.

La Grotta Piazzetta Baldelli 3 ☎0575.630.271. Much like *Dardano*, *La Grotta* is a straight-down-the-line trattoria, albeit with a slightly higher percentage of tourists among the clientiele. Closed Tues.

Osteria del Teatro Via Maffei 5 ☎0575.630.556, ⊛www.osteria-del-teatro .it. Occupying the whole lower floor of a handsome and rambling old house, this is a good-naturedly busy (sometimes frantic) place, featuring delicious homemade pastas on a meat-heavy menu; portions are generous and the prices more than fair – the bill should be around €35 per person. Closed Wed & mid-Nov to mid-Dec.

Preludio Via Guelfa 11 ☎0575.630.104. The food is invariably good and prices surprisingly moderate in this smartly turned-out restaurant. Closed Mon, and lunchtime in winter.

Tonino Piazza Garibaldi 1 ☎0575.630.500. Good antipasti and a wonderful panoramic view from the terrace are the chief attractions of the dependable *Tonino*. Closed Mon evening, plus all Tues in winter.

Bars and cafés

Caffè degli Artisti Via Nazionale 18. For a snack-plus-coffee pit-stop, this place will do nicely.

Caffè del Teatro On the terrace of the Teatro Signorelli. On summer evenings this is a favourite night-time hangout, with live music some weekends.

Caffè-Enoteca La Saletta Via Nazionale 26–28. A glossy café-cum-wine shop, which also does simple meals.

Route 66 Via Nazionale 78. This self-styled "music bar" attracts the youngest crowd in town – the soundtrack is usually loud, and it has occasional DJ nights. It does food too, but it's not the pizzas that make it popular.

Taverna Pane e Vino Piazza Signorelli 27. A good choice if you're after a quick lunch or a light evening meal: the menu offers various types of bruschetta, a wide selection of salamis and cheeses, plus a few more substantial dishes – and the wine list runs to some 550 different vintages. Closed Mon.

Castiglion Fiorentino

Looming high above the road and railway 12km north of Cortona are the walls and massive tower of **CASTIGLION FIORENTINO** – known as Castiglion Aretino until Arezzo became a Florentine holding in 1384. The fortified old town is so far above the train station that it makes more sense to visit by bus; the half-hourly bus from Arezzo to Cortona bowls through here thirty minutes into its one-hour journey, stopping right outside the walls in Piazza Matteotti.

From here the Corso Italia rises to the navel of the *centro storico*, the elegant Piazza del Municipio. There's a modest art gallery, the **Pinacoteca Comunale**, a short distance up the hill behind the Municipio, in Via del Passero (April–Oct Tues–Sun 10am–12.30pm & 4–6.30pm; Nov–March Sat & Sun 10am–12.30pm & 3.30–6pm; €3), with works by Taddeo Gaddi and two fine paintings by Bartolomeo della Gatta. A €5 ticket also gets you into the equally modest archeological museum in the neighbouring library (same hours), where the chief exhibit is a reconstructed fragment of an Etruscan temple. On the same ticket you can visit the excavations of the Etruscan walls underneath the summit of the hill, from which rises the **Torre del Cassero**, Castiglion Fiorentino's landmark tower, built to the orders of Arezzo's pugnacious Bishop Tarlati. (The tower itself is open May–Sept Sun 10am–12.30pm & 4–6.30pm; Tues–Fri in summer and any day except Mon & Sat in winter, visits can be booked at the pinacoteca; €1.50.)

Opposite the Palazzo Comunale is Castiglion's distinguishing feature, a **loggia** – supposedly designed by Vasari – which forms a picture-frame for the hills to the east. Look to the right through the loggia and you'll see the town's major church, the **Collegiata**, which has a *Holy Family* by Lorenzo di Credi to the right of the high altar. The adjoining **Pieve** – currently being converted into a small museum of sacred art – has a Signorelli fresco of the *Deposition*

Four kilometres south of here, the eleventh-century castle of **Montecchio Vesponi** jabs up from the horizon. Commanding a great sweep of the valley, this property was acquired in 1384 by the fearsome *condottiere* Sir John Hawkwood (he of the fresco in Florence's Duomo – see p.97), and is the only one of his numerous ill-gotten residences to survive intact. It's still in private hands.

Farneta, Foiano and Lucignano

About 10km west of Cortona, in the middle of the valley, stands the ancient Benedictine **Abbazia di Farneta** (daily 9am–1pm & 2–4pm). Built largely with stone plundered from a nearby Roman temple dedicated to Bacchus, this beautifully austere building first appeared in local records in 1014, but may have been founded as far back as the eighth century, by the Lombards. Once the most powerful religious house in the Valdichiana, it had fallen into disrepair by 1937, when a remarkable priest by the name of Monsignor Sante Felici arrived here. Over the course of the next sixty years he virtually single-handedly stripped the abbey of the eighteenth-century accretions that had defaced the Romanesque structure, and also excavated the ancient **crypt**, an operation that yielded numerous archeological and paleontological discoveries, including the bones of prehistoric elephants, hippos and rhinos. An engagingly ramshackle little museum used to occupy part of the neighbouring house, but repeated robbery attempts necessitated the transfer of its most precious artefacts – such as an eighth-century Lombard carving of the Crucifixion – to Cortona, while the most spectacular of Monsignor Felici's fossils are now on show in Florence's museum of paleontology.

FOIANO DELLA CHIANA, 4km west of the abbey, sometimes bills itself as "La Città di Carnevale", because it was here, in the 1860s, that allegorical floats were first produced for carnival parades, thereby inaugurating a form of folk art that nowadays is best represented by the Viareggio carnival. Other than at carnival, however, workaday Foiano is far from the most alluring small town in Tuscany. The weathered brick fortifications of the old centre are mildly impressive, and devotees of the art of the della Robbia dynasty might want to take a look at the examples of their output in the churches of **San Michele Arcangelo**, **Santa Maria della Fraternità** and the **Collegiata**, the last of which also houses the last painting by Luca Signorelli. But if none of these appeal, you'd best press on a further 8km to **LUCIGNANO**.

This trim little town is laid out as a concentric pattern of four ellipses, though the density of the centre and its gradients make it difficult to discern the arrangement on the ground. Nucleus of the pattern is the **Collegiata**, an unexceptional church given a touch of panache by the double semicircular staircase leading to its door. Round the back, the **Museo Comunale** (summer Tues–Thurs & Sat–Sun 10am–1pm & 2.30–5.30pm; winter Tues & Thurs–Sun same hours; €3) contains a couple of lesser works by Signorelli and the most arresting artefact on this side of the Valdichiana, an amazing fourteenth-century gilded reliquary made in Arezzo. It's known as the *Albero di Lucignano* or *Albero d'Oro* for its tree-like shape, with gold and silver adornments and branches of coral leafed with crystal, enamels and miniature paintings. Thirteenth- and fourteenth-century frescoes, some of them by Bartolo di Fredi, decorate the adjacent church of **San Francesco**. And that's about it, apart from the inevitable

Medici fortress on the hill to the north, but if you want to stay, book a room at Lucignano's family-run **hotel–restaurant**, *Da Totó*, which occupies a converted monastery on Piazza del Tribunale (☏0575.836.763, ℻0575.836.988; ❸). Tiny it may be, yet Lucignano has two other superb (and not expensive) places to eat: the ✻*Enoteca-Ristorante Il Goccino*, at Via Matteotti 88–90 (☏0575.836.707; closed Mon); and *La Rocca*, Via Matteotti 15–17 (☏0575.836.775; closed Tues).

Monte San Savino

On the opposite side of the Valdichiana from Cortona rises **MONTE SAN SAVINO**, now a market town, once a contentious border post between the territories of Florence, Siena and Arezzo; it was razed in 1325 on the orders of Bishop Tarlati of Arezzo. The town retains a slightly decrepit mix of medieval and Renaissance monuments, but it is not one of Tuscany's more seductive hill-towns. Should you be determined to explore it, however, there are regular trains from Arezzo to the station in the lower town, from where there's the usual bus shuttle; buses from Cortona also periodically cross the valley.

The town was the birthplace of **Andrea Sansovino**, now best remembered as the mentor of Jacopo Sansovino, a crucial figure in Venice's artistic history, who took his teacher's surname. Terracotta was one of his preferred media – the town remains a major producer of majolica – and some of Andrea's best ceramics are in the church of **Santa Chiara**, which stands in Piazza Gamurrini, the square nearest the place where the buses stop. The altarpiece of *SS Lawrence, Roch and Sebastian* was his first major work, while the tabernacle to the left of the high altar was a collaboration with Andrea della Robbia.

Virtually next to the church stands the fourteenth-century Sienese castle known as the **Cassero**, which houses a small tourist office, has a modest three-room **Museo Civico** that's largely given over to ceramics (Sat & Sun 9am–noon & 3–6pm; €1.60), and stages occasional art exhibitions. Also on the square is an obelisk that was raised to honour Monte San Savino's one-time governor, Mattias de' Medici (brother of Grand Duke Ferdinando II); allegedly it cost so much that Mattias forbade any more such ruinous projects.

Continuing down the narrow main street from Piazza Gamurrini you'll pass the **Loggia dei Mercanti**, a collaboration between Sansovino and Antonio da Sangallo the Elder – architect of the Palazzo Comunale opposite. Beyond the Palazzo Pretorio lies the small central square, Piazza di Monte, on both of whose churches Sansovino left a mark. He designed the now crumbling portal of **San Giovanni**, and added the cloister to the fourteenth-century Sant'Agostino, which contains some fifteenth-century frescoes and an altarpiece by Vasari, who ferreted his way into every cranny of the region.

Accommodation is at the one-star *Il Monte*, Via Aldo Moro 5 (☏0575.844.444, ℻0575.844.445; ❶), or the three-star *Sangallo*, Piazza Vittorio Veneto 16 (☏0575.810.049, ⓦwww.sangallohotel.it; ❷).

Travel details

Trains

Arezzo to: Assisi (12 daily; 1hr 35min); Bibbiena (hourly; 50min); Bolzano (5 daily; 7hr 30min); Camucia-Cortona (hourly; 20min); Chiusi (hourly; 1hr); Florence (hourly; 1hr); Foligno (every 2hr; 1hr 50min); Monte San Savino (12 daily; 25min); Orvieto (7 daily; 1hr 20min); Perugia (every 2hr; 1hr 15min); Poppi (hourly; 1hr); Rome (hourly; 1hr 40min); Terni (1 direct daily; 2hr 35min); Teróntola (hourly; 25min); Trento (5 daily; 7hr); Udine (5 daily; 7hr); Venice (5 daily; 5hr 10min); Verona (5 daily; 5hr 15min).

Buses

Arezzo to: Bibbiena & La Verna (1 daily – change at Bibbiena for Poppi & Camaldoli); Città di Castello (at least 12 daily; 1hr 30min); Cortona (hourly; 1hr); Sansepolcro (17 daily; 1hr), some via Monterchi, most via Anghiari; Siena (5 daily Mon–Fri).

Bibbiena to: Badia Prataglia (8 daily Mon–Sat; 40min); Camáldoli (4 daily Mon–Sat 40min); Chiusi Verna (3 daily Mon–Sat; 50min).

Cortona to: Arezzo (hourly; 50min); Castiglione del Lago (7 daily; 1hr); Chianciano (4 daily; 1hr), changing for Montepulciano.

542

Perugia and northern Umbria

CHAPTER 10

Highlights

* **Corso Vannucci, Perugia** Umbria's best *passeggiata*, with some wonderful people-watching. See p.554

* **Collegio del Cambio, Perugia** Medieval chamber decorated with outstanding frescoes by Perugino. See p.556

* **Galleria Nazionale dell'Umbria, Perugia** The region's finest collection of medieval and Renaissance art. See p.557

* **Città di Castello** The Pinacoteca Comunale and Museo Diocesano hold paintings by Raphael, Signorelli, Rosso Fiorentino and others. See p.576

* **Palazzo dei Consoli, Gubbio** A majestic medieval palace, with sweeping views from its belvedere. See p.586

* **Funicular ride, Gubbio** A dizzying six-minute ride over woods and crags into the mountains. See p.592

* **Parco Regionale del Monte Cucco** Wonderful mountain scenery with some great hiking. See p.594

△ The Fontana Maggiore, Perugia

10

Perugia and northern Umbria

Perugia makes for a distinctly uncharacteristic introduction to Umbria. The home of Buitoni pasta and Perugino chocolate, it's a place whose historic core is hidden within a ring of initially off-putting industrialized suburbs, and whose big-city feel, universities and famous summer jazz festival make it wholly different from its bucolic, hill-town neighbours. If you've come to Umbria for the rural experience, you may be tempted to bypass Perugia altogether. Its medieval heart, however, demands at least a day's exploration, two sights alone making the trip more than worthwhile: the **Palazzo dei Priori**, justifiably hyped as one of the greatest public palaces in Italy, and the **Galleria Nazionale dell'Umbria**, which boasts the region's best collection of Umbrian art. And if actually staying in the city doesn't appeal, its highlights can easily be taken in on day-trips from Assisi, Montefalco or other nearby towns.

West of Perugia lies the placid, if unspectacular, **Lago Trasimeno**, a popular magnet for campers and one of the few places in the region where you can put your feet up on a beach. Its nicest town is **Castiglione del Lago**, with brasher **Passignano** the main camping and after-hours resort.

North of Perugia is a moderately pretty and pastoral region centred on the upper reaches of the **Tiber valley**. Road and rail routes follow the river's course, useful mainly for onward forays into Tuscany and the Marche – in particular to Sansepolcro or Urbino for the paintings of Piero della Francesca. Unheralded **Città di Castello** is the only worthwhile Umbrian port of call, a captivating town in which the art gallery contains the region's only painting by Raphael, an artist apprenticed to Perugino, Umbria's pre-eminent Renaissance painter.

East of the Tiber, minor roads climb through swathes of attractively barren country to **Gubbio**, one of Italy's medieval gems and – given Assisi's increasing commercialism – the region's least spoiled hill-town. Much in the town merits comparison with Siena, not least its overbearing civic palace, the **Palazzo dei Consoli**, a magnificent piece of medieval bluster. Churches and galleries abound, and the honeycomb of old streets is riddled with things of interest. Moving east, you come up against the first foothills of the Apennines, their slopes home to a couple of half-forgotten hill-towns, **Gualdo Tadino** and earthquake-shattered **Nocera Umbra**. The mountains behind – **Monte**

N

Sansepolcro

Anghiari

River Tiber

Citerna

Mónterchi

Città di Castello

Monte Santa
Maria Tiberina

Morra

Canoscio

Montone

T U S C A N Y

Umbertide

Cortona

Lisciano

Preggio

Terontola

Tuoro

Castel Rigone

Isola
Maggiore

Passignano
sul Trasimeno

Lago di Trasimeno

Magione

Corciano

Castiglione
del Lago

San
Feliciano

Perugia

Isola
Polvese

▼ Orvieto

Cucco in particular – boast the area's best scenery and are the obvious places to tackle some straightforward hiking.

Perugia is one of the key transport hubs for the region, with direct **trains** from Assisi, Spello, Foligno (for Gubbio and Spoleto), Terni, Narni, Todi, Città di Castello and Teróntola (for Orvieto). A couple of fast trains run direct to Perugia from both Florence and Rome, as do more regular trains from Teróntola on the main Florence–Rome line. The private FCU train line runs throughout the region, from Sansepolcro in the north, through Città di Castello, Perugia and on to Todi (see p.705) and Terni (see p.689). A fast **road** connects Perugia to the A1 *Autostrada del Sole*, with quick links on to Todi, Assisi, Spello and Foligno. **Buses** run to most major centres and many minor ones.

Official websites

Umbria's official tourist websites are Ⓦ www.umbria-turismo.it and Ⓦ www .umbria2000.it. Many of the region's museums and galleries are affiliated to Sistema-museo (Ⓦ www.sistemamuseo.it).

Perugia and Lago Trasimeno

PERUGIA is a place of some style – at least in its old centre – and a city proud of its big-league attractions, its universities, its sights and its football team. A drink on the **Corso Vannucci**, its great central street, reveals a buzz you won't find elsewhere in the region, a sense of dynamism embodied by the cosmopolitan **Università Italiana per Stranieri**, created by Mussolini to improve the image of Italy abroad; now, privately run, it's the country's largest language school. This same dynamism remains evident in Perugia's above-average number of film screenings, concerts and miscellaneous cultural events, and is highlighted further at the July **Umbria Jazz** (ⓦ www.umbriajazz.com), Italy's foremost jazz festival, whose stars have included Miles Davis, Stan Getz and Wynton Marsalis.

In terms of sights, Perugia's interest is essentially medieval, despite its considerable Etruscan heritage. In addition to the **Palazzo dei Priori**, home to the **Galleria Nazionale** and the Perugino-painted **Collegio del Cambio**, there is the **Duomo** and a full quota of churches – the glittering interior of **San Pietro** the most celebrated, the rotunda of **Sant'Angelo** the most ancient. Idiosyncratic one-offs give plenty of reason for wandering the city's streets, the best being Agostino di Duccio's facade for the **Oratorio di San Bernardino** and the Gothic sculpture of **San Domenico**, Umbria's largest church.

Some history

Perugia's command of the Tiber and its major routes has made it the region's main player throughout a long history – albeit not quite as long as early chroniclers made out when they claimed to have traced its foundation to Noah. The easternmost of the twelve key cities of the **Etruscan** federation, Perusia, as it was called, was conquered by **Rome** in 309 BC, later taking the wrong side in the civil war which followed the death of Julius Caesar. Allying itself with Mark Antony, it suffered a debilitating siege at the hands of his opponent Octavius, later the emperor Augustus. It might have survived the ordeal but for the actions of Gaius Cestius, one of the city's less stout defenders, who set fire to his house in a panic-stricken funk. The ensuing conflagration destroyed the city, and Augustus rebuilt it as Augusta Perusia.

The city's passage through the Dark Ages is obscure, though legend claims it was besieged by Totila in 547 and saved from destruction by its bishop, St Ercolano (Herculanus). By 592 it had been absorbed into the **Lombard** Duchy of Spoleto, later emerging as a papal vassal and finally, around 1140, as an independent *comune*.

Medieval Perugia was evidently a hell of a place to be. "The town had the most warlike people of Italy," wrote the historian Sismondi, "who always preferred Mars to the Muse". Male citizens played a game – for pleasure – in which two teams, wearing beaked helmets and clothes stuffed with deer hair, stoned each other mercilessly until the majority on one side were dead or wounded. Children were encouraged to join in to promote "application and aggression". In 1265 Perugia was also the birthplace of the **Flagellants**, who within ten

PERUGIA

Sant'Angelo
Porta Sant'Angelo
Santa Colomba
Santa Caterina
Sant'Agnese
San Benedetto
Sant'Agostino
Porta Bulagaio
Porta Elce
Università per Stranieri
PIAZZA FORTEBRACCIO
Santa Maria Nuova
Porta Pesa
San Severo
San Francesco
Accademia di Belle Arti
Oratorio di San Bernardino
PIAZZA MORLACCHI
PIAZZA DANTI
Duomo
San Filippo Neri
Palazzo dei Priori
Madonna della Luce
Santa Teresa
Collegio del Cambio
Porta Santa Susanna
PIAZZA MATTEOTTI
Sant'Ercolano
Museo Archeologico
PIAZZA ITALIA
Giardini Carducci
Porta Marzia
Santo Spirito
San Domenico
Porta Eburnea
Stazione Sant'Anna
PIAZZA PARTIGIANI
Car Park/ Bus Station
Porta San Pietro
Stadium
PIAZZALE EUROPA
Santa Giuliana

See 'Central Perugia' map

0   200 m

▼ Train Station & Campsites

▶ San Pietro

years had half of Europe whipping itself into a frenzy before the movement was declared heretical. In addition to some hearty scourging, they took to the streets on moonlit nights, wailing, singing dirges and clattering human bones together – all as expiation for the wrongs of the world.

Using its economic muscle and numerous short-lived alliances, the city built up a huge power base, peaking with its **conquest of Siena** in 1358. Around this time the *Priori* (members of the ten leading guilds), noble families and papal agents began vying for control, plunging Perugia into a period when, according to one chronicler, "perfect pandemonium reigned in and about the city". Individual *condottieri* rose briefly from the chaos, the key figures being Biondo Michelotti – stabbed to death in 1398, after five years in power – and the oddly named Braccio Fortebraccio (Arm the Strong Arm), whose eight years of rule brought short-lived stability. The Oddi nobility ran the town until 1488, when the colourful but demented **Baglioni** took over. Their story is the stuff of soap opera: complicated vendettas, incestuous marriages, hearts torn from bodies and eaten, and any number of people murdered on their wedding nights. After one episode was settled with a hundred murders, the bloodied cathedral had to be washed down with wine and reconsecrated. One Baglioni, Malatesta IV, assigned the defence of Florence in 1530, famously sold his services to the enemy, earning the title "world's greatest traitor".

When the last Baglioni, the wimpish Ridolpho, bungled an assassination of the papal legate, it was a cue for the papacy to step in. **Pope Paul III**, one of the more powerful and peculiar pontiffs, razed the Baglioni palaces in 1538, then entered the city demanding that all its nuns line up and kiss his feet. Thus refreshed, he built the Rocca Paolina, a huge fortress that guaranteed church supremacy for three centuries. During the nineteenth-century unification of Italy, Perugia's liberation from the papacy was particularly violent, with numerous citizens massacred by Swiss Guards sent to bolster Church control. Liberation from the Nazis in 1944, courtesy of the British Eighth Army, was considerably less bloodthirsty.

Arrival and information

Arrival in Perugia can be an extremely dispiriting business, its approaches a confusing medley of suburbs, busy roads and hard-to-find parking places. Once in the medieval *centro storico*, however, things improve considerably. The old city revolves around **Corso Vannucci**, a broad pedestrian thoroughfare capped at its northern end by the **Piazza IV Novembre** – home to the Duomo and Palazzo dei Priori – and in the south by **Piazza Italia**, jumping-off point for the city's southern quarters. The twisting medieval alleys off the Corso are initially disorientating, but by dividing the city into western, northern and southern sections you soon get to grips with the layout. You can **walk** everywhere, although you'll cover a fair bit of ground in the course of a day's sightseeing – particularly if you take in sights at the extreme northern and southern ends of town. You should also be prepared for **steep climbs** between Perugia's many levels: lifts and escalators help out only occasionally.

Arrival

Arriving on the state **train** network you'll find yourself well away from the *centro storico* at **Piazza Vittorio Veneto**: it's too far to walk from here – it's all uphill on busy roads – but the centre is an easy bus ride away. Buses #6, #7, #9, #11, #13S, #13D or #15 leave from the forecourt outside the station and arrive ten minutes later in **Piazza Italia** or **Piazza Matteotti**, both equally convenient (the numbering is prone to change, but any bus going to these squares is fine; the bus stop lists the destinations). You can buy a city bus **ticket** (€1 for unlimited journeys in 1hr 10min) from the station newsagents (turn right as you enter the ticket hall from the platforms) or a booth on the left of the forecourt as you exit the station; paying on board costs €1.50, and you must have the right change. You're unlikely to use enough buses to make the Card Turistico (€3.60; valid 24hr) worthwhile. The private FCU rail line between Sansepolcro, Perugia and Terni comes into the more central **Stazione Sant'Anna**, in the southern part of town near the Piazza dei Partigiani **bus terminal**.

The *centro storico* is closed to traffic at most times – and even when open is almost impossible to navigate. The best bet is to follow the signs for Piazza dei Partigiani in the south, where there's a large covered **car park** (hourly tariff). From here you can jump on one of the signed *scala mobile* (escalators) through the weird subterranean Via Baglioni Sotterranea to Piazza Italia. Another good option, in the west, is the parking in Viale Pompeo Pellini (hourly tariff), connected by escalators to Via dei Priori. If you're driving in from the north, you may find the car park in Viale Sant'Antonio more convenient. Out-of-town **buses** arrive at the efficient bus station in Piazza dei Partigiani: to reach the centre simply cross the main road outside the terminal for the ramp leading to the *scala mobile* to Piazza Italia.

Perugia's small **airport**, Sant'Egidio (☎075.592.141, ⊛www.airport.umbria .it), is 18km east, and handles domestic flights to and from Milan (Malpensa) and Rome. An infrequent "Airbus" run by ACAP (☎075.500.9641) meets the main incoming flights, shuttling to Piazza Italia (currently three daily; €2.58). Otherwise, taxis are the only option.

Information

There's a **tourist office** just behind the Palazzo dei Priori in the Sala San Severo, at Piazza IV Novembre 3 (Mon–Sat 8.30am–1.30pm & 3.30–6.30pm, Sun 9am–1pm; ☎075.573.6458, ⊜info@iat.perugia.it). Staff provide a good map, advice on city events and help in finding accommodation and Europcar car rental. A private information office, **Infotourist Point**, on the northeast corner of Piazza Partigiani (Mon–Sat 9am–1pm & 2.30–6.30pm; ☎075.573.2933, ⊛www.infoumbria.com), is a good source of information on organized half- and full-day tours (more information ⊛www.guideinumbria .com); these include half-day trips to Gubbio (€95) and day-trips to Orvieto or Spoleto (both €190).

Accommodation

Perugia has plenty of **accommodation** in all price ranges, though you should reserve ahead as some of the cheapest places may be taken up by long-stay students; book, too, during the July jazz festival, when rates will likely be raised. Prices are otherwise pretty standard year-round, with no real low season. It pays to be in or very near the *centro storico*; you don't want to be out in the suburbs at any price unless you're lucky enough to be staying in an historic hotel such as the *Castello dell'Oscano*. If you're **camping**, it's worth considering travelling into the city from the nicer campsites around Lago Trasimeno (see p.568).

Hotels

Anna Via dei Priori 48 ☎ & ⓕ075.573.6304, ⊛www.albergoanna.it. Central one-star with thirteen rooms and a choice of private or shared bathrooms. ❷

Aurora Viale Indipendenza 21 ☎075.572.4819 or 075.572.4453, ⓕ075.572.4819. A fourteen-room two-star immediately south of Piazza Italia. Basic and clean, with very helpful staff, but on a very busy road. ❸

Castello dell'Oscano Località Cenerente, Strada della Forcella 37 ☎075.584.371, ⓕ075.690.666, ⊛www.oscano.com. This converted four-star hotel has just ten rooms, all part of an amazing castle with full medieval trappings set in acres of parkland 5km north of Perugia. ❼

Eden Via Cesare Caporali 9 ☎075.572.8102, ⓕ075.720.342, ⊛www.hoteleden.191.it. An eighteen-room two-star (all rooms with private bath) in an alley just a few paces west of the Corso. ❸

CENTRAL PERUGIA

ACCOMMODATION
Anna B
Aurora I
Castello dell'Oscano L
Centro Internazionale A
Eden H
Etruria F
Locanda della Posta G
Ostello Spagnoli K
Paola E
Priori C
Rosalba J
Umbria D

CAFÉS & BARS
Bar dell'Accademia 13
Bottega del Vino 8
Caffè di Perugia 18
Caffè Morlacchi 7
Enoteca Provinciale 5
Gelateria Soleluna 20
Il Birraio 2
Pasticceria Sandri 17
Pizza al Taglio 15
Shamrock Pub 11

RESTAURANTS
Cesarino 12
Dal Mi' Cucco 1
Del Sole 19
Falchetto 6
Giancarlo 14
La Taverna 21
Osteria del Gambero 4
Osteria Il Gufo 16
Osteria Turreno 9
Pizzeria Etrusca 3
Pizzeria Mediterranea 10
Scalino 22

Etruria Via della Luna 21 ☎075.572.3730. An eight-room one-star, with and without private bathrooms, perfectly positioned just west of Piazza della Repubblica and the Corso. ❶

Paola Via della Canapina 5 ☎075.572.3816, ⓕ075.573.0236. A popular if slightly peripheral one-star place, but only eight rooms (four shared bathrooms), so be sure to call in advance. It's tricky to find: follow signs for the *Hotel Umbria* from the Corso, go down the steps in the passageway, turn right and follow the second set of steps towards the car park. ❷

Locanda della Posta Corso Vannucci 97 ☎075.572.8925, ⓕ075.573.2562, ⓦwww .umbriatravel.com/locandadellaposta. Central 39-room four-star, and though the five-star *Brufani* just to the south is smarter (and more expensive), this is the first choice in Perugia if you want a treat. Goethe and Hans Christian Andersen are just two luminaries to have stayed here. ❼

Priori Via dei Priori–Via Vermiglioli 3 ☎075.572.3378, ⓕ075.572.3213, ⓦwww .hotelpriori.it. First-choice mid-range hotel – if only because it has 49 rooms, so there's a good chance of finding space; a two-star place tastefully fitted out and well located. Also has a great terrace overlooking the rooftops. Rooms vary in price, so ask to see a selection. ❸

Rosalba Piazza del Circo 7 ☎ & ⓕ075.572.0626, ⓦwww.hotelrosalba.com. An excellent two-star with eleven rooms, all with private bathrooms, south of Piazza Italia. ❷

Umbria Via Boncambi 37 ☎075.572.1203, ⓦwww.hotelumbria.com. An eighteen-room two-star with prices only a whisker higher than the one-star establishments listed above; rooms vary – some are cramped – and come with and without private bath. Breakfast is poor. ❷

Hostels

Centro Internazionale di Accoglienza per la Gioventù Via Bontempi 13 ☎075.572.2880, ⓦwww.ostello.perugia.it. The town's original hostel, perfectly situated two minutes from the Duomo, has 134 beds in four-, six- and eight-bed dorms and a midnight curfew. Closed 9.30am–4pm. Dorm beds €13 plus €2 for sheets if you don't have suitable sleeping bag or sheet sleeping bag.

Ostello per la Gioventù Maria Luisa Spagnoli Località Pian di Massiano ☎075.501.1366, ⓦwww.umbriahostels.org. A newer hostel down near the main FS train station, with its own restaurant and sleeping 186 in four- and six-bed dorms. Dorm beds €15.

Campsites

Perugia's **campsites** *Il Rocolo*, Strada Fontana 1n (☎075.517.8550, ⓦwww .ilrocolo.it; April to mid-Oct) and *Paradis d'Été*, Via del Mercato 29a, Strada Fontana (☎075.517.3121, ⓦwww.well.it; March–Oct) are 5km west of town at Località Colle della Trinità. By car, there are signs off the SS75bis road. By bus, take either the Sulga service from Perugia's Piazza Italia marked "Colle della Trinità", or bus #9 from the station; from the Colle della Trinità stop, the campsites are a short walk uphill.

Corso Vannucci and Piazza IV Novembre

Medieval Perugia hinges around the **Corso Vannucci**, one of Italy's great people-watching streets, its broad expanse packed from dawn to the early hours with a parade of Umbria's shoppers, students, style-makers and followers. Named after the city's most celebrated artist, Pietro Vannucci, better known simply as Perugino, the street has several of the city's key sights, most notably the **Palazzo dei Priori**, still the home of the city's council, as well as the city's loveliest café, *Pasticceria Sandri* (see p.567). At its northern end, the Corso broadens slightly to become the medieval **Piazza IV Novembre**, former site of a Roman reservoir. On one side of the square is the Palazzo dei Priori's northern flank, on the other is the **Duomo**, the religious counterpoint to the palazzo. At the piazza's centre is perhaps the most graceful fountain in Italy, the **Fontana Maggiore**, stunningly restored to as near a pristine state as its 700-year-old sculptures allow.

⑩

Perugia museum pass

The **Card Perugia Città Museo** is a pass in a variety of time and price bands that offers entry to the Cappella di San Severo, Galleria Nazionale dell'Umbria, Museo Archeologico dell'Umbria, Museo Capitolare della Cattedrale di San Lorenzo, Museo delle Porte e Mura Urbiche, Collegio di Cambio, Collegio della Mercanzia, Palazzo Baldeschi al Corso, Pozzo Etrusco, Ipogeo dei Volumni, Centro Servizi Musealì della Rocca Paolina and Palazzo della Penna.

There are four different passes: A (€7, valid for a day and a choice of four sights); B (€12, valid three days for all sights); C1 (€20, valid for a year for all sights); and C2 (€35, valid for a family of four for all sights for year). The passes are available from all participating sights.

The Fontana Maggiore

The **Fontana Maggiore** has quite a pedigree: it was designed in 1277 by Fra' Bevignate, the Silvestrine monk who had a hand in shaping Orvieto's cathedral, and sculpted by the father-and-son team of Nicola and Giovanni Pisano, possibly with help from Arnolfo di Cambio. It was installed to receive the water from the town's new aqueduct, a five-kilometre affair designed by a leading hydraulic engineer of the age, the Venetian Boninsegna. However, as the chronicler Bonazzi observed, "beasts, barrels and unwashed pots and unclean hands were forbidden the use of the water, and indeed it was guarded with such jealous care that it seemed as though the people of Perugia had built their fountain for the sake of beauty only".

The **sculptures** and **bas-reliefs** on the two polygonal basins were part of a carefully conceived decorative scheme designed to illustrate the city's glory and achievements. By some canny calculation none of them line up directly, encouraging you to walk around the fountain chasing a point of repose that never comes. The lower basin has 25 double reliefs, twelve showing the *Labours of the Months*, together with the appropriate sign of the zodiac – December's pig-sticking is particularly graphic. The remaining reliefs include a lion and griffon, Perugia's medieval symbols; four double panels depicting the Liberal Arts; scenes from the Old Testament (note the relief of the large lion and smaller lion being beaten, an allegory expounding the virtues of punishment); and reliefs portraying Roman scenes and two of Aesop's fables. Most of the 24 upper basin statues are by Giovanni Pisano and depict a wide range of characters, among them saints, Old Testament heroes and a variety of allegorical figures representing Victory, Theology and the like. Giovanni also completed the three figures in the basin, believed to represent the three Cardinal Virtues – Faith, Hope and Charity.

The Palazzo dei Priori

The northern end of the Corso is dominated by the gaunt bulk of the **Palazzo dei Priori**, with its majestic Gothic doorway, rows of trefoil windows (from which convicted criminals were thrown to their deaths) and businesslike Guelph crenellations. Often cited as Italy's most impressive civic palace (it's certainly one of the largest), it was begun in 1293 by two local architects and completed in 1443, its impressive effect deriving as much from its sheer bulk as the harmonious beauty created by the buildings around it. Four separate sights are hidden within its precincts: the **Sala dei Notari**, **Sala del Collegio della Mercanzia**, **Collegio del Cambio** and – the star turn – the **Galle-**

ria Nazionale dell'Umbria. All are worthwhile, but orientation within the palazzo can be a little confusing; it's easiest to tackle them in the order given below.

Sala dei Notari

The **Sala dei Notari** (daily 9am–1pm & 3–7pm; Oct–May closed Mon; free), the medieval lawyers' meeting hall, is entered via the fan-shaped steps opposite the Duomo. It's an obvious point of reference, its doorway topped by copies of a bronze Guelph lion and Perugian griffon (the originals are in the Galleria Nazionale; see opposite). Once thought to be Roman, the figures were probably made in 1274 or 1281, making them among the first pieces of large-scale casting in medieval Italy. Latest research, however, suggests the body of the griffon, at least, may be Etruscan, the wings having been added during the thirteenth-century casting. The chains below, according to tradition, were snatched from the gate and gallows of Siena during a raid in 1358. The triple-arched **loggia** is thought to be a remnant of San Severo, a church demolished to make way for the palace in the thirteenth century.

The Sala is one of the oldest parts of the palazzo, dating from the late 1290s – about the same time as the civic palaces in Florence and Siena were being raised. It's a tremendous space, overarched by superb vaulting. Before the lawyers got their hands on it, it was used as a meeting place for the townspeople in times of crisis and decision. Its celebrated **frescoes**, however, were substantially repainted in the nineteenth century, the net result being little more than flashes of colour, fancy flags and swirls. They represent the arms of various *podestà*, or magistrates of the city, from 1297 to 1424, infinitely duller than the hard-to-see thirteenth-century frescoes of scenes from Aesop's Fables and the Old Testament which adorn the upper arches.

Sala del Collegio della Mercanzia

The **Sala del Collegio della Mercanzia** (March–Oct Mon–Sat 9am–1pm & 2.30–5.30pm, Sun 9am–1pm; rest of year Tues–Sat 8am–2pm, Sun 9am–1pm; €1.03; joint ticket with Collegio di Cambio €3.10) is hidden behind an inconspicuous door at no. 15, farther down the Corso side of the palazzo (to the right of the main portal). Since 1390 it has been the seat of the merchants' guild – the city's most important, and a body that survives as a charitable institution to this day. At first glance it amounts to little, but at close quarters the room reveals intricately inlaid wooden panelling, breathtaking fifteenth-century work that is considered some of Italy's finest.

The Collegio del Cambio

The **Collegio del Cambio**, which lies a few doors down at Corso Vannucci 25 (Mon–Sat 9am–12.30pm & 2.30–5.30pm, Sun 9am–12.30pm; €2.60; joint ticket with Collegio della Mercanzia €3.10), was the hall of the town's moneychangers, a guild (founded in 1259) that survives as a charitable body to this day. Its walls are covered with **frescoes** by **Perugino**; these are not only considered his masterpieces, but also reckoned one of the best-preserved Renaissance schemes in the country. The bankers' guild awarded the commission in 1496, about the same time as Perugino was approached to fresco part of the Duomo in Orvieto, an undertaking eventually executed by Luca Signorelli. The city's bankers were determined to have paintings commensurate with their own sense of self-importance, and to this end probably paid Perugino – then at the peak of his powers – more than was on offer in Orvieto. This most likely explains the painter's mysterious disappearance from that city after just five desultory days working in the cathedral.

Having paid their money, the bankers were determined to impose upon the painter their **theme** of choice; Francesco Maturanzio, a leading humanist theorist, was brought in as consultant, and proposed a fusion of classical and Christian culture, painting Christian icons alongside figures of classical myth. Though not an unusual Renaissance conceit, the vigour and uncompromising way in which the themes are yoked together created a distinctly curious juxtaposition. The thesis intended to suggest that there was unity in variety, and that human perfection, expressed by classical art, was obtainable through Christ's example.

Whatever the metaphysical intent, the frescoes certainly succeed aesthetically, unified by Perugino's melancholy tone, idealized and soft-focus figures and mellow landscapes. The paintings cover virtually all the walls and ceiling vaults of the single room, part of which – probably the prophets and sibyls on the right-hand wall (behind the ticket desk) – was painted by Perugino's pupil **Raphael**, then only about 13 years old. Up on the door-side wall there's a famous but unremarkable self-portrait of the master, looking on with sour-faced disapproval – ironically, the only element disturbing the frescoes' beautiful evenness of tone.

The ceiling vaults illustrate the main gods of the classical world: Apollo on his chariot at the centre; Saturn, Jupiter and Mars above the Corso wall; Mercury, Venus and Diana towards the window. Right of the window are portraits of famous Greeks and Romans, real and mythical, with the allegorical figures of Prudence and Justice joined by Cato (symbol of Wisdom), and with Socrates and Trajan, among others, below. The end wall, farthest from the entrance, introduces the Christian strand, with a *Nativity* and the *Transfiguration*, cleaned after having been blackened by smoke from the room's former oil lamps. The right-hand wall shows God amongst the angels, with sibyls to the right and men to the left: Isaac, Moses, Daniel (possibly a portrait of Raphael), David, Jeremiah and Solomon. The lovely little chapel to the rear, the **Cappella di San Giovanni Battista**, is smothered in a frescoed *Life of John the Baptist* (1513–18) by Giovanni di Paolo – like Raphael, a former pupil of Perugino.

The Galleria Nazionale dell'Umbria

The **Galleria Nazionale dell'Umbria** (daily 8.30am–7.30pm; closed first Mon of every month; €6.50; ⓦ www.gallerianazionaleumbria.it), on the fourth floor of the palace complex, is the region's main repository of Umbrian art. Its entrance is through the opulent doorway on the Corso; having pushed past harassed Perugians on their way to do battle with council bureaucracy, you might well find the small lift isn't working, in which case you have to clamber up the stairs, a route once taken by nobles on horseback. Dust has now settled on a long restoration project, which has turned the gallery into one of central Italy's best. Be certain to follow the gallery's prescribed itinerary: after passing through the ticket office rotonda, make for room 2 straight ahead and left. Free guides in several languages are usually available just beyond the ticket office. Note that some paintings may be moved: the gallery seems to be in a constant state of flux, despite the restoration, and plans are in hand to extend the exhibition space across the palace's lower floors. In past years there has been special summer **late opening** (mid-June to mid-Sept until 11pm).

The gallery traces the entire chronology of the Umbrian art canon, from its Byzantine-influenced roots, its parallel development with the Sienese in the thirteenth and fourteenth centuries, through to its late fifteenth-century golden age when Perugia became the main focus of endeavour. The region's premier painters, **Perugino** and **Pinturicchio**, are predictably well covered, as are their imitators, and artists who worked in a late-Renaissance vein and fall outside the confines of the Umbrian school.

Early Umbrian and Sienese schools

Some of the gallery's finest moments have nothing to do with indigenous painters. This is particularly true of early rooms, where the **Sienese** largely hold sway. Amongst a welter of anonymous works, the first highlight is a large *Crucifixion* by the so-called Maestro di San Francesco, one of the gallery's earliest pieces, and painted by the anonymous hand believed to be responsible for some of the superlative frescoes in the nave of the Lower Church in Assisi's Basilica di San Francesco. Also look out for an outstanding *Madonna and Angels* by **Duccio** (1304–08), its static beauty the obvious model for many of the Umbrian works that follow. Other named Sienese masters include Bartolomeo da Siena, Domenico di Bartolo and Taddeo di Bartolo, the last responsible here for three altarpieces, including a *Pentecost* that displays a radical approach to composition, at odds with the more conservative Umbrians to come.

In acknowledging the increasing influence of Tuscan painters on Umbrians as the fifteenth century progressed, the gallery almost allows a pair of paintings by outsiders to steal the show. One is an astounding triptych by **Fra' Angelico**, the *Madonna and Child with Angels and Saints*. Radiant with the painter's gorgeous swathes of blue, it was painted in 1437 for Perugia's church of San Domenico. The other is more extraordinary still: **Piero della Francesca**'s sensational polyptych of the *Madonna and Child and SS Anthony of Padua and John the Baptist with SS Francis and Elizabeth of Hungary*, executed for Perugia's Sant'Antonio monastery between around 1459 and 1468, about the time of his Arezzo cycle. It's full of eccentric compositional nuances, particularly in the small *Annunciation* hinged to the top of the main painting, in which a mannered succession of arches around the Virgin recedes into a blank wall. The predella depicts miracles performed by the saints in the main painting.

Dozens of anonymous early fifteenth-century Umbrian works follow, amounting in many cases to no more than a surfeit of the religious iconography that fills Umbrian paintings without the redeeming dulcet qualities of the Sienese. The better of the Umbrians are Matteo da Gualdo and **Nicolò Alunno**, the latter represented by a *gonfalone*, or painted banner, a genre later to become the special preserve of Perugian painters. Alunno's banner hangs next to a similar work by **Benedetto Bonfigli**, an important mid-period Umbrian painter, who is also represented by a superb *Annunciation and St Luca*; more significantly, he decorated the palazzo's chapel between 1454 and 1480 with surviving fragmentary episodes from the life of Ercolano and Louis of Toulouse, Perugia's patron saints. The frescoes provide a detailed picture of aspects of fifteenth-century Perugia – walls, towers and monuments – that have now largely vanished.

Perugino and the Renaissance

Heralded by a bevy of Perugian contemporaries, **Perugino** marks the apotheosis of the Umbrian school. About a dozen sublime works here encapsulate his immense output; little can detract from the art of a painter talked of by his contemporaries in the same breath as Michelangelo and Leonardo da Vinci. The loveliest painting is probably the *Madonna della Consolazione* (1496–8), a work whose imagery and bravura technique underline just how much Raphael, Perugino's pupil, would take from his master. Almost equally fine are two earlier pieces painted around 1475, a *Pietà* and *Adoration of the Magi*.

The second-ranked Umbrian, and Perugino's occasional collaborator, **Pinturicchio**, is not so well represented, save for the gargantuan *Pala di Santa Maria dei Fossi* (1495), widely considered one of the masterpices of the Umbrian canon. This aside, however, there is little here to compare with the artist's frescoes of Spello's Santa Maria Maggiore (see p.625) or the works in Siena's

Piccolomini library (see p.389). Other rooms contain perfectly good works by followers of Perugino; names to look out for are Sinibaldo Ibi, Giannicola di Paolo and Eusebio di San Giorgio, all fluent interpreters of Perugino's merging of Umbrian and Florentine traditions.

The rest of the gallery ploughs a remorseless course through seventeenth- to nineteenth-century Umbrian offerings, most of them large, gloomy canvases.

The Duomo

Piazza IV Novembre is backed by the plain-faced **Duomo**, or **Cattedrale di San Lorenzo** (Mon–Sat 7am–12.45pm & 4–7.45pm, Sun 7am–1pm & 4–7pm; free). There's been a church on this site for a thousand years, but the cornerstone for the present building was laid in 1345, though the Black Death (1348) almost immediately interrupted subsequent construction. Most of the building was completed late in the following century and even then the facade, which is in the lovely pink stone of most local towns, was left unfinished. Taking a pragmatic approach to the problem, the Perugians stole the marble facing intended for Arezzo's cathedral, though a subsequent hammering from Arezzo brought about its shame-faced return.

To the right of the portal is a bronze statue (1555) of Pope Julius III by Vincenzo Danti, and to the left an unfinished **pulpit** built for the roving St Bernardino of Siena, who was something of a hit with the Perugians. It was here that he preached a Bonfire of the Vanities, urging women to burn their wigs and everyone else to give up books, fine clothes and general good times. To the left are remains of the Loggia Fortebraccio (1423), taken from the house of the city's one-time ruler.

The Baroque **interior** is imposing enough, though short on artworks. Its pride and joy is the Virgin's "wedding ring", a novel relic, housed in the Cappella del Sant'Anello (first chapel on the left). An unwieldy piece of agate, said to change colour according to the character of the person wearing it, the ring was stolen by the Perugians from Chiusi in 1473 and encased in a series of fifteen boxes, fitted like Russian dolls; it's brought out for public edification once a year on July 30. Embedded in the wall nearby are fragments of an altar by Agostino di Duccio (1473); next to them is a lovely painting by Berto di Giovanni showing 1520s Perugia in the background, with a small lunette above by Giannicola di Paolo.

In the right aisle, the first chapel, closed by an iron screen, contains a widely admired *Deposition* painted in 1569 by Barocci, apparently under the influence of poison administered by a jealous rival. More toxin-related mementos are contained in the transepts, where urns hold the ashes of Pope Martin IV, who died in the city after eating too many eels, and Urban IV, who was reputedly poisoned with *aquetta*, an imaginative little brew made by rubbing arsenic into pork fat and distilling the resultant ooze. The most conspicuous piece of art is the *Madonna delle Grazie* attributed to Giannicola di Paolo, on the third pillar of the right nave. Easily recognized by its tinselly votive offerings, it's supposed to have miraculous powers, and mothers still bring their newly baptized children to kneel before it.

The Museo Capitolare della Cattedrale di San Lorenzo

Through the cathedral sacristy (or if it's closed, through a courtyard to the left of the entrance) are the cloisters and **Museo Capitolare**, or Museo dell'Opera del Duomo (Tues–Sun 10am–1pm & 2.30–5.30pm; €3.50), inaugurated in 1923 on the four hundredth anniversary of Perugino's death. It is a rich treasury scattered through 26 rooms with some fine examples of the miniatures for which medieval Perugia was renowned, as well as a *Madonna and Saints* (1484) by Luca Signorelli, and works by Umbrian and Sienese masters such as a fine triptych by Meo da Siena, panels by Andrea Vanni and a *Pietà* by Bartolomeo Caporali. Despite the listed opening hours, note that you often have to apply to the cathedral chapterhouse for entry.

West and east of Corso Vannucci

For a feel of medieval Perugia, the most rewarding streets are to the **west of the Corso**, in particular Via dei Priori, entered through the archway in the Palazzo dei Priori. This curves downhill through a slice of the old city, taking in a succession of little churches and culminating in the Oratorio di San Bernardino, one of Perugia's prime pieces of sculpture. **East of the Corso** there are a couple of extra diversions – not least an impressive Etruscan well and Raphael fresco – in the fine medieval quarter beyond Piazza Danti. Both routes meet up at Piazza Fortebraccio, access point for the city's northern quarters (see p.562).

West of the Corso: Via dei Priori to San Francesco

The steeply sloping **Via dei Priori**, if you're to believe the medieval chroniclers, was a conduit for almost constantly flowing rivers of blood from those killed in the vendettas and intrigues for which Perugia was famous. The side streets, too, have associations with Perugia's gory past, notably **Via della Gabbia**, the first street down on the right, where there once hung a large iron cage used to imprison thieves and wayward clergymen. A journal written in 1492 records the fate of one priest, Angelo di Ferolo, who wound up behind its bars: "It was very cold and there was much snow, and he remained there until the first day of February both night and day and that same day he was brought out dead". You can still make out long spikes on some of the lower walls of the street, used for the heads of executed criminals.

Just beyond, on the left, is the little church of **SS Severo e Agata** (daily 8am–1pm & 3–7pm; free), which was built between 1219 and 1314 on the site of an earlier chapel and retains a sense of its austere Romanesque origins. Inside, a *Crucifixion* dominates the altar wall, possibly from the earlier structure, discovered during restoration work in 1911. There are good fragments of two fourteenth-century Umbrian school fresco cycles on the west and north walls, the latter – *Scenes from the Life of San Severo* – the more intelligible. **San Filippo Neri**, farther down on the right, is a Baroque church worth a look for its high altarpiece, a painting of the *Immaculate Conception* (1662) by Pietro da Cortona, a local star who would go on to make his name in Rome and Florence. On the left of the street as you descend, at no. 52, is the *Bar dell'Accademia* (see p.566).

Further down still is the rarely open **Santi Stefano e Valentino**, a lovely little thirteenth-century church on the right with fragments of frescoes; it puts the ugly **Santa Teresa** opposite to shame. Nearby is the unmissable 46-metre **Torre degli Sciri**, one of the few medieval towers (they reputedly numbered seven hundred) to have survived. Off to the right near here, Via della Cupa leads off towards Via Deliziosa and signs for the Casa di Perugino at no. 17 – not really worth the detour.

Near the end of Via dei Priori comes **Madonna della Luce** (1513–19), dominated by a vault frescoed by G.B. Caporali and an altarpiece by Tiberio d'Assisi, both accomplished followers of Perugino. The tiny chapel takes its name ("Madonna of the Light") from an incident in 1513, when a young barber swore so profusely on losing at cards that a Madonna in a wayside shrine closed her eyes in horror, and kept them closed for four days. The miracle inspired celebrations, processions and the building of this new church. Immediately to the left, the **Porta Trasimena**, or Arco di San Luca, has been one of the principal entrances to the city since Etruscan times.

Bearing right beyond the Madonna della Luce brings you to a welcoming patch of grass, often frequented by students from the art school next door, and conveniently placed for admiring Agostino di Duccio's colourful **Oratorio di San Bernardino** (daily 8am–12.30pm & 3.30–6pm; free). Its richly embellished façade is far and away the best piece of sculpture in the city, an odd but appealing mix of bas-reliefs and coloured marble, commissioned in 1457 by the city's magistrates in gratitude to St Bernardino for trying to bring peace to Perugia. The detail of the carving warrants a close look, especially the lower frieze depicting the Bonfire of the Vanities – a pile of Perugian wigs, books and hosiery elicited by the saint's preaching. The church interior is infrequently open, but contains the tomb of Fra' Angelo, who ordered the oratory's construction, and a high altar fashioned from a fourth-century Christian sarcophagus. Alongside is what's left of **San Francesco**, Bernardino's lodging in the city, and in its time Perugia's most sumptuous church. Started just four years after Francis's death in 1226, it's been laid low by earthquakes and landslips, though the curiously jumbled façade is still just about standing and the interior is often used as a concert hall. From San Francesco, Via Alessandro Pascoli leads east to Piazza Fortebraccio (see p.562).

East of the Corso

Piazza Danti, the pleasant little square behind the Duomo, is the scene of a weekend flower and terracotta market and site of a third-century BC **Pozzo Etrusco**, or Etruscan well, entered at no. 18 (April–Oct Wed–Mon 10am–1.30pm & 2.30–6.30pm, also open Tues in April & Aug; Nov–March Wed–Mon 10.30am–1.30pm & 2.30–5pm; €2.50, includes entry to the Cappella di San Severo and Museo delle Porte e Mura Urbiche, with a week's validity), well worth the few minutes it takes to see. Little in the dim, ancient alley that drops to the entrance hints at the scale of the structure, a massive affair that dramatically illustrates the engineering and technical skills of its Etruscan builders. Its 430,000-litre capacity was sufficient to supply the entire city – water still gathers here from moisture-bearing strata – and was at least 35m deep: the precise depth is impossible to ascertain because of debris at the bottom of the shaft.

Close by is the church of **San Severo** (same hours and ticket as Pozzo Etrusco), the chief sight of this district; take Via Bontempi off the square, then the tiny stepped Via Raffaello curving left, and the church is straight ahead in Piazza Raffaello. Legend claims it was built on the site of a pagan temple to the sun – the spot is east-facing and the town's highest point – which gave its name to the Porta Sole district of the Etruscan city. There would once have been five such districts, spreading down from the temple to five corresponding gates in the outer wall. Most of the church is a Baroque rehash, grafted onto a building that dates from 1007, though one chapel was spared – a survivor that contains one of **Raphael**'s first complete works, a *Holy Trinity and Saints* (1505–8 and 1521), probably painted shortly before (or just after) he settled in Florence in 1505. The fresco, as often in paintings of the Trinity, is on three levels, though the upper level – God the Father – is missing. Notice the figure of Christ, whose nudity echoes the nudity of the heroes of Classical art, and which shows the young Raphael's assimilation of new Renaissance notions. The painter was summoned to Rome to work in the Vatican and never completed the picture: in a poignant piece of artistic irony, the lower panels, depicting *Six Saints*, were painted in 1521 by Perugino, then in his dotage, a year after the death of his erstwhile pupil. Perugino's work shows him at his most stilted, an artist who found a winning formula from which he never moved on, even in old age: Raphael's debt to his master is obvious, but even as a fledgling talent in this fresco he demonstrates his more dynamic approach, not least in the arrangement of his figures: where Perugino's saints stand in a line, face on, Raphael's figures are arranged facing out or sideways, creating a more dramatic compositional effect.

From San Severo, it's easy to continue to Piazza Fortebraccio by way of **Santa Maria Nuova**, a sprawling and much knocked-about church recently restored more or less to its original Gothic appearance (to reach it, return to Via Bontempi and turn left downhill). Its main point of interest is the *gonfalone* in the second chapel on the right; created in 1472 by Bonfigli, it features a view of Perugia under attack from divine thunderbolts. Via Pinturicchio heads on to Piazza Fortebraccio.

In the area above here, the **Porta Sole** proper, there once stood the palace of Cardinal Montemaggiore of Cluny, the city's papal governor from 1372. Though his residence was described by contemporaries as the most beautiful in Italy, he was hated by the locals, described as "that French Vandal, that most iniquitous Nero" – perhaps because he removed bits of the Duomo to aid construction of the palace. Within three years a revolt and siege had sent him scurrying, and the palace was reduced to rubble by a vast catapult dubbed the *cacciaprete*, or priest-hunter.

The northern quarters

The **northern quarters** of the *centro storico* start at **Piazza Fortebraccio**, ten minutes' walk downhill from Piazza IV Novembre, and a similar distance from San Francesco and Santa Maria Nuova. The first route follows Perugia's oldest street, the 2500-year-old **Via Ulisse Rocchi**; the second passes the modern university buildings and goes under the famous raised walkway of **Via del Acquedotto**. However, the best way to tackle this northern part of the city is actually to use this walkway – the views are great and there's no traffic. It can be picked up off Via Baldeschi just north of Piazza IV Novembre, or from just southwest of Piazza Fortebraccio. By following its continuation, Via del Fagiano, you can walk, if you wish, as far as the midway point of Corso Garibaldi near Sant'Agnese. Failing that, walk north from Piazza Fortebraccio and use it to return to the city centre from **Sant'Angelo**, the best of the rather lacklustre sights in the northern quarters: the church is well worth the walk, if only to have a picnic or snooze in its grounds.

Piazza Fortebraccio and Sant'Agostino

Unlovely **Piazza Fortebraccio** is dominated by the **Arco di Augusto**, or Arco Etrusco, a massive gateway whose lowest section represents one of the few remaining monuments to Etruscan Perugia. It dates from the second century

BC, when it was the main entrance to the city. The upper arch and bulwarks were added by the Romans when they recaptured the city in 40 BC; under the arch you can still see the letters spelling out its new name, Augusta Perusia – the first part immodestly large, the latter considerably smaller. The top-storey loggia is a sixteenth-century addition. On the western side of the square, housed in the Palazzo Gallenga, is the **Università Italiana per Stranieri**, founded in 1925 and now a favourite of foreign students keen to bone up on Italian art, language and culture.

A short walk north along Corso Garibaldi brings you out to the half-defunct church of **Sant'Agostino** (Mon–Sat 7.30am–12.30pm & 3.30–6.30pm, Sun 7.30am–12.30; free), originally Romanesque, now botched Baroque, and filled with wistful signs explaining which paintings (fine works by Perugino and others) used to hang in the church before they were spirited to France by light-fingered Napoleonic troops. The missing pictures have been replaced with pretty poor modern art. The church, however, is not entirely ruined: there's a beautiful **choir** (1502), probably based on drawings by Perugino, and patches of fresco in the second and third chapels of the north (left-hand) wall, giving a tantalizing idea of what the place must once have been like. Better still is the fresco *Madonna delle Grazie* attributed to Giannicolo di Paolo in the glassed-off first chapel on the south wall. Adjoining the church is the fifteenth-century **Oratorio di Sant'Agostino**, its ludicrously ornate ceiling erupting in gilt, stucco and chubby plaster cherubs. It's entered from the piazza; Sant'Agostino's sacristan should open up if you ask.

Sant'Angelo

At the end of Corso Garibaldi, tucked into the northern corner of the walls, is the circular **Sant'Angelo** (Tues–Sun 9.30am–noon & 3.30pm–dusk; free), founded in the fifth century as a temple to St Michael the Archangel (hence "Angelo"). One of the oldest churches in Umbria – Spoleto's San Salvatore just pips it for antiquity – it was probably built on the site of a Roman temple, its two rings of pillars deriving from an earlier building (there was once a third set, removed to build the church of San Pietro; see p.565). Further evidence of a pagan predecessor lurks in the high altar, which is cobbled together from Roman fragments. In a touch of decorative subtlety, all the columns of the inner ring are made from a different type of stone, but otherwise the church is beautifully plain, its Baroque additions having been stripped away. The setting, too, is delightful, a grassy and tranquil retreat, the shade of the walls and cypresses outside providing a favourite siesta spot.

Virtually alongside the church is the **Museo delle Porte e delle Mura Urbiche** (April–Oct Wed–Mon 11am–1.30pm & 3–6.30pm plus Tues in April & Aug; Nov–March Wed–Mon 11am–1.30pm & 3–5pm; €2.50, includes entry to Pozzo Etrusco and Cappella di San Severo, with a week's validity). It is housed in the Porta Sant'Angelo, built in the fourteenth century and the largest of Perugia's medieval gateways. The small museum details the history of the city's walls, gateways and other fortifications, but perhaps the best moment comes with the superb view from the top of the gate's tower.

The southern quarters

Perugia's other highlights are grouped together on the southern side of town along **Corso Cavour**, the busy main road out of town towards Assisi, which you can access by walking down from the nineteenth-century **Piazza Italia** across Via Baglioni and the stepped alley off Via Oberdan under the Arco di Sant'Ercolano.

En route, you'll pass the strange octagonal church of **Sant'Ercolano** (now a war memorial), raised between 1297 and 1326 on the spot where the head of Perugia's first bishop miraculously reattached itself after it had been removed by the Goths. A little southwest of this is the **Porta Marzia** (daily 8am–7pm), a superb Etruscan archway above an entrance to **Via Baglioni Sotterranea**, part of an extraordinary complex of submerged medieval streets that can also be accessed from the escalators on the southwest side of Piazza Italia and from Piazza Partigiani. The streets' houses, built over Etruscan ruins, now form part of the foundations for Piazza Italia above, but were once part of the Rocca Paolina, a colossal sixteenth-century papal fortress designed by Sangallo, the remains of which can best be seen coming up on the escalators from Piazza Partigiani (or down from the west side of Piazza Italia). Taking in ten churches and four hundred houses, the Rocca was connected by tunnels to strategic points throughout the city. It was pulled down at Unification, using dynamite and bare hands, by what appears to have been every man, woman and child in the city – and even then the process took thirty years. Trollope, watching the demolition, wrote that "few buildings have been laden with a heavier amount of long-accumulated hatred". Within the Rocca's old confines is **La Rocca Paolina e La Città** (Mon–Fri 2.30–6.30pm, Sat & Sun 10.30am–1pm & 2.30–6.30pm; €1), with modest displays divided into four chronological groups, documenting the fortress's history.

San Domenico

The unmissable landmark on Corso Cavour is **San Domenico**, which, at 122m in length, is Umbria's biggest church. Its unfinished exterior has an attractively melancholy air, with pigeons nesting and grass growing on the pinkish marble, but the interior (begun in 1305) collapsed in the sixteenth century to be replaced by a vast, cold Baroque conversion (1632).

Like Sant'Agostino, however, it's full of hints of past beauties. In the fourth chapel on the right, the Cappella della Madonna del Voto, is a superb **carved arch** by Agostino di Duccio (1459), a fragment of the original church spoilt only by nineteenth-century frescoes and a doll-like Madonna. On the right wall of the first chapel to the right of the high altar is the **tomb of Benedict XI**, another pope who died in Perugia – this time from eating poisoned figs – after ruling for just eight months in 1304. He left to posterity one of the greatest Gothic carvings of its kind in Italy, an elegant and well-preserved piece by one of the period's leading sculptors – Giovanni Pisano, Lorenzo Maitani or Arnolfo di Cambio; nobody knows which, although it's modelled on the tomb of Cardinal de Braye in Orvieto, one of Arnolfo's most influential works (see p.728). Some of the marble work is missing, picked out by troops when a Napoleonic cavalry regiment was billeted in the church. In the next chapel to the right are extensive patches of fresco, another good choir, and – a welcome splash of colour – some impressive stained-glass windows (1411), the largest in Italy after those of Milan cathedral. Also worth hunting out is the *gonfalone* (painted banner) by **Giannicolo di Paolo** in the third chapel in the south transept. It was painted as a votive offering after the plague of 1494 and shows Christ above with the people of Perugia and a view of the city below flanked by saints Dominic and Catherine of Siena. The right wall of the left-most chapel in the north transept has an interesting **fresco of St Sebastian** in which, for once, the saint is not depicted riddled with arrows: the painting instead shows the archers preparing to fire.

It is possible to view **Le Soffitte di San Domenico**, the church's imposing vaults and lofts, which contain works by Giovanni Pisano and Carlo Maderno. Guided visits (Sat & Sun only) are by prior appointment on ☎075.573.1635.

The Museo Archeologico Nazionale dell'Umbria

Housed in San Domenico's cloisters is the **Museo Archeologico Nazionale dell'Umbria**, Piazza Giordano Bruno 10 (Mon 2.30–7.30pm, Tues–Sun 8.30am–7.30pm; €4; the hard-to-find ticket office is on the first floor of the cloister). Before being hammered by Augustus, Perugia was a big shot in the twelve-strong Etruscan federation of cities, which is why the city has one of Italy's most extensive Etruscan collections. The museum has recently undergone a major overhaul, and is definitely worth a visit: there's far more here than the usual run of Etruscan urns and funerary monuments. Particularly compelling are the **Carri Etruschi di Castel San Marino**, some quite exquisite sixth-century BC bronze chariots; a witty collection of eye-opening artefacts devoted to fashion and beauty in the Etruscan era; and a series of bronze helmets and shields. The bewildering **Bellucci Collection** is a private hoard of charms and amulets through the ages: everything from the obvious – lucky horseshoes – to stranger and often more sinister charms such as snakeskins, dried animals, feathers and odd scraps of wool. The exhibits span several thousand years, and form a unique and oddly poignant picture of fears and superstitious hopes across the millennia. Other parts of the museum are still in the process of being updated.

San Pietro

Further south on Corso Cavour, through the double-arched Porta San Pietro (1147), is the tenth-century basilica of **San Pietro**, the city's first cathedral and still the most beautiful and idiosyncratic of its churches. Advertised by a rocket-shaped bell-tower visible for miles around (rebuilt in 1463), it's tangled up in a group of buildings belonging to the university's agricultural department; the entrance is through a doorway in the far left-hand corner of the first courtyard off the road.

The **interior** comes as a shock. Few churches, even in Italy, are so sumptuously decorated, every inch of space being covered in gilt, paint or marble. The effect is appealing, and in the candle lit gloom the church actually feels like a sacred place. That so much of the Romanesque building survives is due to events at Unification, when the church's Benedictine monks sided with the townspeople in their revolt against papal control. Loyalty to the cause of liberation was not forgotten, and when the religious houses were broken up a year later, San Pietro was allowed to keep its patrimony.

The interior's finest single component is the extraordinary **choir** (1526), which has been called the greatest in Italy. All the woodwork here is superb: look out also for the intricately gilded side-pulpits. As for the **paintings**, there's a *Pietà* by Perugino between the first and second altars on the left, three works by Vasari in the Cappella del Sacramento, and a much-praised depiction of *Christ on the Mount* by Guido Reni (located on the left wall of the Cappella Ranieri); the eleven eye-catching frescoes around the upper walls are by a disciple of Veronese. The baffling fresco on the rear wall is a genealogical tree of the Benedictines, collecting together the most eminent members of the order. The best pictures of all are five saints by Perugino and a possible Raphael, gathered in the **sacristy**; you'll probably have to ask the sacristan to let you in.

The Orto Botanico

If you've walked this far, you might want to push on a touch further down the road beyond San Pietro to rest up in the shady and attractive **Orto Botanico**, founded in 1768, at Borgo XX Giugno 74 (Mon–Fri 8am–5pm; free). The gardens divide into two: the medieval section is on the left immediately beyond the church, with the larger botanical section on the right through the Porta San Costanzo.

Eating, drinking and entertainment

Perugia's cuisine is rewarding. While a plethora of fast-food and snack bars cater for the student market, there are several good mid-range **restaurants** and a couple of top-notch ones. There are also plenty of places to **drink**, including the inevitable rash of Irish pubs, but the city's big and busy clubs and discos are all in the suburbs.

There is a permanent covered **food market**, the Mercato Coperto (Mon–Sat 7.30am–1pm), off Piazza Matteotti. An open-air **general market** (Tues & Sat 8am–1pm) operates on the Scala di Sant'Ercolano, near the church of the same name. You can buy other picnic supplies – cheese, hams and so forth – from Giuliano at Via Danzetta 1, a small alley off the east side of the Corso just north of Piazza della Repubblica.

Perugia is strong on events, with films, theatre and concerts packing a page or so each day in the **listings** of the local *Corriere dell'Umbria* newspaper. Posters around the city, in particular near the Università Italiana per Stranieri on Piazza Fortebraccio, give details of concerts and English-language films, which are especially frequent in the April to December term times.

Cafés and bars

Bar dell'Accademia Via dei Priori 52. A good place for a break on a street with several cafés and restaurants. It has a great spread of pastries, and plenty of room to sit at the back.
Bottega del Vino Via del Sole 1 ☏075.571.6181.

A wine bar and shop near Piazza Danti which offers wine by the glass or bottle, along with snacks. Evenings only; until 1am. Closed Sun.
Caffè di Perugia Via Mazzini 10 ☏075.573.1863, Ⓦ www.caffediperugia.it. A pleasantly smart setting with superb vaulted

△ Every July Perugia hosts the world-famous Umbria Jazz festival ceiling from the thirteenth century. All the café staples, plus a restaurant with simple meals, a pizzeria-grill and a wine bar, the last a good early evening retreat. Closed Tues.

Caffè Morlacchi Piazza Morlacchi 8. Smart but student-oriented bar; get to it along Via delle Volte from Piazza IV Novembre. Occasional live music.

Enoteca Provinciale Via Ulisse Rocchi 16–18. Close to the Duomo, this wineshop-cum-bar is the best place to indulge in the local wines; it also does excellent snacks in a room to the rear and has a vast selection of wines to buy by the bottle. Mon 4.30–8.30pm, Tues–Sat 10.30am–2.30pm & 4.30–10pm.

Gelateria Soleluna Via Bonazzi 3. Queues from this ice cream parlour off the Corso often stretch onto the nearby Piazza della Repubblica, especially at the height of the Sunday *passeggiata*. A great choice of flavours and very generous scoops.

Il Birraio Via delle Prome 18. There's no mistaking the beer bias of this odd, modern place, the entrance to which is lined with the copper tanks and vats of an in-house micro-brewery. Tues–Sun 5pm–2am.

Pasticceria Sandri Corso Vannucci 32. The most atmospheric café in Perugia – turn-of-the-century Viennese style with lots of brass, wood panels and frescoed ceilings. Worth at least one cake and cappuccino just for the interior. Closed Mon.

Pizza al Taglio Via dei Priori 3. Small hole-in-the-wall place on the corner with Via della Gabbia, a few steps from the Corso, that does a roaring trade in pizza by the slice to take away.

Shamrock Pub Piazza Danti 18. Predictable but conveniently central Irish pub and restaurant in an alley almost next to the Pozzo Etrusco.

Restaurants

Cesarino Piazza IV Novembre 4–5 ☎075.572.8974. A very central old trattoria-pizzeria that has been around for over thirty years, though sadly it's been modernized a touch recently. Booking is advised, as it attracts students, visitors, locals, Perugia's first-team footballers and politicians alike. Around €25, less for pizzas. Closed Wed.

Dal Mi' Cucco Corso Garibaldi 12 ☎075.573.2511. A variety of set-price menus are available here: the restaurant, as the old local dialect name suggests, presents traditional Perugian dishes. Good value at around €13. Closed Mon.

Del Sole Via Oberdan 28 ☎075.573.5031, ⓦwww.ristorantesole.it. Two large dining rooms under ancient vaults and a terrace with a fine view for summer dining. Food is classic Umbrian (great

antipasti), and a full meal should come in at no more than €30. Tucked away in an alley off the main Via Oberdan. Closed Mon.

Falchetto Via Bartolo 20 ☎075.573.1775, ⓦwww.ilfalchetto.it. Central, reliable restaurant in a simple medieval setting just off Piazza Danti; food is adequate but service can be slapdash. Reasonably priced if you stick to the basics. Closed Mon.

Giancarlo Via dei Priori 36 ☎075.572.4314. Simple but perfectly cooked Umbrian staples, a central location and low prices mean you'll have to book or may have to join a queue to eat at this nononsense trattoria. Closed Fri, and for three weeks during Aug & Sept.

La Taverna Via delle Streghe 8, off Piazza della Repubblica ☎075.572.4128. Tucked away in a small alley, a serious restaurant that often claims the highest rating in the Italian foodie guides that count. Serves a mixture of regional and one-off inventive dishes, plus heavyweight desserts. Wines are overpriced, though, and when the place is full service and food can occasionally suffer. From €30. Closed Mon & late July.

Osteria del Gambero Via Baldeschi 9 ☎075.573.5461, ⓦwww .osteriadelgambero.it. Don't be put off by the English menus: this is a great place that's been in business since 1989 and has picked up a clutch of awards for its traditional cooking. The interior is simple and tasteful; three *degustazione* menus are priced at €25 (vegetarian) or €27 (food of "the territory") and €29 (fish and seafood) with wine. Otherwise €20–25. Closed Sun.

Osteria Il Gufo Via della Viola, junction Via Alessi ☎075.573.4126. The best sort of *osteria*: relaxed atmosphere, old marble tables, open kitchen, traditional regional cooking with the odd dash of innovation. Has just 35 covers, with a few tables on the tiny piazza outside in summer. From €20. Closed Sun & Mon, and a period in Aug & Sept.

Osteria Turreno Piazza Danti 16 ☎075.572.1976. This highly recommended *tavola calda* has been in business for several generations and it shows: the handful of hot dishes each lunchtime are simple but well prepared and very fairly priced. You can buy food to take away or sit outside, at one of a handful of tables by the counter, or in the larger (and rather hidden) seating area to the rear. From €5; for €10 you can get meat, veg, salad, a hunk of bread and a soft drink. Lunch only. Closed Sat.

Pizzeria Etrusca Via Ulisse Rocchi 31 ☎075.572.0762. Located on the hill down to Piazza Braccio Fortebraccio, this is a no-nonsense pizzeria whose keen prices make it popular with students.

PERUGIA AND NORTHERN UMBRIA | Eating, drinking and entertainment

Pizzeria Mediterranea Piazza Piccinino 11–12
℡075.572.1322. A stylish two-roomed pizzeria just a few steps from Piazza Danti and the Pozzo Etrusco, with simple medieval stone walls, a wood-fired oven and pretty brick vaults. From €8. Daily.

Scalino Via Sant'Ercolano 2 ℡075.572.5372. On the corner of Via Oberdan and this narrow stepped alley, *Scalino* is an authentic and old-fashioned pizzeria and trattoria staffed by venerable women and patronized almost entirely by locals. It has a fabulous brick-vaulted dining room and very reasonable prices.

Listings

Books and newspapers Libreria Novecento, Via dei Priori 64, has a good selection of maps, guides and English-language titles. For English newspapers, try the stands along the Corso.

Bus enquiries ASP, Piazza dei Partigiani ℡ or Pian di Massiano ℡075.751.145, ᴡwww.apmperugia.it; SIT ℡0743.212.211; ATC ℡0744.402.900; Sulga ℡800.099.661.

Car rental Avis: airport ℡075.692.9346 or 075.692.9796, train station Piazza Vittorio Veneto 7 ℡075.500.0395; Hertz: train station Piazza Vittorio Veneto 4 ℡075.500.2439 or 0337.650.837.

Changing money Foreign exchange is handled by most of the banks on Corso Vannucci.

Flight enquiries ℡075.592.141, ᴡwww.airport.umbria.it. Tickets ℡075.592.1423.

Lost property ℡075.577.5373.

Medical facilities Late-night pharmacy: Farmacia San Martino, Piazza Matteotti 26 ℡075.572.2335. Hospital: Via Bonacci Brunamonti ℡075.60.81 or

075.57.81. For first aid, call ℡075.578.3422. For an ambulance, call ℡113 or 075.691.9480.

Phones Booths at the post office are open until 11.45pm; the Telecom Italia offices in Via Marconi, Corso Cavour and Corso Vannucci are open 8.30am–10pm.

Police (Questura) ℡075.50.621.

Post office Piazza Matteotti (Mon–Fri 10am–5.30pm, Sat 10am–2pm; ℡075.573.6977).

Student travel CTGS Student Centre, Via del Roscetto 21 ℡075.572.0284 or 075.572.7050.

Study courses For details and prospectuses contact the Università Italiana per Stranieri ℡075.57.461, ᴡwww.unistrapg.it.

Taxis Radio Taxi ℡075.500.4888; Piazza Italia ℡075.573.6092; Corso Vannucci ℡075.572.1979; train station ℡075.501.0800.

Train enquiries Railway station, Piazza Vittorio Veneto ℡89.20.21, ᴡwww.trenitalia.it; FCU private line, Stazione Sant'Anna ℡075.572.9121, ᴡwww.fcu.it.

Lago Trasimeno

The most tempting option near Perugia – whose surroundings are generally pretty bleak – is the reed-fringed **Lago Trasimeno**. An ideal spot to hole up for a few days and swim (if you don't mind murky water), it is the biggest stretch of water on the Italian peninsula and the fourth largest in Italy overall (after Garda, Maggiore and Como), though at times is in danger of drying up completely. With demands on water from agriculture and increased silting, the lake's greatest depth is no more than 7m (average 4.9m) – hence its bath-warm temperature in the summer. It's mostly clean, however, largely because the tourist and fishing industries are the area's economic bread and butter: banks of weed occasionally drift in during the summer, but they're peremptorily taken care of by the council and dumped on the shore. Note that the lake is also easily accessible from, and provides a base for visits to, Cortona (see p.531).

People have lived on or close to Trasimeno's shores since Paleolithic times, though its greatest historical fame dates from 217 BC, when the Romans suffered one of the worst defeats in their history at the hands of **Hannibal** (see p.571). Its strategic position meant that numerous castles and fortified villages grew up on its shores and in the hills around, predecessors of present-day towns

Listings • Lago Trasimeno

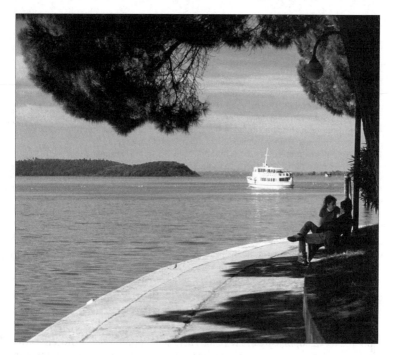

△ Lago Trasimeno

such as Castiglione del Lago. Attempts to regulate the fluctuating water level date back to Roman times, and a number of serious proposals have been put forward to drain the lake altogether. These remained largely in abeyance for much of the late Middle Ages, when the (then) wooded shores were exploited for hunting, and again in the nineteenth century, when the marshy surrounds became a breeding ground for malarial mosquitoes.

These days the main drawback to Trasimeno is its popularity: in high season the lake is covered with speedboats, yachts and windsurfers. If you're after relative seclusion, steer clear of the northern shore – recently opened up by Perugia's autostrada spur – and head instead for the stretches south of Magione and Castiglione, though even here, foreign number-plates are in ever greater evidence. Be warned that **unofficial camping** is not as easy as it looks: commercial sites have grabbed the best spots and much of the remaining shoreline is marshy. If you're just passing through, probably the nicest thing to do is settle down for a long fish lunch at one of the lakefront restaurants in Castiglione, or take a **boat trip** from Passignano, Tuoro or Castiglione to the Isola Maggiore, one of the three islands on the lake.

Passignano

The lake's most accessible point is **PASSIGNANO**, a newish and reasonably attractive resort strung out along the northern shore and served by hourly trains from Perugia and Teróntola (near Cortona). Popular with Italians, the town in summer is often one big traffic jam, Sundays being especially bad. In

Boats on Lago Trasimeno

Boats run roughly twelve times a day throughout the year from **Passignano**'s land-
ing-stage in front of Piazza Garibaldi to the **Isola Maggiore** – either directly (Sun only;
takes 25min) or via **Tuoro** (Mon–Sat; 35min). Boats also shuttle between Passignano
and Tuoro (summer up to 8 daily; 20min), and Passignano and **Castiglione del Lago**
(twice on summer Sat & Sun; 40min). Boats run to the Isola Maggiore from Castiglione del Lago, but with reduced services outside summer (May–Sept 6–8 daily;
Oct–April Sat & Sun 6–8 daily; 30min). To reach **Isola Polvese**, there are boats year-
round from both Passignano (once daily; 55min) and San Feliciano on the eastern
lakeshore (around 9 daily; 10min), about 12km from Passignano.

Typical **ticket prices** are €5.60 return for the trip from Passignano to Isola Maggiore; €4.50 return from Tuoro to Isola Maggiore; and €6.10 return from Castiglione del Lago to Isola Maggiore. For more information, contact APM-Navigazione
(☎075.506.781, ⊛www.apmperugia.it – click on "orari" and then "Navigazione Lago
Trasimeno").

the evenings, though, it's an enjoyable place as people come flooding in from
the surrounding campsites, livening up the bars, discos and fish restaurants. The
waterfront strip is the chief focus, and there's plenty going on in the web of
streets behind as well. Bar two dull Renaissance churches and a bit of a castle,
there's nothing much to see: you can skip the town in the daytime unless it's
to catch a boat.

The **tourist office** is at Piazza Trento e Trieste 6 (June–Sept Mon–Sat
10am–12.30pm & 4–7pm, Sun 10am–12.30pm; Oct–May Fri & Sat 3–6.30pm,
Sun 10am–12.30pm; ☎075.827.635). There are around a dozen **hotels**, most
in the upper bracket. The least expensive options are the fifteen-room one-star
Florida, Via II Giugno 2 (☎075.827.228; ❶), and eleven-room one-star *Del
Pescatore*, Via San Bernardino 5 (☎075.829.6063, ⊜delpescatore@libero.it; ❶),
both comfortable places where all rooms are en suite; or try the larger, smarter
three-star *Trasimeno*, Via Roma 16a (☎075.829.355, ⊛www.hoteltrasimeno.it;
❷). Just 1km north of town in a quiet spot among olives and oaks is the three-
star *Hotel Cavalieri*, Via delle Ginestre (☎075.829.292, ⓕ075.829009, ⊛www
.hotelcavalieri.it; ❸). Some of the 35 rooms have lovely lake views, as does the
dining terrace of its *La Sosta dei Templari* restaurant (closed Tues). There's also an
outdoor pool. The main **campsites** are in the nearby hamlet of San Donato,
notably the *Europa* (☎075.827.405, ⊛www.camping-europa.it; April–Sept).
You can rent **bikes** from Brunello Ragnoni, Via Pompili 61 (☎075.829.239)
and Tecno Motors, Via Natale Ambrogi 6 (☎075.829.6182).

Passignano has plenty of simple **pizzerie** and cheap **restaurants**. If you
want to eat lots of fish, make for the *Cacciatori da Luciano*, Via Nazionale 11
(☎075.827.210; closed Wed – except during summer – & Nov), which also has
an entrance at Via Pompili 11. Otherwise, the best local restaurant is *La Darsena*,
3.5km east at Via Perugina 52 in San Donato (☎075.829.331; closed Wed); it
gets away from the area's obsession with fish (though fish is still available), and
has three-star hotel rooms (❶).

Tuoro sul Trasimeno

The rambling hill-village of **TUORO SUL TRASIMENO**, 4km west of Passignano and a three-kilometre walk from the Trasimeno battlefield, is a quiet but
decidedly dull little place giving road access into the desolate, beautiful mountains north of the lake – the best scenery within easy reach of Perugia.

Hannibal and the Battle of Lago Trasimeno

On the lakeshore west of Passignano is the spot where the Romans suffered the most traumatic defeat in their history, on June 24, 217 BC, at the hands of **Hannibal**. The Carthaginian leader was headed for Rome, having already crossed the Alps and won a sweeping victory at Placentia – though by this stage only one of his famous elephants was still alive. He was accompanied by a battle-hardened army of around 40,000, and was met by a Roman force of some 25,000 men under the consul **Flaminius** (builder of the Via Flamina), close to an amphitheatre of hills above the lake – a location, said the historian Livy, that was "formed by Nature for an ambush".

Things might have gone better for Flaminius if he'd heeded the omens that piled up on the morning of battle. First he fell off his horse, then the legionary standards had to be dug from the mud, then – and this should have been the clincher – the sacred chickens refused their breakfast. (Poultry accompanied all Roman armies in the field, their behaviour or the look of their innards at moments of crisis being interpreted as communications of the will of the gods.) With the chickens against him Flaminius didn't stand a chance. Hannibal lured him into a masterful ambush, ranging his men in the hills above the amphitheatre under the cover of early-morning mist. Meanwhile he sent a small detachment over the hills to the rear of the amphitheatre, allowing Flaminius to see them, thus tricking the Roman commander into thinking he had seen the tail end of Hannibal's army vacating the basin. Thus duped, Flaminius abandoned his marshy position on the lakeshore in favour of the amphitheatre's drier ground. As he marched into the trap Hannibal's men poured down the surrounding slopes, creating havoc among the Roman soldiers – who were marching in a non-battle formation – many of whom barely had time to draw their swords. The only escape lay in a muddy retreat back to the lakeshore, where they were mercilessly pursued and hacked down by Hannibal's men. Two entire legions (16,000 men) were killed, including the hapless commander, run through with a lance. The slaughter lasted for three hours. Hannibal, for his part, is thought to have lost just 1500 men.

Hannibal's sappers had orders to bury the dead where they fell, and recently 113 mass graves, or *ustrina* – deep stone-lined pits with lids – have been discovered. Scientific dating of the remains tallies exactly with the date of the battle. You can follow a poorly waymarked **walk** and **drive** (see below) around the battlefield area, which begins off the minor lakeside road about 1km west of Tuoro.

The SPNT boat company office, on the waterfront at Pontile di Tuoro, Punta Navaccia, is also home to a seasonal **tourist office** (June–Aug daily 9am–1pm & 4–7pm; ☎075.827.157), which has information on two **walking itineraries** around the battlefield: the *Esterno* (16km) concentrates more on the area's scenery, but the *Interno* (8km) – which takes you through the Valle della Battaglia itself – is not terribly exciting, even when you've managed to find its start, which is vaguely signed 1km from Tuoro as a right turn as you drive west on the minor road towards Cortona (the right turn is a long, straight tree-lined road). That said, the various costly-looking observation platforms along the route give an excellent idea of the lie of the land, though it's hard to reconcile the tranquil farm country in front of you with a scene of mass slaughter. A permanent memorial to the carnage exists in the place names of two local hamlets, **Sanguineto** (Place of Blood), which you pass on the battlefield tour, and **Ossaia** (Place of Bones), which lies northwest just below Cortona.

Accommodation is restricted to a single **hotel**, the eight-roomed *Volante Inn*, Via Sette Martiri 52 (☎075.826.107, ✉volanteinn@libero.it; ❶); in the nearby hamlet of Punta Navaccia is the *Punta Navaccia* **campsite**, Via Navaccia 4 (☎075.826.357, ✉navaccia@camping.it; April–Sept).

Castel Rigone

CASTEL RIGONE, 8km east of Passignano, is the outstanding – virtually the only – village in the mountains above the lake. If you have time you can make a neat little driving tour of the area by taking the road north out of Tuoro to Lisciano (13km), then cutting southeast to Castel Rigone via Pian di Marte and Trecine (20km). Castel Rigone itself is a faintly odd little village with superb views and a small, geranium-strewn medieval centre. Most of its incumbents are pensioners, here for the bracing climate and fresh air. There are two smart, rather staid **hotels**, the better of which is the *Relais La Fattoria*, Via Rigone 1 (☎075.845.322, ⓦwww.relaislafattoria.com; ❸), occasionally cited for its **restaurant**, which in reality isn't up to much. A little outside Castel Rigone village is the Renaissance church of **Madonna dei Miracoli**, much lauded but not worth a special visit and somewhat out of place in the overall medieval context.

Castiglione del Lago

CASTIGLIONE DEL LAGO cuts a fine silhouette from other points on the lake, jutting into the water on a fortified promontory. It's a friendly, unpretentious place that can hold your attention for a couple of days – longer if all you want to do is crash out on one of its modest but pleasant **beaches**. These are dotted around the promontory (the best swimming is on the south side) but get extremely busy in summer. It's easy to reach Castiglione by road and rail, though as a lot of the fast trains on the Rome–Florence line no longer stop here, you'll probably end up taking a slower train from Chiusi or Teróntola.

There's little in the town to head for, despite its Etruscan and Roman origins, though the largely sixteenth-century **castle**, or Rocca del Leone (April–Oct daily 10am–1pm & 3–7pm; Nov–March Sat & Sun 10am–4pm; €3) is well preserved, particularly its strange fortified passageway, part of a defensive scheme that in the thirteenth century made it one of Europe's impregnable fortresses. Its design has been attributed to Frate Elias, a controversial Franciscan monk (see p.606) who may also have been responsible for the Basilica di San Francesco in Assisi. The castle ticket also lets you into the ducal **Palazzo della Corgna** in Piazza Gramsci, full of large rooms with ceilings covered in frescoes of Classical subjects. Machiavelli once stayed over here, as did Leonardo da Vinci (in 1503), who made a drawing of the town's fortifications. The castle ramparts offer good views of the lake, and there's a central stage for outdoor summer events. Note that a "**Museo Aperto**" ticket (€6.20) covers entry to the castle and palazzo as well as sights in Panicale (see p.573) and Città della Pieve (see p.731).

You might also hunt down the church of **Santa Maria Maddalena** at the western end of Via Vittorio Emanuele, where the main left altar has a fine *Madonna and Child* by Eusebio di San Giorgio, a follower of Perugino.

Practicalities

The main **tourist office** for the Trasimeno region is in Castiglione's main square, at Piazza Mazzini 10 (Mon 9am–1.30pm, Tues–Sat 9am–1.30pm & 3–7.30pm, Sun 9am–1pm; ☎075.965.2484 or 075.965.2738, ⓔinfo@iat .castiglione-del-lago.pg.it); they have on their books plenty of *agriturismo* choices in the surrounding countryside, a lot of reasonable if characterless **rooms** in private houses, and apartments to rent on a weekly basis.

Hotel prices have shot up to capitalize on the town's increasingly high profile: the top-priced places are the pleasant, family-run three-star *Duca della Corgna*, Via Bruno Buozzi 143 (☎075.953.238, ⓦwww.hotelcorgna.com; ❸), with the three-star *Trasimeno*, Via Roma 174 (☎075.965.2494, ℉075.952.5258; ❸), hot on its heels. The atmospheric *Miralago*, Piazza Mazzini 6 (☎075.951.157, ⓦwww.hotelmiralago.com; ❺), has views of the lake behind. *Fazzouli*, Piazza Marconi 11 (☎075.951.119, ℉075.951.112; ❷), is a modern two-star, though like all these – except the *Miralago* – it's in the newer, lower part of town. Most of the **campsites** are some way north or south; the most highly rated is *Badiaccia*, Via Trasimeno I, 91, Località Badiaccia (☎075.965.9097, ⓦwww.badiaccia.com).

Aside from the summer-only **restaurants** on the promenade, the place to eat game, fish fresh from the lake and other dishes is *L'Acquario*, Via Vittorio Emanuele II 69 (☎075.965.2432; closed Wed; winter also closed Tues) on the old town's main street. Another good option is the *La Fontana* restaurant in the *Miralago* hotel (see above), which in summer has tables in a garden at the rear with pleasant views of the lake. A lovely place for a light meal, snack or glass of wine is *Vinolento*, Via del Forte 75 (☎075.952.5262, ⓦwww.vinolento.it; closed Mon), in a medieval setting with a beautifully frescoed ceiling. The town's lively **market** is on Wednesdays.

Isola Maggiore and Isola Polvese

Regular boats (see p.570) from Passignano, Tuoro and Castiglione make the trip out to **Isola Maggiore**, one of Trasimeno's three islands – a fun ride if you don't mind the crowds. There's a single village of about one hundred people, traditionally known for its lacemaking, and a pretty **walk** round the island's two-kilometre perimeter: follow the quaint brick-paved street from the landing stage to the twelfth-century church of San Salvatore at the top and the path continues beyond. The island is famed for a visit by St Francis in 1211, a forty-day sojourn during which he consumed just half a loaf of bread; a chapel marks the point of his disembarkation, and there's a small Franciscan monastery on the southeast shore. The best outing – and another lovely walk – is through the olive groves to the church of **San Michele Arcangelo**, sited at the island's highest point; the twelfth-century building is decorated with frescoes and has a *Crucifixion* painted by Bartolomeo Caporali in 1460. The island's single **hotel** is the two-star *Da Sauro*, located at the village's northern limit, Via G. Guglielmi 1 (☎075.826.168; ❸); be sure to book ahead, whether it's for a room or for a table in the adjoining and equally popular fish **restaurant** (March–Oct daily; closed Nov–Feb). Alternatively, once everyone's gone home you might discreetly pitch a tent.

Boats also run to the tiny **Isola Polvese**, on which stands the 98-bed *Fattoria Il Poggio* (☎075.965.9550, ⓦwww.fattoriaisolapolvese.com; €17 plus €9.50 for lunch or dinner), with dorm beds, rooms and apartments for rent. It's not far from the jetty, where there is a map showing its location: the owners will generally meet guests and help with luggage. There's no public access to **Isola Minore**, the privately owned third island.

Panicale

The low hills south of Lago Trasimeno make a good scenic backdrop. With your own transport, you could take a detour to **PANICALE**, 5km south of the shore, a village of Etruscan origins which gave birth to the pioneering painter Tommaso Fini, better known as Masolino da Panicale (1383–1440), the master of Masaccio. It's a quiet place for lunch or a stopover, and also breaks your journey if you're walking some of Trasimeno's marked trails. The streets offer picture-postcard views of the lake, plus two easily missed Perugino paintings in the church of **San Sebastiano** (guided tours during opening hours of the tourist office: see below), outside the walls in Viale Belvedere off Piazza Vittoria. Apart from a tiny medieval core, there's little else to the place, save a small museum of religious relics, the Museo degli Arredi Sacri in Via Roma (guided tours during tourist office hours), and the modest Museo del Tulle (June–Aug daily 10am–12.30pm & 4.30–7pm; rest of the year by appointment and guided visit during tourist office hours), a museum in the church of Sant'Agostino devoted to the local tulle fabric.

Panicale's **tourist office** is at Piazza Umberto I 69 (April–Sept daily 10am–12.30pm & 3.30–7pm; Oct–March Fri–Sun 10.30am–12.30pm & 3–5.30pm; ☏075.837.8017). There are two **hotels**, the one-star *Masolino,* Via Roma 7 (☏075.837.180, ℉075.837.151; ●), and the three-star *Le Grotte di Boldrino,* Via Virgilio Ceppari 43 (☏075.837.161, ℉075.837.166, ⓦwww.grottediboldrino .com; ❷); the latter, well furnished with antiques, is built into part of the old medieval walls and surrounded by a garden, with spacious rooms. The hotel **restaurant** offers both pizzas and full meals, though the quality can be erratic. Better might be the *Locanda della Rocca,* in the tiny village of **PANCIANO**, about 4km west of Panicale, Viale Roma 4 (☏075.830.236): it has a great menu, excellent, inexpensive food and lovely views. Also within striking distance of Panicale is the fine *Villa di Monte Solare,* located 14km by road east in the hamlet of Colle San Paolo, at Via Montali 7 (☏075.832.376, ⓦwww.villamontesolare .com; ❺), a lovely 24-room house set amidst olives, vines and woodlands with rooms and common spaces that retain original features such as massive fireplaces, frescoes, antique brickwork and period furniture; meals are also available and there are tennis courts, riding facilities and a pool.

On the map, the main SS220 road below Panicale between Perugia and Città della Pieve looks a good touring proposition; in fact it's a laborious route, spotted by light industry and the odd factory chimney. The only point of interest is the **Santuario di Mongiovino**, a Renaissance temple high above the road, 7km south of Panicale, which looks a good deal more impressive from afar than it does close up.

Northern Umbria

Moving north from Perugia you have two principal options. The most immediately tempting is the thirty-kilometre journey to **Gubbio**, which is among the best-preserved medieval towns in central Italy. This is easily accomplished as a day-trip by car or bus from Perugia, but there's enough in the town and the countryside beyond to warrant an overnight stay, especially if you want to explore the wild upland countryside further east, the best of which is protected by the **Parco Naturale del Monte Cucco**, a mountain park with some excellent hiking trails. Other towns in the remote northeast of the region are rare, and only hilltop **Gualdo Tadino** merits attention – though not a special visit – the only other significant urban centre in the area, Nocera Umbra, having been left little more than a ghost town by the 1997 earthquakes.

The second option from Perugia is to follow the course of the River Tiber (Tevere) towards Sansepolcro, an obvious option if you're heading towards eastern Tuscany or on the trail of Piero della Francesca (see p.517). The river's reaches north of Perugia are pretty and pastoral, and mostly lack the light industry that blights the Valle di Spoleto and stretches of the Tiber further south. However, there is little of major note to see, though if you have time you could take in two artistic diversions at **Montone** and **Morra**, with a fine little art gallery and frescoes by Luca Signorelli respectively. The highlight of the area is **Città di Castello**, an unheralded and relatively little visited town that may not be in quite the same league as Gubbio, but is definitely worth a stop for its pristine medieval centre, outstanding art and trio of fascinating museums.

With your own transport you could combine the region's major towns by visiting Gubbio and then head west on the SS219 road to pick up the SS3bis road north to Città di Castello at Umbertide, a largely modern town with a small medieval core. Public transport connections are slow and infrequent between these two centres, making Città di Castello best seen by rail on the FCU from Perugia if you're without transport.

North from Perugia

The highlight of the area immediately north of Perugia is the abbey of **Santa Maria di Valdiponte** at **MONTELABATE**, on the east side of the valley 16km from Perugia. This monastic foundation once controlled twenty castles in the area, and similar abbeys administered great swathes of the land between Gubbio and the Tiber. Built between the twelfth and fourteenth centuries, the church itself is of rather less interest than the cloisters – which are medieval perfection – and the various artistic treasures, including frescoes by such as Fiorenzo di Lorenzo and Bartolomeo Caporali.

Umbertide

Bombed to the edge of oblivion in World War II, **UMBERTIDE** is now a light-industrial town relieved by a tiny, captivating medieval centre. Artistic attractions are limited to the **Palazzo Comunale** – the best Baroque conversion in Umbria – and a tremendous *Deposition* by Luca Signorelli in the **Museo Comunale di Santa Croce**, just outside the old walls in Piazza San Francesco (June–Sept Fri–Sun 10.30am–1pm & 4–6.30pm; Oct–May Fri–Sun 10.30am–1pm & 3–5.30pm; €3.50). Among a trio of **hotels**, the cheapest is the two-star *Moderno*, Via Nazionale 186 (☎075.941.3759, ℮hotelmoderno@hotmail.com; ❶); rather better – if only because it's more central – is the two-star *Capponi*, Piazza XXV Aprile 19 (☎075.941.2662, ℉075.941.3803; ❶), whose **restaurant** is the standard place to eat.

Monte Corona (693m), 6km south of Umbertide, is topped by the **Badia di San Salvatore**, a good-looking twelfth-century monastery ravaged by a sixteenth-century interior conversion.

Montone and Morra

The castle of Civitella Ranieri rises invitingly northeast of Umbertide, but it's privately owned. More worthwhile is the hill-village of **MONTONE**, 6km north, which harbours a surprisingly good collection of paintings and early medieval sculpture in the **Museo Comunale** (April–Sept Fri–Sun 10.30am–1pm & 3.30–6pm; Oct–March Sat & Sun 10am–1pm & 3–5.30pm; €3.10) in Via San Francesco, housed in the fifteenth-century Gothic former church of

San Francesco. It has some beguiling frescoes from as early as the eleventh century, the best of which are in the apse and depict *Scenes from the Life of St Francis* (1422–23) by Antonio Alberti. The most interesting painting is a *gonfalone* (banner) by Bartolomeo Caporali, the *Madonna del Soccorso* (1481), with a view of fifteenth-century Montone in the foreground.

There's a small **tourist office** in the *comune* at Via San Francesco 1 (Mon–Fri 10.30am–2pm; ☎075.930.6427), plus more information on the village at ⓦwww.montone.net. If you need to **stay**, head for the two-star *Fortebraccio*, Via dei Magistrati 11 (☎ & ℱ075.930.6215; ❷) or the *Locanda dei Capitani*, Via Roma 5–7 (☎075.930.6521, ⓦwww.ilcapitano.com; closed Feb; ❸), just eight rooms in a fine medieval building with a good restaurant (closed Mon) and a veranda for outdoor summer dining. The three-star hotel *Adamo* (☎075.930.6445, ℱ075.930.6146; ❶) is in the hamlet of **CORLO**, midway along the road from Umbertide, and has a reasonable restaurant (closed Thurs). If you're heading east to Gubbio – the most likely reason to be passing through – you might stop off at **Campo Reggiano**, 11km east of Umbertide, for a look at its tiny eleventh-century church and crypt of San Bartolomeo.

West off the main routes towards Città di Castello, accessed via a turnoff at Trestina towards Castiglion Fiorentino, is the village of **MORRA**, with a little-known but superb fresco cycle by Luca Signorelli in the **Oratorio di San Crescentino** (visit with custodian daily 9am–12.30pm & 3–6.30pm; free).

Città di Castello

Umbria's northernmost town, **CITTÀ DI CASTELLO**, is a relatively little-visited spot whose more than passable *centro storico* is a touch spoilt by the industry on its outskirts – mainly tobacco-processing plants, the town being one of Italy's leading producers. On either side of the valley floor, green wooded hills provide a pleasant backdrop, harbouring one of Umbria's larger concentrations of rented villas and farmhouses. At the town's southern edge lies the **Pinacoteca Comunale**, the main artistic reason – along with an excellent diocesan museum – for visiting the town. The old centre is also a pleasant enough place to spend a night, particularly if you devote an evening to sampling the local Colli Altotiberini wines, or happen to catch one of the burgeoning number of festivals.

In the **Pleistocene** age the Tiber valley at this point was submerged beneath an immense lake similar to Lago Trasimeno and the narrow sheet of water that once covered the Vale of Spoleto. Archeological remains suggest a human presence in the region dating back to the Stone Age. An Umbrian town, Tifernum, later developed on the site, giving way in time to a **Roman** trading centre, Tifernum Tiberinum, whose gridiron of streets remains imprinted on the town centre to this day. A bishopric by the sixth century – the Church's seventh-century nickname for the place was *castrum felicitas* (Castle of Happiness) – the town reached its peak around 1500, when the enlightened despotism of the **Vitelli** nobles brought leading artists here, the young Raphael and Signorelli among them. Nemesis arrived in the form of Cesare Borgia, who invited the head of the Vitellis to a banquet, had him strangled and then absorbed the town into the papal domain.

Access is by direct **train** on the private FCU line from Perugia or Terni to the south, or from Sansepolcro to the north; the station is just outside the walls

Map labels and content within the image:

CITTÀ DI CASTELLO

Sansepolcro

0 — 100 m

RESTAURANTS
Amici Miei — 3
Il Bersaglio — 5
Il Postale — 1
Lea — 4
Roma — 2

ACCOMMODATION
Le Mura — D
Residenza
Antica Canonica — C
Tiferno — B
Umbria — A

10

PERUGIA AND NORTHERN UMBRIA | Città di Castello

Train Station (200m)

Garavelle, Seccatoi del Tabacco & 5

to the southeast, five minutes' walk from the centre. Alternatively, you could take a mainline FS train to Arezzo and pick up an ACT bus to Città di Castello, whose **bus station** is in Piazza Garibaldi, on the eastern edge of the *centro storico*. There are **car parks** around the city walls, one of the most convenient being that on Viale Nazario Sauro in the west, linked by a path to the piazza in front of the Duomo.

The Pinacoteca Comunale

The **Pinacoteca Comunale** (April–Oct Tues–Sun 10am–1pm & 2.30–6.30pm; rest of the year 10am–1pm & 3–6; €5), towards the south of the walled town at Via della Cannoniera 22, is housed in the Palazzo Vitelli alla Cannoniera, one of four surviving palaces in Città di Castello formerly owned by the Vitelli, the town's erstwhile overlords. One of the region's more prepossessing buildings, the palazzo was built for Alessandro Vitelli between 1521 and 1532 by Sangallo the Younger and Pier Francesco da Viterbo, and decorated with some beautiful *sgraffito* by Vasari on the garden facade. Inside, the painted stairwells and period furniture complement the paintings, recently restored sixteenth-century frescoes by Cola dell'Amatrice on the stairs and in the first-floor *Salone* being some of the most striking. Not all the palazzo's former guests, however, had time to appreciate the high-class fittings: Laura, one of the Vitelli women, was wont to throw her rejected lovers to their deaths from the windows.

The **gallery** spreads over two floors. One of the highlights is *The Martyrdom of St Sebastian* (1497–8) by **Luca Signorelli** (active in and around the town between 1474 and 1500), the painter of Orvieto's extraordinary fresco cycle (see p.722) and another in Morra, near Città di Castello (see p.576). More compelling still is the damaged but still ravishing processional standard by **Raphael**, the *Creation of Eve* and *SS Roch and Sebastian*. It was painted in about 1503 as a votive offering following an epidemic, Roch and Sebastian being two saints traditionally invoked against the plague. Raphael spent about five years in Umbria and the region once had many works by him. Today the only pieces in Umbria entirely by him are the standard here and the panel in the church of San Severo in Perugia: many of the others were removed to France by Napoleon. A marvellous thirteenth-century *Maestà* by the anonymous Maestro di Città di Castello is also finally ensconced in the gallery, having been backwards and forwards to Florence for restoration since 1969. Other works include **Sienese** and later **Venetian** paintings, among them outstanding pieces by Antonio Vivarini and his brother-in-law Giovanni d'Alemagna (the two often worked in collaboration), as well as versions of the *Madonna and Child* by Spinello Aretino, Neri di Bicci and Andrea di Bartolo. The sculptural high spot is provided by the *Reliquary of St Andrew* (1420), which is graced with two gilded bronze statuettes by the workshop of Lorenzo Ghiberti. There are also ceramics from the **della Robbias**, a lovely sacristy cupboard (1501) in poplar and walnut, and a miscellaneous sculpture collection distinguished by a fourteenth-century marble relief, the *Baptism of Christ*.

The Duomo

Many of Città di Castello's buildings have lost their medieval aspect to later facades, most notably the rather odd-looking **Duomo**, whose half-finished Baroque frontage was begun in 1632 and abandoned some fifteen years later. By 580 the church had already been rebuilt at least once, and further versions followed in the eleventh and fourteenth centuries, and again in 1458, when the building had to be reconstructed virtually from the ground up after an earthquake. Something of its chequered construction history can be seen in the wonderful round **campanile**, which combines an eleventh-century base with a newer Gothic upper level, and in the Gothic lines of the **north portal**, whose carvings include two fine panels, *Mercy* and *Justice* (1339–59). The heavily reworked interior promises little, though if you're lucky enough to find the **sacristy** open (door on the right), take a look at its small annexe containing a handful of paintings.

The Museo del Duomo

The excellent **Museo del Duomo** is entered to the right of the cathedral's dog's-dinner facade at Piazza Gabriotti 3a (Tues–Sun: April–Sept 9.30am–1pm & 2.30–7pm; Oct–March 10am–1pm & 2.30–6.30pm; also open on Mondays that fall on public holidays and daily in Aug 9.30am–1pm & 2.30–7pm; €5). The museum is arranged over two main floors: pride of place on the ground floor, in Sala I, goes to the **Tesoro di Canoscio**, a hoard of paleo-Christian silverware comprising nine plates, eleven spoons and five miscellaneous pieces – some of them beautifully engraved – turned up in the nearby hamlet of Canoscio in 1935 by a farmer ploughing his fields. They were probably made in Constantinople around the sixth century and might have been used to celebrate the Eucharist; it's a shame that their display is a little austere.

In the adjoining Sala II is an almost equally valuable – and visually more striking – *paliotto*, or **gilded altar-relief**, reputedly presented to Città di Castello by Pope Celestine II in 1142. Of quite exquisite detail, the work shows Christ surrounded by symbols and scenes from his life, running from left to right in two orders. The upper order comprises the Annunciation, Visitation, Nativity (note the comical donkey), Adoration of the Magi, Flight from Egypt (first panel bottom left), Arrest of Christ at Gethsemane and the Crucifixion with three saints; below are the four symbols of the Evangelists. In the same room is a superb **Sienese crozier**, dated 1324 and worked in mind-boggling detail: note the tiny statuines of the Virgin and Child and a kneeling bishop in the curl of the crook at the top of the octagonal shaft.

The rest of the ground floor and part of the **upper floor** display religious ephemera such as reliquaries, chalices and crosses spanning some six centuries, plus documents and maps of local buildings. At the top of the stairs, a processional cross contains tiny relics, among them a bone belonging to St Catherine of Siena. Elsewhere upstairs, the early rooms feature a series of good if unexceptional paintings, among them an *Annunciation* by the local painter Francesco da Tiferno (active 1490–1510), a *Madonna* (1492) by the school of Luca Signorelli, and a picture of *St Floridus* (1412), the sixth-century bishop of Città di Castello who rebuilt the Duomo in 580. This sequence is interrupted in **Sala VII** where there are five exceptional paintings. These include the *Madonna and Child with St John* by Pinturicchio, two paintings of angels by Giulio Romano and – the highlight of the show – *Christ in Glory* (1528–30) by Mannerist superstar, **Rosso Fiorentino**, with the figures of the Virgin Mary and her mother, St Anna, on the right, and Mary of Egypt and Mary Magdalene on the left. This would be an exceptional painting were it in the Uffizi or a gallery of similar stature, so it is a treat to find it here. It even warranted comment from Vasari, who thought the figures and items pictured were some of the "strangest things in the world", though in every other respect he considered the work outstanding.

The rest of the town

The third of the town's triumvirate of museums is the fascinating **Collezione Tessile di Tele Umbra**, just off the main Piazza Matteotti at Via Sant'Antonio 3 (Tues–Sat 10am–noon & 3.30–6.30pm, Sun 10.30am–1pm & 3–5.30pm; Oct–March closes 5.30pm; €3.50). The museum is annexed to a not-to-be-missed small textile workshop set up in 1908 by the Franchetti, a local aristocratic family determined to provide employment and keep alive the centuries-old traditions of linen-making in the region; it's still in operation and looks much as it must have done almost a century ago. The museum traces the history of textiles in the Upper Tiber valley, though in many ways it is less interesting than the **workshop** (Mon–Fri 10am–noon & 3.30–6pm; Oct–March closes 5.30pm; same ticket as museum), which still employs local women and still – almost uniquely in Italy – uses traditional hand-worked looms. A small shop sells products made in the workshop.

Palaces

Just east of the Duomo, in Piazza Gabriotti, lies Città di Castello's old civic heart, dominated by the **Palazzo Comunale** (or Palazzo dei Priori), whose unfinished sandstone bulk was begun in 1322 by Angelo da Orvieto, the architect partly responsible for Gubbio's more impressive Palazzo dei Consoli (see p.586). Opposite rises the **Torre Comunale**, or Torre Civica, seat of the town's medieval prison, which can be climbed for some nice views over the rooftops (closed for restoration at time of writing). A graceful fourteenth-century loggia leads out of the square to the **Palazzo del Podestà** (finished 1368), again by Angelo da Orvieto, though much of the medieval work has been obscured by seventeenth-century additions.

You can extend your knowledge of the town's palace architecture by visiting Piazza Garibaldi and the **Palazzo Vitelli a Porta Sant'Egidio**, built in 1540 for Paolo Vitelli, possibly to a design by Vasari, the attribution appearing likely in view of Vasari's involvement with the Palazzo Vitelli alla Cannoniera (Pinacoteca Comunale, see p.578). Its garden frontage provides its best aspect, an outlook that would be improved were the grotto, garden and statues in front of it to be tidied up. The palace now belongs to a bank, but you'll catch a glimpse of the interior if you attend one of the many concerts held here during the summer season. The fifteenth-century **Palazzo Albizzini** (Tues–Sat 9am–12.30pm & 2.30–6pm, Sun 10.30am–12.30pm & 3–6pm; €5), on the same piazza, houses a public collection of paintings donated to the town by the local Alberto Burri (1915–95), a modern artist of international standing. More paintings and sculptures are displayed in the **Seccatoi del Tabacco** (same ticket and hours, except Nov–March Sat & only 10.30am–12.30pm & 3–6pm), colossal buildings on Via Pierucci on the southern edge of town once used to dry tobacco. They're worth visiting for their own sake and provide a breathtaking display space for Burri's work.

Churches

None of Città di Castello's churches can be said to set pulses racing, but taken together they offer a worthwhile medley of miscellaneous treasures. **San Domenico**, a gloomy Gothic affair built between 1271 and 1424, might once have been more tempting, but its Signorelli *Madonna* has been snapped up by the Pinacoteca, while the Raphael *Crucifixion* which once adorned its east nave now resides in London's National Gallery. In their absence you must make do with a set of lovely inlaid choir stalls (1435) and several fifteenth-century patches of local and Sienese fresco. **Santa Maria delle Grazie** (rebuilt in 1587) is almost equally tantalizing, for its main treasure, a painting of the *Madonna delle Grazie* (1456) – the only documented work of Giovanni di Piamonte, also known as a collaborator of Piero della Francesca – is kept hidden in a cupboard on the church's north side and only exhibited on February 2 and August 26. Worthy of interest, though, is a fresco of *The Dormition of the Virgin*, attributed to the Gubbian master Ottaviano Nelli. **San Francesco**, situated on Piazza Raffaello Sanzio, dates from 1273, though its interior bears the all too obvious marks of an eighteenth-century restoration. It, too, once boasted a Raphael (which is now in Milan's Brera gallery) but has to make do with an altarpiece by Vasari, located in the Cappella Vitelli (also by Vasari) off the north aisle. Finally,

San Giovanni Decollato, in Via Sant'Andrea, has frescoes that show the influence of Luca Signorelli, while the nearby **San Michele Archangelo** (Via Sant'Angelo) contains a high altarpiece by Raffaellino del Colle (1480–1566), an accomplished artist active locally in Citerna, Gubbio and elsewhere.

South of the centre

About 2km south of Città, in the hamlet of Garavelle, is one of Umbria's best folk museums, the **Centro delle Tradizioni Popolari** (Tues–Sun: April–Oct 8.30am–12.30pm & 3–7pm; Nov–March 9.30am–12.30pm & 2–5.30pm; €3.50). Situated in Via Marchese Cappelletti, it comprises an eighteenth-century farmhouse, preserved with all the accoutrements of daily life – pots, pans, furniture and so forth, plus a range of exhibits covering wine-making, weaving and carpentry. There's even a blacksmith's forge.

Practicalities

Città di Castello's **tourist office**, in the Logge Bufalini just off Piazza Matteotti (Mon–Sat 9am–1pm & 3.30–6.30pm, Sun 10am–1pm; ☎075.855.4922, ⒺInfo@iat.citta-di-castello.pg.it), deals with the whole Upper Tiber region. The *Residenza Antica Canonica*, near the Duomo, on Via San Florido 23 (☎075.855.6840; Ⓦwww.umbriaholidays.net; ❷), offers good-value mini-apartments with kitchens. The town's best **hotel** is the central four-star *Tiferno*, Piazza Raffaello Sanzio 13 (☎075.855.0331, Ⓦwww.hoteltiferno.it; ❹). Alternatives are the pleasant three-star *Le Mura*, Via Borgo Farinario 24 (☎075.852.1070, Ⓦwww.hotellemura.it; ❷), a renovated rural house near the Pinacoteca – bathrooms are rather small for the price, but there's an appealing little garden with fountain; and the excellent, modern one-star *Umbria*, Via dei Galanti 4 (☎075.855.4925, Ⓕ075.852.0911, Ⓦwww.hotelumbria.net; ❷). The pleasant, rural **campsite** *Montesca* (☎075.855.8566; Ⓕ075.852.0786; May–Sept) is at La Montesca, 1km west.

The best value of several good **restaurants** is ☘ *Amici Miei* (closed Wed), nicely located in a vaulted cellar at Via del Monte 2 (☎075.855.9904). Alternatively, try *Lea*, a locals' favourite at Via San Florido 28 (☎075.852.1678; closed Mon), a short way south of the cathedral. Grander and with more elevated cuisine is ☘ *Il Postale*, Via Raffaele de Cesare (☎075.852.1356; closed Mon & lunch on Sat), where you'll need to spend at least €50 per person to get the best of the creative cooking. For simple meals or pizzas, walk a few steps from Piazza Matteotti to *Roma*, Via Mario Angeloni 2 (☎075.855.3560; closed Sun). *Il Bersaglio* (☎075.855.5534; closed Wed, and 2 weeks in July), 200m southeast of the walls at Via V.E. Orlando 14, is known for its truffle dishes; it's cosy inside, and there is usually the option of at least one *degustazione* menu.

The tourist office can provide details of the town's internationally renowned **Festival delle Nazioni** (Festival of Chamber Music; late Aug & early Sept; Ⓦwww.festivalnazioni.com). An equally well-known **Mercato del Tartufo** – a truffle show and market – is held every November. Piazza Gabriotti is the site of the regular **market** (Thurs & Sat), while Piazza Matteotti has a large monthly **flea market**, the *Fiera del Rigattiere* (3rd Sun of month 8am–8pm).

Around Città di Castello

Beyond Città di Castello you have a choice of three routes: striking east towards Urbino and the Marche, or pressing on into Tuscany, either by heading **north** towards Sansepolcro or **west** towards Arezzo. All are accessible by train or bus from Città di Castello, though only drivers are likely to want to stop en route.

Towards Sansepolcro

North along the Sansepolcro road, 1km east of Lama, you can see faint remains believed to have been a villa owned by Pliny. Some 5km beyond, **SAN GIUSTINO** is a more or less modern settlement, save for the **Castello Bufalani**, a thirteenth-century castle partly converted by Vasari into a splendid villa. Visits are at the discretion of the owners; enquire at the tourist office in Città di Castello. By a quirk of fate, Cospaia, a huddle of houses on the hill outside, was a tiny independent republic until 1826, though there are no visible reminders of its past glories. Sansepolcro (see p.524) lies 5km north of San Giustino.

Monte Santa Maria Tiberina and Citerna

One of the nicest drives out of Città di Castello is to the picture-perfect village of **Monte Santa Maria Tiberina**, atop a hill about 8km west on a minor road. It came under the sway of the Margraves del Colle, descendants of the Franks, in the tenth century, and remained under their control until 1815, having survived as an independent duchy. Until this time it could declare war, strike its own coins and was apparently one of only three places in Europe where duels could legally be fought to the death. Today it's sleepy and pristine, with little to see save a parish church with a fine font and some superb views.

Head west on the SS221 out of Città di Castello and you hit **CITERNA**, a perfect fortified hilltop village whose powerful wooded position attracted attention as late as 1944, when the Nazis destroyed its strategically important castle (leaving only the present little tower). The town dates from Roman times, was rebuilt after barbarian depredations in the seventh and eighth centuries, and achieved high renown in 1849 when Giuseppe Garibaldi, hero of Italian Unification, spent three days here after the unsuccessful Roman uprising of 1848. Today its neat brick houses are spick and span, despite a massive earthquake in 1917 and damage inflicted during both world wars. The fine local church, **San Francesco**, built in 1316 and revamped in 1508, has a grand assortment of gilded wooden altars; a late (1522–23), faded niche fresco by Luca Signorelli and assistants, *Madonna and Child with SS Francis and Michael* (second altar on the right); and the outstanding and extravagantly framed sixteenth-century painting *Madonna and St John the Evangelist* by Raffaellino del Colle (left transept). The busy *Deposition* (1568) in the choir is by the otherwise obscure Alessandro Forzorio from Arezzo. Citerna's **hotel** is the 25-room, three-star *Sobaria*, Via della Pineta 2 (☎075.859.2118; ❷). From Citerna it's a short hop into Tuscany to see Piero della Francesca's *Madonna del Parto* at Monterchi (see p.522).

Gubbio

High, remote **GUBBIO** has the most beautiful medieval appearance of the northern Umbrian towns – indeed it is so well preserved that some Italian guides and the local tourist blurb describe it as the Umbrian Siena. It's not quite that, but the streets are all attractive rosy-pink stone, the monuments worth visiting, and the medieval nooks and crannies as endearing as any in Italy. In many ways it has become the region's loveliest town to explore, since visitor numbers and tacky commercialism have increasingly compromised Assisi's charms. Better still, the countryside around is gorgeous – the forest-covered mountains of the Apennines rearing up behind and the waters of the Camignano gorge running through the town itself (in winter at least). A broad and largely unspoilt plain – bar a cement works to the north – stretches out in front of the town.

ACCOMMODATION

Biagiotti	E	Grotta dell'Angelo	J	Relais Ducale	G
Bosone	I	Locanda della Duca	C	Residenza Le Logge	D
Dei Consoli	B	Locanda del Gallo	H	La Rocca	K
Gattapone	F	Park Hotel ai Cappuccini	A		

RESTAURANTS

Gelateria di Gino	1
Il Campanone	2
La Fornace di Maestro Giorgio	4
San Francesco e il Lupo	5
Taverna del Lupo	3

Gubbio is attracting ever-greater numbers of visitors, and on a summer morning the streets can be very busy. Come even slightly off-season, however, or stay the night, and you'll see it in a different and very much more appealing light.

Some history

Local folklore insists that Gubbio was one of the first five towns built after the Great Flood. It was actually founded by the **Umbrians** around the third or fourth century BC, and may even have been their political and religious capital, later passing to the **Etruscans**, for whom it marked the easternmost limit of their territorial ambitions. Several bronze slabs, the **Eugubine Tablets** – now in the Museo Civico – survive as memorials to both cultures, some of the most important archeological finds of their type (see p.588). The **Romans** followed, building the colony of Iguvium at the edge of the plain, where a sprinkling of monuments and the gridiron plan of their streets survive to this day. Barbarian raids subsequently saw Gubbio's focus move up the hillside, whose steep terraced slopes form the town's present-day heart.

In the medieval period, Gubbio maintained a strategic importance as the pivotal town between Rome and Ravenna, its *comune* achieving a status that rivalled Perugia. According to contemporary chroniclers, the population grew to 50,000 – twice its present number – the town's wealth and size providing not only the wherewithal to build its vast civic palaces, but also the impulse towards artistic and cultural innovation. Umbria's first school of **painting** developed here, as did a **ceramic** tradition that continues today. From about 1350 the papacy and Gabrielli nobility jostled for power, though it was the Montefeltro dukes of Urbino who wrested eventual control, ruling the town virtually unchallenged from 1383 until 1508. Gubbio remained in the Duchy of Urbino until 1624, then became part of the **Papal States**, perhaps one reason why it still feels a town apart, not properly a part of either Tuscany, Umbria or the Marche.

Arrival and information

ASP has roughly hourly **buses** to Gubbio from Città di Castello and Perugia (there are also once-daily direct buses to both Rome and Florence). The nearest **train station** is at Fossato di Vico, 19km south on the Rome–Foligno–Ancona line, from where buses shuttle to Gubbio (Mon–Sat 10 daily, 6 on Sun). Gubbio's **bus terminal** is near the medieval heart of the old town at Piazza Quaranta Martiri; dominating the old town's skyline above the piazza is the colossal bulk of the Palazzo dei Consoli, while on the hill above to the east sits a second landmark, the Basilica di Sant'Ubaldo. The newsagent on the south side of the piazza sells bus tickets as well as a range of maps, including detailed CAI and other sheets that are invaluable if you plan to walk in the nearby hills or the Monte Cucco park (see p.594). By **car**, you'll most likely approach on the meandering cross-country SS298 road from Perugia. Except on Tuesdays, when it's the site of the town's weekly **market**, you can **park** at Piazza Quaranta Martiri; pay at the "Easy Gubbio–Cassa Parcheggio" office a short way up Via della Repubblica on the left. Alternative parking is off Viale del Teatro Romano, close to San Domenico, or further afield in Via del Cavarello near Porta Romana.

There's a **tourist office** at Piazza Odersi 6, off the central Corso Garibaldi (Mon–Fri 8.30am–1.45pm & 3.30–6.30pm, Sat 9am–1pm & 3.30–6.30pm, Sun 9.30am–12.30pm; winter afternoon hours slightly curtailed; ℡075.922.0790 or 075.922.0693, ⊜info@iat.gubbio.pg.it). You can change money at banks or the **post office**, Via Carioli 11 (Mon–Sat 8.30am–6pm).

Accommodation

You shouldn't have any problem finding a **place to stay** in Gubbio, though the place gets busy. The tourist office has details of more than fifty **agriturismo** options dotted around the countryside nearby; there's some great accommodation, for example, in Vallingegno, 14km south, including six two- and three-bed apartments in a converted abbey, the *Abbazia di Vallingegno* (℡075.920.158; ❷). The tourist office also has details of around twenty **rooms** to let, most on nightly or weekly lets, but located outside the town.

Hotels

Biagiotti Via Piccardi 12 ℡075.927.6108. A set of five rooms and one apartment, all with private bathrooms; a good standby if the slightly more expensive – but better – rooms of *Le Logge* almost opposite are full. Daily and weekly deals are available. Rooms and apartment ❶

Bosone Via XX Settembre 22 ℡075.922.0668, ℻075.922.0552. This thirty-room old-world three-star, full of frescoes, medieval vaults and antiques in its common areas, offers a touch of traditional style. Rooms are comfortable enough, but a little tired. You may be obliged to take half-board, but rates are reasonable. ❺ including half-board.

Dei Consoli Via dei Consoli 59 ℡075.927.3335. One of the best locations – in an atmospheric street – and recently revamped, turning nine formerly plain two-star rooms into four-star offerings. Best are the quieter rooms away from the street. ❹

Gattapone Via G. Ansidei 6/Via Beni 11 ℡075.927.2489. First choice mid-range option; a renovated central three-star hotel in a quiet medieval building off Via della Repubblica, with eighteen spacious rooms (small bathrooms) and a peaceful garden. Light sleepers may be disturbed by the bells of San Giovanni nearby. ❹

Grotta dell'Angelo Via Gioia 47 ℡075.927.1747, ℻075.927.3438, ⓦwww.grottadellangelo.it. Reliable eighteen-room two-star in a quiet side-street, with a good, inexpensive restaurant; all rooms are en suite, at prices a few euro lower than the *Locanda della Duca*. ❶

La Rocca Monte Ingino ℡ & ℻075.922.1222, ⓔselenaweb@iol.it. An out-of-town three-star hotel with twelve rooms; to get there without a car, take the funicular or walk up to Monte Ingino and follow the signs from the Basilica. The modern hotel is unexceptional save for the views, for which you pay a little over the odds by comparison with many hotels in town. ❸

Locanda del Gallo Frazione Santa Cristina ℡075.922.9912, ⓦwww.locandadelgallo.it. A great change from the normal run of town hotels, this is a twelth-century aristocratic house converted in a way that fully retains its old medieval appearance, located in peaceful countryside 18km

from town off the main road to Perugia. There's a pool, and rather misplaced Oriental furnishings are the only incongruous note. ❹

Locanda della Duca Via Piccardi 1 ℡075.927.7753. The town's only one-star, with seven rooms. Overlooks the river, and has a reasonable restaurant with a picturesque terrace. Note that for virtually the same price, you can stay in the good rooms at *Residenza Le Logge* on the same street. ❶

Park Hotel ai Cappuccini Via Tifernate ℡075.9234, ⓦwww.parkhotelaicappuccini.it. Major-league hedonism (swimming pool, sauna, garden, gym), in an elegantly converted seven-teeth-century monastery. The downside is the pleasant but out-of-town parkland setting, the size (85 rooms and lots of conference facilities, which work against intimacy) and the price – anything up to €310 for a double room, though off-season rates can be half this. ❾

🏃 **Relais Ducale** Via Montefeltro (formerly Via Ducale)–Via Galeotti 9 ℡075.922.0157, ⓦwww.relaisducale.com. Best upmarket choice. Three converted medieval houses, in a faultless position between Piazza Grande (from where it's signed) and the cathedral, with a lovely terrace and 26 glorious (and varied) rooms decorated with traditional simplicity and elegance. ❻

Residenza Le Logge Via Piccardi 7–9 ℡075.927.7574, ⓔresidenzalelogge@virgilio.it. Very appealing set of four double rooms and two three-bed mini-apartments in a quiet medieval street just off busy Piazza Quaranta Martiri, but well away from its bustle. Clean, comfortable and nicely presented: there's even a small garden. Weekly rates too, from €362 per double. Rooms ❶ Apartments ❷

Campsites

Città di Gubbio Ortoguidone ℡ & ℻075.927.2037. Large hundred-pitch site with a pool in a good setting, 1500m south off the Perugia road. April–Sept.

Villa Ortoguidone Ortoguidone ℡ & ℻075.927.2037. Umbria's only four-star campsite – expensive and with only twelve pitches. Forms part of the *Città di Gubbio* site. April–Sept.

The Town

Piazza Quaranta Martiri makes an obvious place to start a tour of Gubbio; it was named after forty innocent citizens murdered by the Nazis in 1944 as a reprisal for partisan attacks in the surrounding hills; the fighting around Gubbio as the Allies advanced north was especially tough, the battle for the town taking three weeks. After taking in **San Francesco** and its fresco cycles you should head into the medieval town proper, where the vast **Palazzo dei Consoli** houses the town's museum and picture gallery, and then wander the short distance to the adjoining **Duomo**, **Museo Diocesano** and **Palazzo Ducale**, the last based on the Montefeltros' famous palace in Urbino. A lane behind the Duomo – the route taken by competitors during the famous Corsa dei Ceri (see box opposite) – leads up to **Monte Ingino**, a hill-top eyrie which offers lovely views and plenty of picnic and strolling opportunities. Alternatively, you could take in the streets around **San Domenico** and then head east to Porta Romana, where a panoramic funicular also runs up Monte Ingino.

San Francesco and around

In Piazza Quaranta Martiri, slightly stranded from the medieval heart of town, is the town's finest church, Gothic **San Francesco**, possibly designed by Fra' Bevignate, the brains behind Perugia's Fontana Maggiore. Within the recently restored interior is an engaging if faded cycle of **frescoes** painted around 1410 by Ottaviano Nelli (c.1375–c.1444), leading light of the Gubbian school. Ranged around the chapel to the left of the apse, the seventeen panels comprise *Scenes from the Life of the Virgin Mary*. High up in the apse you can just make out early thirteenth-century frescoes showing *Christ Enthroned with Saints*, while the chapel to the right of the apse has still more frescoes, this time fourteenth-century *Scenes from the Life of St Francis*. A small chapel in the sacristy is reputedly the room in which St Francis slept when he visited Gubbio, a sojourn that included his famous taming of a wolf that had been terrorizing the town. The structure is known to have been part of a medieval house belonging to the Spadalonga, family friends of the saint. The simple cloisters beyond still cling to a few fourteenth-century frescoes.

Opposite the church is the distinctive fourteenth-century **Loggia dei Tiratori** (Weavers), Italy's best surviving example of this now rare type of building. Wool was stretched out in the shade of its arches to dry and shrink evenly away from the heat of the sun. The little church to its left is the often-locked **Santa Maria dei Laici**, built in the fourteenth century but altered to dull effect three centuries later. Behind the loggia, Via Piccardi leads just north of a small square containing the church of **San Giovanni Battista**, restored to its thirteenth-century state and distinguished by an oddly elongated campanile. Just off to the west Via Baldassini contains the **Casa di Sant'Ubaldo**, the former home of one of Gubbio's patron saints. Ubaldo, born in Gubbio in 1100, became a bishop and earned his saintly spurs by helping defend the town from Barbarossa in 1155: he's buried in the basilica bearing his name on Monte Ingino.

The Palazzo dei Consoli

Bearing east into the medieval town, along Via della Repubblica, centre-stage is taken by the austere **Palazzo dei Consoli**, a superb building whose crenellated outline and campanile dominate the countryside for miles around. Its western face is particularly impressive, vast buttressing supporting a building that rises almost 100m from the base of the foundations to the tip of the campanile. The plain **facade** is disturbed only by a triple-paired window motif that's unique

The vigil of the feast day of Ubaldo, Gubbio's patron saint, the **Corsa dei Ceri** (May 15) is little known outside Italy, but in Tuscany and Umbria ranks second only to Siena's Palio in its exuberance and bizarre pageantry. The rules and rigmarole of the nine-hundred-year-old ceremony are mind-boggling, but in essence begin with an early-morning Mass and a **procession** through the packed streets of the vast wooden **ceri**, or "candles", removed from Ubaldo's Monte Ingino basilica. Each is dedicated to a particular saint – **Ubaldo**, **Anthony** and **George**. At 10.30am another procession makes its way to the Piazza Grande, where an hour later the four-metre-high *ceri* are raised by members of the town's three traditional confraternities: the builders (represented by St Ubaldo), the artisans (St George) and the peasants (St Anthony). A statue of the relevant saint tops each column.

There follows yet another procession through the streets to show the *ceri* to the townspeople (and TV crews from across Italy). The pillars are then dumped until 4.30pm while all concerned adjoin for a gut-busting fish **lunch** in the Palazzo dei Consoli. Yet another procession ensues, during which the clergy are finally allowed to participate, a journey that takes the *ceri* through just about every last corner of the town.

Back in the Piazza Grande, at 6pm the mayor brandishes a white banner to signal the beginning of a **race**, the climax of the day, which involves carrying the *ceri* back up to the hilltop Basilica di Sant'Ubaldo. No sooner has the race begun than there's a stop at the Porta del Monte. It then resumes up the steep path to the basilica, each confraternity being allowed ten official carriers who have to be replaced every ten minutes – but without stopping. "Race" is something of a misnomer, however, for the *cero* of Ubaldo always wins, the other teams having to ensure they're in the basilica before the doors are shut by the leaders. The *ceri* are then abandoned in the basilica, and the saints brought down in a candlelit procession. Thereafter there's more celebration and a good deal of drinking.

A scholarly debate rages over the origins of the event, generally cited as either a secular feast commemorating the day in 1155 when Ubaldo talked Barbarossa out of flattening Gubbio, or a hangover from some pagan fertility rite. These days the Church claims it as its own, though judging by the very phallic *ceri* and the roar that goes up when they're raised to the vertical in Piazza Grande, there's something more than Christian jubilation going on.

to Gubbio and repeated elsewhere in the town, by a lovely doorway, and by a hole at the top right-hand corner – made to hold the cage, or *gogna* (from *vergogna* meaning "shame"), in which criminals were incarcerated. The little lunette above the door features the *Madonna and Child with John the Baptist and Ubaldo*.

An overbearing gesture of civic pride, the Palazzo dei Consoli took the place of the previous civic headquarters in Via Ducale, which had been embarrassingly overshadowed by a symbol of religious power, the Duomo; this previous headquarters was subsequently lost beneath the foundations of Montefeltro's Palazzo Ducale. Work began on the Palazzo dei Consoli in 1321, probably to the plans of the eminent Gubbian architect Matteo Gattapone. Angelo da Orvieto (active 1334–52), fresh from civic palaces in Città di Castello, may have designed the doorway and its flanking Gothic windows. Construction took a couple of hundred years, during which time vast tracts of the medieval town were levelled, most of the space going to accommodate the huge **Piazza Grande** (or Piazza della Signoria), a windswept belvedere with excellent views, and a suitable setting for this colossal building and for the lesser, unfinished **Palazzo Pretorio** opposite, built to the same Gattapone design.

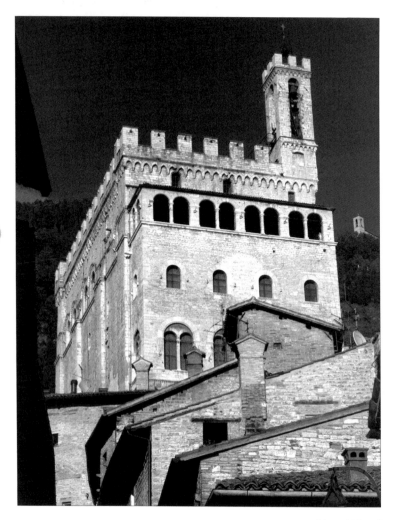

△ Palazzo dei Consoli

The Museo Civico

The cavernous barrel-vaulted Salone dell'Arengo, where the council officers discussed their business, now accommodates a **Museo Civico** (daily: April–Sept 10am–1.30pm & 2–7pm; Oct–March 10am–1pm & 3–6pm; closed during Corsa dei Ceri; €5). Much of this consists of coins and sculptures, scattered like a medieval jumble sale in the main hall, but one of its adjoining rooms off to the left also contains Umbria's most important archeological find, the **Eugubine Tablets**.

Discovered in 1444 by an illiterate shepherd – who twelve years later was conned by the *comune* into swapping the priceless treasure for a worthless piece of land – the tablets consist of seven bronze slabs, four of which probably date from about 200 BC, and three from around 100 BC. They are the most significant extant record of the Umbrian language, believed to have been a vernacular tongue without standard written characters. The bastardized Latin and Etruscan of their texts aimed at producing a phonetic transliteration of the dialect, using the main languages of the day. Gubbio was close to the shrine of the so-called Apennine Jove, a major pagan deity visited by pilgrims from all over Italy, and it's thought the tablets were the work of Roman and Etruscan priests taking advantage of the established order to impose new religious cults in a region where their languages weren't understood. The ritual text – the most important to have survived from antiquity – comprises a prayer divided into stanzas, a list of Gubbio's enemies, and a series of instructions for conducting services and the art of divination from sacrificed animals and the flight of birds. Most importantly, they suggest Romans, Etruscans and Umbrians achieved some sort of coexistence, refuting a long-held belief that succeeding civilizations wiped out their predecessors.

Also worth hunting out in the museum are several key examples of Gubbio's **ceramic tradition**. Its greatest exponent, Maestro Giorgio Andreoli, was born in 1498, and distinguished himself by discovering gold and ruby glazes, the latter – *riverbero* – a colour you rarely see in ceramics as it's extremely difficult to achieve. Unfortunately, Giorgio's sons took the secrets of his unique glaze to their graves; worse still, until recently Gubbio didn't have any examples of the master's work, although in 1991 and 1996, the town managed to purchase auctioned works by public subscription. These two pieces – *Circe* and the *Fall of Phaeton* – are on show in the Sala della Loggetta, from which a corridor leads to Room IV of the Pinacoteca.

The Pinacoteca and the Museo Archeologico

The **Pinacoteca** (same hours and ticket as Museo Civico) is housed in five wonderful medieval rooms at the top of a steep flight of steps on the second floor of the Palazzo dei Consoli. Though the paintings aren't anything special, they trace the development of the Gubbian School, one of central Italy's earliest; names to look out for are Guido Palmerucci and Mello (see p.590). Sienese artists are also represented, notably by Rutilio Manetti, the city's leading follower of Caravaggio, and there's a lovely *Crucifix* by the Maestro di San Francesco (best known for his work in the Basilica di San Francesco in Assisi). The gallery's star painting, *Madonna del Melograno* (Madonna of the Pomegranate) by Pier Francesco Fiorentino, was stolen in 1979 and must now surely be considered lost for good. Don't miss the tremendous views over the Piazza Grande and the lower town from the palace's loggia, entered from the gallery.

The same ticket also allows you into the recently arranged **Museo Archeologico** on the palace's lower floor, entered separately at the rear of the palace (the entrance is signed at the junction of Via dei Consoli and Via Gattapone). This is a rather patchy miscellany, with a good Byzantine sarcophagus and a collection of Roman and Umbrian bronzes, carvings and other archeological displays.

The Duomo

A couple of streets north of the Palazzo dei Consoli, the rather plain thirteenth-century Gothic **Duomo** (usually open daily 9am–6pm, except during services) is redeemed by a fine interior. Immediately noticeable is the strange arched ceiling, a Gubbian speciality known as "wagon vaulting", in which the ten arches are gracefully curved, apparently to emulate the meeting of hands in prayer. There are some fine twelfth-century stained-glass windows, a glitzy Baroque chapel and a wealth of **frescoes** and **panel paintings**. Key works include *Adoration of the Shepherds* by Eusebio di San Giorgio (sixth niche on the north wall), a student of Pinturicchio; the adjoining altarpiece *Santa Maria Maddalena* (1521) by Timoteo Vito; and a painting next door by Sinibaldo Ibi, *Madonna and Child with St Ubaldo and St Sebastian* (1507). In the last niche on the north wall is a beautifully restored picture of St Ubaldo with a lovely green background by the Gubbian painter Benedetto Nucci (1515–87). The **presbytery** contains a superb choir dating from 1549 – sadly, roped off – while the altar (a Roman sarcophagus) conceals the relics of saints Mariano and Giacomo, martyred in 259 in what is now Algeria. Back down the south wall towards the church entrance, the outstanding painting is a *Deposition* by Dono Doni, to the left of which is a good fragment of fresco of *St Sebastian*. Off this side of the church is the gaudy **Cappella de SS Sacramento**, built on the orders of Alessandro Sperelli, a seventeenth-century bishop of Gubbio, who is buried inside.

The Museo Diocesano

A few paces down from the Duomo stands the modest but well-presented **Museo Diocesano** (daily: April–Oct 10am–7pm; Nov–March closes 1hr earlier; €4.50), housed in the old canons' palace. Its prize exhibit is a florid Flemish cope – parts of which were stolen in 1990 – presented to the cathedral by Pope Marcellus II, a former bishop of Gubbio, in 1555: extravagantly embroidered, it portrays scenes from the Passion. There are also a number of frescoes removed from the crypt of the church of Santa Maria dei Laici and other fifteenth-century murals, as well as the interesting *Madonna in Glory*; this painting had long been attributed to Guiduccio Palmerucci, considered Gubbio's earliest documented fourteenth-century painter, but recent restoration has revealed a new signature, *Opus Melli Eugubii* ("a work by Mello di Gubbio", previously unknown artist).

The Palazzo Ducale

Opposite the Duomo – and overshadowing it – is the **Palazzo Ducale** (Mon, Tues & Thurs–Sun 8.30am–7pm; €2), built in 1470 over an earlier Lombard palace and the twelfth-century Palazzo Comunale by Federigo da Montefeltro, the renowned duke of Urbino, and designed as a scaled-down copy of his palace in that town. The architect of the two buildings was probably the same man, Dalmatian-born Luciano Laurana, selected by Federigo after he'd failed to find a suitably bold Florentine designer. The tone is set by the calming Renaissance **courtyard**, close to which a stone staircase leads down to a series of vaulted storerooms and excavations that have revealed the remains of four earlier buildings on the site. Among them are fragments from the tenth century and remnants of the former Palazzo Comunale.

As in Urbino, many of the rooms of the main palace appeal as much for their measured architectural calm as for any surfeit of paintings or furniture. Most are virtually empty, however, and the result is frankly dull, though the views of the town from certain salons make some amends. One room, the **duke's study** (off room 2), was left bare after its intarsia wood panelling was stripped in the nineteenth century (it found its way to the Metropolitan Museum in New York). All the stone-carved windows and doorways are superb, however, as are the fireplaces and cool terracotta floors. The large central **Salone** offers some cracking views of the Palazzo dei Consoli and contains a fireplace that must have worked wonders during Gubbio's mountain-cold winters. Quite what the palace's fine interior will be used for – and it is crying out for something – is unsure.

The northern quarters

Wandering the streets around town you'll soon come across examples of *Porte della Morte* ("Doors of Death") – narrow, bricked-up doorways wedged into the facades of medieval town houses, a conundrum found only in Gubbio, Assisi and southern France. The party line has it they were cut to carry a coffin out of the house and then, having been tainted by death, sealed up – a nice theory, and very Italian, but to judge by the constricted stairways behind the doors, their purpose was probably defensive: the main door could be barricaded, leaving the more easily defended passageway as the only entrance. Gubbio's best examples are in Via dei Consoli. There are dozens of similar picturesque odds and ends around Gubbio's streets, which lend themselves to a slow ramble. Some of the best are in the north: the lanes around San Domenico, and especially along the banks of the Camignano, are the most tempting. Via Baldassini, below Piazza Grande, is also worth a stroll.

En route to these points from Piazza Grande, the **Bargello** – built in 1302 as the medieval police station – in Via dei Consoli is worth tracking down and gives you a chance to survey the adjoining **Fontana dei Matti** (Fountain of the Mad), once Gubbio's prime water source but now undistinguished save for the tradition that anyone walking round it three times will wind up deranged. There's usually someone about wondering whether to give it a go; you qualify for a *patente da matto* ("licence of madness") if you make the run and are simultaneously soaked with water by three locals. Via dei Consoli is home to most of Gubbio's **ceramic shops**, together with Officina Libris, a nice shop selling paper and leather-bound books, at no. 39.

From here you can head east towards the funicular (see p.592) or drop down to look into the nearby church of **San Domenico** (closed at the time of writing for long-term restoration), distinguished by a fine intarsia lectern, or take in the impressive fifteenth-century **Palazzo Beni** and **Palazzo del Capitano del Popolo**, the latter home to an odd little private museum of modern sculpture and medieval torture instruments.

Following the walls anticlockwise back to the Piazza Quaranta Martiri, you could detour to the **Anfiteatro Romano** (daily: April–Sept 8.30am–7.30pm; Oct–March 8am–1.30pm; free). Built in the first century AD, it's one of the largest in the Roman world, at 112m in diameter. It retains its seats and much of the lower arcades – the arena providing the setting for a summer festival of Shakespeare and classical drama. Current excavations are uncovering more remains. Close by is a Roman **mausoleum**, a blockhouse affair 9m high, easily reached from Piazza del Mercato; no one is sure for whom it was intended.

The southern quarters

A path near the Duomo zigzags up Monte Ingino, but the panoramic way up is to take the highly recommended funicular (see p.592). En route to the base station at Porta Romana – walk part of the way on **Corso Garibaldi** for a good view of the large eighteenth-century statue of St Ubaldo at the street's end – you can take in Ottaviano Nelli's masterpiece, the winsome *Madonna del Belvedere* (1413) in the deconsecrated **Santa Maria Nuova**, together with patches of fresco left by his pupils (if the church is shut, try the custodian at Via Dante 66). Little **Sant'Andrea** nearby, probably of eleventh-century foundation and recently restored, is also worth a passing look. Porta Romana itself has a small museum, the **Museo della Ceramica a Lustro di Torre Mediovale di Porta Romana** (daily: June–Sept 9am–1pm & 3.30–8pm; Oct–May 9am–1pm & 3.30–7pm; €2.60) devoted to local ceramics and displays on the mechanics of defending a medieval gateway.

Just outside the walls, the thirteenth-century **Sant'Agostino** is notable for its apse, which is smothered in 26 Nelli frescoes of *Scenes from the Life of St Augustine* (1420); there's a light on the right (south) side alongside a glass casket containing the waxy image of Beato Pietro of Gubbio. The entire church was once frescoed, and tantalizing fragments remain dotted around the walls: the sixth arch-cum-chapel on the right has a particularly good fresco by a follower of Nelli; the third arch has a painting by Nelli and his workshop showing the Madonna with saints, angels and purged souls; and on the north wall the fifth altar features an anonymous *Madonna del Soccorso* (1485) with various Augustinian saints.

Monte Ingino

You can walk to **Monte Ingino** (827m), one of the mountains above Gubbio, from Porta Sant'Ubaldo near the Duomo (a stiff climb) or drive there from Porta Metauro in the north. The most entertaining way to reach the top, however, is courtesy of the six-minute **funicular** from Porta Romana (July & Aug Mon–Sat 8.30am–7.30pm, Sun 8.30am–8pm; June & Sept Mon–Sat 9.30am–7pm, Sun 9am–7.30pm; April & May Mon–Sat 10am–6.30pm, Sun 9.30am–7pm; Oct daily 10am–6pm; March Mon–Sat 10am–5.30pm, Sun 9.30am–6pm; Nov & Dec daily except Wed 10am–5pm; €3 one-way, €5 return). It has open ski-lift type cages holding two people, and affords ample time to admire the view – and to study your cage's welding and bolts, which are all that lie between you and oblivion. Beware the off-season break for lunch (Oct–Dec & March–May daily & June Mon–Sat closed 1.15–2.30pm).

Once you're atop Monte Ingino, the views and a bar are the main attractions. Even better vistas are at hand if you climb up to the **Rocca**. The **Basilica di Sant'Ubaldo**, five minutes from the top station, is not of great interest, though it's revered for the body of the town's patron saint, whose missing three fingers were hacked off by his manservant as a religious keepsake. Inside, you can't miss the big wooden pillars, or *ceri* (candles), featured in Gubbio's annual *Corsa dei Ceri* (see box p.587).

Eating

Gubbio offers some fine small-town cooking. Cheaper **restaurants** can be found at the northern end of Via dei Consoli, along with a good stop for **ice cream** – *Gelateria di Gino*, Via dei Consoli 4. This is also the part of town for **food shopping**: there's a small Despar supermarket at Via Nicola Vantaggi off Piazza Giordano Bruni, plus a good bakery at Via dei Consoli 27 and a fruit and vegetable store two doors below that.

Low-priced restaurants also dot some of the side streets off Corso Garibaldi in the south. First choice is the one attached to *Grotta dell'Angelo* hotel, Via Gioia 47 (T075.927.1747; closed Tues), which has a wonderful cave of a dining room (the *grotta* of its name). Not far away is the inexpensive *San Francesco e il Lupo*, Via Carioli 24, for pizzas or full meals – though service can be sloppy.

You'd do better to make for *Il Campanone* (T075.927.6011; no closing day), near the corner of Via Baldassini and Via Piccardi 21. It has several lovely dining areas – vaulted medieval rooms with crisp white linen and smart red wooden chairs; the moderately priced food is regional. Well known options include the expensive *Taverna del Lupo*, Via Ansidei 21 (T075.927.4368; closed Mon), a more traditional place with medieval interior, and probably a touch better – though occasionally more complacent – than its smaller and less costly upmarket rival, the vaguely modish *La Fornace di Maestro Giorgio*, Via Maestro

Giorgio 2 (☎075.922.1836; closed Tues & lunch on Wed; also closed Feb), sited in the converted workshop of one of Gubbio's medieval master ceramists. The *Bosone Garden* restaurant (closed Wed), attached to the *Bosone* hotel opposite *Maestro Giorgio*, has an interesting menu (including summer barbecues), and, despite the nasty plastic chairs, is the nicest spot for outdoor eating.

Gualdo Tadino

The main centre east of Gubbio is **GUALDO TADINO**, a hill-town that takes its name from the German *Wald* (wood), a throwback to the days of the Holy Roman Empire and Italy's northern European rulers ("Tadino" was only tagged on in 1833). It occupies the site of ancient **Tadinum**, a Roman staging post on the Via Flaminia, and lies close to the site of the battlefield at which Narses, a eunuch and renowned Byzantine general, killed Totila and won a famous victory over the Goths in 552. Later it was the birthplace of **Matteo da Gualdo** (1435–1513), an accomplished but little-known painter (at least outside Umbria) whose works crop up in Assisi, Trevi and Spoleto, as well as in his home town. Today, the town, which sprawls over the lower slopes of the Apennines, has the remote outpost feel of other eastern Umbrian towns. But while the medieval centre is a touch bleak, with little of substance to see, it's quiet and atmospheric, and makes a good base for exploring the beautiful Monte Cucco region (see p.594). Economic well-being flows from the town's renowned **ceramics**, best seen during a big summer exhibition devoted to the craft. The town was badly hit by the 1997 earthquake; accessibility and opening times of all sites remain subject to change for the foreseeable future.

The Town

The Gothic **Duomo** (1256), also known as San Benedetto, is located in the central Piazza Martiri della Libertà, and boasts a facade similar to the one in Todi – the three-tiered arrangement being a recurrent Umbrian design – and a fine carved doorway and rose window: the interior, though, was done to death in the nineteenth century. The little fountain on the building's Corso Italia flank is attributed to Antonio da Sangallo the Elder. Opposite the cathedral is the **Palazzo Comunale**, of eighteenth-century vintage, and close by is the nicely restored **Palazzo del Podestà**. Various works of art left to the cathedral over the years are currently hidden from public view owing to lack of funds and the high probability they'll be lifted by thieves.

Similar worries prevailed in the town's small art gallery, which is closed indefinitely, though most of its works have been moved to the **Museo Civico** (June–Sept Tues–Sun 10.30am–1pm & 4–7pm; April & May Thurs–Sun 10.30am–1pm & 3.30–6pm; Oct–March Sat & Sun 10.30am–1pm & 3–6pm; €3), housed in the imposing Rocca Flea in Via della Rocca, a fine-looking fortress reconstructed by the great Emperor Frederick II. It's arranged in three sections, including an antiquarium with archeological finds from the town and its surroundings; a section devoted to ceramics, which for centuries were the town's economic lifeblood; and a picture gallery, the real reason for a visit. Most of the gallery exhibits are by Matteo da Gualdo, mercilessly lampooned by nineteenth-century critics for his "incorrect drawing", though his brilliant colouring has since restored him to critical favour. However, Matteo's paintings, together with a Sienese *Coronation of the Virgin* by Sano di Pietro, are eclipsed by a sublime polyptych (1471) by **Nicolò Alunno**, whom Berenson described as "the first painter in whom the emotional, now passionate and violent, now mystic and ecstatic, temperament of St Francis's countrymen was revealed".

The church of **San Francesco**, if open (call the Municipio ☎075.915.021 for information), is also pictorially rewarding. Deconsecrated, its airy interior is used for temporary exhibitions, and features frescoes on the *Life of St Julian* (1469) by the school of Ottaviano Nelli (above the west door), a lunette with a damaged *Madonna* (high on the south wall), and a large painted Crucifix in the apse by a follower of the Maestro di San Francesco (see p.607). On the north side of the church also look out for part of a Roman sarcophagus flanked by two winged figures representing Victory, and the unmissable raised fourteenth-century pulpit. Among the apse frescoes is a *Crucifixion* by **Matteo da Gualdo**, who also left a *Madonna and Child with St Francis* in the third arch on the left and another *Madonna and Child* on the pillar between the first and second chapels: the last is the artist's oldest known work. There's another bright Matteo triptych – the *Madonna and Child with St Sebastian and St Roch* – in the church of **Santa Maria dei Raccomandati** in Piazza XX Settembre, close by. If the paintings of Matteo really appeal, it's worth driving to the hill-village of **SAN PELLEGRINO**, 6km northwest off the SS219 Gubbio road, where the church of San Facondino (note the tenth-century tower) has several of his frescoes and a triptych (1465) by Giovanni di Camerino, recovered after its theft.

Practicalities

Given the earthquake-damaged state of Gualdo, the town is best seen as part of a day-trip that might also take in the mountains to the east and north. It's an easy trip by **bus** from Gubbio, and three buses run daily from Foligno (Mon–Sat); **trains** from Assisi, Foligno or Spoleto are frequent, and there's a shuttle bus from the train station to the old centre. The only **hotel** in the *centro storico* is the twelve-room, two-star *Bottaio*, Via Casimiri 17 (☎075.913.230; ❶), though plans are in hand to reconstruct the *Gigiotto* hotel, Via Morone 5 (☎075.912.283, ⓕ075.910.0263), currently the town's most venerable **restaurant** (closed Tues & Nov). For pizzas in the old centre, make for *Baccus* in Vai R. Calai (☎075.910.235; closed Mon). The nearest **campsite** is in the mountains at Valsorda (see below).

Parco Regionale del Monte Cucco

Some of Umbria's best upland scenery is to be found in the mountains east and north of Gualdo on the border with the Marche, much of it protected by the **Parco Regionale del Monte Cucco**. Where this area really scores is in its organized trails and backup for outdoor activities of every kind; if you want to don walking boots without too much fuss, this is the area to do it – and the chances are you won't meet another soul all day. Access is easy, with **buses** from Gualdo to Valsorda and from Perugia, Gualdo, Gubbio and Assisi to Costacciaro.

The southernmost base for exploration of the park is the resort of **VALSORDA** (1000m), 8km northeast of Gualdo. Regular buses run from Gualdo to the village, which is a launching pad for easy hill walks and is a reasonably scenic, if developed, spot in its own right. You can tackle the straightforward trek up **Serra Santa** (1421m), on a track of motorway proportions carved out by pilgrims over the years. From the summit you could then drop into the spectacular **Valle del Fonno** gorge and follow it down to Gualdo. Paths follow the main ridge from Valsorda north and south, and it's feasible to walk all the way to Nocera Umbra.

To get closer to the heart of the mountains, head north from Gualdo past **FOSSATO DI VICO**, a hill-town with the eleventh-century Romanesque San Pietro, and the small Cappella della Piaggiola, which contains some fine frescoes by the school of Ottaviano Nelli. Beyond Fossato the road passes through **SIGILLO** and then, 3km further on, **COSTACCIARO**, a town that looks rather as if it has tried to attract tourists and failed: it is a centre of sorts for the park's outdoor pursuits and access point for the **Grotta di Monte Cucco**, at 922m the fifth-deepest cave system in the world. The cave was explored as early as 1889, but has only recently been opened up by the hundreds of cavers that flock here from all over Europe; over 40km of galleries have now been charted. Above, the huge, bare-sloped Monte Cucco (1566m) is the main playground for walkers.

Practicalities

For **information**, head to the park's administrative office, at Via Matteotti 52 in Sigillo (☎075.917.7326, ⊛www.parks.it/parco.monte.cucco), or to the Centro Escursionistico in Costacciaro (Via Galeazzi; ☎075.917.0400, ⊛www.cens.it). Unusually for Italy, reasonable **maps** are available of the park: the 1:50,000 *Kompass* sheet #665 "Assisi–Camerino" covers the area around Gualdo, and there's a special trail map that you may be able to pick up in Sigillo or Costacciaro; newsagents and bookshops – including the bar-newsagents in Piazza Quaranta Martiri in Gubbio – sometimes stock it, but don't bank on finding a copy.

There's a 44-bed **hostel**, *Università Volo Libero* (☎075.917.0761; €12.91), popular with hang-gliders, about 1km southeast of Costacciaro, at the hamlet of **SCIRCA** on the N3 road. In the past, the Centro Escursionistico has also offered hostel accommodation; call ahead for the latest. The **hotel** *Monte Cucco da Tobia* (☎ & ℻075.917.7194; ●) is a fabled mountaineers' and cavers' hangout in the Val di Ranco east of Sigillo. Also convenient for walkers is the one-star *Cappelloni*, Val di Ranco (☎075.917.7131; May–Sept; ●). In Sigillo, the only hotel is the three-star *Dominus*, Via Matteotti 55 (☎075.917.9074, ⊛www.dominushotel.it; ❷). These three all have **restaurants** (*Monte Cucco*'s big 200-seat place is closed Mon; the *Cappelloni*'s is closed Tues), while in Costacciaro you can eat at the restaurant-rosticceria *Palluconi* in Piazza Garibaldi (no closing day) or the *Bocconera* in Corso Mazzini (closed Wed). The nearest **campsite** for the park is *Rio Verde* (☎075.917.0138, ⊛www.campingrioverde.it; Easter–Sept; ●) at Fornace, 3km north of Costacciaro. It also offers bungalows for two and four people at €20 per person (€25 in July & Aug). Freelance camping is prohibited within the park, but elsewhere you'll have few problems finding a discreet pitch for a tent. At Valsorda, perched at 1010m is the forty-pitch one-star campsite *Valsorda* (☎075.913.261; June–Sept).

Travel details

The excellent website ⊛www.umbriatrasporti.it has links to full and updated timetables for all public transport, including the private FCU and state rail services and the ATC, APM and SSIT bus services.

Trains

Città di Castello to: Perugia (hourly; 50min); Sansepolcro (hourly; 20min).

Fossato di Vico (for Gubbio) to: Foligno (9–13 daily; 45min); Gualdo Tadino (8–11 daily; 10min); Nocera Umbra (8–11 daily; 20min); Orte (10 daily; 1hr 55min); Rome (10 daily; 2hr 40min); Spoleto (10 daily; 1hr 15min); Terni (10 daily; 1hr 30min).

Perugia to: Assisi (hourly; 25min); Città di Castello (hourly; 50min); Deruta (hourly; 30min); Florence (6 daily; 2hr 15min); Foligno (hourly; 40min – for connections to Spoleto, Fossato di Vico, Terni, Narni and Orte); Passignano (hourly; 30min); Sansepolcro (hourly; 1hr 40min); Spello (hourly; 35min); Terni (hourly; 1hr 40min); Teróntola (hourly; 40min – for 6 connections daily to Rome and also Siena); Todi (hourly; 50min).

Buses

Città di Castello to: Rome Tiburtina (1 daily; 3hr 15min); Rome Fiumicino airport (Mon–Sat 1 daily; 3hr 50min); Todi (Mon–Sat 1 direct daily; 2hr).

Gubbio to: Fossato di Vico train station, continuing to Gualdo Tadino and Nocera Umbra (10 daily; 30min); Perugia (Mon–Sat 10 daily, 4 on Sun; 1hr 10min); Rome (1 daily; 2hr 40min).

Perugia to: Ascoli Piceno (1–4 daily; 3hr); Assisi (3–12 daily; 30min); Castiglione del Lago (Mon–Sat 7–9 daily; 1hr 15min); Chiusi (Mon–Sat 5 daily; 1hr 45min); Città della Pieve (Mon–Sat 5 daily; 1hr 30min); Florence (1 daily; 2hr); Gualdo Tadino (Mon–Sat 6 daily, 2 on Sun; 1hr 25min); Gubbio (Mon–Sat 10 daily, 4 on Sun; 1hr 10min); Nocera Umbra (Mon–Sat 1 daily; 1hr 20min); Norcia (1 direct daily; 2hr 50min); Orvieto (1 daily; 2hr 25min); Passignano (Mon–Sat 7 daily; 1hr 10min); Rome (2–6 daily; 2hr 30min); Rome Fiumicino airport (1–3 daily; 3hr); Siena (3–7 daily; 1hr 30min); Spello (Mon–Sat 4 daily; 55min); Spoleto (Mon–Sat 1 daily direct; 1hr 20min); Todi via Deruta (Mon–Sat 3–7 daily; 1hr 15min); Torgiano (Mon–Sat 7 daily; 30min).

Assisi and the
Vale of Spoleto

CHAPTER 11

Highlights

* **Basilica di San Francesco, Assisi** One of Italy's great buildings, and the burial place of St Francis. See p.606

* **Tempio di Minerva, Assisi** An excellently preserved first-century temple front. See p.615

* **Spello** Charming hilltown, whose church of Santa Maria Maggiore hosts a fresco cycle by Pinturicchio. See p.623

* **Monte Subasio** Great walks and drives on the mountain above Assisi, with spectacular views and superb spring flowers. See p.629

* **Bevagna** Captivating village, known for its medieval main square and fine Romanesque churches. See p.632

* **Montefalco** Home of the outstanding Sagrantino Passito wine, plus a major fresco cycle by Benozzo Gozzoli. See p.635

* **Trevi** The most spectacularly sited of the Umbrian hill-towns. See p.639

△ Trevi

Assisi and the Vale of Spoleto

T he **Vale of Spoleto**, the broad plain between Perugia and Spoleto, is Umbria's historic and spiritual heartland: a sweep of countryside that is beautiful in parts and has a majestic focus in **Assisi**. Birthplace of St Francis, Italy's premier saint, this hill-town has been an object of pilgrimage for over seven hundred years, now attracting a staggering five million or more visitors annually. It has also long emerged from the trauma of the 1997 earthquake, which brought the town to worldwide prominence when part of the famous Basilica di San Francesco collapsed, killing four and destroying some minor frescoes.

Quieter hill-towns are just around the corner. **Spello**, the most accessible, remains just ahead of the tourist boom – though the visitors have arrived – and features more art treasures in the shape of Pinturicchio's frescoes in the church of Santa Maria Maggiore. Nearby **Bevagna**, like Spello an outpost on the Roman Via Flaminia, is a tiny, wall-enclosed village locked around a central square that's almost without equal in Umbria. Lording it over the vale is **Montefalco**, a windblown hive of medieval streets that is home to yet another superb fresco cycle – this one by the Tuscan Benozzo Gozzoli – and one of the province's strangest attractions, a quartet of mummified holy corpses. Across the valley is **Trevi**, relatively little visited, but in the throes of a renaissance and perhaps the most perfectly situated of all Italian hill-towns. Mostly modern **Foligno**, the regional capital, has a sprawling, limited provincial appeal and a handsome Duomo, and provides a good standby for accommodation.

Foligno is the centre of the network of transport links throughout the region. The main **rail** link from Rome to Ancona passes through Foligno, whence there are connections to Spoleto, Terni and Narni to the south, Nocera and Gualdo Tadino to the north, and a branch line spur that runs to Teróntola via Spello, Assisi and Perugia. **Buses** radiate from Foligno to the local villages, and

Official websites

Umbria's official tourist websites are Ⓦ www.umbria-turismo.it and Ⓦ www
.umbria2000.it. Many of the region's museums and galleries are affiliated to Sistema-
museo (information ☎ 199.194.114, Ⓦ www.sistemamuseo.it).

there are frequent connections between Perugia, Assisi and points to the south.
Road journeys are quick thanks to the dual carriageway (SS3) between Perugia
and Foligno.

Assisi

ASSISI would be an irresistible target even without its great Basilica and Franciscan sideshow. Visible for miles around, it sits enticingly beneath the whaleback slopes of Monte Subasio, the prominent castle and pink-stoned medieval
houses lording it over the Vale of Spoleto. Millions come as an act of faith, but a
substantial number visit simply to see the sublime paintings in the **Basilica di
San Francesco**, where frescoes by **Giotto** and **Pietro Lorenzetti** comprise
one of the greatest monuments of Italian art. Yet for all the coach parties of

Easter week – Processions and festivities thoughout the week.
Calendimaggio (week following the 1st Tues in May) – Procession to celebrate St Francis's vision of Lady Poverty.
Festa della Voto (June 22) – Procession in medieval costume to celebrate the town's salvation.
Perdono (Aug 1–2) – Pilgrimage to the church of Santa Maria degli Angeli.
Palio della Balestra (Aug 11) – Medieval tournament.
Festa di San Francesco (Oct 3–4) – The big event: a major pilgrimage that draws crowds of pilgrims and ecclesiastics from all over Italy and beyond.
Festa del Corpus Domini (Nov) – Another major procession, through flower-strewn streets.

pilgrims, both religious and secular, Assisi just about remains a town with an uncompromised identity – as an overnight stay, after the car parks have cleared, will reveal. At close quarters, the tacky tourist paraphernalia and religious kitsch are offset by tranquil backstreets, geranium-filled windowboxes and buildings in the muted, rosy stone that distinguishes all the vale's towns. With sufficient enthusiasm you can see almost all the sights in a day, but be warned: this is the third most visited pilgrimage site in Italy (after St Peter's in Rome and Padre Pio's shrine in Puglia).

Assisi's history is not all tied to the Franciscan masthead. Founded by the **Umbrians** – in contrast to Perugia's Etruscan heritage – the town later achieved prominence as Asisium, a **Roman** *municipium*. Thereafter invaders passed it over, attracted by the richer pickings of Perugia, but in the end it fell under the control of that city's monstrous **Baglioni** family. These were characters, said one Franciscan historian, "who did not shudder to murder men, cook their flesh, and give it to the relations of the slain in their prison dungeons". Plague, famine and eventually Church control turned the town into a moribund backwater. However, Francis's elevation to the status of national saint in 1939 managed to reverse its economic decline, and today religious and other tourism have made this a very prosperous town indeed.

Arrival and information

There are roughly hourly **trains** from Foligno (via Spello) and from Teróntola (via Perugia, which is only half-an-hour away) to Assisi's delightful station (℡075.804.0272), virtually rebuilt after the 1997 earthquakes, located in the modern suburb of Santa Maria degli Angeli, 5km southwest of the old town. Roughly half-hourly buses from the station (tickets from the station kiosk) take twenty minutes to reach **Piazza Unità d'Italia** below the Basilica or **Piazza Matteotti**, some by way of Largo Properzio, east of the Basilica di Santa Chiara – from where there's an unreliable escalator to the gateway at Porta Nuova. Both squares are less than five minutes' walk from the heart of the medieval town, **Piazza del Comune**. The town slopes steeply from the Basilica di San Francesco in the west to Piazza Matteotti in the east, so wherever you arrive or stay, you can be faced with a climb.

The main **bus terminal** is in Piazza Matteotti, above and beyond the Duomo. A board in the piazza's northwest corner, on the junction of Via del Comune Vecchio, has a full schedule for bus departures, and there's an electronic display

ASSISI

Cemetery & Car Park

Basilica di
San Francesco

PIAZZA
SUPERIORE DI
S.FRANCESCO

PIAZZA INFERIORE
DI S.FRANCESCO

Porta San
Giacomo

VIA MERRY DEL VAL

Santa
Margherita

VIA METELLI

VIA SANTA CROCE

Santa Croce

VIA METASTASIO

Foro Romano e
Collezione
Archeologica

VIA DEL COLLE

Perugia & campsite

STRADA PIAGGIA S. FRANCESCO

VIA FRATE ELIA

Casa dei
Maestri
Comacini

VIA SAN FRANCESCO

Pinacoteca Comunale

Oratorio dei Pellegrini

VIA S. PAOLO

VIA SEMINARIO

SS. Stefano
e Fortunato

Porta San
Francesco

VIA FONTEBELLA

P. UNITA
D'ITALIA

PIAZZETTA
GARIBALDI

PENNACCHI

VIA DEL FOSSO CUPO

Porta San Pietro

PIAZZA
S. PIETRO

VIA ANCAIANI

VIA BORGO S. PIETRO

San Pietro

VIALE MARCONI

VIALE VITTORIO EMANUELE II

VIA S. APOLLINARE

Porta
Sermentone

ACCOMMODATION

Anfiteatro Romano	F	Ostello della Pace	U
Berti	R	Pallotta	K
Dei Priori	L	Porta Nuova	T
Del Viaggiatore	S	Posta e Panoramic	I
Fontebella	N	Properzio	E
Ideale per Turisti	Q	San Francesco	D
La Fortezza	H	San Pietro	O
La Rocca	C	Sole	P
Le Silve	B	Subasio	G
Lo Scudo	J	Umbra	M
Ostello di Fontemaggio	A		

Train Station, Santa Maria degli Angeli (5km)

next to the ticket and information office, ASP Agenzia (daily 7.30am–9.30pm). Long-distance Sulga buses (☎075.500.9641) to Florence's Piazza Adua, Milan and Naples leave from Piazza San Pietro, at the other end of town (buy tickets on the bus or from the Stoppini travel agent, Corso Mazzini 31).

Parking in central Assisi is virtually impossible. It's best to leave cars at the massive underground car park in Piazza Matteotti or in Piazza Unità d'Italia. There are hundreds of free spaces up by the Rocca, a long walk to the Basilica, and by the cemetery off Viale Albornoz on the road from Porta San Giacomo. Other fringe car parks are located outside Porta Nuova and Porta Moiano. Orange **minibuses** A and B provide connecting services around the town, though in practice you'll find distances are short and that it's easiest to walk. Minibus tickets are sold at shops and newsagents displaying an ASP or *Comune di Assisi* ticket flash.

Information

The **tourist office** is in the pretty (and obvious) old post office building at the western end of the square (April–Oct Mon–Sat 8am–2pm & 3–6.30pm, Sun 10am–1pm & 2–7pm, Sun hours subject to change; Nov–Feb Mon–Sat 8am–2pm & 3–6pm, Sun 9am–1pm; ☎075.812.534 or 075.812.450, ✉info@iat .assisi.pg.it). Staff can help with finding accommodation and provide some useful maps and pamphlets, including a range of individual duplicated sheets with details of trains, buses, private rooms and *agriturismo* options, available on request. There are usually seasonal **summer information offices** in Largo Properzio near Porta Nuova (☎075.816.766) – this is run by Assisi's hoteliers, and has lots of accommodation information – Santa Maria degli Angeli (☎075.812.479), and at the train station (☎075.813.499).

ASSISI AND THE VALE OF SPOLETO | Arrival and information

11

602

RESTAURANTS

Buca di San Francesco	4
I Monaci	3
La Fortezza	H
La Piazzetta dell'Erba	1
Medioevo	5
Pallotta	K
Ristorante La Rocca	C
San Francesco	D

▼ San Damiano

Accommodation

There are getting on for a hundred **hotels** in Assisi, though advance booking is still highly advisable, and essential if you plan to visit over Easter or during the Festa di San Francesco (Oct 3–4) or Calendimaggio (May 21–22). The tourist office can provide full lists of all lodgings, including over fifty **rooms** for rent (ask for the *Extralberghieri*), and will make reservations for you; try to avoid the concentrations of cheaper private rooms and hotels in San Pietro Campagna, Santa Maria degli Angeli and the horribly grim little village of Bastia, 4km out.

The often extraordinarily cheap **pilgrim hostels** (*Case Religiose di Ospitalità*) listed below are open to both women and men and are located in the town proper; these are well known, and so also need to be booked in advance. Most offer singles and doubles and sometimes a couple of dormitory rooms. Costs are from around €20–25 per person, depending on whether rooms have private bathrooms and how many people are sharing a room; doubles all fall around the €50–60 mark. Virtually all provide breakfast for an extra couple of euros, plus very reasonable half- and full-board options.

Hotels

Anfiteatro Romano Via Anfiteatro Romano 4 ℡075.813.025, ℻075.815.110. Good-value one-star hotel, in one of the most pleasant parts of town. Seven rooms, en suite and not. ❶

Berti Piazza San Pietro 29 ℡075.813.466, ℻075.816.870, ℗www.hotelberti.it. Two-star located in a quiet piazza, handy for the Basilica. Rooms have TVs and air-conditioning. ❸

Dei Priori Corso Mazzini 15 ℡075.812.237, ℻075.816.804. Three-star, 34-room hotel, slightly east of Piazza del Comune: rates vary considerably between rooms, but expect to pay €115 for a standard high-season double. ❷–❺

Del Viaggiatore Via Sant'Antonio 14 ℡075.816.297 or 075.812.424, ℻075.813.051. Small, personal, eleven-room two-star above a decent restaurant in the web of streets between Santa Maria Maggiore and Piazza del Comune. ❶

Assisi saw fewer visitors after the **earthquakes** of September 1997 – two major tremors and many aftershocks – which killed four people in the Basilica di San Francesco and destroyed some of the building's less significant frescoes. While the event made world headlines, the damage to Assisi, the Basilica and the rest of Umbria was somewhat overdramatized: the earthquake epicentres were well to the east in Colfiorito and the Marche, and nearby towns Spoleto and Orvieto suffered virtually no ill-effects. Some precautionary scaffolding and buttressing aside, there are now few tangible signs in Assisi that anything happened at all. The important Lower Church of the Basilica has remained open, and the Upper Church – where the partial ceiling collapse occurred – was formally reopened by a representative of the pope in November 1999. All other sights were open at the time of writing, and Assisi's intrinsic medieval charm remains undiminished. Most money has been targeted at the monuments, however, leading to accusations that tourism has taken precedence over the social costs of the disaster. The continued existence of temporary housing on the town's outskirts would certainly seem to suggest that there is more to be done.

Fontebella Via Fontebella 25 ☎075.812.456, ℻075.812.941, ⓦwww .fontebella.com. By far the most elegant and intimate of Assisi's smart hotels, despite its three-star rating and the fact that it is less high profile than the *Subasio*. Try for a room on one of the top two floors for views over the rooftops and the Vale of Spoleto. ❾

Ideale per Turisti Piazza Matteotti 1 ☎075.813.570, ℻075.813.020, ⓦwww .hotelideale.it. Follow signs south from Piazza Matteotti a short way outside the walls to reach this slightly outlying but very reasonable eleven-room two-star hotel: all rooms with private bathroom. Hotel parking is a boon. ❸

La Fortezza Vicolo della Fortezza 19b ☎075.812.418, ℻075.819.8035, ⓦwww .lafortezzahotel.com. Friendly two-star with just seven rooms in a perfect central position just off Piazza del Comune (and a few steps from the *Italia*): the co-owned restaurant is also excellent. ❶

La Rocca Via di Porta Perlici 27 ☎ & ℻075.812.284. A fifteen-room one-star beyond the Duomo at the very end of Via di Porta Perlici. Quiet and with fine views from some rooms; most with own bath. ❶

Le Silve Caparrocchie, near Armenzano ☎075.801.9000, ⓦwww.lesilve.it. This delightful hotel in lovely countryside 10km east of Assisi on the slopes of Monte Subasio makes an excellent, if expensive alternative to staying in town. A traditional, converted rural house (parts of which date back to the tenth century), it sits among fields and woods and offers peace and quiet, a swimming pool, tennis, riding and other activities. ❻

Lo Scudo Via San Francesco 3 ☎ & ℻075.813.196. A small sign outside a pretty medieval house signals this well-placed seven-room one-star; despite its modest rating, all rooms have private bathrooms and you're at the heart of the action. ❷

Pallotta Via San Rufino 6 ☎ & ℻075.812.307, ⓦwww.pallottaassisi.it. Seven-room two-star in a good location between the Duomo and Piazza del Comune: all rooms with private bathroom. The co-owned restaurant just off Piazza del Comune is also good. ❷

Porta Nuova Viale Umberto I, 21 ☎075.812.405, ℻075.816.539, ⓦwww.hotelportanuova.it. Basic thirteen-room three-star standby south of Piazza Matteotti in a quiet area above Basilica di Santa Chiara. ❸

Posta e Panoramic Via San Paolo 17–19 ☎075.812.558, ℻075.816.202. Centrally located two-star with fourteen rooms (all with private bathroom) west of the Duomo – on the street parallel to Via San Francesco. ❶

Properzio Via San Francesco 38b ☎075.813.188, ℻075.815.201, ⓦwww.ristorantesanfrancesco .com. Simple nine-room two-star, handily placed on the main street right by the Basilica. ❷

San Francesco Via San Francesco 48 ☎075.812.281, ℻075.816.237, ⓦwww .hotelsanfrancescoassisi.it. Reliable and conveniently situated three-star hotel just a minute's walk from the Basilica; 45 rooms – some with views – mean there's a good chance of finding space. ❹

San Pietro Piazza San Pietro 5 ☎075.812.452, ℻075.816.332. Large but rather perfunctory three-star hotel with 46 rooms by the gate south of the Basilica. ❹

Sole Corso Mazzini 35 ☎075.812.373, ℻075.813.706, ⓦwww.assisihotelsole.com. Functional two-star hotel with nineteen rooms in a convenient position one minute's walk from the Basilica di Santa Chiara. Also has an eighteen-room annexe at Corso Mazzini 20, so there's a good chance of finding space when others are full. Rooms vary in price by up to €30, so ask to see a range. The cheapest starts at €62. ➋

Subasio Via Frate Elia 2 ℡075.812.206, ℻075.816.691, ⓦwww.hotelsubasio.com. Full of old-world style, this four-star is Assisi's traditional hotel of choice if you're feeling flush: past guests include Marlene Dietrich, Charlie Chaplin and Elizabeth Taylor. Surprisingly unstuffy for all that; the 61 rooms vary considerably, but most have views. ➏

Umbra Vicolo degli Archi 6 ℡075.812.240, ℻075.813.653, ⓦwww.hotelumbra.it. An excellent and very popular mid-market choice, with 25 three-star rooms almost immediately off the southern edge of Piazza del Comune. ➍

Hostels

Ostello di Fontemaggio Strada Eremo delle Carceri 8, at the hamlet of Fontemaggio, 2km east of the town ℡075.813.636 or 075.812.317, ℻075.813.749, ⓦwww.fontemaggio.it. Clean, ten-bed, single-sex dorms at €20 per person; or a choice of fifteen one-star hotel rooms.

Ostello della Pace Via di Valecchie 177 ℡075.816.767. Located in peaceful countryside off the road that leads east from Porta San Pietro and Viale G. Marconi, ten minutes' downhill walk from Piazza Unità d'Italia. Look for the small road (with sign for hostel) off left at the big right-hand bend shortly after the small roundabout junction with Viale Vittorio Emanuele II. Coming from the station by bus, try to be dropped at "Villa Guardi": the hostel is signposted from here. Dorm beds (66 in total in twelve rooms) at €15, plus half- and full-board deals at €26 and €35.

Pilgrim hostels

Casa del Terzario Piazza del Vescovado 5 ℡075.812.366, ℻075.816.377. A definite first choice for location and rooms, though not all rooms have private bathrooms. Closed Nov–March.

Istituto Beata Angelina Via Merry del Val 4 ℡ & ℻075.812.511. Most of the sixteen rooms have private bathrooms; located very close to the Basilica.

Monastero Sant'Andrea Vicolo Sant'Andrea ℡075.812.274, ℻075.815.130. Located in a hard-to-find but excellently situated alley just south of Via San Giacomo and Porta San Giacomo. Take the turn uphill off Via San Francesco by the Casa dei Maestri Comacini. Has forty rooms, half of them en suite.

Monastero San Colette Borgo San Pietro 3 ℡075.812.345, ℻075.816.489. Handy for the Basilica: located just west of the church of San Pietro. Breakfast included, but no half-board or full-board deals; 29 rooms, fifteen en suite.

Monastero San Giuseppe Via Sant'Apollinare 1 ℡ & ℻075.812.332. Located in the southeast corner of town just west of Santa Maria Maggiore. Full board or half board only, at €50 or €45 per person respectively; 32 rooms, all with private bathroom.

Monastero Santo Quirico Via Giovanni di Borino 5 ℡075.812.688. Has fourteen rooms, twelve of which have private bathrooms. Closed at time of writing, but due to reopen.

Suore dell'Atonement Via G. Alessi 10 ℡075.812.542, ℻075.813.723. All twenty rooms offered by the American nuns here have private bathrooms. Breakfast is included.

Private rooms

Annalisa Martini Via San Gregorio 6 ℡075.813.536. Six rooms (three with bathrooms) in the second alley on the left off Via Portica after leaving Piazza del Comune. €38 or €35 with shared bathroom.

Bernardo Pampanini Piazza Matteotti 2 ℡075.813.020. Three doubles in one of the less medieval corners of Assisi, but still convenient for all the sights. €45.

Camere di Santa Chiara Via Sant'Antonio 1a ℡075.815.220. Five doubles, each with bathroom, in a superbly situated alley just south of Piazza del Comune by Sant'Antonio and the Chiesa Nuova. €50.

Cristina Lombardi Via del Comune Vecchio 20 ℡075.816.419. Four singles (two bathrooms) in the pretty street between Piazza Matteotti and Via Porta Perlici. €21.

Il Duomo Vicolo San Lorenzo 2 ℡075.812.742, ⓦwww.hotelsanrufino.it. The best private lodgings in town, located in a tiny flower-decked medieval alley; walk up Via di Porta Perlici from the Duomo and Vicolo San Lorenzo is second on the left. €45.

Marco Gambacorta Via Sermei 9 ℡075.815.206. Six double rooms (three bathrooms) in the small lane immediately north of the Basilica di Santa Chiara off Via Santa Chiara. €40.

Maria Alunni Via dell'Acquario 3 ℡ & ℻075.813.182. Charming proprietress; four spotless, airy rooms and lots of greenery. €40 or €35 with shared bathroom.

Campsites

Fontemaggio Strada Eremo delle Carceri 8 ℡075.813.636, ℻075.813.749. A 244-pitch two-star site alongside the hostel at Fontemaggio and

The Basilica di San Francesco

The **Basilica di San Francesco** ranks second only to St Peter's in Rome as a point of worldwide Catholic pilgrimage, and its cycle of paintings by Giotto has long been considered one of the turning points in Western art, moving from the Byzantine world of iconic saints and Madonnas to one of humanist narrative.

The construction of the Basilica is in two tiers, with the **Upper Church** placed above the **Lower Church**. This posed enormous engineering problems, which were solved by the use of massive arched buttressing that effectively propped up the western end of the town. One of the wonders of early medieval architecture, its creator remains unknown: all the original drawings were burnt in a raid by the Perugians. Most historians presume it to have been the work of Lombard masons, who would have drawn their inspiration from the Gothic churches of southern France. As one of the earliest examples of Italian Gothic, the Basilica exerted great architectural influence, its single-naved Upper Church becoming a model for countless Franciscan churches around the country.

Admission to both parts of the Basilica is free. Both are usually open daily (8.30am–6.50pm; winter closes 5.50pm), except from November to March when both may close for lunch (noon–2pm). The Upper Church may close or have restricted opening on Sundays; both close on holy days. The Lower Church is usually open earlier than the listed time in the mornings (that is, from around 6–6.30am), making this a good time to visit. Indeed, you'd do best to always visit early or late in the day: the crowds at other times can make it hard to get a view of the frescoes, especially in the Lower Church. It's also worth taking a couple of minutes to wander the **cloisters**, entered from the Lower Church. The custodians of the Basilica enforce their **dress code** extremely vigorously: you should always cover your arms and legs. Their repeated exhortations for everybody to remain **silent** seem, sadly, to fall on deaf ears.

The history of the Basilica

The Basilica was conceived, shortly after Francis's death, by the man who had taken over the running of the order a decade or so earlier, one **Elias of Cortona**. Elias, one of the saint's earliest disciples, served as vicar-general of the Franciscans through to 1239, presiding over a series of bitter disputes and schisms, until being deposed and excommunicated. In the early years of the post-Francis order, however, he ran things very much his way, capitalizing on the saint's popular appeal to build the Franciscans into a powerful force, and raising the money to make the founder's Basilica one of the great Christian shrines. To the horror of the more ascetic and zealous followers of the saint – to whom Francis himself was allied in his final years – Elias set about a massive fundraising project, selling religious indulgences across Europe. The "fundamentalist" wing argued that the indulgences were a corruption, and the Basilica's proposed magnificence at odds with Francis's maxim that "small churches should be built, for they ought not to raise great churches for the sake of preaching to the people or for any other reason, for they will show greater humility and give a better example by going to preach in other churches". They pointed out, too, that Francis's choice of **burial site** was intended as a gesture of humility: he had picked one of the most despised spots of medieval Assisi, known as the Colle del Inferno, where criminals were taken for execution. It was to no avail. The burial site was rechristened Colle del Paradiso and a building more ambitious than any in Italy was begun.

While **construction** of the Basilica proceeded, the **political background** became increasingly murky, the strangest twist coming on the day of Francis's canonization. Elias by this time had fallen out with the papacy, which was organizing the ceremony, and as the saint's hearse proceeded through the streets of Assisi, he and a posse burst onto the scene and seized the body. Ignoring the anger of the crowd and the indignation of the papal entourage, they hurried the coffin into the Lower Church and bolted the doors behind them. Prompted perhaps by the fear that his master's remains would be stolen or desecrated (medieval relics had enormous financial and spiritual value), Elias had decided to bury Francis in a **secret tomb** deep within the Basilica. The episode gave rise to a myth, recycled by Vasari, that a vast hidden church had been built below the Basilica, far greater in beauty and grandeur than the churches above. Inside this sealed chamber it was believed the body of the "almost alive saint" hovered above the altar awaiting his call to heaven. The tomb remained undiscovered, or at least unreached, until a two-month search in 1818.

The **1997 earthquakes** could have been catastrophic for the Basilica. In fact, damage was relatively minor, though – in a country where restoration projects can be measured in decades – a third of Umbria's entire 1998 emergency budget for the region's monuments was devoted to state-of-the-art protection for the Basilica in a successful effort to have it reopened for the year 2000 celebrations. What is poignant and ironic is that the Basilica's builders were aware of the problems posed by Umbria's seismic history, and had designed the building with the flexibility to withstand tremors: part of the vaults in the Upper Church collapsed only because tonnes of rubble had accumulated in the hollow ceiling space over the centuries, which generations of restorers had been too lazy to clear. The strengthened and revamped foundations will now withstand, it is hoped, earthquakes of anything up to a most unlikely 12 on the Richter scale.

The Lower Church

The sombre **Lower Church** is the place to begin if you want to follow the architectural and artistic chronology of the shrine. Its convoluted floor plan and low-lit vaults are intended to create a mood of calm and meditative introspection; the low-level natural light has been augmented by fairly discreet spotlighting – a concession that has altered the atmosphere of the chapel, but also makes it possible to study the frescoes and intricate decoration that cover every surface in such density that it really needs several visits to take it all in.

The main nave

The highlights span a century of continuous artistic development. Important but somewhat stilted early works by Byzantine-influenced artists line the walls of the main nave, many credited to the mysterious **Maestro di San Francesco**, the anonymous hand that crops up elsewhere in Umbria. These are the oldest frescoes in the Basilica (1253), the *Scenes from the Passion* (right wall) and *Episodes from the Life of St Francis* (left wall). Faded in places, they have also been partly obliterated by the subsequent opening up of the side chapels, a necessity forced on the Franciscans by the need to accommodate the growing number of pilgrims visiting Assisi.

BASILICA DI SAN FRANCESCO
THE LOWER CHURCH

1 Cappella di San Sebastiano
2 Pulpit (1459)
3 Tomb of Filippo di Courtenay
4 Tomb of Blascio Fernandez
5 Tomb of Cardinal Albornoz (by Gattapone)
   Frescoes (1368) by Andrea da Bologna
6 Life of St Stephen by Dono Doni (1575)
7 Cappella di San Antonio di Padova
   Frescoes (1610) by Cesare Sermei da Orvieto
8 Stairway to the crypt and the Tomb of St Francis
9 Frescoes by Giotto or school of Giotto
10 Right transept: frescoes by Giotto, Cimabue and
   followers
11 Portrait of St Francis (Cimabue?)
12 Five Saints (Martini?) incl. Portrait of St Clare
   (fourth left)
13 Cappella di San Nicola: scenes from the Life of St
   Nicola by Giotto and followers of Giotto

14 Entrance to cloisters, Tesoro and the Upper Church
15 Choir (1471)
16 Vaults of the High Altar by Giotto and/or followers
   of Giotto:
   a St Francis Enthroned
   b Allegory of Obedience
   c Allegory of Poverty
   d Allegory of Chastity
17 Left transept: frescoes by Pietro Lorenzetti
   (assisted by Ambrogio Lorenzetti?)
18 Cappella di S.G. Battista (1288). Madonna and
   Child with SS. Francis and John by Pietro Lorenzetti
19 Sacristy. Relics of St Francis and Madonna
   and Child (Umbrian anon.)
20 Coronation of the Virgin by Puccio Capanna d'Assisi
21 Cappella di San Martino. Scenes from the Life of
   St Martin (1322) by Simone Martini

Don't overlook the church's minor works, notably the little *Madonna Enthroned* (1422) by the Gubbian artist Ottaviano Nelli (on the left as you enter, just right of the Cappella di San Sebastiano), or the **Tomb of Cardinal Albornoz**, built as a temporary resting place for the Spanish firebrand responsible for reinforcing papal power in Umbria. He rebuilt and regarrisoned the castles of Assisi, Narni and Spoleto, among others, and was rewarded for his pains with a tomb in the Basilica (his remains were later removed to Toledo, his home town). The tomb, remarkably, is the work of **Matteo di Gattapone**, the architect responsible for Spoleto's Ponte delle Torri and Gubbio's Palazzo dei Consoli, projects conceived on a far vaster scale.

The Cappella di San Martino

Simone Martini's frescoes in the **Cappella di San Martino**, the first chapel on the left as you enter the nave (no. 21 on the plan), are among the Lower Church's highlights. He worked here in the mid-1310s, shortly after painting the great *Maestà* in Siena, and was given completely free rein: every detail, even the floor and stained glass, came under his control. The panels on the underside of the arch as you enter the chapel were probably painted in 1317. They show eight saints, and were painted to honour St Louis of Toulouse, who had just been sanctified; he is the red-robed figure in the upper left panel, flanked by saints Francis, Anthony and Clare.

In the interior chapel, a far more distinct and insular space than much of the Lower Church, is a complete fresco cycle of the life of **St Martin of Tours**. The father of monasticism in France, Martin was venerated as far afield as Ireland and Africa; here, however, he is featured partly as a sop to the Franciscan friar who commissioned the chapel (the friar had been made cardinal with the title of San Martino ai Monti). The ten-panel cycle starts on the left-hand wall and moves clockwise around the chapel, the lowest four panels representing scenes from the secular part of Martin's life up to and including his conversion, the remaining four wall frescoes and two painted ceiling vaults treating the period after his conversion. Martin was born in 315 in what is now Hungary and brought up in Italy at Pavia. The key event of his conversion – and the first depicted in the cycle – came as a young officer at Amiens, when he gave half his cloak to a beggar, a figure he was later led to recognize as Christ. To the right is the *Dream of St Martin*, in which

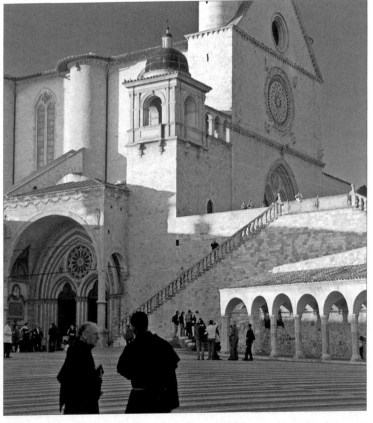

△ Franciscan monks in the lower courtyard of San Francesco

Christ and angels appear to the saint, a panel that mingles secular and sacred iconography amid a panoply of courtly emblems. This trait is continued in the next panel on the right-hand wall, *St Martin is Knighted*, an out-and-out evocation of life at court without religious iconography of any kind. To its right is *St Martin Renounces his Weapons*: "I am Christ's soldier; I am not allowed to fight." Here too, Martini seems to reserve his finest painting for the background – the tents, spears, lances and costumes of the Roman camp and Emperor Julian.

The narrative moves to the second tier back on the left-hand wall, starting with the *Miracle of the Resurrected Child*, another episode never before depicted in Italian art, in which Martin, transported presumably by artistic licence to Siena (the city's Palazzo Pubblico is in the background) raises a child from the dead before its mother and an expectant crowd. Alongside is the *Meditation*, with the saint moved to distraction by contemplation of the Divine, and unmoved by the acolytes trying to direct his attention to the Mass. Round to its right is the *Miraculous Mass*, an unusual subject portrayed here for the first time. Martin has again given a cloak to a beggar, and is about to celebrate Mass when angels appear to present him with a beautifully embroidered piece of material. The next fresco, the *Miracle of Fire*, is damaged, though the sense of the scene is clear: a tongue of flame is forced down the throat of Emperor Valentinian for refusing to give Martin an audience.

The uppermost level depicts two self-explanatory scenes, the saint's death and burial, both distinguished by the exquisite detail of the saint's robes, and by the architectural details that correspond to the moods of the episodes – severe, bare-walled and geometrical around the scene of death, and more ornate in the Gothic chapel that hosts the funeral.

The right transept

Cenno di Pepo, popularly known as **Cimabue** (c.1240–1302), was the first great named artist to work on the Basilica. Vasari's *Lives of the Artists* opens with an account of him, in which he is described as the father of Italian painting, and an obsessive perfectionist, often destroying work with which he was not completely happy. He probably painted in the transepts of the Upper Church between 1270 and 1280, and was active in the Lower Church some time later. His major painting in the Lower Church – where much of his work was later overpainted – is in the **right transept** (right wall), the over-restored *Madonna, Child and Angels with St Francis*, a work that survives from the church's earlier decorative scheme (1280). Ruskin described this painting as the noblest depiction of the Virgin in Christendom. It includes the famous portrait of St Francis, which you'll already have seen plastered all over the town. Next to it, the *Crucifixion* has been attributed to **Giotto**, as have – though with less certainty – the scenes on the end wall and vaults depicting the *Childhood of Christ*. To the left are a half-length *Madonna and Child* and pair of saints, while on the side wall is a set of five saints, all the work of **Simone Martini**. One of the figures – another image much duplicated around town – is believed to be **St Clare**, founder of the women's chapter of the Franciscans (see p.618). The painting shows a clear attempt at the depiction of emotion, the use of light and shade to add verisimilitude to figures, and the creation of a coherent three-dimensional sense of space – all steps on the path trodden with equal certainty by Giotto and Martini's Sienese contemporary, Pietro Lorenzetti.

The vaults over the altar

The question of **Giotto**'s involvement in the Basilica has been at the centre of one of Italy's greatest art history controversies. Certain twentieth-century historians opined that Giotto had never painted in Assisi at all. Some still hold this view, though the modern consensus is that Giotto was indeed responsible for the bulk of the paintings in the Upper Church, executed from about 1295. Authorship in the Lower Church is more dubious, and credit for the allegorical frescoes in the **vaults over the altar** – some of the church's most beautiful and complex – has been taken from Giotto and given to nameless assistants. The same goes for the *Life of Mary Magdalene* cycle (c.1309) in the **Cappella della Maddalena**, the third chapel on the right, as well as the right transept's *Childhood of Christ* (see above). In the hothouse atmosphere of the Basilica during its decoration, however, co-operative efforts must have been commonplace: definitive attributions are all but impossible.

The left transept

Pietro Lorenzetti is represented by a beautiful series of works in the **left transept**. Recent criticism sees the *Six Scenes of the Passion*, on the ceiling of the left-hand transept, as his earliest surviving works, probably painted on a visit to Assisi in about 1314. Restrained, static pieces, they betray the influence of Duccio, an impulse shrugged off when the artist returned to the Basilica in the years 1324–25 and 1327–28. By this time he had absorbed the lessons of Giotto, bringing them to bear on the *Passion of Christ* in the left transept, a cycle he had probably started on his visit ten years earlier.

The frescoes portraying scenes leading up to Christ's crucifixion are comparatively weak. The *Last Supper*, however, in which Christ and the apostles are crowded into a curious hexagonal loggia, reveals a treatment of light and shadow hardly matched during the fourteenth century. The moon and stars light the sky, while to the left is a kitchen illuminated by light from a fire, in which servants unconcernedly scrape food into a dog's bowl – a fine incidental detail paralleled by the two chattering servants to the left of Christ, who are quite oblivious to events before them. The only illumination at the table is from the haloes of Christ and the apostles, a deliberate juxtaposition of material and spiritual light.

Three other panels stand out in the cycle: the *Entombment*, *Crucifixion* and *Deposition*. Dominating almost an entire wall, the *Crucifixion* shows an amazing sense of drama, with Christ raised high above a crowd of onlookers, and closer study reveals carefully observed nuances of character in the crowd. These natural touches recur in the faces of the *Deposition*, less immediately striking but still amongst Lorenzetti's masterpieces for its bold and simple composition. The upper portion of the Cross is completely missing, leaving just the broad horizontal and huge amounts of vacant space, all focusing on the figure of Christ, his limbs bent with rigor mortis.

Lorenzetti also painted in the chapel beyond, the **Cappella di San Giovanni Battista** (no. 18 on the plan), where he left the frescoed triptych of the *Madonna and Child with SS Francis and John the Baptist*. The central panel of stained glass here is attributed to Jacopo Torriti, one of the largely unsung but important Roman artists to have frescoed parts of the Upper Church.

The tomb of St Francis

Before leaving the Lower Church, drop down to the crypt and the **tomb of St Francis**, a spot that remained hidden until 1818. The present tomb, rebuilt in the 1920s, honours Francis's desire for a humble burial, replacing a more elaborate tabernacle raised in the excitement of discovery. Above the main altar is the simple stone coffin that contains the body; at the four corners of the central canopy are the bodies of Francis's earliest key companions, the beatific Leone, Rufino, Masseo and Angelo.

There's a short account of the tomb's fascinating history and discovery (in English) tacked to the bare stone walls.

The Museo del Tesoro

The well-presented **Museo del Tesoro e Collezioni F.M. Perkins** (April–Oct Mon–Sat 9.30am–5pm; donation expected) is entered from doors in the transept behind the main altar. It contains a rich collection of paintings, including 55 masterpieces from the Frederick Mason Perkins Collection, a bequest from an American philanthropist which includes work by Fra' Angelico, Pier Francesco Fiorentino, Luca Signorelli and Masolino. It's also particularly strong on the Sienese, with paintings by Pietro Lorenzetti, Segno di Bonaventura, Bartolo di Fredi and Taddeo di Bartolo. The museum's own original collection contains works by Benozzo Gozzoli and little-known Umbrians like Lo Spagna, Bonfigli and Dono Doni. The remainder of the gallery is crammed with copes, vestments, silverware, reliquaries and the like, given to the Franciscans over the centuries. Pride of place goes to a tapestry of St Francis (1479) and an altar front (1478), both presented by Pope Sixtus IV, the latter with figures by Antonio del Pollaiuolo, together with a series of thirteenth-century Tuscan and Umbrian crucifixes.

The Upper Church

The **Upper Church** is a completely different architectural, aesthetic and emotional experience, its airy Gothic plan intended to inspire celebration rather than contemplation. It feels less a church than a gallery for Giotto's dazzling *Life of St Francis* frescoes, rightly regarded – notwithstanding the odd doubt as to its attribution – as one of the greatest of all Italian fresco cycles. Few signs of earthquake damage remain, save a couple of completely bare vaults, striking memorials to the events of 1997 amid the colour on all sides.

Giotto's Life of St Francis

Giotto's *Life of St Francis* cycle starts from the **far right-hand side** of the nave. Although critics haven't reached a consensus on the date of the frescoes, most believe they are early works, painted with assistants some time around 1296, when Giotto was 29. The style and peripheral narrative content of the last four frescoes has led to their being attributed to the so-called Maestro di Santa Cecilia, who may also have overpainted parts of the first panel.

   Giotto was by far the most important artist to work in the Basilica. Dante immediately recognized his supremacy, and in a famous passage (intended to illustrate the hollowness of earthly glory) wrote: "Cimabue thought to lord it over painting's field. And now his fame is obscured and the cry is Giotto." It seems that Giotto got the commission on the prompting of Cimabue, and that some test pieces in the Lower Church persuaded the friars that Giotto was equal to the task of decorating the upper part of the Basilica. Like many writers and artists of the age, Giotto was a member of the lay **Franciscan Tertiaries**. His frescoes reveal a profound sympathy for the spirit of St Francis and show an almost total rejection of the artistic language of the Byzantines, whose remote icons were highly inappropriate for Francis's very human message. The cycles are full of the natural beauty that moved the saint to profound joy, and the figures are mobile and expressive – aspects of Giotto's art typified by the famous panel **The Sermon to the Birds** (no.15 on our plan). More than any other, this fresco crystallizes the essence of Franciscan humility, with the flock addressed as an indivisible part of God's creation and attending to the saint as distinct from them solely by virtue of the power of speech.

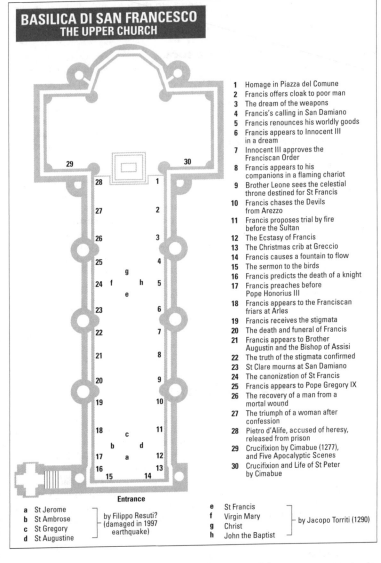

BASILICA DI SAN FRANCESCO
THE UPPER CHURCH

1 Homage in Piazza del Comune
2 Francis offers cloak to poor man
3 The dream of the weapons
4 Francis's calling in San Damiano
5 Francis renounces his worldly goods
6 Francis appears to Innocent III in a dream
7 Innocent III approves the Franciscan Order
8 Francis appears to his companions in a flaming chariot
9 Brother Leone sees the celestial throne destined for St Francis
10 Francis chases the Devils from Arezzo
11 Francis proposes trial by fire before the Sultan
12 The Ecstasy of Francis
13 The Christmas crib at Greccio
14 Francis causes a fountain to flow
15 The sermon to the birds
16 Francis predicts the death of a knight
17 Francis preaches before Pope Honorius III
18 Francis appears to the Franciscan friars at Arles
19 Francis receives the stigmata
20 The death and funeral of Francis
21 Francis appears to Brother Augustin and the Bishop of Assisi
22 The truth of the stigmata confirmed
23 St Clare mourns at San Damiano
24 The canonization of St Francis
25 Francis appears to Pope Gregory IX
26 The recovery of a man from a mortal wound
27 The triumph of a woman after confession
28 Pietro d'Alife, accused of heresy, released from prison
29 Crucifixion by Cimabue (1277), and Five Apocalyptic Scenes
30 Crucifixion and Life of St Peter by Cimabue

Entrance

a St Jerome
b St Ambrose
c St Gregory
d St Augustine
— by Filippo Resuti? (damaged in 1997 earthquake)

e St Francis
f Virgin Mary
g Christ
h John the Baptist
— by Jacopo Torriti (1290)

Giotto's narrative genius cuts straight to the heart of the matter, as seen in the very first panel, **The Homage in Piazza del Comune** (no. 1), in which the universality of Francis's appeal is evoked in a single act of tribute. Moreover, the frescoes display a wealth of everyday detail that made them accessible to the ordinary people of his age. The first people to look at **Francis Offering his Cloak to a Poor Man** (no. 2) would have recognized the world in which it is set as the one they themselves inhabited: the backdrop includes a detailed view of Assisi from the Porta Nuova, along with the Benedictine abbey on

Monte Subasio, now vanished. This attention to the tone and substance of the real world, to its textures and solidity, makes the art of Giotto as revolutionary as Francis's message to the medieval Church.

The choir and the other frescoes

The **choir** is a second focal point. Its 105 inlaid stalls – completed in the fifteenth century – are of immense intricacy and delicacy, most of them depicting famous Franciscans or episodes from their lives. The central throne is a papal seat, the only one in the country outside St Peter's in Rome. Behind the throne, and in the **left transept**, are frescoes by Giotto's probable master, **Cimabue**. These suffered during the ceiling collapse, but were already almost ruined from the oxidation of badly chosen pigments, though the transept's *Crucifixion* remains an impressive composition, its dynamism an obvious departure from static Byzantine order. Giotto and Duccio may have helped on the painting as pupils.

Running around the church immediately above Giotto's Franciscan panels is another much damaged though virtually complete cycle, *Scenes from the Old and New Testaments*. Vasari believed these scenes were by Cimabue, though today they are attributed to artists of the Roman school – **Torriti**, **Rusuti** and **Pietro Cavallini** – who were working in the church around the same time. Before coming to Assisi all three had worked primarily in mosaic, a traditional Byzantine medium, but in the Basilica they turned to fresco, moving, like Cimabue, with cautious innovation towards a freer interpretation of old themes. The *Four Doctors of the Church* in the vaults (saints Jerome, Ambrose, Gregory and Augustine), especially, shows a narrative sense absent in earlier art: cloaks are left thrown over chairs, books lie open as if half-read. The Doctors, moreover, are depicted as characters in their own right, distinct individuals rather than the symbolic representatives of artistic convention. The 1997 earthquake dislodged the St Jerome fresco, which is currently being pieced back together.

To the Piazza del Comune

East from the Basilica, **Via San Francesco** heads off along the ridge of medieval Assisi towards the Piazza del Comune. To each side steep and often stepped alleyways lead down to city gates and peripheral churches, of which **San Pietro** most rewards the diversion. The lanes north of Via San Francesco – in particular **Via Metastasio** – are peaceful and attractive; secreted away in them is a medley of little **churches** – Santa Margherita, Sant'Andrea, Santa Croce: none is any great shakes artistically, but all make pretty diversions. Take this route, however, and you will miss the **Pinacoteca Comunale** (art gallery), which might seem small beer after the Basilica, but contains several interesting frescoes and one or two paintings that would grace any gallery.

San Pietro

Wonderfully restored to its Romanesque-Gothic state, **San Pietro** is a peaceful antidote to the crowds of the Basilica above it. Grass and benches outside offer views over the Vale of Spoleto and of the fine, two-tiered facade – pink below, creamy-white above – with its three huge rose windows. Originally Benedictine, the church dates from the thirteenth century, though it may have been founded as long ago as the second century. The bare interior, mainly Romanesque, also shows the first hints of Gothic in its gently pointed arches and in the ceiling, supported by strange curved vaulting.

The Oratorio dei Pellegrini

At Via San Francesco 11, the **Oratorio dei Pellegrini** (daily 9am–noon & 3–6pm; free) is an exquisite fifteenth-century building that served as part of a hospice for visiting pilgrims. The interior is covered in fetching frescoes, some by the local sixteenth-century artist Matteo da Gualdo, beginning with a faded sample outside under the wooden-eaved exterior. Inside he was responsible for the murals on the altar wall, the vault and side walls being the work of another local artist, Pierantonio Mezzastris. Painted in 1477, the pictures illustrate *Scenes from the Life of St James*, including the comical *Miracle of the Two Hens*, an episode in which the saint restored two dead chickens to life so they could testify to the innocence of a falsely accused pilgrim. Another shows the *Miracle of the Hanged Man*, in which the saint supports an apparently dead man until he is found alive by his parents. Two scenes on the left wall represent episodes from the life of St Anthony Abbot, distributing alms and receiving camels which have brought him and his fellow monks food; the *Three Saints* on the inner face are attributed to Perugino or L'Ingegno, one of his followers. If people are at prayer here – and they often are – you may have to content yourself with a glimpse of the paintings through the glass door.

Close by, at no. 14, is Assisi's finest medieval town house, the headquarters of the masons' guild, known as the **Casa dei Maestri Comacini** (a disproportionate number of the Basilica's builders hailed from Como). A short way beyond the hospice on the right is the arched portico of **Monte Frumentario**, a thirteenth-century hospital – one of the first in Italy. It adjoins the **Fontano di Corletta**, whose inscription warns that the penalty for washing your smalls in the water was one *scudo* and the surrender of your laundry.

The Pinacoteca Comunale

Almost opposite the Oratorio dei Pellegrini in the Palazzo Vallemani is the excellent **Pinacoteca Comunale** (daily: June–Aug 10am–1pm & 2.30–7pm; March–May, Sept & Oct 10am–1pm & 2.30–6pm; Nov–Feb 10.30am–1pm & 2–5pm; €3.50, including admission to the Foro Romano; joint ticket with Foro Romano and Rocca Maggiore €4.50) – well worth the admission, not least for the wonderful paintings moved here on a semi-permanent basis from earthquake-ravaged Nocera Umbra, including the impressive *Immaculate Conception of the Virgin* (1495–1505) by Matteo da Gualdo. This is complemented by many detached frescoes rescued from churches and other buildings around Assisi, among them important works by the Gubbian artist Ottaviano Nelli. Look out for the wonderfully strange fresco by an unknown fourteenth-century Umbrian painter of San Giuliano mistakenly killing his parents, having returned home and mistaken them for his wife and her lover – the artist clearly enjoyed painting the quite unnecessarily graphic and gaping wounds. All the displays are helped by good English commentaries and more works of art are due to be moved to restored medieval rooms on other floors.

Piazza del Comune

Piazza del Comune was built over either the site of the Roman forum or an important sacred area – theories differ. It's a stunning medieval square, lined with plenty of pricey bars from which to people-watch. The tourist office (see p.602) is here, part of the impressive Neo-Gothic former post office, a frescoed mock medieval hall complete with vaulted ceilings.

The piazza is dominated by the **Tempio di Minerva** (Mon–Sat 7.15am–noon & 2–7pm, Sun 8.30am–noon & 2–7pm; free), six Corinthian columns and a pediment from a first-century Roman temple – perfectly preserved and dazzlingly restored. It's as good as any classical monument in Italy, and was the only thing Goethe wanted to see in Assisi. The writer was moved to hyperbole on seeing it – "the first complete classical monument I have seen… so perfect in design… I cannot describe the sensations which this work aroused in me, but I know they are going to bear fruit for ever." He didn't bother with the Basilica, calling it a "Babylonian pile". While the temple is great from the outside, the church behind is a seventeenth-century conversion whose slight lack of interest has been redeemed by a fine recent restoration of its Baroque interior. The restoration uncovered parts of the original pavement and massive wall and terracing to the rear.

Outside, the temple frieze contains reference to two brothers, Gneo Cesio Tirone and Tito Cesio Prisco, who helped finance the temple. It had a chequered history, not least in the early Middle Ages, when it was in such a parlous state that is was described in records as a *casolino* – a little house – and in the thirteenth century, when it passed to the *comune*, who made the lower area a prison and the upper one a council chamber.

To the left of the temple stands the **Palazzo del Capitano del Popolo**, completed in 1282 – though various cod medieval adornments were added in 1927 – and the Torre del Popolo, built in 1305. Notice the measures at the base of the tower, which record standard sizes for stones and other building materials as they were in 1348. On the opposite side of the piazza, the much-restored **Palazzo Comunale** once contained the Pinacoteca Comunale, the sign for which remains, since it forms part of a historic building and as such apparently cannot be removed.

South of the piazza, you might pay quick homage to St Francis's supposed birthplace, a spot commemorated by the unremarkable **Chiesa Nuova** (daily 6.30am–noon & 2.30–6pm; free) – built on land owned by Francis's father at the expense of Philip III of Spain – and a piazza boasting two prominent bronze statues (1984) of Francis's parents.

Foro Romano e Collezione Archeologica

The **Foro Romano e Collezione Archeologica**, entered just off Piazza del Comune at Via Portica 2 (same hours as Pinacoteca Comunale; €3.50, including admission to Pinacoteca; joint ticket with Pinacoteca and Rocca Maggiore €4.50) is unlikely to divert unless you're interested in archeology and Assisi's Roman heritage. It's housed in the crypt of the defunct church of San Nicolò, documented as early as 1097 but demolished in 1926 to make way for the ersatz-medieval post office building. A passage from the museum runs under Piazza del Comune, where excavations are in progress to uncover the Roman remains here without disrupting the piazza above; at present it's rather hard to make any sense of the underground maze, which scholars now believe is not the old Roman forum (as was long believed), but a religious sanctuary linked to the surviving Tempio di Minerva; the forum, it's now thought, may have occupied the present-day site of the Duomo. Dotted around the area are parts of statues and pillars, busts, urns and other Roman and Etruscan fragments, all given added lustre by their strange subterranean setting.

The Duomo, Santa Chiara and the Rocca

Just east of the Piazza del Comune, the Franciscan trail continues with important stops at the **Duomo** and **Santa Chiara**, while up in the northeast corner of the walls a sweep of park leads to the **Rocca Maggiore**, the best-preserved castle in Umbria, with fine views over the city and beyond.

The Duomo

As you emerge from the narrow streets east of Piazza del Comune, you're met by the captivating sight of the **Duomo**, or San Rufino (daily: April–Oct 7am–1pm & 2–7pm; Nov–Feb 8am–1pm & 2–6pm; free), with its typically three-tiered Umbrian facade. Its Romanesque **portal** is a superb piece of carving, guarded by two red marble lions and framed by lilies, leaves, faces, birds, winged crocodiles and a pair of griffons. Look in the lunette for the child being suckled, and its two dour parents. Alongside is a huge, stolid **campanile**, managing somehow to fit into the overall scheme of the church.

According to tradition the first church on the site was built around 412, ostensibly to house the bones of St Rufinus, Assisi's first bishop, martyred some 170 years earlier. Another, better-documented building was raised around 1029 by Bishop Ugone, from which the crypt and present campanile survive. Yet another church – more or less the one that survives today – was begun in 1140 and consecrated in 1253. A small museum, the **Cripta della Cattedrale** or Basilica Ugoniana (daily: April–Oct 10am–1pm & 2–7pm; Nov–Feb 10am–1pm & 2.30–6pm; €3), reached down steps to the right of the facade, contains fragments from these earlier churches. The area was not discovered until 1895, and features remnants of very early frescoes, parts of a Roman wall and conduit and a third-century Roman sarcophagus used as Rufinus's original tomb. Local tradition has it that Bishop Ugone had wanted to bury Rufinus in Santa Maria Maggiore, then the town's cathedral, but the townspeople had argued for the new church. There apparently ensued a literal tug-of-war with the saint's coffin, the bishop and his cohorts pulling one way, the locals the other. The latter clearly triumphed, though the tale is probably more a parable of the ascendancy of the lay city comunes of the time than anything else.

Inside, the main point of interest is the **font** used to baptize St Francis, St Clare and (possibly) the future emperor Frederick II, apparently born prematurely in a nearby village. It's at the near end of the church on the right, fronted by Romanesque statues of a lion and winged ox. Opposite, the beginning of the left aisle contains a little door, which leads to an impressive **Roman cistern**, recent research having led scholars to believe that the cathedral square – rather than Piazza del Comune – was the site of the town's original Roman forum. Various **glass panels** were let into the floor during post-quake restoration to offer insights into the building's earlier incarnations, but they offer little of interest. The church does have a couple of offbeat sights: a terracotta Virgin (left of the altar) which burst into tears in 1494, and a stone knelt on by an angel attending Francis's baptism – he left the imprint of his knee on it. St Rufinus's remains still lie beneath the altar. Off the right (south) nave, there's the small **Museo Capitolare** (same hours and ticket as Cripta), with a passable little collection of paintings, including a fine 1470 triptych by Nicolò Alunno showing scenes from the life of St Rufinus.

The Basilica di Santa Chiara

South of the Duomo, though most easily reached from the Piazza del Comune, is the **Basilica di Santa Chiara** (daily: Easter–Oct 8.30am–7pm; Nov–Easter 8.30am–5pm; free), the burial place of St Clare, St Francis's devoted follower. The church was begun in 1257 and consecrated in 1265, twelve years after her death. It stands on the site formerly occupied by the church of San Giorgio,

St Clare (Santa Chiara) was a close early companion of St Francis and the founder of the **Poor Clares**, the Franciscan nuns. Born in 1182 into a noble family, she had a deeply religious upbringing from her mother, an education which backfired when, enraptured at the age of 17 by the preaching of Francis, she rejected her family and two offers of marriage to live with the saint. In an act of symbolic removal from the world he cut off her blonde hair, the locks of which are still visible in her basilica, and replaced her finery with a rough cassock. A year after her conversion she took her leave of Francis, and – but for the occasional vision – never saw him again until his death.

After initial opposition from the family, Clare's sister, **St Agnes**, joined her in spiritual retreat, and was later joined by her widowed mother. Other young girls from Assisi, similarly inspired by Francis's example, added to the growing community of women, which was soon installed by Francis in the church of San Damiano. In 1215 Clare obtained from Pope Innocent III the "privilege of poverty" – permission for the creation of an order of nuns to live solely on alms and without property of any kind. Over the years the Poor Clares' right to exist was frequently challenged, yet Clare (like Francis) managed to disseminate the movement throughout Europe.

She died on August 12, 1253, outliving Francis by 27 years. She was canonized two years later, and by undignified quirk is now the **patron saint of television**, awarded the honour in 1958 by Pope Pius XII in recognition of her powers: although bedridden, she was able to see and hear the rites of a Christmas service performed by Francis a kilometre away.

where St Francis went to school, where his canonization took place, and where his body lay during construction of the Basilica. Clare, too, was buried in the church until her own resting place was completed.

The church is a virtual facsimile of the Basilica di San Francesco, with its simple facade and opulent rose window. Its engineering, however, wasn't up to the same standards, and the strange buttresses were added in 1351 to prevent its collapse. Before venturing in, wander over to the edge of the piazza in front of the church for some grand views of the Vale of Spoleto and the town's rooftops. The **interior** is dark and almost bare, the result of some zealous early censorship: a seventeenth-century German bishop called Spader, afraid that the nuns might be corrupted by contact with worldly tourists, had its cycle of frescoes obliterated. Only a few patches of earlier Sienese frescoes from the original San Giorgio have survived, mostly in the transepts and cross vaults above the high altar; high in the south transept are *Scenes from the Apocalypse and Life of Christ*, and under them *The Death and Funeral of St Clare*, all the work of a close collaborator of Giotto. The scenes above the high altar, above which hangs a large thirteenth-century Crucifix, show *Scenes from the Life of St Clare*, while the two registers way up in the north transept depict *Episodes from Genesis*. The altar's *Madonna and Child* (c.1265) is probably the work of the Giottesque artist of the south transept. One of the two chapels off the right aisle, the **Oratorio del Crocifisso**, contains the Byzantine Crucifix that bowed its head and spoke to Francis in San Damiano. Alongside are various clothes and oddments that belonged to Clare and Francis, while the body of Clare herself rests in the Baroque horror of the **crypt**.

The Rocca Maggiore

Rising above the town, the **Rocca Maggiore** (daily 10am–dusk; Aug opens 9am; €2; joint ticket with Pinacoteca and Foro Romano €4.50) dates back to Charlemagne, who is supposed to have raised the first defensive walls here after sacking the town. The structure surviving today, with its looming towers, turrets and parapets, owes most to Cardinal Albornoz, who arrived to assert papal authority in 1367, repairing an earlier castle that had been ravaged by repeated skirmishes with Perugia. Church governors reputedly dispensed justice by hanging criminals from the battlements or by throwing them out of a castle window into the ravine. The seductive **medieval streets** leading up to the Rocca from the Duomo are the quietest in Assisi, partly because of their distance from tourist targets, but perhaps as much due to their fierce gradients. The fortress is well worth the climb: the green surrounds provide ideal picnic territory and you'll be rewarded with all-embracing **views** taking in Assisi, Perugia and the Vale of Spoleto across to Montefalco and the Monti Martani.

Outside the walls

The Franciscan trail leads south from Santa Chiara to **San Damiano** and, for the energetic, to a couple of sites farther outside town – the **Eremo delle Carceri** (4km east) and **Santa Maria degli Angeli** in the new town around the station (5km southwest of the old town). San Damiano is well worth the short detour: in a town increasingly undermined by tacky commercialism, it retains an air of calm and dignity.

San Damiano

It was in **San Damiano** (daily 10am–12.30pm & 2–6pm; Nov–March closes 4.30pm; free), in 1205, that Francis received his calling to make repairs, and where he brought St Clare and her followers, "pouring the sweetness of Christ into her ears". Clare remained here till her death, though the nuns left seven years afterwards. After installing the Poor Clares, Francis came to San Damiano just once, towards the end of his life, when – sick and half-blind – he composed the *Canticle of the Sun*. His body rested here briefly after death, fulfilling a promise to Clare that she might see him once more.

Owned by Lord Lothian until 1983, the church now belongs to the Friars Minor, who have kept it in much the same state as it was centuries ago – a condition laid down by Lothian when he made his bequest. Lothian had inherited it in turn from descendants of Lord Ripon, a Catholic convert, who bought it in 1870 when Italy's monastic and most other religious institutions passed to the state. Alone among the places in Assisi with Franciscan associations, this one preserves something of an ideal that is recognizably Franciscan – rural and peaceful in its groves of olives, cypresses and wild flowers, with the pastoral Vale of Spoleto stretching away below. To reach it, walk down the Borgo Aretino from Santa Chiara and then follow the signs through the car park and olive grove – a very steep downhill walk of about fifteen minutes.

Signs point the way round the complex, starting outside with a fresco depicting St Roch – the saint invoked against infectious diseases – proudly displaying a plague sore. The little **balcony** above the main entrance is the point from which Clare, holding aloft the Sacrament, turned back an entire Saracen army that was pursuing Assisi's Guelphs. **Inside**, the nave of the church – which was a Benedictine foundation at least as early as 1030 – is simple and smoke-darkened, with a beautifully decrepit wooden choir and lectern. On the right-hand side is the small window where San Damiano's priest threw the money that Francis offered him to repair the church. Nearby you can see the tiny hole where the saint hid "for a month" from the wrath of his father. Beyond some stairs leading to a terrace and small garden is a vestibule with the woodwormed choir and two frescoes, one a lovely *Madonna and Child* by an unknown Giottesque artist. Up the stairs you reach the **oratory**, and then a small **dormitory**, with a cross and flowers marking the spot where Clare died. A door to the right leads to the **cloisters**, where you may catch a glimpse of the refectory, still equipped with its original table and oak benches.

The Eremo delle Carceri

All over Assisi you'll see pictures of the **Eremo delle Carceri** (daily 6.30am–dusk; free), an active monastery situated in oak woods about 6km east. It can be easily reached by road but the best approach is to follow the footpath – climbing very steeply for the first kilometre or so – from the Porta Cappuccini: outside the gate, turn left along the track of cypresses and then follow the marked path up and to the right behind the Rocca Minore (at the major fork a little way beyond, turn right; sometimes the sign's missing), then, at the top, keep going level and straight until you hit the road just above the monastery. Allow at least an hour, less coming back. A **gratuity** is expected as the monks – who sometimes act as guides – live only off the alms they receive. The monastery is closed for religious festivals.

The hermitage was an early place of retreat for Francis and his followers: the saint caused the well in the courtyard to flow (as depicted by Giotto) and a cell known as the **Oratorio Primitivo** has been identified as that occupied by Francis. There's also a **chapel** containing various unlikely relics: Francis's pillow and a piece of the Golden Gate through which Jesus passed into Jerusalem. The hermitage once owned a lock of the Virgin's hair, too, and some earth from the mound that God used to create Adam, though these treasures have sadly disappeared. With some very low doors and tight corners to negotiate, the whole experience is quite claustrophobic.

On the other side of the church is a dry riverbed, once a torrent until Francis told it to hush because it was spoiling his prayers. It fills up today only when some public calamity is at hand. One of the walls here was built over the so-called *buco del diavolo*, a crevice into which Francis cast a devil by the power of prayer. An old **holm oak**, kept upright by iron stakes, is said to have shaded the saint, and to have been a spot where birds collected to hear his sermons. Beyond this point a lovely **path** ambles into the woods, with plenty of nooks and side tracks where you can escape for a siesta.

Santa Maria degli Angeli

Difficult to miss from almost any point in the Vale of Spoleto, the huge domed basilica of **Santa Maria degli Angeli** (daily 6.30am–8pm; Aug also 9–11pm; free) rises from the new town clustered around Assisi train station – an area to which it has given its name. A majestically uninspiring pile, it was built between 1569 and 1684, then rebuilt after an earthquake in 1832. Its function is to shelter the **Porziuncola** (Little Portion), the hut-cum-chapel that Francis made the centre of the earliest Franciscan movement. Stranded like a doll's house in the church's austere Baroque bowels, it has been embellished with dreadful nineteenth-century frescoes on the outside, but inside there are features claimed to be those of Francis's rough-stone hovel, as well as good fourteenth-century frescoes on the life of the saint.

Bits of the old monastery have been excavated under the **main altar**, site of the saint's death and of Clare's abrupt conversion. Buried in the chapel is Brother Cataneii, one of the earliest Franciscans. He performed so many miracles from beyond the grave, and attracted so many expectant crowds as a result, that Francis implored him in prayer, "Now that we are infected with all these people of the world, I enjoin thee by obedience to make an end of thy miracles and allow us to recover in peace." The miracles stopped. In the garden are descendants of the **rose bushes** into which Francis threw himself while grappling with some immense nocturnal temptation; their thorns obligingly dropped off after contact with his saintly flesh. They now bloom, thornless, every May, their leaves stained with the blood shed that night.

Pilgrims flock to the basilica on August 1–2 for the **Pardon of St Francis**, a visit which guarantees automatic absolution. The pardon recalls a vision of Christ that Francis experienced, when he was asked what might be best for the human soul. Francis replied: forgiveness for all who crossed the threshold of his chapel. The already vast numbers of pilgrims were swelled in the 1920s by the supposed movement of the eight-metre-high bronze Madonna on the facade.

Eating and drinking

Multilingual tourist menus proliferate in Assisi's **restaurants** and prices can be steep. In general, for cheaper and more authentic outlets make for peripheral districts away from the Basilica and Piazza del Comune: the medieval streets leading up from the Duomo to the Rocca are where you'll find the cheapest bars and snacks. **Cafés** and **bars** are dotted around town, with those in Piazza del Comune offering the best people-watching opportunities – and the highest prices. For something quieter, try the *Gran Caffè*, Corso Mazzini 16a: the interior is pleasant, despite the mimsy pastel frescoes and chintzy cherubs. For **ice cream** and **cakes** make for *La Bottega del Pasticceria*, Via Portica 19, a small place a few steps from Piazza del Comune that must have the most mouthwatering window display in Umbria. Pilgrim-bound Assisi has just one in-town **disco**, the *Hermitage*, located under the *Hermitage* hotel, Via degli Aromatari 1.

Restaurants

Buca di San Francesco Via Brizi 1
☎075.812.204. A reputation as the best in town is sometimes belied by erratic quality, though the cooking can be outstanding. As a bonus there's a half-covered outside terrace for summer eating. Closed Mon & two weeks in July.

I Monaci Scaletta del Metastasio, Via Fontebella ☎075.812.512. Entrance in a stepped alley off the north side of Via Fontebella, a few steps down from Piazzetta Garibaldi. Large, friendly place for pastas and pizzas from a wood-fired oven; one of the few places where pizzas are available at lunchtime. Closed Wed.

La Fortezza Vicolo della Fortezza 2 ☎075.812.418. Invariably busy but friendly restaurant, with a high reputation, great food, medieval setting and reasonable prices. However, service can be very slow at busy times. Essential to reserve in summer. Closed Thurs & Feb.

La Piazzetta dell'Erba Via San Gabriele dell'Addolorata 15b ☎075.815.352. Lost in a tangle of alleys and arches a few steps from the Tempio di Minerva, this rustic and informal little place is good for simple, well-cooked meals. It's possible to eat outside in good weather. Closed Mon.

Medioevo Via dell'Arco dei Priori 4b ☎075.813.068. Just south off the Piazza del Comune, this extremely tasteful medieval vaulted dining room is recommended if you want to dress up a touch; the excellent cooking has a vaguely "international" flavour. There is a cheaper and lighter menu at lunch. Closed Wed, and Jan & three weeks in July.

Pallotta Via Volta Pinta 2 ☎075.812.307. Only just off Piazza del Comune, but a very reasonable, unpretentious and welcoming trattoria; book, or arrive before 12.30pm to be sure of getting a place for lunch. Closed Tues.

Ristorante La Rocca Via di Porta Perlici 27. Annexed to the hotel, this is a big, cheap, high-quality locals' place with reasonable food and no frills. Closed Wed.

San Francesco Via San Francesco 52
☎075.813.302. Generally good and original cooking that takes Umbrian basics as its starting point. However, service can be surly and some prices are higher than the food merits. Closed Wed, and two weeks in July & Nov.

Listings

Bike rental Andrea Angelucci, Via Becchetti 31 ☎075.804.2550, ⓦ www.angeluccicicli.it.

Books, maps and guides Eredi di E. Zubboli in the southeast corner of Piazza del Comune is particularly good for guides (in English) and has a small selection of other English-language titles. It also has maps, as does Assisi's oldest shop, San Vignati about 75m away downhill at Via Portica 19.

Bus enquiries ASP, for Assisi and around ☎075.573.1707; SULGA, for Rome & Florence ☎075.500.9641; AMADIO, for Siena and Ascoli Piceno ☎0736.341.838; SPOLETINA, for Foligno, Montefalco and Bevagna ☎0742.670.746 or 0743.212.201. Visit ⓦ www.umbriatrasporti.it for more details.

Car rental Andrea Cuppoloni (with driver only), Piaggia San Pietro 9 ☎075.812.777; Marco Salimbeti, Via San Benedetto 99 ☎075.812.976; or Nicola Corridoni, Via Capobove 9 ☎075.812.409, who also rents cars with a driver.

Exchange Slickest facilities at the automatic machines outside bank branches in Piazza del Comune and Piazza Unità d'Italia; Banca Popolare, Piazza Santa Chiara 19; and Banca Toscana, Piazza San Pietro 6. There are numerous exchange kiosks around town.

First aid Pronto Soccorso, Ospedale di Assisi ☎075.812.824 or 075.813.9227.

Lost property At Vigili Urbani, Vicolo Volta Pinta (Mon–Sat 9am–noon; ☎075.812.820).

Markets Assisi's main market is in Piazza Matteotti (Sat mornings). Piazza Chiesa Nuova hosts an antiques market (Sat & Sun of 2nd week of month).

Police Piazza Matteotti 3b ☎075.812.239, and Piazza del Comune ☎075.812.215.

Post office Largo Properzio 4 ☎075.81.314, and Piazza San Pietro 4 ☎075.815.178.

Taxis Train station ☎075.804.0275; Piazza San Francesco ☎075.812.606; Piazza Unità d'Italia ☎075.812.378; Piazza del Comune ☎075.813.193; Piazza Santa Chiara ☎075.812.600.

Train enquiries ☎075.804.0272 or 075.500.6865, ⓦ www.trenitalia.it.

Travel agent Stoppini, Corso Mazzini 31 ☎075.812.597, sells train and bus tickets, as well as ferry tickets to Sardinia.

The Vale of Spoleto

The **Vale of Spoleto**, or Valle Umbra, describes a graceful arc from Assisi in the north to Spoleto in the south, an almost perfectly flat crescent of land that was once the bottom of Lago Tiberino, a vast, shallow lake like present-day Lago Trasimeno which was eventually drained by the Romans. It has long been an important strategic route, carrying part of the Via Flaminia, a Roman consular road, an artery that either bolstered or prompted the foundation of the area's key towns and villages: **Spello**, **Bevagna**, **Foligno**, **Montefalco** and **Trevi**.

All of these places are essential points of call (with the exception of Foligno, a large and mostly modern provincial town), and all epitomize the qualities that have come to be associated with Tuscan and Umbrian hill-towns: old medieval centres, atmospheric little streets and alleys, fascinating art galleries and excellent restaurants and historic hotels. Around these villages and above the valley floor, the landscapes are hilly and pretty, but on the plain itself intensively cultivated agricultural land is spotted with the ever-increasing blight of modern housing and haphazardly planned industrial concerns. In a car you can avoid the worst of these by following country roads, but on the excellent bus or rail links that provide access to all the towns and villages be warned that you will be faced with the worst of the valley's modern development.

Spello

Ranged impressively on broad walled terraces above the Vale of Spoleto, with the lofty slopes of Monte Subasio beyond, pink-stoned **SPELLO** offers an easily accessible taste of medieval small-town Umbria – and a major art attraction in its superlative frescoes by Pinturicchio in the church of **Santa Maria Maggiore**. It also boasts a few reminders of its Roman past, when as Hispellum it served as a retirement home for pensioned-off legionaries and an important staging post on the Via Flaminia. Later it fell to the Lombards – who destroyed it – then became part of the Duchy of Spoleto. In 1238 it fell to Frederick II (who also destroyed it) and then passed under the yoke of Perugia. Once you're off the main street, the main core of the town is beautifully medieval. Today, despite its proximity to Assisi and Spoleto, it remains relatively quiet, though several new hotels and a rash of chintzy food, wine and trinket shops are testament to increasing numbers of tourists.

Arrival, information and accommodation

Spello is an alternative base for Assisi, with a decent range of accommodation, several good restaurants and a small **tourist office**, Piazza Matteotti 3 (daily 9.30am–12.30pm & 3–5.30pm; closes at 5pm Nov–March; ☎0742.301.009 or 0742.651.408, ⓦwww.comune.spello.pg.it). Regular stopping **trains** serve the town from Foligno and Perugia – check that they really do stop (the station is unstaffed, but there's a ticket machine in the waiting room) – and up to nine **buses** (Mon–Sat) drop off here on the Assisi–Foligno run. The tortuous main street is one-way along its entire length (uphill from Porta Consolare), with the most central **car park** on the right immediately after Sant'Andrea. Alternatively you can walk down from the big car park off Via Cimitero by Porta Montanara. Call for a **taxi** on ☎0742.651.582.

Spello's **accommodation** is rarely too stretched, except in the days around the main festival, the *Infiorita* on Corpus Domni (late May or early June), when the streets are laid with carpets of minutely detailed pictorial scenes created entirely by hand from millions of flower petals. In the weeks leading up to the event you will see people everywhere sitting and talking while they patiently remove petals from stalks. There's also a festival celebrating the area's olive oil in the week before Shrove Tuesday.

Hotels

Alta Villa Via Mancinelli 2 ☎ & ⓕ 0742.301.315. Very comfortable, if rather gaudily luxurious, three-star hotel with 24 rooms, several minutes' walk downhill from the old town (follow the signs from the corner of Piazza Vallegloria). At the top end of its price bracket. ❷

Convento Santa Maria Maddalena Via Cavour 1 ☎0742.651.156 or 0742.301.285. Very pleasant and low-cost rooms almost immediately opposite Santa Maria Maggiore. Ring the bell on the rather anonymous door on the side of the building facing back down the hill. ❶
Del Teatro Via Giulia 24 ☎075.301.140, ⓦwww

SPELLO

▲ Assisi

Collepino & Monte Subasio ▲

Villa Fidelia

Fonte

San Girolamo

San Claudio

Porta Montanara

Santa Maria di Vallegloria

Anfiteatro Romano

PIAZZA VALLEGLORIA

San Severino

Rocca

Porta Prato

San Martino

San Lorenzo

Porta Sant' Angelo

Porta Venere

Palazzo Comunale

Porta di Mastro

PIAZZA D. REPUBBLICA

Sant' Andrea

Pinacoteca Civica

Santa Maria Maggiore

Porta Urbica

Cappella Tega

Santa Ventura

Porta Consolare

Sant'Anna

PIAZZA KENNEDY

Train Station

▼ Bevagna

▼ Foligno

N

RESTAURANTS
Bar Giardino	2
Bar-Gelateria	6
Hosteria de Dadà	4
Il Cacciatore	C
Il Molino	5
La Cantina	3
Pinturicchio	1

ACCOMMODATION
Alta Villa	A
Convento Santa Maria Maddalena	G
Del Teatro	D
Il Cacciatore	C
La Bastiglia	B
Palazzo Bocci	F
Portinaccio	H
Residence San Jacopo	E

0   200 m

.hoteldelteatro.it. Stung by competition from the *Alta Villa* and *Palazzo Bocci*, the owners of the *Cacciatore* opened this superbly appointed intimate three-star hotel with just eleven rooms down the road. It, too, has a pretty breakfast terrace. ➍

Il Cacciatore Via Giulia 42 ☎0742.651.141, ⓦwww.ilcacciatorehotel.com. Good-value and friendly sixteen-room two-star hotel, with fine views from some rooms (although those on the road side are noisy). It's worth staying here just for the superlative panoramic terrace. ➌

La Bastiglia Via dei Mollini 17 ℡ 0742.651.277, ⓦ www.labastiglia.com. Thirty-three smallish but smart four-star rooms in a beautifully restored mill, many of which command a view – plus a fine but fancy restaurant. Some rooms can be ridiculously expensive, but cheaper options are available out of high season. ❺

🏃 **Palazzo Bocci** Via Cavour 17
℡ 0742.301.021, ⓦ www.palazzobocci .com. Tasteful, smart four-star hotel with twenty rooms in a converted, frescoed palazzo just up from Santa Maria Maggiore. A definite first choice if you're doing Umbria in style. The co-owned *Il Molino* restaurant is opposite. ❻

Portonaccio Via Centrale Umbra 46 ℡ 0742.651.313, ℻ 0742.301.615, ⓦ www .albergoilportonaccio.it. If you baulk at the prices in Spello's central hotels and don't mind being outside the walls, make for this big place on the main-road roundabout 100m south of Porta Consolare. ❷

Residence San Jacopo Via Giulia 1
℡ 0742.301.260, ⓦ www.residencesanjacopo.it. An excellent choice if you wish to cook to save, want more room than you'll find in a hotel, or are travelling in a group or as a family. Nine mini-apartments, or *residenze*, are available (above the *Pinturicchio* restaurant), each with linen, TV, private bathroom and kitchen, from €73 for two people, plus €11 for each additional person. ❷

Campsite

Campeggio Subasio Località Sportella ℡ 0742.301.144, ℮ robertoroscini@tiscalinet.it. The nearest campsite, at a height of 840m on the slopes of Subasio. April to early Oct.

The Town

Buses stop at the foot of the town just outside the **Porta Consolare**, one of five Roman gates in the Augustan-era walls that still more or less enclose Spello. The gate is in a slightly sorry state, with an ancient olive tree growing from its crumbling upper reaches – a sixteenth-century fresco in the Comune shows the tower with its trees even then – but it still gives some idea of the glory that was Rome, and retains three original **statues**, figures removed from the town's amphitheatre that local folklore claims depict a family killed by eating poisonous mushrooms. Parts of the old Roman road are also exposed here, while to the left along Via Roma range some well-preserved stretches of the original Augustan-era walls (they are considered some of the best-preserved such walls in Italy). Recently uncovered just west outside the old town walls are some extraordinary mosaics, part of a fourth-century villa. The remains may be extensive, with further treasures to be uncovered, but as they were discovered during the building of a car park, and the car park may well be completed, the fate of the mosaics, and their surroundings, is uncertain at the time of publication.

Inside the gate begins the main street, **Via Consolare–Via Cavour**, which bends and climbs steeply: it has no pavements, so beware – you're forever dodging cars. A couple of minutes' walk (you might take the rubber-surfaced alley on the left as a short cut) brings you to the odd little **Cappella Tega** (always open to view behind glass), half-covered in frescoes from 1461 by a leading Marche-based artist, Nicolò Alunno.

Santa Maria Maggiore

In 1600 Spello had some two thousand inhabitants – compared with around eight thousand today – and a staggering one hundred churches, of which 22 were dedicated to the Virgin. One of the most important of these was **Santa Maria Maggiore** (daily 8.30am–12.30pm & 3–7pm; winter closes 6pm; free), which celebrated both the Virgin's Birth (Sept 8) and the Assumption (Aug 15), the latter alluded to in the inscription *Assumpta Est* below the *Madonna* in the niche on the main portal.

Begun in the twelfth century, the church was remodelled five centuries later to dull effect, the most obvious alterations being the **facade**, which was shifted forward a full nine metres, and the mundane Baroque botch visited on the interior. The facade did keep parts of the original Romanesque portal, however, some of whose fine carving has been attributed to Binello and Ridolfo, the mysterious craftsmen responsible for the strange sculptures on the churches of nearby Bevagna (see p.632). The two columns at the base of the campanile are from an earlier Roman building; Spello's main street follows exactly the course of the old Roman road, and a Roman aqueduct runs beneath it to this day.

Inside is an outstanding Roman **stoup** for holy water, fashioned from the altar tomb (AD 60) of Gaius Titienus Flaccus, a leading light of Hispellum's most important family. The dead man is shown on horseback above an inscription, while in the lower part of the stoup you can still make out a little hollow once used to store his ashes. Another similar tomb – that of a young woman – was moved from the church in the eighteenth century and now supports the cross on top of the campanile.

More fascinating are the paintings by **Pinturicchio** covering the Cappella Baglioni on the left as you enter, vast frescoes which rank with the artist's masterpieces in Siena's Libreria Piccolomini (see p.389) and Rome's Sistine Chapel and Borgia apartments. The paintings were executed in 1501 and glow from restoration work in 1978 that brought out the colourfully decorative detail to stunning effect. Sadly, they are behind glass: you need coins to illuminate them. The barrier also means you can't get a proper look at the chapel's **ceramic pavement** (1566), a faded testimony to the skill of Deruta's medieval craftsmen (see p.715).

The three panels are read from left to right; the ceiling vaults depict the *Four Sibyls*. The **first fresco** features the *Annunciation*, with the Virgin having just

△ Frescoes by Pinturicchio in the Cappella Baglioni

read the prophetic text from the Bible open in front of her. Below and to the right, the obvious hanging painting is a self-portrait of Pinturicchio, and under it a plaque with his name from which dangle brushes, styluses and other tools of the painter's trade. The **central fresco** on the rear wall depicts the *Adoration of the Child*, with the shepherds shown left of Christ and the Magi behind them to the left. Behind the Magi one of the group of armed men amidst the rocks bears an anachronistic detail: a shield with the Baglioni coat of arms (the chapel was commissioned by a prelate belonging to the infamous family in 1500). The painting is also remarkable for its preponderance of symbols, in particular the cross (a prefiguration of Christ's Crucifixion), the peacock (symbolizing eternal life and the incorruptibility of the flesh) and the flask of wine and bread in the bottom right-hand corner (an allusion to the Eucharist). The **final fresco**, the *Disputation in the Temple*, has rather more points of incidental narrative and decorative interest, including a portrait of Troilo Baglioni, the man who commissioned the paintings, who is shown in his black prioral habit at the extreme left. Alongside him stands his treasurer, easily identified by his bag of money, another pictorial reminder of who paid for the frescoes. Over on the extreme right the grisly-featured old woman is an allusion to the "Old Woman of the Cross", the central character in one of Spello's seminal medieval legends. The harridan is said to have tried to fan the mutual hatred of the inhabitants of the upper and lower town, but was vaporized before any bloody encounter could take place by the miraculous apparition of a cross above the town hall in 1346. Pinturicchio also makes an appearance, his name being picked out on the note held by the character in the prominent white headgear in the group to the right of Christ. The artist's hand can also be seen in the disturbing details in the background: the disabled beggars in front of the temple and, more macabre, the tiny figure dangling from a gibbet on the hill-top to the right of the large palm tree.

Elsewhere in the church are a couple of further paintings by Pinturicchio: in the **Cappella del Sacramento**, the chapel to the left of the apse, is a faintly etched angel holding a plaque above a little lavabo; the inscription – *Lavamini et mundi, estote* – means "Wash yourself and be pure." Beyond that, in the canon's room, is an overpainted but beautifully lyrical *Madonna and Child*. Two good late paintings by **Perugino** adorn the two pillars flanking the apse, one a *Pietà*, the other a *Madonna and Child with SS Blaise and Catherine*. The only other worthwhile painting is a single tantalizing fresco of the *Agony in the Garden* (1391) to the left of the large window at the rear of the apse. It's the work of **Cola Petruccioli**, an accomplished early Umbrian painter, and represents all that remains of a complete cycle sacrificed to the apse's blanket of whitewash in the seventeenth century.

The Pinacoteca Civica

Spello's **Pinacoteca Civica** (April–Sept Tues–Sun 10.30am–1pm & 3–6.30pm; Oct–March Tues–Sun 10.30am–12.30pm & 3.30–5.30pm; €2.60) is situated in the old Palazzo dei Canoncini almost beside Santa Maria Maggiore. It reopened in late 2005 after long-term restoration, but parts of the collection are still to be exhibited, and the gallery is likely to remain in a state of flux for some time. The best pieces include the wonderful polychrome wooden statue, *Madonna and Child*, an Umbrian work dating from the end of the twelfth century. Also outstanding is an extraordinary statue of the crucified Christ, its arms hinged to resemble a crude marionette. Such statues, now extremely rare, were used by religious confraternities during Holy Week celebrations: its arms would be opened or folded according to the particular religious celebration.

The gallery's vaguely open-plan arrangement makes it hard to figure out which room is which, but everything is well labelled, making it easy, for example, to track down treasures such as the superb enamelled cross (1398). The central figure depicts the Virgin. Nearby, the little diptych (1391) by Cola Petruccioli, designed as a portable preaching aid for itinerant monks, shows the *Crucifixion* on one panel and the *Coronation of the Virgin* on the other. Two of the gallery's highlights are a pair of early fifteenth-century panels of a triptych by the anonymous Maestro dell'Assunta di Amelia: *St John and the Prophet Isaiah*, and *John the Baptist and Nicholas of Bari*. The original triptych was stolen in 1970, and the main central panel – a *Madonna and Child* – has never been recovered. A similar fate befell another *Madonna and Child*, the central part of a triptych, attributed to Pinturicchio, stolen in the same year from Santa Maria Maggiore, but here the story is happier, for the work was recovered in 2004 and is now exhibited in the gallery.

Even this happy returnee is overshadowed by a still better work, the superbly restored *Crucifixion, Virgin and Saints* by Nicolò Alunno. Nearby is a double-sided *gonfalone*, or banner, probably painted by one of Alunno's assistants. One side depicts the *Madonna della Misericordia* shielding Spello's citizens beneath her cloak, the other the *Miracle of the Cross of Spello*, the event alluded to in Pinturicchio's fresco of the *Disputation in the Temple* in Santa Maria Maggiore.

Elsewhere, look out for the double-sided *gonfalone* (1576) by Lorenzo Doni, depicting a particularly graphic *Martyrdom of St Barbara* on one side and the members of Spello's Confraternity of St Barbara on the other. Also pause in front of the five canvases by Marcantonio Grecchi, especially the *Madonna and Child with St Felix and Andrea Caccioli*; St Felix, an early bishop of Spello, is one of the town's patron saints. The painting's charm lies in the perfectly realized little portrait of Spello held by the two protagonists, the town looking much the same as it does today. The gallery concludes with nineteenth-century works by Benvenuto Crispoldi, an eccentric local dandy.

Sant'Andrea and around

A short distance uphill from the Pinacoteca lies **Sant'Andrea**, its simple thirteenth-century facade hiding a darkly atmospheric interior. Most surfaces are inexpertly painted, though the overall effect is superb, and there is another outstanding **Pinturicchio** – a *Madonna and Child with Saints* in the right transept, executed with Eusebio di San Giorgio. On the extreme right is the figure of St Lawrence, who is shown holding the black griddle on which he was roasted to death. A panel depicting this martyrdom in detail is shown as a luminous square picture rather oddly stitched onto the lower half of his robes. Also look out for the two small panels close to one of the saints (Giovannino), where the painter has proudly transcribed a letter sent to him by Gentile Baglioni (that family again), the bishop of Orvieto. The vast eye-catching Crucifix hanging above the altar is by an unknown fourteenth-century Umbrian follower of Giotto.

The spread of impressive-looking decoration in the apse and elsewhere dates from the nineteenth century and may, it's thought, conceal all sorts of hidden treasures. When the large altar in the left transept was removed for cleaning, areas of important early fresco were revealed behind it, much of which, it appears, had been whitewashed following some long-forgotten plague epidemic. Shortage of funds has as yet prevented any further investigation. In the left transept is another in Umbria's long line of eerily preserved mummies (see p.638 for more on these), this one being the body of the Spello-born beatific **Andrea Caccioli** (1194–1254), one of the earliest followers of St Francis.

A diversion from Sant'Andrea along nearby Via Torri di Properzio (left off Via Cavour) brings you to the best remnant of Roman Spello, the perfectly preserved if slightly forlorn **Porta Venere**, possibly named after a long-vanished temple to Venus: Constantine is said to have built one of Umbria's largest shrines to the goddess in the vicinity. The imposing twin towers flanking the gate might be Roman or medieval; no one's sure.

The rest of the town

Farther up Via Cavour beyond Sant'Andrea, the main **Piazza della Repubblica** is part grotesque twentieth-century, part medieval, with its arched **Palazzo Comunale** boasting a couple of fourteenth-century frescoes by local painters. Farther up again, **San Lorenzo** rates as one of Umbria's more successful Baroque conversions. A mongrel of a church, it had a succession of architects who left a variety of decorative effects, some laughable, like the obviously fake marbles, others more persuasive – as with the *baldacchino*, a bronze canopy copied from Bernini's piece for St Peter's in Rome. The most arresting sight is the minutely realistic statue of St Peter the Martyr, midway down the west wall, complete with trickle of blood from the cleaver delicately planted in his head.

At the top of Spello's main street you'll probably be heartily sick of having to dodge cars, but here you can start to explore the alleys and backstreets that provide the town's typical Umbrian charm. Views from the east side of town are especially good, with lovely panoramas over the bucolic countryside below Monte Subasio. The arch almost opposite San Lorenzo leads to the highest point of the town, occupied by the **belvedere** and **Rocca** – the latter giving the only view you need of the overgrown remains of the first-century Roman amphitheatre to the west.

Beyond the walls, near the amphitheatre, is the half-collapsed twelfth-century church of **San Claudio**, which has a strange Romanesque asymmetry inside and out. It was raised from the ashes of an old Roman building on the same site. A ten-minute walk beyond – also accessible via a country lane which drops down from Piazza Vallegloria – is the prominent but little-known **Villa Fidelia** with a beautiful garden and the miscellaneous Straka-Coppa private collection of paintings, sculptures, old furniture and costumes, together with displays on the Futurists (hours and prices vary according to the temporary exhibitions in progress).

A walk over Monte Subasio

A stiff but wonderful **walk** starts beyond the Rocca at the Porta Montanara. This route is worth climbing just for twenty minutes or so in order to get superb views of Spello and the Vale of Spoleto, though if you follow it the whole way you can reach Assisi (allow a full day for this) via the summit of **Monte Subasio** and/or the Eremo delle Carceri. To find the route, take the second right turn after the Porta Montanara (signposted for Collepino), walk past the olive-oil works on the right, and after 100m take the (initially surfaced) track left at the fountain. The path is marked by the *Club Alpino Italiano*: look for trail no. 50 and red spot markings which run all the way to Assisi. Detailed walking **maps** of the area – and it's advisable to have them – are usually available from the newsagents to the right of San Lorenzo in Spello. You can **drive** on the part-gravel road from the northern end of Spello over Monte Subasio to Assisi (signed "Monte Subasio" and *La Baita*, the latter a panoramic bar-restaurant on a side road halfway up): be certain not to miss the left turn after a couple of kilometres, or you'll end up in Collepino and Armenzano. The **views** are superlative and there are sensational spreads of orchids and narcissi in late May and early June. Once on the top above the trees, you can walk pretty much at will.

Eating and drinking

A good **eating** option is *La Cantina*, Via Cavour 2 (T0742.651.775; closed Wed), a friendly local place set in a vaulted medieval town house serving plenty of regional specialities and wonderful fresh pasta; it suffers from being rather big and unatmospheric on quiet nights. Spello's best restaurant is the flashier and slightly more expensive *Il Molino*, Piazza Matteotti 6–7 (T0742.651.305; closed Tues), with an equally pleasing medieval setting and some good food – as long you avoid the occasional unfortunate pretension to Italian *nouvelle cuisine*. *Il Cacciatore*, Via Giulia 42 (T0742.651.141; closed Mon), has middling food and service, but one of the great Umbrian terraces for summer eating. The cheaper *Pinturicchio* (T0742.301.003; closed Tues) on the left at the top of the main street just past San Lorenzo, is a first-rate trattoria stand-by. Cheapest of all, and good for lunch or a light meal, is the *Hosteria de Dadà*, a small place with six shared tables at Via Cavour 47 (closed Mon). *Bar Giardino*, Via Garibaldi 12, has a huge grassy terrace and tables to the rear, a wonderful spot to soak up the scenery.

The *Bar-Gelateria* on Via Roma opposite the Porta Santa Maria Maggiore serves up **ice cream** and sorbets just a wafer away from perfection. If you're buying picnic supplies, make tracks for the lovely old-fashioned Scarponi **bakery** opposite the *Teatro* hotel at Via Giulia 43. You can buy wine, cheese, ham and the like at numerous tourist-oriented **food shops** around town: one of the best of the more useful stores is Hispellum, Via Cavour 37.

Foligno and around

On public transport, sooner or later you're likely to find yourself passing through **FOLIGNO**, a nodal point for trains and buses. Although this was the place where, in 1472, the first book was printed in Italian – three hundred copies of Dante's *Divine Comedy* – today Foligno is a largely modern place, ringed with factories and concrete sprawl, its star turns bombed during World War II. What remains is a not unpleasant provincial town, though with nothing that would merit a special visit, and certainly nothing to tempt you away from Spello, Bevagna or Montefalco. The town was particularly badly hit by the 1997 earthquakes – the dramatic collapse of the Torre Comunale was broadcast worldwide – and the residue of its medieval heritage is conveniently concentrated in the central **Piazza della Repubblica**. The **Duomo** is the main eye-catcher, the twelfth-century Palazzo Comunale opposite having been ruined by a Neoclassical facade at the beginning of the nineteenth century. Unusually, the church boasts two facades, the south frontage containing one of the most impressive portals in the region: a riot of carving full of zodiac signs, intricate patterning and bizarre animals, as well as a likeness of Frederick II on the left (one of only two in Italy) and a Muslim star and crescent near the apex of the arch. The mosaics of the other facade are a nineteenth-century afterthought. Inside, a panel by Nicolò Alunno in the sacristy is the only feature worth seeking out.

At the western end of the piazza is the **Palazzo Trinci** (1389–1407), the much-altered home of the Trinci, Foligno's medieval big shots and by far the best reason to visit the town. Long-term restoration has revived a fine courtyard, palace frescoes and painted staircase, and a small **archeological museum** (Tues–Sun 10am–7pm; €6) and linked **Pinacoteca Comunale** (same hours and ticket). The key sight is a fine fresco cycle by Gentile da Fabriano whose non-religious themes include the story of the founding of Rome, the Seven Liberal Arts, the Seven Ages of Man, the hours of the day, the cycle of the planets and more. Other high points include a frescoed chapel by Ottaviano Nelli and an *Annunciation* attributed to Benozzo Gozzoli. The only other monument which hints at Foligno's former glory is **Santa Maria Infraportas**, a church of pagan origins in which St Peter is said to have celebrated Mass. The oldest part of the current eighth-century church is the Cappella dell'Assunta off the left nave; the Byzantine mural behind its altar is the town's most precious piece of art.

Practicalities

For Foligno's **tourist office** – at Corso Cavour 126 (April–Oct Mon–Sat 10am–1pm & 4–7, Sun 10am–1pm; Nov–Feb Mon–Sat 10am–1pm & 3–6pm, Sun 10am–1pm; ☎0742.354.459, ✉info@iat.foligno.pg.it) – and **bus station** (Porta Romana), follow Viale Mezzetti west from the **train station** to Piazzale Alunno. Piazza della Repubblica is a short walk along Corso Cavour from here. To get to Montefalco, there are infrequent buses or you could try hitching from the Porta Todi, around Via N. Sauro from Piazzale Alunno.

If hotels in Assisi and Spello are full, you may have cause to try Foligno's **accommodation** options, which are inexpensive but generally not terribly inspiring.

Hotels

Italia Piazza Matteotti 12 ☎0742.350.412, ⓦwww.hotelitaliafoligno.com. A functional three-star place with 35 rooms, very centrally located immediately south of Piazza della Repubblica. ❸
Pierantoni Via Pierantoni 23 ☎0742.342.566, ✉folhostel@tiscalinet.it. A big hostel with around two hundred beds arranged in 39 rooms; dorm bed €15–17.
Summit Hotel Viale Cesare Battisti 1 ☎ & ℱ0742.352.821, ⓦwww.folignohotels.com. Three-star on a busy junction with Piazzale Alunno and

thus convenient for the train station; has 48 rooms, so there's usually something available. ❷
Valentini Via Flavio Ottaviani 19 ☎0742.353.990. A family-run twenty-room two-star just north of the train station – surprisingly pleasant given its position. ❷
Villa Roncalli Viale Roma 25 ☎0742.391.091, ℱ0742.391.001. Best of the upmarket three-star places; a smart seventeenth-century villa with nice garden and pool and Foligno's top gourmet restaurant. ❷

Eating and drinking

Cheap **pizzerie** are numerous. For coffee, drinks, snacks and light **meals**, *La Bottega Barbanera*, Piazza della Repubblica 34 (☎0742.350.672; closed Mon), serves tempting local dishes in charming surroundings – a former *drogheria* with lovely old counter. Even better, and popular with locals, is the small thirty-seat *Il Bacco Felice*, Via Garibaldi 73–75 (☎0742.341.019; closed Mon), set in a library-type salon full of old bottles and books on food and wine; the attention to detail and focus on good ingredients is excellent (co-owner Tiziana has accumulated 32 different types of tomato alone for use in salads and sauces). Equally good – and with a similar approach – is the *Hostaria Sparafucile*, Piazzetta Duomo 30 (☎0742.342.602; closed Wed, Oct & lunchtimes in winter), with a great selection of wines and simple, inexpensive local dishes, served outside in summer.

East of Foligno

Visible from afar from the Vale of Spoleto, the Benedictine **Abbazia di Sassovivo** (interior closed for restoration), 6km east of Foligno, is one of the oldest monasteries in Umbria, dating from 1070. Set in wooded countryside, it also claims the region's finest medieval cloisters, with 128 variegated columns and 58 arches all decorated with mosaics and coloured marbles. The church is dull, save for its eleventh-century crypt, recently restored and now open – along with the cloister and loggia (daily 8.3am–7.30pm; free).

To the north, the SS77 road to Camerino threads through the beautiful **Menotre valley**, a region of small, lost villages and virgin hill country. To explore properly, you'll need transport or the will to hike (plus the invaluable *Kompass* "Assisi-Camerino" map #665). **PALE**, 8km east of Foligno, is the first village you'll come to in the Menotre. It has a castle and a stalactite-crammed cave, the **Grotta di Pale**. Paths cover the 4km to the summit of the craggy **Sasso di Pale** (958m), also accessible from Santa Lucia, 1km on from Pale. The only place of any real size in the valley is **COLFIORITO**, 25km from Foligno, in an area of Umbria that very few tourists see. Once an important Iron Age site, controlling one of the lowest Apennine passes into the Marche, Colfiorito sits at the heart of some extraordinary countryside, mostly marsh and upland plain – rather like the Valnerina – surrounded by fields of grass and mountain peaks. Green and cool in summer, the town has become something of a vacation retreat for locals and is well served by **hotels**, including the three-star *Villa Fiorita*, Via del Lago 9 (T0742.681.326, Wwww.hotelvillafiorita.com; 3), and the small two-star *Valico*, Via Casette di Cupigliolo (T0742.681.385, Wwww .valico.it; 1).

Bevagna

BEVAGNA, shadowed by the Martani hills 8km southwest of Foligno, is even more serene and handsome a backwater than Spello, with a windswept central piazza of austere perfection and two of Umbria's finest Romanesque churches. An Umbrian and then an Etruscan settlement, it became Mevania under the Romans, and a staging post on the Via Flaminia (built in 220 BC) – now the Corso Matteotti, which bisects the town. Its decline dates from the building of a new spur to the Flaminia five centuries later, a road that was routed through Terni and Spoleto rather than Bevagna. After the Roman era it was sacked by Barbarossa, Frederick II, Foligno's Trinci family and, inevitably, Perugia's Baglioni. Today it has scarcely spread beyond its medieval walls, remaining miraculously unscarred by the urban blight of most nearby hill-towns.

The Town

Bevagna's backstreets sooner or later converge on the pedestrianized main square, **Piazza Silvestri**, broad and open after its shadowed surroundings. Every member of this unimprovable arrangement is thoroughly medieval, with the sole exception of the nineteenth-century fountain, and even that blends in perfectly. Two churches face each other across the square, both untouched and creaking with age. The smaller, deconsecrated **San Silvestro** is a magnificent squat example of early Umbrian-Romanesque; its exterior bears a plaque with the date of construction – 1195 – and the name of the builder, Binello, who was also responsible for San Michele opposite, but of whom nothing else is known except for his work on Spello's Santa Maria Maggiore (see p.625). Pieces of Roman remains are woven into the facade, whose upper half is faced in pink Subasio stone and boasts the stump of an unfinished tower. The **interior** – which tends to be open when the rest of the town is shut – is superbly ancient

Bevagna map

in look and feel, with a raised presbytery and sunken crypt. Look out for the capitals of the blunt columns in the nave, which are of an Egyptian order (rather than Doric, Ionic or Corinthian) and were perhaps copied from a Roman temple to distant deities. Britain's Prince Charles has been instrumental in helping raise funds to restore the church. The second church, **San Michele** appears and feels more recent, perhaps owing to its rose window, punched through in the eighteenth century. It is in fact San Silvestro's contemporary and is built to a similar interior plan; its capitals are similarly eccentric, as are the magnificently surreal gargoyles over the main doorway.

The square's third component is the twelfth-century **Palazzo dei Consoli**, distinguished by a broad stone staircase. Infiltrated into it is the delightful nineteenth-century **Teatro F. Torti**, full of minuscule boxes and balconies, one of only a few surviving examples of the tiny provincial theatres that once flourished across Italy. Enquire at the Museo di Bevagna for admittance. Beside is **SS Domenico e Giacomo**, rectangular and workaday, its Baroque interior relieved only by fragments of fresco and two early wooden sculptures. The church's prime position was a gift from the *comune* to the Dominicans for help in rebuilding the town after one of its sackings. Be sure to have a look at the small cloister, reached through the church.

The church of **San Francesco** at the town's highest point claims to have the stone from which St Francis preached his famous sermon to the birds, a discourse that according to the local claim occurred on the road between Bevagna and Cannara (the spot is also commemorated at Assisi's Eremo delle Carceri).

Roman Bevagna

The small **Museo di Bevagna** (June & July Tues–Sun 10.30am–1pm & 3.30–7pm; Aug daily 10.30am–1pm & 3–7.30pm; March–May, Sept & Oct Tues–Sun 10.30am–1pm & 2.30–6pm; Nov–Feb Tues–Sun 10.30am–1pm & 2.30–5pm; €3.50), Corso G. Matteotti 70, devoted to the history of the village, is divided into three modest sections: archeological displays, art and history, and maps, letters and other documents. The paintings are eminently forgettable, but the medley of Roman remains – all found locally – is worth a look. None, though, compares with the impressive black-and-white **Roman mosaic** on the north side of Via Porta Guelfa (free with museum ticket: guided tours depart from museum for mosaics and theatre roughly every twenty minutes). Laid down in the second century, it formed part of a bath complex – hence the associations of its dolphins, lobsters and other sea creatures. To the south, the pillars and half-columns of the **Roman temple** date from roughly the same period. Just to the north, **Porta Cannara**, the best preserved of the town's gates, offers access to a nice stretch of the medieval walls. Farther east on Corso G. Matteotti, be sure to explore Via dell'Anfiteatro, whose diminutive houses follow the line of the former **Roman amphitheatre**, and which gives access to a series of little tunnels that burrow mysteriously into the old under-stage area.

△ Winged gargoyle on the portal of the church of San Michele, Bevagna

Practicalities

From Foligno, three **buses** run to Montefalco via Bevagna (four back from Montefalco), dropping off in the little square immediately to the south of San Silvestro; buy tickets for onward journeys in the bar secreted away in the medieval loggia on the square's eastern edge. The small and irregularly open **tourist office** (℡0742.361.667), below the Palazzo dei Consoli's stone staircase, provides a good map and leaflet on the town, with English translations.

There are several charming **places to stay**. The most central is the one-star *Il Chiostro di Bevagna*, Corso G. Matteotti 107 (℡0742.361.987, ⓦwww .ilchiostrodibevagna.com; ❷), just off Piazza S. Silvestri, in an atmospheric renovated Dominican convent, with an original cloister. The three-star *Palazzo Brunamonti*, Corso G. Matteotti 79 (℡0742.361.932, ⓦwww.brunamonti.com; ❹), is a sumptuous place with a period setting and trompe l'oeil decorations. The luxurious, historic mansion ⚑ *L'Orto degli Angeli*, Via Dante Alighieri 1 (℡0742.360.130, ⓦwww.ortoangeli.it; ❼), with porticoes, gardens and a gourmet restaurant (a fine place to eat), has been in the same family since 1788.

For other **restaurants**, the simple *Enoteca di Piazza Onofri*, Piazza Onofri 1 (℡0742.361.926; closed Wed, Mon–Fri lunchtimes, plus a period in July & Aug), offers light meals based on traditional dishes executed with a slight twist; desserts are usually tiptop (try the *soufflé al cioccolato*). A touch more expensive is the excellent *Ottavius*, Via del Gonfalone 4 (℡0742.360.555; closed Mon & first half of July), wonderfully situated in an old single-vaulted medieval room; the food – great *gnocchi al Sagrantino* and succulent *filetto* – is pure Umbrian. If you have a car, consider driving to nearby Cannara (see below) to eat at the first-rate *Perbacco*. The **bar** just off Bevagna's central piazza – good for ice cream and snacks – has perhaps Umbria's most miserable service and oddest clientele.

Around Bevagna

With your own transport, you can explore the rich agricultural plain surrounding Bevagna. In the hills above the town, clearly delineated on the skyline, is the Renaissance church of **Santa Maria delle Grazie** (rarely open), admirable from below, but by no means worth the journey for a closer look. The most rewarding trip follows the minor road northwest towards Cannara. Some 2km out is the pretty, restored Convento dell'Annunziata, followed by the one-horse hamlet of **CANTALUPO** and the tiny stone chapel of Madonna della Pia. Take a minor left turn 1km beyond and you hit **LIMIGIANO**, a classic fortified hamlet centred on a thirteenth-century church, San Michele. At the crossroads for Cannara, a left turn leads to **COLLEMANCIO**, where 500m north of the village's public gardens are the unexcavated ruins of Urbinum Hortense, a Roman or possibly Etruscan settlement destroyed by Totila in 545. The odds and ends – traces of a temple, pavement and mosaics – merit a wander, while the views over the Vale of Spoleto are superb.

CANNARA itself, stranded mid-plain but sheltered by trees, has three churches, each with significant paintings by major Umbrian artists: **San Giovanni** sports frescoes by Lo Spagna, while **San Matteo** and **San Francesco** have works by Nicolò Alunno. The Palazzo Comunale in Piazza Umberto houses a small **gallery** with frescoes detached from local churches and archeological finds from Urbinium. You'd do well to make a point of **eating** at the exceptional *Perbacco*, Via Umberto I 14 (℡0742.720.492; eves only; closed Mon & 4 weeks during July & Aug), an inexpensive *osteria* at the centre of the village. Everything served is rigorously local, with old-fashioned and sometimes robust dishes you won't find everywhere such as *zampetti con salsa verde* (pigs' trotters) and *piccione in casseruola* (pigeon casserole).

Montefalco

As you'd expect from its name, **MONTEFALCO** ("the Falcon's Mount") commands the Vale of Spoleto. The local tag of *la ringhiera dell'Umbria* ("the balcony of Umbria") may be a touch hyperbolic but the views are nonetheless majestic and past the modern suburbs lies one of the finest hill-towns in the area, a maze of tiny, cobbled streets, with an artistic heritage – including pictures by Perugino and a stunning Gozzoli fresco cycle – out of all proportion to its size.

The town was the birthplace of eight saints, good going even by Italian standards, and began life as a small independent medieval *comune* known as Coccorone. It was destroyed by **Frederick II** in 1249, his only legacy a gate named in his honour, whereafter Montefalco took its new name, supposedly after Frederick's imperial eagle crest. Its chief historical interest lies in a brief interlude in the fourteenth century, when the town became a refuge to Spoleto's papal governors, left vulnerable by the defection of the popes to Avignon. Their munificent presence resulted in the rich decoration of local churches and the commissioning of **Lorenzo Maitani**, who was later to work on the Duomo in Orvieto, to strengthen the town walls (still impressively intact) and to build a fortress for the exiled rulers. Power thereafter devolved to Foligno's Trinci family, to the rapacious Baglioni and eventually to the Church – a cue for several centuries of quiet decline.

Arrival, information and accommodation

Everything is within a few minutes' walk of the main square, Piazza del Comune, home to a **tourist information** office on the south side, La Strada del Sagrantino (daily: April–Oct 8am–1pm & 2–6; Nov–Feb 9am–1pm & 2–6pm; ⊤0742.378.490, ⓦwww.stradadelsagrantino.it). You can also pick up some information at the ticket desk in the San Francesco museum (⊤0742.379.598) on Via Ringhiera Umbra.

Five **buses** daily (Mon–Sat) from Foligno's Porta Romana, and one daily from Perugia (Mon–Sat) stop just outside the walls at the bottom of Via Umberto I in Viale della Vittoria. The **post office** is at the top of Corso G. Mameli virtually on the main square, as is the main bank for **exchange**, Istituto di Credito. The **police station** is in Via A. Gramsci (⊤0742.379.148).

There's no need to spend more than a morning in Montefalco, but it's a peaceful spot to rest up, with two **hotels** in town – the tiny, quaintly old-fashioned *Ringhiera Umbra*, Corso G. Mameli 20 (⊤0742.379.166, ⓦwww.ringhieraumbra .com; ❶), which has a relaxed little restaurant (closed Mon except in summer) in the medieval vaulted room downstairs, and the fancier *Degli Affreschi*, Corso G. Mameli 45 (⊤0742.379.243, ⓕ0742.379.643; ❷), which is a bit closer to the main square. Residents of the latter can use the swimming pool at the ugly modern sister hotel *Hotel Nuovo Mondo*, 2km west of town on the main road. The 🛇 *Villa Pambuffetti*, Via Vittoria 3 (⊤0742.379.417, ⓦwww.villapambuffetti .com; ❻), is a marvellous four-star villa-hotel with park and pool, 100m west of town towards Foligno. Prices are high, but if you're honeymooning, or fancy a night of credit-card madness, this is the place – though make sure you're in the main villa, not the gatehouse. The room to get, if you can, is the one in the old tower, with a 360° view.

The Town

Montefalco's chief attraction, the ex-church of **San Francesco** and its museum, is a stone's throw away from **Piazza del Comune**, the main square, while

Montefalco's **wines** have always been prized within Umbria, but have recently started to achieve wider fame. Their reputation rests not so much on the serviceable *Rosso di Montefalco* as on two powerful reds of mysterious origin, the extraordinary **Sagrantino** and **Sagrantino Passito**. Both are made from the Sagrantino grape, a variety found nowhere else in Europe. Why it should be unique to a tiny area of central Italy is a mystery: it appears in records in the nineteenth century, but experts claim a far more ancient pedigree, some saying it was imported by the Saracens, others that it was introduced by Syrian monks in the seventh century, or perhaps came from Piedmont or Catalonia. Its name may derive from its sacramental use by Franciscan communities who used to cultivate this grape.

Sagrantino is a dry red, usually made with up to five percent of the common Trebbiano Toscano. Sagrantino Passito is similar, with the important difference that it uses semi-dried or *passito* grapes to produce that rarest of drinks – a sweet red dessert wine. Both varieties, in the words of Italian wine guru Burton Anderson, have a remarkable "dark purple-garnet colour, rich, berry-like scent, and warm, rich full flavour". The Sagrantino, he adds, has "voluptuous body" and "staggering strength", qualities to which even the least educated palate will be able to attest after a couple of glasses. There are numerous small producers, with **Adanti** reliable leading exponents of both varieties, their singular *Rosso d'Arquata*, in Anderson's words, "one of central Italy's most original and enjoyable red wines". Any of the many producers in the tiny DOC area, however, should come up trumps, especially Antonelli, Benincasa, Caprai, Rocca di Fabbri and Paolo Bea – the last are producers of what Anderson describes as a "titanic" Sagrantino Passito. The *alimentari* or smart bar-enoteca in Montefalco's main Piazza del Comune contain a superb selection of all the area's wines.

the rest of the town is little more than five minutes' walk from end to end. The only outlying site, **San Fortunato**, is about fifteen minutes' walk away, the stroll relieved by the comprehensively frescoed church of **Sant'Illuminata** en route.

San Francesco

The cavernous fourteenth-century church of **San Francesco** (March–May, Sept & Oct daily 10.30am–1pm & 2–6pm; June & July daily 10.30am–1pm & 3–7pm; Aug daily 10.30am–1pm & 3–7.30pm; Nov–Feb Tues–Sun 10.30am–1pm & 2.30–5pm; €4) hosts one of the great Renaissance fresco cycles, a series of panels on the *Life of St Francis* (1452) by **Benozzo Gozzoli**. Gozzoli, a pupil of Fra' Angelico, has a comparatively lowly place in the pantheon of Florentine artists, but this delightful cycle – which duplicates in its subjects many of Giotto's panels in Assisi – is bold in its colouring and utterly assured of its narrative. It's also of great social interest for its closely observed townscapes: Arezzo is depicted, as is Montefalco (visited by St Francis after his sermon to the birds outside Bevagna). The panels completely fill the apse, with twenty medallions around them depicting famous Franciscans; underneath the main window appear Petrarch, Dante and Giotto, members of the lay tertiary order. Further work by Gozzoli fills the walls and vaults to the right, as well as the first chapel on the left (south) side of the church. The striking but obviously cruder frescoes in the fourth, fifth and sixth chapels on this side are the work of the fifteenth-century Foligno artist Giovanni di Corraduccio.

Elsewhere are displayed paintings by many of the leading lights of the Umbrian Renaissance – Perugino, Nicolò Alunno, Tiberio d'Assisi – and some fascinating little-known characters. Perugino's *Nativity* (1503) on the west wall, in particular, is worth looking out for, as Lago Trasimeno is featured in the background. Works originally commissioned for San Francesco remain *in situ*, with others housed in the excellent **Museo Civico di San Francesco** up the stairs (same hours & ticket). In the gallery look for Francesco Melanzio's *Madonna Enthroned with Six Saints*, the work of a leading local Renaissance painter, and for the two panels – one by Melanzio – showing the *Madonna del Soccorso*. The story, common in Umbria though rarely painted elsewhere, concerns a young mother who, tired of her whingeing child, cries, "Would that the Devil might take you away!", whereupon the Devil appears, prompting the mother to invoke the Virgin to save her infant.

Sant'Agostino

The Augustinians' monastery and church of **Sant'Agostino** is 200m from the Franciscans' power base, across the Piazza del Comune. A simple Gothic hall, begun in 1275, it is typical of the order, designed with a view to minimizing the fripperies and maximizing the preaching space. It has a few excellent frescoes that have survived the damp – including a *Coronation of the Virgin* by Caporali (1522) – but its main interest, lending a distinctly spooky air, lies in its collection of mummies. Midway down the right nave are the first of these – the tiny bodies of **Beata Illuminata** and **Beata Chiarella**, clad in dusty muslin which only half hides their bones, skin and yellow faces. At the top of the left-hand side of the church is another dusty cadaver, propped on one elbow and looking very comfortable in a glass-fronted wardrobe. Known as the **Beato Pellegrino** (Holy Pilgrim), he apparently came to venerate Illuminata and Beata, fell asleep in the church in the position he's in now, and was found dead next morning against a confessional. Immediately placed in a sepulchre, he was found outside it the next day, and refused to stay put on several subsequent occasions. His body and clothes didn't decay for a hundred years. Despite this impressive behaviour, nothing was known of the character, so there was no sainthood, and he was plonked for posterity in his wardrobe.

Santa Chiara

In the church of **Santa Chiara**, five minutes from San Francesco in Via Verdi, the wizened body of St Clare of Montefalco languishes in a transparent casket high up on the altar. The saint – not to be confused with her more famous namesake at Assisi – was born in Montefalco in 1290, became a nun at the age of 6 and embarked on a series of miracles connected with the Passion of Christ. There's a small fresco cycle on her life in a chapel inside the convent (ring the bell on the door to the right of the casket and ask one of the nuns to unlock it). The nuns might also show you around the rest of the adjoining **convent**. On show is a small Crucifix enshrining three of the saint's gallstones (representing the Trinity) as well as the remains of her heart and the scissors with which the relic was hacked out of her, all of which are kept in a cupboard under her body – which is cleverly shared by the main church and this private chapel. The story relates that Christ appeared to Clare, saying the burden of the Cross was becoming too heavy for him; the saint replied she would help by carrying it within, and when she was opened up a cross-shaped piece of tissue was duly found on her heart. Other sights include a miraculous tree that grew from a staff planted by Christ, who appeared again to Clare in the shrubbery. The nuns believe it to be the sole wild specimen of its species in all of Europe; the berries are used to make rosaries, and are said to have powerful medicinal properties.

Sant'Illuminata and San Fortunato

Down Via Verdi from Santa Chiara is the tiny church of **Sant'Illuminata**, worth a visit for its triple-arched Renaissance portico and comprehensively frescoed interior. The standard of painting isn't always high – most works are by the obscure local man Melanzio – but the overall effect is captivating.

Keep heading out of town from here, down the avenue of horse chestnuts, then turn left at the T-junction, and a ten-minute trudge brings you out at the **Monastero di San Fortunato** (closed daily noon–4pm), set amongst ilex woods, the site home to a church since the fifth century. It has noted frescoes on the *Life of St Francis* (1512) by Tiberio d'Assisi – one of Perugino's leading disciples – in its Cappella delle Rose, to the left of the main courtyard. Gozzoli painted the very faded *Madonna and Child with Angels* over the door of the main church (the *St Sebastian* is by Tiberio), the dark fresco of St Fortunatus inside on the left altar, and the three worn tondi on the sarcophagus of St Severus in the little chapel off the right aisle. The St Fortunatus fresco once sat above the remains of Fortunatus himself, whose bones were laid out in a macabre skull-and-crossbones arrangement; at the time of writing they have been temporarily removed. The saint died in 390, and in rotting away proved rather more corruptible than Sant'Agostino's holy personages.

Eating and drinking

For something grander than the *Ringhiera*'s **restaurant**, try the outstanding ⚔ *Coccorone*, set in a medieval building on the corner of Largo Tempestivi and Via Fabbri (☎0742.379.535; closed Wed except in summer), where the chances are you'll have one of Umbria's better meals – great pastas and *crespelli* (rolled pancakes), and superlative *tiramisù*. To find it, follow the off-putting yellow signs for the "Tipical Ristorant". The restaurant in the *Pambuffetti* hotel is also good, though more formal; the dining room is a lovely glass-enclosed space with views onto the garden. This makes it great in summer, but no match in winter for the roaring wood-fire cosiness of the *Coccorone* (the fire usually burns in summer as well – it's used to grill all the meats). Prices, too, are higher in the *Pambuffetti*: you're paying for elegance rather than better food.

You might while away an hour in the **bar-enoteca** in the main square, part of a chic but rather self-conscious little development of craft and food shops; in the cool cellar downstairs from the bar you can drink wine and eat light meals. Otherwise, try the little *Bar Giardino*, signed off the western end of Corso Umberto I. The best place to buy food and wine is the old shop on Piazza del Comune, which has a well-priced stock of truffles, local oils and leading wines.

Trevi

Few people give **TREVI** more than an admiring glance from the train or highway. From across the valley, the town looks merely enticing, but at closer range Trevi has the most stupendous appearance of any town in Umbria, its medieval houses perched on a pyramidal hill and encircled by miles of olive groves renowned for producing central Italy's finest oil. Its daunting inaccessibility is one of the reasons for its easygoing, old-fashioned charm; the feeling is of a pleasant, ordinary provincial town, unspoilt but just beginning – like Spello and Montefalco before it – to feel the first effects of tourism. The town's name, incidentally, has no relation to Rome's celebrated Trevi Fountain, other

Map labels:
TREVI · N · Pinacoteca Comunale · Porta del Bruscito · LARGO DON BOSCO · VIA LUCARINI · VIALE CIUFFELLI · San Martino · Palazzo Valenti · Sant' Emiliano · San Francesco · VIA SAN FRANCESCO · VIA ZAPPELLI · VIA DI SALERNO · Il Terziere · VIA COSTE · Santa Croce · PIAZZA D. TORRE · La Prepositura · PIAZZA DELLA ROCCA · Osteria La Vecchia Posta · Hospital · Antica Dimora alla Rocca · Flash Art Museum · Palazzo Comunale · PIAZZA MAZZINI · PIAZZA GARIBALDI · VIA ROMA · VIA COSTE SAN PAOLO · Roman Wall · VIA CAVOUR · VIA DOGA · Santa Chiara · PIAZZA D. PIAGGIA · VIA S. FABIANO · VIA A. TANTOSATI · San Giovanni Decollato · VIA DELLE GROTTE · Santa Lucia · Trevi Hotel · VIA DELLE FONTI · Bus Stops · Porta San Fabiano · Medieval Wall · Porta Nuova · VIA D. COSTARELLA · Porta del Cieco · VIA D. PIAGGIA · 0 · 100 m · Madonna delle Lacrime · Station

than the fact that it derives, like that of the fountain, from the fact that three roads, or *tre vie*, met here. Olives aside, you might also note Trevi's peculiar black celery (*sedano nero*), in season in October, when a Thursday morning market is devoted to it.

The Town

As with most Umbrian hill-towns, Trevi's chief pleasure lies in tramping the medieval streets, which are obsessively well kept and characterized by complicated patterns of cobblestones. Roman fragments are embedded in the inner of two sets of medieval **walls**, raised when Trevi paraded as a minor independent *comune*.

The key sight is the modern **Pinacoteca Comunale**, or **Raccolta d'Arte di San Francisco** (April–May & Sept Tues–Sun 10.30am–1pm & 2.30–6pm; June & July Tues–Sun 10.30am–1pm & 3.30–7pm; Aug daily 10.30am–1pm & 3–7.30pm; Oct–March Fri–Sun 10.30am–1pm & 2.30–5pm; €3), in the former Convento di San Francesco on Largo Don Bosco, where St Francis's preaching was once interrupted by the braying of an "indomitable ass". The museum is a slick but pleasing affair, and houses a well-presented display of coins, ceramics and Roman fragments, several paintings by Umbrian masters and one outstanding work, a *Coronation of the Virgin* (1522) by Lo Spagna, removed from the church of San Martino (see opposite); it was commissioned by Trevi's medieval governors as a copy of a more famous work by the Florentine Ghirlandaio, mainly because they couldn't afford the real thing. Also look out for *Scenes from the Life of Christ* by Giovanni di Corraduccio, a fifteenth-century painter from Foligno whose frescoes are on display in Montefalco's San Francesco (see p.637). In the same complex is the **Museo della Civiltà dell'Ulivo** (same hours and ticket), a well-intentioned but not entirely successful museum devoted to the history of the olive and olive-oil production: many of its cavernous rooms are all but empty and the half-hearted hands-on displays seem to be aimed mostly at children. The various interpretive boards and their English translations, however, are packed with interesting information – if you can be bothered to wade through the reams of text.

The highest point of the town is **Sant'Emiliano**, comely and recently restored twelfth-century Romanesque on the outside, Baroque horror-show within. Emilianus was an Armenian missionary and bishop of the town cut off in his prime in 302: his feast day (Jan 27) is celebrated by a procession. The only early survivors of the butchery of the building are a captivating *Altar of the Sacrament* (1522) in the second chapel on the left and frescoes by Melanzio, who was active in many villages hereabouts (notably Montefalco) at the start of the sixteenth century. Almost opposite is a very modest gallery of modern art, the **Trevi Flash Art Museum**, Via Lucarini 1 (hours vary; €4).

Outside the walls

A stroll north from Piazza Garibaldi, following the tree-lined Viale Ciufelli left of the hospital complex, offers a superb view of the valley and after ten minutes brings you to the conventual church of **San Martino** (most often open in the morning), site of Trevi's original parish church. It has a lunette above the door by Tiberio d'Assisi plus two pictures in the tabernacles on either side of the presbytery, *St Martin Dividing his Cloak with Beggar* by Tiberio, and a fifteenth-century *Madonna and Child with St Francis and St Antony of Padua* by Mezzastris, a local painter. In the separate Cappella di San Girolamo, to the left of the church, is an important *Assumption and Saints* (1512) by Lo Spagna, another Spoletan artist, and *St Emilianus* by Tiberio d'Assisi.

Most noteworthy of the other peripheral churches is the battered **Madonna delle Lacrime** (undergoing long-term restoration; opening hours variable), just under 1km north of the centre on the minor road towards the Via Flaminia main road, home to a fine *Epiphany with St Peter and St Paul* from 1521 (second altar on the right) by Perugino and a sweep of frescoes (1520) by Lo Spagna in the chapel of the left transept.

Practicalities

Arrive by train, and you have to hope for one of the rare connecting buses to the old town centre, a very steep 4km distant; **buses** from Foligno drop off in **Piazza Garibaldi**, a large square on the east of town just outside the walls, also with parking.

It's a half-minute stroll to the main square inside the walls, Piazza Mazzini, where there's a small and obliging Pro Loco **tourist office** at no. 6 (daily 9am–1pm & 3–6/7pm; ☎0742.781.150, ⓦwww.protrevi.com), and a very helpful Tourist Co-Op (Mon–Sat 8.30am–2pm; ☎0742.780.066, ⓦwww .bedandbreakfastumbria.com). The latter, beneath the Torre Comunale, can organize all manner of accommodation locally, from rooms to villas, as well as a variety of tours and activities: it also has the usual range of maps and general tourist information. Despite the afternoon closing, there's generally someone in the office most of the day. **Hotels** comprise the bland but adequate three-star *Trevi*, Via Fantosati 2 (☎0742.780.922, ⓦwww.trevihotel.net; ❸), and the newer two-star *Il Terziere*, Via Salerno 1 (☎0742.78.359, ⓦwww.ilterziere.com; ❷), which has the bonus of a pleasant garden. The best place to stay, however – and a sign of how Trevi is changing – is the central 24-room *Antica Dimora alla Rocca*, Piazza della Rocca 1 (☎0742.385.401, ⓦwww.hotelallarocca.it; ❹), the sort of smartly renovated historic building (in this case a sixteenth-century palazzo) that has appeared in most Umbrian towns in the last decade or so. The tourist offices have an ever-changing roster of **private rooms** and **apartments** for rent.

For **food**, try the *Osteria La Vecchia Posta*, Piazza Mazzini 14 (Sept–June closed Thurs), or the half-hidden *La Prepositura*, Vicolo Oscura 2a, just below Piazza della Rocca, which has lovely medieval dining areas. In the hamlet of **PIGGE**, 4km south, the *Pescatore*, Via Chiesa Tonda 5 (☎0742.780.483, ⓔmauro .pasq@libero.it; ❶), has nine two-star rooms and a good local **restaurant**, the *Taverna del Pescatore* (☎0742.780.290; closed Wed except in summer).

South to Spoleto

As you move south from Trevi towards Spoleto (see p.648), the Vale of Spoleto becomes increasingly pockmarked with new houses and small factories. It's all the more unexpected, then, to come across the sacred **Fonti di Clitunno** (daily: May–Aug 8.30am–8pm; early Sept 8.30am–7.30pm; late April 9am–8pm; early April & late Sept 9am–7.30pm; late March 9am–1pm & 2–6.30pm; early March & Oct 9am–1pm & 2–6pm; Nov–Feb 10am–1pm & 2–4.30pm; €2), a series of springs revered since Roman times. Originally dedicated to the oracular god Clitunnus, the springs were often used as a party venue by the likes of Caligula and Claudius, even though their major curative effect is allegedly that of removing any appetite for alcohol. Earthquakes over the years have upset many of the underground sources, so the waters aren't as plentiful as they once were, but they still flow as limpid as they did when Byron extolled "the sweetest wave of the most living crystal... the purest god of gentle waters". There's some commercial fuss around the entrance but the springs, streams and willow-shaded lake beyond are languidly romantic, with the occasional coach party the only intrusion on weekdays; at weekends the racket is more intense. Unfortunately, the proximity of the road, with its roaring trucks and buses, comes close to ruining the springs' effect.

A few hundred metres north, and easily missed, is the so-called **Tempietto di Clitunno** (Tues–Sun 9am–dusk; €2), accessible only from the road (not directly from the Fonti). It looks like a miniature classical temple, but is actually an eighth-century Christian church cobbled together with columns from the ruins of Roman temples and villas, all long vanished. Scholars until recently were fooled into thinking it a genuine piece of Roman antiquity, though Goethe was one notable dissenter from the party line. The track that runs below the facade is the remains of the original Via Flaminia. The entrance is to the side; if it's shut, try ringing the bell on the gate. Inside are some faded Byzantine frescoes, dated to the eighth century and said to be the oldest in Umbria, representing Christ, St Peter and St Paul.

Though its position above the Fonti di Clitunno is impressive enough, the main attraction of the small, fortified hamlet of **CAMPELLO** is the fact that it offers accommodation. For **hotel** rooms try either the two-star *Fontanelle*, Via d'Elci 1 (☎0743.521.091, ⓕ0743.275.052, ⓦwww.albergofontanelle.it; ❶), in the hamlet of Fontanelle, or the two-star *Ravale*, Ravale Campello, close to the Fonti (☎0743.521.320, ⓕ0743.520.861, ⓦwww.hotelravale.it; ❷); both have **restaurants** and reasonable rooms. For those equipped with a car or bike, there are superb mountain excursions on the roads northeast of Campello: minor roads follow deep-cut valleys via Pettino and Spina into marvellous countryside, the hills on either side rising to over 1400m at Monte Maggiore and Monte Brunnette.

Travel details

The excellent website ⓦ www.umbriatrasporti.it has links to full and updated timetables for all public transport, including the private FCU and state rail services and the ATC, APM and SSIT bus services.

Trains

Assisi to: Foligno (18–24 daily; 17min), Passignano sul Trasimeno (18–24 daily; 50min); Perugia (18–24 daily; 30min); Spello (18–24 daily; 9min); Terontola (18–24 daily; connections to Chiusi, Orvieto, Arezzo and Florence; 1hr); Tuoro sul Trasimeno (18–24 daily; 55min).

Foligno to: Assisi (18–24 daily; 17min); Fossato di Vico (for Gubbio; 9–13 daily; 45min); Gualdo Tadino (8–11 daily; 40min); Narni (12–16 daily; 1hr 10min); Passignano sul Trasimeno (18–24 daily; 1hr 5min); Perugia (18–24 daily; 40min); Rome (16 daily; 1hr 55min); Spello (18–24 daily; 9min); Spoleto (12–18 daily; 20min); Terni (12–18 daily; 55min); Teróntola (18–24 daily; connections to Chiusi, Orvieto, Arezzo and Florence; 1hr 15min); Trevi (12–16 daily; 7min); Tuoro sul Trasimeno (18–24 daily; 1hr 10min).

Buses

Assisi to: Bastia and Capodacqua (7 daily; 15min); Cannara (4 daily; 30min); Foligno (4 daily Mon–Sat; 50min); Gualdo Tadino (1 daily; 1hr); Norcia (1 daily Mon–Sat, from Santa Maria degli Angeli; 2hr 10min); Perugia (7–10 daily; 40min); Rome (1 daily; 3hr 30min); Santa Maria degli Angeli (every 30min); Todi and Orvieto (1 weekly on Fri).

Bevagna to: Foligno (5 daily Mon–Sat; 30min); Montefalco (4 daily Mon–Sat; 40min).

Foligno to: Assisi (4 daily Mon–Sat; 50min); Bevagna (3 daily Mon–Fri; 20min); Colfiorito (4 daily Mon–Sat; 55min); Giano dell'Umbria (2 daily Mon–Sat; 50min); Montefalco (8 daily Mon–Sat; 30min); Nocera Umbra (4–5 daily Mon–Sat; 30min); Norcia (1 daily Mon–Sat; 1hr 35min); Perugia (7–10 daily; 1hr 20min); Rome (2–3 daily; 3hr); Spello (11 daily Mon–Sat; 20min); Spoleto (4–8 daily; 50min); Trevi (4 daily Mon–Sat; 23min).

Montefalco to: Bevagna (4 daily Mon–Sat; 40min); Foligno (5 daily Mon–Sat; 30min).

Spoleto and the Valnerina

CHAPTER 12

Highlights

✳ **San Salvatore, Spoleto**
The best of Spoleto's
many fine Romanesque
churches. **See p.653**

✳ **Duomo, Spoleto** The
region's prettiest cathe-
dral, celebrated for its
facade and Fra' Lippo
Lippi frescoes. **See p.656**

✳ **Ponte delle Torri, Spoleto** Awe-inspiring medieval aqueduct and bridge
with spectacular views.
See p.661

✳ **The Valnerina** A verdant,
mountain-edged valley
dotted with hill–villages
and spectacular views.
See p.664

✳ **Scenic drive** The
mountain road from

Sant'Anatolia to Mon-
teleone and Cascia is
one of Umbria's most
exhilarating drives. **See
p.665**

✳ **San Pietro in Valle**
Umbria's loveliest abbey,
in a beautiful location,
with works of art dating
from the eighth century.
See p.666

✳ **Norcia** Mountain town
renowned for its ham,
cheese, truffles and other
gastronomic treats. **See
p.670**

✳ **Piano Grande** Glorious
upland plain, centrepiece
of the magnificent Monti
Sibillini national park.
See p.677

△ The Ponte delle Torri, Spoleto

Spoleto and the Valnerina

astern Umbria is in many ways the most enjoyable part of the region, at least in terms of its landscapes, offering superb walking and car or cycle touring amid some of the wildest scenery in central Italy. Its main city and transport hub, **Spoleto**, is one of Umbria's more stimulating bases, its many Romanesque churches and other monuments and a year-round programme of exhibitions and concerts making it an essential feature of any itinerary. Yet for all its medieval and Roman sights, Spoleto is a hill-town far from overwhelmed by its past.

The walking and scenery are at their best in the extreme east of the region, where the spectacular **Monti Sibillini** look down over the **Piano Grande**, a breathtaking highland plain which in spring becomes an expanse of wild flowers. There is sporadic public transport access to these areas from both Spoleto and **Norcia**, a friendly town and the earthquake-prone birthplace of St Benedict, founder of Western monasticism. Equally beautiful, and a little easier to reach, are the villages of the **Valnerina**, an upland valley enclosed by mountains that arc through the region east of Spoleto. Much of the Sibillini and the upper reaches of the Valnerina are best seen using Norcia as a base.

Access to Spoleto is straightforward, as the town lies on the Rome–Ancona **train** line, with links to Terni and Narni to the south, and Foligno, Assisi and Perugia to the north. **Buses** provide feasible links for the main villages of the Valnerina, but not for the trailheads of the Monti Sibillini and Piano Grande; to get the most from the countryside you really need your own transport. If you're driving, note there's a quick road tunnel (not yet marked on most maps) just east of Spoleto off the old minor road over the mountains to Vallo di Nera. The tunnel picks up the Valnerina road a little south of the old Vallo di Nera junction close to Sant'Anatolia di Narco.

Official websites

Umbria's official tourist websites are ⓦ www.umbria-turismo.it and ⓦ www .umbria2000.it. Many of the region's museums and galleries are affiliated to Sistema-museo (information ☎ 199.194.114, ⓦ www.sistemamuseo.it).

N

Trevi

Fonti di
Clitunno

Campello
sul Clitunno

Cerreto
di Spoleto

Triponzo

River Corno

River Nera

Vallo
di Nera

Sant'Anatolia
di Narco

Castel
San Felice

Spoleto

Monteluco

Capanne

Roccaporena

Scheggino

Monte
Coscerno
1685 m

Poggiodomo

Caso

Gavelli

VALNERINA

PARCO

NATURALE

REGIONALE

Monteleone
di Spoleto

Sambucheto

Monte Aspra
1652 m

San Pietro
in Valle †

Ferentillo

River Nera

Montefranco

Arrone

Spoleto

"The most romantic city I ever saw," said Percy Bysshe Shelley of **SPOLETO**, a place that would demand a visit with or without its famous summer **Festival dei Due Mondi**, a contemporary arts jamboree with considerable international kudos. One of the most graceful of all Italian hill-towns, Spoleto maintains a bustling life of its own, a seductively medieval appearance and a superb assembly

SPOLETO & THE VALNERINA

MARCHE

MONTI SIBILLINI

Preci

River Nera

✝ **Abbadia di Sant'Eutizio**

Piedivalle

Campi Vecchio

Monte Argentella
2201 m ▲

PARCO
NAZIONALE
DEI MONTI
SIBILLINI

Castelluccio

Grande

Monte Vettore
2476 m ▲

Piano

Biselli

Serravalle

Norcia

Santa Scolastica

Forca di Presta

Arquata
del Tronto

Forca Canapine

Monte
Serra
1744 m ▲

Savelli

Cascia

LAZIO

Cittareale

Monte Boragine
1829 m ▲

0   5 km

of museums and Romanesque monuments. Its major architectural attractions are in the medieval **Upper Town**, though the largely modern **Lower Town** also boasts three major Romanesque churches. The whole is a relatively compact area and getting around is easy enough on foot – though you don't want to be walking up and down between the Upper and Lower towns too often in the summer heat. Road and transport links make Spoleto a natural base for exploring: even Assisi is an easy day-trip. The one drawback to the place is its ever-increasing popularity; hotels are relatively thin on the ground and, during the height of the summer festival, accommodation is tight and prices inflated.

Of Bronze Age origin, the city was an important **Umbrian** centre, the vast gorge-surrounded crag at its heart an obvious point of strategic importance. Its ancient grandeur is attested to by a series of well-preserved **Roman walls**. Cicero described Spoletium, founded in 241 BC, as Rome's most renowned colony, and it was strong enough to distract and turn away **Hannibal** in 217 BC after his victory at Lago Trasimeno (see p.571) – had it not, history might have been very different, as the Carthaginian general was forced into a damaging excursion into the Marche when an all-but-defenceless Rome lay at his mercy. Strategically sited between Rome and Ravenna, Spoleto prospered while the focus of the Western Empire shifted from one to the other, though its real prominence was to come after 576 when it was established first as a **Lombard** and later as a **Frankish** dukedom. The autonomous **Duchy of Spoleto** eventually stretched to Benevento near Naples, dominating the greater part of central Italy.

During the emergence of the city states it became "the magnificent city, defended by a hundred towers". Its fall from grace came in the shape of **Barbarossa**, who flattened the city in 1155 during an Italian sojourn to restore his imperial authority. This cleared the way for rebuilding, rapid growth and the powerful re-emergence of a quasi-democratic regime (already in existence before 1155) which saw Spoleto at the height of its powers during much of the thirteenth century. Decline and deliverance into the hands of the Church followed a century later, the humdrum years that ensued being relieved in 1499 when the nineteen-year-old **Lucrezia Borgia** was appointed governor by her father, Pope Alexander VI. Apparently she ruled well for the two years she was in nominal charge before being dispatched by her father to conclude the third of her marriages. Thereafter, Spoleto fell into obscurity until the arrival of the festival nearly fifty years ago.

Arrival and information

Regular fast **trains** on the Rome–Ancona or Rome–Perugia routings stop at Spoleto, and there are regular local links with Terni, Orte and Foligno. From the station, city buses shuttle until around 8pm to **Piazza della Libertà** in the Upper Town; buy tickets (€0.80) from the station bar and newspaper stall. Most **inter-town buses**, notably from Montefalco and Perugia, are run by Spolentina (℡0743.212.211); most terminate in the Upper Town at **Piazza Carducci**, just south of Piazza della Libertà, a few in the Lower Town at Piazza Garibaldi. Buses from Norcia and the Valnerina arrive at the train station. It's difficult to **park** in the Upper Town (the likeliest slots are on Via della Rocca). There are large car parks on Via Don P. Bonilli by the stadium and Viale Cappuccini south of the Giardino Pubblico.

The large **tourist office**, Piazza della Libertà 7–9 (April–Oct Mon–Fri 9am–1pm & 4–7pm, Sat & Sun 10am–1pm & 4–7pm; Nov–March Mon–Fri 9am–1pm & 3.30–6.30pm, Sat 10am–1pm & 3.30–6.30pm, Sun 10am–1pm; ℡0743.238.911, Einfo@iat.spoleto.pg.it), can give help on accommodation and details of cultural events, and has a handy pamphlet on walking in the region, including a map for a route into the Monteluco woods, which stretch unbroken some 8km east of town.

Accommodation

For some reason Spoleto's **hotels** charge vastly different prices for different rooms within a single establishment: if the one you're offered seems too expensive, it's worth asking if there's anything cheaper. Several new hotels have opened in recent years, most of them superb historic properties and all in the upper price brackets. Accommodation is very hard to come by during the summer festival (see box p.653).

Hotels

Aurora Via dell'Apollinare 3 ℡0743.220.315, Wwww.hotelauroraspoleto.it. Excellent and very popular mid-range three-star place, in a courtyard just off Piazza della Libertà; fifteen rooms, all with private bathrooms. ❸

Charleston Piazza Collicola 10 ℡0743.220.052, Wwww.hotelcharleston.it. Fancy eighteen-room

three-star with the bonus of a fine Upper Town location, by the church of San Domenico. ❸
Clarici Piazza Garibaldi–Piazza della Vittoria 32 ☎0743.223.311, ⓦwww.hotelclarici.com. Reasonable and comfortable, but rather basic, modern three-star hotel set just outside the Upper Town walls. ❸
Dei Duchi Viale G. Matteotti 4 ☎0473.44.541, ⓦwww.hoteldeiduchi.com. The reliable upmarket four-star alternative to the *Gattapone* (see below), but nowhere near as nice (though rooms are at times a touch cheaper). Comprises 49 perfectly comfortable modern rooms in a hard-to-beat position just off Piazza della Libertà. The best rooms are on upper floors with views south to the hills. ❾
Due Porte Piazza della Vittoria 5 ☎ & ⓕ0743.223.666. A modern fifteen-room two-star in a big, busy and potentially noisy Lower Town piazza, just down the road from the train station. ❶
🏃 **Gattapone** Via del Ponte ☎0743.223.447, ⓦwww.hotelgattapone.it. One of central Italy's nicest and most intimate four-star hotels, where the big-name festival performers tend to stay, with a sublime and (faint road noise apart) peaceful setting looking over to Monteluco. Splash out to enjoy views over the gorge and Ponte delle Torri. Note that there are older and newer parts of this converted country residence: all have views, but you'd do well to ask to see a selection. Newer rooms are better. ❼
Il Panciolle Via del Duomo 4 ☎ & ⓕ0743.45.677. Seven rooms, each with private bathroom, above a nice restaurant in a quietish but convenient part of the Upper Town. A very good two-star option. ❷
Nuovo Clitunno Piazza Sordini 6 ☎0743.223.340, ⓦwww.hotelclitunno.com. The best-value midrange three-star in the Upper Town, just west of Piazza della Libertà. There's a wide price differential among its 35 rooms. ❸
🏃 **Palazzo Dragoni** Via del Duomo 13 ☎0743.222.220, ⓦwww.palazzodragoni .it. This glorious sixteenth-century converted town house is classified as a "Residenza d'Epoca", although for some bureaucratic reason it doesn't make it into Umbria's official hotel listings. This means it remains relatively unknown, so – budget permitting – you have a good chance of snapping up one of its handful of elegant rooms, which are full of frescoes, antique furniture and other perfect period details. A definite first choice in town at the luxury end of the market. ❼
Palazzo Leti Via degli Eremiti 10 ☎0743.223.340, ⓦwww.palazzoleti.com. The *Palazzo Leti*, another "Residenza d'Epoca", opened in 2003 and combines the period splendour of the *Palazzo Dragoni* with the peaceful position and great views of the

(nearby) *Gattapone*. This winning combination is highly tempting, but it doesn't come cheap. ❻
Paradiso Monteluco 19 ☎0743.223.082, ⓦwww .albergoparadiso.net. A faded modern three-star with 21 rooms, in the wooded hills above Spoleto – fine if you don't fancy in-town options or their alternatives on the main road to Terni. It's a long twisting drive up here, however, and so not that convenient for sightseeing. ❷
Villa Redenta Via di Villa Redenta 1 ☎0743.224.936, ⓦwww.villaredenta.com. This Lower Town hotel, a former hostel, has 72 rooms that are inexpensive but far from convenient. From the station, walk the length of Viale Trento e Trieste, the road that stretches away from the forecourt, and turn left at the end onto Via Flaminia Vecchia; the hotel is another seven or eight minutes' walk on the left almost opposite Via delle Lettere. Bus D (every 30min) runs close to the hotel from Piazza della Libertà. ❶

Private rooms and religious houses

Casa Accoglienza San Ponziano Via della Basilica di San Salvatore 2 ☎0743.225.288, ⓦwww .sanponziano.it. Located in the Lower Town far from the centre by the church of San Ponziano – ideal if you want to spend time studying the Romanesque churches on the monastery doorstep. Has 82 beds arranged in 31 rooms; doubles cost €46 (€56 for triples and €64 for generous-sized family four-bed rooms). Half- and full-board deals are available. ❶
Iole Tomassoni Via Cavallotti 9 ☎0743.220.441. Two doubles with bathrooms. €40 per night. ❶
Istituto Bambino Gesù Via Sant'Angelo 4, at junction with Via Monterone ☎0743.40.232. Nine singles and six doubles, all with bathrooms, at a religious institution just southeast and downhill from the central Piazza della Fontana; a simple hotel in all but name. No meals. ❶
La Tirallesca Via Focaroli 12 ☎0743.47.407. Five doubles, all with private bathrooms. €50 per night. ❶

Campsites

Camping Monteluco ☎0743.220.358, ⓔprimaver@caribusiness.it. The nearest campsite to town, just behind the church of San Pietro; very pleasant but tiny (just 35 pitches). April–Sept.
Il Girasole Petrognano ☎0743.51.335, ⓦwww .campingilgirasole.it. A big, flashy affair located 10km northwest of Spoleto (hourly buses from the train station), with a public swimming pool nearby and tennis courts.

The Spoleto Festival

Firmly established as Italy's leading international arts festival, the Festival dei Due Mondi – the Festival of the Two Worlds – came to Spoleto in 1958 when composer Gian Carlo Menotti and his advisers chose the town over thirty other contenders on account of its small venues, outstanding scenery and an artistic, historical and cultural heritage almost without equal. Today the event is generally known simply as the Spoleto Festival.

Menotti's original dream was to combine the best of young Italian and American talent (hence the "Two Worlds" tag), an idea which eventually saw the birth of a sister festival in Charleston, South Carolina. Melbourne in Australia also came on board, albeit in a half-hearted way, to make it an unofficial Festival of the Three Worlds.

Spoleto has a problem, however – namely, what happens when its guru is gone. Menotti is now in his nineties, though the advancing years have done little to mellow his autocratic style: in the past, his relations with Spoleto's town authorities have been strained, the maestro's avowedly independent approach at times having led the council to withhold some of the money it has traditionally ploughed into the festival. Matters weren't helped when Menotti decided to find a niche for his adopted son, Francis ("Chip"), suggesting he should serve as his successor; Chip is now president and artistic director of the festival, his father its founder, the roles prominently emblazoned on literature and websites, just to make things clear.

For information on the festival, visit ⊛www.spoletofestival.it or the office at Piazza del Duomo 8 (℡0743.45.208); or call ℡800.565.600 (toll-free in Italy only). Tickets can be bought online, or there is a box office at Piazza della Libertà 12 (℡0743.44.700 or 0743.220.320; Tues–Sun 10am–1pm & 3–7pm).

The Lower Town

Spoleto's art-festival credentials are immediately established by a rather grotesque monumental **sculpture** by Alexander Calder outside the train station. A relic of the 1962 festival, it serves as a gateway to the **Lower Town**, a quarter much rebuilt after Allies-inflicted bomb damage in the last war. The area does offer a trio of outstanding **Romanesque churches**, however, as well as a handful of Roman fragments. If these don't appeal, catch the city bus or take a taxi from the station to Piazza della Libertà, heart of the old town, tempting from this vantage with its skyline of spires and tiled roofs and splashes of craggy countryside; the fifteen-minute walk is reasonably enjoyable too, once you're beyond the concrete of Viale Trento e Trieste – though not one you want to consider in the heat of a summer afternoon. Head up Corso Garibaldi from Piazza Garibaldi for the most direct approach on foot.

San Salvatore and San Ponziano

One of Italy's oldest churches, **San Salvatore** (daily 7am–7pm; March, April, Sept & Oct closes 6pm; Nov–Feb closes 5pm; free) lies on the edge of the Lower Town, half-hidden in the cemetery, a faintly bizarre attraction in its own right for the glimpse it gives into the Italian way of death. Little has changed in the church since it was built by monks from the eastern Mediterranean in the fourth or fifth century, on a site probably chosen for its proximity to Christian and Neolithic catacombs. Most of the decoration and building materials are Roman and it was conceived when the only models for religious buildings were Roman temples. Not surprisingly, the end result has a distinctly pagan feel, the church's dusty, gloomy **interior** evoking an almost eerie antiquity. The walls are bare, the floors covered in fallen stone, the crumbling Corinthian columns are wedged awkwardly alongside one another and the arches in the nave have been filled in to prevent total collapse. The apse, ringed round with Roman friezes and capitals, is a later addition that gives the church's upper half a crowded and lopsided appearance.

Just a couple of minutes away is twelfth-century **San Ponziano**, dedicated to Spoleto's patron saint. Its Romanesque frontage promises much but delivers little inside. An admiring glance are all the place merits, unless you can tempt the enthusiastic and voluble caretaker out of his house (on the left) to show you the **tenth-century crypt**, a fascinating structure of odd, triangular columns believed to be *metae* (turning posts) from a Roman *circo* (race-track), backed by well-preserved patches of Byzantine fresco.

San Gregorio and Anfiteatro Romano

Across the river in Piazza Garibaldi, **San Gregorio** (daily 9am–noon & 3.30–6pm; closed Sun 12.30–2.30pm; free) dates from 1069 at the latest, but parts look as if they were built yesterday, a result of restoration after years of fire, flood and earthquake damage. Its narrow, porticoed **facade** incorporates a patchwork of fragments filched from Roman remains. The pragmatic mix of materials is most obvious in the tower, its lower half built of massive Roman blocks, the upper of more refined fifteenth-century workmanship. The similarly patchworked portico was a sixteenth-century afterthought, added when the church was heightened to imitate the Duomo in the Upper Town. The **interior** commands most interest, its walls stripped back to their Romanesque state, with substantial frescoes interrupted by a series of intimidating stone confessionals. The frescoes are local fourteenth-century efforts, the best of them in the presbytery, which is raised several metres above the nave, allowing for a **crypt** supported by dozens of tiny, mismatched pillars.

Tradition has it that somewhere under the church are the bones of ten thousand Christian martyrs killed by the Romans in the **amphitheatre** close by; the chapel alongside the portico, the Cappella degli Innocenti, is the favoured candidate for their resting place. Parts of the amphitheatre are still visible in the barracks on Via dell'Anfiteatro. No one seems to mind if you walk straight into the complex, which was formerly a monastery; bear right from the main gateway for the most substantial remains. When the Romans passed on, the huge arena was cannibalized for its stone, first by Totila and then by Cardinal Albornoz for the castle in the Upper Town. What remained was adapted as a medieval shopping arcade, and later bricked up in the courtyard you see today.

The ever-ingenious Romans constructed special gutters to drain blood from the arena into the Tessino river, which ran crimson as a result. The liberal flow of Christian blood is said to have inspired the name for the Roman **Ponte Sanguinario,** now under nearby Piazza Garibaldi. It formed part of the improvements to the Via Flaminia ordered by the Emperor Augustus, remaining in use until the fourteenth century, and rediscovered in 1817. Much remains intact below the piazza, but – contrary to guidebook advice – the site has been shut for years; Spoleto's council has tried to operate regular hours (daily 10am–1pm & 3–5pm), though don't be surprised to find that all you can see is a glimpse of a single arch through closed railings.

The Upper Town

The place to head for first in the **Upper Town** is **Piazza della Libertà**, the terminus for a local and inter-town bus service and home to the large tourist office and post office. Orientation is difficult in the jumble of levels and twisting, narrow streets around, though everything worthwhile is a short walk from Piazza della Libertà. Shops, banks and services are mostly concentrated in **Corso Mazzini**, which runs north from the square, and in **Corso Garibaldi**, which drops down to Piazza Garibaldi. Corso Mazzini is the scene of a rumbustious *passeggiata*, Sunday's walk being a particularly fine spectacle, but for the day-to-day social heart of the town you need to make for **Piazza del Mercato**, site of the old Roman forum.

Piazza della Libertà

For an introduction to Spoleto's much-touted Roman heritage, you only have to cross **Piazza della Libertà** from the tourist office. Here you can look through the railings at the much-restored first-century **Roman theatre**, excavated in 1891 and now used for festival and other performances throughout the summer. Its past includes a grisly episode in 1319 when four hundred Guelph supporters were rounded up by the Spoletans and dumped on the stage with their throats cut; the corpses were then pushed into a pile and burnt. Today it's a trifle overshadowed by the gaudily painted buildings on all sides: the worst of these offenders, the church and convent of Sant'Agata, absorbed much of the stage area in the Middle Ages, the theatre having been damaged and half-buried over the centuries by landslips.

The conventual buildings now house a restoration centre and modest **Museo Archeologico** (daily 8.30am–7.30pm; €4), entered from just down Via Sant'Agata beyond an attractive little medieval loggia. The ticket includes admission to the **theatre**, with its extraordinary vaulted tunnel beneath the tiered seats. You then climb the steps to the museum, which opens with two small rooms, displaying among other artefacts a superb shield, rings and other fragments from a Bronze Age tomb discovered in Piazza d'Armi. Next door to the right is a longer room, graced with a fine fresco, the *Last Supper*, and a well-presented gallery of Roman portrait busts and miscellaneous statuary. A small annexe at the end is devoted to the remarkable Lex Spoletina, a pair of tawny-brown Roman stone inscriptions that forbade the felling of trees in the sacred woods of Monteluco.

Piazza del Mercato

Straddling the entrance to the nearby **Piazza del Mercato** – the old forum – is the **Arco di Druso**, raised in 23 AD by the Spoletan senate to commemorate victories in Germany by Drusus, son of Tiberius and heir to the empire until his early death, courtesy of Caligula. The **walls** hereabouts, and in Via dei Felici, are the city's oldest, built in the sixth century BC by the mysterious Umbrians. Beside the arch is what's described as a **Roman temple and shop**, though you'll need a vivid imagination to see it as anything other than a ditch. However, it's well worth popping into the adjacent church of **Sant'Ansano** (daily 7.30am–noon & 3–6.30pm; Nov–March closes 5.30pm; free) for the Cripta di San Isacco, entered down the stairs to the left of the high altar (where fragments of the temple have been uncovered). As well as containing more persuasive chunks of the temple than lie outside, the crude stone walls are decorated with recently restored frescoes that may date from the sixth century, a time when the spot was home to refugee Christian monks. The main structure dates from the twelfth century.

Nowhere do you get a better sense of Spoleto's market-town roots than in the cosy **Piazza del Mercato**. In the square, old women wash fruit and vegetables in the striking 1746 fountain (its crown embellished with an attractive clock), the men drink in the bars and swap gossip, and tourists make barely a dent in the proceedings. The left-hand crest of the coat of arms atop the fountain monument, built by Carlo Maderno in 1626 for Pope Urban VIII, features three bees, symbols of the Barberini, the Roman family from which Urban hailed. The *alimentari* dotted around the square are a cornucopia of picnic provisions, with a bias towards truffles, oils and sticky liqueurs. The piazza's little open **market** runs in the mornings (Mon–Sat 8.30am–1pm), but there's almost more going on late in the evening when the outdoor tables of the main bar on the west side are the best place for in-town summer drinking.

The Duomo

It's a short walk from Piazza del Mercato to the **Duomo**, or Santa Maria Assunta (daily 7.30am–12.30pm & 3–6pm; Nov–Feb closes 5pm; free), whose restrained and elegant facade is one of the loveliest in Umbria. The careful balance of Romanesque and Renaissance elements is framed by a gently sloping piazza and hanging gardens, with the broad background of sky and open countryside setting the seal on the beautifully unified whole. The lovely, carving-swathed **portico**, an obvious addition, dates from 1491 and is flanked by two little external pulpits, one of which was used by the wandering St Bernardino of Siena to preach to the notoriously wayward Spoletans.

The building was consecrated in 1198, having been commissioned by Pope Innocent III to replace a seventh-century church flattened by Barbarossa. The twelfth-century **campanile** (with fifteenth- and sixteenth-century additions) borrowed much of its stone from Roman ruins, a hotchpotch technique continued in the rest of the building. Architectural details unusual in Italy add interest for the technically minded, most notably the **flying buttresses** tucked out of sight on the side walls; climb to Piazza F. Campello to the right for the best view. Strange, too, are the eight rose windows, clustered around a restored thirteenth-century mosaic of *Christ, the Virgin and St John*.

Less successful transformations were commissioned for the **interior**, where Pope Urban VIII's architect, Luigi Arrigucci, applied great dollops of Baroque midway through the seventeenth century. Urban – named Maffeo Barberini – had been bishop of Spoleto before becoming pope: his impetus and the money of a nephew, another of the town's bishops, financed the works and paid for a Bernini bust of Urban, now in the Museo Diocesano (see p.658). On the first altar on the left, behind glass, stands a brightly restored Crucifix (1187) by Alberto Sotio, the earliest documented Umbrian painter. Walking across to the right-hand side of the church, look in on the **Cappella Eroli** (1497), named after the Spoletan bishop Costantino Eroli: it features Pinturicchio's faded but beautifully lyrical *Madonna and Child with the Baptist and St Stephen*, with a depiction of Lago Trasimeno in the background. In the larger **Cappella dell'Assunta** (or Eroli) adjoining to its right are cruder but nonetheless striking frescoes by the Sicilian Jacopo Santori: that on the left wall shows another Eroli bishop, Francesco, who commissioned the chapel at the beginning of the sixteenth century, kneeling before a separate inset painting of the *Madonna*. The wall to its right has frescoes of saints – *Michael the Archangel* (with sword) and *Lucy*, a popular Spoletan saint: farther right, the wall is adorned with the Eroli family shields.

Back across the church is the **Cappella delle Reliquie**, entered at the top of the left aisle. Restored in 1993, it features impressive intarsia work, vivid painted panels that depict characters from the Old Testament, and some beautifully frescoed ceiling vaults. The vaults and panels are the work of Francesco Nardini, an otherwise little-known sixteenth-century painter. On the right is an outstanding fourteenth-century polychrome wooden statue, the *Madonna and Child*. To its right, behind glass in a gaudy blue-columned frame, is a fragmentary letter in Latin, written by St Francis to Fra' Leone, one of the saint's earliest and most besotted followers (he hoarded virtually every scrap and relic associated with Francis). It is one of only two letters written by the saint to have survived and was written after Francis received the stigmata at La Verna (see p.528), by which time he was virtually blind – hence the shaky handwriting. It salutes Leone and wishes him peace (the word *pacem* is clearly visible near the beginning), urging him to follow his own conscience in matters of faith rather than constantly coming to Francis for advice. It was originally kept in a Spoletan church, but vanished for centuries after its first publication in 1623, mysteriously reappearing in the Vatican archives during the reign of Pope Leo XIII. It was restored to the city in 1904.

All other works of art in the cathedral are eclipsed by the building's original **marble floor**, and by magnificent **frescoes** on the *Life of the Virgin*, painted in 1467 by **Filippo Lippi** and his assistants Fra' Diamanti and Pier Matteo. The newly restored cycle fills the domed apse, starting from the left wall with *The Annunciation* and *The Dormition of the Virgin*, the latter with portraits of the three painters to the right: Lippi is the figure with the white monk's habit over a black tunic. The cycle concludes with the *Nativity* (mostly by Matteo and Diamanti), while above spreads the most glittering scene of all, the *Coronation of the Virgin*. Note the columns and classical motifs separating the panels, many of which Lippi copied directly from old buildings around Spoleto, notably the church of San Salvatore in the Lower Town.

Lippi died shortly after the cycle's completion, the rumour being that he was poisoned for seducing the daughter of a local noble family. The Spoletan cathedral authorities, not too bothered by such moral laxity, were delighted to have someone famous to put in their cathedral, being, as Vasari put it, "poorly provided with... distinguished men". Thus they refused to send the dead artist back to Lorenzo de' Medici, his patron, who had loaned Filippo to Spoleto, reputedly to stop his Florentine philandering. Interred in a **tomb** designed by his son Filippino Lippi, the corpse disappeared during restoration two centuries later, spirited away, according to local legend, by descendants of the compromised girl. The empty tomb is on the left wall of the right (south) transept.

Minor titbits elsewhere in the cathedral include a bronze of Urban VIII by Bernini, too high above the main door to get a good look at, and an icon from Constantinople presented by Barbarossa in 1185 to make amends for having wrecked the town thirty years earlier: it's housed in the chapel below the organ loft to the rear and right of the high altar. If you manage to chat up the sacristan, you might also, if lucky, be able to see the ninth-century **crypt** of San Primiano, part of the earlier church on the site destroyed by Barbarossa.

Sant'Eufemia

Spoleto's most celebrated church is the twelfth-century **Sant'Eufemia** (interior visited with Museo Diocesano; see below), above Piazza del Duomo in Via Aurelio Saffi. The entrance is easily missed, as the church lies inside a courtyard complex off the street; look out for the yellow signs.

The church was probably built in honour of a local bishop, **St Giovanni**, who was martyred by the Goths and reputedly buried here in 980, on a site within both the precincts of the old **Benedictine** monastery and the archbishop's palace. Excavations have revealed that it also lies over the **Lombards'** eighth-century ducal palace, and Roman remains have been found, too. Good use was obviously made of materials from these previous buildings: one of the mismatched columns – that separating the first and second arches on the right – is carved with distinctive Lombard motifs. Many of the mismatched capitals, too, are also clearly from an earlier building. The church is unique in Umbria for its **matroneum**, a high-arched gallery above the aisles (reached from a tiny door at the beginning of the left aisle) which served the purpose of segregating the women of the congregation from the men. Rebuilding took place in the early part of the twelfth century, when northern Italian models were used as inspiration – the current structure bears a striking resemblance, for example, to the church of San Lorenzo in Verona.

Today, Sant'Eufemia is redolent with age and dank solemnity, its walls bare but for the odd patch of **fresco**, notably another *St Lucy* (1455), complete with eyes in a bowl, on the second column on the right (the church was even known as Santa Lucia for several centuries). The only other frills are a stone chair and simple but stunning **altar**, both brought from the Duomo in the thirteenth century. Recently, exhibitions of modern art have begun to be installed in Sant'Eufemia, and you now have to pay to enter the church, the only saving grace being that proceeds go to worthy causes.

The Museo Diocesano

The excellent **Museo Diocesano d'Arte Sacra** (April–Oct Mon & Wed–Sat 10am–1pm & 4–7pm, Sun 10am–12.30pm & 3–6pm; Nov–March Mon & Wed–Sat 10am–12.30pm & 3–6pm, Sun 11am–5pm; €3) occupies the same courtyard as Sant'Eufemia, and displays a wealth of fascinating paintings and other artefacts culled from churches across the diocese. Most of these works – many removed after the 1979 earthquake which ravaged the Valnerina – are due to be returned to their respective churches, though the prevailing view is that they've been in Spoleto for so long that they'll probably remain in the museum.

On the wall to your right as you enter **room 1** is a thirteenth-century triptych of the *Madonna and Child,* juxtaposing three scenes from the life of Christ with a panel (bottom left) showing St Martin dividing his cloak and giving one half to a beggar (later revealed to be Christ). In **room 2**, the strange *Madonna and Child* to your left shows the Child in the brown habit and triple-knotted belt of the Franciscans. Nearby is a thirteenth-century dossal, once used as the rear wall of a confessional, hence its faded appearance and the clear evidence of its having been sawn into pieces at some point. On the wall beside the entrance is a triptych with **St Lucy** depicted to the right of the central panel's *Crucifixion*. The saint, a fourth-century martyr from Sicily, was much venerated in Spoleto and the Valnerina. She was killed for refusing to marry a high-ranking pagan Roman magistrate, the spurned official having her dragged behind two oxen and then boiled alive; on hearing that the magistrate had been captivated by the beauty of her eyes, Lucy is reputed to have torn them out and sent them to her tormentor (hence her usual depiction holding a dish containing a pair of eyes). In the next painting, also a triptych, three episodes from Lucy's life make up the predella: giving to the poor; her denunciation in front of the governor of Syracuse; and her ordeal by oxen. To its left, a triptych with saints **Sebastian** and **Catherine of Alexandria** is attributed to the same painter as the previous work, Bartolomeo da Miranda, active locally in the mid-fifteenth century. Sebastian was often invoked against plague, and this painting was probably a votive offering during an epidemic, a theory reinforced by the green of the Virgin's cloak (as opposed to the more usual blue), a colour symbolizing rebirth as well as being associated with Hope, one of the three Theological Virtues.

Room 3 features the gallery's single greatest painting, a sublime freestanding *Madonna and Child with SS Montano and Bartholomew* (1485) by **Filippino Lippi**. It's strange enough that Lippi, a Florentine, should have painted in

Umbria, and stranger still that the painting should have been commissioned for Todiano, a now almost deserted village lost in the depths of the Valnerina (see p.670). The theory is that it was commissioned by a merchant who left the village and grew wealthy as a result of trade. Bartholomew and Montano are Todiano's patron saints, the latter best known for having tamed a bear and commanded it to take the place of an ox it had devoured. The little scene in the predella shows the bear alongside an ox pulling a plough. The parallel predella scene to the right shows St Bartholomew with his skin slung over his shoulder (the saint was flayed alive). Opposite is another premier painting, *Adoration of the Child* by the Sienese Mannerist **Domenico Beccafumi**, and the room also holds another freestanding Tuscan work, **Neri di Bicci**'s *Madonna della Neve* (1464), an excellent example of a relatively common theme, the *neve* (snow) referring to the miraculous fall of snow in Rome in August which is traditionally said to have marked out the site of the city's ancient Basilica di Santa Maria Maggiore. Its presence here is explained by the strong medieval trading links between Spoleto and Rome.

Left of the Lippi painting, a door leads into **room 4**, where on your left is a *Madonna and Child with SS Sebastian and Leonard*. Sebastian, unusually, is shown holding a clutch of arrows rather than being shot through with them, an allusion to the fact that he recovered from his ordeal by archery (he was martyred by being pummelled to death). St Leonard is rarely portrayed in central Italian art. Little is known of this sixth-century figure, other than that his faith persuaded King Clovis to grant him the right to release any prisoner he met. As a result he is the patron saint of prisoners, who would traditionally have made a votive offering of a shackle to the saint on their release – which is why he is shown in this painting holding a vast leg-iron. Other works here include an *Annunciation* and *Deposition* by Andrea da Caldaroba and a work in a small adjoining room by Sparpane, a rare local painter whose work you can see in Norcia's San Benedetto (see p.674) and in the lonely reaches of the Val Castoriana at Campi Vecchi (see p.670).

Retracing your steps, bear right through the large room beyond room 3, which – like much of the museum building – has a stupendous carved wooden ceiling. Don't let the four gloomy canvases in the far corner distract you from the large bust of Pope Urban VIII by the Baroque genius **Gianlorenzo Bernini**, removed from the cathedral. Past rooms with vestments, a door unexpectedly opens into the upper gallery, or *matroneum*, of Sant'Eufemia, offering a wonderful view of the church.

The museum is in the process of being reorganized, and some works which have been on display in past years had yet to reappear at the time of writing. These include a series of contrasting wooden statues of the Madonna and Child, as well as an unusual statue of Christ with movable arms: like the similar statue in Spello's Pinacoteca, it was used in Easter Week ceremonies, when the arms were extended during processions on Good Friday to mark the Crucifixion: on Easter Sunday the arms were lowered during ceremonies to celebrate the Resurrection. Also to come is an exquisite small *Madonna and Child*, an anonymous Florentine work, and detached frescoes, notably a St Michael with the Devil just visible at the bottom trying to tilt the scales in which Michael is weighing the souls of sinners and the saved.

Most entertaining of these works in limbo are numerous decorated **wooden tiles**, a series of ex-votos painted with often amusing cartoon-like depictions of sick-bed scenes and escapes from perilous (and not so perilous) episodes for which the tiles give thanks. These show events such as women being gored by bulls and a man hanging upside down from a tree and losing his hat, or a precipitous fall from a hayrick (the Virgin, as in other tiles, looks down from a cloud in the top left) and a cart falling from a bridge and hurling its inhabitants into a river.

The Casa Romana and the art galleries

Very near the Museo Diocesano, in a side-street below the Palazzo del Municipio, is the **Casa Romana** (Roman House), entered from Via Aurelio Saffi (daily: mid-March to mid-Oct 10am–8pm; rest of year 10am–6pm, but may close 1–3pm; €2.50 or €6 for combined ticket to Pinacoteca and Galleria d'Arte Moderna). This is a dark and atmospheric little corner excavated between 1885 and 1912 that contains the remains of a house fancifully believed to have belonged to Vespasia Polla, the mother of the emperor Vespasian. Bedrooms, bath and other remnants survive, including swathes of patterned black-and-white mosaic floor.

Note that Spoleto's **Pinacoteca**, which for years was stuck away in the farthest reaches of the Palazzo del Municipio above the Casa Romana, has a temporary home in the Palazzo Rosari-Spada at Piazza Sordini 5 (mid-March to mid-Oct daily 10.30am–1pm & 3–6.30pm; rest of year Wed–Mon 10.30am–1pm & 2.30–5pm; €3 or €6 combined ticket). The collection's highlights are a triptych of the *Madonna delle Grazie* by Nicolò Alunno; a polyptych from the abbey of Sant'Eutizio (with its central panel missing) by Nicola of Siena; a beautifully framed *Madonna and Child* by Antonello da Saliba; a fifteenth-century *Nativity* by Giacomo di Giovannofrio; and several impressive wooden Crucifixes, detached frescoes by Lo Spagna and two elongated panels depicting various saints.

A combined ticket for the Casa Romana also allows you into the **Galleria Civica d'Arte Moderna** (Wed–Mon: mid-March to mid-Oct 10.30–1pm & 3–7pm; rest of the year closes 5pm; €4 or €6 with combined ticket), on the west of town close to Sant'Agostino in the Palazzo Collicola at Piazza Collicola. The collection has works by leading Italian contemporary artists, alive and dead, including Guttoso, Burri, Dorazio and Accardi, plus foreign works from the likes of Calder (he of the railway station sculpture) and a section devoted to the glazed terracotta and other sculptures of Spoleto's own Leoncillo Leonardi (1915–68).

The Rocca

If you do nothing else in Spoleto, take the short walk out to the Ponte delle Torri, the town's picture-postcard favourite. It's best taken in as part of a circular walk around the base of the Rocca, or on the longer trek to San Pietro (see below). The **Rocca** itself is a perfectly endowed castle, with an impressive tally of towers, neatly delineated crenellations and sheer walls. It was built as one of a chain of fortresses with which the tireless Cardinal Albornoz tried to re-establish Church authority in central Italy in the years preceding the Great Schism. Later it became part-fortress, part-holiday home, with several popes staying over, most notably Julius II, sometimes accompanied by Michelangelo, Nicholas V, who fled here from the plague in 1449, and the Sienese Pius II.

The fort's main latter-day function has been as a high-security prison, testimony to the skill of its medieval builders; as many as five hundred prisoners were kept here by the papal authorities between 1817 and 1860; Slavic and Italian political prisoners were held here during the war, while more recent inmates included members of the Red Brigades and Pope John Paul II's would-be assassin, Mohammed Ali Agca. Since its demise as a prison in 1982, two decades and more of stop-start restoration kept the Rocca closed, partly as a result of the scale of the operation, partly through sheer mismanagement. Some £4 million of EU money has been sunk in the project, a condition of the funding (and subsequent grants) being that it should have been open to the public by 1998, when, among other things, a public park and National Museum of the Duchy of Spoleto were due to open (but didn't).

In a classic Italian fudge, areas of the castle are now open, but only as part of a far-from-satisfactory **guided tour** (mid-March to mid-June & mid-Sept to mid-Oct Mon–Fri 10–1pm & 3–7pm, Sat & Sun 10am–7pm; mid-June to mid-Sept daily 10am–8pm; Nov to mid-March Mon–Fri 2.30–5pm, Sat & Sun 10am–5pm; last tours depart an hour before closing time; €4.65): the ticket includes a minibus ride up the surprisingly long and steep approach road and a guide (invariably with limited English), though in the event there is little to be explained: the best bits of the tour are the superb views, the imposing twin courtyards and the quite staggering scale of the building; there is no sign of the much-vaunted museum. Meet at the small wooden ticket office at the start of the castle drive on Piazza F. Campello at the top of Via Aurelio Saffi, just to the left of the large fountain, whose massive stone face marks the end of a Roman and medieval aqueduct.

Highlights of the **interior** start with the **first courtyard**, the Cortile d'Onore, an upper storey supported on vast orange-brick arches and dotted with patches of fresco. The arches are slightly different: one set belong to Gattapone, the original designer, the other to Bernardo Rossellino, Pius II's architect in Pienza (see p.472), who worked here. An arched passage leads to a plainer courtyard beyond, the arch frescoed with six towns in the papal domain, with Spoleto obvious on the right thanks to the depiction of the Ponte Torri, along with Perugia (middle left) and Orvieto (far left), obvious from its cathedral. The missing patches of fresco (two of the four Cardinal Virtues also illustrated are missing) were damaged by fires lit by guards, who sheltered on duty in the passage. The **second courtyard** (used for performances in the summer festival and other events) was once the prison exercise yard: turn round to see the coats of arms above the entrance arch, which belong to Albornoz, Urban V, Eugenius IV – also represented is the monogram of Christ and the crossed keys, symbols of the Church's temporal power, a motif repeated throughout the fortress. Some idea of the castle's past importance, and its illustrious visitors and inhabitants, can be gained from the wealth of other leading family and papal arms around the place – the Barberini bees (particularly in evidence), Medici, Borgia, Colonna, Della Rovere, Piccolomini, Visconti, Aldobandini, Lambertini and many more. The tour also visits rooms on the upper storey of the Cortile d'Onore, impressive more for their size and views than for any surviving frescoes or other artefacts. The exceptions are the bedroom and studio-bathroom, which have well-preserved and pretty courtly scenes from the early fifteenth century appropriate to a bedroom and riding and hunting vignettes in the studio.

The Ponte delle Torri

Within minutes of leaving the shady gardens of Piazza F. Campello you suddenly find yourself in open countryside, with a dramatic view across the Tessino gorge and south to the mountains of Castelmonte. There's an informal little bar, often blaring crackly opera favourites from tinny speakers, about 100m before the Ponte to help you enjoy the view.

This is a good point to look down on a fine stretch of the town's **walls** and the **Ponte delle Torri**, an astonishing piece of medieval engineering with a 240-metre span supported by ten vast arches, the most central ones some 76m high. The site is a notorious lovers' leap. Probably designed by the Gubbian architect Gattapone – the man responsible for Gubbio's Palazzo dei Consoli – it was planned initially as an aqueduct to bring water from Monteluco, replacing a Roman causeway whose design Gattapone borrowed and enlarged upon. In time it became part of the town's defences, providing an escape from the castle when Spoleto was under siege. The remains of what used to be a covered passageway connecting the two are still visible straggling down the hillside. It's possible to walk across the bridge, a highly recommended stroll, with obvious paths on the other side (wind up the stone steps to the right) leading left into lovely ilex woods with superb belvederes overlooking the bridge and gorge. Follow the level path for 1km or so and you bend round an arm of the gorge to emerge in peaceful olive groves.

San Pietro and San Paolo inter Vineas

Accessible on a walking route from the Ponte delle Torri is the church of **San Pietro** (interior 9–11am; to visit 3.30–6.30pm, ring the bell of the custodian in the house adjacent to the church). The facade is the thing to see, visible from the bridge; as you draw close, it reveals a series of twelfth-century **sculptures** that – with Maitani's bas-reliefs in Orvieto – constitute the finest Romanesque carving in Umbria. Partly Lombard in their inspiration, they draw on the Gospels and medieval legend for their complicated narrative and symbolic purpose. Much of the allegory is elusive, but reasonably self-explanatory panels include *A Wolf Disguised as a Friar* before a fleeing ram – a dig at dodgy monastic morals – and, particularly juicy, the *Death of a Sinner* (left series, second from the top). Here the Archangel Michael abandons the sinner to a couple of demons who bind and torture the unfortunate before bringing in the burning oil to finish him off. Compare this with the panel above, the *Death of a Just Man*, where St Peter frees the man of his chains while Michael holds his soul in his scales; the Devil, lashed by the keys of St Peter, tries to tip the scales in his favour and holds a scroll that laments *doleo quia ante erat meus* ("I mourn because he was mine before").

San Paolo inter Vineas, stranded south of the town centre off Viale Giacomo Matteotti, is the least visited of all Spoleto's churches. Mentioned as early as the sixth century by St Gregory the Great, it was rebuilt in the tenth century and has now been restored to its beautifully simple twelfth-century state. It preserves frescoes of the *Creation* and *Prophets* painted before the consecration of the present structure, which makes them among the oldest in the region. If the church is shut, ring for admission at the old people's home next door (daily 9am–2pm).

San Domenico to San Nicolò

Among Spoleto's lesser churches, the massive monastic **San Domenico**, on the town's western margins, warrants a diversion for its colourful pink and white marble banding. Inside – in an interior of stripped-down Baroque – there are some fragments of fresco fossilized in new yellow plaster, the outstanding picture being a large, early fifteenth-century fresco on the southern right-hand wall, *The Triumph of St Thomas Aquinas*. At the back of the church to the right of the presbytery is a small room filled with crude but eye-catching early frescoes; the Cappella dei Montevecchio in the left transept enshrines the umpteenth Nail of the Cross. Close by is the **Galleria Civica d'Arte Moderna**, Piazza Collicola (same hours and ticket as Casa Romana), showing works by leading Italian contemporary artists including Guttoso, Burri, Dorazio and Accardi, plus foreign works from the likes of Calder and a section devoted to the glazed terracotta and other sculptures of Spoleto's own Leoncillo Leonardi (1915–68).

A stroll away in Via Filitteria is the tiny chapel of **SS Giovanni e Paolo**, consecrated in 1174, which has an impressive thirteenth-century fresco outside, and an interior – rarely open – covered in superb frescoes dating from the twelfth century onwards. **San Nicolò**, a couple of minutes north, is impressively Gothic from the outside but long deconsecrated, used as a truffle market and workshop for repairing steam engines, and now a setting for third-rate exhibitions and jumble sales. Alongside is what must have been a beautiful cloister, now restored to a bare semblance of its original state.

Eating and drinking

As you'd expect from its cultural aspirations, Spoleto takes its **food** pretty seriously. The town lies at the heart of renowned olive oil country, the oils of its top producer, Monini, used in kitchens across Italy. These can be bought just about anywhere, but for a **picnic**, stock up at the market and food shops in the Piazza del Mercato: the little shop immediately on the left as you exit the square to the north has an excellent selection, including local wines such as Montefalco's Sagrantino Passito (see p.637), truffle paste and other more rarified products. Another good shop, at the opposite end of the square, is the old-fashioned Salumeria Padrichelli, Via Arco del Druso 22.

The best **bar** in town is the *Vincenzo* on Corso Mazzini – you'll see the big names there during the festival – but for late evenings out-of-doors make for the bar in Piazza del Mercato. On Sunday, late in the afternoon, the region's busiest and most impressive *passeggiata* takes place from the bar in Piazza della Libertà, surging down Corso Mazzini.

Restaurants

Al Druso Via Arco del Druso 25 ℡0743.221.695. Busy trattoria-pizzeria at the southern entrance to Piazza del Mercato. Pizzas and basic meals at keen prices, but no frills. Closed Mon.

Apollinare Via Sant'Agata 14 ℡0743.223.256. Pushes *Sabatini* for the title of Spoleto's best – and first-choice – Upper Town restaurant. The blue and gold upholstery is initially off-putting, but the medieval setting is good and the welcome friendly: the menu is tiny, and the *menù degustazione* excellent value. Don't miss the sublime *caramello* starter – a cheese and truffle delight. Closed Tues.

Del Mercato Piazza del Mercato 29 ℡0743.45.325. Unexceptional but inexpensive and convenient spot on the central square with outside tables. Closed Thurs.

Il Panciolle Largo Muzio Clemente–Via del Duomo 3 ℡0743.45.677. Below the hotel of the same name, this is a good choice for a reliable and reasonably priced, if never over-exciting, meal of Umbrian specialities such as *stringozzi* and fire-grilled meats. Also known for its selection of cheeses. Has a great outside terrace at the back – though the medieval interior with open fire is cosy enough. Closed Wed.

Il Tartufo Piazza Garibaldi 24 ℡0743.40.236. Regarded, rightly, as the best restaurant in Spoleto,

and particularly renowned for its superlative truffle and Umbrian dishes. Piped music, a Lower Town location and high prices work against it, however, though the medieval interior is wonderful; you can eat outdoors in summer, and pick from a couple of *degustazione* menus. Closed Wed.

Osteria del Matto Vicolo del Mercato 3 ℡0743.225.506. A good bet in a tiny alley just off the west side of Piazza del Mercato, if only for the charm of the owner and the decidedly medieval atmosphere. It has a single, cosy dining room, and you can drink wine late into the evening, or settle down for a good light meal or snack. Lunch can be had for as little as €6 and there are set menus at lunch (€14) and dinner (€16).

Pecchiarda Vicolo San Giovanni 1 ℡0743.221.009. A friendly, family-run atmosphere, sprawling outdoor summer pergola and fair prices have made this one of the town's most popular *trattorie*. House red is a cheap and cheerful Sangiovese made by the owner. It's a big and far-from-intimate place, however, and the fact that it's enclosed means there are no views: it's also less central than most listed restaurants. Daily.

Pentagramma Via Martani 4 ℡0743.223.141. Owned by relatives of *Sabatini*'s chef-patron, this medieval vaulted dining room with its out-of-place red-chequered tablecloths specializes in traditional Spoletan staples at middling prices. A relaxed and rather un-Italian bistro atmosphere, but it needs to be busy to be enjoyable. Located immediately off Piazza della Libertà. Closed Mon.

Sabatini Corso Mazzini 54 ☎0743.221.831. Best-known top choice in the Upper Town, though the *Apollinare* perhaps just pips it for quality of cooking. Has a simple, elegant interior and small garden for summer eating, serving interesting, if occasionally over-elaborate variations of local dishes that are more imaginative than in many an Umbrian restaurant; just avoid the house speciality, cheese

risotto. Good wines, which are displayed in lovely old cabinets. Closed Mon.

Sportellino Via Cerquiglia 4 ☎0743.45.230. A good bet in the Lower Town. Walking in, you feel as if you're entering someone's home: it's a simple place with good regional cooking to match: go for *stringozzi*, a chewy local pasta made without eggs, or robust meat dishes such as *coniglio alla cacciatora* (rabbit). Pecorino cheese to finish is excellent and the *antipasti Sportellino* is almost a meal in itself. Closed Thurs & Aug.

Listings

Bike rental Scocchetti Cicli, Via Marconi 82 ☎0743.44.728.

Bookshop English-language titles plus a good stock of guides and maps of the local area at Corso Mazzini 63 (daily 9.30am–1pm & 4.30–8pm; closed Sun "if it's raining").

Car rental Armando Alcidi, a reliable local agency (☎0743.40.221), or Hertz, c/o Via Cerquiglia 144 (☎0743.46.703, ✉hertzspoleto@tin.it), which can

also provide a driver or rent a scooter.

Exchange At the post office, or the banks at the northern end of Via Mazzini.

Markets On Friday, stalls set up in Piazza Garibaldi-Via Cacciatori delle Alpi and Piazza del Mercato, though the latter has a handful of fruit and vegetable stalls most days of the week.

Post office Piazza della Libertà 12 (Mon–Fri 8am–6.30pm, Sat 8am–12.30pm).

The Valnerina

The **Valnerina** is a valley that curves in a broad arc through the east of Umbria, rising in the mountains of the Sibillini and then following a southwesterly course through scenery with a stark, wild beauty which is all the more dramatic after the pastoral hill country to the west. Desolate and sparsely populated these days, the "little valley of the Nera" was once the hub of communications between the kingdom of Naples and the dukedom of Spoleto, and later a bone of contention between the Church and the Holy Roman Empire – which explains its liberal sprinkling of fortified villages. Today, it constitutes a self-contained area of high mountains, steep wooded valleys, lonely hamlets and vast stretches of upland wilderness. Deserted farms bear witness to a century of continuous emigration, and wolves still roam the summit ridges, half-heartedly protected by a Parco Regionale. Few parts of Tuscany or Umbria are so genuine a "forgotten corner".

There is no easy way of visiting the valley's highlights in a straightforward manner. The best approach is from Spoleto, either on the winding scenic road over the mountains that meets the valley just below Vallo di Nera or via the fast tunnel which emerges close to Sant'Anatolia di Narco. You should first head south from either point to see the **Lower Valnerina** and visit the region's main highlight, the abbey of **San Pietro in Valle**. Beyond this the valley loses most of its appeal, becoming more scrappy and built-up in the run past Ferentillo and Arrone towards Terni. A route following the Nera all the way to Terni only makes sense if you are making for Narni, Orte and the road to Rome or the north.

From San Pietro in Valle you should therefore double back and head north – no hardship, as the scenery is delightful – picking one of three options: the slow but very scenic mountain road from Sant'Anatolia di Narco to Monteleone (and then on to Norcia via Cascia and the SS320); the direct but still striking SS396 road to Norcia from just south of Triponzo; or exploring the **Upper Valnerina**, following the SS209 valley road before diverting south towards Norcia via Preci and another fine abbey, **Sant'Eutizio**, and the pretty Val Castoriana (also easily explored using Norcia as a base).

Access to the heart of the region can be very tricky without your own transport, but there are several **bus** services daily from Spoleto east to Norcia on the quickest SS396 route, stopping at most villages along the way. In many cases you'll find a bus waiting at key junctions such as that below **Sant'Anatolia di Narco** to connect with more remote villages to the south and east.

The Lower Valnerina

East of Spoleto, the beautiful and tortuous SS395 road towards Norcia climbs and then – amidst tremendous views – drops to meet the main SS209 running along the floor of the Valnerina at the junction at the hamlet of **Piedipaterno**. This twenty-kilometre route is slow, however, so if you want to have more time to explore the valley, take the tunnel which emerges close to Sant'Anatolia di Narco to the south (see below).

About 1km south of Piedipaterno lies a turnoff left to the village of **VALLO DI NERA**, a self-contained medieval ensemble perched on a hill, the type of fortified village you'll see all the way up and down the valley. In the church of **Santa Maria** in the lower part of the village (the house at no. 4 has the key if the building is shut) are minor but beautiful fourteenth-century apse frescoes. Later, but no less arresting frescoes (1536) adorn the church of **San Giovanni Battista** at the top of the village (try the priest's house next door for access if the church is shut). They're the work of the Sicilian artist Jacopo Santori (or Siculo), who also frescoed one of the Eroli chapels in Spoleto's Duomo (see p.656).

Sant'Anatolia di Narco

Around 2km south on the main road you pass **CASTEL SAN FELICE**, another picture-perfect fortified village, and a couple of kilometres farther arrive at a turnoff to the less alluring **SANT'ANATOLIA DI NARCO**, continually inhabited since the eighth century BC. Take the turn left just before the village (visible on the hill above) at the noisy roadside **bar** and **hotel** *Tre Valli* (☎0743.613.118; ❶), cross the river and look for the small yellow sign 100m or so beyond on the left directing you to the little twelfth-century church of **San Felice**. Its facade bears only the bare essentials – arched doorway, rose window and two pairs of narrow windows. Lumpen red and white marble slabs floor the lovely interior, which is distinguished by a raised sanctuary, an ancient sarcophagus in the crypt, and fifteenth-century frescoes of Christ (in the apse) and the *Adoration of the Magi* (on the left wall of the nave).

From Sant'Anatolia to Monteleone

From Sant'Anatolia a sensational minor road strikes southeast to Monteleone di Spoleto, offering great **views** and cutting across the main mountain ridge. You pass the somnolent little hamlets of **CASO** and **GAVELLI** (1127m), both looking across a vast tree-covered gorge whose scale and appearance are more akin to South America than central Italy. Around 1km past Caso look out on the left for the little bell-tower of **Santa Cristina** (signed), a Romanesque church with a scattering of frescoes. The church of **San Michele** in Gavelli is even better, and one of the extraordinary and unexpected artistic gems so common in Umbria. The entire interior is covered in sixteenth-century frescoes by Lo Spagna, recently restored with the aid of UK-based walking company, ATG-Oxford. If the door is locked, knock at the first house on the left as you climb the lane past the church.

Off-road **walks** from higher up to nearby summits are straightforward, the best target being **Monte Coscerno** (1685m) – the peak on your left as you drive up – reputedly home to at least two pairs of golden eagles. To pick up the track drive about 1km past Gavelli, looking out for a yellow-signed lane back to Gavelli on the right. Opposite this, on the left, a stony track kicks off obliquely uphill. Simply follow this clear, broad path-cum-gravel road gently up, looking out for the one single diversion – an obvious left turn at the pass after about 45 minutes, which will take you on to the breezy open ridge to the **summit**. Continue right for a few metres on the track that starts downwards to get staggering **views** as far as Monte Vettore and the Sibillini.

Scheggino

About 3km south of Sant'Anatolia, and again laid out below a castle, **SCHEG-GINO** is one of the more appealing spots in the region. Much of its charm derives from a couple of canals below the tiny and much-tidied medieval streets. A further fine incentive for stopping, especially at lunch, is an excellent **hotel-restaurant**, *Albergo-Trattoria del Ponte*, Via di Borgo 17 (☎075.61.253, ℱ0743.61.131; ❷; restaurant closed Mon & early Sept). There are twelve modern two-star rooms, cool, quiet and attractive, and a four-room annexe at Via Roma 6. Make a point of sampling the local speciality, trout and truffles, the former plucked from the ice-clear river, the latter harvested by the local Urbani family, top operators in the Italian truffle world (their factory is the yellow building on the left about 1km north of the village). Also check out the fabulous *gelateria*, part of the hotel bar. The only **campsite** for miles around is the *Valnerina* at nearby Valcasana (☎0743.61.115; June–Sept), reached by taking the road east for 1km past the trout farm just outside Scheggino. Halfway there on the left is a great outdoor public swimming pool (late June to Aug).

Abbazia di San Pietro in Valle

From Scheggino, the SS209 continues south 8km to an easily missed turning on the right immediately before the hamlet of Colleponte, signed to the **Abbazia di San Pietro in Valle** (daily 10am–noon & 2–5pm; free; if it's closed ring at the custodian's house, signed on the left midway up the two-kilometre approach road). Set high on the hillside near a thickly wooded cleft, this is one of central Italy's finest abbeys and one of Umbria's few memorials to the Lombards' dukedom of Spoleto. At the time of writing considerable restoration work was under way: more ominously, the abbey buildings, which have been in private hands since 1860 (the abbey church is a state-owned national monument) have been part-converted into a hotel, a development that can only be to the long-term detriment of this perfect medieval ensemble.

In **Roman** times there was probably a pagan temple on the site, later replaced by a series of small hermitic communities. Meanwhile, in Spoleto, the sixth Lombard Duke of Spoleto, **Faroaldo II**, who reigned between 703 and 720, experienced a vision in which St Peter told him to found a monastery in his honour at a place in which he would discover a lone and disconsolate monk. While hunting some time later he came across a recently bereaved monk, and so duly founded an abbey, but also abdicated his throne in favour of the monastic life. At his death eight years later he was buried in the abbey, his tomb a magnificent Roman **sarcophagus** which survives to this day to the right of the high altar. The abbey became a mausoleum for many of the Spoletan Lombard dukes, the last to be buried here being Franco Vinigisio, who abdicated in 822.

The abbey was sacked by a **Saracen** raiding party in 881 and restored in 991, when a series of fortresses were built to lend it added protection. One of these, **Umbriano**, can still be seen on the opposite side of the valley; fanciful legend has it that it was the first settlement ever founded in Umbria. Thereafter the abbey became one of the most powerful religious houses in the region, controlling vast tracts of land and dominating the lives of thousands of people. In 1234 it passed from the Benedictines to the **Cistercians**, but by 1300 had become so corrupt that Boniface VIII was forced to transfer responsibility for its operation to Rome. In 1484 Innocent VIII sold its land and feudal rights to Franceschetto Cybo and his descendants, who took the title of Count of Ferentillo: it remained in their domain until 1730, passing through other minor aristocratic hands until 1860, when the church was appropriated by the newly formed Italian state and the buildings sold to the local Costanzi family, still the current owners.

The abbey ⚲**hotel** (☎0744.780.129, ⓦwww.sanpietroinvalle.it; ⑤) is a lovely place to stay, even if you can't help but feel its presence has taken something from this glorious spot. You can also stay in **SAMBUCHETO**, the hamlet at the foot of the approach road, where the nine-room *Ninfa del Nera* sits on the busy main road, Via del Monastero 3 (☎0744.780.172; ①); it also has a **restaurant**, though you'd be better advised to aim for the *Del Ponte* in nearby Scheggino (see p.666).

The church

The highlight of the complex is the **church**, much of which survives from two separate periods of building – the eighth and twelfth centuries, the earlier date probably having yielded the transept, the three apses and parts of the rough mosaic pavement behind the main altar.

As you enter via the main rear door there is a small conical **stone altar** on your right, a pagan altar dating back to the first century BC. On the left is a series of medieval and Roman fragments from the earliest buildings on the site. The rear wall has two accomplished sixteenth-century **frescoes**, *The Madonna of Loreto* and *The Madonna and Child with St Sebastian*. Out of the door immediately off the right side of the church is a faultless two-tiered **cloister**, usually decked out with a profusion of flower-filled pots; the custodian should open the door for you to see two exquisite ninth-century statues of saints Peter and Paul, flanking the portal. Moving down the church you cross a **stone division** set into the floor, flanked by two small pillars: this marked the point beyond which those who had not been baptized were forbidden to progress.

Up above, covering most of the side walls, are two breathtaking, if badly faded, **fresco cycles**. Painted in 1190, they are considered some of the most important paintings of their period in Italy, being amongst the first attempts to move away from the stylized influence of Byzantine painting; the artist is unknown. Most of these precocious pictures are biblical scenes, showing a startling sense of invention and composition, full of narrative detail and attempts at light and shade unique for their time. Those on the left-hand wall are from the Old Testament, those on the right from the New.

The **Old Testament** scenes are better preserved, and are worth studying. They are arranged in three tiers, and progress left to right from the top tier down. The **first tier** comprises the *Creation of the World, Creation of Adam, Creation of Eve* (who is shown emerging from Adam's rib, with the four Rivers of Paradise – looking like fish – at Adam's side), *Adam Naming the Animals, Original*

Sin, *God's Warning*, and *The Expulsion from Paradise*. The **second tier** comprises the *Sacrifice of Cain and Abel, Cain Slaying Abel, God's Warning to Noah, The Construction of the Ark, Noah Giving Thanks to God, Abraham and the Three Angels, The Sacrifice of Isaac*, and *Isaac and Jacob*. Only one fresco survives of the lowest tier, its theme unclear.

The **New Testament** scenes on the opposite wall depict, in the badly faded **upper tier**, angels and Old Testament characters. The **second tier** has seven better-preserved panels, from left to right *The Shepherds being told of Christ's Birth, Journey of the Magi, Epiphany, Departure of the Magi, Massacre of the Innocents, Baptism of Christ*, and the *Wedding at Cana*. The **lowest tier** has four panels that can be clearly made out: *Christ's Entry into Jerusalem, The Last Supper, The Washing of the Feet*, and *Calvary*.

The church's magnificently preserved **altar** is a still more significant artefact, being one of only a tiny handful of dated works of art anywhere in Italy of Lombard vintage – its age is obvious even from a cursory glance at the almost Celtic figures and motifs that decorate its two main faces. It was carved by Ursus, the left of the two crude figures depicted in the lower front section (his signature is still clearly visible): the other figure is Ilderico, Duke of Spoleto between 739 and 742, who commissioned the piece.

To each side are well-preserved Roman **sarcophagi**, the right-hand specimen – Faroaldo's tomb – especially appealing, backed by some of the gloriously coloured Giottesque frescoes (c.1320) that dot much of the apse and shallow transepts.

In the **left transept**, look for the tiny fresco on the side wall depicting Faroaldo's vision of St Peter: the duke is shown lying in a canopied bed while his companions play dice to the right. The capitals in the apse are probably from the original Roman building on the site, likely crowning fluted columns that are now concealed under the plasterwork of subsequent centuries. Three other carved sarcophagi lie elsewhere in the church, along with odd stone fragments around the walls, including a bas-relief of a monk, brought from Syria by refugee Christians in the seventh century.

On your way out of the abbey (the route currently lies around the back of the church rather than through the cloister) take a look at the twelfth-century **campanile**, similar to the Lombard-influenced towers common in Rome and Lazio, and distinguished by fragments and reliefs salvaged from the eighth-century church.

The Upper Valnerina

In the **Upper Valnerina** north of Piedipaterno is **TRIPONZO** ("Three Bridges"), an ancient hamlet whose prominent marking on the map belies its size – just a shop and a couple of houses. Nonetheless, it was mentioned by Virgil, who talked of the Nera's creamy waters, an allusion to the sulphurous springs that feed into the river here. Just before Triponzo, the SS396 heads off through a tunnel into the deep **Corno valley** on the way to Norcia, the scenery becoming increasingly wild amid steep mountains cut by tempting deserted side valleys. On this road, there are **hotels** at the hamlet of **BISELLI** – the three-star *Dei Cacciatori* (℡0743.822.347, ℱ0743.822.237; closed for periods in Dec & Jan; ❷) – and 2km farther on at the larger village of **SERRAVALLE**, the good two-star *Italia* (℡ & ℱ0743.822.320; ❶).

Preci

In the Nera valley, 12km north of Triponzo lies the fortified village of **PRECI**, a likeable place, despite some terrible damage in the 1997 earthquake. Aim to

The surgeons of Preci

Preci was once famous for its thirty families of surgeons, who from the twelfth to the mid-eighteenth century handed down their medical knowledge and hearsay from generation to generation. Over the years their patients included such luminaries as Pope Sixtus V, Sultan Mehmed the Conqueror and Elizabeth I of England. Their most notorious sideline was the castration of young boys foolish enough to show operatic potential, a spin-off that developed from the technique of using castration to prevent death from hernia – an area of expertise that the Preci surgeons picked up from their work on pigs. The methods employed were entirely empirical: if something didn't work and the patient died, another approach was tried the next time. Their only classroom was the operating table, more often than not the patient's kitchen table. Crude anaesthetic – a jug of rum or strong wine – would be administered, with boiling vinegar used as a post-operative antiseptic. Though some of Preci's surgeons gained a reputation for their skill in extracting kidney stones, most of the doctors were quacks, and when the papacy introduced more stringent licensing of medical practitioners the end of the tradition was swift: not one of Preci's sawbones was granted a licence.

arrive in time for lunch at the first-rate *Il Castoro*, an inexpensive **restaurant-pizzeria** in Via Roma (☏0743.939.248; closed Thurs in winter, and a period in Nov). The **hotel** *Agli Scacchi* (☏0743.99.221, ⓦ www.hotelagliscacchi .com; ❷) has a pool but occasionally unreliable plumbing. Nearby at the hamlet of **CASTELVECCHIO** is a beautifully sited and top-grade rural **hotel** and **campsite**, *Collaccio* (☏0743.939.084, ⓦ www.ilcollaccio.com; ❷), with a friendly, English-speaking owner, pool and riding, cycling, tennis and hanggliding. There are wooden chalets for rent that sleep four to six people (€490 weekly in summer) and a farmhouse with hotel rooms (❷), as well as a cheap **restaurant** serving huge portions.

From Preci, the most direct route to Norcia continues up the valley past Piedivalle to the Forca d'Ancarano pass (see below). A longer alternative runs north through Visso (in the Marche), then onwards by the desolate and stunning road over the Passo di Gualdo (1496m) and through Castelluccio (see p.677).

Abbazia di Sant'Eutizio

Some 2km south of Preci, signposted off the Norcia road at Piedivalle, is the rambling monastic complex of **Abbazia di Sant'Eutizio** (irregular opening hours, but generally daily 10am–noon & 3–5pm; free). It was one of the cradles of the **Benedictine** movement, which helped preserve much of Western learning though the depredations of the Dark Ages. Initially the site of a Roman building, then a cemetery for hermits who had lived in the hills, it became a community that eventually controlled over a hundred churches and local castles, its domain extending as far as the Adriatic. After years of neglect and near-ruin it has been extensively restored, thanks largely to the efforts of a single monk based in Norcia. The effect is perhaps a little too polished and tidy, but there's no denying the beauty and tranquillity of the place, nor its seminal place in the history of the Benedictines.

Its Romanesque **church**, built in 1190, has a fourteenth-century apse and gallery and, inside, a *Crucifixion* by Nicola da Siena (1461) above the high altar. The altar houses the sepulchre of St Eutizio, one of the early hermits, who was known for his missionary zeal and for his ability to induce rain; when there's a drought, locals still parade his tunic round the fields. Crawling through the specially constructed tunnel below the altar is supposed to guarantee relief from all manner of back ailments. Down in the **crypt** are a couple of vast sandstone columns, perhaps remnants of the original Roman building on the site. Steps behind the abbey church, to the right of the fountain, lead to the **caves** of the earliest monks; according to Gregory the Great, it was in these grottoes that Benedict – in conversation with Eutizio and a fellow hermit, Spes – discovered his religious vocation.

From Campi to Norcia

The road south from the Abbazia di Sant'Eutizio runs for 15km through delightful and pastoral country, the Castoriana and Nida valleys, which once made up one of the most important north-to-south trading routes in this part of the Apennines. It passes little medieval hamlets such as Piedivalle and **CAMPI**. Just before the latter is the church of **San Salvatore**, a double-fronted Romanesque beauty gleaming from restoration work necessitated by the 1979 earthquake that ravaged the Valnerina (the fault line runs along this valley, more or less in front of the church). It's rarely open, but the interior is smothered with frescoes by Giovanni and Antonio Sparapane, a fifteenth-century dynasty of painters active around Spoleto and the Valnerina.

Above is the village of **CAMPI VECCHI**, arched across the wooded hillside to the north; to reach it drive through Campi and keep your eyes open for the yellow sign directing you to **Sant'Andrea**, the church clearly visible at the side of the village, its portico framing one of the loveliest views in the area. The key to the church is kept by a woman in the village – with your back to the building, walk down the steps and take the lane right in the little piazza: the house is about four down on the right. The custodian may also regale you with stories of the cholera pit beneath the church and the evil princess buried under the inverted Roman inscription on the facade, as well as show you the beautifully kept interior; leave a generous tip. She also holds the key to the chapel of **Santa Maria di Piazza**, in the same little street as her house, about 50m down on the right but so broken and well disguised you could walk past it. The vaults are covered in several superbly well-preserved and accomplished frescoes on the *Life of the Virgin*, the work of the Sparapane. Other areas of frescoes have been revealed on the whitewashed walls, but there's no money at present to pay for their restoration.

Across the valley, **ABETO** and **TODIANO** villages appear invitingly over the woods and hilly ridges – but, though they were once stuffed with paintings and other works of art (now in Spoleto's Museo Diocesano), they've become weirdly and almost completely deserted. Continuing on the road to Norcia, 4km south of Piedivalle beyond Sant'Angelo, you climb to 1008m at **Forca d'Ancarano**, a pass which affords spectacular views over surrounding mountains before the precipitous drop down to Norcia.

Norcia

Noted on the one hand as the birthplace of St Benedict – founder of Western monasticism – and on the other as one of Italy's great culinary capitals, **NORCIA** is small, walled and stolid, the only place of substance in eastern Umbria. Its air of faint desolation and low, sturdy houses are a world away from the bucolic towns to the west, a contrast explained by the constant threat of earthquakes. Thick-walled and heavily buttressed, Norcia's buildings have been

△A shop in Norcia selling truffles and other local produce

compulsorily stunted since 1859, when a law forbade the raising of houses over 12.5m high. The last tremor, a particularly violent one, was in 1979; outside town you'll see ranks of temporary housing, ready for the next big one. At the same time Norcia is a prosperous and likeable place, the sort of town where everything works and everybody knows everyone else. Its streets are relieved by glimpses of the mountains, views of which unfold unexpectedly at many corners. The town can serve as the base for some good trips into the **Monti Sibillini** and **Piano Grande** (see p.677) and north to the Castoriana valley and abbey of **Sant'Eutizio**. A new road through the mountains into the Marche (emerging just above Arquarta del Tronto) also looks set to open up the area.

Norcia has been inhabited since prehistoric times, thanks to its abundant springs, fine agricultural land and a vital position commanding one of the lowest east-to-west routes across the Apennines. Ancient Norcia was the northernmost town of the **Sabines**, contemporaries of the Umbrians, before becoming Nursia, a minor Roman *municipio* (290 BC). After the attentions of sixth-century barbarians, recovery took a long time to come – and when it did, **earthquakes** periodically discouraged long-term development. For five centuries before Italian Unification, though, the town was effectively a frontier post between the Papal States and the kingdom of Naples, making it a safe haven for bandits and refugees from opposing sides. Papal reaction was to build the **Castellina** in 1554, a huge, blunt fortress that dominates the town centre. Thereafter Norcia and the surrounding countryside was drained by emigration, a trend that continues today, but whose effects have been tempered by the success of its small food-processing concerns.

Arrival, information and accommodation

Norcia is well served by **buses** from Spoleto, Terni, Perugia, Foligno and Assisi; they drop off at the Porta Romana, from where it's a straight walk on Corso Sertorio to the central **Piazza San Benedetto**. There's no tourist office; the offices of the *Vigili Urbani*, located under the arches of the Palazzo Comunale, often

Though disconcertingly turd-like in appearance, weight for weight **truffles** are one of the world's costliest foodstuffs – only saffron costs more. Norcia is one of Italy's truffle capitals, home to the fabled black truffle – *Tuber melanosporum* – pursued with a great deal more fanfare in France. (Italy's other mushrooming heartland is the countryside around Alba, nestled in the Piedmontese hills, but there the prize is the *Tuber magnatum*, the white truffle.)

Truffles have been known, if not understood, since ancient times. The first written record dates from the 5th century BC. They were enjoyed by the Babylonians, the Greeks and the Romans, who consumed them as much for their reputed aphrodisiac qualities as their gastronomic allure. Plutarch believed they were mud cooked by lightning; Juvenal that they were the product of thunder and rain. Pliny, bewildered by their origins, considered them Nature's greatest miracle. In the Middle Ages they were considered a manifestation of the Devil. And no wonder, for here was a plant apparently without root, branch, or stem; without leaf, fruit or flower; lacking, in fact, all visible means of growth.

Truffles are actually subterranean fungi of the class *Ascomycetes*, part of the *Tuber* genus, a species which over the course of 100 million years has disappeared underground, probably as part of an evolutionary defence against the weather. Their underground existence precludes photosynthesis, meaning they rely for nutrients on a symbiotic relationship with the roots of certain trees, most commonly the oak, hazel, beech and lime. Unlike a normal mushroom, their spores are spread not by the wind, but by truffle-eating animals such as rodents, deer, slugs and wild boar – and to ensure they're snuffled up, they need to advertise their presence.

And this is where the truffle's famous perfume – and dogs and pigs – come in. The fungi mature slowly, often over the course of several months, attaining their final dimensions – anything from the size of a pea to the size of a football – over a few days during the spring. Only when ripe – from about November onwards – do they give off their distinctive perfume, and only then for about ten days, thus ensuring they're snaffled up only when laden with viable spores. Thereafter they become poisonous and rot.

Pigs and truffles once went together, pigs being foremost among the sleuths inclined to nose them out (goats, foxes, ferrets and – in Russia – even bear cubs are used). Pigs love truffles – at least female ones do – for among the volatile compounds exuded by the truffle is one that resembles the musky pheromones of the wild boar. This is all well and good, but not only are sows huge and difficult to manage, they're also prone to attacks of sexual frenzy when close to a truffle. Dogs are therefore now preferred, and can be worth anything up to £2500 when trained.

There are countless **types of truffle**. Nine are edible, though only six are well known and commercialized. Four are considered a delicacy, and of these two are found in quantity around Norcia and Spoleto. Varieties mature at different depths and at different times of the year, so that April and May are the only times of the year when fresh truffles are not available. Umbria's most common type is the **tartufo**

have **maps** and information on the town, while in the southeast corner of Piazza San Benedetto and just outside the Porta Ascolana are *tabacchi* that sell **walking maps** and **guides** – handy if you're going on into the Sibillini. The hotel bar in Castelluccio (see p.677) also usually has copies. There is a park office for the Sibillini national park at Via Solferino 22 (June–Sept daily 9.30am–12.30pm & 3.30–6.30pm; rest of the year mornings only; ℡0743.817.090; ⓦ www.sibillini .net), which offers plenty of information on both the town and the mountains.

First **accommodation** choice on a budget is the *Casa Religiosa San Bene-detto*, Via delle Vergini 13 (℡0743.828.208; ❶); all 35 rooms have bathrooms,

nero, gathered from a few centimetres below the ground [...] and mid-March. More prized is the **tartufo pregiato**, avai[...] Rarer are the two summer and autumn **scorzone** variet[...]

But why all the fuss? The fungi's perfume has been [...] ripe cheese, garlic, methane and armpits. But for e[...] truffle's unique and subtle flavour. Elizabeth David, [...] *Food*, called them the "most delicious of all foods any[...] famous nineteenth-century French gastronome, stated that [...] can be no truly gastronomic meal".

The truffle's mystery, its seemingly spontaneous appearance and [...] tence, is also important. So, too, is the rarity and thrill of the hunt – it's [...] gourmet food, indeed one of the only foods of any description, that can't be gr[...] to order. The truffle is gloriously unpredictable, a fact that has made commercial cultivation something of an agricultural Holy Grail. One tree will yield truffles while its apparently identical neighbour will not – and nobody knows why.

Money also plays its part. Many a *cavatore*, or truffle-hunter, sells either directly to a restaurant, or, more likely than not, to an agent working for Signor Urbani, king of the truffle world, whose small company, based in Scheggino (see p.666), a village a few kilometres from Norcia, controls 65 percent of the world's truffle trade. Truffles, after all, are big business: a kilo of white Alban truffles could be yours for around £1990; an equivalent quantity of Beluga caviar costs around £1750. Black truffles, of the type found in France and Umbria, retail at around £300 a kilo. So valuable are the finds that it's not unusual for people to hunt at night equipped with a torch and trowel, searching a spot where dogs have sniffed out their prey earlier in the day.

Every aspect of truffle exploitation is **controlled by law**, from hunting and final sale to the ownership of land rights and the precise definition of varieties, but in practice most people moonlight (literally), with only those working for large producers being obliged to obey the bureaucratic niceties. Old-timers say this free-for-all, a relatively recent phenomenon, is ruining the business as newcomers ravage old beds for short-term gain, thereby destroying yields not only for a season, but for years to come.

You'll find shops all over Norcia selling truffle paste, truffles under oil (to preserve them), and truffle-flavoured oils, cheeses, liqueurs, pâtés – even truffle chocolate. For the real thing, however, head for the *Grotta Azzurra*'s tremendous restaurant, a temple to Umbrian cuisine (see p.50).

If you enjoy truffles you'll be in exalted company – Louis XVIII, Napoleon, Churchill and Rita Hayworth were all passionate devotees of the mysterious tuber. So, too, however, was the unfortunate Duke of Clarence. In 1368, so the story goes, the hapless duke, approaching his wedding night and a frisky Italian wife with some trepidation, so gorged on white truffles – anxious to enlist their aphrodisiac support – that he collapsed and died before he could test their amatory powers. Where the truffle is concerned, therefore, the watchwords are eater beware.

and there are good half- and full-board deals available. Or there is a **hostel**, the *Ostello Norcia*, Via Ufente 1b (☎0743.817.487 or 0349.300.2091; ⓦwww .montepatino.com; beds €15), sleeping 52 people in two- four-, five- and ten-bed rooms. The eight rooms of the one-star *Da Benito*, Via Marconi 5 (☎0743.816.670, ⓦwww.hotelbenito.it; ❶), are adequate and central, but if you can afford the extra get a room at the livelier *Grotta Azzurra*, Via Alfieri 12 (☎0743.816.513, ⓦwww.bianconi.com; ❹), the best, busiest and friendliest hotel in town. Under the same management is the *Salicone* (☎0743.828.076, ⓦwww.bianconi.com; ❻), just outside the walls at Porta Romana, a very smart

NORCIA

Porta
San Giovanni

Sant'Antonio

Porta
Romana

San Giovanni

Tempietto

Police

Oratorio di Sant'
Agostinuccio

Porta
Santa
Lucia

Porta
Palatina

Sant'
Agostino

PIAZZA
GARIBALDI

PIAZZA
V. VENETO

San
Francesco

Palazzo
Comunale

Porta
Orientale

Castellina
(Museo
Civico)

PIAZZA
SAN
BENEDETTO

San
Benedetto

Porta
Ascolana

Duomo

Porta
del Colle

ACCOMMODATION

Casa Religiosa	
San Benedetto	**B**
Da Benito	**D**
Grotta Azzurra	**E**
Ostello Norcia	**C**
Salicone	**A**

| 0 | 100 m |

RESTAURANTS

Bar Vignola	**3**
Taverna de' Massari	**1**
Trattoria del Francese	**2**

Stadio

Hospital

▼ Castelluccio & Piano Grande

three-star hotel with some of the best sports facilities in central Italy: all sorts of leading soccer, volleyball, basketball and other sports teams from across Europe have come to train here. You'll also spot three or four modern hotels outside the Porta Romana. A short walk out of town to the east offers scope for freelance **camping**.

The Town

The main **Piazza San Benedetto** is a large, open area with something of a *High Noon* atmosphere in mid-afternoon, but at other times is the lively focus of the town's comings and goings. It's presided over by a statue of a suitably severe and disapproving Benedict, erected in 1880 on the 1400th anniversary of his birth and these days liberally adorned with football flags, hats and scarves after victories by the *Azzurri* (the Italian national team) or Milan or Juve. In earlier centuries the square was the site of a bullring and a place of execution for witches, traitors, adulterers and necromancers.

San Benedetto

The piazza's most arresting sight is the church of **San Benedetto**, built, according to legend, over the house where Benedict and his sister, St Scholastica, were born; it's more likely to have been the site of a Roman temple, as the square itself was the site of the forum. Despite repeated post-earthquake reconstructions, the facade – sole survivor from the 1389 original – remains an attractive, two-tiered affair, its design typical of several churches in the region (notably San

Francesco and Sant'Agostino in Norcia itself). It features a lovely Gothic portal, rose window, niche statues of Benedict and Scholastica and a fourteenth-century campanile to the rear. During Norcia's blast-furnace summers the newer arched gallery (1570) to the right provides welcome shade, and it has a drinking fountain too. Notice also the unusual old stone measures, used for selling or distributing wine and olive oil when the gallery was used as a market.

On the left as you enter the church is a good restored niche **fresco** – possibly the work of Francesco Sparapane, one of a dynasty of local fifteenth-century painters – of *SS Barbara and Michael*, with a *Madonna and Child* above. The only other worthwhile painting is Filippo Napoletano's *St Benedict and Totila* (1621), located in the left arm of the left transept. Down in the **crypt**, excavated as recently as 1910, the little apse at the head of the left aisle is traditionally held to be the place where Benedict and Scholastica were born. It's half-covered in faded frescoes depicting the *Annunciation, Nativity* and other scenes. Stone fragments of a late Roman edifice are visible closed off nearby, making this by far the most evocative part of the church.

La Castellina

Across the square from San Benedetto is the unmissable **Castellina**, an extraordinarily gaunt fortress with no concessions to architectural subtlety. The superb granite lions outside came originally from the crypt of San Benedetto. It was built on the site of a Benedictine priory and Norcia's old parish church for Pope Julius III by the usually sophisticated Vignola and now houses the town's **Museo Civico**. The whole complex was shut for decades until 1996, when superb restoration work on the castle and its interior was completed. Regular hours have proved hard to establish (currently it should be open May–Sept Tues–Sun 10–1pm & 4–7.30pm plus unspecified winter hours; @www.artenorcia.net); if it's open, both the building and the handful of top-quality exhibits are well worth the admission (€4). Most of the rooms, which look down prettily onto the square, are taken up with **sculptures**, the highlights being a rare thirteenth-century *Deposition* – five figures in all – a *St Sebastian* (minus arrows) and a poignant life-size glazed terracotta *Madonna* by Andrea della Robbia. Among the **paintings** look out for a bizarre *Risen Christ* (1460) by Nicola da Siena, in which a near-naked but curiously sexless Christ is shown stepping forcefully from his marble sepulchre. There is also a lovely picture attached to a casket lid of Benedict and Scholastica, the former shown holding a painted church, as well as a beautifully restored *Madonna and Child with Saints* by Giacomo di Giovannofrio, the Virgin sitting atop a gloriously decorated throne beneath a coffered Renaissance vault.

The Duomo and the Palazzo Comunale

Almost beside the Castellina is the largely uninteresting sixteenth-century **Duomo**, its less-than-dominating position a result of comparative modernity, its forlorn interior the legacy of countless earthquakes. It does have one outstanding work, however, the Cappella della Madonna della Misericordia, located at the end of the north aisle and consisting of an ornate altar (1640–41) of inlaid marble whose appearance, so at odds with central Italian work of the period, has led experts to attribute it to Francesco Duquesnoy, a noted sculptor in the employ of the Neapolitan court. At the heart of the altar is an early sixteenth-century painting, probably by Francesco Sparapane, the *Madonna and Child with SS Benedict and Scholastica*. Benedict is shown pointing to a painted miniature of Norcia, whose prominent Gothic campanile no longer exists, having collapsed in the eighteenth century.

Completing Piazza San Benedetto's ensemble is the now superbly restored **Palazzo Comunale**, oddly but beautifully multicoloured, and based around a 1492 portico and later additions which blend delightfully to create the town's most distinctive building.

The rest of the town

Northeast of Piazza San Benedetto is the **Tempietto**, or **Edicola** (literally "Kiosk"), one of the town's more unusual buildings. Built in 1354 by Vanni Tuzi, it's a small arched structure, decorated with bas-reliefs and open to the street on all sides. Its purpose is unknown, but it may have been commissioned in honour of San Felicianus, who evangelized Norcia, as a shrine to be used in Holy Week processions – hence the signs of the Passion which figure among its decoration; possibly it was used as a *contra pestum*, a votive offering against the plague (an epidemic ravaged much of Italy at the time that the work was built).

Beyond is a quarter of town that fell into disrepair during the Middle Ages and was taken over by shepherds from Castelluccio. Adopting it as their own, they built small houses – complete with stalls for their sheep – amidst a jumble of streets that contrasts with the central grid. Look out for the church of **Sant'Antonio Abate** – the shepherds' saint, invoked to protect their flocks – and the nearby **San Giovanni**, known for its wooden ceiling and magnificent Renaissance altar of the *Madonna della Palla*, located on the right wall; the arched and gilt marble surround frames a painting of the eponymous Madonna (1469), so-called because someone is supposed to have kicked a ball (*palla*) against the painting, causing the Virgin's expression to change miraculously at an act of such wanton sacrilege.

Food shops

Piazza San Benedetto's other main component is its **food shops**, no small consideration in a town renowned for its culinary delights. Anything that can be done to a pig, food-wise, the Norcians apparently do, and better than anyone else – which is why you'll see butchers in other parts of Italy called *Un Norcino*. Sausages, salami, hams and wild boar, reputedly the country's best, are all in abundance, as are less appetizing non-porcine delicacies such as mountain ram and sausage-filled sacs claiming to be mules' testicles. On this theme it's worth noting that Norcian butchers in the past had a notorious sideline, namely the castration of young boys, a skill passed down by the surgeons of Preci (see p.669) and honed by their work on similarly luckless pigs. A leg-crossing contemporary account survives which describes the procedure: [boy] would be "drugged with opium or some other narcotic, placed in a very hot bath, until he was in a state of virtual insensibility. Then the ducts leading to the testicles were severed, so that the latter in the course of time shrivelled and disappeared." The only castrato to make a recording, Domenico Mustafa, who died in 1912 having also been director of the Sistine Chapel choir, was a Norcian graduate.

Local mountain **cheeses** are excellent too – two years old and never in a fridge – and if finances permit you could indulge in the area's **black truffle**. The season runs from January to April, but all year you can sample the foul truffle *digestivo* called *Amaro di Tartufo*, truffle *grappa*, and even truffle chocolates. The Bar Vignola, with outside tables, between San Benedetto and the Castellina, is a good place to indulge in these or more standard refreshments. The shop to the left, one of the town's more pungent, offers a good selection of genuine products (don't be put off by the cheerful sales patter of the owner), as does Moscatelli, midway down Corso Sertorio on the left as you head towards the walls. Best of all, off the piazza and round the bend to the east behind San Benedetto, is the generations-old Ansuini, Via Anicia 105, surely one of the best food shops in this or any other Italian region.

The church of **Sant'Agostino**, located in Via Anicia, is half-filled with surprisingly accomplished and well-preserved frescoes, those on the entrance wall depicting, among other things, the grisly martyrdoms of several saints. Also make time for the tremendous wooden ceiling of the **Oratorio di Sant'Agostinuccio** just behind Piazza Palatina.

Eating and drinking

You'd be foolish not to try local specialities in Norcia's **restaurants**, the most lauded of which – in most Italian foodie guides – is the *Trattoria del Francese*, Via Riguardati 16 (℡0743.816.290; closed Fri), which in the event turns out to have a rather tatty trattoria atmosphere. You'd do far better to make for the medieval dining halls of the ⅄ *Grotta Azzurra*, Via Alfieri 12 (℡0743.816.513), complete with huge fire, suits of armour and tapestries, for probably one of the best meals you'll eat in Umbria – treat yourself to *risotto al tartufo* or *tagliolini al tartufo*, the latter the classic way to tackle a truffle, or, if finances allow, indulge in their award-winning marriage of truffle and steak, *Filetto del Cavatore* ("Fillet of the Truffle-Hunter"); Castelluccio lentils, mountain mushrooms, cheeses and hams are also to be sampled. For a change, try the *Taverna de' Massari*, Via Roma 13 (℡0743.816.218; closed Tues), or one of the more affordable *pizzerie* in the back streets (a couple are set into the walls just south of the Porta Ascolana).

The Piano Grande and the Monti Sibillini

The mountainous landscape east of Norcia is one of the most distinctive in all Italy, with its centrepiece the eerie **Piano Grande**, an upland prairie devoid of any feature save sheep, hang-gliders and the odd bedraggled haystack. Surrounded on all sides by the sheer and barren mountains of the **Monti Sibillini**, the Piano Grande forms a colossal amphitheatre that's often swathed in a dense, early morning mist. Gazing down on this wilderness from the remote hamlet of **Castelluccio**, it's easy to imagine the hazards for the unsuspecting traveller in past centuries. Papal rulers forbade crossing the plain during winter, and even today the bells of Castelluccio toll on gloomy days to guide shepherds across its desolation. The plain was a key set on Zeffirelli's glutinous Franciscan epic, *Brother Sun, Sister Moon*, and is also famous for being – reputedly – the world's largest football pitch, having hosted a match between two teams of a hundred players each; the home side went down by twelve goals to one.

Late spring to early summer is the best period to visit the *piano*, when it blazes with an extraordinary profusion of wild flowers. In about mid-May crocuses and narcisi bloom, giving way in early June to buttercups, wild tulips and fritillaries, followed by poppies and cornflowers in late June/early July. These are only approximate timings though, and can vary by up to two weeks. Woven into the floral carpet are rare Alpine flora, including the *Carex buxbaumi*, an Ice-Age relic discovered in 1971 and believed to be unique. On the mountains around can be found further rarities such as Apennine edelweiss (found elsewhere only in parts of the Abruzzo), the martagon lily, bear's grape, Apennine potentilla and the Alpine buckthorn – but you don't need to be an expert to enjoy the startling spectacle.

Castelluccio

An isolated farming village at 1452m, **CASTELLUCCIO** is one of Italy's highest continually inhabited settlements, and the only habitation for many

△ Castelluccio, with Monte Vettore behind

kilometres around. As well as its appeal as a belvedere onto the grasslands and a trailhead for **mountain walks**, the village attracts rabid attention from **hang-gliders**, drawn by the Sibillini's treeless slopes. There are likely to be several campervans parked in the windblown square. A couple of bars have smartened themselves up, as has the long-established hang-gliding school, signs of change that benefit the locals hardly at all – most of the hang-gliding jocks camp and spend little money locally.

The place has made few other concessions to tourism and the feel is of an uncompromising and bleak working village. The almost incestuously inter-related population has dropped from 700 in 1951 to around 150 today, most of whom are migrant shepherds, many of them Sardinians or former Yugoslavs, who spend the winter months down in Norcia. The most immediately noticeable thing in the village is its **graffiti**, daubed in thick white paint on huge walls; this forms a kind of social document for the community, the pieces – often malicious and some going back generations – recording stories and myths about local people. Wander up to the **parish church**, which has a marvellous fresco cycle on the left wall describing the life of St Anthony Abbot, patron saint of shepherds and their flocks. On the arch outside the church to the right as you look down to the Piano Grande is a Fascist plaque, of a type long ago removed from other, less remote towns and villages in Italy, which salutes the Duce, "refounder of the Italian Empire".

Practicalities
Castelluccio is served by two **buses** a week on Norcia's market day only – Thursday – currently departing Norcia's Porta Ascolana at 6.25am and 1.30pm; the return bus leaves Castelluccio at 2.20pm.

It's well worth booking **accommodation** in advance. There's only one hotel, the two-star *Sibilla* (℡0743.870.113; ❶; hotel closed in winter), an Alpine-looking building in the village centre with just eleven double rooms (ask for one with views over the Piano Grande – half of them look onto the scrappy car park piazza). The *Sibilla* has a **restaurant** which, though less appealingly rustic, serves up remarkably good food. Castelluccio's shops, such as they are, have only the most basic supplies, though fruit and bread vans visit regularly – except in winter, when the place is frequently cut off by snow. On the Norcia–Arquata road 8km south of Castelluccio, on the pass at the southern edge of the Piano Grande, is the smartly refurbished *Forca Canapine* (℡0743.823.005; ⓦwww.hotelcanapine.com; ❷), a huge pink building that is an excellent base for walks in all directions. Rooms are plain but clean, with what must be some of the smallest bathrooms in Italy.

Camping anywhere in the hills around is no problem; there's plenty of grassy flat ground a stone's throw from the village. Farther afield, be sure to take enough water, as the limestone hills have no surface source. For **hang-gliding** information contact the *Scuola di Volo* just north of the village. The bar of the *Sibilla* and *Bar del Capitano*, on the southern edge of the village with a great belvedere over the Piano Grande, can provide **walking information** and maps and books on the area.

Walking in the Sibillini

The **Monti Sibillini** are the only really wild mountains of Tuscany and Umbria, and the most precious natural environment for many hundreds of miles. The northernmost of the big Apennine massifs, they run north–south for about 40km, their summit ridge marking both the Umbrian border and the watershed between the Adriatic and Tyrrhenian seas. In **Monte Vettore** (2476m) they have the third-highest point on the peninsula, a massive, barren mountain that rises above the Piano Grande with majestic grandeur. The Sibillini have been designated a **national park**, a status that sadly exists more on paper than on the ground, with no binding laws to stop hunting or building.

According to local tradition, the mountains were home to one of the three ancient **sibyls** – the wise women with oracular powers who were supposed to have foretold the coming of Christ. Later misogynist versions of the sibyl myth transformed them into temptresses possessed by the Devil – those lured to the sibyls' caves were doomed to remain trapped there until the Day of Judgement – which perhaps explains why these mountains have a reputation for necromancy and Satanism. By happy coincidence the code for the *Kompass* map to the area is 666, the Devil's number.

Hiking in the Sibillini is superb, whether you fancy casual day hikes or more demanding backpack ventures. Unlike the Alps or Abruzzo there are few marked paths – these are not yet well-known mountains – and you're unlikely to meet many people other than shepherds. The Club Alpino Italiano (CAI) has discreetly tagged a few trails, with a view ultimately to creating a continuous path on the summit ridge.

The 1:50,000 *Kompass: Sibillini* **map** is adequate and widely available, though locally you should be able to pick up the better 1:25,000 *Montevettore* produced by *Universo* and the *Unione Italiana Sport Popolare*, or the similiar CAI map. **Paths** marked on maps do generally exist but in good weather the hills are so open (bar a few glorious beech woods) that you can wander pretty much at will, at least on the western, Umbrian side of the mountains. This is less true on the eastern flanks (in the Marche), which are dotted with dangerous crags and screes. However, around Castelluccio and the western ramparts the worst you'll have to contend with are some of the steepest grass slopes you'll ever come across. For enthusiasts or emergencies there are several **mountain huts** (marked on maps), none with services and often in a poor state.

The hikes

Castelluccio is the best base for **day hikes**, with trails leaving from the village in all directions. **Monte Vettore** via Forca di Presta (8km east of Castelluccio on the road to the Marche) is the obvious big target, returning along the ridge via Quarto San Lorenzo and Forca Viola. This is a pretty tough full day's outing, which you could take at a more leisurely pace by starting at the summer-only **refuge** at *Forca di Presta* (☎0743.99.278 or 0743.99.165; always call in advance). Sited at 1500m, the *rifugio* is a source of basic food, maps and information.

Another good walk from Forca di Presta or Castelluccio, mainly downhill through woods, takes you to **ARQUATA DEL TRONTO** in the Marche, a smallish place with two **hotels**, the better of which is *Ca' Martina* (☎0743.99.261; ❶), on a side road just north of the village, well placed for the paths on and off the hills. A third rewarding hike is to strike across country from Castelluccio to Norcia, a route comfortably accomplished in a day, though the route-finding here requires a little more diligence: paths to the ridge (around 1800m) are straightforward, but the drop from the ridge can be a bit of scramble if you miss the path. Trails lower down, which you'll easily pick up, are much better.

For a quick and easy glimpse of the scenery **north of Castelluccio** follow the *strada bianca* (gravel road), for about twenty minutes, past the *Scuola di Volo*, round the corner into the Valle Canatra and on to the Fonte Valle Canatra. It's an all-but-level stroll which you could prolong by following the obvious cart track to the head of the lovely pastoral valley and the open plains under Monte delle Rose (1881m). This is good camping territory. Another excellent, straightforward and not overly demanding walk is to leave Castelluccio on the upper *strada bianca* west and then follow the rough road and clear path along the ridges of the Piano Grande's western rim (Colle Tosto, Monte Vetica, and others), overnighting at *Forca Canapine* (see "Practicalities" above).

A more ambitious and longer hiking route is to cross over the ridge **east of Castelluccio** into the Marche, where the best-known walk runs to the

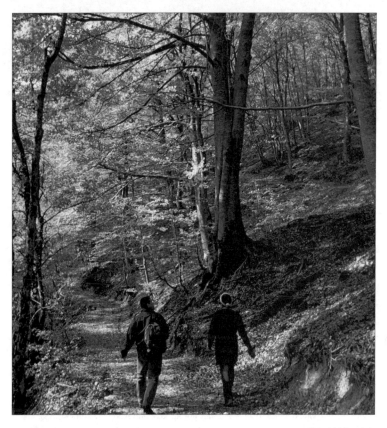

△ Gola del Infernaccio

Lago di Pilato, an idyllic spot under Monte Vettore. This is supposedly the burial place of Pontius Pilate, the story being that Pilate's body was dispatched from Rome on a cart pulled by two oxen, which traipsed through wild country and then plunged into the lake, disappearing without trace. The legend has made the lake the heart of the mountains' supposed necromantic practices; Norcians used to sacrifice animals here, and humans too, so it is said, to placate the demons and protect themselves from storms and bad weather. When the area was part of the Papal States a wall was built by the Church to prevent access to the lake, and stones inscribed with occult symbols have been found on the shores. In many recent summers the lake has all but dried up, putting in danger an endemic crustacean (*Chirocephalus marchesonii*), which used to stain the water red, a colouring anciently attributed to the blood of Pilate.

From Lago di Pilato, another superb trail runs under the main ridge along the Valle del Aso to the hamlet of **FOCE**: the combined trek from Castelluccio to the lake and then to Foce makes a perfect day's walk. The only problem is you'll have to haul yourself back over the mountains if you're returning to Castelluccio the next day, so this is a route for seasoned hikers. East of Foce, **MONTE-**

MONACO in the Marche makes another good Sibillini walking base. A nice medieval village in itself, it provides a starting point for walks up Monte Sibilla (2173m) and the spectacular yet easy hike in the **Gola del Infernaccio** (Hell's Canyon). This is a huge gorge complete with cliffs and crashing river, which opens out into a broader upland where an upper track takes you to the **Eremo di San Leonardo**.

Cascia and around

CASCIA, 18km south of Norcia, figures large on the map but is disappointing in actuality, only recommendable to pilgrims in search of **St Rita**. Her presence – and the stupendously ugly twentieth-century Basilica – dominates both the new and the earthquake-damaged hill-town, which was abandoned for a time in the eighteenth century. Little known elsewhere, Rita has a massive cult following in Italy, especially amongst women, for whom she is a semi-official patron saint. Thousands come annually to venerate her shrine.

Rita's Basilica in the old town is a monument to religious vulgarity probably without equal – a piece of Fascist architectural brutalism that attempts to place Byzantine and Romanesque elements in a modern context, and in doing so produces a fantasy in white marble that might sit more happily in Disneyland. Rita's exhumed and mummified body lies behind grilles on the left (northern) side of the basilica, surrounded in the half-gloom by flickering candles and votive offerings, whose appeals for the saint's salvaging of impossible situations include the pennants of several Italian football teams. The interior is smothered in extravagant stonework – all bearing the robust, strong-lined bludgeoning of

St Rita

St Rita experienced – and survived – the kind of hardships borne by women throughout history, which is the main reason for her appeal, and also why she's sometimes known as the "saint of the impossible". Born in 1381, a poor child of aged parents, she was forced to marry at 15 and endured eighteen years of mistreatment from an alcoholic husband. Having weaned himself from the bottle and repented his past, the husband died in a brawl a few weeks later. Rita's children, for the most part wretched wasters, both died attempting to avenge their father.

Beaten, widowed and childless, Rita sensibly thought it about time she became a nun. Her knowledge of the marital bed, however, made this impossible; only a relaxation of convent rules allowed her to become an Augustinian, a development held up as one of her "impossible" miracles. No sooner had she joined than she developed a sore in the middle of her forehead, an excrescence so foul-smelling that none of the nuns would come near her. This supposedly developed when a thorn fell from a crown of thorns as she was praying to a statue of Christ, and so was regarded by her companions as a kind of stigmata. The smell abated only once – to allow her to join her companions on a week's visit to Rome to meet the pope; on their return the odour returned as virulent as ever.

Rita died in 1457, but the process of her beatification was laborious, hampered by doubts as to the veracity of her miracles, by the fact that she was a woman (and one with a past), and doubtless by the size of her grassroots support, a groundswell the papacy feared beyond their control. The proclamation of her beatification finally came in 1628, and her elevation to sainthood as late as 1900, and then only in the wake of a huge public campaign.

Fascist masonry – and the vaulted ceiling and cupola glow with garish painting-by-numbers frescoes. The altar is surrounded by what appears to be gold barbed wire and is surmounted by a large golden egg. Visitors are taken in groups to Rita's original Augustinian monastery, now annexed to the building, for a view of the cell in which she died, a vine that grew from her walking stick and a rose – which Rita coaxed into life out of season – transplanted from her garden in Roccaporena (see below).

Cascia's other sights are few, and many are still under restoration following a catastrophic earthquake in 1979. **San Francesco** on the main Piazza Garibaldi, begun in 1425 but rebuilt almost completely in 1925, houses a fourteenth-century Gothic choir, a fresco of the *Madonna and Child* by a fifteenth-century Umbrian artist – on the west entrance wall – and more early local frescoes around the pulpit. Walk along the level main street from here and you come to **Santa Maria**, the town's oldest church (founded in 825), a large airy space, still with a medieval atmosphere of sorts, and the place where Rita was baptized (the font is at the top of the left nave in a special chapel left of the choir). On the west wall are frescoes of the *Deposition* by Nicola da Siena and *St Michael Weighing the Souls of Sinners and the Saved*. At the beginning of the right nave is a *Nativity* in which the Madonna seems to be sleeping on a large air-bed.

Continue past Santa Maria and through the gateway to the right; the road downhill soon brings you to the excellent **Chiesa-Museo di Sant'Antonio Abate** just outside the walls in Via Porta Leonina (Aug & Dec 24–Jan 6 daily 10.30am–1pm & 3–6pm; mid-March to April & mid-Sept to Oct Sat & Sun 10.30–1pm & 3–6; May–July Fri–Sun 10.30am–1pm & 3–6pm; Nov–March Sat & Sun 10.30am–1pm & 3–5pm plus other days during special exhibitions; joint ticket with Palazzo Santi €3). This contains two excellently preserved fresco cycles: the fifteenth-century, sixteen-panel cycle on the *Life of St Anthony* by the Maestro della Dormito di Terni, and *Stories of the Passion and the Life of Christ* (1461) by Nicola da Siena. The presbytery holds a precious sixteenth-century group of wooden statues depicting Tobias and the Angel. The **Museo Comunale di Palazzo Santi** (same hours and ticket), in the town centre on Via Gaetano Palombi, is divided into a predictable archeological section, with finds from the surrounding area, and an art gallery with paintings removed from local churches and an outstanding collection of rare medieval wooden statues. The ticket office is also striking, part of an eighteenth-century pharmacy.

Practicalities

Cascia's **tourist office** in the central square, Piazza Garibaldi 1 (Mon–Sat 9am–1pm & 3.30–6pm; summer also Sun 8.30am–12.30pm; ☎0743.71.147, ℮info@iat.cascia.pg.it), is the main office for eastern Umbria, including the Valnerina, Norcia and the Piano Grande, and so can be worth a visit for maps and pamphlets.

Of the huge, pilgrim-oriented **hotels**, the best for general purposes is the basic one-star *Centrale*, Piazza Garibaldi 36 (☎0743.76.736; ❶); a little more up-market is the three-star *Cursula*, Viale Cavour 3 (☎0743.76.206, ☻hotelcursula .com; ❷), which has Cascia's best **restaurant**.

Roccaporena and the Corno valley

Cascia's countryside is considerably more rewarding than the town. If you want a quick taste – and to stay on the St Rita trail – the trip to Roccaporena, the saint's birthplace, admirably fits the bill. The best way to get here is to take the marked and well-worn **Sentiero-Passeggiata di Santa Rita**, a perfectly level path that contours above the Corno gorge for 6km between Cascia and the village. The track can be picked up in the centre of town through the forecourt of the *Delle Rose* hotel: drop down into the underground car park, walk through it and take the gate 100m beyond, slightly to the left when you emerge. After 4km – you simply follow the same track all the way, with no diversions left or right – cut down to cross the river on a track that branches off right just after a ruined house and the point where a large pipe crosses the river: you'll know if you've gone too far as the track, which has been following an underground aqueduct, becomes too narrow to walk on. The last kilometre is on the road.

The surreal little village of **ROCCAPORENA** sits at the bend of a deep-sided, heavily wooded valley, dominated by a soaring vegetation-shrouded crag, the **Scoglio di Santa Rita**. Perched on the needle-point summit is a tiny chapel, tiring to reach but with magnificent views. In the village, a small but often pilgrim-thronged place devoted almost entirely to Rita, the parish church of **San Montano** has the graves of Rita's family, and is the spot where she concluded her unfortunate marriage. More people make the pilgrimage to the **Orto di Santa Rita**, site of the saint's now rather tatty garden, an unlikely spot for horticulture given its barren, cliff-edge location. It's well signed, on the valley side opposite the Scoglio, the spot marked by a modern bronze statue of the saint, on and around which are often dozens of invocations scrawled on scraps of paper. The obvious place to **stay** is the three-star *Hotel Roccaporena-Casa del Pellegrino* (☎0743.7549, ⓦ www.roccaporena.com; ➋), an institutional but spotless and comfortable pilgrims' hotel. It also has a cheap, canteen-like **restaurant**, more or less the only place in the village to eat.

The Corno valley and Monteleone

There are plenty of opportunities for **walks** into the hills from Roccaporena, and particularly along the wooded arm of the **Corno valley** that makes a dog's-leg turn to the south. To pick up paths simply follow the gravel road beyond the *Casa del Pellegrino*, which climbs quickly, becoming a cart track after a couple of kilometres. East 1km into the valley, it's worth making a brief detour to the hamlet of Capanne, for its views and small fifteenth-century church. An hour's walk northwest from there, over upland, leads to the lonely **Madonna delle Stelle**, a restored monastery which you can also reach more easily from the Borgo Cerreto–Monteleone road.

MONTELEONE itself, on the only road south into Lazio, is a fine, if in parts earthquake-battered medieval village surrounded by grand hill country and noted for woodcarving and delicacies such as olives, wine and truffles. The main sight is the church of **San Francesco**, graced with an exceptional Gothic door, and scattered with artistic and archeological fragments excavated from a massive Neolithic necropolis nearby. The village is best known, however, for *farro*, a crude grain that finds its way into soups – *zuppa di farro* – across the Valnerina. *Farro* is reputedly what wheat would be like had it not been improved over the centuries: the Romans and Etruscans used it as a staple grain, and allegedly fed it to their soldiers before they went into battle.

Travel details

The excellent website ⓦ www.umbriatrasporti.it has links to full and updated timetables for all public transport, including the private FCU and state rail services and the ATC, APM and SSIT bus services.

Trains

Spoleto to: Arezzo (8 daily; 2hr 10min); Florence direct (8 daily; 2hr 30min–3hr); Foligno via Trevi (12–18 daily; 20min; connections for Spello, Assisi, Perugia and Teróntola); Fossato di Vico (for Gubbio; 9–13 daily; 1hr 10min); Narni (10–17 daily; 40min); Nocera Umbra (8 daily; 40min); Orte (10–17 daily; 55min; additional connections to Rome and Florence); Perugia direct (15–20 daily; 45min); Rome (10–17 daily; 1hr 15min–1hr 45min); Terni (10–17 daily; 30min).

Buses

Note that all buses between Spoleto and Norcia and Cascia run via Sant'Anatolia di Narco; Cascia services to and from Norcia, Spoleto or Rome require a connection at Serravalle.

Cascia to: Foligno (Mon–Sat 1 direct daily; 2hr); Norcia (Mon–Sat 5–8 daily, 1 on Sun; 40min); Roccaporena (1–3 daily; 15min); Rome (Stazione Tibertina; Mon–Sat 2 daily, 1 on Sun; 3hr); Spoleto (Mon–Sat 5–7 daily, 3 on Sun; 1hr 5min).
Norcia to: Borgo Cerreto via Campi, Preci and Triponzo (Mon–Sat 1 daily, currently leaves 1.25pm; 1hr); Cascia (Mon–Sat 5–8 daily, 1 on Sun; 40min); Castelluccio via Forca Canapine (2 on Thurs; 50min); Perugia (Mon–Sat 1 direct daily, currently leaves 6.15am; 2hr 30min); Rome (Stazione Tibertina; Mon–Sat 2 daily, 1 on Sun; 3hr); Spoleto (Mon–Sat 5–7 daily; 3 on Sun; 55min).

Spoleto (train station or Piazza Vittoria) to: Cascia (Mon–Sat 5–7 daily, 3 on Sun; 1hr 5min); Foligno (Mon–Sat 4 daily; 50min); Monteleone (Mon–Sat 1 daily, runs via Caso and Gavelli; currently departs 1.05pm); Montefalco (Mon–Sat 3–4 daily; 1hr); Norcia (Mon–Sat 5–7 daily, 3 on Sun; 55min); Perugia (Mon–Sat 1 direct daily via Spello and Santa Maria degli Angeli; 1hr 40min; additional connections at Foligno); Scheggino (Mon–Sat 4 daily with change at Sant'Anatolia di Narco; 40min); Terni (Mon–Sat 5 daily; 45min).

Orvieto and
southern Umbria

* **Narni** Compact hill-town with outstanding cathedral, medieval streets and Romanesque churches. See p.696

* **Amelia** This tiny hill-town is part-enclosed by some of Italy's oldest and mightiest walls. See p.702

* **Todi** A main piazza of medieval perfection: imposing palaces, a lovely cathedral and a fascinating museum. See p.705

* **Duomo, Orvieto** Umbria's most spectacular cathedral, with the finest facade in Italy and an outstanding and influential fresco cycle by Signorelli. See p.720

* **Underground Orvieto** Guided tours into the labyrinth below the town. See p.726

* **Pozzo di San Patrizio, Orvieto** This colossal well is a dazzling example of medieval engineering. See p.728

△ Amelia

⑬

Orvieto and southern Umbria

S**outhern Umbria** features two of the province's most illustrious hill-towns – **Orvieto** and **Todi**. Each has become a little too popular for its own good, but they are essential visits, the former for Italy's richest Gothic cathedral, the latter for the atmosphere, museum, main square and stunning high-altitude location. Often bypassed in the rush to these star attractions are a number of smaller but still enjoyable centres, notably **Narni** – occupying a promontory above the River Nera – and **Amelia**, whose encircling walls are among the most redoubtable in the country.

Terni, a transport hub and the province's largest supply centre after Perugia, is the area's low spot, a grim industrial city whose most valuable role is as the southern gateway to the **Valnerina**. Buses up the valley pass close to the most celebrated landscape attraction in this part of Umbria, the **Cascate delle Marmore** – a partly artificial waterfall that nonetheless provides an impressive spectacle.

Mainline **trains** from Terni head north to Spoleto and south to Narni, connecting with the Rome–Florence route (and Orvieto trains) at **Orte**. The most enjoyable ride is provided by the Ferrovia Centrale Umbra (FCU), a private single-track line that runs from Terni to Perugia, and then on to Città di Castello and Sansepolcro. Using spartan two-carriage trains, this fills the gaps left by the state network, rattling through lovely countryside to provide access to Todi, and to minor halts like **Deruta**, heart of the region's ceramic tradition. Good **road** links follow almost identical routes: if you're driving or hitching, the big junction with the A1 at Orte – an obvious gateway in and out of the region – offers options in all directions.

Terni

TERNI, the southernmost major town in Umbria, was the unlikely birthplace of **St Valentine**, patron saint of lovers and bishop of the town until his martyrdom in 273 – but a less romantic city would be hard to imagine. Prewar Terni formed the cradle of Italy's industrial revolution, claiming the country's first steel mill and producing the world's first viable plastic; its

Map labels:

▲ Arezzo & Florence

TUSCANY

Città della Pieve

Montegabbione
Montegiove
Pornello
Marsciano
Parrano
San Venanzo
Fratta Todina
Fabro
Ficulle
Monte Castello di Vibio

▲ Monte Peglia

Prodo

River Tiber (Tevere)

Castel Viscardo
Orvieto
Lago di Corbara
Civitella del Lago

A1

Baschi

Bolsena

Civita
Bagnoregio

Lago di Alviano

Lago di Bolsena

LAZIO

River Tiber (Tevere)

Alviano
Lugnano in Tevere

Attigliano

Bomarzo

Orte

0   10 km

Viterbo

armaments and steel industries made it a target for Allied bombing in 1944. During over a hundred air raids, most of the town – including the best part of its Roman and medieval heritage – was reduced to rubble. These days Terni is no longer a manufacturing powerhouse, though postwar rebuilding has put the arms and chemical industries back on their feet: the gun that allegedly shot Kennedy was made here.

ORVIETO & SOUTHERN UMBRIA

Bettona

Spello

Deruta

Foligno

Castelleone

Bevagna

Gualdo
Cattaneo

Montefalco

Trevi

Collazzone

Giano dell'
Umbria

Todi

Massa
Martana

Sant'Anatolia
di Narco

Spoleto

Scheggino

Acquasparta

Avigliano
Umbro

Portaria

San Pietro
in Valle †

Carsulae

San
Gemini

Ferentillo

Pollino

Amelia

Terni

Arrone

Marmore

Piediluco

Narni

Lago di
Piediluco

LAZIO

Stroncone

N

Otricoli

To give the town credit, it does its best: the piazzas are clean and often filled with sculpture; cultural life is rich and varied, with an offshoot of the **Umbria Jazz** festival held here around Easter (with a preponderance of spirituals and gospel music); and the arrival of **film-makers** and production companies, increasingly put off by high costs in Rome, has seen the growth of Terni as a movie production centre: the Centro Multimediale di Terni was involved,

St Valentine

Terni's tourist literature treads carefully around the subject of St Valentine, talking of his "delicate tradition" – delicate, that is, because there are doubts about whether he ever existed and exactly whose body it is that pilgrims venerate in the Basilica di San Valentino, 2km south of Terni. The uncertain identity of the corpse, however, didn't stop someone stealing the saint's head as a love-token in 1986; it was found three years later, wrapped in newspaper, under a park bench at the Cascate delle Marmore.

According to the delicate tradition, Valentine was elected first bishop of Terni in 197 AD and attempted to bring converts to Christianity – then still outlawed – by encouraging the religious marriage of young people. It's also said that star-crossed lovers would turn to him for advice, drawn by his open-mindedness and his custom of giving them flowers from his garden. His most famous success was the union of Sabinus and Serapia, two lovers – he pagan, she Christian – barred from marriage by their lack of a shared faith. Valentine comforted them with the assurance that their souls would never be separated; when the young Serapia died, he converted Sabinus and thus achieved the reunion of the lovers when Sabinus died soon after. Another theory suggests the saint's feast day was the same day on which birds in Umbria were traditionally thought to mate.

Evidence of Valentine's other qualifications for sainthood is scarce, though after his martyrdom in Rome, his head is said to have rolled 93km from its place of execution. Oddly enough, his following in Italy is considerably less than in the "unromantic" Anglo-Saxon countries.

among others, with Roberto Benigni's *Life is Beautiful*, much of which was shot in a local suburb. The best times to be in Terni are **May Day** – celebrated with unusual vigour and a parade of floats by this committed left-wing town – and **St Valentine's Day** (Feb 14), marked by a festival, market and evening Latino disco. The **International Piano Festival** is a high-class event held in June.

The Town

There's little to see in Terni, and what there is is usually lost amongst modern buildings. Perhaps the best reason for leaving the train station is the new **Pinacoteca Comunale "O. Metelli" e "Museo A. De Felice"** in the Neoclassical Palazzo Gazzoli, Via del Teatro Romano 13 (Tues–Sun 10am–1pm & 4–7pm; €3.80). Its star turns are *The Marriage of St Catherine* by Benozzo Gozzoli, the *Pala dei Francescani* by Piermatteo d'Amelia, and a *Crucifixion* by the Folignese artist Nicolò Alunno, along with works by several key moderns – Chagall, Braque, Picasso, Ernst, Kandinsky and Miró. Contemporary works are arranged in a separate section of the gallery. There's also a generous helping of canvases by Orneore Metelli (1872–1938), an impoverished shoemaker from Terni who chronicled his daily life in colourful and appealing naive paintings. The same ticket gives you admission to the Mostra Permanente di Paleontologia, Largo Liberotti (Tues, Fri & Sat 9am–1pm & 4–7pm), a very modest collection of fossils.

The greenest parts of a grey city are the gardens of its southwest quadrant around San Salvatore and the Roman amphitheatre. **San Salvatore**, off the shapeless sprawl of Piazza Europa, is the town's most interesting church, featuring a rotunda that was long believed to have been a Roman temple to the sun, but has recently been dated to the eleventh century. Nonetheless, excavations have revealed extensive remains from Roman buildings on the site. The portico dates from the twelfth century, and the chapel – which has frescoes by an unknown Umbrian painter – from two centuries later. Two blocks west are the remains of the **Roman amphitheatre**, built in AD 32 to hold ten thousand spectators; comprehensively ruined, it's home to the town's bowls club. Just north of San Salvatore is the church of **San Francesco**, started on a Romanesque plan in 1265 and defined by its campanile, a fourteenth-century addition featuring vivid ceramics. In the centre, off Via Cavour, are **Sant'Alò**, a twelfth-century church built by the Knights of Malta, and the **Palazzo Spada**, the last work of Antonio da Sangallo the Younger, who died in Terni in 1546.

Practicalities

Terni is a major **rail** junction, with trains running on the state network from Rome, Orte (connection-point from Orvieto and Florence), Spoleto, Foligno (connection-point from Assisi, Spello and Perugia) and Rieti. There's also the private FCU train line, which shares the state railway station, with hourly trains from Todi, Perugia, Città di Castello, Sansepolcro and stations en route. ATC **buses** leave from the forecourt near the train station to numerous local villages, and to Narni, Todi, the Cascate delle Marmore, Piediluco, Arrone, Ferentillo, Triponzo, Spoleto, Orvieto, Viterbo and Scheggino.

You can **change money** at Terni's train station ticket office (daily 7am–7pm) and at the post office, Via del Plebiscito (Mon–Sat 8.10am–6pm, last Sat of month closes noon). From the train station, head 300m along Viale della Stazione to the seventh turning on the right, for the **tourist office**, Viale Cesare Battisti 7a (Mon–Sat 9am–1pm, Tues & Fri also 3–6pm; ☎0744.423.047, ⓦwww.provincia.terni.it or ⓦwww.comune.terni.it). The regional tourist office covering the Lower Valnerina, Narni and Otricoli is in the same building.

Accommodation

Hotels

Brenta Viale Brenta 12 ☎0744.283.007. Central 23-room one-star hotel with a restaurant. Extremely cheap but also pretty basic; not all rooms have private bathrooms. ❶

Brenta II Via Montegrappa 51 ☎ & ⓕ0744.273.957. A middling modern two-star hotel with 23 rooms, each with bathroom but little else in the way of frills, in a quiet, backwater neighbourhood, across the river to the east. ❶

De Paris Viale Stazione 52 ☎ & ⓕ0744.58.047,

ⓦwww.hotelparis.it. Large 63-room three-star hotel that offers better value than the nearby four-star *Michelangelo Palace*. The facilities are good, but the modern rooms are somewhat soulless; very convenient for the station, however, if you're just passing through. ❸

Garden Viale Bramante 4 ☎0744.300.041, ⓦwww.gardenhotelterni.it. Not central, but top-of-the-range luxury in a modern and large four-star hotel close to the exit from the *superstrada*, with swimming pool, flower-filled balconies and all the frills. ❺

Eating and drinking

Terni puts on a rather better showing with its **restaurants**: there are a couple of top-grade gastronomic venues, numerous cheap and serviceable *trattorie* and dozens of pizza-by-the-slice and fast food outlets. *Tacitus*, Piazza Tacito, is a good local trattoria a few minutes' walk south of the station (closed Fri) – you'll pass it en route to the tourist office. For something just as good, try the tiny *La Piazzetta*, Via del Leone 34 (☎0744.58.188), with a long menu of reliable regional dishes (closed Sun & 2 weeks in Aug). Also first rate is *Il Gatto Mammone*, Vico Catina 15 (☎0744.400.863; closed Sun & Aug), a little more expensive and imaginative in its cooking. The city's oldest **bar** is the *Pazzaglia*, Corso Tacito 10, a great source of **cakes and pastries**, including *l'amour polenta*, the house speciality.

The Lower Valnerina

Terni is the ideal point of entry for the **Lower Valnerina** and on to Norcia and the Sibillini: drive or take a bus along the SS209, which follows the valley into its upper reaches (see p.668). Buses from Terni go as far as Triponzo (see p.668), via Piedipaterno, where you could link up with bus connections on to Norcia or Spoleto. The lower valley's highlight is undoubtedly the Abbazia di San Pietro in Valle (see p.666), 18km north of the city, but on the way you'll pass a number of fine natural diversions, such as the **Marmore waterfalls** and **Lago di Piediluco**. Scenery is generally scrappy until **Ferentillo**, however – when the hills start to rise in impressive fashion – so there's an argument for simply ignoring the valley's lower reaches until you hit San Pietro.

Cascate delle Marmore

The first stop of interest in the valley comes just 6km southeast of Terni at the **Cascate delle Marmore** (access by train or buses from Terni's Piazza Dante), which at 165m are among the highest waterfalls in Europe. They were created by the Romans in 271 BC, when they diverted the River Velino into the Nera during drainage of marshlands to the south. Further channels were cut in 1400 and 1785, both with the intention of draining Rieti's plain without flooding Terni, though the falls' major boost came with the damming of Lago di Piediluco in the 1930s to satisfy industrial demand for hydroelectric power. Terni's power-station complex is the largest hydroelectric plant in Italy.

Pictures of the falls in full spate adorn most Umbrian tourist offices, but what they don't tell you is that the water can be diverted through turbines at the flick of a switch, leaving a none-too-spectacular trickle. **Flow times** are notoriously variable (July & Aug Mon–Fri noon–1pm, 5–6pm & 9–11pm, Sat 11am–1pm & 3–11pm, Sun 10am–1pm & 3–11pm; June Mon–Fri 4–5pm & 9–11pm, Sat 11am–1pm & 3–11pm, Sun 10am–1pm; mid-March to May & Sept Mon–Fri noon–1pm & 4–5pm, Sat 11am–1pm & 4–9pm, Sun 10am–1pm & 4–9pm; Oct Sat 11am–1pm & 4–8pm, Sun 10am–1pm & 3–8pm; Nov to mid-March Sun 3–4pm) – in general, evenings and Sunday mornings are likeliest, especially during July and August when there's an impressive *son et lumière*.

There are two **observation points**: the belvedere in Marmore village, and the SS209 road down below. A steep and frequently muddy path connects the two, starting 100m downstream of the falls, and there are swimming pools at the bottom of the cascade when the water's turned off. The green and luxuriant setting, tumbling water and acres of gleaming marble add up to a spectacular show – shame about the factories around the corner.

Marmore has a **campsite**, the *Marmore*, at the nearby hamlet of Campacci (℡0744.389.792; April–Sept).

Lago di Piediluco

Surrounded by steep, thickly wooded hills, **Lago di Piediluco** is rather like a miniature alpine lake: its waters are dark and deep, a bit murky for swimming and in places unsafe, though the fringes are edged with the odd beach. Piediluco **train station** is on the southwest edge of the lake, 3km southeast of Marmore and about 1km from **PIEDILUCO** village on the north shore. The station is a perfect access point if you want to put up a tent on the southern, less-visited shore or to walk the scenic minor road (no vehicle access) – reached by walking through the quarry by the station – to **Monte Caperno**, where there's a quay for boats serving Piediluco village, and a famous **echo** that's constantly being tried out. It reproduces with perfect clarity phrases up to four seconds in length, the stock Italian test phrase being lines from the mystic poet Jacopone da Todi (see p.711): *"Per te, amor, conumone languendo e vo stridendo, per te abbracciare"* ("I'm pining for you, my darling, and looking forward to embracing you").

Piediluco village is a major sailing and canoeing centre, always crowded at weekends with people escaping from Terni. **Accommodation** can be tight. Head for the two-star *Lido*, Piazza Bonanni 2 (☎0744.368.354, ℗0744.368.292; ❸), or the smart three-star *Casalago*, Mazzalvetta 3 (☎0744.368.421, ℗0744.368.425; ❸), overlooking the lake. The **campsite** *Il Lago* (☎0744.369.199, ℮c.marmore@cuoreverde.com; April–Oct), at Strada di Valle Spoletina 1d in nearby Ara Marina, is large and often busy. Note that nearby Labro, whose medieval houses look attractive from a distance, is owned lock, stock and barrel by Belgians and operates only as a holiday village. For **food**, try the small, inexpensive, family-run *Tavoletta*, Via Forca 4 (☎0744.368.196; closed Mon–Wed and periods in June, Oct & Dec).

Arrone and Montefranco
North up the valley, **ARRONE** and **MONTEFRANCO** are the first of several fortress villages. Montefranco has the better of the views, but portions of its medieval centre are in ruins, and there's little cheer either in the shape of food and drink, or from its inhabitants. Across the valley Arrone sits atop a rocky pinnacle, crowned by an inviting little tower. The village's alleys again lack the sparkle of their distant promise, though the church of **Santa Maria Assunta** in the central Piazza Garibaldi contains recently uncovered sixteenth-century frescoes. These include apse frescoes (1544) by Jacopo Siculo, whose work you can also see in the Duomo in Spoleto, and scenes from the *Life of the Virgin* (1516) by Giovanni di Spoleto and Vincenzo Tamagni, inspired by Lippi's frescoes in the apse of the same cathedral.

With transport you could make the scenic drive from Arrone to **POLINO**, a twelve-kilometre succession of hairpins through dense forest to Umbria's smallest *comune* – just a couple of hundred people, a tiny castle and one nameless trattoria. Press on and you reach **COLLE BERTONE** (1232m), a minor winter resort in good walking country. There's a small **hotel** here, perched idyllically at 1241m, *La Baita* (☎0744.789.132; ❶).

Other local **accommodation** is scarce. Near Arrone on the main road, look for the two-star *Rossi*, Isola 7, Castel del Lago (☎0744.388.372, ℗0744.388.305; ❶); its **restaurant** (closed Fri) is one of the better around. At Racognano, on the SS209 near Montefranco, there's the ritzier three-star *Fontegaia* (☎0744.388.621, ℗0744.388.598; ⓦwww.hotelfontegaia.it; ❸), also with a restaurant. A cheaper place to eat is the *Rema* (closed Mon) on the Polino road from Arrone.

Ferentillo and its mummies
FERENTILLO is rapidly becoming the **free-climbing** capital of Italy, its crags swarming at weekends as new and more difficult routes are pioneered. The village itself sprawls across two rocky hillsides, guarded by twin fourteenth-century towers, and merits a stop for one of Umbria's more grotesque ménages – a collection of mummies. These are to be found propped up in the **Museo delle Mummie** in the crypt of San Stefano on Via della Torre, signposted off the main road (daily: April–Sept 9am–12.30pm & 2.30–7.30pm; March & Oct 9am–12.30pm & 2.30–6pm; Nov–Feb 10am–12.30pm & 2.30–5pm; €3), on the east side of the Nera in the Precetto quarter. Now behind glass and viewed on guided tours – a precaution taken after a head was stolen – the corpses were simply dumped in the crypt and preserved by accident, apparently dried by their bed of sandy soil and a desiccating wind from the south-facing windows. The

characters are a curious mix: two French soldiers hanged during the Napoleonic wars; a bearded dwarf; a mother who died in childbirth (the child displayed alongside her); a papal soldier, bolt upright with his gun, housed in the case of a grandfather clock; a lawyer shot in a local feud over a farm; a farmer whose gun backfired in the same feud and blasted a hole in his stomach; and a hapless Chinese couple who came to Italy in 1880 for their honeymoon and died of cholera. To round things off there's a pile of leering skulls with a mummified owl perched in their midst.

You wouldn't necessarily want to stay locally, though there is a good three-star **hotel**, the eleven-room *Monterivoso*, a converted mill at Via Case Sparse 5 in the nearby hamlet of Monteriviso (℡0744.780.772, ⓦwww.monterivoso .it; ❷) – though you'd do better staying 6km north at the abbey of San Pietro (see p.667). There's a good **restaurant**, the *Piermarini*, Via della Vittoria 53a (℡0744.780.714; closed Sun evening, Mon & three weeks in Aug & Sept), whose interesting cooking ventures beyond the more usual Umbrian standards.

Narni

NARNI is an intimate, unspoilt hill-town that juts into the Nera valley on a majestic spur crowned by another of Cardinal Albornoz's formidable citadels. It lies half an hour by train midway between Terni and Orte; from the latter, it's a spectacular trip through a tree-filled gorge. The fortress draws an admiring glance before you see the welter of chemical works around Narni Scalo, the new town that's grown up around the station – thankfully almost invisible from the medieval centre. Old Narni's stage-set medievalism is even more complete than Perugia's or Assisi's, its quiet piazzas, Romanesque churches – notably the **Duomo** and **Santa Maria in Pensole** – and labyrinth of ancient streets and stepped passageways forming one of Italy's most congenial townscapes. There are also vestiges from the time when Narni was the Roman colony of Narnia, established in 299 BC – one of the first in Umbria – and a linchpin in Rome's defences, standing close to the Tiber valley and the undefended road to the capital. It was the birthplace in AD 32 of the Roman emperor Nerva, and of Erasmo da Narni, better known as Gattamelata (1370–1443), one of the greatest of all medieval mercenaries.

San Giovenale is the focus of Narni's main **festival**, during which a fortnight of festivities lead up to the **Corsa dell'Anello**, held on the second Sunday in May. On the Saturday evening of that weekend a torchlit procession takes place. The next day, contestants from the town's three medieval quarters compete to thrust a lance through a ring (*anello*) suspended in Via Maggiore.

Arrival, information and accommodation

Buses from nearby towns as well as the station arrive at Piazza Garibaldi, where there's an ATC office for bus information and tickets and limited **parking** (there are more spaces on the approach to the square in Via Roma). Frequent **trains** from both Terni and Orte (where you can pick up connections to Orvieto on the Rome–Florence line) arrive at Narni Scalo station. From the station forecourt buses run into town; buy tickets on board or from the station news kiosk. You may have to wait, but don't be tempted into the long and tedious walk. The **post office**, Via Vittorio Emanuele 40, has a foreign exchange facility.

The **tourist office** is at Piazza dei Priori 3 (summer Mon–Fri 9.30am–12.30pm & 4–7pm, Sat 9.30am–12.30pm & 4.30–7.30pm, Sun 10am–12.30pm

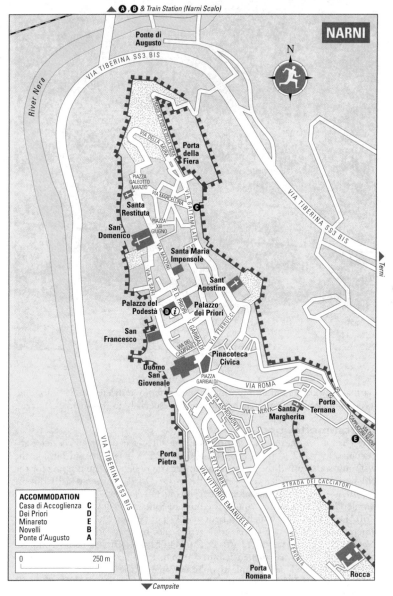

ACCOMMODATION
Casa di Accoglienza   C
Dei Priori   D
Minareto   E
Novelli   B
Ponte d'Augusto   A

0   250 m

& 4.30–7.30pm; variable winter hours; ☎0744.715.362, ✉info@iat.narni.tr.it).
Ask here for details of **Narni Sotterranea** ("Underground Narni"; ⓦwww
.narnisotterranea.it), partly inspired by the similar excellent enterprise in Orvieto (see p.726). It involves guided tours of some of the town's ancient subterranean chambers and tunnels, notably those around San Domenico, Santa Maria
Impensole and the Roman "Formina" aqueduct that brought water to Piazza

△Side street in Narni

Garibaldi. Tours are rather impromptu, and currently restricted to Saturdays and some Sundays, but more may be introduced, especially in summer.

Accommodation

The cheaper of the two town **hotels** is the three-star *Minareto*, Via dei Cappuccini Nuovi 32 (℡0744.726.343, ℻0744.726.284; ❶), situated outside the walls just southeast of the Porta Ternana; but you're better off plumping for the old-world finery of the very central three-star *Dei Priori*, Vicolo del Comune 4 (℡0744.726.843, ⓦwww.loggiadeipriori.it; ❸). A cheaper alternative is the simple *Casa di Accoglienza*, run by the nuns of Santa Anna at Via Gattemelata 74 (℡0744.715.217; ❶), which has beds at €17 per person. The alternatives – for emergencies only – are hotels in Narni Scalo: by the station, the three-star *Novelli*, Via della Stazione 12 (℡ & ℻0744.751.004; ❷), has had a complete renovation, which has turned it into a comfortable and inexpensive place to stay. However, its location, unless you're coming off the train, is hardly perfect. There's a **campsite** 5km south at Monte del Sole, on the road to Borgaria (℡ & ℻0744.796.336; April–Sept).

The Town

The circuitous bus route from Narni Scalo to the medieval town allows a brief view of the Roman **Ponte di Augusto**, a solitary arch built in 27 BC in the middle of the river (a second collapsed in 1855), remnant of a bridge which in its day was 30m high and spanned 160m, a product of Augustan-era renovations to the Via Flaminia. In the eighteenth century this was one of the key sights on the Grand Tour – Corot, among others, painted the scene (the picture is in the Louvre) – but now is so lost among the lower town's development that you could easily miss it completely: the best viewpoint is provided by the train from Orte, just before you pull into Narni.

Piazza Garibaldi is the town's rather oddly shaped and disjointed social hub; its ancient name, Piazza del Lago, hints at one reason for the strangeness, for the square was once a medieval cistern (or *lacus*), built over a Roman cistern fed by an aqueduct from the surrounding hills. Note the piazza's restored fountain (1527), decorated by imaginary animals. From the square, the main street, Via Garibaldi (and its continuation, Via Mazzini), leads north to the heart of the old town – still built on the old Roman grid – through an arch in the city walls, following the course of the Via Flaminia, whose construction in 220 BC set the seal on Narni's importance.

The Duomo

The Duomo, or **Cattedrale di San Giovenale** (daily 8.30am–12.30pm & 3.30–7pm; free), fronting Via Garibaldi's first bend, was built around 1047 and named after Narni's first bishop, who was buried in accordance with Roman custom outside what were then the town walls in 376. Other religious worthies buried on the site include San Cassio, interred here in 558. By the ninth century (perhaps earlier), a chapel had been built which provided the basis for the 1047 church – by then within the town's medieval borders. It was consecrated in 1145 by Pope Eugenius III and amended over the years so that it is now an intriguing mix of accretions from most centuries since. Its facade is small and unassuming, cramped by surrounding buildings and by the Lombard-influenced portico, which dates from 1492 (with later additions). The portal, laced with carvings, dates from the twelfth century.

Inside, the church has a slightly lopsided feel, owing to the addition of an outer south aisle in the fifteenth century. The extravagant Baroque altar is over-shadowed by gold-leafed **pulpits** on either side of the nave and an intricate **screen** – all mainly late fifteenth-century works, but incorporating fragments of Romanesque and paleo-Christian reliefs. The Cosmati pavement is also attractive, while elsewhere parts of the original church show through, chiefly in the patches of fresco – notably a little niche *Madonna and Child* on the west (rear) wall and in the apse behind the choir. The little wooden summer **statue** (1474) representing St Anthony Abbot near the rear wall at the start of the left aisle is by the Sienese master Vecchietta, who may also have been responsible for *San Giovenale*, a painting of Narni's patron saint on the last pillar of the right aisle.

Giovenale's tomb lies in the cellar-like chapel midway down the south aisle, the extraordinary **Sacello di San Giovenale e San Cassio** (also known as the Oratorio di San Cassio). It's shielded by a Cosmatesque marble screen and pillars, possibly from the presbytery of the Romanesque church here rebuilt in 1322, and a relief of *Two Lambs adoring the Cross*, together with two thirteenth-century niche statues of the *Pietà* and *San Giovenale*. An important piece of early Christian architecture, the chapel dates from 558; its crude, age-blackened walls contain a ninth-century **mosaic** of Christ high up on an inner wall, the oldest in the region. Inside are more Cosmati fragments and reliefs, together with the eighth- or ninth-century sarcophagus used as Giovenale's tomb: the stones beyond the tomb represent part of the original Roman wall. The tomb of Cassio and his wife, Fasta, is above the chapel entrance. The couple's remains, along with those of Giovenale, were stolen by the Tuscans in 850 and languished for a time in Lucca.

The Pinacoteca Civica

The **Palazzo Vescovile** alongside the Duomo, a seventeenth-century former bishop's palace, is probably destined to house the town's **Pinacoteca Civica**. Years in the planning and execution, it will collect work currently held in the Palazzo del Podestà and various churches around town; there will also be a section devoted to the gold and silverware from the cathedral treasury. In the collection, the influence of Tuscan artists in the region is acknowledged in Benozzo Gozzoli's *Annunciation* (1451–2) and a tabernacle attributed to the school of Agostino di Duccio. One section will be devoted to San Girolamo, an important former Franciscan convent 13km southeast of Narni that was once home to the town's best painting, Domenico Ghirlandaio's *Coronation of the Virgin* (currently on view in the Palazzo del Podestà; see below), commissioned for the convent in 1486 by Cardinal Eroli, a cleric who was also busy in Spoleto (see p.656). Other works from the convent include detached fifteenth-century frescoes, a painted terracotta bust of St Bernardino of Siena attributed to the Sienese artist Vecchietta, and a lunette attributed to Pier Matteo d'Amelia frescoed with a *Madonna and Child and SS Francis and Giralomo*. The best of the cathedral treasury's exhibits are six bronze chandeliers and a pair of eighteenth-century reliquaries.

Piazza dei Priori

Via Garibaldi continues through a vibrant residential centre, following the line of the old Roman Cardo Maximus past Via del Campanile on the left, which provides a glimpse of the cathedral's fifteenth-century campanile (built on a Roman base). It soon emerges into the **Piazza dei Priori**, a perfect little civic square where pride of place goes to the fourteenth-century **Palazzo dei Priori** and its loggia, designed by the Gubbian Matteo Gattapone, the architect responsible for Gubbio's Palazzo dei Consoli and Spoleto's vast Ponte delle Torri. Next to its high arches and Roman inscription is a little exterior pulpit, built for the peripatetic St Bernardino. The striking Palazzo Sacripante alongside is covered in medieval reliefs.

Opposite the Palazzo dei Priori is the **Palazzo del Podestà**, or Palazzo Comunale, cobbled together by amalgamating three town houses and adding some token decoration. The thirteenth-century Romanesque sculptures above the main door are worth a glance, as are the numerous Roman fragments of the courtyard. In the Sala di Consiglio, or Sala Consigliare (Fri–Sun & public hols 10am–1pm & 3–7pm; free) is displayed the best of the works destined for the Pinacoteca Civica (see above): these include Gozzoli's *Annunciation* and the majestic *Coronation of the Virgin* (1486) by the Florentine Domenico Ghirlandaio. The latter is the town's pride and joy, and it was so admired by the authorities of Todi and Trevi that they commissioned cheaper copies by the local artist Lo Spagna. Another small room nearby contains paintings removed from San Domenico, the town's former picture gallery, among them a double-sided standard dated 1409 by the anonymous Maestro di Narni showing the *Dormition* and *Coronation of the Virgin*.

The rest of the town

Beyond the piazza, Via Mazzini passes after 50m the inconspicuous but lovely church of **Santa Maria Impensole** (daily 8.30am–12.30pm & 3.30–7.30pm; free). A simple basilica, unchanged since it was built in 1175, it was sited over a pagan place of worship that in turn was the site of a cemetery and then a Roman-era house with two still extant cisterns. It has an enchanting triple-arched Romanesque portico and a beautiful carved frieze around the square doorways. The interior is plain save for a few simple carvings and capitals, though interesting rooms below the nave with Roman remains are occasionally open, including one with a sixth-century tomb.

The ex-church of **San Domenico**, a slightly forlorn building a short way farther down Via Mazzini, is now home to Narni's archives and public library (Mon–Thurs 9am–1pm & 3.15–6pm, Fri 9am–1pm; free). It's worth dropping by for the wealth of medieval fresco fragments around the walls and the funerary wall monument (1494) to Gabriele Massei, crafted by followers of Agostino di Duccio. You could also try asking in the library to view the Roman **aqueduct** that lies below the building. Behind the church to the left, at the beginning of Via Aurelio Saffi, a small **garden** with fragments of an old tower offers great views down into the Nera gorge: the distinctive building way down below is the recently restored twelfth-century Benedictine **Abbazia di San Cassiano** (generally open to the public on Sun).

The northern tip of the town is graced with more gardens and good views, as well as steep little streets leading down to Via Gattamelata; no. 70 is reputedly the birthplace of the eponymous *condottiere* (mercenary). Towards the street's southern end lies the tatty, water-stained church of **Sant'Agostino**, its large, bare portal concealing an interior with a redoubtable fourteenth-century stone altar and a few medieval faded frescoes amidst half-hearted Baroque. The best fresco, to the right of the main door, is a *Madonna Enthroned with SS Lucy and Apollonia* (1482) by the accomplished local artist Pier Matteo d'Amelia, best known as one of Fra' Filippo Lippi's two assistants on the apse frescoes in Spoleto cathedral. Also spare a moment for the fresco fragments in the apse, which depict a variety of saints.

Returning to Piazza Garibaldi and heading south takes you into a warren of little streets, worth wandering for their own sake. At the top of this quarter lies the **Rocca** (irregular opening; free), a massive affair lording it over the town and surrounding country. It's reached by Via del Monte, a street that threads through the *terziere di Mezule*, one of the three areas into which the medieval town was divided. The castle was commissioned by Cardinal Albornoz in the 1370s and is attributed to Gattapone, responsible for the town's Loggia dei Priori; it formed a link in the chain of fortresses by which Albornoz sought to reassert papal authority across Umbria. The park around the castle is a perfect spot for a picnic and siesta.

Eating and drinking

Virtually the only proper **restaurant** in the heart of Narni's old town is the classy *La Loggia*, Vicolo del Comune (☎0744.722.744; closed Mon & late July). **Pizzerie** and bars are gathered on Piazza Garibaldi, and there are good snacks at *Il Forno* bakery off Piazza del Popolo. The best restaurant around lies 15km south in the hilltop hamlet of **San Vito**, *Monte del Grano*, Strada Guadamello 128 (☎0744.749.143; closed Mon & mid-Jan to mid-March; Tues–Fri eves only). It's small and has a fine reputation, so booking is usually essential; service, food and ambience all justify the high price tag, though not all the innovative dishes are a complete success. There are two cheaper top-rate places closer to town: in **Testaccio**, 2km south of Narni on the old Rome road, is *Il Cavallino*, Via Flaminia Romana 220 (☎0744.761.020; closed Tues & 2 weeks in July), a popular place that's been run by the same family for three generations; while in wooded, hilly country 8km south of town near the hamlet of **Moricone** is *Da Sara*, Strada Calvese 55–7 (☎0744.796.138;), a typical rural trattoria with a small bar-*osteria* alongside (both closed Wed).

Amelia and around

AMELIA, 11km west of Narni Scalo, sits perched on top of a sugarloaf hill, its position and surrounding countryside the nicest for some distance around. The town is as delightful as its setting, enclosed by some of the oldest and mightiest **walls** in Italy. Formed from vast polygonal blocks joined without mortar, they are up to 4m wide and 8m high. Parts are known to have belonged to an Umbrian acropolis of the fifth century BC, though the Roman historian Pliny claimed the town was formed in the eleventh century BC, three centuries before Rome. The Romans took advantage of the fortifications in 90 BC when they used the town, then named Amerina, as a staging post on the Via Amerina, one of nine military roads linking Etruria to the Via Flaminia. Thereafter the town within the walls was all but destroyed by Totila, and later history followed a predictable course through rule by the nobility and slow decline.

The Town

Access is through one of the four original gates: the main entry is the **Porta Romana**. The walls can be seen from a small park to the left of the gate, and from the pleasant two-kilometre path that starts here and encircles the town. Immediately inside the gate stands the church of **San Francesco**, also known as SS Filippo e Giacomo, its typically plain-faced facade relieved by a rose window of 1401. Inside, the Cappella di Sant'Antonio contains six tombs belonging to members of the Geraldini family, the clan that held sway over Amelia for long periods during the Middle Ages. One family member, Alessandro (1455–1525), achieved fame as one of the key advocates in the Spanish court of Columbus's 1492 expedition to the New World. The monuments (1477) on the top right, to Matteo and Elisabetta Geraldini, are the work of Agostino di Duccio. Next door at Piazza Augusto Vera 10 is the ex-Collegio Boccarini, with a beautiful courtyard and double loggia, home to the **Museo Archeologico di Amelia**, Piazza Augusto Vera 10 (July & Aug daily 10.30am–1pm & 4.30–7.30pm; April–June & Sept daily 10.30am–1pm & 4–7pm; Oct–March Fri–Sun 10.30am–1pm & 3.30–6pm; €4). The star exhibit is a bronze statue discovered locally in 1963 of the Roman general Nerone Claudio Druso, better known as Germanico, a nephew of Tiberius who died in mysterious circumstances in AD 17. There's also a picture gallery of paintings removed from local churches and palaces.

From San Francesco, the spiralling Via della Repubblica draws you to **Piazza Marconi**, a lovely old square from where the stepped Via del Duomo leads steeply to the town's summit, site of a panoramic cathedral square. A small park here offers the best views. The most striking feature of the **Duomo**, a Romanesque church ruined by Baroque superfluities and nineteenth-century frescoes, is a twelve-sided **tower**, dated 1050 and claimed by some to symbolize the Apostles, by others to represent the signs of the zodiac. It's studded with Roman fragments and originally served as the town's principal civic tower. Inside, flanking the second chapel on the right are two standards reputedly won from the Turks at the Battle of Lepanto. The first chapel in the north aisle holds the *Tomb of Giovanni Geraldini* (1476) by Agostino di Duccio, and the first column on the right was the one against which St Fermina, the local patron saint, is said to have been martyred. A distinctive **octagonal chapel** is attributed to Antonio da Sangallo, its two funerary monuments to Ippolito Scalza, who played a key role during the construction of Orvieto's Duomo.

You might also investigate the uncovered frescoes and *sinopie* in **Sant'Agostino**'s sacristy in Via Cavour, thought to date back to the year 1000, showing four saints, red star motifs and floral decoration. Amelia's attraction otherwise is the typically Umbrian mix of views, medieval streets and close-at-hand countryside. You could walk the short distance to **Monte San Salvatore**, worthwhile for its views and a tiny ninth-century chapel, or head for the nearby rural church of **Madonna delle Cinque Fonti**, supposed site of a St Francis sermon.

Practicalities

Buses run to Amelia from Terni and Orvieto, as well as from the two nearest train stations, Narni Scalo and Orte. Beside the Porta Romana is the **tourist office**, Via Orvieto 1 (Tues–Sat 9.30am–12.30pm & 2.30–6.30pm, Mon & Sun 9.30am–12.30pm; Nov–March closes 5.30pm; ℡0744.981.453, ✉info@iat .amelia.tr.it). A minibus shuttle runs between here and the centre. There's also a lift from a lower car park to the upper town, letting you out near the post office.

On the main approach road, 2km from the walls, is one of two local **hotels**, the three-star *Scoglio dell'Aquilone*, Via Orvieto 23 (℡0744.982.445, ✉scoglio dellaquilone@tiscalinet.it; ❶). The other, with a good restaurant (closed Mon except July & Aug), is the three-star *Anita*, Via Roma 31, 200m from the turnoff on the Narni road (℡0744.982.146, ℻0744.983.079; ❷). Another option is the one-star, ten-room *Amerino*, Via Amerina 54 (℡0744.989.667; ❷), at **Fornole**, midway to Narni. The nicest of the lot is the small seven-room *Il Carleni*, Via Pellegrino Carleni 21 (℡0744.983.925, ⊛www.ilcarleni.com; ❹), a "historic residence" with pretty garden, good views and a restaurant. In town, too, there is an excellent youth hostel, the *Giustiniani*, Piazza Mazzini 9, (May–Sept; ℡0744.978.673, mobile ℡339.261.0398, ⊛www.ostellogiustiniani.it; ❷), which has dorm beds at €15.50 and two-, four- and six-bed rooms and family rooms at €17 per person.

Il Carleni is also very good for inexpensive **food** and in summer there's the chance to eat outside. You might also try the restaurant in the *Anita*, or *La Tavernetta* pizzeria on Via della Repubblica in the old centre. At **Gabelletta**, 3.5km northeast on the Foce road, is *La Gabelletta*, Via Tuderte (℡0744.982.159; closed Mon & late July), a large, courteous and highly rated restaurant. Be sure to indulge in Amelia's speciality, a teeth-rotting combination of white figs, chopped nuts and chocolate known as *fichi girotti*, available from local bars.

Lugnano in Teverina

The run along the back roads between Orvieto and Amelia (possible by bus) is a treat, offering plenty of oak forests and the chance to catch one of southern Umbria's Romanesque highlights, the twelfth-century **Santa Maria Assunta** in **LUGNANO IN TEVERINA**. Fronted by an exotic, restored portico (1230), the church has finely carved twin pulpits and has somehow hung onto a triptych by Nicolò Alunno in the apse. The interior also has plenty of lovely carved capitals, a reconstructed *cantoria* and a Cosmatesque floor, while the beautifully pillared crypt features a fine sculpted screen and further Cosmati marble work. From Lugnano it's well worth heading to **BOMARZO**, 17km south in Lazio. Ten minutes' walk from the village is the **Parco dei Mostri** (opening times vary; phone ℡0761.924.029), a sixteenth-century theme park of fantasy and horror devised by the hunch-backed Duke of Orsino that's become one of the area's primary tourist attractions.

Otricoli

The medieval streets and fresco-dotted church of Santa Maria in **OTRICOLI**, 15km south of Narni, are eclipsed by the remains of **Otriculum** (unrestricted access; free), a collection of Roman ruins within easy walking distance. To reach them, take the main road that bypasses the village, head downhill for 200m and follow the signposted track that strikes off right towards the Tiber. Unusually the settlement has no walls, having served more as a pleasure garden than a defensive site; it was built as a sort of holiday village for Rome's hoi polloi, who cruised in by boat on the Tiber. The colony is still largely unexcavated and draped in clinging undergrowth; the best of the visible remains are a partly buried amphitheatre, a succession of twin-level arches and the rambling ruins of some small villas, cisterns and bathhouses. Turner stopped off here to paint the scene (a work now in the Tate Gallery) and in the sixteenth century Montaigne described the spot as "infinitely pleasant". It may not stay that way for much longer: so far, no more than a trickle of tourists visit but plans to make this an archeological park mean it may be headed for the big time. In the meantime there's a small **Museo Antiquarium** in the village, Via Vittorio Emanuele 13–15 (April–Sept Sat & Sun 10.30am–12.30pm & 3.30–6pm; Oct–March Sat & Sun 10.30am–12.30pm; free) with a small collection of finds from the site. You can find **rooms** in the village at the one-star, seven-room *Umbria*, Via Roma 72 (T0744.709.013; ●).

⑬ Carsulae and around

The hills flanking the SS3bis main road north of Narni and the parallel road and FCU rail line from Terni harbour a number of typical Umbrian villages, of which the most substantial is **CESI**, 12km northwest of Terni and known as *la ringhiera della valle Ternana* ("the balcony of the Terni valley"). In addition to a handful of churches and a ruined fort, it offers a fine walk to the church of Sant'Erasmo and on to the summit of Monte Torre Maggiore.

The building of the Via Flaminia from Rome to Ancona confirmed this region's importance as the crossroads of Italy; colonies along its route were to evolve into modern-day Narni, Terni, Spoleto and Spello. Some settlements, however, such as **CARSULAE**, 15km north of Terni, were abandoned after earthquakes and civil war. In its day, this particular pile of stones was known as the Pompeii of central Italy, its beauty praised by both Tacitus and Pliny the Younger. To get there, take the first junction for San Gemini Fonte on the main Todi–Terni road (ie before the tunnel heading south), and then just before San Gemini Fonte (not before plain San Gemini) take the dusty signposted track to the ruins, the largest Roman site in Umbria.

The site (daily: April–Sept 8.30am–7.30pm; Oct–March 8.30am–5.30pm; free) is today dominated by a church, **San Damiano**, made from materials filched from the ruins; other precious marbles went to build local houses. Behind the church you can follow a long stretch of the original **Via Flaminia**, complete with grooves made by chariots, to a substantial arched gateway, built by Trajan; beyond the arch, on the left, is a large square Roman tomb. Walking back on the Flaminia, you'll see the site of the **Basilica Forense** (law courts) off to the left; behind it, across a modern lane rise the remnants of the **amphitheatre**, built in the hollow of a natural depression. Behind the arena is a **theatre**, its orchestra still impressively intact, and to its rear a spread of ruins still awaiting excavation. Back across the site, behind San Damiano and the Flaminia, are the **forum**, composed of numerous low walls, and the vague outlines of baths, a well and two temples.

PORTARIA, 3km north of Carsulae, is an inviting-looking village, clearly visible from the SS3bis, straggling along the cliffs on the eastern side of the valley. It's worth driving up for bird's-eye views over the valley. To the west, **SAN GEMINI** and **ACQUASPARTA** are both spa towns, each with passable medieval centres: the churches of San Francesco and San Nicolò in the former are the main draws. San Gemini has the two-star **hotel** *Duomo*, Piazza del Duomo 4 (T0744.630.015, Wwww.gruppobacus.com; ❷), currently being added to and improved (but open): it will emerge as a four-star with spa in 2007.

The high, wooded hills west of Acquasparta shelter a handful of windblown hamlets amid empty country – this is a real stretch of unknown Umbria. Driving round the hills, though rewarding, is a slow business; if you're going west there's no petrol almost until you reach Orvieto. **MONTENERO** has the best of the many castles in the area, and virtually every other village boasts a Romanesque church; the best are Santa Maria at **QUADRELLI**, and San Martino and Santa Vittoriana in **DUNROBBA**. In **AVIGLIANO** is the two-star **hotel** *Antica Lanterna*, Via Matteotti 31 (T & F0744.933.104, Wwww.anticalanterna.it; ❶), which also has a decent restaurant (closed Tues).

Todi

TODI provides a graphic illustration of what has happened in much of Umbria over the last two decades. Once a sleepy, simple agricultural centre, it became a favoured retreat for foreign expats and Rome's arts and media types, attracted as much by the town's considerable rustic charms as its relative proximity to the Italian capital. These days the transformation is all but complete: Todi is firmly on the tourist trail and has been smartened up to within a whisker of its life. Gentrification is manifest in a scattering of estate agents, shuttered holiday homes and the revamped and decidedly high-profile **Todi Festival** – ten days of music, ballet and other arts at the beginning of September. The final straw came when an American university study proclaimed it the world's most amenable place in which to live: the few remaining unrestored farmhouses and villas were duly snapped up. Don't be put off, for the town is still unmissable, with much charm and many sights, notably an impressive **Piazza del Popolo** and the churches of **San Fortunato** and **Santa Maria della Consolazione**, though perhaps what lingers most in the memory is its position 410m up, a stunning and daunting prospect from below.

Iron Age remains suggest some three thousand years of continual habitation. Tradition has it the Umbrian town was built where an eagle dropped a tablecloth snatched from a local family – hence the eagle and cloth in the town's insignia. More certain is the **Etruscan** heritage: coins bearing the name Tutare ("border") suggest a town of some independence during pre-Roman rule, probably one of several outposts used by the Etruscans to defend their frontier along the Tiber. Necropolises all round Todi have yielded some of the finest Etruscan treasures, most of them – including a famous bronze statue of Mars – shipped off to Rome. Ancient Roman rule came (in 42 BC) and went, leaving little except a second set of walls and indistinct ruins. The town's heyday was the thirteenth century, when as a free *comune* – one of Umbria's first – it managed to annex Amelia and Terni, hold its own in skirmishes with Spoleto, Narni and Orvieto, and build a third set of walls and crop of civic palaces. The two small eaglets under the wings of the Todi eagle on some of the town's coats

ORVIETO AND SOUTHERN UMBRIA | Todi

13

of arms represent the towns of Amelia and Terni. The **Atti** were the leading noble family, overseeing – in tandem with the Church's representatives – a period of decline interrupted only by a flicker of sixteenth-century prosperity that produced more palaces and Todi's great Renaissance church of Santa Maria della Consolazione.

Arrival, information and accommodation

Access to Todi by public transport can be a headache. The town has two **train** stations on the FCU line between Terni (33km) and Perugia (41km), but both are in the middle of nowhere and connecting buses can involve a longish wait. The Ponte Rio station, 6km distant, is marginally closer, and has a more reliable shuttle minibus to the old town (Linea C; around 12 daily Mon–Sat; tickets from the station ticket office); the other station is Ponte Naia. Buses back to Ponte Rio station leave from Piazza Jacopone – between Piazza del Popolo and San Fortunato – fifteen minutes before each train departure.

From Perugia, **buses** are more convenient: there are around six daily (Mon–Sat, more on school days), the last return bus leaving at 5pm. Most stop in Piazzale della Consolazione next to Santa Maria della Consolazione. From here to the centre, you can take an orange minibus (Linea A), or follow the marked footpath that strikes off Viale della Consolazione, 20m beyond the corner on the right. Buy tickets for the minibuses and long-haul buses from the unlikely-looking stall that sells nuts and snacks. Some inter-town buses – plus a once-daily service to Rome – continue to (and leave from) Piazza Jacopone. Get tickets and information from the fruit shop in the piazza next to the *Ristorante Jacopone*.

By car, you'll be hard pressed to navigate Todi's narrow streets and one-way system, never mind find a central **parking** place. The best plan is to leave your car outside the walls at Porta Perugina, Piazzale della Consolazione or Porta Romana. There are limited paid places in Piazza del Mercato Vecchio.

Todi's **tourist office** is in the southeast corner of the main square at Piazza del Popolo 36 (April–Oct daily 10am–1pm & 4–7pm; Nov–March Mon–Sat 10am–1pm & 3–5, Sun 10am–1pm; ☎075.894.5416, ✉info@iat.todi.pg.it).

Hotels

Agricola Todini Collevalenza ☎075.887.122. One of the numerous *agriturismo* places near Todi. Three-room option 11km southeast of Todi on the Massa Martana road, where the high rates buy you swimming, riding, archery and other diversions. ❹

Bramante Via Orvietana 48 ☎075.894.8381, ⓦwww.hotelbramante.it. This long-established but rather faded four-star hotel, a converted medieval convent beyond Santa Maria della Consolazione, had its thunder stolen by the opening of the *Fonte Cesia*. Its only advantages are easier parking, slightly airier rooms and a pool and tennis courts looking over the Umbrian countryside. ❼

🏃 **Fonte Cesia** Via Lorenzo Leoni 3 ☎075.894.3737, ⓦwww.fontecesia.it. Definite first choice in Todi if finances allow: beautiful converted palazzo on several levels, with excellent restaurant, good service and very comfortable rooms: the central four-star is also the only one of Todi's hotels within the walls. ❻

🏃 **Relais Todini** Località Collevalenza ☎075.887.182, ⓦwww.relaistodini.com. A glorious restored thirteenth-century hilltop castle 9km south of Todi, beautifully appointed with just twelve rooms and period fittings, antiques, oil paintings, pastel colour scheme, wood and stone floors and walls. Facilities include tennis courts and a swimming pool. ❺

Tuder Via Maestà dei Lombardi 13 ☎075.894.2184, ⓦwww.hoteltuder.com. Functional three-star in an uninspiring modern, built-up district, ten minutes' relatively unpleasant walk from Porta Romana. ❸

Villa Luisa Via Angelo Cortesi 147 ☎075.894.8571, ⓦwww.villaluisa.it. Relatively posh, if uninspiringly modern three-star that boasts a pleasant garden but has a far-from central location, a short distance beyond the *Tuder*. ❹

B&Bs and rooms

Le Vetrate Via G. Matteotti 136 ☎0347.119.1071, ✉leonhard78@virgilio.it. Todi's only in-town bed-and-breakfast option near the bottom of the hill towards the Porta Romana; just one double room with private bathroom. ❸

San Lorenzo Tre Via San Lorenzo 3 ☎075.894.4555. Very comfortable rooms in a pleasantly and elegantly furnished town house in the street parallel to Via del Duomo just east of the cathedral. ❹

Religious houses

Convento di Montesanto Viale Montesanto ☎075.894.8886, ✉montesanto@libero.it. Occasionally accepts guests in eighteen double rooms. Check availability in advance. ❶

Convento Sacro Cuore Via Cesia 5 ☎075.894.2358, ⓕ075.943.082. Has five three- and four-bed rooms, at around €31 person. Check availability. ❷

Santissima Annunziata Via San Biagio 2 ☎075.894.2268, ✉smrtodi@libero.it. Monastery with 34 rooms for women, couples and families, from €28 per person. Check availability. ❶

The Town

All Todi's main sights are within a few minutes' walk of each other, though the southeast part of the town around Porta Romana involves a long downhill hike, as does the walk to **Santa Maria della Consolazione**. From the bus terminus, the minibus drops you at the central **Piazza del Popolo**, home to the cathedral and an outstanding **museum**; walking up via the footpath leaves you in the municipal gardens, near the church of **San Fortunato**. Like many a hill-town, random exploration is one of Todi's pleasures.

A combined ticket (€6) is available for the Museo-Pinacoteca di Todi, the Cisterne Romane and the campanile of San Fortunato. However, note that this represents only a very modest saving over individual tickets.

Piazza del Popolo

The **Piazza del Popolo** is often described as the most perfect medieval piazza in Italy – and with full justice, even if the cars detract slightly from the overall effect. Flanked by a range of palazzi and a superb Duomo, it's enough to take the breath away, however many other Italian hill-towns you've seen. Originally the site of the Roman forum, it is built above a surviving complex of Roman cisterns (see p.710).

The **Duomo** (daily: summer 8.30am–12.30pm & 3–7pm; winter 8.30am–12.30pm & 2.30–5.30pm; free), atop a broad flight of steps added in 1740, represents a merging of the last of the Romanesque and the first of the Gothic forms filtering in from France in the early fourteenth century. Construction started at the beginning of the twelfth century, on the site of a Roman temple to Apollo, and continued intermittently until the seventeenth. The square, three-tiered **facade**, recently restored, is inspired simplicity, with just a sumptuous rose window and ornately carved composite doorway (1513 and 1639) to embellish the pink weathered marble – the classic example of a form found all over Umbria and the Abruzzo. The exterior sides of the church are more complicated and it's worth walking down adjoining side streets for glimpses of arches, windows and bulging buttresses.

The **interior** has some impressive nineteenth-century stained glass in the arched right-hand aisle, a lovely font (1507), an exquisite fourteenth-century *Madonna and Child* and, at the end of the aisle, a fetching altarpiece by Perugino's follower Giannicolo di Paolo. Nothing, however, matches the **choir**, carved with incredible delicacy and precision by a local father-and-son team between 1521 and 1530; a nice touch are the panels at floor level near the front which depict the tools used to carve the piece – though you may have to run the gauntlet of church attendants to get a close look. The rear west wall is defaced by a dreadful sixteenth-century *Last Judgement* (derived from Michelangelo's Sistine Chapel fresco). Underground, there's a mildly interesting crypt-cum-passageway (€0.80), entered from the top of the north aisle, scattered with Roman and possibly Etruscan fragments; pay at the little wooden kiosk midway down the north (left) aisle. The little cells in the corridor were used as tombs until the nineteenth century.

The piazza's other key buildings are a trio of thirteenth-century public palaces, squared off near the Duomo in provocative fashion – the *comune*'s aim being to put one over on the Church. The **Palazzo del Capitano**, built around 1290, and the adjoining **Palazzo del Popolo**, dating from 1213 (one of Italy's earliest civic palaces), are the most prominent, thanks mainly to their external staircase, which looks like the set of a thousand B-movie swordfights. Several films have in fact been shot in Todi, which offers the twin attractions of scenographic authenticity and proximity to Cinecittà, Italy's major film studios across the border in Lazio. Most notable was the ill-fated *Cleopatra* with Elizabeth Taylor.

The upper floor of the Palazzo del Capitano houses the town's superb modern museum, the **Museo–Pinacoteca di Todi** (Tues–Sun: April–Oct 10.30am–1pm & 2.30–6.30pm; Nov–March 10.30am–1pm & 2–5pm; open Mon on public holidays; €3.50), which brilliantly weaves an open-plan sequence of rooms into the existing medieval structure. A guide in English to buy or borrow is usually available at the ticket desk (which has a window with a fabulous view). Before entering the gallery proper, take a look at the poignant painting by the ticket desk of Todi near the Porta Romana as it appeared in the early twentieth century: the walls are completely unsullied by modern building, the only incongruous detail a single very old-looking motor car.

△ Frescoed salon in the Museo-Pinacoteca di Todi

The first area of the museum, the **Museo della Città**, delves into Todi's history, with lots of individually interesting paintings and artefacts. Look out in particular, in Section IV, for the large painting (1592) of Todi's patron saints and protectors (including Fortunato defending the town from the Goths) by Pietro Paolo Sensini. Todi's *Book of Martyrs* lists no fewer than 853 saints and martyrs who had some sort of connection with the town (plus 53 Servants of God): only five were elevated to the position of patron saints – Fortunato, Callisto, Cassiano, Degna and Romana. Along the wall to the left are several extremely old statues and carvings, some going back to the eighth century, opposite an eye-catching painting depicting various branches of the Benedettoni family, singled out because they were descendants of Jacopone da Todi (see box on p.711).

This area's greatest oddity is the saddle of Anita Garibaldi, left behind when she passed through the town in an advanced state of pregnancy and could no longer bear the discomfort it caused her: it's rather hidden immediately by the exit as you leave the "Museo della Città" part of the gallery.

The sections that follow are devoted to archeology, coins and medals (including an important collection of Republican and Imperial-era **Roman coins**), medallions and fabrics. In many cases the rooms are more alluring than their exhibits, particularly the lovely **salon** devoted to ceramics, which was frescoed in 1367 on the orders of the town's priors when it became their home: most of the surviving pictures date from the seventeenth to the twentieth centuries, and include portraits of illustrious Todians and a map by Sensin (1612) of the territory once controlled by the town. Numerous individual exhibits merit a closer look, none more so than the museum's star painting: the sumptuous **Coronation of the Virgin** (1507) by Lo Spagna which greets you as you walk into the picture gallery. The predella of the painting was appropriated by Napoleon in 1811 and now resides, sadly, in the Louvre.

Elsewhere in the piazza outside, the restored **Palazzo dei Priori**, built between 1293 and 1337, was the seat of Todi's various rulers and is now the town hall – note the eagle coat of arms, complete with tablecloth; if you can look like you're on council business you should be able to peek inside. A recently opened minor attraction on the west side of the piazza (signed off the square down a small alley) are the **Cisterne Romane** (April–Oct Tues–Sun 10.30am–1pm & 2.30–6.30pm, open Monday on public holidays; Nov–March Sat, Sun & public holidays 10.30am–2.30–5pm; €2), the well-preserved remains of the colossal Roman (and probably Etruscan) cisterns beneath the piazza. There isn't much to see, but the cisterns' scale graphically illustrates the Romans' engineering acumen.

The best place to enjoy the piazza's streetlife above ground is from the **bar** down on its southwest corner, a locals' local in contrast to the smarter place midway down the piazza's western side – though the latter does a good line in sandwiches and enjoys more sunshine. Finally, for some wonderful **views** of the surrounding countryside, wander to **Piazza Garibaldi** just alongside the square. The statue here (1890) is of Giuseppe Garibaldi, while the scenically perfect cypress is supposed to have been planted to celebrate Garibaldi's visit to Todi with his wife (see above) in 1849.

San Fortunato

The single most celebrated site after the piazza is the enormous **San Fortunato** (summer daily 8.30am–12.30pm & 3–7pm; winter Tues–Sun 9.30am–12.30pm & 3–5pm; free), set above some half-hearted gardens a stroll south of the piazza. Its disproportionate size is testimony to Todi's medieval wealth, and the messy-looking and squat facade – an amalgam of Romanesque and Gothic – reflects the time it took to build the church (1292–1462). Lorenzo Maitani was commissioned to decorate the facade as he did Orvieto's Duomo, and the story goes that the burghers of that town, unable to stomach the prospect of a rival church, took out a contract on his life. If true, it was money spent too late, because this florid **doorway** stands good comparison with that in Orvieto, all arched swirls and carved craziness. The Annunciate angel in the niche to the left of the portico is outstanding, and has been attributed to the Sienese sculptor Jacopo della Quercia. Look out for some of the smaller details, especially the tiny figures – small jokes, you suspect, on the part of the sculptor – which are hidden in the twists of the portal's spiral columns.

The light, airy **interior**, recently highlighted by cleaning and several controversial coats of whitewash, marks the pinnacle of the Umbrian Gothic tradition

Jacopone da Todi

Fra' Jacomo dei Benedetti, known to all as Jacopone, was among Italy's leading medieval poets, a trenchant critic of the papacy, and the probable author of what became one of Christendom's most famous carols, the *Stabat Mater Dolorosa*. For much of his life he displayed an eccentricity perhaps unequalled by any of Italy's crazed medieval mystics. Born in Todi in 1228, he pursued the life of decadence that seems the birthright of those ultimately destined for sainthood – gambling, feasting, cavorting in fine clothes and rarely levering himself out of bed before midday. After training as a lawyer in Bologna, however, he returned to Todi a respectable attorney. Aged about 38 he married Vanna, a young, rich and deeply devout member of the Umbrian aristocracy. A year after the marriage, Vanna was attending a local public festival when the platform on which she was sitting gave way. Injured, she was carried from the scene by Jacopone, who, tearing away her fine clothes, found she had been wearing a hair shirt beneath her *haute couture*. Seconds later she died in his arms.

Jacopone was inconsolable, shocked at both Vanna's death and his ignorance of her deep devotion. The experience became the catalyst for his own conversion and deliberate abasement. He sold his house, gave his wealth to the poor, distanced himself from family and friends and tramped Todi's streets dressed in rags, often spending days on all fours. He appeared at a niece's wedding dressed in tar and feathers. He added soil and wormwood to his food, to make it repugnant, and demanded to be given the most menial tasks. He also requested that when he died his "grave" should be the belly of a wolf so that his "relics" would be merely excrement. Applying to join the Franciscans, who had recently been established in Todi by Francis himself, he was rejected because his behaviour was deemed too extreme even by the Franciscans' exacting standards; it was to be many years before they allowed him into their community.

Spurned, Jacopone wandered Umbria's countryside for a decade, deliberately remaining cold, hungry, thirsty and dirty to atone for his sins. He also began to compose the poems and *laude* (hymns) for which he was to become famous, writing 211 in all and becoming, in the words of one modern authority, "the most popular and the most inspired of the poets of the Franciscan tradition". He also wrote the influential *Donna del Paradiso*, a powerful dialogue on the grief of the Virgin at the Crucifixion. The work spread throughout Italy, and would inspire the Passion plays, some of the country's first theatrical creations since the Romans.

Jacopone also achieved considerable fame for his outspoken criticism of the papacy. Boniface VIII, one of the most vice-ridden of popes, was a regular visitor to Todi, where he had a reserved stall in the cathedral. One of his favourite tricks was to have the tongues of heretics nailed to doors. Jacopone bravely – if tactlessly – said of him: "Blasphemous tongue, that has poisoned the world,/There is no kind of ugly sin/In which you have not become infamous." He was imprisoned for his eloquence, lucky to escape with his life, and remained incarcerated for five years in the papal dungeons of Palestrina, near Rome. Only the election of Pope Benedict XI in 1303 secured his release. Returning to Todi, he joined a Franciscan convent at Collazzone, north of Todi, where he contrived to die on Christmas Day, 1306. Todi remembers him with a piazza and the vast mausoleum in the crypt of San Fortunato.

of large vaulted churches. The style was based on the smaller, German-influenced "barn" churches common in Tuscany, distinguished – as here – by a single, low-pitched roof with naves and aisles of equal height. (San Domenico in Perugia is another, less successful example.) Note the grey stone brackets, added to correct the increasingly alarming lean of the supporting pilasters. The two battered stoups may date from an earlier church on the site. At the rear sits an excellent

choir (1590), heavier and with more hints of the Baroque than the one in the Duomo, as well as a few scant patches of fresco – the *Madonna* by **Masolino di Panicale** (1432) in the fourth chapel on the right is a good if somewhat battered example of this painter's rare work. The sixth chapel on this side contains further good fresco fragments of the Crucifixion and scenes from the life of St Francis from around 1340 by an unknown Umbrian follower of Giotto.

It is possible to climb the 153 steps of the church **tower** for some fine views (Tues–Sun: April–Oct 10.30am–1pm & 3–7pm; Nov–March 10.30am–1pm & 2.30–5pm; open Mon on public holidays; €1.50); the entrance is on the north aisle. Be sure to pay homage to the **tomb of Jacopone da Todi** in the crypt, which was built in 1596 on the orders of Bishop Angelo Cesi to house this tomb and those of the town's five patron saints. Cesi was one of a family who managed to retain control of the town's clergy for decades, holding the bishopric continually from 1523 to 1606 – probably not unconnected with the fact that one of the Cesi, Paolo Emilio, managed to become Pope Paul III. The **cloisters** are outside and to the right of the church.

Note that a quiet lane leads from the right of the church into **public gardens**, full of shady nooks and narrow pathways, and an enjoyable spot for a siesta or picnic on the route to Santa Maria della Consolazione. On this western edge of town, there's also a kids' playground and a very small **Rocca** of Albornoz vintage, both far less noteworthy than the views, which are extensive, if often obscured by haze. At the gardens' western end a zigzag path cuts down to Viale della Consolazione for the church.

Santa Maria della Consolazione

Many architectural cognoscenti rate **Santa Maria della Consolazione** (daily except Tues: April–Oct 9am–1pm & 2.30–6pm; Nov–March 10am–12.30pm & 2.30–6pm; free) as one of the best Renaissance churches in Italy. Inspired by an apparition of the Virgin on the site and completed in 1607, the project was initiated a century earlier, probably by the virtually unknown Cola da Caprarola, possibly using one of Bramante's drafts from St Peter's in Rome. The church's use of alternating types of window in the cupola – known as rhythmic bays – is a Bramante trademark. Over the years, virtually every leading architect of the day had his say in the design of the church, including Sangallo, Peruzzi and Vignola. Tantalizingly, a picture from 1489 of the church was also found among the architectural drawings of Leonardo da Vinci, pre-dating Caprarola's involvement. Whatever the church's convoluted and mysterious origins, it eventually came to conform to most of the precepts articulated by Alberti, the great theoretician of Renaissance architecture: a Greek-cross floor plan (purity of form and proportion), isolation in an open piazza, a white or near-white finish (purity again), high windows (cutting off from earthly contact) and a preference for statuary (again of greater "purity" than painting).

The rest of the town

For a reminder of ancient Todi, take a look at the so-called *nicchioni* (niches) in **Piazza del Mercato Vecchio**, sited just below Piazza del Popolo; cisterns and walls aside, they constitute more or less all that's left of the Roman colony. The town's proud of them, but they don't amount to much: four slightly overgrown arches, which perhaps formed the wall of an Augustan basilica. Two minutes' walk down from here brings you to **San Ilario** (also known as San Carlo), an ancient Lombard chapel well off the beaten track, and all too often locked to protect a fresco of the *Madonna della Misericordia* by Lo Spagna. Just beyond the church, adjoining a crumbling, flower-strewn arbour, is the **Fonte Scarna-**

becco (1241), an unusual arched fountain that was Todi's lifeblood and social meeting place before piped water.

Just inside the medieval walls at Porta Romana are the churches of **San Filippo**, dull except for frescoed panels on the right-hand wall, and the more interesting **San Nicolò**, distinguished by a striking wooden ceiling, three imposing Gothic arches and two small Umbrian frescoes on the left-hand wall. You might also drop in on thirteenth-century **Santa Maria in Camuccia**, two minutes off Via Roma, recently reunited with its priceless, stolen twelfth-century wooden Madonna. Two beautifully fluted Roman columns flanking the entrance are the most substantial parts of a large collection of Roman pieces dug up from under the church; for a look at the minor pieces, chat up the resident priest – the stuff is in his quarters.

Eating and drinking

Todi's most enjoyable **restaurant** for lunch is the *Umbria* (℡075.894.2737; closed Tues), behind the tourist office; prices are rather high and service can be slow and offhand, but the panorama across what seems like half of Umbria from the outside terrace makes it all worthwhile; in season arrive early or book to be sure of an outside table. Inside, the appeal is considerably reduced, especially if you have to sit in one of the stuffy, smoke-filled side rooms. An excellent alternative, in a less appealing situation but with a cosy brick-vaulted interior and creative cooking, is *Antica Osteria della Valle*, Via Ciufelli 19 (℡075.894.4848; closed Mon), a little way down from San Fortunato. Otherwise, *Le Scalette* (℡075.894.4422; closed Mon), directly opposite, offers a small panoramic terrace and less imaginative food at similar prices.

Cheaper options include the friendly *Cavour*, Corso Cavour 21–23 (℡075.894.3730; open daily), not as pleasantly old-fashioned as it used to be and with an unfortunate tendency to piped music, but with good, basic food (including pizzas) and outside dining on a fine panoramic terrace. Cheaper still is the spartan *Giubilei Italo*, a pizzeria-*rosticceria* in Piazza Bartolomeo d'Alviano, 100m from Piazza del Popolo (℡075.894.2645; closed Mon after 8pm). Opposite this is the *Pianiggiana*, a good **bar** with outside tables, though the couple of bars in Piazza del Popolo give you more to look at.

South of town, locals head to *La Mulinella*, 3km away near the sports centre, Pontenaia 29 (℡075.894.4779; closed Wed & part of Nov), a family-run place where matriarch Irma changes the menu regularly without straying too far from regional staples. In summer, you can sit in the garden and look up to Todi.

Listings

Exchange At the post office, or the bank across the road from the square on Piazza del Popolo's southeast corner.
Hospital Via Giacomo Matteotti ℡075.88.581.
Police Carabinieri: Via Sant'Agostino 77 ℡075.894.2323. Municipal police: Via Mazzini 2

℡075.895.6843.
Post office Piazza Garibaldi 4 (Mon–Fri 8am–6.20pm, Sat 8am–1.20pm).
Taxis Piazza Garibaldi ℡075.894.2375 and Piazza Jacopone ℡075.894.2525.

Along the Tiber valley

North of Todi, the Tiber valley broadens out to a plain, edged with low hills and dotted with light industry. It's not an area where you'll want to spend a lot of time – and most people tear through (or crawl along on the FCU train). A few of the castles, villages and Romanesque churches, however, are worthwhile if you're in no hurry to get to Perugia.

The west bank of the Tiber

The spectacularly sited **MONTE CASTELLO DI VIBIO** is 12km from Todi, off the N397. This eagle's nest of a village dominates the countryside, and its castle was one of a reputed 365 fortresses that formed a defensive screen around Todi. There's little to see, save extraordinary views and the usual maze of medieval alleyways. It does, however, have a lovely little 99-seat **theatre** (Sat & Sun 9.30am–noon & 3/4pm–5.30/6.30pm; or by appointment ☎075.878.0307; free), built in 1808 in celebration of the French Revolution and restored in 1993. The village makes an excellent base away from the crowds, thanks to the twenty-room three-star **hotel** *Il Castello*, Piazza G. Marconi 5 (☎075.878.0560, Ⓦwww.hotelilcastello.it; ❹), superbly converted from a sixteenth-century patrician town house.

Below Monte Castello the walled village of **FRATTA TODINA** is guarded by another castle, strengthened in the fifteenth century by the local warlord Braccio Fortebraccio as a garrison for his troops. Near the centre of the village is a Franciscan monastery, which features in many of the stories and legends of the order. Moving north, Marsciano is the region's main town, modern and without interest. **CERQUETO** has Perugino frescoes of *St Sebastian* (1478) in its parish church, and other damaged works attributed to the artist at the edge of the village in the Maestà di Santa Lucia. There are impressive castle remains 1km away at Sant'Elena.

East of the Tiber

GIANO DELL'UMBRIA, a perfect fortified hamlet ringed by olive groves and pastoral countryside, served by at least two buses daily (Mon–Sat) from Foligno, lies 23km northeast of Todi along a looping detour off the N316. Its central parish church has a widely revered fourteenth-century fresco fragment of the *Madonna and Child*. Take the road south of the village, fork left at the junction after about 1km and you'll come to the only **hotel** for a long way, the two-star *Park Hotel* (☎0742.90.551; ❷), with seven rooms and a cavernous dining room. The only **campsite**, the *Pineta di Giano*, is opposite the hotel at Colle

Romanesque churches east of the Tiber

Almost any of the hill-villages you choose east of the Tiber will be quiet and boast a Romanesque church. Most of these are built over the graves of early monks and martyrs, the Tiber and Naia valleys having been amongst the earliest to be colonized by Christians fleeing Roman persecution; this area and the region south towards Terni thus formed the springboard of Umbria's monastic tradition. Perhaps the most rewarding churches are those you come upon by accident, in crumbling hamlets or in the midst of the ilex woods that blanket surrounding hills. The following are outstanding: Viepri (in the village of the same name north of Massa Martana), Abbazia and Villa di San Faustino (key kept in house next door to villa; catacombs and funerary basilica still being excavated on the site are usually open Tues, Thurs & Sat 9am–1.30pm); Santa Maria in Partano, in which the high altar is made from an old Roman altar (south of Massa Martana; key kept in house to right of church); San Terenzano (outside village of same name; interior usually closed, but crypt entered by stairs from exterior usually open); and the eleventh-century Abbazia di SS Fidenzio e Terenzio (interior usually closed).

del Gallo, Montecerreto (☎0742.930.040; April–Sept); it has a swimming pool and a beautiful site, backed by the tree-covered slopes of the Monti Martani. Several paths run up to the summit ridge, which has magnificent views as far as Todi and, in May and June, exceptional carpets of wild flowers. There's an excellent little-known and inexpensive **restaurant**, *Il Buongustaio* (closed Wed), immediately within Giano's walls at the village's southern entrance.

North of Giano, the unfortunately named Bastardo is a modern mess with nothing to recommend it. **GUALDO CATTANEO**, just beyond, is by contrast an enticing medieval hill-village dominated by a circular tower-cum-castle built in 1494 by the Borgia Pope Alexander VI. Its name comes from the Saxon word for forest, *wald*. Virtually every hamlet within a ten-kilometre radius has a castle, those at Barattano, Cisterna, Pozzo and Sargano being particularly outstanding. Some hamlets have both a castle and a Romanesque church, as at **MARCELLANO**, with its frescoed twelfth-century church of Sant'Angelo, and **GRUTTI**, whose name derives from the nearby grottoes of early Christians. Slightly north are two more short-stop villages. **COLLAZZONE** has good views and medieval streets, with scenic roads around through olives and oak forest. The parish church in **CASTELLEONE**, over towards Deruta, has frescoes by Matteo da Gualdo, a fifteenth-century Umbrian more usually active farther north.

Deruta and Madonna dei Bagni

DERUTA is best known for its **ceramics** – much of it handmade, hand-painted and by general consent among Italy's best. The Romans worked the local clay, but it was the discovery of distinctive blue and yellow glazes in the fifteenth century, allied with the Moorish-influenced designs of southern Spain, that put the town firmly on the map. Some fifty workshops traded as far afield as Britain, and pieces from Deruta's sixteenth-century heyday have found their way into the world's major museums. Designs these days are mainly copies, with little original work; if you're serious about this sort of thing, avoid the roadside stalls and head for the workshops of the new town for the best selection and prices. The **old town** on the hill isn't particularly compelling, apart from the **Museo Regionale della Ceramica** alongside the church of San Francesco (July–Sept daily 10am–1pm & 3.30–7pm; April–June daily 10.30am–1pm & 3–6pm; Oct–March daily except Tues 10.30am–1pm & 2.30–5pm; €3). The best material is on the second floor, with ceramics from the Renaissance period: elsewhere you'll find exhibits from just about every era from the Roman period to the present day. The ticket also admits you to the tiny **Pinacoteca** in Piazza dei Consoli (closed for restoration of uncertain duration), where the high spots are a detached, damaged but rare fresco (1478) by Fiorenzo di Lorenzo and a *Madonna and Child* and *gonfalone* by Nicolò Alunno. **San Francesco** was largely ruined in the eighteenth century and is distinguished only by the tiniest fragments of – fourteenth-century fresco.

The rarely open church of **MADONNA DEI BAGNI**, 2km south of Deruta, is the one sight on the main SS3bis road that's definitely worth a detour. Its walls are covered with hundreds of votive tiles left by pilgrims over the last three centuries, yielding a unique insight into the peculiarities of religious belief and the changes in daily life. The most entertaining are those offered as thanks for escapes from dangerous and not so dangerous corners – fire, flood, famine, a fall from a cow, a bite from a donkey. They also represent an offbeat record of the area's thriving ceramic tradition. Sadly, a hundred tiles were stolen in 1980, so opening hours are curtailed as a result: the best time to try is on Saturday morning, when it's not unknown for coach parties to show up.

Torgiano

TORGIANO, 8km north of Deruta, though a fairly dull town, is home to Umbria's finest wines, all of them produced by **Giorgio Lungarotti**, first of the new breed of Italian producers. A self-made man and now something of a national celebrity, he's put together an interesting and extensive **Museo del Vino** in the suitably atmospheric cellars of the Palazzo Graziani-Baglioni, Corso Vittorio Emanuele II (daily 9am–1pm & 3–7pm; Oct–March closes 6pm; €4, joint ticket with Museo dell'Olivo €7; ⓦ www.lungarotti.it). Early sections look at the origins of viticulture, followed by documentation relating to wine-making in the Middle Ages. Subsequent rooms are devoted to Vin Santo, commerce, the legal niceties of wine-making, cultivation, wine mythology and more, everything well labelled in English. The less persuasive **Museo dell'Olivo e dell'Olio**, Via Garibaldi 10 (same hours; €4, joint ticket €7) traces the story of olives and local olive cultivation. An excellent selection of **wines** are sold at good prices in the enoteca beside the Museo del Vino, and in shops and restaurants across Umbria and beyond; any bottle with the Lungarotti name should be good, but particular labels to look out for include Lungarotti's Rubesco, Torre di Giano, Chardonnay and Castel Grifone. You can buy the cheaper Torgiano wines in most Italian supermarkets, but the Rubesco Riserva, which rates as one of Italy's very finest, is rather more elusive.

Orvieto

ORVIETO sits on a spectacular tabletop of volcanic tufa whose sheer sides fall 325m to the vine-covered valley floor – a cliff-edged remnant of the four volcanoes whose eruptions also bequeathed the soils that produce Orvieto's occasionally fine wines. Out on a limb from the rest of Umbria, the town is perfectly placed between Rome and Florence to serve as a historical picnic for tour operators, and tourists flood here in their millions in high season, drawn by the **Duomo** – one of the greatest Gothic buildings in Italy and home of some sublime frescoes by Luca Signorelli. Once these have been admired, Orvieto is not as exhilarating as some Umbrian towns, though the *centro storico*, the views and the renowned white **wine** are enough to justify a night's stop.

The city is one of the most ancient in Italy, thanks to its irresistible site. Bronze and Iron Age tribes were present before it became an **Etruscan** settlement, later named Volsinii Veteres, or Velzna, in around the ninth century BC. Eventually it became a leading member of the twelve-strong Etruscan federation, and possibly the site of the Etruscans' principal religious shrine, the Fanum Voltumnae. In 264 BC (possibly earlier), the **Romans** ravaged the town and displaced the Etruscans to present-day Bolsena, or Volsinii Novi – the place they abandoned becoming known as Urbs Vetus (the Old City), thus Orvieto. Its medieval influence was considerable, the independent *comune* challenging Florence and eventually claiming land as far as Monte Amiata in the north and to the coast at Orbetello in the west. Power and prestige remained high until the usual internecine squabbling, the **Black Death** of 1348 sounding the town's effective death knell. It passed to the Church for good a hundred years later and became something of a papal home from home: 32 popes in all stayed in the city. One of them, Gregory I, even met **Edward I** of England here on Edward's return from the Crusades.

A single ticket, the Carta Orvieto Unica (€12.50), provides admission to the Signorelli frescoes in the Duomo's Cappella di San Brizio, Orvieto Underground, the Museo Claudio Faina and Torre del Moro. It also allows you one trip on the funicular and one bus journey, plus five hours' worth of parking at the Campo della Fiera car park beneath the walls at the southwest corner of Orvieto (from where escalators run up to town). You can buy the ticket at the tourist office and the Parcheggio della Funicolare, or funicular car park (℡0763.302.370), by the railway station in Orvieto Scalo.

Arrival, information and accommodation

Fast **trains** on the Rome–Florence run tend to bypass Orvieto, so you may well have to change at Orte or Chiusi to a slower connecting service; from Perugia (86km), change at Teróntola. Orvieto's station is in the grim new town of Orvieto Scalo, a twisting three-kilometre drive from the old centre. From the station forecourt, a wonderful restored nineteenth-century **funicular** (Mon–Sat every 10min 7.20am–8.30pm, Sun every 15min 8am–8.30pm; €0.80) runs up to Piazza Cahen in the old town, from where it's a pleasant five- or ten-minute walk along Corso Cavour to the centre. Minibuses (free with a funicular ticket; otherwise €0.80) shuttle every few minutes from the top station to Piazza del Duomo – either direct (bus A) or via Piazza della Repubblica (bus B). After 8.30pm, buses replace the funicular. Inter-town **buses** take you to Piazza Cahen, Piazza XXIX Marzo or Piazza della Repubblica, depending on the service; some terminate at the train station.

Cars are prohibited in the old town at certain times, but even when they're not, finding a parking space is a tall order. There are car parks in Piazzale Cahen and off Via Roma just to the west, or you could use the big free car park on the east side of the station and take the funicular. Better still, aim to park at Campo della Fiera, below the southwest corner of the old town, where you can pick up local buses (Linea B or C) on their run from the station to Piazza della Repubblica; pedestrian lifts and escalators up to the centre (exiting near Via Garibaldi and Via Ripa Medici) also run from this point.

The **tourist office**, Piazza del Duomo 24 (Mon–Fri 8.15am–1.50pm & 4–7pm, Sat 10am–7pm, Sun 10am–6pm; variable and shorter winter hours; ℡0763.341.772, ⓦ www.comune.orvieto.tr.it), has plenty of maps and information, as well as details of private rooms and a dozen or so **agriturismo** options nearby. The town has also seen the rapid growth of a B&B sector, with central rooms mostly at around €65–85, depending on the time of year. You can get details from the tourist office or on their website (click on "dove dormire"). There are also plenty of cheap, modern but characterless hotels in the unlovely Orvieto Scalo. All but one of the local **campsites** are some way out.

Hotels

Corso Corso Cavour 343 ℡0763.342.020, ⓦ www.hotelcorso.net. A good, but relatively pricey three-star hotel, part of a fine and recently renovated medieval town house with nine bright, spacious rooms (some with panoramic terraces) in a fairly quiet and convenient position. ❸

Duomo Vicolo di Maurizio 7 ℡0763.341.887, ⓦ www.orvietohotelduomo.com. An excellent central sixteen-room three-star option. In a peaceful and perfect location, one alley north of the Duomo, but the tile floors make rooms and corridors very noisy if you have heavy-footed neighbours. ❹

Filippeschi Via Filippeschi 19 ℡ & ℻ 0763.343.275. Moderately priced fifteen-room three-star in a convenient central location just west of Piazza della Repubblica. ❸

Grand Hotel Italia Piazza del Popolo 13 ℡0763.342.065, ⓦ www.grandhotelitalia.it. The biggest central hotel, with 45 three-star rooms; likely to have space in an emergency. ❸

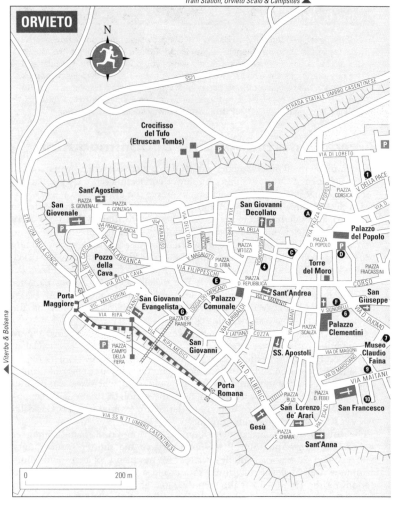

ORVIETO

N

Crocifisso
del Tufo
(Etruscan Tombs)

Sant'Agostino

San
Giovenale

Pozzo
della
Cava

Porta
Maggiore

San Giovanni
Evangelista

San
Giovanni

Porta
Romana

Gesù

San Giovanni
Decollato

Torre
del Moro

Sant'Andrea

Palazzo
Comunale

SS. Apostoli

Palazzo
del Popolo

San
Giuseppe

Palazzo
Clementini

Museo
Claudio
Faina

San Lorenzo
de' Arari

San Francesco

Sant'Anna

0   200 m

La Badia Località La Badia ☎0763.301.959,
ⓦwww.labadiahotel.it. Most Umbrian towns
now have a luxurious, out-of-town option: this is
Orvieto's, a converted abbey 5km south on the
Bagnoregio road. It's not as grand as some newer
conversions, however, and could do with a revamp,
especially some of the relatively austere rooms.
This said, the grounds (with good views of Orvieto)
are lovely, and there are all the usual smart facilities, including tennis courts and a pool. ❻
Maitani Via Lorenzo Maitani 5 ☎0763.342.012,
ⓕ0763.342.011. The most traditional and most
central of Orvieto's quartet of four-star hotels

– and with forty rooms there's a good chance of
space. ❹
Palazzo Piccolomini Piazza Ranieri 36
☎0763.341.743, ⓦwww.hotelpiccolomini.
it. You have two choices for doing Orvieto in style:
the traditional *Maitani* (see above) and this
central thirty-room four-star, converted in 1997 from
a sixteenth-century palace and, in the manner of the
Fonte Cesia in Todi or *Palazzo Bocci* in Spello, one of
the breed of very stylish, tasteful and refined historic
hotels which the region does extremely well. ❻
Posta Via Luca Signorelli 18 ☎0763.341.909,
ⓦwww.orvietohotels.it. The only inexpensive two-

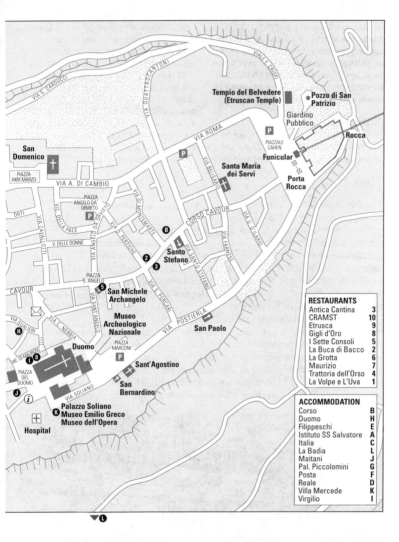

RESTAURANTS

Antica Cantina	3
CRAMST	10
Etrusca	9
Gigli d'Oro	8
I Sette Consoli	5
La Buca di Bacco	2
La Grotta	6
Maurizio	7
Trattoria dell'Orso	4
La Volpe e L'Uva	1

ACCOMMODATION

Corso	B
Duomo	H
Filippeschi	E
Istituto SS Salvatore	A
Italia	C
La Badia	L
Maitani	J
Pal. Piccolomini	G
Posta	F
Reale	D
Villa Mercede	K
Virgilio	I

star choice amongst the central hotels; faded and rather charmingly old-fashioned medieval house just two minutes from the Duomo, with a garden and twenty cool, quiet and pleasant rooms with and without private bathrooms. ❶

Reale Piazza del Popolo 25 ℡0763.341.247, ⓦwww.orvietohotels.it. Slightly less expensive 31-room three-star than the nearby *Italia*, but only if you go for one of the handful of lower-grade rooms without private bath. ❸

Virgilio Piazza del Duomo 5–6 ℡0763.341.882, Ⓕ0763.343.797. Often celebrated for its perfect position, but in fact only a handful of the relatively

modest thirteen three-star rooms actually have (side-on) views of the Duomo. And rooms looking on to the piazza are likely to be noisy on summer evenings. ❸

Religious houses

Istituto SS Salvatore Via Piazza del Popolo 1 ℡0763.342.910, Ⓔistitutosansalvatore@tiscalinet .it. You can stay cheaply with the nuns in this central Dominican convent, but the minimum stay is generally two nights and there's a 10pm curfew (9pm autumn & winter). Has fifteen rooms with and without bathrooms, with doubles from €45. ❶

Villa Mercede Via Soliana ☎0763.341.766, ⓔvillamercede@orvienet.it. It's harder to imagine a cheaper bed close to the cathedral than in this simple but perfectly situated twelve-room religious house, where doubles (all en-suite) are €68. Minimum stay is two days, and there is a 10pm curfew (9pm in autumn and winter). ❷

Campsites

Il Falcone Località Vallonganino 2a, Civitella del Lago ☎0744.950.249, ⓔilfalcone@tin.it. A well-run two-star site with a friendly owner, overlooking Lago di Corbara. Although it's 10km or so from Orvieto, you can pick up supplies in Civitella or eat at the Bar-Pizzeria, Via Italia 16, or in the restaurant Da Crespino, Via degli Atti, Montecchio ☎0744.951.017. Open April–Sept. Another campsite on the lake, the Orvieto, was closed at the time of writing.

Scacco Matto ☎0744.950.163, ⓕ0763.950.373. Basic one-star site, also by Lago di Corbara; take the bus for Civitella del Lago (two daily) or Narni (six daily; alight at Baschi). Has a few ❷ rooms to rent as well. Open April–Sept.

The Duomo

The historian Jacob Burckhardt described Orvieto's **Duomo** (daily 7.30am–12.45pm & 2.30–7.30pm; March & Oct closes 6.15pm; Nov–Feb closes 5.30pm; free; Cappella di San Brizio has different hours and an admission charge, see p.722; ⓦwww.opsm.it) as "the greatest and richest polychrome monument in the world"; Pope Leo XIII called it the "Golden Lily of Italian cathedrals", adding that on the Day of Judgement it would float to Heaven carried by its own beauty. Though the cathedral's overall effect might be a bit rich for some tastes, it rates – with Assisi's Basilica di San Francesco – as one of the two essential sights in Umbria.

The monumental **facade** of the Duomo is just the right side of overkill: a riot of columns, spires, bas-reliefs, sculptures, dazzling colour, colossal doorways and hundreds of capricious details held together by four enormous fluted pillars. Many have compared it to a painted triptych in an elaborate frame. Some 52m high and recently cleaned and overhauled, it is a stunning spectacle from the piazza, particularly at sunset or under floodlights. Most of the basic work was accomplished by **Lorenzo Maitani** (see box), but such illustrious names as

△ Bas-reliefs, depicting Hell, on the facade of Orvieto's Duomo

Construction of the Duomo

Church tradition holds that the Duomo was built to celebrate the Miracle of Bolsena, which occurred in 1263. The protagonist, a young Bavarian priest, was on a pilgrimage to Rome to shake off his disbelief in transubstantiation (the idea that the body and blood of Christ are physically present in the Eucharist). While he celebrated Mass in a church near Lago di Bolsena, blood started to drip from the Host onto the *corporale*, the white linen cloth that covers the altar, "each stain severally assuming the form of a human head with features like the Volto Santo, the face of the Saviour". The linen was whisked off to Pope Urban IV, who was holed up in Orvieto to escape the literal and political heat in Rome. He proclaimed a miracle and a year later Thomas Aquinas, then teaching in Orvieto's San Domenico, drew up a papal bull instigating the feast of Corpus Domini.

The cornerstone of the Duomo was not put in place for another 25 years (laid by Pope Nicholas IV on November 13, 1290) and Aquinas's bull makes no specific mention of Bolsena, so it's likely that the raising of the Duomo was as much a shrewd piece of political pragmatism as a celebration of a miracle. The papacy at the time was in retreat and the Umbrian towns – not least Orvieto – at the height of their civic expansion. Thus it seems likely that the building of this awe-inspiring cathedral, in one of the region's most powerful towns, was a piece of political muscle-flexing to remind errant citizens of the papacy's power.

It was, indeed, miraculous that the Duomo was built at all. Medieval Orvieto was so violent that at times the population considered abandoning the city altogether. Dante wrote that its family feuds were worse than those between Verona's Montecchi and Cappelli, inspiration for Shakespeare's murderous Montagues and Capulets in *Romeo and Juliet*. The building was also dogged by a committee approach to design, the plans being modified continually to accommodate changes in architectural taste. At least the site posed no problems: the city's highest point was previously home to an Etruscan temple and Orvieto's first cathedral, Santa Maria Prisca. Even today, the cathedral continues to dominate the skyline for miles around.

The architect is unknown, though it seems possible that it was Arnolfo di Cambio, designer of Florence's Duomo. At Orvieto the plan initially was for a simple and orthodox Romanesque church, but in the early years of work a local architect's extravagant departures into the Gothic brought the structure close to collapse, leading to the call-up in 1310 of the Sienese master, Lorenzo Maitani. In the course of three decades he guided the construction at its most crucial stage and produced the magnificent carvings on the facade. Though building dragged on for over three hundred years, exhausting 33 architects, 152 sculptors, 68 painters and 90 mosaicists, the final product is a surprisingly unified example of the transitional Romanesque-Gothic style.

Andrea Pisano and Andrea Orcagna – responsible for much of the rose window – also had a hand in design and construction.

The four pillars at the base are among the highlights of fourteenth-century Italian **sculpture**. The work of Maitani and his pupils, they depict episodes from the Old and New Testaments in staggering detail: lashings of plague, famine, martyrdom, mutilation and murder. The panels read from left to right, starting with the Creation on the left-most pillar. The stories in stone here are wonderfully graphic and self-explanatory, but the delicacy of the carving, especially of the trees, which have the intricacy of coral, is extraordinary. Look in particular at the scene of Eve emerging from Adam's rib (second tier), the casting out of Adam and Eve (fourth tier) and Cain slaying Abel (fifth tier, right-hand panel), the last especially powerful. The second pillar has the stories of Abraham and David, and the third, scenes from the lives of Christ and the Virgin. Many details, it appears, were created partly to point an accusing finger at Orvieto's moral slackers, as the extraordinary fourth and final pillar makes clear, with its depictions of the Last Judgement, Hell and Paradise, and the damned packed off to eternal fire, brimstone and the company of an awful lot of snakes.

Maitani was also responsible for the four large bronzes of the symbols of the Evangelists across the first tier, and for the angels over the beautiful central **doorway**. These, however, together with the *Madonna* in the lunette, have been removed for restoration and will probably be replaced by copies: the originals are lined up for display in the Museo dell'Opera. The **mosaics**, the facade's showiest aspect, are mostly eighteenth- and nineteenth-century additions, replacements for originals nabbed by Rome. Only the four examples in the corners of Orcagna's huge **rose window** (1359), have any vintage, completed around 1388. The central bronze doors, by Emilio Greco, were made as recently as 1965, and in the best traditions of the Duomo were added after much talk and controversy.

The Cappella di San Brizio

At first, little save the colossal scale grabs your attention in the Duomo's interior – which is far less cluttered than the similar cathedral in Siena – a few snatches of fresco in the scalloped side niches, and the work immediately on your left as you enter, a heavily restored *Madonna and Child* (1425) by Gentile da Fabriano, with a very sickly-looking Jesus. However, in the right transept – the **Cappella di San Brizio** – are **Luca Signorelli**'s superlative paintings of the Last Judgement (1499–1504), one of Italy's great fresco cycles and one that had a profound influence on Michelangelo's version in the Sistine Chapel, painted forty years later. The cycle is on view again after years of restoration (April–Sept Mon–Sat 9am–12.45pm & 2.30–7.15pm, Sun 2.30–5.45pm, except Sun July–Sept closes at 6.45pm; March & Oct Mon–Sat 9am–12.45pm & 2.30–6.15pm, Sun 2.30–5.45pm; Nov–Feb Mon–Sat 9am–12.45pm & 2.30–5.15pm, Sun 2.30–5.45pm; €5). **Tickets** are not available in the cathedral, but must be bought from the tourist office.

Several painters tackled the chapel before Signorelli. **Fra' Angelico** made a start in 1447, completing two of the ceiling's eight vaults, *Christ in Glory with Angels* (marked as 1 on our plan) and *The Prophets* (3), with the assistance of **Benozzo Gozzoli**, whose hand can be seen in the angels of the latter panel. Angelico, it appears, suggested the frescoes' central theme, the Last Judgement, but was then called to Rome to work in the Vatican, never to return. The murder of a local grandee involved in financing the project, Arigo Monaldeschi, then brought work on the Duomo to one of its periodic halts. **Perugino** popped up forty years later and disappeared for reasons unknown – never to return – after working for just five days. Signorelli saved the day, graciously restoring Fra' Angelico's work and completing the vaults according to the original plan.

Work then started in earnest on the walls, all but the lowest of which are crowded with passionate and beautifully observed muscular figures, creating an effect that's both realistic and almost grotesquely fantastic at the same time. Seven main episodes are painted in the eight panels of the vaults and the twelve floor-level groups of frescoes. The first is the **End of the World** (9) on the entrance wall, the last of the major episodes painted (1503–4). In the lower right foreground are depicted Eritrea, a sibyl, shown holding a book of prophecies, while alongside is the Prophet David, who is shown asserting the veracity of the prophecies. Behind them an earthquake brings down a temple and three youths fall prey to brigands; in the background ships are tossed on a

CAPPELLA DI SAN BRIZIO, ORVIETO

Altar Wall

Right Wall

Left Wall

Entrance

1. Christ in Glory with Angels
2. The Apostles
3. The Prophets
4. Portents of the Last Judgement
5. The Martyrs
6. The Patriarchs
7. The Doctor of the Church
8. The Virgins
9. The End of the World
10. The Preaching of the Antichrist
11. The Resurrection of the Dead
12. Inferno
13. Purgatory
14. The Calling of the Saved
15. Paradiso

16. Monument to Cardinal Ferdinando Nuzzi (d. 1717)
17. Portrait of Tibullus
18. Pietà, SS. Faustino and Pietro Parenzo, and Martyrdom of the Saints by Luca Signorelli
19. Ovid and four tondo scenes from Metamorphoses
20. Portrait of Claudian
21. Scenes from Ovid's Metamorphoses
22. Scenes from Dante's Purgatorio
23. Portrait of Statius
24. Portrait of Dante: Medallions here and around and joining panels show scenes from Cantos 1–11 of Purgatorio
25. Cappella Gualtieri (1736); painting of Saints (1724) by Ludovico Muratori
26. Portrait of Sallust: Medallions – Classical scenes and grape harvest
27. Empedocles (?) and The End of The World

sea convulsed by a tidal wave brought on by the earthquake. High up on the left you see the fall of the rebel angels, many of whom unleash thunderbolts of fire which fall on a terrified crowd below. A putto in the panel's centre holds a sign with the mark of the Opera del Duomo (OPSM), a reminder of the cathedral works committee responsible for commissioning and overseeing the project.

The first lunette panel on the wall left of the entrance depicts one of the cycle's most powerful works, the **Preaching of the Antichrist** (10), the iconography of which is unique (the subject itself is very rare in Italian painting). It derives from a text whose precise authorship is unknown, but which unites elements from St Augustine's *City of God*, ancient millennial texts – the world was widely expected to end in the year 1000 – and the *Golden Legend* of Jacopo da Varagine (also the inspiration for Piero della Francesca's Arezzo cycle: see p.517). The Antichrist is shown preaching and bears the image of Christ, albeit one that displays a demonic demeanour, with a devil whispering in his ear. Various historical figures stand amidst the crowd to the left and right of the Antichrist, designed to represent all colours, creeds and conditions of the human family: Signorelli has portrayed himself with Fra'Angelico behind (in the black of a Dominican monk) in the left foreground, both apparently unperturbed by the garroting taking place in front of them. Also present in the left-hand group are Dante (rear right, in profile with red hat), Cesare Borgia (on the extreme left of the group with beard, blond hair and red hat) and Pius II, the corpulent fellow in yellow behind the figure with hands on hips alongside the Antichrist. Also here is the figure of Signorelli's mistress, who jilted him during the time the frescoes were being painted, and as punishment is prominently portrayed in the foregound of the group as a prosti-tute taking money. Groups of Franciscan and Dominican monks can be seen to the rear and right of the Antichrist trying to calculate the precise date of the end of the world – one counts off three and a half years with his fingers, the 1290 days that the reign of the Antichrist was expected to endure. The two other group vignettes behind the monks to right and left show a false miracle and the execu-tion of two penitents. In the background is the Temple of Solomon, while in the heavens, the Archangel Michael is seen preventing the ascension of the Antichrist and unleashing a storm of fire onto the corrupt below.

The sequence then moves to the first lunette on the right wall with the **Resurrection of the Dead** (11), summoned by the trumpets of the angels depicted on high. Signorelli here departs from convention, painting the fig-ures emerging dramatically from the bare earth rather than from tombs, the traditional iconography employed in depictions of this scene. Note the small scratched figures at the centre of the panel, probably drawn by Signorelli to illustrate some point to the cathedral committee. The adjoining lunette on the right wall depicts **Inferno** (12), probably Signorelli's first completed fresco in the chapel.

On the altar wall right of the window is the **Punishment of the Damned, or Purgatory** (13), which in its portrayal of the damned inevitably draws on Dante's *The Divine Comedy*, but also utilizes the iconography of pagan works such as the battle scenes carved on the reliefs on Trajan's Column in Rome. Signorelli's mistress is again prominently painted, this time as the figure at the centre of the picture being carried by a flying winged devil. The panel left of the window shows the **Calling of the Saved** (14), a portrayal that includes two of Orvieto's saintly protectors, Costanzo and Brizio, at its centre; St Michael weighing the souls; and angels serenading and guiding the elected to **Paradiso** (15), the scene portrayed in the adjoining lunette on the left wall. In this last mural, Paradise's peace and harmony are symbolized by a heavenly choir of nine angel musicians and – in the centre – by two angels who scatter roses and camellias. These flowers were painted onto dry plaster, a less durable technique than the more usual practice of adding paint to wet plaster, hence their faded appearance. The altarpiece, incidentally, is the *Madonna di San Brizio*, an anony-mous work held by tradition to have been painted by St Luke, but in truth probably executed towards the end of the fourteenth century.

The outstanding **frescoes and medallions** (numbered 16 to 27) on the lower parts of the walls are also by Signorelli and include portraits of Homer, Dante, Ovid, Virgil, Horace, Lucan, Empedocles and others, together with episodes from classical myth, notably Ovid's *Metamorphoses* and Dante's *Divine Comedy*. Of particular note is the *Pietà with SS Faustino and Pietro Parenzo* (18) in the recess on the right. Vasari claimed that the figure of the dead Christ was a close portrait of Signorelli's own son, Antonio, who died from the plague in 1502 while the artist was employed on the frescoes.

Everything here has a didactic purpose, further illustrating or drawing allusions to the main theme of the frescoes above. Dante's *Divine Comedy* – which is frequently evoked – forms an obvious corollary, with its themes of salvation and damnation. Elsewhere, however, Signorelli uses Classical myth and literary figures to his own ends; Empedocles (27), for example, is shown in shocked contemplation of the end of the world, though he in fact never prophesied such an event. Some critics believe this is actually a figure of a common man who has not converted to Christianity, and looks on at the horrors that await him as one of the damned. The separate portrait of Stazio (23) is used in a similar way. The figure looks towards the chapel's high altar as if receiving spiritual illumination, but Dante writes that while the poet converted to Christianity, he kept his conversion and subsequent faith a secret. Throughout the Middle Ages the figure was therefore a symbol of salvation and also of only partial redemption – just the sort of character who would have been compromised, to say the least, come the Day of Judgement.

The Cappella del Corporale and the apse
The artistic pyrotechnics of the Cappella di San Brizio rather overshadow the opposite transept's **Cappella del Corporale**, which contains the sacred *corporale* of the Miracle of Bolsena, usually locked away in a massive, jewel-encrusted casket on the left designed in 1358 as a copy of the facade. On the chapel walls are extensive **frescoes** (1357–64) by a local artist, Ugolino di Prete Ilario, depicting episodes from the *Miracle of Bolsena* (right-hand wall) and various *Miracles of the Sacrament* (opposite). The chapel also houses (on the right) the glorious freestanding *Madonna dei Raccomandati* (1339) by the Sienese painter Lippo Memmi.

Ugolino covered the entire **apse** in frescoes (1370–84) of scenes from the *Life of the Virgin*, many of which were touched up by Pinturicchio, who was eventually kicked off the job for "consuming too much gold, too much azure, and too much wine".

The rest of the town

Nothing in Orvieto can quite live up to the Duomo, but then nor can much else in central Italy, though the piazza has a tremendous Etruscan museum, the **Museo Claudio Faina**, and a couple of other worthwhile sights. The dark tufa used as building stone around town can make parts seem a little dour during aimless exploration, particularly in poor weather, but some of the town's peripheral corners provide attractions that more than justify the walk – **San Giovenale** and the strange **Pozzo di San Patrizio** in particular. Trying to arrange a logical itinerary is difficult, but as distances are modest the walking's not too onerous – though be warned that the town drops sharply away on its western side, so expect a steep walk back to the centre from this area.

Underground Orvieto

Cut into the crag below the town are the fascinating Grotte della Rupe, an extraordinary honeycomb of caves, wine cellars, aqueducts, quarries and tunnels used – and added to – since Etruscan times. A staggering 1200 separate caves have been found beneath Orvieto, around a third of the entire area under the town having been excavated at one time or another. Guided tours in English are run by Orvieto Underground, leaving from the tourist office (daily 11am, 12.15pm, 4pm & 5.15pm; €5.50; ℡0763.344.891, ℡339.733.2764 or ℡347.383.1472, ⓦwww.orvietounderground .it); call for details or to make advance bookings (although you can just turn up and hope to get on a tour). The Pozzo della Cava, Via della Cava 26 (Tues–Sun 8am–8pm; ⓦwww.pozzodellacava.it; €3 or €2 for holders of tickets for buses, funicular, Pozzo di San Patrizio or Museo Emilio Greco), is a large smooth-sided Etruscan-era well, one of about forty found around the town. It's a slightly cynical money-making exercise – it used to be free – but striking enough if you haven't time for the full underground tour.

Piazza del Duomo

Beside the Duomo stands the **Palazzo Soliano**, or Palazzo dei Papi, begun for Pope Boniface VIII in 1297. For years it has been home to the **Museo dell'Opera del Duomo**, a museum that was closed for years and has only recently been reopened after restoration on a rather ad hoc basis. For the current situation, contact the tourist office or nearby Opera del Duomo office at Piazza del Duomo 26 (℡0763.343.592) or visit ⓦwww.opsm.it. Highlights of the museum collection include some topnotch paintings, notably a self-portrait by Signorelli, a *Madonna and Child* (1268) by the influential early Tuscan painter Coppo di Marcovaldo, and five parts of a polyptych from San Domenico by the Sienese master Simone Martini. Among the sculptures are wooden and marble Madonnas by Nino, Giovanni and Andrea Pisano, a lovely font filled with Escher-like fishes, and unfinished but important pieces by Arnolfo di Cambio.

On the ground floor of the museum is a section devoted to **Emilio Greco**, who created the Duomo's bronze doors in the 1960s (daily 10.30am–1pm & 2.30–7pm; Oct–March 10.30am–1pm & 2–5.30pm; €2.50, joint ticket "*biglietto cumulativo*" with Pozzo di San Patrizio €4.50). On display are nearly a hundred works donated to the city by the artist. None of them is profoundly interesting unless you're a Greco enthusiast: peek through the door beyond the ticket office and you'll see enough of the exhibits to know if you want a closer look.

The Palazzo Papale, beyond the cathedral's east end, houses the unremarkable **Museo Archeologico Nazionale** (daily 8.30am–7.30pm; €2, joint ticket with Necropoli Etrusca, or Crocifisso del Tufo €3), which contains fourth-century BC Greek vases, two reconstructed painted tombs with their original murals and other Etruscan artefacts excavated during digs at Orvieto's own Cannicella and Crocifisso del Tufo tombs.

The Museo Claudio Faina

You're better off spending your money on the **Museo Claudio Faina** (incorporating the Museo Civico and Museo dei Ragazzi) opposite the Duomo (April–Sept daily 9.30am–6pm; Oct & March daily 10am–5pm; Nov–Feb Tues–Sun 10am–5pm; €4.50), reopened after a renovation project which has turned a previously dull museum into a wonderful showcase for one of Italy's leading private archeological collections. It's worth the admission price simply for a view of the Duomo from the upper floor. The core of the collection is 34 vases given in the nineteenth century to Mauro Faina, a Perugian count,

⑬

ORVIETO AND SOUTHERN UMBRIA | Orvieto

726

by Princess Maria Bonaparte, Napoleon's grandniece (the count had been a regular "visitor" to the princess's home). Over the years Faina, together with his nephew, added obsessively to the collection, which was left to the city in 1954. The exhibits spread over 22 rooms on two upper floors of the Palazzo Faina (plus a small ground-floor civic collection), arranged in a modern museum setting that would be the envy of far grander galleries.

Highlights include three vast, sixth-century BC Attic **amphorae** (room 6) attributed to Exekias, one of antiquity's finest vase painters – their presence in Orvieto testimony to the town's prosperity at the time. Also famous is the so-called **Vanth group** (rooms 11, 18 and 22), the name given to a collection of pots made locally in the last two decades of the fourth century BC. Vanth was an important female divinity associated with the Etruscan underworld, often portrayed with two serpents around each arm and, in the manner of medieval saints, with symbols such as keys, taper, mantle and scroll, the last partially unrolled to reveal the name of the goddess. As here, she was often portrayed greeting the recently deceased on their arrival in the underworld.

There are also many black *bucchero* **vases** (rooms 10, 11 and 14), so-called because at the time of their discovery they were thought to resemble vases from South America known to the Spanish as *bucaro*. The black colour was imparted in the kiln, where the firing process oxidized iron compounds in specially chosen clay. Quality declined around the fifth century BC, the result of insufficiently pure clays, a shortfall that resulted in *bucchero grigio*, or grey ware (gradually replaced by simple black-glazed pottery). A similar falling-off of quality occurred with the familiar black-figure Attic vases (rooms 11, 13 and 16), invented in Corinth around 700 BC, and made by painting a figure in black silhouette before incising detail so that the lighter-coloured clay beneath showed through. Such pottery was wildly popular throughout the Mediterranean, but no market was as large as Tyrrhenian Etruria. It was eventually replaced by Attic red-figure pottery (rooms 11, 14, 17 and 18), invented in Athens around 530 BC, in which figures and decorative details were composed in the clay and the rest of the pot painted black. The museum also has a large collection of coins, bronzes and miscellaneous funerary objects.

West to San Giovenale

The tiny Romanesque **San Lorenzo de' Arari** (or dell'Ara), a short walk west of the Duomo, was built in 1291 on the site of a church destroyed by monks from nearby San Francesco because the sound of its bells got on their nerves. Four restored frescoes (1330) on the left of the nave depict traumatic scenes from the *Life of St Lawrence*, including execution by roasting, and there's a Byzantine-influenced *Christ Enthroned with Four Saints* in the apse. An Etruscan sacrificial slab rather oddly serves as the altar (*arari*) from which the church derives its name.

From nearby Piazzale Cacciatore there's a good **walk** around the city's southern walls along **Via Ripa Medici**, with views over to a prominent outcrop of rock in the mid-distance, part of the old volcanic crater. En route, stop by the excellent **Enoteca Regionale**, Via Ripa Serancia 16 (Mon–Sat 9am–1pm & 3–7pm; wine-tasting tours mid-April to mid-Sept daily 11am & 5pm, rest of year daily 4pm; check for latest times; ☎0763.393.529). To learn more, or to visit local vineyards, contact the Consorzio Tutela Vino, Corso Cavour 36 (☎0763.343.790).

Ten minutes or so farther west – with a big drop to the Porta Maggiore and a climb up again – is the ancient **San Giovenale**, set amid rustic surroundings on the western tip of Orvieto's plateau (you might also approach this part of town from Piazza della Repubblica and the northwest tangle of streets to avoid the slopes). New studies have established the previously accepted date of its foundation – 1004 – as the date of its first restoration. It's not much to look at from outside, but the musty interior is a distinctive hybrid of a church, the thirteenth-century Gothic transept, with its two pointed arches, standing rather oddly a metre above the rounded Romanesque nave. Beautiful thirteenth- and fifteenth-century **frescoes** cover all available surfaces; they include a *Tree of Life* to the right of the main door and the macabre *Calendar of Funeral Anniversaries* partly covered by the side entrance.

Make the walk worthwhile by taking in the glorious **view** from the town wall just to the west, or by following the wall-top lane (Via Volsinia II) down towards the Porta Maggiore. Otherwise, from San Giovenale back to the centre of town, Via Malabranca and Via Filippeschi are the best preserved of the medieval streets.

Piazza della Repubblica and around

Back in the heart of town, **Sant' Andrea**, in **Piazza della Repubblica**, is worth a look for its twelve-sided campanile, odd patches of fresco and pieces of Roman and Etruscan city in the crypt. For an overview of the town, climb the medieval **Torre del Moro** not far east of the church at Corso Cavour 87 (daily: May–Aug 10am–8pm; March, April, Sept & Oct 10am–7pm; Nov–Feb 10.30am–1pm & 2.30–5pm; €2.60). The bell up here is engraved with the 24 symbols of Orvieto's medieval guilds and was cast in 1316; it's been tolling every fifteen minutes ever since. Not to be missed nearby, on the corner of **Piazza del Popolo**, is Alda, Via San Leonardo 18, an exceptional antique shop housed in a sensational space: two former churches, San Carlo and San Bernardo, which are covered in superb frescoes. The place is virtually unknown to outsiders and keeps irregular hours; to be sure of getting a peek, visit on market days (Thurs & Sat) in the piazza, when the owners are almost always on hand.

Northeast of Piazza del Popolo, **San Domenico** stands next to a Fascist-era barracks – far and away the ugliest building in the town. Half of the church, built between 1233 and 1264 (and thus Italy's first church to be dedicated to St Dominic) was sliced off during the construction of the barracks. The principal artwork is the *Tomb of Cardinal de Braye* (died 1281) a pioneering work by Arnolfo di Cambio in the Cappella Petrucci, entered via a door on the south (right) wall. This defined the format of wall tombs for the next century, showing the deceased lying on a coffin below the Madonna and Child, within an elaborate architectural framework.

The Pozzo di San Patrizio and the Rocca

Orvieto's novelty act is the huge cylindrical well known as the **Pozzo di San Patrizio** (daily 10am–6.45pm; Oct–March closes 5.45pm; €3.50, joint ticket with the Emilio Greco section of the Museo dell'Opera del Duomo €4.50), signposted beside the funicular terminus in Piazza Cahen east of the centre. Pope Clement VII commissioned it from Antonio da Sangallo the Younger two years after the Sack of Rome, which he'd been forced to flee disguised as a greengrocer. An attack on Orvieto was expected from the imperial troops, and the well was designed to guarantee the town's water supply during a siege. The attack never materialized – which was fortunate, as it took ten years of digging to hit water. It was while in Orvieto that Clement took the fateful decision not to annul Henry VIII's marriage to Catherine of Aragon.

The well is a virtuoso piece of engineering, 13m wide and 62m deep, and takes its name from a supposed resemblance to the Irish cave where St Patrick died at the ripe old age of 133. Water was brought to the surface by donkeys on two broad 248-step staircases, cannily designed in a double helix so that they never intersect. Half the well is carved from solid tufa, half is brick-lined, and the whole thing is lit by 72 strange windows cut from the spirals into the central shaft. In Italy, skinflints are said to have "pockets as deep as the Pozzo di San Patrizio".

The direct recipient of the water from the *pozzo* was the nearby **Rocca**, built in 1364 by Cardinal Albornoz, the papal fireband recruited to restore Church authority across central Italy. Views from the ruins are wonderful; nearby are the small but pleasant **public gardens**, one of Orvieto's few patches of green and home to the prominent remains of an Etruscan temple, the **Tempio del Belvedere**. The castle itself was built over the only stratum of travertine in the town, a robust piece of rock that escapes the landslips which strike the tufa with increasing regularity. Defoliation, the collapse of ancient sewers, the lowering of the water table and the intensification of traffic culminated in disastrous slips during 1977 and 1979, finally prompting the approval of vast funds from the European Union. Miles of tunnels and caves dating back to the Etruscans still honeycomb the rock, a labyrinth once used for quarrying, burials and the fermenting of wine; the subterranean conditions were said to be responsible for the excellence of Orvieto's vintages. Modern methods now make a drier product, better selling but less exalted than the traditional semi-sweet *abboccato*.

The Necropoli Etrusca

The **Necropoli Etrusca, or Crocifisso del Tufo** (daily 8.30am–7pm; Oct–March closes 5pm; €2, joint ticket with Museo Archeologico €3) – a set of sixth-century BC Etruscan tombs – are well worth a look: walk or drive down the town's approach road from Piazza Cahen (or from Porta Maggiore on the town's west side) to the small car park on the south side of the road and follow the signs. There are rows of massive and sombre stone graves (more are being excavated), though none has the grandeur or the paintings of the more famous necropolises in Tarquinia or Cerveteri. Still visible, however, are Etruscan inscriptions above the tomb entrances, thought to refer to the names of the erstwhile occupants.

Eating and drinking

Orvieto's tourist traffic once inflated prices in the town's many **restaurants**, and for years it has had fewer genuine culinary high spots than neighbouring towns. Over the past few years, however, a crop of good small **trattorie** has opened, together with a selection of excellent more upmarket places. Cheaper **pizzerie** are mostly clustered together at the very eastern end of Corso Cavour. For **ice cream**, the best bet is the *Gelateria Pasqualetti*, which has outlets to the left of the cathedral as you face it at Piazza del Duomo 14, and at Corso Cavour 56.

There are plenty of **bars**, with obvious key sites for watching the world go by in front of the Duomo and in Piazza della Repubblica, though the most prestigious bar in town, founded in 1917, is *Montanucci* at Corso Cavour 21. Also good, if only because it's quiet and you can while away a siesta in the shade of two fine trees outside, is the *Bar del Teatro* in Piazza Fracassini. If you want to buy food for **picnics** or to take home, head for La Gastronomia Carraro, Corso Cavour 101, or Enoteca La Loggia, Via Mercanti 6, which has a good selection of wine and jams, preserves and other produce. La Bottega del Tortellino, Corso Cavour 147, produces great fresh pasta. If all you want is pizza on the hoof, there's a *pizza taglia* (by the slice to take away) outlet at Via Signorelli 9.

Antica Cantina Corso Cavour/Piazza Monaldeschi 18–19 ☎ 0763.344.746. One of the best places on the Corso, reasonably priced and with a self-pro-claimed old-fashioned trattoria atmosphere and food *come una volta* ("as it was in the past"). Very popular with locals, especially at lunch. There is a set menu at €18 and a handful of outside tables. Closed Wed.

CRAMST also known as *Al San Francesco*, Via Lorenzo Maitani 15/Via B. Cerretti 10 ☎ 0763.343.302. Very popular with locals, this is a co-operatively run 400-seat canteen affair, offering a choice between a restaurant (evenings) and self-service trattoria; very good value. Closed Sun.

🏃 Etrusca Via Lorenzo Maitani 10 ☎ 0763.44.016. A fairly serious and tradi-tional-looking restaurant with a medieval vaulted dining-room – first choice in this category, with relaxed atmosphere and service and surprisingly fair prices for top-notch Umbrian specialities. Be sure to go downstairs to see the wine cellars, carved out of solid tufa. Closed Mon & mid-Jan to mid-Feb.

Gigli d'Oro Piazza del Duomo ☎ 0763.341.903. Cooking here is hardly original, but the quality's always high: what you're paying for, though, are elegant surroundings and the pleasure of dining in the shadow of the Duomo. Closed Wed.

I Sette Consoli Piazza Sant'Angelo 1a ☎ 0763.343.911. Highly rated by Italian restaurant guides for its more than usually reasonable food (it has only 35 covers), but the dining room is a little austere. A *degustazione* menu, with three wines and five courses, is available at €40. Fine if it's busy, but

otherwise *La Volpe e L'Uva* should be your first choice among the new-wave *trattorie*. Closed Wed, dinner on Sun & a period in Feb or March.

La Buca di Bacco Corso Cavour 299–301. Almost opposite *Antica Cantina*, mildly more formal but also in the first rank of Orvieto's traditional restau-rants. Closed Tues.

La Grotta Via Signorelli 5 ☎ 0763.341.348. Just off Via del Duomo and a few steps down from the hotel *Posta*, this is a good-value and friendly trat-toria, offering reliable Italian staples. Closed Tues & parts of late Jan & late July.

🏃 La Volpe e L'Uva Via Ripa Corsica 1 ☎ 0763.341.612. A very good and popular trattoria offering traditional cooking – the menu, if anything, is almost too long – and great value for money. A touch bigger and cheaper than *I Sette Consoli*, and an awful lot more relaxed and welcoming, although there are still only two rooms (one for non-smokers). Closed Mon, Tues & March.

Maurizio Via del Duomo 78 ☎ 0763.341.114. The smart-looking, modern interior may be off-putting, but the food here is good if you're prepared to pay for more than just the basics. Well known, but somewhat overtaken by newer and cheaper rivals. Closed Tues.

Trattoria dell'Orso Via della Misericordia 16–18 ☎ 0763.341.642. Friendly and very snug two-roomed place with simple interior and a handful of tables. This is Orvieto's oldest restaurant, and little has changed over the years, certainly not the traditional and excellent local cooking; good value for money. Closed Mon & Tues.

Listings

Hospital Località Ciconia, Orvieto Scalo ☎ 0763.3071.
Police Carabinieri: Piazza Angelo d'Orvieto 6 ☎ 0763.341.9550; Polizia Municipale: Piazza della Repubblica ☎ 0763.340.088.

Post office Via Cesare Nebbia, off Corso Cavour (Mon–Sat 8.10am–6pm, last day of the month 8.10am–noon).
Taxis Piazza Matteotti 15, Orvieto Scalo ☎ 0763.301.903. Piazza della Repubblica ☎ 0763.342.613.

Around Orvieto

The environs of Orvieto are not the most compelling in Umbria. However, if you have transport and time to spare, **Monte Peglia** might make you dally en route to Todi or Perugia, as might the **Lago di Corbara** on the way to Todi, and **Città della Pieve** if you're heading to Montepulciano.

The road west to Lago di Bolsena – which lies across the border in Lazio – gives some of the best **views** of Orvieto: it's where the postcard shots are taken from and where Turner set up his easel for a landscape that now resides in the Tate in London. The wooded pocket of countryside around Castel Giorgio is pretty enough, but only worth bothering with if you're in a car.

Monte Peglia

Monte Peglia is the name for the triangular expanse of wild, sparse land that rises between the Chiani valley and the Tiber, northeast of Orvieto. With its hilltop hamlets, olive groves, vines, herds of white oxen and miles of deserted roads and tracks, this is the archetype of pastoral lowland Umbria. Villages marked on the maps often turn out to be no more than scattered farms, many of them abandoned. You'll get the best quick taste of the area on the circuitous and beautifully deserted SS79bis road from Orvieto Scalo to Todi. Superb initial views peter out as the road climbs through hairpins into densely wooded hill country – though, haze allowing, there are occasional glimpses as far as Perugia. The picturesque castle at **PRODO** is perhaps the best vantage point. The best of the scenery is north of this road and something of a wildlife haven, its high point the summit of Monte Peglia itself (837m).

Lago di Corbara

The scenic SS448 from Orvieto to Todi passes medieval Baschi and runs along the flattish southern shore of **Lago di Corbara**, before taking off into an unexpectedly dramatic gorge for the rest of the route on to Todi. Close to the lake's southern tip, enclosed on three sides by water, stands *La Penisulo*, Pian delle Monache 138 (☎0744.950.521; ❹), a beautiful **hotel–resort** set in a twenty-acre estate; it has twelve rooms in converted nineteenth-century farm buildings, a pool and lots of opportunities for outdoor activities (they'll even rent you a car). Beyond, midway down the shore, is the *Vissani* **restaurant** (☎0744.950.206, ⓦwww.casavissani.it; closed Sun eve, Wed & Thurs lunch, and 4 weeks during July & Aug), rated by virtually every Italian gastronomic guide as one of the finest in Italy; booking is obligatory and you'll need to be ready to part with around €150 a head. Be prepared to dress the part and expect considerable formality, not to say a rather precious attitude. Further east, the lakeside scenery improves considerably, the strange purple-red rocks of the gorge contrasting with the forested slopes. The road's fairly quiet, with plenty of camping and picnic opportunities as the valley flattens out towards Todi.

Città della Pieve

You can easily see **CITTÀ DELLA PIEVE**, 41km north of Orvieto on the A1 (or 47km via the prettier, winding SS47), in an hour, despite the vague enticement of the distant view. Travelling by rail, it's definitely not worth the long haul up from the train station, unless you're a committed fan of **Perugino**, the town's most illustrious son, born here in 1446. Straggling impressively along its 500-metre-high ridge, the town, founded by the Etruscans, consists of tiny, red-brick houses (there being no local building stone) and narrow streets, one of which, Via della Baciadonna, claims to be the narrowest in Italy – the width of a woman's kiss, the name suggests (or so narrow that you are pressed so close you have no option but to kiss anyone you pass).

Via Garibaldi and Via Vittorio Veneto make up the main east–west axis, meeting in the linked central squares of Piazza Gramsci and **Piazza del Plebiscito**, where you'll find the seventeenth-century **Duomo**. This has a couple of late works that show Perugino in his worst light, the *Baptism of Christ* (1510) on the first altar of the north (left) aisle, and the *Madonna Enthroned with SS Peter, Paul, Gervasio and Protasio* (1514) in the apse: the original ninth-century parish church, or *pieve* (which gave the town its name), on the site of the Duomo, was dedicated to the last two saints. The same square contains the **Torre del Pubblico**, thirteenth-century Romanesque at the base (built in travertine) and fifteenth-century Gothic higher up. Also here are the Palazzo dei Priori and, opposite the Duomo, the **Palazzo della Corgna** (daily: June–Sept 9.30am–1pm & 4–7.30pm; Oct–May 10am–12.30pm & 3.30–6pm; €3), begun in 1551 for Ascanio della Corgna, whose uncle, Pope Julius III, had thoughtfully made him governor of the town for life. It contains some half-decent sixteenth-century frescoes by Salvio Savini and Pomarancio, the second another painter born in the town. At the foot of the main stairs is a small sandstone **obelisk**, thought to be an Etruscan sundial from the sixth century BC.

Also worth a look is the **Palazzo Bandini** and its fine Renaissance portal behind the Duomo, which fronts Via Roma, the first right turn as you walk up Via Vittorio Veneto to the northeast from the cathedral square. Continue down Via Roma and through Porta del Vacciano (or Romana) and 200m from the square, after passing a church on the right dedicated to Giacomo Villa, a seventeenth-century beatific, you come on your left to **Santa Maria dei Servi** (rarely open), which contains Perugino's *Deposition* (1517), an important late fresco damaged when monks erected a choir screen nearby. Greater damage was done to Città's artistic patrimony by foreigners, not least by Napoleon, who removed cartloads of the town's other Peruginos to the Louvre.

The **Oratorio di Santa Maria dei Bianchi** (same hours and ticket as Palazzo Corgna) is reached by returning to the main Piazza del Plebiscito and continuing north on Via Pietro Vannunci. The Perugino here, *The Adoration of the Magi*, is one of his masterpieces; note Lago Trasimeno in the background. It was painted in just 29 days in 1504, perhaps, claim some critics, with the assistance of Perugino's pupil, the young Raphael. Perugino initially asked for 200 florins for the work, then said he'd be happy with half that as he was a native of the town; in the end the confraternity which owned the Oratorio (it exists to this day as a charitable institution) paid him just 75. Two letters from the artist displayed with the painting document the financial wrangling. If the building is shut, try asking at the custodian's house, Via Pietro Vannucci 42.

Practicalities

The **tourist office** is at Piazza del Plebiscito 1 (Mon–Sat 10.30am–12.30pm & 4–6/7pm; ☎0578.299.375). Città della Pieve makes a peaceful enough stop and has a two-star **hotel**: the *Vannucci*, Via Icilio Vanni 1 (☎0578.299.572, ⓔhvannucci@supereva.it; ❶), located not far after the church of San Francesco beyond the eastern end of Via Vittorio Veneto. It has a garden and a restaurant, though the best **place to eat** in town is *Serenalla*, Via Fiorenzuola 28 (☎0578.299.683; closed Wed), a family-run place off Via Vittorio Veneto. Another hotel a touch farther out (in the same direction as the *Vannucci*: turn right at the fork after San Francesco) is the three-star *Piccolo Eden*, Via Santa Lucia 53 (☎0578.297.065, ⓕ0578.297.066, ⓦwww.cdpieve.com; ❶), where they'll lend you a bike to run into town or explore farther afield.

Travel details

The excellent website ⓦwww.umbriatrasporti.it has links to full and updated timetables for all public transport, including the private FCU and Trenitalia state rail services and the ATC, APM and SSIT bus services.

Trains

Narni to: Foligno (9–13 daily; 55min; connections for Assisi, Nocera Umbra, Gualdo Tadino, Fossato di Vico – for Gubbio – and Perugia); Fossato di Vico (5 daily; 1hr 45min); Gualdo Tadino (5 daily; 1hr 35min); Nocera Umbra (5 daily; 1hr 10min); Orte (12–16 daily; 15min; connections for Rome, Orvieto, Chiusi, Arezzo and Florence); Rome direct (10 daily; 1hr); Terni (12 daily; 15min).

Orvieto to: Arezzo (14–20 daily; 1hr 20min); Castiglione del Lago (14–20 daily; 40min; connections to Siena, 1hr 30min and additional connections to Castiglione del Lago, 10min); Florence (14–20 daily; 1hr 30min); Orte (14–20 daily; 40min; connections to Narni, Terni, Spoleto and Foligno); Rome (14–20 daily; 1hr–1hr 30min); Teróntola (7–10 daily; 50min; connections to Perugia).

Terni to: Foligno (18–23 daily; 40min; connections for Assisi, Nocera Umbra, Gualdo Tadino, Fossato di Vico – for Gubbio — and Perugia); Fossato di Vico (5 daily; 1hr 30min; additional connections at Foligno); Gualdo Tadino (5 daily; 1hr 20min; additional connections at Foligno); Narni (12 daily; 15min); Nocera Umbra (5 daily; 1hr; additional connections at Foligno); Orte (12–16 daily; 30min; connections to Rome, Orvieto, Chiusi, Arezzo and Florence); Perugia Ponte San Giovanni/Sant'Anna (10–16 daily; 1hr 30min; connections at Sant'Anna for FCU services to Città di Castello and Sansepolcro; connections at Ponte San Giovanni for Trenitalia services to Teróntola and Foligno); Rome direct (12–16 daily; 50min–1hr 20min); Spoleto (12 daily; 20min); Todi (10–16 daily; 40min).

Todi to: Perugia Ponte San Giovanni/Sant'Anna (10–16 daily; 1hr 30min; connections at Sant'Anna for FCU services to Città di Castello and Sansepolcro; connections at Ponte San Giovanni for Trenitalia services to Teróntola and Foligno; 45min); Terni (10–16 daily; 40min).

Buses

Amelia to: Avigliano (3 daily Mon–Sat, 1 connecting to Todi via Dunarobba; 25min); Lugnano in Teverina (Mon–Sat 10 daily, 1 on Sun; 20min); Narni (10 daily Mon–Sat, 1 on Sun; 25min); Orvieto (5–7 daily Mon–Sat; 1hr 15min); Terni (10 or more daily Mon–Sat, 1 on Sun; 50min).

Orvieto to: Amelia (5–7 daily Mon–Sat; 1hr 15min); Bolsena (2 daily Mon–Sat; 50min); Corbara/Civitella del Lago (1 daily Mon–Sat; 50min); Lugnano in Teverina (7 daily Mon–Sat; 1hr); Narni (5 daily Mon–Sat; 1hr 40min); Perugia (1 daily; 2hr); Terni (5 daily Mon–Sat; 2hr); Todi (1 daily Mon–Sat; 1hr 30min).

Narni to: Amelia (10 daily Mon–Sat, 1 on Sun; 25min); Orvieto (5 daily Mon–Sat; 1hr 40min); Otricoli (8 daily Mon–Sat; 30min).

Terni to: Amelia (10 or more daily Mon–Sat, 1 on Sun; 50min); Cascata delle Marmore (15-plus daily Mon–Sat, 11 on Sun; 40min); Ferentillo (17 daily Mon–Sat, 12 on Sun; 40min); Lugnano in Teverina (8 daily Mon–Sat, 1 on Sun 1hr 10min); Orvieto (via Baschi, Guardea, Montecchio and Amelia; 5 daily Mon–Sat; 2hr); Piediluco (9 daily Mon–Sat, 6 on Sun; 35min); Scheggino (8 daily Mon–Sat, 5 on Sun; 50min); Todi (via Sangemini, Acquasparta or Avigliano; 3 daily Mon–Sat; 1hr).

Todi to: Deruta (3 daily Mon–Sat; 40min); Marsciano (2 daily; 30min); Orvieto (1 daily Mon–Sat; 1hr 30min); Perugia (3 daily; 1hr); Terni (3 daily Mon–Sat; 1hr).

for FCU services to Città di Castello and Sansepolcro; connections at Ponte San Giovanni for Trenitalia services to Teróntola and Foligno; 45min); Terni (10–16 daily; 40min).

Contexts

Contexts

The historical background: Tuscany

A comprehensive history of Tuscany in its medieval and Renaissance heyday would consist in large part of a mosaic of more or less independent histories, as each of the region's cities has a complex story to tell. In an overview such as this, fidelity to the entanglements of central Italy's past is impossible. Instead, within a broad account of the main trends in the evolution of Tuscany, we have concentrated on the city that emerged as the dominant force – Florence. The brief reviews of the other major towns – Siena, Pisa, Arezzo, Prato, Pistoia and so on – are supplemented by background given in the appropriate sections of the guide. Similarly, crucial episodes in the history of Florence and its culture – for instance, the ascendancy of Savonarola – are covered in greater detail in the chapter on that city.

Etruscans and Romans

The name of the province of Tuscany derives from the **Etruscans**, the most powerful civilization of pre-Roman Italy. There's no scholarly consensus on the origins of this people, with some experts insisting that they migrated into Italy from Anatolia at the start of the ninth century BC, and others maintaining that they were an indigenous tribe. All that's known for certain is that the Etruscans were spread thoughout central Italy from the eighth century BC, and that the centre of gravity of their domain was in the southern part of the modern province, roughly along a line drawn from Orbetello to Lago Trasimeno. Their principal settlements in Tuscany were Roselle, Vetulonia, Populonia, Volterra, Chiusi, Cortona, Arezzo and – most northerly of all – Fiesole.

It seems that the Etruscans absorbed elements of those cultures with whom they came into contact, thus their trade with Greek settlements produced some classically influenced art that can be seen at its best in Florence's archeological museum and in Cortona. The Etruscan language has still not been fully deciphered (a massive translation programme is under way in Perugia), so at the moment their wall paintings and terracotta funerary sculptures are the main source of information about them, and this information is open to widely differing interpretations. Some people have inferred an almost neurotic fear of death from the evidence of their burial sites and monuments, while others – most notably D.H. Lawrence – have on the contrary intuited an irrepressible and uncomplicated vitality.

There may have been an Etruscan settlement where Florence now stands, but it would have been subservient to their base in the hill-town of Fiesole. The substantial development of Tuscany's chief city began with the **Roman** colony of Florentia, established by Julius Caesar in 59 BC as a settlement for army veterans – by which time Romans had either subsumed or exterminated most Etruscan towns. Expansion of Florentia itself was rapid, with a steady traffic of trading vessels along the Arno providing the basis of accelerated growth in the second and third centuries AD.

This rise under the empire was paralleled by the growth of **Siena**, **Pisa** and **Lucca**, establishing an economic primacy in the north of Tuscany that has endured to the present. According to legend Siena was founded by the sons of Remus, supposedly fleeing their uncle Romulus, while the port at Pisa was developed by the Romans in the second century BC. Lucca was even more important, and it was here that Julius Caesar, Crassus and Pompey established their triumvirate in 56 BC.

Barbarians and margraves

Under the comparative tranquillity of the Roman colonial regime, **Christianity** began to spread through the region. Lucca claims to have been the first Christian city in Tuscany – evangelized by a disciple of St Peter – though Pisa's church of San Pietro a Grado is said to have been founded by Peter himself. In Florence, the church of San Lorenzo and the martyr's shrine at San Miniato were both established in the fourth century.

This period of calm was shattered in the fifth century by the invasions of the **Goths** from the north, though the scale of the destruction in this first barbarian wave was nothing compared to the havoc of the following century. After the fall of Rome, the empire had split in two, with the western half ruled from Ravenna and the eastern from Constantinople (Byzantium). By the 490s Ravenna was occupied by the Ostrogoths, and forty years later the Byzantine emperor Justinian launched a campaign to repossess the Italian peninsula.

The ensuing mayhem between the Byzantine armies of Belisarius and Narsus and the fast-moving Goths was probably the most destructive phase of central Italian history, with virtually all major settlements ravaged by one side or the other – and sometimes both. In 552 Florence fell to the hordes of the Gothic king **Totila**, whose depredations so weakened the province that less than twenty years later the **Lombards** were able to storm in, subjugating Florence to the duchy whose capital was in Pavia, though its dukes preferred to rule from Lucca.

By the end of the eighth century Charlemagne's **Franks** had taken control of much of Italy, with the administration being overseen by imperial **margraves**, again based in Lucca. These proxy rulers developed into some of the most powerful figures in the Holy Roman Empire and were instrumental in spreading Christianity even further, founding numerous religious houses. Willa, widow of the margrave Uberto, established the Badìa in Florence in 978, the first monastic foundation in the centre of the city; her son Ugo, margrave in turn, is buried in the Badìa's church.

The hold of the central authority of the Holy Roman Empire was often tenuous, with feudal grievances making the region all but ungovernable, and it was under the imperial margraves that the notion of an autonomous Tuscan entity began to emerge. In 1027 the position of margrave was passed to the **Canossa** family, who took the title of the Counts of Tuscia, as Tuscany was then called. The most influential figure produced by this dynasty was **Matilda**, daughter of the first Canossa margrave. When her father died she was abducted by the German emperor Henry III, and on her release and return to her home territory she began to take the side of the papacy in its protracted disputes with the empire. The culmination of her anti-imperialist policy came in 1077, when she obliged the emperor Henry IV to wait in the snow outside the gates of Canossa before making obeisance to Pope Gregory VII. Later friction between the papay, empire and Tuscan cities was assured when Matilda bequeathed all her lands to the pope, with the crucial exceptions of Florence, Siena and Lucca.

Guelphs and Ghibellines

Though Lucca had been the titular base of the imperial margraves, Ugo and his successors had shown a degree of favouritism towards **Florence** and over the next three hundred years Florence gained pre-eminence among the cities of Tuscany, becoming especially important as a religious centre. In 1078 Countess Matilda supervised the construction of new fortifications for Florence, and in the year of her death – 1115 – granted it the status of an independent city. The new *comune* of Florence was essentially governed by a council of one hundred men, the great majority drawn from the rising merchant class. In 1125 the city's increasing dominance of the region was confirmed when it crushed the rival city of Fiesole. Fifty years later, as the population boomed with the rise of the textile industry, new walls were built around what was then one of the largest cities in Europe.

Not that the other mercantile centres of Tuscany were completely eclipsed, as their magnificent heritage of medieval buildings makes plain. **Pisa** in the tenth and eleventh centuries had become one of the peninsula's wealthiest ports and its shipping lines played a vital part in bringing the cultural influences of France, Byzantium and the Muslim world into Italy. Twelfth-century **Siena**, though racked by conflicts between the bishops and the secular authorities and between the nobility and the merchant class, was booming thanks to its cloth industries and its exploitation of a local silver mine – foundation of a banking empire that was to see the city rivalling the bankers of Venice and Florence on the international markets.

Throughout and beyond the thirteenth century Tuscany was torn by conflict between the **Ghibelline** faction and the **Guelphs**. The names of these two political alignments derive from Welf, the family name of Emperor Otto IV, and Waiblingen, the name of a castle owned by their implacable rivals, the Hohenstaufen. Though there's no clear documentation, it seems that the terms Guelph and Ghibelline entered the Italian vocabulary at the end of the twelfth century, when supporters of Otto IV battled for control of the central peninsula with the future Frederick II, nephew of Otto and grandson of the Hohenstaufen emperor Barbarossa (1152–90). Within the first few years of Frederick II's reign (1212–50), the labels Guelph and Ghibelline had changed their meaning – the latter still referred to the allies of the Hohenstaufen, but the Guelph party was defined chiefly by its loyalty to the papacy, thus reviving the battle lines drawn up during the reign of Matilda.

To muddy the waters yet further, when Charles of Anjou conquered Naples in 1266, alliance with the anti-imperial French became another component of Guelphism, and a loose Guelph alliance soon stretched from Paris to Naples, substantially funded by the bankers of Tuscany.

Ghibelline/Guelph divisions approximately corresponded to a split between the feudal **nobility** and the rising **business classes**, but this is only the broadest of generalizations. By the beginning of the thirteenth century the major cities of Tuscany were becoming increasingly self-sufficient and inter-city strife was soon a commonplace of medieval life. In this climate, affiliations with the empire and the papacy were often struck on the basis that "my enemy's enemy is my friend", and allegiances changed at baffling speed: if, for instance, the Guelphs gained the ascendancy in a particular town, its neighbours might switch to the Ghibelline camp to maintain their rivalry. Nonetheless, certain patterns did emerge from the confusion: Florence and Lucca were generally Guelph strongholds, while Pisa, Arezzo, Prato, Pistoia and Siena tended to side with the empire.

As a final complicating factor, this was also the great age of **mercenary** armies, whose loyalties changed even quicker than those of the towns that paid for their services. Thus **Sir John Hawkwood** – whose White Company was the most fearsome band of hoodlums on the peninsula – is known today through the monument to him in Florence's Duomo, but early in his career was employed by Ghibelline Pisa to fight the Florentines. He was then taken on by Pope Gregory XI, whom he deserted on the grounds of underpayment, and in the end was granted a pension of 1200 florins a year by Florence, basically as a form of protection money. Even then he was often absent fighting for other cities whenever a fat purse was waved in his direction.

Medieval Florence before the Medici

In this period of superpower manoeuvring and shifting economic structures, city governments in Tuscany were volatile. The administration of Siena, for example, was carried out by various combinations of councils and governors and in 1368 its constitution was redrawn no fewer than four times. However, Florence provides perhaps the best illustration of the turbulence of Tuscan politics in the late Middle Ages.

In 1207 the city's governing council was replaced by the **podestà**, an executive official who was traditionally a non-Florentine, in a semi-autocratic form of government that was common throughout the region. It was around this time, too, that the first **arti** (guilds) were formed to promote the interests of the traders and bankers, a constituency of ever-increasing power. Then in 1215 Florence was riven by a feud that was typical of the internecine violence of central Italy at this period. On Easter Sunday one **Buondelmonte de' Buondelmonti**, on his way to his wedding, was stabbed to death at the foot of the Ponte Vecchio by a member of the Amidei clan, in revenge for breaking his engagement to a young woman of that family. The prosecution of the murderers and their allies polarized the city into those who supported the *comune* – which regarded itself as the protector of the commercial city against imperial ambitions – and the followers of the Amidei, who seem to have politicized their personal grievances by aligning themselves against the *comune* and with the emperor.

These Ghibellines eventually enlisted the help of Emperor Frederick II to oust the Guelphs in 1248, but within two years they had been displaced by the Guelph-backed regime of the **Primo Popolo**, a quasi-democratic government drawn from the mercantile class. The *Primo Popolo* was in turn displaced in 1260, when the Florentine army marched on Siena to demand the surrender of some exiles who were hiding out in the city. Though greatly outnumbered, the Sienese army and its Ghibelline allies overwhelmed the aggressors at **Montaperti**, after which the Sienese were prevented from razing Florence only by the intervention of Farinata degli Uberti, head of the Ghibelline exiles.

By the 1280s the balance had again moved back in favour of Florence, where the Guelphs were back in control – after the intervention of Charles of Anjou – through the **Secondo Popolo**, a regime run by the *Arti Maggiori* (Great Guilds). It was this second bourgeois administration that definitively shifted the fulcrum of power in Florence towards its bankers, merchants and manufacturers – whereas in Siena, the second richest city in Tuscany, the feudal families retained a stranglehold for far longer. Agitation from the landed nobility of the countryside around Florence had been a constant fact of life until the *Secondo Popolo*, which in 1293 passed a programme of political reforms known as the *Ordinamenti della Giustizia*, excluding the nobility from government and investing power in the **Signoria**, a council drawn from the *Arti Maggiori*.

Strife between the virulently anti-imperial "Black" and more conciliatory "White" factions within the Guelph camp marked the start of the fourteenth century in Florence, with many of the Whites – Dante among them – being exiled in 1302. Worse disarray was to come. In 1325 the army of Lucca under **Castruccio Castracani** defeated the Florentines and was about to overwhelm the city when the death of their leader took the momentum out of the campaign. Then in 1339 the Bardi and Peruzzi banks – Florence's largest – both collapsed, mainly owing to the bad debts of Edward III of England. The ultimate catastrophe came in 1348, when the **Black Death** destroyed as many as half the city's population.

However, even though the epidemic hit Florence so badly that it was generally referred to as the Florentine Plague, its effects were equally devastating throughout the region, and did nothing to reverse the economic – and thus political – supremacy of the city. Florence had subsumed Pistoia in 1329 and gained Prato in the 1350s. In 1406 it took control of Pisa and thus gained a long-coveted sea port, and five years later Cortona became part of its territory. From this time on, despite the survival of Sienese independence into the sixteenth century, the history of Tuscany increasingly becomes the history of Florence.

The early Medici

A crucial episode in the liberation of Florence from the influence of the papacy was the so-called **War of the Eight Saints** in 1375–78, which brought Florence into direct territorial conflict with Pope Gregory XI. This not only signalled the dissolution of the old Guelph alliance, but had immense repercussions for the internal politics of Florence. The increased taxation and other economic hardships of the war provoked an uprising of the industrial day-labourers, the **Ciompi**, on whom the wool and cloth factories depended. Their short-lived revolt resulted in the formation of three new guilds and direct representation for the workers for the first time. However, the prospect of increased proletarian presence in the machinery of state provoked a consolidation of the city's oligarchs and in 1382 an alliance of the city's Guelph party and the **Popolo Grasso** (the wealthiest merchants) took control of the *Signoria* away from the guilds, a situation that lasted for four decades.

Not all of Florence's most prosperous citizens aligned themselves with the *Popolo Grasso*, and the foremost of the well-off mavericks were the **Medici**, a family from the agricultural Mugello region whose fortune had been made by the banking prowess of Giovanni Bicci de' Medici. The political rise of his son, **Cosimo de' Medici**, was to some extent due to his family's sympathies with the *Popolo Minuto*, as the members of the disenfranchised lesser guilds were known. With the increase in public discontent at the autocratic rule of the *Signoria* – where the Albizzi clan were the dominant force – Cosimo came to be seen as the figurehead of the more democratically inclined sector of the upper class. In 1431 the authorities imprisoned him in the tower of the Palazzo Vecchio and two years later, as Florence became embroiled in a futile and domestically unpopular war against Lucca, they sent him into exile. He was

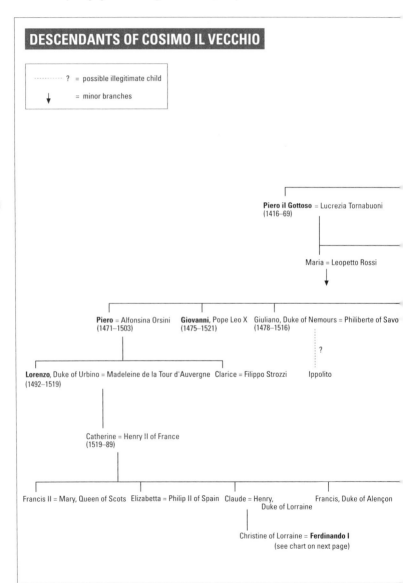

DESCENDANTS OF COSIMO IL VECCHIO

⌐⌐⌐⌐⌐ ? = possible illegitimate child

↓ = minor branches

Piero il Gottoso = Lucrezia Tornabuoni
(1416–69)

Maria = Leopetto Rossi
↓

Piero = Alfonsina Orsini   **Giovanni**, Pope Leo X   Giuliano, Duke of Nemours = Philiberte of Savo
(1471–1503)   (1475–1521)   (1478–1516)
                                                                      ⋮ ?

Lorenzo, Duke of Urbino = Madeleine de la Tour d'Auvergne   Clarice = Filippo Strozzi   Ippolito
(1492–1519)

Catherine = Henry II of France
(1519–89)

Francis II = Mary, Queen of Scots   Elizabetta = Philip II of Spain   Claude = Henry,   Francis, Duke of Alençon
                                                                        Duke of Lorraine

Christine of Lorraine = **Ferdinando I**
(see chart on next page)

away for only a year. In 1434, after a session of the *Parlamento* – a general council called in times of emergency – it was decided to invite him to return. Having secured the military support of the Sforza family of Milan, Cosimo became the pre-eminent figure in the city's political life, a position he maintained for more than three decades.

Cosimo il Vecchio – as he came to be known – rarely held office himself, preferring to exercise power through backstage manipulation and adroit invest-

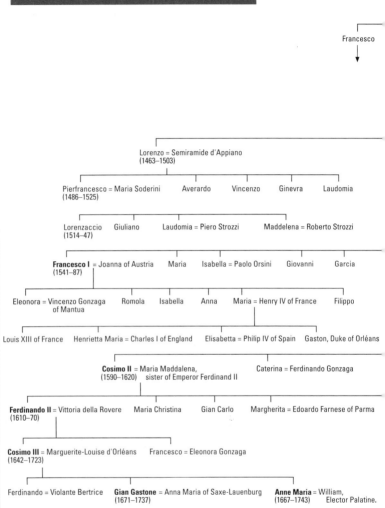

DESCENDANTS OF LORENZO DE' MEDICI

Francesco

Lorenzo = Semiramide d'Appiano
(1463–1503)

Pierfrancesco = Maria Soderini   Averardo   Vincenzo   Ginevra   Laudomia
(1486–1525)

Lorenzaccio   Giuliano   Laudomia = Piero Strozzi   Maddelena = Roberto Strozzi
(1514–47)

Francesco I = Joanna of Austria   Maria   Isabella = Paolo Orsini   Giovanni   Garcia
(1541–87)

Eleonora = Vincenzo Gonzaga   Romola   Isabella   Anna   Maria = Henry IV of France   Filippo
       of Mantua

Louis XIII of France   Henrietta Maria = Charles I of England   Elisabetta = Philip IV of Spain   Gaston, Duke of Orléans

Cosimo II = Maria Maddalena,   Caterina = Ferdinando Gonzaga
(1590–1620)   sister of Emperor Ferdinand II

Ferdinando II = Vittoria della Rovere   Maria Christina   Gian Carlo   Margherita = Edoardo Farnese of Parma
(1610–70)

Cosimo III = Marguerite-Louise d'Orléans   Francesco = Eleonora Gonzaga
(1642–1723)

Ferdinando = Violante Bertrice   **Gian Gastone** = Anna Maria of Saxe-Lauenburg   **Anne Maria** = William,
                     (1671–1737)   (1667–1743)   Elector Palatine.

ment. His extreme generosity to charities and religious foundations in Florence was no doubt motivated in part by genuine piety, but clearly did no harm as a public relations exercise – even if it didn't impress the contemporary who recorded that his munificence was due to the fact that "he knew his money had not been over-well acquired".

Dante, Boccaccio and Giotto in the first half of the fourteenth century had established the literary and artistic ascendancy of Florence, laying the

C

CONTEXTS | The historical background: Tuscany

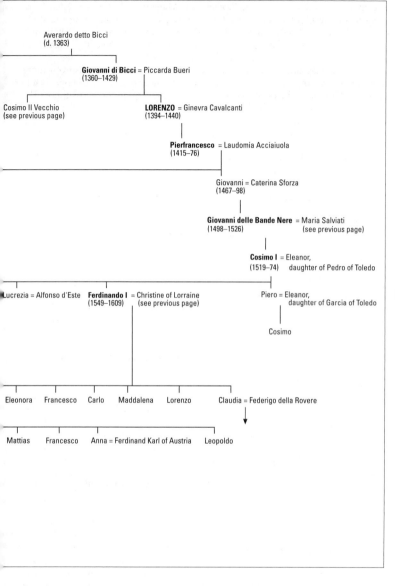

Averardo detto Bicci
(d. 1363)

Giovanni di Bicci = Piccarda Bueri
(1360–1429)

Cosimo Il Vecchio
(see previous page)

LORENZO = Ginevra Cavalcanti
(1394–1440)

Pierfrancesco = Laudomia Acciaiuola
(1415–76)

Giovanni = Caterina Sforza
(1467–98)

Giovanni delle Bande Nere = Maria Salviati
(1498–1526)   (see previous page)

Cosimo I = Eleanor,
(1519–74)   daughter of Pedro of Toledo

Lucrezia = Alfonso d'Este   Ferdinando I = Christine of Lorraine
(1549–1609)   (see previous page)

Piero = Eleanor,
daughter of Garcia of Toledo

Cosimo

Eleonora   Francesco   Carlo   Maddalena   Lorenzo   Claudia = Federigo della Rovere

Mattias   Francesco   Anna = Ferdinand Karl of Austria   Leopoldo

foundations of Italian humanism with their emphasis on the importance of the vernacular and the dignity of humanity. Florence's reputation as the most innovative cultural centre in Europe was strengthened during the fifteenth century, to a large extent through Medici patronage. Cosimo commissioned work from Donatello, Michelozzo and a host of other Florentine artists, and took advantage of the 1439 Council of Florence – a conference of the Catholic and Eastern churches – to foster scholars who were familiar with the literatures of the ancient world. His grandson **Lorenzo il Magnifico** (who succeeded Piero il Gottoso, the Gouty) continued this literary patronage, promoting the study of the classics in the Platonic academy that used to meet at the Medici villas. Other Medici were to fund projects by Botticelli, Michelangelo, Pontormo – in fact, most of the seminal figures of the Florentine Renaissance.

Lorenzo il Magnifico's status as the *de facto* ruler of Florence was even more secure than that of Cosimo il Vecchio, but it did meet one stiff challenge. While many of Florence's financial dynasties were content to advise and support the Medici, others – notably the mighty Strozzi clan – were resentful of the power now wielded by their fellow businessmen. In 1478 one of these disgruntled families, the Pazzi, conspired with Pope Sixtus IV, who had been riled by Lorenzo's attempt to break the papal monopoly of alum mining. This **Pazzi Conspiracy** resulted in an assault on Lorenzo and his brother Giuliano during Mass in the Duomo; Lorenzo was badly injured and Giuliano murdered, an outcome that only increased the esteem in which Lorenzo was held. Now that the plot had failed, Sixtus joined forces with the ferocious King Ferrante of Naples to launch a war on Florence, and excommunicated Lorenzo into the bargain. Taking his life in his hands, Lorenzo left Florence to persuade Ferrante to leave the alliance, a mission he somehow accomplished successfully, to the jubilation of the city.

The wars of Italy

Before Lorenzo's death in 1492 the Medici bank failed, and in 1494 Lorenzo's son Piero was obliged to flee following his surrender to the invading French army of Charles VIII. This invasion saw the commencement of a bloody half-century dominated by the so-called **Wars of Italy**.

After the departure of Charles's troops, Florence for a while was virtually under the control of the inspirational monk **Girolamo Savonarola**, but his career was brief. He was executed as a heretic in 1498, after which the city continued to function as a more democratic republic than that of the Medici. In 1512, however, following Florence's defeat by the Spanish and papal armies, the Medici returned, in the person of the vicious **Giuliano, Duke of Nemours**.

Giuliano's successors – his equally unattractive nephew Lorenzo, Duke of Urbino, and Giulio, illegitimate son of Lorenzo il Magnifico's brother – were in effect just the mouthpieces of Giovanni de' Medici (the Duke of Nemours' brother), who in 1519 became **Pope Leo X**. Similarly, when Giulio became **Pope Clement VII**, he was really the absentee ruler of Florence, where the family presence was maintained by the ghastly Ippolito (illegitimate son of the duke of Nemours) and Alessandro (illegitimate son of the duke of Urbino).

The Medici were again evicted from Florence in the wake of Charles V's pillage of Rome in 1527, Pope Clement's humiliation by the imperial army providing the spur to eject his deeply unpopular relatives. Three years later the pendulum swung the other way: after a siege by the combined papal and imperial forces, Florence capitulated and was obliged to receive Alessandro, who was proclaimed **Duke of Florence**, the first Medici to bear the title of ruler. Though the sadistic Alessandro lost no opportunity to exploit the immunity that came from his title, in the wider scheme of Italian politics he was a less powerful figure than his ancestors. Tuscany was becoming just one more piece in the vast jigsaw of the Habsburg empire, a superpower far more interventionist than the medieval empire of Frederick II could ever have been.

The later Medici

After the assassination of Alessandro in 1537, power passed to another **Cosimo**, not a direct heir but rather a descendant of Cosimo il Vecchio's brother. The emperor Charles V, now related to the Medici through the marriage of his daughter to Alessandro, gave his assent to the succession of this seemingly pliable young man – indeed, without Habsburg consent it would not have happened. Yet it turned out that Cosimo had the clear intention of maintaining Florence's role as the regional power-broker, and he proved immensely skilful at judging just how far he could push the city's autonomy without provoking the imperial policy-makers.

Having finally extinguished the subversive threat of the Strozzi faction at the battle of **Montemurlo**, Cosimo went on to buy the territory of Siena from the Habsburgs in 1557, giving Florence control of all of Tuscany with the solitary exception of Lucca. Two years later Florentine hegemony in Tuscany was confirmed in the Treaty of Cateau-Cambrésis, the final act in the Wars of Italy. Soon after, though, the new Habsburg emperor, Philip II, installed a military outpost in the Orbetello area to keep Tuscany under scrutiny.

Imperial and papal approval of Cosimo's rule was sealed in 1570, when he was allowed to take the title **Cosimo I, Grand Duke of Tuscany**. In European terms Tuscany was a second-rank power, but by comparison with other states on the peninsula it was in a very comfortable position, and during Cosimo's reign there would have been little perception that Florence was drifting inexorably towards the margins of European politics. It was Cosimo who built the Uffizi, extended and overhauled the Palazzo Vecchio, installed the Medici in the Palazzo Pitti, had the magnificent Ponte Santa Trìnita constructed across the Arno and commissioned much of the public sculpture around the Piazza della Signoria.

Cosimo's descendants were to remain in power until 1737, and aspects of their rule continued the city's intellectual tradition: the Medici were among Galileo's strongest supporters, for example. Yet it was a story of almost continual if initially gentle economic decline, as bad harvests and recurrent epidemics worsened the gloom created by the shift of European trading patterns in favour of northern Europe. The half-century reign of **Ferdinando II** had scarcely begun when the market for Florence's woollen goods collapsed in the 1630s, and the city's banks simultaneously went into a terminal slump. The last two male Medici, the insanely pious **Cosimo III** and the drunken pederast **Gian Gastone** – who was seen in public only once, vomiting from the window of the state coach – were fitting symbols of the moribund Florentine state.

To the present

Under the terms of a treaty signed by Gian Gastone's sister, Anna Maria de' Medici, Florence passed in 1737 to the **House of Lorraine**, cousins of the Austrian Habsburgs. The first Lorraine prince, the future Francis I of Austria, was a more enlightened ruler than the last Medici had been and his successors presided over a placid and generally untroubled region, doing much to improve the condition of Tuscany's agricultural land and rationalize its production methods. Austrian rule lasted until the coming of the French in 1799, an interlude that ended with the fall of **Napoleon**, who had made his sister Elisa Baciocchi Grand Duchess of Tuscany.

After this, the Lorraine dynasty was brought back, remaining in residence until the last of the line, Leopold II, consented to his own deposition in 1859. Absorbed into the new **Kingdom of Italy** in the following year, Florence became the **capital** in 1865, a position it held until 1870, when Rome – having at last become part of the otherwise united country – took over the role.

Italy's unpopular entry into World War I cost thousands of Tuscan lives, and the economic disruption that followed was exploited by the regime of Benito **Mussolini**. The corporate Fascist state of the 1920s did effect various improvements in the infrastructure of the region, but Mussolini's alliance with Hitler's Germany was to prove a calamity. In 1943, as the Allied landing at Monte Cassino was followed by a campaign to sweep the occupying German forces out of the peninsula, Tuscany became a battlefield between the Nazis and the **partisans**. The districts around Monte Amiata and the Val d'Órcia sheltered particularly strong partisan groups, and many of the province's hill-towns had their resistance cells, as numerous well-tended war memorials testify.

Yet, as elsewhere in Italy, the loyalties of Tuscany were split, as is well illustrated by the case of Florence, an ideological centre for the resistance but also home to some of Italy's most ardent Nazi collaborators. Wartime Florence in fact produced one of the strangest paradoxes of the time: a Fascist sympathizer in charge of the British Institute and a German consul who did so much to protect suspected partisans that he was granted the freedom of the city after the war.

Although most of the major monuments of Tuscany survived the war – sometimes as a result of pacts between the two sides – there was inevitably widespread destruction. Grosseto, Pisa and Livorno were badly damaged by Allied bombing raids, while Florence was wrecked by the retreating German army, who bombed all the bridges except the Ponte Vecchio and blew up much of the medieval city near the banks of the Arno.

Postwar Tuscany

Tuscany is a prosperous and conservative region that in the past has tended to return right-of-centre members of parliament. On a local level, however, **communist** and other left-wing support is high, the party's record in the war and subsequent work on land reform maintaining a loyal following. Until recently, the communists were effectively excluded from national government by the machinations of the now-defunct Christian Democrat party (which, like the old Socialist party, was undone by the corruption scandals of the early 1990s). By contrast, the communist party and newer left-wing parties projected themselves – and continue to project themselves – as the grassroots opposition to the centralization and corruption of Roman politics. It's a strategy that has been particularly successful in Tuscany, which has clung onto an image of itself as a state within the state. Since the 1970s the town halls of the region have been governed predominantly by communist-led coalitions, forming the heartland of the so-called "red belt" of central Italy.

Despite migration from the land in the 1950s and 1960s, the **economy** of Tuscany has been adroitly managed. The labour-intensive vineyards, olive groves and farms continue to provide a dependable source of income, boosted by industrial development in the Arno valley and around Livorno and Piombino. Production of textiles, leather goods and jewellery have brought money into Prato, Florence and Arezzo, while wine has brought untold prosperity to previously moribund towns such as Montalcino and Montepulciano. But **tourism** plays an uncomfortably large and ever-increasing part in balancing the books of these and other historic centres. This is a mixed blessing, sheer weight of numbers in places such as Florence, Siena and San Gimignano (and many others) over-burdening an already creaking infrastructure and – worse – undermining the charm and damaging the historic and artistic treasures that attract visitors in the first place.

The historical background: Umbria

Although the history of Umbria overlaps with that of Tuscany in the eras of the Etruscans and the Romans, the emergence of self-governing cities marks a divergence between the economically dynamic Tuscan region and landlocked, more inward-looking Umbria. As with the summary of Tuscan history, what follows is but a sketch of what is an immensely complex story, more details of which are to be found in the accounts of the various Umbrian towns.

Pre-Roman Umbria

Over 1500 years before the birth of Christ, a large-scale migration of primitive tribes from central Europe and the east brought permanent settlers to the marshy lowlands around Terni and Perugia. As time went by, these tribes started to move away from the plains in favour of the uplands around Norcia, giving rise to the first of the **hill-towns** that were eventually to dominate the entire region.

By the eighth century BC these peoples were absorbed by the larger and more sophisticated tribes that followed them from the north. These gradually formed themselves into three distinct groups: the Samnites, the Latins (who later became the Romans), and the **Umbrians**. All three had common cultural roots, spoke dialects of a shared language, and between them occupied all but the southernmost tip of the Italian peninsula. The Umbrians' own territory extended far beyond the region's present boundaries, including the best part of what is now Tuscany and the Marche – a vast area for a people of whom almost nothing is known. Only the Eugubine Marbles found near Gubbio yield any clues as to the religion or language of what was clearly a cogent civilization. Other than these, the Umbrians' only memorials are the walls still standing, more or less intact, in a dozen-odd cities in the region.

When the **Etruscans** began to encroach on these cities, their predominantly agricultural inhabitants retreated quietly into the mountains and carried on life much as they had done before. In time they started to trade and intermarry with their new neighbours and the two cultures became more or less indistinguishable. By 700 BC Etruscan influence in Umbria extended as far east as the Tiber, and in some isolated cases – Gubbio for example – some way beyond it. All aspects of their life point to a sophisticated and ordered social set-up, with a political system formed around a confederation of cities, of which two – Perugia and Orvieto – were situated in what is now Umbria.

Roman Umbria

The first time Umbria appears in **Roman** records is in 309 BC, the occasion being Perugia's defeat at the hands of the Roman consul Fabius. The battle marked the beginning of the end for the Etruscan cities, and though some continued to cling to independence, by the second century BC most had become reluctant allies of the Romans. Any vestiges of autonomy were stripped away when Perugia was defeated a second time, a consequence of the power struggle that followed the murder of Julius Caesar in 44 BC. This effectively amounted to a confrontation between the consul Mark Antony, his brother Lucius, and **Octavius**, Caesar's great-nephew. In 40 BC the dispute reached crisis point, and while Antony was preoccupied with Cleopatra in Egypt, Octavius succeeded in harrying Lucius from Rome. Lucius, unhappily for the citizens of Perugia, decided to take refuge within their walls – an action that resulted in the city's destruction at the hands of Octavius.

Octavius went on to proclaim himself **Emperor Augustus**, and with this proclamation the Imperial Age began. Under his rule, Umbria continued to enjoy a period of prosperity that had begun with the opening of the **Via Flaminia** in 220 BC. The new road linked Rome to the Adriatic coast and to the cities of the north, and gave Umbria immense strategic importance. It superseded the Tiber as the focal point of the region and brought in its wake a massive increase in trade and prosperity: colonies were built from scratch or on the sites of Umbrian and Etruscan settlements, land was drained and roads constructed. Umbria – named as such for the first time – became a unified and thriving province.

Early Christianity and the barbarian invasions

Christianity spread quickly in Umbria, thanks mainly to Roman lines of communication. By the first century AD towns such as Spoleto and Foligno had become bishoprics, and within 200 years most towns had Christian communities. As religious practice increasingly adhered to the monastic pattern established in the eastern Mediterranean, it was in Umbria's remote countryside, however, rather than its cities, that Christianity found its most enduring home. The first recorded **monastery** was founded at Monteluco, near Spoleto, by Julian, a Syrian from Antioch. From such beginnings was born the extraordinary religious and monastic tradition in Umbria that was to culminate with St Francis, nearly a millennium later.

St Benedict, the most significant of Umbria's early saints, was born in Norcia in 480 AD, within a few years of the deposition of the last Roman Emperor, and at the very moment that the first Barbarian invaders from the north were turning towards Italy. The order he founded and the rule he drew up to guide its members were of incalculable importance in ensuring the survival of Western culture in the tumult that followed the fall of Rome. The rule aimed to move men to a perfect love of God through a combination of prayer, study and work, thus ensuring that countless monks were quietly working, studying and preserving aspects of learning that might otherwise have vanished for good.

As the **Goths** and **Huns** plundered the country, Umbria succumbed to the consequences of plague and famine. The only order in these desperate times came from the clergy, who began to take over the civic functions formerly carried out by the Roman state. Bishops took it upon themselves to become generals, frequently instigating resistance to the invaders. While on the face of things their achievements seemed negligible, in that virtually every Umbrian city was razed to the ground, they won increasing respect for themselves and the Church they represented.

After the death of their leader, Totila, at Gualdo Tadino, the Goths were replaced by the Lombards, who by 571 had established three principalities in Italy, the central one of which contained most of Umbria and had Spoleto as its capital. This Dukedom of Spoleto was to achieve great importance throughout central Italy, despite being cut off from the Lombard kingdom centred on Pavia to the north by a narrow corridor of territory controlled by the Byzantines – a ribbon of land running from the Adriatic to Rome, including Narni, Amelia, Terni and Perugia. This buffer-state remained a thorn in the Lombards' side for 300 years, though in Umbria it had the effect of guaranteeing the Dukedom of Spoleto considerable independence of action, a habit that in the coming years would be a hard one to break. The Lombards generally adopted the manners and customs of the local people, establishing an order which brought a short-lived increase in artistic and commercial initiative. Acknowledging the increasing growth of Christianity, they built monasteries alongside those of the Benedictines.

In 754 the growing power of the papacy as a force in Italian politics was illustrated by Pope Stephen III's appeal to the **Franks** to rid Italy of the Lombards. The Franks took up the invitation, first under Pepin the Short, and then under his more famous son, **Charlemagne**. By 800 the Lombards and Byzantines had both been driven out of the country.

Between the empire and the papacy

The papacy received great tracts of land from Charlemagne, who in return demanded that Pope Leo III crown him emperor of the new **Holy Roman Empire**. Peace reigned while Charlemagne lived, but the harmony between papacy and empire disappeared within a few years of his death. The divisions amongst his successors and their preoccupations in northern Europe again left much of Italy prey to invasion and conflict. The papacy was no healthier, weakened by the rival claims of powerful families; with no central authority, it was not long before the whole country reverted once more to chaos.

The anarchy of the next few years set the tone of events for centuries to come. Many towns and old Roman centres, such as Carsulae (near Todi), unsuited to the rigours of constant invasion and siege, were either abandoned or destroyed, to be replaced by **fortified villas** and **castles**, for which the region's hilly terrain was ideal. Around these fortresses developed independent and self-sufficient communities, creating a pattern of isolated, ambitious hill-towns, each with an eye on the territory of its neighbour.

Throughout this period Italy was the scene of a complicated, confused and constantly shifting conflict between the parties of the empire and the papacy, the **Guelphs** and **Ghibellines** (see p.739). As elsewhere, Umbrian towns frequently switched their allegiances, exacting new measures of independence from whomever ruled them at the time, in exchange for promises of loyalty. Yet of all its cities, only Perugia ever really came to merit attention on a national scale. It had become a free *comune* in 1139, owing its wealth to trade links with Rome and the burgeoning economic power of Florence, and was soon the prime mover in any machinations that affected the region as a whole.

Occasionally, however, the Umbrians were distracted from their squabbles by events taking place in the world at large. In 1152, for example, the truce between the empire and the papacy produced by the Concordat of Worms was shattered by the election of a new and ambitious emperor: Frederick Hohenstaufen. His determination to reassert the power of the empire in Italy spelt doom for the Umbrian cities, who soon had cause to fear the man better known by his Italian nickname of **Barbarossa**. As he marched south, some towns, such as Assisi, took his side while others, such as Perugia, tried to stand up to him; the majority – of which Spoleto was the most notable example – were partly or completely destroyed.

Like Charlemagne before him, Barbarossa was unable to ensure the survival of the authority he had imposed on the empire. After his death Pope Innocent III set about exploiting the anti-imperialist feeling aroused in Italy by the ferocity of his campaigns, and to ally it with the collective guilt at the capture of Jerusalem by the infidel Saladin in 1187, hoping thereby to resurrect papal fortunes. When he came to Umbria, however, he met with little success, cities such as Perugia and Spoleto being quite happy to accept new powers of autonomy, but turning obstructive when papal governors were sent to oversee them.

Medieval communes and war lords

In 1308 the papacy moved to Avignon, and the outlook for the Church grew even more bleak from 1387 until 1417, when Europe was divided in its support for rival popes in Rome and France. The power vacuum that resulted from this **Great Schism** was the single most important factor in allowing the development of democratic communes in central Italy. At the same time, the influence of the older noble families was eclipsed by the emergence of a mercantile class, brought to prominence by the increase and diversification of trade. With the influx of new money and new men, secular building took place on an unprecedented scale, giving the rapidly expanding cities the appearances that they have largely retained to the present day.

Liberal and sophisticated constitutions were drawn up to administer the new towns, of which **Spoleto**'s, instituted at the end of the thirteenth century, serves as a typical example. Originally civic issues were decided by a show of hands in the *arringo*, a general assembly of all adult males convoked in the central piazza. By 1296, when a new constitution was drawn up, the size of the population had made such an arrangement impracticable, and the role of the *arringo* was reduced to a body that could express opinions, but no longer take decisions. The legislative function was taken over by a General Council elected from the twelve parishes that made up Spoleto's administrative districts. Final executive and judicial power lay with the **podestà**, a kind of troubleshooter elected for a year and often brought in from outside the city – as in Tuscany. He was answerable to the **capitano del popolo**, a police chief and appeals judge who was also responsible for the day-to-day running of the administration. Below him were a host of elected minor officials, all of whom were, in the manner of contemporary Italian bureaucracy, constrained by rigid job specifications.

The theory was reasonable, but the practice was often rather different. First, the cities spent so much time arguing with their neighbours that their administrations were obliged to be almost constantly prepared for war. Second, towns were plagued by continual dissent from within as Guelphs and Ghibellines fought each other, most of them citing their allegiances to distant authority merely as an excuse to wipe out local rivals and seize power. Citizens soon came to realize that a strong executive was the only means to combat such disorder, and began to accept the domination of forceful individuals, usually the heads of the strongest **noble families** of the moment, or the person who could muster the largest private army – in most cases one and the same man.

At about the same time, other powerful individuals began to figure in Umbria's affairs: the **condottieri**, or itinerant private soldiers hired to fight battles on behalf of their citizens. Most of them were English or French refugees from the Hundred Years' War, or German and Swiss stragglers from the imperial armies. Some were astute enough to form themselves into efficient bands and soon found in Umbria a healthy market for their services. The cities were losers in every way in these contracts, wasting money on unreliable allies while property was destroyed and land plundered. Added to this, there was the everyday chaos produced by warring noble families, whose disputes were often settled in bloodshed worthy of Jacobean tragedy. Taking into account the normal range of calamities, such as plague and famine, which could strike the medieval world at any time, life in Umbria should have been intolerable.

But against this background of violence and suffering, the artistic and intellectual life of the region went from strength to strength. The same subtle changes being wrought throughout northern Italy that were to culminate in the **Renaissance** were also taking place in Umbria. In religion, St Francis had almost single-handedly revitalized man's relations to the divine. In painting, Cimabue, Giotto and their followers had introduced a naturalism that left behind the stilted beauty of the Byzantines. A university was founded in Perugia as early as 1308, and the first edition of Dante's *Divine Comedy* was printed not in Florence, but in Foligno.

Papal consolidation and the Risorgimento

Gradually the infighting exhausted the cities, and the **papacy** – which out of choice or necessity had largely stood back from the centuries of bloody disorder – seized the opportunity to exert its power. One by one the cities fell: Spoleto in 1354 to the crusading Cardinal Albornoz; Foligno in 1439, when the ruling Trinci family surrendered to soldiers of Pope Euginius V; Spello in 1535, after 150 years of despotic rule; and Gubbio in 1624, handed over to Urban VIII by the last of the ruling Montefeltro.

The old civic administrations were replaced by papal governors and for the two centuries before Unification Umbria slumbered under the rule of the Church. Although order was restored, peace and papal rule were no guarantee of prosperity. The isolation that had once served the region so well now began to tell against it. Absentee landlords – amongst whom the papacy figured large – collected rents but took little interest in land management, so that the soil deteriorated and with it the agriculture on which Umbria depended. Such industry as existed was agriculture-based and so shared in its stagnation, and in any case it was cut off from the prosperous markets to the north by poor communications. To anyone surveying the Umbrian scene at the end of the eighteenth century it would have seemed as if very little had changed in almost 500 years.

Matters improved somewhat in the upheaval that followed the French Revolution and the rule of **Napoleon**, when the French organized the region into two districts and tried to encourage economic growth. In the more liberal atmosphere of the times, a more free-thinking class of merchants emerged, which the return of papal rule after Napoleon's death could do little to repress. By the time of the battle for the Unification of Italy, this spirit had found broader and more popular support, and Umbria welcomed **Garibaldi**'s troops into Perugia on September 11, 1860.

Unfortunately, when trade barriers between the regions were abolished the Umbrian economy was subjected to the rigours of free competition, with which it was ill-equipped to deal. Traditional craft and agricultural industries crumbled in the face of industrialization in the north. Private wealth remained idle, or was invested in the north, while the state failed to make the improvements to the region's infrastructure that might have halted the agricultural decline.

Umbria in the twentieth century

In the first years of the twentieth century the Italian economy as a whole was on an upswing, and for a while things began to look up for Umbria as well, with light industry appearing in the region for the first time. But this flicker of prosperity came to an abrupt end when the small **Banca di Perugia**, which had been largely responsible for funding the new investments, was swallowed by the Banca Commerciale, which preferred to invest in the more profitable and less risky ventures in the north.

Where the capital went, the people went too. Although in 1911 half the region's population was illiterate, they did not need education to know that their future lay outside Umbria. Thousands **emigrated** to America or to the new factories of Turin and Germany, leaving a population at home who increasingly saw socialism as the answer to the region's ills. By 1919, Umbria's scattered left-wing parties commanded 48 percent of the vote and had established control of many local and regional councils. Hopes of reform, however, were quickly dashed by the rise of Mussolini, even if the preparations for war did put some energy into the regional economy.

World War II left Umbria relatively unscathed until the German retreat up the peninsula, when the key strategic corridors – between Lago Trasimeno, Perugia and Orvieto – made it the seat of bitter fighting. Resistance groups were active in the hills above the main valleys, with the area around Gubbio seeing particularly intense partisan activity.

Postwar emigration rates were higher than ever. Only when central government devolved more power to the regions did Umbria begin to prosper. Political control by now was in the hands of the Communist Party, which carefully directed funds at co-operative ventures and projects appropriate to the region's special needs, with transport, agriculture and latterly tourism as the main priorities. Road and rail links at last provided an economic lifeline to Rome and the north.

Finally, and perhaps most importantly, the last few decades have seen the birth of what can only be described as a new pride and enthusiasm in Umbria. There is still poverty and there are still problems but there is also a powerful sense of vigour and community which seems determined to overcome them. It is a spirit that even the most casual visitor cannot fail to notice, manifestly obvious in the region's extraordinary range of cultural events, the diversity and skill of its craftspeople, the Umbrians' own obvious pride in their countryside and their heritage, and a host of more minor signs that at last point to progress.

A directory of artists and architects

Agostino di Duccio (1418–81). Born in Florence, Agostino served as a mercenary before turning to sculpture. Having possibly studied with Jacopo della Quercia, he carved the altarpiece for Modena cathedral then returned to Florence in 1442. His masterpiece is the Tempio Malatestiano in Rimini, on which Alberti and Piero della Francesca also worked. The best example in this region of his marble relief work, with its emphasis on linear grace, is the Oratorio di San Bernardino in Perugia. He returned to Florence briefly in the 1460s, a period during which he spoiled the marble block that was to become Michelangelo's *David*.

Alberti, Leon Battista (1404–72). Born illegitimately to a Florentine exile, probably in Genoa, Alberti was educated in Padua and Bologna. One of the most complete personifications of the Renaissance ideal of universal genius, he was above all a writer and theorist: his *De Re Aedificatoria* (1452) was the first architectural treatise of the Renaissance, and he also wrote a tract on the art of painting, *Della Pittura*, dedicated to his friend Brunelleschi. His theory of harmonic proportions in musical and visual forms was first put into practice in the facade of Santa Maria Novella in Florence, while his archeological interest in classical architecture found expression in the same city's Palazzo Rucellai, his first independent project. Even more closely linked to his researches into the styles of antiquity is the miniature temple built for the Rucellai family in the church of San Pancrazio. His other buildings are in Mantua and Rimini.

Albertinelli, Mariotto (1474–1515). A colleague of Fra' Bartolommeo in the workshop in San Marco, Albertinelli abandoned painting to be an innkeeper. His best work is the Uffizi *Visitation*.

Alunno, Nicolò (1430–1502). The greatest of the purely Umbrian painters before Perugino, Alunno was probably the pupil of the Venetian Carlo Crivelli, whose bright colouring and precise contours are a feature of his work. Emotionally more intense than Perugino, he usually rejects the conventional dulcet pastoralism of Umbrian art for a bleaker landscape such as that around Gubbio and Foligno.

Ammannati, Bartolomeo (1511–92). A Florentine sculptor-architect, much indebted to Michelangelo, Ammannati is best known for his additions and amendments to the Palazzo Pitti and for the graceful Ponte San Trìnita (though in all likelihood this was largely designed by Michelangelo). He created the fountain in the Piazza della Signoria, with some assistance from his pupil Giambologna, and the Bargello contains some of his pieces made for the Bóboli gardens.

Andrea del Sarto (1486–1530). The dominant artist in Florence at the time of Michelangelo and Raphael's ascendancy in Rome. His strengths are not those associated with Florentine draughtsmanship, being more Venetian in his emphasis on delicacy of colour and the primacy of light. He made his name with frescoes for two Florentine churches in the San Marco district – the Scalzo and Santissima Annunziata. For a period in the 1510s he was in France, and the received wisdom is that his talent did not develop after that. However, two of his other major works in Florence date from after his return – the *Last Supper* in San Salvi and the *Madonna* *del Sacco* in the cloister of the Annunziata. His major easel painting is the *Madonna of the Harpies* in the Uffizi.

Arnolfo di Cambio (c.1245–1302). Pupil of Nicola Pisano, with whom he worked on sculptural projects in Bologna, Siena and Perugia before going to Rome in 1277. The most important of his independent sculptures are the pieces in Florence's Museo dell'Opera del Duomo and the *Tomb of Cardinal de Braye* in San Domenico in Orvieto. The latter defined the format of wall tombs for the next century, showing the deceased lying on a coffin below the Madonna and Child, set within an elaborate architectural framework. However, Arnolfo is best known as the architect of Florence's Duomo and Palazzo Vecchio, and various fortifications in central Tuscany, including the fortress at Poppi.

Bandinelli, Baccio (1493–1560). Born in Florence, Bandinelli trained as a goldsmith, sculptor and painter. He perceived himself as an equal talent to Michelangelo and to Cellini, his most vocal critic. Despite manifest shortcomings as a sculptor, he was given prestigious commissions by Cosimo I, the most conspicuous of which is the *Hercules and Cacus* outside the Palazzo Vecchio. Other pieces by him are in the Bargello.

Beccafumi, Domenico (1484/6–1551). The last great Sienese painter, Beccafumi was in Rome during the painting of the Sistine chapel ceiling and Raphael's *Stanze*. He returned to Siena in 1513, when his work showed tendencies that were to become prevalent in Mannerist art – contorted poses, strong lighting, vivid artificial coloration. His decorative skill is especially evident in his illusionist frescoes in the Palazzo Pubblico and the pavement of the Duomo.

Benedetto da Maiano (1442–97). Florentine sculptor, best known for his portrait busts in the Bargello and the pulpit in Santa Croce.

Botticelli, Sandro (c.1445–1510). Possibly a pupil of Filippo Lippi, Botticelli was certainly influenced by the Pollaiuolo brothers, whose paintings of the *Virtues* he completed. The mythological paintings for which he is celebrated – including the *Birth of Venus* and *Primavera* – are distinguished by their emphasis on line rather than mass, and by their complicated symbolic meaning, a reflection on his involvement with the Neo-Platonist philosophers whom the Medici gathered about them. In the last decade of his life his lucid, slightly archaic style suffered from comparison with the more radical paintings of Michelangelo and Leonardo da Vinci, and his devotional pictures became almost clumsily didactic – a result, perhaps, of his involvement with Savonarola and his followers.

Bronzino, Agnolo (1503–72). The adopted son of Pontormo, Bronzino became the court painter to Cosimo I. He frescoed parts of the Palazzo Vecchio for Eleanor of Toledo, but his reputation rests on his glacially elegant portraits, whose surface brilliance makes no discrimination between the faces of the subjects and their apparel.

Brunelleschi, Filippo (1377–1446). Trained as a sculptor and goldsmith, Brunelleschi abandoned this career after his failure in the competition for the Florence baptistery doors. The main product of this period is his contribution to the St James altarpiece in Pistoia. He then devoted himself to the study of the building techniques of the Classical era, travelling to Rome with Donatello in 1402. In 1417 he submitted his design for the dome of Florence's Duomo, and all his subsequent work was in that city – San Lorenzo, the Spedale degli Innocenti, Cappella Pazzi (Santa Croce) and Santa Spirito. Unlike the other great architect of this period, Alberti, his work is based on no theoretical premise, but rather on an empiricist's admiration for the buildings of Rome. And unlike Alberti he oversaw every stage of construction, even devising machinery that would permit the raising of the innovative structures he had planned.

Buonarroti, Michelangelo (1475–1564). See first colour insert.

Buontalenti, Bernardo (c.1536–1608). Florentine architect, who began as a military architect to the papacy. Much of his later output was for the court of the Medici – the grotto of the Bóboli gardens, the gardens of the villa at Pratolino and tableaux for court spectaculars. Less frivolous work included the Fortezza del Belvedere, the facade of Santa Trìnita, the villa Artimino and the fortifications at Livorno.

Castagno, Andrea (c.1421–57). The early years of Castagno's life are mysterious, and the exact year of his birth is not known. Around 1440 he painted the portraits of some executed rebels in the Bargello, a job that earned him the nickname "Andrea of the Hanged Men". In 1442 he was working in Venice, but a couple of years later he was back in Florence, creating stained glass for the Duomo and frescoes for Sant'Apollonia. His taut sinewy style is to a large extent derived from the sculpture of his contemporary Donatello, an affinity that is especially clear in his frescoes for Santissima Annunziata. Other major works in Florence include the series of *Famous Men and Women* in the Uffizi and the portrait of *Niccolò da Tolentino* in the Duomo – his last piece.

Cellini, Benvenuto (1500–71). Cellini began his career in Rome, where he fought in the siege of the city by the imperial army in 1527. His sculpture is greatly influenced by Michelangelo, as is evident in his most famous large-scale piece, the *Perseus* in the Loggia della Signoria. His other masterpiece in Florence is the heroic *Bust of Cosimo I* in the Bargello. Cellini was an even more

accomplished goldsmith and jeweller, creating some exquisite pieces for Francis I, by whom he was employed in the 1530s and 1540s. He also wrote a racy *Autobiography*, a fascinating insight into the artistic world of sixteenth-century Italy and France.

Cimabue (c.1240–1302). Though celebrated by Dante as the foremost painter of the generation before Giotto, very little is known about Cimabue – in fact, the only work that is definitely by him is the mosaic in Pisa's Duomo. He is generally given credit for the softening of the hieratic Byzantine style of religious art, a tendency carried further by his putative pupil, Giotto. Some works can be attributed to him with more confidence than others; the shortlist would include *The Madonna of St Francis* in the lower church at Assisi, the *Passion* cycle in the upper church, the *Maestà* in the Uffizi and the crucifixes in Santa Croce (Florence) and San Domenico (Arezzo).

Civitali, Matteo (1436–1501). Probably self-taught sculptor from Lucca, where all his important work is to be found.

Daddi, Bernardo (c.1290–1349). A pupil of Giotto, Daddi combined the solidity of his master's style with the more decorative aspects of the Sienese style. His work can be seen in the Uffizi and Santa Croce in Florence.

Desiderio da Settignano (c.1428–64). Desiderio continued the low relief technique pioneered by Donatello in the panel for the Orsanmichele *St George*, and carved the tomb of Carlo Marsuppini in Santa Croce, Florence. Better known for his exquisite busts of women and children, a good selection of which are on show in the Bargello.

Donatello (c.1386–1466). A pupil of Ghiberti, Donatello assisted in the casting of the first set of Florence Baptistery doors in 1403, then worked for Nanni di Banco on the Duomo. His early marble *David* (Bargello) is still Gothic in its form, but a new departure is evident in his heroic *St Mark* for Orsanmichele (1411) – possibly produced after a study of the sculpture of ancient Rome. Four years later he began the intense series of prophets for the Campanile, and at the same time produced the *St George* for Orsanmichele, the epitome of early Renaissance humanism, featuring a relief that is the very first application of rigorous perspective in Western art.

In the mid-1520s Donatello started a partnership with Michelozzo, with whom he created the tomb of Pope John XXIII in the Florence Baptistery, a refinement of the genre initiated by Arnolfo di Cambio. He went to Rome in 1431, possibly with Brunelleschi, and it was probably on his return that he made the classical bronze *David* (Bargello), one of the first nude statues of the Renaissance period. Also at this time he made the cantoria to be placed opposite the one already made by Luca della Robbia, the pulpit for Prato cathedral (with Michelozzo) and the decorations for the old sacristy in Florence's church of San Lorenzo – the parish church of his great patrons, the Medici.

After a period in Padua – where he created the first bronze equestrian statue since Roman times – he returned to Florence, where his last works show an extraordinary harshness and angularity. The main sculptures from this period are the *Judith and Holofernes* (Palazzo Vecchio), the *Magdalene* (Museo dell'Opera del Duomo) and the two bronze pulpits for San Lorenzo.

Duccio di Buoninsegna (c.1255–c.1318). Though occupying much the same pivotal position in the history of Sienese art as Giotto does in Florentine art, Duccio was a less revolutionary figure, refining the stately Byzantine tradition rather than subverting its conventions. One of his earliest works was ordered by Florence's church of Santa Maria Novella – the *Maestà* now in the Uffizi – but the bulk of his output is in his home city. Despite frequent ructions with the civic authorities, for refusing to do military service among other transgressions, in 1308 he received his most prestigious assignment, the painting of a *Maestà* for Siena's Duomo. The polyptych no longer exists in its original form, but most of the panels are now in Siena's Museo dell'Opera del Duomo. This iconic image of the Madonna, with its rich use of gold and decorative colour, was to profoundly influence such painters as the Lorenzettis and Simone Martini, while the small scenes on the back of the panels reveal a less frequently acknowledged mastery of narrative painting.

Fra' Angelico (1387/1400–55). Born in Vicchio, Fra' Angelico joined the Dominican order in Fiesole, near his home town and later entered their monasteries in Cortona and Foligno. His first authenticated painting dates from the mid-1420s, but the first one that can be definitely dated is a *Madonna* he produced for the linen guild of Florence in 1433. Three years later the Dominicans took over the San Marco monastery in Florence, and soon after he embarked on the series of frescoes and altarpieces now displayed in the museum there. In the mid-1440s he was called to Rome to work on the Vatican, after which he worked at Orvieto, served for three years as prior of the monastery in Fiesole, and returned to Rome around 1452, where he died. For all their sophistication of technique, Fra' Angelico's paintings, with their atmosphere of tranquil piety, seem to belong to a less complex world than that inhabited by Donatello, his contemporary. His altarpieces of the Madonna and Saints – a genre known as *sacre conversazione* – were, however, extremely influential compositions.

Fra' Bartolommeo (c.1474–1517). Fra' Bartolommeo's earliest known work is the Raphael-influenced *Last Judgement* painted for the San Marco monastery in Florence in 1499. The following year he became a monk there, then in 1504 became head of the workshop, a post previously occupied by Fra' Angelico. In 1514 he was in Rome, but according to Vasari was discouraged by Raphael's fame. The works he later produced in Florence had an influence on High Renaissance art, with their repression of elaborate backgrounds and anecdotal detail, concentrating instead on expression and gesture.

Francesco di Giorgio Martini (1439–1501/2). Sienese painter, sculptor and architect, whose treatise on architectural theory was circulated widely in manuscript form; Leonardo had a copy. Employed for a long period by Federico da Montefeltro – also a patron of Piero della Francesca – he probably designed the loggia for the Palazzo Ducale in Urbino and the church of San Bernardino. The church of Santa Maria degli Angeli in Siena and the Palazzo Ducale in Gubbio might be by him; the one Tuscan building that was certainly designed by him is Santa Maria del Calcinaio in Cortona, one of the finest early Renaissance structures in Italy.

Gaddi, Taddeo (d.1366). According to tradition, Taddeo Gaddi worked with Giotto for 24 years, and throughout his life barely wavered from the precepts of his master's style. His first major independent work is the cycle for the Cappella Baroncelli in Santa Croce, Florence. Other works by him are in Florence's Uffizi, Accademia, Bargello and Museo Horne.

Agnolo Gaddi (d.1396), Taddeo's son, continued his father's Giottesque style; his major projects were for Santa Croce in Florence and the Duomo of Prato.

Gentile da Fabriano (c.1370–1427). Chief exponent of the International Gothic style in Italy, Gentile da Fabriano came to Florence in 1422, when he painted the gorgeous *Adoration of the Magi* now in the Uffizi. In 1425 he went on to Siena and Orvieto, where the intellectual climate was perhaps more conducive than that in the Florence of Masaccio; he finished his career in Rome.

Ghiberti, Lorenzo (1378–1455). Trained as a goldsmith, painter and sculptor, Ghiberti concentrated on the last discipline almost exclusively after winning the competition to design the doors for Florence's baptistery. His first set of doors are to a large extent derived from Andrea Pisano's earlier Gothic panels for the building, yet his workshop was a virtual academy for the seminal figures of the early Florentine Renaissance, Donatello and Uccello among them. The commission took around twenty years to complete, during which time he also worked on the Siena baptistery and the church of Orsanmichele in Florence, where his Baptist and St Matthew show the influence of classical statuary. This classicism reached its peak in the second set of doors for Florence's baptistery (the Gates of Paradise) – taking the innovations of Donatello's low relief carving to a new pitch of perfection. The panels occupied much of the rest of his life but in his final years he wrote his *Commentarii*, the main source of information on fourteenth-century art in Florence and Siena, and the first autobiography by an artist.

Ghirlandaio, Domenico (1449–94). The most accomplished fresco artist of his generation, Ghirlandaio was the teacher of Michelangelo. After a short period working on the Sistine Chapel with Botticelli, he came back to Florence, where his cycles in Santa Trìnita and Santa Maria Novella provide some of the most absorbing documentary images of the time, being filled with contemporary portraits and vivid anecdotal details.

Giambologna (1529–1608). Born in northern France, Giambologna – Jean de Boulogne – arrived in Italy in the mid-1550s, becoming the most influential Florentine sculptor after Michelangelo's death. Having helped Ammannati on the fountain for the Piazza della Signoria, he went on to produce a succession of pieces that typify the Mannerist predilection for sculptures with multiple viewpoints, such as the *Rape of the Sabines* (Loggia della Signoria) and the *Mercury* (Bargello). His workshop also turned out scores of reduced bronze copies of his larger works; the Bargello has an extensive collection.

Giotto di Bondone (1266–1337). It was with Giotto's great fresco cycles that religious art shifted from being a straightforward act of devotion to the dramatic presentation of incident. His unerring eye for the significant gesture, his ability to encapsulate moments of extreme emotion and his technical command of figure modelling and spatial depth brought him early recognition as the greatest artist of his generation – and even as late as the sixteenth century artists were studying his frescoes for their solutions to certain compositional problems. Yet, as with Cimabue, the precise attribution of work is problematic. In all probability his first major cycle was the *Life of St Francis* in the upper church at Assisi, though the extent to which his assistants carried out his designs is still disputed. The Arena chapel in Padua is certainly by him, as are large parts of the Bardi and Peruzzi chapels in Santa Croce in Florence. Of his attributed panel paintings, the Uffizi *Maestà* is the only one universally accepted.

Gozzoli, Benozzo (1421–97). Though a pupil of Fra' Angelico, Gozzoli was one of the more worldly artists of the fifteenth century, with a fondness for pageantry that is seen to most impressive effect in the frescoes in Florence's Palazzo Medici-Ricardi. His celebrated cycle in Pisa's Camposanto was all but destroyed in World War II; his other surviving fresco cycles include the *Life of St Francis* in Montefalco and the *Life of St Augustine* in San Gimignano.

Guido da Siena (active mid-thirteenth century). Guido was the founder of the Sienese school of painters, but his life is one of the most problematic areas of Siena's art history. A signed painting by him in the Palazzo Pubblico is dated 1221, but some experts think that the date may have been altered, and that the work is from the 1260s or 1270s – a period when other pictures associated with him are known to have been painted.

Leonardo da Vinci (1452–1519). Leonardo trained as a painter under Verrocchio, and it is said that his precocious talent caused his master to abandon painting in favour of sculpture. Drawings of landscapes and drapery have survived from the 1470s, but the first completed picture is the *Annunciation* in the Uffizi. The sketch of the *Adoration of the Magi*, also in the Uffizi, dates from 1481, at which time there was no precedent for its fusion of geometric form and dynamic action. Two years later he was in the employment of Lodovico Sforza of Milan, remaining there for sixteen years. During this second phase of his career he produced the *Lady with the Ermine* (Kraków), the fresco of the *Last Supper* and – probably – the two versions of *The Virgin of the Rocks*, the fullest demonstrations to date of his so-called sfumato, a blurring of tones from light to dark. Innumerable scientific studies and military projects engaged him at this time, and he also made a massive clay model for an equestrian statue of Francesco Sforza – never completed, like so many of his schemes.

When the French took Milan in 1499 Leonardo returned to Florence, where he devoted much of his time to anatomical researches. It was during this second Florentine period t he was commissioned to paint 'sco of the *Battle of Anghiari* in the main hall of the Palazzo Ducale, where his detested rival Michelangelo was also set to work. Only a fragment of the fresco was completed, and the innovative technique that Leonardo had employed resulted in its speedy disintegration. His cartoons for the *Madonna and Child with St Anne* (Louvre and National Gallery, London) also date from this period, as does the most famous of all his paintings, the Louvre's *Mona Lisa*, the portrait of the wife of a Florentine merchant. In 1506 he went back to Milan, thence to Rome and finally, in 1517, to France. Again, military and scientific work occupied much of this last period – the only painting to have survived is the *St John*, also in the Louvre.

Lippi, Filippo (c.1406–69). In 1421 Filippo Lippi was placed in the monastery of the Carmine in Florence, just at the time Masaccio was beginning work on the Cappella Brancacci there. His early works all bear the stamp of Masaccio, but by the 1530s he was becoming interested in the representation of movement and a more luxuriant surface detail. The frescoes in the cathedral at Prato, executed in the 1550s, show his highly personal, almost hedonistic vision, as do his panel paintings of wistful Madonnas in patrician interiors or soft landscapes – many of them executed for the Medici. His last work, the *Life of the Virgin* fresco cycle in Spoleto, was probably largely executed by assistants.

Filippino Lippi (1457/8–1504) completed his father's work in Spoleto – aged about twelve – then travelled to Florence, where his first major commission was the completion of Masaccio's frescoes in Santa Maria del Carmine (c.1484). At around this time he also painted the *Vision of St Bernard* for the Badìa, which shows an affinity with Botticelli, with whom he is known to

have worked. His later researches in Rome led him to develop a self-consciously antique style – seen at its most ambitious in Santa Maria Novella.

Lippo Memmi (d.1357). Brother-in-law of Simone Martini, Lippo Memmi was his assistant on the Uffizi *Annunciation*. His major work is the *Maestà* in the Palazzo Pubblico in San Gimignano, and he may also have been responsible for the dramatic New Testament frescoes in the Collegiata of the same town.

Lorenzetti, Ambrogio (active 1319–47). Though Sienese, Ambrogio spent part of the 1320s and 1330s in Florence, where he would have witnessed the decoration of Santa Croce by Giotto and his pupils. He's best known for the *Allegory of Good and Bad Government* in the Palazzo Pubblico, which shows painting being used for a secular, didactic purpose for the first time, and is one of the first instances of a landscape being used as an integral part of a composition rather than as a mere backdrop. The Uffizi *Presentation of the Virgin* highlights the difference between Ambrogio's inventive complexity and the comparative simplicity of his brother's style (see below). There's a fine altarpiece by him in Massa Maríttima as well.

Lorenzetti, Pietro (active 1306–48). Brother of Ambrogio, Pietro Lorenzetti was possibly a pupil of Duccio's in Siena. His first authenticated work is the altarpiece in Arezzo's Pieve di Santa Maria (1320); others include frescoes in Assisi's lower church, in which the impact of Giotto is particularly noticeable, and the *Birth of the Virgin* in Siena's Museo dell'Opera del Duomo, one of the best demonstrations of his skill as a narrative painter. It's probable that both the Lorenzettis died during the Black Death.

Lorenzo Monaco (1372–1425). A Sienese artist, Lorenzo Monaco joined the Camaldolese monastery in Florence, for which he painted the *Coronation of the Virgin*, now in the Uffizi. This and his other earlier works are fairly conventional Sienese-style altarpieces, with two-dimensional figures on gold backgrounds. However, his late *Adoration of the Magi* (Uffizi), with its fastidious detailing and landscape backdrop, anticipates the arrival of Gentile da Fabriano and fully fledged International Gothic.

Lo Spagna (1450–1528). Possibly of Spanish origin – hence the name – Lo Spagna spent much of his life in Umbria. Like many of his contemporaries he came under the influence of Raphael, who spent at least five of his formative years in the region.

Maitini, Lorenzo (c.1270–1330). Sienese architect and sculptor, Maitini was the only local artist to challenge the supremacy of the Pisani. In 1310 he was made supervisor of Orvieto's Duomo, for which he designed the biblical panels of the facade – though it's not certain how much of the carving was actually by Maitini. Virtually nothing else about him is known.

Martini, Simone (c.1284–1344). The most important Sienese painter, Simone Martini was a pupil of Duccio but equally influenced by Giovanni Pisano's sculpture and the carvings of French Gothic artists. He began his career by painting a fresco counterpart of Duccio's *Maestà* in the city's Palazzo Pubblico (1315). Soon after he was employed by Robert of Anjou, King of Naples, and there developed a sinuous, graceful and courtly style. In the late 1320s he was back in Siena, where he probably produced the portrait of Guidoriccio da Fogliano – though some experts doubt its authenticity. At some point he went to Assisi, where he painted a cycle of *The Life of St Martin* in the lower church. In 1333 he produced a sumptuous *Annunciation* for the Siena duomo; now in the Uffizi, this is the quintessential fourteenth-century Sienese painting, with its immaculately crafted gold surfaces and emphasis on fluid outline and bright coloration. In 1340 Martini travelled to the papal court of Avignon, where he spent the rest of his life. It was at Avignon that he formed a friendship with Petrarch, for whom he illustrated a magnificent copy of Virgil's poetry.

Masaccio (1401–28). Born just outside Florence, Tomasso di se Giovanni di Mone Cassai – universally known as Masaccio – entered the city's painters' guild in 1422. His first large commission was an altarpiece for the Carmelites of Pisa (the central panel is now in the National Gallery in London), which shows a massive grandeur at odds with the International Gothic style then being promulgated in Florence by Gentile da Fabriano. His masterpieces – the *Trinity* fresco in Santa Maria Novella and the fresco cycle in Santa Maria del Carmine – were produced in the last three years of his life, the latter being painted in collaboration with Masolino. With the architecture of Brunelleschi and the sculpture of Donatello, the Carmine frescoes are the most important achievements of the early Renaissance.

Maso di Banco (active 1340s). Maso was perhaps the most inventive of Giotto's acolytes, and his reputation depends chiefly on the cycle of the *Life of St Sylvester* in Santa Croce, Florence.

Masolino da Panicale (1383–1447). Masolino was employed in Ghiberti's workshop for the production of the first set of baptistery doors, and the semi-Gothic early style of Ghiberti conditioned much of his subsequent work. His other great influence was the younger Masaccio, with whom he worked on the Brancacci chapel.

Michelangelo see first colour insert.

Michelozzo di Bartolommeo (1396–1472). Born in Florence, Michelozzo worked in Ghiberti's studio and collaborated with Donatello before turning exclusively to architecture. His main patrons were the Medici, for whom he altered the villa at Careggi and built the Palazzo Medici, which set a prototype for patrician mansions in the city, with its rusticated lower storey, smooth upper facade, overhanging cornice and inner courtyard. He later designed the Villa Medici at Fiesole for the family, and for Cosimo de' Medici he added the light and airy library to the monastery of San Marco. In the Alberti-influenced tribune for the church of Santissima Annunziata, Michelozzo produced the first centrally planned church design to be built in the Renaissance period.

Mino da Fiesole (1429–84). Florentine sculptor, perhaps a pupil of Desiderio da Settignano, Mino is known chiefly for his tombs and portrait busts; there are examples of the former in Fiesole's Duomo and the Badìa in Florence, and of the latter in the Bargello.

Nanni di Banco (c.1384–1421). A Florentine sculptor who began his career as an assistant to his father on the Florence Duomo, Nanni was an exact contemporary of Donatello, with whom he shared some early commissions: Donatello's first *David* was ordered at the same time as an *Isaiah* from Nanni. The finest works produced in his short life are his niche sculptures at Orsanmichele (especially the *Four Saints*) and the relief above the Duomo's Porta della Mandorla.

Nelli, Ottaviano (active 1400–44). The artist that brought the International Gothic style to Umbria; his intricate and glittering paintings can be seen in Foligno, Assisi and Gubbio.

Odersi, or Oderigi (1240–99). The founder of the Umbrian school, little is known of Odersi except that he was a friend of Giotto and worked mainly in Gubbio. A handful of his miniatures survive, though Dante called him *l'onor d'Agobbio* ("the pride of Gubbio") and stuck him in Purgatory as punishment for an obsession with art that left him no time for anything else.

Orcagna, Andrea (c.1308–68). Architect-sculptor-painter, Orcagna was a dominant figure in the period following the death of Giotto, whose emphasis on spatial depth he rejected – as shown in his only authenticated panel painting, the Strozzi altarpiece in Santa Maria Novella. Damaged frescoes can be seen in Santa Croce and Santo Spirito, but Florence's principal work by Orcagna is the massive tabernacle in Orsanmichele. Orcagna's brothers Nardo and Jacopo di Cione were the most influential painters in Florence at the close of the fourteenth century: the frescoes in the Strozzi chapel are by Nardo.

Perugino (1445/50–1523). Born Pietro di Cristoforo Vannucci in Città della Pieve, Perugino was the greatest Umbrian artist. Possibly a pupil of Piero della Francesca, he later trained in Florence in the workshop of Andrea Verrocchio, studying alongside Leonardo da Vinci. By 1480 his reputation was such that he was invited to paint in the Sistine Chapel, filling the east wall with his distinctive gently melancholic figures; today only one of Perugino's original three panels remains. In 1500 he executed his greatest work in Umbria, a fresco cycle commissioned by the bankers' guild of Perugia for their Collegio di Cambio. This was probably the first occasion on which he was assisted by his pupil Raphael – and the moment his own career began to wane. Vasari claimed that he was "a man of little or no religion, who could never bring himself to believe in the immortality of the soul" and the production-line altarpieces that his workshop later turned out were often lacking in genuine passion. Yet he was still amongst the most influential of the Renaissance painters, the catalyst for Raphael and mentor for a host of Umbrian artists. In Tuscany he is best seen in the Uffizi and in the church of Santa Maria Maddalena dei Pazzi.

Piero della Francesca (1410/20–92). Piero was born in Borgo Sansepolcro, on the border of Tuscany and Umbria. In the late 1430s he was in Florence, working with Domenico Veneziano, and his later work shows the influence of such Florentine contemporaries as Castagno and Uccello, as well as the impact of Masaccio's frescoes. The exact chronology of his career is contentious, but much of his working life was spent in his native town, for which he produced the *Madonna della Misericordia* and the *Resurrection*, both now in the local Museo Civico. Other patrons included Sigismondo Malatesta of Rimini and Federico da Montefeltro of Urbino, of whom there's a portrait by Piero in the Uffizi. In the 1450s he was in Arezzo, working on the fresco cycle in the church of San Francesco, the only frescoes in Tuscany that can bear comparison with the Masaccio cycle in Florence. He seems to have stopped painting completely in the early 1470s, perhaps to concentrate on his vastly influential treatises on perspective and geometry, but more likely because of failing eyesight.

Piero di Cosimo (c.1462–1521). One of the more enigmatic figures of the High Renaissance, Piero di Cosimo shared Leonardo's scholarly interest in the natural world but turned his knowledge to the production of allusive mythological paintings. There are pictures by him in the Uffizi, Palazzo Pitti, Museo degli Innocenti and Museo Horne.

Pietro da Cortona (1596–1669). Painter-architect, born Pietro Berrettini, who with Bernini was the guiding force of Roman Baroque. The style was introduced to Florence by Pietro's ceiling frescoes in the Palazzo Pitti. His last painting is in his home town.

Pinturicchio (1454–1513). Born Bernardino di Betto in Perugia, Pinturicchio was taught by Perugino, with whom he collaborated on the painting of the Sistine Chapel. His rich palette earned him his nickname, as well as Vasari's condemnation for superficiality. Most of his work is in Rome but his last commission, one of his most ambitious projects, was his *Life of Pius II* for the Libreria Piccolomini in Siena.

Pisano, Andrea (c.1290–1348). Nothing is known of Andrea Pisano's life until 1330, when he was given the commission to make a new set of doors for the Florence baptistery. He then succeeded Giotto as master mason of the Campanile; the set of reliefs he produced for it are the only other works definitely by him (now in the Museo dell'Opera del Duomo). In 1347 he became the supervisor of Orvieto's Duomo, a job later held by his sculptor son, Nino.

Pisano, Nicola (c.1220–84). Born somewhere in the southern Italian kingdom of the emperor Frederick II, Nicola Pisano was the first great classicizing sculptor in pre-Renaissance Italy; the pulpit in Pisa's baptistery (1260), his first masterpiece, shows clearly the influence of Roman figures. Five years later he produced the pulpit for the Duomo in Siena, with the assistance of his son Giovanni (c.1248–1314) and Arnolfo di Cambio. Father and son again worked together on the Fonte Gaia in Perugia, which was Nicola's last major project. Giovanni's more turbulent Gothic-influenced style is seen in two other pulpits, for San Andrea in Pistoia and for the Pisa Duomo. The Museo dell'Opera del Duomo in Siena has some fine large-scale figures by Giovanni, while its counterpart in Pisa contains a large collection of work by both the Pisani.

Pollaiuolo, Antonio del (c.1432–98) and **Piero del** (c.1441–96). Though their Florence workshop turned out engravings, jewellery and embroideries, the Pollaiuolo brothers were known mainly for their advances in oil-painting technique and for their anatomical researches, which bore fruit in paintings and small-scale bronze sculptures. The influences of Donatello and Castagno (Piero's teacher) are evident in their dramatic, often violent work, which is especially well represented in the Bargello. The Uffizi's collection of paintings suggests that Antonio was by far the more skilled artist.

Pontormo, Jacopo (1494–1556). See p.174.

Quercia, Jacopo della (1374–1438). A Sienese contemporary of Donatello and Ghiberti, della Quercia entered the competition for the Florence baptistery doors which Ghiberti won in 1401. The first known work by him is the tomb of Ilaria del Carretto in Lucca's Duomo. His next major commission was a fountain for Siena's main square, a piece now reassembled in the loggia of the Palazzo Pubblico; before that was finished (1419) he had begun work on a set of reliefs for Siena's baptistery, a project to which Ghiberti and Donatello also contributed. From 1425 he expended much of his energy on reliefs for San Petronio in Bologna – so much so, that the Sienese authorities ordered him to return some of the money he had been paid for the baptistery job.

Raphael (1483–1520). With Leonardo and Michelangelo, Raphael Sanzio forms the triumvirate whose works define the essence of the High Renaissance. Born in Urbino, he joined Perugino's workshop some time around 1494 and within five years was receiving commissions independently of his master. From 1505 to 1508 he was in Florence, where he absorbed the compositional and tonal innovations of Leonardo; many of the pictures he produced at that time are now in the Palazzo Pitti. From Florence he went to Rome, where Pope Julius II set him to work on the papal apartments (the Stanze). Michelangelo's Sistine ceiling was largely instrumental in modulating Raphael's style from its earlier lyrical grace into something more monumental, but all the works from this more rugged later period are in Rome.

Robbia, Luca della (1400–82). Luca began as a sculptor in conventional materials, his earliest achievement being the marble cantoria (choir gallery) now in the Museo dell'Opera del Duomo in Florence, typifying the cheerful tone of most of his work. Thirty years later he made the sacristy doors for this city's Duomo, but by then he had devised a technique for applying durable potter's glaze to clay sculpture and most of his energies were given to the art of glazed terracotta. His distinctive blue, white and yellow compositions are seen at their best in the Pazzi chapel in Santa Croce, the Bargello, and at Impruneta, just outside Florence. The best work of his nephew, Andrea della Robbia (1435–1525), who continued the lucrative terracotta business, is at the Spedale degli Innocenti in Florence and at the monastery of La Verna. Giovanni della Robbia (1469–1529), son of Andrea, is best known for the frieze of the Ceppo in Pistoia.

Rossellino, Bernardo (1409–64). An architect-sculptor, Rossellino worked with Alberti and carried out his plans for the Palazzo Rucellai in Florence. His major architectural commission was Pius II's new town of Pienza. As a sculptor he's best known for the monument to Leonardo Bruni in Santa Croce – a derivative of Donatello's tomb of John XXIII in the baptistery. His brother and pupil Antonio (1427–79) produced the tomb of the Cardinal of Portugal in Florence's San Miniato al Monte, and a number of excellent portrait busts (Bargello).

Rosso Fiorentino (1494–1540). Like Pontormo, Rosso Fiorentino was a pupil of Andrea del Sarto, but went on to develop a far more aggressive, acidic style than his colleague and friend. His early *Deposition* in Volterra (1521) and the roughly contemporaneous *Moses Defending the Daughters of Jethro* (Uffizi) are typical of his extreme foreshortening and tense deployment of figures. After a period in Rome and Venice, he eventually went to France, where with Primaticcio he developed the distinctive Mannerist art of the Fontainebleau school.

Sangallo, Antonio da, the Elder (1455–1534). A Florence-born architect, Antonio da Sangallo the Elder produced just one major building, but one of the most influential of his period – San Biagio in Montepulciano, based on Bramante's plan for St Peter's in Rome. His nephew, Antonio the Younger (1485–1546), was also born in Florence but did most of his work in Rome, where he began his career as assistant first to Bramante then to Peruzzi. He went on to design the Palazzo Farnese, the most spectacular Roman palace of its time. In Tuscany his most important building is the Fortezza da Basso in Florence. Giuliano da Sangallo (1445–1516), sculptor, architect and military engineer, was the brother of Antonio the Elder. A follower of Brunelleschi, he produced a number of buildings in and around Florence – the Villa Medici at Poggio a Caiano, Santa Maria delle Carceri in Prato (the first Renaissance church to have a Greek-cross plan) and the Palazzo Strozzi, the most ambitious palace of the century.

Sassetta (c.1392–1450). Sassetta was basically a conventional Sienese painter, though his work does show the influence of International Gothic. Works by him are on show in Siena, Assisi and the Uffizi.

Signorelli, Luca (1450–1523). Though a pupil of Piero della Francesca, Signorelli is more indebted to the muscular drama of the Pollaiuolo brothers and the gestural vocabulary developed by Donatello. In the early 1480s he was probably working on the Sistine Chapel with Perugino and Botticelli, but his most important commission came in 1499, when he was hired to complete the cycle begun by Fra' Angelico in Orvieto's Duomo. The emphasis on the nude figure in his *Last Judgement* was to greatly affect Michelangelo. Shortly after finishing this cycle he went to Rome but the competition from Raphael and Michelangelo drove him back to his native Cortona, where he set up a highly proficient workshop. Works are to be seen in Cortona, Arezzo, Monte Oliveto, Perugia, Sansepolcro and in the Uffizi and Museo Horne in Florence.

Sodoma (1477–1549). Born Giovanni Antonio Bazzi, Sodoma arrived in Siena in 1501, having become familiar with the work of Leonardo da Vinci during a four-year spell in Milan. His major work was begun four years later, a cycle of 31 frescoes at Monte Oliveto. He later won contracts to work in Rome, though the work he commenced in the Vatican was handed over to Raphael.

Spinello Aretino (active 1370s–1410). Probably born in Arezzo, Spinello studied in Florence, possibly under Agnolo Gaddi. He harks back to the monumental aspects of Giotto's style – thus paradoxically paving the way for the most radical painter of the next generation, Masaccio. His main works are in Florence's church of San Miniato al Monte and Santa Caterina d'Antella, just to the south of the city.

Uccello, Paolo (1396–1475). After training in Ghiberti's workshop, Uccello went to Venice, where he worked on mosaics for the Basilica di San Marco. He returned to Florence in 1431 and five years later was contracted to paint the commemorative portrait of Sir John Hawkwood in the Duomo. This trompe l'oeil painting is the first evidence of his interest in the problems of perspective and foreshortening, a subject that was later to obsess him. After an interlude in Padua, he painted the frescoes for the cloister of Santa Maria Novella (c.1445), in which his systematic but non-naturalistic use of perspective is seen at its most extreme. In the following decade he painted the three-scene sequence *Battle of San Romano* (Louvre, London National Gallery and Uffizi) for the Medici – his most ambitious non-fresco paintings, and similarly notable for their strange use of foreshortening.

Vasari, Giorgio (1511–74). Born in Arezzo, Vasari trained with Luca Signorelli and Andrea del Sarto. He became the leading artistic impresario of his day, working for the papacy in Rome and for the Medici in Florence, where he supervised (and partly executed) the redecoration of the Palazzo Vecchio. His own house in Arezzo is perhaps the most impressive display of his limited pictorial talents. He also designed the Uffizi gallery and oversaw a number of other architectural projects, including the completion of the massive Madonna dell'Umiltà in Pistoia. He is now chiefly famous for his Tuscan-biased *Lives of the Most Excellent Painters, Sculptors and Architects*, which charted the rebirth of the fine arts with Giotto and the process of refinement that culminated with Michelangelo.

Veneziano, Domenico (1404–61). Despite the name, Domenico Veneziano was probably born in Florence, though his preoccupation with the way in which colour alters in different light conditions is more of a Venetian concern. From 1439 to 1445 he was working on a fresco cycle in Florence with Piero della Francesca, a work that has now perished. Only a dozen surviving works can be attributed to him with any degree of certainty and only two signed pieces by him are left – one of them is the central panel of the so-called *St Lucy Altar* in the Uffizi.

Verrocchio, Andrea del (c.1435–88). A Florentine painter, sculptor and goldsmith, Verrocchio was possibly a pupil of Donatello and certainly his successor as the city's leading sculptor. A highly accomplished if sometimes over-facile craftsman, he ran one of Florence's busiest workshops, whose employees included the young Leonardo da Vinci. In Florence his work can be seen in the Uffizi, Bargello, San Lorenzo, Santo Spirito, Orsanmichele and Museo dell'Opera del Duomo.

Books

Most of the books recommended below are currently in print, and those that aren't shouldn't be too difficult to track down through second-hand bookstores or websites such as ⓦwww.alibris.com and ⓦwww.abebooks.com. Wherever a book is in print, the UK publisher is given first in each listing, followed by the publisher in the US, unless the title is available in one country only, in which case we have specified the country concerned. If the same publisher produces the book in the UK and US, the publisher is simply named once. We've added ⚑ to signify titles that are especially recommended.

Travel books and journals

Charles Dickens *Pictures from Italy* (Penguin). The classic mid-nineteenth-century Grand Tour, recording the sights of Emilia, Tuscany, Rome and Naples in measured and incisive prose.

Wolfgang Goethe *Italian Journey* (Penguin). Revealing for what it says about the tastes of the time – Roman antiquities taking precedence over the Renaissance.

Edward Hutton *Florence; Country Walks About Florence; The Valley of the Arno; A Wayfarer in Unknown Tuscany; Siena and Southern Tuscany; Cities of Umbria; Assisi and Umbria Revisited; The Cosmati* (all out of print). A Tuscan resident from the 1930s to 1960s, Hutton was nothing if not prolific. Some of his prose adds a new shade to purple, but his books, between them, cover almost every inch of Tuscany and Umbria and are packed with assiduous background on the art and history.

Henry James *Italian Hours* (Penguin). Urbane travel pieces from the young James; perceptive about particular monuments and works of art, superb on the different atmospheres of the great Italian cities.

D.H. Lawrence *Etruscan Places* (included in *D.H. Lawrence and Italy*, Penguin). Published posthumously, these are Lawrence's provocative musings on Etruscan art and civilization – which he considered more or less ideal ("ripe with the phallic knowledge", etc). Penguin UK also publishes a volume entitled *Sketches of Etruscan Places and other Italian Essays*, which contains material omitted from the first edition of *Etruscan Places*, plus an essay on Florence.

Mary McCarthy *The Stones of Florence* (Penguin, o/p; Harvest). Written in the mid-1960s, *Stones* is a mix of high-class reporting on the contemporary city and anecdotal detail on its history – one of the few accounts that doesn't read as if it's been written in a library.

H.V. Morton *A Traveller in Italy* (Methuen; Da Capo). Morton's leisurely and amiable books were written in the 1930s (long before modern tourism got into its stride), and their nostalgic charm has a lot to do with their enduring popularity. But this title – recently reissued – is also packed with learned details and marvellously evocative descriptions.

Iris Origo *War in the Val d'Orcia* (Allison and Busby; Godine). A stirring account of Origo's activities in the last war, hiding partisans and Allied troops on her estate near Montepulciano. In her biography *Images and Shadows* (John Murray, o/p; Godine), Origo expands on her Tuscan residence, with some intriguing insights into peasant life in the 1930s.

Tobias Smollett *Travels through France and Italy* (Oxford University Press, o/p). One of the funniest travel journals ever written – the apotheosis of Little Englandism, calling on an unmatched vocabulary of disgust at all things foreign.

Matthew Spender *Within Tuscany: Reflections on a Time and Place* (Penguin, o/p in UK). Recollections of twenty years of living in Tuscany – refreshingly free of the condescension and smugness that besets most "Brits abroad" memoirs.

History and society

General

Harry Hearder *Italy: A Short History* (Cambridge University Press). The best one-volume survey of the country from prehistory to the present.

Giuliano Procacci *History of the Italian People* (Penguin; Harper & Row o/p). A comprehensive if indigestibly dense history of the peninsula, charting the development of Italy as a nation state and giving a context for the story of Tuscany and Umbria.

Medieval

Adrian House *Francis of Assisi* (Pimlico; Paulist Press). A much-needed modern biography that brings to life a saint who is respected by Christians and non-believers alike. House doesn't dodge difficult issues, such as Francis's relationship with St Clare or the possible causes of his stigmata, and provides an entertaining account of his early, apparently dissolute, life.

Iris Origo *The Merchant of Prato* (Penguin; Godine). Based on the massive documentation of Francesco di Marco Datini's business empire, this is a wonderfully lively re-creation of domestic life in fourteenth-century Tuscany.

Frances Stonor Saunders *Hawkwood: Diabolical Englishman* (Faber). Fascinating study of the rapacious mercenary captain whose private army terrorized vast tracts of Italy in the late fourteenth century, in the wake of the miseries of the Black Death. More than an excellent biography, this book is a vivid reconstruction of a hellish period of Italian history.

Daniel Waley *The Italian City Republics* (Longman, o/p). Excellent general account, which gives much prominence to Florence and its Tuscan rivals.

Florence and the Renaissance

Harold Acton *The Last Medici* (Thames & Hudson, o/p). Elegant biography of the least elegant member of the dynasty, the perpetually inebriated Gian Gastone.

Gene A. Brucker *Renaissance Florence* (University of California Press). Concentrating on the years 1380–1450, this brilliant study of Florence at its cultural zenith uses masses of archival material to fill in the social, economic and political background to its artistic achievements.

Jacob Burckhardt *The Civilization of the Renaissance in Italy* (Penguin). A pioneering nineteenth-century classic of Renaissance scholarship – the book that did more than any other to form our image of the period.

Eric Cochrane *Florence in the Forgotten Centuries 1527–1800* (University of Chicago Press o/p). Massively erudite account of the twilight centuries of Florence; intimidating in its detail, it's unrivalled in its coverage of the years when the city's scientists were more famous than its painters.

J.R. Hale *Florence and the Medici* (Weidenfeld & Nicolson, UK). Scholarly yet lively, this covers the full span of the Medici story from the foundation of the family fortune to the calamitous eighteenth century. Vivid in its re-creation of the various personalities involved, it also presents a fascinating picture of the evolution of the mechanics of power in the Florentine state.

Christopher Hibbert *The House of Medici: its Rise and Fall* (Perennial). More anecdotal than Hale's book, this is a gripping read, chock-full of heroic successes and squalid failures.

Christopher Hibbert *Florence: The Biography of a City* (Penguin; Norton, o/p). Yet another excellent Hibbert production, packed with illuminating anecdotes and fascinating illustrations – unlike most books on the city, it's as interesting on the political history as on the artistic achievements, and doesn't grind to a standstill with the fall of the Medici.

Mary Hollingsworth *Patronage in Renaissance Italy* (Johns Hopkins University Press, o/p). The first comprehensive English-language study of the relationship between artist and patron in *quattrocento* Italy's city-states. A salutary corrective to the mythology of self-inspired Renaissance genius.

George Holmes *Florence, Rome and the Origins of the Renaissance* (Oxford University Press). Magnificent – and costly – portrait of the world of Dante and Giotto, with especially compelling sections on the impact of St Francis and the role of the papacy in the political and cultural life of central Italy.

Luaro Martines *April Blood: Florence and the Plot Against the Medici* (Pimlico; Oxford University Press). A thorough and engrossing account of the most notorious conspiracy in Florentine history.

Paul Strathern *The Medici: Godfathers of the Renaissance* (Pimlico, UK). Like Hibbert's book, this is a pacy and well-researched narrative of Florence's most famous family, but gives a little more space to the various luminaries (Michelangelo, Galileo etc) who were drawn into their orbit.

Siena, Assisi and Perugia

Edmund G. Gardner *The Story of Siena*; **Margaret Symonds & L. Duff Gordon** *The Story of Perugia* and *The Story of Assisi*. Published in Dent's "Medieval Towns" series in the 1920s, these pocket encyclopedias contain lots of anecdote and historical detail you won't find elsewhere.

Judith Hook *Siena: A City and its History* (Hamish Hamilton, o/p – but available in Siena). This superb study of the city and its art concentrates on the medieval heyday but also takes the story through to the present, and includes a good analytical section on the Palio.

Contemporary Italy

Paul Ginsborg *Italy and its Discontents* (Penguin; Palgrave). If you want to understand contemporary Italy's baffling mixture of dynamism and ideological sterility, this book – lucidly argued and formidably well-informed – is an essential read. There is no better book on the subject.

Tobias Jones *The Dark Heart of Italy* (Faber; North Point Press). Written during a three-year period in Parma, and comprising essays dealing with aspects of modern Italian society, from the legal and political systems to the media and football. Bewildered and fascinated at every turn, Jones reveals a culture in which evasiveness and ethical malleability are as significant as the much-celebrated virtues of vivacity, charm and sophistication – a culture exemplified above all by the character of Silvio Berlusconi, in effect the owner of the Italian state. An affectionate but clear-eyed corrective to the sentimentalizing claptrap perpetrated by so many English and American expats.

Charles Richards *The New Italians* (Penguin; Michael Joseph, o/p). An affectionate and very well-informed survey of modern Italy, with plenty of vivid anecdotes that illustrate the tensions within a culture that is at once deeply traditional yet at the same time enthralled by the trappings of modernity.

Frederic Spotts & Theodor Wieser *Italy: A Difficult Democracy: A Survey of Italian Politics* (Cambridge University Press). Authoritative and highly readable account of religion, social history and economics in postwar Italy.

Art and architecture

Harold Acton *The Villas of Tuscany* (Thames & Hudson, o/p). Huge and lavishly illustrated tome, with good architectural and historical background on most of the major Tuscan villas – many of them the homes of Sir Harold and his chums.

Frederick Antal *Florentine Painting and its Social Background* (Harvard University Press, o/p). Very authoritative – if less than enthrallingly written – study of patronage in early Renaissance Florence.

Charles Avery *Florentine Renaissance Sculpture* (John Murray, o/p). Dependable introduction to the milieu of Donatello and Michelangelo.

Michael Baxandall *Painting and Experience in Fifteenth-Century Italy* (Oxford University Press). Invaluable analysis, concentrating on the way in which the art of the period would have been perceived at the time.

Malcolm Bull *The Mirror of the Gods: Classical Mythology in Renaissance Art* (Penguin). Scores of illustrious academics have devoted themselves to decoding the meaning of the multitude of Renaissance artworks that are derived from classical mythologies, and Malcolm Bull is here arguing (in essence – this is a book of many arguments), that most of them have been barking up the wrong tree. He contends that there is no coherent philosophy underlying this use of pagan imagery, and that such art was marginal – and not in an entirely negative sense. A provocative, exciting and demanding study.

Keith Christiansen *Painting in Renaissance Siena* (Abrams, o/p; Metropolitan Museum o/p). The fullest study of the subject.

Vincent Cronin *The Florentine Renaissance* and *The Flowering of the Renaissance* (Pimlico in UK, o/p).

Concise and gripping narrative of Italian art's golden years – the first volume covers the fifteenth century, the second switches the focus to sixteenth-century Rome and Venice.

Rona Goffen *Renaissance Rivals* (Yale). It's a truism that the cultural history of Renaissance Italy is to a large extent a history of competition – between artists, between individual patrons and between the various city states. However, Rona Goffen's masterly book, published in 2003, is revelatory in its analysis of the depth and the complexity of the antagonisms involved in the production of high art in this period. Concentrating above all on the work of Michelangelo, Leonardo, Raphael and Titian, and making incisive use of a wealth of documentation, from poetry to legal contracts, she illuminates a world in which painters, sculptors and architects were ceaselessly endeavouring to supersede their contemporary rivals and the exemplars of the ancient world.

Richard Goy *Florence: the City and its Architecture* (Phaidon). Published in 2002, this book presents a fresh approach to a subject about which you might think there's nothing new to say. Instead of writing a doggedly sequential history, Goy has constructed a book that uses multiple perspectives to illuminate the architecture of Florence: the first section summarizes the city's development up to the unification of Italy; part two looks at the influence of the two chief "nuclei of power" – the Church and the State; part three analyses the fabric of the city according to building type (palazzi, churches, fortifications, etc); and the final section looks at the changes that Florence has undergone in the last century and a half. Encompassing everything from the Baptistery to the football stadium, and magnificently illustrated, this is a clear first choice.

J.R. Hale (ed.) *Concise Encyclopaedia of the Italian Renaissance* (Thames & Hudson, o/p in UK). Exemplary reference book, many of whose summaries are as informative as essays twice their length; covers individual artists, movements, cities, philosophical concepts, the lot.

Frederick Hartt & David Wilkins *History of Italian Renaissance Art* (Prentice Hall). If one book on this vast subject can be said to be indispensable, this is it. In view of its comprehensiveness and the range of its illustrations, it's a bargain.

Michael Levey *Early Renaissance* (Penguin, o/p). Precise and fluently written account from former director of the National Gallery, and well illustrated; probably the best introduction to the subject. Levey's *High Renaissance* (Penguin, o/p) continues the story in the same style.

Michael Levey *Florence: A Portrait* (Pimlico; Harvard). An often illuminating analysis of the city's history, and its artistic history in particular, with snippets and details missed by other accounts.

Anna Maria Massinelli and Filippo Tuena *Treasures of the Medici* (Rizzoli; Vendome). Illustrated inventory of the Medici family's collection of jewellery, vases and other *objets d'art*, published to celebrate the 500th anniversary of the death of Lorenzo il Magnifico, perhaps the clan's most compulsive collector. Not the first book to buy for your Florentine library, but definitive in its field.

Peter Murray *The Architecture of the Italian Renaissance* (Thames & Hudson; Schocken). Begins with Romanesque buildings and finishes with Palladio – useful both as a gazetteer of the main monuments and as a synopsis of the underlying concepts.

Diana Norman *Painting in Late Medieval and Renaissance Siena* (Yale). First published in 2003, this concise and well-illustrated book explicates the evolution of Sienese art from the thirteenth century to the middle of the sixteenth, finishing with the work of Beccafumi, the last Sienese painter of any magnitude.

John Shearman *Mannerism* (Penguin, o/p). The self-conscious art of sixteenth-century Mannerism is one of the most complex topics of Renaissance studies; Shearman's brief discussion analyses the main currents, and never succumbs to oversimplification or pedantry.

Giorgio Vasari *Lives of the Artists* (Penguin). This two-volume abridgment is the fullest available translation of Vasari's classic (and highly tendentious) work on his predecessors and contemporaries. Includes essays on Giotto, Brunelleschi, Leonardo and Michelangelo. The first real work of art history, and still among the most revealing books on Italian Renaissance art. Oxford University Press publishes a newer and briefer one-volume selection.

Individual artists

James A. Ackerman *The Architecture of Michelangelo* (University of Chicago). A concise, scholarly and highly engaging survey, which will make you see Michelangelo's architecture with fresh eyes.

Charles Avery *Donatello: An Introduction* (Murray, o/p; Icon, o/p). A perfectly serviceable book that does exactly what its title suggests, but there is a gap in the market for a more substantial English-language study of this titanic figure of the Renaissance.

Charles Avery *Giambologna* (Phaidon). This is the best survey of the career of the pre-eminent sculptor of the Mannerist period, an artist who can be seen as the successor of Michelangelo and precursor of Bernini. Though a little dogged in its approach – an overview of the career, followed by thematic chapters devoted to "Monumental statues", "Religious sculpture", "Marble fountains" etc – Avery's book is admirably comprehensive (every single sculpture is covered) and beautifully illustrated, with plenty of detailed close-ups of the major pieces and fascinating examples of the clay models that Giambologna created while sketching out his ideas.

Umberto Baldini and Ornella Casazza *The Brancacci Chapel* (Thames & Hudson, o/p; Abrams, o/p). Written by the chief restorers of the Brancacci cycle of frescoes by Masaccio, Masolino and Filippino Lippi, this luscious book is illustrated with magnificent life-size reproductions of the freshly cleaned masterpieces.

Luciano Bellosi *Duccio: The Maestà* (Thames and Hudson). Published in 1999, this superb production aims to present "a very direct experience of Duccio di Buoninsegna's masterpiece", and it does just that, with page after page of the highest quality details from the greatest of all Sienese paintings. The analytical essay that precedes the reproductions is a useful introduction to the work, but essentially this is a book to contemplate rather than to read.

Kenneth Clark *Leonardo da Vinci* (Penguin). Old-fashioned in its reverential connoisseurship, but still highly recommended.

Bruce Cole *Giotto and Florentine Painting 1280–1375* (HarperCollins o/p). Excellent introduction to the art of Giotto and his immediate successors.

Carlo Ginzburg *The Enigma of Piero* (Verso). Art history as detective story, on a quest to decipher Piero's *Baptism*, the Arezzo cycle and the *Flagellation*. Provocative, ingenious and often utterly eccentric.

Ludwig Goldscheider *Michelangelo: Paintings, Sculpture, Architecture* (Phaidon). Virtually all monochrome reproductions, but an extremely good pictorial survey of Michelangelo's output, covering everything except the drawings.

Anthony Grafton *Leon Battista Alberti* (Penguin; Harvard University Press). A fascinating study of one of the central figures of the Renaissance, Grafton's book illuminates every aspect of Alberti's astonishingly versatile career, which encompassed not just the visual arts and architecture, but also music, law, science and literature. Invaluable, not just as a portrait of an amazing man, but as an introduction to the whole culture of *quattrocento* Italy.

James Hall *Michelangelo and the Reinvention of the Human Body* (Chatto & Windus; Farrar, Straus & Giroux). A provocative and frequently brilliant study of Michelangelo, arguing for the essential modernity of Michelangelo's unprecedented emphasis on the male nude. Not all of Hall's observations are wholly convincing, but on almost every page there's an insight that will make you look afresh.

William Hood *Fra Angelico at San Marco* (Yale University Press). Maintaining this imprint's reputation for elegantly produced, scholarly yet accessible art books, Hood's socio-aesthetic study of the panel paintings and frescoes of Fra' Angelico is unsurpassed in its scope.

Anthony Hughes *Michelangelo* (Phaidon). This was one of the first titles in Phaidon's "Art & Ideas" series, a project which aims to present well-illustrated overviews of the work of individual artists and art movements, written by scholars but in a style that's accessible to all. *Michelangelo* is a superb advertisement for the series, giving a clear narrative while delineating the social and cultural milieu, and explaining clearly the key issues of style, technique and intepretation.

Martin Kemp *Leonardo* (Oxford University Press). Kemp is one of the world's leading Leonardo scholars, but he wears his learning lightly in this brief study, which is primarily concerned with revealing the intellectual preoccupations that unite the artist's multifarious creations.

Ross King *Brunelleschi's Dome* (Penguin). The tale of one of the most remarkable feats of engineering in European history – the design and construction of the dome of Florence's cathedral. King is good on the social and intellectual atmosphere, and has a thriller-writer's sense of pace.

Marilyn Aronberg Lavin *Piero della Francesca* (Phaidon). Another title in Phaidon's "Art & Ideas" project, this is the best English-language introduction to this most elusive of major Renaissance artists. Marilyn Aronberg Lavin is perhaps the world's leading authority on the subject, but this overview is perfectly pitched for the general reader, and benefits from having been published after the restoration of the Arezzo cycle, so its illustrations are uniquely accurate.

Charles Nicholl *Leonardo: The Flights of the Mind* (Penguin). Leonardo left more than 7000 pages of manuscript notes, and Nicholl's dazzling biography is founded on an intensive study of these largely unpublished writings. The result is a book which is both a highly persuasive portrait of this elusive genius, and a compendious reconstruction of the milieu in which he worked.

Jeffrey Ruda *Fra Filippo Lippi* (Phaidon). First published in 1993, Ruda's monograph is a fine achievement, combining a biographical study of the most wayward of early Renaissance masters with a consistently illuminating analysis of the paintings, which are reproduced in gorgeous large-format colour plates. The paperback edition is an abridged version of the hardback (the catalogue of Lippi's output is reduced to a list of key works), but it's as thorough as any lay reader could want, and astonishingly inexpensive for a production of this quality.

John White *Duccio: Tuscan Art and the Mediaeval Workshop* (Thames & Hudson, o/p). The fullest study of the Sienese master available in English, concentrating on his art in the context of medieval workshop practices.

Alison Wright *The Pollaiuolo Brothers: the Arts of Florence and Rome* (Yale). As painters, sculptors and goldsmiths, the Pollaiuolo brothers ran one of the busiest workshops in fifteenth-century Florence. Wright's book is a thorough and superbly illustrated study of the business of art production, as well as giving an unimprovable guide to the brothers' highly varied and innovative output.

Literature

Dante Alighieri *The Divine Comedy* (Oxford University Press, 3 vols). No work in any other language bears comparison with Dante's poetic exegesis of the moral scheme of God's creation: in late medieval Italy it was venerated both as a book of almost scriptural authority and as the ultimate refinement of the vernacular Tuscan language. There are numerous translations; the Oxford University Press version is in prose, but it has the advantage of presenting the original text opposite the English, and has exemplary notes.

Ludovico Ariosto *Orlando Furioso* (Penguin). Barbara Reynolds has done a fine job in this two-volume verse translation of Italy's chivalric epic, set in Charlemagne's Europe. Oxford University Press produces a one-volume prose translation.

Giovanni Boccaccio *The Decameron* (Penguin). Set in the plague-racked Florence of 1348, Boccaccio's assembly of one hundred short stories is a fascinating social record as well as a constantly diverting and often smutty comedy.

Benvenuto Cellini *Autobiography* (Penguin). Shamelessly egocentric record of the travails and triumphs of the sculptor and goldsmith's career; one of the freshest literary productions of its time. Oxford University Press also publishes an excellent translation, under the title *My Life*.

Niccolo Machiavelli *The Prince* (Oxford University Press). A treatise on statecraft which actually did less to form the political thought of Italy than it did to form foreigners' perceptions of the country; yet there was far more to Machiavelli than the *Realpolitik* of *The Prince*, as is shown by the selection of writings included in Viking's superb anthology *The Portable Machiavelli*.

Petrarch (Francesco Petrarca) *Selections from the Canzoniere* (Oxford University Press). Often described as the first modern poet, by virtue of his preoccupation with worldly fame and secular love, Petrarch wrote some of the Italian language's greatest lyrics. This slim selection at least hints at what is lost in translation.

Leonardo da Vinci *Notebooks* (Oxford University Press). Miscellany of speculation and observation from the universal genius of Renaissance Italy; essential to any understanding of the man.

Tuscany and Umbria in English fiction

Michael Dibdin *Ratking* (Faber; Vintage). Crime time in Perugia. Best of the Italy-set books of an author who sometimes tries a little too hard to underline just how much he knows about the country.

George Eliot *Romola* (Penguin). Weighty tale of fifteenth-century Florence; researched to the hilt, but will probably remain the great unread Eliot novel.

E.M. Forster *Where Angels Fear to Tread* (Penguin; Vintage) and *Room with a View* (Penguin; Bantam). The settings are, respectively, San Gimignano and Florence, the milieu uptight Edwardian English society in Forster's two perfectly formed Italian novels.

Magdalen Nabb *Death in Springtime*, *Death in Autumn*, and many other titles (Soho Press). Florence is the locale for many of Nabb's brilliant thrillers, based on a good knowledge of the city's low life and the Sardinian shepherds who dabble in a spot of kidnapping in the hills.

Michael Ondaatje *The English Patient* (Bloomsbury; Vintage). At the close of World War II, a badly burned English aviator sees out his days in a wrecked Tuscan villa, attended by a cast of characters who come from widely differing backgrounds yet all think and speak in high-flown lyrical language. Some find Ondaatje's prose hypnotic, others find it portentous.

Barry Unsworth *After Hannibal* (Penguin; Norton). Unsworth lives in Umbria, which is where this black comedy is set. Where lesser writers resort to rose-tinted fantasies, Unsworth evokes the reality of expat existence.

Flora and fauna

Hermann Heinzel, Richard Fitter & John Parslow *The Birds of Britain and Europe* (Collins). Best-known general guide, with plentiful maps and illustrations.

Lionel Higgins & Norman Riley *Field Guide to the Butterflies of Britain and Europe* (Collins, o/p). Amply illustrated and detailed handbook.

C.J. Humphries, J.R. Press & D.A. Sutton *Trees of Britain and Europe* (Philips; Hamlyn). A thoroughly reliable and straightforward guide.

Oleg Polunin & Antony Huxley *Flowers of the Mediterranean* (Chatto & Windus, o/p). Excellent guide, with colour pictures, line drawings and concise reference list as aids to identification.

Thomas Schauer *Field Guide to the Wild Flowers of Britain and Europe* (Collins, o/p). Comprehensive handbook with good drawings and detailed descriptions.

Christopher Grey Wilson & Marjorie Blamey *Alpine Flowers of Britain and Europe* (Collins, o/p). Full account of mountain flora, particularly useful as a handbook for the Monti Sibillini, Orecchiella and Alpi Apuane.

Hiking guides

Stefano Ardito *A Piedi in Umbria* (Edizione Iter). One of a series by the doyen of Italian backpackers.

Antonio Arrighi and Roberto Pratesi *A Piedi in Toscana* (Edizione Iter, 2 vols). Useful route guides for walkers, with basic maps. Widely available in Italy.

Wine and food

Burton Anderson *Vino: the Wines and Winemakers of Italy* (Little, Brown, o/p). The definitive book on Italian wines, detailing production methods, grape varieties, climates and geology, and written in a light-hearted and readable style.

Burton Anderson *The Pocket Guide to Italian Wines* (Mitchell Beazley o/p; Simon & Schuster o/p). Excellent handbook for selecting rarer or vintage wines on the spot.

Burton Anderson and others *Chianti* (Edizioni Grafica Comense o/p). Comprehensive handbook to the wines, producers, and restaurants of the region.

Leslie Forbes *A Table in Tuscany* (Penguin, o/p). Regional recipes presented in the format of a facsimile manuscript, illustrated with colourful drawings.

Marcella Hazan *Classic Italian Cookbook* (Papermac; Ballantine o/p). Marcella features a fair number of Tuscan recipes and issues the kind of instructions that inspire total confidence.

Hugh Johnson *Tuscany and its Wines* (Mitchell Beazley). Johnson's knowledge of the subject is sound, and the photographs almost qualify as oeno-porn.

Elizabeth Romer *The Tuscan Year: Life and Food in an Italian Valley* (Orion; North Point). An engaging mix of recipes and background on countryside traditions.

Janet Ross and Michael Waterfield *Leaves from our Tuscan Kitchen* (Penguin, o/p). Classic vegetarian recipes, first published in 1899.

Language

Language

Italian

The ability to speak English confers prestige in Italy, and there's often no shortage of people willing to show off their knowledge, particularly in the main cities and resorts. However, in more remote areas you may find that no one speaks English at all.

Wherever you are, it's a good idea to master at least a little Italian, a task made easier by the fact that your halting efforts will often be rewarded by smiles and genuine surprise. In any case, it's one of the easiest European languages to learn, especially if you already have a smattering of French or Spanish, which are extremely similar to Italian grammatically.

Pronunciation

Easiest of all is the **pronunciation**, since every word is spoken exactly as it's written, and usually enunciated with exaggerated, open-mouthed clarity. The only difficulties you're likely to encounter are the few consonants that are different from English.

c before e or i is pronounced as in church.

ch before e or i is hard, as in cat.

sci pronounced as in sheet.

sce pronounced as in shelter.

g is soft before e or i, as in geranium; hard before h, as in garlic.

gn as in onion.

gl is softened (the g is silent), as in stallion.

h is not aspirated, as in honour.

When **speaking to strangers**, the third person is the polite form (ie *Lei* instead of *Tu* for "you"); using the second person is a mark of disrespect or stupidity. It's also worth remembering that Italians don't use "please" and "thank you" half as much as we do: it's all implied in the tone, though if you're in any doubt, err on the polite side.

All Italian words are **stressed** on the penultimate syllable unless a stress mark – ´ or ` – denotes otherwise. Note that the ending *-ia* or *-ie* counts as two syllables, hence *trattoria* is stressed on the i. Generally, in the text we've added stress marks whenever it isn't immediately obvious how a word should be pronounced, though you shouldn't assume that this is how you'll see the words written in Italian: quite often they're omitted altogether. For example, in *Maríttima*, the mark is on the first i, but on Italian maps it's often written as *Marittima*. **Accents** look similar to stress marks – generally ` – but they have the function of altering a word's final vowel sound, as in *sì* or *caffè*, and can never be dropped.

Italian words and phrases

The Basics

good morning	buongiorno
good afternoon/evening	buona sera
good night	buona notte
hello/goodbye (informal)	ciao
goodbye (formal)	arrivederci
yes	sì
no	no
please	per favore
thank you (very much)	(molte/mille) grazie
you're welcome	prego
alright/that's OK	va bene
excuse me (apology)	mi scusi/prego
excuse me (in a crowd)	permesso
sorry	mi dispiace
How are you? (informal)	Come stai?
How are you? (formal)	Come sta?
I'm fine	bene
Do you speak English?	Parla inglese?
I don't understand	Non ho capito
I don't know	Non lo so
I'm here on holiday	Sono qui in vacanza
I live in…	Abito a…
I'm…	Sono…
English/Scottish	inglese/scozzese
Welsh/Irish	gallese/irlandese
American (m/f)	americano/a
Canadian/New Zealand	canadese/nuova zelandese
Australian (m/f)	australiano/a
Mr…	Signor…
Mrs…	Signora…
Miss…	Signorina…

(use *il Signor, la Signora, la Signorina* when speaking about someone else)

What time does it open/close?	A che ora apre/chiude?
How much?	Quanto?
How much does it cost?	Quant'è?
What's it called in Italian?	Come si chiama in italiano?
Where?	Dove?
Where is/are…?	Dov'è…?/Dove sono…?
When?	Quando?
What?	Cosa?
What is it?	Cos'è?
How many?	Quanti?
Why?	Perchè?
It is/There is	È/C'è
Is it…?/Is there…?	È…?/C'è…?
here/there	qui/la
good/bad	buono/cattivo
big/small	grande/píccolo
cheap/expensive	económico/caro
early/late	presto/ritardo
hot/cold	caldo/freddo
near/far	vicino/lontano
quickly/slowly	velocemente/lentamente
slowly or quietly	piano
with/without	con/senza
more/less	più/meno
enough, no more	basta
wait a minute!	aspetta!
today	oggi
tomorrow	domani
day after tomorrow	dopodomani
yesterday	ieri
now	adesso
later	più tardi
in the morning	di mattina
in the afternoon	nel pomeriggio
in the evening	di sera
What time is it?	Che ora è?/Che ore sono?

Some signs

entrance/exit	entrata/uscita
free admission	ingresso líbero
open/closed	aperto/chiuso
closed for restoration	chiuso per restauro

closed for holidays	chiuso per ferie	WC	bagno
pull/push	tirare/spingere	vacant/engaged	libero/occupato
do not touch	non toccare	arrivals/departures	arrivi/partenze
danger	perícolo	platform	binario
beware	attenzione	cash desk	cassa
out of order	guasto	to let	affítasi
no smoking	vietato fumare	go or walk	avanti
ring the bell	suonare il campanello	stop	alt
drinking water	acqua potabile	customs	dogana
gents/ladies toilet	signori/signore	first aid	pronto soccorso

Accommodation

Is there a hotel nearby?	C'è un albergo qui vicino?	Could I see another room?	Potrei guardare un'altra camera?
Do you have rooms free?	Avete camere libere?	How much is it?	Quanto costa?
I'd like to book a room	Vorrei prenotare una camera	Is breakfast included?	È compresa la prima colazione?
I have a booking	Ho una prenotazione	half/full board	mezza pensione/ pensione completa
a single/double room	una camera singola/ doppia	Do you have anything cheaper?	Ha niente che costa di meno?
Do you have a room...	Ha una camera...	Can I see the room?	Posso vedere la camera?
for one person	per una persona	I'll take it	La prendo
for two/three people	per due/tre persone	Can we camp here?	Possiamo fare il campeggio qui?
for one night	per una notte		
for two/three nights	per due/tre notti	Is there a campsite nearby?	C'è un camping qui vicino?
for one week	per una settimana		
for two weeks	per due settimane	tent	tenda
with a double bed	con un letto matrimoniale	cabin	cabina
with twin beds	a due letti	youth hostel	ostello per la gioventù
with a shower/bath	con una doccia/un bagno	porter	il facchino
		lift	ascensore
with a balcony	con una terrazza	key	la chiave
hot/cold water	acqua calda/freddo		

Restaurants

I'd like to reserve a table	Vorrei riservare una tavola	I'm a vegetarian (m/f)	Sono vegetariano/a
		I'd like...	Vorrei...
Have you a table for two?	Avete una tavola per due?	It's good/delicious	È buono/squisito
		The bill, please	Il conto, per favore
I'd like to order	Vorrei ordinare	Is service included?	Il servizio è incluso?

Travelling

bus	autobus/pullman	train station	stazione ferroviaria
bus station	autostazione	ferry	traghetto
train	treno	hydrofoil	aliscafo

ferry terminal	stazione maríttima	How long does it take?	Quanto ci vuole?
port	porto	What number bus is it to…?	Que número di autobus per…?
ship	nave		
A ticket to…	Un biglietto a…	How do I get to…?	Come arrivo a…?
one-way	solo andata	How far is it to…?	Quant'è lontano a…?
return	andata e ritorno	Can you give me a lift to…?	Mi può dare un passaggio a…?
Can I book a seat?	Posso prenotare un posto?		
What time does it leave?	A che ora parte?	left/right	sinistro/destro
		go straight ahead	sempre diritto
When is the next train to…?	Quando parte il prossimo treno per…?	turn to the left/right	gira a destra/sinistra
		Can you tell me when to get off?	Mi può dire scendere alla fermata giusta?
Do I have to change?	Devo cambiare?		
Where does it leave from?	Da dove parte?	Next stop please	La prossima fermata, per favore
What platform does it leave from?	Da quale binario parte?	bicycle	bicicletta
		hitchhiking	autostop
How many kilometres is it?	Quanti chilometri sono?	on foot	a piedi

Driving

car	macchina	slow down	rallentare
Where's the road to…?	Dov'è la strada a…?	road closed/up	strada chiusa/guasta
parking	parcheggio	no through road	vietato il transito
no parking	divieto di sosta/sosta vietata	no overtaking	vietato il sorpasso
		crossroads	incrocio
one-way street	senso único	speed limit	limite di velocità
no entry	senso vietato		

Numbers

1	uno	19	diciannove
2	due	20	venti
3	tre	21	ventuno
4	quattro	22	ventidue
5	cinque	30	trenta
6	sei	40	quaranta
7	sette	50	cinquanta
8	otto	60	sessanta
9	nove	70	settanta
10	dieci	80	ottanta
11	undici	90	novanta
12	dodici	100	cento
13	tredici	101	centuno
14	quattordici	110	centodieci
15	quindici	200	duecento
16	sedici	500	cinquecento
17	diciassette	1000	mille
18	diciotto	5000	cinquemila

Italian menu reader

Meals and courses

la colazione	breakfast	zuppe/minestre	soups
pranzo	lunch	secondi	main courses
cena	evening meal	contorni	vegetables
antipasti	starters	dolci	desserts
primi	first courses	menù degustazione	tasting menu

General terms

il cameriere	waiter	maionese	mayonnaise
il menù/la lista	menu	marmellata	jam (jelly)
la lista dei vini	wine list	olio	oil
un coltello	knife	olive	olives
una forchetta	fork	pane	bread
un cucchiaio	spoon	pane integrale	wholemeal bread
senza carne	without meat	panino	bread roll/sandwich
coperto	cover charge	panna	cream
servizio	service charge	patatine	crisps (potato chips)
aceto	vinegar	patatine fritte	chips (french fries)
aglio	garlic	pepe	pepper
biscotti	biscuits	pizzetta	small cheese and tomato pizza
burro	butter		
caramelle	sweets	riso	rice
cioccolato	chocolate	sale	salt
focaccia	oven-baked snack	uova	eggs
frittata	omelette	zucchero	sugar
grissini	breadsticks		

Cooking terms

affumicato	smoked	al Marsala	cooked with Marsala wine
arrosto	roast		
ben cotto	well done	Milanese	fried in egg and breadcrumbs
bollito/lesso	boiled		
brasata	cooked in wine	pizzaiola	cooked with tomato sauce
cotto	cooked (not raw)		
crudo	raw	al puntino	medium (steak)
al dente	firm (not overcooked)	ripieno	stuffed
ai ferri	grilled without oil	al sangue	rare (steak)
fritto	fried	allo spiedo	on the spit
grattuggiato	grated	surgelato	frozen
alla griglia	grilled	umido	steamed/stewed

Pizzas

calzone folded pizza with cheese, ham and tomato

capricciosa literally "capricious"; topped with whatever they've got in the kitchen, usually including baby artichoke, ham and egg

cardinale ham and olives

frutta di mare seafood; usually mussels, prawns and clams

funghi mushrooms; the tinned sliced variety, unless it specifies fresh (*funghi freschi*)

margherita cheese and tomato

marinara tomato, anchovy and olive oil

napo/napoletana tomato

quattro formaggi "four cheeses", usually including mozzarella, fontina and gruyère

quattro stagioni "four seasons"; the toppings split into four separate sections, usually including ham, green pepper, onion, egg, etc

Antipasti

antipasto misto	mixed cold meats and cheese
caponata	mixed aubergine, olives, tomatoes
caprese	tomato and mozzarella salad
crostini	mixed chicken liver canapés
insalata di mare	seafood salad
insalata di riso	rice salad
insalata russa	Russian salad (diced vegetables in mayonnaise)
melanzane in parmigiana	aubergine in tomato and Parmesan cheese
peperonata	green and red peppers stewed in olive oil
pomodori ripieni	stuffed tomatoes
prosciutto	ham

crostini di milza	minced spleen on pieces of toast
donzele/donzelline	fried dough balls
fettuna/bruschetta	garlic toast with olive oil

finocchiona	pork sausage flavoured with fennel
pinzimonio	raw seasonal vegetable in olive oil, with salt and pepper
prosciutto di cinghiale	cured wild boar ham
salame toscano	pork sausage with pepper and cubes of fat
salsicce	pork or wild boar sausage

Umbrian antipasti

prosciutto di'Norcia	cured ham from Norcia
salame mezzafegato	sausage spiced with a mixture of pine nuts, pork liver, candied orange, sugar and raisins
schiacciata	flat bread baked with olive oil, or flavoured with onions or cooked greens
torta al testo	unleavened bread baked on a stone slab

Primi

Soups

brodo	clear broth
minestrina	any light soup
minestrone	thick vegetable soup
pasta fagioli	pasta soup with beans
pastini in brodo	pasta pieces in clear broth
stracciatella	broth with egg

Pasta

cannelloni	large tubes of pasta, stuffed
farfalle	literally "butterfly"-shaped pasta

LANGUAGE | Italian menu reader

fettucine	narrow pasta ribbons
gnocchi	small potato and dough dumplings
maccheroni	tubular spaghetti
pasta al forno	pasta baked with minced meat, eggs, tomato and cheese
penne	smaller pieces of rigatoni
rigatoni	large, grooved tubular pasta
risotto	cooked rice dish, with sauce
spaghettini	thin spaghetti
tagliatelle	pasta ribbons (another word for fettucine)
tortellini	small rings of pasta stuffed with meat or cheese
vermicelli	"little worms" (very thin spaghetti)

Pasta sauce (salsa)

arrabbiata	spicy tomato sauce with chillies
bolognese	tomato and meat
burro	butter
carbonara	cream, ham and beaten egg
funghi	mushrooms
matriciana	tomato and cubed pork
panna	cream
parmigiano	Parmesan cheese
peperoncino	olive oil, garlic and fresh chillies
pesto	green basil and garlic sauce
pomodoro	tomato sauce
ragù	meat sauce
vongole	clam and tomato sauce

Tuscan primi

acquacotta	onion soup served with toast and poached egg
cacciucco	fish stew with tomatoes, bread and red wine

carabaccia	onion soup
garmugia	soup made with fava beans, peas, artichokes, asparagus and bacon
gnocchi di ricotta	dumplings filled with ricotta and spinach
minestra di farro	wheat and bean soup
minestrone alla fiorentina	haricot bean soup with red cabbage, tomatoes, onions and herbs
panzanella	summer salad of tomatoes, basil, cucumber, onion and bread
pappa al pomodoro	tomato soup thickened with bread
pappardelle	wide, short noodles, often served with hare sauce (con lepre)
pasta alla carrettiera	pasta with tomato, garlic, pepper, parsley and chilli
penne strasciate	quill-shaped pasta in meat sauce
ribollita	winter vegetable soup, based on beans and thickened with bread
risotto nero	rice cooked with cuttlefish (in its own ink)
zuppa di fagioli	bean soup

Umbrian primi

manfrigoli	rustic pasta made from emmer, a coarse type of wheat introduced into the region by the Romans
minestra di farro	tomato, wheat and vegetable soup
pici/stringozzi/ceriole	thread-like spaghetti, usually served with garlicky tomato sauce
spaghetti alla norcina	spaghetti with an oily sauce of black truffles, garlic and anchovies
umbrici	large, heavy noodles

L

LANGUAGE | Italian menu reader

Secondi

Meat (carne)

agnello	lamb
bistecca	steak
cervello	brain
cinghiale	wild boar
coniglio	rabbit
costolette	chops
cotolette	cutlets
fagiaon	pheasant
faraona	guinea fowl
fegatini	chicken livers
fegato	liver
involtini	meat slices, rolled and stuffed
lepre	hare
lingua	tongue
maiale	pork
manzo	beef
mortadella	salami-type cured meat
ossobuco	shin of veal
pernice	partridge
pancetta	bacon
pollo	chicken
polpette	meatballs
rognoni	kidneys
salsiccia	sausage
saltimbocca	veal with ham
spezzatino	stew
tacchino	turkey
trippa	tripe
vitello	veal

Fish (pesce) and shellfish (crostacei)

acciughe	anchovies
anguilla	eel
aragosta	lobster
baccalà	dried salted cod
calamari	squid
céfalo	mullet
cozze	mussels
dentice	dentex
gamberetti	shrimps
gámberi	prawns
granchio	crab
merluzzo	cod
ostriche	oysters
pescespada	swordfish
póoipo	octopus
sarde	sardines
sgombro	mackerel
sogliola	sole
tonno	tuna
triglie	red mullet
trota	trout
vóngole	clams

Tuscan secondi

arista	roast pork loin with garlic and rosemary
asparagi alla fiorentina	asparagus with butter, fried egg and cheese
baccalà alla livornese	salt cod with garlic, tomatoes and parsley
bistecca alla fiorentina	thick grilled T-bone steak
cibreo	chicken liver and egg stew
cieche alla pisana	small eels cooked with sage and tomatoes, served with Parmesan
lombatina	veal chop
peposo	peppered beef stew
pollo alla diavola/ al mattone	chicken flattened with a brick, grilled with herbs
scottiglia	stew of veal, game and poultry, cooked with white wine and tomatoes
spiedini di maiale	skewered spiced cubes of pork loin and liver, with bread and bay leaves
tonno con fagioli	tuna with white beans and raw onion
trigile alla livornese	red mullet cooked with tomatoes, garlic and parsley
trippa alla fiorentina	tripe in tomato sauce, served with Parmesan

anguilla alla brace	grilled eel
anguilla in úmido	eel cooked with tomatoes, onions, garlic and white wine
frittata di tartufi	black truffle omelette
gobbi alla perugina	deep-fried cardoons (like artichokes) with meat sauce
lepre alle olive	hare cooked with herbs, white wine and olives
palombe/palombacci	woodpigeon, usually spit-roasted

pollo in porchetta	chicken cooked in the same way as suckling pig
porchetta	suckling pig cooked in a wood oven with fennel, garlic, mint and rosemary
regina in porchetta	Lago Trasimeno carp, cooked as above
salsiccia all'uva	pork sausage cooked with grapes
tegamaccio	freshwater-fish stew with white wine and herbs

Vegetables (contorni) and salad (insalata)

asparagi	asparagus
basílico	basil
capperi	capers
carciofi	artichokes
carciofini	artichoke hearts
carotte	carrots
cavolfiori	cauliflower
cávolo	cabbage
cetriolo	cucumber
cipolla	onion
fagiolini	green beans
finocchio	fennel
funghi	mushrooms
insalata mista	mixed salad
insalata verde	green salad
melanzane	aubergine

orígano	oregano
patate	potatoes
peperoni	peppers
piselli	peas
pomodori	tomatoes
radicchio	chicory
spinaci	spinach
zucchini	courgettes

fagioli all'olio	white beans served with olive oil
fagioli all'uccelletto	white beans cooked with tomatoes, garlic and sage
frittata di carciofi	fried artichoke flan

Sweets (dolci), fruit (frutta), cheese (formaggi) and nuts (noce)

amaretti	macaroons
ananas	pineapple
anguria/coccómero	watermelon
arance	oranges
banane	bananas
cacchi	persimmons
ciliegie	cherries
fichi	figs
fichi d'India	prickly pears
fontina	northern Italian cooking cheese

fragole	strawberries
gelato	ice cream
gorgonzola	a soft blue cheese
limone	lemon
macedonia	fruit salad
mandorle	almonds
mele	apples
melone	melon
mozzarella	bland soft white cheese used on pizzas
nespole	medlars

parmigiano	Parmesan cheese	frittelle di riso	rice fritters
pecorino	strong hard sheep's cheese	meringa	frozen meringue with whipped cream and chocolate
pere	pears	necci	chestnut-flour crêpes
pesche	peaches	panforte	hard fruit, nut and spice cake
pignoli	pine nuts	ricciarelli	marzipan almond biscuits
provolone	strong hard cheese		
ricotta	soft white sheep's cheese	schiacciata alla fiorentina	orange-flavoured cake covered with powdered sugar, eaten at carnival time
torta	cake, tart		
uva	grapes		
zabaglione	dessert made with eggs, sugar and Marsala wine	schiacciata con l'uva	grape- and sugar-covered bread dessert
zuppa inglese	trifle	zuccotto	sponge cake filled with chocolate and whipped cream

Tuscan dolci

brigidini	anise wafer biscuits
buccellato	anise raisin cake
cantucci/cantuccini	small almond biscuits, served with Vinsanto wine
castagnaccio	unleavened chestnut-flour cake containing raisins, walnuts and rosemary
cenci	fried dough dusted with powdered sugar

Umbrian dolci

cialde	paper-thin sweet biscuits
fave di morte	almond biscuits
pinoccate	pine nut biscuits
serpentone/torcolato	almond and dried fruit dessert in the shape of a coiled snake (*torcolo*)

Drinking essentials

aperitivo	pre-dinner drink	caffè	coffee
digestivo	after-dinner drink	cioccolata calda	hot chocolate
vino rosso	red wine	frappé	milkshake made with ice cream
vino bianco	white wine		
vino rosato	rosé wine	frullato	milkshake
spumante	sparkling wine	ghiaccio	ice
secco	dry	granita	iced drink with coffee or fruit
dolce	sweet		
birra	beer	latte	milk
litro	litre	limonate	lemonade
mezzo	half-litre	selz	soda water
quatro	quarter-litre	spremuta	fresh fruit juice
Salute!	Cheers! (toast)	succo di frutta	concentrated fruit juice with sugar
acqua minerale	mineral water		
aranciata	orangeade	tazza	cup
bicchiere	glass	tè	tea
bottiglia	bottle	tonico	tonic water

Glossary

Artistic and architectural terms in English

Apse Semicircular recess at the altar, usually eastern, end of a church.

Architrave The lowest part of the entablature.

Atrium Inner courtyard.

Basilica Originally a Roman administrative building, adapted for early churches; distinguished by lack of transepts.

Belvedere A terrace or lookout point.

Capital Top of a column.

Chancel Part of a church containing the altar.

Cornice The top section of a classical facade.

Cosmati work Decorative mosaic work on marble, usually highly coloured, found in early Christian Italian churches, especially in Rome. Derives from Cosma, a common name among families of marble workers at the time.

Crypt Burial place in a church, usually under the choir.

Cupola Dome.

Cyclopean walls Fortifications built of huge, rough stone blocks.

Diptych Twin-panelled painting.

Entablature The section above the capital on a classical building, below the cornice.

Ex-voto Artefact designed in thanksgiving to a saint. The adjective is ex-votive.

Fresco Wall-painting technique in which the artist applies paint to wet plaster for a more permanent finish.

Intarsia Inlaid stone or wood.

Loggia Roofed gallery or balcony.

Lunette Semicircular space in vault or ceiling.

Narthex Vestibule of a church.

Nave Central space in a church, usually flanked by aisles.

Polyptych Painting on several joined panels.

Portico Covered entrance to a building.

Predella Small panel below the main scenes of an altarpiece.

Reliquary Receptacle for a saint's relics, usually bones. Often highly decorated.

Stucco Plaster made from water, lime, sand and powdered marble, used for decorative work.

Triptych Painting on three joined panels.

Trompe l'oeil Work of art that deceives the viewer by tricks of perspective.

Artistic and architectural terms in Italian and Latin

Ambo A kind of simple pulpit, popular in Italian medieval churches.

Anfiteatro Amphitheatre.

Badìa Abbey.

Baldacchino A canopy on columns, usually placed over the altar in a church.

Baluardo Bastion.

Battistero Baptistery.

Borgo Medieval suburb or hamlet.

Caldarium The steam room of a Roman bath.

Campanile Bell-tower, sometimes detached, usually of a church.

Campo Square.

Camposanto Cemetery.

Cantoria Choir loft.

Cappella Chapel.

Castello Castle.

Cenacolo Last Supper.

Chiesa Church.

Chiostro Cloister.

Ciborium Goblet for communion wafers; or another word for baldacchino.

Collegiata Church just below the hierarchy of a cathedral.

Contrada Ancient quarter of a town.

Cortile Galleried courtyard or cloister.

Decumanus Maximus The main street of a Roman town. The second cross-street was known as the Decumanus Inferiore.

Duomo/Cattedrale Cathedral.

Fonte Fountainhouse.

Fortezza Fortress.

Gonfaloni Painted flags or standards.

Maestà Madonna and Child enthroned.

Matroneum Women's gallery in early church.

Municipio Town hall.

Palazzo Palace, mansion, or block of flats.

Palazzo del Podestà Magistrate's palace.

Palazzo del Popolo/Palazzo Pubblico/Palazzo Comunale Town hall.

Pantocrator An image of Christ, usually portrayed in the act of blessing.

Piano Nobile Main floor of a palace, usually the first (upstairs).

Pietà Image of the Virgin mourning the dead Christ.

Pietra dure Hard or semiprecious stones used for decorative inlay.

Pieve Parish church.

Pinacoteca Picture gallery.

Porta Gate.

Putti Cherubs.

Rocca Castle.

Sala dei Priori Council chamber.

Santuario Sanctuary or chancel.

Sgraffito Decorative technique whereby a layer of plaster is scratched to form a pattern.

Sinopia Sketch for a fresco, applied to the wall.

Teatro Theatre.

Tempio Temple.

Thermae Baths, usually elaborate buildings in Roman villas.

Tondo Round painting or relief.

Torre Tower.

Some common Italian words

Alto Upper.

Autostrada Motorway.

Bagno Bath or spa; also WC.

Basso/Scalo Lower.

Biblioteca Library.

Centro storico Historic centre.

Comune An administrative area; also the local council or town hall.

Corso Avenue or boulevard.

Festa Festival, holiday.

Fiume River.

Giardino/Orto Botanico Botanical garden.

Golfo Gulf.

Lago Lake.

Lungomare Seafront road or promenade.

Mare Sea.

Mercato Market.

Ospedale Hospital.

Paese Place, area, or village.

Passeggiata The customary early-evening walk (sometimes applied to a promenade).

Piano Plain.

Questura Main police station.

Sottopassagio Subway.

Spiaggia Beach.

Strada Road.

Acronyms

AAST Azienda Autonoma di Soggiorno e Turismo.

ACI Automobile Club d'Italia.

APT Azienda Provinciale di Turismo.

CAI Club Alpino Italiano.

EPT Ente Provinciale di Turismo (provincial tourist office); see also APT and AAST.

IVA Imposta Valore Aggiunto (VAT/sales tax).

RAI The state TV and radio network.

SS Strada Statale; main road (eg SS18).

TCI Touring Club d'Italia; map and guide publishers.

Travel store

WHEREVER YOU ARE,

WHEREVER YOU'RE GOING

WE'VE GOT YOU COVERED!

Rough Guides Travel Insurance

Visit our website at www.roughguides.com/insurance or call:

- UK: 0800 083 9507
- Spain: 900 997 149
- Australia: 1300 669 999
- New Zealand: 0800 55 99 11
- Worldwide: +44 870 890 2843
- USA, call toll free on: 1 800 749 4922

Please quote our ref: *Rough Guides books*

Cover for over 46 different nationalities and available in 4 different languages.

COLUMBUS
Travel Insurance

ROUGH
GUIDES

Small print and

Index

A Rough Guide to Rough Guides

Published in 1982, the first Rough Guide – to Greece – was a student scheme that became a publishing phenomenon. Mark Ellingham, a recent graduate in English from Bristol University, had been travelling in Greece the previous summer and couldn't find the right guidebook. With a small group of friends he wrote his own guide, combining a highly contemporary, journalistic style with a thoroughly practical approach to travellers' needs.

The immediate success of the book spawned a series that rapidly covered dozens of destinations. And, in addition to impecunious backpackers, Rough Guides soon acquired a much broader and older readership that relished the guides' wit and inquisitiveness as much as their enthusiastic, critical approach and value-for-money ethos.

These days, Rough Guides include recommendations from shoestring to luxury and cover more than 200 destinations around the globe, including almost every country in the Americas and Europe, more than half of Africa and most of Asia and Australasia. Our ever-growing team of authors and photographers is spread all over the world, particularly in Europe, the USA and Australia.

In the early 1990s, Rough Guides branched out of travel, with the publication of Rough Guides to World Music, Classical Music and the Internet. All three have become benchmark titles in their fields, spearheading the publication of a wide range of books under the Rough Guide name.

Including the travel series, Rough Guides now number more than 350 titles, covering: phrasebooks, waterproof maps, music guides from Opera to Heavy Metal, reference works as diverse as Conspiracy Theories and Shakespeare, and popular culture books from iPods to Poker. Rough Guides also produce a series of more than 120 World Music CDs in partnership with World Music Network.

Visit www.roughguides.com to see our latest publications.

Rough Guide travel images are available for commercial licensing at www.roughguidespictures.com

SMALL PRINT

Rough Guide credits

Text editor: Ruth Blackmore
Layout: Dan May
Cartography: Ed Wright and Katie Lloyd-Jones
Picture editor: Jj Luck
Production: Katherine Owers
Proofreader: Amanda Jones
Cover design: Chloë Roberts
Photographers: Dylan Reisenberger and James McConnachie

....

Editorial: **London** Kate Berens, Claire Saunders, Geoff Howard, Polly Thomas, Richard Lim, Clifton Wilkinson, Alison Murchie, Karoline Densley, Andy Turner, Keith Drew, Edward Aves, Nikki Birrell, Helen Marsden, Alice Park, Sarah Eno, David Paul, Lucy White, Joe Staines, Duncan Clark, Peter Buckley, Matthew Milton, Tracy Hopkins, Ruth Tidball; **New York** Andrew Rosenberg, Steven Horak, AnneLise Sorensen, Amy Hegarty, Hunter Slaton, April Isaacs, Sean Mahoney
Design & Pictures: **London** Simon Bracken, Diana Jarvis, Mark Thomas, Harriet Mills; **Delhi** Madhulita Mohapatra, Umesh Aggarwal, Ajay Verma, Jessica Subramanian, Amit Verma, Ankur Guha, Pradeep Thapliyal

Production: Sophie Hewat, Aimee Hampson
Cartography: **London** Maxine Repath; **Delhi** Manish Chandra, Rajesh Chhibber, Jai Prakash Mishra, Ashutosh Bharti, Rajesh Mishra, Animesh Pathak, Jasbir Sandhu, Karobi Gogoi, Amod Singh
Online: **New York** Jennifer Gold, Suzanne Welles, Kristin Mingrone; **Delhi** Manik Chauhan, Narender Kumar, Shekhar Jha, Rakesh Kumar, Chhandita Chakravarty
Marketing & Publicity: **London** Richard Trillo, Niki Hanmer, David Wearn, Demelza Dallow, Louise Maher, Jess Carter; **New York** Geoff Colquitt, Megan Kennedy, Katy Ball; **Delhi** Reem Khokhar
Custom publishing and foreign rights: Philippa Hopkins
Manager India: Punita Singh
Series editor: Mark Ellingham
Reference Director: Andrew Lockett
PA to Publishing Director: Megan McIntyre
Publishing Director: Martin Dunford

Publishing information

This sixth edition published June 2006 by **Rough Guides Ltd**,
80 Strand, London WC2R 0RL
345 Hudson St, 4th Floor,
New York, NY 10014, USA
14 Local Shopping Centre, Panchsheel Park,
New Delhi 110017, India
Distributed by the Penguin Group
Penguin Books Ltd,
80 Strand, London WC2R 0RL
Penguin Putnam, Inc.
375 Hudson Street, NY 10014, USA
Penguin Group (Australia)
250 Camberwell Road, Camberwell,
Victoria 3124, Australia
Penguin Books Canada Ltd,
10 Alcorn Avenue, Toronto, Ontario,
Canada M4V 1E4
Penguin Group (New Zealand)
Cnr Rosedale and Airborne Roads
Albany, Auckland, New Zealand
Cover concept by Peter Dyer.

Typeset in Bembo and Helvetica to an original design by Henry Iles.

Printed and bound in Italy by Legoprint

© Jonathan Buckley, Mark Ellingham and Tim Jepson 2006

No part of this book may be reproduced in any form without permission from the publisher except for the quotation of brief passages in reviews.

820pp includes index

A catalogue record for this book is available from the British Library

ISBN 1-84353-676-5

ISBN 13: 9781843536765

SMALL PRINT

The publishers and authors have done their best to ensure the accuracy and currency of all the information in **The Rough Guide to Tuscany & Umbria**, however, they can accept no responsibility for any loss, injury, or inconvenience sustained by any traveller as a result of information or advice contained in the guide.

1   3   5   7   9   8   6   4   2

Help us update

We've gone to a lot of effort to ensure that the sixth edition of **The Rough Guide to Tuscany & Umbria** is accurate and up to date. However, things change – places get "discovered", opening hours are notoriously fickle, restaurants and rooms raise prices or lower standards. If you feel we've got it wrong or left something out, we'd like to know, and if you can remember the address, the price, the time, the phone number, so much the better.

We'll credit all contributions, and send a copy of the next edition (or any other Rough Guide if you prefer) for the best letters. Everyone who writes to us and isn't already a subscriber will receive a copy of our full-colour thrice-yearly newsletter. Please mark letters: "**Rough Guide Tuscany & Umbria Update**" and send to: Rough Guides, 80 Strand, London WC2R 0RL, or Rough Guides, 4th Floor, 345 Hudson St, New York, NY 10014. Or send an email to **mail@roughguides.com**
Have your questions answered and tell others about your trip at
www.roughguides.atinfopop.com

Acknowledgements

Tim Jepson would like to thank Duncan and Amanda Baird, Marella Caracciolo, Michael Sheridan and Yasmin Setha, as well as Nicholas Harrison for extra updating, and editor Ruth Blackmore.

Readers' letters

Thanks to all the readers who have taken the time to write in with comments and suggestions (and apologies if we've inadvertently omitted or misspelt anyone's name):

Len Amaral, Mike Appleton, Lance Ashdown, Jean Austen, Colin Aylott, Linda Baker, Paul Barker, Clive Barham Carter, Gerry Barton, Giacomo Benedetto, Alan Bennett, Rolf Bergman, Massimo Biancucci, Ruth Bohin, Susan Boucher, Elizabeth Cary Blum, Ian Bookless, Judy Cahusac, Jeremy Carne, Stacie Carr, Angela Chattoe, Steve Cheetham, David Claridge, Suzanne Cosgrave, Justine Cottage and Mike Curry, George Craig, Suzanne Dalton, Ronald Davison, Hans Deseure, Thomas Dickie, Gerry Donnelly, Sarah Elgie , A. Firman, David Gardner, Suzanne Garner, Dr Robert Gibson, Anne Goodchilde, David Grant, Niall Greene, Daniel Happell, Gert Haverkate, Sandra Harris, Pam Henson, John and Jan Hilary, Martin Hillman, Louise Hirasawa, Geoffrey and Vivian Hobbs, Neville B. Holland, Dr J M Jagger, Allan Jeans, Anthony Jennings, Ross Johnson, Colin and Ann Jones, Mary Lake, Jean Lang, Ted Leverton, Ian Loudon, Chiara Mazzarri, David R. Mears, Jill Millar, John Millest, Suki Morys, Mark Newcomb, Barry Newsome, Michael Ng and Lisa C. Fong, Robin Mekell-Redwood, Christina Murphy, Norma Padoan, Luisa Pastore, Michael and Monica Pennington, Paul A. Pontecorvo, Jeff Ravetto, Jean and Alec Roberts, Nicolas Robinson, Simon Rowntree, Steve Sears, Ann Scott, Graham Scott, Jeanette Shapiro, Petrina and Michael Slaytor, Colin Smith, Julia Speht, Matthias Stephan, Susan Street, Fiona Towers, Sheila Trenholm, Anthony del Tufo, Brigitte Verhage, Susan Webster, Edward Windus, Martin Wright.

Photo credits

All photos © Rough Guides (Dylan Reisenberger colour introduction, chapters 2–5 & 7–13; James McConnachie chapters 1 & 6 and Palio colour insert) except the following:

Cover
Front picture: Abbazia di Sant'Antimo Church, Montalcino © Getty.
Back picture: Neptune fountain, Piazza della Signoria, Florence © Alamy.

Introduction
Painted shop sign, Pienza, Val d'Órcia, Tuscany © Dylan Reisenberger.
Cellini's *Perseus* © Rough Guides (James McConnachie).
Val d'Órcia, Tuscany © Dylan Reisenberger.

Things not to miss
02 *Adoration of the Magi*, Gentile da Fabriano (c.1370–1427) © Scala – Ministero Beni e Att. Culturali.
03 Duomo, Siena © Rough Guides (James McConnachie).
05 Taddeo Gaddi (c.1300–1366) *Annunciation to the Shepherds*, Santa Croce, Florence © Scala – Ministero Beni e Att. Culturali.
06 Duomo, Pienza © Dylan Reisenberger.
07 Barga © Dylan Reisenberger.
09 Interior view of the Sagrestia Nuova at San Lorenzo, Florence © Alinari Archives/Corbis.
10 Piazza del Duomo © Rough Guides (James McConnachie).
13 *Perchè No!* gelateria © Rough Guides (James McConnachie).
14 View from Monti dell'Uccellina, Torre di Collelungo, Maremma, © SIME/Spila Riccardo.
18 Volterra Balze © Stone/Getty.
19 Rooftops of Cortona © Nick Higham/Alamy.
21 Farmhouse, Val d'Órcia © Dylan Reisenberger.
25 *La corsa dei ceri*, San Ubaldo quarter, Gubbio © CuboImages srl/Alamy.
26 Piero della Francesca (1415/20–1492) *Legend of the Cross: Battle of Heraclius and Khosrow*, San Francesco, Arezzo © Scala – Ministero Beni e Att. Culturali.

Black and whites
p.40 Detail of *Night*, from the Tomb of Giuliano de' Medici by Michelangelo Buonarroti © Massimo Listri/Corbis.
p.260 View from Passo de Tambura, beneath Monte Tambura, over lower mountains towards Carrara and the sea, in the Alpi Apuane © Dylan Reisenberger.
p.291 A nun talks with parishioners outside a church in Barga © Dylan Reisenberger.
p.316 The Certosa di Pisa © Scala.
p.325 Wooden case holding bottles of Ornellaia 1989, Bólgheri © Cephas Picture Library/Alamy.
p.331 Island of Elba © Frank Chmura/Alamy.
p.402 Ambrogio Lorenzetti, *Madonna and Child*, Pinacoteca Nazionale, Siena © Scala – Ministero Beni e Att. Culturali.
p.478 Shop selling typical local produce, Pienza © Dylan Reisenberger.
p.486 The Church of San Biagio, Montepulciano © Dylan Reisenberger.
p.566 Performers on the Alfa Soul Stage during Umbria Jazz in Perugia © Stock Italia/Alamy.
p.626 Fresco paintings by Bernardino Pinturicchio, Cappella Baglioni © Elio Ciol/Corbis.
p.681 The Gola dell Infernaccio © CuboImages srl/Alamy.

Colour insert: Michelangelo
Giuliano Bugiardini (1476–1555): Portrait of Michelangelo Wearing a Turban, Casa Buonarroti, Florence © Scala – Ministero Beni e Att. Culturali.
Michelangelo: *Prisoner known as Atlas*, Accademia, Florence © Scala – Ministero Beni e Att. Culturali.
Michelangelo: *Battle between Centaurs and Lapiths*, Casa Buonarroti, Florence © Scala – Ministero Beni e Att. Culturali.
Michelangelo: *Tomb of Giuliano de' Medici* © Massimo Listri/Corbis.
Michelangelo: *Holy Family* © David Lees/Corbis.

Colour insert: The Palio
All photographs © Rough Guides, with thanks to the Comune di Siena and APT Siena.

Colour insert: Landscape
Wild boar © blickwinkel/Alamy.
Tuscan countryside © Tim Jepson.
Piano Grande © Tim Jepson.

SMALL PRINT

Selected images from our guidebooks are available for licensing from:
ROUGHGUIDESPICTURES.COM

Index

Map entries are in colour.

INDEX

W

Y

INDEX

Map symbols

maps are listed in the full index using coloured text

Railway	⚔	Battlefield
Motorway	⚲	Church (regional maps)
Road	◉	Accommodation
Road tunnel	▣	Restaurant
Steps	⚠	Campsite
Pedestrianized road	✉	Post office
Footpath	ⓘ	Tourist office
River	⊞	Hospital
Ferry route	✡	Synagogue
Chapter division boundary	🅿	Car park
Regional boundary	★	Bus stop
Mountains		Building
Mountain peak		Church (town maps)
Point of interest		Park
Town wall		Cemetery
Gate		Beach
Castle		Forest